U.S. Dept. of State.

**Foreign Relations of the
United States, 1961–1963**

Volume XXII

# Northeast Asia

*Editors*      Edward C. Keefer
David W. Mabon
Harriet Dashiell Schwar

*General Editor*    Glenn W. LaFantasie

United States Government Printing Office
Washington
1996

r

*JX 233*
*. A3*
*1961-1963*
*Vol. 22*

DEPARTMENT OF STATE PUBLICATION 10320

OFFICE OF THE HISTORIAN

BUREAU OF PUBLIC AFFAIRS

For sale by the U.S. Government Printing Office
Superintendent of Documents, Mail Stop: SSOP, Washington, DC 20402-9328
ISBN 0-16-045206-6

# Preface

The *Foreign Relations of the United States* series presents the official documentary historical record of major foreign policy decisions and significant diplomatic activity of the United States Government. The series documents the facts and events that contributed to the formulation of policies and includes evidence of supporting and alternative views to the policy positions ultimately adopted.

The Historian of the Department of State is charged with the responsibility for the preparation of the *Foreign Relations* series. The staff of the Office of the Historian, Bureau of Public Affairs, plans, researches, compiles, and edits the volumes in the series. This documentary editing proceeds in full accord with the generally accepted standards of historical scholarship. Official regulations codifying specific standards for the selection and editing of documents for the series were first promulgated by Secretary of State Frank B. Kellogg on March 26, 1925. These regulations, with minor modifications, guided the series through 1991.

A new statutory charter for the preparation of the series was established by Public Law 102–138, the Foreign Relations Authorization Act, Fiscal Years 1992 and 1993, which was signed by President George Bush on October 28, 1991. Section 198 of P.L. 102–138 added a new Title IV to the Department of State's Basic Authorities Act of 1956 (22 USC 4351, *et seq.*).

The statute requires that the *Foreign Relations* series be a thorough, accurate, and reliable record of major United States foreign policy decisions and significant United States diplomatic activity. The volumes of the series should include all records needed to provide comprehensive documentation of major foreign policy decisions and actions of the United States Government, including facts that contributed to the formulation of policies and records that provided supporting and alternative views to the policy positions ultimately adopted.

The statute confirms the editing principles established by Secretary Kellogg: the *Foreign Relations* series is guided by the principles of historical objectivity and accuracy; records should not be altered or deletions made without indicating in the published text that a deletion has been made; the published record should omit no facts that were of major importance in reaching a decision; and nothing should be omitted for the purposes of concealing a defect in policy. The statute also requires that the *Foreign Relations* series be published not more than 30 years after the events recorded.

The editors of this volume, which was compiled in 1992, are convinced that it meets all regulatory, statutory, and scholarly standards of selection and editing with the exception of the compilation on Japan, the reasons for which are explained in the section on Declassification Review. Although this volume records policies and events of more than 30 years ago, the statute of October 28, 1991, allows the Department until 1996 to reach the 30-year line in the publication of the series.

*Structure and Scope of the Foreign Relations Series*

This volume is part of a subseries of volumes of the *Foreign Relations* series that documents the most important issues in the foreign policy of the 3 years (1961–1963) of the administration of John F. Kennedy. The subseries presents in 25 print volumes and 5 microfiche supplements a documentary record of major foreign policy decisions and actions of President Kennedy's administration.

This volume presents documentation on U.S. policy toward North Asia, including compilations of China, Japan, Korea, and a small compilation on possible recognition of Mongolia. A separate microfiche supplement presents additional documents on China, Japan, and Korea.

*Sources for the Foreign Relations Series*

The *Foreign Relations* statute requires that the published record in the *Foreign Relations* series include all records needed to provide comprehensive documentation on major foreign policy decisions and actions of the U.S. Government. It further requires that government agencies, departments, and other entities of the U.S. Government cooperate with the Department of State Historian by providing full and complete access to records pertinent to foreign policy decisions and actions and by providing copies of selected records. The editors believe that in terms of access this volume was prepared in accordance with the standards and mandates of this statute.

The editors had complete access to all the retired records and papers of the Department of State: the central files of the Department; the special decentralized files ("lot files") of the Department at the bureau, office, and division levels; the files of the Department's Executive Secretariat, which contain the records of international conferences and high-level official visits, correspondence with foreign leaders by the President and Secretary of State, and memoranda of conversations between the President and Secretary of State and foreign officials; and the files of overseas diplomatic posts. Certain intelligence-related files maintained in the Bureau of Intelligence and Research became available to Department historians only after this volume was compiled, but the editors were able to examine them before the volume went for publication. They believe that information in these records was covered adequately in the volume, at least before declassification decisions, and therefore it was unwarranted to delay publication of the volume. Arrangements have been made for Department historians to have full and timely access to these records for future volumes.

The editors of the *Foreign Relations* series also have full access to the papers of Presidents Kennedy, Johnson, and Eisenhower and other White House foreign policy records. Presidential papers maintained and preserved at the Presidential libraries include some of the most significant foreign affairs-related documentation from other federal agencies including the National Security Council, the Central Intelligence Agency, the Department of Defense, and the Joint Chiefs of Staff. Also of special value at the Kennedy Library are the papers of Roger Hilsman, Director of the Bureau of Intelligence and Research at the State Department and later Assistant Secretary of State for Far Eastern Affairs, transcripts of telephone conversations of Under Secretary of State George Ball, and the Papers of James C. Thomson, Jr., who served in a series of key staff assistant roles. Averell Harriman's papers at the Manuscript Division of the Library of Congress, which include material from Harriman's tenure as Assistant Secretary of State for Far Eastern Affairs and then as Under Secretary of State for Political Affairs, constitute another important source.

Department of State historians also have access to records of the Department of Defense, particularly the records of the Secretary of Defense and his major assistants, and to the Maxwell Taylor Papers and the Lyman Lemnitzer Papers at the National Defense University. Those Joint Chiefs of Staff records that were not available in White House, State, or Defense records, were obtained from the Joint Staff of the Joint Chiefs of Staff on a request basis.

Since 1991, the Central Intelligence Agency has provided expanding access to Department of State historians to high-level intelligence documents from those records in the custody of that Agency. This access is arranged and facilitated by the History Staff of the Center for the Study of Intelligence, Central Intelligence Agency, pursuant to a May 1992 memorandum of understanding. This access arrangement was concluded in connection with the research of volumes for the 1961–1963 triennium and in order to enlarge the scope of coverage as required by the 1991 law. The highly sensitive and security-protected records of the CIA do not lend themselves easily to historical research. Department of State and CIA historians continue to work out the procedural and scholarly aspects of identifying the key portions of the intelligence record. The variety of documentation made available to Department of State historians and ultimately selected for publication in the volumes has expanded. The editors of the volume made particular use of the files of Directors Allen W. Dulles and John A. McCone as well as special collections of records in the custody of the Center for the Study of Intelligence at the Agency.

All of this documentation has been made available for use in the *Foreign Relations* series thanks to the consent of these agencies, the assistance of their staffs, and especially the cooperation and support of the National Archives and Records Administration. The List of Sources, pages XVII–XXIV, lists the particular files and collections consulted and cited in this volume.

*Principles of Document Selection for the Foreign Relations Series*

In preparing each volume of the *Foreign Relations* series, the editors are guided by some general principles for the selection of documents. Each editor, in consultation with the General Editor and other senior editors, determines the particular issues and topics to be documented either in detail, in brief, or in summary. Some general decisions are also made regarding issues that cannot be documented in the volume but will be addressed in a microfiche supplement or in bibliographical notes.

The following general selection criteria are used in preparing volumes in the *Foreign Relations* series. Individual compiler-editors vary these criteria in accordance with the particular issues and the available documentation. The editors also tend to apply these selection criteria in accordance with their own interpretation of the generally accepted standards of scholarship. In selecting documentation for publication, the editors give priority to unpublished classified records, rather than previously published records (which are accounted for in appropriate bibliographical notes).

*Selection Criteria (in general order of priority):*

1. Major foreign affairs commitments made on behalf of the United States to other governments, including those that define or identify the principal foreign affairs interests of the United States;

2. Major foreign affairs issues, commitments, negotiations, and activities, whether or not major decisions were made, and including dissenting or alternative opinions to the process ultimately adopted;

3. The decisions, discussions, actions, and considerations of the President, as the official constitutionally responsible for the direction of foreign policy;

4. The discussions and actions of the National Security Council, the Cabinet, and special Presidential policy groups, including the policy options brought before these bodies or their individual members;

5. The policy options adopted by or considered by the Secretary of State and the most important actions taken to implement Presidential decisions or policies;

6. Diplomatic negotiations and conferences, official correspondence, and other exchanges between U.S. representatives and those of

other governments that demonstrate the main lines of policy implementation on major issues;

7. Important information that attended Presidential decisions and policy recommendations of the Secretary of State;

8. Major foreign affairs decisions, negotiations, and commitments undertaken on behalf of the United States by government officials and representatives in other agencies in the foreign affairs community or other branches of government made without the involvement (or even knowledge) of the White House or the Department of State;

9. The main policy lines of intelligence activities if they constituted major aspects of U.S. foreign policy toward a nation or region or if they provided key information in the formulation of major U.S. policies, including relevant National Intelligence Estimates and Special National Intelligence Estimates as may be declassified;

10. The role of the Congress in the preparation and execution of particular foreign policies or foreign affairs actions;

11. Economic aspects of foreign policy;

12. The main policy lines of U.S. military and economic assistance as well as other types of assistance;

13. The political-military recommendations, decisions, and activities of the military establishment and major regional military commands as they bear upon the formulation or execution of major U.S. foreign policies;

14. Diplomatic appointments that reflect major policies or affect policy changes.

*Scope and Focus of Documents Researched and Selected for Foreign Relations, 1961–1963, Volume XXII*

The documentation printed in this volume focuses on the formulation of U.S. policy toward North Asia, particularly the most significant aspects of U.S. political, economic, and military relationships with the Governments of Japan, Korea, and the Republic of China on Taiwan. Also included is documentation on U.S. policies toward the People's Republic of China and Mongolia, with which the United States had no official diplomatic relations.

President Kennedy in conjunction with key advisers made the major foreign policy decisions during his presidency, and the editors tried to document his role as much possible. The role of White House and National Security Council Staff members in providing information and advice to the President grew during this period. The editors accordingly selected memoranda that presented to the President the views and recommendations of his White House advisers. Formal approved policy papers were rare in the Kennedy administration, and internal discussions between the President and his advisers were not always recorded.

The editors sought to document Presidential decisions by drawing upon the best material available. The Department of State continued to play a leading role in formulating foreign policy and providing advice on foreign policy matters to the President, and it played the principal role in exchanges of view and negotiations on policy matters with foreign governments. The volume includes documentation on a range of lesser policy decisions that did not reach the President or were resolved in the Department of State or other foreign affairs agencies.

The microfiche supplement to this volume contains additional documents on the subjects dealt with here. Where appropriate these documents are cited in the volume.

*Editorial Methodology*

The documents are presented chronologically according to Washington time or, in the case of conferences, in the order of individual meetings. Incoming telegrams from U.S. Missions are placed according to time of receipt in the Department of State or other receiving agency, rather than the time of transmission; memoranda of conversation are placed according to the time and date of the conversation, rather than the date the memorandum was drafted.

Editorial treatment of the documents published in the *Foreign Relations* series follows Office style guidelines, supplemented by guidance from the General Editor and the chief technical editor. The source text is reproduced as exactly as possible, including marginalia or other notations, which are described in the footnotes. Texts are transcribed and printed according to accepted conventions for the publication of historical documents in the limitations of modern typography. A heading has been supplied by the editors for each document included in the volume. Spelling, capitalization, and punctuation are retained as found in the source text, except that obvious typographical errors are silently corrected. Other mistakes and omissions in the source text are corrected by bracketed insertions: a correction is set in italic type; an addition in roman type. Words or phrases underlined in the source text are printed in italics. Abbreviations and contractions are preserved as found in the source text, and a list of abbreviations is included in the front matter of each volume.

Bracketed insertions are also used to indicate omitted text that deals with an unrelated subject (in roman type) or that remains classified after declassification review (in italic type). The amount of material not declassified has been noted by indicating the number of lines or pages of source text that were omitted. Entire documents withheld for declassification purposes have been accounted for and are listed by headings, source note information, and number of pages not declassified in their chronological place. The amount of material omitted from this volume because it was unrelated to the subject of the volume, however, has not been delineated. Brackets that appear in the source text are so identified by footnotes.

An unnumbered source note to each document indicates the document's source, original classification, distribution, and drafting information. This note also provides the background of important documents and policies and indicates if the President or his major policy advisers read the document. Every effort has been made to determine if a document has been previously published, and this information has been included in the source footnote.

Editorial notes and additional annotation summarize pertinent material not printed in the volume, indicate the location of additional documentary sources, provide references to important related documents printed in other volumes, describe key events, and provide summaries of and citations to public statements that supplement and elucidate the printed documents. Information derived from memoirs and other first-hand accounts have been used when appropriate to supplement or explicate the official record.

*Advisory Committee on Historical Diplomatic Documentation*

The Advisory Committee on Historical Diplomatic Documentation, established under the *Foreign Relations* statute, reviews records, advises, and makes recommendations concerning the *Foreign Relations* series. The Advisory Committee monitors the overall compilation and editorial process of the series and advises on all aspects of the preparation and declassification of the series. Although the Advisory Committee does not attempt to review the contents of individual volumes in the series, it does monitor the overall process and makes recommendations on particular problems that come to its attention.

*Declassification Review*

The final declassification review of this volume was completed in 1995. The compilation on China had no documents denied in full and excisions amount to 1.1 percent of the documentation originally selected for publication. The editors believe it is a thorough, accurate and reliable record of major United States foreign policy decisions and significant diplomatic activity.

In the compilation on Japan, 13.5 percent of the material selected for publication was not declassified. The Office of the Historian prepared a compilation for Japan of 65 documents, 3 for the 1958–1960 period and 62 for 1961–1963. Nine documents were denied declassification, despite full use of the appeal process for 3 of them. The denied material relates to ramifications and arrangements arising from certain aspects of the Mutual Security Treaty of 1960 and concern and actions of the U.S. Government in response to the political situation in Japan during the years 1958–1960. The Advisory Committee on Historical Diplomatic Documentation has examined the denied documents and concluded that this published compilation does not constitute a "thorough, accurate, and reliable documentary record of major United States foreign policy decisions," the standard set by Public Law 102–138 of October 28, 1991 (22 USC 4351, *et seq.*). The Advisory Committee will continue to seek declassification of the documents withheld.

In the compilation on Korea, 5.9 percent of the documentation originally selected was withheld; four documents were denied in full. All four originated in the Department of Defense and concerned a high-level debate about potential alternative methods of defending the Republic of Korea against the threat from China and North Korea. While it was an interesting deliberation, the debate did not eventuate in any policy recommendation and never moved beyond the theoretical stage. Therefore, the editors believe that the compilation on Korea is an accurate and reliable record of U.S. policy decisions toward Korea as well as of significant diplomatic activity with the Republic of Korea.

The Division of Historical Documents Review of the Office of Freedom of Information, Privacy, and Classification Review, Bureau of Administration, Department of State, conducted the declassification review of the documents published in this volume. The review was conducted in accordance with the standards set forth in Executive Order 12356 on National Security Information, which was superseded by Executive Order 12958 on April 20, 1995, and applicable laws.

Under Executive Order 12356, information that concerns one or more of the following categories, and the disclosure of which reasonably could be expected to cause damage to the national security, requires classification:

1) military plans, weapons, or operations;
2) the vulnerabilities or capabilities of systems, installations, projects, or plans relating to the national security;
3) foreign government information;
4) intelligence activities (including special activities), or intelligence sources or methods;
5) foreign relations or foreign activities of the United States;
6) scientific, technological, or economic matters relating to national security;
7) U.S. Government programs for safeguarding nuclear materials or facilities;
8) cryptology; or
9) a confidential source.

The principle guiding declassification review is to release all information, subject only to the current requirements of national security and law. Declassification decisions entailed concurrence of the appropriate geographic and functional bureaus in the Department of State, other concerned agencies of the U.S. Government, and the appropriate foreign governments regarding specific documents of those governments.

*Acknowledgements*

The editors wish to acknowledge the assistance of officials at the John F. Kennedy Library of the National Archives and Records Administration, in particular Suzanne Forbes, and other officials of specialized repositories who assisted in the collection of documents for this volume.

Harriet Dashiell Schwar collected, selected, and edited the compilations on China and Mongolia; David W. Mabon prepared the Japan compilation, and Edward C. Keefer prepared the compilation on Korea. David Mabon planned the volume and conducted the review under the general supervision of Editor in Chief Glenn W. LaFantasie. Edward C. Keefer oversaw the final steps in the editorial and publication process. Vicki E. Futscher did the copy and technical editing and Barbara-Ann Bacon of the Publishing Services Division oversaw the production of the volume. Paul Zohav prepared the index.

**William Z. Slany**
*The Historian*
*Bureau of Public Affairs*

July 1996

# List of Kennedy Administration Volumes

Following is a list of the volumes in the *Foreign Relations* series for the administration of President John F. Kennedy. The year of publication is in parentheses after the title.

**Print Volumes**

| | |
|---|---|
| I | Vietnam, 1961 (1988) |
| II | Vietnam, 1962 (1990) |
| III | Vietnam, January–August 1963 (1991) |
| IV | Vietnam, August–December 1963 (1991) |
| V | Soviet Union |
| VI | Kennedy–Khrushchev Exchanges (1996) |
| VII | Arms Control and Disarmament (1995) |
| VIII | National Security Policy |
| IX | Foreign Economic Policy (1995) |
| X | Cuba, January 1961–September 1962 |
| XI | Cuba, October 1962–December 1963 |
| XII | American Republics (1996) |
| XIII | Western Europe and Canada (1994) |
| XIV | Berlin Crisis, 1961–1962 (1994) |
| XV | Berlin Crisis, 1962–1963 (1994) |
| XVI | Eastern Europe; Cyprus; Greece; Turkey (1994) |
| XVII | Near East, 1961–1962 (1995) |
| XVIII | Near East, 1962–1963 (1995) |
| XIX | South Asia (1996) |
| XX | Congo Crisis (1995) |
| XXI | Africa (1996) |
| XXII | Northeast Asia (1996) |
| XXIII | Southeast Asia (1995) |
| XXIV | Laos Crisis (1994) |
| XXV | General; United Nations |

**Microfiche Supplements**

Arms Control; National Security Policy; Foreign Economic Policy; General and United Nations (Volumes VII, VIII, IX, XXV)
Cuba; American Republics (Volumes X, XI, XII)
Western Europe; Berlin (Volumes XIII, XIV, XV) (1995)
Near East; Congo; Africa (Volumes XVII, XVIII, XX, XXI)
Northeast Asia; Laos (Volumes XXII, XXIV)

# Contents

# List of Sources

## Unpublished Sources

### Department of State

*Decimal Central Files.* Through January 1963, the Department of State continued to use the decimal central file system familiar to users of previous volumes of the *Foreign Relations* series. The following files were most useful in compiling this volume through January 1963:

#### China

303: representation in the United Nations
411.93: U.S. trade with China
493.00: general issues concerning trade with China
611.93: political relations between the United States and China, including both U.S-ROC relations and the U.S.-PRC ambassadorial talks
661.93: Sino-Soviet relations
793.00: political affairs and conditions in China, including the mainland and Taiwan
793.5: Chinese military affairs, including the mainland and Taiwan
793.5–MSP: mutual security program in the Republic of China
793B: political issues concerning Tibet
893.00: economic affairs and conditions in China

#### Japan

033.1100–KE: visits abroad of Attorney General Robert F. Kennedy
102.201: the Joint Chiefs of Staff
294.1141: U.S. claims on Japan
394.41: conferences or negotiations on trade and commercial treaties
411.006: U.S. import restrictions
411.9441: U.S.-Japan trade relations
411.946: U.S. restrictions on imports from Japan
494.0012: conditions affecting Japanese imports
611.94: U.S.-Japan relations
611.9441: U.S.-Japan consular functions
611.9442: U.S.-Japan Treaty of Friendship, Commerce and Navigation
611.9494: U.S.-Japan aviation negotiations
693.94: Sino-Japanese relations
794.5: Japanese defense affairs
794C.0221: U.S. forces in the Ryukyus
811.0094C: U.S. economic aid to the Ryukyus

#### Korea

033.95B11: visits of South Korean officials to the United States
110.15–HA: foreign travel of Assistant Secretary of State Harriman
120.1590: special missions to East Asia
294.9541: Japanese claims against South Korea
601.95B11: diplomatic representation of South Korea in the United States
611.95B: political relations between the United States and South Korea

611.95B7: military and defense agreements between the United States and South Korea
694.95B: political relations between Japan and South Korea
700.5–MSP: U.S. mutual security program, general
795.00: political affairs and conditions in Korea
795B.00: political affairs and conditions in South Korea
795B.5: national defense affairs in South Korea
795B.5–MSP: mutual security program in South Korea
795B.56311: U.S. bases in South Korea
811.0095B: U.S. economic aid to South Korea
895B.00: Economic matters and conditions in South Korea
895B.00 FIVE YEAR: South Korea's Five Year Economic Plan
895B.05: capital in South Korea
895B.10: financial matters in South Korea

### Mongolia

611.93C: political relations between the United States and Mongolia
793C.02: question of recognition of Mongolia

Subject-Numeric Central Files. In February 1963 the Department adopted a subject-numeric central file system. The following files for February through December 1963 were most useful in compiling this volume:

### China

DEF CHINAT: armed forces of the Republic of China; defense of Taiwan
POL CHICOM: political affairs and conditions on the China mainland
POL CHICOM–US: U.S. policy toward the People's Republic of China and the U.S.-PRC
    ambassadorial talks
POL CHICOM–USSR: Sino-Soviet relations
POL CHINA: political affairs and conditions in China, including both the mainland and
    Taiwan
POL CHINAT: political affairs and conditions in Taiwan
POL CHINAT–US: political relations between the United States and the Republic of China
POL TIBET: political issues concerning Tibet

### Japan

E 1 JAPAN–US: general U.S.-Japanese economic relations
DEF 1 JAPAN: general Japanese defense policy
DEF 4 JAPAN–US: U.S.-Japan defense agreements
DEF 6 US: U.S. armed forces
DEF 7 JAPAN–US: U.S.-Japan defense visits and missions
DEF 15 JAPAN–US: U.S. bases and installations in Japan
DEF 15 RYU IS–US: U.S. bases and installations in the Ryukyus
DEF 19–3 JAPAN: Japanese defense organizations
FN 5 JAPAN: Japanese financial laws and regulations
FN 12 JAPAN: Japanese balance of payments, including military offset program
FT 11–5, JAPAN: Japanese voluntary trade controls
ORG 7 OSD: visits abroad of Department of Defense officials
POL JAPAN–US: general U.S.-Japan political relations
POL RYU IS–US: general U.S. political relations with Ryukyuan authorities
POL 19 RYU IS: administration of the Ryukyus

### Korea

DEF 6 S KOR: armed forces of South Korea
DEF 16 S KOR–US: U.S. bases and installations in South Korea
E 1–1 S KOR: economic stabilization in South Korea
E 2–2 S KOR: economic review in South Korean

POL S KOR: general policy, South Korea
POL KOR–US: general U.S.-South Korean relations
POL 12 S KOR: political parties in South Korea
POL 14 S KOR: elections in South Korea
POL 15 S KOR: government in South Korea
POL 26 S KOR: coups in South Korea
POL 33–4 JAP–KOR: Japanese-Korean territorial waters dispute

**Mongolia**

POL 16 MONGOLIA: question of recognition of Mongolia

*Lot Files.*

Conference Files: Lot 65 D 366

Records of official visits by heads of government and foreign ministers to the United States and international conferences attended by the President or Secretary of State, 1961, as maintained by the Executive Secretariat.

Conference Files: Lot 65 D 533

Records of official visits by heads of government and foreign ministers to the United States and international conferences attended by the President or Secretary of State, 1962, as maintained by the Executive Secretariat.

Conference Files: Lot 66 D 110

Records of official visits by heads of government and foreign ministers to the United States and international conferences attended by the President or Secretary of State, 1961–1964, as maintained by the Executive Secretariat.

EA/J Files: Lot 68 D 373

Files on Japanese economic affairs, 1961–1966, as maintained by the Office of East Asian Affairs, Bureau of Far Eastern Affairs.

FE Files: Lot 64 D 25

Files of the Bureau of Far Eastern Affairs, 1962.

FE Files: Lot 65 D 6

Files of the Bureau of Far Eastern Affairs, 1963.

FE/EA Files: Lot 65 D 93

Files of the Office of East Asian Affairs, Bureau of Far Eastern Affairs, 1960–1961.

FE/EA Files: Lot 65 D 235

Files of the Office of East Asian Affairs, Bureau of Far Eastern Affairs, 1961–1962.

FE/EA Files: Lot 66 D 224

Files of the Office of East Asian Affairs, Bureau of Far Eastern Affairs, 1961–1962.

FE/EA Files: Lot 66 D 225

Files of the Office of East Asian Affairs, Bureau of Far Eastern Affairs, 1964, with some files pertaining to China, Japan, and Korea for previous years.

FE/RA Files: Lot 65 D 486

Files of the Office of Regional Affairs, Bureau of Far Eastern Affairs, 1962.

FE/RA Files: Lot 67 D 200

Files of the Office of Regional Affairs, Bureau of Far Eastern Affairs, 1963–1964.

Geneva Talks Files:  Lot 71 D 368

Files relating to the U.S.-China ambassadorial talks at Geneva and Warsaw for the years 1955–1962, as maintained by the Office of Chinese Affairs and later by the Office of East Asian Affairs and the Office of Asian Communist Affairs.

Geneva Talks Files:  Lot 72 D 415

Files relating to the U.S.-China ambassadorial talks at Geneva and Warsaw for the years 1955–1968, as maintained by Asian Affairs and the Office of Asian Communist Affairs.

INR/EAP Files:  Lot 90 D 99

National Intelligence Estimates and Special National Intelligence Estimates for East Asia for 1952–1985, as maintained by the Office of Analysis for East Asia and the Pacific in the Bureau of Intelligence and Research.

INR/EAP files:  Lot 90 D 110

National Intelligence Estimates and Special National Intelligence Estimates for East Asia, 1952–1985, as maintained by the Office of Analysis for East Asia and the Pacific in the Bureau of Intelligence and Research.

Policy Guidelines:  Lot 67 D 396

Master file of Guidelines for Policy and Operations papers for 1961–1966.

Presidential Correspondence:  Lot 66 D 204

Correspondence between the President and Secretary of State and heads of government and foreign ministers for 1953–1964, as maintained by the Executive Secretariat.

Presidential Memoranda of Conversation:  Lot 66 D 149

Memoranda of conversation between the President and foreign visitors, 1956–1964, as maintained by the Executive Secretariat.

ROC Files:  Lot 71 D 517

Top Secret files relating to China for 1954–1963, maintained by the Office of Chinese Affairs and later by the Republic of China desk in the Office of East Asian Affairs.

ROC Files:  Lot 73 D 39

Top Secret files for 1954–1968, maintained by the Office of Chinese Affairs and later by the Office of East Asian Affairs and the Office of Republic of China Affairs.

ROC Files:  Lot 75 D 76

Political files for 1954–1973, maintained by the Office of Chinese Affairs and later by the Office of East Asian Affairs and the Office of Republic of China Affairs.

ROC Files:  Lot 79 D 120

Top Secret files for 1961–1972, maintained by the Republic of China desk in the Office of East Asian Affairs and later by the Office of Republic of China Affairs.

Rusk Files:  Lot 72 D 192

Files of Secretary of State Dean Rusk, 1961–1969, including texts of speeches and public statements, miscellaneous correspondence files, White House correspondence, chronological files, and memoranda of telephone conversations.

Secretary's Memoranda of Conversation:  Lot 65 D 330

Memoranda of the Secretary's and Acting Secretary's conversations, 1961–1964.

Secretary's Staff Meetings: Lot 66 D 147

Minutes of the Secretary of State's staff meetings and memoranda of Chester Bowles telephone conversations, as maintained by the Executive Secretariat.

State–JCS Meetings: Lot 70 D 238

Memoranda of conversations between the members of the Joint Chiefs of Staff and representatives of the Department of State, 1959–1963, as maintained by the Executive Secretariat.

S/P Files: Lot 70 D 199

Files of the Policy Planning Council, 1963–1964.

S/S Country Files: Lot 70 D 209

Policy Guidelines Papers and ancillary materials as maintained by the Executive Secretariat.

S/S Files: Lot 66 D 150

Briefing books and files on a variety of subjects maintained by the Executive Secretariat, 1960–1965, including material on the Offshore Islands Working Group, 1962.

S/S Files: Lot 66 D 219

Briefing books and files on a variety of subjects maintained by the Executive Secretariat, 1962–1965, including material on the Offshore Islands Working Group, 1962.

S/S–NSC Files: Lot 70 D 265

Files pertaining to National Security Council meetings, including policy papers, position papers, administrative documents, but not minutes of the meetings themselves, for 1961–1966, as maintained by the Executive Secretariat.

S/S–NSC Files: Lot 72 D 316

Files of National Security Action Memoranda (NSAMs), 1961–1968, maintained by the Executive Secretariat.

S/S–NSC (Miscellaneous) Files: Lot 66 D 95

Miscellaneous files of the National Security Council, including records of actions, 1947–1963, as maintained by the Executive Secretariat.

S/S Policy Guidelines Files: Lot 67 D 396

Department of State Policy Guidelines papers and related materials for the years 1961–1966.

State–JCS Meetings: Lot 70 D 328

Records of the meetings of the Joint Chiefs of Staff and representatives of the Department of State for the years 1959–1963, maintained by the Executive Secretariat.

Warsaw Talks Files: Lot 73 D 210

Files relating to the U.S.–China ambassadorial talks at Warsaw for the years 1955–1971, maintained by the Embassy at Warsaw and later by the Office of People's Republic of China and Mongolia Affairs.

## National Archives and Records Administration

### Record Group 59, General Records of the Department of State

S/P Files: Lot 67 D 548

Records of the Policy Planning Council for 1957–1961.

S/P Files: Lot 69 D 121

Records of the Policy Planning Council for 1962.

**Record Group 84, General Records of the Departament of State**

Taipei Embassy Files:  FRC 66 A 878, Item 114 (Lot 65 F 163)
    Classified Embassy subject files for 1961.

Taipei Embassy Files:  FRC 67 A 1450, Item 12 (Lot 66 F 113)
    Classified Embassy subject files for 1962–1963.

**Record Group 319, Records of the Army Staff**

Assistant Chief of Staff, G–2 (Intelligence), "Secret" Incoming and Outgoing Messages, 1961–1963
    Intelligence reports on China, 1961–1963, filed under Taiwan.

## Dwight D. Eisenhower Library, Abilene, Kansas

Whitman File
    Papers of Dwight D. Eisenhower as maintained by his personal secretary, Ann C. Whitman.

## Lyndon Baines Johnson Library, Austin, Texas

National Security File
    Aides' Files

Rusk Appointment Books

Vice Presidential Security File

Waldron Papers
    Papers of Robert Waldron, a member of Vice President Johnson's party during Johnson's trip to Asia in 1961.

## John F. Kennedy Library, Boston, Massachusetts

Ball Papers
    Papers of George W. Ball, Under Secretary of State for Economic Affairs, 1961, and Under Secretary of State, 1961–1963, consisting of records of telephone conversations during his tenure as Under Secretary.

National Security Files:
    Departments/Agencies Series
    Clifton Series
    Countries Series:  China, Japan, Korea, Outer Mongolia, Poland, Ryukyus, Tibet, USSR
    Trip Series
    Meetings and Memoranda Series

President's Appointment Books

President's Office Files:  China, Korea, Outer Mongolia, Ryukyus

Hilsman Papers
    Papers of Roger Hilsman, Jr., Director of the Bureau of Intelligence and Research, Department of State, 1961–1963; Assistant Secretary of State for Far Eastern Affairs, 1963.

Thomson Papers

> Papers of James C. Thomson, Jr., Special Assistant to the Under Secretary of State, 1961; Special Assistant to the President's Special Representative for Africa, Asia, and Latin America, 1961–1963; Special Assistant to the Assistant Secretary of State for Far Eastern Affairs, 1963.

## Agency for International Development

Administrator Files: Lot 286–65–481

> Files of the AID Administrator for 1961–1962.

Administrator Files: Lot 286–67–1530

> Files of the AID Administrator for 1962–1965.

## Central Intelligence Agency

Director of Central Intelligence Executive Registry: Job 80–B0176R

> Official files of Allen W. Dulles, 1953–1961

Director of Central Intelligence, McCone Files: Job 80–B01235A

> Files of John A. McCone, 1962–1965.

## Library of Congress Manuscript Division

Harriman Papers

> Papers of W. Averell Harriman, Ambassador at Large, 1961; Assistant Secretary of State for Far Eastern Affairs, 1961–1963; Under Secretary of State for Political Affairs, 1963

## National Defense University, Washington, D.C.

Lemnitzer Papers

> Papers of General Lyman L. Lemnitzer, Chairman of the Joint Chiefs of Staff, 1960–1962.

Taylor Papers

> Papers of General Maxwell D. Taylor, Military Adviser to the President 1961–1962, and Chairman of the Joint Chiefs of Staff, 1962–1964.

## Seeley G. Mudd Manuscript Library, Princeton University, Princeton, New Jersey

Stevenson Papers

> Papers of Adlai E. Stevenson, Representative at the United Nations, 1961–1965.

## Washington National Records Center

### Record Group 330, Records of the Office of the Secretary of Defense

OSD Files: FRC 65 A 3464

> Files of the Secretary and Deputy Secretary of Defense and their assistants for 1961.

OSD Files:  FRC 66 A 3529

Top Secret files of the Deputy Secretary of Defense and his assistants for 1961–1963.

OSD Files:  FRC 66 A 3542

Files of the Secretary and Deputy Secretary of Defense and their assistants for 1962.

OSD Files:  FRC 69 A 3131

Files of the Secretary and Deputy Secretary of Defense and their assistants for 1963.

OSD Files:  FRC 71 A 3470

Files of Secretary of Defense Robert S. McNamara, 1961–1968.

OSD Files:  FRC 71 A 6489

Miscellaneous records of the Secretary and Deputy Secretary of Defense and their assistants, 1951–1966.

OASD/ISA Files:  FRC 64 A 2382

General and country files of the Assistant Secretary of Defense for International Security Affairs for 1961.

OASD/ISA Files:  FRC 65 A 3501

General and country files of the Assistant Secretary of Defense for International Security Affairs for 1962.

OASD/ISA Files:  FRC 67 A 4564

General and country files of the Assistant Secretary of Defense for International Security Affairs for 1963.

OASD/ISA Files:  FRC 69 A 926

Top Secret files of the Assistant Secretary of Defense for International Security Affairs for 1961–1963.

# List of Abbreviations

**ACW,** anti-aircraft warfare
**AC&W,** aircraft control & warning
**AEC,** Atomic Energy Commission
**AID,** Agency for International Development
**AIDTO,** telegram indicator for messages from USOM to AID
**ARTY,** artillery
**ASW,** anti-submarine warfare

**BADGE,** base air defense ground environment
**BNS,** battalions

**CA,** circular airgram; Office of Chinese Affairs, Department of State
**CAF,** Chinese Air Force (Republic of China)
**CAS,** Controlled American Source
**ChiCom,** Chinese Communist(s)
**CIA,** Central Intelligence Agency
**CIB,** Combined Intelligence Board ·
**CIC,** Counterintelligence Corps
**CINCPAC,** Commander in Chief, Pacific
**CINCPAC POLAD,** Political Adviser to the Commander in Chief, Pacific
**CINCUNC,** Commander in Chief, United Nations Command
**CJCS,** Chairman, Joint Chiefs of Staff
**CMDR,** Commander
**CNO,** Chief of Naval Operations
**CODEL,** Congressional delegation
**COMUSJAPAN,** Commander, United States Forces, Japan
**COMUSKOREA,** Commander, United States Forces, Korea
**COMUSTDC,** Commander, United States Taiwan Defense Command
**CPG,** Central People's Government
**CPR,** Chinese People's Republic
**CUSA,** Council for United States Aid (Republic of China)
**CY,** calendar year

**DAG,** Development Assistance Group
**DCI,** Director of Central Intelligence
**DCM,** Deputy Chief of Mission
**DEF,** defense
**Deptel,** Department of State telegram
**DL,** Development Loan
**DLF,** Development Loan Fund
**DMZ,** Demilitarized Zone
**DOD,** Department of Defense
**DRP,** Democratic Republican Party (Republic of Korea)

**E,** Bureau of Economic Affairs, Department of State
**EA,** Office of East Asian Affairs, Bureau of Far Eastern Affairs, Department of State
**EA/J,** Officer in Charge of Japanese Affairs, Office of East Asian Affairs, Bureau of Far Eastern Affairs, Department of State
**EAP,** East Asia and Pacific
**ECM,** electronic countermeasures

**ECONCOM,** Economic Committee
**EEC,** European Economic Community
**Embtel,** Embassy telegram
**E.O.,** Executive Order
**E/OR,** Office of International Resources, Bureau of Economic Affairs, Department of State
**E/OT,** Office of International Trade, Bureau of Economic Affairs, Department of State
**EPB,** Economic Planning Board

**FA,** food allocation
**FBI,** Federal Bureau of Investigation
**FE,** Bureau of Far Eastern Affairs, Department of State
**FE/EA,** Office of East Asian Affairs, Bureau of Far Eastern Affairs, Department of State
**FonMin,** Foreign Minister
**F.R.,** *Federal Register*
**FRC,** Federal Records Center
**FROKA,** First Republic of Korea Army
**FY,** fiscal year
**FYI,** for your information

**G,** Deputy Under Secretary of State for Political Affairs
**GARIOA,** Government and Relief in Occupied Areas
**GATT,** General Agreement on Tariffs and Trade
**GIO,** Government Information Office (Republic of China)
**GNP,** Gross National Product
**GOJ,** Government of Japan
**G/PM,** Deputy Assistant Secretary of State for Politico-Military Affairs
**GRC,** Government of the Republic of China (Taipei)
**GRI,** Government of the Ryukyu Islands

**HE,** high explosives
**HICOM,** High Commissioner (of the Ryukyu Islands)

**IBRD,** International Bank for Reconstruction and Development (World Bank)
**ICA,** International Cooperation Administration
**ICBM,** inter-continental ballistic missiles
**ICC,** International Control Commission (Vietnam)
**ICRC,** International Committee of the Red Cross
**IDA,** International Development Association
**IMF,** International Monetary Fund
**INR,** Bureau of Intelligence and Research, Department of State
**IO,** Bureau of International Organization Affairs, Department of State
**IPI,** International Press Institute
**ISA,** Office of the Assistant Secretary of Defense for International Security Affairs
**ISA/FE,** Far East Division, Office of the Assistant Secretary of Defense for International
    Security Affairs

**JAEC,** Japanese Atomic Energy Commission
**JCP,** Japan Communist Party
**JCRR,** Joint Commission on Rural Reconstruction (Republic of China)
**JCS,** Joint Chiefs of Staff
**JCSM,** Joint Chiefs of Staff Memorandum
**JFY,** Japan fiscal year
**JIC,** Joint Intelligence Committee
**JSP,** Japan Socialist Party

**KBS,** Korean Broadcast Service
**KCIA,** Korean Central Intelligence Agency
**KMT,** Kuomintang
**KST,** Korean Standard Time
**kw,** kilowatt

**L,** Office of the Legal Adviser, Department of State
**LCM,**  landing craft, mechanized
**LDC,** less developed countries
**LDP,** Liberal Democratic Party (Japan)
**L/FE,** Assistant Legal Adviser for Far Eastern Affairs, Department of State
**LOG COMD,** Logistics Command
**L/SFP,** Assistant Legal Adviser for Special Functional Problems
**LST,** landing ship, tank
**LTA,** Long Term Agreement (on cotton textiles)

**M,** Under Secretary of State for Political Affairs
**MAAG,** Military Assistance Advisory Group
**MAC,** Military Armistice Commission
**MACE,** a surface-to-air missile
**MAF,** Ministry of Agriculture and Fisheries
**MAP,** Military Assistance Program
**MC,** Marine Corps
**MCST,** Mutual Cooperation and Security Treaty
**MDC,** Military District Commander
**MFN,** most favored nation
**MITI,** Ministry of International Trade and Industry (Japan)
**MND,** Minister of Defense
**MP,** Military Police

**NA,** Office of Northeast Asian Affairs, Bureau of Far Eastern Affairs, Department of State
**NATO,** North Atlantic Treaty Organization
**NEFA,** Northeast Frontier Agency
**niact,** night action, immediate reply
**NIE,** National Intelligence Estimate
**NK,** North Korea
**NOFORN,** No foreign distribution
**NSAM,** National Security Action Memorandum
**NSC,** National Security Council
**NT,** New Taiwan

**OECD,** Organization for Economic Cooperation and Development
**OP,** Operations Plan
**OSD,** Office of the Secretary of Defense
**OSD/ISA,** Office of the Assistant Secretary of Defense for International Security Affairs
**OTF,** Office of International Trade and Finance, Bureau of Economic Affairs, Department of State
**OTF/TA,** Trade Agreements Division, Office of International Trade and Finance, Bureau of Economic Affairs, Department of State

**PACOM,** Pacific Command
**PIO, EUSA,** Public Information Office, Eighth U.S. Army
**POL,** politics; petroleum, oil, and lubrication
**POLAD,** Political Adviser
**P.L.,** Public Law

**PRC,** People's Republic of China
**Pri Min,** Prime Minister

**QR,** quota restriction

**reftel,** reference telegram
**rep,** representative
**ROK,** Republic of Korea
**ROKA,** Republic of Korea Army
**ROKAF,** Republic of Korea Armed Forces
**ROKG,** Republic of Korea Government
**rptd,** repeated

**SA,** Stabilization Assistance
**SAM,** surface-to-air missile
**SCNR,** Supreme Council for National Reconstruction
**SECTO,** series indicator for telegrams from the Secretary of State or his party to the Department of State
**sens,** sensitive
**SG,** Steering Group
**SHAPE,** Supreme Headquarters, Allied Powers, Europe
**SIOP,** Single Integrated Operations Plan (for use of strategic nuclear weapons)
**SNIE,** Special National Intelligence Estimate
**SOF,** Status of Forces
**SOFA,** Status of Forces Agreement
**S/P,** Counselor and Chairman of the Policy Planning Council, Department of State
**SROKA,** Second Republic of Korea Army
**S/S,** Executive Secretariat, Department of State
**SSN,** nuclear ballistic missile submarine

**TDC,** Taiwan Defense Command
**TEA,** Trade Expansion Act
**TIAS,** United States Treaties and Other International Agreements
**TOPOL,** series indicator for telegrams from the Department of State to the Permanent Representative at the North Atlantic Council, Paris
**TOSEC,** series indicator for telegrams to the Secretary of State or his party from the Department of State

**U,** Under Secretary of State
**UK,** United Kingdom
**UN,** United Nations
**UNC,** United Nations Command
**UNCMAC,** United Nations Command, Military Armistice Commission
**UNCURK,** United Nations Commission for the Unification and Rehabilitation of Korea
**UNGA,** United Nations General Assembly
**unn,** unnumbered
**UNP,** Office of United Nations Political and Security Affairs, Bureau of International Organization Affairs, Department of State
**U/PR,** Chief of Protocol, Department of State
**USA,** United States Army
**USAF,** United States Air Force
**USARPAC,** United States Army, Pacific
**USCAR,** United States Civil Authority, Ryukyus
**USDEL,** United States Delegation
**USFK,** United States Forces in Korea

**USG,** United States Government
**USIA,** United States Information Agency
**USIB,** United States Intelligence Board
**USIS,** United States Information Service
**US MP,** U.S. Military Police
**US MPS,** United States Military Personnel
**USN,** United States Navy
**USOM,** United States Operations Mission
**USSR,** Union of Soviet Socialist Republics
**UST,** United States Treaties (series)
**USTDC,** United States Taiwan Defense Command

**ZENRO,** Japanese trade union grouping

# List of Persons

**Ainsworth, Thomas W.,** Officer in Charge of Japanese Affairs, Bureau of Far Eastern Affairs, Department of State, from August 1963

**Amory, Robert,** Deputy Director for Intelligence, Central Intelligence Agency, until March 1962

**Anderson, Admiral George W.,** USN, Chief of Naval Operations, August 1961–August 1963

**Asakai, Koichiro,** Japanese Ambassador to the United States, until winter 1963

**Bacon, Leonard L.,** Deputy Director, Office of Northeast Asian Affairs (East Asian Affairs after December 1961), Bureau of Far Eastern Affairs, Department of State, until August 1963; thereafter Acting Director

**Ball, George W.,** Under Secretary of State for Economic Affairs February–December 1961; thereafter Under Secretary of State

**Bane, David M.,** Director of the Office of Northeast Asian Affairs, Bureau of Far Eastern Affairs, Department of State, until May 1961

**Battle, Lucius D.,** Executive Secretary of the Department of State March 1961–May 1962

**Beam, Jacob D.,** Ambassador to Poland and U.S. Representative at U.S.-PRC Ambassadorial talks through November 1961

**Bell, David E.,** Director of the Bureau of the Budget January 1961–December 1962; thereafter, Administrator of the Agency for International Development

**Berger, Samuel D.,** Ambassador to Korea after June 1961

**Bohlen, Charles E.,** Special Assistant to the Secretary of State until September 1962

**Bonesteel, General Charles H.,** USA, Assistant to the Chairman of the Joint Chiefs of Staff 1960–1961; Commanding General, 7th Corps, 1961–1962; Director of Special Studies, Office of the Chief of Staff of the Army, 1963

**Bowles, Chester A.,** Under Secretary of State January–December 1961; President's Special Representative and Adviser on African, Asian, and Latin American Affairs, and Ambassador at Large, December 1961–June 1963; Ambassador to India from July 1963

**Brubeck, William H.,** Deputy Executive Secretary, Executive Secretariat, Department of State, August 1961–May 1962; Special Assistant to the Secretary of State and Executive Secretary May 1962–July 1963; thereafter, member of National Security Council staff

**Bruce, David K.E.,** Ambassador to the United Kingdom from March 1961

**Bundy, McGeorge,** Special Assistant to the President for National Security Affairs from January 1961

**Bundy, William P.,** Deputy Assistant Secretary of Defense for International Security Affairs January 1961–November 1963; thereafter, Assistant Secretary of Defense for International Security Affairs

**Burke, Admiral Arleigh A.,** USN, Chief of Naval Operations until August 1961

**Cabot, John M.,** Ambassador to Poland and U.S. Representative in U.S.-PRC Ambassadorial talks from March 1962

**Caccia, Sir Harold,** British Ambassador to the United States until October 1961

**Carter, Lieutenant General Marshall S.,** USA, Deputy Director of Central Intelligence, after April 1962

**Cary, Major General John B.,** USAF (ret.), member of the Institute for Defense Analysis

**Chang, Myon,** Prime Minister of Korea until May 1961

**Chang Yo-yong (Chang Do Young), Lieutenant General,** ROKA, Chief of Staff, Republic of Korea Army; Chairman of the Military Revolutionary Committee from May 16, 1961; Chairman of the Supreme Council for National Reconstruction until July 1961

**Chayes, Abram,** Legal Adviser, Department of State, from February 1961

**Ch'en Ch'eng,** Vice President of the Republic of China; Premier until December 1963

**Ch'en Yi (Chen Yi),** Foreign Minister of the People's Republic of China

**Chiang Ching-kuo,** General, Minister without Portfolio and Deputy Secretary General of the National Defense Council of the Republic of China

**Chiang Kai-shek,** President of the Republic of China

**Chou En-lai (Zhou Enlai),** Premier of the People's Republic of China

**Christopher, Warren,** Special Consultant to the Under Secretary of State for Economic Affairs; Chairman of the United States Delegation for Cotton Textile Negotiations held in Tokyo August 22–September 12, 1961

**Cleveland, J. Harlan,** Assistant Secretary of State for International Organization Affairs from February 1961

**Cline, Ray S.,** Central Intelligence Station Chief in Taipei until June 1962; thereafter, Deputy Director for Intelligence, Central Intelligence Agency

**Clough, Ralph N.,** Counsellor of Embassy and Deputy Chief of Mission in the Republic of China from August 1961

**Connelly, John,** Secretary of the Navy January–December 1961; Governor of Texas from January 1963

**Dean, Sir Patrick,** United Kingdom Permanent Representative at the United Nations

**De Gaulle, Charles,** President of France

**DeSilva, Peer,** Attaché and Special Assistant to the Ambassador in Korea until July 1962

**Dillon, C. Douglas,** Secretary of the Treasury from January 1961

**Dobrynin, Anatoliy,** Soviet Ambassador to the United States

**Drumright, Everett F.,** Ambassador to the Republic of China until March 1962

**Dulles, Allen W.,** Director of Central Intelligence until November 1961

**Dutton, Frederick G.,** Special Assistant to the President until November 1961; thereafter Assistant Secretary of State for Congressional Relations

**Eisenhower, Dwight D.,** President of the United States until January 20, 1961

**Fearey, Robert A.,** First Secretary of Embassy in Japan until September 1961; Officer in Charge of Japanese Affairs, Bureau of Far Eastern Affairs, Department of State, October 1961–August 1963; thereafter Acting Deputy Director of the Office of East Asian Affairs

**Felt, Admiral Harry D.,** USN, Commander in Chief, Pacific

**FitzGerald, Desmond,** Head of the Far Eastern Division, Directorate of Plans, Central Intelligence Agency

**Forrestal, Michael V.,** member of the National Security Council Staff from 1962

**Fukuda, Hajima,** Japanese Minister of International Trade and Industry from July 1962

**Fulbright, J. William,** Democratic Senator from Arkansas and Chairman of the Senate Foreign Relations Committee

**Galbraith, John Kenneth,** Ambassador to India April 1961–July 1963

**Gilpatric, Roswell L.,** Deputy Secretary of Defense from January 1961

**Grant, Lindsey,** Officer in Charge of Mainland Chinese Affairs, Office of East Asian Affairs, Bureau of Far Eastern Affairs, Department of State, from February 1962

**Green, Marshall,** Counselor and Consul General at the Embassy in Korea until November 1961; Consul General at Hong Kong until September 1963; thereafter Deputy Assistant Secretary of State for Far Eastern Affairs

**Gudeman, Eduard,** Under Secretary of Commerce, 1961–1963

**Habib, Philip C.,** Counselor for Political Affairs at the Embassy in Korea from January 1962

**Hamilton, Fowler,** Administrator of the Agency for International Development September 1961–December 1962

**Hansen, Kenneth R.,** Assistant Director, Bureau of the Budget

**Haraldson, Wesley C.,** Director of the AID Mission in Taiwan

**Harriman, W. Averell,** Ambassador at Large February–November 1961; Assistant Secretary of State for Far Eastern Affairs December 1961–April 1963; thereafter, Under Secretary of State for Political Affairs

**Heinz, Rear Admiral Luther C.,** USN, Director, Far East Region, Office of the Assistant Secretary of Defense for International Security Affairs

**Herter, Christian A.,** Secretary of State until January 20, 1961

**Hilsman, Roger, Jr.,** Director of the Bureau of Intelligence and Research, Department of State, February 1961–April 1963; thereafter Assistant Secretary of State for Far Eastern Affairs

**Holdridge, John H.,** Officer in Charge of Chinese Political Affairs, Bureau of Far Eastern Affairs, Department of State, until June 1962

**Home, Lord (Alexander Frederick Douglas),** British Foreign Secretary until October 1963

**Hood, Viscount Samuel,** Minister of the British Embassy in the United States until December 1962

**Howze, General Hamilton H.,** USA, Chief, U.S. Military Advisory Group, Korea, 1959–1961; Commander in Chief, United Nations Command, Korea, 1963

**Hughes, Thomas L.,** Deputy Director of the Bureau of Intelligence and Research, Department of State, until April 1963; thereafter Director

**Ikeda, Hayato,** Prime Minister of Japan

**Il Kwon Chung,** Korean Ambassador to the United States

**Janow, Seymour J.,** Assistant Administrator for the Far East, Agency for International Development

**Jenkins, Alfred LeS.,** Regional Planning Advisor, Bureau of Far Eastern Affairs, Department of State, until October 1961

**Johnson, Lyndon B.,** Vice President January 1961–November 1963; thereafter President

**Johnson, Robert H.,** member of the National Security Council staff until February 1962; member of the Policy Planning Council, Department of State, after August 1963

**Johnson, U. Alexis,** Deputy Under Secretary of State for Political Affairs from April 1961

**Kaysen, Carl,** member of the National Security Council staff June–December 1961; thereafter Deputy Special Assistant to the President for National Security Affairs

**Kennedy, John F.,** President of the United States January 1961–November 22, 1963

**Khrushchev, Nikita Sergeyevich,** Chairman of the Council of Ministers of the U.S.S.R. and member of the Presidium of the Supreme Soviet

**Killen, James S.,** Director, USOM Korea after August 1961

**Kim Chong-pil (Kim Chong-p'il),** Lieutenant Colonel, ROKA, Director, Korean Central Intelligence Agency until January 1963

**Kim Hong-il,** Foreign Minister of the Republic of Korea from May 1961 until sometime before November 1961

**Kim Yong-sik,** Foreign Minister of Korea from March 1963

**Kirk, Admiral Alan G.,** USN (ret.), Ambassador to the Republic of China July 1962–April 1963

**Kohler, Foy D.,** Assistant Secretary of State for European Affairs until August 1962; thereafter Ambassador to the U.S.S.R.

**Komer, Robert W.,** member of the National Security Council staff from January 1961

**Koren, Henry L.T.,** Director of the Office of Northeast Asian Affairs, Bureau of Far Eastern Affairs, Department of State, July–December 1961; thereafter Director of the Office of Southeast Asian Affairs

**Kosaha, Zentaro,** Japanese Minister of Foreign Affairs until July 1962

**Labouisse, Henry R.,** Director of the International Cooperation Administration March–October 1961

**Lemnitzer, General Lyman L.,** USA, Chairman of the Joint Chiefs of Staff until September 1962

**MacDonald, Donald S.,** Officer in Charge of Korean Affairs, Bureau of Far Eastern Affairs, Department of State, until August 1962

**Macmillan, Harold,** British Prime Minister until October 1963

**Magruder, Brigadier General Carter B.,** USA, Commander in Chief, United Nations Command, Korea, until 1961

**Manhard, Phillip W.,** Officer in Office of Korean Affairs, Bureau of Far Eastern Affairs, Department of State, until June 1962; thereafter Deputy Political Adviser to CINC-PAC

**Manning, Robert J.,** Assistant Secretary of State for Public Affairs from April 1962

**Mansfield, Michael J.,** Democratic Senator from Montana and Senate Majority Leader

**Mao Tse-tung (Mao Zedong),** Chairman of the People's Republic of China

**Martin, Edwin M.,** Assistant Secretary of State for Economic Affairs until May 1962

**Martin, Edwin W.,** Director of the Office of Chinese Affairs, Bureau of Far Eastern Affairs, Department of State, until September 1961

**McConaughy, Walter P.,** Ambassador to Korea until April 1961; Assistant Secretary of State for Far Eastern Affairs April–December 1961

**McCone, John A.,** Director of Central Intelligence from November 1961

**McGhee, George C.,** Counselor of the Department of State and Chairman of the Policy Planning Council February–December 1961; Under Secretary of State for Political Affairs December 1961–March 1963; thereafter Ambassador to the Federal Republic of Germany

**McGovern, George,** Special Assistant to the President and Director of Food for Peace 1961–1962; Democratic Senator from South Dakota from January 1963

**McNamara, Robert S.,** Secretary of Defense from January 1961

**Meloy, General Guy S.,** USA, Commander in Chief, United Nations Command, Korea, 1961–1963

**Melson, Vice Admiral Charles L.,** Commander, Taiwan Defense Command, from May 1962

**Morgan, Thomas E.,** Democratic Congressman from Pennsylvania and Chairman of the House Committee on Foreign Affairs

**Nitze, Paul H.,** Assistant Secretary of Defense for International Security Affairs January 1961–November 1963

**Norred, Christopher A.,** Officer in Charge of Korean Affairs, Office of East Asian Affairs, Bureau of Far Eastern Affairs, Department of State, after August 1962

**Ohira, Masayoshi,** Japanese Minister of Foreign Affairs from July 1962

**Pak Chung-hui (Park Chung Hee, Pak Jung-Hui), Major General,** ROKA, Deputy Commander, Second Republic of Korea Army; Deputy Chairman of the Military Revolutionary Committee, May 1961; Member of the Supreme Council for National Reconstruction, May 1961; Chairman of the Supreme Council, July 1961; Acting President of the Republic of Korea from October 1963; President after December 14, 1963

**Parsons, J. Graham,** Assistant Secretary of State for Far Eastern Affairs until March 1961

**Peterson, Avery,** Deputy Assistant Secretary of State for Far Eastern Economic Affairs until February 1963
**Popple, Paul M.,** Officer in Charge, Government of the Republic of China Affairs, Office of East Asian Affairs, Bureau of Far Eastern Affairs, Department of State, from June 1962

**Reischauer, Edwin O.,** Ambassador to Japan from April 1961
**Rhee, Syngman,** President of the Republic of Korea until April 1960
**Rice, Edward E.,** Deputy Assistant Secretary of State for Far Eastern Affairs from January 1962
**Rostow, Walt W.,** Deputy Special Assistant to the President for National Security Affairs until December 1961; thereafter Counselor of the Department of State and Chairman of the Policy Planning Council
**Rusk, Dean,** Secretary of State from January 1961

**Salans, Carl F.,** Attorney Adviser, Office of the Assistant Legal Advisor for Far Eastern Affairs, Department of State
**Sato, Eisaku,** Japanese Minister of International Trade and Industry July 1961–July 1962
**Saunders, Harold H.,** member of the National Security Council staff
**Shen Chang-huan,** Foreign Minister of the Republic of China
**Sheppard, William,** Regional Director, Office of Far Eastern Operations, International Cooperation Administration, until August 1961
**Shima, Shigenobu,** Japanese Deputy Vice Minister for Foreign Affairs, 1961–1962; Vice Minister, 1963
**Smith, Bromley,** Acting Executive Secretary of the National Security Council until August 1961; thereafter Executive Secretary
**Smoot, Vice Admiral Roland N.,** USN, Commander, Taiwan Defense Command, until May 1962
**Sneider, Richard L.,** Officer in Charge of Japanese Affairs, Office of Northeast Asian Affairs, Bureau of Far Eastern Affairs, Department of State, until August 1961
**Song Yo-chan,** Prime Minister of Korea after May 1961
**Steeves, John M.,** Deputy Assistant Secretary of State for Far Eastern Affairs until January 1962
**Stevenson, Adlai E.,** Representative to the United Nations

**Takeuchi, Ryuji,** Japanese Vice Minister of Foreign Affairs; Japanese Ambassador to the United States from 1963
**Talbot, Phillips,** Assistant Secretary of State for Near Eastern and South Asian Affairs, from April 1961
**Taylor, General Maxwell D.,** USA, President's Military Representative until October 1962; thereafter Chairman of the Joint Chiefs of Staff
**Thomson, James C., Jr.,** Special Assistant to the Under Secretary of State, April–December 1961; Special Assistant to the President's Special Representative, and Adviser on African, Asian, and Latin American Affairs, December 1961–June 1963; Special Assistant, Bureau of Far Eastern Affairs, from August 1963
**Thompson, Llewellyn E.,** Ambassador at Large from October 1962
**Trezise, Philip,** Deputy Assistant Secretary of State for Economic Affairs from October 1961
**Tsiang, Ting-fu,** Republic of China Representative at the United Nations until July 1962; Ambassador to the United States from January 1962
**Tubby, Roger W.,** Assistant Secretary of State for Public Affairs March 1961–April 1962
**Tyler, William R.,** Senior Deputy Assistant Secretary of State for European Affairs May 1961–July 1962; thereafter Assistant Secretary of State for European Affairs

**Vettel, Thelma,** Special Assistant, Office of Northeast Asian Affairs (East Asian Affairs after December 1961), Bureau of Far Eastern Affairs, Department of State, from August 1961

**Wang Ping-nan (Wang Bingnan),** Ambassador from the People's Republic of China to Poland

**Williams, G. Mennen,** Assistant Secretary of State for African Affairs from February 1961

**Wright, Admiral Jerauld,** USN (ret.), Ambassador to the Republic of China from June 1963

**Yager, Joseph A.,** Director of the Office of Chinese Affairs, Bureau of Far Eastern Affairs, Department of State, September–December 1961; Director of the Office of East Asian Affairs December 1961–August 1963; thereafter member of the Policy Planning Council

**Yeh, George K.C.,** Republic of China Ambassador to the United States until November 1961

**Yil Hyung Chyung,** Foreign Minister of Korea until May 1961

**Yun Po-sun,** President of the Republic of Korea until June 1962; candidate for President, October 1963

**Zhou Enlai,** see Chou En-lai

# China

1. Telegram From the Department of State to the Embassy in the Republic of China

Washington, January 12, 1961, 8:40 p.m.

310. Deliver following message to President Chiang, advising date time delivery.[1]

"Personal and Confidential. January 12, 1961.

Dear Mr. President:

I have read with profound appreciation the kind sentiments which you have expressed in your letter of December 14[2] regarding my work and United States assistance to the Republic of China during the past eight years. The close and fruitful relations that have existed between our two countries during this period have been a source of great gratification to me. As I made clear during my visit to Taiwan last June, I have been deeply impressed by the fortitude with which the Republic of China, under your dedicated leadership, has resisted Communist aggressive threats and pressures and by the energy and skill with which your government has moved to promote the economic and social development of Taiwan. I am proud that the United States through its military and economic assistance programs has been able to help the Republic of China develop its military and economic strength.

I am pleased to know that discussions between representatives of our two countries have continued in Taiwan in pursuance of our conversations in June and my reply to certain points raised by you at that time which was conveyed to you by Ambassador Drumright in August. In this connection I am glad to tell you that, after careful consideration of your request for the delivery of several C–130 or other transport planes, I have authorized the delivery to your Government of one C–130B at this

---

Source: Department of State, Central Files, 793.5–MSP/1–1261. Confidential; Presidential Handling. Drafted by Deputy Director of the Office of Chinese Affairs LaRue R. Lutkins; cleared by Assistant Staff Secretary to the President Colonel John S.D. Eisenhower, Deputy Assistant Secretary of State for Far Eastern Affairs John M. Steeves, and Under Secretary for Political Affairs Livingston T. Merchant; and approved by Raymond L. Perkins of the Executive Secretariat.

[1] Telegram 390 from Taipei reported that the message would be delivered to Chiang that afternoon. (Ibid., 793.5–MSP/1–1461)

[2] For text, see *Foreign Relations*, 1958–1960, vol. XIX, pp. 747–749.

time.[3] You will appreciate, I am sure, that in view of the large number of countries which look to the United States for military equipment, as well as the requirements of our own armed forces, it is difficult to make immediately available to your Government more than one of these aircraft. However, if in the light of your experience with this aircraft it should become apparent that another of the same type could be effectively utilized, I am confident that the United States Government would give serious consideration to a further request from you.

In closing, I wish to reiterate my deep admiration for a staunch and courageous ally and my hope that the friendly ties that unite the Chinese and American peoples and the solidarity of our two countries will be strengthened even further in the future.

With the Season's Greetings,

Sincerely yours,

Dwight D. Eisenhower"

Foregoing is reply to following letter from Chiang to President delivered by Chinese Embassy here:

[Here follows the text of Chiang's letter of December 14, 1960.]

White House desires text President's letter not become public.

**Herter**

---

[3] The C–130B was not sent. A memorandum of January 24, 1962, from Deputy Assistant Secretary of Defense William P. Bundy to Secretary of Defense McNamara states that the Department of State had delayed action because of "certain reservations about the probable use to which the C–130 would be put" and that arrangements were made to substitute a C–54, which was delivered on August 28. (Washington National Records Center, RG 330, Records of the Office of the Secretary of Defense, OSD Files: FRC 66 A 3542, 091 China)

---

## 2.    Editorial Note

At the 475th meeting of the National Security Council on February 1, 1961, there was some discussion pertaining to China. According to NSC Action No. 2397A, Director of Central Intelligence Allen W. Dulles noted the "serious agricultural situation in Communist China" in the course of briefing the Council on world developments. Subsequently, there was brief discussion of a possible change in U.S. policy to permit U.S. oil companies to provide bunkering to foreign ships carrying food to the People's Republic of China under Chinese charter. NSC Action No. 2397C records this as follows:

"The Council discussed a possible change in U.S. policy relating to the bunkering of Free World ships under Communist Chinese charter, provided such ships were carrying only food and paid cash. The President requested that the Secretary of State study this question further, particularly whether any such change in policy could be at the request of the Canadian Government." (Department of State, S/S–NSC (Miscellaneous) Files: Lot 66 D 95)

No other record of the discussion at this meeting has been found except handwritten notes by Joint Chiefs of Staff Chairman General Lyman L. Lemnitzer, which add nothing substantive to this. (National Defense University, Lemnitzer Papers, Box 29)

A memorandum of February 1 from Special Assistant to the President Frederick G. Dutton to President Kennedy states that Secretary of the Treasury C. Douglas Dillon was requesting the President's approval of a "State–Treasury decision to authorize U.S. oil companies to bunker ships with Chinese Communist charter carrying food from Australia, Canada and elsewhere to the Chinese mainland because of the famine." He recommended that the request should be informally denied. The memorandum reads in part as follows: "Although a decision either way on this is not critical, I conclude that the action proposed by State and Treasury (a) raises unnecessary possibilities of domestic political attack for the new Administration (without adequate countervailing advantages in a substantive sense), and (b) most decisive with me, would be a poor symbolic or actual first step toward a new policy vis-à-vis Red China. Certainly a better 'First small gesture'. . . an important consideration in a change of major controversial policy . . . could be picked than this one to presage new attitudes toward trade with Red China markets." (Kennedy Library, National Security Files, Countries Series, China) No formal request from Dillon or from Dillon and Rusk has been found.

Dutton sent a copy of his memorandum to McGeorge Bundy, the President's Special Assistant for National Security Affairs, on February 3 with a handwritten note which reads as follows:

"To Bundy—This was sent to the President at Dillon's request before and without knowledge of NSC interest in the question. The President said that all requests by U.S. companies should be denied when application by them is made. No advance announcement. Fred"

National Security Action Memorandum No. 3 from Bundy to Rusk, dated February 3, reads as follows:

"In the light of information received from the Secretary of State at the National Security Council on February 1, 1961, the President initially requested that the Department of State give further study to the question of the possible change in U.S. policy on the bunkering of free world ships under Communist Chinese charter, when such ships are carrying food and pay in cash, but on further consideration he has now indicated that in his view there should be no such change in policy at the present time." (Department of State, NSAM Files: Lot 72 D 316, NSAM 3)

## 3.     Memorandum of Conversation

Washington, February 3, 1961, 3:10–3:40 p.m.

SUBJECT

Problems Related to China

PARTICIPANTS

The Secretary
Dr. George K. C. Yeh, Ambassador, Chinese Embassy
Dr. Yi-seng Kiang, Minister Plenipotentiary, Chinese Embassy
Mr. John M. Steeves, Deputy Assistant Secretary for Far Eastern Affairs
Mr. Edwin W. Martin, Director, Office of Chinese Affairs

The Chinese Ambassador called this afternoon at the Secretary's request. After an exchange of amenities, the Ambassador said that for the sake of convenience and clarity, he had put what he wanted to say in writing; he then handed the attached informal memorandum[1] to the Secretary, indicating that it was neither a démarche nor a note.

After reading the memorandum, the Secretary said that he would like to make two points. The first was that the new Administration fully intends to meet United States commitments under the Mutual Defense Treaty[2] and to continue support under it. Secondly, it will take an interest in efforts to promote economic and social development in Taiwan and hopes to play a substantial part in them.

The Secretary went on to say with reference to the question of recognition of Communist China (which had been raised in the Ambassador's memorandum) that he could not see any prospect that this question would arise in any form which would make such a development pos-

---

Source: Department of State, Central Files, 793.00/2–361. Secret. Drafted by Martin and approved in S on February 8. The time of the meeting is from the Secretary's Appointment Book. (Johnson Library)

[1] The memorandum, headed "Remarks made by Ambassador George C. Yeh to the Secretary of State at their meeting in the State Department at 3 p.m., February 3, 1961," is not printed.

[2] For text of the Mutual Defense Treaty between the United States and the Republic of China, signed at Washington on December 2, 1954, and the related notes signed on December 10, 1954, by Secretary of State John Foster Dulles and then-Foreign Minister Yeh, see 6 UST 433.

sible. There was no indication from Peiping that the Chinese Communists were interested in bringing this about, and we ourselves had no intention of taking any initiative. As the Ambassador knew, Peiping says that the United States has to abandon his Government. We, of course, will not do that.

With regard to the problem of Chinese representation in the United Nations, the Secretary recalled that he had indicated in the hearings before the Senate Foreign Relations Committee that we faced a very complicated parliamentary situation in the United Nations.[3] It was clear, however, that support was running out for the moratorium, not only because of the admission of a great many new States, but for other reasons as well. For example, some of our Latin American friends were worried about the failure of the United Nations to recognize a de facto regime on the Chinese mainland since in Latin America there was sometimes a succession of de facto regimes. The parliamentary situation in the United Nations was complicated by the fact that with respect to the new states neither the GRC nor the United States has a great deal of political capital or influence on this issue. If the Chinese representation this year came up as a simple credentials question, our position would be technically weak, since the issue could be decided by a bare majority. The Secretary said that the Administration was assuming that the Chinese representation issue had been dealt with for the resumed General Assembly[4] and therefore had not canvassed the present voting situation thoroughly in view of other pressing matters. He asked whether Ambassador Yeh had heard anything from Ambassador Tsiang on the current voting situation.

Ambassador Yeh replied that he had been in touch with Ambassador Tsiang on this subject. It was their conclusion that the moratorium should not be given up lightly without further research into the possibilities of maintaining it through the next (16th) General Assembly. After pointing out that the Chinese had lost only one and one half votes on the moratorium in the 15th General Assembly, Ambassador Yeh acknowledged that the behavior of the African states was disturbing. Although assurances had been received from eleven African states in writing that they would support the moratorium in the 15th General Assembly, after their delegations had come to New York, and had been worked on by the Indians and by other Africans such as Sekou Toure, they had decided to abstain. They had sent a verbal note to the Chinese indicating that in their

---

[3] Rusk testified before the committee on January 12. For text of his comments on this subject, see *Nomination of Dean Rusk, Secretary of State-Designate: Hearing Before the Committee on Foreign Relations, United States Senate, Eighty-seventh Congress, First Session* (Washington, Government Printing Office, 1961), pp. 7 and 33–34.

[4] The General Assembly decided in Resolution 1493 (XV), adopted on October 8, 1960, not to consider at its 15th session any proposals on the question of Chinese representation; the resolution was adopted by a vote of 42 to 34, with 22 abstentions. For documentation concerning this issue, see *Foreign Relations, 1958–1960*, vol. II, pp. 1–463 ff.

own interests, after talking with other countries, they had decided not to take sides on this cold war issue. Ambassador Yeh emphasized, however, that his Government was working on the African countries. It had established diplomatic relations with eleven of them. There were a few Chinese Ambassadors roving about Africa with credentials in their pockets ready to establish relations in order to prevent the Chinese Communists from getting in. Moreover, a GRC agricultural mission was presently touring Africa. The Ambassador hoped that as a result of these Chinese efforts, the GRC would be able to get the support of Liberia and four or five of the former French colonies for the moratorium. He thought there would be twenty or twenty-five abstentions. Thus, it might still be possible to make a moratorium work in the next General Assembly.

The Secretary commented that the outcome might be influenced by events between now and next General Assembly, e.g., by developments in Laos or by pressures from the north into Southeast Asia. The Ambassador agreed.

Taking the Secretary's mention of Laos as his cue the Ambassador expressed the hope that the ICC would not be revived as this might bring Souvanna Phouma[5] back. The Ambassador emphasized the strategic importance of Laos, with particular reference to the security of Viet-Nam and Thailand. The Secretary agreed that it was important to prevent Laos from falling under Communist domination. The Ambassador said that while he appreciated the United States desire to obtain a broad base for its policy in Laos, he would like to point out that the free Asian countries no longer look to the French or the British, but to the United States for leadership. He felt that the French, who harbored some resentment against United States influence in Laos, do not care about keeping the Communists out of Laos. The British want peace in Laos regardless of the political trends, and believe that the Lao cannot be taught anti-Communism. The Secretary said that any shift outwards from Laos of our point of contact with the Communists would of course be disadvantageous. The Ambassador, in passing, commented that in Thailand Sarit[6] was anti-Communist, but that Pote Sarasin,[7] because of his position in SEATO, had to maintain good relations with the British and French, while the Thai Foreign Minister did not want to stick his neck out.

The Secretary said that he thought it was most unfortunate that the Chinese irregulars had come into northwest Laos from Burma. He stressed that anything which gave the Chinese Communists a pretext to intervene in Laos was not only a great disservice to Laos, but also to the mobilization of opinion in support of resistance to the Communists

---

[5] Former Prime Minister Souvanna Phouma.

[6] Thai Prime Minister Thanarat Sarit.

[7] Secretary General of the Southeast Asia Treaty Organization Pote Sarasin.

there. He asked Ambassador Yeh to tell his Government not to play that role. The Ambassador said he would report the Secretary's concern to his Government. He recalled that his Government had helped evacuate many of the irregulars several years ago.[8] The Secretary replied that he was aware of this and he also was aware that the GRC had agreed not to have any further connections with the irregulars, but unfortunately it was still supplying them by air-drop. The Ambassador said that he was aware that the GRC had air-dropped medicines and doctors to the irregulars last fall, but he was not aware of any supply of arms and ammunition. He would personally be very unhappy if he felt that such supplies were going in. However, he was certain that his Government was not pursuing a policy of sustaining and strengthening the irregulars, who were not good fighters. The Secretary said that the irregulars were not under discipline and were not an effective fighting force. They simply opened up, by their presence in the area, possibilities of counter-pressures from the Communists. Ambassador Yeh said the irregulars had been under pressure since December between the Chinese Communists and the Burmese. In connection with the demarcation of the Sino-Burma border the Burmese had given the Chinese Communists the right of hot pursuit against the irregulars. Elements of two Chinese Communist divisions had been identified in Burma.

The Secretary asked if the irregulars were not remnants of the Chinese Army. The Ambassador said they were not, but were originally in Lung Yun's[9] army in Yunnan. They had fled across the border into Burma when the Chinese Communists occupied Yunnan. Their commander, Li Mi, was not with them at the time. He subsequently went to Bangkok without the permission of the Chinese Government and had led these forces back into Yunnan, where they occupied 16 hsien. They were subsequently driven back into Burma by the Communists and were accompanied by some 75,000 men, women and children from Yunnan. The Secretary asked the Ambassador to impress upon his Government the importance of cleaning up the irregulars situation.

The Ambassador drew the attention of the Secretary to the last paragraph of his memorandum[10] and asked whether the Secretary might be

---

[8] Several thousand Chinese Nationalist irregular troops were evacuated in 1953–1954; for related documentation, see *Foreign Relations, 1952–1954*, vol. XII, Part 2, pp. 1–242 ff.

[9] Lung Yun was a former warlord in Yunnan Province.

[10] The last paragraph expressed the hope that Rusk would make a statement in the near future that U.S. policy in regard to "the China question" remained unchanged and that the United States would continue to support the position of the Republic of China internationally and in the United Nations. On February 6 in response to a question at a press conference about the Chinese representation issue, Rusk stated, "The essence of the problem is that we have strong commitments to our ally, the Government and people of Formosa: the National Government of China. That commitment is firm, and, of course, the other side looks upon that as a major obstacle."

able to make a statement on China policy in the near future. The Secretary said he thought that he had done that in the Senate hearings. He had expressed his support there for the Mutual Defense Treaty. He would, however, give further thought to the matter.

With reference to the Warsaw talks[11] (mentioned in the Ambassador's memorandum), the Secretary said there was no significance to our postponement of the talks until March.[12] We had nothing on the agenda for February, and did not think we had anything in particular to raise in March. As the Ambassador knew these talks had declined to about the same level as the meetings of the Military Staff Committee at the United Nations. The Ambassador said that he hoped that the Department could continue to keep the Chinese Embassy informed of what might transpire at the Warsaw talks.

The Ambassador said that he had the duty to convey a true picture of what was going on both to Taipei and to Washington, and he hoped the Secretary would have confidence in him so that he could perform this duty intelligently. He said that Taipei has been under some misapprehensions and he hoped that the Secretary would take an early occasion to repeat the statements he made in the Senate hearings. The Secretary said that the problem the Chinese Government faced in the United Nations was not with the United States. Ambassador Tsiang would have to continue to work hard on this problem. Ambassador Yeh mentioned that the GRC had a problem in connection with ECOSOC. The Secretary replied that he was not familiar with this particular problem, but in general he thought that the question of Chinese representation, which was a highly political issue, should be resolved in the General Assembly and the Security Council, and not in the subsidiary bodies of the United Nations.

---

[11] Reference is to the ongoing series of talks at the ambassadorial level between representatives of the United States and the People's Republic of China, which were held between August 1955 and December 1957 in Geneva and after September 1958 in Warsaw. For documentation, see *Foreign Relations, 1955–1957*, volume III and the Supplement thereto, and ibid., 1958–1960, volume XIX.

[12] Telegram 781 to Warsaw, January 26, instructed the Embassy to request postponement of the meeting scheduled for February 2 until March 7. Telegram 1064 from Warsaw, January 28, reported that the Chinese had agreed to the postponement. (Department of State, Central Files, 611.93/1–2661 and 611.93/1–2861, respectively)

4.   Memorandum From the Assistant Secretary of State for Far
     Eastern Affairs (Parsons) to Secretary of State Rusk

Washington, February 19, 1961.

SUBJECT

Review of Warsaw Ambassadorial-Level Talks and Suggested Approaches to
Chinese Communists at Forthcoming Meetings

In my memorandum of January 24 (Tab C),[1] I stated that FE would
prepare for you a study summarizing the recent course of the ambassadorial-level talks in Warsaw between the United States and the Chinese
Communists, together with suggestions for possible ways in which we
might proceed in forthcoming meetings. The promised summary
(broadened to include a brief review of all major developments which
have occurred since bilateral talks began in June 1954) and the suggestions on possible approaches in forthcoming meetings are transmitted
herewith (Tabs A and B, respectively).[2]

In my opinion the over-all review of the record demonstrates that
Peiping has not regarded the ambassadorial-level meetings primarily as
a channel in which to adjust differences with us through genuine negotiations, but rather as a vehicle for demanding major political concessions
from us—first, the withdrawal of United States forces from the Taiwan
area, and to a lesser extent, the granting of some form of de facto United
States diplomatic recognition to the Peiping regime—as the price for any
concessions on its part. Our own immediate objectives have been much
less: namely, securing the release of American prisoners and an agreement renouncing the use of force. When it became evident to the Peiping
regime in the latter part of 1955 that we were not prepared to pay its price,
Communist China simply ceased to honor the sole agreement reached in
the talks (a commitment by each side to release "expeditiously" all

---

Source: Department of State, Central Files, 611.93/2–1961. Secret. Drafted by Officer
in Charge of Chinese Political Affairs John H. Holdridge.

[1] The tabs are not attached to the source text. In the reference memorandum, not
printed, Parsons suggested postponing the next ambassadorial meeting in Warsaw from
February 2 to March 7 so that Rusk could have time to review the course of the talks and
determine what use he wished to make of this channel. (Ibid., 611.93/6–3061)

[2] Neither printed. Tab A was a summary of bilateral talks. Tab B discussed possible
approaches for the talks. In case a decision was made to introduce new subjects for discussion, it suggested probing the Chinese position on disarmament and nuclear control,
sounding out the Chinese reaction to a possible U.S. offer of food assistance, and introducing the topic of an interchange of scholars. It also suggested reintroducing the issue of a
possible exchange of newsmen, noted that progress on the issue of renunciation of force
was unlikely, and recommended raising the issue of the five U.S. civilians imprisoned in
China and U.S. military personnel missing since the Korean conflict as a matter of record
although it was not expected that discussion would be fruitful.

detained personnel of the other side) and became increasingly intransigent in its insistence that no improvement in its relations with the United States could be effected except on its terms. In particular, I call your attention to Peiping's statement of September 13, 1960[3] that it will no longer discuss "minor matters," but will devote itself to such "fundamental issues" as securing United States consent to "withdraw all its armed forces from China's territory Taiwan and the Taiwan Strait area."

Nevertheless, it is my belief that despite the rigid and hostile stance of the Chinese Communists, we have derived the following distinct political and psychological gains from the talks:

1. We have been able to cite to United States and world public opinion that we are not "ignoring 650 million people," as has frequently been charged, but have actually been dealing with the Chinese Communists on a regular basis on matters of common concern. (Unfortunately, the effectiveness of this argument has been watered down by the obvious sterility of our exchanges with the Chinese Communists over the last two years.)

2. As a result of long and patient negotiations with the Chinese Communists on various issues, we have been able to an appreciable extent to place the onus for the tense relations between the United States and Communist China where it belongs, on the Chinese Communists themselves. For example, the talks have aided greatly in publicizing the Peiping regime's detention of five American prisoners in contravention of its commitment to release all such persons. The record has also helped emphasize the fact that Peiping in effect demands the surrender of Taiwan in return for any improvement in Sino-American relations, and has made it plain to interested parties, especially journalists, that the Chinese Communists are adamantly opposed to the admission of American newsmen to the China mainland under conditions which would permit objective reporting on conditions there.

3. The talks have apparently acted as a partial damper on Chinese Communist military actions against Taiwan, i.e., since August 1955 Peiping has resorted to force in the Taiwan Strait area only during a period when the talks were not in session, and the subject of renunciation of force was not being actively pursued by us. After having failed to gain Kinmen (Quemoy) through its attacks of August–September 1958, Peiping then took the initiative in proposing that the meetings be resumed.

4. The continuation of the talks minimizes the chance of third parties' attempting to set themselves up as middlemen between Peiping and ourselves, thereby further complicating our relations with the regime.

5. The talks constitute a direct, private means of communications between the United States and Communist China which we have been able to use to bring up a wide array of topics, even after the Chinese Com-

---

[3] For text, see *Peking Review*, September 14, 1960.

munists released the statement mentioned above refusing to discuss "minor matters." (In my judgment, for all practical purposes we can disregard Peiping's statement, and my view is shared by Ambassador Beam in Warsaw.)

This last feature of the talks is one which could be of considerable significance to United States policy interests. Should the Chinese Communists ever moderate their hostility toward the United States and sincerely seek to adjust the differences between us, the private nature of the talks might well facilitate progress by obviating any loss of "face" to the regime through such a reversal. By like token, if we ourselves should desire to sound out the Chinese Communist attitude and intentions regarding major world issues (including disarmament and nuclear control), or expand our efforts to find reasonable grounds for an understanding with the Peiping regime, the ambassadorial-level contact provides us with a convenient, rapid, and entirely confidential channel to the leaders of that regime. In my mind these factors alone amply justify continuation of the talks quite apart from the other advantages I have cited. Conversely, cessation of the talks would probably be interpreted by world opinion and by the Chinese Communists themselves as a negative gesture betokening a United States unwillingness to seek settlement of its disputes with Peiping by peaceful negotiations. In the psychological as well as practical sense, we are certainly in a better position vis-à-vis the Chinese Communists with the talks still continuing than we would otherwise be.

Admittedly little of a substantive nature has been gained in the most recent phase of the talks, but I do not feel that we should assess the value of the meetings solely in terms of what tangible results are gained. Moreover, it is conceivable that your assumption of office may provide the Chinese Communists with a justification for responding more positively to our overtures, whether on matters already under discussion or on entirely new subjects. It is in this light that I have appended the list of suggested topics and approaches for use in forthcoming meetings (Tab B) for your comment or approval. The next meeting is now scheduled for March 7, and I would greatly appreciate having your views on the conduct of the talks far enough in advance so that draft instructions can be prepared and cleared with the Departmental offices concerned.[4]

---

[4] A February 21 memorandum from Under Secretary Chester Bowles to Rusk reads as follows:

"On the basis of FE's presentation, I recommend that the Warsaw talks be continued provided the Chinese Communists are willing to continue these conversations without insisting upon immediate discussion of the so-called "fundamental issues." It seems that the conversations provide certain minor advantages to us at the present time and might be even more useful in the future. However, I think it is obvious that we are not prepared at this moment to discuss with the Chinese Communists such matters as the status of Taiwan, disarmament and nuclear controls, etc."

## 5.    Telegram From the Department of State to the Embassy in the Republic of China

Washington, February 22, 1961, 8:07 p.m.

401. For Ambassador from Secretary. Ref [*less than 1 line of source text not declassified*] messages dated February 19 and 20 from Taipei.[1]

Please see President Chiang at earliest practicable moment and impress upon him utmost seriousness USGov regarding KMT irregulars in Burma and Laos.

1. It is imperative that GRC make immediate arrangements to evacuate all KMT personnel who are willing to return to Formosa, especially those who were transported into area with GRC assistance during past three years. Further, all irregulars unwilling return Formosa should be disarmed and resettled as civilians to small groups in any neighboring country other than Laos willing to receive them. Maintenance and identity as a large organized group must cease.

2. USGov would consider it a major infraction of expressed and implicit obligations of GRC to USGov if supplies of US origin are henceforth furnished KMT irregulars by US type aircraft.

3. Recent activities GRC regarding these irregulars, contrary to earlier understanding that GRC would accept no further responsibility for personnel not evacuated in 1953–54, plus failure GRC to inform USGov of such activities imposes a severe strain on hitherto friendly relations between our two countries.

4. We find it incomprehensible that GRC should recklessly create situation which imposes upon itself formidable international political burdens at time when it can least afford them. Further such action severely

---

Source: Department of State, Central Files 793.551/2–2261. Top Secret; Niact; Eyes Only. Drafted by Rusk and approved by Parsons. According to a memorandum of February 21 from Director of the Department of State Executive Secretariat Walter J. Stoessel, Jr., to Ralph A. Dungan of the White House staff, this telegram was sent as a result of a discussion that morning between Rusk and Kennedy. At Rusk's suggestion, Stoessel attached a February 20 memorandum from Rusk to Kennedy, enclosing a paper entitled "United States Efforts To Effect Cessation of Government of Republic of China's Support of Chinese Irregulars in Burma–Laos Border Area." (Kennedy Library, National Security Files, Countries Series, China)

[1] The February 19 message, not found, is summarized in the paper cited in the source note. It reported that in response to earlier representations by the Ambassador on the subject, President Chiang had offered to withdraw all Chinese military forces from Burma but wanted the irregulars in Laos to remain there. The February 20 message from [*text not declassified*] in Taipei [*text not declassified*] reported that he had told General Chiang Ching-kuo that day that this would not be acceptable and had urged repatriation of the irregulars from both Burma and Laos; Chiang Ching-kuo argued against this in the "angriest" and "most heated" exchange [*text not declassified*] had ever had with him. The message is filed with a covering note of February 21 [*text not declassified*] to Military Aide to the President Brigadier General Chester V. Clifton. (Ibid.)

limits any effective political help which USGov might be able render to GRC in its difficult situation.

5. USGov will not bargain with respect to reabsorption KMT personnel in Formosa but would be willing to ask assistance other necessary governments regarding arrangements to liquidate problem.

6. USGov must enter reservations to GRC's denial that arms equipment or supplies furnished to GRC for other purposes were improperly used pending results further investigation.

7. GRC must be aware that other nations will hold US directly responsible for GRC actions in this situation in view of close military and other relationships between our two countries. GRC must understand that USGov is determined to protect its reputation and good faith and will, if necessary, do so at cost of GRC. USGov is considering steps it might take to reduce cooperation with GRC in order make clear its complete disassociation from these activities but believes that most effective solution would be steps taken publicly and vigorously by GRC to liquidate situation. This would be better solution for both.

8. USGov hopes that this serious threat to otherwise good relations will not be permitted to continue; we would find it difficult to believe that GRC would underestimate gravity of problem and fail to act with greatest vigor.

FYI. Greatly appreciate your previous strenuous efforts this matter. If position outlined above sounds severe, it is intended to be. GRC would make serious miscalculation if it supposes we would not back it up. End FYI.

**Rusk**

## 6.    Memorandum of Conversation

Washington, February 24, 1961, 1–2:45 p.m.

SUBJECT

   China

PARTICIPANTS

   The President
   Prime Minister Menzies of Australia
   Ambassador Beale of Australia
   The Secretary of State
   Assistant Secretary of State Parsons

Referring to his conversation in Secretary Rusk's office,[1] the Prime Minister went over much of the same ground. He expressed his concern that the moratorium was no longer a useful device for dealing with the question of Chinese representation in the United Nations. Speaking in anticipation of his visit to the United Kingdom for the Commonwealth Conference, he mentioned that down the line in the Foreign Office he felt there was disregard of the Chinese Nationalists and that this colored British attitudes. The Secretary and the President both referred to recent public statements, notably by Lord Home, and it was intimated that it would be helpful if the British refrained as much as possible from public expressions prior to consultation with us. There had not been opportunity for such discussions yet.

Prime Minister Menzies made it clear that in his view Formosa should not be abandoned. Secretary Rusk again mentioned that the issue should be dealt with, not as a matter of credentials, but of membership. Mr. Menzies reiterated that regardless of our views on the substance of the problem, it was even more important that the United States not suffer defeat and isolation on this matter.

The President several times mentioned the deep feeling which the Chinese issue engendered here, saying that it extended broadly throughout both parties. It should not be dealt with in such a way as to cause

---

Source: Department of State, Presidential Memoranda of Conversation: Lot 66 D 149. Secret; Limit Distribution. Drafted by Parsons and approved by S and by the White House on March 27. The meeting was held at the White House. The source text records only the discussion of China. A memorandum of the entire conversation is filed with a covering memorandum of March 2 from Stoessel to Dungan. (Ibid., Central Files, 033.4311/3–261)

[1] According to a memorandum of this conversation, Menzies suggested that they consider some sort of package proposal, which might include a seat for the Chinese Communists in the General Assembly and in the Security Council, with a separate independent existence and seat in the General Assembly for the Chinese Nationalists. Rusk stated that it would be "disastrous" for the United States and the United Nations to treat the China issue as a credentials question. (Ibid., 793.00/2–2461)

harmful divisions and controversy here. He alluded to former President Eisenhower's strong feeling and continued interest in this subject. The President also said that were Communist China to be seated in the United Nations, American support for the United Nations might very well be forfeit. These points, effect on the United States and effect on the United Nations, which we desired to support, were basic in the President's thinking on this subject. Were it not necessary for these reasons strongly to oppose the Chinese Communists, who maintained an attitude of hostility to the new administration, the admission of Red China would be relatively a matter of indifference. No one was doing very well with the Communist Chinese in their present isolation. However, so far as our own bilateral situation was concerned, there was no intention to recognize Communist China, which, for its part, was in no mood to deal with us except on its terms.

There was discussion of the Chinese irregulars in Burma, a problem which was viewed in the context of Chiang Kai-shek's preoccupation with a return to the mainland. None of those present thought that he was likely to give up this mystical aim. Also discussed was the question of the effect on the Chinese minorities in southeast Asian countries if Communist China were to gain admission to the United Nations. Mr. Menzies thought this effect would be less, and perhaps manageable, if the Republic of China on Formosa were maintained as a country in being with support from our side. The President expressed interest in learning on what other occasions the Chinese Communists had expressed themselves, as Chou En-lai had to Edgar Snow, against the two Chinas thesis. He was told that this was a longstanding and constantly reiterated position.

Prime Minister Menzies pointed out that the China issue was not just a question between the two blocs — it was a conflict between two sets of ideas that were fundamentally different. In this context it involved everyone — not just the major powers. He reiterated that, right or wrong, in Australian opinion, Australia would support the United States position, as it did not wish to see the United States defeated or isolated on this. In the context of further statement by the President of our determination not to permit abandonment of the Republic of China and to take a strong position against the admission of Communist China to the United Nations, Mr. Menzies asked if he could quote the Secretary to the British to this effect. He thought perhaps the President should be left "above these storms." The President nodded agreement to Mr. Rusk's suggestion that it would be useful for Prime Minister Macmillan to know privately that these were the President's views as well as his own. Mr. Menzies said it would be most useful for him to be able to speak in this vein in London.

## 7.    Telegram From the Embassy in the Republic of China to the Department of State

Taipei, February 25, 1961, 9 p.m.

513. For Secretary. Deptels 401[1] and 412 and Embtel 510.[2] President Chiang summoned me to his residence at 5 p.m. today. Foreign Minister was present. President was calm in attitude and conciliatory in approach.

President started by saying that Foreign Minister had reported in detail to him yesterday on my representations of same date to Foreign Minister. President went on to say relations and cooperation between China and US had heretofore been as close and harmonious as possible. Nothing should be done, he said, by one country to cause harm to the other or to make difficulties. If any difficulty arose it was up to two governments to make adjustments and for each to help the other.

President then said that when I had made previous representations (February 7),[3] irregulars were in midst of engagements with Burmese and ChiCom forces. He believed at time no harm was being done to US interests. Moreover, attempts at that time to evacuate irregulars would have affected fighting spirit and morale of forces. In view of these factors, President said he felt at time he could do or say nothing regarding evacuation. President added hatred of irregulars for ChiComs was such, his attempts at that time to persuade irregulars to withdraw would have been to no avail. What was true of irregulars was true of all patriotic Chinese civilian and military alike—a common hatred of and enmity for ChiComs.

President continued as follows: But after irregulars withdrew from Mong Pa Liao and more particularly after plane incident in northern Thailand on February 15,[4] he for first time realized situation was actually causing inconvenience and embarrassment to US. GRC had therefore ceased airdrops thereafter. He had felt bad after Burmese and ChiComs

---

Source: Department of State, Central Files, 793.551/2–2561. Top Secret; Priority; Eyes Only.

[1] Document 5.

[2] Telegram 510 from Taipei, February 24, reported that when Ambassador Drumright requested an appointment with President Chiang, Foreign Minister Shen told him Chiang was busy. Drumright gave Shen the substance of telegram 401 in the hope that this would prepare Chiang for swift action and make the confrontation less embarrassing. (Department of State, Central Files, 793.551/2–2661) Telegram 412 to Taipei, February 24, directed Drumright to renew his request to see the President personally. (Ibid., 611.93/2–2461)

[3] Reported in telegrams 459 and 461 from Taipei, February 7 and 8. (Ibid., 751J.00/2–761 and 751J.00/2–861)

[4] A Chinese Nationalist plane apparently seeking to drop supplies to irregular units in Burma was shot down by Burmese fighter aircraft on February 15 and crashed on the Thai side of the border; see the paper cited in the source note, Document 5.

had seized opportunity to embarrass US. He was especially sorry about demonstrations before US Embassy in Rangoon.

President then said GRC is prepared to evacuate "those elements responsive to our influence" to Taiwan since their presence where they now are is of no benefit to GRC and a cause of embarrassment to US. But there was one matter of which US Government should be aware: There are irregulars not responsive to GRC orders. With regard to such elements, GRC will disassociate itself from and no longer supply them. President then said inasmuch as such elements may want to continue struggle, they may refuse to disarm.

President summed up that foregoing was what he had decided to do. As to arrangements, he said details would be subject to discussions between two governments. He said he would look to US Government for assistance in carrying out arrangements. He concluded his statement with request that I promptly take up implementing details with Foreign Ministry.

I thanked President for his response which I knew to be painful and difficult one, adding I thought it appropriate to our requirements. I said I was at disposal of Foreign Ministry to help in working out evacuation. I urged speed in implementation of evacuation and asked President to use his influence to get greatest number to lay down arms. He responded faster evacuation carried out the better but repeated what he had said earlier about determination of some irregulars to fight on no matter what he might say or do. I also suggested early GRC discussions with Laos and Thailand and he said these would be taken care of.[5]

After concluding with President, I had a conversation with Foreign Minister who leaves February 27 for visit of about one week's duration to Korea and Japan.

Minister Shen stated he had gone to see President yesterday as soon as he could put into Chinese representations I had made to him yesterday (he took them down almost verbatim). After a long discussion with President, Shen and several high officials including President's Secretary General Chang Chun and President's son Chiang Ching-kuo had met until 2 a.m. to hammer out recommendations for President. Shen had reported early this morning to Vice President-Premier and then had met

---

[5] A report of a similar conversation with Chiang Ching-kuo was sent to President Kennedy with a covering memorandum of February 25 from Allen Dulles. (Kennedy Library, President's Office Files, China, Security 1961)

for further long session with President. It was not until 1 p.m. that President had taken decision he communicated to me at 5 p.m.[6]

Shen said to his knowledge this was first time President had ever acknowledged irregulars in Burma were of no benefit to GRC cause. He said he was sure President meant what he said and would sincerely cooperate to return to Taiwan those willing to come back. He was also certain no further attempt would be made to supply irregulars who choose to remain behind.

Shen was obviously relieved and pleased with outcome of what has been until recently an obscure nightmare to him. I believe he played an important role in bringing President around and I congratulated him warmly.

I asked Shen if he had any idea what cooperation would be required of us and he said he frankly could not say. He said he had been so busy working on President he had not yet had time to give implementing measures thought. He seemed to agree orders would have to go to irregulars through military channels and he appeared to think this would be done through hands of Chiang Ching-kuo. He also agreed GRC would find it necessary to discuss evacuation and asylum problems with Lao and Thai Governments but said proposals would require some thought and care.

In response to my urging that speedy implementation be undertaken, Shen intimated Chiang Ching-kuo would be instrumental in this regard. He suggested in his absence I keep in touch with Vice Foreign Minister Hsu and perhaps Chiang Ching-kuo. At close of conversations Shen urged that both governments exercise greatest care regarding publicity. Apparently having in mind assurances made in 1953 and 1954, he said he believed both governments should avoid statements harmful to other and which could give comfort to Communists who would do all in their power to create difficulty and embarrassment. In this regard, Shen also obviously had in mind difficulty GRC would have in ever admitting it had sent forces or arms to Burma in violation of earlier pledges. I believe GRC is hopeful public statements regarding disarming and evacuation of irregulars be kept to absolute minimum. I hope we can meet GRC wishes in this respect.

---

[6] An unsigned memorandum for the record, March 31, states that when Rusk's message (see Document 5) arrived in Taipei on February 23, Drumright showed it to [text not declassified], who had been discussing the subject regularly with Chiang Ching-kuo, and asked him to convey the seriousness of the U.S. demand to Chiang Ching-kuo, in the hope that he might persuade his father to agree without a difficult confrontation or loss of face. The memorandum states that Drumright and [text not declassified] agreed the use of this procedure, involving close cooperation between them, was the best way to get U.S. views, especially unpalatable ones, to Chiang Kai-shek without the embarrassment and formality of diplomatic admonitions by the Ambassador. (Kennedy Library, National Security Files, Countries Series, China)

We recognize here only first step has been surmounted and we face a long and rocky road to completion of implementation of President's new assurances. I propose to press matters through Foreign Ministry and Chiang Ching-kuo where necessary. I would of course appreciate Department's guidance in fulfilling this task.

I assume Department will inform Vientiane, Bangkok and Rangoon as appropriate of developments reported in this message. Successful evacuation and/or resettlement will be dependent in considerable measure on level of cooperation accorded by Lao and Thai Governments.

**Drumright**

## 8.    Memorandum From Robert W. Komer of the National Security Council Staff to the President's Special Assistant for National Security Affairs (Bundy)

Washington, March 1, 1961.

SUBJECT

Quick Thoughts on China

Let's face it; China problems may not wait for careful, leisurely review. With new UN session coming up, with Brazil wavering, with test ban talks resuming they may begin hitting us all too soon.

Hence, as I see it we should prod State to get started pronto on broad-scale rethinking exercise. Perhaps "task force" approach useful here. Do mention 5–10 year focus.[1]

As to publicity, since it almost inevitable that we'll have to change some aspects our China policy, shouldn't we give a few public hints we're rethinking now, lest we later look like being dragged into such changes, with resultant loss of favorable impact on rest of world. I realize Congressional and US[2] reaction a real problem here but this will be just as great later as now.

My own horseback guess is we must disengage, as skillfully as we can, from unproductive aspects our China policy, e.g., UN membership

---

Source: Kennedy Library, National Security Files, Countries Series, China. Secret. Also sent to Deputy Special Assistant to the President Walt W. Rostow.

[1] This sentence is handwritten on the source text.

[2] The letters "US" are handwritten on the source text in the place of the letters "VP", which are crossed out.

where we're likely to get clobbered and later on Offshores in order ratio-nalize our posture for long term struggle with hard-line CPR.

If we move soon we may be able get UK, India, etc. buy enough of a "two Chinas" policy to make Peiping refuse UN membership, thus gain-ing us credit for being reasonable while shifting onus to intransigeant CPR.

This one is going to be painful as hell to us. But I'm convinced that, with due regard to domestic political realities and importance preserv-ing Taiwan asset, the longer we wait the more painful (and costly) its going to be.[3]

**Bob K.**

---

[3] Komer elaborated his views in a 41-page paper, dated April 7 and entitled "Strategic Framework for Rethinking China Policy." It recommended "a middle road, aimed at the existing goal of long-run containment of the CPR" and called for "greater tactical flexibility, and disengagement from the least productive aspects of our China policy in order to ratio-nalize it for the long pull." It recommended acceptance of PRC membership in the United Nations "if we can't keep it out and can exact a satisfactory price" and Nationalist with-drawal from the offshore islands. (Ibid.)

---

## 9.    Memorandum of Conversation

Washington, March 3, 1961, 1–3 p.m.

SUBJECT

China

PARTICIPANTS

The President
Secretary Rusk
Prime Minister Holyoake of New Zealand
Mr. McIntosh, Secretary for External Affairs of New Zealand
Assistant Secretary Parsons
Mr. White, The Chargé d'Affaires, a.i.

The President opened this subject with a reference to recent public British statements bearing on the Chinese representation matter, a sub-ject which we had not yet had opportunity to discuss in depth privately

---

Source: Department of State, Central Files, 793.00/3–361. Secret. Drafted by Parsons and approved in the White House on March 27. The meeting was held at the White House. A memorandum of conversation between Prime Minister Holyoake and Secretary Rusk is ibid.

with the British. He emphasized that however the matter might be handled in the United Nations, it was important to assure that there be no abandonment of the Republic of China on Formosa. Referring to the loss of support for the moratorium procedure, the President said that in connection with the other means of handling this question there were three important dangers from the American viewpoint which must be avoided.

First, the matter must be dealt with in such a way as not to cause loss of support in this country for the United Nations, which could be the outcome if the Chinese Communists were to gain admission. Second, China questions must be dealt with in such a way as not to cause deep divisions within our nation, and he mentioned former President Eisenhower's strong views on the China question and the risks that a national debate on the subject might entail, including the risk of mounting isolationist sentiment. Third, he pointed out the damage which would be done to United States prestige if we were to suffer a defeat on this issue and implied that a weakening of United States leadership would have most unfortunate effects not only within this country but abroad in the free world as well. He emphatically agreed with a remark that along the periphery of Asia a weakening of the United States position or a defeat could have the most serious repercussions as respects the continued independence of the smaller countries, which, of course, would affect the security of other nations as well.

The President said that he thought of the China issue in terms of United States national interest and he was not particularly concerned by legalisms or theory in relation to the China problem. He had come into office with perhaps a more open mind on this issue and had been prepared to take such steps as might be possible to bring about a less tense atmosphere and to make it possible to seek some sort of a developing relationship. If he had found that there were, in fact, possibilities, he would have been prepared to tackle the very deepseated and emotional opposition throughout this country from such groups as the Committee of One Million,[1] because he felt that if he could show that new steps were in the national interest they would be accepted in the end and that they would be the right thing. However, it quickly became apparent that the Chinese Communists were just as hostile to the new administration as they were to the old, and were attacking him personally already. Their attitude indicated that they did not wish to be on better terms with us but preferred to maintain an intransigeant position. The possibilities, therefore, seemed very limited indeed. Thus, the United States position

---

[1] Reference is to The Committee of One Million Against the Admission of Communist China to the United Nations. Numerous petitions that the committee sent to Congress in the spring and summer of 1961 to be forwarded to the White House are in Department of State, Central File 303.

remained substantially unchanged and certainly there was no question at all of diplomatic recognition.

Mr. McIntosh inquired whether there was any interest here in an idea emphasized in the London *Economist*, of using Japan to explore some approach for better relations with Communist China, thus avoiding a direct commitment of United States prestige. The President answered in the negative and commented briefly on the Japanese position, which was one of desiring some sort of relation with its neighbor, China, but not at the risk of alienating the United States and impairing Japan's security. The President went on to indicate that we were going to make some limited exploratory gestures such as by raising the question of exchange of journalists in the Warsaw talks but we had to recognize that all the indications were that the Chinese Communists were not willing to take a position which could facilitate a solution of major questions such as the Chinese representation issue.

Prime Minister Holyoake wondered whether the question would get any easier with the passage of time and whether we might not have to recognize early in the new administration that the seating of the Chinese Communists would have to be faced. The President replied that this would depend on what the consequences might be in terms of our national interest and particularly the effect on Formosa and the Asian countries. If it were worthwhile, he would, he replied, be willing to face this difficult issue domestically. He referred in this connection to the strength of feeling in Congress among members of both parties.

---

## 10.    Telegram From the Department of State to the Embassy in Poland

Washington, March 4, 1961, 8:43 p.m.

931. Following is guidance for 103rd meeting:

1. Begin your presentation with following prepared statement: "Mr. Ambassador, since last meeting a new administration has taken over

---

Source: Department of State, Central Files, 611.93/3–461. Confidential; Limit Distribution. Drafted by Holdridge, except paragraph 6, which was drafted by Robert G. Sturgill of the Disarmament Administration; cleared by Parsons and cleared in draft in the Bureau of Security and Consular Affairs, the Bureau of Public Affairs, the Legal Adviser's Office, the Disarmament Administration, and the Department of Defense; approved for transmission and signed by Rusk. A memorandum of March 2 from Parsons to Rusk enclosing the draft telegram for his approval states that it was drafted in accordance with Rusk's oral comments to Parsons on his February 19 memorandum (Document 4).

conduct of affairs of United States Government. This administration is firmly committed to cause of freedom. It also recognizes that far-reaching differences exist between basic concepts of our two sides. Developments such as statement issued December 6, 1960 following 'Moscow Conference of Representatives of Communist and Workers' Parties,' and in particular official comments issued by your side since January 20 criticizing new United States administration, have made us even more aware of basic differences between us. In all frankness we are not encouraged by lack of civility displayed by your side toward United States and its government. Nevertheless, for our part we are willing to overlook what your side has said and follow procedure of discussing differences between us in manner which would avoid mutual recrimination and be more conducive to cause of peace. We believe that if your side will follow suit, these discussions can then deal with specific points in ways which would accord with best interests our two sides."

2. Continue along lines that in our view most productive first step toward improving conduct of talks would be to resolve problem of Americans imprisoned by Wang's side. As Wang may have observed, USSR's release of American airmen held by it[1] has helped bring about climate of civility between US and USSR. Although we do not underestimate extent of basic differences dividing us, we regard this climate of civility as being preferable to one of rancor and bitterness, and as opening up possibility for improvement in US-USSR relations. If Wang's side can deal with matter of imprisoned Americans in spirit similar to that of USSR, practical obstacle to better relations between Wang's side and ours can be eliminated.

3. Tell Wang that further step toward improving relations between our two sides would be his side's admission of American newsmen. Remind Wang that his side did not interpose question of agreed announcement in admitting Edgar Snow, who had validated passport issued by United States Government. We would be pleased to see his side admit in same fashion any or all of remaining newsmen who are eligible receive such passports, and to facilitate process of selection will provide him with complete list of newsmen who as of this moment have been designated by their organizations to make trip. (At this point hand Wang newsmen list, as transmitted in separate telegram.)[2] Invite Wang provide us with list of his side's correspondents who desire entry into United States, and assure him that we will take under immediate consideration the issuance of visas to these individuals once they apply. You may tell

---

[1] Reference is to the release on January 25 of two members of the crew of a U.S. RB–47 aircraft, which had been shot down on July 1, 1960.

[2] Telegram 930 to Warsaw, March 4. (Department of State, Central Files, 611.93/3–461)

Wang that in this way we believe arrangement can be worked out whereby his side's correspondents can be admitted to United States in numbers which would be equal to number of American newsmen admitted by his side. Foregoing approach intended satisfy Wang's side's insistence on reciprocity while at same time honoring United States immigration laws, which must, of course, be complied with. In our judgment this approach provides simple and workable means of effecting travel of newsmen, and we urge Wang's side give it full consideration.

4. In event Wang raises question of Taiwan and reiterates call for United States withdrawal, mention that throughout history of talks we have never sought to compel his side abandon its claim to Taiwan. We have attempted only to gain his side's agreement to press its claim by peaceful means rather than by threat or use of force. Accordingly, renunciation of force is fundamental ingredient in any constructive and meaningful discussions between us on this issue, and our past position this subject remains unchanged.

5. Conceivable that Wang may raise topic of food shortages on China mainland and accuse United States of attempting magnify situation for propaganda purposes. If so, cite press conference remarks President Kennedy January 25 to effect that United States has no intention of offering food merely to make propaganda efforts.[3] However, in case there is serious desire for food or need for food on part of Wang's side, then United States would be glad to consider answering need. If people's lives are involved, United States will always do what it can to help on purely humanitarian grounds. (Conversely, in unlikely contingency that Wang should actually express interest in receiving United States food aid, inform him you will refer any request for same to Department.)

6. In unlikely event that Wang should raise subject of nuclear test negotiations, respond as follows:

If Wang should depose a formal statement on an agreement to discontinue testing you should refer to continuing interest of United States Government in disarmament in all its aspects and accept statement, with an indication that it will be transmitted to Washington for study. If Wang should inquire generally about progress of negotiations you should respond in general terms that negotiations are to resume on March 21 and that we are hopeful that Soviet concessions to permit adequate on-site inspection and other features of effective control will make possible

---

[3] Kennedy stated that if there was both a desire and a need for food, "the United States would be glad to consider that need, regardless of the source." He added, however, that the Chinese Communists had recently been exporting food and had been expressing "a rather belligerent attitude" toward the United States. The President concluded: "there is no indication, direct or indirect, private or public, that they would respond favorably to any acts by the United States." For text of these remarks, see *Public Papers of the Presidents of the United States: John F. Kennedy, 1961*, p. 15.

an early agreement on suspension of testing as envisaged in joint US-UK declaration of March 29, 1960.[4]

In very unlikely event that Wang should raise question of applicability of an agreement to Peiping we should refer to United States draft treaty article which provides for the accession of additional states "whose accession the (Control) Commission or Preparatory Commission finds would contribute to the achievement of the purposes of the treaty and which deposits an instrument of ratification or an instrument of acceptance in accordance with the provisions" of the treaty. We should refer also to our position on phasing of installation of system, according to which control posts would be extended to all of Asia exclusive of the USSR in a second phase to begin within one year after the treaty enters into force and to be completed within five years after treaty enters into force.

If Wang should raise question of an atom-free zone in Far East we should, without disclosing any particular United States interest in such a zone, try to ascertain what part, if any, of the Chinese mainland they would propose to include in such a zone.

7. Counter any charges raised by Wang to extent you deem necessary, using guidance or procedures employed in previous instructions.

**Rusk**

---

[4] For text of this declaration, see *Public Papers of the Presidents of the United States: Dwight D. Eisenhower, 1960–61*, pp. 318–319.

---

## 11.     Telegram From the Embassy in Poland to the Department of State

Warsaw, March 7, 1961, 5 p.m.

1254. Beam–Wang Talks. 103rd meeting one hour 25 minutes.[1]

Wang led off in brief mild statement with reference to fact this was first meeting of new year and that new administration had assumed

---

Source: Department of State, Central Files, 611.93/3–761. Confidential; Niact; Limit Distribution. Repeated to London, Moscow, and Hong Kong.

[1] Beam sent recommendations for the next meeting in telegram 1255, March 7, commented on the March 7 meeting in telegram 1262, March 8, and sent a detailed, apparently verbatim report of the meeting in airgram G–351, March 10. (Department of State, Central Files, 611.93/3–761, 611.93/3–861, and 611.93/3–1061, respectively)

office in US. Said despite lack of progress past five years hoped US Government now prepared make new constructive proposals. All that was needed to improve relations was for US to withdraw from armed occupation of Taiwan. Concluded that even though Taiwan problem had not been settled past 11 years it surely would be during next 11 years and sooner it was settled the better.

I responded with paragraph 1 Deptel 931,[2] continuing with paragraphs 2, 3 and 4.

Wang expressed disappointment my presentation contained no positive proposal concerning Taiwan. Regarding prisoners he pointed out that although RB–47 flyers had been released, U–2 pilot Powers still held. Added that this side had taken several steps such as release of 11 US flyers in 1955 in effort improve atmosphere but US had failed respond. Furthermore, US continued place obstructions in way of Chinese wishing return their country. Regarding newsmen he declared he had put forward reasonable proposal September 6[3] and we should reconsider our attitude to that proposal. He returned list of newsmen I had handed him saying until Taiwan problem solved, it was very difficult make progress on other issues.

I pointed out that far from failing to respond to Chinese Communist release of 11 flyers US had already before that occurred removed all restrictions on departure Chinese from US. I said his allegations Chinese being prevented from leaving were unsupported by any evidence and reminded him that we had yet to receive any complaint on behalf of a Chinese from Indian Embassy. On newsmen I expressed hope that his negative response was not final word regarding our new proposal and urged that his side give it further consideration. I added that in view interest this subject in US my government reserved right to make public statement. Wang was silent as to possibility public statement by his side.

Next meeting April 18, 2 p.m.

**Beam**

---

[2] Document 10.
[3] See *Foreign Relations*, 1958–1960, vol. XIX, pp. 715–716.

## 12.    Draft Memorandum from the Counselor of the Department of State (McGhee) to Secretary of State Rusk

Washington, March 10, 1961.

SUBJECT

A New Basic Approach to the GRC

There is attached a paper[1] proposing that the U.S. should seek to arrive at a new basis in its relations with the GRC under which we would be willing to support Taiwan, but not the GRC's mainland ambitions. It is a principal thesis of this paper that continued pursuit of those ambitions would endanger both the GRC's base on Taiwan and the U.S. itself.

The best long-term political and military defense of Taiwan will require that the GRC continue to be represented in the UN; that a consensus be developed in the free world that the people on Taiwan are entitled to a separate existence from the mainland; and that the U.S. commitment to defend Taiwan be spread among our allies. We would hope to use the widespread conviction among members that Taiwan deserves continued representation in the UN, and the ChiComs' objection to sitting in that body with another Chinese regime, to transfer to their backs the monkey of unreasonable opposition, and thus keep them out. We see the liquidation of the dangerous confrontation around the offshores as a means whereby the civil war might be turned into a period of a de facto peace, with 100 miles of blue water between the contestants, in which the needed free-world consensus about Taiwan's right to a separate future might grow; and would seek to use evacuation of the offshores as an inducement which might be offered our allies for sharing our commitment to defend Taiwan.

We recognize that bringing about the readjustments we propose will at best be a most difficult task: President Chiang is too deeply and publicly committed to a return to the mainland to publicly disavow that ambition; and his leadership cannot be greatly damaged without also disrupting the GRC itself. Hence those readjustments will only be possible if we give all possible consideration to the requirements of his "face"; hold out the inducements of greater U.S. assistance; and be prepared to press on the sensitive nerve which is GRC dependence on us for its continued existence.

---

Source: Department of State, S/P Files: Lot 67 D 548, China, 1959–1961. Secret. It is not clear whether the memorandum was sent to Rusk. The source text is an unsigned copy. A handwritten note dated March 10 reads: "Discussed with IO/FE/L. IO and FE to prepare papers."

[1] Not printed; dated March 10 and entitled "A New Basic Approach to the GRC."

The underlying memo does not have FE concurrence. It was discussed with officers of FE in an earlier version[2] which envisaged an overall approach to the GRC: We felt that a new administration can most easily alter policies while it was new; that our two governments might as well reach a basic understanding sooner rather than later; and that some elements in an overall approach can be mutually supporting. It is the feeling in FE, which faces the difficult practical problems of dealing with the GRC, that we should not embarrass chances of getting it to cooperate in the UN membership problem by presenting it at the same time with the much larger dose of bitter medicine which evacuation of the offshore islands would represent. The memo in its present form does not choose between these alternatives, but they need to be faced as alternatives and a choice made.

---

[2] The earlier version, dated March 6, is attached to the source text. A handwritten notation indicates it was not cleared in FE and was not sent. Another handwritten notation states that a memorandum of March 10 from Parsons to McGhee suggested an FE/S/P task group to discuss differences with an FE draft paper.

---

## 13.    Memorandum of Conversation

Washington, March 14, 1961, 10:35 a.m.–12:15 p.m.

SUBJECT

US/UK Bilateral Talks: China and Chinese Representation in the UN

PARTICIPANTS

*US*

The Secretary
The Under, Secretary
George C. McGhee, Counselor
Foy D. Kohler, Assistant Secretary for European Affairs
Harlan Cleveland, Assistant Secretary for International Organization Affairs
James K. Penfield, Acting Assistant Secretary for African Affairs
John M. Steeves, Deputy Assistant Secretary for Far Eastern Affairs

---

Source: Department of State, Secretary's Memoranda of Conversation: Lot 65 D 330. Secret; Limit Distribution. Drafted by Swihart and approved in U on March 31. The time of the meeting is from the Secretary's Appointment Book. (Johnson Library) A U.S.-British agreed minute of this conversation is in Department of State, Conference Files: Lot 65 D 366, CF 1832.

William C. Burdett, Director, Office of British Commonwealth and Northern
  European Affairs
James W. Swihart, Officer in Charge, U.K. and Ireland Affairs

*UK*

Ambassador Caccia
Viscount Hood, Minister
Denis A. Greenhill, Counselor
R. T. D. Ledward, Counselor
Charles D. Wiggin, First Secretary

The Secretary began the discussion by observing one can always
hope that the U.S. and the U.K. could get together on the problem of
China. In 1949, perhaps, an argument could have been made for either
the U.S. or U.K. position. Now it was a tragedy that we had divergent
policies. We see no prospect at this time of U.S. recognition of Communist China. Peiping continues its extreme hostility toward this country
and its attitude to the new Administration is equally uncompromising. It
continues to take the position that Formosa must become a part of Communist China. We feel the possibility of any change in the situation is up
to Peiping and not to us. During the last Warsaw talks there was no
indication of any change in their position. It was reiterated that the U.S.
must get its troops off Formosa which is Peiping's traditional way of
pressing for our abandonment of Formosa. They refused to accept a list
of names for an reciprocal exchange of newspapermen, and they will not
release our prisoners. Despite these circumstances we plan to continue
the contact in Warsaw in order to have a forum for some sort of "dialogue". We believe that Peiping at an appropriate stage might be brought
into the nuclear testing and disarmament talks. If they go successfully, it
would be essential to have them included in the discussions and to sign
any agreements reached. We have a bilateral security agreement with
Formosa. We expect to stand by it and would use force to prevent Formosa from being taken over by the mainland. Our position is not just
because of public opinion here but is based also on the strategic situation
and the attitudes of our Far East Allies. We recognize this position in
itself constitutes an obstacle to normalization of our relations with Peiping. We hope others throughout the Free World will in time recognize the
necessity of the maintenance of Formosa's independence. We are concerned about the off-shore islands problem and will have to take a look at
what can be done about it. We regret that Admiral Radford and Mr. Robertson were not successful in their efforts.[1]

Ambassador Caccia responded the British have always understood
our position. They agree the blame for the situation is Peiping's and the

---

[1] Reference is to a mission to Taiwan in April 1955 by JCS Chairman Admiral Arthur
W. Radford and Assistant Secretary of State for Far Eastern Affairs Walter S. Robertson. For
documentation, see *Foreign Relations, 1955–1957*, vol. II, pp. 445–543 ff.

latter's demands would be too large to swallow. The U.K. agrees furthermore that millions of people "should not be handed around". The offshore islands present a different problem from a legal standpoint from
that of Formosa which is legitimatized by the Cairo declaration. The Secretary commented he wouldn't want to spell out the legal problems as far
as the Cairo declaration is concerned but he would not suppose that
under it, Peiping could really make any claim to Formosa.

The Ambassador at this point inquired whether we might agree to a
joint assessment about the following:

A) The political and economic strength of China.
B) Sino-Soviet differences and ways of exploiting them.
C) Probable future trends in Chinese foreign relations, particularly
with Japan.

The Secretary agreed. It was understood that the two intelligence
communities would be asked to participate in these assessments. The
Under Secretary observed that if for any reason we were to agree to discuss possible recognition of Communist China with Peiping, the very
first question we would be asked would be to give up Formosa. Right at
that point the talks would have to stop. The Ambassador thought this
was a good point and one we should make clear around the world. The
Under Secretary agreed and believed if really understood, we would be
in a stronger position in the eyes of world opinion.

The Secretary then turned to the subject of Chinese representation in
the UN. He stated we cannot as of this moment spell out the full parliamentary position. We do not seek as an objective of U.S. policy Peiping's
admission to the UN. Our objective would be to put ourselves in a reasonable light and position in the UN and then leave the problem of Peiping to others. We would not wish to move from what many call our
unrealistic attitude to an unrealistic position. If the question of a seat for
China comes up as a credentials matter regardless of the vote, the outcome would have an unrealistic result. There are two organisms each
claiming they represent all of China. Neither has control over the areas it
claims; each have the attribution of statehood and population criteria for
admission to the UN. We, therefore, do not look upon the problem as procedural or technical but rather one of a wide-range political character. We
believe it would be disastrous if the matter were settled on a procedural
vote. It is fundamental to the United States that Formosa retain a seat in
the United Nations. If this is unacceptable to Peiping then they are at
fault. We don't believe we should have to pay the ticket for Peiping's
admission at Formosa's expenses. If Peiping won't accept admission
under these conditions, then that is their choice and we would not be
responsible. There is a further complication on how the matter is handled
in the General Assembly and the Security Council. On the assumption it
couldn't be dealt with satisfactorily as a credentials matter, the outcome

in the General Assembly would probably be satisfactory. This would not be true in the Security Council. The Ambassador inquired how we proposed to proceed, was the moratorium to be continued? etc. The Secretary replied we would have to look at the situation closer to the time. What he had just previously said, however, was based on the assumption that the moratorium has exhausted itself. Unless, because of some new crisis, the situation changes by September, it would appear that the moratorium has "run out of votes". The Ambassador asked how we prevent the problem from not being handled as one of "who sits in China's seat". Could we be sure we would succeed? Heretofore, the moratorium has been handled as a procedural problem at the U.S. request, i.e., a simple majority vote. The Secretary thought that the moratorium had truly been a procedural problem whereas the other involves the important question which country is entitled to sit in the UN. The Ambassador again inquired how we expected to get the votes and wouldn't we have to line up other governments. The Secretary answered there obviously would have to be consultation, but closer to the time. He observed we would like to start with the U.K. vote. Lord Hood felt that if everyone knew beforehand the U.S. was prepared to see the admission of Peiping so long as Formosa could remain in the UN then it might be possible to get the necessary votes. The Ambassador added there remained the question who would get the Security Council seat. The Secretary observed this issue couldn't be settled by any action of the General Assembly. Its action would have to be confined to the seating of a member in the General Assembly. The Ambassador asked whether Formosa would continue on the Security Council. The Secretary replied affirmatively.

Mr. Steeves commented that if the moratorium is licked then such countries as Malaya and others would for the first time begin to think twice before throwing Formosa out of the Security Council. The Ambassador commented that the U.K. would be in the following position if the question of who is entitled to China's Security Council seat came to a vote: The U.K. would have to vote for Peiping because it recognizes that Government. If we had any ideas how the Formosa seat could be retained despite the fact the U.K. would have to vote for Peiping, he would be interested in hearing about them. The Secretary commented the problem could be relieved by the U.K.'s recognition of Formosa. The Ambassador replied they could not do this because the U.K. would be thrown out of Peiping. He believed, therefore, the U.S. should try to get Peiping's agreement to two delegations. Mr. Cleveland inquired whether the British felt an offer of conditional membership to Peiping was salable subject to the requirement that Formosa retain its membership in the UN. The Ambassador thought this was doubtful but possibly worth exploring. He thought it very important that we should be making our position known to others soon so it could be realized the U.S. wasn't just standing pat on the moratorium anymore. The Secretary said that for us the problem is not one of finding a place for Formosa, it was rather does the United Nations wish to find a place for Peiping. He added our own tactics will depend somewhat on studies presently underway in Formosa. We will not take our marching orders as a result of these studies but it will be helpful to know whether Formosa continues to take the position that Peiping should not be admitted to the UN. The Secretary observed that we do not expect to consult unduly until our views have crystallized more. The present exchange with the British was because of our exceptionally close relations. He stressed its confidential nature.

Lord Hood inquired if we were content to accept a UN majority decision to admit Peiping so long as Formosa remained, then what would the situation be in the Security Council? The Secretary felt it was possible to visualize both having seats in the General Assembly but that in the Security Council, we would find it difficult to accept that the problem was a credentials matter. If considered on a procedural vote, the Republic of China would probably vote against it. The matter might then be referred to the International Court. If we get into a wrangle in the Security Council, then there would be pressure to open the entire membership of the Security Council. The Ambassador wondered whether there would not be some advantage to starting all over again. Inasmuch as no government represents all of China, perhaps Formosa might stand down or aside and then we could have a new negotiation about membership in the Security Council. The Secretary thought this might be possible and in fact might be the only chance to renegotiate Security Council membership. Mr. Steeves felt the best we could hope for would be that Formosa might choose not to exercise its right to a Security Council seat while the Security Council membership was being renegotiated. The Ambassador reiterated his fear of any breakdown between us if events reached a point whereby the U.K. would have to vote for Peiping's admission. The Secretary asked whether this was because Peiping would break relations with the U.K. or because of the logic of the situation. The Ambassador replied the latter. Mr. McGhee inquired what would be the U.K. attitude to a resolution stating that Formosa should retain membership in the UN. The Ambassador replied that as long as we didn't oppose Peiping's admission he thought the U.K. could abstain. Mr. McGhee asked whether Chiang's position on the off-shore islands was a critical matter to the U.K. The Ambassador replied yes. Chiang's withdrawal from the off-shore islands would have a helpful effect on world public opinion. The Secretary asked whether HMG has a positive policy to seat Peiping in the UN or whether its policy is "to be on a better wicket in the UN". The Ambassador replied the latter. The West has been losing ground and the moratorium has run out of support. The Secretary said then if there was a reasonable posture in the UN and Peiping turned it down, could we assume that the British would not be overly bothered. The Ambassador agreed. The Secretary added that if the dead-lock were on "another basis" would the British feel happier. The Ambassador again agreed.

Mr. Ledward commented that the U.K. would have more difficulty if Peiping had to apply for membership in the UN than if Formosa had to apply. The Secretary observed something quite new might be possible. He pointed out that after the partition of India both India and Pakistan had seats in the UN; India retaining its seat and Pakistan was admitted as a new nation. It was possible the UN could pass a resolution in effect saying what is now one country has become two countries. As for the Security Council problem we might respond to the interest of new countries in renewing the membership of the Security Council. A study could be undertaken. We would be in no hurry.

## 14.    Memorandum of Conversation

Washington, March 17, 1961, 11:30 a.m.–12:10 p.m.

SUBJECT

Chinese Representation

PARTICIPANTS

The Secretary
Dr. George K. C. Yeh, Chinese Ambassador
Mr. C. C. Lai, First Secretary Chinese Embassy
Mr. E. W. Martin, Director Office of Chinese Affairs

Ambassador Yeh called on the Secretary at the latter's request this morning. The Secretary opened the conversation by inquiring whether Ambassador T.F. Tsiang had returned to New York. Ambassador Yeh explained that Dr. Tsiang had not gone to Taipei for consultation; he had remained in New York in order to consult with Ambassador Stevenson on the prospects for using the moratorium again. Ambassador Yeh expressed the view of his government that the moratorium should not be given up lightly but that steps should be taken to see how many votes could be obtained in support of it.

---

Source: Department of State, Central Files, 303/3–1761. Secret. Drafted by Martin and approved in S on April 6. The time of the meeting is from the Secretary's Appointment Book. (Johnson Library)

The Secretary responded that he was not surprised that the GRC hoped to continue the moratorium. However, he thought that the GRC should consider alternatives. He pointed out that a growing number of United Nations members feel that the subject of Chinese representation should at least be discussed in the General Assembly. There was also a feeling among members that the moratorium was running out of votes and they were losing patience with it. Thus it looked as though the subject was going to come up for debate in the next General Assembly. (It had, of course, been decided for the resumed General Assembly.)

The Secretary emphasized that there would be no change in the bilateral relations between the United States and China. The United States would continue to recognize the GRC. On the other hand, there was no prospect that Peiping would be recognized both because of its own policy and of United States policy.

The United Nations problem was more complicated, however; the parliamentary situation there was very difficult. To us the most disastrous result would be to have the issue treated as a credentials question—as a question of which delegation should be seated in China's seat. If the moratorium expires, it means that a majority of members want to have the issue discussed, not necessarily that the majority wants Peiping to replace the GRC in the United Nations. A serious parliamentary threat, which we must guard against, is the technical possibility that a bare majority would decide that this is a credentials matter. We think it is not simply a credentials matter but an important matter of far reaching implications. The seating of the Peiping regime is not an objective of policy of some members who vote for the seating of Peiping or against the moratorium. The Ambassador asked if the Secretary was thinking of the United Kingdom. The Secretary said he was thinking of a number of countries. He indicated we should try to get away from the present deadlock which involves a considerable risk and produce another deadlock but on a more advantageous position. At this point the GRC should consider its attitude on this key question. How does it feel on the choice between an all-or-nothing position, on the one hand, and the determination to remain a member of the United Nations, on the other? If the GRC takes an all-or-nothing position, it is likely that a majority of United Nations members will insist on dealing with the issue as a credentials question. If the GRC concentrates on retaining its position in the United Nations, however, then the prospect is that Peiping will refuse to take up membership on the grounds that the GRC is still in the United Nations, and a deadlock will ensue for which Peiping will bear the responsibility. The Secretary said that if the issue were decided to be an important matter, there would probably not be a two-third's majority for any solution. The key point is the GRC's attitude on the question of all-or-nothing.

The Ambassador said he would faithfully report what the Secretary had said to his government. He regarded it as being very important. He could not answer the Secretary's question as to whether his government would take an all-or-nothing approach or concentrate on remaining in the United Nations. Although he could not give his government's answer to this question, as a personal footnote he could point out that in response to a strong recommendation on his part the GRC had instructed its Chargé d'Affaires to remain in Senegal (at least temporarily) even though the Senegal Government had decided to recognize Communist China.[1] Thus, for the time being any way, the GRC had not taken an all-or-nothing attitude in Senegal. The Ambassador also recalled the situation which had arisen in Melbourne in the 1956 Olympic Games. Dr. Yeh, who was then Foreign Minister, had decided to send a GRC team to Melbourne despite the presence of the Chinese Communists. As a result, Peiping withdrew from the Olympics. The Ambassador emphasized that in these personal footnotes he was not suggesting what his government's policy would be on the United Nations question. However, these were cases where his government had determined to participate regardless of whether the Chinese Communists came or not.

The Secretary emphasized that the GRC's attitude was crucial in the determination of how to deal with the subject in the United Nations. He noted that Peiping had made acknowledgement of its claim to Formosa a condition to United Nations membership. If the United Nations insists that the GRC retain an independent seat this would represent a major breach in Peiping's claim to Formosa, and require a major shift in Peiping's policy for it to accept United Nations membership.

Ambassador Yeh said he felt sure his government would not want to leave the United Nations in favor of Peiping but would stay on because it has a right to be there. However, the GRC would not want to change its national name. At the San Francisco Conference, the name Republic of China had been deliberately chosen instead of China by the Chinese delegation. Former Ambassador Koo had remarked at the time that this choice of name might be important as a criterion in the future (the Ambassador noted that the Chinese delegation had included Communist representatives). The Secretary doubted that much could be rested on this point in the United Nations. Dr. Yeh agreed, but reiterated the importance that the GRC attached to retaining its own name. If the Peiping government were voted in, it should be in its own name as the "People's Republic of China".

The Ambassador analyzed briefly the voting in the 15th General Assembly on the moratorium, pointing out that the favorable votes had decreased from 44 to 42, with the loss of Cuba and Ethiopia, and the abstentions had increased from 9 to 22, including 14 African states. The

---

[1] Telegram 602 from Dakar, March 15, reported that Senegal's Prime Minister had informed the GRC Chargé on March 14 that Senegal had decided to recognize the PRC but that it did not intend to establish diplomatic relations with the PRC and hoped the GRC would maintain its Embassy in Dakar. (Department of State, Central Files, 793.02/3–1561)

GRC had established diplomatic relations with 11 African states. He thought that some of these 11 would vote for the moratorium. Probably Brazil's vote might be lost, and Mexico and Pakistan would abstain. He asked the Secretary if the United Kingdom would part ways with the United States. The Secretary replied that it would be difficult for the United Kingdom to continue to support the moratorium formula, but we could find some other formula which would result in a deadlock. The United Kingdom and others who don't feel it is an objective of their policy to bring Peiping into the United Nations could vote for it. A number of countries now feel that there is an unreality about the present situation, but we could get a good deal of help from them if we could develop a reasonable proposal which would bring about a deadlock and shift the onus to Peiping. Ambassador Yeh asked if this would mean putting the question on a two-third's basis since the Chinese Communists could not get a two-thirds majority in their favor. The Secretary indicated this might be one alternative on the parliamentary trail. He emphasized that the GRC should mobilize international support for the conservation of what it has on Formosa even from those who already recognize Peiping.

The Ambassador asked what countries had indicated that they were tired of the moratorium. The Secretary said we do not have a complete list but he pointed out that the principal opposition comes from among those delegations where we have the least political capital. Ambassador Yeh remarked that those who say we must discuss the issue want to see Red China come in. The Secretary said he didn't know about that and cited the fact that President Quadros of Brazil had made clear that he was interested in discussing the issue but was not committed on admission of Communist China. Ambassador Yeh said that, according to his information, Quadros was thinking about recognizing Peiping at the time he issued his instructions to his United Nations delegation but he had since changed his mind. In closing the Ambassador expressed the hope that while these discussions were going on between his government and the United States American officials would refrain from making public statements on the issue. The Secretary emphasized that we were being pressed on this matter and we had to make decisions soon. It was therefore very important that the GRC reach a decision on the question he had earlier put to the Ambassador.[2]

---

[2] Ambassador Yeh called on Secretary Rusk on March 22 requesting more detailed information on the U.S. position. Yeh stated that he had received telegrams from Taipei indicating that his government would face extreme difficulties in agreeing to any "two Chinas" formula. He gave Rusk several questions and asked for his comments, but Rusk replied that the questions were procedural ones deriving from broad policy issues; the real question was whether the GRC would insist on an all-or-nothing approach. When Yeh stated that he could not present a plan to his government without saying how it would work, Rusk replied that the United States was not presenting a plan; the nature of any plan that was worked out would depend upon the GRC attitude. (Memorandum of conversation, March 23; ibid., 303/3–2361) See the Supplement.

## 15. Telegram From the Embassy in the Republic of China to the Department of State

Taipei, March 20, 1961, 7 p.m.

571. For first time since I came to Taiwan three years ago, I sense a feeling among high GRC authorities that USG is looking for some way out of China impasse at their expense. Thus far this "feeling" appears not to have seeped down to lower official levels or to general public. This attitude has its genesis in US election campaign and accompanying debates, change of administration, and public utterances of well known Americans who have become high officials and who are felt in position to influence US policy. Uneasiness has been heightened by what is believed to be US disposition to reach accommodation with ChiComs if only latter would unbend, and US shift toward advocacy of neutral Laos. Issue of sharpest focus currently however is UN representation. GRC authorities are deeply disturbed because they consider new administration has not come out unreservedly in support of GRC on this issue. They see US Government as fearful of its ability to preserve moratorium formula and prepared to toss in towel. There are officials here, and they are thought to include those in highest circles, who are coming to believe USG is prepared to plump for "two Chinas". That there are responsible Chinese officials prepared to believe this preposterous and mistaken idea is testimony to decline taking place in their confidence in United States. It is also reflective on their extreme sensitivity to mere thought of any solution smacking of "two Chinas" which would be contrary to their fundamental doctrine of return to mainland and liberation of compatriots.

As I interpret thinking of GRC officials, they believe maintenance of moratorium formula remains best tactic and they profess to believe if only USG will place shoulder to wheel wholeheartedly and unreservedly, moratorium will win again. Because of repugnance for "two Chinas" GRC is most reluctant to advance or discuss alternatives suggestive in any way of "two Chinas". Even if some such tactic were adopted with a view to keeping ChiComs out UN, there are officials here who believe that once door is opened other pressures would be applied by powers intent on ChiCom admission which would force GRC to leave UN. Point to remember here is that GRC would prefer to be out of UN to representing only Taiwan.

We are clearly faced with a problem of great delicacy and one on which GRC may not find it possible to yield at all. I believe it will be very difficult to sell GRC officials on any formula with a "two Chinas" con-

Source: Department of State, Central Files, 611.93/3–2061. Secret; Priority; Limit Distribution.

notation even if for tactical purposes only. Any approaches we make in this direction must be handled with utmost subtlety and tact lest GRC be driven in desperation to withdrawing from UN and going it alone. In my view, leadership here is quite capable of such course of action if pushed too hard or driven into corner. Of course such state of affairs would shake stability of Taiwan and could give ChiComs opportunity they have sought for years to take Taiwan without a struggle.

I have been engaged recently in almost daily talks with Foreign Minister and Vice Foreign Minister. Subject of UN representation has invariably come up and I have done my best to assure them of constancy of US position, of US opposition to "two Chinas" and of US opposition to ChiCom admission to UN. On March 18 I spoke of Secretary's desire for GRC's idea of solution and urged that one be provided.

Foregoing was prepared prior to receipt of Deptel 471[1] which appears to pose problem in acute form. Foreign Minister told me today without going into substance of Secretary's talk with Ambassador Yeh, that he wished to explore representation issue with me in day or two.

**Drumright**

---

[1] Dated March 18; it summarized the conversation recorded in Document 14. (Department of State, Central Files, 793.02/3–1861)

---

16.    **Memorandum From the Deputy Assistant for Special Operations to the Secretary of Defense (Lansdale) to Secretary of Defense McNamara**

Washington, April 3, 1961.

SUBJECT

China

The recent strong comments by Allen Dulles about troubles inside China[1] should give pause to all of our policy makers. "The Great Leap Forward" in China apparently has landed it in the soup.

I have talked with some of his staff most concerned with China, with "China hands," and with Chinese friends. They picture a China weak-

---

Source: Washington National Records Center, RG 330, OSD Files: FRC 65 A 3464, 091 China. Secret. Also sent to Deputy Secretary of Defense Roswell L. Gilpatric, and copies were sent to Lemnitzer and Nitze.

[1] Not further identified.

ened by overwork and malnutrition, a political regime being forced by growing discontent to start relaxing its stringent rules, and clear indications of more trouble to come. It might well be the time to initiate some actions inside China and to keep the pressures on.

The immediate troubles in China stem from malnutrition and exhaustion. Unlike historic natural disaster areas in China, 1961 also includes North China. Millet and wheat are not on the market. There is similar shortage of rice in the south. And, this has happened prior to the usual "starvation period" of April–May. A combination of an economy dislocated to fit a political theory, bad weather, and floods brought this about.

Last year was a bad year. This year is worst. Next year might continue the trend. 1958, a good crop year, produced 212-million tons of grains (wheat, millet, rice). The estimate for 1961, with some 50-million more mouths to feed, is about 180-million tons of grains. Meat, fish, and oils are disappearing from Chinese diets. Conditions have reawakened the old Chinese political saying, "Three bad harvests and the mandate from heaven changes."

Intelligence estimates now being compiled probably will describe the Chinese people as tired from the long hours of work under the commune system, weak from hunger, but taking their suffering with resignation. Despite trouble in the Army in Shantung and the granary riots there, in Hankow, and on Hainan not long ago, it is not believed that China is on the point of general rebellion. Chinese are realists and know that they would have little chance of succeeding—unless helped from the outside.

There is little information on the morale of the Army. Since the military have been a favored class under the Communists, get their rations even when the people starve, and are under the strong control of Lin Piao,[2] it is probable that the Army is still effective. However, a strong psychological campaign could change this. There are reports that Army men are sending part of their rations home. Some observers feel that Mao wouldn't dare undertake an adventure with his Army now, despite his threats to do so.

In summary, Defense responsibilities for our national security dictate that we should make sure that the U.S. takes a hard look at our policy towards China at this time. Holding back from permitting probing actions inside China, feeling that our Seventh Fleet can be looked upon merely as a diplomatic pawn, or giving undue weight to Chou En-lai's political gambits, might well be exactly the wrong thing to do today. The threat of China has hung heavy over our heads in Asia. It may well be that we can start changing this in 1961.

---

[2] Minister of Defense in the People's Republic of China.

## 17.    Special National Intelligence Estimate

SNIE 13–61                                                Washington, April 4, 1961.

THE ECONOMIC SITUATION IN COMMUNIST CHINA

### The Problem

To assess current Chinese Communist economic difficulties, with special reference to the food situation, and to estimate their economic and political consequences: (a) over the next few years, and (b) in the event 1961 should prove a poor crop year.

### Conclusions

1.  The Chinese Communist regime is now facing the most serious economic difficulties it has confronted since it consolidated its power over mainland China. As a result of economic mismanagement, and, especially, of two years of unfavorable weather, food production in 1960 was little if any larger than in 1957—at which time there were about 50 million fewer Chinese to feed. Widespread famine does not appear to be at hand, but in some provinces many people are now on a bare subsistence diet and the bitterest suffering lies immediately ahead in the period before the June harvests. The dislocations caused by the "Leap Forward" and the removal of Soviet technicians have disrupted China's industrialization program. These difficulties have sharply reduced the rate of economic growth during 1960 and have created a serious balance of payments problem. Public morale, especially in rural areas, is almost certainly at its lowest point since the Communists assumed power, and there have been some instances of open dissidence. (Paras. 7–25)

2.  The Chinese Communist regime has responded by giving agriculture a higher priority, dropping the "Leap Forward" approach in industry, and relaxing somewhat the economic demands on the people. Perhaps the best indicator of the severity of the food shortage has been Peiping's action in scheduling the importation of nearly three million tons of food-grains during 1961, at a cost of about $200 million of Communist China's limited foreign currency holdings. (Paras. 26–30)

3.  While normal crop weather in 1961 would significantly improve farm output over the levels of 1959 and 1960, at least two years of average

Source: Department of State, INR/EAP Files: Lot 90 D 110. Secret. According to a note on the cover sheet, the Central Intelligence Agency and the intelligence organizations of the Departments of State, the Army, the Navy, the Air Force, the Joint Staff, and the National Security Agency participated in the preperation of this estimate. All members of the USIB concurred in this estimate except the representatives of the AEC and the FBI, who abstained on the grounds that the subject was outside their jurisdiction.

or better harvests will be required to overcome the crisis and permit a restoration of the diet to tolerable levels, some rebuilding of domestic stocks, and the resumption of net food exports. If Soviet technicians in large numbers do not return to China, industrial production is likely to increase about 12 percent annually, as compared with about 33 percent in 1959 and 16 percent in 1960. (Paras. 31–35)

4. If 1961 is another poor crop year the economic and political effects for Communist China are likely to be grave. There probably would be no increase in gross national product (GNP) in 1961, and growth prospects for later years would also be affected. Unless there were substantial food imports, malnutrition and disease would become widespread, and a considerable amount of starvation probably would occur. Public disaffection probably would become a major problem for the regime, perhaps forcing it to undertake a massive campaign of threats and terror. It is unlikely even in these circumstances, however, that public disaffection could threaten continued control of China by its present leadership. (Paras. 38–40)

5. We do not believe that Peiping would accept food offers from the US even under conditions of widespread famine. (Para. 42)

6. We do not believe that even famine conditions would, in themselves, cause Peiping to engage in direct military aggression. Such difficulties probably would, however, prompt Peiping to avoid actions which would exacerbate its relations with Moscow. (Paras. 40–41)

[Here follow paragraphs 7–42, comprising the discussion portion of the estimate, and a map showing China's agricultural areas.]

## 18.    Memorandum of Conversation

Washington, April 5, 1961, 3 p.m.

### THE PRESIDENT'S MEETINGS WITH PRIME MINISTER
### MACMILLAN
#### Washington, April, 1961

SUBJECT

United Nations: Chinese Representation Problem

PARTICIPANTS

| US | UK |
|---|---|
| The President | The Prime Minister |
| The Secretary of State | Lord Home |
| The Secretary of the Treasury | Ambassador Caccia |
| Ambassador Stevenson | Sir Frederick Hoyer Millar |
| Ambassador Bruce | Sir Patrick Dean |
| Mr. Dean Acheson | The Honorable Peter Ramsbotham |
| Mr. McGeorge Bundy | Mr. Philip de Zulueta |
| Mr. Walt W. Rostow | Mr. John Russell |
| Mr. Charles E. Bohlen | Mr. A.C.I. Samuel |
| Mr. George C. McGhee | |
| Mr. Harlan Cleveland | |
| Governor Williams | |
| Mr. William C. Burdett | |
| Mr. James W. Swihart | |

The President stated it is a fact that there is a division between us on China.[1] He would, however, like to stress the importance of this issue to this country. When he last saw President Eisenhower on January 19 the latter stated that he hoped to support him on all foreign policy issues but would feel it necessary to return to political life if the Chinese commu-

---

Source: Department of State, Conference Files: Lot 65 D 366, CF 1833. Secret. Drafted by Swihart. A notation on the source text indicates it was uncleared. The meeting was held at the White House. According to Kennedy's Appointment Book, those present for this portion of the discussion, which took place between 4:30 and 6:10 p.m. were Kennedy, Rusk, Stevenson, Bruce, Cleveland, Steeves, Kohler, and Bohlen, and on the British side, Macmillan, Home, Caccia, Permanent Under Secretary of Foreign Affairs Sir Frederick Hoyer Millar, Representative to the United Nations Sir Patrick Dean, Cabinet Secretary Sir Norman Brook, and Macmillan's private secretary Philip de Zulueta. (Kennedy Library, President's Appointment Books) Macmillan visited Washington April 4–8; see vol. XIII, pp. 1035–1039.

[1] Secretary Rusk and Lord Home discussed this issue on April 4. A memorandum of the conversation by Deputy Assistant Secretary for European Affairs Ivan B. White is in Department of State, Conference Files: Lot 65 D 366, CF 1833. See the Supplement. Cleveland and Deputy Legal Adviser Leonard C. Meeker briefed the President on the subject at breakfast on April 5. Meeker's record of the conversation is in Department of State, Central Files, 303/4–561. See the Supplement.

nists were admitted to the United Nations.[2] If they are brought in a great wave of distrust about the United Nations would arise. We could not acquiesce in their admission. The problem then is how to prevent us from being defeated in the United Nations and to prevent increasing communist prestige throughout the world. Even though we differ, we assume the UK does not want the US public to distrust the United Nations nor to increase communist prestige. We have been considering various alternatives. There is the position of Formosa in the General Assembly and in the Security Council. There is the problem if there are to be two China's in the UN, would Communist China be willing to join.

Ambassador Stevenson observed that assuming the objective to keep Taiwan in the United Nations we have been considering various possibilities. Our first objective is to avoid action by simple majority on a credentials vote. On this issue we believe we would be defeated. One possibility would be to have a proposal for a resolution which stated that Communist China was eligible for admission. This would take a two-thirds vote. We would abstain. Whether Taiwan would we don't know. But at this point we doubt, however, such a resolution would get a two-thirds vote. Also, it might look as a delaying tactic by putting Communist China at the mercy of the Republic of China's veto. There is the question also of the Security Council seat problem. Another approach is the successor nation one. This would take the form of a resolution stating that two states have succeeded to China's seat. The Prime Minister asked whether this would be the same as the India and Pakistan example. Ambassador Stevenson said it was somewhat different; India kept its seat and Pakistan got a new seat. Under the successor nation theory Communist China could apply for admission. Another possibility which has occurred to us would be for the US to make it clear it backs Taiwan as a sovereign country with a right to a seat in the United Nations and let others worry about Peiping. The last alternative we have considered would be to amend the United Nations Charter. In our view probably the best way is for a resolution stating Communist China is eligible to apply for admission. This leaves the problem of the Security Council seat in abeyance for a while. We recognize that the moratorium device has had its day and that something must be done. Lord Home stressed the UK understands the US position. In fact, it does not particularly want Communist China in the United Nations but as the UK has recognized Communist China it would have to vote for it in any credential vote. The UK would be happy to cooperate on any resolution we would want. Never-

---

[2] The January 19 meeting between Kennedy and Eisenhower is summarized in separate memoranda, both dated January 24, by Kennedy's adviser Clark M. Clifford and Secretary of Defense-designate Robert S. McNamara. Neither records any discussion of China. (Department of State, Rusk Files: Lot 72 D 192, White House Correspondence, 1/61–11/63, and Washington National Records Center, RG 330, OSD Files: FRC 65 A 3464, respectively)

theless, he felt none suggested were practical unless Formosa became a separate independent country without any pretense of any rights to the mainland. The President asked whether it was important whether China and Communist China both claim to represent all of China, or whether the use of the name China for either or both was essential. Patrick Dean doubted any formula would be acceptable to most members that did not recognize Communist China as in effect China. The Secretary thought the name would have no great importance. We are presently negotiating with Peiping in Warsaw and, the President added, will soon be in the 14 Nation Committee.[3] The President reiterated we could not support Red China's admittance to the UN. We needed to find a formula for keeping them from wanting to get in. We believe we are in the best position to defend Formosa's position of having a right to be in. The Secretary thought that if we could get a reasonable position so that the world could see that Communist China has impossible conditions for admission which we could not accept, this would be salutary. The President felt although the fact may be that Formosa should be a separate country the Republic of China won't admit it. He inquired what were the UK's views as to the effect of a defeat of the US on a direct vote, particularly in Southeast Asia. Lord Home thought the effect would be bad. The Secretary remarked that Americans would pick up the tally vote and wonder why we had not put more pressure on countries voting for Red China. Lord Home reported that at the recent Commonwealth Conference only Menzies was not in favor of seating Communist China in the UN. The Prime Minister wondered whether it is important what people called themselves. He recalled that the King of England called himself the King of France for many years when in fact he had no such position. He wondered whether we couldn't express it in terms of the truth. There are two countries, each claiming control of the other. Couldn't we have a resolution which would find both should be in the United Nations, a resolution which appealed to everyone along the lines of the successor state theory. Lord Home reiterated that if they both called themselves China there would be difficulty. The President asked whether some other UN members don't have claims over other areas also. Sir Patrick Dean observed there are some, India in particular, who want the Security Council enlarged. Possibly, therefore, some resolution might succeed and we could get their help if they understood we are working on the Security Council enlargement problem. Ambassador Stevenson thought we could get a two-thirds vote this fall on a successor state resolution. The Prime Minister felt this would leave only the problem of name. Ambassador Caccia pointed out such a resolution would name only two states and the question of name would be up to the countries concerned. The

---

[3] Reference is to the proposed 14-nation conference on Laos.

President suggested that Sir Patrick Dean and Ambassador Stevenson work together on this problem and that either through correspondence or the next time the Prime Minister and he were together they take a look at the results. In the meantime we want to avoid a major defeat during the next year. He added that we would of course have to stay arm's length away from any resolutions of the sort we have been discussing. Lord Home felt it was necessary to devise a most ingenious resolution. Ambassador Stevenson thought this was not too difficult. It would merely state that two countries have succeeded to the rights of China and automatically they would have the right to be members in the United Nations. This would leave unresolved the Security Council problem. He added he thought there would be enough support for such a resolution. Lord Home thought that if Formosa were dropped from the Security Council such a resolution would get more support. The Secretary thought that later on we could put the interest of others in Security Council membership into the pot for consideration which would help drag out this problem. The President said it would be best from our standpoint if Red China were not admitted this year. He would like to see if we could not address ourselves to a resolution they would not be likely to accept. If they were admitted it would raise incalculable problems for us. Furthermore, from a purely domestic political point of view it did not look good for a new administration to have allowed Chinese Communist admission so soon. The Prime Minister wondered whether a resolution which in effect said that there were many changes and many new members since the UN had started and that therefore a committee should be set up to consider the problem of divided countries and enlargement of the Security Council. The Secretary commented that the latter might help but he doubted the former. The Prime Minister said that Communist China really knows the UK would not support their taking over eight million people. He suggested we should consider first a delaying resolution and secondly a successor nation resolution. The President reiterated we would have to stay way in the background as far as a successor state resolution was concerned. Sir Patrick added the UK would have to be careful too. The Prime Minister thought it could be farmed out to a neutral.[4]

---

[4] Kennedy and Rusk later raised the subject of Chinese representation in an April 8 meeting with Macmillan. According to a memorandum of conversation by Burdett, Kennedy stressed the political sensitivity of the China problem, and Rusk indicated that any change in U.S. policy would be particularly difficult if it appeared to be made "because of the eloquence of our friends from London." Macmillan replied that in his public comments he would emphasize the complicated nature of the issue. He added that further relaxation of multilateral restrictions on trade with China would tend to mute criticism in the British business community. (Department of State, Conference Files: Lot 65 D 366, CF 1833) See the Supplement.

## 19.    Telegram From the Department of State to the Embassy in the Republic of China

Washington, April 5, 1961, 9:26 p.m.

500. Following summary Ambassador Yeh's call on Secretary April 3 based on uncleared memcon.[1] Conversation centered on Chinese Representation issue, but Yeh first handed Secretary letter for President Kennedy from President Chiang[2] together with copy of translation for Secretary to read. In portion devoted to Chinese Representation letter recalls ROC's role as founding member of United Nations and its record faithful adherence to obligations of charter. From its own standpoint ROC's continued membership in United Nations means preservation its rightful status and its moral position as true representative of Chinese people in community of nations, while from United Nations standpoint ROC's continued presence assures United Nations of Chinese peoples uninterrupted cooperation with other free nations in safe-guarding positions and principles of United Nations charter. Admission of Chinese Communist regime, however, would not only run counter to wishes of people of mainland, but also extinguish their hope of liberation. Letter states further: "My Government cannot possibly accept the so-called 'two-Chinas' or any other arrangement that would affect the character of the Republic of China's right of representation in the United Nations . . . there is no room for patriots and traitors to live together." Letter expresses gratitude for United States Government's staunch support of GRC in United Nations in past years and sincere hope for continued cooperation in devising ways and means to bar Chinese Communists from United Nations membership.

After reiterating some of foregoing arguments orally Ambassador Yeh put forward GRC proposal that United States and GRC canvass United Nations members see how many oppose and how many favor moratorium and how many reserve their position. Also suggested ascertain how many countries basically oppose entry of Communist China. He suggested next two months be spent in accumulating and analyzing these data, then Governments could meet again and go over whole problem. Yeh said he had explained to GRC United States intention to block

---

Source: Department of State, Central Files, 303/4–561. Secret; Limited Distribution. Drafted by Martin, cleared by Assistant Secretary of State for International Organization Affairs Harlan Cleveland, and approved by Steeves.

[1] Drafted by Martin; not printed. (Ibid., 303/4–361)

[2] Dated April 1; not printed. The letter is in the Kennedy Library, National Security Files, Countries Series, China, Chiang Kai-shek Correspondence; a translation is in Department of State, Presidential Correspondence: Lot 66 D 204, Chinese Officials Correspondence with Kennedy/Johnson.

Communist China's admission, but he emphasized that any tactic which implied two-Chinas would meet terrific opposition both within ROC and among overseas Chinese. In this connection he stressed Dulles–Chiang Joint Communiqué of October 1958[3] was furthest GRC could travel in this direction. He also mentioned constitutional problem arising from any situation implying separate mainland.

Secretary felt there were two points on which GRC wholly isolated.

1—On recognition of GRC as in any sense de facto Government of all China.

2—On issue that support of GRC means active support of continuing civil war or regaining mainland.

Yeh agreed, but expressed hope that this issue would not be raised. Secretary pointed out people want to know what they are supporting. Yeh felt this question answered in Joint Communiqué of 1954 [1958]. Secretary said implication Chiang's letter was that Chinese Representation question would be dealt with by moratorium formula, which could be decided by a bare majority. If moratorium failed, same bare majority could treat issue as credentials matter and seat Communist China. In reply to Ambassador's comment that if moratorium failed effort could be made treat issue as important question requiring two thirds vote, Secretary said if both GRC and Peiping regime take view that it is only question who sits in China's seat, it would be very hard to argue it is anything but procedural matter. Yeh pointed out he was not saying moratorium formula would work, but GRC wanted to wait longer before making definite assessment. Cleveland suggested that if we wait too long we may go beyond point where still possible get majority for some alternate formula.

In reply Secretary's comment he gathered from Chiang's letter there no change in GRC's attitude toward problem since 1949, Yeh replied this correct so far as GRC's being in United Nations with Peiping regime. However he understood our purpose was not to get Peiping regime into UN but to block it. Secretary confirmed this as a purpose but said we could not think about it efficiently without knowing GRC's position. He said there was point of difference in United States and GRC attitudes. GRC would rather keep its position as is at risk of losing it. Yeh rejoined that it would risk losing it in order to adhere to principles. Secretary said if GRC took risk and lost it would be out of UN, but United States would still be there with loss to our position. Thus we had to think separately about our own interests which were different from GRC's on this point.

---

[3] Reference is to the joint communiqué issued at Taipei on October 23, 1958, at the conclusion of meetings between President Chiang and Secretary Dulles. For text, see *Foreign Relations*, 1958–1960, vol. XIX, pp. 442–444.

Ambassador said GRC's proposal was to think further on matter and explore possibility another formula which would not mean volte-face for GRC. Perhaps we would be helped by international situation. Secretary said we would have think about problem some more.

When Yeh asked what British want, Secretary said if issue posed as credentials question (as implied by Chiang's letter) they would have to go along with Peiping. However we are trying think of way of avoiding that issue being posed. Cleveland said we wanted build majority on simple proposition that GRC should stay in UN. This difficult if GRC says there are worse things than being out of UN. It probable we could get majority in UN in support of letting Peiping regime stay out because GRC was there thus shifting onus to Peiping.

**Rusk**

---

### 20.    Memorandum From the Acting Assistant Secretary of State for Far Eastern Affairs (Steeves) to Secretary of State Rusk

Washington, April 15, 1961.

SUBJECT

United Nations Chinese Representation Tactics and Offshore Islands Problem

REFERENCE

Mr. McGhee's Memorandum of April 3, 1961 (Tab A)[1]

I agree with Mr. McGhee that in working out our tactics on Chinese representation in the United Nations we should not consider this issue in vacuo but in relation to the other important problems which we face in the area, and that the offshore islands are one of the most important of these. To the extent feasible, it would clearly be desirable to handle the representation issue in a way that will not jeopardize our long-run purpose of disengaging from these islands. For the following reasons, how-

---

Source: Department of State, Central Files, 303/4–1561. Secret. Drafted by Lutkins, cleared in draft by Sullivan, and initialed by Rusk, indicating that he had seen it.

[1] McGhee's April 3 memorandum to Rusk commented on a March 24 memorandum from Legal Adviser Abram Chayes to Cleveland and a March 28 memorandum from Parsons to Cleveland on the Chinese representation issue. (All are ibid., S/P Files: Lot 67 D 548, China, 1959–1961)

ever, I am not persuaded by the arguments advanced by Mr. McGhee in this connection on behalf of the successor state formula as opposed to the FE–IO proposal that Communist China be required to apply for United Nations membership as a new state.

Mr. McGhee argues that following the tactical approach proposed by FE and IO would mean that we would have to expend our bargaining power with the GRC in an effort to gain its cooperation, leaving us little leverage for use in seeking to effect GRC evacuation of the offshore islands. The weakness of this argument, in FE's view, is that we possess very limited practical leverage vis-à-vis the GRC on the offshore islands question in any case. President Chiang has repeatedly made it clear both privately and publicly that he will not abandon this territory, but will defend the islands regardless of United States support. Retention of the islands is a matter integrally related to the GRC's national existence, as it conceives it, and in FE's opinion no inducements we could offer or pressures we might threaten to exert would at this time serve to alter its position.

Secondly, in seeking to persuade the GRC to adopt a posture in the United Nations necessary to ensure the success of the new state tactic advocated by FE and IO we would certainly have to expect to use up some bargaining power, as Mr. McGhee points out. The important point, however, is that, assuming we deal with it with understanding, tact, and patience, there is some chance that the GRC will in the end be willing to cooperate with us in employing this tactic. On the other hand in FE's judgment, there are definite limits to the GRC's tactical flexibility, and we see virtually no chance of its accepting the successor state formula which envisages automatic seating of Communist China. If faced with the prospect of action embodying such an approach, the GRC would probably withdraw from the United Nations (at least from the General Assembly), leaving a clear field to Peiping. FE can see no bargaining counters available to us that would be sufficient to induce the GRC to cooperate with us on the basis of this formula.

Lastly, Mr. McGhee's memorandum suggests that the leading role that the United States would have to play in seeking to handle the Chinese representation issue in the tactical manner proposed by FE and IO would create a maximum of domestic political difficulty for the Administration. In my opinion any such difficulty would be mild compared to that involved in adopting the successor state approach. The latter would require the United States at least to acquiesce in the automatic seating of Communist China, which would be certain to evoke strong criticism from a large segment of the American people. Under the FE–IO formula, on the other hand, the United States would be free to maintain its stand that Communist China is not qualified for membership in the United Nations and to oppose its seating.

## 21.    Letter From President Kennedy to President Chiang

Washington, April 17, 1961.

DEAR MR. PRESIDENT: I have received your thoughtful letter of April 1,[1] which was brought to Washington by Ambassador Yeh following his consultations in Taipei. I am grateful for your kind words of greeting and wish to reciprocate them fully. I appreciate also your careful exposition of the views of the Government of the Republic of China with regard to the problem of Chinese representation in the United Nations and other problems facing the nations of the free world.

My government is keenly aware of the expansionist aims of world communism and of the particular threat posed by its sustained efforts to divide the free world. The Republic of China faces most directly the threat of communist aggression. Here the Communists do not conceal their aims, but rather they proclaim their "right" to attack Taiwan. I assure you, Mr. President, that my Government will faithfully adhere to its commitments under the Mutual Defense Treaty between our countries.

We are mindful of Communist attempts to manipulate the United Nations so that it may serve as an instrument in their drive for world domination. We will continue to use every opportunity to strengthen the United Nations as the best means of preserving genuine world peace and protecting the independence of small nations.

One of our major objectives in the United Nations is the maintenance of the status of the Republic of China as a member of the organization. Our problem is not one of objectives, on which we agree, but rather on the choice of tactics to attain those objectives. We have indicated to Ambassador Yeh, with whom we are in close consultation, our serious doubt that sufficient support remains to carry the moratorium procedure successfully in the next General Assembly, and are giving urgent consideration to other tactical means of assuring success in attaining our objectives. These exchanges with Ambassador Yeh have been most useful. We will continue to consult closely with him in the interest of both our countries and of the free world.

In the long run, the free world can best meet the challenge of communism by strengthening its democratic institutions and making them

---

Source: Department of State, Presidential Correspondence: Lot 66 D 204, Kennedy/Johnson Correspondence with Chinese Officials. Confidential. Limit Distribution. The letter was pouched to Taipei on April 24. It was drafted in the Office of Chinese Affairs, except the last sentence which was added in the White House, and was sent to the White House with a covering memorandum of April 14 from Rusk stating that it had been drafted to take advantage of the occasion to reassure Chiang of U.S. support. (Ibid., Central Files, 303/4–1461)
[1] See footnote 2, Document 19.

more responsive to the aspirations of the peoples of the world. In this connection, the American people have become increasingly aware of the significant social and economic progress that has been achieved in Taiwan during recent years in spite of the heavy burden imposed by the requirements of defense against Communist aggression. The United States Government has supported these successful endeavors and will continue to do so as free China demonstrates in its accelerated economic growth program that a nation can advance the material welfare of its people while maintaining its great traditions.

Please accept my best wishes for continued success in your high office in the service of the Chinese people. My wife joins me in extending greetings to you and Madame Chiang.

Sincerely,

**John F. Kennedy**[2]

---

[2] Printed from a copy that indicates President Kennedy signed the original.

---

## 22.   Telegram From the Embassy in Poland to the Department of State

Warsaw, April 18, 1961, 5 p.m.

1509. Beam–Wang talks. 104th meeting one hour forty minutes.[1] I opened with paragraphs 1, 2 and 3 of Deptel 1125.[2] Wang replied his side indeed desired improve relations as he had stated last meeting but it was now three months since new administration had taken office in Wash-

Source: Department of State, Central Files, 611.93/4–1861. Confidential; Niact; Limit Distribution. Repeated to Taipei, Hong Kong, and Moscow.

[1] Beam commented on the meeting and sent recommendations in telegram 1518, April 19, and transmitted a detailed, apparently verbatim report in airgram G–427, April 21. (Ibid., 611.93/4–1961 and 611.93/4–2161, respectively)

[2] Telegram 1125, April 14, transmitted Beam's instructions for the meeting. The paragraphs under reference instructed him to state that the United States had consistently sought to improve relations and that it had never demanded that Wang's side abandon its claim to Taiwan but only that it should not press its claim by threat or use of force, to express appreciation for the news that one U.S. national imprisoned in China (Robert E. McCann) was to be released, and to state that there was great public concern over the situation of the imprisoned Americans and that their release would improve the atmosphere of the talks and eliminate a practical obstacle to better relations between the two countries. (Ibid., 611.93/4–1461)

ington and they have seen no signs of any change in US policy. US still occupied Chinese territory Taiwan and its military forces had made nine additional incursions into China's territorial sea and air. If US would only renounce use of force against China and withdraw from Taiwan relations would improve. His government had noted US had been massing military strength in South China; and had been interfering in Laos instigating use of "KMT remnant forces" against Laotian people.

I briefly restated US position on Taiwan and denied his allegations concerning Laos pointing out US had encouraged evacuation Chinese irregulars to Taiwan. I then referred to our newsmen proposal at last meeting[3] expressing hope his side might now accept.

Wang repeated charges US violating Geneva accords and interfering in Laos. Then restated Chinese Communist position on Taiwan drawing analogy with US civil war. Of correspondents he said US refusal accept their September 6, 1960 proposal and attempt after last meeting to shift blame to Peiping proved US unwillingness exchange correspondents and improve relations with his country.

I pointed out Wang had glossed over growing Soviet aid to Pathet Lao rebels but suggested our differing views on Laos could probably not be reconciled here and expressed hope peaceful solution would be reached through actions now underway elsewhere. I then presented new draft agreed announcement on newsmen in accordance paragraph 4 reftel.[4]

Wang said our job is to find means of settling Taiwan issue. If US would end armed occupation Taiwan the remaining internal matter could be readily settled. Then question of use of force would not arise. Regarding our latest proposal on correspondents he reserved position until next meeting.

I then inquired regarding Tora as instructed paragraph 5 reftel[5] to which Wang said they had no information. I urged that should any information come to their attention they let us know.

Next meeting May 25, 2 p.m.[6]

**Beam**

---

[3] See Document 11.

[4] Paragraph 4 authorized Beam to expand his March 7 proposal by accepting the language of a Chinese draft agreed announcement of September 12, 1957, modified to take the form of parallel unilateral statements of intentions of the two governments, thus avoiding the "governments agree" formulation of the Chinese draft. Beam transmitted the text of the draft he intended to give Wang in telegram 1497, April 17. (Department of State, Central Files, 611.93/4–1761) For text of the Chinese draft of September 12, 1957, see *Foreign Relations, 1955–1957*, vol. II, p. 601, footnote 2.

[5] Paragraph 5 instructed Beam to renew an earlier inquiry for any information concerning the crew members of the yacht *Tora*, which had disappeared in the Taiwan Strait in July 1958.

[6] Telegram 1695 from Warsaw, May 19, reported that the date had been changed to June 29 at Chinese request. (Department of State, Central Files, 611.93/5–1961)

23.    **Memorandum From Robert W. Komer of the National Security Council Staff to the President's Special Assistant for National Security Affairs (Bundy)**

Washington, May 2, 1961.

*Operation Candor with the GRC*

Without accepting Ambassador Drumright's extravagant statements (Taipei 639, 21 April),[1] he nevertheless makes his case that acute apprehension amounting to a crisis of confidence is gripping the GRC.

Taipei's natural fears about the new Administration have been fed by a series of minor developments (outlined by FonMin Shen in above cable, e.g. Outer Mongolia) which, though not intended to spook them prematurely, have, in their highly uncertain frame of mind, apparently had this effect. While such fears may be partly put on, Taipei seems half-convinced we're going to sell it out.

This situation creates both an imperative need to reassure Chiang and an opportunity (in the process of doing so) to bring some pressure to bear. We cannot afford to let GRC morale drop too far because of our silence; at the same time Chiang's uncertainty should put him in a more receptive mood.

Our main thrust must be to convince Chiang that we have in no whit altered our determination to support Free China. If possible we should provide tangible evidence by announcing our willingness to underwrite a long-term GRC development plan (in line with new foreign aid approach).

But we must also stress the necessity, in terms of our long-term interests and theirs, of rethinking those aspects of our policy which have reached the point of diminishing returns, i.e. UN membership and the Offshore Islands. We must both face the fact that (unless the ChiComs get so belligerent, e.g. in Laos, as to fix themselves) most Free World countries will no longer support us on these issues.

---

Source: Kennedy Library, National Security Files, Meetings and Memoranda Series, Staff Memoranda, Robert W. Komer. Secret. Also sent to Rostow.

[1] Telegram 639 reported that Foreign Minister Shen had indicated in a meeting with Drumright that he believed the United States was moving toward a "two Chinas" policy. Drumright commented that this feeling would fester until the United States convinced the GRC that it had no such intention. He predicted that if such a policy was adopted, the GRC would "try to go it alone" rather than sacrifice its "sacred basic objective" of liberating the mainland; without U.S. support, however, Taiwan would fall into Communist hands in a few years. He urged "utmost circumspection" in making any changes in China policy, for "a single misstep could lead to irreparable loss to US as well as GRC." (Department of State, Central Files, 611.93/4–2161)

On UN membership, if we don't come up with a way to shift the onus to Peiping, a UN majority is liable to vote it in and Taipei out. As to the Offshores, they offer a standing invitation to ChiCom pressure on terms so adverse that we are being compelled to rethink our policy.

These harsh realities do not mean that we are playing the UK's game; we ourselves think that Free China's own interests require that it liquidate those issues on which it will inevitably lose sooner or later, and which divert world attention from Peiping's own aggressive policies. We do not intend to desert Chiang, but we feel entitled, as his chief supporter, to insist that he rationalize his position for the long pull.

In sum, we had better act to reassure the GRC promptly, an opportunity we can also use to put him on notice. Another Kennedy–Chiang letter might suffice, but a VP stop in Taipei if he's going to Saigon might be better.[2] At any rate urge you raise at planning lunch and see if State has anything in mind.[3]

**Bob K.**

---

[2] Reference is to a projected trip by Vice President Johnson to Southeast Asia.

[3] An attached note of the same date from Komer to Bundy and Rostow recommended that they raise the subject at lunch with Deputy Under Secretary of State for Political Affairs U. Alexis Johnson and ask him what steps the Department was contemplating to reassure Chiang since the timing of the Vice President's projected trip was uncertain. No record of such a discussion has been found.

---

### 24.    Editorial Note

In Dean Rusk's *As I Saw It*, he describes a "long, private talk" with President Kennedy in May 1961 on the subject of China. According to Rusk's account, he asked Kennedy if he wanted the State Department to explore possible changes in China policy, and the two sketched out some options: "Recognize both Chinas, the so-called two-Chinas approach; work quietly behind the scenes for reconciliation between Peking and Taipei; and sit tight and await further developments."

Rusk states that he and Kennedy agreed that "American China policy in the year we took office, indeed for many years, did not reflect Asian realities." After referring to the problem of Chinese representation, he continues as follows:

"Not surprisingly, Kennedy ruled out any changes in our China policy. With his razor-thin victory in the November elections—he used to attribute his win to 'Cook County, Illinois'—he felt he lacked a strong mandate from the American people. Consequently, he was very cautious about selecting issues on which to do battle. And any change in China policy would have been one hell of a battle. In fact, just before Dwight Eisenhower left office, he told Kennedy that although he would support him on foreign policy in general, he would strongly oppose any attempt by the new administration to recognize Peking and seat mainland China at the United Nations.

"Also, such contacts as we had with Peking were not promising. Simply put, the Chinese Communists didn't seem interested in improving U.S.-Chinese relations. As far as Kennedy was concerned, then, adopting a more realistic China policy became a future task, not a present one. Fearing the issue might divide Congress and the American people, he decided the potential benefits of a more realistic China policy didn't warrant risking a severe political confrontation. He could have been cut to ribbons politically by the China Lobby, the Republicans, and many members of Congress. We would have had great difficulty implementing a two-Chinas policy.

"I agreed with Kennedy's reasoning and his conclusions, and I told him so. But as I was leaving the Oval Office, he called, 'And what's more, Mr. Secretary, I don't want to read in the *Washington Post* or the *New York Times* that the State Department is thinking about a change in our China policy!' I went back to the department, and when Adlai Stevenson, Chester Bowles, and others would drop by to talk about China and especially their hopes for a two-Chinas policy at the UN, I stonewalled them and played the role of the 'village idiot.' I didn't tell them about my talk with the president because I would have read about *that* in the *Washington Post* or the *New York Times*. Nor did I initiate any new studies on China policy; in that leaky Kennedy administration even that would have gotten to the press." (*As I Saw It* by Dean Rusk, as told to Richard Rusk (New York: W.W. Norton, 1990), pages 282–284)

According to Kennedy's and Rusk's Appointment Books, their only private meeting in May was on May 5. Rusk's Appointment Book (Johnson Library) indicates that he was alone with the President from 1:10 to 1:25 p.m.; according to Kennedy's (Kennedy Library), Rusk was alone with him from 1:05 to 1:10 p.m. No other record has been found of this conversation.

## 25.    Memorandum From the Deputy Under Secretary of State for Political Affairs (Johnson) to Acting Secretary of State Bowles

Washington, May 10, 1961.

SUBJECT

U.S. Policy Toward the Chinese Civil War

There are attached the papers prepared by S/P[1] and FE[2] on the foregoing subject sent to me for review.

First, no one can possibly quarrel with the objective of attempting to end the civil war. It represents a very real danger to peace in the area and could well involve us in hostilities not of our own choosing and making. Therefore, I see no reason that we should not continue to strive towards the objective, but I am very doubtful that we should attempt to bring severe pressure on the GRC in this regard unless and until we have some reason to believe that Peiping would be responsive. To do so would only produce severe strains on our relationship with the GRC without any practical result, for it takes two to end a war.

As I mentioned the other day, one of the objectives of my talks with the Chinese Communists which began in Geneva in 1955 was de facto to accomplish the result of ending the war by obtaining from the Chinese Communists a reciprocal renunciation of force in the area. The Chinese Communists were undoubtedly aware that they would at that time have been able considerably to embarrass us by accepting such a proposition, for it was by no means certain that the GRC would agree. However, the

---

Source: Department of State, Central Files, 611.93/5-1061. Top Secret.

[1] The memorandum of May 10 from Deputy Counselor and Vice Chairman of the Policy Planning Council George A. Morgan to Bowles states that it was prepared in response to a May 4 request from Bowles for discussion of "the pros and cons of terminating the Chinese civil war." It declared that while there would be many advantages in adopting such a policy, "tantamount to a two-China policy," it would be foolhardy to embark on it without plans for coping with adverse GRC reactions, bringing about an evacuation of the offshore islands, and ensuring Congressional and public support. It recommended (1) further study of the question on an urgent basis and (2) in the meantime, keeping GRC operational activities against the mainland to a minimum.

[2] The May 10 memorandum from Assistant Secretary of State for Far Eastern Affairs Walter P. McConaughy to Bowles stated that although FE agreed with the recommendations of the Morgan memorandum, FE was unable to associate with it in its entirety because: developments in Laos and Vietnam made it a bad time to embark upon such a policy, efforts to persuade the GRC to accept it would fail and have unfortunate consequences, the PRC would not drop its claim to Taiwan, and since PRC hostility to the United States was "an inescapable fact of life" pressures should be increased in order to exploit current PRC economic difficulties. It concluded that rather than seeking the unrealistic goal of persuading both sides to abandon their aspirations, "we should concentrate our efforts on seeking to insure that neither side resorts to large-scale use of force to realize their objectives."

Chinese Communists resolutely refused and are still continuing to refuse such a proposition. It is my own feeling that the imperatives of the Chinese revolution and their internal situation render it virtually impossible for them to do so.

As I also mentioned the other day, I probed as deeply as I know how on their attitude toward the off-shore islands. Neither at that time, nor I understand subsequently, have they either publicly or privately shown the slightest interest in GRC evacuation of the off-shores but have consistently linked those islands with their whole attitude toward Taiwan. Therefore, however logical and practical it might seem that an evacuation of the off-shores would tend to reduce tensions in the area, Chinese Communist attitudes do not give the slightest indication that this would in fact result. However, the military weakness of the exposed position of the GRC in the off-shores is obvious and I believe we should continue to urge their evacuation on that ground.

I agree with the FE memorandum that the very raison d'etre of the present group in the GRC is their claim to return to the mainland and, unrealistic though this may be, I do not think we can any more expect them to renounce the principle than we could for West Germany to renounce the principle of German reunification. I fear that this is one of those issues which only time can solve, and more time is needed. In the meanwhile, we continue to do all we can to prevent its exploding into hostilities which involve us. In this connection, the Congressional Resolution on the off-shore islands[3] gives the President discretionary authority and is not a commitment on our part.

The aspect of our China policy that has most bothered me is that the necessity of defending the position of the GRC in the United Nations and other international organizations all too often becomes the controlling factor in our decisions and greatly limits our freedom of choice. I would hope that, as our policy on China evolves, we could work out a formula that could much more effectively cope with this aspect.

In summary, I certainly see no objection to S/P continuing to explore more fully the practicability of a policy aimed at terminating the Chinese civil war and hopefully, with some fresh thinking, some new ideas can be developed. The formidable difficulties should not deter us from trying.[4]

---

[3] Reference is to the Joint Resolution approved on January 29, 1955, or P.L. 84–4; 69 Stat. 7). For text, see *Foreign Relations, 1955–1957*, vol. II, pp. 162–163.

[4] Bowles initialed the Morgan memorandum on June 9, indicating his approval of the recommendation for further study. A notation on the memorandum indicates that no decision was taken on the second recommendation.

26.    **Telegram From the Embassy in the Republic of China to the Consulate General in Hong Kong**

Taipei, May 15, 1961, 9 p.m.

134. Codel Johnson for Crockett.[1] Summary follows of conversation between Vice President Johnson and President Chiang on afternoon of May 14. As agreed with Vice President's party, Embassy will send detailed memorandum of conversation to Department under cover of limited distribution despatch[2] stating that memorandum has not been reviewed by Vice President.

After initial exchange of greetings, Vice President handed President Chiang letter from President Kennedy.[3] As is his usual custom, President Chiang did not ask for immediate translation of letter. Substance of letter was, however, covered fully by Vice President in subsequent discussions.

President Chiang expressed his pleasure over Vice President's visit to Taiwan and stated Vice President's trip has given Asian people great hope. Vice President stated that principal purpose of trip is to make clear firmness of US policy and to gain further understanding of situation in Asia. Vice President pointed out it is very important that United States Government and free Asian governments have accurate information concerning one another's intentions. President Chiang agreed.

Vice President said President Kennedy is man who believes in keeping commitments. President Chiang commented that with President

---

Source: Johnson Library, VP Security File, VP Johnson's Trip—Far East, May 1961. Secret; Priority; Limit Distribution. Repeated to the Department as telegram 717 from Taipei. (Department of State, Central Files, 033.1100 JO/5–1561) Also repeated to Bangkok.

[1] Vice President Johnson was in Hong Kong following a May 14–15 visit to the Republic of China in the course of a trip to South and Southeast Asia. Documentation on his visit is ibid., 033.1100 JO, and Conference Files: Lot 65 D 366, CF 1880. For text of the joint communiqué issued at Taipei on May 15, see *American Foreign Policy: Current Documents, 1961,* pp. 947–948. For text of Johnson's May 23 report to Kennedy on his trip, see U.S. Department of Defense, *United States-Vietnam Relations, 1945–1967,* vol. 11, pp. 159–166.

[2] Despatch 612, May 16. (Department of State, Central Files, 033.1100 JO/5–1661) Despatch 655 from Taipei, June 9, transmitted Chinese records of this and two subsequent conversations between Johnson and Chiang. (Ibid., 033.1100 JO/6–961)

[3] Dated May 8, it reads in part as follows:

"I wish to take this opportunity, Mr. President, to reiterate that my Government will continue to stand solidly behind the Mutual Defense Treaty between our two countries in meeting the challenge posed by the Chinese Communists in the Taiwan area. I also wish to assure you that my Government has no intention of recognizing the aggressive and tyrannical communist regime in Peiping. My Government, furthermore, remains opposed to the seating of the Chinese Communist regime in the United Nations and, as I emphasized in my letter of April 17 [Document 21] to you, regards it as important that the position of the Republic of China in the United Nations should be maintained." (Department of State, Presidential Correspondence: Lot 66 D 204) See the Supplement. The letter was drafted in the Department of State and sent to the White House with a May 8 covering memorandum from U. Alexis Johnson to Rostow. (Department of State, Central Files, 793.11/5–861)

Kennedy at head of free world he is confident concerning success of both general free world struggle and of China's own struggle in particular.

Vice President said he wished to make clear US has no intention whatsoever of recognizing Communist China. Policy of present US administration is to love one's friends and to hate one's enemies.

President Chiang asked Vice President Johnson how he had found situation in South Vietnam. Vice President replied that he and President Diem had discussed number of positive proposals made in letter from President Kennedy to President Diem.[4] President Chiang expressed opinion that as the result of Vice President's visit the situation in South Vietnam may become stabilized. Vice President observed that democratic system frequently makes slow start but then is hard to stop. Totalitarian governments, however, sometimes enjoy early successes. Recent Communist successes in Laos were reason for President Kennedy asking him to make present trip. President had also sent his brother-in-law and sister[5] to take look at situation in Asia in which President is intensely interested.

Vice President explained that he had been sent on his current mission first to reassure allies who wish to stand up to communism and second to try to strengthen existing programs or to create new programs which will help those allies to do so. By time trip has been completed, Vice President said, he expects President Diem will have sent representative to Washington with additional suggestions designed to increase military strength in South Vietnam. Also, he and members of his party will have greater understanding of the situation in Asia and he is confident program will be evolved that will make possible all out effort resist evil force of communism.

Vice President expressed his admiration for excellent job which Vice President Chen had told him is being done on Taiwan. He commented particularly on achievements in education, and on high living standard. He also commented favorably on sincere friendship of Chinese people for United States and on interest of Chinese leaders in development of science. In latter connection, President Chiang congratulated VP on space flight of Commander Shephard. President expressed skepticism concerning Soviet claims for its space flight. Vice President contrasted full television coverage of Commander Shepard's flight with limited information provided by Russians on their space venture.

---

[4] The text of Kennedy's May 8 letter to South Vietnamese President Ngo Dinh Diem is printed in *United States-Vietnam Relations, 1945–1967,* vol. 11, pp. 132–135. Other documentation pertaining to Johnson's May 11–13 visit to South Vietnam may be found in *Foreign Relations, 1961–1963,* vol. I, pp. 135–157.

[5] Stephen and Jean Kennedy Smith.

Vice President said he believes President will soon recommend to Congress: (1) better coordinated, practical and more useful economic aid programs; (2) considerable increase in strength of United States conventional forces; and (3) all out effort in the space field.

Vice President mentioned recent visits of Adenauer and Macmillan to Washington and coming trip of President Kennedy to confer with President De Gaulle. Vice President said that President Kennedy is anxious United States consultations with friendly leaders not be limited to Europe or to either large or small countries. Vice President said that is why he is in Taipei. VP said that US has tried very hard to induce French and British to give greater support to this part of world but that they have been most reluctant to do so. VP said he hoped information obtained and objectives developed on trip would enable US government to be more persuasive with French and British than it has been thus far.

Vice President said any new approach to Southeast Asia should involve effort build maximum strength in Vietnam and perhaps also substantial SEATO assistance in Thailand. SEATO members might be asked to make substantially increased contributions. Thus when decision is made concerning Laos, we will know where we are going in Thailand and Vietnam and area will be source of strength. Vice President said since present approach is not working it is very important to find new plan which will stop free world giving up and moving back. President Chiang commented that this was precisely his own view.

In summing up, Vice President said he had tried: (1) to express his appreciation of developments on Taiwan and to state attitude of US toward President Chiang and his government, toward Chinese Communists, toward issue of recognition of Chinese Communists and toward question of admission of Chinese Communists to United Nations; and (2) to give some ideas on how US is approaching program for Southeast Asia. Vice President said he would like President Chiang's opinion on latter subject. He had no doubt concerning his views on former subjects.

President Chiang expressed admiration for Vice President's statement concerning US position and his analysis of situation. President said he wished to speak very frankly as between allies and friends. Vice President encouraged him to do so.

President Chiang first thanked US govt and American people for their support which has enabled his government to consolidate Taiwan as base for carrying out fight against communism. President expressed regret time did not permit lengthy exchange of views and said he would state briefly points which he wished to make and would elaborate on them if Vice President wished.

President Chiang said his first point is that developments in Laos have proved that SEATO is not much more than empty shell. Reverses in Laos have weakened confidence of Asian members in SEATO and may also have affected their confidence in American leadership. He agreed with Vice President that something different must be done to save situation.

Complaint, President said, is that none of friendly Asian nations concerned will believe that Britain or France can be persuaded to take more positive stand in Southeast Asia. Suspicion exists, he said, that these two countries joined SEATO more to hinder than to help. Free Asian leaders recall colonial record of British and French and cannot believe that they have had change of heart. Also, presence of British and French in SEATO permits Communists to charge that SEATO is merely instrument to perpetuate Western colonial interests. President stated situation in Laos may be charged largely to British and French obstructionism. It is high time, he said, to give up hope that Britain and France will play active role in any anti-Communist alliance in Asia.

Turning to another point, President said that, despite United States bilateral security agreements with several Asian nations, united policy under positive leadership is lacking. He expressed hope that US would supply this policy and this leadership. United States, he said, has expended considerable effort in Asia but this effort does not add up to strength it should have produced. General reappraisal of United States policy is required. United States policy in Asia should be based on giving effective aid to nations involved in struggle against communism. President criticized US concept of maintaining fire brigade to rush here and there putting out fires. He said there is no need to supply US forces. Local Asian peoples can do job. President Chiang also urged that new positive policy in Asia apply to entire area. Effort to solve problems in one country, such as Laos, separately should be discontinued. Vice President asked President Chiang what US should have done in Laos that it has not done. Madame Chiang responded by asking whether it was true that US advisors in Laos had worn civilian clothes, had been responsible for only administrative aspects of aid, and had not been permitted to train Laotian forces. Vice President said she was correct and had put her finger on source of difficulty. Weak spot in Laos, he said, was failure of French to perform their job effectively. Vice President said United States government has made clear to French and other governments that US is concerned with freedom everywhere—not just in some areas. We have told French, he said, that we cannot see why we must argue with them about Laos.

Vice President Chen said it is often asked why Pathet Lao can fight and troops of Lao government cannot although both are Laotian. Answer, he said, is very simple. Pathet Lao are supported by Russian airlift, Chinese Communist advisors, and North Vietnamese reinforcements. Lao government is in effect being attacked by several governments. To meet this free world forces must be organized in coordinated manner. We must have unified planning, execution, and command.

Vice President Johnson asked President Chiang whether he would favor sending Pakistan, Filipino, and American forces into Thailand or Vietnam as sign we mean business. President Chiang suggested that, if Thailand were willing, Thai troops be sent into Laos to defend key points along Mekong River such as Vientiane, Luang Prebang, and Tak Hok. US, he said, should give Thais logistical support, supply planes and train Thai pilots. Vice President commented Thais might be interested in this approach if men in US uniform were at their side which was what President Chiang said US should not do. President Chiang agreed and said he has been and still is of opinion that US policy in Asia should not be based on getting US forces involved.

Vice President expressed interest in continuing conversation during and after dinner that evening. President Chiang agreed.

(Notes on conversations between Vice President Johnson and President Chiang on evening of May 14 and morning of May 15 were taken by member of Vice President's party. Embassy understands party will report to Washington on those conversations).[6]

**Drumright**

---

[6] According to transcripts based on notes taken by Robert Waldron of Johnson's party, on May 14 Chiang stressed the need for coordinated action in Asia, and he and Johnson discussed a draft joint communiqué. On May 15 Chiang complained that in the past the United States had sometimes not placed enough trust in his government. He predicted "an explosion or collapse on the China Mainland" within 1 or 2 years and urged regular U.S.-GRC consultations to agree on common policies and to study the situation on the mainland "so that more effective steps and measures can be worked out to hasten the overthrow of the Communist regime." Johnson stressed the importance of taking an affirmative approach in public statements on his visit, emphasizing the economic and educational progress in Taiwan. (Johnson Library, Waldron Papers)

## 27.    Memorandum of Conversation

Washington, May 24, 1961, 4:57–6:32 p.m.

SUBJECT

Chinese Representation in the UN

PARTICIPANTS

The President
The Secretary of State
Ambassador Adlai E. Stevenson
Assistant Secretary Harlan Cleveland

The following is a summary of consensus and action and not a detailed record of a meeting which lasted about an hour and a half, covering several subjects.

As a result of the briefing by Alexis Johnson and others on May 23, in connection with the President's trip to Paris,[1] the President indicated his familiarity with the general lines of the State Department's current thinking on Chinese Representation, as set forth now in the memorandum for the President on that subject, dated May 24, 1961.[2]

In the course of discussion of this subject, the Secretary handed the President a talking paper for his prospective conversation with Henry Luce.[3] The Secretary recommended that the President discuss the matter with Mr. Luce on the basis of the analysis of the problem contained on Page 1 of the talking paper, and the analysis of the precarious state of the moratorium formula contained in the Annex to the talking paper; but not to get into detail on the "successor nation" or other specific formulas for the handling of parliamentary tactics in the UN next fall.

Ambassador Stevenson emphasized the importance of not saying for domestic consumption that the purpose of the exercise is to keep the

---

Source: Kennedy Library, National Security Files, Countries Series, China. Secret. Drafted by Cleveland. A note on the source text indicates it was not cleared by the President or the Secretary. The time of the meeting is from Kennedy's Appointment Book. (Kennedy Library) The meeting was held at the White House.

[1] For documentation concerning President Kennedy's May 31–June 2 visit to Paris, see vol. XIII, pp. 656–667.

[2] Not further identified, but see Document 28.

[3] Editor and publisher Henry R. Luce. The paper, unsigned and undated, stated that the U.S. objective was to find a proposal that would retain membership for Nationalist China on terms that the Chinese Communists would reject, that this objective could not be explained to the American public without damaging the U.S. case with other governments, and that "Whether the Nationalists can be kept in the UN by this means, therefore, depends heavily on the understanding and restraint of leaders of public opinion, particularly those who agree with us that it is extremely important not to damage the prospects of the Government of the Republic of China by acting in such a way as to make inevitable a credentials fight in which the Nationalists could be defeated." (Kennedy Library, President's Office Files, Countries Series, Communist China)

Chinese Communists out of the UN, since that would make any proposal of ours, providing for a procedure whereby the Chinese Communists could under certain conditions take a seat in the UN, seem hypocritical.

The President asked Ambassador Stevenson what he really thought about the matter of Communist China, should we want them in the UN? Ambassador Stevenson said no, he did not want them in the UN; but that this subject should not be one on which the U.S. sustained a major loss, on a question which we had staked the whole of our prestige and leadership.

The President emphasized his view that the U.S. should not take the lead in building the coalition for the kind of "two Chinas" formula proposed in the State Department memorandum. He was clear that the Chinese Nationalists are in real danger of being thrown out of the UN, and that our objective is to keep them in; the Department's proposal seems the best arrangement in the circumstances, but it would require a good discussion with key political figures in the U.S. before the U.S. Government could take the lead in putting it forward internationally.

The President said he would ask Henry Luce and others whether they have any better ideas about how to keep the Nationalists in the UN, given the circumstances as described in the analysis of the voting situation on the moratorium. But we could not take the major leadership in promoting even the best formula through diplomatic consultations, without its leaking to the press, and stirring up political controversy in the United States which would adversely affect the foreign aid bill and other objectives of his Administration. While, therefore, informal discussions could proceed in diplomatic channels and with key figures in United States opinion, including President Eisenhower, the President's reaction was that the Government cannot bring this subject formally to the surface for a couple of months at least.

The Secretary reported that the Australian Ambassador had been in to visit him the previous day,[4] and had volunteered on behalf of his government to take some initiative in this field if we thought that would be helpful. The President's reaction was that it would be useful to discuss the formula we have developed with the Australians and perhaps the British, and see if it could be floated internationally as from them.

The President also emphasized the importance of getting the Chinese Nationalists to cooperate as much as possible, since their views and attitudes will be influential with some segments of American opinion on this kind of subject. He suggested that further conversations with the Chinese Ambassadors to the UN and to Washington might be helpful in

---

[4] A memorandum of the conversation, dated May 23, is in Department of State, Central Files, 303/5–2361.

this regard.[5] In the course of this discussion a brief summary of the discussions with Ambassadors Tsiang and Yeh was provided to the President.[6]

There was some discussion of the Security Council aspects of the China Representation issue; the potential delays and difficulties that might stand in the way of resolving early the matter of the Chinese seat on the Security Council were described by the Secretary. These included the uncertainty of whether a substitution of the Communists for the Nationalists in the Security Council was a vetoable proposition, and the possibility that this whole question would become a part of the larger question of changing the composition of the Security Council, which would require revision of the Charter and ratification by member states, including the United States Senate.

The President thought that it would be just as well not to get on the Security Council aspects in the near future; he suggested to Ambassador Stevenson that in discussion of Chinese Representation it would be better not to have a well developed position on the Security Council stage, and to discuss the matter for the time being in its General Assembly context. In this connection, he emphasized once again the political dynamite locked up in this issue.

---

[5] Stevenson met with Chinese Ambassador to the United Nations T.F. Tsiang on June 1. He told Deputy Assistant Secretary of State for International Organization Affairs Woodruff Wallner in a June 5 letter that he had told Tsiang that "we hoped his Government would be able to refrain from actions or statements which, *by affecting our own domestic climate,* might limit our tactical maneuverability." (Ibid., 303/6–261)

[6] Telegram 3129 from USUN, May 17, reported on a meeting between Stevenson and Tsiang that day. (Ibid., 303/5–1761) A meeting of May 18 among Cleveland, McConaughy, Yeh, and Tsiang is recorded in a memorandum of conversation of that date. (Ibid., 303/5–1861) The discussions are summarized in Document 28.

## 28.    Memorandum From Secretary of State Rusk to President Kennedy

Washington, May 26, 1961.

SUBJECT

China and the United Nations

*Basic Elements of the Problem*

Informal discussions among the delegates in New York, and our own formal discussions with the Government of the Republic of China, have somewhat clarified the alternatives open to us on the Chinese representation issue—by narrowing them.

It now seems clear that there is potentially a majority vote in the Assembly for two propositions:

a. that the Government of the Republic of China should remain a member of the United Nations; and
b. that the People's Republic of China should become a member of the United Nations.

Our judgment is that we cannot postpone substantive voting on the China question in the General Assembly beyond the 16th session of the General Assembly this fall. The moratorium can no longer be relied upon.

It is, further, our judgment that if the Assembly is asked to choose between the Chinese Communists and the Chinese Nationalists as occupants of a single China sent in the Assembly, a majority of the General Assembly would vote to seat the Chinese Communists. Such a vote would, moreover, find a number of important countries, including friends and allies, on the opposite side of the fence from the United States. You will remember that Prime Minister Macmillan and Lord Home said as much in the discussions with you on April 5 and 6, 1961.[1]

It seems clear that the best way to avoid having the Chinese Nationalists thrown out of the United Nations in a vote against our position, which might have extremely adverse effects on American public opinion about the United Nations, is to develop some form of "Two Chinas" proposal which can command wide support in the United Nations. To this

---

Source: Department of State, Central Files, 303/5–2661. Secret. No drafter is indicated on the source text but an attached covering memorandum of May 25 from Cleveland to Rusk indicates that it was drafted in the Bureau of International Organizational Affairs. A handwritten note on the source text states that the original was returned to the Secretary and sent at his request to Deputy Under Secretary Johnson on May 29.

[1] See Document 18 and footnote 4 thereto. No record has been found of any discussion of China on April 6.

end early consultation, well before the opening of the General Assembly on September 19, will be required.

*Chinese Position*

We have discussed the problem with Ambassador George Yeh and Ambassador T.F. Tsiang, who represents the GRC at the United Nations.[2] This discussion and reports from Embassy Taipei have made it clear that, in connection with the problem of finding a practical alternative to the moratorium, the GRC will not take any action implying acceptance of a "Two Chinas" concept.

The "New Member" approach was thoroughly explored with the Chinese Ambassadors. In addition to the difficulties they found with the "Two Chinas" implications, they said this approach was unacceptable on two other grounds. First, the GRC could not make any public declaration foregoing its right to use the veto on membership applications. Secondly, the position of the GRC in the Security Council would be in jeopardy. The "Successor States" approach was also discussed. Although the two Ambassadors made it clear that this proposal was also unacceptable, they indicated that if the majority of the General Assembly voted to accept a resolution based on a "Successor States" approach, they "could do nothing about it." A "Successor States" approach would not require any affirmative action by the GRC. They stated however, that they would be "greatly surprised" if the United States were to sponsor such a resolution.

*Suggested Solution*

The attitude of the Republic of China, in our judgment, renders the "New Member" approach politically unfeasible. We have therefore prepared an alternative designed to eliminate the need for any public declaration of agreement or acquiescence by the GRC or any affirmative action by it. This is a marriage of the "Successor States" approach and the "New Member" approach.

Under this alternative the General Assembly would adopt a resolution: (a) noting the significant political changes which have taken place in China since 1945 and the fact that governmental authority in the territory which was under Chinese administration when China became a member of the United Nations, is now exercised by the Government of the Republic of China with its seat of government in Taipei and by the Central People's Government of the People's Republic of China with its seat of government in Peking, (b) affirming the continuing membership of the Republic of China in the United Nations, and (c) expressing the Assembly's willingness to consider credentials of a delegation of the

---

[2] See footnote 6, Document 27.

PRC, as a member of the United Nations in addition to the Republic of China, upon being informed by the CPG of the PRC that it has accepted the Charter of the United Nations and the obligations of membership. This expression by the Assembly would be based on the proposition that the PRC is not to be regarded as a UN Member unless it elects to regard itself as already a UN Member (in accordance with a decision under Article 55 of the Chinese Communist Common Program) and informs the UN that it accepts the Charter and the obligations of membership. We believe that the U.K. could support this proposal, that the GRC could tolerate it, that it would find wide support in the General Assembly, and that the Chinese Communists would reject it. This approach should result in the continued exclusion of the Chinese Communists who have been strongly opposed to a "Two Chinas" concept. It should also serve to shift the onus for their exclusion to the Chinese Communists themselves.

Securing a reliable majority in support of the above proposal would require active US consultation with many other governments during the next three months. When the resolution came to a vote in the General Assembly, the US could, in theory, vote against or abstain on parts of the resolution or on the whole resolution. However, there are some strong considerations for our voting in favor: voting in favor would make a major contribution to our holding together a large coalition. It would also avoid our appearing to be dissatisfied with the outcome and treating the result as a defeat for the United States. Finally, US strong and open support for the resolution would maximize the chances of Chinese Communist refusal to come into the United Nations. The decision on how we would vote on such a resolution need not be taken at this time.

*Security Council Problem*

The foregoing approach leaves open the question of which China should sit in the Security Council. There would undoubtedly be considerable pressure in the General Assembly at the time the membership question was raised to give the seat to the Chinese Communists, but we believe we could avoid any definitive recommendation on this point in the General Assembly resolution on the grounds that the issue is one which should be decided by the Security Council itself if and when there are physically present in the United Nations two claimants for the same permanent seat.

However, if the Chinese Communists should agree at some point to take up their seat in the General Assembly on the foregoing basis, it is unlikely that they could be kept out of the Security Council for any extended period of time. That time period could probably be prolonged somewhat by getting this question involved with the question of enlarging the Security Council and proposing the addition of India or other states as permanent members.

*Recommendations:*

Taking into account the foregoing analysis and the exploratory discussion held with you on May 24 (summary attached), I request authorization to proceed on the following basis:

1. That you approve in principle the proposals for a solution of the China problem in the United Nations along lines outlined above.

2. That you authorize consultations on a confidential basis with China, the U.K. and Australia. The purpose of talking with the Chinese would be to seek their acquiesence. The object of consulting with the British is to get their cooperation. As to the Australians, we should seek to have them take the lead at an early date in presenting the proposed course of action "as their own" in private consultations with selected key delegations. In this way, it might be possible for soundings to be taken on the above course of action without the US directly being connected with such a proposal at the outset.

Once consultations begin along the above lines, however, press leaks are inevitable. Consultations with a limited number of key Congressional leaders, therefore, should be undertaken at an early stage, preferably in advance of the proposed consultations with the U.K., Australia and China, and certainly before Australia begins its own broad consultations.

It is important for us to face realistically the fact that an indefinite deferral of an active US role is dangerous because weeks of hard negotiations and consultations will be needed to develop the stable majority required to avoid the substitution of Communist China for the Republic of China in the United Nations.

3. That you authorize us to consult, informally and confidentially, with various other friendly governments who would be influential in determining how the General Assembly deals with this issue, such as Canada, Norway and Japan. As part of the preparation for your conversations with the Japanese Prime Minister, it is important for the Japanese to focus on this problem and the complex procedural issues involved. It is our impression that the Japanese have not yet done so.

**Dean Rusk**[3]

---

[3] Printed from a copy that indicates Rusk signed the original.

## 29.    Editorial Note

During the Vienna meeting of President Kennedy and Chairman of the Soviet Council of Ministers Nikita S. Khrushchev, June 3–4, 1961, there was some discussion pertaining to China. Khrushchev raised the subject during a June 3 conversation in which the two leaders were accompanied only by their interpreters. A memorandum of the conversation by U.S. interpreter Alexander Akalovsky reads in part as follows:

"Mr. Khrushchev then said that he wanted to say a few words about China. At the same time, he wanted to emphasize that he had not been authorized or requested to speak on China's behalf. He said he simply wanted to set forth his thinking on the problem. He said that US relations with China were very aggravated. Obviously they could not be improved until the United States ended the occupation of Taiwan. The most realistic policy would be that of recognizing China and having China admitted as a member of the United Nations. What kind of United Nations is it when it does not have among its members a nation numbering 600 million people? On the other hand, it should be clear that China would never join the United Nations if Chiang Kai-shek were to be still there. This would be a discrimination against China's rights. There is no question that at some point China will gather its strength and liberate Taiwan. If the Soviet Union were in China's place, it would probably have attacked Taiwan long time ago. The Soviet Union supports the policy of reunification of China's territory. As a matter of fact, the United States itself signed a document recognizing Taiwan as part of China. Mr. Khrushchev said that he did not know whether the United States was ready for a change in its policy toward China. The relations between Chiang Kai-shek and Mao Tse-tung are an internal affair of China, and neither the US nor the USSR should interfere. This would be a reasonable course and it would promote a peaceful development of the situation. Mr. Khrushchev said that he was glad that there were voices in the United States asking for a change in US policy toward China, but said that he did not know how that policy would develop. He reiterated that he had not been requested by the Chinese to speak on their behalf."

After addressing other Khrushchev statements, Kennedy replied as follows:

"The President said that even before he had assumed office China had made strong attacks against the United States and himself personally, and this has been going on like a drumbeat ever since. At the same time the USSR was cordial and expressed the hope that our relations would improve. The President said that he recognized that China was a forceful nation, that its population was one quarter of the world, and that it might still further increase its strength. He also recognized that bad relations between the United States and China affected world relations in general. However, if the United States were to withdraw from Taiwan, it would have a strategic problem. It would be confined to its shores and its strategic position in Asia would be greatly impaired. This is a problem of security for the United States."

Khrushchev replied that "this was an interesting conception with which he could not agree" and declared that although the Soviet Union sympathized with socialist countries, its policy toward capitalist countries was one of non-interference, and that Kennedy's argument regarding Taiwan sounded "strange."

Kennedy interjected that "the situation should be viewed in the light of Chinese hostility." Khrushchev replied that "the Chinese cannot reconcile themselves with US bases on Taiwan." After some remarks about U.S. bases near the Soviet Union, he returned to the subject of China:

"Thus, Mr. Khrushchev continued, the President's argument only fortifies the views of the Chinese. The US will not leave Taiwan and force will have to be used. This is a sad thing indeed. Referring to Chinese statements, Mr. Khrushchev said that the Chinese were against US policy, but then the Soviet Union has also criticized US policy. Mr. Khrushchev said that he had not spoken against the President personally and would not wish to do so. He said he wanted to improve relations between the two countries with the President in the White House, but he may turn out to be wrong. In that event he would have to criticise the President too. The best thing for the United States would be to recognize China because diplomatic relations alone impose certain obligations. The United States could continue to support Chiang Kai-shek, but of course only morally. The Chinese position is correct and the United States should settle its differences with China. The USSR certainly hopes that this will take place. Mr. Khrushchev reiterated that if the USSR had been in China's shoes, it would have acted long time ago. He again referred to the fight against Americans in the Far East and against the French, the British, and Germans in other areas of Russia during the Civil War. He said that this fight had been carried on until its victorious end and that any country would do the same. Such wars are not aggressive, they are holy wars."

Kennedy turned to other subjects, but Khrushchev soon renewed the subject of China:

"Referring to Taiwan, Mr. Khrushchev recalled the President's remark that withdrawal of US troops from that area would affect US strategic posture. This, he said, might be true, but what about the Chinese position—how should they regard the occupation of Taiwan? If the United States proceeds from such an assumption, Mr. Khrushchev said, he will be forced to doubt whether the United States really wants peaceful co-existence or is simply seeking a pretext for warlike developments.

The Soviet Union sympathizes with the Chinese and this seems to be the only solution. There is no other way out. After all, the United States might even occupy China and say that this would improve its strategic position. This would be true. But it would be the policy of Dulles, a policy of strength. Times have changed and such policy is doomed to failure. If the US wants to dictate its conditions, that is inconceivable today. No improvement of relations would be possible in such circumstances." (Department of State, Conference Files: Lot 66 D 110, CF 1901)

There was a brief exchange pertaining to China the next morning, when Kennedy, urging a nuclear test ban, cited "a Chinese proverb saying that a thousand-mile journey begins with one step." According to Akalovsky's memorandum of conversation,

"Mr. Khrushchev rejoined by saying that the President apparently knew the Chinese very well but that he too knew them quite well. To this the President replied that Mr. Khrushchev might get to know them even better. Mr. Khrushchev retorted that he already knew them very well." (Ibid.) Documentation on the Vienna meetings, is in volume V.

---

### 30.  Memorandum From the Counselor of the Department of State (McGhee) to Secretary of State Rusk

Washington, June 15, 1961.

SUBJECT

The Offshore Islands Issue and Related Problems

I attach a study (Tab A)[1] on the offshore islands and other problems, involving the Government of the Republic of China (GRC), on which that

---

Source: Department of State, S/P Files: Lot 67 D 548, China. Top Secret. Concurred in by McConaughy. Filed with a June 29 covering memorandum from Rusk's Special Assistant Emory C. Swank noting that Rusk had approved the first of the recommendations but had taken no action on recommendations 2, 3, and 4. A handwritten note on Swank's memorandum reads in part: "I spoke to McConaughy, Alex Johnson & Swank. All agreed that the Secretary probably withheld action on 2, 3, & 4 because of current delicate situation."

[1] Dated June 15 and titled "U.S. Policy towards the GRC—the Necessity for Decision," it declared that the principal problems between the United States and the GRC stemmed from its over-riding objective of reestablishing its rule over all of China. It concluded that the United States could not expect that the GRC leadership would soon abandon its ambition to return to the mainland and that the only other readjustment that would make it possible to damp down the civil war and promote "conditions under which Taiwan's long-term viability might be promoted more effectively" would be evacuation of the offshore islands.

issue has immediate bearing; and the pertinent portions of an earlier paper examining the offshore islands problem in greater detail (Tab B).[2]

On the basis of the conclusions of this study, I make the recommendations which follow:

*Recommendations:*[3]

1. We should, without prematurely giving outside indication of our aim or ruling out the possibility that new GRC-Chinese Communist hostilities may sometime become in our interest, adopt a policy designed: (a) to bring about maximum damping down of the GRC-Chinese Communist civil war, and (b) to leave minimum chance that we may become unnecessarily involved in it through different US and GRC interpretations of our respective obligations under the mutual defense treaty.

2. We should, recognizing the difficulties it will impose in our relations with the GRC, adopt as a policy objective bringing about GRC evacuation of the offshore islands.

3. FE should, in consultation as may be necessary with other elements in the Department and elsewhere in the Government, formulate such plans for your approval and subsequent action as may be needed to implement these policies, including plans for preliminary steps designed to provide circumstances most favorable to GRC acquiescence in the evacuation of the offshore islands and indication as to how the requisite approach might best be made.

4. That you should determine when, after the Chinese membership issue has been dealt with in the next UNGA, this approach should be made.

---

[2] Dated June 28, 1960, and titled "Taiwan Straits and Offshore Islands Problem." Regarding this paper, see *Foreign Relations*, 1958–1960, vol. XIX, p. 695, footnote 1.

[3] Rusk initialed approval of recommendation 1 on June 29. The other recommendations were neither approved nor disapproved.

## 31.    National Intelligence Estimate

NIE 43–61                                          Washington, June 20, 1961.

### PROSPECTS FOR THE GOVERNMENT OF THE REPUBLIC OF CHINA[1]

### The Problem

To estimate the prospects for the Government of the Republic of China (GRC) over the next two or three years, with particular reference to its international position.

### Conclusions

1. The GRC is likely to be faced this year with abandonment or failure of the UN moratorium on discussion of the question of Chinese representation. It does not necessarily follow, however, that Peiping would replace the GRC or achieve any representation in the UN this year. Many countries are moving towards a preference for a two-Chinas formula. Both Taipei and Peiping have rejected such a formula and each has stated that it will not accept dual representation. If any Chinese Communist membership in the UN appeared imminent to the GRC, the latter would threaten to withdraw. If Communist China achieved membership in both the General Assembly and the Security Council, we believe the GRC would withdraw from the UN. In less drastic cases however, the GRC might not carry out the threat to withdraw, if only to attempt to prevent Peiping's actually filling a proffered seat. (Paras. 12–15, 27)

2. The GRC's principal objective will continue to be to regain control of the mainland. The GRC leaders believe that now is a good time to agitate the question of taking probing actions against the mainland in order

---

Source: Department of State, INR/EAP Files: Lot 90 D 110, NIE 43–61. Secret. According to a note on the covering sheet, the Central Intelligence Agency and the intelligence agencies of the Departments of State, the Army, the Navy, the Air Force, and the Joint Staff participated in the preparation of this estimate. All members of the USIB concurred in this estimate except the representatives of the AEC and the FBI, who abstained on the grounds that the subject was outside their jurisdiction.

[1] Intelligence Board document USIB–D–15.2/73, June 21, titled "Post-Mortem on NIE 43–61," states that on June 20 the Board noted findings set forth therein and requested members of the Board to take such action as they deemed appropriate. The findings state that production of the economic section of NIE 43–61 had caused great difficulty; interpretations of Taiwanese economic developments varied "substantially" both in the field and in Washington. The major remaining gaps concerned such questions as GRC intentions with respect to unilateral use of GRC forces to exploit discontent on the mainland, the possibility of an attack on the mainland intended to embroil the United States in war, the genuineness of GRC threats to "go it alone" rather than give up the back-to-the-mainland policy, and the succession question. (Ibid.)

to capitalize on the economic distress and other sources of discontent there. Although we doubt that they would commit forces to such a mission in the face of specific US objections, the possibility cannot be ruled out that they might, without consulting us, undertake airdrops or raids at any time. (Para. 25)

3. Most GRC leaders now believe that their best chance of regaining the mainland would come in the wake of a war between the US and Communist China. We believe, however, that there is only a remote chance of their trying to provoke such a war. (Para. 23)

4. Politically conscious Taiwanese are generally opposed to GRC rule of Taiwan, but inadequate leadership and organization minimize their threat to the regime. GRC security forces are almost certainly more than adequate to cope with any domestic troubles. Mainlander-Taiwanese relations will almost certainly come under increasing strain. (Paras. 30–33)

5. With the help of large-scale US aid, the GRC has made substantial economic progress, and economic development has acquired momentum. Some negative factors such as growing unemployment, an extremely rapid population growth, and a recent decline in productive investment threaten this trend. Whether sufficient economic growth can be maintained over the long run depends largely on the course of US policy and aid and on the ability and willingness of the leadership to adapt to the requirements of prolonged existence on Taiwan. (Paras. 34–38)

6. Over the next few years the GRC will probably suffer setbacks, particularly those growing out of the enhanced international position of Peiping. The ability of the GRC to ride out these next few years will depend largely upon the manner and pace at which the setbacks come and in considerable degree upon the role of the US. We believe that, as long as US economic support and military protection are assured, the GRC can survive these setbacks and can adjust, however reluctantly, to a gradual series of changes. (Para. 28)

7. If the GRC leaders were faced with a major change in US policy such as a US decision to use the extreme pressures that would be necessary to force the evacuation of the offshore islands, advocacy of the acceptance of a two-Chinas formula, or formal recognition of Communist China, the bitterness and psychological shock would be profound, whatever guarantees or explanations the US might give. Some mainlanders on Taiwan would seek accommodation with the Communists, or advocate precipitating a war with Communist China, or seek refuge elsewhere in the Free World; however, we believe that most would resign themselves to making the best of a future on Taiwan. The surviving government would probably be less disciplined and more corrupt and less stable than the present one; Communist subversion would probably

become a problem. However, given continued US aid and protection, Taiwan would probably continue as a part of the Free World. (Paras. 39–46)

[Here follow paragraphs 8–48, comprising the Discussion portion of the estimate, in five sections entitled "Introduction," "International Problems," "GRC Reactions to Its Changing International Status," "Domestic Problems," and "Contingencies," and Appendix A, "Military," Appendix B, "Political Tables," and a map of East China and Taiwan showing army strengths.]

---

**32.    Telegram From the Embassy in the Republic of China to the Department of State**

Taipei, June 21, 1961, 1 p.m.

824. At tea yesterday honoring former MAAG Chief, President Chiang asked me to remain for private talk. Madame Chiang was present.

1. President first alluded to Thomas Liao case.[1] He has just read Amb Yeh's cable notifying US decision to admit Liao and had not yet had time to go over case with Foreign Minister. I interrupted to say Foreign Minis-

---

Source: Department of State, Central Files, 793.00/6–2161. Secret. Rusk and Bundy discussed this telegram in a telephone conversation at 8:51 a.m. on June 21. Notes of the conversation by Rusk's secretary, Phyllis Bernau, read in part as follows:

"The Sec returned the call and B said he was just going in with the early morning reports and he thinks the most stimulating is the backfire to Drumright. The Sec said he is drafting a personal message to him from the Sec. The problem is government in Taiwan wants us to act like a satellite. The Sec thinks we should talk it over fully—he is thinking of suggesting the FM come over—they are in sort of a pathological state of mind and are not satisfied unless we follow every one of their points. B asked if the Sec expects political backfire here. The Sec said some but he thinks the Amb here is sensible enough not to go too far in that direction." (Ibid., Rusk Files: Lot 72 D 192, Telephone Calls)

[1] Thomas Liao, self-styled "President of the Republic of Formosa in exile in Japan" and leader of the Formosan Democratic Independence Party, had sought admission to the United States at intervals since November 1950 but had been denied a visa. After Senator William Fulbright urged granting Liao a visa in a March 30 letter to Rusk, Rusk referred the question to the Legal Adviser's office, which concluded on May 19 there were no legal grounds for denial. On June 13 the Department informed Ambassador Yeh of the decision to grant a visa to Liao. The case is discussed in memoranda of April 5 and June 26 to Bowles from his Special Assistant James C. Thomson, Jr. (Ibid., Central Files, 793.00/4–561 and 790.00/6–2661, respectively)

ter had discussed case with me previous day and on basis of conversation I had cabled report to Washington (Embtel 818).[2] Speaking with emphasis and at times in tone of indignation, President said it was incomprehensible to him that US would admit Liao in face of his past actions and clear motivations, persistent and recorded GRC opposition to this action, and without consulting GRC in advance re action proposed to be taken. He could only conclude State Department unaware of profound implications of its action to admit Liao. President termed Liao action an unfriendly act taken in utter disregard of interests of friendly ally. Admission of Liao would be regarded locally as step on part of USG to promote "two Chinas" and as effort to promote Liao's scheme for an independent Taiwan at cost of GRC. US action to admit Liao was not only incomprehensible but inconsistent with US defense and aid commitments to GRC. Admission of Liao would create confusion and misunderstandings among Chinese people. Liao and other adherents of an independent Taiwan would be encouraged to stir up trouble at cost of stability of Taiwan. Burdens of GRC would thus be magnified at time when it imperative that US and GRC stick together in face of growing Communist danger.

2. President then raised Outer Mongolian issue.[3] He had meant to leave this and their representation issue to Foreign Minister, but introduction of Liao case at this juncture impelled him to express some views on these issues as well. In proposing to establish relations with Outer Mongolia, US was becoming involved in what Chinese regarded as issue of high importance to them. Here again US was proposing to take action portending incalculable consequences to friendly ally without opportunity for advance consultation; advance notification was far from adequate in such an important issue. Establishment of US relations with Outer Mongolia would not only be of tremendous benefit to Communist Bloc but would do irreparable harm to GRC interests. USG was handling Outer Mongolian and Liao issues in a manner that would not be worthy of a master-satellite relationship, let alone relationship supposed to exist between friendly allies with mutual interests. Continued US ignoring of rights and interests of friendly and loyal ally could produce very serious consequences.

3. President raised as third point China representation issue. He said he regarded US proposals advanced thus far for dealing with this issue

---

[2] Dated June 20. (Ibid., 793.00/6–2061)

[3] The Embassy informed the Foreign Ministry on June 1 that the United States was opening talks in Moscow concerning the possible establishment of diplomatic relations with Outer Mongolia. On June 5 Foreign Minister Shen told Drumright the GRC considered this a "very unfriendly act" and gave him an aide-mémoire urging reversal of the decision. The text of the aide-mémoire was transmitted in telegram 767, and the conversation was reported in telegram 768, both dated June 5. (Ibid., 303/6–561) For related documentation, see Documents 198–200.

as not only ineffectual but as a plan to bring about a "two Chinas" arrangement in UN. GRC would have no part of such proposals and would withdraw from UN rather than be party to them. If US adhered to existing proposals, GRC would in actual fact be "driven" to leave UN. In President's view US would have to bear responsibility for this action.

4. President said Liao development, following in wake of Outer Mongolian and China representation attitudes of US administration, led him to suspect that despite protestations of support, USG is actually embarked on a calculated change of its China policy. If this should unfortunately be borne out by further unfavorable development of foregoing and other important issues, US-GRC relations could be seriously prejudiced with unfortunate results to security and other interests of both countries. President said "honor" was most precious quality. It had led him to Taiwan when all was lost on mainland. "Honor" would be his main guideline if he should again be put to crucial test. To this quality he linked "principle, responsibility and integrity." He would rely on these moral qualities to see him through any crisis.

5. President started conversation as if it were to be private, unofficial person-to-person talk, but he ended by requesting that I pass his observations to Department. I assured him I would do so.[4]

6. I made no attempt at a point-by-point rebuttal of President's observations. I did, however, deny his implication of a calculated change in US China policy. I also stated I believed Liao decision had been taken because of outside pressures and was not to be construed as evidence of US support of an independent Taiwan. President clearly was not convinced by my argumentation.

7. *Comment:* President's observations mirror GRC disapproval of US actions in three separate areas. GRC believes US is taking unilateral decisions of great importance to GRC in disregard of GRC interests. Beyond this GRC sees US handling of Laos problem as weak and ineffectual and as probably portending weakening of US determination to defend free Asian nations. Moreover, GRC believes US is not showing required leadership to rally free nations and is in fact waging a losing battle against communism.

---

[4] Drumright reported in despatch 691, June 26, that Foreign Minister Shen had conveyed "supplementary" views from Chiang to him at Chiang's direction on June 23, but the substance was similar to that transmitted in telegram 824. Subsequently, Drumright was given Chinese records of the chief points made by Chiang and Shen. He enclosed translations of those records with despatch 691, noting that this was an unusual procedure, probably done at Chiang's direction. (Ibid., 793.00/6–2661) Chiang Ching-kuo elaborated on his father's statements in June 23 conversation, in which he stressed GRC concern at the U.S. decision to grant a visa to Liao and stated that because of this he was cancelling a planned July trip to the United States. (TDCS 3/478,643, dated June 23; Kennedy Library, National Security Files, Countries Series, China)

Lack of GRC confidence in US firmness and consistency of policy has been growing, although Vice President's visit brought temporary relaxation. Chiang touched on three points of immediate concern to GRC. In his mind all add up to "two Chinas" and seating of Chinese Communists in UN. Clearly, Chiang will leave UN rather than be forced into "two Chinas" arrangement. It is clear too that Chiang will use veto to bar Outer Mongolia from UN no matter what eventual cost may be to GRC.

Liao case has hardened Chiang's determination and roused deep suspicion of US motivations. Although inherently least important of three issues raised, Chiang regards it as of highest personal importance. If Liao is admitted and allowed to engage in anti-GRC political activity in USA, Chiang will be convinced it represents USG-supported conspiracy against him and his regime. Liao's actions could conceivably lead to a virtual suspension of GRC-US relations. Here on Taiwan Chiang would almost certainly impose pervasive security measures that would cripple promising social programs in being and probably seriously set back accelerated economic program. Our relations with GRC counterparts would be undermined and our influence diminished or destroyed.

If Liao is allowed liberty of political action in USA Chinese Communists will seize upon this as golden opportunity to create division between mainlanders and Taiwanese. Liao would be held up of course as US agent. Communists would no doubt redouble hitherto ineffective attempts to influence and subvert Taiwanese.

I can only urge from here that we reconsider our position on the points raised by Chiang in hope of stopping drift toward breakup of friendly relations and mutual confidence that have hitherto existed. As admission of Liao can only be gained at tremendous cost, I would hope a decision would yet be taken to exclude him. We are also at an impasse over Outer Mongolia's admission to UN by abstention method. On China representation, I believe we should conduct a careful survey of possibility of a successful moratorium jointly with GRC before taking any decision to rule it out. If GRC could be satisfied moratorium would fail, perhaps GRC would find it advantageous to adopt some passive tactic that would still keep Chinese Communist from UN.

**Drumright**

## 33.    Telegram From the Department of State to the Consulate General in Geneva

Washington, June 23, 1961, 1:14 p.m.

2222. Eyes only for Harriman[1] from the Secretary. I was very much interested in your suggestion (Confe 210)[2] about the possibility of your having a quiet discussion with Chen Yi. I certainly share your feeling that we should attempt avoid unnecessarily strained personal relations with ChiCom Delegation which might leave us at disadvantage in dealing with ChiComs as compared with attitude of other key Western delegations. Our posture should be polite and correct at all times. Nevertheless, while I believe a discussion between you and Chen Yi might be useful at some point in the Conference I rather doubt that it would be of particular benefit at this point, inasmuch as friendly delegations should be able to fill us in on Chinese attitudes. It seems unlikely that such a meeting could be kept secret, since the Chinese Communists might consider it advantageous as a means of increasing their prestige and making us appear weak and anxious, to leak the fact that you had taken the initiative to approach them. The repercussions of our taking the initiative for such a private meeting on our Asian SEATO allies as well as on the governments of the divided Asian countries would be adverse, particularly if there seemed to be no tangible advantage to us from the discussion. The Canadians and French who occupy far less important roles in the Far East than ourselves can hold such meetings with Chen Yi without these risks.

I would be glad to receive your further thoughts on this matter particularly if developments at the Conference should warrant our taking this significant step.

In meanwhile I suggest you and members your delegation gradually adopt a "correct" attitude in and out of Conference toward Chen Yi and other members Chinese Communist Delegation generally not taking initiative toward additional contacts but also not rebuffing any Chinese Communist initiative. However, if you feel it useful there would be no objection to testing Chinese Communist response by having Steeves

---

Source: Department of State, Central Files, 751J.00/6–361. Secret. Drafted by Martin; cleared by McConaughy, Johnson, and, with revisions, by Bowles; and approved for transmission and signed by Rusk.

[1] W. Averell Harriman was heading the U.S. delegation at the International Conference on the Settlement of the Laotian Question.

[2] Telegram Confe 210, June 17, suggested that Harriman meet quietly with PRC Foreign Minister Chen Yi, who headed the Chinese delegation, to discuss controversial Laotian questions directly with him. (Department of State, Central Files, 751J/6–1761)

make casual and informal approach to Wang Ping-nan in delegates lounge or any other such occasion where both happen to be present.[3]

**Rusk**

---

[3] Harriman reported in telegram Confe 279 that Steeves had spoken to Wang Ping-nan at a reception, and Wang expressed the hope that efforts could be made to normalize relations but stated that the United States should take the initiative "because we are the ones who have been wronged." Steeves introduced Harriman and Mrs. Harriman to Wang, and they shook hands with Chen Yi and exchanged a few words. (Ibid., 751J.00/6–2661) Rusk states in his memoir that when he was in Geneva at the beginning of the conference in May 1961 he "discreetly" suggested a private meeting with Chen and Chen refused, but he and Chen shook hands and exchanged pleasantries at a reception. ( As I Saw It, p. 287)

## 34.    Editorial Note

U.S. Representative at the United Nations Adlai Stevenson met with President Kennedy and Secretary of State Rusk on June 26, 1961. A memorandum of June 27 from Stevenson to Rusk enclosed brief memoranda of subjects discussed by Stevenson and Kennedy after Rusk's departure. The memorandum of discussion of Chinese representation in the United Nations reads as follows:

"The President wants a fresh count on the moratorium together with explanations about Ireland, Norway, Sweden, Denmark, Upper Volta and Laos. He instructed me to say to the Senate Committee this morning if and when asked that policy of the Administration was to keep the People's Republic of China out, but that we had grave misgivings about whether the moratorium could prevail again.

"He instructed me to talk with Cabot Lodge and Mr. Donovan of Harry Luce's office to try to enlist their understanding for a change, if necessary. He has also asked me to see Roy Howard for the same purpose; the approach being to get his advice because he is so friendly with Chiang. He also asked me to have a similar talk with Jerry Wadsworth.

"I am to let the President know the results following my meetings with Lodge, Donovan and Howard.

"He is instructing Drumright to return at once preparatory to taking a firm position with Chiang Kai-shek.

"The President seemed astonished that we could possibly lose on a credentials vote by a simple majority. The President requests a simple memorandum explaining the 'successor state' approach to be used as a talking paper. I understand IO will prepare such a memorandum for him." (Department of State, Central Files, 304.11/6–2761)

A July 3 letter from Stevenson to the President reported on several matters that they had discussed on June 26. Stevenson enclosed a memorandum explaining the "successor states" approach and another with the latest USUN estimate of a vote on the moratorium. He reported that he had talked with former Representative at the United Nations and 1960 Vice-Presidential candidate Henry Cabot Lodge, editorial director of Time, Incorporated, Hedley W. Donovan, and former president of Scripps-Howard newspapers Roy W. Howard; he stated that Howard had been very cooperative and would try to use his influence on Chiang not to veto the admission of Mongolia.

He also enclosed a memorandum summarizing Lodge's view that the United States should press for the moratorium again and, if it failed, should introduce a resolution stating that the General Assembly would be willing in the future to consider representation for Communist China when it changed its ways. The memorandum also stated the USUN view that an effort to extend the moratorium for another year would fail, undermining U.S. ability to win support for other important issues, and that following such a defeat, the United States would not be able to obtain a two-thirds majority for a resolution such as Lodge (and, according to Stevenson, Henry Luce) proposed. Stevenson concluded the memorandum with an argument for the successor states approach and enclosed a draft resolution. (Ibid., 320/7–361)

A memorandum of June 30 from Battle to Bundy responded to Kennedy's request for a brief explanation of the "successor state" approach. (Kennedy Library, National Security Files, Countries Series, China) A July 9 memorandum from Rusk to Kennedy responding to Kennedy's request for another estimate of the possibility of sustaining the moratorium resolution stated that while it might be possible, there was very great risk in attempting to sustain it. (Ibid.)

## 35.    Memorandum From the President's Special Assistant for National Security Affairs (Bundy) to President Kennedy

Washington, June 26, 1961.

SUBJECT

The Secretary of State on Liao and the Generalissimo

As I was talking with Dean Rusk on other matters,[1] I raised directly with him your question as to the level at which the Liao case had been decided in the Department. He at once told me that he had decided it himself, after long and careful consideration. He weighed the following considerations:

(1) That to deny a visa to a political refugee is contrary to our traditions, and to do this because of pressure, even from a friendly government, is still worse.

(2) This matter has been pressed urgently with the Department over a long period of time by Senator Fulbright and others.

(3) Liao will not in fact make anything like the amount of noise in the United States that the Chinese claim.

(4) The case is not in itself as important to the Chinese as they are now saying, and the fuss on this particular issue will die down.

More broadly, the Secretary agrees strongly with you that Drumright is not representing our point of view effectively. While it has to be borne in mind that his recall at this time will probably confirm the Generalissimo's worst suspicions, the Secretary still agrees with you and is proceeding with plans for his recall for consultation. On the result of this consultation, as I understand it, would hang a decision on his return.

The Secretary is planning himself to have a prompt and serious talk with the Chinese Ambassador here, and will let you know what comes of that. He also thinks that we ought to arrange to get either Chiang's son, Ching-kuo, or the Foreign Minister over here promptly, and on that visit he would hope to have your direct and forceful participation.

Meanwhile, the Chinese attitude makes it harder than ever for us to put our weight behind a "successor states" proposal for the UN, and as

---

Source: Kennedy Library, National Security Files, Countries Series, China. Secret.

[1] The conversation took place at 1 p.m. on June 24. According to notes prepared in Rusk's office, Bundy told Rusk the President "had taken him to task" about the Chinese representation problem, thought Drumright "should be recalled," and was wondering if the decision on the Liao visa was made with Rusk's knowledge. Rusk stated that the visa decision was his own judgment. Bundy said the President "was startled to see all that flap over one man." Rusk said there had been nothing in the press, and Bundy replied that Kennedy's information came from a cable. Bundy asked if the President should see Yeh; Rusk said he should see the Foreign Minister if he came, but not the Ambassador. (Department of State, Rusk Files: Lot 72 D 192, Telephone Calls)

time passes, the prospect of an effective operation on this line gets weaker. In other words, the Chinese are hard at work creating exactly the situation they should wish to avoid, and that is what the Secretary will tell the Ambassador.

McG. B.[2]

²  Printed from a copy that bears these typed initials.

---

## 36.    Memorandum From the Joint Chiefs of Staff to Secretary of Defense McNamara

JCSM–425–61                                Washington, June 26, 1961.

SUBJECT
   A Strategic Analysis of the Impact of the Acquisition by Communist China of a
   Nuclear Capability (U)

1. The Joint Chiefs of Staff have had prepared a strategic analysis of the impact of the acquisition by Communist China of a nuclear capability. A copy of this analysis is attached.[1]

2. The Joint Chiefs of Staff conclude that:

   a. The attainment of a nuclear capability by Communist China will have a marked impact on the security posture of the United States and the Free World, particularly in Asia.

   b. The United States should use the time that is still available to counter this impact through coordinated political, psychological, economic, and military actions.

3. The military impact of this capability will continue to be reflected in appropriate strategic plans. Because of the scope and importance of the problem, the Joint Chiefs of Staff recommend that:

   a. This analysis be referred to the Department of State for consideration of the nonmilitary points in the required actions.

---

Source: Washington National Records Center, RG 330, OSD Files: FRC 65 A 3464, 471.61 China Reds. Secret. A note on the source text indicates it was seen by McNamara.

¹ The analysis, attached as an appendix to the memorandum, is not printed. It estimated that Communist China might test a nuclear device between 1962 and 1964 and, in another 2 years, might have a small stockpile of weapons with aircraft that could reach targets in Asia. It predicted that China would move as rapidly as possible to develop ballistic missiles, but uncertainty about the likelihood of Soviet assistance for such an enterprise caused uncertainty in the estimate of the length of time required. It estimated that without Soviet assistance, China could produce a missile with a range of 200–500 miles by 1968–1970 but could not produce an ICBM until well after 1970. See the Supplement.

b. A combined State–Defense–Central Intelligence Agency–United States Information Agency Plan be developed to insure that appropriate, timely and coordinated national action is taken with respect to this problem.

For the Joint Chiefs of Staff:
**L. L. Lemnitzer**
*Chairman*
*Joint Chiefs of Staff*

---

37.    **Telegram From the Embassy in Poland to the Department of State**

Warsaw, June 29, 1961, 7 p.m.

1930. Beam–Wang Talks. 105th meeting 1 hour 20 minutes.[1]

Wang opened saying in two months since last meeting US had not only not taken steps to improve relations with his country but instead seemed to be trying to worsen these relations. Visit of Vice President Johnson to Taiwan showed the US Government was set upon continuing interfere in Chinese internal affairs and make Taiwan stronghold for conducting anti-Communism in Asia. Furthermore, US planes and ships continued intrude into China's territorial sea and air. If US really wanted to live in amity with China as President Kennedy had said in Paris US must stop interfering in Chinese internal affairs and cease occupying Taiwan.

I briefly refuted his allegations and stated our position along lines paragraph two, unnumbered Deptel June 26.[2]

---

Source: Department of State, Central Files, 611.93/6–2961. Confidential; Priority; Limit Distribution. Repeated to Taipei, Hong Kong, and Moscow. Received at 5:49 a.m. on June 30.

[1] Beam sent his comments and recommendations for the next meeting in telegram 1932, June 30, and sent a detailed, apparently verbatim report of the meeting in airgram G–572, June 30. (Both ibid., 611.93/6–3061)

[2] Reference is to telegram 1519 to Warsaw, June 26. It instructed Beam to take a low-key approach and avoid polemics. Paragraph 2 instructed him to reject Wang's thesis that the essence of the issue between the two sides was the "withdrawal of U.S. forces from Taiwan and the Taiwan Straits," to remind Wang of the original agenda of the talks, to stress the continuing U.S. concern about American prisoners in China and missing and unaccounted-for servicemen, to assert that the question of renunciation of force was a fundamental one, and to tell Wang that the United States had repeatedly put forward constructive proposals on these and other topics, such as newsmen. (Ibid., 611.93/6–2661)

Brushing aside my statement concerning imprisoned Americans with assertion his side had consistently carried out agreed announcement Wang reiterated Taiwan was central issue and since his side was injured party it was up to US to take next step. They had hoped new administration would alter situation but so far no such indication. Regarding newsmen they had studied US proposal but found it unacceptable. Newsmen exchange must be brought about in such manner as to promote solution of problem of withdrawal US forces from Taiwan. He urged acceptance their September 1960 proposal.

Further give and take on Taiwan issue followed. Then I again urged him to accept our latest proposal which differed little from their proposal of 1957[3] and did not contain political condition as their September proposal did. Wang replied they had once thought solution Taiwan problem [apparent omission] and they had made proposals to end. Such efforts had proved futile and they had reached conclusion that only when progress was made on main problem could agreement be reached on other matters. I told him my government reserved right to make public statement concerning our newsmen proposal.

I then mentioned food parcel proposal along lines paragraph four, unnumbered Deptel June 26[4] to which Wang replied that although China was suffering from effects of several years of natural calamities it was overcoming its difficulties by its own efforts including purchase of food stuffs abroad and did not require "relief" from any quarter. I emphasized proposed arrangement was to be purely private but he repeated that no "relief" was required. Next meeting August 8, 2 p.m.[5]

**Beam**

---

[3] Reference is to a draft agreed announcement proposed by Wang on September 12, 1957, under which both governments would agree "to give permission, on an equal and reciprocal basis," for correspondents to enter their respective countries. For text, see *Foreign Relations, 1955–1957*, vol. III, p. 601, footnote 2.

[4] Paragraph 4 of telegram 1519, cited in footnote 2 above, instructed Beam to state that many private U.S. citizens had asked permission to send food parcels to individual Chinese on the China mainland, that the U.S. Government proposed to grant such permission on humanitarian grounds, and that it hoped Wang's side would be willing to receive such parcels, which would be purchased and sent by private individuals.

[5] Telegram 120 from Warsaw, July 20, reported that the meeting had been postponed until August 15 at U.S. request. (Department of State, Central Files, 611.93/7–2061)

38. **Telegram From the Embassy in Poland to the Department of State**

Warsaw, June 30, 1961, 4 p.m.

1934. Beam–Wang Talks. After regular 105th meeting[1] Wang invited me to adjoining apartment for a cup of coffee and conversation which lasted hour and half with only interpreters each side present.

He began by saying move or gesture by US required for Laos solution. He put particular stress on two points. First, if US withdrew forces and advisers from Laos he was "certain Pathet Lao attacks would stop". Secondly, he said his side not satisfied with Souvanna Phouma original idea to exclude Boun Oum and Nosavan from Cabinet. Intimated his side willing to have latter two in Cabinet since representation three factions necessary in new government in order "to accord with realities situation".

Wang led up to above by long exposé Laos developments saying Souvanna Phouma "who belonged neither to East nor West" only possible chief of government. Pathet Lao which had started as very small force now a growing national movement which must be given rightful role. ChiComs had 500 mile frontier with Laos and would not tolerate hostile government. ChiComs had never intervened or exerted pressure in Laotian affairs nor had they been accused of doing so at present Geneva conference.

Wang then complained about alleged remarks by Vice President Johnson in Taiwan that Marshal Chen Yi "insignificant figure who spoke only from prepared texts." Regretted this as personal attack especially when US representative Geneva had complimented Chen Yi on elevated tone of debate. Stressed continued presence Chen Yi at Geneva sign of ChiCom patience and restraint.

Wang then switched to Chiang Kai-shek who he asserted (contrary to recent ChiCom propaganda) had been mistrusted in early days by General Stilwell[2] and President Roosevelt. He appealed to US withdraw forces from Taiwan area following which there would be peaceful settlement with Chiang. Mentioned former Kuomintang representatives now generals on Chinese mainland and said Chiang would be eligible for even higher position and be taken care of in honorable fashion. Inciden-

Source: Department of State, Central Files, 611.93/6–3061. Secret; Priority; Limit Distribution. Repeated to Taipei and Geneva.

[1] See Document 37.

[2] Lieutenant General Joseph W. Stilwell, chief of staff to Generalissimo Chiang Kai-shek in the latter's role as Supreme Commander of United Nations forces in the China Theater, 1942–1944.

tally said he himself involved in 1936 kidnapping of Chiang whom Chi-Coms on humanitarian grounds decided not to kill him.

Wang emphasized his personal friendship with General Stilwell when latter military attaché 1938 as well as with other Americans. 600 million Chinese could not understand US support Chiang Kai-shek as representing China.

Wang said had he had heard Adlai Stevenson would undertake mission shortly to convince Europeans on need "successor state" solution for Chinese representation next UN whereby GRC and ChiComs would become "successor states" to former China, GRC remaining on SC and ChiCom obtaining GA seat. He scorned this as ridiculous. I replied not competent discuss Laos beyond pointing out we required guarantees for neutral independent Laos through ICC supervision effective cease-fire and assurances country would be able remain independent and neutral. Pathet was not to be regarded as neutral because of character outside support. I said Chiang Kai-shek one of oldest allies whom we would not abandon and whom we recognized as head Government Republic of China. As to Taiwan area, pointed out US not asking ChiComs abandon their case or even expecting them cease political activities but were asking them join in renunciation of force in interest removing risk of hostilities. Recalling Wang asked for US gesture said there was one ChiComs could usefully make on grounds justice and advantage. While US prisoners might seem small issue to Wang it was major question with US public and their release would yield immediate and measurable benefits in improving atmosphere. As to Stevenson, said not informed about such mission and knew of no change in US position.

After his presentation which was obviously prepared Wang said little in reply to my remarks. He said Steeves and Harriman had indicated willingness have another talk with him and with Chen Yi in Geneva and that he looked forward to this. He recalled he had exchanged dinners with Johnson[3] in Geneva 1955 at which frank private talks had been held "without obligation either side".[4] He stated that he considered this meeting in Warsaw in similar light.

*Comment:* Wang's unusual initiative in proposing informal tete-a-tete probably had its origin in desire to exploit his presence on ChiCom delegation Geneva. It seems likely he will follow it up with Steeves and perhaps seek opportunity for further informal exchanges at Geneva. Wang probably expects me to respond with invitation to similar informal get-together, as he referred to value of social exchange between him and

---

[3] U. Alexis Johnson, then Ambassador to Czechoslovakia, represented the United States in the ambassadorial talks in Geneva, 1955–1957.

[4] For Johnson's reports of his discussions with Wang over dinner on August 22 and 28, 1995, see *Foreign Relations,* 1955–1957, vol. III, pp. 58–60 and 70–71.

Johnson in 1955. This might be useful to us at some appropriate future time, subject to Department's prior clearance.

On ChiRep matter, Wang appeared wish spike any new move our part in UN which would advocate less than SC membership for Chi-Coms. He did not, however, specifically put his government on record as refusing sit with GRC in UN under any conditions whatsoever.

Wang was at pains to adopt friendly, persuasive, at times almost cajoling mood. He returned constantly to theme that two governments should reconcile views and could do so. He noted his government had often had many critical things to say of US but that we should take this in good grace as it was for our own benefit. He contrasted this with "flattery" of Syngman Rhee,[5] Chiang Kai-shek and certain Japanese toward US which, he asked, was of what real benefit. Throughout conversation he was relaxed, attempted humorous sallies, and interjected reminiscences.

**Beam**

---

[5] Former President of the Republic of Korea.

---

39.  **Memorandum From the President's Special Assistant for National Security Affairs (Bundy) to President Kennedy**

Washington, July 7, 1961.

I had a long talk last night with Ray Cline, who is the head of CIA in Taiwan.[1] He is I think the ablest officer in any service on the island, and he is the one who has the closest confidence of the Generalissmo and his son, Chiang Ching-kuo.

Cline reports that the Chinese Nationalists are more disturbed about their relation to the U.S. than at any time in the past five years. They live in a queer world in which only the U.S. stands between them and disaster, and in which therefore the faintest indication of a change in U.S. attitudes can seem like a matter of life and death. Moreover, they are used to Republicans and fearful of Democrats.

---

Source: Kennedy Library, National Security Files, Countries Series, China. Secret. The memorandum bears no indication that it was seen by Kennedy.

[1] For Ray Cline's recollections of his years in Taipei, see *Secrets, Spies and Scholars: Blueprint of the Essential CIA* (Washington: 1976), pp. 172–181. See also Cline, *Chiang Ching-kuo Remembered: The Man and His Political Legacy* (Washington: 1989), pp. 15–99.

They have been deeply shocked by the U.S. position on Outer Mongolia. They were also disturbed by the Liao incident, and of course most of all by the possibility of U.S. support for a two-China position in the UN. But according to Cline, what has particularly troubled them in all three cases is that they did not feel consulted in the process. Our earlier and successful pressure on the matter of Chinese Nationalist forces in Burma bothered them less, Cline says, because it was handled by private communication—which Cline himself was our most effective persuader. The Department of State has been sending stern lectures to Chiang (I attach a sample, together with Chiang's response, Tab A),[2] instead of talking with him ahead of time about hard problems. The fact that the Department is right does not make its pills more palatable.

The net result, according to Cline is that the Chinese Nationalist Government now feels deeply uneasy about the U.S., and is preparing dangerous adventures of its own, up to and including a suicidal landing on the mainland. Their intransigence on Outer Mongolia, moreover, threatens to make any manageable solution of the UN problem unlikely. The Generalissimo personally cancelled Chiang Ching-kuo's visit to the U.S., Cline reports, and if present trends cannot be reversed, he foresees a grievous split.

What makes all this so sad is that *in fact* we have no intention of deserting Chiang and every reason to support real progress in Formosa. Yet we seem headed for the same impasse Marshall and Acheson got into— and with equally bad political results at home and abroad.

Cline makes the following suggestions:

1. The Chinese suspicion is currently directed more at the State Department than at you, and reassurance directly from you can do more to encourage the Generalissimo than any other course. At my invitation he has drafted a possible letter which would move in this direction, and while it would need to be checked closely with Dean Rusk, it seems to me a highly promising start. (Tab B)

2. Our own interest in a mission in Outer Mongolia is pretty small, and Cline thinks we could back off from this with no great loss of face. He doubts whether in any case our mission would get any very attractive facilities and he does not see why we need to put a mission in Outer Mon-

---

[2] The tabs are not attached to the source text. According to a marginal note, Tab A was telegram 715 to Taipei, June 30, and telegram 5 from Taipei, July 2. The former instructed Drumright to meet with Chiang and respond to the views reported in Document 32; it instructed him to assure Chiang of U.S. support but to lay out the U.S. views on Chinese representation, Mongolia, and the Liao visa issue. Telegram 5 from Taipei reported that Drumright had done so in a July 1 conversation with Chiang, who had replied that the GRC had not ruled out the possibility of an alternative to the moratorium but that it would withdraw from the United Nations rather than accept a "two Chinas" arrangement. (Department of State, Central Files, 611.93/6–2961 and 611.93/7–291, respectively) See the Supplement.

golia when our real concern is simply not to oppose its admission to the United Nations. He agrees with me, however, that we must try to persuade the Chinese Nationalists not to veto Outer Mongolia admission.

3. The Liao visa does not need to be withheld but we can give assurance that Liao will not be treated to any official notice or support.

4. On the UN issue, we both think that Dean Rusk's proposal of a move from the moratorium to a straight debate on the merits has real promise. Even Cline believes that we could lose such a debate and not bother our Chinese friends very much, because it would be an honest defeat on what they would call an issue of principle. The same thing would hold with respect to domestic opinion—and in any case we might not lose on the merits if the case is strongly made. Opposition on this one is likely to come from Adlai.

5. A great sustaining dream of the Chinese Nationalists is of course a return to the mainland, and in Cline's view we could at once recapture great support from Chiang if we would join with him in certain reconnaissance probes on the mainland. This is, of course, a lot to ask of us, although no U.S. troops would be involved, but there is at least a case for a study of this possibility with more sympathy than has yet been given it. I will have more on this after the weekend.

In sum, Cline gives me the strong impression of being a tough, flexible, wholly *American* observer of this very difficult situation. He will be here until Tuesday[3] if you should want to see him.

McG. B.[4]

---

[3] July 11.
[4] Printed from a copy that bears these typed initials.

### 40.    Telegram From the Commander in Chief, Pacific (Felt) to the Joint Chiefs of Staff

Honolulu, July 10, 1961, 4:48 p.m.

110248Z. US-GRC relations. A. Dept State Instruction No. CA–10880 June 16, 1961[1] B. COMUSTDC 100645Z July PASEP.[2] C. [*less than 1 line of source text not declassified*] July 10.[3]

1.    COMUSTDC has been studying for several months the problem of what will be the effect on the GRC if it appears that acceptance of two-China solution is imminent. He has not been able to coordinate his studies with the Embassy but has discussed the essentials of his concern with the Ambassador. The latter, emphasized the political nature of the problem and indicated that COMUSTDC was perhaps out of his field. In our opinions, it is the essence of prudence for COMUSTDC to continue to be concerned.

2.    His study develops 3 possible GRC courses of action:

A. Unilateral military action by the GRC,
B. GRC accommodation with Communist China,
C. Negotation with the U.S. to salvage best possible concessions for mainlander element resident on Taiwan.

3.    Further study is required before a recommendation can be forwarded. However, it is clear that the U.S. should anticipate GRC actions in case of a two-China decision and should develop our own courses of action to meet future contingencies.

4.    Ref. A promulgates a statement of United States China policy which presents U.S. policy intentions and lines of action with respect to GRC and Red China. This paper is reassuring. On the other hand, a rash

---

Source: Department of State, Central Files, 793.00/7–1161. Top Secret. Also sent to JCA to pass for information to JACE, AJCC, Fort Richie, Maryland. Repeated for information to PACAF, CINCPACFLT, CINCUSARPAC, and COMUSTDC.

[1] The reference instruction, sent to all U.S. diplomatic and consular missions, stated that its purpose was to counteract the widespread expectation that the new U.S. administration would make a rapid and substantial change of U.S. policy toward China, and it set forth the basic U.S. position as guidance for discussion with foreign officials and other interested persons. (Ibid., 611.93/6–1661) See the Supplement.

[2] It stated the view of Taiwan Defense Command Commander Vice Admiral Roland N. Smoot that Chiang Kai-shek might undertake independent major action against the mainland if his forces were in the highest possible state of readiness, mainland conditions were at the worst possible level, and he believed U.S. policy was changing so as to foreshadow reduced U.S. support. (Department of State, Central Files, 611.93/7–1161) See the Supplement.

[3] Not found. [*text not declassified*] circulated as TDCSDB–3/647,621, July 19, referred to [*text not declassified*] (TDCSDB–3/647,522) as reporting the training of airdrop teams. (Kennedy Library, National Security Files, Countries Series, China)

of stories has appeared in U.S. newspapers reporting that the U.S. is weighing an offer to admit Peiping to the UN Assembly. We note the difference between policy statement suggested by Senator Goldwater and Mr. Nixon's advice to shoot down unofficial reports that State is considering a change in U.S. policy. Senator Scott[4] has called attention to the fact that some advisers are favoring admission of Red China to the UNGA and keeping Nationalist China on the Security Council. These papers add to the Gimo's concern and apprehension.

5. Ref. B reports kinds of unilateral military action which might be taken by the GRC. We have been observing for many months the GRC training programs for dropping large groups of special forces. We are conversant with the development of their plans for utilization of special forces. Adm Smoot informs me that Mr. Ray Cline is in Wash DC with Amb Drumright. I recommend strongly that you make arrangements through CIA to meet with Cline. He has been working with Chiang Ching-kuo for a long time.

6. Ref C is pertinent.

[4] Senator Hugh Scott of Pennsylvania.

## 41. Highlights of Discussion at Secretary of State Rusk's Planning Meeting

Washington, July 13, 1961.

CONTINGENCY PLANNING FOR A POSSIBLE OFFSHORE
ISLANDS CRISIS

The Under Secretary chaired the meeting.

The paper under consideration was one of July 10, 1961, prepared primarily by FE:CA and entitled "Contingency Planning for Possible Renewed Chinese Communist Attack on the Offshore Islands".[1]

Source: National Archives and Records Administration, RG 59, S/P Files: Lot 67 D 548, Secretary's Policy Planning Meetings. Secret. Drafted by Edward E. Rice of the Policy Planning Council. The meeting was one of a series of such meetings held irregularly by the Secretary and principal officers of the Department.

[1] A copy of the paper as revised on July 14 is ibid., China.

It was brought out in preliminary discussion that the Chinese Communists have the capability of taking the offshore islands, though the military price would probably be high. They could also, at any time, start a renewed crisis which might be intended for other purposes rather than actual capture of the GRC positions there.

There followed considerable discussion of the desirability of bringing about a GRC evacuation, though the paper under consideration is based on the assumption that the GRC remains wholly committed to remaining on the islands. The comment was made that, in issues such as this one, US policy revolves around points fixed by our supposed satellites and that recovery of US freedom of decision would impose costs which cannot be fully weighed, but which would undoubtedly be considerable.

One participant suggested that, while the paper envisages handling another crisis much like the last, the situation is now different in at least three respects: (1) We have a different President who has made different statements on the subject; (2) there is a different situation in Europe (Berlin), with consequent greater need for solidarity with our (NATO) allies; and (3) it will not be possible next time to keep the issue out of the UN.

Another pointed out in rebuttal: (1) Whatever the President may have said about the offshore islands' evacuation, they are still under GRC occupation; (2) while the greater solidarity needed in NATO suggests we press for evacuation of the offshore islands, there is also a different situation in Asia which, it might be argued, operates in the opposite direction; and (3) the paper does envisage our taking a new crisis immediately to the UN.

There was some disagreement on this last matter. One participant agreed we would need to *consider* taking the issue to the UN but pointed to the pitfalls we might encounter in handling it there. Another believed a new offshore crisis could not be kept out of the UN and that we had best take the initiative in order to have a better chance of controlling the way the issue might be handled. (Still another indicated, after the meeting broke up, that the UN appeared the only suitable vehicle for handling the issue in a non-belligerent context. During the last crisis we agreed to resume Ambassadorial talks, which are still continuing although our exchanges about Taiwan and the Strait have reached a sterile impasse. If a crisis now broke out despite the Warsaw talks, we might need to seek a different forum. The UN should provide that different forum.)

It also was brought out there is need for a contingency plan in case of a pro-Communist military coup on Taiwan. The FE planning advisor agreed, and made note of the requirement.

## 42.    Letter From President Kennedy to President Chiang

Washington, July 14, 1961.

DEAR MR. PRESIDENT: Vice President Johnson has brought to my attention your thoughtful letter of June ninth,[1] and I have decided to reply directly to you myself because to my distress a number of misunderstandings seem to have arisen recently between our two governments. Our countries plainly have so much in common that it is quite intolerable for us to permit any relationship to exist except the kind of closest cooperation and confidence appropriate between old and trusted friends.

It seems to me essential for us to resolve outstanding difficulties promptly and work out together suitable courses of action on the many grave problems confronting us at this time. It would of course be most effective if you could yourself come to see me or if I could go to Taipei. The weight of responsibilities on both of us and, indeed, my schedule of official visits here, make this seem impracticable. Therefore, I urge that you send to Washington a fully trusted representative to speak for yourself and your government in talks with me and other American officials concerning the critical decisions we need to take on strategy and tactics in the United Nations this fall. I had looked forward to seeing your son, General Chiang Ching-kuo, anticipating that he would be able to speak frankly and fully for you on these matters on his projected visit to the United States. I would still be delighted to see him if he can come in the near future, but in any case I urge you to designate someone in whom you repose great confidence to come to see me so that we can have the benefit of your considered views. In all these conversations, of course, we would continue to rely for diplomatic advice and guidance on your competent Ambassador, George Yeh, who has represented you most skillfully in exchanges of views to date here in Washington.

---

Source: Department of State, Central Files, 611.93/7–1461. Top Secret; Eyes Only. Filed with a covering note of the same date from Bromley Smith of the White House staff to U. Alexis Johnson. Drafted in the White House and revised in the Department of State. A July 11 memorandum from Bundy to Johnson states that the draft "responds to the President's own sense of the situation, as I understand it." Johnson returned the revised draft with a July 14 memorandum stating that the changes were "relatively minor" and "directed primarily to somewhat cutting back on the making of commitments to Chiang and thus preserving our freedom of action." Both memoranda, together with the draft with handwritten revisions, are ibid., Presidential Correspondence: Lot 66 D 204. See also Document 43.

[1] In his June 9 letter to Johnson, Chiang argued vigorously against the U.S. intention to seek diplomatic ties with Mongolia, declaring that such a move would indicate that the United States was "retreating from principles in the global struggle against world Communism" and would be viewed as paving the way for a "two Chinas" arrangement. (Department of State, Central Files, 611.93/6–991)

My staff has pointed out to me that some concern was caused in Taipei by the announced decision in principle to grant a visa to Thomas Liao. Our view was that he could make less propaganda unfavorable to the Republic of China if he visited the United States without any official attention than if we continued to exclude him. It is of course difficult under our political and legal system to deny entry to anyone without very serious cause. In view of your concern, however, we have instructed our Embassy in Tokyo to withhold his visa for the time being[2] and we will not issue it until we have had further talks with you about the best way to handle the matter. I assure you that Liao will receive no official encouragement or attention from the United States Government nor, of course, any sponsorship of his visit.

On the issue of Outer Mongolia, I wish to inform you that the United States Government is merely exploring the possibility that some strategic advantage for the Free World might be gained by sending Western diplomatic representatives to this region between Soviet Russia and Mainland China. We are not committed to this line of action and can of course defer United States recognition indefinitely if that seems wise. Actually our main concern is with the United Nations, where our primary need is to avoid letting the Outer Mongolia issue adversely affect the vote on the much more vital matter of Chinese representation in the United Nations. Our hope is that you can find some way to avoid the necessity of your delegation at the United Nations vetoing the entry of Outer Mongolia to the United Nations. We fear the consequences a veto probably would have on the attitude of the African states which unfortunately seem to have acquiesced in the Soviet linkage of the admission of Mauretania and Outer Mongolia. Working out a reasonable position on this complex matter is one of the main tasks that we should set for ourselves if you can send someone to give us the benefit of your ideas on the subject.

On the broader problem of Chinese representation, we must promptly reach a meeting of the minds. We have informally explored a variety of schemes, none of them too satisfactory. We are anxious to get the benefit of your judgment on all of the alternatives. We are convinced that, unfortunately, the moratorium will fail if presented again this fall. We should compare detailed notes on this point, but I am afraid this is likely to be the case. We should consider parliamentary tactics to employ that would insure that the issue comes up in the right context and that it

---

[2] In telegram 214 to Tokyo, July 22. (Ibid., 793.00/7–2261) A July 14 memorandum from U. Alexis Johnson to Legal Adviser Abram Chayes and McConaughy stated that the President had decided that "for reasons of national policy" Liao should not be given a visa "*at this time.*" The memorandum stated that Liao should not be told he had been denied a visa but that his application would remain under active consideration; the purpose was to delay granting a visa but to retain flexibility for future action. (Ibid., 793.00/7–1461)

will be considered a substantive rather than a procedural matter. In any case, it is of high importance that your government and mine reach an understanding on the positions most advantageous for us to adopt.

I need not remind you that my primary aim is to support the Republic of China in every possible way and to oppose the entry of the Chinese Communists into the United Nations. Vice President Johnson made these points clear, I know, when he visited you and delivered my letter to you[3] a few weeks ago. The key points made in my letter are expressions of the policy of the United States Government and will not change. Our difficulties are in finding ways to carry out those policies in the face of determined enemies and troublemakers. You can help us there by drawing on your long experience in dealing with the Chinese Communists as well as your knowledge of Asian psychology and temperament generally. With a common goal and good understanding we should be able to map a course that will work to the advantage of our two countries.

Please let me know your reaction to these views and particularly whether you can send to Washington a plenipotentiary representative or representatives in the near future.[4]

With great respect,

Sincerely,

John F. Kennedy

---

[3] Dated May 8; see footnote 3, Document 26.

[4] The letter was transmitted to Taipei in telegram 29, July 14. (Department of State, Central Files, 611.93/7–1461) Telegram 60 from Taipei, July 19, reported that Drumright had delivered the letter to Chiang on July 18. Chiang expressed pleasure and told Drumright he was thinking of sending Vice President Ch'en Ch'eng to Washington. (Ibid., 611.93/7–1961)

## 43.    Letter From Secretary of State Rusk to President Kennedy

Washington, July 15, 1961.

DEAR MR. PRESIDENT: In the attached memorandum of July 12 you asked Assistant Secretary McConaughy for an explanation of the lack of substance in the draft reply to President Chiang Kai-shek's letter to the Vice President.[1]

I am replying myself because, although I had not personally seen the text of the draft, its general nature was determined with my knowledge and full concurrence.

It does not seem to me appropriate for a Vice President to become deeply involved in the particulars of highly controversial topics which we have outstanding with other governments. These involve the most careful negotiations and discussion, making full use of diplomatic channels and, where necessary, direct communications between foreign ministers or heads of government. In the case of President Chiang Kai-shek's letter to the Vice President, it was my view that the subjects could better be dealt with in detail on the spot by Ambassador Drumright, and I personally approved a telegram (#715 of June 30, attached)[2] instructing the Ambassador to discuss the topics raised in the letter to the Vice President prior to the Ambassador's return for consultation. It was also my view that, following Drumright's return, a communication from you to President Chiang Kai-shek would be appropriate.

Assistant Secretary McConaughy discussed the nature of the reply with the Vice President's staff, as well as with the White House staff. It was our understanding that the Vice President preferred to avoid a substantive reply to the Generalissimo.

---

Source: Kennedy Library, National Security Files, Countries Series, China Subjects, Chiang Kai-shek Correspondence. Personal. The source text bears a note in Bundy's handwriting: "President has seen and disagrees." The letter was drafted by Rusk, based in part on a draft memorandum from Rusk to Kennedy prepared by McConaughy. Rusk elaborated on the points in McConaughy's draft and added the second and last paragraphs. (Department of State, Presidential Correspondence: Lot 66 D 204, Kennedy/Johnson Correspondence with Chinese Officials)

[1] The draft letter, prepared in the Office of Chinese Affairs, was sent to the White House with a July 6 covering memorandum from Battle to Bundy. (Ibid., Central Files, 611.93/7–661) The draft was enclosed with Kennedy's July 9 weekend reading and returned to the White House with a note by Kennedy: "Chiang's letter shows the depth of his feeling on Outer Mongolia, and the draft answer is, in my view, an excellent example of how not to deal with the problem." (Kennedy Library, National Security Files, Countries Series, China)

Kennedy's July 12 memorandum, attached to the source text, reads in part: "I can think of no letter that would have had a more disastrous effect. It almost appears to be an intended rebuff as it deals with none of the questions that were raised in Chiang Kai-shek's letter and does not have any substantive expressions of good will, which I believe are rather necessary at this time."

[2] Not attached to the source text; see footnote 1, Document 39.

It was not our intent that the draft reply serve as a rebuff to President Chiang. We had hoped instead to assure him that the questions he raised were being given the most serious attention, a point reinforced by Ambassador Drumright's representations.

Although judgments may vary about the precise language proposed in the draft, I believe that it was an appropriate reply under all the circumstances and that the Generalissimo would have considered it so.[3]

Faithfully yours,

**Dean Rusk**

---

[3] The final letter from Johnson to Chiang, July 12, was almost identical to the draft cited in footnote 1 above. It assured Chiang that U.S.-GRC relations would continue to be governed by the letter and spirit of their joint communiqué but was otherwise non-substantive. It was transmitted in telegram 28 to Taipei, July 14. (Department of State, Central Files, 611.93/7–1461)

---

## 44.    Memorandum of Conversation

Washington, July 28, 1961, 11 a.m.–1:05 p.m.

SUBJECT

Conference at White House on China Representation at United Nations and Outer Mongolia-United Nations Membership Application

PARTICIPANTS

The President
The Secretary
Mr. George W. Ball, Under Secretary for Economic Affairs
Mr. Walter P. McConaughy, Assistant Secretary for Far Eastern Affairs
Mr. Harlan Cleveland, Assistant Secretary for International Organization Affairs
Ambassador Everett F. Drumright
Mr. McGeorge Bundy, Special Assistant to the President
Mr. Walt W. Rostow, Deputy Special Assistant to the President
Mr. Robert W. Komer, The White House
Mr. Robert W. Rinden, Acting Director for Chinese Affairs

With respect to the China representation issue at the United Nations, the Secretary recommended the "important question" device as

---

Source: Kennedy Library, National Security Files, Countries Series, China. Secret. Drafted by Rinden and approved in S on August 8 and by the White House on August 10. According to Kennedy's Appointment Book, other participants were present for part of the discussion, which included Southeast Asia as well as preparations for Ch'en Ch'eng's visit. (Kennedy Library)

the best tactic to use since it offered us a reasonable chance of getting a clear, blocking one-third. In response to the President's question whether Ambassador Stevenson thought this tactic would get us more votes than the moratorium, the Secretary said that Ambassador Stevenson thought that it would. He said that any "two Chinas" proposal was unacceptable to the GRC.

The President asked about the usefulness of the Swedish proposal for a commission to study the problem and report back to the 17th United Nations General Assembly.

Mr. Cleveland said that the GRC was allergic to the Swedish proposal because of its fears about the composition of the commission.

The Secretary thought GRC fears were well founded as the Commission would likely recommend some sort of two Chinas solution.

The President asked that some variant of the Swedish proposal, acceptable to the GRC, be devised. He said that to use only the "important question" device would be too transparent a blocking measure. It was important, he declared, to formulate a more attractive proposal, apparently moving towards a final solution of the China representation issue. Nigeria and certain other countries would be willing to support us on the China representation issue if we presented a proposal offering suitable rationale.

Mr. Rusk said that, in view of United States interest and the damage to the United Nations that might result, the China representation issue was, on its merits, an important question.

The Secretary said that there are governments who recognize Peiping but do not want Peiping in the United Nations. They would vote against United Nations membership for Peiping if they had a justification to use vis-à-vis Peiping. He thought that the proposal for a commission to study the China representation issue might be more attractive to such countries if the commission were also to look into the problem of the allocation of United Nations seats, not just the problem of the China seat. No one, however, he said, would be fooled by whatever device we used.

In reply to the President's question as to what Ambassador Stevenson and his USUN colleagues thought about the various proposals, Mr. Cleveland said that they seemed to prefer the "successor state" formula. The President was concerned to have Ambassador Stevenson's agreement on the proposal to be used as he would have to carry the fight in the United Nations.

Mr. Cleveland said that there was also the timing problem; other countries want to know what we will do before they will decide their position. In response to the President's query when the United States proposal should be floated, the Secretary said that it should be deferred until after the talks with Premier Ch'en.

The President said that, as the moratorium was impossible, to fight for it would be the ultimate futility. What we must work on now is the "important question" and what to add to it in order to win.

We must also convince the GRC the United States and GRC have a common objective: to keep the Chinese Communists out of the United Nations. We want to give away as little as possible of the GRC position in order to attain our common purpose. The GRC must recognize that there is good faith on both sides and that there is no ambiguity in the United States position. If we were defeated on the China representation issue, it would be almost as bad for the United States as the GRC. Some friendly countries like Nigeria, Pakistan and Great Britain say they can't vote with us, and Japan says we can't win. But we can't allow ourselves to be beaten; we must do what we have to in order to win. The GRC will be asked to give up as little as is essential to winning.

With respect to Outer Mongolia's United Nations membership application, the President said the GRC must not veto the application. He also indicated that United States recognition of Outer Mongolia should be put aside in the interests of victory on the China representation issue.

The Secretary said that we did not want to organize abstentions to defeat the Outer Mongolian membership application although we and the GRC would abstain. There was the possibility that, in addition to Mauritania, Kuwait and Sierra Leone might also be involved. In any case, if Mauritania was kept out of the United Nations, we would infuriate the Africans and our goose would be cooked.

## 45.   Memorandum of Conversation

Washington, July 31, 1961, 11 a.m.–12:40 p.m.

SUBJECT

Chinese Representation in the United Nations

PARTICIPANTS

| | |
|---|---|
| General Ch'en Ch'eng, Vice President, GRC | President Kennedy |
| | Vice President Johnson |
| Dr. Shen Ch'ang-huan, Foreign Minister, GRC | Secretary Rusk |
| | Mr. Ball, Under Secretary for Economic Affairs |
| Dr. George K.C. Yeh, Chinese Ambassador to US | |
| | Mr. McConaughy, Assistant Secretary, FE |
| Dr. T.F. Tsiang, Chinese Permanent Representative to the UN | Mr. Cleveland, Assistant Secretary, IO |
| | Ambassador Drumright |
| Dr. Hu Ch'ing-yu, Advisor, Ministry of Foreign Affairs, GRC | Mr. Rostow, White House Staff |
| | Mr. Rinden, Acting Director, CA |
| Mr. James Shen, Director, Government Information Office, GRC | Mr. Mehlert, Interpreter |

The President said that he wanted to say something about United States policy with regard to China in the United Nations. United States policy is to take every means to prevent the Chinese Communists from entering the United Nations. This is the basis of our policy.

If Red China were to gain admission into the United Nations these effects would follow:

1. The GRC would no longer be a member. This would adversely affect its international position, as well as its bilateral relations with a number of countries who now recognize it.

2. It would have a detrimental effect on the attitude of overseas Chinese in Southeast Asia and elsewhere.

3. Such a success for the Communists—when we face them in Southeast Asia and Berlin—would give impetus to their prestige at a difficult and important time for us. It would be a very damaging blow to United States prestige and would hurt the United States position in Southeast Asia, Pakistan, Iran and Turkey. So the United States and the

---

Source: Kennedy Library, National Security Files, Countries Series, China. Secret. Drafted by Rinden. The time of the meeting is from Kennedy's Appointment Book. (Ibid.) Vice President Ch'en Ch'eng visited Washington July 31–August 3. Briefing materials for the Ch'en visit are ibid., National Security Files, Countries Series, China; President's Office Files, China Security; and Department of State, Conference Files: Lot 65 D 366, CF 1939. A memorandum of conversation on U.S.-Chinese cooperation in Southeast Asia is in the Kennedy Library, National Security Files, Countries Series, China. A copy of Chiang's July 28 letter to the President is in Department of State, Central Files, 303/8–1561. See the Supplement for both.

GRC have the same position on this question: to use every means to keep the Chinese Communists out of the United Nations. On this we are in whole agreement.

So the matter which concerns us is how to get a majority plus one in order to carry out this policy. We do not want to lose by three or four votes. This is a question that does not involve just the GRC; it involves the United States equally.

Vice President Ch'en said that while en route to the USA he was gratified to learn that the United States Senate had passed a resolution opposing entry of Communist China into the United Nations.[1]

The President said the problem is to get votes in the United Nations; there is no problem to get votes on this matter in the United States Congress.

Vice President Ch'en said that because the United States and the GRC are defending one position of common interest it is easier to find means to realize the objective.

The President emphasized that this was a matter of vital importance to the United States and the GRC and that, given the background of this situation, it would be extremely inimical to United States interests if the Chinese Communists should enter the United Nations.

The President said we must be realistic in counting votes in the United Nations. We must be careful not to count votes we don't have. We don't want to be beaten in the United Nations by a few votes. This is a matter that will be won or lost in a very close vote.

At 12:30 the conference adjourned for the President's luncheon in honor of Vice President Ch'en.

---

[1] The Senate adopted S. Con Res. 34 on July 25 by a vote of 76 to 0. The House of Representatives concurred by a vote of 395–0 on August 31. The resolution reaffirmed U.S. support for the Republic of China and opposition to seating the Chinese Communist regime in the United Nations, "so long as that regime persists in defying the principles of the United Nations Charter". For text, see 75 Stat. 965.

## 46.    Memorandum of Conversation

Washington, August 1, 1961, 10:04–11:35 a.m.

SUBJECT

United States-China Relations

PARTICIPANTS

| | |
|---|---|
| General Ch'en Ch'eng, Vice President, GRC | President Kennedy |
| Dr. Shen Chang-huan, Minister of Foreign Affairs, GRC | Vice President Johnson |
| | Secretary Rusk |
| | Mr. McConaughy, Asst. Sec., FE |
| Dr. George K. C. Yeh, Chinese Ambassador | Mr. Cleveland, Asst. Sec., IO |
| | Ambassador Drumright |
| Dr. T. F. Tsiang, Chinese Permanent Representative to the United Nations | Mr. Walter Rostow, White House Staff |
| | Mr. Rinden, CA |
| Dr. Hu Ching-yu, Advisor, Ministry of Foreign Affairs | Mr. Calvin Mehlert, Interpreter |
| Mr. James Shen, Director, Office of Information | |

Regarding China representation at the United Nations, the President said that we are in agreement on strategy, that is, on our objective. We now have to decide what tactics would be best to get the necessary majority in the United Nations. Vice President Chen replied that at breakfast with Secretary Rusk there had not been adequate time to arrive at agreement on all points. He hoped to talk further with the Secretary this afternoon.[1]

The Secretary said that at the breakfast meeting we had discussed the precarious situation on the moratorium and thought that we might go for the important question. If we would get enough votes to carry this proposal, the GRC would go along. Some thought was also given to deferring the China seat issue until the problem of reallocating seats in the United Nations and its organizations had been resolved.

The President said that what we have to worry about is this year. We don't know what the Chinese Communists may do in the next 12 months. The coming 12 months may present us a different problem and a different solution. Many things may happen—for example, as a result of the dispute between India and China. He said: "Let's win this one." Next year we may fight them on another basis.

---

Source: Kennedy Library, National Security Files, Countries Series, China. Secret. Drafted By Rinden. The time of the meeting is from Kennedy's Appointment Book. (Ibid.)

[1] A record of the discussion at the breakfast meeting is in Department of State, Central Files, 611.93/8–161. A record of a 4 p.m. meeting between Rusk and Ch'en is ibid., 303/8–161. See the Supplement for both.

The President said that last year Pakistan had not voted against us because of a special plea from President Eisenhower. The Pakistanis, however, made clear that last year was the last time they would accede to our request on this matter. Nigeria is friendly to the United States but, in accordance with the general Commonwealth position, it will vote against us this year. Brazil also has had a change of attitude.

The Secretary said that at the breakfast meeting he had explained that the United States position with regard to Outer Mongolia was one of great flexibility and that we were in no rush for bilateral relations with Outer Mongolia. We were much concerned, however, about the effect Outer Mongolia would have on voting in the United Nations.

The President said he had read over the 1955 correspondence between the GRC and the US concerning United Nations membership for Outer Mongolia.[2] He noted that President Chiang Kai-shek had replied that, as Outer Mongolia was not an independent state, the GRC could not agree to United Nations membership for Outer Mongolia. The interest of the United States now is the effect the Outer Mongolian question will have on votes in the United Nations with respect to China representation. How many votes can we lose or gain from Africa in this regard? As the Secretary has said, we are suspending talks on bilateral relations with Outer Mongolia.

Ambassador Yeh said that the last time he was in Taiwan, President Chiang asked him if United States plans to establish relations with Outer Mongolia were based purely on improving the United States position vis-à-vis the China representation issue—or did the United States have other motives?

The President said that these bilateral talks had taken place in order to seek a solution to the deadlock over Mauritania and Outer Mongolia. Last year the United States could not decide if Outer Mongolia was independent. Now we are not going ahead on the question of United States–Outer Mongolia relations because of the GRC's feelings regarding Outer Mongolia.

The Secretary remarked that the intelligence community felt that we needed more information on remote areas but that this consideration had been a relatively small part of the problem. Perhaps President Chiang's idea was that United States relations with Outer Mongolia was a step toward United States recognition of Peiping. However, it was nothing of the kind. The dominant problem is the fact that the entire African community is terribly troubled over the question of United Nations membership for Mauritania. The Soviet Union's linking Mauritania and Outer Mongolia has involved 10 to 15 votes on China representation.

---

[2] For texts of President Eisenhower's messages of November 22 and 28 to Chiang and Chiang's messages of November 26 and December 3 to Eisenhower, see *Foreign Relations, 1955–1957,* vol. XI, pp. 388–424, passim.

Ambassador Tsiang said that the GRC would prefer to rely on abstentions to keep Mauritania out of the United Nations rather than to use the veto. In any event, some African states would feel that we were ganging up on Mauritania if the abstentions device was used. Nonetheless, there is a difference in abstaining and in vetoing, but it is impossible to express this difference in number of votes. He had advised his government not to veto the Mauritanian United Nations application but to use the abstention method.

President Kennedy said the question is: what will be the effect on the Africans of a group of abstentions?

Ambassador Tsiang said that in May 1961 he was in Taipei. It was unfortunate then that the question of United States recognition of Outer Mongolia had generated suspicions on Taiwan and had stiffened the GRC attitude against United States recognition of Outer Mongolia. The United States attitude on Asia appears different from its attitude on Europe. In the latter case, it says "thus far and no further," but in Asia it seems prepared to retreat still more.

President Kennedy replied that since 1945 we had fought in Asia but not in Europe.

Ambassador Tsiang asked whether the United States could adopt an attitude toward Outer Mongolia such as it had adopted toward the Baltic states.

The President said that we have suspended our bilateral talks with Outer Mongolia.

Ambassador Tsiang asked if the United States could go further than merely suspending the negotiations.

The President said it would be best to let these negotiations on Outer Mongolia die out during the Berlin situation.

Ambassador Tsiang asked, if the United States could not make a public statement about Outer Mongolia, could the United States assure the GRC that the United States policy is the same towards Outer Mongolia as toward the Baltic states.

The Secretary said that the United States would have to think about that.

The President said that we accepted the GRC views on the non-independence of Outer Mongolia and we will not continue our negotiations with it. The question is what should we do about Outer Mongolia in the United Nations?

Vice President Chen said that he was fully aware of the relationship between the Outer Mongolia question and China representation at the United Nations. He had discussed this with President Chiang and the Cabinet more than once. The GRC is governed by one overriding consideration in its relationship with the United States. The GRC does not want to add to United States difficulties or see United States prestige suffer. The GRC has no suspicion of wicked motives on the part of the United States. However, each country has its own difficulties and historical background. He would like to explain the GRC position on Outer Mongolia. The GRC is not dominated by emotions. It has objectively considered the problem and taken considerable regard for internal repercussions in the GRC. Ambassador Drumright in Taipei had been kept fully informed of the Chinese attitude and in Washington Ambassador Yeh had been kept fully informed so that he could convey GRC views to the United States Government.

Outer Mongolia is clearly one of the Soviet Union's creations. The Asian countries recognize this and the United States at the United Nations had declared Outer Mongolia did not have the attributes of a sovereign state. The GRC feels United States recognition of Outer Mongolia would greatly add to Soviet and Communist world prestige. The GRC is concerned about the effect of this on its compatriots on the China mainland and other peoples behind the iron curtain. The United States, as the leader of the free world, should consider whether any of its actions would add to the prestige of the Soviet Union and the Communist world. Internally, the GRC's people are pledged to a policy of fighting Communism and countering Russia. This policy was formulated by the Kuomintang, adopted by the GRC government and endorsed by the GRC legislative branch. The GRC's feeling in this regard is shared by a number of Asian countries.

Vice President Chen said he believes he can control his own cabinet. However, just before his departure from Taipei for Washington, a meeting was held of representatives of the five Yuans. At this joint conference the Vice President represented the Executive Yuan and heard the unanimous views on Outer Mongolia of the representatives of the other four Yuans. Their united view was that the GRC must use all means under the United Nations Charter to block Outer Mongolia's entry into the United Nations.

The President said that Vice President Chen, as a military man, should know that it is easy to send instructions to the field but at the General Assembly the ambassadors of the GRC and the United States would have to carry the fight on China representation. In the United States there had been Congressional resolutions on keeping the Chinese Communists, as well as Outer Mongolia, out of the United Nations. The real question was how to do this.

The Secretary said that United States and GRC policies towards Africa are important. He had been impressed by the progress the GRC had made in Africa. The African bloc in the United Nations is as important now as the Latin American bloc. GRC relationships with the African states can greatly strengthen its position in the United Nations. The United States has a great stake in Africa.

The President said that, in seeking to keep the GRC in the United Nations and Outer Mongolia out, we must recognize the close relationship between the United Nations membership applications of Outer Mongolia and Mauritania. In this regard he said, "You can't have everything."

Some people on Taiwan may think that United States recognition of Outer Mongolia is a backhanded way of recognizing Peiping. This is not true. The only concern of the United States is to win on Chinese representation in the United Nations—to get the majority of votes on this question. We can't let those who don't understand this situation direct our strategy or we will end up beaten, the President said.

The Secretary asked Vice President Chen if it wouldn't be better to have Outer Mongolia than Communist China in the United Nations.

Ambassador Yeh said that we wouldn't want either. He offered assurance that none of the Chinese present had any sneaking suspicions of the United States. Otherwise, Vice President Chen wouldn't have come to Washington.

Vice President Chen said with reference to President Kennedy's statement about GRC misunderstanding of United States motives that, if he had ever had any suspicions, these suspicions had been completely dissipated after the talks with President Kennedy and Secretary Rusk. He knows President Kennedy is dealing with vast world problems, and he doesn't want to waste President Kennedy's time. Therefore, he suggests that Secretary Rusk, Foreign Minister Shen and other United States and GRC officials work out the technical details. He prefers the Outer Mongolian problem to be handled at this level.

Vice President Chen said that, in the continuing struggle between Communism and freedom, the GRC does not want to help the Communist world. It is important for the free world to achieve greater solidarity and stronger organization in facing Communist bloc. What is needed is a permanent staff set-up among the free countries of Asia. The GRC has drawn up a plan toward this end. As soon as the document is translated into English, the Secretary will be given a copy.[3] The organization proposed would do much to solidify and unify anti-Communist forces in

---

[3] The text of the proposal, "An Outline Proposal for a Collective Security Organization of the Anti-Communist Countries in the Western Pacific Area," codenamed Taiping, was enclosed with instruction CW–1777 to CINCPAC and five Embassies, August 25. (Department of State, Central Files, 790.5/8–2561) A November 21 memorandum from McConaughy to Rusk recommended against the proposal. (Ibid., 790.5/11–2161) Steeves informed Minister Kiang on December 19 that the United States considered that the objectives of the Chinese proposal could best be gained through existing liaison machinery. (Ibid., 790.5/12–1961)

Asia. If this plan could be adopted as soon as possible it would relieve the United States of some worries. This plan will not lead to requests from the GRC for more money. It is conceived in the interest of the United States and the free world.

The President said that Secretary Rusk would look at this proposal after it had been given to him in English translation.

It was an extremely difficult task to maintain understanding among all United States allies such as India and Pakistan or France and Tunisia, the President observed.

The President emphasized that the United States and the GRC must be sure to have the best possible intelligence on China mainland conditions.

Vice President Chen said he fully shared the President's anxiety about having accurate information on mainland conditions. In this connection, he had brought some materials concerning political, social, economic and military conditions on the mainland, but these materials have yet to be translated. The GRC still keeps in touch with its people on the mainland and gets information from them.

The President referred to the GRC concern over issuance of a United States visa to Thomas Liao and suggested that Secretary Rusk could discuss this later with the Chinese representative.

Vice President Chen said that Liao was a nonentity and that he did not attach much importance to the Liao case. However, in Taiwan some people had the impression the Americans wanted to bring him to the United States and build him up.

The President said that we don't want to make Liao important. In fact, scarcely anyone in the United States had heard of him.

Vice President Chen assured the President that the Liao case was no problem.

The Secretary said that at present possibly 500 people in the United States had heard of Liao. However, if the human rights issue were raised in his case, 100 million Americans might hear of him.

The President mentioned that Senator Fulbright was interested in the Liao visa case.

Ambassador Yeh said that Liao had taken Senator Fulbright's reply to him and had mimeographed copies made for distribution to Liao sympathizers in Japan.

The Secretary said that we are agreed on the basic relationships between the United States and the GRC, notably as set forth in the Mutual Defense Treaty of 1954 and the accompanying exchange of notes on the use of force by agreement only.

The President said that close consultation between our two governments on any actions that may bring on a military response is also most important.

Ambassador Yeh said that the GRC agreed. It was in this connection that the GRC had suggested joint staff meetings.

The President said that we must be careful not to get involved in actions on the China mainland which are based on hope and not facts. Therefore we need reliable information.

Ambassador Yeh said the GRC had "never acted contrary to the Treaty and never intends to."

Vice President Chen assured the President that "China's word is gold." He said that "we don't go back on our word." The Vice President reiterated that our common struggle with Communism will be long, and so we must stick together. We must look at these problems in the same spirit.

The GRC does not intend to suggest the replacement of SEATO but rather to make it more effective by including anti-Communist countries who have forces to fight Communist aggression. Both the United States and GRC are working on parallel lines, such as in intelligence work on the China mainland. They should pool their efforts with those of other Asian countries. The two countries should use psychological warfare as a substitute for military action. The GRC is seeking to strengthen its psychological warfare.

Vice President Chen said that, as a result of his work in Youth organizations on the China mainland many years ago, there were 30,000 potential agents on the China mainland who were loyal to him. They were lying low for the time being but would respond when the time came for action.

The President asked what method of communication the GRC had with the underground. The Vice President said that small radio sets had been used, but this method had been stopped recently. The best way now was for these agents to send messages back to Taipei through Macao and Hong Kong. The Vice President said that the GRC cannot rely completely on these agents on the mainland in the absence of an over-all organization. The GRC tactic vis-à-vis the Communists is to counter organization with organization.

Vice President Chen said that his faith in his mainland compatriots' eventual liberation had never been shaken because of his communication with them. His faith was not based on mere hope but on his continuing relationships with these mainland units.

47.    Editorial Note

On August 2, 1961, President Kennedy attended a dinner given by Vice President Ch'en in his honor at the Mayflower Hotel in Washington. Three memoranda of conversation drafted by interpreter Calvin Mehlert, all dated August 2, record aspects of the conversation. According to one, Kennedy requested that Ch'en take the following message to President Chiang:

"The United States Government wishes to do its utmost to maintain the position of the GRC at the September General Assembly and to prevent the seating of Communist China. The United States must not be defeated in the United Nations on this issue. No matter what differences may arise between the United States Government and the GRC on the best means to be used at the United Nations to avoid a defeat on the Chinese representation issue, it should be remembered that on fundamental questions the United States Government and the GRC are united."

Ch'en replied that the GRC did not wish to see the prestige of the United States damaged and would take no steps that might result in injury to the U.S. position. (Kennedy Library, National Security Files, Countries Series, China)

A second memorandum of conversation records conversation between Kennedy and Ch'en concerning various topics, including a question from Kennedy to Ch'en whether the GRC armed forces were not becoming over-age; Ch'en replied that the problem had been solved by conscription and that the average age was 25. A third memorandum records some discussion between Kennedy and Mehlert in which the President inquired about the attitude of the Chinese Communists at Geneva and in the Warsaw talks. (Ibid.)

## 48.    Memorandum of Conversation

Hyannis Port, Massachusetts, August 5, 1961.

SUBJECT

U.S. Strategy in the 16th General Assembly

PARTICIPANTS

The President
Ambassador Adlai E. Stevenson
Arthur Schlesinger, Jr., Special Assistant to the President
Harlan Cleveland, Assistant Secretary of State

[Here follows discussion of a possible Presidential speech to the General Assembly and other issues before the United Nations.

*Chinese Representation*[1]

Ascertain by intensive consultations (in New York and through diplomatic channels at government level around the world) what proposition can command a majority vote in the General Assembly.

*Action:* IO

*Including* an explicit arrangement with the French Africans as to their affirmative action of ChiRep if we are able to get Mauritania's membership application past the Soviet veto in the Security Council.

*Action:* USUN

Proposition to be floated will include two elements for a start:

a. the procedural proposition that ejecting the Chinese Nationalists or seating the ChiComs requires a two-thirds General Assembly vote as an "important" matter. (Watch out for pitfall of two-third requirement for *acceptance* of GRC credentials.)[2]

b. the procedural step of establishing a committee of the Assembly to study Chinese representation in the context of proposals for enlarging

---

Source: Kennedy Library, Papers of Arthur Schlesinger, Jr., Box WH22, Subject File, U.N. Speeches, 8/3/61–8/11/61. Confidential. Drafted by Cleveland. The memorandum states that it records two discussions, one in the middle of the day and one late in the afternoon. For Schlesinger's account of the conversation, see *A Thousand Days*, pp. 479–481.

[1] An August 31 memorandum from Cleveland to Rusk reports that at the August 5 meeting with Stevenson, Schlesinger, and himself, the President had requested them to "ascertain by intensive consultations what proposition could command a majority vote in the General Assembly that would keep the Chinese Communists out of the United Nations and the Republic of China in." (Department of State, Central Files, 303/8–3161)

[2] In an August 7 telephone conversation, Ball asked Stevenson about the Hyannis Port meetings. Stevenson said that the President was "flexible on the China thing" and that both he and the President felt an investigating committee had more promise than "'important question' gambit which could be turned against us on credentials." (Kennedy Library, Papers of George Ball, China (Taiwan))

the Councils. (Composition of such a committee would, of course, be highly important, and should reflect the relative strength in the General Assembly of the Peking recognizers (33) and the Taipei recognizers (49).)

Ambassador Stevenson gave his opinion that these propositions would not be sufficient, and that something like the successor state idea should also be in the picture.

The President said he realized the committee or any other means of postponement might only lead in time—next year, perhaps—to a Two-China proposal or even to ChiCom admission in some form. But he wanted to avoid taking any major step along this road this year. He also was determined that the United States was not to be defeated on this issue in the United Nations. Based on discussions with Chen Cheng this past week, the President fears that Chiang Kai-shek may be in what Mr. Schlesinger called a "gotterdammerung" mood, ready to pull the house down on himself—and on us in the process. Nevertheless, we had to keep on trying to persuade him that in the interest of protecting his UN seat (a national interest of the U.S. as well as of the GRC) some tactical adjustments would be required as we went along. One notable adjustment is the non-use of the GRC veto on the admission of Outer Mongolia.

The President wants to send a letter to Chiang this next week on this matter. Chiang's friends in this country, notably Roy Howard and Henry Luce, should also be enlisted in this effort of persuasion.

*Action:* FE

[Here follows discussion of unrelated issues.]

*Membership.* While no decision was recommended at this stage on just how to vote when the Mongolia–Mauritania issue comes up in the Security Council, the President did not exclude the option of voting for the Mongolia application if we could be assured that as a consequence the French Africans would stand with us on Chinese representation.

[Here follows discussion of unrelated issues.]

*Tibet.* Ambassador Stevenson expressed the opinion that the legal grounds for objection to China's action in taking over the administration of Tibet were relatively weak.

[Here follows discussion of unrelated issues.]

## 49.    National Intelligence Estimate

NIE 10–61                                             Washington, August 8, 1961.

### AUTHORITY AND CONTROL IN THE COMMUNIST MOVEMENT

#### The Problem

To assess the cohesion of the Sino-Soviet Bloc and among the parties of the world Communist movement, to identify trends in the degree of Soviet control, and to estimate the future implication of these trends.

#### Summary and Conclusions

*General Considerations*

1.  According to Communist doctrine, it would be impossible for conflicts of interest to disturb in any basic way the relations between Communist parties in the international movement. This is so, it is argued, because the class interests which are the source of international conflict among non-Communist states have been suppressed by the new social order, and have been replaced by the fundamental identity of views and harmony of interests of the "classless" society. In fact, however, the appearance of unity in the Communist movement has been due, not so much to the absence of conflicts of interest, as to the overwhelming authority exercised by Moscow. This authority has rested on the great military and economic power of the USSR, on its historical precedence as the first Communist state, on the long personal ascendancy of Stalin over the international Communist movement, and on the tradition of dictatorial centralism in that movement. (Paras. 13–18)

2.  In the period since World War II a number of developments have demonstrated the falsity of the simplistic Communist theory of natural harmony among Communist parties. When the Communist parties of Eastern Europe achieved state power they naturally acquired new interests and attitudes different from those they had reflected as small conspiratorial groups wholly dependent on the protection and support provided by Moscow. Yet they were small states in Moscow's immediate sphere of power; therefore, whatever pretensions to independence they

---

Source: Department of State, INR/EAP Files: Lot 90 D 110, NIE 43–61. Secret. According to a note on the covering sheet, the Central Intelligence Agency and the intelligence agencies of the Departments of State, the Army, the Navy, the Air Force, the Joint Staff and the FBI participated in the preparation of this estimate. All members of the USIB concurred in this estimate on August 8 except the representative of the AEC who abstained on the grounds that the subject was outside his jurisdiction.

may have had were bound to be extremely circumscribed. The achievement of state power by the Chinese Communists was a different matter, however, because it meant that for the first time Communist theory on state relations had to be applied to the relations between two great powers. (Paras. 14–16)

3. Beyond this, there was in the postwar period a considerable growth in the number and in the size of Communist parties all over the world. Among them there were wide variations in the cultural and political environments in which they operated, in their tactical problems, and in the degree of their Marxist-Leninist sophistication and training. Over the years, moreover, there has been a tendency for a number of the more important non-Bloc parties to be increasingly concerned to see that their own local points of view are considered in policy deliberations of the international movement. (Paras. 14, 39–40)

4. All these developments have tested not only the theory of unity, but also the authority of the Soviet Party over other parties which was the practical reality on which the appearance of unity was built. In the best of circumstances it was bound to become increasingly difficult for Moscow to maintain the unity of so large and varied a movement with so wide a range of differing views and interests. In addition, these events have aggravated the frequent conflicts between the requirements of the foreign policy of the Soviet state and those of the international Communist movement. Altogether, it is evident that Communist political institutions, like all other institutions, are subject to pressures for change and are in fact changing. (Paras. 13–21, 34–40, 59)

*Disciplinary Problems in the Communist Movement*

5. Stalin's authority over the international Communist movement was tested almost as soon as the new Communist states came into existence at the end of World War II. Challenged by Yugoslavia in 1948, he failed either to impose discipline or to prevent Yugoslavia's subsequent survival as an independent Communist state. When the Chinese Communists achieved state power in 1949—like the Yugoslavs, largely by their own efforts—they inevitably acquired a special status in the Bloc. After Stalin died and his awesome aura of personal authority over the parties disappeared, his less eminent successors attempted to overcome the abuses of his brutal and open control by substituting a more flexibly exercised but still decisive influence. These experiments were cut short, however, by the Eastern European upheavals of 1956, which showed that the balance between influence and outright control would be a difficult one to strike. (Paras. 13–15, 19–21)

6. Since 1956, when Peiping helped Moscow to restore its badly shaken authority in Eastern Europe, China has become an increasingly important factor in the direction of the movement, and has developed pretensions as an authoritative source of Communist doctrine. When the

Chinese leaders resorted in 1960 to open politics in their policy disagreements with Moscow, and also lobbied openly among Communists against Soviet policies, the Soviets responded by, in effect, putting the Chinese on trial before the other parties, first at Bucharest and later at the November conference in Moscow. Nevertheless, during the Sino-Soviet dispute of 1960 the Chinese were able to bring a successful challenge to Soviet authority and to establish the formal principle of mandatory consultation among the parties on matters of general Communist policy. (Paras. 16, 21–28)

*Prospects for Soviet Authority*

7.  Since the 81-party conference of November 1960, the Soviets and the Chinese have continued, within limits, their separate efforts to preserve and expand their own authority in the movement. It seems to us unlikely that the two major parties will be able for some time to come to resolve their differences and achieve a stable arrangement for directing the Communist movement. On the other hand, an open rupture between them appears to us equally unlikely. We believe that the course of their relations will be erratic, cooperative at some times and places, competitive at others. (Paras. 35, 38, 59–62)

8.  In this situation the Soviet Party possesses enormous advantages, because of its greater military and economic power, and also because of its traditional authority and prestige within the movement. The ability of the Chinese Party to contend for leadership is currently limited by China's serious internal difficulties. The Soviets retain some opportunity to exert pressure by virtue of China's relative economic and military weakness, though this apparently was not very effective in the dispute of 1960. Because of the present preponderance of Soviet power, Moscow will probably be able, though with increasing difficulty, to maintain its primacy in the Communist movement for some time to come. The Soviet leaders will endeavor to maintain the substance of their former authority by exercising pressure and influence bilaterally upon other parties, by confronting their rivals with strong majority coalitions at international gatherings, and sometimes by shrewd adjustments of Soviet policies in order to undercut Chinese criticisms. Because the role of personalities has figured in some degree in the Soviet-Chinese difficulties, the appearance of new leaders in either country could have an important influence on the further course of their relations. (Paras. 60–62)

9.  In these circumstances, the other parties will almost inevitably be tempted to bargain between Moscow and Peiping in order to obtain greater advantages for themselves. Within certain parties which develop serious prospects of achieving power, and which therefore must make important tactical choices, conflicting brands of advice may tend to intensify factionalism. In the long run, some of the parties in Eastern

Europe, or factions within them, may attempt to develop further the autonomy conceded by Stalin's successors. In the Asian satellites, where Chinese influence is already strong and has a good prospect of increasing if China's power continues to grow, the regimes will be better able to bargain with both Communist great powers for economic and political support. (Para. 63)

*Implications for Policy Toward the West*

10. It is evident that the international Communist system, for decades little more than an instrumentality of Soviet policy, is being changed, because of the forces of nationalism and diversity within it, into a movement reflecting an appreciable diffusion of power. While the altered relationships within the Communist movement and the decline in Soviet authority have not altered the fundamental hostility of the Communists toward the non-Communist world, we believe that these developments are having an important influence on Communist policy. They have already diminished to some extent the flexibility of Soviet policy towards the West, and the Soviet Party will probably encounter increasing difficulties in its efforts to coordinate general Communist policy. These difficulties may not be as serious in times when events generally favor Communist interests, but they may again erupt into open polemic during periods of adversity, or even at times when fundamental decisions are required for the exploitation of unfolding opportunities. (Paras. 59, 65)

11. The development of the relationship between the USSR and China, and the evolution of the international Communist movement generally, will obviously be of profound significance for the security and interests of the West. In the long run Chinese power, assertiveness, and self-interest might increase so far as greatly to impair the common policy with the USSR, and even lead the Soviets to believe that they had more in common with the ideological enemy than they have today. For some time to come, however, the most likely prospect is that the USSR and China will maintain their relationship in something like its present form. It will be an alliance which is from time to time troubled and inharmonious, but which nevertheless preserves sufficient unity to act in concert against the West, especially in times of major challenge. However, present trends as described in this paper point to an increasing complexity, diversity, and interplay of forces within the Communist system, and to a remarkable survival of old-fashioned impulses of nationalism. (Para. 67)

12. These trends may have various effects. They may from time to time result in more aggressive anti-Western policies intended to hold the forces of disunity in check. They may enable certain parties, free from the restrictions of a rigid, general Communist line, to pursue more effective policies in local situations. But eventually, if such trends persist, they may considerably diminish the effectiveness of the Communist move-

ment as a whole. This would give the West opportunities for maneuver and influence which could provide important advantages in the world struggle. (Para. 68)

[Here follow paragraphs 13–68, comprising the Discussion portion of the estimate, in four sections entitled "Development of Relations Among the Communist Parties," "Current Relations Among the Bloc Parties," "The Non-bloc Parties," and "The Outlook."]

---

## 50.    Telegram From the Department of State to the Embassy in Poland

Washington, August 13, 1961, 6:24 p.m.

221. Eyes only for the Ambassador from the Secretary. Supplemental to other instructions being sent to you on informal meeting with Wang,[1] if you find atmosphere propitious and believe useful purpose might be served I would have no objection to your expanding your remarks to include following line: You could frankly state that you are returning to Washington for Selection Board duty, that while here you will of course be discussing with your superiors future relations with Communist China and that for your background in doing so you would welcome Wang's views in some depth, particularly on the following questions. In asking the following questions you would disclaim having any instructions on these points and couch your remarks in purely personal terms.

---

Source: Department of State, Central Files, 611.93/8–1361. Secret. Drafted by U. Alexis Johnson; approved and signed by Rusk. An attached memorandum of August 13 from the duty officer in the Executive Secretariat states that at Johnson's request, copies had been distributed only to him and Rusk. A memorandum of the same date from Johnson to Rusk states that he had discussed the draft telegram with McConaughy, who was in full agreement, and that "its base is somewhat narrower than what we first discussed" but that Johnson thought it would help to "fill the need" and "somewhat offset the danger inherent in the fireworks that will be taking place at the UN during the period there are no Warsaw meetings." It also assured Rusk that the message would be sent through a secure channel with no distribution. (Ibid.)

[1] Telegram 220 to Warsaw, August 13, authorized Beam to reciprocate Wang's informal approach at the June 29 meeting (see Document 38). It declared that the unique value of the ambassadorial talks was their potential for reducing tension on a bilateral basis and that "we believe most promising approach lies in realistic, flexible efforts to make progress on practical questions between two sides." No progress would result from demands for surrender on fundamental issues, but progress in solving problems that might seem minor in themselves could contribute to the step-by-step improvement of relations. (Department of State, Central Files, 611.93/7–2761) See the Supplement.

You might preface your remarks by stating that Peking of course has its view of the world and the presumed historical imperatives of its "revolution", while the US also has its views on the subject. Also, we of course each have our own views on the problem of Taiwan. While these cannot now be reconciled, it should be perfectly clear to Wang that regardless of our domestic differences with respect to Taiwan and Communist China he must take it as a fact that no American administration ever could or would consider turning the people of Taiwan against their will over to Communist China. However you do assume that the Peking leaders have some concern for the welfare and fate of the great people of China. You know the USG certainly has a strong concern and sense of responsibility for the future and fate of the American people. Recognizing these facts, you wonder whether there are not some common points of interest between the two governments that can be identified and cooperation undertaken, or is it the view of Peking that the only outcome is an eventual holocaust involving our two peoples. It is the view of the USG that such need not be the case. You would hope that this is also ChiCom view in spite of seeming meaning ChiCom public doctrine and therefore, that there is at least common interest in avoiding war.

If this is case you wonder what implications ChiComs would draw therefrom. It is your view that if ChiComs accept this thesis it is important to look for even smallest opportunities to improve atmosphere between two countries. It is for this reason you have been laboring point of prisoners and newsmen. However, ChiCom response has consistently been pegged to unrealistic demands on Taiwan, etc. This is hardly way to make any progress. You wonder whether ChiComs see any realistic steps that could be taken. If so you would like to explore and discuss while in Washington.

For example, you understand that through ChiCom ConGen, Geneva, ChiComs have invited Dr. Samuel Rosen of New York to demonstrate his unique surgical technique for relief of common form of deafness. Under present conditions USG had no choice but to discourage his travel. However, if ChiComs are still interested you would be willing further explore matter on your return to Washington. Does Wang think issuance of passport to Dr. Rosen would be helpful and if so is there any gesture ChiComs could make now or later? You are not seeking to bargain or enter into agreements but rather to see whether in quiet way there are reciprocal small steps that can be taken by two governments that would offer some hope of relieving present complete impasse in relations. Therefore, prior to your return to Washington you would welcome any thoughts Wang may have in this regard and if he desires would be willing again informally to meet with Wang prior to your departure.

If you think desirable there would be no objection to your inviting Wang to your residence or other secure place for informal meeting if this could be handled in manner that would avoid publicity. In this event, of course, recognize you may have to accept similar return invitation from him.

You should transmit any reply on this portion your conversation "Eyes Only".

**Rusk**

---

**51.    Telegram From the Embassy in Poland to the Department of State**

Warsaw, August 15, 1961, 5 p.m.

279. Beam–Wang Talks. 106th meeting; 52 minutes.[1]

I opened with paragraphs 1, 2, 3 of Deptel 215.[2]

Wang replied there had been no settlement real issues during course these talks and US policy headed opposite direction. US Government trying worsen Sino-US relations with President's invitation Chen Cheng's visit. Noted communiqué reiterated US support GRC "usurpation" China's UN seat. Only with US support was "Chiang Kai-shek clique" able be entrenched Taiwan and in UN seat. No indication change this policy. Noted US Senate resolution also pledged support Chiang-Kai-shek usurpation China's UN seat. Stated since August 11 ChiCom spokesman had issued 158th through 165th series warnings indicating US trying to worsen relations through intrusion Chinese territory and territorial waters. Stated Berlin crisis used as pretext for increasing military expenditures and some US leaders state global action may be taken. Increasingly blatant hostility toward Chinese people one part of this. Above in contravention my opening statement. American suggestions for exchange newsmen were a mockery; such exchange could not be con-

---

Source: Department of State, Central Files, 611.93/8–1561. Confidential; Niact; Limit Distribution. Repeated to Taipei, Hong Kong, and Moscow.

[1] Beam sent a detailed, apparently verbatim report of the meeting in airgram A–116, August 18. (Ibid., 611.93/8–1861)

[2] Telegram 215, August 11, provided guidance for the formal portion of the meeting. Paragraphs 1, 2, and 3 instructed Beam to tell Wang he had to return to Washington for temporary duty for about 3 months, to urge release of the four remaining imprisoned American civilians, and to urge Wang's side to reexamine this and other U.S. proposals as ways of reaching agreement on practical questions. (Ibid., 611.93/8–1161) See the Supplement.

sidered during the exchange of Vice Presidential visits between US and GRC. Cannot skip main issue: Seizure of Taiwan by US. This also applies newsmen question. Chinese have had sincere desire for success since inception these talks but no response from US. Rather US has had policy of hostility even more undisguised. Chance of success depends on change in US occupation of China's territory Taiwan.

I replied I could not accept his unwarranted attack on meeting between President Kennedy and Vice President Chen Cheng. Stated Wang had once again attacked our ally of long standing. US bound to GRC by sympathy and common interest; only natural and reasonable two countries should survey international scene in spirit mutual understanding reflected by this communiqué. Communiqué presents assessment international situation which Wang leaders should consider carefully and thoughtfully if indeed they thought to contribute lessening tensions in Far East. Rejected Wang accusation US warships and planes intrude ChiCom waters stating we governed by international law not unilateral ChiCom determinations. Re newsmen regretted our proposal was rejected as designed decrease tensions.

Wang replied could not accept my explanation meeting between President and Chen Cheng. No real peace in Far East mainly because US occupying Chinese territory Taiwan which has upset peace. Reiterated US must change policy.

I replied that threat and use of force against GRC is real point at issue. US and GRC have treaty relations and defense alliance. US forces in Taiwan as result. Basically we have asked for renunciation of force which would bring peace to area. Unfortunately Wang side rejected this and tension continues. I then continued with substance paragraph 4 Department telegram 215.[3]

Wang replied Old China represented by Chiang Kai-shek regime ended when People's Republic China inaugurated. Only US support enables Chiang Kai-shek eke out existence on Taiwan. Cannot be regarded as state for represents no people. Taiwan is only province of PRC. No right to conclude treaty with foreign power therefore treaties with US are null and void. In these talks ChiComs have earnestly sought ways and means settle issues. Basic position is to realize ChiCom territorial integrity. US occupation this part China territory stands in way final realization China territorial integrity. US Government has used force against China to obstruct reunification China. Therefore not China but US should initiate realistic, practical steps remove obstacles.

---

[3] Paragraph 4 instructed Beam to make his presentations as brief as possible while keeping the record clear and, if appropriate, to point out that the two sides remained as far apart as ever on fundamental issues, reinforcing the U.S. view that the best approach to the talks was to try to reach agreement on practical concrete questions; the United States did not expect Wang's side to give up their position on fundamental issues and did not believe they seriously expected the United States to do so.

I replied GRC recognized as sovereign government by majority nations world. Many nations have interest in GRCs protection and integrity. Present situation in which threats proceed from Wang's side are of great interest to world from standpoint maintenance peace in area. US trying to devise formula and means remove threat and regrets unsuccessful till now. Wang replied have told you many times Chiang Kai-shek regime would not last one day without US support. No rationalization by you can change fact US is occupying Chinese territory. It righteous enterprise on part Chinese people to work for unification of country. Chinese people not threatening anyone; rather US threatens Chinese people. Such abnormal situation cannot be allowed continue forever.

I replied I had nothing further and sought advance agreement press announcement next meeting. Wang appeared surprised at openended announcement and asked if agreeable to set date some time December subject to latter change if necessary. I agreed and we set date next meeting December 5, 2 p.m.

**Beam**

---

52. **Telegram From the Embassy in Poland to the Department of State**

Warsaw, August 16, 1961, 10 a.m.

281. Beam–Wang talks. At beginning of informal conversation over coffee after formal 106th August 15 meeting, Ambassador Wang and I exchanged remarks on Geneva Laos conference. Wang stated Ambassador Harriman had told him in Geneva he would like to have meetings between American and Chinese delegations in order to exchange views on means of solving the Laos question. Wang said he told Harriman that his side would not refuse to participate in any exchange of views. When I asked Wang if he were going back to Geneva, he replied he had many things here to take care of before he could return. After we had exchanged a few more general remarks concerning Laos conference, I made presentation outlined in Deptel 220,[1] speaking from pencilled notes.

---

Source: Department of State, Central Files, 611.93/8–1661. Secret; Priority; Limit Distribution. Repeated to Hong Kong, Taipei, and Geneva for FECON. Received at 11:05 a.m.

[1] See footnote 1, Document 50. Concerning Laos, telegram 220 instructed Beam to tell Wang that the United States hoped that a "genuinely neutral, independent Laos" would emerge from the Geneva discussions but that it would not enter an agreement which was only a "thinly veiled screen for eventual commie takeover Laos."

Wang replied: There have always been many problems between us. In these ambassadorial talks we have a very heavy responsibility to solve them. No one is willing to be responsible for a mission that has failed. A famous British diplomat, Neville Henderson, once wrote a book, *Failure of a Mission*, which described a diplomat's unfortunate experience along this line. You have said that you appreciate the candid statements which I had made during our previous informal meeting. Then I explained that Chinese people did not intentionally set themselves against American people and all of our leaders, including Chairman Mao, Premier Chou and Foreign Minister Chen, have said many times that Chinese people are friendly to American people. We hope that US policy can be built on realistic foundations and that US will be able to change its former methods. (At this point, Wang entered into discussion of why he felt the "Chiang Kai-shek regime" had fallen despite fact that US had given large amounts of aid. He attributed this defeat to the "personal dictatorship" of Chiang and to his policy of "action against the people's interest". Likewise Rhee had been thrown out by Korean people despite US aid. Wang predicted that some day he and I would be discussing the fate of Taiwan just as we today were discussing the past defeat of Chiang Kai-shek on mainland of China.)

Wang continued:

I remember after Chiang Kai-shek had evacuated to Taiwan, President Truman stated that Taiwan problem was Chinese internal affair and that US had no intention to meddle therein.[2] If US had held to this non-interference principle, we believe Sino-American relations would be different from what they are today. We also believe that US policy toward Taiwan is of no benefit to US but rather detrimental to its best interest. China will never threaten US interests and will never expand outwards. This is because not only does China have sufficient resources and territory for its own development, but also (and this is not least important) because socialist system forbids expansionist policy. China and US were located on opposite sides of world. Being such a long way apart, there is no reason why there should be any direct clash between us.

We don't believe war settles anything. We oppose war and advocate peace. The big powers, including China and US, should seek to adjust their differences in order that world peace be maintained. Basis of Chinese foreign policy is adherence to the five principles. These should be applied to Sino-American relations. Thus, we have advocated creation of a nuclear free zone in Pacific.[3] Furthermore, it is not true as you have just

---

[2] Reference is to a statement made by Truman on January 5, 1950. For text, see *Public Papers of the Presidents of the United States: Harry S. Truman, 1950*, pp. 11–12.

[3] A message from PRC Premier Chou En-lai to the Sixth World Conference Against Atomic and Hydrogen Bombs and for Total Disarmament, July 30, 1960, called for making the Asian and Pacific area a nuclear-weapon-free zone. The text is printed in *Documents on Disarmament, 1960*, pp. 180–181.

alleged, that Chinese people or government are deliberately opposed to US or are trying to create discord between China and US. Since the Chinese people are injured party, it is normal that they manifest their feeling of being wronged. Just as people of Tunisia, so Chinese people want to regain their own territory and to restore their territorial integrity.

Mr. Ambassador, your return to US provides you opportunity to make a new appraisal of Sino-American relations and for your government to adopt more positive approach. We believe if your government takes over-all view, it will be seen that wisest move by the US Government would be to normalize relations with us. We hope something useful will come out of your discussions in Washington and that on your return you will be able to take positive steps to change present state of affairs between us.

I believe many US statesmen are aware of this situation. I had an opportunity to talk with Senator Humphrey at Geneva, he told me he hoped someday he might visit China in order to contribute to promotion of better relations between our two countries. He told me also he had campaigned consistently for Chinese participation in international disarmament talks.

To express a willingness to promote better relations is one thing, but to adopt real measures to this end is another. One must prescribe correct medicine for the treatment of a particular disease; it is not enough merely to apply a panacea like tiger balm. In India I learned a saying which went something like this: I want to live, but, I must also live and let live. We believe reason will prevail. Thus I am happy for this opportunity to exchange views with the Ambassador before he returns to Washington. Despite long interval before our next meeting, I hope that when you return, we shall be in a position to make progress.

Wang then inquired concerning Alex Johnson, asking if he were not now in Washington in a high position.

I said he was now Deputy Under Secretary of State.

**Beam**

53.   Telegram From the Embassy in Poland to the Department of
      State

Warsaw, August 16, 1961, 1 p.m.

282. Eyes only for the Secretary. Although Wang did not respond positively to first part my informal presentation (Embtel 281)[1] I considered occasion sufficiently favorable to proceed with expansion of remarks suggested in Deptel 221[2] which I emphasized was purely personal contribution advanced to see if impasse could in some way be broken.

I concluded by informing Wang that, after short holiday, I should return to Warsaw on August 28, to stay here until September 2 when I would depart for Washington. I told him that, had he any response to make to my presentation, I would be available to meet with him privately some time between August 28 and September 2.

Wang replied: I also think both sides should seek out common ground. It is most important both countries act responsibly in field of international affairs in order that peace be preserved. It is duty of both of us to resolve quarrels and strife between us. Concern which you have expressed concerning war with regard to Taiwan, however, is superfluous. We have said many times Taiwan is an internal matter for China in which US has no right to interfere. If the US were to act in conformance with President Truman's statement and not interfere, then I believe greater half of Taiwan problem would be solved. Once Taiwan problem is normalized then basic issues between China and US can be solved. It is unwise for US Government to pay so much attention to small advantages only to lose important ones. For example, US persistence in its economic blockade against China has not prevented our reconstruction; on contrary, this blockade only hurts US economy. In similar way, US opposition to restoration to China of its legal position in UN does not prevent development of our friendship with peoples of the world but it does do great harm to US prestige. Perhaps you do not now share my views but I believe day will come when you will realize this truth.

I haven't heard about desire to have Dr. Samuel Rosen go to China. I will look into this matter and if it is necessary to have another conversation with you, I will let you know.

I then explained again to Ambassador Wang that this was apparently case in which Chinese doctors hoped to have Doctor Rosen visit China in order to demonstrate his new technique to them but that failing

---

Source: Department of State, Central Files, 611.93/8–1761. Secret; Priority.
[1] Document 52.
[2] Document 50.

any small gesture of concession from ChiComs side we had to discourage visit. I then once again expanded on our conviction that if both sides will seek resolution of small practical questions, this would promote relaxation of tension and maintenance peace.

I also took up his frequent reference to January 1950 statement by President Truman that US regarded resolution of Taiwan problem as internal affair of Chinese. I said outbreak of Korean war had changed the opinion of the American people concerning the ability of small nations in Asia to withstand by themselves external aggression. Basing himself on this new conviction of the American people, President Truman in June of 1950 had made second statement[3] which took completely altered situation into account.

The meeting broke up with both of us assuring the other that despite the obvious seriousness of our differences, we must all exert every effort to resolve the problems between us.

*Comment:* With excellent interpreters on both sides and with reiteration of the theme through formal meeting and both halves of informal talk, Wang could hardly have failed to get the point of our approach. His fallback on classic ChiCom position was to be expected as initial reaction but he was far from hostile and at end he felt himself obliged to pay tribute to idea of efforts toward improvement. Since ChiComs will doubtless wish weigh our suggestions in light many other factors, I question if I shall hear from Wang before my departure September 2. Interesting he did not belabor ChiCom UN membership issue, probably for reasons of pride and desire show lack of concern. Significant also he wished avoid appearance of rupture of talks by insisting on tentative date three months hence for next meeting.

**Beam**

---

[3] Reference is to a statement made by Truman on June 27, 1950; for text, see *Public Papers of the Presidents of the United States: Harry S. Truman, 1950,* p. 492.

54.    Memorandum From the President's Special Assistant for
National Security Affairs (Bundy) to President Kennedy

Washington, August 22, 1961.

SUBJECT

The Chinese Representation Issue

Your memorandum of August 21st[1] asks for information as to where this stands and emphasizes that we must find a winning position. The attached cable[2] gives a pretty good statement of our current view. It has gone to all our missions and responses are being collected and tabulated. So far only about a third of the answers are in, but they suggest that this position is worth holding for the moment.

The nut of this proposal, as you know, is that we will seek a majority for the "important question" position and then expect to have a blocking one-third against any resolution that would admit representation. We have sweetened this proposal with the notion of a commission to study the broader problems of criteria for UN membership and the composition of the Security Council and the Economic and Social Council. This commission would report a year later.

Until we have more responses to this circular, and until we see what happens on the Outer Mongolian issue, I see no basis for a change in our current stand. The Outer Mongolian question may come up next week, and we are keeping the heat on the Chinese Nationalists. In particular, I am seeing Ambassador Yeh this afternoon to emphasize to him that your letter to the Generalissimo[3] was not merely a docile statement of the views of the wicked State Department, but an expression of a policy which you yourself strongly hold. The Chinese Nationalists are trying to hint that you are their friend and cannot really mean what your letter says. They are also suggesting that the Congress may not agree with you, and I shall say a few words to George about that, too.

McG. B.[4]

---

Source: Kennedy Library, National Security Files, Countries Series, China. No classification marking.

[1] Not found.

[2] Not attached to the source text. The reference is apparently to circular telegram 253, August 12. (Department of State, Central Files, 303/8–1261)

[3] The letter, August 15, urged strongly against a GRC use of the veto to block Outer Mongolian membership in the United Nations and stated that if the GRC agreed not to veto, the United States would abstain. (Ibid., Presidential Correspondence: Lot 66 D 204, Kennedy/Johnson Correspondence with Chinese Officials) See the Supplement. The letter was transmitted in telegram 117 to Taipei, August 15; telegram 167 from Taipei, August 17, reported that Drumright had delivered the letter that day. (Ibid., Central Files, 303/8–1561 and 3–03/81761, respectively)

[4] Printed from a copy that bears these typed initials.

55.    **Memorandum From the President's Special Assistant for National Security Affairs (Bundy) to the Deputy Under Secretary of State for Political Affairs (Johnson)**

Washington, August 22, 1961.

As we agreed, I talked to Ambassador Yeh this afternoon. I found him extraordinarily understanding and clear about the issues. I began by emphasizing to him the President's letter[1] represented not only the views of the Department of State, but the most careful and considered judgment of the President himself. He took the point.

We then turned to what we might be able to get in return if in fact his government should decide not to veto, and there ensued the discussion which I reported to you on the telephone. On the basis of that telephone conversation, I have made it plain to Ambassador Yeh that if, in fact, his government can give us private assurance that it will not veto Outer Mongolia, we will be glad to join with the Republic of China in attempting to get maximum support for our position on Chinese representation from French-African states. Ambassador Yeh particularly emphasized his hope that in this politicking we could point out that this is a case of Soviet blackmail and that while we are prepared to be helpful in this case, French-African states ought not to get in the habit of putting heat on us on the Chinese representation issue every time the Soviets put the heat on them.

Ambassador Yeh pointed out to me that it might be reassuring to his government if it could hear the same noise from Ambassador Drumright that he was hearing from me, and accordingly I suggest that it may be useful for you to send a dispatch to Drumright, in whatever form you think right, to back up what seems to me to have been a fruitful conversation.[2] Ambassador Yeh told me that it was his private impression that President Chiang has not yet made up his mind but will do so in the next two or three days. Yeh is most anxious that his own strong support for a change in his government's position should not be reported in any way to Taipei, and therefore I hope your dispatch to Drumright may avoid reference to my conversation with Yeh.

McGeorge Bundy[3]

---

Source: Kennedy Library, National Security Files, Countries Series, China. Secret.

[1] See footnote 3, Document 54.

[2] Telegram 129 to Taipei, August 23, instructed Drumright to tell the Foreign Minister that if the GRC would give private assurances that it would refrain from vetoing Outer Mongolian membership, the United States would approach African states and in return for this GRC concession, solicit their support for the U.S. position on Chinese representation. (Department of State, Central Files, 303/8–2361)

[3] Printed from a copy that bears this typed signature.

## 56.   Editorial Note

A paper entitled "The Offshore Islands: Alternative Courses and Probable Consequences," drafted by Edward E. Rice of the Policy Planning Council and dated August 22, 1961, was sent on August 25 to McGeorge Bundy, who had requested such a paper, and to Secretary of State Rusk. The paper discussed the offshore islands problem and set forth four alternative courses of action which it summarized as follows:

"Theoretically at least, the US might: (a) acquiesce in continued GRC occupation of the offshore islands without extending our present commitments; (b) acquiesce, and in addition extend to the offshores an unequivocal US defense commitment; (c) use all suitable means now at our disposal in an effort to bring about early evacuation of the offshore islands; or (d) pursue the objective of bringing about a GRC evacuation over an extended period of time, using such means as are now at hand or may become available in a patient campaign which we would hope to keep sufficiently low-keyed to avoid a damaging crisis." (National Archives and Records Administration, RG 59, S/P Files: Lot 67 D 548, China)

Policy Planning Council Chairman George C. McGhee sent a copy to McGeorge Bundy, with a covering memorandum of August 25, noting that the paper "as requested," set forth the alternatives and their estimated consequences but made no recommendation. (Kennedy Library, National Security Files, Countries Series, China) He sent a copy to Rusk with a covering memorandum of the same date noting that the paper had been prepared at Bundy's request with terms of reference that precluded making a recommendation between the alternatives, but, "As probably can be determined from reading, there is no question that S/P recommends the fourth alternative." (National Archives and Records Administration, RG 59, S/P Files: Lot 67 D 548, China) There is no indication of any reaction from Rusk or Bundy. Under Secretary of State Chester Bowles praised the paper in a September 12 memorandum to McGhee, and Under Secretary of State for Economic Affairs George W. Ball praised it in a September 25 memorandum to McGhee, which expressed agreement that the fourth alternative was the only feasible one under the existing circumstances. (Ibid.)

A handwritten note of December 29 from Rice to Walt W. Rostow, who had succeeded McGhee, stated that McGhee had "decided this should be held up pending settlement of Chi Rep issue in UN" and asked if Rostow wished to take any action. A note of April 7, 1962, in an unidentified handwriting states that Rostow had not done so. (Both ibid.)

## 57.    Telegram From the Embassy in Poland to the Department of State

Warsaw, September 2, 1961, 2 p.m.

402. Eyes only for the Secretary. Met with Wang at his Embassy September 1, 4 p.m. unobserved. (Deptel 321.)[1]

I opened with a short statement emphasizing this was private meeting between us.

Wang referred our last meeting and stated would like give his position noting I had suggested we meet again prior my return US. Said at last meeting he had put forth clearly position his government and therefore had doubts necessity of such meetings over such short space of time. He first noted since last meeting international situation had changed significantly. US had undertaken series moves and military provocations leading to dangerous military-like atmosphere. This could not help but affect today's meeting and would like to express several points of his own opinions about these moves with hope I would take these to Washington. He wished explain his point of view clearly and so had prepared text of his remarks.

He then started reading lengthy prepared Chinese text. Stated that lately US and its allies with the pretext of the Berlin crisis had caused situation approaching war by sending military contingent to West Berlin, as well as other provocative acts of West German revanchists vis-à-vis GDR. Said "I would like to ask you whether this is to lead to the calling forth of military conflict in Europe." Noted the realization in South Vietnam of so-called storm plan increase of military forces and training of troops in Far East for despatch to neutral Laos, and asked whether this aimed at eruption of war in Indochina. Noted maneuvers of US Marines in Okinawa and land maneuvers in South Korea, stating these further increased tension in Northeast Asia. Accused US military airplanes and warships of gradually more frequent violations Chinese territory. In connection with maneuvers of Chiang Kai-shek forces on Matsu and Quemoy asked whether these actions preparatory to landing on China coast. Stated that they could not help but take these very seriously and

---

Source: Department of State, Central Files, 611.93/9–261. Secret; Priority; Eyes Only. Received on September 3.

[1] Telegram 321, August 31, replied to telegram 378 from Warsaw of the same date. In it, Beam reported that the Chinese Embassy had just telephoned that Wang would be happy to receive Beam at his Embassy the next day. Beam stated that his visit could be arranged unobtrusively, although the Poles would be aware of it since Wang was dean of the diplomatic corps in Warsaw. Beam doubted that he would be willing to come to the U.S. Embassy first. (Ibid., 611.93/8–3161) Telegram 321, drafted by Johnson and cleared by Ball, replied, "No objection your visit to Wang's Embassy as unobtrusively as possible. In fact, we feel might be advantages your meeting Wang there." (Ibid.)

issued very strong warning. Would like to take occasion to voice his personal concern about dangerous policies of my government and expressed hope I would bring his point of view to attention my government. War policy present administration had improved upon that of late Secretary Dulles and leads to an increasingly rapid isolation of the US on international scene. Observed people had hoped Democratic Administration and particularly President Kennedy could have changed US policy to one of peace. This was particularly so since President had emphasized his strategy of peace during campaign. But now he noted US Government does not have intention of turning away from path of war but on contrary approached gradually closer to it. US Government had already decided to step onto path of war. These steps have significantly been accelerated, not only does US prepare for atomic war but also has preparations for limited war. US has set time bomb in heart of Europe and various countries in Asia, Africa and South America. Occupation by US on Taiwan leads to especially dangerous military threat greatly increasing threat of war against China.

Desired tell me frankly this type of policy could only lead to worsening international situation. This course was meeting with greatly stronger opposition from people of world including people of US. Chinese value peace and are fighting to create peaceful international conditions. China and US are two great powers and both have responsibility for peace throughout world. War will not bring any advantages whatever and he convinced I would agree with his view. Both countries should make every effort take advantage these contacts and extend greatest efforts to this end. Talks already numbered 106 but up to now no progress achieved. Facts show that reason for this is US interference in international affairs China and Taiwan. Believed betterment of Chinese-US relations required above all solution this basic problem.

Noted that during our discussions on August 15[2] I had said no US Government could ever turn Taiwan over to China and remove US forces from Taiwan. This was evidence US wished continue these talks as means to further aggressive policies of the US and does not have least intention resolve basic problem by means of negotiation. Indications are US Government intends to worsen these basic differences by means of these negotiations. Said at previous meeting I had utilized US responsibility towards Chiang Kai-shek as pretext for US occupation Taiwan and threatened ChiComs with war. Doubted if I really believed that type pretext and it had no significance.

US responsible for existence Chiang Kai-shek and facts show he is US creature. This is intervention in China internal affairs, equivalent to

---

[2] See Documents 51–53.

situation between Japanese Tojo Government and Manchukuo. This is humbug. At same time situation is important responsibility for China. Again reminded me that US position will never be accepted by China and that if US does not recognize this it will be a great historical mistake. Problem of Taiwan is principal problem between China and US. Without resolution will be difficult to resolve other problems. Repeated he wished me to bring this to attention of Washington and again desired state China very much wished to resolve various problems between China and US peacefully and he hoped we would put forth constructive propositions looking toward the removal of US forces from Taiwan.

He then stated we had already agreed that the next meeting would be December 5. But in view of the serious situation we should maintain contact and be prepared for it (contact) at moment's notice. In response our questions to clarify this point, he stated 107th meeting still on agenda for December 5 and added that if important matters arise in interim they would communicate.

I realized he had made an extraordinary response to my approach. I categorically believed [denied?] false accusations he had made against my government. His remarks about President surpassed bounds of common politeness. Recrimination not helpful but was bound to point out that chief problem of today is action from Communist side threatening peace all over world. This was my necessary answer since Wang had chosen to broaden area of discussion.

I corrected his statement about what I had said concerning Taiwan, reiterating no American Government would turn Taiwan over to mainland against will of its people. US forces in Taiwan area, [apparent omission] this being purpose of my personal suggestions to him. Reiterated necessity finding common ground on matters of mutual interest and advisability making progress, even in small matters, as means breaking impasse. Rejection my suggestions matter of personal regret. Danger was situation would get worse but both sides still have time to consider and I hoped Wang would make personal effort to have my previous suggestions reviewed.

I also doubted usefulness this kind of private talks if they continued in this sense and reminded him he took initiative in starting them. I had hoped his initiatives here and in Geneva might be constructive and so had attempted to offer constructive response. While great effort required on both sides, was worthwhile to relieve tensions in order avoid far greater dangers. Asked Wang if he believed statement US using these talks to further aggressive policies. Would have to report this remark to my government and let it draw its own conclusions.

Thereafter there followed an exchange of the type customary at formal meetings regarding status Chiang Kai-shek government. Nothing new was said.

*Comment:* Wang obviously read from prepared governmental statement which completely reversed more conciliatory attitude he had displayed at previous private meeting Sunday Geneva. He seemed slightly embarrassed and made effort to be cordial on my departure.

**Beam**

## 58.    Editorial Note

On September 5, 1961, President Kennedy discussed the question of Chinese representation in a meeting at the White House with Secretary of State Rusk, Representative to the United Nations Stevenson, Assistant Secretary for International Organization Affairs Cleveland, Special Assistant to the President for National Security Affairs Bundy, Special Counsel to the President Theodore C. Sorensen, and Special Assistant to the President Schlesinger.

A memorandum of action taken at the meeting, drafted by Cleveland and dated September 5, reads in part as follows:

"a. In the Secretary of State's memorandum of September 5 to the President on Chinese Representation in the United Nations, the President was asked two policy questions:

"(i) Do you believe that Ambassador Stevenson should now be authorized to make it known informally to other delegations that the United States does not preclude the possibility that a General Assembly study committee would recommend for the consideration of the General Assembly at its 1962 session an essentially "two Chinas" solution based on the successor state approach? and

"(ii) Are you prepared to authorize Ambassador Stevenson to vote affirmatively in the Security Council on the application for UN membership of the Mongolian People's Republic, if in his judgment such a vote will substantially assist him in developing support among the French African states for the U.S. position on Chinese Representation?

"The President answered 'yes' to both of these questions. He expressed again his judgment of the importance of keeping the Chinese Communists out of the United Nations this year.

"b. The President said he wants to write President Chiang Kai-shek a further letter, in which he would lay stress on the United States interests in the Chinese Representation question and therefore on the related matter of the Mongolian and Mauritanian applications for UN membership.

"c. Individuals in the United States who are particularly close to the GRC will be brought into the discussion. The President will talk to Congressman Walter Judd. The Secretary of State will follow up Henry Cabot Lodge's call to him on the Outer Mongolia issue, with a view to further discussions with Henry Luce on the matter. Ambassador Stevenson will speak to Roy Howard of Scripps-Howard." (Filed with a covering memorandum of September 6 from Battle to Bundy; Department of State, Central Files, 301/9–661)

Rusk's September 5 memorandum cited above reported that the Department had conducted exploratory discussions concerning a two-pronged approach, combining a resolution declaring any change in China's representation an "important question" with the establishment by the General Assembly of a study committee to consider criteria for U.N. membership and related problems. The consultations thus far had indicated that there was no certainty of obtaining the required majority for either proposal. Rusk stated that the Department would continue its efforts for the two-pronged approach but that a further "sweetener" might have to be added. He posed the two policy questions quoted in Cleveland's memorandum of action, recommending in favor of the second but stating his view that the first step was not yet necessary. (Ibid., 303/9–561)

For Schlesinger's account of the discussion, see *A Thousand Days*, pages 483–484.

---

**59.    Telegram From the Department of State to the Embassy in the Republic of China**

Washington, September 6, 1961, 10:40 p.m.

158. For Ambassador. Present following letter from President Kennedy to Chiang Kai-shek as soon as possible.[1]

"Dear Mr. President:

I have given careful thought to your letter of August 26.[2] I will not conceal from you my deep disappointment that you would utilize the

---

Source: Department of State, Central Files, 303/9–661. Secret; Priority; Limit Distribution; Verbatim Text. Drafted by Officer in Charge of General Assembly and United Nations Organization Affairs Alfred Wellons and Deputy Director of the Office of United Nations Political and Security Affairs William B. Buffum; cleared by McConaughy, Cleveland, and Bundy; and approved and signed by Rusk.

[1] Telegram 226 from Taipei, September 7, reported that the letter had been delivered to the Foreign Ministry that day for transmittal to Chiang. (Ibid., 303/9–761)

[2] Transmitted in telegram 195 from Taipei, August 27. (Ibid., Presidential Correspondence: Lot 66 D 204) See the Supplement.

veto in circumstances that would prevent the admission not only of Outer Mongolia but also of Mauritania to the United Nations.

It is clear that even though we share the common goal of preventing the admission of the Chinese Communists to the United Nations you are not persuaded that a veto on Outer Mongolia would inevitably have very serious consequences for the Chinese representation question. Briefly, the United States has concluded that a satisfactory resolution of this question may prove the decisive element in determining whether we can prevent the replacement of the GRC by the Chinese Communists in the United Nations this fall. I am sure you must be in possession, through your able representative in New York, of the same hard facts that lead us to this conclusion.

This matter is of such vital importance to the United States that if we are unable to reach agreement I am sure you will understand that we must reserve our freedom to pursue whichever avenue we consider best calculated to advance the objective which we both seek. (Appropriate complimentary close.)"

**Rusk**

## 60.   Memorandum From Secretary of State Rusk to the Representative to the United Nations (Stevenson)

Washington, September 13, 1961.

SUBJECT

Representation of China in the United Nations

Following is a summary of the standing instructions on the Chinese representation issue, which were worked out during your two recent visits to Washington. They have been approved by the President.

U.S. objectives in the 16th General Assembly are twofold: To keep Communist China out and Nationalist China in the United Nations.

Your instructions are to attempt to accomplish these objectives by the following steps:

---

Source: Kennedy Library, National Security Files, Countries Series, China. Secret. A September 13 covering note from Rusk to Stevenson noted that this memorandum contained "the revisions we discussed." Stevenson's draft is in Princeton University, Seeley G. Mudd Manuscript Library, Stevenson Papers, Previously Embargoed Files, Box 3, Kennedy.

1. Induce several countries broadly representative to inscribe on the General Assembly an item entitled "Representation of China". Use your own judgment as to the countries and the title of the item. If you cannot induce other countries to take this initiative, the United States should inscribe the item promptly.

2. Attempt to get the General Assembly to declare that any change in the representation of China is an "important question" within the meaning of Article 18 of the Charter. My understanding is that such a decision requires a simple majority vote and that an important question requires a two-thirds vote.

3. Persuade the Assembly to appoint a committee to consider criteria for UN membership (including the question of Chinese representation) and the composition of the Security Council and ECOSOC; and to report to the next General Assembly a year hence. We strongly prefer one committee rather than a special committee on Chinese representation.

4. You are authorized to say—privately, if believed essential—that the United States does not exclude the possibility that the study committee would recommend to the 1962 session a successor state solution if that becomes necessary.

5. The U.S. objective is to head off any consideration of the representation of China as a credentials question requiring a simple majority vote. If the foregoing proposals are rejected by the Assembly and a defeat of U.S. objectives, stated above, appears imminent you should then seek instructions as to whether we should adopt the successor state approach.

6. When the applications of Outer Mongolia and Mauritania come before the Security Council, you are authorized to abstain or vote for the admission of Outer Mongolia to thereby assist with the election of Mauritania, assuming that these elections take place at a time when you deem the support of the French-African States necessary in the larger question of Chinese Representation.[1]

**Dean Rusk**

---

[1] In a September 13 telephone conversation between Ball and Stevenson, Ball expressed concern that Nationalist supporters in Congress were not prepared for the possibility of a U.S. defeat on the Chinese representation issue and that Stevenson could "get badly hurt in this." Stevenson said he "had tried to protect himself by a memo." (Notes of telephone conversation; Kennedy Library, Ball Papers, China (Taiwan))

## 61.   Telegram From the Department of State to the Embassy in the Republic of China

Washington, September 17, 1961, 4:59 p.m.

189. Eyes only for the Ambassador from the Secretary. Your 237[1] caused me to review Embassy telegrams since Chen Cheng's return. With one or two exceptions (such as your 183 on DCM's conversation Vice FonMin)[2] record is thin on reports of efforts by Embassy to impress upon GRC views of USG as well as suggestions or actions to prevent or modify mood reported your 237. We expect frank and accurate reporting from Ambassadors on attitude host government but such reporting in turn becomes point of departure for maximum effort Embassy as well as Dept. to search for means for giving effect to US policy.

If GRC is determined to "go down with ship" rather than compromise on Outer Mongolia this is GRC decision for which we will share no responsibility and we shall make it quite clear if necessary that GRC elected to commit political suicide in UN despite our best efforts.

If GRC dissatisfaction with US is mounting reverse is equally true. If we have applied persistent pressure on Outer Mongolia issue it is for no other purpose than to marshall support on ChiRep issue. Of course we are consulting other governments on ChiRep issue but with none so fully or in so timely a fashion as with GRC. Their complaint this score is not on failure consult but our inability agree with them at every point.

President personally has spent enormous effort to mobilize international support for GRC. It has been a principal topic of conversation with the many distinguished statesmen whom he has seen since January 20. Department's effort has been equally intensive. We cannot accept GRC doubts our motives and must ask that you react sharply to any such implications by GRC officials.

We had not supposed we have failed to clarify what we will do in SC on Outer Mongolia. Our vote on that question will be used to support

---

Source: Department of State, Central Files, 303/9–1161. Secret; Priority. Drafted and approved by Rusk and cleared by Johnson. A copy was sent to Bromley Smith with a covering memorandum of September 18 from Deputy Executive Secretary of the Department Melvin L. Manfull stating that it had been circulated in the Department on a "show" basis to Bowles, Johnson, and McConaughy and requesting that it receive similar handling at the White House. (Kennedy Library, National Security Files, Countries Series, China)

[1] Telegram 237, September 11, reported a GRC mood of "deep gloom and dissatisfaction mixed with determination to go down with ship rather than compromise over Outer Mongolia and ChiRep issues" and mounting GRC dissatisfactions with the United States. (Department of State, Central Files, 303/9–1161) Telegram 236 from Taipei, September 11, transmitted the text of a September 10 letter from Chiang Kai-shek to Kennedy, which stated that agreeing to Outer Mongolian U.N. membership would be yielding to "international blackmail" and that such an abandonment of the GRC moral position would be such a "fatal blow" that continued U.N. membership would not compensate for it. (Ibid.)

[2] Dated August 24. (Ibid., 303/8–2461)

GRC on over-riding question ChiRep. That means we will not share responsibility losing African votes on ChiRep by negative vote or by organizing abstentions. We will cast affirmative vote if necessary to clarify this point. President and I made this entirely clear to Chen Cheng.

It is sign of increasing isolation GRC from reality that they persist in disregarding best advice their own representatives and best friends abroad. It is patent absurdity for GRC to conclude that inability USG to persuade enlarged and changed membership UN is due to lack of US effort. If we cannot persuade GRC, whose primary support is US, to meet us on any of several significant matters whom can we persuade?

If GRC officials are tempted to give signal for expressions frustration and anger at US, they would make fundamental error in supposing what GRC thinks of US is sole preoccupation both sides. Someone in Taipei would be well advised to begin to worry about what US thinks about GRC. We have seen very little investment by GRC in US-Chinese relations.

We will do everything we can to help GRC in its difficult position except to join it in reckless policy which insures its own defeat. If leadership GRC cannot break through its own mythology and give leadership to its own people on course necessary to preserve its international position, our ability to help them is severely limited.

Urge you to make entirely clear to GRC gravity of their situation. We wish to give them strongest possible support because of fundamental common interests but we also want support from them.

**Rusk**

---

## 62.   Special National Intelligence Estimate

SNIE 13–2–61                                   Washington, September 28, 1961.

### COMMUNIST CHINA IN 1971

### The Problem

To estimate the position of Communist China as a world power 10 years from now, in the light of its probable political, economic, scientific, and military strengths and weaknesses.

---

Source: Department of State, INR/EAP Files: Lot 90 D 110. Secret. According to a note on the covering sheet, the Central Intelligence Agency and the intelligence agencies of the Departments of State, the Army, the Navy, the Air Force, and the Joint Staff, and the AEC participated in the preparation of this estimate. All members of the USIB concurred in this estimate on September 28 except the representative of the FBI, who abstained on the grounds that the subject was outside his jurisdiction.

## Note

This estimate is based on what now appears to be the most probable course of the important factors likely to affect Communist China's industrial, scientific, and military growth over this period. Primary factors are the race between food production and population growth, and the Sino-Soviet dispute. Since these and many other factors could develop in a number of different ways, our judgments are necessarily tentative, particularly in view of the dearth of information on current conditions and the degree of the recent disruption of Peiping's long-range plans. However, a "contingency" section considers the effect of unanticipated developments in the primary factors of agriculture and Sino-Soviet relations. For both the main estimate and the contingencies it has been assumed that neither general war nor major international war in the Far East has occurred.

## Conclusions

1. In 1971 mainland China will probably continue to be under the control of a ruthless, determined, and unified Communist leadership which remains basically hostile to the US. Communist China's position as one of the major power centers of the world will have been greatly strengthened. Communist China will probably have more than 850 million people and will continue to have the world's largest standing army and military reserve. It is likely to be among the top three nations in the production of coal, steel, and electric power. (Paras. 5, 9, 14, 18)

2. By 1971 the Chinese Communists are likely to have a modest stockpile of domestically produced nuclear weapons. They will be producing short-range and probably medium-range missiles, and it may be that they will have a submarine-launched missile capability. The possibility cannot be excluded that they can produce an operational intercontinental ballistic missile system with thermonuclear warheads by 1971.[1][2] (Para. 15)

3. At the same time its people will continue to subsist on a barely adequate diet in good years, suffering shortages in bad years. Although impressive advances will have been made in science and technology, the quality, diversity, and technological level of production still will be considerably below that of Japan, the USSR, and the industrial nations of the West. (Paras. 6–11, 14)

---

[1] These estimates of Communist China's missile and nuclear capabilities in 1971 are preliminary and tentative, subject to revision after intensive analysis in the forthcoming SNIE 13–4–61, "Chinese Communist Advanced Weapons Capabilities." [Footnote in the source text. SNIE 13–4–61 was apparently never completed.]

[2] The projections in this paragraph assume continued Soviet cooperation at somewhere near the present level. The contingencies of a marked increase or decrease in Soviet cooperation are discussed in paragraphs 24 and 25. [Footnote in the source text.]

4. As Communist China's strength grows, relations with the USSR will become an increasingly difficult problem. Communist China will become even less restrained in taking political or military action independent of the USSR. It is likely, however, that their common commitment to the Communist cause, and, especially, their common enmity toward the anti-Communist world will preserve sufficient unity to enable Moscow and Peiping to act in concert against the West, especially in times of major challenge. (Para. 17)

[Here follow paragraphs 5–18, comprising the Discussion portion of the estimate; paragraphs 19–25, entitled "Contingencies"; and Appendix A. The contingencies considered were agricultural failure and a major change either for the better or for the worse in Sino-Soviet relations. Appendix A discussed the estimate's prediction of GNP growth averaging 6–8 percent per year.]

---

**63.    Telegram From Secretary of State Rusk to the Department of State**

New York, September 29, 1961, 12:45 p.m.

Secto 52. Following based on uncleared memcon:[1]

Following a brief exchange with Ambassador T.F. Tsiang in Delegation Lounge yesterday,[2] Secretary called in FonMin Shen and Ambassador Yeh this morning to review current status of prognostication re vote on ChiRep issue.[3]

---

Source: Department of State, Central Files, 303/9–2961. Secret; Priority. Repeated to Taipei.

[1] SecDel/MC/62, September 29. (Ibid., Conference Files: Lot 65 D 366, CF 1957)

[2] Secto 3 from USUN, September 18, reported that Rusk had urged against a GRC veto of Outer Mongolian membership in a meeting with Shen and Tsiang that day. (Ibid., Central Files, 303/9–1861)

[3] Rusk discussed this with McConaughy in a September 28 telephone conversation recorded by Phyllis Bernau, which reads in part as follows: "The Sec wondered about one last message to Taipei—if this takes the course it appears to be on if they veto OM and the African states vote with the SU and Peiping will be seated and the GRC will be evicted. Then GRC would get indignant at us—if all this happens we will make it publicly clear they elected to commit suicide and there will be a review of our relations. This is not just Outer Mongolia but a question of having *anyone* including us with them. The Sec will not take anything from them on this issue if they get themselves unseated in the face of their veto of OM. We are going to make this so clear that the American people will lose their interest out there. Somebody there should worry about it. M thinks Chiang is irrational on this but probably we should put it forward to him. M thinks he will take it as a threat though. The Sec said it is a threat. The issue is lost if they pursue this line of events." (Ibid., Rusk Files: Lot 72 D 192, Telephone Calls)

Shen said that following Secretary's conversation with Tsiang yesterday matter had again been reported to Taipei with as yet no comment. He reviewed for the Secretary again the reasons for GRC's obduracy on Outer Mongolian issue.

Secretary said that he wanted to be absolutely sure that GRC fully appreciated the gravity of the situation which we faced and its long-reaching consequences. He pointed out that should GRC's recalcitrance on the Outer Mongolia veto issue result in GRC's departure from the UN, there could well be feeling in Taiwan that GRC's humiliation due to lack of effort on part of US. In order to protect our position we would have no alternative but to review the facts and disassociate ourselves completely from GRC position. Secretary emphasized point that choice before US was between acquiescence to entry of Outer Mongolia or Peking and in this dilemma our position was clear. He reviewed again for the Minister and the Ambassador the tremendous investment in effort which the United States had expended in mobilizing support for GRC. United States also had much at stake in the outcome of this vital issue. If appreciation of this fact were completely disregarded by the GRC an unfavorable outcome could unfortunately affect our future relations.

Although FonMin Shen seemed to appreciate situation now facing GRC, he followed the line that bowing to Soviet blackmail on this issue would seriously undermine morale and public support for GRC domestically. He seemed to take unrealistic refuge in possibility that African groups, such as Brazzaville body, would not vote in unison and that the GRC's position may thus still be salvaged on the "important question" even though they exercise their veto or abstain in the SC on Outer Mongolia. In response to the query as to their exact position as of today, Shen said it was to use the veto if necessary if sufficient abstentions in the Security Council would not preclude Outer Mongolia's entrance.

**Rusk**

## 64.  Telegram From the Department of State to the Embassy in the Republic of China

Washington, October 2, 1961, 10:12 p.m.

221. Your 286, rptd USUN 38.[1] I hope I am correct in my impression that my conversation with T.S. Tsiang and Chen at New York last week[2] has resulted in Chiang's being in a mood to change his mind on the vote on the Outer Mongolia issue if he is provided with what he would consider satisfactory answers on the specific points raised by him with you. (Incidentally, you should have no hesitancy in assuring Chiang that what I said to Tsiang and Chen accurately reflects full views of the President.) We have therefore sought to provide you with bona fide assurances which may have desired results. You should avoid any impression that we are in any way backing away from the statements which I made to Tsiang and Chen.

We have added impression that Chiang has never fully appreciated international repercussions both to US and GRC which would result from situation in which Chinese might find themselves out of UN. You should do everything possible emphasize that this is not simply matter of seat in international organization in which Chiang has only peripheral interest but impinges on every phase of GRC relations abroad, including ability of United States to defend them.

You are commended for your generally excellent replies to Chiang's seven numbered questions. However, believe you should make further comment, drawing on following supplementary statements addressed to numbered questions:

1. No additional comment.[3]

---

Source: Department of State, Central Files, 611.93/10–261. Secret; Niact; Limit Distribution. Drafted by Johnson, McConaughy, and Rusk; cleared by Director of the Office of United Nations Political and Security Affairs Joseph J. Sisco and William P. Bundy; and approved for transmission by Rusk. Repeated to USUN.

[1] Telegram 286, October 2, reported a conversation that day between Drumright and President Chiang. Drumright stressed that U.S. policy with respect to Outer Mongolia was aimed at furthering U.S. and GRC mutual interests. Chiang posed seven questions and also asked whether the United States had a fixed position on Outer Mongolia; Drumright gave preliminary replies to the questions and commented that the conversation showed Chiang's suspicions and resentment but also disclosed anxiety about possible deterioration of GRC-U.S. relations and a new willingness to consider a compromise solution. (Ibid., 611.93/10–261) Telegram 216 to Taipei, September 29, had instructed Drumright to call on Chiang to reaffirm the substance of Rusk's conversation that day with Shen and stress the gravity of the situation. (Ibid., 303/9–2961)

[2] See Document 63 and footnote 2 thereto.

[3] Question 1 was: "Is it true that if GRC vetoes Mongolia US will vote for OM's admission?" Drumright replied that Kennedy and Rusk had reserved freedom of action on this, but that if an affirmative vote was cast, it would be done to satisfy the African states and assist the GRC on the representation issue.

2. Question of "White Paper" has not been considered here. However, as already noted we would certainly be obliged inform American public of our reasons for divergence with GRC in event of veto but this would not be for purpose of censuring or criticizing. Also in our minds is near certainty that American inability to follow GRC would lead to seriously critical stories from Taipei which we would be compelled to answer. It is well to emphasize that one basis of our concern is a deterioration in the public opinion attitudes beyond control of governments.[4]

3. Department's announcement that it had suspended exploration of question of establishing relations with Outer Mongolia[5] was made in light of existing world situation. This means we had reached conclusion that further approaches toward Outer Mongolia at this time would be detrimental to United States and free world interests. GRC veto of Outer Mongolia would not in itself change our conclusion. While we could not make long-term commitment affecting other times and circumstances we have no present plan to reopen question direct OM-US relations.[6]

4. USG will absolutely not sever relations GRC, but loss of GRC international status through defeat in UN would inevitably color US-GRC relations. For example, we must assume that GRC would lose most if not all of its friends in Africa, and as a consequence its seat in UN; hence joint plans such as "Operation Vanguard"[7] would be futile. Moreover, we would find it impossible successfully defend GRC's position in international organizations of all types after suffering defeat in major battle of retaining GRC seat in UN. Not only GRC position, but US leadership in world would suffer seriously as result. We are glad to note that Chiang seems to appreciate importance of preservation of US prestige and influence in present world struggle. We would also find it impossible arrest "band wagon" trend toward recognition of Communist China among nations now well disposed toward GRC, many of which have told us they will recognize Peiping if GRC loses UN seat.[8]

---

[4] Question 2 was: "Is it true that if GRC vetoes OM, USG will issue 'white paper' criticizing or censuring GRC?" Drumright referred to Rusk's discussion with Shen but stated that he saw no possibility of the issuance of a statement directed specifically at criticism of the GRC.

[5] See Document 200.

[6] Question 3 was: "Is it true that if GRC vetoes OM, USG will move to recognize and establish relations with OM?" Drumright replied that the exploratory talks could conceivably be resumed at a later date but that such a decision would not be related to a GRC veto.

[7] Reference is to a plan to provide GRC technical assistance to African countries with joint U.S.-GRC financing. (Memorandum of conversation between Martin and Kiang Yi-seng, June 20; Department of State, Central Files, 893.0070/6–2061)

[8] Question 4 was: "Is it true that in event GRC vetoes OM, USG will sever relations with GRC?" Drumright replied in the negative but pointed out that the loss of the UN seat would impair the GRC's international status, which the United States was anxious to preserve.

5. In addition to points you made it should be recognized that US ability to prevent such development is directly related to preservation GRC position in UN. You might also add in order to make important distinction between official attitude of USG and inevitable deterioration of public opinion in US and other countries that USG considers Mutual Security Treaty fundamental relationship based upon genuine common interests but that official policy this matter needs full support of US public opinion and general understanding world opinion if it is to be fully effective.[9]

6. Any news reports to effect that USG has favored consideration Outer Mongolia before Mauritania manifestly incorrect.[10]

7. On whole ChiRep and Outer Mongolia issue, US has consulted GRC in detail and on day-to-day basis both here and in New York more intensively than with any other single ally on vital common interests. Further, USG has spent far more time in highest level consultations with leaders other governments in ChiRep problem than on any other single issue.[11]

You should find opportunity to explain to Chiang that we have been severely handicapped in recent discussions ChiRep with other governments because they cannot believe that if we ourselves were really serious that GRC could possibly veto Outer Mongolia. This does not mean that they consider GRC our satellite but cannot understand how GRC could throw such barrier in the way when USG is making maximum effort on basis that ChiRep is a fundamental issue both for USG and GRC.

Security Council adjourned this afternoon without acting on membership application of Outer Mongolia. We therefore have period of few additional days to bring about change in GRC position. Hope you can make best possible use of this time.

**Rusk**

---

[9] Question 5 was: "If GRC vetoes OM and ChiComs are admitted to UN, is it part of your policy that present status of Taiwan will disappear and will then be regarded as ChiCom territory?" Drumright replied that a leading U.S. concern was to prevent such a development and that the best way to prevent it was to preserve the GRC position in the United Nations.

[10] Question 6 was: "SC last week agreed Mauritanian application would be considered before that of OM. Is there any credence in news reports that USG now favors OM consideration first?" Drumright pointed out that the United States had voted to give precedence to Mauritania and that he would be surprised if this position were reversed.

[11] Question 7 was: "US started exploratory talks with OM without prior consultation and took some forms of action on ChiRep issue without prior consultation. Does this mean USG is committed to independent course of action on Outer Mongolia and ChiRep issues?" Drumright stated that in general, there had been consultation but divergence of views over Outer Mongolia had occasioned difficulties, and the United States accordingly reserved freedom of action on that issue.

65.    Memorandum From the President's Special Assistant for
        National Security Affairs (Bundy) to President Kennedy

Washington, October 4, 1961.

I telephoned George Yeh about Chiang and Outer Mongolia, and he
urgently asked me to come over for a talk. I did, and he spelled out the
feelings and response of his government in recent months with extraordinary candor.[1] His account is as follows:

Vice President Chen went back from Washington with a conviction
that you personally were committed to strong support of Chiang and
maintenance of this U.S. policy. He found Secretary Rusk "cagey." This
account was persuasive to the Generalissimo, and it still colors his whole
approach to U.S. policy. Your first effort, after the Vice President's visit, to
shift Chiang on Outer Mongolia was not effective, but it did not change
his regard for you. Indeed, he was getting the same arguments from all
the professionals in his own government, except the Foreign Minister.
Then the Chinese Government undertook a campaign of persuasion
with the Brazzaville group, and was discouraged to find no responsive-
ness whatsoever. As Yeh put it, "The Africans were interested in Mauritania and not at all in our problem."

As the moment of choice came closer, and estimates of the voting
became more and more narrow, the Chinese professionals continued
their pressure on their own government, but without avail. Then last
week the Secretary of State had his stern conversations with Tsiang and
the Foreign Minister in New York. Yeh reports that these conversations
deeply shook the Generalissimo. I think myself that the Secretary is probably right in his belief that this shaking is what has moved Chiang to his
present apparent willingness to reconsider the veto. The Secretary said
that if the division persisted, it might affect the "basic relationships" of
the two countries. This phrase above all others is what led Chiang to his
series of anguished questions to Drumright.

Yeh said to me in the strongest terms that a message of friendliness
and encouragement from you might well be decisive, and I told him that
you had asked to get in touch with him precisely to deliver such a
message. I made it clear that there was no difference in policy between
you and the Secretary, and that you associated yourself with his estimate
of the seriousness of the situation. But I also said that neither you nor Mr.

Source: Kennedy Library, National Security Files, Countries Series, China. Top
Secret.
    [1] A memorandum for the files dated October 4 by Arthur H. Rosen of the Office of
Chinese Affairs summarizes the highlights of the meeting between Bundy and Yeh the previous evening as told to Rosen that day by Chinese Embassy Political Counselor C.C. Lai,
who was present. (Department of State, Central Files, 303/10–461)

Rusk had any intention of shifting away from the basic treaty relation between our two countries, and I went further by emphasizing your own great respect and regard for the Generalissimo as a heroic figure, and your sense of close personal partnership in purpose with him. I said that he could be assured that our whole object in this affair was to prevent the admission of Communist China for as long as possible, and that this seemed to us to be in the common interest of our two countries. I said that you would deeply regret any misunderstanding that might have occurred inadvertently in any of our conversations, and I indicated that we would hope to be able to work together more closely and without misunderstandings if we could reconcile this particular difference over Outer Mongolia.[2] All of this Yeh undertook to report to his government, and indeed I said some of it at his suggestion in order to take advantage of his obvious agreement with us that the thing to do is to use every reasonable instrument to insure that the Generalissimo does, in fact, change his mind.

I believe that this conversation serves the purpose which Drumright has in mind in the attached message, just received from Taipei.[3] But perhaps we could also send the special personal message as he suggests in the last paragraph.[4] The Department agrees to this—the "10–10" celebration next week offers an admirable time for a warm personal message from you, and a draft will be prepared for your decision.

**McG. B.**[5]

---

[2] According to Rosen's memorandum cited in footnote 1 above, Bundy stated that the President "now feels that our initial, rather casual move toward recognition talks with Outer Mongolia was ill-advised" and that the President had instructed Rusk and Stevenson "to use all possible means to block admission of the Chinese Communists and protect the GRC in the United Nations."

[3] Drumright urged in telegram 287 from Taipei, October 4, that Kennedy send a personal message to Chiang, and that in return for a GRC commitment not to veto Outer Mongolian admission, the United States give a return commitment to abstain. (Department of State, Central Files, 303/10–461)

[4] It suggested an especially warm and personal message to Chiang for the 50th anniversary of the 1911 Chinese revolution on October 10.

[5] Printed from a copy that bears these typed initials.

## 66.    Telegram From the Department of State to the Embassy in the Republic of China

Washington, October 5, 1961.

225. Your 287[1] and 289.[2] Following message from President Kennedy to President Chiang should be delivered soonest:

"October 5, 1961.

"I have sent you separately my warm congratulations on the occasion of the Fiftieth Anniversary of the Chinese Revolution,[3] and I hope by now you will also have received my informal message to you delivered by my assistant Bundy to Ambassador Yeh.[4] I want to take this one more opportunity, however, to state in the strongest terms my regard for your statesmanship, my support for the alliance that binds our two countries, my personal approval of the reassurances recently conveyed by Ambassador Drumright in response to your seven questions, and my appreciation for your understanding of the importance to me of the need to keep Communist China out of the United Nations.

"In particular I want to make it clear that while Secretary Rusk spoke for me in outlining the difficulties we might face if we met defeat on the issue of Communist China in the United Nations after a veto of Outer Mongolia, neither he nor I would ever intend to state such a concern to a trusted ally in tones of threat; we have meant rather to indicate clearly how forces beyond our control might bring trouble to both our countries in such an event. I believe that we can bridge our honorable differences on this matter of Outer Mongolia—you by avoiding a veto, and we by avoiding any new diplomatic initiative toward that country in the existing circumstances—and if we can do these things in the light of the common needs of the free people, we shall be fairly on the way to increased

---

Source: Department of State, Central Files, 303/10–461. Top Secret; Niact; Eyes Only. The time of transmission is illegible on the source text. Drafted at the White House and approved by Manfull. Repeated to USUN for Stevenson. Notes by Phyllis Bernau of a telephone conversation that day between Rusk and Bundy indicate that the telegram was drafted by Bundy and cleared by Rusk and Kennedy. (Ibid., Rusk Files: Lot 72 D 192, Telephone Calls)

[1] See footnote 3, Document 65.

[2] Telegram 289, October 4, reported a conversation between Drumright and Acting Foreign Minister Hsu Shao-chang, who told Drumright that President Chiang's senior foreign policy advisers had been informed of Rusk's responses to Chiang's questions and that their consensus was that a message from Kennedy to Chiang would be most effective in influencing him not to veto Outer Mongolian admission. (Department of State, Central Files, 303/10–461)

[3] For text of the message, dated October 5, see *Public Papers of the Presidents of the United States: John F. Kennedy, 1961*, p. 650.

[4] See Document 65.

effectiveness together, an effectiveness based on personal trust and understanding as well as on the true interests of our nations.

"John F. Kennedy"

Rusk

---

## 67.    Telegram From the Embassy in the Republic of China to the Department of State

Taipei, October 6, 1961, 8 p.m.

299. Called on President Chiang this afternoon and handed him message conveyed via Deptel 225.[1] Also conveyed text double tenth message transmitted via Deptel 227.[2]

Chiang expressed deep appreciation not only for President Kennedy's written message but also for oral message conveyed through Bundy to Ambassador Yeh. He said both touched and moved him deeply.

Chiang then shifted from foregoing into long, involved eloquent statement of troubles he faces here if he commits volte-face on Mongolian question. For one thing, Prime Minister, in face of unanimous Legislative Yuan resolution enjoining government to use all means to bar Mongolia, will be obliged by constitution to submit resignation as Prime Minister. But worse still, Chiang says he faces even more formidable job explaining reversal to officialdom, armed forces and public. If not handled adequately and properly, he said government will be endangered, morale sapped and will and purpose of government and people dissipated. He said it is particularly important to preserve idea government is not retreating from fundamental policy (mainland recovery) or weakening in its determination to oppose communism to end.

He added that his task is painful and onerous. Only two men can put it across—President Kennedy and himself. It was this conviction which was behind instruction he transmitted yesterday to Ambassador Yeh to

---

Source: Department of State, Central Files, 303/10–661. Top Secret; Niact; Limit Distribution. Received at 12:55 p.m.

[1] Document 66.

[2] Dated October 5. (Department of State, Central Files, 793.00/9–1661)

seek public statement from President Kennedy reaffirming US strong support of GRC and pledging US use of all means, including SC action if necessary to bar ChiComs from UN (Embtel 293).[3] Armed with such a statement, Chiang said he believed he could carry it with Legislative Yuan and public opinion; without it, he would face serious trouble. Chiang indicated that if President Kennedy would issue such a supporting statement he would be prepared to forego veto. Left unsaid but plainly implied was impression he could not go ahead without supporting statement.

At this point, I conveyed to Chiang substance of Deptel 226[4] which I had earlier passed to Acting Foreign Minister Hsu. However, President insisted that only a fresh statement from President Kennedy would suffice for his purposes. I then said perhaps Ambassador Stevenson could make some such statement in SC when Mongolian issue considered, but he said this would not be sufficient.

In face of Chiang's adamant position, I then told him I would report to Washington. He asked that his views be passed President Kennedy.

*Comment:* There is no doubt that Chiang is faced with a troublesome predicament even if he does embroider on it to a certain extent. He desperately wants statement from President Kennedy on which he can pin his defense of volte-face. He also wants JFK's assurances as reassurance to Chinese people that admission of OM this year will not be followed by that of Red China next year. I concede that this argument has substance and I agree that a carefully worded statement from JFK could be helpful in solving his dilemma.

If requested statement is not forthcoming, possibility exists that Chiang will refuse to go ahead on Mongolia. Consequently, it is my judgment that we should in this case stretch a point and try to meet his request.

At its discretion Department repeat to USUN.

**Drumright**

---

[3] Telegram 293, October 5, informed the Department that Acting Foreign Minister Hsu had informed the Embassy of Chiang's message to Yeh. (Ibid., 303/10–561)

[4] Telegram 226, October 5, instructed Drumright to inform Hsu that a public statement on the Chinese representation issue did not appear necessary or desirable at that time; statements of U.S. support had been made as recently as the joint statement issued by Kennedy and Ch'en on August 2. (Ibid.) For text of the joint statement, see *Public Papers of the Presidents of the United States: John F. Kennedy, 1961*, pp. 545–546.

## 68.    Telegram From the Department of State to the Embassy in the Republic of China

Washington, October 7, 1961, 5:15 p.m.

237. Please inform President Chiang at the earliest opportunity that his views reported in your 299[1] have been conveyed to President Kennedy and sympathetically considered by both President and Secretary.

The President plans to make it clear at his forthcoming press conference on October eleventh that the United States continues to be strongly opposed to the entry of Communist China into the United Nations and continues to give its strong support to the continued representation of the Republic of China in all UN bodies.[2]

The President has considered the specific suggestions which President Chiang has put forward for supplementary comments and his conclusion is that specific mention of the Security Council in relation to the Chinese Communists or of a possible veto by the United States would be damaging to our common position in the UN at this time.[3] We are collecting support on the issue of the "important question," and mention of the Security Council or of the veto would both weaken that support and suggest some fear that we might lose in our current effort.

The President wishes, however, to extend once more to President Chiang and through him to all appropriate officers of the GRC his assurance that the purposes of the United States, and his own political objective in this matter, are precisely to prevent admission of Communist China and to sustain the position of the Republic of China both in the United Nations and in the international community.

---

Source: Department of State, Central Files, 303/10–661. Top Secret; Niact. Drafted by Bundy; cleared by Johnson, Wallner, Director of the Office of Chinese Affairs Joseph A. Yager, and in substance by Rusk; and approved by McConaughy and the President. Repeated to USUN. According to notes prepared in Rusk's office, Bundy called Rusk on the morning of October 7 and told him that Kennedy had agreed to make a statement at a press conference. In a subsequent call to Johnson, Rusk said he thought "it might be worth it so we don't give him any excuse on question of losing 8–10 votes." (Ibid., Rusk Files: Lot 72 D 192, Telephone Calls)

[1] Document 67.

[2] At this point, the following sentence is crossed out on the source text: "The President will also make clear his conviction that this policy can be successfully sustained in the UN."

[3] Drumright reported in telegram 307 from Taipei, October 8, that when he conveyed the substance of telegram 237 to Hsu, the latter expressed the view that it would not satisfy President Chiang, who had sent new instructions to Shen and Yeh directing them to press for supplementary assurances. (Department of State, Central Files, 303/10–861) Telegram 239 to Taipei replied that it was considered neither appropriate nor necessary for the President to go beyond the terms used in telegram 237, and telegram 240 to Taipei informed Drumright, "High quarters our Govt near end of their patience over repeated GRC demands on President in connection handling of ChiRep issue." (Both dated October 8; ibid.)

As you know, the Chinese delegation at the United Nations has already begun to seek assurances from the Brazzaville group of support in the event that the GRC withdraws its veto of Outer Mongolia. These soundings have produced wide African support for GRC on ChiRep issue but if after such conversations the veto of Outer Mongolia were to be reasserted, the effect would be most damaging. Thus it may be useful to suggest that GRC, having begun to change its course, can now reassert veto only at a still higher price to itself and to us. This last point should perhaps be made indirectly to others, rather than to President Chiang himself. It should in no way be presented as a threat from USG.

**Rusk**

### 69.   Editorial Note

The Chinese representation issue was discussed at White House daily staff meetings on October 9, 10, and 11, 1961, each of which was recorded in a memorandum for the record by Colonel Julian J. Ewell of the White House staff. His October 9 memorandum records the discussion of the subject as follows:

"Mr. Bundy mentioned the divergency of approach between Stevenson and the Administration (I think here he means the State Department) on the ChiCom membership in the UN for next year. Mr. Stevenson seems to be working to smooth the way for the ChiCom to become members with the U.S. gaining as much political advantage as possible, whereas the Administration policy seems to be to keep them out. The President, regardless of any personal views he may have, probably cannot afford to be officially associated with a two China idea. This was followed by a long discussion of how the Berlin and Chinese Communist situations are somewhat the same, i.e., how far do you go in recognizing an existing fact? It was also noted that the Chinese Nationalists seem to have exposed to public scrutiny their more flexible position on the Outer Mongolia situation." (National Defense University, Taylor Papers, Box 24, Daily Staff Meetings)

The relevant portion of Ewell's October 10 memorandum reads as follows:

"The Chinese Nationalists have allowed the Taipei newspapers to discuss the possibilities of a flexible policy on the Outer Mongolia question. This is taken as an indication that the Chinese Government has finally decided on a flexible attitude. Mr. Bundy remarked that the Nationalists evidently want us to agree to veto ChiCom entry into the

UN under any circumstances. A very complex argument followed, with Komer persuasively arguing that we have to adjust to a two China situation without antagonizing all the neutrals, while keeping the Nationalists in the UN. Mr. Bundy, possibly acting as the devil's advocate, advanced the thought that a U.S. veto might not be a bad idea, that we are gradually getting into a situation where we will have to veto some matters and we might as well do it on an issue where the President could make a move which would be popular with a large element of public opinion. I really didn't follow this discussion in all its turns and twists." (Ibid.)

Ewell's October 11 memorandum records the following comments concerning the subject:

"Chiang has backed off on a flexible policy in regard to Outer Mongolia. State is trying to get him back, either through the Ambassador or, preferably, through the Chinese Ambassador, who has been called back for consultation." (Ibid.)

---

## 70.    Memorandum From Secretary of State Rusk to President Kennedy

Washington, October 10, 1961.

SUBJECT

Chinese Representation

Ambassador Yeh informed the State Department this afternoon that he has received a telegram from Vice President Chen Cheng containing the following points: (1) after prolonged consideration the Chinese Government still feels that President Kennedy would best save the Chinese Government's situation by including in his reply to a question at his coming press conference reference to the use of the veto by the United States in the Security Council if necessary to prevent the admission of Communist China; (2) if the Chinese position on Outer Mongolia's UN application were to be changed, Vice President Chen would resign;[1] (3) if

---

Source: Kennedy Library, National Security Files, Countries Series, China. Confidential. The source text is not dated, but the Department of State file copy is dated October 10 and indicates that it was drafted by Sisco. A marginal note indicates that Rusk gave the original to Bundy on October 10. (Department of State, Central Files, 303/10–1061)

[1] Telegram 313 from Taipei, October 11, reported Chiang and Ch'en had agreed that if the GRC were to change its position on Outer Mongolia, Ch'en would have to resign as Prime Minister. (Ibid., 303/10–1161)

President Kennedy is unable to include in his press conference statement a reference to the United States veto of Communist China, the Chinese Government will not change its original instructions to its UN Delegation on the Outer Mongolia issue—that is, the Chinese Delegation would veto Outer Mongolia if there was no other way to prevent Outer Mongolia's admission to the UN; and (4) the Chinese Government would not want to place the US Government or President Kennedy in any difficulty but hopes that President Kennedy can consider the need for the requested reference in his press conference statement in order to save the face of President Chiang and the Chinese Government.

A subsequent telegram received by Ambassador Yeh from Vice President Chen this afternoon instructs Ambassador Yeh to assure the State Department and, if possible, the White House that the position taken by the Chinese Government on Outer Mongolia has nothing to do with its attitude toward President Kennedy, which remains one of friendliness and respect. The Chinese Government's position, this message states, has been taken entirely for internal reasons. This message also expressed the hope that President Kennedy can suspend what he is prepared to say at the press conference on October 11 because what he has prepared would not improve the position of the Government in Taipei.

We have considered carefully once again the Chinese request in light of the foregoing. We have concluded that it would not be desirable for the United States to make a press statement of the kind requested by the Chinese. There are two principal reasons supporting this conclusion.

First, such a statement would tend to establish the premise that the United States had already suffered two defeats: (1) our proposals in the General Assembly had not received the required support and (2) the United States does not have seven affirmative votes for a proposal which it favors in the Security Council. The fact that the new Administration would have found it necessary to make such a statement would be regarded as defeatist and help to generate this kind of an atmosphere in the General Assembly.

Secondly, an indication by the United States of its intention to use the veto to oppose the admission of Red China to the United Nations would seriously undermine our present tactical plan at the General Assembly designed to establish the precedent that any change in the Chinese representation question is an "important one" under the Charter and providing for the establishment of a committee to make recommendations on this and related questions. A United States statement of intention to use the veto in this way would tend to preclude in the eyes of a number of delegations a possible recommendation by the study committee in favor of a two China solution. Our study committee would then be conceived of not as a serious study proposal designed to make constructive recommendations, but rather as an empty one-year moratorium gimmick. It would not be viewed as a serious proposal, and therefore our statement would tend to diminish considerably the voting support we can hopefully expect.[2]

**Dean Rusk**

---

[2] Rusk met with Yeh on October 11 and stated that there were two objections to a public reference to a possible U.S. veto on Chinese representation. First, it would be an empty gesture, if the issue arose in a framework in which the veto could be used, the GRC would also have the veto; second, and more important, it would imply that "the jig is up in the General Assembly." (Memorandum of conversation, October 11; ibid.) See the Supplement.

---

71.    **Message From the President's Special Assistant for National Security Affairs (Bundy) to the Chief of the Central Intelligence Agency Station in Taipei (Cline)**

Washington, October 11, 1961.

The President is prepared to give private reassurance to the Generalissimo that if at any time a U.S. veto is what will be effective in preventing Chinese Communist entry into the UN, the United States will use that veto. This assurance, however, must be kept wholly private for the powerful reason that public disclosure of such a U.S. pledge at this time would be deeply damaging to the common cause at the UN. There we are debating on the important question issue and we will lose many votes—and also indicate fear of defeat—if there is any public discussion of a veto.

The President wants this assurance conveyed to Chiang in the most effective way and by the best possible person. On the evidence of recent days I am inclined to yourself or to George Yeh who has been extraordi-

---

Source: Kennedy Library, National Security Files, Countries Series, China General, CIA Cables 7/61–10/16/61. Top Secret; Eyes Only. The message, headed "To Mr. Ray Cline From McGeorge Bundy at the President's Direction," is the first of a series of messages between Bundy and Cline sent through CIA channels. The source text does not indicate the time of transmission. An October 13 message from Bundy to Cline (Out Smilax 3) instructed Cline to use the slug Smilax for future messages in the series. (Filed with a covering memorandum of October 14 from Dulles to Bundy; ibid.) Copies of all the messages in the series through October 17 were sent from the White House to the Department of State on that date. (Filed with a memorandum of October 18 from Stevenson to Rusk; Department of State, Central Files, 303/10–1861)

narily helpful and is now returning for consultation. Suggest urgently you consult with him and then decide how to communicate the President's assurance.

We recognize that what President Chiang now faces is a domestic political problem, in which private assurances may not be useful. But we are completely persuaded that any public statement mentioning the veto would be intolerably destructive of his purposes and ours alike.

We leave it to you to decide after discussion with Yeh whether the President's assurance could be conveyed in such a way as to allow President Chiang to use it privately with reliable key figures. But there should be no leak, and this Government would have to deny any rumors about reassurance on the veto, in order to protect its position at the UN.

You will note that the President does not promise a veto in all circumstances. This is because our best experts report that in some circumstances, such as a straight credentials vote; a veto would not be possible. Thus, in fact, the veto is not the cure-all that Chiang appears to think it is. The point of our assurance is that the President will use whatever weapons seem likely to work, including the veto, and you may put the matter in this way if it seems more persuasive.

The President has great trust in you and wishes to leave you free to convey these assurances.

The State Department is informed, but Ambassador Drumright is not, and at this stage we prefer that he not be included unless you find it urgent for reasons not apparent here.

Yours by candlelight for scholarship and skullduggery.

## 72.   Message From the Chief of the Central Intelligence Agency Station in Taipei (Cline) to the President's Special Assistant for National Security Affairs (Bundy)

Taipei, October 14, 1961.

Eyes only for McGeorge Bundy from Ray Cline. This is my Smilax 3 per 6943.[1]

After consultations with George Yeh and many hours talk 14 October with Chiang Ching-kuo who was constantly referring substance to Gimo we hammered out a draft of proposed confidential understanding between President Chiang and President Kennedy which Gimo has seen and will agree to if advised it is acceptable to President Kennedy.

2.   Draft understanding is verbatim as follows:

A.   US will not vote for admission of Outer Mongolia to UN.

B.   President Kennedy will at early opportune time to be agreed issue public statement as follows:

"The United States has always considered the GRC the only rightful government representing China and has always given full support to the position and to all the rights of that government in the UN. Therefore the United States firmly opposes the entry of the ChiComs into the UN or into any of the components of the UN."

C.   President Kennedy will give President Chiang the following private assurance through diplomatic channels:

"I wish to assure you that if at any time a US veto is necessary and will be effective in preventing Chinese Communist entry into the UN, the US will use that veto."

This assurance will be given with the explicit understanding that it must be kept wholly private since public disclosure of such a pledge at this time would adversely affect the common US-GRC interest in preserving the free world position in the UN and keeping the ChiComs out of that organization.

---

Source: Kennedy Library, National Security Files, Countries Series, China, General, CIA Cables 7/61–10/16/61. Top Secret; Eyes Only. Transmitted from the Central Intelligence Agency to the White House, where it was received at 9:01 a.m. on October 14. It does not indicate the time of transmission from Taipei.

[1] Reference is apparently to Bundy's Out Smilax 3 message, cited in footnote 1, Document 71. Cline's first message in this series, sent on October 13, reported that he had discussed the subject of Bundy's October 11 message with Chiang Ching-kuo and had arranged to discuss it with George Yeh. In his second message, sent on October 14, Cline reported that he had talked to Yeh, who was to see Chiang Kai-shek that day, and commented that he thought a public statement by Kennedy coupled with the proposed private assurances would persuade Chiang to withhold the veto. (Ibid.)

D. The GRC will not use the veto against Outer Mongolia's admission to the UN.

3. If you advise me these four points are acceptable to President Kennedy then Gimo will invite me for private conference where he will definitely commit himself to this reversal of position on Outer Mongolia. Strongly urge approval of wording on public statement as this is by far most innocuous of many formulations discussed. It seems to me reiteration of technical juridical position of US on ChiRep issue.

4. Gimo says he expects great local political difficulties including necessity Prime Minister to resign. Gimo will have big convincing job to do. Therefore requests one week's time for this job between US public statement and resumption UN Security Council consideration Outer Mongolia. If draft proposal approved by two Presidents public statement should be made soon thereafter providing only Gimo is informed of timing in advance via this channel.

5. Gimo says private assurance should not be in form of letter because in China this would imply lack of trust between two correspondents. In fact Gimo says he is willing approve this difficult change in GRC policy only because he has great confidence in friendship of President Kennedy and wishes build close personal understanding between two men. Suggest private assurance be delivered orally by Ambassador Drumright as diplomatic message from President Kennedy.

6. Since now have Gimo's concurrence in principle will brief Ambassador Drumright at earliest opportunity in accordance your authorization received today.[2]

7. If President Kennedy approves this draft proposal and notification reaches me during next twelve hours believe Gimo will see me 15 October and give his firm commitment, this line of action.

---

[2] Bundy's Out Smilax 3 message, cited in footnote 1, authorized Cline to inform Drumright.

**73.    Message From the Chief of the Central Intelligence Agency Station in Taipei (Cline) to the President's Special Assistant for National Security Affairs (Bundy)**

Taipei, October 16, 1961.

Eyes only for Bundy from Cline. This is my In Smilax 5.

1. Presented statement of policy outlined my Smilax 3[1] as amended my Smilax 4[2] to President Chiang 0900–1000 16 Oct. Sending by separate message Smilax 6[3] for the record verbatim text my presentation.

2. President Chiang responded as anticipated that his policy views on the points covered are identical with those of President Kennedy. Said he appreciated Kennedy's personal intervention in matter and had full confidence these policy undertakings are in common interest. Noted he expects gravest political difficulties in carrying out this policy reversal but will personally see that it is done properly.

3. My presentation included as footnote the following: "President Kennedy observes that the U.S. will not vote for admission unless circumstances make it clear that it somehow would be essential to the success of this whole maneuver in support of the GRC." Gimo said he hoped U.S. would not find it necessary to vote for admission Outer Mongolia and in any case trusts President Kennedy would give him prior warning if this is proposed.

4. The Gimo asked me to tell President Kennedy that he desperately needed one week to ten days to reverse GRC political stand on Outer Mongolia after President Kennedy's public statement and before vote in UN Security Council. Suggested delegations at UN work out this timing.

---

Source: Kennedy Library, National Security Files, Countries Series, China General, CIA Cables 7/61–10/16/61. Top Secret. The source text was transmitted from the Central Intelligence Agency to the White house, where it was received at 1:25 a.m. on October 16. No time of transmission is on the source text.

[1] Document 72.

[2] Received at the White House on the evening of October 14. It stated that Cline would change the verbs in each of the four points in his draft proposal from "will" to "should," would preface them with a statement that Kennedy had instructed him to convey to Chiang as a friend the following statement of policy on some key issues confronting the two countries at the United Nations, and would omit the phrase "at this time" from point two. The changes were in accordance with suggestions sent by Bundy in an October 14 message to Cline, which stated in part that it would be preferable "not to think of this as a confidential understanding, but rather as a private exchange of statements of policy". Bundy's Out Smilax 5, dated October 15, conveyed Kennedy's approval and authorized Cline to proceed. (All in Kennedy Library, National Security Files, Countries Series, China, General, CIA Cables, 7/61–10/16/61)

[3] Received on October 16. (Ibid.) See the Supplement.

5. Gimo requested advance notice exact time of President Kennedy's public statement

6. Following background gives insight into GRC policy process. In my marathon talks with George Yeh and Chiang Ching-kuo on 15 October it emerged that Gimo had committed himself to me through his son but still had not disclosed this fact to George Yeh who still late on 15 Oct was discussing with me how to persuade Gimo of points we had worked up and which already had been sent to Washington. Chiang Ching-kuo asked me not to give game away before final approval from Washington. Obviously Gimo was hoping George Yeh's protracted arguments would serve to persuade other top officials that what Gimo had already decided was right. Interestingly George Yeh said by late 15 October he was convinced big majority responsible leaders already persuaded Gimo should not use veto on Outer Mongolia.

7. Gimo requested me not to tell any Chinese that this understanding was worked out through me and Chiang Ching-kuo. Evidently he felt this politically undesirable for variety reasons but his stated reason was he highly valued this private channel for frank exchange of views with President Kennedy and wished to preserve its privacy.

8. At Gimo's request through young Chiang did not brief Ambassador Drumright prior receipt your final approval for fear he inadvertently tip off Foreign Ministry which was then being kept in dark. Consequently briefing Drumright immediately 16 October.

9. Thanks for opportunity "to Smilax" the Gimo and for your excellent guidance and support. Yours by the midnight oil of the lamps of China.[4]

---

[4] Cline's final Smilax message, Smilax 7, received at the White House on October 25, reported a conversation with Chiang Ching-kuo on the political procedures involved in reversing the GRC position on the veto of Outer Mongolia. Cline reported that Chiang Kai-shek had specifically asked him to thank Bundy for his help in finding a solution to the problem. He concluded, "Obviously this channel should not be overworked but in view of Gimo's attitude it can be used whenever you feel it is needed." (Kennedy Library, National Security Files, Countries Series, China, General, CIA Cables, 10/17/61–11/5/61)

## 74.    Telegram From the Department of State to the Embassy in the Republic of China

Washington, October 16, 9:09 p.m.

259. Eyes only for Ambassador Drumright. Following instruction is from the President:

At earliest opportunity you should seek meeting with President Chiang and inform him orally of this private assurance from me. "I wish to assure you that if at any time a US veto is necessary and will be effective in preventing Chinese Communist entry into the UN, the US will use that veto." You should tell him that this assurance is given privately because of the unfavorable impact that public disclosure would have on our common position at the UN. This is my policy, and President Chiang is entitled to know it, but any public use of this assurance would force a diplomatic denial here.

You should also inform President Chiang that I now plan to make a strong public statement of support for GRC in UN in following terms Wednesday, Oct. 18. "The US has always considered the Government of the Republic of China the only rightful government representing China and has always given full support to the position and to all the rights of that government in the UN. Therefore, the US firmly opposes the entry of the Chinese Communists into the UN or into any of the components of the UN."[1]

Finally you should convey my warmest personal regards to President Chiang and indicate to him my understanding of the difficult political problems he is dealing with and my thanks for his trust in me. End Instruction.[2]

**Rusk**

---

Source: Department of State, Central Files, 303/10–1661. Top Secret; Niact; Eyes Only. Drafted by Bundy, cleared in substance by Rusk and U. Alexis Johnson, and approved by McConaughy.

[1] Telegram 276 to Taipei, October 19, transmitted the text of a statement identical to this one that had been released that day by Kennedy's Press Secretary Pierre E.G. Salinger in response to a press inquiry. (Ibid., 793.02/10–1961)

[2] Telegram 339 from Taipei, October 17, reported that Drumright had met with Chiang and conveyed to him Kennedy's private assurance, the public statement he planned to make, and the other points in telegram 259. It reported that Chiang said he would have to reveal the assurance in confidence to a few officials in order to obtain support for the policy change and that he would be able to take steps to reverse position only after Kennedy made his public statement. After Drumright pointed out that speed was necessary because of pressure for an early meeting of the Security Council, Chiang stated that he would accept responsibility that the GRC would abstain on the question of Outer Mongolian membership, and he urged U.S. abstention. (Ibid., 303/10–1761)

75.    Editorial Note

A memorandum of October 16, 1961, from Special Assistant to the President for National Security Affairs McGeorge Bundy to the President reads in part as follows:

"We are going to get a blast from Adlai on our assurances to Chiang. He feels greatly distressed not to have been consulted, especially about our private assurance that we will use the veto if necessary and effective. Harlan Cleveland briefed him on this yesterday at the Secretary's direction, and Adlai spent the day muttering about resignation. He will be writing you direct to ask for an appointment Monday." (Kennedy Library, National Security Files, Countries Series, China, General, CIA Cables, 7/61–10/16/61)

A memorandum of October 18 from Representative to the United Nations Stevenson to Secretary Rusk objected to the proposed public statement on Chinese representation. The first paragraph reads as follows:

"The timing of this statement could not be worse. It could cause us acute trouble in sustaining our good faith in asking for a study committee and prejudice our chances of winning approval. It will be interpreted by many as excluding the chance of a compromise policy next year, such as the successor state approach. Others will interpret it, coming at this time, as confirmation that our proposal for a study committee is insincere and only a device to postpone. I will not comment here on other possible effects on confidence in our leadership in the United Nations."

Stevenson suggested a revision of the language of the second sentence of the statement and suggested a supplementary statement which could be used to explain and enlarge upon the President's statement. (Ibid.)

Handwritten notes prepared by Stevenson for a meeting with the President criticize the "deal with Chiang" on the veto as unnecessary, against Chiang's own interests, and "grossly dishonest". One point reads, "Diminishes chances of a compromise pol. next year—2 China policy." A handwritten notation indicates that Stevenson discussed the subject with Kennedy at Newport, Rhode Island, on October 22. No record of the meeting has been found. (Princeton University, Seeley G. Mudd Manuscript Library, Stevenson Papers, Previously Embargoed Files, Box 2, Chiang Kai-shek, 1961)

Bundy's memorandum to Kennedy cited above also stated that he thought there was one "loose end" in the communications through Cline. He attached a draft cable to Cline, which he intended to check with Rusk. The draft message pointed out that the Chinese representation question might not present itself in a form subject to the veto, that the veto of one proposal might result in another proposal that was still less desirable but not clearly subject to the veto, and that the use of the veto might therefore not be effective in all cases. It stated that President Kennedy wanted to be sure that President Chiang did not mistake his assurance for an unconditional guarantee, and it suggested that Cline consult with Ambassadors Yeh and Drumright as to whether this was sufficiently clear to President Chiang or whether "the danger of misunderstanding and consequent breakdown of partnership next year" was grave enough to make further action necessary. The memorandum bears a handwritten note stating that at Rusk's request the draft message was not sent.

On October 25 the United Nations Security Council recommended the admission of the Mongolian People's Republic to the United Nations by a vote of 9–0 with 1 abstention (United States). The Republic of China did not participate in the voting. (U.N. doc. S/4968) Mongolia was admitted to the United Nations by General Assembly Resolution 1630 (XVI), adopted by acclamation on October 27. The Republic of China did not participate in the voting.

On December 1 Australia, Colombia, Italy, Japan, and the United States introduced a draft resolution deciding that any proposal to change the representation of China was an important question. The resolution was adopted on December 15 as Resolution 1668 (XVI) by a vote of 61 to 34 with 7 abstentions. The text of the resolution is printed in *American Foreign Policy: Current Documents, 1961*, page 145.

---

**76.    Draft Paper Prepared in the Policy Planning Council**

Washington, October 26, 1961.

U.S. POLICY TOWARD CHINA

[Here follow a table of contents and 111 pages of text.]

*V.    Recommendations*

Although a variety of considerations converge in some of the following recommendations, they have been arranged, for purposes of convenience, in related groups.

---

Source: Department of State, Central Files, 611.93/10–2661. Top Secret. Drafted by Rice, according to a memorandum of January 4, 1962, to Ball from Robert W. Barnett of the Foreign Economic Advisory Staff in Ball's office, which forwarded the paper to Ball with Barnett's comments and the suggestion that Ball read the paper's recommendations. (Filed with a covering memorandum of February 21 from Barnett to Harvey; National Archives and Records Administration, RG 59, S/P Files: Lot 69 D 121, China) A memorandum of December 11 from Harriman to Rostow conveyed the Bureau of Far Eastern Affairs comments on the paper. (Department of State, Central Files, 611.93/12–1161)

## A. Basic Strategy

(1) We should pursue toward mainland China the general policy of seeking: (a) to hold ajar the door to a more satisfactory relationship with the US, (b) to mute our shared hostility, (c) to transfer to Communist China the onus for it, and (d) at the same time to build more effective barriers to the expansion in Asia of the Sino-Soviet bloc.

## B. Manifestations of a Humanitarian Concern for the Chinese People

(2) We should proceed to lift the embargo on exports to Communist China of foodgrains (including flour) and medicines, and consider, in the light of other recommendations contained herein, whether trade with Communist China should not be put on a comparable basis with trade with the Soviet Union.

(3) If recommendation (2) is accepted in whole or part, we should adopt a policy of giving bunkering facilities at least to all ships coming to our ports with cargo for Communist China which is restricted to foodstuffs (or other items from which we lift the embargo).

(4) We should explain changes in the embargo, and the modification of bunkering restrictions, in terms of putting concern for the welfare of the Chinese people above our differences with the regime which rules them.

(5) When that may appear warranted by a situation of more acute privation on the mainland than now exists there, and provided Communist China has been abstaining from new commitments to export foodstuffs from its own stocks, we should extend an offer of foodstuffs to Communist China on a grant basis. Any supply of US grain to Communist China should be accompanied, in the unlikely event that it is accepted, by safeguards against subsequent Chinese Communist charges about its suitability for human consumption.

(6) We should actively seek to share with Communist China information about medical advances likely to be helpful to the Chinese people.

(7) We should supply consistently, by radio or otherwise, weather information including typhoon warnings derived from our weather satellites.

## C. Removal of Unnecessary Provocations

(8) We should review US and GRC special operations against the Chinese mainland and thereafter desist ourselves, and try to keep the GRC from carrying out, ones which we conclude are likely to be more provocative than is justified by the anticipated return.

(9) We should review and revise US practices to ensure that our planes and ships do not without sufficient reasons, based on intelligence needs and operational requirements, penetrate Chinese Communist territorial waters and airspace.

*D. Negotiation and Communication with Communist China*

(10) We should continue the Ambassadorial talks.

(11) We should continue the policy of non-recognition of Communist China.

(12) We should determine what conditions we would set for recognition of Communist China and be prepared to restudy the question of recognition whenever altered circumstances, such as ones involving changes in the actions and apparent objectives of the Chinese Communist regime, and its own attitude toward diplomatic relations with us, may appear to justify such reconsideration.

(13) We should continue the present policy of attempting to keep Communist China out of the United Nations.

(14) We should initiate a study having as its aims the formulation of alternate objectives to be sought when and if it may become apparent that our aim of keeping Communist China out of the UN is no longer realistic, the tactics required to achieve those objectives, and the best timing for the initiation of the relevant efforts.

(15) We should consider the inclusion of Communist China in disarmament negotiations importantly involving its military capabilities if and when it may appear that substantive progress with the Soviet Union is likely.

(16) We should explore the feasibility of including Communist China in case of renewed negotiations for a nuclear test ban despite the likelihood that its response would be negative.

(17) We should endeavor to assure that any invitation to Communist China to participate in negotiations for disarmament or a nuclear test ban be portrayed in terms such that the onus for any refusal to participate would rest on the Chinese Communists.

(18) We should avoid hasty responses to Communist Chinese statements, no matter how provocative, as well as a shrill tone and any unnecessary vituperation in our own statements.

(19) Without exerting undue pressure, we should continue to seek access to Communist China by US correspondents and, within the limits set by concern for the safety of Americans in a country where we cannot afford them diplomatic protection, pursue the objective of gaining access to Communist China for other qualified American observers, scientists, scholars and, if trade is resumed, businessmen.

(20) We should utilize potentially useful Chinese Communist declarations, such as the self-imposed restrictions inherent in the five principles enunciated at Bandung, in contexts which may permit us to mobilize support for holding the Chinese Communists to them.

### E. Military and Nuclear

(21) We should increase the non-nuclear military capabilities we maintain in the western Pacific area, including capabilities related to counter-guerrilla operations.

(22) We should develop and covertly disseminate in Asia such propaganda as may tend to reduce the impact which will be made there by the first Chinese Communist nuclear explosion, and to lessen its contribution to the belief that Communism provides a superior blueprint for national development.

(23) We should avoid statements or actions which unnecessarily contribute to the view that Communist China's military strength and expected acquisition of nuclear weapons make it too powerful for its neighbors to resist.

(24) We should promote and support Japanese and Indian leadership of and assistance to other Asian states in the field of peaceful uses of atomic energy and materiels, and widest possible recognition of that leadership.

(25) We should ascertain what bilateral measures, such as training indigenous forces in the use of US nuclear weapons and stationing nuclear missiles in the respective countries, or in the case of Japan perhaps eventually on ships at sea, seem feasible and best adapted to reducing Communist China's opportunities to use nuclear blackmail against its Asian neighbors.

(26) We should endeavor to turn the prospective Chinese Communist acquisition of a nuclear capability to positive account as the rationale for rapprochements between Japan and the ROK, and of India with Pakistan, and their closer mutual involvement in such contexts as integrated air-defenses of the Korea–Japan area and of the Indian sub-continent.

(27) We should investigate the alternatives to stationing nuclear weapons on US-held bases close to the Chinese mainland, such as their transfer to US-held territories farther to the east.

(28) We should endeavor to convert pressures which may develop against our retention of bases in countries such as Japan to pressures for the development of independent indigenous military capabilities, and assumption of corresponding responsibility in respect of regional defense arrangements, as necessary prerequisites for any phasing downward of the military presence of the US.

### F. Protecting the States on Communist China's Periphery

(29) We should take steps designed to ensure that the requirements for preventing Thailand and other threatened Asian states from being successfully subjected to the Maoist cycle of infiltration and insurrection are analyzed, that the results are embodied in country-plans, and that

they are met through the efforts of the threatened states, the US, and other cooperating countries.

(30) We should, as a matter of urgency, determine what change we should promote in the international relationships of the mainland states of southeast Asia, including relationships toward each other, in the interests of their survival in the face of Communist China's growing power and the threat to them of ambiguous forms of Communist aggression.

(31) We should promote widest possible international recognition that bloc instigation and support of internal violence of the type now underway in Southeast Asia constitutes aggression directed at the national independence of the states involved, and endeavor to translate this recognition into appropriate inhibitory international action both within and outside the United Nations.

(32) We should, starting in FY 1963, program for the ROK economic aid of kinds and in amounts which appear required to put and keep it on the road to economic viability, and be prepared to accept the risks inherent in phasing down the size of ROK forces to levels which can be ROK supported.

(33) We should use our influence on and aid to Taiwan as means not only of protecting that island through our alliance with the GRC, but also of progressively promoting the timely emergence there of government based on popular consent and minimizing our over-identification with the GRC as it is now constituted and motivated.

(34) We should work, within the limits which the need for a continued useful relationship with the GRC will allow, for the damping-down of the GRC-Chinese Communist civil war and the evacuation of the offshore islands, considering as a first step seeking a major reduction in the garrisons on purely military grounds.

(35) We should, in dealing with Chiang, accept the risks inherent in pressing for change, in place of those which are implicit in letting the GRC pursue present courses, make appropriate elements of our aid conditional so it can be used as a lever in pressing for change, and time pressures for major specific changes so they occur in the context of maximum assurance of continued over-all US support.

(36) We should prepare for the contingency that Communist China may embark on a more aggressive but still sub-belligerent course, which might both require and make internationally acceptable the application to it of maximum pressure short of war, by a study exploring what forms of pressure might be applied, evaluating how much each element might contribute, and estimating how effective the totality might be if all acceptable components were combined.

### G. The Sino-Soviet Split

(37) We should continue study of the measures we might best take in order to take advantage of the present Sino-Soviet split in the interests of widening it further or of otherwise exploiting it.

### H. Internal and External Adjustment for an Altered Course

(38) We should center responsibility within the Department of State for affairs related to mainland China (and perhaps for the rest of Communist Asia as well) in an office different from that responsible for relations with the GRC.[1]

(39) We should make such official efforts to inform the US public in regard to Chinese affairs, including facts regarding influences exerted directly on US public opinion by the GRC, as prospective changes in policies toward it may promise to require.

(40) We should consult with appropriate allies and other friendly countries, including especially Japan, in advance of altering courses toward either Chinese regime, in the interests of securing maximum international understanding and support for US policy in an area where we are now too largely isolated.

---

[1] On December 26 the Office of Chinese Affairs and the Office of Northeast Asian Affairs were consolidated into the Office of East Asian Affairs, comprising sections for Japanese Affairs, Korean Affairs, Republic of China Affairs, and Mainland China Affairs (including Hong Kong and Macau). The Harriman memorandum cited in the source note noted that this recommendation had "already been anticipated" in the impending reorganization.

---

### 77.   Editorial Note

At the 493d meeting of the National Security Council on November 15, 1961, Director of Central Intelligence Allen W. Dulles and Deputy Director for Intelligence Robert Amory briefed the Council on Sino-Soviet relations and the situation in China, and there was some related discussion. A record of the meeting, probably drafted by the Vice President's military aide Howard L. Burris, describes this portion of the meeting as follows:

"Mr. Dulles opened the meeting with the reading and discussion of a prepared report on the Soviet-Chinese rift. Following the presentation the President asked for the basis of the current impasse between Russia and Albania. Mr. Dulles replied that it was obviously ideological since Albania was one of the smallest countries in Europe with the lowest per capita income and possibilities and potential in general. Mr. Amory then discussed the current food and agricultural shortages in Communist China and brought out the fact that Chinese advances have been generally retarded across the board because of crop shortages. The deficient diet has tended to diminish efficiency in other fields of endeavor. Production generally is on the decline. A brief outline of the size and disposition of Chinese armed forces was given. The President then asked what routes of movement are available for these troops from China to North Viet Nam. Mr. Amory pointed out and described the condition of railway and roads of access and cited the generally inadequate aspects of these avenues. Mr. Dulles cautioned that it should not be assumed that the Chinese setbacks as well as the ideological rift were such that the Soviets and Chinese would not be able nor willing to engage jointly any nation which threatened Communist interests." (Johnson Library, Vice Presidential Security File, National Security Council (II))

The record of the subsequent discussion, which concerned Vietnam, is printed in volume I, pages 607–610.

---

**78.   Telegram From the Embassy in Poland to the Department of State**

Warsaw, November 28, 1961, 6 p.m.

924. Beam–Wang talks. 107 meeting.[1] 1 hour 50 minutes.

1. Nothing new emerged. Wang slightly less caustic. Opened saying since last meeting US had continued statements hostile to PRC and aggressive activities all round its periphery. Complained of US military exercises in collaboration with GRC and around Okinawa and of aggressive acts South Vietnam and Laos. Attacked US for preventing PRC from rightful representation UN, disrupting activities Geneva conference on Laos, alleged plans establish Northeast Asia alliance and US occupation Taiwan. Reasserted that sooner or later US must withdraw its forces from

---

Source: Department of State, Central Files, 611.93/11–2861. Confidential; Priority; Limit Distribution. Repeated to Taipei, Hong Kong, Geneva, and Moscow.

[1] Beam commented on the meeting and sent recommendations for the next meeting in telegram 927 from Warsaw, November 29, and sent a detailed, apparently verbatim report of the meeting in airgram A–391, December 1. (Ibid., 611.93/11–2961 and 611.93/12–161, respectively)

Taiwan and Straits. Quoted Montgomery there is only one China with seat in Peking. Repeatedly referred to President Kennedy's statements on China as proof US has no intention abandoning hostile attitude towards CPR and Chinese people. Contrasted with Chen Yi's offer raise talks to Foreign Minister level.[2] Said had been 15 serious violations Chinese territory since last meeting.

2.   Above emerged during some half dozen exchanges in which I followed guidelines Deptels 774[3] and 786.[4] Near close I said both sides have certain interests viewed as vital which so far irreconcilable. This why we had considered it best concentrate on those areas where it seemed reasonable and just agreement might be possible. Wang ignored my statements re imprisoned Americans, missing servicemen and exchange of newsmen. Returned to picture of China as injured party with American occupation Taiwan and military activities on mainland periphery constituting aggression. When I observed world had become too small and its tools of destruction too absolute permit any but peaceful avenue, Wang responded 650 million Chinese people could not be frightened.

3.   After some discussion during which Wang insisted on specific date, I agreed on February 6 for next meeting with clear understanding this may be altered either direction depending on arrival my successor.[5] Wang's goodbye to me was gracious.

**Beam**

---

[2] Ch'en Yi's suggestion was made in a press interview on October 11. President Kennedy responded at a press conference that day that the United States was in communication with the Chinese Communists at Geneva and at Warsaw. He continued, "But we have not seen any evidence as yet that the Chinese Communists wish to live in comity with us, and our desire is to live in friendship with all people. But we have not seen that attitude manifested." (*Public Papers of the Presidents of the United States: John F. Kennedy, 1961*, p. 658)

[3] Telegram 774 to Warsaw, November 22, instructed Beam to review the current situation concerning the talks and to declare that while the U.S. side had proposed practical measures to reduce tension, Wang's side had carried on a "campaign of obstruction" amounting to "negation of the essential concept of these talks." It instructed Beam to tell Wang that Beam's successor as Ambassador at Warsaw would also succeed him as U.S. representative in the ambassadorial talks and would get in touch with Wang after he arrived in Warsaw to arrange the next meeting. (Department of State, Central Files, 611.93/11–2261)

[4] Telegram 786, November 24, provided guidance on Southeast Asia for use if necessary to rebut charges. (Ibid., 611.93/11–2461)

[5] The meeting date was subsequently changed to March 1. Telegram 1012 to Warsaw, January 26, proposed a date of March 6, since Beam's successor, John M. Cabot, would not arrive in Warsaw until near the end of February. Telegram 1178 from Warsaw, January 29, reported a Chinese counterproposal of March 1 because Wang had to return to China immediately thereafter to attend a meeting. (Ibid., 611.93/1–2662 and 611.93/1–2962)

### 79.    Memorandum From the Ambassador to India (Galbraith) to the Under Secretary of State for Economic Affairs (Ball)

New Delhi, November 30, 1961.

I am addressing the three of you on a matter which requires your immediate and urgent attention. The issue, which is one on which my ideas are conclusively formed, involves the continuation of a series of adventures launched under the past Administration [*1-1/2 lines of source text not declassified*]. It keeps going an activity started by the last Administration but about which that Administration had manifested sufficient uneasiness to halt. The reasons for the operation, which in my view were never sufficient, have diminished in value and now depend in part, as in the case of Cuba, on the fact that men have been trained, action is under way and now must be continued and in part on intelligence yield.

*History*

The history of the operation extends back over several years. At the time of the ChiCom takeover in Tibet, refugees came out which included quite a few able-bodied men. A group of these were taken to a special establishment [*less than 1 line of source text not declassified*] where they were trained in guerrilla tactics. [*5-1/2 lines of source text not declassified*] The stated purpose was to prevent the consolidation of the hold of the Chinese on Tibet, draw off Chinese resources into the insurrection there and keep in the public eye the image of Chinese aggression in the area.

At the time of the U–2 attempt in the summer of 1960 President Eisenhower became aware or conscious of the operation [*1-1/2 lines of source text not declassified*]. The number east of Lhasa was built up to the neighborhood of about 1000. Pressure to supply them developed. I became aware of plans [*less than 1 line of source text not declassified*] last spring shortly before coming to India. By that time the political and economic return could only be defended in the most modest terms. [*2 lines of source text not declassified*] The operation had been strongly opposed by my predecessor, Ellsworth Bunker. Richard Bissell described it as of marginal yield. It seemed particularly unfortunate in the light of the then unsettled state of the Laos situation. I raised the matter with the President one morning at breakfast, [*2-1/2 lines of source text not declassified*].

[*1 paragraph (8 lines of source text) not declassified*][1]

---

Source: Department of State, Central Files, 691C.93B3/11–3061. Secret; Eyes Only for Under Secretary Ball. Also sent to Harriman and McGhee.

[1] Galbraith urged in telegram 2518 from New Delhi, April 28, directed to Kennedy, Rusk, Bowles, and Bundy, that the operation should be abandoned, [*text not declassified*], and any U.S. connection with the force in Nepal should be severed and the latter encouraged to disperse. (Ibid., 793B.00/4–2861) Bowles replied in a letter of May 12 [*text not declassified*], Galbraith would be fully consulted. (Ibid.)

Meanwhile, training continued. The [*less than 1 line of source text not declassified*] groups have come under the leadership of the people trained [*less than 1 line of source text not declassified*] and they are regarded as being much more competent than those eliminated west of Lhasa. Forays into Tibet have occurred. And pressure to supply them has built up. Under Alexis Johnson as Deputy Under Secretary it has had a measure of success. Two or three days ago I had a peculiarly insulting telegram from Johnson saying [*less than 1 line of source text not declassified*] that my objections were known and had been rejected.[2] This was presumed to take care of the promised consultation. I immediately cabled Bundy and the President through intelligence channels[3] and I may add sent some homely truths to Johnson. These have assuaged my anger but have not left me any easier in my mind as to the operation. The objections, which are in all circumstances numerous and compelling, [*8-1/2 lines of source text not declassified*].

[*4 paragraphs (34 lines of source text) not declassified*]

Against these overwhelming objections the gains are negligible. [*2 lines of source text not declassified*] This hope has of course disappeared. It was once thought that the operations would keep the Chinese from consolidating their hold on Tibet. Of this there is no chance. The operations cover a few square miles of an incredibly vast area. Finally, it is argued that by keeping alive the resistance, the Chinese aggression in Tibet is kept before world opinion. Again, the fact that this is confined to a few acres destroys this case. And it is further destroyed because little news leaks out even of these operations. Finally, it must be urged that there is intelligence yield. [*5 lines of source text not declassified*]

The truth is that the operation continues because it got started. [*4 lines of source text not declassified*]

This argument holds in effect that we must inherit and carry out faithfully the mistakes of the previous Administration. (Rather more faithfully than Eisenhower in fact because he cancelled the support operations after the U–2.) [*3-1/2 lines of source text not declassified*]

[*1 paragraph (6 lines of source text) not declassified*][4]

I should be sorry about this for my relations with CIA in this matter have been wholly satisfactory. They have discussed it candidly and at all levels and, while arguing for their own objectives, have not asserted the

---

[2] A copy of the message from Johnson to Galbraith, undated, is in the Kennedy Library, National Security Files, Countries Series, Tibet.

[3] A copy of the message, from Galbraith to Bundy for the President, dated November 27, is ibid. Galbraith sent a copy of his November 30 memorandum to Bundy with a covering letter of December 2, noting, "My intention is to deter but I do not wish to overkill." (Ibid.)

[4] The text of the letter, which Kennedy sent to all U.S. Ambassadors on May 29, is printed in Department of State *Bulletin,* December 11, 1961, pp. 993–994.

172 Foreign Relations, 1961–1963, Volume XXII

priority of these over the larger political considerations which it is our task to consider and which have not been considered.

Yours faithfully,

**John**

I am very serious abut this. Do get it under control.[5]

**JG**

---

5 The postscript was handwritten by Galbraith. Telegram 1913 to New Delhi, December 5, from Bundy to Galbraith, reported that Kennedy had decided the [*text not declassified*] should continue. (Department of State, Central Files, 793B.00/12–561) A December 9 memorandum from Bundy to Kennedy recommended [*text not declassified*]. (Kennedy Library, National Security Files, Countries Series, Tibet) DCI John McCone discussed Tibet with Kennedy on January 7, and according to his memorandum of the meeting, [*text not declassified*] preliminary discussions were underway. (Central Intelligence Agency, DCI (McCone) Files, Job 80–B01285A, Meetings with the President)

---

**80. Special National Intelligence Estimate**

SNIE 13–3–61                                        Washington, November 30, 1961.

## CHINESE COMMUNIST CAPABILITIES AND INTENTIONS IN THE FAR EAST

### The Problem

To estimate Communist China's objectives in the Far East, its assessment of its own position, and its capabilities and likely courses of action over the next two years or so; and to consider how these might be affected by the contingency of an open break in relations between the Chinese and Soviet Communist Parties.

---

Source: Department of State, INR/EAP Files: Lot 90 D 110, SNIE 13–3–61. Secret. According to a note on the covering sheet, the Central Intelligence Agency and the intelligence agencies of the Departments of State, the Army, the Navy, the Air Force, and the Joint Staff participated in the preparation of this estimate. All members of the USIB concurred in this estimate on November 30 except the representatives of the AEC and the FBI, who abstained on the grounds that the subject was outside their jurisdiction.

Conclusions

1.  Communist China almost certainly does not intend to attempt the open military conquest of any other Far Eastern country during the period of this estimate. Communist China's leaders believe that they can eventually achieve their objectives in the area at far less cost and risk through the techniques of Communist political warfare. When Peiping believes the circumstances are right, it will endeavor to supplement the more conventional forms of political warfare with guerrilla and terrorist action by indigenous forces, supported and guided by Peiping. (Paras. 23, 25)

2.  In any case, the Communist Chinese will seize every opportunity to undermine US standing and to generate anti-American feeling in the Far East. They will strive to promote discontent and instability in the pro-Western countries of the area. (Para. 24)

3.  Peiping has no compunctions about openly using its military forces to extend its control when it can do so with little or no risk. It will continue its refusal to renounce the use of force for the seizure of Taiwan and the offshore islands, but we believe that concern over retaliation by the US will deter it from attempting a military conquest of Taiwan or the offshore islands during at least the period of this estimate. However, the Chinese might undertake limited military action in the strait area to test Nationalist Chinese defenses and to probe US determination or to call world attention to what it terms "the danger to peace caused by the US occupation of a part of China's territory." (Paras. 26–27)

4.  Peiping's reluctance to launch a military invasion in the Far East will almost certainly not prevent it from reacting vigorously to any US or SEATO action which Peiping believed threatened its security. For example, if SEATO (or US armed forces alone) came to the defense of Laos or South Vietnam, Peiping's reaction would probably be to increase its aid to the Pathet Lao and the North Vietnamese while deploying substantial Chinese regular forces along its own southern border. In the more extreme situation where a SEATO or US action constituted a threat to North Vietnam which the North Vietnamese forces could not counter, the Chinese Communists would almost certainly intervene overtly with their own forces;[1] should such action appear to threaten the Communist position in northern Laos, the Chinese Communists would probably intervene overtly with their own forces. (Para. 28)

5.  If Sino-Soviet relations were to deteriorate, for example to the present level of Albanian-Soviet relations, Communist China's military

---

[1] Peiping's probable reactions to a number of intermediate courses of US action in South Vietnam are considered in SNIE 10–4–61, "Probable Communist Reactions to Certain US Actions in South Vietnam," dated 7 November 1961. (Top Secret, Limited Distribution) [Footnote in the source text. SNIE 10–4–61 is ibid.: Lot 90 D 99.]

capabilities would be somewhat reduced and Peiping would have much less confidence that it could count on the Soviet nuclear umbrella. Perhaps most important, such an open Sino-Soviet break would also reduce Communist China's capabilities for political warfare, at least in the short run. The very foundations of communism would be shaken and Sino-Soviet rivalry for dominant influence in the other Communist parties of Asia would have a disruptive effect on these parties and would substantially weaken them as instruments of subversion for the time being. (Paras. 30–31)

[Here follow paragraphs 6–31, comprising the Discussion portion of the estimate, in six sections entitled "Objectives," "Peiping's Estimate of the Situation," "Capabilities for Military Action and Subversion," "Foreign Policy," "Likely Courses of Action," and "The Contingency of a Sino-Soviet Split"; and a military annex with three tables and a map.]

---

81.    **Letter From the Under Secretary of State (Ball) to the Director, Food for Peace (McGovern)**

Washington, December 6, 1961.

DEAR GEORGE: Your memorandum of November 3 to Chester Bowles[1] came at a time when we were actively considering the question of foodstuffs for the people of mainland China. The Chinese Communists have admitted to Viscount Montgomery[2] and others that the 1961 harvest will be disappointing for the third successive year. Thus it would seem likely that Peiping's prospects for feeding its expanding and already undernourished population may become very grim in the early months of next year.

At Mr. Bowles' request, a statement of the recommended United States position was prepared in the Department's Bureau of Far Eastern Affairs. A copy of that statement is enclosed.[3] As you will see, our salient conclusions are these: first, that there is no change in the presumption

---

Source: Department of State, Central Files, 893.03/12–661. Secret. Drafted by Lindsey Grant of the Office of Chinese Affairs. Concurred in by the Bureau of Economic Affairs, the Legal Adviser's Office, and the Agency for International Development.

[1] This memorandum requested a statement of policy concerning "overtures of food assistance to Red China." (Ibid., 893.03/11–361)

[2] British Field Marshal Bernard Law Montgomery.

[3] Not found attached; presumably it was the statement of policy set forth in a November 21 memorandum from McConaughy to Ball, which Ball approved on December 6.

that the Chinese Communists will not ask for United States help and
would refuse it if offered; second, that the United States should not take
the initiative in offering such relief; third, that the United States Government should not now prejudge its reaction in the unlikely event that a
Chinese Communist request is received, but that certain important criteria as to whether to offer relief and the manner of doing so can now be set
forth.[4]

I enclose also a copy of a telegram which we sent to Ambassador
Everton in Rangoon, in response to a suggestion which he relayed from
U Nu to the effect that the United States provide wheat to Communist
China by means of a triangular PL 480 Title I deal through Burma.[5] I
believe that our telegram succinctly sets forth the Department's thinking
on the issue.

I should be much interested in learning your thinking on the problem.

Sincerely,

**George W. Ball**[6]

---

[4] The memorandum stated that consideration should be given only to a firm,
although not necessarily public, Chinese request for food, only to the direct supply of food
as a humanitarian gesture rather than to a sale or quasi-commercial arrangement, and only
to an arrangement in which relief foodstuffs would actually reach those in need.

[5] Telegram 296 to Rangoon, November 27, approved by Rusk, stated that such a proposal would "be bound to create an extremely sensitive political problem for this country"
and that "This consideration has added force in a period when Peiping seems to be splitting
even from Moscow in pursuance of a more aggressive policy, and when our own contacts
with the Chinese Communist authorities show no inclination or desire on their part to
lessen the threat or reduce tensions in the area. Southeast Asia is now exposed to a particularly vigorous penetration effort by the Communist bloc." (Department of State, Central
Files, 811.0093/11–2761) Further documentation on this proposal is ibid., 811.0093 and FE/
EA Files: Lot 65 D 93, Trade with Communist China, 1961.

[6] Printed from a copy that indicates Ball signed the original. Ball had assumed the
position of Under Secretary of State between the drafting of the letter and its signature.

## 82.    Memorandum From James C. Thomson, Jr., to the Assistant Secretary of State for Far Eastern Affairs (Harriman)

Washington, January 12, 1962.

SUBJECT

> Secretary's Policy Planning Meeting, January 2, 1962: Discussion of the Sino-Soviet Conflict and U.S. Policy[1]

In your meeting with Mr. Bowles earlier this week you requested that I pass on my recollections of the discussion that took place at the Secretary's Policy Planning Meeting on January 2. The paper under discussion was "The Sino-Soviet Conflict and U.S. Policy."[2] Here are the major comments, gathered from my notes on the meeting:

1. The Secretary termed the paper a highly important document and asked Mr. Rostow to make some introductory comments.

2. Mr. Rostow said that the Moscow–Peking split is clearly an historic and unprecedented development; however, (a) no one knows what to do about it, and (b) there is urgent need for a hard intelligence effort on the subject as we have little knowledge of the Chinese agricultural situation, of differences within the Chinese leadership, or of the impact of the split on other Communist parties.

3. Mr. Rusk proposed (a) that the Department arrange for the Council on Foreign Relations to put together at once a study group on the 22nd Party Congress whose major aim would be to examine, under this cover, the Sino-Soviet split; (b) that the Department establish a study group within NATO on the same subject for the same purpose; and (c) that we submit a sanitized version of the paper under discussion to Capitol Hill for use by the Foreign Relations and Foreign Affairs Committee chairmen. Mr. Hilsman commented that such studies were already under way, to some extent, at Harvard, Columbia, and Brookings.

4. Mr. Rusk asked to what extent the split involved a move toward the type of diversity we face within NATO. Mr. Bohlen commented that

---

Source: Department of State, Central Files, 661.93/1–1262. Thomson was Special Assistant to the President's Special Representative and Adviser on African, Asian, and Latin American Affairs, Chester Bowles.

[1] Another record of the meeting, drafted by Mose L. Harvey of the Policy Planning Council, is ibid., S/P Files: Lot 69 D 121, Secretary's Policy Planning Meetings. See also James C. Thomson, Jr., "On the Making of U.S. China Policy, 1961–9: A Study in Bureaucratic Politics," *The China Quarterly*, No. 50, April/June 1972, pp. 226–227.

[2] Reference is to a December 19 draft prepared in the Policy Planning Council. It declared that the Sino-Soviet conflict had reached a "critical stage," that the basic issue was one of supremacy within the Communist camp, that its ultimate source lay in a clash of national interests, and that it was likely to continue, perhaps until there was a "decisive break" in the world Communist movement. (Kennedy Library, Thomson Papers, Box 15, Far East, Communist China, Sino-Soviet Conflict and U.S. Policy, 4/30/62) Related drafts are in Department of State, S/P Files: Lot 67 D 548, USSR, 1961.

the evolving situation was not in fact a parallel to the divisions that exist within NATO.

5.  Mr. Rostow stressed the complex implications of the split for U.S. policy. He stated that it was essentially a favorable event for us, but in concrete situations it posed a variety of new and difficult problems (e.g., Southeast Asia).

6.  There was a general discussion as to what constitutes a "complete break," and whether a complete break is what we want to bring about. Mr. Rostow said that we must be careful not to build our intelligence effort around the concept of a "break"; there are too many varieties of breaks possible; we need a graduated system of analysis.

7.  Mr. Talbot noted the effects of the deepening rift on bilateral conflicts in his region and elsewhere. For instance, we see India moving somewhat closer to the USSR while Pakistan shows some signs of accommodation with Communist China. The result, he said, will be intensification of bilateral conflicts in many parts of the world. Mr. Rice agreed that global competition between China and Russia would be an inevitable outgrowth of the break.

8.  Mr. Bohlen said the essense of the quarrel is that the Russians have become the Mensheviks, while the Chinese are Bolsheviks. Mr. Bohlen added that the serious implications of the conflict are well understood by such orthodox leaders as Molotov: If you start changing the ideology you inevitably end up by changing the structure. Such a realization accounts for the opposition Khrushchev is encountering within the USSR.

9.  Mr. Chayes said that, historically, the break must be in our favor, as are all breaks in monoliths. He raised the question of the rift's effect on Outer Mongolia and the off-shore isles.

10.  Mr. Rusk asserted that this paper could be taken as a strong argument for establishing diplomatic relations with Outer Mongolia.

11.  Mr. Rostow discussed Yugoslav interest in polycentrism within the bloc. The Sino-Soviet conflict provides a temptation to Yugoslavia to "play the game" within the bloc; but such activities tend to destroy the position the Yugoslavs have built as a Communist neutral. In this regard, he pointed out that the Yugoslavs are reestablishing relations with the Indian Communist Party.

12.  Assuming that we favor polycentrism, Mr. Martin asked why we should consider providing any assistance at all to the Chinese Communists. Economic adversity would tend to increase tensions between Peiping and Moscow and therefore operates in our favor. Perhaps we should aim to support right-wing deviationists (Tito) but not left-wing deviationists (the Chinese).

13. Mr. Rusk agreed. He pointed out that Peiping combines old-fashioned Chinese imperialism as well as left-wing Communist deviationism.

14. Mr. Tubby suggested that, in view of the break, we place more emphasis on our struggle against Chinese nationalism and Russian nationalism rather than our struggle against communism.

15. Mr. Harvey commented that there had been two types of Soviet attempts to force their decisions on the Chinese: first, by making USSR party decisions binding on other parties (rejected by the Chinese), and second by making Communist World Congress decisions binding on other parties (the Chinese say such decisions must be unanimous to be binding). As a result of these two failures, Mr. Harvey said, the monolith no longer exists.

16. Mr. Rusk said that this might be true, but what if their objectives remain the same? Mr. Harvey replied that their objectives are no longer the same.

17. Mr. McGhee said that the West is moving from diversity towards unity while the Communists are disintegrating from a monolith into diversity. He added that the resulting internal competition within the Communist system now acts as an escape valve for energies that were originally focused entirely on us.

18. Mr. Rostow said that there are three elements of such competition within communism: (a) competition in third countries through local Communist parties; (b) competition over the central issue of who gets nuclear weapons and what type of control is to be exercised over them (a national fight on degrees of sovereignty similar to conflicts within NATO); and (c) probable competition within the Chinese Communist hierarchy, which is not likely to retain its present monolithic form as the old leaders are replaced.

19. Mr. Hilsman added that INR is preparing two relevant studies, one on Chinese Communist leadership, and one on Chinese nuclear capability.[3]

20. Mr. McGhee said that the new era of diversity affords us possibilities for leverage within Communist parties outside of the bloc.

21. Mr. Rostow said that the paper implies one major decision which may be forced on us any day now: what do we do if Mao dies and there is a crisis within the Chinese leadership? Do we give them a vision of the possibility of better relations with us if they calm down? Or do we buckle them in even more tightly with the Russians?[4]

---

[3] Neither found.

[4] A marginal notation in Harriman's handwriting reads: "Stalin—'We can't supply' capital needs".

22. Mr. Rusk said that we face two immediate needs: (a) a review of possible USSR divergencies on specific issues that have arisen since 1950 (for instance, the Korean war negotiations); and (b) a study of the rift's effect on post-Goa bilateral situations (such as the conflict between Guatemala and Great Britain over British Honduras). He added that we must be careful not to overemphasize Chinese Communist military and economic power. The key question is "power where"? Relative Chinese power on the North India border, for instance, is considerably less than Chinese power elsewhere. Also, we must relate our evaluation to the resources available and the jobs to be done. Mr. Rusk added that we should give some attention to the tradition of the turnover of governments in China throughout the centuries: for instance, what constitutes the Mandate of Heaven, and when does a government lose it?[5]

23. Mr. Rice responded that the Mandate of Heaven will be lost when the party,[6] army, and security forces are no longer responsive to orders from the top. There is no evidence as yet of such a development on the Mainland.

24. Mr. Rusk raised additional questions regarding the possible recrudescence of Chinese warlordism and regionalism. He felt that such factors should be studied in the perspective of Chinese history.[7]

---

[5] A marginal notation in Harriman's handwriting reads: "Can't consider China in any more exactly [illegible] context". Another reads: "Never before a Communist Party organization."

[6] A marginal notation in Harriman's handwriting reads: "Party selects leader."

[7] A marginal notation in Harriman's handwriting reads: "Is there any sign of warlordism? Isn't he overhopeful?"

## 83.    Letter From Secretary of State Rusk to the Dalai Lama

Washington, January 17, 1962.

YOUR HOLINESS: I thank you on behalf of President Kennedy and myself for your letters, which Mr. Gyalo Thondup delivered when he called at the Department of State.[1]

It has been heartening to have new proof, in the adoption by the United Nations General Assembly of the resolution concerning Tibet,[2] that most of the countries of the world join in the condemnation of the brutality and oppression which the Chinese Communists impose on the Tibetan people, and in the conviction that the principle of self-determination should apply to the people of Tibet.

The Chinese Communist authorities have publicly denounced the General Assembly's adoption of the resolution concerning Tibet. They have taken the position that "no foreign countries or international organizations, the United Nations included, have any right to meddle" in any aspect of the situation in Tibet. Their belligerence even toward countries which they had previously described as friendly has been evident in recent months. In these circumstances it will clearly not be easy to find effective means of halting the Chinese Communists' actions against the Tibetan people.

We are nevertheless determined to continue our efforts to help achieve a just and peaceful solution of this tragic problem. We are also hopeful that provisions may be expanded and improved for the assistance of those Tibetans who have had to take refuge outside their homeland. Your counsel, and that of your representatives, is always most welcome in these matters.

Respectfully yours,

**Dean Rusk**[3]

---

Source: Department of State, Central Files, 793B.00/1–1762. Drafted by Thomas W. Ainsworth of the Mainland China desk.

[1] A letter of October 17 from the Dalai Lama to President Kennedy is filed with a January 17 covering memorandum from Battle to Bundy. (Ibid.) The letter to Rusk has not been found. The Dalai Lama's brother, Gyalo Thondup, delivered the letters when he met with U. Alexis Johnson on December 18; a memorandum of that conversation is ibid., 793B.00/12–1861.

[2] Resolution 1723 (XVI) was adopted by the General Assembly on December 20 by a vote of 56 (including the United States) to 11, with 29 abstentions. The text is printed in *American Foreign Policy: Current Documents, 1961*, pp. 1641–1642.

[3] Printed from a copy that indicates Rusk signed the original.

84.    Memorandum From Robert W. Komer of the National
       Security Council Staff to the President's Special Assistant for
       National Security Affairs (Bundy)

Washington, January 29, 1962.

*Return to the Mainland*

This one is going to be quite a problem in 1962. Peiping's still acute economic crisis, the deepening Sino-Soviet schism, the aging Chiang's own feel that the GRC's own position is eroding, and finally Chiang's continuing apprehensions over US policy are all leading him to consider more and more a final gamble. There are renewed indications of GRC preparations for at least probing operations. Now Gimo himself has asked Cline whether time ripe for discussing whole issue with JFK (TDCS DB 3/649, 215 attached).[1]

Before fobbing Chiang off, let's at least consider his case. Certainly Peiping is feebler than at any time since it consolidated the 1947–49 revolution. It is obviously on its own, with the Soviets using a slow-down if not cessation of economic and military aid as a means to bring Mao back into line. Food shortage continues into third year, and we recently had good indications [*less than 1 line of source text not declassified*] that even the army's capabilities have been affected.[2] Moreover, the GRC *is* probably a wasting asset—so we too must consider whether or not to use it before it declines past the point of no return.

Ed Rice's excellent study on "return to the mainland"[3] concluded that it could only be successful if there were a major revolution in Red

---

Source: Kennedy Library, National Security Files, Countries Series, China, Return to Mainland, 1/62–5/62. Top Secret. Filed with a covering note of the same date from Komer to Bundy which reads as follows:

"We have two problems coming up re China: (1) probable ChiCom [*ChiNat*] approach on return to mainland; (2) question of food sales to ChiComs.

"These are of course two sides of same coin. We shouldn't start down either road without at least considering the other. Attached is a think piece on first road. I come out negative—but I don't think we should necessarily turn around and sell food to ChiComs. Will discuss these problems at State, but food issue at least is already on way to high-level decision."

[1] Dated January 26, it summarized a January 24 conversation with Chiang Kai-shek during which Chiang proposed an exchange of views on the circumstances under which GRC intervention on the mainland might be feasible and necessary or desirable. (Ibid.) The conversation was reported in more detail in telegram 270057Z from CIA to JCS. (Ibid.) See the Supplement.

[2] An appraisal of the documents under reference was sent to Kennedy with a January 9 covering memorandum from McCone. (Kennedy Library, President's Office Files, China Security, 1962–63) A number of them were published in translation in J. Chester Cheng, ed., *The Politics of the Chinese Red Army* (Stanford: Hoover Institution, 1966).

[3] Reference is apparently to a July 14 paper entitled "Unrest and Uprisings in Mainland China." (Kennedy Library, National Security Files, Countries Series, China)

China (even though one initially regional in character), which Chiang could support. The consensus to date has been that this is unlikely, even in Red China's present desperate state. But we must now ask ourselves whether GRC action might not precipitate such a revolution.

There are two broad options. One would be a major landing in South China designed to put several divisions ashore with adequate air cover and seize a bridgehead. Into it we would pour more divisions and air support. One bonus effect might be the impact on Communist operations in SEA. But many objections loom. First, Chiang simply lacks the resources (except for an unopposed landing in an area already in revolt). Thus he would need substantial US air cover, air and sea lift, and logistic support. I can't see this in the cards for us without some tremendous provocation by the ChiComs, such as their overt intervention in SEA.

In any case, if we made a major attempt to retake South China, the Chinese would almost certainly appeal for Soviet aid and the USSR would grant it in good measure. The Soviets would recognize that so long as they confined themselves to defending the ChiCom regime, most of world opinion would be with them; they would not in a period of nuclear stand-off be running unacceptable risk of US retaliation against the USSR itself. So why should they accept the major reverse involved in a successful western counter-attack in China, particularly since they would see an opportunity to re-establish their influence over Peiping. For all these reasons I cannot see us getting involved in even a local war with the USSR over China.

This leaves the option of local probing operations, initially small but if these prove out then on a gradually increasing scale, designed to see whether the GRC couldn't gin up a local revolution. Although Chiang might ask us to back the first option above, I suspect he would settle for our support or even tacit acquiescence in such probes. The GRC apparently has enough well-trained forces for small scale operations, although they are deficient in lift. There is some appeal in a probing operation designed to find out whether the ChiCom position is as brittle as some think. Moreover, the Soviets might not regard such probes as justifying their counter-intervention, but would prefer to let Peiping stew in its own juice, counting on a Peiping appeal to Moscow if the situation got out of hand.

But let's look further at this proposition. Assuming that it were successful and that a revolt of some size could be ginned up, we would then be faced with the circumstances described under first option above. The GRC would argue for a major campaign, with substantial US support. So our very success would lead to a situation in which Peiping, humbling itself, would have to turn to the Soviets for aid. Then we'd have a major US/USSR war in China which, even if it did not spread, we'd be unlikely to win. Also, what if the GRC failed, even after an initial success? Assuming that the failure were visible enough, it might mean the end of the GRC's pretensions as "the only legitimate government" of China. In fact, the backlash of an unsuccessful attempt would only undermine further the GRC's international position and make it even more difficult for us to preserve it as an independent government on Taiwan. Chiang might be willing to take this gamble, but should we?

There is, of course, a third possible outcome between failure and complete success. In effect the GRC could stir up enough unrest in South China to deplete further ChiCom resources and energies and to make even more difficult Peiping's economic recovery. However, even this could lead the ChiComs to make their peace with Moscow (at least temporarily—most of us feel that, whatever happens, Sino-Soviet tie will never be the same again).

Note that my argument against unleashing Chiang is not based on any value judgment as to whether the ChiComs are now weak enough to make the odds favorable—*it is based on my contention that, no matter how weak the ChiComs are, the Soviets won't let us succeed.* Before discarding the possibility on these grounds, however, let's ask ourselves what happens once Peiping recovers from its current predicament (as is likely, short of some further pressure on it). Since this recovery will probably coincide with ChiCom acquisition of their first home-grown nuclear weapons, it is a gloomy prospect indeed. Therefore, we should at least consider any option which might prolong Peiping's time of troubles so as to allow Japanese and Indian strength to grow and to buy time to strengthen such peripheral areas as SEA, Korea, etc.

The above becomes doubly relevant when we might go in the opposite direction and sell food to the ChiComs. Harriman is looking into bona fides of Seattle firm's claim ChiComs want to buy 400,000 tons of grain on normal commercial basis.[4] His inclination is to go ahead, largely because ChiCom dollars spent for food leave that much less for industrial buildup. But let's think thrice before we start down this road: (a) ChiCom needs are so much greater than piddling 400,000 tons that this feeler, if valid, is just to see whether we'll play; (b) Gimo will surely blow his top if we start feeding ChiComs when he wants to push them over; (c) what about effect on new trade bill passage if we start trading with Chi-Coms at this point?

---

[4] Reference is to an application by a Seattle firm for an export license to export wheat and barley to China and North Korea. A memorandum of January 25 from Martin and Harriman to McGhee outlined the situation and expressed doubt as to whether a bona fide Chinese order existed. (Department of State, S/S–NSC Files: Lot 70 D 265, NSC Standing Group, January 26, 1962) According to the Record of Actions at a meeting of the NSC Standing Group on January 26, the Standing Group noted that the Central Intelligence Agency would seek to obtain further information and the Department of State would prepare recommendations. (Ibid.) Further information concerning the proposed sale is ibid., Central File, 493.119.

*After considering all these factors, I still come down on the side of keeping the Gimo on a tight leash.* Prospects for success in a major spoiling operation directed at Red China are highly problematical, particularly since the Soviets have the counter-option of checkmating us at any time they choose. They might let Peiping stew awhile to teach it a lesson, but if things got bad enough they wouldn't hesitate to step in. If they did so, we would have succeeded in pushing Peiping and Moscow together again, in effect postponing the day when the two giants of the Communist world may be at each other's throats instead of ours. Moreover, bad as things are on the mainland, there is no evidence of any feeling that the GRC could make them better (even if we could get across that it would bring with it huge quantities of US food and other aid).

If backing Chiang in a last dramatic gamble is against our interests, let's start thinking now about the painful task of dissuading him. Drumright and Cline feel that we will shortly get a major approach from the GRC. Instead of waiting for it, there might be some advantage in jumping first by telling them how we look at the situation.

State did attempt a minor operation of this sort in asking Drumright to tell Gimo we hoped his New Year's Day speech call for "return to the mainland" in 1962 meant no change in policy, and reminding him of the required prior consultation with US.[5] Drumright replied that this would only outrage Chiang and revive his latent apprehensions about new administration's China policy.[6] So State told Drumright merely to talk with the Foreign Minister.[7] This won't quite do if we are going to have the necessary impact on the Gimo. We need to be more forthright and honest and to have some trade goods at hand, perhaps more development aid. We may also need a special envoy to carry this word (Harriman?), since Drumright can't do it effectively.

*Recommendation:* That we tell State President has noted indications of quickening ChiNat interest in a return to mainland, doubts GRC would have much success, and would like State's views, including whether we should attempt to forestall any upcoming Chiang approach to him (see attached).[8]

**Bob K.**

---

[5] The message was sent in telegram 410 to Taipei, January 8. (Ibid., 793.00/1–862)

[6] Drumright replied in telegram 525 from Taipei, January 11. (Ibid., 793.00/1–1162)

[7] The message was sent in telegram 424 to Taipei, January 17. (Ibid.) Drumright met with Shen on February 9. He reported the conversation in telegram 569, February 13. (Ibid., 793.00/2–1362)

[8] Attached was a draft memorandum from Bundy to Rusk, apparently not sent.

## 85.    Editorial Note

A memorandum of February 6, 1962, to President Kennedy from Chester Bowles argued that the Chinese food crisis might offer an opportunity to lessen "the danger of Chinese expansionism" and offered the non-Communist world an opportunity "to gain some important leverage in its economic relations with the Peiping regime." He suggested beginning with "a highly confidential effort to explore Chinese Communist attitudes." He was about to leave on a trip to the Middle East and Asia, and he suggested that he stop in Rangoon to discuss the subject with Burmese Prime Minister U Nu. (Kennedy Library, President's Office Files, China Security)

Bowles states in a memoir that he met with Kennedy before his departure and asked him if the United States would be prepared "to sell a limited amount of wheat to the Chinese on an emergency basis for hard currency and without political conditions" and "if China would agree not to attempt to change its existing borders by force (without necessarily forfeiting its claims to territories outside its present borders)," whether it would be prepared "to offer much larger quantities of wheat on a continuing, low interest, long-term basis?"

According to Bowles, Kennedy "readily agreed" to the first proposal, suggesting as much as 3 to 5 million tons. Concerning the second proposal, Kennedy said that "if some reliable means of communication could be opened up," he would consider an agreement to sell 10 to 12 million tons of American wheat annually on a long-term, easy-credit basis, "provided China agreed to abandon its present military-political pressures on its neighbors." Bowles states that Kennedy agreed that Bowles could advance these proposals with U Nu, describing them as proposals that he had discussed in general terms with the President but which had not been formally approved. Bowles was not able to meet with U Nu, however; the latter's government was overthrown the day before Bowles was scheduled to leave New Delhi for Rangoon. (*Promises to Keep: My Years in Public Life, 1941–1969* (New York: Harper & Row, 1971), pages 470–471)

According to Kennedy's Appointment Book, Bowles met with Kennedy for 25 minutes on February 6. (Kennedy Library) No other record has been found of the conversation.

### 86.   Telegram From the Embassy in the Republic of China to the Department of State

Taipei, February 28, 1962, 2 p.m.

596. For Governor Harriman. No doubt you have seen reports transmitted [*less than 1 line of source text not declassified*] of further approaches made [*less than 1 line of source text not declassified*] and William Bundy on occasion of latter's recent visit to Taiwan.[1] These proposals by President Chiang and his son are regarded here as a further, more concrete approach to USG and as indicating Chiang's desire for consultations at high level and his hopes for US assent to plan he is suggesting or some feasible modification thereof. Chiang's latest approach also suggests quickening of his resolve to "do something about mainland" in months ahead. I have reviewed Chiang's latest approach together with [*less than 1 line of source text not declassified*], Commander TDC and Chief MAAG. There was agreement that USG must soon take cognizance in one form or another of Chiang's latest suggested plans. It was agreed that best choice of action as of now would be [*less than 1 line of source text not declassified*] to continue discussions. In doing so he should attempt without commitment to obtain specific details of Chiang's latest plans for consideration by US authorities. Once specific plans were obtained, [*less than 1 line of source text not declassified*] US military authorities here would study them for feasibility and pass their views to higher US authorities for consideration. Consensus was that in discussing problem with Chiang and his son a sympathetic attitude on our part would be desirable as to keep GRC side engaged and thus permit US side to study proposals and submit observations and counter proposals. There was general agreement that cold shouldering or ignoring of Chiang's proposals was least desirable course of action and could lead to undesirable actions and consequences. It was also consensus that in discussing problem further GRC side should be pressed to present concrete intelligence to support its estimates of mainland conditions and possibilities of sparking uprising among people. (In this respect it was concluded that Chiang is predicat-

---

Source: Department of State, Central Files, 793.00/2–2862. Secret; Roger Channel. Received at 1:40 p.m.

[1] Bundy's message, dated February 24, to McNamara and McGeorge Bundy reported a meeting the previous evening with Chiang Kai-shek, in which Chiang argued for a counterattack on the mainland. He declared that the GRC did not want U.S. participation but "tacit agreement" and perhaps secret or indirect logistic support; Bundy was noncommittal and stressed the importance of joint consultations. (Filed with a February 24 covering memorandum from Desmond FitzGerald of the CIA to Bundy; Kennedy Library, National Security Files, Countries Series, China) See the Supplement. A Chinese record of Bundy's conversation with Chiang Kai-shek and a conversation with Chiang Ching-kuo is summarized in TDCSDB–3/649, 521. (Kennedy Library, National Security Files, Countries Series, China)

ing his plans of touching off uprising on assumptions rather than realistic intelligence appraisals.)

In light of foregoing discussion it was agreed [*less than 1 line of source text not declassified*] continue discussions with Chiang and his son designed to elicit further concrete details. In doing so [*less than 1 line of source text not declassified*] make it clear continuing talks implied no new commitments. [*less than 1 line of source text not declassified*] also discreetly keep to fore requirement on part of GRC to observe restraints set forth in Mutual Defense Treaty and related agreements.

Although Chiang is quite obviously reluctant to discuss this problem with me, I expect to touch on it when I see him before departing Taiwan.[2] I shall [not] accept Chiang's plan in its present form, [but] I would hope that it would be possible for Washington to respond in such way as not to constitute a flat negative. Otherwise, we risk possibility of Chiang's jumping off on his own on some risky adventure.

**Drumright**

---

[2] Telegram 429 to Taipei, January 23, reported that since Drumright was completing his 4 years of service in Taipei, the Administration had decided to replace him. It instructed him to hold this information closely and stated that he would be informed before the White House announcement so that he could give the Chinese Government 24 hours advance notice. (Department of State, Central Files, 123–Drumright, Everett F.)

---

87.   **Telegram From the Embassy in Poland to the Department of State**

Warsaw, March 1, 1962, 7 p.m.

1336. Cabot–Wang talks. 108 meeting two hours 15 minutes.[1] Re Deptel 1114.[2]

---

Source: Department of State, Central Files, 611.93/3–162. Confidential; Priority; Limit Distribution. Repeated to Taipei, Hong Kong, Geneva, Stockholm, and Moscow.

[1] Cabot commented and sent recommendations for the next meeting in telegram 1337, March 3, and sent a detailed, apparently verbatim report of the meeting in airgram A–496, March 2. (Ibid., 611.93/3–362 and 611.93/3–262, respectively)

[2] Telegram 1114, February 22, transmitted Cabot's instructions for the meeting. It stated that in Cabot's first session as U.S. representative, he should direct his effort to the two items most closely identified with the original agenda: the detained American civilians and renunciation of force. (Ibid., 611.93/2–2262)

(1) After initial civilities and handing Wang letter (reference telegram paragraph 1),[3] I opened with substance paragraph two reference telegram.[4] Long silence followed during which Wang nervously shuffled papers, which I interpret as bearing out prediction paragraph three reference telegram.[5]

(2) After welcoming me, Wang observed serious disputes exist between our two countries affecting not only our relations but peace in Far East. Attached significance and hope to fact this first talk of new year and my first participation. Reviewed briefly history of return of prisoners question with nothing new in arguments, stressing would be abnormal for sovereign country allow criminals go unpunished. Also covered US "occupation" Taiwan. Wang charged we were still retaining some Chinese in US.

(3) I countered with part of substance paragraph two Deptel 774[6] and paragraph three reference telegram, adding that if Wang felt US failed apply agreed announcement 1955 fully, we would welcome names any Chinese who wish return mainland and have failed do so. Specifically covered pertinence Powers release[7] (to which Wang did not return). Answered Taiwan charge paragraphs four and five reference telegram.

(4) Wang made distinction between civilians and convicts. Then requested US make serious reappraisal policy toward China. Accused US of coercion in UNGA Chinese representation and insisting on discussion Tibet which internal matter. UN declaring China as aggressor Korea was ignominious time in history UN for US was aggressor and is now preparing for nuclear war. Eight serious warnings aircraft and ship intrusions since last meeting. Accused US direct participation in war in Vietnam and torpedoing Laos agreement. Our activities SEA were threat to China. Relations US and China already deteriorated seriously but could improve. Key is withdrawal from Taiwan after which other questions could be readily settled.

---

[3] The letter confirmed Cabot's designation as U.S. representative to the Ambassadorial talks.

[4] Paragraph 2 declared that it was impossible to reconcile the continued detention of U.S. civilians with the agreed announcement of September 10, 1955. For texts of the announcements made by both sides on that date, see Foreign Relations, 1955–1957, vol. III, pp. 85–86.

[5] Paragraph 3 began: "Limiting opening statement to prisoners issue should make it relatively awkward for Wang to make logical transition to propaganda accusations concerning United States policy in Far East which have been mainstay of his recent presentations."

[6] See footnote 3, Document 78.

[7] Reference is to the Soviet Union's release of Francis Gary Powers on February 10; see volume V. Telegram 1114 suggested that Cabot note the release of Powers and, if queried as to its relevance, state that it showed other Communist authorities found means consistent with judicial sovereignty to release an imprisoned American.

(5) I said majority governments of world did not agree Chinese Communist regime was legal government of China. My impression was it came to power by force and maintained self by force. Rebutted charges against US policy SEA along lines Deptel 786.[8]

(6) In saying Chinese people rejected Chiang, Wang referred my personal observations of Chinese welcome to Communist forces in Shanghai. I denied noting evidences any jubilation and referred [refuted] earlier claim our relations with Chiang were master-slave.

(7) Wang asked what sort freedom exists in US where "progressive" organization not even allowed exist? I said our constitution guarantees right engage in peaceful political activities any group. There followed brief banter concerning freedom in general on which meeting ended in relatively friendly atmosphere with agreement April 5 for next meeting.

(8) Polish News Agency took brief movies at conference and on arrival and departure at behest US news.

**Cabot**

---

[8] See footnote 4, Document 78.

---

## 88.    Telegram From the Embassy in the Republic of China to the Department of State

Taipei, March 6, 1962, 2 p.m.

615. Department for Secretary. When I saw President Chiang today to bid him farewell[1] he brought up subject of mainland. This gave me

---

Source: Department of State, Central Files, 793.00/3–662. Secret; Roger Channel. Repeated to Manila for Harriman. Received at 1:44 p.m. Harriman was in the Philippines for a conference of U.S. Chiefs of Mission in East Asia, after which he planned to visit Taipei.
[1] Telegram 616 from Taipei, March 6, reported that Drumright had called on Chiang and told him of his impending departure on March 8. Chiang's reaction was that Drumright's withdrawal must represent a basic departure in U.S. policy; Drumright assured him that this was not the case. (Ibid., 611.93/3–662)

opportunity to set forth US position along lines Deptel 486.[2] I urged need on both sides for utter frankness, full exchange of views, development of maximum possible intelligence resources re mainland and attitudes of people. I urged need above all for joint agreement respecting use of force against mainland.

I said as evidence of our desiring exchange views a USG estimate of mainland situation[3] had been handed his son yesterday. Chiang said he had not yet seen our estimate but would read it with interest. I said we would welcome up-to-date GRC estimate, and in this regard stressed need for concrete mainland intelligence.

I told Chiang Governor Harriman would be prepared to discuss mainland problem in general, and urged him to bare his views frankly to Harriman.

Chiang expressed view small-scale operations would fail and thus upset his plans, whereas I said USG skeptical that larger-scale operations could succeed at this juncture. I said there seemed to be a difference of aims. We wanted small-scale operations to test reactions and gather intelligence whereas Chiang wanted large-scale operation to touch off explosion. Chiang did not dissent from this analysis, but asserted he is confident now is time to act and any delay may allow Communists to retrieve situation. I responded it seemed most important to choose right time and method, adding it my belief mainland deterioration would continue and perhaps open up better opportunities. I also urged Chiang to have regard for whole world situation, US responsibilities, et cetera. With so many problems, US naturally cautious about opening new major front. I also said Communist adventures in Southeast Asia or elsewhere might develop in such ways as to open opportunities toward mainland.

*Comment:* Discussion, in which Foreign Minister was only other participant, took place friendly atmosphere, nevertheless, it was utterly clear that Chiang is bent on taking some kind of action this year against mainland and that it will take skillful, adept responses on our part to channel his actions in directions we deem appropriate to situation.

**Drumright**

---

[2] In telegram 486, March 1, Harriman replied to Drumright's message in telegram 596 (Document 86). It stated that the Department and Central Intelligence Agency concurred in Drumright's recommendation that Cline should continue discussions with Chiang Ching-kuo and press the GRC to supply concrete intelligence to support its views. The thrust of his talks was to be willingness to discuss GRC plans with no implication of commitment, skepticism concerning the possibility of successful military action under existing circumstances, and concern over the disastrous effect of an unsuccessful military venture; he was to stress the GRC obligation to obtain U.S. concurrence before taking any military action. It stated that Harriman was prepared to discuss the subject in general terms but not in detail when he saw Chiang Kai-shek. (Department of State, Central Files, 793.00/2–2862)

[3] Not further identified.

89. Message From the President's Special Assistant for National
Security Affairs (Bundy) to the Chief of the Central
Intelligence Agency Station in Taipei (Cline)

Washington, March 6, 1962.

We have received the reports of your conversations and those of my
brother with high authorities in Taipei. The President is instructing Averell Harriman to review those matters at the highest possible level during
his visit to you March 14–15. Meanwhile, we think it important that an
interim response be made along following lines, and you should make
this response in such a way as to indicate, without flatly saying so, that it
represents the views of the highest authorities here:

1. The United States is most appreciative of this full information on
the political assessments of the Generalissimo. Such information is
obviously the more important and valuable when the matter is one of
such significance as a projected mainland effort.

2. We continue to base our policy in this matter on the understanding embodied in the exchange of notes of December 10, 1954, between the
U.S. Secretary of State and the Chinese Minister of Foreign Affairs. In
accordance with the terms of this understanding, the United States
remains wholly confident that any "use of force will be a matter of joint
agreement." The responsibilities and interests of both governments
make it imperative that this agreement be the basis of all discussion. The
interest of the highest authorities here in restating this matter derives
simply from an earnest desire for clear understanding that all discussions of our common hopes for the future freedom of the mainland must
rest upon this premise.

3. The intelligence available to us, and separately reported to you,
creates a grave question in our minds as to the timeliness of the particular
proposals discussed in the recent conversations. We believe that a first
step in further consultation should be a careful joint study of the
information available to our two governments.

---

Source: Kennedy Library, National Security Files, Countries Series, China, Return to
Mainland, 1/62–5/62. Secret. Filed with a March 6 covering memorandum from Bundy to
U. Alexis Johnson requesting Department of State clearance for the message and stating
that it was to be sent through intelligence channels. A handwritten note on the source text
indicates that it was approved by telephone. The source text does not indicate the time of
transmission.
Cline replied in a March 7 telegram that Bundy's message had been "most helpful."
Cline had conveyed the substance to Chiang Ching-kuo without attribution to anyone in
Washington and had conveyed Bundy's comments in paragraph 5. Cline noted that while
President Chiang and Chiang Ching-kuo were pleased about Harriman's visit, the GRC
was "somewhat apprehensive" over what the press was treating as the "strangely abrupt
resignation and departure" of Drumright. (Ibid.)

4. Finally, you should emphasize that Harriman is not merely the Assistant Secretary of State with responsibilities for this area. He is also a statesman of long experience and proven friendship for the Government of China. He has the President's full personal confidence, and will be empowered to speak in the most direct and authoritative way for the President himself.

5. If you think it appropriate, I should be glad if you would express my personal respects to the appropriate Chinese authorities and say that, at the President's direction, his staff continues to take a most active and sympathetic interest in relations with the Government of China.

---

**90.    Draft Message From President Kennedy to the Assistant Secretary of State for Far Eastern Affairs (Harriman)**

Washington, March 9, 1962.

In your conversations with Generalissimo, I hope you will make it clear that you come with my full authority and that you and I have discussed together the question of ChiNat return to the mainland. You may want to begin by indicating that you and I have repeatedly shown our own support for GRC and therefore count on full understanding by Generalissimo of our position, as follows:

1. We continue to assume that all discussions of return to the mainland are governed by the understanding in the exchange of notes between U.S. Secretary of State and Chinese Minister of Foreign Affairs dated December 10, 1954. We know that understanding on this point has been excellent so far, but we should never omit straight-forward repetition of it.

2. We believe that most careful study is necessary of both intelligence and operational planning for proposed new venture. You may draw, if you wish, on the Cuban misadventure as proof of the dangers of

Source: Kennedy Library, National Security Files, Countries Series, China, Return to Mainland, 1/62–5/62. Secret. Filed with a March 9 covering memorandum from Bundy to U. Alexis Johnson that reads as follows: "This draft has the President's approval, and, subject to any changes that you may suggest, I hope it may go promptly to Governor Harriman." The source text and the covering memorandum bear no indication of approval or objection and no transmission time. The message was not sent through Department of State channels; it was presumably sent through [text not declassified].

bad intelligence, and of decisions based more on hope than reality. You should emphasize our insistence on continued detailed study and exchange of views.

3. Our earlier approval of 20-man drops[1] was heavily connected with the fact that we were not involved. 200-man teams with U.S. air support are a wholly different matter, and while we too will await results of further study, you should indicate that support for such drops would be a major shift in policy for us and would have to be supported by compelling evidence.

If you concur, you should indicate that it still seems best to us to think in terms of smaller actions which might in themselves increase our knowledge of the possibilities. The smaller the action, and the more completely it is handled by the GRC, the more likely our agreement.

You should of course make it clear that we would like nothing better than the downfall of the mainland regime, and we are fully aware of the advantages such a change would bring in the whole world situation. But it is one thing to desire a result and quite another to make sound judgment on proposed measures to bring that result about.

The more you can learn from the Generalissimo about his precise estimate of the situation, the better, but you should make it clear to him that solid evidence is more interesting to us than eloquently expressed hopes.

---

[1] An unsigned paper, evidently a draft of a March 30 memorandum from Hilsman to Harriman, states that a plan developed by the GRC [text not declassified], providing for six 20-man teams to be airdropped into South China, was approved in the third week of July 1961 by "a U.S. intragovernmental committee" (presumably the Special Group) and by the President. (Department of State, FE/EA Files: Lot 65 D 235, GRC Mainland Recovery, January 1962) Hilsman's March 30 memorandum omits this point but states that the United States had suggested 20-man probes in mid-1961 in response to GRC plans for 200–300 man airdrops; a few months later, when preparations were complete, the GRC declined to carry out the probes on the ground that they would be too small to be useful. (Library of Congress Manuscript Division, Harriman Papers, Kennedy–Johnson Administrations, Subject Files, China) See the Supplement.

## 91.  Memorandum for the Record

Washington, March 12, 1962.

The Chinese Ambassador[1] came in today, accompanied by the Chinese Minister. The Ambassador seemed to want only to pay a formal call, probably arising from my relations with George Yeh last summer. I took the occasion to raise with him the matter of GRC plans to return to the mainland. I told him that we were most appreciative of the Chinese Government's willingness to keep us informed, and I indicated that our own intelligence did not give us much hope that the time was ripe for any such operations. I also reiterated our belief that our discussions and relations on this question should be governed by the exchange of notes of December 1954 between Dulles and Yeh. I said that it seemed to me that our interests were so deeply joined together in this issue that we must be sure to agree together before any action is taken. Finally, I indicated that we of course would like nothing better than the end of Communist domination on the mainland, and would always be alert to any real opportunity. But I referred to the Cuban episode, indicating that both our governments must be careful not to mistake hopes for realities.

The Ambassador indicated that his government would be glad to receive our analysis of the matter, and he said he could add that, on the premises of the basic attitude I have described, he thought we could count on serious attention to our views. He nevertheless asked us to understand how deeply the return to the mainland is the purpose of life of his people.

In conclusion, I mentioned to him the letter of Pearl Buck on food for the mainland, and asked him what the position of his government would be if there were such a request. He said his government was caught in a dilemma. If it opposed the sale of food, it would be attacked on humanitarian grounds and might also lose popular support on the mainland. But if it approved of them, it might be encouraging the political and military reinforcement of the mainland regime. In this situation his government had so far refrained from expressing an opinion on Australian and Canadian sales. He obviously was much interested in what we might or might not do, but I confined my own remarks to saying that this question had not yet arisen. The Ambassador did indicate that he believed the conditions laid down by Mrs. Buck would prove unacceptable to Peking.

**McGeorge Bundy**

---

Source: Kennedy Library, President's Office Files, China Security, 1962–63. Top Secret. Filed with a covering note to Kennedy's secretary, Evelyn Lincoln, stating that it was for the President. Bundy sent a copy to Battle with a March 13 covering note indicating that it was for limited distribution. (Department of State, Central Files, 793.00/3–1262)
[1] Ambassador Tsiang had replaced Yeh as Ambassador to the United States while continuing to represent the Republic of China at the United Nations.

## 92. Telegram From the Embassy in the Republic of China to the Department of State

Taipei, March 15, 1962, 3 p.m.

629. Eyes only for President and Secretary. From Harriman.[1] In two conversations March 14 with President Chiang of about an hour each before and after dinner with Madame Chiang and Chargé present[2] we discussed at length his strategy for return to mainland. After exchange of rather warm reminiscences about Cairo, President Roosevelt, Chungking, etc., in which I underlined President Kennedy's friendly attitude, he led off by saying mutual defense pact called for consultation on action to be taken, and expressed confidence President Kennedy was sympathetic with his objectives and would do nothing to deter or prevent him from acting. He asked me to assure President Kennedy he would not do anything behind back of US Government nor anything detrimental or harmful to US. I reminded him twice need not only for consultation, but also agreement. He responded the second time that he hoped our conversation would deal with political problem of how to achieve our common objectives, rather than discuss legal position.

Chiang said he had heard US intelligence sources had reported GRC about to take action in month's time. He said, laughing, not to worry that he had no such intent.

I replied that I had heard rumor to that effect, but did not take seriously since I knew he was aware his forces could not be prepared for such rapid action.

Chiang said help must be given first to people on mainland so they could rise against Communist regime only then would GRC move in to support them. He now concerned with first stage, for which he needed transport from US to carry out drops over mainland. He said he did not wish to go into technical details, which could be studied by US and GRC military [less than 1 line of source text not declassified]. He obviously did not want to risk turn down of request for planes through me direct to President.

He then presented strong plea for US understanding and cooperation. People on mainland ripe for revolt. Although outer fabric of ChiCom regime might look solid, once pierced there would be massive uprisings and defections. He did not desire intervention by US troops.

Source: Department of State, Central Files, 793.00/3–1562. Secret; Priority; Roger Channel.

[1] Harriman visited Taipei March 14–15. A general report of his visit was sent in despatch 355 from Taipei, March 20. (Ibid., 123 Harriman, W. Averell)

[2] A memorandum of both conversations, drafted by Clough, is ibid., 793.00/3–1462.

Chiang repeated several times that he would not act lightly, but only on definite assurance of success. If he had no such assurance he would not act. Present opportunity was heaven-sent and must be taken or it would be lost forever. Things could not get much worse on mainland and by next autumn would have reached decisive stage. When eruption occurred GRC would have to act.

I told Chiang I knew President Kennedy would be glad to learn of the caution with which he approaching matter. One mistake could be disastrous.

Chiang said he realized a reverse would have serious consequences, said he had high sense responsibility and situation called for greater caution. He was not impatient, but people and armed forces were and unless action taken soon he might lose control and things might begin to happen not according to plan. This would be matter of great regret.

I told him I had no fear his control. I congratulated him on Taiwan's progress and urged expansion of Taiwan's technical assistance program to other Asian and African countries. Chiang said he would be glad to do so.

We had some discussion regarding Moscow–Peiping rift. Chiang expressed view it was largely personal clash between Mao and Khrushchev. I explained in my opinion differences dated back to Stalin's time and were fundamental. Chiang felt Soviets would not intervene in China. I stated firmly that I was sure Soviets would if US forces involved. At that point he agreed and said that was why he planned on use only of Chinese forces.

Chiang asked for frequent consultation on mainland problem. I said President Kennedy wished to keep in closest touch and exchanges of views could be held as often as Chiang thought necessary.

I said that I found it odd for an American to be advising a Chinese to be patient. He seemed to take this in good part.[3]

**Clough**

---

[3] Harriman sent an additional message to the President in telegram 1471 from Bangkok, which commented that Chiang "obviously wanted me to accept his concept that return to mainland was Chinese affair and his only obligation was consultation, not prior agreement, with us. When he failed in that, he undertook to impress me with the care and caution with which he was approaching the undertaking. He avoided making any specific request for aircraft, I felt, because he did not want to get a turn-down direct from the President. He called Admiral Felt back to see him the next morning and repeated the request already mentioned by his son to [less than 1 line of source text not declassified] namely five C–130's. If his request is granted, he will consider that the operation he has in mind will be approved although he has no direct evidence that it will succeed. The most optimistic estimate I have heard from any American is ten to one against achievement its objective." (Ibid., 793.00/3–2362)

93.  Memorandum From Acting Secretary of State Ball to
     President Kennedy

Washington, March 23, 1962.

SUBJECT

   Visa Case of Thomas W.I. Liao

You will recall that Thomas W.I. Liao, self-styled "President of the Republic of Formosa in Exile," was denied a United States visa prior to 1961 because it was believed that his anticipated activities in the United States would be prejudicial to the national interest under Section 212(a)(27) of the Immigration and Nationality Act. It is clear that Liao's main purpose in seeking admission to the United States is to press his cause on Americans and to build up support for it among Taiwanese groups here. The Government of the Republic of China (GRC) is well aware of Liao's activities and plans and would take strong exception to his entry into the United States.

For several years the Department has been under continuing pressure from Senator Fulbright to admit Liao on the grounds that his continued exclusion is incompatible with our traditional attitude regarding the right of dissenters to be heard in the United States. In May 1961 the Department concluded that Liao should no longer be excluded on the grounds cited above, and decided to admit him. In response to a subsequent GRC protest the Department replied that we would defer issuing a visa until we had discussed with the GRC the best way of handling his admission.

You ordered this deferral to minimize difficulties we then faced with the GRC, particularly in connection with the Chinese representation issue in the United Nations. At no time was the GRC given reason to believe that Liao would be barred permanently. During your discussions with Vice President Chen Cheng on August 1, 1961, the point was made to him that Liao's presence in the United States would go virtually unnoticed, but that his continued exclusion might make him a figure of national prominence. Recent publicity in the *New York Times* and *Look* magazine have borne out this contention.

Liao's entry would under any circumstances cause at least a temporary worsening in our relations with the GRC, and in particular would anger President Chiang. We believe, however, that the anticipated adverse GRC reaction could be reduced if Liao's admission were to come when our relations with the GRC are otherwise reasonably tranquil.

Source: Kennedy Library, National Security Files, Countries Series, China. Confidential.

Since the Chinese representation issue is not active in the United Nations, it appears that the next few weeks may afford us an opportunity to admit Liao with a minimum adverse impact. The Department has accordingly decided to admit Liao to the United States under the conditions set forth below, subject to your approval.

In order to lessen the effect on GRC sensitivities of Liao's activities in the United States, the Department proposes to require that he comply with the provisions of the Foreign Agents Registration Act. Should he attempt to establish his "government's" headquarters here, we would inform him that the United States Government does not tolerate the existence of such regimes in this country, and that he must either desist or face deportation. With such leverage over Liao, the Department believes we could safely admit him at an early date and so control his activities as to minimize the impact on our relations with the GRC.

We would, of course, want Liao out of the country prior to the opening of the next General Assembly, when his presence might be damaging to our effort to sustain the GRC's position in the United Nations, and possibly seriously affect our relations with the GRC. The Department would therefore propose to request the Immigration and Naturalization Service to limit Liao's stay to a three month period. We would also inform the GRC of our decision, and of the actions we would take to minimize the effect of his activities here.[1]

**George W. Ball**

---

[1] A memorandum of March 27 from Bundy to Rusk states that the President had considered the Department's memorandum and "does not believe that it makes sense to admit Liao at present and considers it still to be true that his anticipated activities in the United States would be prejudicial to the national interest." (Ibid.)

---

94.   **Memorandum From the Deputy Assistant Secretary of State for Far Eastern Affairs (Rice) to the Assistant Secretary of State for Far Eastern Affairs (Harriman)**

Washington, March 28, 1962.

SUBJECT

Recommendation for Meeting Between You and Ray Cline of CIA[1]

---

Source: Department of State, Central Files, 793.00/3–2862. Top Secret. Drafted by Holdridge.

[1] A note on the source text in Harriman's handwriting instructed his secretary to arrange a meeting with Cline. A note in another handwriting states that a meeting was arranged for Saturday, March 31, at 11 a.m.

As you may know, the CIA Station Chief in Taipei, Ray Cline, was called back to Washington for consultation shortly after your visit to Taipei. At my request, Mr. Cline called on me March 27 to brief me on his recent discussions with Generalissimo Chiang Kai-shek concerning Chiang's plans for mainland operations, and to give me his own impressions of the alternatives for United States policy which these plans entail. In essence, Cline expressed the view that the situation leaves us with but two courses of action, as follows:

1) To give Chiang a flat "no" in his request for United States support of several clandestine operations against the China mainland involving airdrops of 200 to 300-man teams. According to Cline, this alternative would unquestionably evoke a bitter reaction from Chiang which might lead to anti-American demonstrations, disruption of American [*less than 1 line of source text not declassified*] and other programs on Taiwan, and, conceivably, "desperation" attacks by the GRC against the mainland in hopes of involving the United States. Cline also reported that in such circumstances the Generalissimo might ultimately resign as President of the GRC, thus causing political chaos on Taiwan and in US-GRC relations.

2) To temporize by agreeing to furnish suitable aircraft and other support for one GRC operation of approximately 50–100 men against the mainland. Cline anticipated that it might require from six to twelve months before the operation could actually take place, thanks to the delay needed to add proper electronic counter-measure equipment to the aircraft (either C–130's or C–123's) and to complete adequate planning and training for the operation. During this time we would, of course, be in constant touch with the GRC on the feasibility of the project. We would also be able [*1 line of source text not declassified*] and, if deemed necessary, to make plans for dealing with successors to Chiang Kai-shek if we subsequently were to decide that we should discontinue our support of his plans and the consequences noted in 1, above, should develop. On the other hand, if we should wish to avoid a showdown with Chiang at the end of the period of grace, we could possibly find ways to bring about further delays in GRC moves against the mainland.

Cline indicated that he greatly wishes to discuss these considerations in person with you prior to his return to Taipei, both to have the opportunity for a fuller exploration of the implications and to be able to assure Chiang Kai-shek that the detailed information he brought about their plans and views have been passed to high officials of the United States Government, including yourself. His departure for Taipei is presently set for the evening of March 29, but he is prepared to put off his return until the evening of March 31 if he could meet you briefly in the interval. I strongly recommend that you see him at your earliest convenience.

Meanwhile, CIA is preparing a paper for you setting forth the alternatives outlined above in greater detail.[2]

---

[2] TDCS DB–3/649, 714, March 23, reported conversations with Chiang Kai-shek and Chiang Ching-kuo. On March 21 Chiang Kai-shek requested Kennedy's private assurance of continued U.S. support for the GRC, secret U.S. support for GRC clandestine operations to contact and assist resistance forces, and secret U.S. support for GRC military action to support such forces when and if both sides agreed that the proposed action was feasible and timely. He renewed an earlier request for planes capable of transporting large armed teams to selected target areas. On March 22 Chiang Ching-kuo elaborated on these requests and stated that President Chiang thought the U.S.-GRC Mutual Defense Treaty infringed GRC sovereignty and freedom of action and should be re-examined. (Kennedy Library, National Security Files, China Cables) See the Supplement.

---

## 95.    Special National Intelligence Estimate

SNIE 13–3–62                                   Washington, March 28, 1962.

### PROBABLE CONSEQUENCES OF CHINESE NATIONALIST MILITARY OPERATIONS ON THE CHINA MAINLAND

#### The Problem

To evaluate the intentions and capabilities of the Government of the Republic of China (GRC) to undertake limited military operations on the China mainland in 1962 and to estimate the prospects for and consequences of such operations.

---

Source: Department of State, INR/EAP Files: Lot 90 D 110, SNIE 13–2–62. Secret. According to a note on the cover sheet, the Central Intelligence Agency and intelligence organizations of the Departments of State, Defense, the Army, the Navy, and the Air Force and the Joint Staff participated in the preparation of this estimate. All members of the USIB concurred with this estimate on March 28 except the representatives of the AEC and the FBI, who abstained on the grounds that the subject was outside their jurisdiction.

An April 4 letter from Hilsman to Clough, enclosing a copy of the estimate, states that it was generated largely as a result of Harriman's and his own talks in Taipei and that the major problem was estimating GRC capabilities for independent operations. (Ibid.) Hilsman visited Taipei on March 8. His conversation with Chiang Ching-kuo on that date was reported in telegram 620 from Taipei, March 8. (Ibid., Central Files, 793.00/3–862) A more detailed account is in a memorandum for the record by Hilsman, dated March 19. (Kennedy Library, Hilsman Papers, Box 1, China, Planning on Mainland Operations, 3/62) See also Roger Hilsman, *To Move a Nation: The Politics of Foreign Policy in the Administration of John F. Kennedy*, pp. 312–314.

Conclusions

1. Public dissatisfaction and demoralization are widespread in Communist China and there has been some weakening of discipline among local officials and low-level party cadres. Nevertheless the regime's control apparatus is still intact and effective. Present indications are that the regime will continue to be able to isolate and repress any likely internal challenge to its authority. (Paras. 5–7)

2. Even if GRC special forces teams could be successfully established on the mainland, they would almost certainly be destroyed in a short time. Very few people, and no significant military units, would be likely to join the GRC forces in the absence of clear military success—which we believe would be impossible without large-scale US support. (Para. 17)

3. US refusal to support or sanction the GRC proposals for special forces operations would place additional strains on US-GRC relations. We believe that the GRC leaders, despite their limited capabilities, might undertake some kind of special force operations against the mainland in 1962 even without US approval. (Para. 9)

4. If the GRC were or undertake military operations on the mainland, with or without US support, Communist China and the USSR would launch major propaganda and political campaigns against the GRC and the US. Peiping might undertake some retaliatory action in the Taiwan Strait area. Moscow would be most unlikely to alter its policies toward Communist China or the US so long as the GRC operations met with no notable success. In the unlikely event that Communist control of the mainland were threatened, the Soviet leaders would almost certainly support the regime to the extent necessary to put down the rebellion, while exploiting the opportunity to attempt to bring Peiping's policy and outlook in line with that of the USSR. (Paras. 18–21)

[Here follow paragraphs 5–22, comprising the Discussion portion of the estimate, in three sections, headed "The Situation on the Mainland," "GRC Intentions and Capabilities," and "Consequences of the Proposed GRC Military Operations on the Mainland."]

## 96.    Telegram From the Embassy in the Republic of China to the Department of State

Taipei, March 30, 1962, 3 p.m.

658. For Harriman. Embassy, US military and CAS continue receive indications that serious preparations for attack on mainland are steadily proceeding. Press campaign, which reached high pitch at time your visit, has abated only a little and will be again stimulated by President Chiang's Youth Day message (Embtel 657).[1] Members country team are concerned that campaign may be acquiring momentum of its own which would make it increasingly difficult for Chiang to apply restraint should he wish to do so. We are particularly concerned as to effect campaign may be having on state of mind of officer corps and are urgently seeking information this subject. Top economic officials whom Yager saw during visit here expressed guardedly and obliquely, but unmistakably, their deep disquiet over increasing threat to economic stability arising from very large advances being made to military for undisclosed purposes.[2]

There is no clear indication as to timing of possible action against mainland. Current evidence of GRC thinking points to early fall as most likely target date, but we doubt Chiang has reached any decision. US attitude likely have important influence on decision. On one hand we should avoid encouraging GRC in preparations for early overt military action against mainland. On other hand, we should avoid such flat opposition to GRC proposals and objectives which create serious risk of unilateral desperate lunge to take advantage of conjunction of circumstances which Chiang almost certainly regards as unique and most unlikely to recur. This likely prove extraordinarily difficult balancing act, for we believe Chiang to be deadly serious in his determination to take action and he can be expected to try to edge us steadily in direction of agreeing to larger operations, threatening unilateral action if we do not go along. Nevertheless, he is not reckless man and recognizes only too clearly how dependent he is on US support. So long as he is satisfied US

---

Source: Department of State, Central Files, 793.00/3–3062. Secret; Roger Channel.

[1] Dated March 29. (Ibid., 793.00/3–2962)

[2] Despatch 363 from Taipei, March 27, reported that Director of the Office of East Asian Affairs Joseph A. Yager met on March 23 with Finance Minister C.K. Yen and Economic Affairs Minister C.T. Yang. It reads in part as follows: "Both these officials spoke quite frankly of the economic consequences of plans underway for some kind of operations against the mainland. Minister Yang also indicated that loss of confidence by mainlanders in U.S. policy toward China, rising in part out of last year's UN debate and the Outer Mongolia issue, has caused those responsible for the government to hasten planning for mainland recovery at the expense of Taiwan's economy. Feeling that U.S. economic aid and political support are no longer assured, these people believe they must move while they yet can. Meanwhile, what happens to the local economy is not significant." (Ibid., 611.93/3–2762)

Government is fundamentally in sympathy with his objectives, has no intention of changing its China policy and shows willingness to at least study plans for action against mainland, I think it unlikely, for the next few months at least, that he would resort to unilateral assault. Of course, substantial uprising on mainland would change situation entirely and create enormous pressure on him to act immediately.

Believe following courses of action would be appropriate US response to present situation:

1. Take steps to discourage excessive press publicity on mainland attack theme. Yager has already spoken to Vice Premier, CAS to Chiang Ching-kuo and political counselor Deputy Secretary General of Kuomintang on this. Recommend I be instructed take up with Foreign Minister, pointing out dangers of building up premature expectations in Taiwan, of tipping hand to ChiComs, and unnecessarily alarming other countries to detriment of GRC international position.

2. Have CAS examine in detail and discuss with GRC proposal for 200–300 man drops or alternative smaller clandestine operations against mainland. Cline will have discussed this thoroughly on current visit to Washington.

3. Request opportunity for US military to make detailed examination GRC planning going beyond clandestine operations. Chiang's offer in conversation with you to make details his planning available could be used as basis for request. Admiral Smoot much concerned at extensive GRC planning and preparations now going on which his officers have no access, but which might have profound effect on combined planning for defense of Taiwan and Penghus for which he bears responsibility. We believe US scrutiny GRC offensive planning would inject greater realism into thinking on this subject and ultimately would affect Chiang's own thinking. Admittedly, US-GRC study and discussion of GRC offensive planning might be taken to imply degree of US commitment to offensive concept. There would have to be clear and unmistakable disclaimers of any such US commitment. If time should come, as it well may, when we have to express flat opposition to a proposed GRC offensive action, we would be in far better position to do so on basis of unrealistic nature their plans, which we had studied in detail, rather than solely on basis of our differing judgments of likely mainland response.

4. Make démarche on economic situation, aimed in first instance at seeking more information on military spending, but expressing concern at threat to stability of economy if it continues. We will send separate cable shortly containing more detailed recommendation.

5. Consider urgently in Washington proposing to GRC a program of substantially increased [less than 1 line of source text not declassified] probing activity against mainland to produce better intelligence on state of Chinese Communist controls and to increase chances for perfection. Pro-

gram should cover as broad of a spectrum as possible, [5 lines of source text not declassified].

Believe foregoing series of actions, while it would exert only limited initial restraining influence on GRC preparations for mainland attack, would serve at least to postpone any decision for unilateral action and would place us in better position to oppose such action later.

**Clough**

## 97.  Memorandum for the Record

Washington, March 31, 1962.

SUBJECT

White House Meeting on GRC Plans

The meeting was in the Cabinet room. Present were the President, the Secretary, McGeorge Bundy, Ray Cline, General Pat Carter[1] (who by the way looks pretty good) and Mike Forrestal. McCone is out of town. The Secretary began, tossing the ball immediately to Ray Cline. Cline's presentation focussed attention on whether the operation would succeed rather than how we handle the GRC. Our maps[2] came in handy. The Secretary intervened with great vigor and a strong opinion, that this operation just wouldn't wash, etc., the plan was nonsense, and the idea that we could keep it covert was also nonsense. The GRC hand would show and so would the American hand. I said that the issue really was not whether or not the Chinese Nationalists could get back into the Mainland. They couldn't. The issue was whether we reject the plan outright or whether we temporize. My fear was that if there were an outright rejection, the GRC would immediately start a public campaign to arouse the China lobby. There was also a great danger in temporizing, i.e., that we get ourselves more and more committed to the GRC in the familiar pattern of the covert operations in Indonesia and Cuba.

---

Source: Kennedy Library, Hilsman Papers, Box 1, China—Planning on Mainland Operations, 3/62. Top Secret. According to Kennedy's Appointment Book, the meeting was held from 10:30 to 11:25 a.m. (Ibid.) Hilsman describes this meeting briefly in *To Move a Nation*, pp. 314–315.

[1] Deputy Director for Central Intelligence Lieutenant General Marshall S. Carter, USA.

[2] Not further identified.

Harriman, by the way, beforehand was very worried that the Secretary would recommend outright rejection. Harriman prefers temporizing.

The President proposed preparing two C–123's in the United States.

Ray Cline said that he had to take back something tangible. The President then suggested that we also train Chinese crews here in the United States in the operation of these planes.

Mr. Cline said that this would be satisfactory.

The Secretary agreed providing that the planes were prepared in this country and not sent to Taiwan before a further decision was made.

The President said that Cline should make it clear to the GRC that no commitment was being made other than to prepare the planes and be willing to consider their use in the light of the intelligence available in October. The President also instructed Mr. Cline to get a commitment from the GRC that there would be no further public discussion of a return to the Mainland.

I suggested that another commitment be obtained to permit American participation in the other planning that the GRC was doing.

McGeorge Bundy made the point very strongly that Ray Cline was to tell the GRC that with the appointment of a new Ambassador the United States intended to transfer to the Ambassador the special role formerly played by the CIA.

[Here follows discussion of other subjects.]

RH

## 98.   Memorandum to the Chief of the Central Intelligence Agency Station in Taipei (Cline)

Washington, March 31, 1962.

On your return to Taiwan you should be guided by the following statement of the U.S. position, and should make it clear to those with whom you deal.[1]

1.   The United States would view with great satisfaction any developments on the Mainland of China in which freedom might be restored to the Chinese people.

2.   We do not, however, now have the kind of hard[2] evidence to support the feasibility of activities on the scale recently discussed with Governor Harriman and you.

3.   It is necessary that we conduct jointly further investigation of conditions on the Mainland and that we increase our mutual consultations on detailed planning for the future.

4.   In order to achieve the above objectives, the United States favors probing operations and specifically the joint training, equipping, and supervising of the formation of probing teams of the type previously authorized. In this connection, and because of the difficulties of airborne operations,[3] it is suggested that greater emphasis be placed upon the possibility of using seaborne raids on the coast.

5.   You are also authorized to maintain close liaison with GOC on[4] planning and preparation for larger scale clandestine operations on a contingent basis involving up to a maximum of 200 men in a single airdrop, but it is essential that all responsibility for the preparation and

---

Source: Kennedy Library, National Security Files, Countries Series, China, CIA Cables, 3/62–4/62. Top Secret. A draft of this memorandum marked "Not for signature," bearing handwritten revisions, some of which are in Kennedy's handwriting is ibid. A March 31 memorandum from Bundy to Cline reads in part as follows: "The memorandum of instruction is as agreed and has the explicit concurrence of the Secretary and Mr. Harriman. The President specifically asked that you talk from it without handing it to any Chinese." (Ibid.) A draft letter from Kennedy to President Chiang, a paper headed "Memorandum on GRC Mainland Operations Planning," and a draft paper for oral delivery, all unsigned and undated, are filed with a March 30 note from Bundy to Harriman. (Ibid.) Bundy's March 31 memorandum to Cline states that Kennedy was not signing the letter to Chiang.

[1] On the draft cited above, this sentence was added in Bundy's handwriting.

[2] On the draft, the words "the kind of hard" were added in a handwriting that is probably Kennedy's.

[3] On the draft, the words "and because of the difficulties of airborne operations" were added in an unidentified handwriting.

[4] On the draft, the words "engage in joint" are crossed out and the words "maintain close liaison with GOC on" appear in an unidentified handwriting.

execution of such operations rest with the GOC.[5] The United States will, concurrently with such planning, prepare two C–123 aircraft in the United States and train the Chinese crews in this country. Such preparation and training will take about six months and the planes will be made available to the GOC when and if there is agreement between us that an operation is feasible and timely. It must be understood that we are preparing the capability for this operation—but have made no decision at this time to proceed with it.[6]

6. The planning in this area must be kept very quiet. Further talk along the lines of recent published articles will jeopardize any future operations. The United States will continue publicly to deny that there is any joint consultation on this subject.

7. The President is grateful for the message sent through Governor Harriman that the Generalissimo would continue to exercise great caution in these matters and would not act lightly.[7]

---

[5] On the draft, this sentence originally ended with the words "single airdrop." A marginal notation in Kennedy's handwriting reads, "but this should be R.O.C." The second clause was added in an unidentified handwriting. Message CAP 5172–62 from Bundy to Cline, April 2, asked him to confirm his understanding that this sentence referred to one single air drop involving a maximum of 200 men. In a message of April 4, Cline confirmed that this was his understanding and stated that his impression was that subsequent operations might be studied in accordance with paragraph 3, but that their detailed planning and preparation for execution would require further authorization. (Both ibid.)

[6] On the draft, this sentence was added in Kennedy's handwriting.

[7] A copy of this memorandum in the files of the Bureau of Intelligence and Research bears McGeorge Bundy's typed signature. (Department of State, INR Historical Files, Special Group Files, S.G. 112, February 20, 1964)

---

**99.   Editorial Note**

On April 2, 1962, Policy Planning Council Chairman Walt W. Rostow sent Secretary of State Rusk a paper entitled "U.S. Policy Re the Sino-Soviet Conflict," with a covering memorandum stating that it represented a "communal effort" of a group of policy and intelligence officers. The paper states that its recommendations were based on the conclusion in NIE 11–5–62, "Political Developments in the USSR and the Communist World," dated February 21, that "Sino-Soviet relations are in a critical phase just short of an acknowledged and definitive split. There is no longer much chance of a fundamental resolution of differences. In our view, the chances that such a split can be avoided in 1962 are no better than even." For text of NIE 11–5–62, see volume V.

The paper recommended (A) psychological exploitation of the dispute through the dissemination of information concerning its development, (B) a judicious increase in official U.S. attention to the dispute, (C) negotiations with the Soviet Union with the objective of finding and capitalizing on areas of overlapping interest, (C) (*sic*) declarations and concrete military measures to make it clear to the Chinese Communists that aggressive Communist actions would be countered resolutely and effectively, (D) efforts to open new lines of communication to Communist China and to offer it opportunities, possibly including grain sales, "to secure benefits from better relations with us in exchange for modifications in its behavior," and (E) consideration of the desirability of seeking Chinese participation in disarmament negotiations. (National Archives and Records Administration, RG 59, S/P Files: Lot 69 D 121, USSR)

The paper was discussed at a meeting with Rusk on April 17; no record of the meeting has been found. In an April 30 memorandum to Rostow, Rusk approved portions of recommendations (A) and (B) but made no decisions on the other recommendations. (Kennedy Library, Thomson Papers, Far East, Communist China, Sino-Soviet Conflict and U.S. Policy, 4/30/62)

---

## 100.  Draft Memorandum From Secretary of State Rusk to President Kennedy

Washington, April 4, 1962.

SUBJECT

United States Policy on Shipments of Medicines and Food Grains to Communist China

At the January 26, 1962, meeting of the National Security Council Standing Group it was agreed that the Department of State should sub-

---

Source: Department of State, Central Files, 411.9341/4–462. Secret. Drafted by Rice on April 4, but it was attached to an April 3 memorandum from Harriman to Rusk stating that after prolonged study and discussion, the Department had reached a general consensus embodied in the four recommendations in the "draft" memorandum. Harriman noted that Johnson dissented from the third recommendation but stated that he thought the recommendations represented "a modest proposal which should not be further reduced." (Ibid., 411.9341/4–362) McGhee forwarded the package under an April 5 memorandum recommending approval. (Ibid., 893.49/4–562)

mit to you recommendations regarding possible sale of food grains to Communist China.[1]

In formulating such recommendations we have sought to take into account the background facts of China's international crises and its dispute with the U.S.S.R.; the Cuba precedent in the context of exports of both food and medicines; humanitarian concern of Americans for the plight of suffering people, whatever the character of the regime under which they live; the clearly demonstrated determination of the Chinese Communist leadership not to accept American charity; restrictions imposed by U.S. legislation; the desirability of having Communist China's foreign exchange used for food purchases rather than industrial development; availability of non-U.S. sources of supply; the undesirability of our seeming to be motivated unduly by commercial considerations; Communist China's international behavior; the known unwillingness of China's present principal suppliers to attach political conditions to sales of foodstuffs to Communist China, together with the near certainty that Communist China would reject efforts explicitly to establish such a connection; the probable domestic and foreign repercussions of now changing present policy; the needs to retain flexibility and to bring about a more fruitful dialogue between Communist China and the U.S.; the long-term possibility of a different relationship between the U.S. and Communist China; and the related undesirability of establishing a record of unwillingness to supply food to the Chinese people when they badly need it and if it cannot be obtained elsewhere.

Against this background we have formulated four recommendations. In considering them we would point out that adopting the second recommendation may serve useful purposes vis-à-vis the American people and world opinion, but would probably be regarded by the leaders of Communist China as principally designed to call attention to their and their country's failures of policy and performance. Especially if it were accompanied by propaganda fanfare, it would inhibit the dialogue intended to be promoted by the third recommendation.

The following are our recommendations:

1. The Department of Commerce should forthwith place shipments of medicines to all destinations under general license (on the

---

[1] See footnote 4, Document 84. The application that prompted the Standing Group discussion was rejected on March 23. A March 26 memorandum from Rice to Harriman quotes the text of a Department of Commerce announcement that day stating there was no evidence that the order was based on a request from the governments concerned. Rice's memorandum states that according to Chayes, the decision was made at a meeting on another subject that day among Kennedy, Dillon, Secretary of Commerce Luther Hodges, Chayes, and Martin and that its purpose was to forestall a prospective Congressional resolution opposing any grain sales to Communist China. (Department of State, FE Files: Lot 64 D 25, Communist China)

grounds that the U.S. Government should not place obstacles between such medicines and the human beings who may need them).

2.  The U.S. Government should make known, but without accompanying propaganda exploitation, that it has not been our policy to deny licenses for the export of food parcels to Communist China, and that the Department of Commerce henceforth also will license bona fide private gift shipments of food, or food grains, to that country.

3.  Ambassador Cabot, in his talks with Wang Ping-nan in Warsaw, should state:

a.  The U.S. Government has been told that the Chinese Communist regime is interested in the purchase of U.S. grains. We have reason to doubt whether such interest does exist. However, if there is such interest, we are curious to know why, since the Chinese Communist regime has not exhausted possibilities of meeting its needs from other free world suppliers;

b.  United States legislation now precludes our Government's selling grain to Communist China on credit terms as favorable as those offered by other suppliers;

c.  If the Chinese Communists were able to finance United States grain purchases, given the foregoing legal restrictions, they should also be able to finance the equivalent purchases from other suppliers;

d.  The U.S. Government is not now interested in modifying the relevant policies from commercial or financial motives, and could not justify revision of trade control policies for humanitarian motives so long as Chinese needs can be met by other principal suppliers;

e.  It could reconsider the matter at such times as it may become evident that mainland China's needs cannot be met elsewhere; and

f.  The U.S. Government would not propose to make propaganda capital out of the fact of an approach to us for food grains.

4.  The Department of State should inform the Governments of Australia, Canada and France that the U.S. Government has considered but has not adopted proposals which would have put the United States in competition with those countries as suppliers of grain to mainland China; that we do not expect or ask them in present circumstances to attach extraneous conditions to their supply of food grains to Communist China; that it might, however, be possible to deter deeper Chinese Communist external involvement at the expense of the free world if the Peiping regime were to recognize that there would be a relationship between the direction of any important change in its external behavior and continued availability to it of non-bloc food grains, and that we

would hope those Governments would at an appropriate time find suitable means of conveying this fact to the Chinese Communists.[2]

**Dean Rusk**[3]

---

[2] In a meeting with the Canadian and Australian Ambassadors on January 16, Ball conveyed U.S. interest in "any potential lever which might be useful as a possible restraint on any aggressive intentions of Communist China." He emphasized that he was not suggesting that Canadian and Australian wheat sales should be stopped and that "it might even develop that increased sales would be found useful." (Ibid., Central Files, 493.009/1–1662)

[3] Printed from a copy that bears this typed signature.

---

## 101. Telegram From the Embassy in Poland to the Department of State

Warsaw, April 5, 1962, 7 p.m.

1547. Cabot–Wang talks. 109th meeting two hours forty minutes.[1] Reference: Department telegram 1314.[2]

1. In opening Wang attacked US Far East policies as predicted, with emphasis on alleged US occupation Taiwan as basic to our strained relations. After rebutting as instructed, I spoke of the problem of dogma at bottom of much of our misunderstandings, along lines paragraphs 2 and 3 reference telegram.[3] Covered American prisoners issue in terms paragraph 4.[4] Wang did not respond to this point.

2. Wang said no one doubts American people want peace but world cannot believe US Government following policy of peace. It did

---

Source: Department of State, Central Files, 611.93/4–562. Secret; Priority; Limit Distribution. Repeated to Taipei, Hong Kong, Geneva, Stockholm, and Moscow.

[1] Cabot commented and sent recommendations for the next meeting in telegram 1548, April 6, and sent a detailed, apparently verbatim report of the meeting in airgram A–563, April 7. (Ibid., 611.93/4–662 and 611.93/4–762, respectively)

[2] Telegram 1314, April 3, conveyed Cabot's instructions for the meeting. (Ibid., 611.93/4–362)

[3] Paragraph 2 declared that Wang's side had labeled the United States as an enemy because of dogma rather than facts. Paragraph 3 declared that it would be in the interests of both sides if they were to take an objective look at the situation.

[4] Paragraph 4 urged fulfillment of the 1955 agreement to release imprisoned U.S. civilians in the interest of reducing international tensions.

during Roosevelt era but not since. Said US had organized military blocs taking China, Soviet Union and all socialist countries as targets; had hundreds of military bases around world; sent troops into Lebanon, Cuba, Laos and South Vietnam; and now, against world opinion promises resume nuclear tests. I rebutted these points. Wang further claimed Chinese Communist policy not simply determined by theory and dogma, but primarily on basis actual relations between countries and on facts. Spoke with feeling of century of humiliation China had suffered and said Chinese people capable of judging from history which nations treated China equally and which otherwise. China will no longer be subjected to insults from foreigners or intimidated by foreign power. No one would prevent China from exercising its legitimate rights under name of so-called defensive measures.

3. I said not only Roosevelt but succeeding Presidents had all been freely elected by American people and all have striven to represent peace-loving policies of American people. After World War II US largely disarmed but unfortunately [garble] many others had not. Outlined Communist hostility which forced us to join with other free nations in defense. Spoke of our constant efforts in interest disarmament.

4. Wang returned again to difference between desires American people and policy of government. I said representatives of people in Congress had repeatedly and in overwhelming majority showed intention of American people resist aggression by Chinese Communists, stressed importance studying sequence of events in Far East which show US defensive moves always in response Communist provocation.

5. In speaking of seven serious warnings of sea and air intrusions since last meeting, Wang complained specifically of US ships in territorial waters Yung Hsing Island which did not withdraw after warning flashed. I said I would be glad to inquire as to the circumstances of this alleged invasion. Request guidance in answering for next meeting.

Nothing new introduced in long, futile meeting.

Next meeting May 17.

**Cabot**

## 102. Memorandum From the Deputy Under Secretary of State for Political Affairs (Johnson) to Secretary of State Rusk

Washington, April 6, 1962.

SUBJECT

United States Policy on Shipments of Medicines and Food Grains to Communist China

As Governor Harriman's memorandum of April 3[1] to you on the foregoing subject notes, I am not able to concur in the third recommendation in the draft Memorandum for the President, that is, the proposal that Ambassador Cabot, in his talks with Wang Ping-nan in Warsaw should take the initiative in indicating a willingness to reconsider our policy on the sale of grain to Communist China at such time as it may become evident that Mainland China's needs cannot be met elsewhere. Among my reasons are the following:

1. Basically, I feel that our posture toward Communist China should be one of receptivity toward any initiatives they may take for improvement of relations with us, but, at least for the time being, not to make further overtures of our own. Our previous and most recent overtures have been most rudely rejected.

2. Chinese Communist hostility toward us is based on our policy with respect to Taiwan. All other issues, including trade, are very peripheral. There is little hope of any useful dialogue between ourselves and the Chinese Communists until there is some change in their attitudes in this regard. There is as yet no sign of any such change.

3. The Chinese Communists have consistently taken the position that they could afford to wait and that, without their making any concessions, the pressure of events would require unilateral adjustments of U.S. policy, viz. outside pressures with respect to the UN and Taiwan, and our own commercial pressures with respect to trade. Now to make such an even tentative approach to them with respect to grain will tend to convince them that their policy is paying off and that we are being forced to react to the pressures of our commercial grain interests. All they have to do is to continue to wait and we will continue to move in their direction.

---

Source: Department of State, Central Files, 611.93/4–662. Secret. Drafted by Johnson. Copies were sent to Ball, McGhee, and Harriman. Ball forwarded the memorandum to Rusk along with Documents 100 and 104, with a covering memorandum of April 9 stating that he shared Johnson's reservations and thought "it would be a mistake to interject the possibility of grain sales into the Warsaw talks." (Ibid., 411.9341/4–962)

[1] See the source note, Document 100.

4.  Our expressed willingness to permit gift shipments of food, as suggested in the second recommendation, and which will in all probability again be blocked by Chinese Communist unwillingness to permit such shipments, will do all that is necessary at this time to remove any onus on the United States for hunger in China and place the onus where it properly belongs, on the Chinese Communist Government.

5.  I am satisfied that, if and when the Chinese Communists have a genuine interest in the purchase of American grain, we will unmistakably know it—not directly, for they will never mention it in Warsaw, but rather indirectly.

---

**103.  Telegram From the Embassy in the Republic of China to the Department of State**

Taipei, April 10, 1962, 2 p.m.

684.  Embtel 662[1] and Deptel 544.[2] I spoke to Foreign Minister Shen April 9 along lines reftels. I explained I had delayed requesting appointment with him because decline in press attention to subject I wished discuss with him reduced urgency and because he was so fully occupied last week with visit of Malagasy President. Although tone of press had moderated lately, I thought he would wish to know US Government had been concerned at rising crescendo of press attention to counterattack theme. I added I knew from his prompt and effective reaction to Lien Ho Pao story April 7 (Embtel 682)[3] that he was fully aware of problem.

Shen replied he fully agreed that press had played up counterattack too sensationally. He assured me GRC had not instigated press to do this,

---

Source: Department of State, Central Files, 793.00/4–1062. Secret.

[1] Telegram 662, March 31, expressed concern about the consequences of the press campaign and public statements in recent weeks on the "counterattack" theme, stated that several U.S. officials in Taipei had spoken critically to GRC leaders about the campaign, and recommended a more formal démarche by Clough to Foreign Minister Shen. (Ibid., 793.00/3–3162)

[2] Telegram 544, April 2, authorized Clough to make the approach he had recommended to Shen. (Ibid.)

[3] Telegram 682, April 7, reported that Shen had told Clough the Foreign Ministry was denying a news story that day quoting Ambassador Tsiang as stating that Presidents Chiang and Kennedy were giving serious consideration to the question of a counterattack. (Ibid., 793.00/4–762)

as was demonstrated by fact that Government papers treated subject in a much more sober and calm manner than independent press. He had personally made effort to restrain press. At secret meeting for Foreign Affairs Committee of Legislative Yuan he had tried to dampen speculation about political significance of Drumright's resignation, publication of 1943 papers,[4] etc. He also held background briefing March 27 for publishers and editors of newspapers at which he not only argued vigorously that there was no basis for speculation regarding possible change in US policy, but also urged pressmen not to agitate unduly counterattack question, particularly US relationship to it. He pointed out to publishers that no possible good could come from causing questions to be put to US spokesmen regarding US attitude toward counterattack, for those spokesmen could not possibly under present circumstances respond in any way helpful to GRC objectives. Shen expressed appreciation at my having raised subject with him and added he thought our two governments had common interest in avoiding excessive press attention to counterattack theme. He said of course subject could not be totally ignored by press in Taiwan, but it should not be sensationalized.

Comment: Moderating of press discussion counterattack past two weeks probably due in part to Shen's efforts and others reportedly undertaken by KMT Fourth Section (FCT 7683) helped by preoccupation of press with Malagasy President's visit. Believe MOFA particularly alive to dangers and will do what it can to influence press as well as other party and government officials. We will watch situation closely and seek to head off build-up of any further campaign. We have been warning prominent visiting American officials in advance of questions they may expect from local newsmen on arrival and believe this has helped to keep temperature down.

**Clough**

---

[4] Reference is to *Foreign Relations*, 1943, China, which was released on March 20, 1962. Telegram 501 to Taipei, March 8, suggested that in case Chiang raised the subject of the volume's pending release with Harriman, the latter could point out that the volume had been printed for release in 1957 and had been withheld from publication since that time, but pressure for its release had been intensifying, and the Department considered that further withholding would be more damaging to U.S. and GRC interests than its release. (Department of State, Central Files, 611.00/3–862) Chiang did not raise the subject with Harriman.

## 104.   Memorandum From the Assistant Secretary of State for Far Eastern Affairs (Harriman) to Secretary of State Rusk

Washington, April 13, 1962.

SUBJECT

United States Policy on Shipments of Medicines and Food Grains to Communist China

I would like to respond to the arguments contained in Mr. Johnson's memo to you of April 6,[1] which Mr. Ball has supported. Mr. Johnson objected to the proposal, advanced in the memo on the foregoing subject which I sent you through Mr. McGhee on April 3,[2] that Ambassador Cabot let the Chinese Communists know we could reconsider our present policy against selling food grains to mainland China if and when it became evident that its needs could not be met by purchases elsewhere.

Whether such reconsideration resulted in a decision to sell, or not to do so, would of course have to depend on the whole set of surrounding circumstances. I think we should not indicate actual willingness to sell foodstuffs to Communist China unless the Peiping regime takes the initiative—lest we seem to be anxious for commercial profits. I also believe that we should not exploit any such initiative by them for purposes of political propaganda. This accords very closely with what the President said in his January 25, 1961, news conference[3] in the context, however, of sending food through the United Nations, CARE, or a similar organization. He alluded to some circumstances which militated against our supplying food to Communist China, but he also expressed concern for hunger anywhere, a willingness to give careful consideration to any indication of a desire for food from the United States and disinterest in offering it as a mere propaganda gesture.

Since then, the Chinese Communists have come considerably closer to exhausting other sources of grain. Nevertheless, a statement of the sort proposed, in the Warsaw talks, might well be brushed aside, perhaps rudely. The Chinese Communist leadership has made a part of its stock in trade the portrayal of the US as an enemy of the Chinese people. I am against giving them ammunition by our acts or failures to act: We should not live up to their picture of us. Moreover, we do not know what inner battles may be going on now and may occur in the future within the Chi-

---

Source: Department of State, FE Files: Lot 64 D 25, Communist China. Secret. Drafted by Rice.

[1] Document 102.

[2] See the source note, Document 100.

[3] See footnote 3, Document 10.

nese Communist leadership: Internal and external difficulties must surely be breeding differences within that leadership. Evidence that the US would be willing to play a part in moving our relationship away from one of implacable mutual hostility might strengthen the hand of any elements which might favor doing so, now or later. Whether it did or not, I think we should not have our historical record be one of having refused to sell food to a people in a period when food was greatly needed. That would be a record which might one day rise to haunt us.

Against this perspective, I am not impressed by the argument that we should, "at least for the time being, not make any overtures of our own". If we are ever to make them, we can do so more gracefully now than, say, after the Chinese Communists have exploded a nuclear device—when overtures might be interpreted as motivated by apprehension.

The move we suggest is a small one, but our choice seems to be between immobility and steps which are few and small. I cannot believe that a policy of immobility can serve us well in a world where change is the rule.[4]

Personal for the Secretary. I feel strongly about this and if need be wish to have a chance to discuss it with you. It's my hunch that it would be what the President wants. W.A.H.[5]

---

[4] The grain sales issue was discussed in the context of Sino-Soviet relations at an April 17 meeting with Rusk; see Document 99. When Battle asked whether he should arrange another meeting with Rusk on these subjects, Harriman replied affirmatively, adding, "I certainly don't want to see the rigid policies of the past foisted on the President. I think he is strongly for the less rigid attitude as far as the grain issue is concerned." (National Archives and Records Administration, RG 59, S/P Files: Lot 69 D 121, China) An April 23 memorandum from Rostow to Battle suggested meeting with Rusk on the basis of Document 100 and Harriman's April 13 memorandum but not until Hilsman could respond to questions Rusk had raised about possible divisions in the Chinese leadership and recent Sino-Soviet developments. (Department of State, Central Files, 411.9341/4–2362)

[5] The postscript, the last paragraph, is typed on the source text, but a typed note on the source text indicates that the postscript was handwritten and only on the Secretary's copy.

## 105.   Message From the President's Special Assistant for National Security Affairs (Bundy) to the Chief of the Central Intelligence Agency Station in Taipei (Cline)

Washington, April 17, 1962.

In response to your priority telegram which has been discussed with President[1] the difficulty of your task is well understood here and your efforts to convey our position to the GRC are greatly appreciated.

The USG position must be that it stands on what is outlined in the President's seven-point statement. We cannot safely get ourselves in the position of negotiating on this.

In the light of the above our comments on the GRC ABC formulation are as follows:

Point A goes further than the seven-point statement in that it commits the United States to a drop of a 200 man unit with only the date subject to discussion and joint agreement. The statement only contemplated studying the feasibility of such a drop, preparing two aircraft for possible GRC use and making them available only if hard evidence is obtained to support the conclusion that such an operation would succeed.

In connection with the lack of hard evidence no mention is made of point four of the seven-point statement.

The statements in Points B and C that the United States Government and the GRC will "study" subsequent clandestine and open military actions and "jointly decide" their "execution and timing" could be interpreted to commit the United States to approve such actions in advance and by implication to support them. The seven-point statement made no mention of subsequent actions.

We recognize your problem is conveying this position effectively and we suggest that you hang your report on the difficulty which we have in the United States Government in asking the President in matters of this kind to approve two different formulations of policy. After all, in

---

Source: Kennedy Library, National Security Files, Countries Series, China, CIA Cables, 3/62–4/62. Top Secret. No time of transmission is indicated on the source text.

[1] An April 14 message from Cline to Bundy reported that Chiang Kai-shek had agreed to postpone the target date for possible action against the mainland from June until October and to work with U.S. officials to achieve a common understanding of the requirements of the mainland situation but that he wanted reassurance of the following: agreement on October 1 as the beginning date of the initial airdrop, agreement to begin joint study of plans for secret or open military operations to follow up a successful airdrop, and agreement that the execution and timing of an initial airdrop and subsequent action would be decided jointly by the two governments in the light of circumstances at that time. (Ibid.) See the Supplement.

logic, if in fact the three-point formulation is the same as the seven-point formulation, it is not necessary, and if there is a difference, there would be danger of misunderstanding not only with our good friends in Taiwan but within the Administration itself.[2]

---

[2] An April 19 message from Cline to Bundy stated that although Bundy's message had "plunged Chiang Ching-kuo and Gimo into another trough of despair and made me sweat blood trying to resell seven points," Chiang Ching-kuo had told him that day that "Gimo willing accept seven points as basis close study and cooperation during next few months" and had authorized senior staff discussions of GRC clandestine and military plans. He added, "For moment situation under control but believe me it was close thing. Cooperative relationship liable come unstuck if not given sympathetic attention this end and tangible signs of active interest from Washington." (Filed with an April 23 memorandum from Forrestal to Harriman; Library of Congress Manuscript Division, Harriman Papers, Kennedy–Johnson Administrations, Subject Files, China) See the Supplement.

---

## 106.  Telegram From the Department of State to the Embassy in the Republic of China

Washington, April 29, 1962, 10:23 a.m.

594. Embtels 737[1] and 716.[2] Department agrees imperative induce GRC curb military spending but recognizes appeals to GRC economic officials of limited effect. Therefore Chargé should request immediate appointment with Vice President who concerned Taiwan economic development and may be able induce President to exert restraint on military spending. Chargé should make following points to Vice President:

---

Source: Department of State, Central Files, 793.5/4–2662. Secret; Niact; Limit Distribution. Drafted by Herbert E. Horowitz of the ROC desk and Yager; cleared in draft by Harriman and with the Agency for International Development, in substance with the Department of Defense, and by U. Alexis Johnson and Bundy; and approved by Rice. Repeated to CINCPAC.

[1] Telegram 737, April 26, reported that GRC leaders had approved a military preparedness plan which would cost NT $2.48 billion and special taxes and other revenue measures to finance it. Clough commented that the program violated a basic commitment of the accelerated development plan and created a completely new setting in which to consider applications for AID financing. (Ibid., 793.5/4–2662)

[2] Telegram 716, April 20, commented on a situation reported in telegram 713, dated April 19. The latter reported that the Embassy had learned that during the previous year, the Ministry of National Defense had been allotted approximately NT $1 billion in special advances, about half of which had been spent on "extra preparedness measures." (Ibid., 793.5/4–1962) Telegram 716 commented that the problem was not only the threat to economic stability and growth posed by these expenditures but how to respond to the GRC decision that the prospects of relatively early action against the mainland were good enough to warrant urgent and extensive preparations, even at the risk of substantial damage to other GRC objectives. (Ibid., 793.5/4–2062)

(1) United States Government deeply concerned over threat to economic stability of Taiwan posed by alarming increase in military expenditures now taking place and proposed. Such spending cannot in our view be justified on ground of military necessity. While we appreciate GRC desire to be prepared for eventual return to mainland, our best intelligence convinces us that Chinese Communist security controls have not yet deteriorated to point where attacks at present time or in immediate future could have any hope of success. Current and projected military spending could in fact seriously damage GRC base on Taiwan and impair GRC efforts achieve ultimate goal. (Might recall Chen's theme that efforts Taiwan's economic development justified by importance as base for mainland recovery.) Emphasize loss of confidence in currency that can result from inflation threat, possible undoing of fiscal and exchange reforms of last several years, impact of diversion of resources from development purposes, undermining of program induce foreign investment, and adverse effect Four Year Plan and Accelerated Development Program. (We believe Vice President much concerned all these points.) He undoubtedly mindful that all Chinese bear scars disastrous war and post-war inflation on mainland, and that resumption sharp inflation could have grave repercussions public confidence in government.

(2) United States Government deeply disappointed over failure of GRC to keep it adequately informed concerning recent increased military expenditures despite repeated requests by United States officials for such information. United States Government also disturbed over apparent intention of GRC to confront United States Government with plan of military preparedness as fait accompli in disregard of close US-GRC partnership that has hitherto existed in matters affecting security of Taiwan.

(3) In view extent United States commitment in building GRC military and economic bastion on Taiwan we consider it our duty as well as right to insist that:

(a) Formal adoption of plan of military preparedness described Embtel 737 be deferred until United States Government can have adequate opportunity to express its views.
(b) GRC inform United States Government fully on extent and nature recent and proposed extraordinary military expenditures.
(c) Mutual consultations be held as soon as possible with view toward minimizing adverse effect recent increase this spending on economy and limiting level of spending in future months.

Immediately following Chargé's talk with Vice President, Commander Taiwan Defense Command, Chief MAAG, AID Mission Director, [less than 1 line of source text not declassified] should brief their principal GRC contacts on points made by Chargé to Vice President and emphasize seriousness with which United States Government views recent sharp increase in military spending. Chief MAAG and AID Mission Director should express as personal opinion view that failure to check such spending may force re-examination of United States aid programs. If question arises [*less than 1 line of source text not declassified*] USG position on mainland operations recently conveyed to President Chiang [*less than 1 line of source text not declassified*] remains unchanged.

To further impress GRC with urgency we view this problem, Harriman will call in Ambassador Tsiang and make démarche parallel to that of Chargé. Chargé should inform Department in advance time his appointment with Vice President.

FYI: Department and other agencies concerned are considering additional steps that may be required if approaches described above do not produce desired results. Country team recommendations are requested in this regard. Also, additional information on level and nature of GRC military spending beyond that reported Embtel 737 should be reported as soon as it becomes available.

AID Mission should assess effects on economy and make appropriate recommendations soften impact military spending. Pending outcome of discussions on military spending, nothing should be said to GRC concerning prospects for $30 million non-project loan. End FYI.

Defense and AID concur in this message.

**Ball**

---

## 107. National Intelligence Estimate

NIE 13–4–62                                          Washington, May 2, 1962.

PROSPECTS FOR COMMUNIST CHINA

The Problem

To estimate the prospects for Communist China over the next several years with emphasis on the viability of the regime and trends in its foreign policy.

---

Source: Department of State, INR/EAP Files: Lot 90 D 110, NIE 13–4–62. Secret. According to a note on the cover sheet, the Central Intelligence Agency and intelligence organizations of the Departments of State, Defense, the Army, the Navy, and the Air Force and the Joint Staff participated in the preparation of this estimate. All members of the USIB concurred with this estimate on May 2 except the representatives of the AEC and the FBI, who abstained on the grounds that the subject was outside their jurisdiction.

NIE 13–4/1–62, June 29, not printed, supplemented NIE 13–4–62 with more extended discussion and supporting information concerning economic, military, and internal security matters. (Ibid.)

## Conclusions

1. The future course of events in Communist China will be shaped largely by three highly unpredictable variables: the wisdom and realism of the leadership, the level of agricultural output, and the nature and extent of foreign economic relations. During the past few years all three variables have worked against China. In 1958 the leadership adopted a series of ill-conceived and extremist economic and social programs; in 1959 there occurred the first of three years of bad crop weather; and in 1960 Soviet economic and technical cooperation was largely suspended. The combination of these three factors has brought economic chaos to the country. Malnutrition is widespread, foreign trade is down, and industrial production and development have dropped sharply. No quick recovery from the regime's economic troubles is in sight. (Paras. 5–14)

2. Economic disasters have brought widespread disillusionment and disaffection in their wake, but we believe that widespread organized resistance to the regime is unlikely to develop. In any case, the regime's monopoly on arms, organization, and communications is probably sufficient to crush any incipient uprising. Communist China's armed forces have experienced setbacks in their modernization program and logistical capabilities, but, although there has been some decline in morale, they will probably remain loyal to the regime. We believe that by the end of the decade the Chinese Communists will have a limited nuclear weapons and missile capability.[1] (Paras. 21–24)

3. We believe that over the next few years Communist China will follow relatively conservative and rational policies of the kind recently instituted, that the odds favor improved crop weather, and that increased trade with Western Europe and Japan will partially compensate for the severe reduction in Soviet economic and technical cooperation. We therefore believe that the most likely prospect is for slow recovery and a gradual resumption of economic growth. However, there is also a possibility that the economic depression will continue, bringing increasing problems for the regime, and there is a slimmer possibility of fairly rapid recovery and economic expansion. In any case, over the longer run, given communism's demonstrated inefficiency in agriculture, it is possible that the regime will founder on a failure to solve China's chronic food problem. (Paras. 15–20)

---

[1] See NIE 13–2–62, "Chinese Communist Advanced Weapons Capabilities," dated 25 April 1962. The Assistant Chief of Naval Operations (Intelligence), Department of the Navy, believes that a reliable estimate of the Chinese Communist program in the development of nuclear weapons cannot yet be made. His footnote to paragraph 38 of NIE 13–2–62 contains the rationale for his position. [Footnote in the source text. NIE 13–2–62 is ibid., INR/EAP Files: Lot 90 D 99. See volume VIII, p. 274, for a summary.]

4.  We believe that the US will continue to face a hostile Communist China which will be constantly probing for weaknesses, trying to push the US out of the Western Pacific, and causing trouble wherever else it can. Meanwhile China will probably continue to promote the image of being a strong but peaceful nation, while covertly providing tactical guidance and material aid, to the extent of its capabilities, to leftist revolutionary movements in Asia, Africa, and Latin America. Outside the Far East these capabilities are limited by China's poverty, relative international isolation, and difficulties with the USSR. Communist China almost certainly does not intend to attempt the open military conquest of any Far Eastern country during the period of this estimate, although it would almost certainly be willing to take military action to defend Communist interests in North Vietnam and North Korea and, probably in Laos. (Paras. 26–35)

[Here follow paragraphs 5–35, comprising the Discussion portion of the estimate, in two sections, headed "Introduction" and "Prospects," and a map entitled "Communist China."]

## 108.  Telegram From the Department of State to the Embassy in the Republic of China

Washington, May 4, 1962, 8:10 p.m.

614.  Department's 594, sent CINCPAC unnumbered.[1] Harriman called in Chinese Minister Kiang this afternoon to express deep concern of USG over GRC military preparedness program.[2] Harriman explained that in view of importance of subject he had expected to meet with Amb.

Source: Department of State, Central Files, 793.5/4–2662. Secret; Priority; Limit Distribution. Drafted by Yager, cleared in draft by Harriman, and approved by Rice. Repeated to CINCPAC.

[1] Document 106.

[2] In a telephone conversation on May 3, Harriman and Michael Forrestal of the NSC staff briefly discussed Harriman's plan to talk to the Chinese Ambassador. According to notes of the conversation made in Harriman's office, Forrestal stated that he and Bundy were opposed to sanctions but thought "nothing at all wrong with being quite firm [about] our inability to be of any really useful help to them if they do not tell us what they are doing." Harriman replied, "We can't let them stop their growth—the example they are giving compared to mainland China." (Library of Congress Manuscript Division, Harriman Papers, Kennedy–Johnson Administrations, Telecons)

Tsiang, but Ambassador Stevenson had asked that Amb. Tsiang not be called away from his duties as Security Council Chairman during discussion delicate Kashmir question. Urgency of business at hand made delay undesirable.

Harriman said USG is very disturbed over large increase in military spending of nature only vaguely known to us. We are shocked that such program has been undertaken without consulting us despite our past close working relationship. We were further disturbed by unsympathetic response of Vice President Chen when problem of increased military spending was raised with him by our Chargé few days ago.[3] Harriman said we are concerned over possible inflationary effect of new program or, even if program covered by new taxes, by diversion of resources from investment necessary to maintenance of strength and growth of Taiwan economy needed to meet future possible emergency or exploit opportunity. Jeopardizing this strength seems to us most unwise. GRC appears to be disregarding past common understandings, including declaration in 19 point economic reform program of January 1960[4] to effect military expenditures would be kept at current level. Harriman emphasized that he spoke for highest levels of USG in requesting that new military preparedness program be held in abeyance until it can be reviewed by US and discussed by responsible US officials in Taipei. He asked that our Chargé and other appropriate senior US officials be given fullest information on new program as soon as possible.

Harriman also noted we would want opportunity to analyze effect of new taxes. Harriman further noted concern of USG over new upsurge in publicity in Taipei on return to mainland in connection with new taxes and stated this publicity appears to violate past GRC assurances that such publicity will be minimized.

Kiang responded Chinese Embassy has received no official report on new program. He promised to report fully views expressed by Harriman and will urge early reply.

---

[3] Clough reported the conversation in telegram 766 from Taipei, May 2. (Department of State, Central Files, 793.5/5–262) Telegram 770 from Taipei, May 4, reported similar conversations between other U.S. and GRC representatives. (Ibid., 793.5/5–462) Clough commented in telegram 775, May 4, that although the reaction had been essentially negative, this might change as the full import of the representations sank in. He noted that Chiang Ching-kuo had been more forthcoming and might affect an improvement in the GRC attitude. (Ibid.)

[4] Reference is to the "Accelerated Economic Growth Program" dated January 14, 1960, enclosed with a letter of that date from K.Y. Yin, Vice Chairman of the Council for U.S. Aid, to Haraldson. Paragraph 9 stated the GRC intention to maintain defense expenditures (in constant dollars) at the current level, "at least in the immediate future." (Washington National Records Center, RG 84, FRC 66 A 878, Taipei Embassy Files: Lot 65 F 163, 500—Accelerated Program for Taiwan) See Foreign Relations, 1958–1960, vol. XIX, p. 649, footnote 2.

Harriman stated mere reply would not be sufficient. What is required is action in terms of immediate discussions in Taipei with appropriate American officials.

**Ball**

## 109. Telegram From the Embassy in Poland to the Department of State

Warsaw, May 17, 1962, 7 p.m.

1846. Cabot–Wang Talks. 110 meeting one hour 40 minutes.[1] Re Department telegram 1540.[2]

1. I opened with general statement on US disarmament policy and reasons therefor, after which I handed Wang documents as instructed reference telegram.[3] I continued with substance paragraphs two and three on our activities vicinity Paracels and on imprisoned Americans.[4]

2. Wang replied he failed to see evidence USG wants disarmament or peace, asking why we continued occupy Taiwan and intrude into Chinese territory with increasing tempo. Mentioned *De Haven* surveillance over period one week during which alleged three intrusions. Said Chinese people keenly resent these intrusions which show US accustomed to brutally trampling on sovereignty other countries and has contempt for elementary code international conduct. Gave ChiCom version history Paracels and reiterated sovereignty claim. In claiming we had well

---

Source: Department of State, Central Files, 611.93/5–1762. Confidential; Priority; Limit Distribution. Repeated to Taipei, Hong Kong, Geneva, Stockholm, and Moscow.

[1] Cabot commented and sent recommendations for the next meeting in telegram 1852, May 18, and sent a detailed, apparently verbatim report of the meeting in airgram A–638, May 18. (Ibid., 611.93/5–1862)

[2] Telegram 1540, May 14, conveyed Cabot's instructions for the meeting. (Ibid., 611.93/5–1462)

[3] Reference is to a U.S. proposal submitted to the Eighteen-Nation Disarmament Committee in Geneva on April 18; the text is in *Documents on Disarmament, 1962*, vol. I, pp. 351–382.

[4] Paragraph 2 of telegram 1540 instructed Cabot to state that the U.S. Government did not recognize the claim of Wang's side to the Paracels, that U.S. ships and aircraft in that area had operated on the high seas according to a U.S. policy of avoiding measures likely to increase tension, and that U.S. ships would continue to exercise their freedom to sail the high seas. Paragraph 3 instructed him to raise the issue of the imprisoned Americans.

earned label of imperialists, said we were main enemy of peoples of whole world.

Claimed some of our forces Taiwan were combat forces. Said top priority in our talks was US occupation Taiwan and this question could not be dismissed no matter how we attempted distort picture. Said his side favored general and complete disarmanent but US policies real obstacle to attainment. Claimed President Kennedy openly declared US ready strike first with nuclear weapons in preventive war.

3. I said throughout period of difficulty with Wang side we have tried pursue policy of peace but have been compelled protect ourselves and allies from aggressive moves his side. We do not occupy Taiwan and I would be glad next time to say more of the character of our military personnel there. Answered *De Haven* accusation accordance reference telegram.[5] Expressed gratification at statement Wang's side favors general and complete disarmament which precisely what we want. Again reminded Wang of aggressions his side, notably Korea. Said while we seek disarmament, we would not disarm unilaterally. Said to best my knowledge and belief President had not spoken of and never intended speak of preventive war.

4. Wang then launched into carefully prepared, lengthy standard upside-down account of Korean War.

5. I said facts re Korea so clear to world, not necessary go into detail but it was clear North Korea, with connivance Wang's side, committed aggression.

Next meeting July 12.

Informal meeting re Laos reported following telegram.[6]

**Cabot**

---

[5] Telegram 1540 instructed Cabot that if Wang raised the subject of an alleged intrusion into Chinese territorial waters by the USS *De Haven*, Cabot should reply that, in accordance with the U.S. policy of avoiding measures likely to increase tension, the *De Haven* had stayed outside even the 12-mile limit claimed by Wang's side.

[6] Cabot reported in telegram 1847, May 18, that after the formal meeting he met with Wang privately, with only interpreters present, and stated U.S. views on Laos as set forth in telegram 1550 to Warsaw, May 15. (Department of State, Central Files, 611.93/5–1862 and 611.93/5–1562, respectively)

## 110. Memorandum for the Record

Washington, May 17, 1962, 5:36 p.m.

SUBJECT

White House Briefing on China

PRESENT

The President, Mr. Bundy, Mr. McCone, Mr. Cline

1. The President opened the discussion by inquiring about news reports from Taipei of GRC support for the Phoumi Government. Mr. Cline reported that the news accounts were indicative of general moral and political support and did not reflect any material support of any consequence since the GRC fully understood U.S. wishes with respect to Laos and did not want to encourage Phoumi to resist U.S. policy. In fact, the GRC said they were advising Phoumi to accommodate to U.S. policy, whether it was right or wrong. They wished us to understand, however, that they felt a coalition in Laos would lead to a communist takeover even as it had in China years ago.

2. With respect to the China Mainland situation, Mr. Cline said, the GRC felt that the ChiCom system of public security controls was beginning to crumble, as evidenced recently in the astonishing throng of hungry refugees arriving by the thousands on the Hong Kong border. This tended to confirm the Gimo in his belief that the time was ripe or soon would be for establishing a beach-head in South China and encouraging popular resistance against the ChiComs and winning back sizable parts of the Mainland through defections from the armed forces, whose morale is certainly being lowered by the food situation and popular disillusionment with the ChiCom regime. The Gimo asked that President Kennedy be advised of his views on this situation, which is of great strategic importance to the U.S. as well as to the GRC. The President said that he recognized that if the ChiCom regime could be destroyed, it would tremendously alter the situation in Asia to the advantage of the Free World and that he did not want to dismiss this possibility altogether even though it seemed unlikely at this time.

3. Mr. Cline explained that the Gimo's main concepts, which he wished to be conveyed to the President, were as follows:

a. A strategic agreement between President Kennedy and President Chiang on policy and courses of action in Asia was essential to the welfare and interest of both the U.S. and the GRC.

Source: Central Intelligence Agency, DCI (McCone) Files, Job 80–B01285A, DCI Meetings With the President. Secret. The time of the meeting is from the President's Appointment Book. (Kennedy Library) Bundy is not listed as a participant in the President's Appointment Book.

b.  The GRC feels it is essential for it to plan and prepare for both clandestine and military actions to support anti-Communist resistance forces on the Mainland, but it recognizes that any action of this kind should be purely a GRC responsibility with no direct U.S. participation or sponsorship.

c.  Any sizable operations against the Mainland, whether clandestine or open military in character, must be jointly decided upon by the U.S. Government and the GRC in the light of the circumstances and conditions obtaining at the time of proposed execution of the operation; all preparations in the meantime are purely contingent in character.

d.  In the light of the situation on the Mainland, the GRC is obliged to take certain prudent military preparedness measures to be ready to intervene in case the situation deteriorates to the point where the U.S. agrees that action is in Free World interest.

e.  The psychological pressure in the top ranks of the GRC, particularly among the military, to do something positive to take advantage of the lowering of morale on the Mainland is intense, and the Gimo will increasingly encounter dissatisfaction and even internal opposition that will be hard to contain if he continues to postpone taking action against the Mainland; he has promised to take no action until 1 October, but it will be very difficult to postpone beyond this date even though the U.S. insists.

f.  In the event further delays are necessary, it would help a great deal to explain this to his own military leaders if the Gimo could point to increased military strength being supplied by the U.S. even though its use was contingent on U.S. agreement; thus enough C–123's to carry the 200-man team we have agreed to prepare for clandestine launch (5 aircraft—i.e. ECM configured C–123's—rather than the 2 set aside for this purpose) ought to be given to the GRC, as well as about 16 B–57's, which would be needed to neutralize IL–28 bombers if hostilities broke out, and a considerable number of LST's (75–100,000 tons, which would be 20–25 vessels) for amphibious forces. The provision of any of these items would convince people actual preparations were being made and would permit further delays to be weathered more gracefully.

g.  The Gimo considers good U.S.-GRC relations are vital, and he regrets the recrimination over recent budget and tax provisions the GRC has made to cover the military expenditures the GRC has felt it essential to make ($62 million for FY 62 and FY 63) to be prepared for the contingency of an open invasion of South China by GRC armed forces in the next 18 months. These fiscal measures will be coordinated with the U.S. Embassy and U.S. military aid officials, but the Gimo feels that the discussion should be in terms recognizing the right of the GRC to make prudent preparations in its own national security interest.

h.  The Gimo said he was reluctant to get into detailed coordination of these matters because he felt many U.S. officials were totally unsympathetic with what the GRC considered its national interest in assisting the Chinese people throw off the yoke of the ChiCom regime if they were able and willing to do so. He said he was willing to discuss and explain anything and to accept U.S. advice if it was sympathetically given, preferably privately and off the record. He said that he particularly hoped President Kennedy would understand that threats of reprisals and pressures in the form of restricting U.S. aid to the GRC would be counter-productive and would in fact only destroy the prestige of the Gimo's Government and might cause instability and anti-Americanism in Taiwan. He wished the President to know that he thought it was a mistake for the U.S. to use open threats delivered through diplomatic channels against any Asian leaders, as it caused them to lose face and either resist U.S. advice or to become discredited with their own people. He thought the U.S. State Department was increasingly inclined to threaten economic pressures against any friendly government which disagreed with the U.S. It might be necessary to use this kind of diplomatic and economic pressure on some small and ineffective nations, although he doubted its wisdom, but in any case the Gimo wished earnestly and with the friendliest of purposes to advise the President that such pressures on the GRC would only serve to weaken Sino-American cooperation and injure our common interests. If this heavy-handed pressure could be avoided, the Gimo felt sure that a reasonable accommodation could be worked out on any issues in dispute.

**Ray S. Cline**[1]
*Deputy Director (Intelligence)*

---

[1] Printed from a copy that bears this typed signature.

---

**111.  Editorial Note**

A memorandum of May 25, 1962, from Rusk's Special Assistant Charles E. Bohlen to the President's Special Assistant for National Security Affairs, McGeorge Bundy, responded to a May 24 note from Bundy that President Kennedy had requested the opinion of Ambassador to the Soviet Union Llewellyn E. Thompson concerning two papers: NIE 11–5–62, "Political Developments in the USSR and the Communist

World," dated February 21, and comments on it by Ambassador to Yugoslavia George F. Kennan, conveyed in despatch 636 from Belgrade, April 11.

For information concerning NIE 11–5–62, see Document 99. Kennan's comments in despatch 636 read in part as follows:

"In summary, it seems to me that Chinese-Soviet relations bid fair to receive, in the coming period, a certain easement through the combined effect of two separate sets of frustrations: those suffered by the Chinese in the effort to realize their ambitious internal programs, and those suffered by Khrushchev in his effort to establish 'peaceful coexistence' with the West as a real and effective alternative of policy which would give him greater flexibility in his relations with other bloc parties. The greater modesty of aspiration which will be inflicted on both parties by these failures should make it easier rather than harder for them to get on together. Particularly is this true so long as the world is divided into opposing military camps with the tendency running to increased bipolarity. It is flexibility in the international situation, more than anything else, that will bring out the latent divisions within the bloc. An environment of continued sharp, military bipolarity will leave the two partners little choice but to repress their differences and carry on." (Department of State, Central Files, 101.21–NIS/4–1162)

In his memorandum to Bundy, Bohlen stated that he had requested Thompson's comments on the two papers and proceeded to state his own views, which he summarized as follows:

"In the first place, the NIE paper on which Kennan comments, dates from February of this year, when the situation in regard to the Sino-Soviet dispute was somewhat different. I am inclined to agree with George that it is somewhat too optimistic in speaking of the odds on the avoidance of an open split 'during 1962' are not better than even. Since that time, as you know, there have been certain indications in Sino-Soviet relations pointing towards a desire to agree to disagree and avoid the consequences of a further exacerbation of these differences and the dangers of a split, with all that that would entail. However, there is not the slightest sign that any adjustment of the basic elements of that dispute have been or are in process of adjustment. I, therefore, tend *in general* to agree with George's questioning of the validity of so absolute a statement as contained in the NIE in question."

After more detailed comments on Kennan's views, he concluded as follows:

"In regard to this whole matter, there should be one word of caution added; namely, that there is very little that the United States can do profitably to its interests in regard to this dispute. It is, of course, true that some agreement with the Soviet Union in any important area, and I have particularly in mind Berlin and Germany, would be useful, but in view of the insufficiency of our knowledge of the real factors in operation between these countries, we certainly should not predicate any policy on the fact of the Chinese-Soviet dispute. There is little question but that we are observing a deep process of evolution inside the Soviet camp, the outcome of which cannot possibly be accurately determined at this time, but at the present moment, I see very little basis for any shift in our current policy because of these developments." (Kennedy Library, National Security Files, Countries Series, USSR) See the Supplement.

Thompson replied in telegram 3070 from Moscow, May 26, that he had not yet received Kennan's comments. He commented on NIE 11–5–62 in part as follows: "Though I agree with basic line of NIE 11–5–62 I believe it somewhat exaggerates likelihood Sino-Soviet break and consider this borne out by events since this paper written. Similarly believe it underestimates possibilities of at least temporary accommodations between the two parties. For example should Khrushchev find his leadership of Soviet Party threatened and have possibility maintain his position by temporary accommodations to Chinese policy he would not hesitate adopt it; even if accord were reached believe it would be temporary in view of fundamental nature of issues." (Department of State, Central Files, 101.21–NIS/5–2662)

---

## 112.    Draft Paper Prepared in the Department of State

Washington, May 28, 1962.

SUBJECT

   Food Grains for Mainland China

*The Problem:*

   To determine what action the US should take in view of the current chronic food shortage on mainland China.

*Discussion:*

   1. It is not in the US interest to bail Peiping's present leaders out of their current difficulties. Making large quantities of grain available to them on longer-term easy credit terms would tend to do so.

---

Source: Department of State, Central Files, 893.03/5–1362. Secret. No drafting information is indicated on the source text. Filed with a May 31 memorandum from Brubeck to Harriman, which refers to it as "the third draft, May 28, which was used by the Secretary as a basis for his discussion with the President on this subject." According to Brubeck's memorandum, the first two drafts, May 24 and 25, were discussed at a May 24 meeting and a May 25 Standing Group meeting. Neither the drafts nor any record of the Standing Group meeting has been found. Handwritten notes of the May 24 meeting, chaired by McGhee, are ibid., S/S–NSC Files: Lot 70 D 265, NSC Standing Group, May 25, 1962. Rusk met with Kennedy on May 29 to discuss grain for China. (Kennedy Library, President's Appointment Book; Johnson Library, Rusk Appointment Book) No record of the meeting has been found.

2. It is, however, against our interests to establish an historical record of having stood between hungry people and foodstuffs which we have in abundant surplus: This is not our traditional attitude and might well be held against us in future relations with China.

3. There are bound to be among Chinese Communist leaders some who are basically more, and others who are less, antagonistic towards the US, or some who may believe in a tough policy towards the US and others who may see advantages to China in a more conciliatory policy. By inaction we would strengthen the hand of those advocating a line of maximum antagonism; by suitable action we might encourage those who are at the less hostile end of the spectrum—however narrow the spectrum.

4. It is not possible to identify individual leaders among the Chinese Communists as being dissident elements to whom a separate channel of communication should be sought.

5. The Chinese Communist regime would find it repugnant to accept gift shipments of Free World grain. Repugnance would be greatest if the gift were from the US Government.

6. Preliminary information from the Department of Agriculture suggests Communist China probably will within the months immediately ahead exhaust all substantial non-US sources of Free World grain. The principal Free World grain suppliers are states which would welcome a less rigid US policy towards China. While they might have mixed feelings about our supplying grain to Communist China, regret at such development would be tempered if their own stocks were low.

7. GRC objections might give us difficulties, but the GRC should not be permitted to veto action on our part taken in our own interest.

8. The refugee influx into Hong Kong which has occurred this month has dramatized hunger on the mainland.[1]

*Recommendations:*

We should instruct Ambassador Cabot at Warsaw to inform Wang Ping-nan, at the earliest opportunity, that:

(1) Reports of widespread hunger on the Chinese mainland have led to concern among Americans, who retain feelings of human friendliness towards the Chinese people.

(2) We are aware that food grains appear to be entering a period of tight supply. Should the Chinese Communists decide to advise us that

---

[1] In early May the number of mainland Chinese apprehended crossing the land frontier into Hong Kong had suddenly increased from the usual 100–200 per month to more than 2,000 in one 24-hour period. Telegraphic reports from Hong Kong on this subject are in Department of State, Central File 793.00. Telegram 1294 from Hong Kong, May 21, attributed the sudden influx of refugees to hunger and dissatisfaction, combined with the failure of demoralized local officials to enforce the usual rigid discipline. (Ibid., 793.00/5–2162)

they wished to procure US food grains, we would be prepared to reconsider present US policies and discuss the matter.[2]

***

[2] Telegram 1655 to Warsaw, May 30, reported that Cabot would probably be instructed to raise a new item of business at his next meeting with Wang. It stated that the item should be raised as soon as it was possible to do so in a normal and low-key manner and asked whether a U.S. request for a meeting about the middle of June rather than on July 12 as scheduled would seem unusual. (Ibid., 611.93/5–3062) The Embassy replied that since the meeting had been scheduled after July 1 at U.S. request, changing the date would indicate something unusual. (Telegrams 1947 and 1962 from Warsaw, May 31 and June 2; ibid., 611.93/5–3162 and 611.93/6–262, respectively) Telegram 1680 to Warsaw, June 4, agreed that the date should not be changed. (Ibid.)

***

## 113.  Memorandum From the Director of the Bureau of Intelligence and Research (Hilsman) to Secretary of State Rusk

Washington, May 29, 1962.

SUBJECT

GRC Operations Against The Mainland

This paper is in response to a request from Governor Harriman for a review of the situation with examination of various US policy alternatives and their probable consequences.

*I. The Problem*

Present GRC policy consists of closely interrelated political and military objectives focusing on recovery of the Chinese mainland. The political goals are continued assurance of US support for the GRC as it is now constituted and guarantees that the US will not drift toward a "two-China" policy. Militarily the GRC seeks increased US material support and eventual US involvement in an attempt to regain control of China.

Chiang Kai-shek believes that an uprising on the mainland is possible and that the GRC can gain control of such a revolt, perhaps initiat-

***

Source: Kennedy Library, National Security Files, Return to the Mainland, 1/62–5/62. Secret; Noforn. Filed with a covering memorandum of the same date from Brubeck to Bundy stating that it might be of interest and use to those attending the meeting on GRC matters that afternoon and an unsigned note to Bundy dated May 31 which stated, "FYI. Secretary had on his copy 'President should see.'"

ing it through small-scale military action. However the GRC recognizes that even if a spontaneous uprising should occur, re-gaining control of the mainland would be impossible without significant increases in the GRC forces and eventual US participation, at least at the logistical level. A summary of GRC efforts to win increased US support for operations against the mainland is included in an appendix attached herewith.[1]

US estimates challenge the basis of GRC planning on three counts: (1) there is almost no chance that a mainland uprising would extend beyond a single province, (2) there is even less likelihood that such an uprising would follow GRC leadership, and (3) should a GRC-sponsored uprising actually threaten the Chinese Communist regime, Russian intervention would almost certainly be forthcoming. Thus GRC efforts face either quick defeat or short-lived success. The accompanying risks for US policy range from political embarrassment to a war of escalation.

*II. Chiang's Position*

President Chiang probably sees that the US has no present intention of supporting a GRC attack. Under the circumstances, he can attempt independent action or he can hope for a change in the situation which would cause the US to re-examine its policy. This change could come from increased tensions in Southeast Asia or from growing unrest in Communist China. Having waited thirteen years, he probably feels that unilateral action is not yet necessary. Waiting, however, requires that he keep the US committed to support of the GRC, and if possible, to strengthening its forces. At the same time, he must avoid confronting the US with a basic decision wherein a later US re-examination would be foreclosed through refusal of any further support for preparations against the mainland.

As evidence of this delaying tactic, Chiang apparently decided in mid-April to put off all offensive action until after September since no US support was forthcoming this spring and the environment might prove more auspicious in the fall. The Laotian crisis undoubtedly strengthened this hope. Although possibly disappointed that US troops did not enter Laos, GRC leaders probably see the deployment of US forces in Thailand as indicating a stronger anti-communist stand than was originally anticipated in Taipei. While this may reduce GRC suspicions of US actions as foreshadowing the abandonment of Chiang, it increases the likelihood that the GRC will exploit this more determined US posture by stepping up its requests for material support.

The recent flood of refugees into Hong Kong provided further encouragement for GRC hopes that a sudden breakdown of Chinese

---

[1] Not printed, but see the Supplement.

Communist controls will unleash ever widening disturbances. Even though the exodus has ended, at least for the moment, it is probably regarded in Taipei as proof of the unrest to be exploited in the very target-areas selected for proposed GRC airdrops.

*III. US Policy Alternatives*

The US may respond to GRC demands for support in its mainland aspirations in any of four general ways: acquiescence, outright refusal, temporizing, and polite postponement.

*Acquiescence* to GRC demands would relieve immediate US-GRC pressures. The GRC would feel encouraged to exploit mainland unrest as it saw fit, regardless of subsequent US warnings. Defeat would end Chiang's hopes forever, removing this thorn in US-GRC relations. Success, if prolonged beyond a few days, would reveal the weakness of Communist China. If Soviet intervention proved necessary, Peiping's claims to Asian leadership would be thoroughly discredited. Against these favorable considerations must be weighed the certainty of US political involvement and the consequent embarrassment of relations with Asian and European allies. Should UN censure strike at the GRC, US interests would be affected. This combination of military and political setbacks might compel Chiang to resign, with no certainty of his successor's ability to rule Taiwan as the Republic of China. Should GRC operations against the mainland be prolonged, the civil war might spread or escalate. Hong Kong and Laos would be vulnerable to Chinese Communist counter-pressures. Soviet intervention might confront the US with abandonment of its ally or thermonuclear war.

*Outright rejection* would eliminate the ambiguity in US-GRC relations. Direct or indirect revelation of this move would lessen the US embarrassment should Chiang go it alone. Indications of a GRC intent to violate the mutual defense treaty obligations requiring joint approval of offensive military operations could be answered with graduated sanctions through the withholding of US economic and military aid. This open confrontation of US-GRC interests, however, might strain relations to the breaking point. Chiang might strike against the mainland with whatever force he could muster in hope of winning a toehold. This would buy time for appealing directly to his countrymen and for building political pressure within the US to force a reversal of policy. Should he not go it alone, Chiang might submit a token resignation in symbolic protest against the US position, hoping that the domestic US response would force a change of policy. Throughout this political crisis in US-GRC relations, Peiping would intensify its efforts to collapse GRC morale, alternating between renewed threats of force and offers of amnesty for those who rejoined the motherland.

*Temporizing* would delay an explicit US response concerning our ultimate intentions while offering material and political tokens of our sympathetic support for Chiang's goals. We would insist that two pre-requisites for offensive operations were (1) clear indication of sufficient support on the mainland to guarantee GRC success and (2) demonstration of GRC realism in planning both the attack and the subsequent pacification. This would ease US-GRC tensions somewhat, depending upon the levels of material assistance accompanying our temporizing. We would have an opportunity to influence GRC planning and would probably improve our information on GRC preparations for attack. So long as no significant revolt occurred on the mainland, only minor crises would arise as each GRC request won partial and delayed US agreement. Should a revolt begin, US involvement would have become almost inextricable even if unilateral GRC action in violation of treaty obligations provided legal justification for disengagement. In the eyes of many in the GRC, Asia, and the US itself, our public identification of American policy and interest with Chiang, buttressed by our material support for his forces, would require further support now that the opportunity for regaining China lay at hand. Regardless of the risks identified with the acquiescence alternative above, personal and institutional pressures might well override previous intentions. Should we disavow the GRC action, many observers would conclude that the US nerve had weakened at the last moment. Other allies might lose confidence in the US resolve to make genuine sacrifices for their interests. The possibility of a GRC fait accompli on the basis of these overall considerations cannot be wholly discounted.

*Polite postponement* permits the US to insist that overriding considerations connected with the unstable Southeast Asian situation compel complete suspension of all steps in preparation against the mainland, pending resolution of the Laotian crisis. Not only would GRC exacerbation of mainland unrest jeopardize our joint interests through possibly provoking Peiping to countermoves in Laos, but any indications of eventual action against the mainland might persuade Peiping to raise the stakes in Southeast Asia as a counter against subsequent GRC action. Thus even token material support would be denied on the basis of its possible effect on Chinese Communist authorities. The GRC would insist that its forces could help beleaguered Southeast Asian states by keeping Chinese Communist planners insecure and that in case of a deepening crisis in Laos, diversionary attacks in support of local uprisings could only strengthen Free Asia's security. Since the US position did not foreclose eventual assistance for mainland operations, GRC protests might not strike too acrimonious a note. Requests for equipment would reoccur, and should a coalition government eventuate in Laos, GRC pressures would mount. Uncertainty as to the eventual US position, however, might caution against extreme demands with tolerable levels of tension characterizing US-GRC relations.

## 114.    Memorandum From the Assistant Secretary of State for Far Eastern Affairs (Harriman) to the Under Secretary of State for Political Affairs (McGhee)

Washington, May 29, 1962.

SUBJECT

Offshore Islands

1.   The considerations set forth in your memorandum of April 19[1] have prompted FE to take a fresh look at the Offshore Islands problem. As you know, this is a question which has come under review on several occasions during the past few years. We agree that evacuation of the islands should be a United States objective and that this should preferably be brought about before the Chinese Communists have nuclear weapons.

2.   At this juncture we see only two possibilities to bring about GRC evacuation of the Offshores: the offer of an exceedingly attractive inducement, or the application of extreme pressures to compel withdrawal. I believe the price for either alternative would be exorbitant.

3.   We might urge withdrawal in order to regain mobility for the troops so that they could be used in an attack on the mainland. The proposal would have to be coupled with a firm United States commitment at least to agree to a GRC counterattack against the mainland and perhaps also to give it full support. Otherwise the GRC would regard it as only a ploy. These assurances the United States Government is obviously not prepared to give, and I perceive no change in circumstances in the near future which might make such an offer feasible.

4.   The application of extreme pressures on the GRC, such as the threat of flat disavowal of the GRC's claim to the mainland, cessation of military assistance, and/or possible denunciation of our Mutual Defense Treaty might compel GRC withdrawal from the Offshores. Given the current urge for the GRC to go in the opposite direction—to return to the mainland—such a result would require stronger pressures than ever before. Such extreme pressures would involve the very real risk of provoking the GRC into a desperate and possibly suicidal attack against the mainland. Alternatively, these pressures might lead to the

---

Source: Department of State, Central Files, 893.1901/5–3062. Secret. Drafted by Arthur H. Rosen of FE/EA, Yager, and Rice.

[1] McGhee's April 19 memorandum to Harriman suggested a review of the offshore islands problem, commenting that "if the GRC and/or US are ever to disengage from the offshore islands this should be done before Communist China's detonation of a nuclear device, which is expected by 1963–64." (Ibid., 893.1901/4–2062)

resignation or involuntary removal from office of President Chiang Kai-shek, quite probably followed by a period of dangerous political instability. This period of instability might even end in Communist control of Taiwan.

5. This being said, it should also be remarked that Peiping's fundamental national interest would argue strongly against actual use of nuclear weapons against the Offshore Islands. The Chinese Communists have made much of the propaganda theme that Americans used the atomic bomb only against Asians. For the Chinese Communists to use the nuclear weapon against fellow Chinese would do them irretrievable psychological and political damage around the world and among Chinese everywhere. Even if the Communists were willing to accept this damage, they would probably estimate that this course of action would precipitate a nuclear exchange with the vastly superior forces of the United States. A Communist China with some nuclear capability might, however, be bolder and more inclined to take risks—against the Offshore Islands and elsewhere.

6. We shall, of course, remain alert for any developments which might reasonably offer hope of inducing the GRC to withdraw from the Offshores. We would point out that the Offshore Islands policy of the GRC is inextricably connected with its other policies, of which that calling for the return to the mainland is central. Accordingly, the alteration in circumstances which made evacuation possible would have to be radical. If we are to alter the circumstances instead of waiting on events, we shall have to alter radically main policies towards the GRC. The Offshore Islands may well become a side issue in a perhaps inevitable showdown over the whole project of return to the mainland. If the timing of such a showdown is to be decided by the United States, the decision will have to be made on the basis of domestic as well as external political considerations, and at the highest level.[2]

---

[2] McGhee replied in a memorandum of May 30, filed with the source text, that he realized "the present critical situation in China would perhaps argue against any fundamental change in our present relations with the GRC" but assumed Harriman would give the matter continuing review.

## 115. Memorandum for the Record

Washington, May 29, 1962.

SUBJECT

Presidential Conference on Taiwan

At 5:30 p.m. on Tuesday, May 29, 1962 the President conferred in the Cabinet Room with the following persons: Deputy Under Secretary U. Alexis Johnson; Assistant Secretary Harriman; General Carter; Desmond FitzGerald; Assistant Secretary of Defense Paul Nitze; Mr. Bundy, and Mr. Forrestal.

Mr. Johnson reported that a meeting had been held in his office on May 22nd the results of which were summarized in a memorandum dated May 28, 1962 and a draft telegram attached thereto (copies of which are attached to this memorandum).[1] Mr. Johnson explained that the GRC had recently requested two more C–123's, 70–100,000 tons of LST's and 16 B–57's.[2] The purpose of the draft telegram was (1) to answer this request and (2) to indicate that after his arrival in Taipei Ambassador Kirk would be the principal United States spokesman on all major policy matters between this Government and the GRC.

Admiral Kirk, in response to a question from the President, said the 70,000 tons of LST's would be the equivalent of approximately 35 ships, each capable of carrying a platoon of tanks or an enlarged infantry company.

---

Source: Kennedy Library, National Security Files, Countries Series, China. Top Secret. Drafted on May 31. The meeting was held at Kennedy's request, as conveyed in a May 18 memorandum from Bundy to Rusk. (Department of State, Central Files, 793.00/5–1862) Another record of the meeting is in a memorandum for the record by Desmond FitzGerald, Chief of the Far East Division in the CIA Operations Directorate. (Central Intelligence Agency, DCI (McCone) Files, Job 80–B01285A, DCI Meetings With the President)

[1] The attached May 28 memorandum from Brubeck to Bundy reported on a May 22 meeting of State, Defense, CIA, and White House representatives. The draft telegram stated that the substance of Chiang's May 15 meeting with Cline had been passed to Kennedy, that Kirk would be prepared to discuss Chiang's request for additional airlift when he arrived in Taipei, and that Kirk would have full responsibility as the President's representative for handling all major policy problems. It also stated that the initial reaction to Chiang's request for landing ships and bombers was not favorable but further GRC intelligence effort on the mainland and further U.S.-GRC consultation would be desirable. Brubeck's memorandum stated that it had been agreed that Kirk should tell Chiang that five C–123's would be prepared but would remain in the United States until it was decided to use them.

[2] The requests were summarized in an unsigned and undated memorandum enclosed with an April 20 memorandum from the CIA Deputy Director for Plans to Bundy. (Kennedy Library, National Security Files, Countries Series, China, CIA Cables, 3/62–4/62)

Both Mr. Johnson and Admiral Kirk suggested that we had no information that a drop of a 20-man team or a 200-man team on the mainland of China could survive. It was more likely, according to Admiral Kirk, that this request was being made simple as a means of dragging us into GRC plans for an invasion of the mainland.

The President stated that he did not want the GRC to be able to say that just as they were prepared to go to the mainland, the United States flunked out. The President would rather be in the position of saying that hard intelligence indicated that a landing on the mainland was doomed to failure, or that the GRC had refused to cooperate in getting the essential intelligence on internal conditions on the mainland.

Mr. Johnson and Admiral Kirk both suggested, and the President agreed, that the CIA should prepare a list of specific actions to be taken in order to secure more intelligence on the mainland. This would have the purpose of stimulating the GRC either to collect the necessary intelligence, or, if they refused, of building a record of non-cooperation.

The President agreed with Admiral Kirk that we should not contemplate taking any public action, such as sending ships or bombers, without hard intelligence.

Mr. Johnson observed in connection with joint planning with the GRC we should remember that their security might not be too effective. We must assume, he said, that some of the planning could leak to the Russians.

In response to a question from the President, General Carter and Mr. FitzGerald both said that the five C–123's which would be prepared would also be of use to their agency in other areas. The ECM equipment will have to be engineered, which will take some time.

No decision was taken on the proposal to send two C–123's without the ECM equipment to Taiwan for training purposes.

The President read the draft telegram with the changes in ink[3] and approved its transmission. He noted that Admiral Kirk expected to be in Taipei on June 28th.

**Michael V. Forrestal**[4]

---

[3] The copy attached to the source text bears no handwritten revisions and is apparently the final revised version. An earlier draft is attached to another copy of the Brubeck to Bundy memorandum cited in footnote 1 above. (Ibid., General)

[4] Printed from a copy that bears this typed signature.

**116.   Telegram From the Central Intelligence Agency Station in Saigon to Director of Central Intelligence McCone**

Saigon, June 7, 1962.

IN 47381. To McGeorge Bundy for passage to President. To Hilsman for SecState. To Lansdale for SecDef.

1. Following is memo conversation of Director with Chiang Kai-shek 5 June 62.[1]

"Memorandum for the record of a discussion between President Chiang Kai-shek and Mr. McCone on Tuesday June 5, 1962.

The meeting extended from 10:00 to 12:30 pm. After an exchange of pleasantries the entire substance of the conversation dealt with the question of President Chiang's intention to launch operations of various types with the object of destroying the Chinese Communist regime and liberating his people.

The Generalissimo made it abundantly clear that for the past thirteen years his sole purpose, and that of the GRC, had been to prepare for a victorious return to the Mainland. To this end he had created on Taiwan a government which represented free China, built a military machine capable of exploiting the deterioration of Communist control on the Mainland, worked to create an expectation of deliverance among the Chinese people now under Communist rule, and maintained faith in ultimate victory among his adherents on Taiwan.

The President then declared his conviction that conditions on the Mainland had so deteriorated that operations on a reasonable scale, if properly executed, would be supported by the populace and would succeed in establishing control of an area which by further efforts on a larger scale would expand over all of South China and would ultimately topple the Communist regime. This belief, he said, was shared by all his followers on Taiwan giving rise to almost irresistible pressure upon him to act. This pressure, plus his own deep feeling of responsibility to his people on the Mainland, had impelled him to now prepare for initial operations. These were originally scheduled to take place in April–May of this year. He had been persuaded by the United States Government to postpone these attempts for six months. However he could not delay beyond this time and will have to be fully prepared to act in October. He

Source: Kennedy Library, National Security Files, Countries Series, China. Top Secret; Operational Immediate. No time of transmission is indicated on the source text but it was received at 3:13 a.m.

[1] McCone visited Taipei in connection with a trip to Southeast Asia. The memorandum transmitted in this telegram is in Central Intelligence Agency, DCI (McCone) Files, Job–80 B01285A, DCI Far East Trip, 2–14 June 1962. Briefing materials and other materials relating to McCone's visit to Taipei are ibid.

therefore strongly urged that all preparations be made during the intervening months so that his people on Taiwan and his followers on the Mainland would know that he was prepared and would act if conditions existent in October warranted action.

The Generalissimo then stated:

1. That under no circumstances would he undertake a reckless operation or one which did not offer a reasonable chance of success. Any move made by the GRC to recover the Mainland would be carefully thought through and properly planned.

2. He would not undertake any formal military operations without consultation and concurrence with the United States Government.

Mr. McCone questioned the Generalissimo on the term "formal military operations," asking whether prospective drops of several teams of two or three hundred men constituted in the Generalissimo's opinion a formal military action. The Generalissimo responded that in his opinion such drops would not fall under the definition of formal action and would therefore not require U.S. concurrence. Large-scale amphibious operations, by contrast, would constitute a formal military action and would, under the terms of the treaty, require concurrence. Mr. McCone took exception to this position, stating it was his view that a two hundred man drop was a sizeable operation and one which would be attributable to both the United States Government and the GRC. Therefore any such operation must be fully coordinated and agreed between the USG and GRC. It was finally agreed that the sizeable airdrop operation would require consultation and concurrence.[2]

Mr. McCone went on to stress the vital importance of success in any operation on a major scale such as large air drops. Failure in such an attempt would be a catastrophic setback to the GRC, place the future of Formosa in doubt and the net result would be to give added momentum to the Communist movement in China and Southeast Asia. He repeatedly expressed concern that a large air drop or sizeable amphibious operation would encounter large, well-equipped Chinese Communist military forces loyal to the regime and the ChiNat forces would be destroyed and the civilians who joined the insurgent effort slaughtered as they were in Hungary. He therefore again emphasized the importance of gathering hard intelligence before launching any sizeable attack on the Mainland and urged that Communist combat units in the southern and central provinces were prime targets for penetration and intelligence efforts. Mr. McCone indicated that if the Generalissimo felt that

---

[2] This sentence was not in the telegram as received but was added to the source text in accordance with a CIA request conveyed in a June 12 memorandum from Desmond Fitz-Gerald to Thomas A. Parrott of the White House Staff, filed with the source text. The memorandum cited in footnote 1 above does not include this sentence.

commitments of food would help to neutralize or disaffect Communist military units his views should be discussed with Ambassador Kirk promptly on his arrival.

President Chiang agreed that an intense intelligence effort should be initiated (and apparently has given orders to this effect) but went on to point out that in his opinion intelligence alone could not provide all the information needed to gauge the chances for success in that reconquest of the Mainland by the GRC was a revolutionary movement which would gather momentum as it succeeded. True knowledge of the Mainland reaction, he contended, could only be gained after a sizeable military operation had been launched, an area secured, and the people together with their local leaders given reason to hope for relief from oppression. In any other situation popular resistance to the Communists would continue to be passive.

At this point the Generalissimo spoke of his dilemma with regard to obtaining United States Government approval for his actions, indicating that this area always presented him with an uncertainty and therefore foreclosed proper dynamic planning of operations. He went so far as to state that he could conceive of a situation under which he would have to free himself of the restrictions imposed on him in his role as head of state by stepping down to a position from which he could lead an independent revolutionary movement. Mr. McCone interpreted this not as a threat but as a reflection upon earlier days when the Generalissimo had taken similar steps on the Mainland.

At no point during the conversation did the Generalissimo say or intimate that he felt that the United States had an obligation to join him with American combat forces nor did he indicate that he expected such assistance; however he made it abundantly clear he expected the U.S. to give him logistic support even though there was no formal obligation to do this. In discussing the question of American support for GRC efforts to recover the Mainland Mr. McCone advised the Generalissimo that two C–123 aircraft were being prepared, that training for GRC aircrews had been approved, and that the GRC request for three additional C–123's was under consideration. Mr. McCone indicated that Ambassador Kirk would be able to advise the Generalissimo concerning these three additional aircraft when he arrived in Taipei. Mr. McCone said that no decision had been reached concerning provision of B–57 bombers and LST's for GRC but that President Chiang's request for these weapons would be considered when an agreement had been reached concerning the operations in which they would be used. Mr. McCone pointed out that this was actually a matter beyond his competence as Director of Central Intelligence.

The discussion throughout was exploratory and very frank (President Chiang stated that the exchange was the most complete in many years) but at no time was the question of U.S. policy taken up, nor did the Generalissimo ask or Mr. McCone volunteer information about what the U.S. position might be under hypothetical future circumstances. All this was left for subsequent discussions with Ambassador Kirk and it was made perfectly clear that Mr. McCone's mission had to do only with intensifying the intelligence effort as a preface to any larger decision or action."

2. HULA: Please pass CINCPAC. TAMI: Please pass to Clough.

---

**117. Telegram From the Embassy in the Republic of China to the Department of State**

Taipei, June 15, 1962, 7 p.m.

968. Joint Embassy–AID message. Purpose of this message is to take stock of situation and outline our thoughts on appropriate course of action re special military expenditures program and US aid to GRC following Janow visit.[1]

Believe combination of delay in action on economic assistance programs and emphatic views expressed to senior GRC officials has convinced latter we are seriously concerned at possible adverse effect of military preparedness program on economy and has served to warn them effectively against any future action of this sort without adequate consultation. Postponement of long term Title I[2] agreement and cutback of program loan also served this purpose.[3] Economic Ministers were especially worried; they probably heard Janow's recommendations

---

Source: Department of State, Central Files, 811.0093/6–1562. Confidential.

[1] Seymour J. Janow, Assistant Administrator for the Far East in the Agency for International Development, visited Taiwan June 4–6.

[2] Reference is to Title I of P.L. 480, the Agricultural Trade Development and Assistance Act (approved July 10, 1954; 68 Stat. (pt. 1) 454), as amended.

[3] Ambassador Tsiang called on AID Administrator Fowler Hamilton on May 31 to request an early decision on a pending nonproject (program) loan and a new P.L. 480, Title I agreement. Hamilton told him the increased GRC military budget necessitated a reappraisal of the basis for aid. Telegram AIDTO 456 to Taipei, June 2, summarizes the conversation and states that the nonproject loan authorization was being reduced from $30 to $20 million. (Department of State, Central Files, 811.0093/6–162) A memorandum of the conversation and other related material is in Washington National Records Center, Agency for International Development Files, Administrator Files: Lot 286–65–481, China, Nationalist, FY 1962)

Embassy telegram 921[4] (i.e., to proceed with reduced program loan and interim Title I agreement) with more relief than dismay. We believe conversations during Janow visit and subsequently will strengthen their hand in holding special expenditures down to surtax revenues. They may even be able, with help of our continued prodding, to cut back planned civilian procurement under preparedness program or stretch out into FY 1964.

Re public concern at delay in approval aid program, statements made at Janow departure[5] supported by interim Title I signing[6] did fill psychological need for affirmation US aid continuing as well as promise to meet immediate assistance needs.

Problem now as we see it is to find ways of continuing to emphasize US concern that adverse effect of military preparedness program on economy be minimized and of inducing GRC to reduce or stretch out future military spending. Situation appears to require coordinated action along three lines:

1. Re economic assistance we should continue proceed with caution not only to assure that approved programs are in accord with new situation but also to maintain impression that we are not relaxed in accepting non-performance of commitment to restrain defense expenditures and continue to be concerned that expenditures and economic impact be minimized. In this line would suggest no action for time being on long-term Title I agreement, proceeding with deliberation in implementation program loan, and parallel attitude with respect to smaller aid projects.

2. MAAG review of information provided by MND on special expenditures shows very small proportion of purchases to date are items programmed for future MAP delivery. Action with respect such items and other elements military expenditures will be discussed with Chief MAAG on his return from Washington appropriate recommendations made.

3. We should seek authoritative reaffirmation GRC still considers valid its commitment to limit military expenditures as specified under 19

---

[4] In telegram 921, June 5, Janow reported that he had seen the President, Vice President, Foreign Minister, and ministers concerned with economic affairs and he recommended proceeding with the $20 million program loan and in interim P.L. 480 agreement. (Department of State, Central Files, 811.0093/6-562)

[5] Janow's June 6 statement pledged continuing assistance for the GRC economic development program and in it he declared, "I look to Taiwan as one of the success stories of Asia in the postwar years." (Filed with a June 7 memorandum from AID Executive Secretary Donald B. Easum to Kaysen; Kennedy Library, National Security Files, Countries Series, China)

[6] Telegram 940 from Taipei, June 9, reported that notes amending the Title I P.L. 480 agreement were exchanged that day. For text of the notes, see TIAS 5090; for text of the agreement they amended, signed at Taipei on April 27, 1962, see 13 UST 461.

points and that other commitments there stipulated which form basis of accelerated development program must also be honored. In effect this would be a return to the status quo ante after special preparedness program. This might be appropriate topic for Ambassador Kirk to take up with President Chiang following review of US attitude regarding special expenditures program and present mainland return prospects.

**Clough**

## 118.   Memorandum for the Record

Washington, June 18, 1962.

SUBJECT

The Director's Meeting with the President, 18 June

1. The Director and the Deputy Director (Plans) met with the President at 4:05 P.M., 18 June, to report on the trip to Southeast Asia.

2. The President opened the conversation by asking if we knew where Joseph Alsop had got his information about the build-up of Chi-Com divisions in the Fukien area. We said that we did not know [2 lines of source text not declassified]. The President asked whether it would not be desirable to conduct an investigation as to how Alsop had acquired this knowledge. The Director commented that he did not think an investigation would be fruitful but that he would like to take the matter under advisement for consideration with USIB.

[Here follows discussion of an intelligence operation, not identified in the memorandum.]

4. The Director described his conversations in Taiwan with Chiang Kai-shek, the President having stated that he had read with interest the Director's report from the field on this subject. When the Director had finished, the President wondered out loud what Chiang would do if he were told flatly that the United States would not support him in any mili-

---

Source: Central Intelligence Agency, DCI (McCone) Files, Job 80–B01285A, DCI Meetings With the President. Secret; Eyes Only. Prepared by Richard Helms. The meeting concluded at 4:54 p.m. (Kennedy Library, President's Appointment Book)

tary operation against the Mainland. It was agreed that Chiang might then "go it alone." DD/P described Chiang's belief that the Soviets would not intervene as long as the ChiNats conducted their military operations south of the Yangtse River. The President mused about this and expressed the opinion that Soviet air support could readily be brought to bear on the side of the ChiComs. No conclusions were reached on what should be done to support Chiang, although the Director expressed the view, already presented to the Secretary of State and the Secretary of Defense, that the United States Government should start to stockpile air and amphibious equipment while maintaining control over it.[1]

[Here follows discussion of Vietnam, Laos, and Cuba.]

**RH**
*Deputy Director (Plans)*

---

[1] McCone met separately with Rusk and McNamara earlier on June 18. According to records of the conversations drafted by Helms, McNamara "did not seem to feel that amphibious equipment should be stockpiled until it became clear that ChiNat intelligence-gathering missions demonstrated that an attack on the Mainland had some chance of success." Rusk did not comment on Chiang's proposals. (Central Intelligence Agency, DCI (McCone) Files, Job 80–B01285A, DCI Meetings With the President)

---

**119. Memorandum From the Director of the Bureau of Intelligence and Research (Hilsman) to Secretary of State Rusk**

Washington, June 18, 1962.

SUBJECT

Chinese Communist Troop Movements

*I. Chinese Communist Intentions*

Reports of additional troop movements over the weekend lead us to take a somewhat more serious view of Chinese Communist intentions than we did initially.

---

Source: Kennedy Library, National Security Files, Countries Series, China. Secret; Noforn; Limited Distribution. Filed with a covering memorandum of the same date from Forrestal to Bundy, which reads as follows: "I will check with Averell to see if he agrees with this rather alarmist estimate. I will also ask CIA what its guess is." A note in Bundy's handwriting on Forrestal's memorandum reads, "Hold for 6 pm meeting." Reference may be to the June 20 meeting recorded in Document 122.

In brief, our conclusions are as follows:

1. We still feel that the primary purposes of the reported movements are to deter the Chinese Nationalists from attacking the mainland and to ensure that defenses opposite Taiwan are adequate for all contingencies.

2. However, we are now inclined to believe it is also likely that the Chinese Communists have decided to exploit the troop movements politically by creating a new offshore island crisis. To the Chinese Communists a new crisis may appear useful for several reasons: to exacerbate the visible strains in relations between the U.S. and Nationalist China; to divert attention from domestic economic difficulties and justify stringent measures at home; and to demonstrate that Peiping's power and interests are something the world must reckon with.

3. We cannot rule out the possibility that the Chinese Communists are preparing for a sudden, all-out effort to take either or both Quemoy (Kinmen) and Matsu, perhaps utilizing equipment not available in 1958. However, in the absence of evidence that the Chinese Communists are massing the necessary transport (e.g. motorized junks), we do not think a sudden, all-out attack is either imminent or likely.

## II. Implications for the U.S.

This Chinese Communist military buildup opposite Kinmen and Matsu brings to the forefront not only the problem of the offshore islands themselves but also of Chiang Kai-shek's intentions to "counterattack" the mainland. A direct confrontation of the U.S. and Chinese Nationalist interests seems very likely.

If the Chinese Communists attack, the US will be faced with pressure from Chiang, from his friends in Southeast Asia, and from his friends here in the United States to participate in the defense of the islands. A decision will be immediately required on whether or not the attack is a preliminary to an attack on Formosa, as specified in the Formosa Resolution, and Chiang undoubtedly will make public all sorts of "intelligence" designed to show that it is.

If the Chinese Communists do not actually attack, but create a 1958-style politico-military crisis, the situation is only slightly better. Chiang's demands will be urgent, and if support is not forthcoming, they will undoubtedly become both public and strident.

The Chinese Communists have considerable incentive to exacerbate US-Chinese Nationalist relations and can begin at any time. Chiang, on the other hand, has always had among his high priority objectives involvement of the US in reconquest of the mainland. Once the Chinese Communists are in position, he may provoke an attack or in other ways take the initiative to exploit the situation for his own purposes.

Thus the initiative would appear to be with the Chinese, either Communist or Nationalist, once Peiping's troops are fully in position. If preventive or interposing action should be necessary to safeguard US interests, it would appear that such action may be a realistic alternative for only a very limited time.

Tab A attached[1] analyzes the military factors bearing upon Kinmen's vulnerability to invasion and blockade.

Tab B attached[2] presents an analysis of political, economic, climatic, and military factors from the standpoint of the Chinese Communists.

---

[2] Entitled "Kinmen: The Costs of Capture"; not printed.
[3] Entitled "The Situation Viewed from Peiping"; not printed.

---

## 120.   Memorandum for the Record

Washington, June 19, 1962.

SUBJECT

Meeting with the President, 1800 hrs, 19 June 1962[1]

1. In attendance were the following: The President, General Taylor, and Messrs. McGeorge Bundy, Forrestal, McCone and Knoche.

2. Knoche described in considerable detail the nature of the evidence of Chinese Communist military buildup in the Taiwan Strait area. [5 lines of source text not declassified]

3. The extent of buildup was described. In response to his questions the President was told that so far only 15 jet fighters, no bombers, have moved in, but that we expect more.

4. There was a discussion of the status and capability of the ChiCom navy in the Taiwan Strait area. The distinction was made between Matsu, the taking of which would require modern amphibious equipment, and Quemoy, which is in effect a river-crossing and could be assaulted with the myriad of junks and other assorted craft in the area. Mr. McCone described the topography and fortification of Quemoy.

---

Source: Central Intelligence Agency, DCI (McCone) Files, Job 80–B01285A, DCI Meetings With the President. Top Secret; [classification indicator not declassified]; Eyes Only. Prepared by E.H. Knoche.

[1] According to Kennedy's Appointment Book, the meeting began at 6:01 p.m. and ended at 6:17 p.m. (Kennedy Library)

5.   General Taylor cited the security surrounding Chinese Communist military movements in the Korean War and asked if we didn't think that the Chinese were being more "open" in this case. Knoche's reply was that the information is reliable deduction [2 *lines of source text not declassified*].

6.   A brief discussion of past Taiwan Strait crises ensued, with various comments concerning events in August–September 1958. The President asked Forrestal to check to see what decisions were made by the NSC at that time.

7.   General Taylor suggested, and it was later agreed, to hold a meeting with the President at 6:00 p.m., 20 June, with representation from State, Defense and CIA.[2]

8.   Mr. McCone showed the President and General Taylor a copy of the message sent from the DCI to Chiang Kai-shek outlining the danger and requesting the Generalissimo's evaluation of Communist intentions.[3]

E.H.K.
*Assistant to the Director*

---

[2] See Document 122.
[3] Not further identified

---

121.   **Telegram From the Department of State to the Embassy in the Republic of China**

Washington, June 19, 1962, 8:23 p.m.

754. Eyes only Chargé. You should request early appointment with President (or in event he is not available Vice President) and inform him as follows: (1) GRC is of course aware evidence of large build-up of Chinese Communist forces in Fukien Province. Very real possibility exists that Chinese Communists intend full scale attack against some of off-shore islands. (2) In this situation it is most important that GRC not give Communists any pretext for such attack either by any public statements by GRC officials or by any GRC actions. (3) US will of course expect to

---

Source: Department of State, Central Files, 793.00/6–1962. Secret; Priority: Drafted by Yager; cleared by Allen Evans, Deputy Director for Research in the Bureau of Intelligence and Research, and in draft by Harriman; and approved by Rice.

consult closely with GRC on appropriate measures to be taken in light of developing military situation.[1]

Ball

---

[1] Clough reported in telegram 991 from Taipei, June 21, that President Chiang was ill but that he had an appointment with Vice President Ch'en on June 22. (Ibid., 793.00/6–2162) He reported in telegram 995, June 22, that he had seen Ch'en, who "assured me GRC would act very carefully and would not provide Chinese Communists with pretext for attack." Ch'en declared that the Chinese Communist buildup might be for offensive or defensive purposes and urged that the United States and the GRC should increase their alertness and prepare for the possibility of aggressive action. (Ibid., 793.00/6–2262)

---

## 122.  Record of Meeting

Washington, June 20, 1962, 6–7:30 p.m.

The meeting opened with John McCone giving pretty much the SNIE;[1] the only difference was that he read that last sentence[2] and didn't put the right emphasis on the purely military considerations. But this was all right; I was in the President's office right after the meeting; he

---

Source: Kennedy Library, Hilsman Papers, Box 1, China—Offshore Islands Crisis, 6/62. No classification marking, but the first page is marked "T.S. File." The document is apparently a transcript of an oral briefing by Hilsman of the meeting, which was held at the White House. A summary record of the meeting is in a memorandum for the record by Cline; according to it, the participants included Kennedy, Vice President Johnson, the President's Military Representative General Maxwell D. Taylor, Bundy, Forrestal, Ball, U. Alexis Johnson, Harriman, Hilsman, McCone, McNamara, Lemnitzer, Felt, and Kirk. (Central Intelligence Agency, DCI (McCone) Files, Job 80–B01285A, DCI Meetings With the President) A June 20 memorandum from Taylor to the Director of the Joint Staff describes this meeting as a briefing of the President on China and suggests that DOD/JCS representatives include in their presentations the answers to several questions which "have Presidential interest" concerning the possibility of a Communist attack on the offshore islands, the ability of the Nationalists to defend them, and U.S. assistance that might be necessary for a successful defense. (National Defense University, Taylor Papers, Box 17, Folder 11, Miscellaneous)

[1] SNIE 13–5–62, "Chinese Communist Short-Range Military Intentions," dated June 20. [text not declassified] it stated that the Chinese Communists had moved seven army divisions, with possibly five more on the way, across the Strait from Taiwan, representing "the largest such movement since the Korean War." The scale and urgency of the troop movements appeared too large to be merely a demonstration to deter GRC raids. The SNIE concluded that the movements were either defensive, designed to put pressure on the offshore islands, or intended for a surprise attack on the Chinmens. (Central Intelligence Agency Files, Job 79–R01012A, ODDI Registry) See the Supplement.

[2] The last sentence reads: "The scale and urgency of the military movements, taken by themselves, strongly support this last possibility."

asked Mac Bundy, George Ball, and I to step in, and McNamara and I noticed that on the coffee table he had the CIB,[3] SNIE, and our paper of a couple of days ago[4] and he had it all right there, and he was as well informed as anybody around the table by and large.

McCone finished and McNamara charged in with all guns blazing, and charged in hard and with contempt in his voice for the intelligence community and he said this was pretty silly, and of course McNamara understands the facts and figures business, this is his business; so he said there were 300 motorized junks, and 1300 sailing vessels, take 50 men each; this means that the most you can do is 100,000; you'd have to go back, and couldn't move heavy equipment; with LST's and he thinks this is for the birds; now, of course, this puts CIA in a terrible position because McCone had presented it in a way, and the President asked questions, so that obviously the President was looking at this one as that which he had to be most fearful of; and McNamara jumped all over him; then Lemnitzer came in and the same thing; downgrading it, the idea of the third possibility; very heavily, and Lemnitzer, he said there are three possible explanations for this; maybe they will attack Taiwan, and nobody even suggested this; and to draw people away from Southeast Asia; to try to get us out of SEA; they jumped all over this and McNamara said he had several recommendations to make; he wanted to bring two more SAC U–2s into Formosa; we gotta have intelligence; have no intelligence; implications that CIA has been doing a lousy job, make judgments on the wrong facts; McCone didn't defend himself very well, talked a little bit about the weather problems, and President asked—can't you fly lower and got off into a kind of hassle about the technique of getting air photos, with CIA not much in focus. He didn't defend himself very well.

McNamara was—if you wanted to lose a few lives, you might still do it subtleties—and I wasn't about to step in at that point, to defend a course of action, I had busily fought his people all morning. And then even Kirk spoke up that this was quite an operation, and he is an amphibious warfare expert, but he ended up on the right note saying if you wanted to spend enough lives, you could probably do it. The nearest Defense came off the better of this exchange. Mac Bundy asked if there was anybody in this Intelligence [community?] and USIB who was taking the line that it was possible for it to be a surprise attack; was it potential Pearl Harbor and Mr. McCone said no one did. And this amazed me for this is exactly what Fitzh[5] was arguing. So I didn't say anything to that but it looked awfully funny with Defense (Lemnitzer and McNamara)

---

[3] Presumably the June 20 issue of the Current Intelligence Bulletin, a coordinated daily intelligence summary; not found.

[4] Presumably Document 119.

[5] Possibly Desmond FitzGerald.

joining hands here; opposing this thing that the Defense (Navy and Army) Navy supported the Army a little bit; this was weird, and McNamara did say that he hadn't had a chance to get together with his people (intelligence) and that will be interesting when that happens. McNamara recommended keeping the 4th Carrier in the Pacific which it was due to come back apparently moving a couple of carriers into the Straits, bringing two more U–2s to Formosa; I didn't quite get the reason for this and it was some time before that it turns out that his real reason is not a bad one; which is, that if there is a clear day that we deploy all 4 simultaneously and make the most of it. These are SAC having ChiNat pilots; cause they have 4—Ray Cline raised the possibility of deploying them and hiding them in the hangar, but they said, put them in Okinawa, Clark Field or someplace like that.[6]

The funny thing is that there was a hassle between McNamara and Lemnitzer on one side and McCone on the other; one thing that made the State Department look good was that I spoke up to the JIC estimate and a couple of things; after the meeting I said a couple of more things; but I was keeping my head down in this one because there was almost nothing that I could say to correct McNamara or Lemnitzer without appearing to defend a position we wouldn't ourselves support; and there was no possible way for me to put him in perspective without looking like I was defending something we wouldn't want to defend.

You know that it was going to be an all-out Pearl Harbor assault on Quemoy right away, which would go against all our feeling about caution; so I kept my mouth shut on this one; and I supplied some things about the JIC and some factual data but didn't intervene at this point.

The State Department looked a little bad in that the President said well, we've got to get straight what we want to say to the Russians and what we want to say to the Chinese Communists and how we want to say

---

[6] Cline's memorandum cited in the source note states that McNamara and the JCS recommended "(a) augmentation of carrier strength by retaining fourth carrier in 7th Fleet which had been due to return to the United States; (b) deployment of carriers closer to Taiwan; (c) all-out reconnaissance effort by F–101 and high-altitude photo-recce aircraft based on Taiwan; (d) doubling high-altitude force to permit maximum effort."

All the measures were approved except the last, which was to be considered. The memorandum states that Kennedy "raised the possibility of deploying U.S. air units to the area," but McNamara thought it unnecesary. The carrier returned to the United States early in July. (Telegram from Kaysen to Kennedy in Mexico City, June 29; Kennedy Library, National Security Files, Countries Series, China)

it; and we had spent half an hour in Ball's office going over the papers;[7] the trouble was that Harriman wasn't completely satisfied with the papers his boys had produced and so he didn't speak up and Ball didn't come in and say we've got it; so we looked like we hadn't done our home work; or at least on this one, which puzzled me because I didn't know why . . . (exchange of conversation).

Now Yager is going to work out the contingencies with Defense;[8] I have the impression Yager is nervous about INR's role here; is that right (addressed Peaslee).[9] I don't think he is [as] willing to have us participate as Rice and Koren. Harriman is perfectly clear—and he doesn't feel that way.

Afterwards I took occasion to chat with McNamara and to give him some political reasons to support his own position. To get a little back in his good graces. So this was very friendly little chat with McNamara, Ball, and myself. I went in with the President and Mac and talked about the press guidance, where I got these instructions; the President is having Salinger do it[10] and wants us to do this.

Now, we went back to George Ball's office afterwards and got ourselves in line; Harriman would like two decisions at the moment; one is a decision that we will in fact restrain Chiang; how far we are prepared to go on this one; and how much we are prepared to tell the Russians on this one. But he also wants advance permission to support the defense of the

---

[7] Lists of measures that might be taken before any attack on the islands and measures that might be taken after an attack were sent to Ball on June 20 with a covering memorandum from Harriman. The first included proposals to try to deter an attack by approaching the Soviet Ambassador or by calling a meeting at Warsaw to warn that an attack could lead to wider hostilities. The second proposed that the U.S. response to an attack should be calculated "to localize the conflict and terminate it as swiftly as possible with the islands still in GRC hands." Direct U.S. involvement should be avoided if possible and, if unavoidable, should be limited to the minimum necessary to prevent Communist seizure of the islands, with no use of nuclear weapons. (Department of State, ROC Files: Lot 71 D 517, Offshore Islands (Misc) 1962)

[8] An interdepartmental Offshore Islands Working Group representing the State and Defense Departments, Central Intelligence Agency, and White House, met irregularly between June 21 and July 17. Participants at the first meeting included Harriman, Hilsman. Nitze, Cline, and Forrestal but participation was usually at a somewhat lower level. Unsigned notes of the meeting and extensive contingency planning papers produced under its stimulus are ibid., S/S Files: Lot 66 D 150, Offshore Islands Contingency Planning Papers, Vol. II, and Offshore Islands Chronology, Vol. III.

[9] Alexander L. Peaslee, Chief of the Asian Communist Division in the Bureau of Intelligence and Research.

[10] According to notes of a June 21 telephone conversation between Harriman and House Foreign Affairs Committee Chairman Thomas E. Morgan, Harriman stated that the President had decided rather late in the evening to let Salinger tell "some responsible people" about the situation; most of the White House press corps had left, and Salinger talked to the Associated Press and United Press reporters. (Library of Congress Manuscript Division, Harriman Papers, Kennedy–Johnson Administrations, Chronological Files, Telephone Conversations)

islands if the Chinese Communists attack it. Not nuclear weapons or anything like that but to make—if Chinese Coms do attack Quemoy and Matsu that the US helps the Chinese Nationalists to the extent of making it awfully expensive for them.

He wants these two decisions so he can talk to Dobrynin; he doesn't want to threaten Dobrynin; just wants to ask a question at stage one.

A somewhat more harmonious message through the British to the Chinese Communists but in stage two with Dobrynin he wants to be able to tell him the first time around with Dobrynin—he'd like to know what our decisions are and just say, just ask him, what about this and say here we are, peace in Southeast Asia, Laos agreement, and what are your boys doing out there.

Exactly why Harriman wants it faced. (others talking)

He may not and may not get it in this point of the scenario.

That could be. Well the exercise right now; what Harriman and FE are doing right now is what he would be saying to Dobrynin. In the meantime Yager and Company and Nitze are going to do contingency planning, various contingencies; McNamara has the idea that in 1958 we didn't let them bomb the airfields from which the planes were taking off, we ought to let them bomb those airfields this time. Pretty major step and he wouldn't necessarily recommend it, but he is thinking about it. This was just in chatting.

I don't know what we do.

### 123.   Memorandum for the Record

Gettysburg, June 21, 1962.

SUBJECT

Briefing of General Eisenhower in Gettysburg, Pa., at 11 a.m. to 12:30 p.m. on June 21, 1962

Persons present were: General Eisenhower, Lt. Colonel John Eisenhower, Director McCone, and Mr. Forrestal.

---

Source: Kennedy Library, National Security Files, Countries Series, Laos. Top Secret. Drafted by Forrestal on June 22 and revised on July 16 to incorporate suggestions by Lieutenant Colonel John Eisenhower. Forrestal's original draft is filed with a copy of a June 22 memorandum, which he sent to John Eisenhower enclosing his draft and inviting the latter's comments. (Ibid., China) A copy is also filed with John Eisenhower's June 26 reply suggesting several revisions. (Eisenhower Library, Eisenhower Post-Presidential Papers, Augusta–Walter Reed Series, Memorandum of Conference)

Director McCone briefed General Eisenhower on recent intelligence indications of a substantial military buildup by the Chinese Communists in Fukien Province (see SNIE 13–5–62).[1] General Eisenhower speculated whether this buildup could be a reaction to statements by the ChiNats that they intended operations against the Mainland. Director McCone said that this was a possibility. However the purpose of the buildup was not definitely known, but (according to the SNIE) could be (a) response to fear of landings from Taiwan; (b) resumption of a campaign of pressure on the Offshore Islands similar to that which occurred in 1958; and (c) a deliberate assault on the Offshore Islands in the immediate future. Director McCone said that the urgency and scale of the military preparations strongly supported the last possibility.

General Eisenhower gave his opinion that the disposition of Chi-Com forces in Fukien Province would indicate whether their intentions were defensive or offensive. A defensive posture would probably involve a spreading out of military units up and down the coast with reserves fanned out in the rear echelons. An offensive posture would suggest a heavy concentration of troops in the immediate vicinity of the target.

General Eisenhower also emphasized that an invasion of Quemoy could hardly be carried out without an intensive artillery bombardment in advance. He said that he estimated that such a barrage would probably have to be continued for at least 72 hours, although possibly by an extremely heavy effort a "time-on-target" type barrage would shorten the time. General Eisenhower recollected the bombardment and the investing of the island of Pantelleria during the campaign in the Mediterranean. Despite intensive naval and air bombardment lasting for 3 or 4 days, relatively little actual damage was done to the gun emplacements on the island. Nevertheless the garrison on the island surrendered without resisting a landing, because their morale had been badly shaken and because communications and utilities had been destroyed.

General Eisenhower then turned to the diplomatic problems involved in the defense of the Offshore Islands. He recalled that in 1958 the ChiComs had made numerous propaganda statements to the effect that it was their intention to recapture Taiwan. In the light of these statements it was possible for his Administration to construe an attack upon Quemoy and Matsu as the first stage of an attack upon the Mainland. General Eisenhower recalled that his and Mr. Dulles' statements indicated this intention, but he never made a categorical statement to this effect. General Eisenhower observed that today the President's position was somewhat more difficult, because there has so far been less propa-

---

[1] See footnote 1, Document 122.

ganda relating the current buildup to a conquest of Formosa. Under these circumstances the President might wish to go back to Congress for the authority to commit the United States to the defense of the Offshore Islands.[2] Of course with Congress in session, time was not so much of a problem. Also, if the ChiComs attack Taiwan by air or if they came in too close on reconnaissance, the original resolution would suffice as basis for our intervention.

In response to a question from Mr. Forrestal, General Eisenhower said that the United States could probably aid in the defense of Quemoy by non-combative means, such as supply, as we had done in 1958, without resorting to Congress, although consultations with the leadership would be desirable.

General Eisenhower also observed that it would be hard to stay out of the defense of Quemoy if the action there was prolonged and bloody.

General Eisenhower said that he approved the idea of a warning to the ChiComs to the effect that in the event of an attempt by them to begin operations against Taiwan, "the U.S. would do its part."

The former President recollected that he had asked Chiang to evacuate civilians from the Islands of Quemoy and Matsu and make them into strong island fortresses, using a minimum number of troops to do so. Director McCone observed that the Island of Quemoy had been historically a fortress for Chinese who had been driven off the Mainland and consequently was of considerable psychological importance to Chiang. General Eisenhower observed that such a fortress would be of value only for defensive purposes and not profitably used as staging areas for an attack upon the Mainland.

Director McCone asked whether General Eisenhower had supported Chiang's return to the Mainland. General Eisenhower replied that the policy of his Administration was to avoid that question. His policy was composed of the following elements: (1) the preservation of the security of Taiwan and the Pescadores; (2) support of Chiang in order to support the morale of the overseas Chinese; (3) maintenance of Chiang's ability to conduct operations on the Mainland but always under our complete control. Former President Eisenhower recalled that he had revised President Truman's orders to the 7th Fleet ("unleashing Chiang") as a warning to the ChiComs that aggressive acts on their part might be countered by activities on their own territory.

General Eisenhower summed up by saying that he was delighted to have been given this briefing. The general feeling he had was that we should be intensely watchful and alert—on the qui vive. There was time to decide the U.S. reaction.

---

[2] At this point, Forrestal's original draft included the following sentence: "General Eisenhower did not feel that this was a necessity."

## 124.    Memorandum From Acting Secretary of State Ball to President Kennedy

Washington, June 21, 1962.

SUBJECT

Suggested Diplomatic Action in Connection with Chinese Communists Build-up

*Approach to Russians*

I would suggest that Harriman be authorized to call in Dobrynin (preferably at lunch) and informally request information on what the Soviets know about ChiCom troop movements in the Fukien area and what their objectives are. He would state that because of the agreement between the President and Khrushchev on Laos, we had assumed Khrushchev had no desire for military action at this time over the off-shore islands. Harriman would indicate to the Ambassador that in case the Soviets or ChiComs were concerned regarding rumors of ChiNat preparations for mainland invasion, the U.S. had no intention of supporting such a move under existing circumstances. He would point out that ChiNats had agreed not to take any offensive action without full consultation and prior agreement on the part of the United States.

In this connection, he would also note that in our meetings with the Chinese Communists since 1955, we have consistently been urging agreement that force not be used by either side to change the existing situation, and of course we continue to adhere to that position.

On the other hand, he would mention the defensive treaty with the GRC and, therefore, refer to the dangers of any aggressive action on the part of the ChiComs. The conversation should be more of an inquiry than a démarche.

*Approach to Chinese Communists*

We should make sure that the Chinese Communists do not act under a misunderstanding of our intentions.

While approach to the ChiComs might be made through Ambassador Cabot to [Chinese] Communist Ambassador Wang, I think it would be better to try to use the British Embassy in Peiping, both because the ChiCom response could be faster and because the ChiComs might be more willing to talk frankly with the British.

---

Source: Kennedy Library, National Security Files, Countries Series, China. Secret. The source text does not indicate the drafter, but the Department's record copy indicates that it was drafted by Ball. (Department of State, Central Files, 793.5/6–2162) The source text bears a handwritten note: "OK'd by the President. M.K." A memorandum of June 22 from Bundy to Ball notified him of the President's approval. (Ibid., 793.5/6–2262)

Subject to your approval, I propose that we call in the British Ambassador and discuss with him the Chinese Communist military build-up in Fukien. If the British Ambassador believes that an approach by their Embassy in Peiping to the Chinese Communists would be useful, we could suggest to him the line that might be taken.

The British might call the attention of the Chinese Communists to the Mutual Defense Treaty between the U.S. and the GRC and to the 1955 Formosa Resolution giving the President of the United States the authority to use U.S. armed forces to defend the off-shore islands, if he judges such action is required or appropriate in assuring the defense of Taiwan and the Pescadores. The Chinese Communists might be advised that in view of the strength of the GRC garrisons on the off-shore islands, any effort to take them would be a major operation which could not easily be limited to the immediate vicinity of the islands. Serious risk of wider hostilities involving U.S. forces would therefore arise.

If the Chinese Communists were to raise with the British the report of GRC plans to attack the China mainland, the British might respond by stating that it is their understanding that the United States Government has no intention of supporting such an attack under existing circumstances. The British might also call attention to the Exchange of Notes between the U.S. and the GRC in December 1954 which requires the GRC to obtain agreement of the U.S. in any offensive action by GRC military forces. In this connection, they might also note that in our meetings with the Chinese Communists since 1955, we have consistently been urging agreement that force not be used by either side to change the existing situation, and of course we continue to adhere to that position.

*Consultation with Allies*

In addition to consultation with the British I think we should move immediately to inform the Australians and New Zealanders of our concern over the Fukien build-up. As soon as the situation becomes clear we should consult on a similar basis with the Japanese Government.

*Congressional Consultation*

Presumably you will wish to advise the leadership of the possible implications of ChiCom actions. I shall await your instructions as to any approaches you may wish us to make with other members of Congress.

**George W. Ball**[1]

---

[1] Printed from a copy that indicates Ball signed the original.

## 125.   Memorandum From the Director of the Bureau of Intelligence and Research (Hilsman) to the Assistant Secretary of State for Far Eastern Affairs (Harriman)

Washington, June 21, 1962.

SUBJECT

   US Posture, Nationalist Chinese Interests, and Chinese Communist Intentions

We have considered the effects of alternative US decisions to defend or not to defend the offshore islands in the event of eventual communist attack. We assume the decision is made in the near future and under present circumstances (i.e., there is an ominous Communist Chinese buildup but no offensive action against the offshore islands) and a decision of such magnitude would become known to Peiping and Taipei whether or not the US so intended. Our last assumption is that Peiping's intentions are offensive and at the very least involve a phased, probing approach to possible ultimate attack.

Our conclusion is that there are clearcut disadvantages in making any firm decisions on US defense of the offshore islands under present circumstances.

—A decision *not to defend* risks encouraging Chinese Communist efforts to seize the islands, a lessening of possible Soviet influence for restraint, and grave worsening of US-GRC relations.

—A decision *to defend* risks increased GRC efforts to involve us even more deeply in their counter-attack actions as well as a tightening of the Sino-Soviet alliance.

Continued ambiguity as to US intentions coupled with a military posture capable of interpretation by the Chinese Communists as preparatory to defense of the islands, while offering the GRC no exploitable assurances, combines the advantages of plausible deterrence and preparedness with maximum flexibility and maneuverability for the US. It avoids a sharp worsening of US-GRC relations and possibly serious domestic US repercussions, while keeping the Chinese Communists seriously in doubt as to the ultimate risks involved in a grab for the offshore islands.

The primary justification for a decision to be made at this time *not to defend* the offshore islands would be a policy decision to bring about GRC withdrawal from the islands.

Correspondingly the primary justification for a decision to be made at this time *to defend* the offshore islands would be a policy decision to give full support to the GRC.

---

Source: Department of State, FE Files: Lot 64 D 25, Communist China. Secret.

It is generally agreed that the Chinese Communist military buildup opposite Taiwan and the offshore could be, from the *military* point of view, compatible with Chinese intentions to:

1. Defend against a possible GRC attack on the mainland (with or without US support),
2. Initiate a political-military crisis on the order of that of the 1958 shelling of Kinmen (Quemoy), or
3. Attack one or more of the offshore islands for the purpose of seizing it by military means.

However aggressive Peiping's intentions may be, its actual course of actions as the situation develops will be significantly affected by a number of factors (other than purely military considerations) which include the posture of the US, the attitude and actions of the GRC, and the relationship between Peiping and Moscow. In our view, the most important single factor in Peiping's eyes will be the posture and apparent intentions of the US simply because the risk of direct confrontation with US military power is the most critical single limitation on Chinese Communist freedom of action in the situation.

*If We Now Decide Not to Defend the Offshore Islands.*

Convincing evidence that the US would not participate in the defense of the offshore islands would sharply reduce the risks Peiping would see in an attack on the islands. It would at the same time reduce the likelihood that Moscow could exert any restraining influence on Peiping since the latter would regard Soviet support as less likely to be required.

In this situation, the Chinese Communists would be encouraged to launch intensive propaganda and subsequently artillery barrages against one or more of the islands in the expectation of reducing them to surrender through blockade and attrition of troop morale without the necessity of launching an amphibious assault. Such a probe would also constitute a further test of the firmness of the US decision not to defend the islands. If the US continued to show no evidence of supporting the GRC through logistic and other assistance to maintain their island positions, and if Peiping became convinced its probing tactics would not be successful, the Chinese Communists might be emboldened to accept the lessened but still formidable military costs of an amphibious assault. (Even if Peiping's intentions are strictly defensive, evidence that the US would not defend the islands could cause them to move over to the offensive.)

The GRC would react to the US decision with horrified disbelief. "The GRC attaches great political and psychological importance to the offshore islands. Nationalist leaders are convinced that the islands must be held not only to assist the defense of Taiwan, but more importantly to maintain their claim to be a national government, to prevent a serious blow to morale, and to preclude any further decline in the prestige and international position of the GRC." [NIE 43–61, June 20, 1961][1]

The GRC would view the US decision as a fundamental change in its China policy implying adoption of a "two-China" position, as an unwarranted and cowardly retreat under communist threat of force, and as an invitation to Peiping to apply further force not only in the Taiwan Straits but also elsewhere in the Far East.

The GRC would probably calculate that the decision was not immutable. It would mobilize all its political resources to attack the decision not only on the grounds cited above but also as vitiating the impact of the 1958 Joint Resolution of Congress as a deterrent to communist attack on the offshores and on Taiwan itself. The GRC would reassert its determination to defend the offshores to the last man, whatever the consequences, and might take actions designed further to prove its determination, e.g., reinforcements of the offshores and further military mobilization on Taiwan. It would put the offshores themselves on intensified alert and might respond sharply to Chinese Communist shelling (for example, by returning HE for propaganda). It would probably welcome an escalation of military activity at the offshores but would be cautious about altering the levels or terms of conflict in ways that the US might regard as dangerously provocative.

The GRC would probably anticipate that the US would seek to persuade it to withdraw from the offshore islands without bloodshed, and its position (as above) would be intended in part to forestall any such attempt. If the US nevertheless did seek to persuade the GRC to withdraw, ". . . the GRC would refuse, banking on US reluctance to use its leverage. We believe that the GRC leaders would eventually yield, but only when they were convinced that the US would in fact use whatever means were necessary to force compliance—e.g., drastic curtailment of economic, military and diplomatic support." [NIE 43–61]

If the Chinese Communists eventually launched an attack on the offshore islands, the GRC would desperately attempt to reverse the US decision and agree to evacuate the islands only if utter defeat were imminent.

*If We decide Now to Defend the Offshore Islands*

US commitment to defend the offshore islands would, at the very least, diminish any doubts Peiping may have that an attack on the islands could result in a direct clash with the US. The Chinese Communists would in consequence become very cautious in their approach. At the

---

[1] Document 31. All brackets are in the source text.

same time, however, Peiping's concern over the likelihood of a GRC-US attack on the Chinese mainland would almost certainly be aggravated by the sudden hardening of a position the US had previously maintained ambiguously. This concern would be communicated to and probably shared to an increased extent by the Soviet Union, even should we attempt to relieve Soviet anxieties about our offensive intentions against Communist China. Aside from the anticipated propaganda exploitation by the bloc of anxieties among US allies and others about the extended US commitment, there might well be at least a temporary tightening of the Sino-Soviet military alliance. This could carry with it attendant risks of escalation in the event of any GRC or Chinese Communist moves to take advantage of the apparently increased support from their allies.

The GRC would welcome the knowledge that the US had decided to help defend the offshore islands as further commitment to the GRC cause and as offering new hope that it might involve the US in offensive actions against the mainland.

The GRC would attempt to place greater reliance on US military and logistic capabilities for the defense of the offshores and to devote more of its own resources to other operations. Therefore the GRC could be expected to seek US assistance in launching airdrops or even amphibious strikes on the mainland outside the area of Chinese Communist buildup. Knowledge of Chinese Communist strength and readiness would make the GRC cautious about any action without definite US support, but the GRC might either provoke an incident with the Chinese Communists which would be calculated to engage US forces, or might be less careful to avoid such an incident in their patrols and probes along the coast.

The GRC might seize on any appropriate Chinese Communist military action, such as shelling the offshores with high explosives, to argue that the activity was preliminary to an assault and that the US should take preemptive measures such as air strikes at military positions in the immediate area or even at supporting airfields and communications lines. The GRC would probably not contemplate independent strikes against the mainland but would increase pressures on the US to provide planes and equipment for later airdrops or amphibious landings.[2]

---

[2] Hilsman elaborated on his views in a June 21 telephone conversation with Forrestal. According to notes of the conversation, Hilsman stated, referring to a cable from Hong Kong, "We think there is a lot in this that the mainland people are running scared, and that we have got to leave them a way out. This memo I will send you [presumably a copy of the one printed here] doesn't make it clear that one of our concerns is to give the ChiComs a way of saving face." (Kennedy Library, Hilsman Papers, Box 8, Memoranda of Telephone Calls) Telegram 1503 from Hong Kong, June 21, conveyed a report that Chinese Communist leaders, beset by domestic problems and fearing U.S.-fomented external attacks, had lost their confidence. (Department of State, Central Files, 793.00/6–2162) See the Supplement.

126. **Letter From the Assistant Secretary of Defense for International Security Affairs (Nitze) to the Under Secretary of State for Political Affairs (McGhee)**

Washington, June 21, 1962.

DEAR GEORGE: This is in reply to the Department of State request of 17 April 1962 for Department of Defense comments on the draft Guidelines paper on the Republic of China.[1]

On the basis of a review by the Joint Chiefs of Staff and interested elements of the Office of the Secretary of Defense, it is the Department of Defense opinion that, from a military viewpoint, with the exception of the treatment given U.S. policy with respect to the GRC-held Offshore Islands, and subject to certain other modifications, the paper provides an adequate basis of U.S. foreign policy and operational guidance toward the Republic of China. The specific JCS recommendations on the draft paper are set forth and explained in the first inclosure to this letter.[2]

We recognize that there are some compelling arguments in support of a policy of seeking an eventual voluntary GRC withdrawal from the Offshore Islands. Nevertheless, before a policy decision on this matter is made, we believe that full consideration should be given at the highest level of the government to the judgments of the Joint Chiefs of Staff regarding both the military significance of the Offshore Islands and their defensibility. The views of the JCS, which were furnished Governor Harriman as an attachment to a letter from Bill Bundy on 5 May 1962,[3] were reaffirmed by the JCS in their recent review of the draft Guidelines paper under consideration. I am attaching as a second inclosure a copy of a JCS memorandum of 6 June 1962 (minus attachment) setting forth the latest military judgment of the Joint Chiefs on this question.

---

Source: Department of State, Central Files, 611.93/6–2162. Secret.

[1] The April 17 memorandum, not found, apparently forwarded for comment a March 1962 draft paper entitled "The Republic of China: Department of State Guidelines for Policy and Operations." (Ibid., Policy Guidelines Files: Lot 67 D 396, China Nationalist)

[2] Not printed; it is entitled "Recommended Changes in the Draft Guidelines Paper on the Republic of China."

[3] The JCS memorandum of April 6, enclosed with Bundy's May 5 letter, recommended that the United States seek to preserve the status quo of the Nationalist-held offshore islands by providing GRC forces with equipment and training to assist them in defending the islands and that the United States be prepared to support the GRC in the defense of the islands with U.S. forces "to the extent required" to ensure the defense of Formosa and the Pescadores. (Department of State, Central Files, 794A.5/5–562) See the Supplement.

The Department of Defense fully shares the JCS view that a policy decision involving a change of the U.S. position with respect to the continued GRC presence on these islands[4] should receive Presidential approval. Accordingly, I recommend that until a policy decision on this matter is obtained in connection with the President's review of the new statement of Basic National Security Policy,[5] references to the eventual withdrawal of the GRC from the Offshore Islands be deleted from the Guidelines paper. Should you feel, on the other hand, that this question must be addressed in the Guidelines document, I recommend that the paper, or at least those sections dealing with an eventual GRC withdrawal from the islands, be referred to the President in a manner that will permit the JCS and the Department of Defense to present possibly differing viewpoints.[6]

Sincerely,

**Paul**

**Enclosure[7]**

**Memorandum From the Joint Chiefs of Staff to Secretary of Defense McNamara**

JCSM–429–62                                    Washington, June 6, 1962.

SUBJECT

Guidelines of US Policy Toward the Republic of China (U)

1.   Reference is made to a memorandum, dated 21 April 1962, from the Deputy Assistant Secretary of Defense (ISA),[8] requesting comments or views on the subject paper.

---

[4] U. Alexis Johnson commented in a memorandum of June 26 to McGhee:

"Incidentally, I find it surprising that Defense now feels there is not a policy of *seeking* the withdrawal of the GRC from the Offshore Islands. I thought this had been a consistent policy since 1955, even though it may not have been formally reaffirmed by this administration." (Department of State, Central Files, 611.93/6–2662)

[5] See Document 129.

[6] A letter of June 30 from McGhee to Nitze reads:

"I think you will agree that it would be inopportune now to raise for discussion the question of longer-term US policy towards the Offshore Islands. I also think we could not expect to settle such a question by exchanging correspondence about a Guidelines paper.

"Accordingly, instead of considering issuance of the Republic of China Guidelines paper now, we are withdrawing it from interagency consideration." (Department of State, Central Files, 611.93/6–2162) No "Guidelines" paper on China was ever approved.

[7] Secret.

[8] A copy of the memorandum from Deputy Assistant Secretary Bundy to the Chairman of the Joint Chiefs of Staff is filed with the original copy of the JCS memorandum and a copy of Nitze's letter of June 21. (Washington National Records Center, RG 330, Records of the Office of the Secretary of Defense, OSD Files: FRC 66 A 3542, 091. China.)

2.  The Joint Chiefs of Staff consider that the draft Guidelines of US Policy Toward the Republic of China are in general consonance with US strategic objectives for the Far East except for the paragraphs dealing with the Government of the Republic of China (GRC) Offshore Islands. With respect to the Offshore Islands, the subject paper does not show a proper appreciation of the strategic and military importance of this Island complex to the defense of Taiwan/Penghus and to the attainment of US forward strategic objectives in the Pacific.

3.  The Offshore Islands are closely bound to the defense of Taiwan/Penghus, which form an important link in the defensive chain extending from the Aleutians to Australia. It is of the greatest importance that our policy guidelines recognize this as US policy regarding the GRC. The Offshore Islands themselves have significant military assets. They block the two most important ports between Shanghai and Canton from which the ChiComs could mount an amphibious attack against Taiwan/Penghus. They provide a source of early warning for the air defense of Taiwan/Penghus, and they serve as excellent visual reconnaissance and psychological warfare bases. The withdrawal from a valuable strategic location that enhances our own forward strategy and reduces ChiCom ability to mount an invasion force is militarily unsound. Further, the Offshore Islands are of paramount importance, politically and psychologically, in the minds of Asians as a symbol of successful resistance against communist aggression. Moreover, in event of war involving the United States and China, the Offshore Islands could be a valuable asset in military operations against the South China mainland. Retention of these islands together with the maintenance of the GRC position on Taiwan/Penghus will continue to pose a serious obstacle to the attainment of the communist objective of occupying all Nationalist held territory.

4.  The major islands of the Offshore Islands complex are defensible provided the GRC is given adequate US support. Without US support, the GRC would not be able to defend the Offshore Islands for any prolonged period against a determined ChiCom attack. The Offshore Islands are of significant strategic, military, political and psychological importance to the United States. A GRC defeat here would damage greatly the US prestige and would lessen the credibility of the US determination to stand firm against communist encroachment elsewhere.

5.  The Joint Chiefs of Staff recommend that the subject paper enunciate a firm policy with regard to support of the GRC in the retention of the Offshore Islands as an integral part of our forward strategy in the Pacific.

6.  In view of the importance of this guideline to US forward strategy in the Pacific, the Joint Chiefs of Staff recommend that this paper,

modified as indicated in the Appendix,[9] be referred to the National Security Council.

For the Joint Chiefs of Staff:
**L.L. Lemnitzer**[10]
*Chairman*
*Joint Chiefs of Staff*

[9] The appendix was not sent with the source text. (Ibid.)
[10] Printed from a copy that indicates Lemnitzer signed the original.

---

## 127. Memorandum of Conversation

Washington, June 22, 1962.

PARTICIPANTS

Ambassador Anatoliy F. Dobrynin, USSR
W. Averell Harriman, FE

I asked Ambassador Dobrynin to come to my house for a drink at 6 o'clock Friday, June 22. I first gave him Vientiane's 1783[1] (unclassified) reporting Souvanna's announcement that agreement had been reached between the three factions and that the Government of the National Union would be installed tomorrow. I said I thought Mr. Khrushchev would consider this "good news" (this reference to his opening phrase in the message to the President on the Khong-khay agreement among the Princes, June 12).[2] After some little discussion of the message and his query as to who the two Phoumis were (General Phoumi Nosavan[3] and Phoumi Vongvichet[4]), he agreed that this was good news and Mr. Khrushchev would be gratified. I pointed out, however, that there were a

---

Source: Kennedy Library, President's Office Files, China Security, 1962–63, Secret. Sent to Kennedy on June 24 with a covering note from Bromley Smith.

[1] Dated June 22. (Department of State, Central Files, 751J.00/6-2262)
[2] For text of Khrushchev's June 12 message to Kennedy, see volume V. Also printed in Department of State *Bulletin*, July 2, 1962, p. 12.
[3] Deputy Premier and Minister of Finance in the new Laotian Government.
[4] Pathet Lao delegate at the Geneva Conference on Laos and Minister of Information and Tourism in the new Laotian Government.

number of other steps which we would have to watch carefully, such as the withdrawal of North Viet-Nam troops and the integration of military force within Laos. I suggested that this would mean continuation of close cooperation between us. He said that he agreed and would be ready to discuss any matters that might arise. He said that Pushkin[5] and I had worked together closely and the relationship established by our governments should continue in the future. I said I hoped that Mr. Pushkin would not create any difficulties in Geneva. He asked whether there was much left for agreement. I replied that the declaration of the Laotian Government was important as the international agreement and protocol were based on it. He again commented that we should have continued cooperation to achieve our mutual objectives. He said that he considered that the fulfillment of the agreement between Mr. Khrushchev and President Kennedy on Laos was most important and he hoped this would lead to understanding in other fields.

I then turned to mainland China. I said we had assumed Mr. Khrushchev was interested in other areas of the Far East, not simply Laos. We were surprised by the build-up of Chinese Communist forces in Fukien and asked him what he knew about it. He said that he had no information other than what he had seen in the press. I said that such information as we had was generally in line with the press reports and that we had no knowledge of the ChiCom intentions. I asked him whether he thought the move was precautionary against possible attack by Chiang Kai-shek or a build-up for an attack on the off-shore islands. Again he replied that he had no information.

I said I assumed Mr. Khrushchev did not want to see a major military engagement break out in the Pacific and, therefore, we considered it important that Mr. Khrushchev should know the U.S. Government's attitude. Since there had been a good deal of talk from Taipei regarding Chiang Kai-shek's intention to invade the mainland, I thought Mr. Khrushchev should understand that Admiral Kirk was not being sent as Ambassador because of his experience in amphibious warfare. Dobrynin commented that he had read of this speculation. I explained that Admiral Kirk had been selected because of his standing and the confidence that President Kennedy had in him; also, that we had no intentions under existing circumstances of giving Chiang encouragement or support for an attack on the mainland. It seemed important for Mr. Khrushchev to understand this. I pointed out further that an agreement had been reached between Mr. Dulles and President Chiang Kai-shek which was still in effect, namely, that the ChiNats would take no offensive action without full consultation and prior agreement on the part of the United States. I also stated that in our meetings with the ChiComs since

---

[5] Georgi M. Pushkin, Soviet Deputy Foreign Minister for Southeast Asia and Deputy Chief of the Soviet delegation at the Geneva Conference on Laos.

1955 we had consistently been urging agreement that force not be used by either side to change the existing situation and of course we continue to adhere to that position. He said he felt sure Mr. Khrushchev would be glad to learn this. In reply to his question, I told him that Cabot was seeing Wang in Warsaw Saturday[6] & would give him same information I was giving Dobrynin.[7]

I then continued that if for any reason the ChiCom build-up was of a more ominous character, Mr. Khrushchev should understand our treaty with the GRC and I referred to the dangerous situation arising from any aggressive action on the part of the ChiComs. With an air of surprise, he commented "you wouldn't help defend the off-shore islands?" I replied, "why not?" "But these islands are Chinese territory," he asserted. I said we believed in peaceful settlement of differences but we could not stand by if the ChiComs took aggressive action.

He then raised the whole question of Formosa and asked whether we were prepared to carry out the Cairo agreement.[8] I pointed out that this was an agreement with Chiang Kai-shek, not with the ChiComs. When he attempted to argue further, I asked whether Mr. Khrushchev was prepared to hand over East Germany to Adenauer. He asked if I could tell him anything about our policy toward China. I replied that there was no change from the position President Kennedy had taken last October.[9] When he tried to probe into the possibility of change in that position, I said that this was not an appropriate time for a discussion of the future of China and that we should concentrate on the question before us, namely, why the ChiComs were reinforcing their position in Fukien. He said that the Soviet Government maintained Taiwan was part of China and would support that position. I said I was familiar with Mr. Khrushchev's attitude as he had told me in June, 1959.[10] We then discussed this meeting in some of its sober, as well as some of its amusing aspects. Before leaving, he reiterated the importance of Laos and said he hoped we would have further discussions such as the one we had this afternoon. I replied that I would not hesitate to talk with him about the developments and agreed that it was of great importance that our two governments keep in close contact. He left to dress for dinner with the Swiss Ambassador.

---

[6] June 23.

[7] This sentence appears in Harriman's handwriting on the source text.

[8] Reference is to the Cairo Declaration, the communiqué issued by President Roosevelt, Generalissimo Chiang, and British Prime Minister Winston Churchill on December 1, 1943.

[9] The reference is unclear. For text of remarks made by Kennedy at a press conference on October 11, see *Public Papers of the Presidents of the United States: John F. Kennedy, 1961*, p. 658.

[10] Harriman met with Khrushchev in Moscow on June 23, 1959; regarding that conversation, see *Foreign Relations, 1958–1960*, vol. XIX, p. 568.

128. **Telegram From the Department of State to the Embassy in the United Kingdom**

Washington, June 22, 1962, 9:25 p.m.

6895. For Bruce from Harriman. Acting Secretary called in British Ambassador morning June 22 to inform him we unclear whether Chi-Com troop concentrations Fukien offensive or defensive and therefore wished notify Peiping soonest as follows:

U.S. wishes attention Peiping called to Mutual Defense Treaty between US and GRC and to 1955 Formosa Resolution giving President authority to use US armed forces to defend offshore islands, if he judges such action is required or appropriate in assuring defense of Taiwan and Pescadores. Peiping further advised that in view of strength of the GRC garrisons on offshore islands, any effort to take them would be a major operation which could not easily be limited to immediate vicinity of islands. Serious risk of wider hostilities involving US forces would therefore arise.

Re reported GRC plans to attack mainland, USG has no intention of supporting such an attack under existing circumstances. Attention called to Exchange of Notes between US and GRC in December 1954 which requires GRC to obtain agreement of US in any offensive action by GRC military forces. In this connection Peiping might also note that in our meetings with Chinese Communists since 1955, we have consistently been urging agreement that force not be used by either side to change the existing situation, and of course we continue to adhere to that position.

Acting Secretary added that parallel approach to be made by Harriman to Dobrynin afternoon 22nd and requested British convey above representation to Chinese.

Ormsby Gore agreed transmit remarking FonOff might state UK itself very concerned. Pointed out no British Chargé presently Peiping and FonOff approach Chinese Chargé London best alternative. This agreed to, in view importance time question. Presence Secretary in London 24th added advantage, since as Ormsby Gore noted, it might not be possible reach Chinese Chargé before 25th.

**Ball**

---

Source: Department of State, Central Files, 793.5/6–2262. Secret; Limit Distribution. Drafted by Bacon, cleared by Yager and Tyler, and approved by Harriman. Repeated to Taipei, Hong Kong, Warsaw, and Rome for the Secretary.

## 129.   Editorial Note

During the first few months of 1962, a series of draft statements entitled "Basic National Security Policy" was prepared in the Policy Planning Council under the supervision of its Director, Walt W. Rostow. None of the drafts was approved. The final papers were a 185-page draft dated June 22, which was sent to the President, and a shorter version dated August 2. The June 22 paper called for a "carrot" and "stick" approach to Communist China. It stated in part:

"We will use force to deter or deal with the Chinese Communists' military or indirect aggression wherever it occurs; we will not otherwise ourselves initiate aggression against Communist China; but we may not be content to meet Chinese Communist harassments of the free community, if these harassments expand, wholly within the borders of that community."

It also stated:

"Concurrently, we should leave ajar possibilities for expanding commercial, cultural and other contacts with Communist China, by making clear that the bar to the entrance of Communist China into more normal relations with the U.S. is its basic unwillingness to modify its present aggressive policies."

Concerning Taiwan, it stated in part:

"a. We should use our influence and aid to promote the emergence on Taiwan of a political process increasingly based on popular consent, and to support economic development on an effective long-term basis.

"b. We should work, within the limits which a useful relationship with the GRC will allow, for a dampening-down of the GRC-Chinese Communist civil war. It remains an objective of U.S. policy: (i) to disengage U.S. and GRC prestige from the defense of the offshore islands, if and when this can be done without damage to our position in the Far East; (ii) to persuade the GRC through means which include aid and support for its position on Taiwan either to withdraw its forces from the islands or to regard the islands as outposts to be garrisoned in accordance with the requirements of outpost positions, again if and when this can be done without damage to our position in the Far East."

Concerning the Sino-Soviet split, it stated that while there was little the United States could do to promote it, the United States should "at least avoid measures which might have the effect of healing it." It further stated that the United States should not lose sight of the fact that both states, whether closely knit or not, would continue to be "basically hostile to us though perhaps in different degrees and in different ways." (Department of State, S/P Files: Lot 69 D 121, BNSP Draft 6/22/62)

Documentation concerning various draft statements of Basic National Security Policy are in volume VIII. The complete text of the June 22 draft is in the Microfiche Supplement to that volume.

## 130.    Telegram From the Consulate General at Hong Kong to the Department of State

Hong Kong, June 22, 1962, 7 p.m.

1525. On basis of limited info as to latest movement ChiCom forces to Fukien Province, ConGen sees this build-up as being essentially defensive in character reflecting ChiCom fears of ChiNat attacks on mainland, increased concern over reliability of populace and possibly apprehension over US intentions toward China as result recent US military moves in SE Asia.

In moving force into Fukien Province, ChiComs probably seek to (A) deter attack on mainland by Chiang's forces or cope with attack should it materialize; (B) provoke US and others to dissuade Chiang from attack; (C) shore up internal security situation particularly along coastal areas most directly exposed to possible ChiNat activity; and (D) divert national attention away from internal malaise and toward a common adversary. Peiping may have in mind provoking USG into disavowing any involvement in threatened GRC military attacks against mainland, thereby smothering possible expectations in China that USG prepared to support return of GRC. (Note relationship to how ChiComs used British closure of Hong Kong to mainland refugee influx in dissuading people from further efforts go to Hong Kong.)

If there is any new concentration of ChiCom forces now pointing toward offshore islands, this is probably aimed at (A) throwing Chiang's return-to-mainland preparations off balance; (B) calling world attention to possible conflict over these controversial islands; and (C) causing USG to disclaim support for offshores defense and otherwise seeking to weaken US-GRC relations and undermine GRC.

In making moves to date, ChiComs probably have not yet determined whether or not they would carry actions to point of actually attacking offshore islands. May be moving into posture where that alternative open to them. We continue to believe, as we have since 1958 offshore crisis, that Peiping sees the GRC occupation of these islands as providing certain clear benefits, namely, avoid crystalization "two China" concept; but in light of present mood as analyzed Congentel

---

Source: Department of State, Central Files, 793.54/6–2262. Secret; Priority. Repeated to Taipei, Tokyo, Moscow, London, and CINCPAC for POLAD.

1512[1] they may feel impelled to act against offshores because of their own nervous state of mind, their desire to score some victory to overcome current disillusionments and setbacks and to internal benefits of having country on war footing.

Green

---

[1] Telegram 1512, June 21, reported signs of "mounting political unrest" conveying an impression of "dispirited people and bewildered leadership." It cautioned, however, "We continue to doubt the people are prepared to challenge military and police power which is feared and can be broadly deployed to cope with possible disorders. Significant that attitude of refugees recently pouring into Hong Kong reflected no readiness of people on mainland to translate dissatisfaction into political action or to opt for return of GRC rule." (Ibid., 793.00/6–2162) See the Supplement.

---

**131.  Telegram From the Embassy in Poland to the Department of State**

Warsaw, June 23, 1962, 8 p.m.

2136. Deptels 1827,[1] 1828.[2] Had a two hour talk with Ambassador Wang this afternoon.[3] He started by referring to situation in Southeast

---

Source: Department of State, Central Files, 611.93/6–2362. Secret; Niact; Limit Distribution. Repeated to London, Hong Kong, Taipei, and Rome for the Secretary. A copy of this telegram, along with Document 127, was sent to Kennedy with a June 24 note from Bromley Smith which reads: "Ball and Harriman believe the Chinese Communist démarche was made because of anxiety that the Nationalists might invade. They believe the Communists are also concerned about local unrest in the area into which Communist troops have been moved." (Kennedy Library, President's Office Files, China Security, 1962–1963)

[1] Document 128 was repeated to Warsaw as telegram 1827.

[2] Telegram 1828, June 22, replied to telegram 2127 from Warsaw of the same date, in which Cabot reported that Wang had invited him to tea at 4 p.m. the next day, and he had accepted. Telegram 1828 stated that Wang's invitation provided an opportunity to pass through him the message being sent through London; it instructed Cabot to "first exhaust everything Wang has on his mind" and then repeat that message. (Both in Department of State, Central Files, 793.5/6–2262) Wang had invited Cabot to a private conversation at tea on June 15, but the Chinese Embassy had telephoned that day to say that Wang had to postpone the meeting because of illness. (Telegrams 2057 and 2064 from Warsaw, June 14 and 15; ibid., 611.93/6–1462 and 793.5/6–1562, respectively)

[3] Cabot sent a detailed report of the meeting in airgram A–718 from Warsaw, June 29. He added that the meeting had been held in a reception room in the Chinese Embassy. Wang's interpreter Ch'iu Ying-chueh, served as interpreter for both sides; U.S. Embassy officer William A. Buell took notes. (Ibid., 611.93/6–2962) See the Supplement.

Asia. He expressed concern about our military build-up in South Vietnam and forces in Thailand. He mentioned that the three Princes agreement in Laos offered favorable conditions for peaceful settlement in Laos and easing Southeast Asia situation.

Wang then said his government wished to call attention to situation in Taiwan area. Chiang Kai-shek clique was preparing invasion Chinese Mainland and this preparation had support US Government. He then discussed at some length military preparations on Taiwan including increase US military and economic aid. He said US playing with fire, such attack would not benefit US and US would bear responsibility for it.

Replying I expressed pleasure at Laos settlement and consequent reduction of tension. With reference to troops in Thailand, we had always made clear this a temporary measure. With reference to Vietnam, we were giving military help to legitimate government in view of outside intervention in South Vietnam. I then referred to situation in Taiwan area. I said that I was authorized to state that US Government had no intention of supporting any GRC attack on Mainland under existing circumstances. I pointed out GRC committed not to attack without our consent. I then noted ChiCom military build-up opposite Taiwan and said if this defensive, it was unobjectionable. However, I invited his side's attention to our formal treaty with GRC and to 1955 resolution re defense of Taiwan and Pescadores. I said that any effort to take off-shore islands would require major military operation which could not be easily limited and in such event there was serious danger US forces would become involved. Wang requested me to repeat my last statement which made in close paraphrase of Department's telegram. I then referred to our repeated proposals for agreement renouncing use of force by other side to which we continued to adhere. I summarized by saying we had no intention of committing or supporting aggression against his side anywhere.

Wang then repeated charge that Chiang Kai-shek planning attack. He referred to Chiang's repeated boasts that he would return to Mainland and to military aid we had furnished Chinese Nationalists over the years. He said that without US support, Chiang would not dare to attack. Wang emphasized ChiCom military strength and denied ChiComs were interfering in South Vietnam.

Replying I said I could not speak for GRC but reiterated we had no intentions of supporting attack on Mainland under existing circumstances. If GRC forces invaded Mainland it would be contrary to their commitments to us and I said I did not believe they would do it. I said with regard to South Vietnam that I had merely stated that there had been foreign intervention there, which had been certified by ICC. If Wang side would discourage such intervention we would not have to send military aid to legitimate government of South Vietnam.

Wang referred to ChiCom proposals for renunciation of force. He reiterated that without US support, Chiang would not dare to attack. Replying I pointed out that tension we were discussing existed precisely in Taiwan Straits area and that our proposals for renunciation of force specifically included that area whereas theirs did not. Wang stated Chi-Com opposed to Two China concept. Reverting to an earlier remark by Wang that our talks could not continue if an attack were made, I said that such attack if made by GRC would be without support of US. It would seem to me most important under those circumstances for our talks to continue in order to restore peace. We would clearly disassociate ourselves from any such attack.[4]

Wang said that a simple statement of disassociation would not suffice. I pointed out that I was sure we would disassociate ourselves in word and deed from any attack and would seek to restore peace. I then asked for assurances from him that ChiComs would not attack Taiwan. There was a long pause and Wang then replied question of ChiCom attack does not arise. The question is of Taiwan organizing an attack on Mainland. I regretted that it was not possible to have reciprocal assurances. He replied "we have not faced the problem on our side by seeking a settlement by force, but should an invasion take place, the character of whole situation would change." I then reminded Wang again of our commitments to GRC.

*Comment:* Although discussion throughout was serious, atmosphere not particularly tense. I think this summary of conversation, which comes from almost word for word transcript made by Embassy officer, gives flavor better than anything I can add. Wang was relaxed and friendly when offering us tea after formal exchange. Wang's first statement was made from prepared text but later ones were extemporaneous. I was unable to reach any conviction as to whether his démarche was made because of genuine anxiety on ChiCom part that GRC might invade Chinese Mainland with US support or whether statement was attempt to pin responsibility on us in planned ChiCom aggression against GRC.

Transcript of conversation by next pouch.

**Cabot**

---

[4] According to Cabot's report of the meeting in airgram A–718, Wang said that if an attack occurred, the United States "would certainly be held responsible for it" and the issue would be one involving China and the United States.

## 132.  Memorandum of Conversation

SET/MC/33                                    London, June 24, 1962, 8 p.m.

### SECRETARY'S EUROPEAN TRIP
(June 18–28, 1962)

PARTICIPANTS

| United States | UK |
|---|---|
| Secretary of State | Prime Minister Macmillan |
| Ambassador Bruce | Lord Home, Foreign Minister |
| Mr. Bohlen | Edward Heath, Lord Privy Seal |
| Mr. Kohler | Sir Harold Caccia |
| | Sir Evelyn Shuckburgh |
| | Mr. Ian Samuels |

SUBJECT

China

The Secretary opened the conversation on China by referring to the ChiCom military build-up opposite Taiwan. We felt that this was probably of a defensive nature, responsive to the talk from Taiwan on "return to the mainland." He could assure the British, however, that Peiping knows that the United States will not allow an attack on the mainland. He then commented on the question of food for mainland China. He felt that an initiative on our part in this connection would play into Peiping's hands. Our people had calculated that to provide simply an additional 100 calories a day to bring consumption from 1300 to 1400 calories (as against a normal requirement of 2200–2300) would alone cost in the range of $700 million per year. This was a difficult question and one on which the United States could not act unless it were possible to reverse the Food for Peace slogan to "Peace for Food."

The Prime Minister replied vehemently that he simply did not understand United States policy on China. We did not even admit that China existed. He wondered what our long-run policy was. He regarded it as indefensible by any logic. He said the Peiping regime obviously are China. The United States had "a fellow from Taiwan" sitting in China's seat in the UN. He admitted that we had come out of the last session very well, but only because we had "bullied all the South Americans" into voting for us. The British, he said, do a good business with the Chinese Communists. They had, for example, sold them fourteen Viscounts. The British are an island, they live on trade.

---

Source: Department of State, Central Files, 110.11–RU/6–2462. Secret; Limit Distribution. Drafted by Kohler and approved in S on June 28. The conversation was held at Carleton Gardens.

The Secretary commented that the UK traded with the Chinese Communists while we furnish the gendarmes to keep them from misbehaving. If the choice had to be made, he would say frankly we were much closer to the East Germans than to the Chinese Communists. He commented that we would be faced with an appalling prospect if the Chinese government changed and the food problem became ours. He added that we are maintaining regular contact with the Chinese Communists through the Warsaw talks but that we had got nothing from these, not even a few American prisoners.

Lord Home then referred to the question of American troops in Southeast Asia and asked what should be done about these. The Secretary replied that these were like NATO troops. They posed no threat for the Chinese Communists if Peiping behaved. Our troops had no intention of going north. Lord Home then asked whether if the situation remained quiet in South Vietnam it might be possible to work out an arrangement along the lines of the Laos settlement. The Secretary replied that the two situations were not comparable. He then commented that there could be two interpretations of Khrushchev's purpose in Laos. Possibly it could be that he wanted to show us that agreement was possible. On the other hand, he may have wanted to show the other Communist parties that his "peaceful coexistence" policy was a way to advance the Communist cause. He felt that the situation still had to be carefully watched. We were worried about the possible course of development, especially during Souvanna's absence from the country.

## 133.  Memorandum of Conversation

SET/MC/38                                      London, June 25, 1962, 11 a.m.

### SECRETARY'S EUROPEAN TRIP
June 18–28, 1962

PARTICIPANTS

| United States | Great Britain |
|---|---|
| The Secretary | Lord Home |
| Ambassador Bruce | Sir Harold Caccia |
| Mr. Bohlen | Sir Evelyn Shuckburgh |
| Mr. Kohler (for the beginning) | Mr. Joseph Godber |
| | Mr. Ian Samuel |
| | [Ramsbotham, Mason][1] |

SUBJECT

China

The Secretary said that last night they had talked about letting Peiping know that there would be no attack. He said the Peiping regime had broadcast an article which described these measures as defensive. In addition, from their information, the scale does not indicate offensive action, which was confirmed by the air dispositions and the fact that there were no assault boats being assembled.

Turning to the question of food,[2] the Secretary pointed out that President Kennedy had deliberately left this question open.[3] We did not see how food from outside could have much effect on the general situation in China but he said, however, we did not exclude the possibility of partici-

---

Source: Department of State, Central Files, 110.11–RU/6–2562. Secret; Limit Distribution. Drafted by Bohlen and approved in S on July 3. The conversation was held at the Foreign Ministry.

[1] Brackets in the source text.

[2] Lord Home raised the question of sending food to China in a May 20 message to Rusk, who replied noncommittally in a May 22 letter to British Ambassador David Ormsby Gore. (Both in Department of State, Central Files, 893.49/5–2262) A British aide-mémoire of May 29 conveyed a suggestion by former Japanese Prime Minister Yoshida for an international consortium to provide food to China. (Ibid., 893.49/5–2962) On June 12 Rusk authorized discussion of the proposal with the British Embassy. (Memorandum from Harriman to Rusk, ibid., 893.02/6–1262) Yager subsequently indicated to Ledward U.S. willingness to discuss the proposal, but by that time British interest had apparently subsided. (Memorandum of conversation, July 9; ibid., 893.49/7–962)

[3] Kennedy stated on June 14, in response to a question asked at a meeting with the headquarters staff of the Peace Corps, that U.S. policy was "to do nothing on the food until there is some indication that the Chinese Communists desire it" and to "consider it on an independent basis at that time." (*Public Papers of the Presidents of the United States: John F. Kennedy, 1962*, pp. 487–488)

pating in some general humanitarian action. He felt that it would be essential politically in the United States to have some indication from the Chinese communists that they were relaxing their tactics of pressure on India and elsewhere in order to get it through the Senate.

Lord Home remarked that their recent Chargé in Peiping had said that nothing would induce the Chinese to ask for aid. He said he felt there was nothing to do in the circumstances but be ready to consult together if any request was received. He mentioned that Averell Harriman had suggested that the UK should talk to the Chinese about the off-shore islands but that they were not in very good odor in Peiping at the moment. He wondered if it would be worthwhile. He said they would be prepared to do so if necessary, but doubted the desirability of doing it now. He said the new Chargé would be going to Peiping in the latter part of July. The Secretary suggested that he might be briefed to be ready to act if and when it was necessary and the British agreed.

The Secretary mentioned, in this connection, that Ambassador Cabot in Poland, discussed this matter with the Chinese Ambassador. In fact, Wang had brought it up. He said it was our impression that the Chinese communist leadership was less arrogant and less confident than previously.

Mr. Bohlen mentioned certain intelligence indications that we had had of a certain dampening-down of the Chinese-Soviet dispute in recent months.

Lord Home said that the Chinese refugees trying to get into Hong Kong had been very interesting and appeared to reveal that the provincial authorities were not in complete control, but that when the national government had taken over the matter the action was very quick. The Secretary said that we felt that the unrest in China might have been a factor in the military buildup off Taiwan. Lord Home remarked that they had that information; that there had been no censorship of letters coming from overseas from Chinese who had written urging their relatives to come out.

Sir Harold Caccia said that on his trip through China he had found them less arrogant but no less sensitive. The Secretary remarked that the Chinese nationalists had withdrawn their plan to put in a new SC representative,[4] which was good news since this was a very poor time to bring this up. He mentioned that ten years ago, to Wellington Koo, that the Chinese could not get seven votes in the Security Council, which had caused them to drop the matter then.

---

[4] Documentation concerning GRC interest in naming a new Security Council representative as well as a new Permanent Representative to replace Tsiang is in Department of State, Central File 303.

Turning to the question of the General Assembly this fall, the Secretary mentioned that our people in New York felt that it would follow very much the lines of last year. They had found little enthusiasm for the study commission, but thought it was well to keep it alive for possible use in the future.

Mr. Godber said that he thought this time it would be less procedural than last year and would concentrate more on the central question—that is, who would represent China. He felt that the study group might be a means of stiffening the interest in this question.

### 134.   Memorandum From Secretary of Defense McNamara to President Kennedy

Washington, June 25, 1962.

Yesterday the Joint Staff prepared the attached answers[1] to the seven questions related to the defense of the Offshore Islands which General Taylor sent to me Saturday.[2] Time did not permit the development of a complete answer to question 1. b.: "What would be the likely pattern of the attack and what the outcome?" We will continue to explore this subject.

General Lemnitzer has concurred in the Joint Staff's statements. I, too, share their views, with one exception. The answer to question 5. b.[3] implies that the defense of the Offshore Islands may require the use of tactical nuclear weapons, and that the U.S. should be prepared to use such weapons. I believe that with full U.S. support the Islands can be effectively defended without tactical nuclear weapons; in any event, I am not ready to recommend their use for that purpose.

RMcN

---

Source: Kennedy Library, National Security Files, Countries Series, China. Top Secret.

[1] The attachment, entitled "Questions Related to the Defense of the Offshore Islands," is not printed, but see the Supplement.

[2] June 23. Taylor's memorandum stated that the President anticipated the probable need for an early meeting with the Congressional leadership on the subject of the threat to the offshore islands and wanted answers by June 25 to the seven questions that Taylor attached to provide him with background for such a discussion. (Kennedy Library, National Security Files, Countries Series, China)

[3] Question 5 asks about circumstances in which atomic weapons might be used.

## 135.    Memorandum for the Record

Washington, June 26, 1962.

NSC MEETING HELD ON TUESDAY, JUNE 26, 1962 AT 10:30 AM.

Meeting was a formal NSC meeting called for the purpose of hearing a report from Governor Adlai Stevenson on the problems confronting the US delegation to the United Nations during the fall meeting of the General Assembly. Governor Stevenson made the following points:

[Here follows paragraphs 1–5, Stevenson's review of various subjects.]

6. In answer to a question by the President the Ambassador stated that if the Chinese Communists continue their strident attitude, their quarrels with India, etc., the Chinese representation problem would be less of an issue than in recent years. However, if Chiang's provocative statements concerning returning to the Mainland are repeated, they will cause problems and embarrassments to the US in the UN. Stevenson expressed doubt as to the reason for the military buildup, indicating he thought it might be due to domestic implications.

He stated that the Soviet resolution[1] if presented as in the past would be soundly defeated, but that if they changed the resolution (which he thought was unlikely) to merely recognition of ChiComs and not the expulsion of the ChiNats, they might succeed in getting sufficient support to pass the resolution.

7. In answer to another question by the President with respect to responding to an attack on Quemoy, Stevenson stated that he, like others, wished that Chiang was out of the Islands and therefore the problem removed. He implied but did not specifically advise, a declaration by the President to the effect that we would not assist in the defense of Quemoy. He suggested that the President state that the US "had no intention of supporting Chiang's adventures on the Mainland." Stevenson went on to state that many delegations of the UN felt that Chiang was in trouble politically in Taiwan, and that leadership of the ChiNats was passing to other and perhaps more extreme and militant hands.

---

Source: Central Intelligence Agency, DCI (McCone) Files, Job 80–B01285A, DCI Meetings with the President. Secret; Eyes Only. Drafted by McCone. Kennedy's Appointment Book lists the time of the meeting as 10:40 a.m.–12:10 p.m. It lists 30 persons present, including Kennedy, Johnson, McNamara, and Ball. (Kennedy Library) Lemnitzer's notes of the portion of the meeting here printed are similar in substance. (National Defense University, Lemnitzer Papers, Box 29)

[1] The Soviet draft resolution introduced October 27, 1961, would have immediately removed "the representatives of the Chiang Kai-shek clique who are unlawfully occupying the place of China in the United Nations" and invited the Government of the People's Republic of China to send representatives. (U.N. doc. A/L.360; printed in *American Foreign Policy: Current Documents, 1961*, p. 144)

[Here follows discussion of other subjects.]

**John A. McCone**[2]
*Director*

---

[2] Printed from a copy that bears this typed signature.

---

### 136.  Memorandum From the President's Military Representative (Taylor) to President Kennedy

Washington, June 26, 1962.

SUBJECT

JCS Reply to Questions related to the Defense of the Offshore Islands

I have just read the memorandum of 25 June from the Secretary of Defense and the Joint Staff replying to your questions bearing on the defense of the Offshore Islands.[1]

In their reply, the Joint Staff appear to consider a classic amphibious operation mounted against the Offshore Islands as the principal threat from the ChiComs. This thought underlies the estimate in paragraph 1 a of one to four months as needed to mount a major attack. It also finds expression in paragraph 1 b, where the anticipated pattern of attack includes a considerable air and artillery preparation prior to any attempt to land. The same thought is found in 1 c, where the possibility of a surprise attack receives a low rating.

Personally, I am not at all sure that this kind of deliberately phased attack is the most likely or the most dangerous to the defense of the Offshore Islands. Because of the shallow depth of the water around Chinmen, it will be impossible to get heavy weapons ashore during the assault phase. The attack will inevitably depend on masses of lightly armed infantrymen, supported by air and artillery from the mainland. The pattern of the assault is likely to resemble that of the ChiComs in

---

Source: National Defense University, Taylor Papers, Box 47, Quemoy–Matsu 1962. Top Secret.

[1] See Document 134 and footnotes 1 and 2 thereto.

1949 rather than any American amphibious landings of World War II. The amphibious shipping will probably consist largely of rafts, sampans and junks employed in large numbers and with little order.

It seems likely that the ChiComs would make every effort to exploit surprise in making their attack. Under the cover of the very bad weather which is common during this season of the year, and utilizing small craft always in the area, it is entirely possible for the ChiComs to make a quick jump across the narrow water passage separating Chinmen from the mainland and establish a substantial beachhead in the course of a single night. The Defense Intelligence Agency considers that the landing craft required for an attack on the Chinmens or Matsu could be marshalled within 24 or 48 hours, and that the ChiComs could launch an attack on the Offshore Islands with little or no warning.

This or any other major attack will be extremely costly to the Chi-Coms and, if they have sensible leadership, the adventure should not prove attractive. However, we probably do not think like Chinese and their eventual decision may run counter to what seems sensible to us. The prize to them would be the elimination of a large part of Chiang's best troops, a serious blow to ChiNat and U.S. prestige worldwide, and a great lift to the ChiCom home front. On the other hand, a reverse for the ChiComs would greatly increase the already serious internal situation and would exact a heavy price in military assets.

**Maxwell D. Taylor**[2]

---

[2] Printed from a copy that bears this typed signature.

---

## 137.   Editorial Note

On June 26 and 27, 1962, U.S. press and wire services carried reports from "informed sources" about the June 23 meeting between Ambassadors Cabot and Wang. The evening of June 26 a Department of State spokesman gave a statement to the press confirming that Cabot and Wang had met on June 23, that Wang had raised accusations, and that Cabot had "reiterated our opposition to the use of force and our oft-repeated proposal for the mutual renunciation of the use of force in the Taiwan Strait area." The statement was approved by Kennedy. (Kennedy

Library, National Security Files, Countries Series, Poland, Ambassadorial Talks) Press reports are summarized in telegram 786 to Taipei, June 27. (Department of State, Central Files, 793.00/6–2762)

President Kennedy opened his press conference on June 27 with a statement concerning the situation in the Taiwan Strait area. He stated that there had been large movements of Chinese Communist forces into that area and declared, "Our basic position has always been that we are opposed to the use of force in this area." In the event of "aggressive action" against Quemoy and Matsu, he declared, "the policy of this country will be that established 7 years ago under the Formosa Resolution. The United States will take the action necessary to assure the defense of Formosa and the Pescadores."

After quoting a statement he had made in October 1960 supporting the Eisenhower administration position, he continued as follows:

"Under this policy sustained continuously by the United States Government since 1954, it is clear that any threat to the offshore islands must be judged in relation to its wider meaning for the safety of Formosa and the peace of the area.

"Exactly what action would be necessary in the event of any such act of force would depend on the situation as it developed. But there must be no doubt that our policy, specifically including our readiness to take necessary action in the face of force, remains just what it has been on this matter since 1955." (*Public Papers of the Presidents of the United States: John F. Kennedy, 1962*, page 510)

Under Secretary of State Ball and National Security Adviser Bundy discussed a draft of the President's statement in a June 27 telephone conversation, recorded in a memorandum of the conversation prepared in Ball's office. (Kennedy Library, Ball Papers, China (Taiwan)) On June 28 Kennedy telephoned Ball and expressed concern about a report by Max Frankel in that day's *New York Times*. According to a memorandum of conversation prepared in Ball's office, Kennedy thought the Frankel report indicated that "somebody really high up is leaking because it was interpreted in very sophisticated terms." (Ibid., China (Peking))

Kennedy commented on his press conference statement at a June 28 meeting with McCone, recorded in a memorandum by Helms, which reads in part as follows:

"[Kennedy] explained that he had made his statements at the Press Conference in the context of restating United States policy and emphasizing the 'defensive' nature of our treaty commitment. He said that he saw no useful purpose in changing United States policy until such a time as we had some specific reason for so doing, i.e., the possibility of deterioration on the Mainland to a point where it was felt desirable to support Chiang in a military operation. In other words, he indicated that he was not pre-judging developments but simply wanted to prevent the ChiComs from making propaganda capital out of any apparent change in United States posture." (Central Intelligence Agency, DCI (McCone) Files, Job 80–B01285A, DCI Meetings With the President)

138.  **Telegram From the Department of State to the Embassy in the Republic of China**

Washington, June 28, 1962, 8:58 p.m.

793. Eyes only Clough. In connection with the statements made at his press conference yesterday the President wishes you to convey to Chiang Kai-shek his strong feeling that is of utmost importance that both the United States and the GRC avoid giving the appearance of contemplating any aggressive action against the mainland at this time. Unless we both agree that conditions justify it we are not prepared to take action and therefore we must not appear aggressive. Invasion at this time obviously would not be successful and it is important that the Communists be regarded as the aggressors. Any departure from this principle can only play into the hands of the Communists by weakening our international position in the defense of Quemoy and Matsu and make us appear to be the instigators of military action. This can only complicate our position no matter which way the situation develops in the future.

Use your discretion whether to delay delivery of this message until the arrival of Ambassador Kirk.[1]

**Ball**

Source: Department of State, Central Files, 793.00/6–2862. Top Secret; Roger Channel. Drafted by Forrestal; cleared by Bundy and in draft by Rice; and approved by Joseph W. Scott, Deputy Director for Coordination in the Bureau of Intelligence and Research. Repeated to CINCPAC eyes only for Kirk, who was en route to Taipei.

[1] Clough replied in telegram 1 from Taipei, July 2, that he was unable to see Chiang, who was recovering from surgery, and was therefore waiting for Kirk to deliver the message directly. (Ibid., 611.93/7–262)

---

139.  **Telegram From the Embassy in the Republic of China to the Department of State**

Taipei, July 4, 1962, 2 p.m.

16. At one hour interview with President Chiang July 4[1] at which Madame Chiang, Foreign Minister, Director GIO and Chargé were pres-

Source: Department of State, Central Files, 793.00/7–462. Top Secret; Roger Channel. Repeated to CINCPAC. Received at 6:47 a.m.

[1] Kirk reported in telegram 8 from Taipei, July 3, that when he presented his letter of credence to Foreign Minister Shen on July 3, Shen told him that Chiang wanted to meet with him privately on July 4 prior to Kirk's formal presentation of credentials the following day. (Ibid., 611.93/7–362)

ent, I said President Kennedy had asked me to convey to President Chiang how very concerned President Kennedy was that no action be taken by GRC which could be used as pretext by Communists to accuse us around the world of being aggressors. I emphasized how important it was for aggressive action to be clearly defined as coming from other side. I said this would have important bearing on whatever we decided to do in future. I added we were particularly concerned about Quemoy and Matsu and wanted to make it clear to the world that we are not being aggressive in that area. Chiang replied he fully appreciated US position and assured me GRC would not initiate anything against Communists in Quemoy and Matsu area. However, he thought Communists might take action against one of the smaller offshore islands. ChiComs would wait and see how US reacted before attacking anywhere beyond Quemoy and Matsu areas.

Chiang then inquired whether I had any message for him concerning the discussions of military material which had taken place between our intelligence people. I replied President felt unable to go very far in planning because of lack of hard intelligence on real situation inside Communist China. However, I was authorized to assure President Chiang two C–123s would be ready in October and three more between January and February. The other material requested was still under consideration.

Chiang said he had read in press that US had assured ChiComs at Warsaw that US would not assist GRC return to Mainland. Was this correct and if so, what was nature of assurances given? I replied that this was not correct, that what the US had proposed to ChiComs as in the past was a mutual renunciation of force.

Chiang asked if I had seen Khrushchev's statement that USSR would support ChiComs in Taiwan area.[2] I replied I doubted very much USSR would intervene in any operation in Taiwan Straits. Chiang replied he also believed USSR would not intervene. Unfortunately, report of Warsaw talks together with Khrushchev's statement couldn't help having adverse effect on morale here. I said most westerners discounted Khrushchev's threats. Chiang replied this was appreciated by people at high level in government but not by people in general.

Chiang emphasized need for US and GRC to be prepared for ChiCom offensive action against offshore islands, which he expected within the next six months. He then went on to express pleasure at my assign-

---

[2] Reference is to a July 2 speech by Khrushchev. Telegram 12 from Moscow, July 2, reported that it had included "sharp denunciation provocations directed against CPR by Chiang Kai-shek with Pentagon support. Khrushchev in apparent riposte President's press conference warned anyone attempting attack CPR will be dealt crushing blow by CPR with solid support mighty socialist camp. Recalled alleged similar provocations 4 years ago and stern Soviet warning at that time." (Ibid., 761.13/7–262)

ment here and said that as soon as he had recuperated from further medical treatment beginning July 5, he hoped to consult closely with me. I said I was always at his disposition and added that he could count on the US fully complying with its commitments to GRC provided GRC did not undertake any unilateral action. Chiang assured me GRC would not undertake any unilateral action, but would continue to consult very closely with US.

I concluded interview by explaining reasons why 1,000 Marines withdrawn from Thailand. Chiang commented he thought this would have adverse effect on morale of people in area, as Laos problem was far from solved, but admitted that he was not fully abreast of situation.

Interview was very friendly throughout. Points on which Chiang particularly concerned were reported assurances given by US at Warsaw and US response to his request for matériel. Full memcon by pouch.[3]

**Kirk**

---

[3] A memorandum of the conversation was enclosed with airgram A–18, July 11. (Ibid., 611.93/7–162)

---

## 140.   Telegram From the Embassy in the Republic of China to the Department of State

Taipei, July 5, 1962, 6 p.m.

22. Following presentation credentials President Chiang had me come to his office for conversation at which Foreign Minister, Secretary General Chang Chun and DCM were present. He said that since he was going into hospital this afternoon and would not be available for a few days he wanted to make some additional comments related to our conversation of July 4.

Chiang said he first wished President Kennedy to understand he would not undertake any unilateral action but would cooperate sincerely with the US and fully coordinate his policy with us. He recognized

---

Source: Department of State, Central Files, 611.93/7–562. Top Secret; Roger Channel. Repeated to CINCPAC for POLAD.

that President Kennedy had many problems to deal with and he certainly would not do anything which would add to these problems. He hoped US Government would on its part also keep in mind importance of maintaining morale of Chinese people and armed forces and their confidence in GRC. Cabot–Wang conversation and Khrushchev declaration had caused much uneasiness in mind of people and Armed Forces. Press in Hong Kong and Taipei reflected this apprehension. I replied Khrushchev could hardly be expected to say anything other than what he said. On basis our own sources of information we feel Khrushchev does not want war in Taiwan Straits and therefore are not too much concerned.

Chiang said top GRC officials shared our view but propaganda effect on people was bad. I suggested GRC make use of its press to reassure its people. Chiang responded that they lost no opportunity to assure people of US support but clarification from Washington would carry greater weight. He expressed hope Ambassador would strengthen work of [1 *line of source text not declassified*] and that plans for strengthening GRC Air Force and Navy being discussed by this committee could be carried out. GRC would then be in position counter doubts in Armed Forces as to US support by pointing to what US is doing.

I pointed out relations between our two governments are governed by 1954 treaty which guarantees defense of Taiwan and Pescadores and such related territories as US President may find necessary to defense of Taiwan and Pescadores. US maintains forces in this area and is fully prepared to use them in support of its treaty obligations. Treaty does not say we will support GRC counterattack against mainland and it would be mistake to create impression in minds of people that US has any such obligations. If time comes when two governments mutually decided conditions are suitable for invasion that will create a new situation, but at present US commitment is limited to support of defensive nature.

Chiang replied both he and Chinese people fully understand defensive nature of treaty relationship. However, he hoped Ambassador Kirk could not only help maintain but also strengthen morale of GRC Armed Forces. If morale dampened, this would be loss both to US and GRC.

I remarked that I did not think either Khrushchev's statement or Cabot–Wang talk should be taken so seriously as President Chiang appeared to regard them. Chiang replied that news from US often produced far greater effect than people in Washington imagine. At time when ChiComs showing force he did not expect US publicly announce its support for GRC counter-attack—that would obviously be impossible—but neither did he see necessity of declaring to enemy US would not help GRC. Foreign Minister interjected that President was not so much complaining about past actions as expressing hope care would be taken in future.

Chiang concluded by saying he hoped he would not need too long a rest, but that in meantime Vice President and Foreign Minister were always available. Full memcon follows.[1]

**Kirk**

---

[1] Enclosed with airgram A–18; see footnote 3, Document 139. In telegram 3 from Geneva to Taipei (repeated to Washington as telegram 29), July 9, Harriman commended Kirk's handling of his July 4 and 5 conversations with Chiang and added, "In second talk it would appear that he is using morale in Taiwan as excuse to get US step by step publicly involved in support of possible invasion. President's June press conference clearly states position we must maintain." (Department of State, Central Files, 611.93/7–962)

---

### 141.   Special National Intelligence Estimate

SNIE 13–5/1–62                          Washington, July 5, 1962.

CHINESE COMMUNIST SHORT-RANGE MILITARY INTENTIONS

The Problem

To assess the significance of the Chinese Communist military buildup in the Foochow Military Region facing the Taiwan Strait.

Note

This Estimate supplements SNIE 13–5–62, "Chinese Communist Short-Range Military Intentions," dated 20 June 1962, on the same subject.[1]

The Estimate

1.   At the time when SNIE 13–5–62 was approved on 20 June, Chinese Communist armed forces had moved into the Foochow Military

---

Source: Department of State, INR/EAP Files: Lot 90 D 110, SINE 13–5/1–62. Secret. According to a note on the cover sheet, the Central Intelligence Agency and intelligence organizations of the Departments of State, Defense, the Army, the Navy, and the Air Force participated in the preparation of this estimate. All members of the USIB concurred with this estimate on July 5 except the representatives of the AEC and the FBI, who abstained on the grounds that the subject was outside their jurisdiction.

[1] See footnote 1, Document 122.

Region in large numbers. There had been no public announcement of the move, and no propaganda manifestations by the Chinese Communists which appeared to have any relationship to it. Neither were there any other clear indications of the purposes and motivations which might lie behind it. The Chinese Communists did have sufficient reason to take seriously the possibility of incursions by GRC forces in the coming months, and they had of course not abandoned their claims to Taiwan and the offshore islands.

2. Soon after 20 June news of the Chinese Communist military buildup appeared in the Western press, accompanied by statements of concern about Peiping's intentions. Chinese Communist propaganda then began vigorously to attack the Chinese Nationalists and the US, accusing them of a concerted intention to invade the mainland, but placing no stress on the "liberation" of the offshore islands or Taiwan. No movements of major military units into the Foochow Region were noted subsequent to 17 June. On 23 June Chinese Communist Ambassador Wang sought out US Ambassador Cabot in Warsaw, probably in order to discover what he could of US intentions. He was told that the US would not support a Chinese Nationalist attack on the mainland under present circumstances, and was also warned of the risks involved in a Chinese Communist attack on the offshore islands. US statements and Press Conference remarks by the President reaffirmed earlier declarations of US policy on the issues involved. Movements and increased readiness of US forces accompanied these statements.

3. Although these developments have changed the situation considerably they still do not permit a firm estimate of the motivations which lay behind the military buildup. A plausible interpretation is that the Chinese Communist leaders were seriously concerned with the possibility of a GRC incursion, perhaps with US support, on the mainland at a time of considerable unrest, and that they accordingly moved enough forces into the area to deter such incursions, to cope with them if they occurred, and to be in a position to attack the offshore islands if such a course seemed desirable, possibly in connection with repelling Nationalist landings on the mainland. They may also have had various expectations of political profit to be made when the troop movement became known, the reactions to it registered in the world, and the US attitude tested. This interpretation of the Chinese motives does not exclude the possibility that offensive action was under consideration prior to the US reactions.

4. Whatever the original motivations of the Chinese Communist military buildup may have been, world attention has been focused again on the Taiwan Strait issue, and a declaration of attitude and policy has been issued by the US. Publicly, the Chinese Communists proclaim their disbelief in the US disclaimer of support for GRC intrusion on the mainland, and they probably do remain somewhat uncertain of US intentions.

Yet the US statement probably diminished their fears of such attacks. It must also have encouraged them to hope for serious friction between the US and the GRC. Finally the Chinese Communists have used the situation to try to arouse the mainland population from its lethargy and perhaps to reduce the chances of local support for any possible Chinese Nationalist landing.

5.  The magnitude and scope of the military buildup have increased the offensive as well as the defensive capabilities of the Chinese Communists, and we still cannot dismiss the possibility of a full-scale assault on the offshore islands. However, the element of surprise has been largely lost, and the risks of the enterprise have been confirmed by US policy statements and precautionary measures. For the near future, therefore, we think that the odds are against such an attack. The Chinese Communists might undertake raids or small-scale attacks on one or another of the smaller islands held by the Nationalists, but there would be danger of escalation even in such actions and we doubt they would consider the gains worth the risk.

---

**142.  Telegram From the Department of State to the Embassy in the Republic of China**

Washington, July 7, 1962, 1:59 p.m.

16. 1. In call on Secretary today[1] Amb. Tsiang first asked if Secretary had discussed Chinese Communist military buildup in his recent talks with Lord Home.[2] Secretary said this subject discussed only briefly in response to Home's question concerning significance of reported buildup. Secretary had told Home this difficult to judge but from nature of movements and content of Chinese Communist propaganda, immediate all out Chinese Communist attack did not appear likely.

2.  Tsiang said Chinese opinion in Taiwan and elsewhere has been alarmed by reports that "Rostow paper"[3] calls for "two-Chinas" policy,

---

Source: Department of State, Central Files, 793.00/7–762. Secret; Limit Distribution. Drafted and approved for transmission by Yager and cleared by U. Alexis Johnson. Repeated to Geneva for Harriman.

[1] A memorandum of the conversation, dated July 10, is ibid., 793.00/7–1062.
[2] See Documents 132 and 133.
[3] Reference is to the draft Basic National Security Policy paper; see Document 129. Articles in the *Chicago Tribune* of June 17 and 18 about the "Rostow document" are reprinted in *Executive Sessions of the Senate Foreign Relations Committee, Together With Joint Sessions With the Senate Armed Services Committee (Historical Series)*, Volume XIV, Eighty-seventh Congress, Second Session, 1962 (Washington: Government Printing Office, 1986), pp. 553–558.

cessation of US opposition to UN membership for Chinese Communists, US recognition of Chinese Communists, and US effort to neutralize Taiwan. Tsiang asked if some effort might be made to clear air. Secretary replied that he understands Senate Foreign Relations Committee plans to publicize Rostow testimony[4] which will clarify situation. Tsiang asked whether Secretary could also make clarifying statement in press conference. Secretary replied that if question arises in press conference he will of course be responsive.

3.  Tsiang next referred to question of GRC military action against China mainland. He assured Secretary that GRC will not engage in any adventurist policy and that GRC will live up to its obligation to consult US before any military move. At same time, Tsiang stated, GRC cannot sit idly by if worsening mainland economic situation leads to large scale uprisings. Tsiang asked whether US could not adopt "more or less flexible attitude" on this problem or at least not make public statements which Chinese Communists can exploit to deprive mainland people of hope.

4.  Secretary responded that whether fundamental change in mainland situation will occur cannot now be predicted. We have no information indicating change in disparity between GRC and Chinese Communist forces or weakening in control of Chinese Communist regime. Under present circumstances we cannot adopt flexible position. We do not want to build up expectations in absence of evidence that they can be fulfilled. Also USG must be very careful not to mislead own people.

5.  Secretary said great weakness is lack of firm accurate information on mainland situation. Tsiang said if US has such information President Chiang would certainly consider it carefully. GRC realizes its own intelligence is spotty. Secretary said we would be glad to share such information but collection difficulties are well known.

6.  At conclusion of call Tsiang repeated hope that US could adopt more flexible attitude or at minimum not make unfavorable public statements. Secretary replied problem is always not to be misleading or confusing. Our first obligation is to our own people. Secretary added we will continue to watch situation and will consider statements made by Tsiang. He did not want to give impression, however, that there would be any major change in our publicly stated position. For years we have declared that issues in Taiwan Strait must be resolved without resort to force.

**Rusk**

---

[4] Ball and Rostow testified on June 26 at an executive session of the Senate Committee on Foreign Relations. For a transcript of the testimony, see ibid., pp. 558–611. The committee considered releasing Rostow's testimony (ibid., pp. 612–613) but did not do so at that time.

**143.    Telegram From the Embassy in Poland to the Department of State**

Warsaw, July 12, 1962, 6 p.m.

83. Cabot–Wang Talks. 111th Meeting.[1] One hour thirty minutes. Department telegram 45.[2]

1) Wang opened saying favorable developments Laos should have been starting point toward relaxation tensions but US continuing aggravate tensions Southeast Asia and Taiwan Straits. Said Bowles and other officials had announced US building up military crescent in western Pacific encircling China. This was "insolent" scheme which Chinese people deeply resented. Considered US troops Thailand threat security Laos and neighboring states. Enumerated further alleged encroachments air space and territorial waters by US resulting to date in 209 serious warnings. Wang specifically said we in error in claim *De Haven* had not entered Chinese Communist territorial waters. Concluded saying long-standing Sino-American dispute subject to settlement by US withdrawal from Taiwan.

2) I replied US gratified progress re Laos and pointed out we have already withdrawn some forces from Thailand which we would not be likely to do so if we had aggressive intent of which Wang's side accuses us. Said could not understand why we were accused of increasing tensions after what I told Wang under instructions in recent private meeting. Said I regretted use of word "insolent" for our endeavor to defend ourselves and friends against attack. Continued with substance paragraph (1) reference telegram, adding observations re import ICC findings and adding three quotes from Mao's writings glorifying military force to indicate Communist support military activities Southeast Asia was in line with very policy of Chinese Communist regime. Followed with statements re imprisoned Americans and newsmen exchange accordance paragraphs (3) and (7) reference telegram.

---

Source: Department of State, Central Files, 611.93/7–1262. Confidential; Priority; Limit Distribution. Repeated to Taipei, Hong Kong, Geneva, Stockholm, and Moscow.

[1] Cabot commented in telegram 84, July 13, that the atmosphere of the meeting was "matter of fact" and that the talks continued to offer a "useful safety valve." (Ibid., 611.93/7–1362) He sent a detailed report of the meeting in airgram A–51, July 20. (Ibid., 611.93/7–2062)

[2] Telegram 45, July 7, instructed Cabot to deny the charges Wang was expected to make on the theme of U.S. "occupation" of Taiwan and alleged encouragement of GRC counter-attack plans, to reaffirm U.S. willingness to join in a mutual renunciation of force, and to reiterate U.S. readiness to carry out its obligations under the U.S.-GRC mutual defense treaty. It also instructed him to urge release of the Americans imprisoned in China and to urge consideration of earlier U.S. proposals for travel of newsmen between the two countries. (Ibid., 611.93/7–762)

3) Wang then virtually repeated his opening speech, adding comment re letter from prominent Americans appearing *NY Times* April 16 as evidence American people not behind our Vietnam policies. Said Chinese people do not want war with US so question renunciation force between us does not arise. Said exchange newsmen was old question first raised by Chinese side. US obstruction prevented agreement.

4) I said I had already answered Wang's repetitious observations but was pleased in tribute he paid to freedom of expression in America. Said seemed to me test of aggressive intent simply made; not only had Wang's side refused agree to mutual renunciation force but while we had unilaterally informed his side we would not support use of force in Taiwan Straits area under present circumstances, Wang had refused give reciprocal assurance his side would not use force. Would seem to be clear which side thinking of using force and which side not. Refuted Wang claim we had obstructed newsmen exchange.

Next meeting August 23.

**Cabot**

---

## 144.    Telegram From the Embassy in the Republic of China to the Department of State

Taipei, July 27, 1962, 6 p.m.

102. Attitude displayed by Chiang Ching-kuo[1] not unexpected and may have been subtle way of conveying his father's reaction to my two talks July 4th and 5th.[2] While somewhat emotionally expressed, perhaps on certain levels there does exist a desire to force the issue of our real intentions, i.e. are we or are we not willing to provide bombers and landing craft as an earnest of our trust in GRC and our desire to help GRC

---

Source: Department of State, Central Files, 793.56/7–2762. Secret; Roger Channel.

[1] Reference is apparently to a July 11 conversation between Chiang Ching-kuo [*text not declassified*]. A July 12 telegram enclosed with a July 13 memorandum from Desmond FitzGerald to Thomas A. Parrott of the White House staff reported that Chiang, stating that he was speaking personally without instructions, expressed concern that nothing had come of the discussions of GRC mainland recovery planning and "emphatically expressed disappointment" in the lack of a U.S. reply to GRC requests for landing craft and bombers. He declared that nothing would alter U.S.-GRC friendship but expressed concern that lack of U.S. action in support of GRC planning would make Chiang Kai-shek's position increasingly difficult. (Kennedy Library, National Security Files, Countries Series, China)

[2] See Documents 139 and 140.

recover mainland. If yes, then when—if no, we are to remain "good friends".

Possibly I am expressing this thought too crudely and furthermore it may not be the desire of the Generalissimo to put the question to the test at this time.

Nevertheless it is evident that US position is thought to be equivocal with unspoken misgivings over our attitude on the "two-Chinas" question and latent concern over possibility of US support for third force on mainland or elsewhere.

Our response that request for B–57's and landing craft "under consideration" has been taken as indicating unwillingness to take positive action. Nevertheless, I see no reason to let the issue be forced upon us in immediate future. I think we can continue to delay until all implications size and import this request for large amounts war material obviously of an offensive character are fully digested. Its aggressive nature is self-evident and its release to GRC cannot be concealed.

We are making careful study here on aspects phases 1, 2, and 3 GRC plan dated 1 June 1962.[3] This will take some time but we believe we see some possibility making phase 1 serve to ease tensions now incipient in delays on decision supplying debatable material and at same time we think we can put on brakes in matters of large scale drops of 200 or more so as to keep control of velocity of movements proposed by GRC. When we arrive at definite conclusions, suitable report and recommendations will be submitted.

Kirk

---

[3] Reference is apparently to a GRC outline plan for the second stage of counterattack on the mainland, given to U.S. officials on May 23 and reported in CIA report TDCS DB–3/650, 315, May 25. Phase 1 called for airborne and maritime commando raids of varying sizes against targets on the Fukien and Kwangtung coasts to support the initiation of resistance movements; phase 2 envisioned assault landing at several points to carry out conventional warfare operations and provide a base for spreading the resistance movement; phase 3 called for the advance of GRC troops deeper into Fukien and Kwangtung. (Ibid., China, Return to Mainland, 1/62–5/62)

## 145. Telegram From the Department of State to the Embassy in the Republic of China

Washington, July 28, 1962, 8:52 p.m.

85. Eyes only for Ambassador. Following is paraphrase of report of hour-long conversation between Malcolm MacDonald[1] and Chen Yi which took place at Geneva week of July 15–21.[2]

Chen conceded that harvests for current as well as past three years have been bad. These bad harvests have brought ChiCom Govt and people great difficulties. While seven provinces seriously affected and large parts population have rather too little to eat, nobody is starving because China for first time in its history has a proper national organization for the distribution of food in all areas of the country. The Chinese, given time, will overcome these difficulties. Grain purchases from Canada and Australia had helped. However only the Chinese themselves, by improving their agriculture and growing much more food, could solve the national problem.

The Peking Government, Chen said, wants international peace so that it may be left free to get on with the vast tasks of improving the peoples' standard of living and of national development. While some of their critics think ChiComs wish to be aggressive in this or that neighboring country, ChiComs do not entertain such desires. Since they must mobilize all their resources for internal development, they do not want to get involved in any wars, big or small. The Laos agreement is, therefore, welcome to them. They hope that it will lead to an improvement elsewhere in Southeast Asia, and they hope that foreign intervention in Laos can be brought to an end, the civil war there stopped, and a truly neutral government maintained by the three Laotian political forces. Peoples, such as some of those of Africa and South America, who are striving for independence have been promised help by the Chinese. Help, which the Chinese are prepared to give, will be forthcoming in ways which will be peaceful. All peoples who are not yet independent are being advised by the Chinese to strive for the achievement of their goals through peaceful means such as political or diplomatic negotiations.

---

Source: Department of State, Central Files, 893.49/7–2862. Secret; Eyes Only. Drafted by William J. Cunningham of the Office of East Asian Affairs and approved by Rice. Also sent to New Delhi.

[1] Head of the British delegation at the International Conference on Laos.

[2] A copy of the report was given to Harriman on July 20. (Library of Congress Manuscript Division, Harriman Papers, Kennedy–Johnson Administrations, Subject Files, China) Rusk sent the text to Kennedy and Ball in Secto 3 from Geneva, July 20, noting that the conversation was "of some considerable interest." (Department of State, Conference Files: Lot 65 D 533, CF 2134)

Success of the Laotian conference, Chen said, demonstrated that patient diplomatic negotiation can settle international questions. Signature of the agreement by both Chinese and American representatives is a step forward in relations between China and America.

Chen said that contrary to what many critics of China had asserted, the massing of troops opposite Quemoy and Matsu was not intended to divert the attention of the Chinese people from domestic difficulties or to unnecessarily excite them about foreign threats. Chiang Kai-shek's loud announcements of his intentions of attacking the mainland caused the Chinese to feel it necessary to dispose troops on the mainland opposite Taiwan. The number of prominent American military figures visiting Taiwan recently has also caused them concern.

Chen said that American assurances that neither support nor encouragement would be given Chiang Kai-shek to attack the mainland had been conveyed to the Chinese Ambassador in Warsaw by the American Ambassador. The Peking Government appreciated this assurance. Though it was a good step forward, it was not, by itself, enough. Chiang Kai-shek's dynasty had fallen long ago, and the Americans therefore should abandon their support for him in Taiwan. The Chinese can never accept that Taiwan is not a part of the rest of China.

The Chinese would not use force in an attempt to settle this question. They will not attack Quemoy and Matsu, though they easily could do so, nor will they take military action against Taiwan, though they could do so. Ultimately, the Americans will have to realize that they should abandon Chiang Kai-shek's cause. The Taiwan question has remained unsettled for thirteen years and it may be necessary to wait another thirteen years, but the Chinese will be patient.

Chen criticized some aspects of American policy but not so virulently as MacDonald might have anticipated. He said, in reply MacDonald's comments that he realized that the Administration could not ignore lobbies and other interests in Congress and elsewhere which are hostile, and that Americans feel very strongly about Communist China. But he said that here again the Chinese were ready to be understanding and patient. MacDonald said that the present US administration on a number of Asian questions such as that of Laos had modified the policies of the previous administration. It understands and accepts the neutrality of some other Asian countries as well. Chen asked whether MacDonald thought the President and Harriman are sincere in their Laotian policy and whether the other modifications MacDonald mentioned are also sincere. MacDonald's reply was emphatically affirmative, and Chen then said he was inclined to think the same. MacDonald told him that alterations in policy could only take effect gradually in a country with a constitution like America. Chen said the American government's policies and difficulties should be understood by the Chinese and that they should patiently hope for a gradual improvement in relations.

Chen nodded sagely when MacDonald observed that it was Chinese policy on some matters which had driven the west in general and the Americans in particular to strong criticism, and that the Chinese should do things which would impress the sincerity of their peaceful intentions upon the Americans and the British.

Chen said he understood from the former ChiCom Chargé in London that Lord Home would be glad to meet Chen in Geneva, and Chen said he hoped there would be time for him to have a talk with Lord Home, as he wanted to discuss ways of further improving relations between China and Great Britain. He considered them quite good now, thought they could be steadily improved, and believed that China and Britain can bring about general improvement in the international atmosphere through cooperative effort. Chen said he was in a hurry to get back to Peking to help tackle urgent problems confronting the government and would be in Geneva only until the 25th. MacDonald promised to report this to Lord Home, who would have to leave Geneva a day prior to Chen's own anticipated departure date.

**Rusk**

---

146. **Letter From the Counselor of the Department of State (Rostow) to the President's Military Representative (Taylor)**

Washington, July 31, 1962.

DEAR MAX: You may have missed this Airgram from Hong Kong[1] which represents, I think, a line of thought many of us share.

One implication of the situation in China which, I believe, should be brought home to the President is this: whether Chinese development has been retarded for "tens of years" (page 3), it is pretty clear that for the

---

Source: National Defense University, Taylor Papers, Box 44, Other Far East. Secret.
[1] Airgram A–60 from Hong Kong, July 18, entitled "Implications for U.S. Policy of Latest Developments in Communist China," summarized reports of a deteriorating situation on the China mainland and estimated that although there seemed to be no imminent threat to the Communist Party's retention of power, the weakened economy would "deter Peiping from large-scale overt military adventures" but not from less ambitious efforts. It concluded that the United States should continue to restrain the GRC from attacking the mainland while continuing its general posture of containing Chinese Communist expansionism. (Department of State, Central Files, 793.00/7–1862) See the Supplement.

1960's Communist China is not going to be a major industrial and military power. Over the foreseeable future, we do not, therefore, face in Southeast Asia historical pressure which should lead us to any fatalism about losing that region. The Chinese situation should strengthen our will to pursue a policy which would deny South Viet Nam, Thailand—and Laos, too—to the Communists over the indefinite future; and we should pursue this policy with inner confidence.

Sincerely yours,

**Walt**

---

147. **Memorandum From Michael V. Forrestal of the White House Staff to the President's Special Assistant for National Security Affairs (Bundy)**

Washington, August 3, 1962.

SUBJECT

GRC War Plans

I attach the full version of the GRC war plan which I spoke to you about the other day.[1] It was received in Taipei on May 23rd and sent to Washington on June 1. The Agency summarized it by cable on May 25 and again on July 20 and 23. As a result it didn't get the kind of attention that I would have hoped had I known about it.

One can speculate that the existence of this document in Taiwan may have come to the attention of the ChiComs, and if so, may have some connection with their buildup during the month of June. I don't think the Agency agrees with me on this, but it's a thought which I cannot quite get rid of.[2]

---

Source: Kennedy Library, National Security Files, Meetings and Memoranda Series, Staff Memoranda, Michael V. Forrestal. Top Secret and Personal. A note in Bundy's handwriting reads, "Hold for meeting on China this PM. MGB."

[1] See footnote 3, Document 144.

[2] Forrestal stated in an August 7 memorandum to Bundy that when he was in Hong Kong on July 22, an officer of the Consulate General told him that when Forrestal and Harriman were in Hong Kong in March, a journalist had asked the officer to arrange an interview with Forrestal, stating that he wanted to confirm a story he had "picked up in Taipei from the 'Naval Auxiliary Communications Center'" to the effect that the United States had recently agreed to assist the dropping of GRC teams on the China mainland that fall. (Kennedy Library, National Security Files, Meetings and Memoranda Series, Staff Memoranda, Michael V. Forrestal)

I think you should look at the phases set out on page 2, paragraph B. You will note that Phase 1 in effect is the program for the 200-man drop, which we have already agreed to prepare, although not necessarily to implement. Phase 2 is obviously a consequence of Phase 1.

This document, together with conversations I had in Taipei[3] with Admiral Kirk, his DCM and CAS Station Chief has brought me to suspect that we may have made a mistake last May in going along with Ray Cline's proposals for the 200-man teams. I think there is a significant difference between the 20-man drop concept, which is more clearly in intelligence collection operation, and the 200-man drop concept, which comes close to the first stage of active military operations.

I visualize a situation where the 200 men have been dropped on a hillside and are in the process of collecting a certain amount of support. Meanwhile the People's Army of Liberation (or whatever they call themselves) begin marching in regimental strength from its base some distance away towards our 200 men. Several days go by and in the meantime there have been a certain amount of defections, and our 200 men are joined by say a thousand or so mainland Chinese.

At this point the regiment arrives and our 200 men augmented call the Gimo, who calls us, for help. What do we do?

Admiral Kirk suggested that we should try to find a time when we could go to the Gimo and be more frank with him. We should point out, perhaps, that the President of the United States cannot surrender his decision whether or not to commit his country to major military action to any other person, no matter who may be allied with us; and by the same token the President cannot put another person in a position to force the United States into such an action. (Vide de Gaulle.)

Thus, we will do everything necessary for the defense of Taiwan. We will help in doing everything possible to obtain intelligence information on the situation on the Mainland, both for the benefit of the GRC and also to put ourselves in the position to make an intelligent decision when the occasion arises. But we must stop short of deliberately supplying an offensive capability under circumstances which makes it possible for others to take the ultimate decision away from us.

A possible time for having Admiral Kirk go to the Gimo with such thoughts would be at the end of the year when a decision to permit a 200-man drop has to be taken.

The consequences of any frank talk with the Gimo would, I understand, be fairly sharp in Taiwan and perhaps also in Congress if the GRC decided to make a public noise about it. But I think that such a noise is far

---

[3] According to Forrestal's August 7 memorandum he was in Taipei on July 23.

more endurable than the prospect of being caught in a sequence of events over which we have less and less control.

MVF

---

148. **Message From the Assistant Secretary of State for Far Eastern Affairs (Harriman) to the Ambassador to the Republic of China (Kirk)**

Washington, August 8, 1962.

Out 63801. For Kirk from Harriman. Agree with excellent analysis of our problem with Chiang contained your In 39469[1] and concur in course of action you propose with following modifications and comments:

1. In order to minimize possibility of adverse reaction by Chiang, your response on landing ships and bombers should not take form of final turn-down. You should clearly state our unwillingness provide these items under present circumstances, but at same time indicate willingness to reconsider negative decision should changed circumstances warrant.

2. Only two C–123s should be brought to Taiwan in support of small drop program. Bringing larger number to Taiwan might unduly stimulate GRC hopes of US concurrence in 200-man drops which we oppose under present circumstances. Also, if as seems possible ChiComs have knowledge of 200-man drop proposal, appearance of several C–123s on Taiwan might increase tension in area.

---

Source: Kennedy Library, National Security Files, Countries Series, China. Secret. The source text does not indicate the transmission time. The message was approved in an August 8 meeting with the President, recorded in a memorandum for the record by McCone, dated August 9. (Central Intelligence Agency, DCI (McCone) Files, Job 80–B01285A, Box 6, DCI Meetings with the President)

[1] Reference is to an August 3 message from Kirk to Harriman recommending that the response to the GRC request for bombers and landing craft should be "either temporizing or frankly negative." He argued that much preparatory work would be necessary to determine whether overt military action would have any chance of success, and it was essential to give Chiang and his advisers a realistic appreciation of the problems involved. He was "inclined" to state frankly that the United States could not agree to supply the requested items "under present circumstances" and to press for intensified intelligence work and a contingency study of GRC capability for an amphibious assault. (Kennedy Library, National Security Files, Countries Series, China, Cables)

3. Assume that GRC rather than joint US-GRC propaganda intended. FYI. Our own propaganda of course will be tailored to our own objectives. End FYI.

4. Regarding your statements that it seems imperative test "as soon as possible" whether mainland deterioration has proceeded point where small clandestine teams could survive and that we should persuade GRC undertake small team drops, would offer following comments: (A) from our viewpoint the need so to test situation is not pressing in the time sense per se, but only in the context of anticipating, containing and diverting GRC pressures for larger-scale operations; and (B) although we do not object to 20-man team drop we would not want press any drops on GRC, in view contents FCT 7903.[2] We would of course support any such drops up to 20 men which they propose.[3] Assume you also have in mind smaller drops as well.

5. We leave to your judgment desirability encouraging contingency study of capability GRC as presently equipped undertake amphibious assault in support widespread uprising on mainland. While such study may generate additional requests for US equipment we recognize it may be essential bring home to President Chiang and his advisors realistic appreciation problems involved in overt amphibious operations. Assume your purpose is educational and that every effort will be made to avoid any appearance of joint planning. However, we would oppose similar study capabilities launch amphibious assault as diversionary measure in event ChiCom attack on offshore islands. GRC should not be encouraged think of such assault as acceptable response to such attack. US effort in event of such attack would be to localize and dampen down hostilities.

6. Regarding Chiang's possible renewal threat resign: You are probably aware he resigned, early in 1948, but did not fully relinquish control. His recently reported statement he might resign and head a revolutionary movement, if actually made, appears to have posed implicit threat he might free himself from responsibility for govt's international commitment without giving up ability to influence relevant acts of govt. However, he could not, in good faith to us, thus separate authority from responsibility. Against this background we wonder whether reported statement was more than threat designed influence us to support his programs for return to mainland.

7. This cable was cleared with highest authority.

---

[2] Not found.

[3] According to a memorandum by McCone of an August 22 meeting among the President, Taylor, and himself, he outlined a Chinese Nationalist proposal for a 20-man drop to gather intelligence and recommended U.S. support of the mission, and the President approved. (Central Intelligence Agency, DCI (McCone) Files, Job 80–B01285A, Box 6 DCI Meetings with the President)

### 149.  Telegram From the Embassy in Poland to the Department of State

Warsaw, August 23, 1962, 7 p.m.

354. Cabot–Wang Talks. 112th Meeting.[1] One hour 48 minutes. Department telegram 257.[2]

1. I opened, observing not only is first item our original agenda still at issue since implementation by Wang's side of agreed announcement incomplete but we having great difficulty making any progress re "other practical matters now at issue". Followed with substance paragraphs one, three, two, five and six reftel.

2. Wang said lack of progress in talks due US hostility toward China. Referred to my mentioning last meeting that GRC had stated it would rely principally on measures other than force to achieve objectives whereas Wang's side unwilling so state. Wang said China could not "sign such an agreement". Said my comment that if ChiComs could not pledge themselves to such renunciation, we would remain ready carry out our obligations to GRC contained implied threat. No one would be cowed by threats. Taiwan being Chinese territory this was strictly internal matter. Means Chinese would use re Taiwan was no business of US. This was absolutely not a subject for discussion at Ambassadorial level talks between two countries. Said while Taiwan was internal matter, the international dispute which exists between China and US, like other international disputes, should be settled without use of threat of force. Fact is US has already used force in occupying Taiwan. Therefore in dispute between China and US, US alone should denounce use of force and withdraw Seventh Fleet. US refused consider Chinese draft agreement September 22, 1958.[3] US is aggressor since its forces are in area. Since US has already used force, how can Chinese agree to anything which would

---

Source: Department of State, Central Files, 611.93/8–2362. Confidential; Priority; Limit Distribution. Repeated to Stockholm, Moscow, Taipei, and Hong Kong.

[1] Cabot commented and made recommendations for the next meeting in telegram 365, August 14, and sent a detailed, apparently verbatim report of the meeting in airgram A–165, August 25. (Ibid., 611.93/8–1462 and 611.93/8–2562, respectively)

[2] Telegram 257, August 17, instructed Cabot to argue that recent statements by Wang's side were contradictory, that Wang's statement at the last meeting that if the United States would withdraw its forces from Taiwan "the knot in Sino-American relations would be undone" showed that the hostility of Wang's side toward the United States was based on national territorial interests rather than on ideological grounds, that only persons "dangerously isolated from and unaware of realities of present-day world" could seriously argue, as Wang's side did, that if his side attacked Taiwan by force it would be an internal affair, and that release of American civilians would give the American people some cause to believe Wang's side was interested in reducing tensions with the United States. (Ibid., 611.93/8–1762)

[3] For text, see Foreign Relations, 1958–1960, vol. XIX, p. 257.

make US armed occupation Taiwan perpetual and legalized? Said our treaty with Chiang was worthless and US would be held responsible for consequences its activities. Sooner or later we would be thrown out of Taiwan if we refused quit now. Hoped US would not make mistake of failing recognize determination Chinese people liberate Taiwan.

3.  Wang continued saying wished speak of important matters. All evidence pointed to continuation military activities of US in vicinity North China territorial waters. From 0235 on 14 April to 0031 on 21 April destroyer *De Haven* intruded into territorial waters from Chien-Li-Yen to Ping Island. From 0310 to 2008 on 22 May US destroyers encroached Northeast Tsingtao. From 0500 to 2335 on 12 June another US destroyer was in vicinity territorial sea between Ping Island and Chao-Lien Island. On morning 9 July US destroyer came close to Cheng-Shan-Tou and Tung-Lien Island in territorial waters. On 17 August US destroyer operated in vicinity East of Jung-Cheng Bay, east of Tsingtao. Wang said this matter had gone too far to be tolerated. Under instructions was making serious protest once more and US would be held responsible for all consequences.

4.  Wang expressed surprise that after June 23 private meeting State Department had made disclosures of subjects discussed after which there followed heavy press coverage. Said he had never divulged anything to press.

5.  I gave historical refutation Wang's claim American Government hostile to China, adding US not threatening anyone and desired peace in all parts of the world. Again denied we occupying Taiwan. US is judge of its treaty commitments and considers treaty with GRC valid. Referred to Wang's repeated mention our ships being "vicinity of" or "near" territorial waters. Pointed out this not illegal and said I had in past been informed no incursion into territorial waters had occurred. Re press leaks made conciliatory statement and expressed conviction Wang had not given information anymore than I had.

6.  Wang said determination whether rapprochement can be brought about between our countries depended on a lot of concrete actions. Long as US occupies Taiwan, continues to deprive Chinese of rights in UN, and tries isolate China, he can hardly talk about US friendship for Chinese people. His Government had formally issued statement re territorial limits September 4, 1958[4] but US ships and aircraft had continued encroachment despite repeated protests. He then launched into long dissertation re territorial waters. Said US in 1793 had proclaimed three-mile limit and if "unilateral" claims were involved, US had taken

---

[4] For text, see *American Foreign Policy: Current Documents, 1958*, p. 1199; also printed in *Peking Review*, September 9, 1958, p. 21.

lead in such. Said neither of our proposals at 1958 Law of Sea Conference[5] had obtained sufficient backing and asked on what grounds we should try to impose three-mile limit on others. I suggested question of territorial limits throughout world was vast one beyond scope these talks. Wang said in absence standard limit universally recognized, each sovereign country had right adopt limit whether three, six or twelve miles.

Next meeting October 11, Wang said Adviser Yao Kuang being transferred and would inform us later as to successor.

**Cabot**

---

[5] Reference is to the U.N. Conference on the Law of the Sea, which met at Geneva, February 24–April 27, 1958. For documentation on U.S. policy with respect to the conference, see *Foreign Relations*, 1958–1960, vol. II, pp. 641–708.

---

**150. Telegram From the Embassy in the Republic of China to the Department of State**

Taipei, August 23, 1962, 5 p.m.

216. For Harriman from Kirk. Deptel 128.[1] I have discussed rubber boats question further with Commander TDC, Chief MAAG and [*less than 1 line of source text not declassified*]. We recognize, as stated Embtel 146,[2] that GRC doubtless hopes to use these boats along with MAP-supplied equipment in eventual attack on mainland. However, we do not believe that supplying these boats will significantly increase either GRC capabilities for unilateral action or likelihood that GRC will take unilat-

---

Source: Department of State, Central Files, 793.56/8–2362. Secret; No Distribution Outside Department.

[1] Telegram 128 to Taipei, August 16, was a message from Harriman to Kirk concerning whether an export license should be granted for a GRC order for 200 rubber assault boats. It noted reasons for believing the GRC wanted the boats for use from the offshore islands and stated that granting an export license might undermine U.S. policies of "attempting prevent provocations from offshores" and "localizing any new offshores crisis if it breaks out." It concluded, however, that the question had to considered in the context of other problems and stated, "If after considering foregoing you personally want license issued, we will do so." (Ibid., 793.56/8–662) Other documentation concerning this issue is ibid., 793.56.

[2] Dated August 6. (Ibid., 793.56/8–662)

eral action. We also agree GRC authorities unlikely engage in sporadic and reckless adventures with such inadequate equipment as rubber boats. In any case, US cannot effectively deny such boats to GRC, for they could be obtained Japan or elsewhere if US continued withhold license.

Withholding of license increasingly provoking acid comments from Chinese military to MAAG that US does not trust GRC to keep its pledged word. Minister Defense Yu in discussing issue with Chief MAAG Sanborn[3] August 21 pointed out GRC had committed itself not to attack mainland without US agreement, and continued withholding of license on such minor item as rubber boats could only be interpreted as demonstrating serious lack of trust in an ally. He said US and GRC had reached "psychological impasse" over this question.

We may soon have to respond to GRC request for bombers and landing craft. I do not think it is wise to complicate our handling of that problem by further delay in licensing item which represents only relatively slight increment to GRC lift capability which they could obtain in any case without our help. I therefore recommend going ahead with the licensing. TDC, MAAG [*less than 1 line of source text not declassified*] concur.

Kirk

---

[3] Major General Kenneth O. Sanborn.

---

## 151.   Memorandum of Conversation

Taipei, September 6, 1962, 10–11:30 a.m.

PARTICIPANTS

President Chiang Kai-shek
Foreign Minister Shen Chang-huan
Director of Government Information Office James Shen (Interpreter)
Ambassador Alan G. Kirk
Deputy Chief of Mission Ralph N. Clough

---

Source: Library of Congress Manuscript Division, Harriman Papers, Kennedy–Johnson Administrations, Subject Files, Kirk, Alan G. Secret. Drafted by Clough. Attached to a September 10 letter from Kirk to Harriman. A letter of September 21 from Kirk to Harriman enclosed a copy of the GRC record of the conversation, which was of a revision of Clough's memorandum.

PLACE

Yang Ming Shan Official Residence

Ambassador Kirk opened the conversation by mentioning the various changes of top personnel in U.S. Agencies. He took the occasion to point out that all heads of U.S. Agencies in Taiwan operated under his general direction in accordance with President Kennedy's directive of May 29, 1961.[1] He said he would like to present two of the new agency heads to President Chiang at the President's convenience. The President replied that he would be glad to receive them and that a time would be set. Ambassador Kirk went on to say that cooperation between the U.S. and GRC in the fields of economic aid, military aid and diplomatic cooperation seemed to be going forward smoothly. President Chiang commented that they found U.S. Agencies most cooperative.

Ambassador Kirk said that the Chinese Communist build-up on the Fukien Coast appeared to be completed and the forces in that area were substantially stronger than they had been prior to June 1962. We thought their purpose was probably defensive but the possibility of aggressive action could not be excluded.

Ambassador Kirk said that the U.S. Government had noted an improvement in GRC intelligence, but it was still essential for both U.S. and GRC intelligence agencies to work harder. It would be very difficult for President Kennedy to make sound decisions without good and up-to-date intelligence.

President Chiang replied that there could be little of what the U.S. Government regarded as "hard" intelligence until and unless there was action against the mainland. The GRC had many sources of intelligence which had not been revealed to the United States. Even if these should be revealed he was afraid they would not be taken at face value. Many such sources were based on oral arrangements and would not become known, visible or tangible until action took place.

Ambassador Kirk said that the United States Government had been following closely GRC plans for an early small air drop. Although U.S. intelligence people had some reservations concerning the desirability of the area chosen, they were cooperating closely with the GRC in the preparations. Ambassador Kirk added that this drop, the first since 1959, should test the vulnerability of the Chinese Communists and produce intelligence obtainable in no other way. He said he assumed that the drop had not taken place within the last couple of days because of the typhoon.

---

[1] For text of the letter which President Kennedy sent on that date to all U.S. Ambassadors, see Department of State *Bulletin*, December 11, 1961, pp. 993–994.

President Chiang replied that there had been two typhoons, one right after the other, which had flooded the drop area and created many mountain freshets. Therefore, it was necessary to postpone the drop for a few weeks. Ambassador Kirk said that was the reason we had been uneasy about the area because there were so many rice paddies, canals, and so forth. He remarked that when the 101st Airborne Division was air-dropped into Normandy many soldiers landed in the flooded area behind Utah Beach. This force was very embarrassed by finding itself landing in deep water. President Chiang replied that was also the GRC's concern and that was why they had called off the planned drop.

The Ambassador told the President that in order to facilitate the small drop program the U.S. Government now intended to send two C–123 aircraft to Taiwan as soon as they were ready and the crews trained. Five Chinese crews had already departed for the United States for training. The President commented that this was good and he expressed his thanks.

Ambassador Kirk inquired whether his understanding was correct that the purpose of these air drops was to test whether underground resistance elements could be contacted. The President replied that it was. The Ambassador said only if such actions were successful could we consider going further.

President Chiang said it was more important for us to explore and locate weak points on the other side where one or two thinly garrisoned or undefended cities could be seized by means of a large air drop. Unless the GRC were able to do that it would be difficult to rally large numbers of people to rise against the regime. In such an event the Chinese Communist armed forces, especially the officers with whom the GRC has established contacts, would be able to rise. One or two cities must be seized before this could take place. One reason the Communists transferred away from the coast troops previously stationed there was because the Communists were afraid they were becoming too friendly with the local people. However, their transfer does not halt the contact between these troops and the GRC. [3-1/2 lines of source text not declassified] The reason this information was not passed to the U.S. was to enable the U.S. to stay clear of the Communist charge that U.S. "imperialism" was meddling in Chinese affairs.

Ambassador Kirk said the United States Government still feels action had best be limited to small air drops, to which President Chiang replied that this matter could be discussed further.

The Ambassador said President Kennedy's view was that United States actions must be peaceful and defensive. Although the President had made a careful study of the GRC requested for bombers and landing craft he did not feel justified in making such items available at the present time as they would certainly appear to be aggressive in character. If circumstances warranted it the United States Government would, of course, be willing to reconsider the GRC request.

President Chiang inquired what the U.S. attitude would be in case of a large-scale rebellion on the mainland. Ambassador Kirk replied that that would have to be judged at the time. He could not predict what the U.S. Government's attitude would be but he was sure that the situation would be examined very closely to see what opportunities arose. Ambassador Kirk continued that the U.S. Government was ready to examine the GRC proposals for overt action. We have been working very closely with the GRC through the 420 Committee on intelligence matters. Overt invasion of a whole continent was quite another thing which would require a close study of GRC plans and preparations.

President Chiang said that the GRC should, of course, keep the U.S. Government informed and consult with it. However, if the U.S. Government should continue to stop the GRC from going ahead with its plans the time might come when the government would find it difficult to keep the people and army under control, especially since the government had started to collect the special defense surtax and had told the people what it was for. If there were still no action after a certain lapse of time the people would lose confidence in the government. The report that the United States Government had given the Chinese Communists assurances that the U.S. would not help the GRC had created an unfortunate impression in the minds of people that the GRC would be unable to act.

Ambassador Kirk commented that the U.S. position was limited to that set forth in the 1954 treaty, according to which neither side was to take action without the agreement of the other. Agreement meant examination of the facts and agreement on action to be taken. It did not mean the extension of a blank check to go ahead. What facilities did the GRC possess for really making a landing on the continent? Ambassador Kirk said he had participated in a couple of such landings and knew what was involved.

President Chiang said of course the GRC is ready to abide by any agreement it signed. However, there is a question of whether or not the treaty concluded in 1954 is still applicable. Times and circumstances have changed. Strict adherence to the treaty would enable the Chinese Communist regime to prolong its life and continue to suppress the Chinese people because the GRC was being bound hand and foot and prevented from going to their aid. Thus, the treaty favors an enemy instead of an ally. It is all very well for the United States to say that the GRC must stand by its agreement regardless of changes in the situation, but it is hard for the President to tell this to the people. The U.S. interpretation of the treaty is causing resentment in certain places and giving rise to a feeling that the GRC's ally is not helping the GRC but helping its enemy. This is very difficult for the people and the armed forces to accept. Does the United States intend to hold to this position indefinitely?

Ambassador Kirk replied that the treaty works both ways. Treaties are of course always subject to revision. This could be studied if President Chiang desires to propose it. However, this is a serious matter. Does President Chiang propose to denounce the treaty, and therefore desire that U.S. military and other aid be halted? He didn't quite understand President Chiang's meaning. President Chiang responded that that was a policy for the United States Government to decide.

The Ambassador said that in addition to proposing increased cooperation in the intelligence field, we had been considering the advisability of a study group to consider plans for overt action against the mainland, keeping in mind that this would be action against a continent and not an island. He wanted the President to know that he had been busy about many matters other than official calls during the past two months and was now prepared to suggest such a study group. Perhaps President Chiang would like to consider it.

The President said that the GRC must, of course, keep the U.S. Government informed and consult with it, but the U.S. Government must realize the great importance of the feelings of the people and armed forces. The hopes of the people on the mainland are such that it is impossible to deny them indefinitely. They hope for deliverance, preferably with U.S. assistance. The U.S. may succeed for a time in keeping this feeling down but not indefinitely. The U.S. Government could state publicly that the question of the GRC's return to the mainland is a Chinese domestic affair. Instead the U.S. Government has taken on itself the responsibility of preventing the GRC from going back. This could not go on indefinitely. Eventually it would be difficult for any government to keep things under control. The GRC is ready to abide by the treaty but when things change the treaty must be reconsidered. He knows Ambassador Kirk has been working hard, that he is staunchly anti-Communist, and that he is sympathetic with GRC aspirations.

Ambassador Kirk said that President Chiang, in raising questions about the treaty, had moved to a higher plane than the Ambassadorial level. If he were not satisfied with the terms, perhaps his Ambassador should take this up in Washington.

President Chiang responded that he had spoken at some length on the treaty because it had been brought up by Ambassador Kirk. Revision or annulment of the treaty was one thing, but it was another to let the world know that under the treaty the GRC is not free to do this or that. This was not doing the United States any good and was creating resentment. The U.S. could have said if a large-scale uprising took place on the mainland this was an internal matter. Instead the U.S. Government was letting it be known that under the treaty the GRC was not free to attack the mainland.

Ambassador Kirk reminded the President that President Kennedy had heavy world-wide responsibilities. Just as President Chiang was responsible to the Chinese people, so President Kennedy was responsible to his own people. He has as heavy a responsibility as any head of state. The treaty of 1954 provides that agreement is necessary.

President Chiang replied that he was fully aware of President Kennedy's heavy responsibilities. He wished to assure him through the Ambassador that he would not do anything lightly. He would do nothing harmful to the prestige of the President or the United States. All the President needs to do is to say that the GRC action against the China mainland is entirely a domestic matter. Such a declaration would also discourage, if not prevent, any overt Soviet participation. He wished to reiterate his assurances that he would do nothing contrary to the provisions of the treaty but he wished the United States Government would devise ways of helping the GRC do its duty to its own people without violating the provisions of the treaty. There must be ways and means of doing this.

Ambassador Kirk said that the United States has responsibilities to its other allies in NATO and elsewhere. It could hardly send bombers and landing craft to Taiwan in secret. Such action would be regarded as aggressive.

The President said he did not have this equipment in mind when he suggested that the U.S. try to find ways and means to help. What he really had in mind was an appeal for a greater area of understanding between the U.S. and the GRC. The last thing which the U.S. should wish to foster is the idea that the U.S. is beginning to be a friend to the Chinese Communists while binding its ally hand and foot. The U.S. should not permit the Chinese people to get the impression that the U.S. did not distinguish between an enemy and an ally. The U.S. was even holding up the export of goods the GRC wished to purchase with its own money. This was in effect applying an embargo to the GRC. He wondered whether such an embargo was applied to the enemy. He said he was speaking very frankly to the Ambassador as a friend rather than as an Ambassador.

Ambassador Kirk replied that it was unnecessary to reiterate the friendship between the United States and China which had a background of over a hundred years. As was well known, for a long time all U.S. trade with Communist China had been prohibited. There was no reason to say that the U.S. was being friendly to an enemy. It was just that President Kennedy and his advisors were unable to agree at the present time to GRC plans and hopes, taking into account the world situation.

President Chiang said he hoped that the longer Ambassador Kirk remained the deeper his insight would be into the importance of the problem of the China mainland. What happened there would have a vital affect on the rest of the world. It was for this reason that he felt it necessary to speak as frankly as he did.

Ambassador Kirk then explained in more specific terms that what he had proposed earlier was the organization of two groups. One to handle covert intelligence operations, and the other to study overt operations. The first group existed already in the form of the Joint Intelligence Committee (JIC), while the second also existed, but in a somewhat vague status, in the form of the 420 Committee. What we were proposing was that expert personnel be added to the 420 Committee so that it would be possible to examine GRC capabilities with its present equipment for amphibious operations in the event of a mainland uprising. The President said that he would welcome the organization of such a group. The Ambassador said this suggestion of a study group needed reflection and examination prior to acceptance, and then inquired who would probably act as responsible head of the group on the GRC side. Would it be the President himself, the Vice President, the Defense Minister or someone else? President Chiang replied this would have to be given consideration. Perhaps it would be the Defense Minister. He inquired who would head the American element of the group. The Ambassador replied that he himself would.

On getting up to leave, Ambassador Kirk mentioned that General Taylor was arriving the following day and offered to bring him to call on President Chiang if convenient. The President replied that he would be glad to receive him.[2]

---

[2] General Taylor visited Taiwan September 7–9 as part of a visit to several East Asian countries that he made prior to assuming the position of Chairman of the Joint Chiefs of Staff. He met with President Chiang on September 8. Telegram 403 from Taipei, September 17, reported that Chiang's main points were that peasant resistance groups were forming on the mainland, that Khrushchev would not help Mao in case of trouble on the mainland because the animosity between them was so sharp, and that the Soviet Union would not intervene if Communist rule was overthrown in the part of China south of the Yellow River. (Department of State, Central Files, 120.1590/9–1762) For Taylor's comments on his visit to Taiwan, see Document 153.

## 152. Telegram From the Department of State to the Embassy in the Republic of China

Washington, September 13, 1962, 8:06 p.m.

236. Deptel 232.[1] Sept 13 Dept officer informed Counselor Chinese Embassy our serious concern GRC terrorist activities near Hong Kong and Macao and requested that our views be transmitted GRC.

Dept officer stated Ambassador Kirk had already made two approaches FonMin on this subject, but that no response had been received and terrorist activities had continued. Therefore, we now felt constrained to bring matter up with Chinese Embassy here in order emphasize seriousness of our concern.

After reviewing in general terms series of bombing incidents and representations made by Hong Kong and Macao authorities, Dept officer reiterated points made by Ambassador Kirk and strongly stressed our belief that these activities should be terminated immediately. Dept officer stressed our conviction that our position on this matter not in opposition GRC interests, but in common interest both US and GRC.

Counselor stated he understood seriousness of matter, and said that our views would be transmitted to his government with appropriate emphasis on degree US concern.

**Rusk**

---

Source: Department of State, Central Files, 793.00/9–1362. Confidential. Drafted by Popple and approved by Yager. Repeated to Lisbon, London, Hong Kong, and CINCPAC for POLAD.

[1] Telegram 232, September 12, reported that the Department considered the GRC reaction to Kirk's previous approaches on the subject of terrorist activities near Hong Kong and Macau far from satisfactory and intended to raise the matter with the Chinese Embassy. (Ibid., 793.00/9–1162) Telegram 195 to Taipei, August 30, had instructed Kirk to meet with the Foreign Minister and express U.S. concern over recent reports of Nationalist-sponsored terrorist activities in the Hong Kong–Macau area. (Ibid., 793.00/8–2962)

### 153.   Paper Prepared by the President's Military Representative (Taylor)

Honolulu, September 20, 1962.

IMPRESSIONS FROM TAIWAN

*1. MAP Objectives*

The MAAG mission which is currently in effect in Taiwan is stated in the following terms:

a. Continue to assist the Chinese to develop a military force which is capable of:

(1) Maintaining internal security;
(2) Deterring a Communist attack; or
(3) Defeating such an attack if short of an all-out Communist effort.
(4) Assisting US forces extensively in the event of a general war in the Far East.

The foregoing language emanates from The Military Assistance Planning Document and is applicable to Korea as well as to Taiwan. Because of the open-ended nature of objective (4), under this language, it is possible to justify the maintenance of a ChiNat force structure of almost any size. Where there is no mention of the defense of the Off-shore Islands as a specific objective, the language is broad enough to provide for this mission.

Although guidance such as the foregoing does not offer precise guidelines to assist the MAAG, it is my opinion that the dollar ceiling of $160 million MAP per year has resulted in establishing reasonable priorities consistent with the most pressing needs of the defense of Taiwan, the Penghus and the Off-shore Islands. However, it would be useful in justifying this program to Congress to have more precise objectives, devoid of the open-ended features noted above. It is interesting also to note that the foregoing statement of mission is not the same as that contained in the CINCPAC Military Assistance Plan, FY 64–68, another example of the need for a thoroughgoing overhaul of the statements of MAP objectives in all the countries visited thus far.

---

Source: National Defense University, Taylor Papers, Box 48, Far East Trip, September 1962. Top Secret. This was one of a series of papers written by Taylor concerning his East Asian trip. It is summarized in the Taiwan section of a message that Taylor sent to Rusk, McNamara, Lemnitzer, Bundy, and Ewell in telegram 200410Z from CINCPAC, summarizing his conclusions from the trip. That message incorporates almost all of the first three sections of this paper and the last two paragraphs of section 5. (Kennedy Library, National Security Files, Trips and Conferences Series, Maxwell D. Taylor Trip to the Far East)

2.  *Possible New MAP Objectives for Taiwan*

If a revision of the statement of objectives is undertaken I would suggest stating the mission as follows:

a. The maintenance of Chinese National military forces to accomplish:

(1) Internal security.
(2) The defense of Taiwan, the Penghus and the Off-shore Islands with such U.S. assistance as may be agreed.
(3) The maintenance of an expeditionary force of three divisions for use elsewhere in the Western Pacific.

The effect of taking such objectives would have little effect upon the Air Force and Navy as now planned. In the case of the Army, it would reduce the military requirement to not more than 15 divisions, of which three would receive special treatment. The priorities in the hardware program would thus be:

a.  Modernized air defense (semi-automatic AC&W, introduction of the F104G, more SAM).
b.  Army and Navy equipment related to the defense of the Off-shore Islands.
c.  Modernization of three divisions.
d.  Modernization of the remaining 12 divisions.

Items which should not be included in the revised program would be: tanks in any significant number; amphibious lift beyond the present one division level; and any ASW capability directed at the ChiCom submarine threat (this to remain a U.S. responsibility).

3.  *Air Defense*

As in the case of Japan and Korea, the most pressing military problem in Taiwan is the provision of a modernized air defense. Here the conditions are as elsewhere—the growing threat of an improving ChiCom air force equipped with airplanes generally superior to those in the hands of our Allies and deployed in depth on an extensive land mass. The restricted areas of Japan, South Korea, Okinawa and Taiwan offer vulnerable targets to this superior, modernized ChiCom air force. In all areas arises the question of how to offset this danger.

I am impressed with the need to study this problem, not by individual country but as an entity consisting of the entire Western Pacific area. In planning for AC&W, it is highly important that any new system introduced to one country be made common to all. In all countries, we are faced with the problem of introducing a high performance, all-weather interceptor, usually the F104G. Based upon justifiable military requirements, it is quite easy to run up an excessively high bill for interceptors which will require an improved AC&W to exploit their full capability. Thus, there are two heavy bills in the offing.

In contemplating the foregoing prospect, one is inclined to ask whether there may not be some better solution to offset the ChiCom air superiority in the Far East. I believe that we should look at the possibility of a higher reliance upon surface-to-air and surface-to-surface missiles as a more effective response to the threat. The exact mix of surface-to-air missiles and interceptors for each country is a problem for the experts to determine. However, any SAM-interceptor combination is purely defensive and offers no deterrent to the aggressive employment of the ChiCom air force. If, on the other hand, the ChiCom knew that we had their airfields zeroed in by surface-to-surface missiles or Polaris type missiles, the situation would improve to our advantage. Further, these missiles should be publicized to be appreciated by ChiComs and others. Before embarking upon a large and costly program for improved local air defense, we should evaluate closely present plans versus a solution based largely on missiles supplemented by carrier aircraft.

4.   *Defense of the Off-shore Islands*

A visit to Kinmen provides visible evidence of the determination of the ChiNats to defend the Off-shore Islands to the last ditch. Whether this is sensible or not is academic. The ChiNats are on the Off-shore Islands and intend to stay. Their defenses are impressive and could be overcome only at a prohibitive cost to the ChiComs.

In discussing the most dangerous kind of attack against Kinmen, I found the Chinese officials in general accord. They believe that a surprise attack under cover of darkness or bad weather would be the most likely to succeed, particularly if the ChiComs treated the situation as a river crossing rather than an amphibious landing. In the former case, they would bring small craft in numbers down to the coast from inland without producing any detectable alteration of activity in the coastal waters. After assembling secretly, they would have a good chance of crossing quickly the narrow waters separating Kinmen from the mainland and of establishing a foothold before the ChiNats could react effectively. Such a landing would probably be accompanied by parachute drops throughout the island. The outcome, in my judgment, would be uncertain. But, even if the island were taken, the price exacted from the ChiComs would make it a Pyrrhic victory.

All American officials contacted in Taiwan agreed that the U.S. should recognize, however reluctantly, that the ChiNats will continue to hold and defend the Off-shore Islands. The Islands are valuable as outposts for the main defense of Taiwan and the Penghus, as the site of early warning radar and as a symbol of the determination of the ChiNats some day to return to the mainland.

## 5.   The Return to the Mainland

In an hour's discussion with Chiang Kai-shek, the President showed his unshakable confidence in the readiness of the mainland to receive his liberating forces. He does concede, however, the need for a preparatory phase in which the people of the mainland would be given assurance of assistance and of arms in case they rose in revolt. The parachute drops which he desires to make are for this purpose. He regrets that the US withholds assistance from his grand design and explains our reluctance as fear that our assistance might provoke Khrushchev into initiating World War III.

I assured him that, personally, I had no such fear but that we Americans could not forget the experience of Cuba where overly optimistic friends had undertaken an expedition of liberation in anticipation of a friendly uprising ashore which did not occur. It was natural for us to ask for hard evidence before sharing the Gimo's confidence. The President assured me that he had ample agent reports to support his view, but offered to produce nothing tangible.

It is becoming increasingly difficult to respond to the Gimo's demands to be allowed to try to return to the mainland. Local U.S. officials feel that some U.S. participation in realistic studies of possible landings would help to show the Gimo and his associates the vast military requirements for a return to the mainland. I understand that such planning is underway and hopefully will demonstrate the magnitude of the problem. While I am doubtful that this exercise will deflate the optimism of the Gimo, it should have a salutary effect upon his advisors.

It may be that we are storing up trouble for ourselves in not being more frank with the Gimo in stating what our intentions are and are not with regard to supporting him in a return to the mainland. He has considerable justification to retain his hopes as long as we give a certain approval to his maintenance of a force structure justified only if he is indeed going to assault the mainland. Furthermore, we have allowed him to raise his special budget for defense purposes, while continuing to help him to meet the deficit in his over-all budget. It must be hard for him to believe that there are not some situations in which we will see him ashore.

## 154. Telegram From the Embassy in Poland to the Department of State

Warsaw, September 20, 1962, 7 p.m.

562. Cabot–Wang talks. 113th meeting.[1] One hour forty minutes. Deptel 404.[2]

1. Wang opened saying meeting called because he was instructed launch strongest protest re intrusion American U–2 September 9 on espionage mission and demand US stop such flagrant aggression. Said reconnaissance solely directed by US which held fully responsible for it. Said whole world knows this and ChiComs possess ample evidence prove it. Referred to June 23 meeting when US indicated no intention attack China and would not support Chiang in such. Said plane intrusion not consistent with pledge not to attack China by armed force and it evident this latest aggressive act was important step by US to incite Chiang attack Mainland. If present administration any different in China policy from previous two, it is that it is more adventurous and irresponsible as evidenced by U–2 incident. Stressed gravity of this "act of war provocation undertaken by USG."

2. Wang continued saying 214 warnings re encroachments issued since 1958. U–2 plane is fourth US espionage aircraft shot down by ChiComs. Said matters could not go on this way indefinitely. We are playing with fire heading toward war. Demanded US "rein in horse in coming to edge of precipice," stop provocations and sit down to talk seriously regarding withdrawal US forces from Taiwan and Taiwan Strait. Said

---

Source: Department of State, Central Files, 611.93/9–2062. Secret; Priority; Limit Distribution. Repeated to Taipei, Hong Kong, Geneva, Stockholm, and Moscow.

[1] The meeting was held at Chinese request. Telegram 517 from Warsaw, September 15, reported the request for an emergency meeting on September 17. (Ibid., 611.93/9–1562) Since Cabot was out of the country, the U.S. Embassy suggested September 21. Telegram 525 from Warsaw, September 17, reported that both sides had agreed to announce that day that they would meet on September 20. (Ibid., 611.93/9–1762) Cabot subsequently acceded to a Chinese request that this be considered a special, unnumbered meeting. (Telegram 749 from Warsaw, October 18; ibid., 611.93/10–1862)

Cabot commented and sent recommendations for the next meeting in telegram 564, September 21, and sent a detailed, apparently verbatim report of the meeting in airgram A–240, September 22. (Ibid., 611.93/9–2162 and 611.93/9–2262, respectively)

[2] Telegram 404, September 18, provided guidance for the meeting in the expectation that Wang would charge the United States with responsibility for GRC U–2 overflights of the Chinese mainland. (Ibid., 611.93/9–1762) A Chinese Nationalist-piloted U–2 aircraft was shot down over the mainland on September 9. Circular telegram 414, September 9, states that the Department of State had that day issued a statement that two U–2's had been sold to the GRC by the Lockheed Aircraft Corporation in July 1960 and that an export license had been issued. (Ibid., 793.5622/9–962) President Kennedy reiterated this at a September 13 press conference. (*Public Papers of the Presidents of the United States: John F. Kennedy, 1962,* p. 675)

September 18 US destroyer again operated in waters off Tsingtao on hostile reconnaissance mission. This is sixth such operation since April. Said Chinese cannot ignore this for long and was instructed protest this state of affairs.

3. I responded along lines paragraphs 3, 4 and 6[3] reference telegram and in doing so observed that Wang had repeatedly indicated in these talks ChiCom intention to overcome GRC by any means including use of force and asked whether he then expected GRC to take no precautions against ChiCom declared purpose. Continued with substance paragraph 9 reference telegram and last portion paragraph 8.[4]

4. Wang said U–2 espionage could not be denied, was yet another provocation against China which raised extreme indignation of Chinese people. Said attempt portray supply of U–2 to China as commercial transaction did not fool anyone. Said U–2 stationed in many parts of world for espionage purposes and it well known all under direct control of US. Asked how those stationed in Taiwan could be exception. Said Senior official Japanese Defense Board had said U–2s never previously been turned over to foreign country but were under direct control US military. Said in fact all "criminal activity" over Mainland was organized by CIA branch in Taiwan. Quoted *New York Times* September 10 and September 13 re photo reconnaissance activities of US and *Time* articles September 14 to effect US has no plans to ground U–2s and has not made pledge refrain from flying over other nations except for USSR.

5. I said it was necessary consider historical development our dispute if it was to be in proper perspective. Reminded Wang our difficulties really began when ChiCom troops in defiance UN resolution fought our troops in Korea who were there in pursuance UN resolution. That made clear problem was international one. Referred again to our treaty with GRC which we intended carry out. Said as long as his side displayed aggressive attitude, it was logical for a state threatened and for friends of that state to take due precautions. Said his side had not only threatened use of force but has used force repeatedly against GRC. Asked how he could consider flight of unarmed plane over Mainland as act of provocation. Said I had no intention giving Wang any information as to any military collaboration we may be furnishing GRC but would

---

[3] Paragraph 3 suggested that Cabot observe that an "air of aggrieved innocence" was ill suited to those who reiterated their intention to overcome the GRC by any means. Paragraph 4 stated that the GRC purchased the U–2's directly from the manufacturer and that what it did with them was its own affair. Paragraph 6 declared that the argument that U.S. manufacture of aircraft made the United States responsible for their use was untenable.

[4] Paragraph 9 stated that no U.S. naval vessels had been within 12 miles of any land held by Wang's side. Paragraph 8 stated that in the absence of international agreement, the United States protested all claims of a 12-mile limit as unilateral assertions but that in the interest of avoiding incidents, it did not as a general practice exercise its legal rights with regard to passage and overflight to the full limits.

say his statements seriously distorted. Referring to Wang's claim his side had never sent aircraft into US airspace, reminded him ChiComs had however sent many divisions their soldiers to fight US in Korea. Said this was vastly more aggressive act than anything Wang had alleged re US activities. Assured him statement in June 23 meeting continued to be policy my government.

6. Wang said could by no means accept "various justifications" for intrusion U–2. Re origin our dispute, said it was US armed occupation Taiwan and US aggression Korea which brought crisis in Far East. Since then US not only has not stopped its aggressive acts against China but stepped them up. Said it was not true US naval vessels had not entered territorial waters China. Tsingtao area was special objective of reconnaissance and US vessels had gone back and forth in this area in prolonged reconnaissance. This was deliberate provocation. Repeated in detail his accusations re U–2. Said to prevent recurrence U–2 incident and relax tension US should order all American high-altitude planes from Taiwan, withdraw CIA branch from Taiwan, withdraw Task Force of 13th Air Force, and all other forces.

7. I said did not recall we had ever complained re supplies sent Wang's side by Soviets. If carried Wang's argument to logical conclusion, he might complain to US because some of weapons they used in capturing Mainland cities were of US manufacture. Repeated we were not occupying Taiwan but were there by agreement and degree our support was question to be decided between US and GRC. I pointed out absurdity Wang's charge of aggression in connection unarmed aircraft over Mainland. Wang replied it was matter of the sovereignty of a given state to lay down breadth its territorial waters which were sacred and inviolable. Intruding aircraft whether combat or reconnaissance is aggression and cannot be tolerated by sovereign state. Said he did not know what US would say if foreign aircraft intruded into its airspace. I said we had both made our positions clear and saw no point in further repetition.

Next meeting October 25.[5]

**Cabot**

---

[5] The next meeting was postponed at Chinese request until December 13. Telegram 719 from Warsaw, October 15, reported that the Chinese Embassy had requested the postponement, saying that Wang planned to go to China. Telegram 532 to Warsaw of the same date approved the postponement. (Both ibid., 611.93/10–1562)

## 155.    Editorial Note

On November 10, 1962, Director of Central Intelligence John A. McCone met with Secretary of State Dean Rusk to discuss several subjects, including the question of [*text not declassified*] Tibet. McCone summarized the meeting in a memorandum for the record, dated November 13; the portion pertaining to Tibet reads as follows:

"I reviewed with the Secretary the plan CIA had developed [*7 lines of source text not declassified*] in an effort to free Tibet of the ChiCom occupation. I said this objective was a stated policy of the United States adopted about 1958 and supported by CIA. I had gathered from discussions at the Special Group some doubt as to whether this policy remained valid—some doubt as to whether the United States really wished to exercise effort to free Tibet of Chinese Communist occupation, and if there was an inclination to change this policy, I wished to know it promptly [*less than 1 line of source text not declassified*].

"I said that objectives and viewpoints expressed by Secretaries Harriman and Martin and Ambassador Galbraith restrained and frustrated long range plans developed in support of U.S. policy and because of the weight given to these viewpoints, I felt that here again we were not operating on a policy line but were acting from day to day in a manner considered best by an individual of the State Department. [*5-1/2 lines of source text not declassified*] I therefore stated that we will make no move whatsoever until there is a policy determination on this matter." (Central Intelligence Agency, DCI (McCone) Files, Job 80–B01285A DCI Memos for the Record)

Ambassador Galbraith had objected to projected CIA plans in a message of November 5, which argued that the United States should not risk possible exposure of such activities "unless it is necessary to do so in order attain major objective, and unless there is no other feasible way in which achieve desired result" and asserted that the current proposal failed on both counts. (Attached to a November 15 memorandum from Parrott to Bundy; Kennedy Library, National Security Files, Countries Series, Tibet)

A November 16 message from Bundy to Galbraith states that the Special Group had considered how best to employ the CIA [*text not declassified*] and had concluded as follows:

"[*1 paragraph (3 lines of source text) not declassified*]
"[*5 lines of source text not declassified*] CIA intends to initiate a program of active contingency planning [*2-1/2 lines of source text not declassified*]. No active operations will be undertaken until such plans have been worked out." (Ibid.)

## 156.   Telegram From the Consulate General at Singapore to the Department of State

Singapore, November 13, 1962, noon.

287. For Harriman. Reference: Consulate General telegram 282.[1] Conversation with Malcolm MacDonald on Nov 12, mentioned reftel, concentrated primarily on internal situation Communist China, US-ChiCom relations and Sino-Indian border dispute. MacDonald prefaced remarks by stating he had been allowed to visit every place he requested with exception of Jehol which hosts said was too far away. (MacDonald wished trip to Jehol because of historic interest.) Said he saw "hundreds of thousands" of Chinese, communes, factories, iron and steel mills and believes has obtained true and accurate picture of Mainland conditions and of attitudes of ChiCom leaders on matters discussed below.

*1. Internal Situation*

MacDonald convinced that ChiCom leaders have gone through an "agonizing reappraisal"; that they have learned their lesson, and that, although they know the country is still vulnerable to nature, they have become more practical, more realistic and more patient. He says this for three reasons: (A) Leaders miscalculated speed with which country, particularly peasants, could enter modern age. Chou En-lai told him their plans had been over-ambitious. He saw factories which were built two or three years ago and are now closed, although he was assured they would reopen as soon as primary problem of agriculture was ameliorated. (B) Withdrawal of Soviet technicians. Neither Chou nor Chen Yi would acknowledge any indebtedness to these technicians but MacDonald believes it an essential element of the necessity for reappraisal. Chinese technicians he saw were excellently trained but young and inexperienced. (C) Three bad harvests which undoubtedly caused real hardship and suffering. According to MacDonald agriculture has first priority with those industries related to it given only slightly lower priority. Iron and steel mills are going full blast with a slight balance in favor of iron smelt as ChiCom leaders now realize peasants not only prefer but will have to use hand implements for "decades and decades." He visited

---

Source: Department of State, Central Files, 793.00/11–1362. Confidential; Priority. A notation on the source text in Harriman's handwriting apparently indicates that he wanted a copy sent to the President.

[1] Telegram 282, November 8, reported a luncheon conversation with Malcolm MacDonald, who had just visited the People's Republic of China; he had lengthy discussions with Chou En-lai and Chen Yi. MacDonald commented briefly on his visit and arranged to meet with Acting Consul General Robert Donhauser on November 12. (Ibid., 793.00/11–862)

mills at Nanchang and Wuhan. At Loyang he saw factory producing 50 tractors a day, 15,000 per year. Irrigation and chemical fertilizer plants are others high on priority list.

Turning to communes MacDonald said he thought they were smaller; 10,000 or less was average commune. Communes have fewer functions than formerly and peasants, to whom cadres must now pay heed, have more influence in handling agricultural problems. Overall planning for area is still function of communes, but production team or brigade is village unit. Peasants have no more land, but agricultural produce and livestock have increased because of better grain and stock. Peasants allowed to sell some produce on free market.

In summation MacDonald said people on the whole looked "hale and hearty" (there were "good spring and fall harvests"); that they appeared reasonably content because regime was giving them a little more of everything and they were better off than they ever had been, but that it would take years, which leaders realized, for Communist China to become modern nation. He ruefully remarked that he had planned write series of articles on internal situation for London *Observer* but had decided against it, thereby losing 1500 pounds, because he would have to paint "too favorable a picture."

### 2. US-ChiCom Relations

Chou told MacDonald he was pleased with results of Geneva Conference on Laos but that since that time there had been marked deterioration in US-ChiCom relations: there were US soldiers in civilian dress still in Laos; US had troops in Taiwan, Thailand and Vietnam and now giving military aid to India. US was encircling China. (Here MacDonald made obvious observation to me that ChiCom leaders were intensely nervous about their national security.)

MacDonald told Chou that since new administration there had been some changes in US policy toward Asian nations which had gained world-wide acceptance and approval and suggested US scholars and journalists be permitted travel throughout country in order inform American public of true facts. Chou replied that US refused reciprocal arrangements, that it imposed restrictions on Chinese; that there were Chinese in prison [garble] which was reason for his holding prisoners and that unless US agreed to reciprocity on all questions he was not prepared to budge. In this connection MacDonald has impression ChiComs do not rule out completely some type of exchange of scholars and journalists but it would be impossible effect until after Indian border dispute settled.

Chou raised Warsaw talks and GRC (see reftel).[2] Said most Taiwanese wished be joined with Mainland but he was "patient" and was not going attempt "violent" solution. On other hand Chiang was "internal matter" not for outside (i.e. US) interference. MacDonald said Chou obviously wished assure him privately Peiping had no intention of invading Taiwan but would never state so publicly.

### 3. Sino-Indian Relations[3]

On this subject MacDonald differentiates between discussion and monologue. Chou and he were discussing Sino-UK relations which Chou said were good (trade, Hong Kong, UK vote in UN, although he disliked UK support for retention of seat for Taiwan).[4] Chou took exception to UK position that Peiping was aggressor in border dispute. Stated he realized UK must support India as member of Commonwealth but did not have to charge Chinese aggression. He wished to go to conference table but India had made impossible demands prior to discussions, particularly since territory under dispute was not Indian but Chinese. MacDonald, of course, upheld UK position. He thinks that ChiComs again are concerned with internal security and believes they consider they must have control of roads in that area to maintain military control of Tibet. Also that ChiComs do not wish go beyond border incident stage because of concern for their own domestic internal problems. He believes they will attempt subversion in Bhutan, Nepal, Sikkim, Ladakh and elsewhere in SEA but at this time they definitely will not attempt large scale military aggression anywhere in Asia.

### 4. Other Items

(A) MacDonald believes ChiComs intensely resentful of Soviet withdrawal of technicians. At every opportunity emphasis was placed on Chinese having to "go it alone." While he never queried them directly on subject, he sensed a real defiance of USSR and a fiercely independent attitude. (B) MacDonald did not see Mao but from films he saw of him thinks he looked old. (C) When asked about succession, MacDonald

---

[2] Concerning the Warsaw talks telegram 282 reported, "Chou stated Warsaw talks had been going on for seven years 'with no results' but that he was prepared have them continue for another seven years." Concerning the GRC, it reported that Chou had said the Taiwan question was the business of the Chinese alone, had given MacDonald the impression that "hidden contacts exist between GRC leaders and ChiComs," and had "emphasized his old line that Taiwan would have nothing to fear from mainland takeover and would survive as minority political group."

[3] For documentation relating to the Sino-Indian border conflict of October–November 1962, see volume XIX.

[4] On October 30 the General Assembly rejected a Soviet draft resolution by a vote of 42 in favor (including the United Kingdom) to 56 against (including the United States), with 12 abstentions. It would have removed "the Chiang Kai-shek representatives" from all U.N. organs and invited the People's Republic of China to send representatives to occupy China's place. (U.N. doc. A/L.395)

stated Chou, Chen Yi and "their school" were in the ascendancy and, subject to death, would certainly remain so. (*Note:* These two were only ChiCom bigwigs MacDonald saw. He, of course, knew of Liu Shao-chi and others but was not prepared to comment on them.)

MacDonald reiterated he would write letter to you and ask that his communications to London be sent Washington.[5] He will be in North Borneo next ten days and then plans return Singapore for short while. Will be happy answer any questions you may have at that time. Will then proceed to New Delhi and London, thence Canada.

Since you requested personal report[6] this telegram and reftel have not been sent other interested posts.

**Donhauser**

---

[5] A letter of November 12 from MacDonald to Harriman, together with copies of telegrams from MacDonald, which the Foreign Office had made available to the Embassy in London, may be found in Library of Congress Manuscript Division, Harriman Papers, Kennedy–Johnson Administrations, Subject Files, MacDonald, Malcolm.

[6] Requested in telegram 189 to Singapore, November 7. (Department of State, Central Files, 110.15 HA/11–762)

---

**157. Paper Prepared in the Policy Planning Council**

Washington, November 30, 1962.

US POLICY TOWARD COMMUNIST CHINA

I.

*Purpose:* This paper proposes specific policy decisions and actions designed to secure maximum benefit to the US from the changing situation in Communist China.

---

Source: National Archives and Records Administration, RG 59, Records of the Department of State, S/P Files: Lot 69 D 121, S/P Record Copies. Top Secret; Sensitive Handling. A handwritten note on the source text indicates that it was discussed by the Planning Group on December 4. No drafter is indicated on the source text, but the paper is derived from two longer papers of November 15 and 19, both entitled "A U.S. Policy Toward Communist China," drafted by Mose Harvey of the Policy Planning Council. (Ibid., China) According to a November 28 memorandum from Rostow to Planning Group members, the longer papers were based in part on discussions over several months by an interagency group. (Ibid., Harvey, M., Chron)

According to Rostow's November 28 memorandum one of the papers on which this one was derived had been discussed by senior officers of the Department and, while there was disagreement on some points, there was general agreement that the policy approach recommended in the paper was sound. No other record of that discussion or the December 4 discussion has been found.

## II.

*Background:* Strong elements of instability exist in Communist China in consequence of economic difficulties and worsening relations with the USSR. To these must be added the inevitable problem of succession as the aging veterans of the long-march, who still absolutely dominate the leadership, pass from the scene. While we cannot be sure of the long-run effects of these disruptive forces, there is a good probability they will result in either a lasting erosion of the capability of the regime to effect its communist goals at home and abroad or in a basic change in orientation. This probability is sufficiently great to justify tailoring US policy to give it full play. There is also a possibility that the Chinese Communist leadership, frustrated in many directions, will launch massive aggression across their borders. Although they have thus far moved with considerable caution, this contingency deserves steady policy attention.

## III.

*Basic Policy Requirements:* Our broad aims should be: (a) to avoid actions, and to seek to induce others to avoid actions, that would reduce pressures operating on the regime as it is presently constituted and oriented, or would force the regime and the Soviets back into a close association; and (b) within the limits of these requirements, to maintain flexibility adequate to enable us to encourage and capitalize on any movement toward significant favorable change within China.

To effect these aims we have need for: (a) maximum cooperation from allied and friendly governments; (b) appreciation of our objectives and the rationale therefor by the Congress and the American public; and (c) minimal restraints on our freedom of action in consequence of our alliance with the Nationalist regime on Taiwan.

The specific tasks we face are: (a) to refine and make more effective our present policy of keeping the regime under pressure; (b) to isolate touchstones of change in Communist China that would justify changes, small or large, in US policy; (c) to maintain lines of communication that will enable us to send signals as to our policy and intentions regarding developments in China and to receive signals that may be forthcoming from within China; (d) to respond to any concrete indications of change in ways that would encourage movement toward a favorable reorientation but would not contribute prematurely to a relief from pressures operating on the regime; and (e) given convincing evidence of a basic shift in Chinese policies and purposes, to be prepared to adjust our own policies to the extent necessary to nail down the shift and to use it as a basis for seeking a lasting resolution of the China problem.

IV.

*Recommended Policy Decisions and Actions:* At the present stage[1] decisions and actions should encompass the following:

*A. Essential Foundations*

1. We should formally adopt as the governing principles of our China policy:

a. Continued firm US opposition to any relaxation of pressures on or compromises with the Peiping regime unless and until concrete evidence is given of an intention on the part of Peiping to alter its aggressive policy and actions and to modify its stance of active hostility toward the US and the non-communist world.

b. A willingness on the part of the US to meet any specific move by Peiping toward relaxation with an appropriate corresponding move of its own, although not necessarily in kind.

c. Readiness of the US to settle on an across-the-board basis its differences with China if and when any regime in power convincingly demonstrates by its policies and conduct, at home and abroad, an intention to devote its energies and resources to meeting the legitimate needs of the Chinese people and to establish on a lasting basis good relations with the US, its Asian neighbors, and the western world generally.

2. Following adoption of these principles, we should:

a. Take the initiative in explaining to key allied governments the US position and the underlying rationale. We should seek to develop a sober appreciation of the great advantage the Free World derives from even a temporary preoccupation of Communist China with its internal problems, and of the possibility that prolonged failures of the regime to solve those problems can lead to a break of truly historical importance for the Free World cause.

b. Inform the American public more fully of the problems and opportunities incident to our China policy. Our aim should be an understanding that our stance of reciprocal hostility, which will be maintained as long as necessary, is not an end in itself but a means to effect changes in China that will enable us to live at peace with whatever regime is in power.

c. Systematically seek to reconcile the Chinese Nationalists to the fact that our China policy must necessarily serve the broad interests of

---

[1] The recommendations made here do not cover all of the measures necessary to meet the policy requirements set forth under III above. They are limited to those necessary to get the policy under way. As the situation develops and various contingencies arise, appropriate additional steps can be taken within the framework of this policy plan. The recommendations also do not cover present policies which require no changes under the plan. [Footnote in the source text.]

the US and the Free World generally rather than the interests of the Taipei regime alone. We should clarify our policy toward Nationalist military action against the mainland along lines set forth in paragraph B8 below. We should reaffirm our lasting resolve to protect the security of Taiwan proper, but should at the same time prepare the way for general policy adjustments which we may come to consider desirable and necessary and which would not affect Taiwanese security. (Should Chiang pass from the scene at an early date, we should press on the successor regime this educational campaign with special vigor.)

d. Take advantage of appropriate opportunities that might be offered in the Warsaw talks to elaborate our basic thinking re problems affecting US relations with China and the circumstances that could contribute to their resolution.

*B. Maintenance of Pressures on an Unregenerate Regime*

3. In the interest of keeping the Peiping regime under pressure unless and until it demonstrates a change of heart, our primary need will be to continue present policies encompassing territorial containment, support for peoples threatened by either direct or indirect Chinese aggressions, direct military confrontation at various crisis points, preservation of and support for the Nationalist regime on Taiwan, differential trade treatment by the US and such friendly powers as the US can influence, and attempts at maximum political isolation. It is important, however, that we maintain an added alertness to frustrate maneuvers by Peiping, or even by our friends, to break the line, and that we introduce certain refinements and tactical variations in our policies to make them more effective.

4. A continuing need is to stay on top of Chinese trade relations with western countries. Since 1960, Chinese trade with bloc countries has precipitously declined. Trade with the west has at the same time increased, now equalling more than 50 percent of the total. This proportional change has so far not involved a substantial shift from bloc to western suppliers; the phenomenon reflects simple abstinence with regard to bloc goods, particularly machinery, while large supplies of grain have been procured in the west. The Chinese have, however, shown interest in developing western alternatives to bloc sources. While some shifts to the West may be desirable, we should attempt to prevent any net improvement in the Chinese situation as a result.

a. We should make representations to all allied and friendly governments to discourage liberalization of present trade practices, particularly opposing grants of long term credits. In addition to utilizing the rationale of our own China policy in these representations, we should place special emphasis on the lessons to be drawn by the Free World from Chinese attacks on India.

b. We should raise with the Canadians, Australians and French question about grain sales to China in the context of the Chinese attack on India. In addition to discouraging any improvement in credit terms, we should lay foundations for a possible end to shipments in case China renews the border conflict with India.[2]

c. We should take added steps to influence the Japanese to move slowly in developing its trade with China. Although neither the current level of Sino-Japanese trade, nor the currently indicated level for the near future, is apt to affect significantly conditions in China, the potential is quite important, particularly if Japan should allow long-term credits or enter into intricate developmental barter arrangements. The "lesson of India" as well as other considerations should be kept constantly before the Japanese.

d. We should explore possibilities, and the advantages and disadvantages, of denying to China petroleum from western sources should Peiping, either on its own initiative or as a result of Soviet action, attempt to shift from the Soviet market.

e. Should large-scale Chinese attacks against India be resumed, we should explore possibilities of a total western embargo against China.

5. We should subject the regime to a more forthcoming psychological drive. In particular:

a. We should encourage a full and continued public airing in the US and abroad of Communist China's troubled situation and dimmed prospects, but in a way that would not suggest a special campaign, which might be counter-productive.

b. We should supply US missions, particularly in the under-developed countries, with documentary and intelligence data on developments in Communist China, and should instruct missions to arrange to keep appropriate government officials and influential private citizens informed of these developments on a continuing basis.

c. We should push diligently and begin early implementation of the project already underway to minimize the impact of a possible Chinese explosion of a nuclear device.

d. In continuing to oppose Communist China's admission to the UN, UN subsidiary organizations, and other international organizations, we should tailor our arguments to reflect the basic principles of our China policy as outlined under IV 1. above.

e. US officials should increasingly stress publicly US concern for the welfare and progress of the Chinese people. We should emphasize

---

[2] According to a CIA study of November 27, grain shipments from western sources contributes appreciably to the strength of the regime. Grain shipments, in fact, appear the only economic lever the western world has against the regime. [Footnote in the source text.]

our willingness to help, with the rest of the civilized world, the Chinese people if and as the attitudes, policies and—by implication—make-up of the ruling regime make this feasible.

6. It is especially important that we continue to do whatever may be necessary to deny to Peiping, or to Communist elements generally, cheap successes in Asia.

7. We should maintain, and if circumstances warrant step up, the pressures resulting from our military presence in the Taiwan Strait, Korea, and South East Asia.

8. We should avoid ourselves, and insist that the Nationalists avoid, military operations against the mainland on a scale and of a nature that would risk costly losses, furnish an effective rallying point for the regime, invite a dangerous counter-move by the regime (e.g., an all-out attack on the Offshores), or place us in the position of having to back a losing ally or lose prestige. We should, however, support continued or even substantially increased small-scale probes and clandestine operations by the Nationalists which could be useful for intelligence purposes, particularly as a means of testing the temper of communist-armed forces and of the public, and possibly for keeping the regime off balance. We should not, however, give such countenance to these operations as would suggest, or escalate into, US commitments to sanction increasingly pretentious Nationalist efforts. We should instead gradually make clear to the Nationalist regime that the only circumstance in which we envisage the possibility of their return to the mainland would be one wherein they had in effect been invited to do so by strong forces within China, which had already declared themselves against the communist regime.

*C. Touchstones for US Policy Changes*

9. While pursuing a policy of pressures on an unregenerate regime, we should maintain a constant alert for direct or indirect indications of changes in the attitudes and policies of the rulers and should react in ways designed to further movement toward a genuine reorientation.

a. The weight we attach to apparent signals should be heavily influenced by the composition of the dominant element in the leadership at the time. As a general rule:

—We should be wary of any gestures or maneuvers emanating from a leadership still subject to Maoist control; we should not ignore Maoist moves, but should limit our responses to atmospherics designed to test how far Mao is prepared to go; we should especially avoid responses involving exchange of relief from pressures or important prestige gains for atmospherics or commitments revokable at will.

—In case movement occurs in a "regular" succession situation (i.e., Mao had apparently died or been incapacitated), we should match step with step, going as far and as fast as the new leadership is willing to, but still exercising care not to get ahead of the game.

—Should it be apparent that a coup had been effected against Mao or Maoist elements in the leadership, we should assume optimum chances of progression to a basic reorientation and shape our policies accordingly.

b. Our evaluation of Chinese moves should accord with their implications for a basic change in orientation of the ruling regime rather than for a simple "relaxation of tensions".

—The prime test should be whether moves involve changes in attitude and policies toward the US. This derives from the fact that hostility toward the US, as the leader of the "imperialist" camp, is the keystone of the Chinese revolutionary ideological system.
—We should be little impressed by overtures to "second" capitalist powers, e.g., Japan, India, or even the UK, unless accompanied by gestures the US, as these could well be undertaken as a means of relieving pressures or as a maneuver in the revolutionary game.
—We should also be little impressed by a revival of the "Bandung spirit" or other steps involving renewed play upon "peaceful coexistence."

c. With regard to specifics, we should look for and react favorably to: moves involving a marked change in propaganda treatment of the US, a change of stance regarding Taiwan, de-emphasis of the "national liberation" theme for SE Asia, overtures to the US for renewed trade relations, relaxation of restrictions on contacts with the non-communist world, and proposals looking toward negotiations with the US without the "pre-conditions" of the past.

d. Our evaluation of moves in the international sphere should be importantly influenced by whether there are indications of an accompanying relaxation of militancy on the domestic front.

10. Our responses to Chinese moves should aim at moving the process of change forward rather than wrapping up immediate advantages. Until the game gave promise of decisive results, US reaction should be guarded, designed to keep the dialogue going, but stopping short of anything that would give the regime important advantage or restrict our own freedom of action to match in kind any sudden reversal.

11. We should not initially expect or even seek formal agreements or negotiated quid pro quos. For some time at least, reliance should be on parallel tracks of reading and sending signals. The principal area of maneuver on our part should be in the trade field. Beginning with only token steps to meet token gestures on Peiping's part, we should be prepared to move progressively to a point where our trade policies toward mainland China would correspond to those toward members of the Soviet Bloc. Another area of maneuver that should be opened up once substantial progress had been demonstrated would be military confrontation. If, for example, Chinese propaganda attacks on the US should be significantly reduced we might pull our naval forces back from the

Taiwan Strait and operate behind rather than forward from Taiwan. Given a more decisive move on the Chinese side, say significant efforts to stabilize the situation in Southeast Asia, we might respond by inducing the Nationalists to evacuate the Offshores.

*D. Contingency Planning for Disaster Situation*

12. Although current indications do not suggest the likelihood of an early turn in China that would lead to chaotic conditions, the magnitude of the problems that would arise in this event, specifically in connection with emergency relief, made desirable a comprehensive study of the scale and urgency of requirements that would result and of the possibilities with regard to meeting them.

---

**158.   Telegram From the Embassy in Poland to the Department of State**

Warsaw, December 13, 1962, 7 p.m.

968. Cabot–Wang Talks. 113th Meeting.[1] 2 hours 20 minutes. Deptels 530 and 695.[2]

1. After confirming previous agreement (Embtel 749)[3] that this would be only 113th meeting and I would open, I covered American prisoners and exchange newsmen in accordance numbered paragraph 3 first reference telegram and 1 second reference telegram.[4] Wang said essential objective our meetings Washington try to settle question of restoration

---

Source: Department of State, Central Files, 611.93/12–1362. Confidential; Priority; Limit Distribution. Repeated to Taipei, Hong Kong, Geneva, Stockholm, and Moscow.

[1] Cabot sent his comments and recommendations in telegram 972, December 14, and sent a detailed, apparently verbatim report of the meeting in airgram A–478, December 15. (Ibid., 611.93/12–1462 and 611.93/12–1562, respectively) He sent further recommendations in telegram 1182, February 1. (Ibid., POL CHICOM–US)

[2] Telegram 530 to Warsaw, October 13, reported that it had been necessary since June to reemphasize the gap between the two sides on basic issues in order to make clear that the United States had not changed its commitment to the GRC but that since that point had been made, Cabot should return to concrete issues and should limit his opening presentation to the prisoner and newsmen issues. (Ibid., 611.93/10–1362) Telegram 695 to Warsaw, December 7, reaffirmed those instructions with some modifications. (Ibid., 611.93/12–762)

[3] See footnote 1, Document 154.

[4] Paragraph 3 of telegram 530 reiterated the U.S. position on the prisoner issue. Paragraph 1 of telegram 695 instructed Cabot to refer to Chou En-lai's statement to Malcolm MacDonald that the United States wished to impose restrictions on Chinese journalists that they would not accept on American journalists visiting China (see Document 156) and to counter by referring to previous discussions.

Taiwan to Mother Land. Since US persisted in policy of hostility and refused accept reasonable proposals, no progress made. Wang said during first stage of talks Chinese thought pending resolution of main issues, we could deal with some minor problems. Therefore, during 1956 and 1957 his side had many proposals, e.g. lifting of trade embargo, exchange of persons and cultural intercourse, rendering of judicial aid by both sides, and exchange of newsmen. Claimed his side had not distorted record re newsmen but we had rejected his reasonable proposal of September 6, 1960. Only after our side had raised obstacles to solution various concrete matters had his side concluded pending settlement to basic issue between two sides no progress could be made.

2. Wang continued saying 9 more serious warnings issued since previous meeting. Complained US had engaged with ChiNats in big parachute maneuver in Taiwan and it was matter of public knowledge that armed agents sent to mainland in attempt prepare ground for invasion were all trained and equipped by US. Enumerated series of visits by high-ranking US military officers to Taiwan recently. Said General Taylor quoted *Christian Science Monitor*, US would probably use tactical nuclear weapons in any conflict with Communist China. *Washington Post* also reported many US military men advocated nuclear weapons should be used in fighting in Asia. Said our claim US would not be responsible if Chiang attacked mainland without our consent was obvious attempt to prepare ground in advance for shirking our responsibility in backing invasion.

3. Wang continued accusing US of meddling India massive military aid and instigating India to carry on extensive war against China. Our apparent design was to utilize India to strike at China and keep her engaged in a new direction.

4. I said I scarcely thought matter of American prisoners was side issue as implied in Wang's remarks. We feel strongly these men should be released under the one real agreement reached in these talks. We have tried honorably carry out our side of bargain.

5. Re newsmen, I said Wang's proposal would in effect have us abandon solemn treaty with GRC. Did not see how he could consider proposal reasonable or expect us do any such thing. Again denied we occupying Taiwan. Re parachute maneuver I said it was true we furnished certain military training advice. In view our defense treaty, we see no impropriety in this.

Re alleged agents sent to mainland reminded Wang his side had repeatedly refused renunciation force in area China and has repeatedly used force in that area. Could scarcely expect other side remain passive under circumstances. Said position I expressed to him last June remained that of my government re mainland invasion.[5]

6. I said Government and people of US were shocked by open aggression his side against India. Followed with substance paragraph 2 second reference telegram[6] and paragraph 7 first reference telegram.[7]

7. In response my request for details, Wang listed by areas and dates alleged intrusions serious warnings 215 through 221. I promised report these to my government but assume they are available to Department through NCNA broadcasts and *Peoples Daily*.

8. Re prisoners, Wang said not a single American civilian in China and desiring to return was being detained. Four American "convicts" are serving sentences. They committed offenses against Chinese law and it is natural that they must serve their sentences. Claimed there were number of Chinese desiring to return but being obstructed.

9. Re Sino-Indian border, Wang said this question was legacy of history. Chinese Government had consistently advocated fair and reasonable solution through peaceful means. Peace-loving nations and people throughout world urging India accept proposals made by Chinese Government. Said our Secretary of State and Ambassador to India had been abetting and exhorting India to carry out its military venture. Said we had openly announced recognition of illegal McMahon line despite fact that Secretary Herter in 1959 indicated US would not recognize that line.[8] Asked whether words of Kennedy Administration or Eisenhower Administration were to be believed.

10. After reiterating familiar line re Taiwan, Wang then (in response to my mention of Kuo Mo-jo's speech) said ChiComs almost daily had to put up with all sorts offensive comments, attacks, and vilifications made by American publications and high-ranking members US Government

---

[5] Telegram 530 to Warsaw instructed Cabot to state, if Wang mentioned Chiang Kai-shek's threats of action against the mainland, that he had explicitly stated the U.S. position concerning attack on the mainland and had nothing to add to or subtract from that statement.

[6] Paragraph 2 of telegram 695 authorized Cabot to state that the purpose of U.S. aid to India was to "help India resist efforts by Wang's side to impose its views concerning boundary by force of arms. United States would wish to see peaceful solution, but one which Indians can accept with honor."

[7] Paragraph 7 of telegram 530 reported that Kuo Mo-jo, President of the PRC Academy of Sciences and a member of the Standing Committee of the National People's Congress, had charged in a September 26 speech that Kennedy had surpassed Hitler and Tojo in savagery and tyranny; it called this "highly offensive to American people" and instructed Cabot to ask Wang whether it represented the view of the authorities on his side.

[8] Reference is apparently to Secretary of State Christian A. Herter's statement at a press conference on November 12, 1959, that the United States had taken no position on the Sino-Indian border dispute since the question had not previously arisen. For text, see *American Foreign Policy: Current Documents, 1959*, pp. 1190–1191.

against policies social system and leaders his country. It was his side which had most to complain about on this subject.

11. I said if Wang would furnish particulars on Chinese desiring go to mainland but allegedly obstructed, my government would be pleased investigate. Added if Wang's side wished under present circumstances to alter arrangement whereby Indian Embassy is its agent on this question, I am sure my government would have no objection. Said we had never agreed because persons had been convicted constituted reason for them not to be released under agreed announcement. Re Indian border, I said we were not trying to establish what is right and wrong, but what is clear is that his side by military action had taken territory which had long been in Indian hands. We had furnished arms of which he spoke only after heavy fighting had broken out. Added penultimate sentence paragraph 6 first reference telegram.[9]

Next meeting February 22.

**Cabot**

---

[9] The sentence reads as follows: "Apparent position of Wang's side may be summed up in few words: 'Aggression consists in preventing his side from using armed hostilities to accomplish its objectives.'"

---

159. **Telegram From the Department of State to the Embassy in the Republic of China**

Washington, December 26, 1962, 5:27 p.m.

446. Embtel 567.[1] Dept concurs in your proposal see Vice President at earliest opportunity for purpose forestalling possibility GRC may mis-

---

Source: Department of State, Central Files, 793.5/12–2262. Secret. Drafted by Popple and Rice, cleared with the Legal Adviser's Office and the Agency for International Development Program Coordination Staff, and approved by Harriman. Repeated to CINCPAC for POLAD.

[1] Telegram 567, December 22, referred to GRC plans to equip an additional airborne regiment and build 100 LCMs, to be paid for out of the special preparedness budget, and stated that the MAAG had not been informed about the LCMs until procurement had been initiated and it acquired the information independently. The telegram further reported that MAP materials had been diverted without prior consultation, and a promise of replacement was given only after a MAAG inquiry. Lest U.S. silence be misconstrued as a change in the U.S. position on military action against the mainland, Kirk proposed to discuss the matter with Ch'en. (Ibid., 793.5/12–2262)

construe silence for change in our position on military action against mainland. Agree your making that portion of presentation proposed to be made as under instructions per penultimate paragraph reftel,[2] and that you should remind GRC that on basis information so far furnished we do not perceive any material alteration in situation on mainland.

You will, of course, wish to avoid creating impression that our assessment conditions there would necessarily provide the key to our agreeing to a GRC effort to return to the mainland. While we think it highly unlikely that the mainland regime's control will soon deteriorate to a drastic extent, there is possibility such deterioration may eventually occur and that circumstances might then still be such that we could not agree to a GRC counterattack. In such a situation, it would add to our difficulties if we had meanwhile overplayed mainland conditions as decisive factor.

You should also point out that unilateral decision divert MAP materials from agreed purposes for which furnished would constitute violation Mutual Defense Assistance Agreement Feb 9, 1951,[3] and that such diversions, [as] well as military expenditures which we learn of after event, can have only adverse impact on economic planning and implementation US military and economic assistance to GRC, and may handicap our gaining Congressional support for it.

Unilateral diversions MAP materials would under abovementioned agreement justify reduction or cessation future deliveries. This is fact you may allude to in your discretion as personal observation. However, we think it would be undesirable for you also make personal observation that you assume FY 63 MAP was cut partly as reaction to special preparedness budget.[4] It was cut because of urgent requirements elsewhere and in view of fact substantial deliveries to GRC remained in pipeline. Having made the observation might constrain us, should GRC fail improve performance, from going ahead with sizable increase FY 64 MAP.[5]

**Rusk**

---

[2] In it, Kirk proposed stating that the United States continued to "view with uneasiness this excessive military expenditure burden" and that it saw "no reason to assume any imminent military action against mainland justifies such imbalance of national economy."

[3] Effected by an exchange of notes at Taipei, January 30 and February 9, 1951; for text, see 2 UST (pt. 2) 1499.

[4] Kirk had suggested this in telegram 567 from Taipei; see footnote 2 above.

[5] Kirk reported in telegram 575 from Taipei, January 1, 1963, that he had met with Ch'en the previous day and had stressed the need for full exchange of information. (Department of State, Central Files, 793.5/1–163) Telegram 592 from Taipei, January 9, 1963, reported that further information had made the previously reported diversion of MAP materials seem doubtful, and that this was taken into account in the meeting with Ch'en. (Ibid., 793.5/1–963)

## 160.    Editorial Note

Negotiations for a Status of Forces agreement concerning U.S. forces in the Republic of China had begun in August 1955 and continued intermittently through May 1960 without reaching agreement; see *Foreign Relations, 1955–1957*, volume II, pages 607–610; ibid., volume III, pages 282–283; and ibid., 1958–1960, volume XIX, pages 732–733. A second series of negotiations began on January 7, 1963, with a GRC counterdraft of May 11, 1960, as the basis for discussion, except that discussion of Article XIV on criminal jurisdiction was based on a U.S. proposal of March 1960. As in the earlier negotiations, Article XIV proved to be the greatest source of difficulties. The 16th meeting of the second series of negotiating sessions, held on September 30, was the last formal session in 1963. Subsequent informal discussions also failed to reach agreement. Documentation on this subject is in Department of State, Central File 611.937 through January 1963, thereafter in file DEF 15–3 CHINAT and DEF 15–3 CHINAT–US.

## 161.    Telegram From the Embassy in the Republic of China to the Department of State

Taipei, January 10, 1963, 5 p.m.

595. For Governor Harriman from Kirk. During visit Foreign Minister Shen at his home (he suffering from a severe cold) I brought up informally the current Peiping propaganda onslaught about the 9 teams recently obliterated by ChiComs.[1] Broadcasts from Peiping were being pretty factual to identities of prisoners and of sources of their equipment

---

Source: Department of State, Central Files, 611.93/1–1063. Top Secret.

[1] A PRC Public Security Ministry communiqué of December 29 declared that nine groups of "U.S.–Chiang Kai-shek agents" had been "wiped out" in the past 3 months. A January 11 memorandum from Director of the Bureau of Intelligence and Research Thomas L. Hughes to Harriman summarizes the report as follows: Communist press commentary attacking the United States as the moving force behind the infiltration, and Nationalist press reports "confirming" that 172 guerrillas had been "killed" but claiming that others were active on the mainland. (Kennedy Library, National Security Files, Countries Series, China) Information concerning the nine Nationalist teams is summarized in a memorandum of January 14 from Desmond FitzGerald to Thomas Parrott, attached to a memorandum of January 15 from Parrott to Bromley Smith. (Ibid.)

and I pointed out United States was being pilloried as villain of this act with scanty attention to ChiNats. Furthermore it appeared these broadcasts were being directed to many parts of the world and again US accused of aggressive action. Shen said he also had become aware of this heavy propaganda attack from Peiping and deplored its virulence with some regret ChiNats captives had fallen into trap.

Then I pointed out that President Kennedy held strongly view that United States must do nothing now to be accused of aggressive action in Taiwan Straits area, that as I had stressed to Generalissimo in my earliest talks (July 4 and 5) furnishing by US of B57's plus large numbers landing craft was not consistent with above basic attitude, and that our position must continue to remain steadfastly of such nature.

Also I remarked that repeated claims by "highest sources" here that ChiNats were penetrating mainland with guerrillas, agents, etc. in preparation for "counter offensive"[2] was having result (press sources) of Peiping expecting ChiCom populace increase vigilance against such efforts, especially along coastlines. Added that my personal view was concentration ChiCom armies abreast Taiwan last summer was direct response to ChiNats bellicose assertions that return to mainland was imminent. I also noted that this ChiNat publicity created pressure on Department spokesman to comment on guerrilla question and that such pressure could scarcely produce results pleasing to either my government or his. I left with Minister copy of Department spokesman's statement January 9.[3]

Foreign Minister had little to say except that results small probes were disappointing and Peiping making most of opportunity, and that he appreciated friendly manner in which topic had been broached. Added that statement by Ministry National Defense spokesman January 8[4] had been surprise to him.

**Kirk**

---

[2] Telegrams 593 and 596 from Taipei, both January 10, reported extensive reports to this effect in the press. (Department of State, Central Files, 793.00/1–1063)

[3] Telegram 473 to Taipei, January 10, transmitted an excerpt from the transcript of the Department of State January 9 press briefing in which spokesman Lincoln White, in response to a question about U.S. policy concerning Chiang Kai-shek's desire to return to the mainland, referred to the joint communiqué of October 23, 1958 (cited in footnote 3, Document 19), and Kennedy's comments at his June 27 press conference (see Document 137). (Department of State, Central Files, 793.00/1–1063)

[4] Telegram 593 from Taipei, cited in footnote 2 above, reported that a Defense Ministry spokesman had stated on January 8 that the GRC "had many times sent large groups of guerrillas to mainland" and that "feverish activity was proof that GRC underground forces have dealt them serious blows."

## 162. Editorial Note

Director of Central Intelligence John A. McCone and the President's Special Assistant for National Security Affairs McGeorge Bundy had some discussion pertaining to China in a meeting in Bundy's office on January 10, 1963. A memorandum for the record by McCone, January 11, reads in part as follows:

"Bundy then brought up the question of the estimate of Chinese Communist nuclear capability, with its current status, and what was the present estimate of when the ChiComs would explode a device. He stated that the President felt that this was probably the most serious problem facing the world today and intimated that we might consider a policy of indicating now that further effort by the Chinese Communists in the nuclear field would be unacceptable to us and that we should prepare to take some form of action unless they agreed to desist from further efforts in this field. Bundy said that he felt the President was of a mind that nuclear weapons in the hands of the Chinese Communists would so upset the world political scene it would be intolerable to the United States and to the West. Apparently this subject was also discussed at Nassau, although this was not stated. We discussed in some detail the estimate. DCI pointed out to Bundy that all facts upon which the estimate was based were most uncertain; we knew very, very little about the ChiCom production of uranium, their metal plants, their gaseous diffusion plants; that we knew nothing whatsoever about their reactors, we knew nothing about their chemical separation plants and, finally, their weapon developments. McCone advised Bundy of his program for an intense intelligence effort in this field, which had been discussed in recent days with DD/P."

McCone noted:

"It appeared to me that Cuba and the Communist China nuclear threat are two issues foremost in the minds of the highest authority and therefore should be treated accordingly by CIA." (Central Intelligence Agency, DCI (McCone) Files, Job 80–B01285A, Box 2, DCI Memos for the Record)

The estimate to which Bundy referred has not been identified. The reference to Nassau is to the December 18–21 meeting between President Kennedy and Prime Minister Macmillan. Records of their conversations in Department of State, Conference Files: Lot 65 D 533, CF 2209, do not reveal any discussion of this subject. Documentation on the Nassau meeting is in volume XIII, pages 1091–1123.

Bundy told Assistant Secretary Harriman in a January 16 telephone conversation that Kennedy wanted a long-range estimate on Communist China's potential military strength, especially nuclear strength, with thought given to possible U.S. responses. Harriman and Bundy agreed to set up an interdepartmental working group. (Library of Congress Manuscript Division, Harriman Papers, Kennedy–Johnson Administrations, Chronological File, Telephone Conversations)

Further documentation bearing on U.S. concern about the Chinese nuclear weapons program is included in volume VII.

### 163.  Memorandum by the Deputy Director for Intelligence (Cline)

Washington, January 14, 1963.

MEMORANDUM

Sino-Soviet Relations

1. Attached is a CIA memorandum[1] dealing with the status and implications of the Sino-Soviet dispute. The paper points out that the ideological conflict between the two Communist parties and the divergence of the national policies of the two governments are already so fundamental that, for most practical purposes, a "split" has already occurred. From the viewpoint of most of the rest of the world, the USSR and China are now two separate powers whose interests conflict on almost every major issue.

2. A formal and definitive break between Moscow and Peiping would obviously have many important advantages for the West. However, the emergence of a separate Asian Communist Bloc under the leadership of China could have grave implications for U.S. security interests in the Far East because of Peiping's militant and intense anti-Western line.

**Ray S. Cline**

---

Source: Kennedy Library, National Security Files, Countries Series, USSR. Secret.

[1] The attached CIA memorandum, OCI No. 0581/63, dated January 14, entitled "Sino-Soviet Relations at a New Crisis," is not printed.

## 164. Editorial Note

President Kennedy addressed the National Security Council at its 508th meeting on January 22, 1963. An unsigned summary of his remarks prepared by a Department of State official reads in part as follows:

"He expressed great concern about the possibility of the Chinese Communist nuclear capability. He thought a test ban agreement might produce pressure against development of such a capability. Any negotiations that can hold back the Chinese Communists are most important, he said, because they loom as our major antagonists of the late 60's and beyond." (Department of State, Central Files, 711.5/1–2263)

For text of his remarks, see volume VIII, pages 457–462.

Assistant Secretary of State for Far Eastern Affairs Harriman commented on the President's NSC statement in a January 23 letter to Kennedy. It reads in part as follows:

"To my mind, the most important matter in the interest of our security which you touched upon was the question of attempting to prevent Red China from obtaining nuclear capability, and the possibility of working with the Soviets to this end. They undoubtedly would want a similar understanding regarding West Germany.

"This matter has come up in a general way in conversations I have had with several Russians. They always indicated Kremlin concern over the remilitarization of Western Germany, and particularly over the possibility of her obtaining independent nuclear capability. In this connection, I have usually suggested that the Soviets must have similar concern regarding Red China."

After comments relating to Germany, the letter continues as follows:

"As far as China is concerned, in a conversation with one Russian representative, I asked what was the use of our coming to an agreement on a test ban without Red China. He replied that if the United States and the Soviet Union agreed, world opinion would prevent China from acting independently. The earnest manner in which he spoke gave me the impression that what the Kremlin had in mind was that with such an agreement, together we could compel China to stop nuclear development, threatening to take out the facilities if necessary. In any event, I was glad to learn that you put this subject so high on your priority list."

Harriman also wrote: "We are making progress in Taiwan in regaining our 'independence.'" He noted that Ambassador Kirk was to return to the United States for surgery, and stated, "While he is here, I hope we would have a chance to talk with you about Red China, including the future of Taiwan. The Generalissimo seems to be becoming a bit obstreperous and we need some guidance." (Library of Congress Manuscript Division, Harriman Papers, Kennedy–Johnson Administrations, Subject Files, John F. Kennedy)

## 165.  Memorandum of Conversation

Washington, February 4, 1963, 12:05–1 p.m.

PARTICIPANTS

Mr. McGeorge Bundy
Ambassador Alan G. Kirk

After the usual exchange of friendly remarks, I said that we were facing the period of spring fever, that the bellicose statements of the Gimo and others publicly announcing this was the year and that they were ready to go, time was ripe, now or never; and that we knew pretty well what was going on in terms of building LCMs, training parachutists to form an airborne division, etc.

The Embassy plus AID, MAAG and MAP, plus the service attachés, plus Taiwan Defense Command (TDC) ought to warn us of impending unilateral action in forces, but I said it is possible for the Chinese to make a quick airlift employing all their available C–46's, C–47's, etc., lifting 5 and 10 thousand men. This kind of force could take off in the dark or early dawn. We would have considerable trouble in detecting it and certainly in stopping it.

While the Gimo protests that he would never violate the terms of the Mutual Defense Treaty, that he was a man of honor, that he resented the Ambassador referring to that Treaty every time (three times) I saw him, yet we are all uneasy. In fact, the Gimo sent a message by Admiral Felt to the effect that President Kennedy should be informed that the Gimo would never violate his word, etc. etc. (I was informed of this after the event.) This poses some problems about the propriety of military and other personalities allowing themselves to be drawn into conversations by the Gimo on political matters. After all the American Ambassador is the channel for such things, and military and others should not allow themselves to be trapped in any such discussions nor serve as a medium of transmission of messages indirectly to the President of the United States. In fact, Mr. Bundy and I discussed how to deal with the paper that Admiral Felt was given at the airport in Taipei, which was the Chinese interpreter's paper as to what the Gimo had said to Admiral Felt.[1] This requires some careful thought as to exactly what should be done by

---

Source: Library of Congress Manuscript Division, Harriman Papers, Kennedy–Johnson Administrations, Subject Files, Kirk, Alan G. Secret; Limit Distribution. Drafted by Kirk.

[1] Reference is apparently to the Chinese record of a January 15 conversation between Admiral Felt and President Chiang, filed as an attachment to a January 30 memorandum from Forrestal to Harriman, which states that Bundy had given it to him on January 29 after talking to Felt. (Ibid., Michael V. Forrestal)

Washington, whether to ignore it or send out word that no such type of messages should be accepted for transmission behind the back of the United States Ambassador. (This is a bit delicate, i.e., do we do it through the Department of Defense or do we do it through the Chinese Ambassador or directly to the Gimo via the Chargé?)

Regarding Vice Admiral Melson's visit on the day after my own departure (January 19),[2] it seems to me this was not wholly incorrect as after all Vice Admiral Melson was on the Blue Lion Committee and I must assume, as the cable shows, the meeting was an elaboration of my own report of my talk with the Gimo on the 16th.[3] The important item in this conversation of Admiral Melson's was point no. 6, i.e., that there would be no breach of the Treaty if the Chinese Government decided to land two divisions on the mainland to gain a foothold.[4] The argument was that it was a "sovereign right" on their part and not anything to do with the United States, that the United States would not be involved. It does, however, pose the serious question of what is to happen if those divisions get in trouble and have to be rescued. Mr. Bundy agreed that it poses a serious problem and how to stop a large operation of this kind was difficult. A direct warning not to do such a thing in advance might be ignored or might be hard to deliver in person to the Gimo.[5] On the other hand, it would not be unreasonable to assume the Chinese Communists

---

[2] Melson's conversation of January 19 with Chiang, with no one else present except a Chinese interpreter, was reported in a message that Clough sent to Harriman on January 21 [text not declassified], filed as an attachment to a January 21 memorandum from William E. Colby of the Central Intelligence Agency to Forrestal. (Kennedy Library, National Security Files, Countries Series, China) See the Supplement.

[3] According to a memorandum of the conversation that Clough transmitted with a January 23 letter to Harriman, Kirk discussed with Chiang the work of the Joint U.S.-GRC committee to study GRC capabilities for a landing on the mainland (Blue Lion Committee), which he and Chiang had agreed on September 6, 1962 (see Document 151), to establish. (Library of Congress Manuscript Division, Harriman Papers, Kennedy–Johnson Administrations, Subject Files, Kirk, Alan G.)

[4] Clough's January 21 message to Harriman, cited in footnote 2 above, reported that Chiang had given Melson an unsigned paper entitled "Important Principles Guiding the Landing of Chinese Government Forces on the Mainland" with six points. The first four points concerned the size of forces to be landed and the area where landings might be made. Point 5 stated that the United States should not be involved. Point 6 reads as follows:

"This kind of military action is China's domestic affair, and is the exercise of her sovereign right as an independent nation, and as such it has absolutely nothing to do with any other country."

[5] Clough's January 21 message to Harriman, cited in footnote 2 above, stated that he was to meet with Shen the next day and intended to state that "any action of the character contemplated in Chiang's paper must be a matter of joint agreement as provided by treaty." Harriman replied in a January 21 message, filed with Clough's, concurring in Clough's proposed statement, authorizing him to state that he was acting under instructions, and adding that he should make it clear that the United States would not agree to a modification of the Treaty and exchange of notes. See the Supplement. No record has been found of Clough's January 22 meeting with Shen, but he evidently discussed Point 6 with him. A February 15 letter from Clough to Kirk states that he had heard nothing further from Shen about Point 6. (Department of State, FE/EA Files: Lot 66 D 224, R.C., ORG 1)

might use air attack either to bomb China troops coming by sea or to bomb the port of embarkation and airfield on Taiwan. The question then arises: should the 7th Fleet come to the succor of the Chinese Nationalists or the defense of Taiwan itself? Possibly the ChiComs would refrain from overt attack on Taiwan, the Penghus, or the Offshore Islands in order not to embroil the United States.

Nevertheless, the U.S. Government must have some plan as to what is to be done on our part in the event the Gimo exercises "sovereign rights" and does something of this kind to our definite discomfiture.

In this connection, we then discussed the delivery of the C–123's and mentioned the hassle on the alleged bad faith of the United States in not making all five of them available on Taiwan *now*.[6] My position was that the first two should be delivered when they are completely prepared but I was strongly against sending the other three out this spring or summer. Were all five to be on Taiwan, it seems to me a definite risk that they would be employed for large drops with or without our concurrence. If "large drops" were made somewhere inland carrying between two and three hundred Chinese troops, to seize a town or an area disaffected, and then get into trouble, the Gimo would want to go and bail them out willy-nilly. Here again we are in trouble. Consequently, Mr. Bundy and I felt it would be better to give them the two C–123's as soon as fully ready but not to send the other three until after next fall after the summer period of tension has passed. While we both knew that the other three 123's might be employed for different types of operations elsewhere, my feeling was they must stay outside the control of the Gimo, i.e., at Okinawa or possibly Clark Field.

I explained that I was under constant pressure to agree that certain things could be done by the Gimo with his own money from his special preparedness tax. Some of these things did not involve the United States. My position had been consistently that use of these sums to buy equipment in other areas used up the resources of foreign exchange, were definitely inflationary to the economy of the Island, and objectionable from many points of view. Here I remarked that it should be remembered that the Vice President, Mr. Chen Cheng, had assured me that special preparedness tax would expire 30 June 1963, and would not be renewed.

We talked about the success of my country team, which I explained was due to the caliber of U.S. military or civil people in charge. They were harmonious and outstanding, we shared our points of view, and worked together shoulder to shoulder. All these men understand they are working for the President of the United States and not for the President of China.

---

[6] Kirk discussed the C–123's with Shen on January 10 in the conversation partially reported in Document 161. That portion of the discussion is recorded in a memorandum of conversation dated January 31 and transmitted in a letter of that date from Clough to Harriman. (Department of State, Central Files, 611.93/1–3163)

## 166.  Memorandum of Conversation

Washington, February 4, 1963, 4:35–5:05 p.m.

PARTICIPANTS

The President
Ambassador Alan G. Kirk

After kind inquiries on the part of the President about my health, I said at once to him that I was in trouble this spring and summer and I was afraid he might be in trouble too; that the spring fever trouble was on, and the Gimo, now 76, having recovered from an operation similar to my own, having promised the people he would return to the mainland sooner or later, felt that now he must go. The Gimo speaks of the morale of his troops and the necessity of not keeping everybody at fever pitch too long. Then I explained that the gist of our study of the Chinese military plan for the invasion of the Mainland had been given to the Gimo by me on January 16. He had insufficient attack force for sea lift, air cover, supply and everything that went to make an invasion of a continent possible. I said further that from high sources we knew the Chinese military and other authorities were counting on dragging the United States into the party. The President then asked if they got ashore, could they stick? And I said, no, not without our help. He asked if the recent teams had been successful and I said all nine had been captured. They had lasted 7 to 10 days, that the Peiping Government had accused the United States of fostering the whole operation, that of course the equipment captured with the team was made in the United States and such was being exploited to our disadvantage.

I explained in connection with the Blue Lion study that I had said to the Gimo that 20 years had elapsed since the amphibious operations of the last war and that one must be prepared for different kinds of tactics now. The Gimo had agreed but said the ChiComs were not up-to-date in such matters. Whereupon the President questioned what the Gimo thought about India. Were the ChiComs ok? I replied the Gimo had said it was not the question of ChiCom superiority, the Indians were no good whatever.

We then touched on the C–123's and I said only two should go now, that despite the hassle over matters of good faith or not good faith, that is what we said we would give and that is all we will give. That I was opposed to sending five to Taiwan as the ChiNats would then try to make

---

Source: Library of Congress Manuscript Division, Harriman Papers, Kennedy–Johnson Administrations, Subject Files, Kirk, Alan G. Secret; Limit Distribution. Drafted by Kirk. The meeting was held at the White House.

a large drop of 250 to 300 men and then we would have to send a fire rescue party to get them out. The President said, how many men can they take? The Chinese would pack from 250 to 300 men in them willy-nilly. Again I reiterated that the Gimo and his cohorts would expect the United States to come to the rescue and we would then be dragged in whether we wanted to or not. Further, I said I am sure that the Gimo et al. based everything on dragging us in.

I touched briefly upon our experience with the Gimo as the war in Asia drew to a close, when he flatly rejected our advice not to attack the ChiComs north of the Yellow River nor pursue them westward. The Gimo tried to regain Manchuria and lost his armies and their equipment. He went westward and again met disaster. He misgoverned the area south of the Yangtze and was detested by the local Chinese. He complained the U.S. let him down, and I felt if he ever did get back on the Mainland he would be ungrateful to the United States, and be very difficult to handle.

I told the President I had difficulty in seeing the Gimo, that he fobbed me off, felt that I did not understand the Chinese, and that I always brought up the Treaty. I further said that visitors were occasionally given messages to convey to President Kennedy in indirect means of a type that really should be sent through the U.S. Ambassador. It showed the Gimo could not get very far with me and he tried other and devious means of getting around, an old Chinese trick.

At the end I pointed out we had a difficult personality in the Gimo, age, health, glory, obstinate, etc. The President was good enough to say he had excellent reports about the mission and was gratified. I replied that my people all understood they were working for the President of the United States and nobody else. The President asked if I liked living conditions in Taiwan and I said not very much. That I wanted to get back as soon as I could, that I wanted to be there before the spring fever advanced; that I would be ambulatory after a little while and would be available if he wanted to send anyone out to Bethesda to talk with me.

## 167.    Letter From President Kennedy to President Chiang

Washington, February 15, 1963.

DEAR MR. PRESIDENT: Ambassador Kirk has just returned to Washington and has told me about a misunderstanding which he feels has needlessly complicated the channels of communication between our Governments. In these critical times, I feel strongly that it is of the utmost importance that these channels remain as clear as humanly possible. I have made a special effort in my Administration to insure that my Government speaks with one voice. Consequently, where it appears that there has been a failure of understanding, I am most anxious to take the measures necessary to overcome it.

Since Ambassador Kirk will be confined for a while in the hospital, I have directed [1-1/2 *lines of source text not declassified*] to discuss a proposal[1] with your representative which I hope will satisfy the [*less than 1 line of source text not declassified*] needs of both our Governments. Later, Ambassador Kirk will return to his post in Taipei, and I hope you will be able to explore with him at some length and in some detail the larger issues which concern us both.

I know you feel as I do that between nations with such a historic friendship as ours, the greatest good is to be obtained through a frank and continuous discussion of common problems. Please consider that Ambassador Kirk is my personal representative in the most intimate sense and is unusually well equipped to carry on a frank exchange of views on my behalf.

I was especially happy to learn from Ambassador Kirk that you have fully regained your health and strength after your illness of last year.

Pending Ambassador Kirk's return to Taipei, do not hesitate to write me your thoughts through our Chargé, Mr. Clough, to whom I am entrusting the delivery of this letter.

Sincerely,

**John Kennedy**

---

Source: Department of State, Presidential Correspondence: Lot 66 D 204, Kennedy/Johnson Correspondence with Chinese Officials. Secret. Filed with a covering note from Bundy to Brubeck requesting that it be shown to Yager before its transmittal by pouch. Transmitted to Taipei by pouch on February 15.

[1] According to a March 5 memorandum [*text not declassified*] the proposal [*text not declassified*] reported on March 1 that he had discussed it with Chiang Ching-kuo on February 28. The memorandum indicates that the proposal was to send the C–123 planes at issue to Taiwan and that they would remain under U.S. control and ownership for use in South Vietnam with GRC crews; they would be used in mainland operations only in case of joint agreement. (Kennedy Library, National Security Files, Countries Series, China) The February 14 memorandum and the March 1 report have not been found.

## 168.    Telegram From the Embassy in Poland to the Department of State

Warsaw, February 20, 1963, 6 p.m.

1299. Cabot–Wang talks. 114th meeting.[1] 2 hours 10 minutes. Deptel 967.[2]

1. Wang opened saying since last meeting USG had increased tension in Taiwan Straits area and furthered hostile acts in Asia as whole. Serious warnings 222 through 230 issued and special emphasis given activities destroyer *Edgar Holm* (?) off Fukien and Kwang Tung coasts and its entry into territorial waters east of Leichou Peninsula at 0705 on December 19. Wang termed this outrageous provocation and demanded our side put an end to such.

2. He then accused us of jointly planning and organizing recent "Chiang gang" activities against Mainland. Said they had abundant evidence establish our complicity these matters. Complained we had set up guerrilla section under MAAG for such purposes. Also complained of "blue sky" joint maneuvers and of increased aid in form F104Gs and new U–2 planes despite President's earlier saying we had no plans to sell further U–2s.

3. Wang made quite a point of fact ChiComs would hold USG exclusively answerable for Chiang harassments large or small now or in the future. Also claimed we were trying to turn Sino-Indian dispute into another front against China and at same time were urging Japan to join with South Korea in setting up Northeast Asia military bloc to serve our purposes in preparing for nuclear war.

4. I said I had to disagree with practically everything Wang had said. Said I would report warnings as usual (assume Department has them already) and especially the one alleged clear intrusion into territorial waters. Followed with substance paragraph two[3] reference telegram

---

Source: Department of State, Central Files, POL CHICOM–US. Confidential; Priority; Limit Distribution. Repeated to Taipei, Hong Kong, Stockholm, Moscow, and Geneva. Received at 5:46 a.m. on February 21.

[1] Cabot commented and sent recommendations in telegram 1303, February 21, which referred to the conversation as "another exercise in futility." He sent a detailed, apparently verbatim report of the meeting in airgram A–668, February 22. (Both ibid.)

[2] Telegram 967, February 14, transmitted guidance for the meeting. (Ibid.)

[3] Paragraph 2 of telegram 967 instructed Cabot to reject the charges of U.S. air and sea intrusions which Wang had made at the last meeting, noting that the United States did not recognize the Chinese claim to the Paracel Islands and that two of the islands cited by Wang were not under the control of his side.

on alleged intrusions, then substance paragraphs 1,[4] 3[5] and 4[6] reference telegram on Mainland operations, Laos and prisoners.

5. Wang reiterated claim CPR sovereignty Paracels and repeated accusation US participation in recruiting, training, and dispatch of agents to Mainland. Said our accusation continued activity in Laos was pure fabrication. Said US had not yet withdrawn all its military forces from Laos and it is US which should be condemned for maintaining troops there. Said illegal persecution by India of Chinese nationals was not at all to be compared with China's retention of mere handful of American "criminals". Wang then warned US against sending aid to India saying this would prove not to be in our interest.

6. I said we could not accept Wang's seeming view our ships and planes do not have right be on high seas in neighboring waters to Chinese territorial waters. I mentioned Wang's complaining that US ship movements in that area were not "normal." I said I thought we could both agree on fact that conditions in that area were not normal either but those conditions have to be met. I pointed out several governments claim Paracels. As for Laos we had scrupulously observed all provisions Geneva agreements and regretted ICC had been obstructed from observing activities in Communist-controlled areas. Said we could not accept warning about giving aid to India. US will consult its own interests in this matter. I then covered newsmen subject in accordance reference telegram.

7. Wang repeated since CPR regarded Chiang clique as no government at all but puppet taking refuge behind US bayonets, CPR would hold USG exclusively responsible for attacks against Mainland on Chiang's part whether large or small. Concluded by saying we had obstructed agreement re newsmen by refusing accept their reasonable proposal of September 6, 1960, designed to seek eliminate estrangement between two governments by settling peacefully subject of withdrawal

---

[4] Paragraph 1 instructed Cabot to reply to the anticipated charges of U.S. responsibility for GRC commando operations by stating that the United States was not involved in any such operations. It further stated:

"FYI: Omit reference our proposal for renunciation force and related assurances. We wish to see if Wang brings up. If he specifically asks whether our position unchanged, direct reply to mutual renunciation force, but avoid reiteration of assurances given at June 23, 1962 meeting."

[5] Paragraph 3 instructed Cabot to tell Wang that the United States had received reliable reports that Wang's side had been sending arms and ammunition to Pathet Lao forces and that Chinese workmen building roads from Yunnan into Laos were working under the supervision of armed Chinese military engineers, although foreign troops were banned from Laos under the 14-nation Geneva agreements.

[6] Paragraph 4 pointed out that the Agreed Announcement of September 10, 1955, had provided that civilians of both sides who desired to return to their own countries could do so and stated that if some of the Chinese listed by Wang had not returned, it was not because of any U.S. obstruction.

all US armed forces from Taiwan area. I said we sincerely wanted news-men exchange but could not be expected to accept conditions his side try-ing to impose. Having agreed we had both made our points of differences quite clear to the other and further elaboration not necessary now, agreed meet again April 17.

Cabot

## 169.  Draft Memorandum From the Ambassador at Large (Thompson) to Secretary of State Rusk

Washington, February 26, 1963.

SUBJECT

Policy re treatment of Sino-Soviet conflict

I have reviewed our policy on treatment of the Sino-Soviet conflict by United States officials which is contained in Circular Airgram 5667, November 22, 1962.[1] This airgram was not sent to me for clearance, and I had not previously seen it. There are some statements in it with which I would disagree, but doubt that these are serious enough to attempt to clear a revision.

There are several points to which I draw your attention, however, since they bear on the problem of the extent to which United States offi-cials should initiate public discussions of this problem. For example, on

---

Source: Department of State, Central Files, POL 1 CHICOM–USSR. Confidential. The memorandum was routed through Harriman, Tyler, and McGhee. A covering note to them reads: "To save time, I put down my own thoughts on this, but if you would rather have a meeting and work out an agreed paper, I would be glad to do so." Harriman returned it with a brief memorandum of March 1 agreeing that the circular should have been cleared with Thompson and stating there seemed to be no need for a meeting. Thompson appar-ently did not pursue the matter further.

[1] The airgram, sent to all U.S. missions, stated that official treatment of the Sino-Soviet conflict should "(a) insure world opinion aware inconsistency relations communist countries and opportunities this offers West (b) furnish rationale for policy changes US may find desirable in view dispute (c) deny communists monopoly in interpreting their problems and (d) counter communist efforts paper over seriousness differences and there-fore maintain fiction of non-existent monolithic unity." It cautioned against exaggerating the dispute's impact on cold war problems or suggesting that U.S. interests were better served by one party than the other. (Ibid., 661.93/11–2262)

page three of the airgram, it is stated "A general understanding of what is taking place in the communist world would serve both to give impetus to the fragmentation of the communist movement and to diminish the effectiveness of the communist appeal. Accurate publicity given the dispute would exacerbate problems of discipline in the world communist movement and in individual parties." My own view is that strong emphasis by United States officials tends to increase the pressure of the other communist parties upon the Soviets and Chinese to patch up the quarrel and get together. It seems to me there has been ample publicity in the press about this problem.

The airgram states that officials should avoid any suggestion that the United States is taking sides in the dispute. While I think this is debatable in view of the fact that the Chinese are advocating a more militant, aggressive policy against the West, and the United States in particular, the airgram, in fact, appears to be taking the Chinese side, particularly in the *Major Points of Stress*, beginning at the bottom of page four. Point one, in particular, states that the great issue in the conflict is the question of Moscow's authority over the communist camp. While it is scarcely our business to assess blame, we surely should not come down on the side of the Chinese who advocate a policy much more dangerous for us, at least in the short run, than that advocated by the Soviets.

The paper also omits any mention of some of the causes of conflict, such as Soviet concern over the Chinese population explosion, psychological antipathy, etc.

In any event, all I would suggest for the present is that you issue a directive to Mr. Manning, a draft of which is attached,[2] that in approving speeches, he keep in mind the inadvisability of giving the impression that we are embarking on a special campaign to exploit the conflict.[3]

---

[2] Not found. Harriman's memorandum cited in the source note above concurred with his proposed directive, and an unsigned note attached to the source text indicates that it was sent to Manning.

[3] A note on the source text, apparently from a member of Thompson's staff, states that an airgram suggesting the need for some caution in public statements on the subject was under preparation. Reference is apparently to CA 9675, March 7. (Ibid., POL CHICOM–USSR)

### 170. Message From the Chargé in the Republic of China (Clough) to the Assistant Secretary of State for Far Eastern Affairs (Harriman)

Taipei, March 2, 1963.

[document number not declassified] Reference: [document number not declassified].[1] Pass following to Dept of State for Governor Harriman from Clough:

1. President's letter[2] and proposal concerning C–123's appear to have been received very well by President Chiang and Chiang Ching-kuo. [less than 1 line of source text not declassified] I believe ill-feeling aroused by C–123 issue has been substantially removed and that arrangements for use of three of these aircraft in Vietnam can be made without too much difficulty.

2. It seems to me quite clear that in Chiang's feeler regarding treaty[3] he referred to September conversation with Ambassador,[4] at which Chiang pled for U.S. devise some means by which he could fulfill his obligation to rescue Chinese on mainland without involving U.S. or violating his treaty obligations. We have had other recent indications that Chiang feels frustrated by limitations placed on him by 1954 exchange of notes and is groping for means to gain greater freedom of action. To what extent he really hopes to get greater freedom of action and to what extent his objective is a public posture of greater freedom of action is unclear. What he seems to be seeking is formula by which U.S. would agree in advance, or perhaps only appear to agree in advance, not to oppose his taking armed action against mainland and once GRC action was underway, to publicly declare a hands-off policy and disclaim any responsibility for it.

3. It is clearly not in U.S. interest under present circumstances to give Chiang greater freedom of action. Consequently, believe we should avoid getting into discussion of subject with him if possible, as outcome could only be unfavorable to his hopes and likely to result in intensifying

---

Source: Kennedy Library, National Security Files, Countries Series, China, Cables. Secret; Priority. The message was transmitted in telegram [document number and text not declassified]. Filed with a covering memorandum of March 11 from Forrestal to Bundy.

[1] Not printed.

[2] Document 167. No record has been found indicating when Clough gave it to Chiang.

[3] The memorandum [text not declassified] in footnote 1, Document 167, quotes an oral message from Chiang Kai-shek that Chiang Ching-kuo had given [text not declassified] on March 1. It reads in part as follows: "The President again wished to give assurances that he had no intention of shirking on the treaty and related agreements but felt something had to be done to solve the mainland problem within the framework of the treaty."

[4] See Document 151.

his feeling of frustration. Yes, I think it important to find means of exploring his purposes more deeply.

4.  Recommend, therefore [*less than 1 line of source text not declassified*] be instructed respond to Ching-kuo as follows on this point: Questions relating to treaty should, of course, be taken up through diplomatic rather than intelligence channels. However, Ambassador is away and it would be undesirable in any case put forward any formal proposal which Washington could not accept. Some informal discussion seems called for, as we do not understand why existing treaty and exchange of notes do not provide acceptable framework for action against mainland if circumstances should permit. Perhaps Ching-kuo or Foreign Minister could give Chargé a more detailed explanation of President Chiang's thinking.

5.  If Chiang responds to foregoing suggestion it would not only provide opportunity to explore further his thinking but also to repeat U.S. position regarding treaty and exchange of notes, without the risk to Chiang's face inherent in confrontation between Chiang and Ambassador.[5] (End of message)

---

[5] A March 6 message from Harriman to Clough, attached to the source text, agreed that Chiang should not be given greater freedom of action, concurred in the suggested response to Chiang Ching-kuo, and stated that if the proposed talks with Chiang Ching-kuo or the Foreign Minister took place, Clough should discourage any GRC thought of requesting revision of the treaty or related agreements. No record of [*text not declassified*] response to Chiang Ching-kuo been found. Clough reported subsequent meetings with Shen, and Chiang Ching-kuo which touched on related subjects in letters of May 29 and June 24 to Hilsman. (Department of State, Central Files, POL 1 CHICOM–US) Clough's May 29 letter to Hilsman is in the Supplement.

---

## 171.  Editorial Note

Telegram 616 to Taipei, March 22, 1963, informed the Embassy that President Kennedy was considering a brief trip to the Western Pacific in October, including a 1-day visit to Taiwan. It instructed Chargé d'Affaires Ralph Clough to inquire whether such a visit would be convenient. The fact that the President was considering it was not to be made public, since the trip was necessarily contingent on his other responsibilities. (Department of State, Central Files, POL 7 US/KENNEDY) Telegram 724 from Taipei, March 26, reported that Clough had informed Foreign Minister Shen Chang-huan, and telegram 727, March 28, reported that

President Chiang had asked Shen to extend a warm welcome to President Kennedy on his behalf. (Ibid.) Telegram 867 from Taipei, June 17, transmitted a letter of invitation from Chiang to Kennedy. (Ibid., Presidential Correspondence: Lot 66 D 204, Chinese Officials' Correspondence with Kennedy/Johnson)

Documentation concerning planning for the contemplated trip to Asia is in the Kennedy Library, National Security Files, Trip Series, President's Proposed Far East Trip. A memorandum of a November 19 meeting among Kennedy, Assistant Secretary Hilsman, and other officials and a memorandum of the same date by Hilsman indicate that Kennedy was still thinking of going to Asia, including Taiwan, in the spring of 1964, although he thought he might limit the trip to Japan and perhaps Korea in case of unfavorable developments in Indonesia. (Department of State, FE Files: Lot 65 D 6, POL 7, Visits and Mtgs, Oct.–Dec. 1963)

---

## 172.  Memorandum From the Ambassador to the Republic of China (Kirk) to President Kennedy

Washington, March 29, 1963.

SUBJECT

Decisions Facing United States vis-à-vis Chiang Kai-shek

1.  The basic situation as of now seems to require decisions on our part as to what we are going to do in the event of:

a.  A minor harassing invasion of the Mainland,

b.  Build up of minor forces successfully landed on the Mainland,

c.  Chinese attempts to succor or relieve beleaguered forces from a. and b. above, by large-scale operations.

2.  The fundamental questions confronting the United States Government are:

a.  Whether the retention of the island of Taiwan in friendly hands is vital to the interests of the United States in the Western Pacific and

---

Source: Kennedy Library, President's Office Files, China Security, 1962–63. Top Secret. Filed as an attachment to a note of April 1 from Forrestal to Kennedy which calls it Kirk's "swan song." Because of illness, Kirk did not return to Taipei.

b.  How and when are we going to make it clear to President Chiang that a feeble attempt to assault the Mainland, with the intention of involving the United States Government in a first-class war with the Chi-Coms, cannot and will not be tolerated.

3. a. It would appear that the decision as to whether or not Taiwan is "vital" to our interests needs to be reviewed. This would require re-examination and a decision taken at the highest level.

b.  The United States is committed, of course, to the Mutual Defense Treaty of 1954 together with its accompanying Exchange of Notes. The GRC in turn is committed thereby not to use force against the Mainland without our "agreement." This obligation the Generalissimo is currently trying to escape.

4.  A major revolt on the Mainland against the ChiCom authorities of Peking of real magnitude may warrant military action by the United States Government to overthrow Communism on the Mainland of China. Decision in this matter would require very complete intelligence as to what was happening on the Mainland. We must be aware from the "Tibetan Papers" that sharp unrest did occur in north China (Honan) in 1960. Apparently at the time it was not known to our own Government or to the Government of Chiang Kai-shek. Despite contrary claims, it is my opinion intelligence sources from the Mainland of China are very inadequate. In the major Communist states, such as the Soviet Union, to acquire accurate information of disorders, discontent, revolt, revolution, etc., has been found most difficult if not impossible. It should be further noted that as of now no major political character of the ChiCom Party has defected. Similarly no highly placed officer in the ChiCom armed forces has defected. Consequently claims made by the Generalissimo and others of his Government that widespread discontent does exist must be looked at askance.

5.  On the other hand, there is a theory expressed from time to time by the Minister of National Defense, Mr. Yu Ta-wei, as well as General Chiang Ching-kuo, to the effect that any landing anywhere would produce a "detonation" resulting in widespread acclaim and adhesion to the forces of Nationalist China which would result in overthrow of the government of Peking. With this point of view it is hard to agree. The masses of the people in China are lacking in food, clothing, weapons, cohesion and leaders. Invading forces would be obliged to come equipped to supply these missing resources on a vast scale in order for their presence to generate widespread uprising of the people, assuming "the masses" had the will to revolt.

6.  In the military sphere we know from studies made by "Blue Lion" and other papers submitted by Embassy Taipei that the Chinese military regime is so deficient in the elements necessary for a successful invasion of a continent as to warrant grave skepticism on our part of any

success. Probably the greatest handicap to a successful landing on the Continent would be the deficiency of air power. It is well-known that the Allied invasion of Normandy in 1944 with the subsequent outrunning of the German forces in Western Europe had the paramount advantage of complete control of the air. In addition, of course, masses of artillery, tanks, guns, manpower and supplies of all kinds enabled the Allies to create a juggernaut which overran the Germans, and under the protection of our own formidable air umbrella. Besides all the above, the French Resistance, properly equipped, organized and instructed, played a most important part (blowing bridges, railroad tracks, etc.).

7. The United States assistance to Chinese military and economic sectors has been restricted to war matériel designed for defense and not for offense. The Chinese Air Force has no long-range bombers. Their fighters are modern but short-ranged. Their air-lift capacity is very limited, and their supplies of bombs, shells and ammunition have been furnished for defense rather than offense.

8. It is true that the Chinese Air Force demonstrated a marked superiority over the ChiCom Air Force in the battle of 1958 for the Off-shore Islands, and this was due more to their tactical skill than to their use of sidewinder missiles supplied by the United States Air Force. On the other hand, one must assume that the ChiCom Air Force is now equipped with later-type MIG fighters and would have learned in these past 4-1/2 years to improve their own tactics. Thus, an air battle over the coast of Mainland China would result in a battle of attrition in which the Chinese Air Force would be gradually whittled down. The ChiCom air bases withdrawn some distance from the coastline would now be more difficult to attack by the Chinese Air Force.

9. While some 20 years have elapsed since the Allied major amphibious landings of World War II and it may be presumed that the technique of such operations now would be different, yet it still appears that the sea-lift for troops, replacements, ammunition, etc., would still be needed in this or any Mainland invasion. Here again the Chinese military machine has but meager resources. Embassy Taipei has reported recently on the numbers of landing craft of all types plus merchant shipping under Chinese Government control plus stocks stored on Taiwan. It is at once obvious that the scale of a major invasion of a continent requires vastly more than now in the hands of the Generalissimo.

10. The Chinese Navy is woefully deficient in gunfire capacity to cover the landing as well as to protect replacement convoys.

11. The latest estimate from Embassy Taipei would indicate a sea-lift of about 32,000 troops. An air-lift of 5–10,000 may also be possible. In each of these cases it should be realized that for a short haul across the Strait of Formosa the Chinese could readily overload shipping and aircraft beyond the standards used by the Western Allies in World War II.

12. In the papers thus far produced on the subject of Chinese capabilities very little mention is made of the ChiComs' reactions. We do know from the defector [*less than 1 line of source text not declassified*] that in the summer of 1962 there were two schools of thought in ChiCom military circles. The first was to crush the attempted invasion at the shoreline and the second was to allow the invasion force to make some penetration inland in order to destroy or capture the invaders plus all their accompanying equipment.

13. On the other hand, it seems most unlikely that, were the invading forces to make any significant progress inland, the ChiComs would not resort to the normal offensive strategy of attacking the bases on Taiwan from which these forces were supplied, or attacking the air fields used by the Chinese Air Force.

14. This does not necessarily mean an invasion of Taiwan. The government at Peking might be loath to undertake any operations against Taiwan which would result in US intervention. Nevertheless, such a possibility should not be overlooked and ChiCom bombing squadrons should be expected to make attacks by day or night on these staging areas or air fields whose precise locations are undoubtedly known to the Peking military authorities.

15. Here the question arises of what the United States Government would feel called upon to do. It might be the Government of Peking would disclaim any intent to invade the island of Taiwan, but bombing of such character would undoubtedly result in considerable damage to installations on the island of Taiwan plus the people living there. American personnel would not escape serious punishment. Casualties to our own people would be expected to produce a sharp reaction in the United States—not only on the part of the Government but of the people and of the Congress. Retaliation on our part by our armed forces could scarcely avoid intrusions over the Mainland territory of Communist China. Such hostile action by United States forces would undoubtedly produce a reaction on the part of the Government of Peking. Thus, open warfare between the United States Government and the Government of Peking would eventuate. Consequently there arises the very delicate question as to whether such would not be the opening phase of World War III—a disaster for the world.

16. From this estimate it will be seen that I myself am strongly opposed to giving President Chiang Kai-shek any leeway whatsoever in his attempt to circumvent his Treaty with the United States.

a. I further believe that it is necessary that we take steps now to make it clear to Chiang Kai-shek that we will have no part of this.

b. I believe we might properly make some public statements in the near future that we do not intend to recede from our declared position that we will defend Taiwan but we will not countenance aggression initiated by the Chinese Government now on Taiwan. I believe such a step would be an acceptable method lying between the (a) stern warning not to do it and given on a short notice or (b) using US military forces to intervene once an invasion had been started by the Gimo.

I consider it most inadvisable to allow the Generalissimo to have any private way of conveying to the United States Government that he is going to take any measures of an aggressive nature with or without our sanction.

c.  I disagree with the point of view held by President Chiang Kai-shek that Soviet Russia would not intervene to sustain a Communist regime in China. I myself was US Ambassador to the USSR when the Sino-Soviet Treaty of 14 February 1950[1] was signed; and its Article I is highly pertinent. Khrushchev could not afford a different type of government on Mainland China, even if only in the areas south of the Yangtze River. While a change in the personalities of the governing authorities in Peking might be welcomed in Moscow, a complete overthrow of Communist domination would be intolerable—especially if the United States shared therein.

d.  I find it impossible to believe a Chinese invasion of the Mainland could now occur without the whole world—friend and foe alike—blaming the United States for allowing the Sino-American Defense Pact to be violated. I see no way in which that Treaty can be circumvented; short of its denunciation or public abrogation, the Treaty stands before our Allies, all neutral nations, and all of the Communist bloc as a solemn pledge of the United States. To condone or to camouflage the evasion of its articles would impugn our good faith, our honor, and our self-respect. Furthermore, we should be well aware of our inability to reason with General Chiang Kai-shek in the 1944–49 period, when he lost the Mainland.

**Alan G. Kirk**

---

[1] Reference is to the treaty of friendship, alliance, and mutual assistance signed at Moscow on that date. For text, see UNTS 226:5; also printed in *American Foreign Policy: Basic Documents, 1950–1955*, pp. 2463–2465.

### 173.    Letter From President Kennedy to President Chiang

Washington, April 11, 1963.

DEAR MR. PRESIDENT: I have read your letter of March fifteenth[1] with great interest. I appreciate your full and frank expression of your views on problems of deep concern to both of our countries. I know that you would want me to respond with equal candor.

China occupies a special place in the hearts of the American people. No news could give Americans greater joy than to learn that, after thirteen long years of suffering, the people of mainland China have freed themselves from Communist oppression. Our hopes for the early liberation of the Chinese people, however, cannot be permitted to cloud our judgment of what is possible or to lead us into ill-considered actions that would not work, would end only in disaster for you and might precipitate a situation that neither of us want.

Despite the arguments set forth so cogently in your letter, I do not believe that we possess sufficient information to make firm judgments on vital questions such as the will and ability of the Chinese people to rise up successfully against their Communist masters. Also, I do not see how, given the long and close association of our two Governments and the Treaty and related agreements which bind us, the United States Government could be absolved from responsibility for actions which your Government might take against the Communist-held mainland.

Under these circumstances, the United States Government must exercise care in concerting with your Government on a program of action against the Chinese Communists. We can and will continue to work closely with you in checking the expansion of Chinese Communist political and diplomatic influence and in supporting the international position and influence of the Republic of China. We can and will continue to

---

Source: Department of State, Presidential Correspondence: Lot 66 D 204, Chinese Officials Correspondence with Kennedy/Johnson. Top Secret; Eyes Only. Drafted by Yager. The draft was sent to Bundy with a covering memorandum of April 4 from Acting Department of State Executive Secretary William B. Connett, Jr., stating that it reflected an April 3 discussion in Bundy's office. (Ibid.) The letter was transmitted in telegram 659 to Taipei, April 12, which stated that a parallel message from McCone to Chiang Ching-kuo was being sent [text not declassified]. (Department of State, Central Files, POL 15–1 US/ KENNEDY) Clough reported in telegram 764, April 18, that both letters were delivered that day. (Ibid.) A draft message from McCone to Chiang Ching-kuo is in the Kennedy Library, National Security Files, Countries Series, China Subjects, Chiang Kai-shek Correspondence.

[1] Chiang's letter argued that growing unrest on the mainland and the deepening rift between Mao and Khrushchev created an unprecedented opportunity and urged consultation on a plan to give his government "adequate support for the deliverance of our compatriots from despotic rule." (Department of State, Presidential Correspondence: Lot 66 D 204, Chinese Officials Correspondence with Kennedy/Johnson) See the Supplement.

give you needed assistance in your most important effort to create on Taiwan a model of dynamic economic development in contrast to the misery and stagnation prevailing under Communist rule on the mainland.[2] And, I need scarcely add, we will without question honor our defensive commitments under the Mutual Defense Treaty. Given our present estimate of the situation, however, we cannot acquiesce in military action against the China mainland.

It was in order to facilitate close consultations on the entire range of problems of common concern to China and the United States that I appointed a man of such unusual professional qualifications as my Ambassador in Taipei. Although regrettably Admiral Kirk will not be able to return to his post for reasons of health, I have asked another outstanding Naval Officer to succeed him. I hope that you will feel free to exchange views with Admiral Wright in a spirit of utmost frankness and trust, so that we can maintain the high degree of cooperation needed to cope successfully with the problems and dangers that lie ahead. Admiral Wright enjoys my complete confidence and has direct access to me at all times on either a formal or an informal basis.

As a final personal note, I should like to say that I fully understand and appreciate your feeling of sorrow as you contemplate the bitter fate that has temporarily befallen the greater part of the Chinese nation. I also share your faith that, true to their long and glorious history, the Chinese people will one day overcome their present oppressors and take their proper leading place in the community of free nations.

With kindest regards,

Sincerely,

**John Kennedy**

---

[2] In telegram 754 from Taipei, April 15, Clough expressed concern at the lack of any reference to continued U.S. support for the GRC armed forces and commented that the implication that U.S. support might be terminated could intensify Chiang's view that he must act soon. (Department of State, Central Files, POL 15–1 US/KENNEDY) Telegram 664 to Taipei, April 15, replied that no such implication was intended, and Clough could so inform Chiang Kai-shek. (Ibid.) In telegram 764, cited in the source note above, Clough reported that he had informed Foreign Minister Shen and Chiang Ching-kuo.

## 174. Memorandum of Conversation

Washington, April 15, 1963.

SUBJECT

    Return to the Mainland

PARTICIPANTS

    General S.M. "Tiger" Wang, Chinese Delegation to the UN (Military Staff
    Committee)
    Chinese Air Attaché, Col. Hsiung-sheng Hwang
    Deputy Under Secretary, Mr. U. Alexis Johnson

General Wang, whom I have known for a long time, called on me today. He said that he had spent about 40 days in Taiwan and was extremely concerned over the attitudes that he found there on the question of the return to the mainland. He said that we should not underestimate or minimize the problem. He impliedly agreed with my observations that an attempt could only result in disaster but emphasized that the leadership on Taiwan is in an increasingly desperate frame of mind and feels that it is "this year or never", regardless of the risks. He implied that we had not been sufficiently blunt in talking with Taiwan and that, unless we were more blunt than in the past, they may misinterpret our attitude.

In reply to his direct question as to my "personal view" as to what the reaction of the United States Government would be in the event they were to seek to mount an invasion of the mainland without concurrence of the United States, I said that the reaction would be uniformly most seriously adverse. I said that we had, in our treaty with the GRC, undertaken very clear and definite obligations with respect to the defense of Taiwan, and the GRC had in turn undertaken very definite obligations with respect to us. If the GRC disregarded its reciprocal obligations it could not but call into question the validity of the obligations we had undertaken. I had Colonel Hwang translate this so that there would be no misunderstanding.

In reply to his direct question, I said that, in spite of the undoubted economic difficulties Peking was having, we had no information whatever which would indicate its hold on the mainland had weakened sufficiently to give any hope whatever that a landing by the GRC could be

Source: Department of State, Central Files, DEF CHINAT. Confidential. Drafted and approved by Johnson. Copies were sent to McGeorge Bundy, Nitze, Taylor, and McCone. (Kennedy Library, National Security Files, Countries Series, China; Washington National Records Center, RG 330, Records of the Office of the Secretary of Defense, OASD/ISA Files: FRC 67 A 4564, 092, Republic of China)

successful. I pointed out that the first indication of the weakening of Peking's hold would be the GRC ability successfully to carry out extensive intelligence operations on the mainland. He, as a soldier, well appreciated the importance of intelligence and nothing that he had said, or other information that I had, indicated any increased GRC capability in this regard. General Wang admitted that this was correct.

General Wang also said that many people and "scholars" in Taiwan were saying that the question of the GRC seeking to land on the mainland was purely an "internal matter". I said that this, of course, was also exactly what I had heard from Wang Ping-nan at Geneva for three years, and was the consistent Peking line. I said that I could not see how Taiwan could take this attitude without also reviewing whether it desired to maintain its treaty relationship with the United States. Under our present treaty, what affected the security of Taiwan affected the United States, and for Taiwan to undertake offensive operations against the mainland clearly involved the security of Taiwan. Apart from the attitude of the GRC, the security of Taiwan was of great interest to the United States and we had invested heavily in its maintenance.

In reply to General Wang's question on the outlook for military aid this next year, I pointed out the extreme resistance that aid was meeting in the Congress this year, the Clay Report,[1] and said that it seemed to me doubtful that the present level could be maintained.

While General Wang's influence is now limited, I spoke to him as I did with the hope that something of what I was saying would get back through him and/or Colonel Hwang.

---

[1] Reference is to the report of a committee chaired by General Lucius D. Clay entitled *The Scope and Distribution of United States Military and Economic Assistance Programs: Report to the President of the United States from the Committee to Strengthen the Security of the Free World, March 20, 1963* (Washington: Government Printing Office, 1963). The committee's recommendations are also printed in *American Foreign Policy: Current Documents, 1963,* pp. 1148–1163.

175.  Telegram From the Embassy in Poland to the Department of State

Warsaw, April 17, 1963, 6 p.m.

1607. Cabot–Wang Talks. 115th Meeting[1] 2 hours 20 minutes. Deptel 1245.[2]

(1) I opened with substance Deptel 1251[3] on Laos followed with *Agerholm* portion paragraph seven reference telegram,[4] and paragraph two (handling Wang letter enclosing identifying information on deportees).[5] I then reminded Wang of our interpretation agreed announcement re prisoners but added quite apart from this, would be gratifying receive word of promised review of their cases. Concluded with substance paragraph one reference telegram, giving Wang pouched materials on wrecked vessels.[6]

(2) Wang expressed appreciation for information re missing fishing boats and promised later reply concerning deportees. Added for moment Chinese nationals may still apply at Indian Embassy Washington.

(3) Wang spoke of serious warnings 231 through 239. Said our nonrecognition their sovereignty over Paracels and other islands expose US

---

Source: Department of State, Central Files, POL CHICOM–US. Confidential; Priority; Limit Distribution. Repeated to Taipei, Hong Kong, Stockholm, Moscow, and Geneva.

[1] Cabot commented on the meeting in telegram 1608, April 18. He noted that the "list of US sins re Taiwan, Mainland, Laos and Vietnam unusually long, and Wang was considerably shriller and more vehement than usual, also more mendacious." He stated that since his own initial presentation had been "relatively moderate," he subsequently "spoke rather sharply" and "having rejected Wang's warning about Laos, I gave him in turn a veiled warning." (Ibid.) He sent a detailed report of the meeting in airgram A–846, April 20. (Ibid.)

[2] Telegram 1245, April 12, provided guidance on a number of subjects. (Ibid.)

[3] Telegram 1251, April 15, provided guidance concerning Laos. (Ibid.) Telegram 1260 to Warsaw, April 16, noted a Chinese Communist statement that day charging the United States with responsibility for the current Laos crisis and instructed Cabot to make a presentation on Laos in his opening statement. (Ibid.)

[4] Paragraph 7 concerned Chinese Communist charges of U.S. intrusions since the last meeting. It stated that Wang's protest at the last meeting on the *Edgar Holme* evidently referred to the USS *Agerholm*, which at the time indicated was at least 20 miles from the nearest land.

[5] Paragraph 2 asked Cabot to raise three deportation cases with Wang, suggesting that he introduce them as coming under agenda item one, although no similar cases had been raised in that context. The cases concerned three deportable individuals who wished to go to mainland China; Cabot was to ask whether the authorities there were willing to admit them. It also suggested that he ask Wang what services if any his side currently expected the Indian Embassy in Washington to perform with regard to travel of Chinese persons, noting that this was intended as a practical inquiry, not as a needle on Sino-Indian relations.

[6] Paragraph 1 instructed Cabot to give Wang information concerning several small wrecked vessels washed ashore at Okinawa and neighboring islands in late January and early February.

designs commit aggression against his country and is part of US pattern to abet Chiang in invasion of mainland. Gave long line "brass hats" recently visiting Taiwan as indication insidious scheme brewing against mainland, as was also joint military operations Southern Formosa. Asked why guerilla section established under Military Advisory Group, why transport carriers recently supplied Chiang, why training schools for agents in Tamsui and Hualien established, if we did not plan abet invasion. GRC would not survive single day without US occupation Taiwan and responsibility for GRC actions placed by PRC where it belongs: On US.

(4) Turning to Laos, Wang said evidence indicates US should be held responsible for assassination Quinim.[7] US has brought officers of Chiang gang to Plaine Des Jarres and neutral police officer has been assassinated. Recent fighting and assassinations engineered and masterminded by US which has involved SEATO protection in violation Geneva accords. US has concealed nine hundred military personnel and thousands of troops of satellite states in Laos, continues air drop agents in rear of Lao patriotic forces. US has stepped up suppression South Vietnamese people and is trying to get Philippine troops to take part in Vietnam war. US has introduced rocket-firing helicopters and used noxious chemicals. US continues incite India oppose China and plans supply it with missiles. Ambassador Galbraith has made "scheming trip" to Chinese-Sikkim border. At SEATO meeting Rusk did not conceal his hostility to Southeast Asian countries and China. US will be held responsible for consequences if war rekindled in South-East Asia. Wang said was instructed give me and through me to my government serious warning urging US to rein in horse at edge of precipice and stop playing with fire (sic).

(5) I covered remainder paragraph seven reference telegram except for FYI, then spoke at some length on our relations with GRC, stressing defensive nature of alliance, but should occasion arise—which we hope will not—we would honor our commitments. No plans for invasion mainland included. We will continue send "brass hats" consult re defense Taiwan. I continued with denial US complicity Laos assassinations and stressed we had lived up to Geneva agreements. Said chemicals we have used in Vietnam were defoliants, harmless to humans. Followed with substance paragraph five reference telegram on aid to India.

(6) Wang responded with supremely dry lecture of history of Paracels, ending with observation omission reference no sovereignty of

---

[7] Quinim Pholsena, Lao Foreign Minister, was assassinated on the night of April 1 by a guard at his residence.

islands in Japanese Peace Treaty (concocted single-handedly by US) was insidious maneuver linked with our Treaty of Alliance with Chiang.

(7) Wang stressed we faced with dangerous prospect in Laos. US must strictly abide by Geneva accords if it does not want to see renewed conflict and US must stop interference in internal affairs and withdraw all military personnel. Chinese especially shocked by US employment Chiang bandits create trouble in Laos. This was something Chinese people could never tolerate or permit. In speaking again of chemical warfare Vietnam arousing indignation of world, mentioned Bertrand Russell letter and protest in NY Times by 62 Americans.

(8) I made obvious rejoinders including observation our Treaty with GRC had followed ChiCom use of force against our troops in Korea.

(9) Wang cited January 31 ICC report as proving Pathet Lao skirts clean. I said this belated investigation was after careful Pathet Lao preparation and did not alter its record of obstruction ICC activities.

In view planned leaves Wang suggested August 7 for next meeting. I voiced no objection but stated I assumed should urgent cause for meeting arise on either side, presumably we could meet earlier.

**Cabot**

---

## 176.  National Intelligence Estimate

NIE 13–63                                              Washington, May 1, 1963.

### PROBLEMS AND PROSPECTS IN COMMUNIST CHINA

#### The Problem

To establish where Communist China now stands in its domestic situation and foreign policies, to identify the major problems it faces, and to estimate probable developments over the next two years or so and, where possible, further ahead.

Source: Department of State, INR/EAP Files: Lot 90 D 110, NIE 13–63. Secret. According to a note on the cover sheet, the Central Intelligence Agency and intelligence organizations of the Departments of State, Defense, the Army, the Navy, the Air Force, and the NSA participated in the preparation of this estimate. All members of the USIB concurred with this estimate on May 1 except the representatives of the AEC and the FBI, who abstained on the grounds that the subject was outside their jurisdiction.

Conclusions

A. Communist China's domestic situation appears slightly improved from its recent grievous state. To a considerable extent this improvement reflects relatively moderate, pragmatic policies which have replaced the excesses of the "leap forward" and commune programs. With good luck and good management, the economy could within the next couple of years resume a rapid rate of growth approaching that of the First Five-Year Plan, though it is likely to fall short of this. A critical question over the next five years will be whether the Chinese Communist leadership will sustain a pragmatic course in the face of its strong ideological compulsions. Unsound doctrinaire policies, bad weather, and other unfavorable factors could combine to cause complete economic stagnation. (Paras. 1–6, 11–17)

B. Though discontent will persist and could increase if the economic situation deteriorates, we do not believe that dissidence will pose any serious threat to the regime in the next two years. (Para. 10)

C. Communist China's economic difficulties and the drastic reduction of Soviet cooperation have lessened the relative effectiveness of Communist China's military establishment. Nevertheless, Peiping still has by far the strongest Asian army, and this is sufficient to support the kind of relatively cautious foreign policies Peiping has actually been conducting or is likely to conduct during the next two years. It will almost certainly not have a militarily significant nuclear weapons system until well beyond this period.[1] (Paras. 18–23)

D. Peiping's dispute with Moscow springs from basic issues of incompatible national and party interests, and the Chinese Communists show no signs of relenting. Public polemics may be damped down on occasion, but we do not believe a fundamental reconciliation will take place. The Chinese will almost certainly continue to attempt to expand their influence at Soviet expense in the underdeveloped countries and to turn Communists throughout the world against Khrushchev and his policies. A formal schism could occur at any time, although the chances are reduced by each party's great anxiety to avoid the onus of having split the world Communist movement. (Paras. 24–30)

E. Communist China's foreign policy will probably continue generally along current lines. Peiping will remain passionately anti-American and will strive to weaken the US position, especially in east Asia, but is unlikely knowingly to assume great risks. China's military force will

---

[1] This question will be discussed in detail in NIE 13–2–63, "The Chinese Communist Advanced Weapons Program", (Top Secret) to be published soon. [Footnote in the source text. The estimate under reference was published as SNIE 13–2–63, "Communist China's Advanced Weapons Program," July 24, 1963. A portion of the text is printed in volume VIII, pp. 492–494.]

probably not be used overtly except in defense of its own borders or to assert territorial claims against India. Subversion and covert support of local revolutions will continue to be Peiping's mode of operation in southeast Asia and, to a necessarily more limited degree, elsewhere in Asia and in Africa and Latin America. (Paras. 31–40)

[Here follow paragraphs 1–40, comprising the Discussion portion of the estimate, Annex A, "Economic", comprising 343 paragraphs, Annex B, "Order of Battle Tables", and two maps.]

---

## 177. Memorandum From the Assistant Secretary of Defense for International Security Affairs (Nitze) to Secretary of Defense McNamara

Washington, May 11, 1963.

The attached paper[1] was prepared by my staff and has my full support. It does not, however, meet head on the considerations you and General Taylor advanced during Thursday's N.S.C. meeting[2] which related more to the general problem of dealing with the ChiCom military problem than to the specific Korean problem.

As I remember it, General Taylor said we should not permit ourselves to become engaged with the hordes of China, that any military contest with Communist China should be nuclear; your view was that our present strategy calls for the use of nuclears against the ChiComs and, therefore, conventional capabilities in the Far East, beyond counterinsurgency, have a low priority; and the President said that just as in Europe we would use nuclears if there were no other way of avoiding defeat, so would we in the Pacific.

To my mind, and as I understood the President to suggest, there is no substantial difference in the grounds for policy toward the East or

---

Source: Washington National Records Center, RG 330, Records of the Office of the Secretary of Defense, McNamara Files: FRC 71 A 3470, Korea. Top Secret. The source text does not indicate the drafter. Marginal notations on the source text in McNamara's handwriting are illegible.

[1] Document 303.

[2] Reference is to the May 9 NSC meeting. (Kennedy Library, National Security Files, Meetings and Memoranda Series, NSC Meetings )

toward the West, toward Russia or toward China. If a policy of giving the President maximum options in Europe makes sense, it would also seem to make sense in the Pacific. If a policy of giving the other side time to make the decision to back down makes sense in Cuba, I don't see why it doesn't make sense in Korea. If a policy of getting our allies to reduce, over time, the conventional imbalance in Europe makes sense, I don't see why a similar policy doesn't make sense in the Pacific. The ChiComs non-nuclear power, particularly her air power, is certainly vastly inferior to that of the Warsaw Pact. We can't foretell the exact relationship between Peiping and Moscow that will emerge, but to my mind it is equally doubtful, or more doubtful, that the U.S.S.R. would stand aside while we defeated China with nuclear weapons, than if we did so with non-nuclear weapons. The more important point, however, is that the Soviets might have less reason to restrain the Chinese in aggressive action if our only possible response were a nuclear response which the circumstances might make politically difficult for us and thus of dubious credibility.

## 178.  Editorial Note

At President Kennedy's press conference on May 22, 1963, a reporter noted that there had been "considerable discussion in the Far East that Chiang Kai-shek might be preparing to invade the mainland of China" and asked how the U.S. Government would view such an attempt. The President replied that the treaty relationship under the Mutual Defense Treaty provided for "very close consultation between the two governments before any such action would be taken." He continued: "As a practical matter, this of course does involve the United States, and we have expressed our views to the Government of Formosa on the matter." (*Public Papers of the Presidents of the United States: John F. Kennedy, 1963*, pages 422–423)

## 179.    Memorandum From the President's Special Assistant for National Security Affairs (Bundy) to President Kennedy

Washington, May 27, 1963.

SUBJECT

Your visit from Admiral Wright[1]

Wright is making essentially a courtesy call before proceeding to Taipei. But he needs a strong indication of your own interest in keeping a sharp eye on the Nationalist government. I had a short talk with him last week in which he two or three times indicated a feeling that we ought to be more understanding of the Nationalists desires, and I think there is a perceptible danger that he might be captured by that government if he does not have it very clearly in mind that his mission is to act in the wider U.S. interest.

Because of Kirk's firmness in presenting unpalatable conditions, the Generalissimo did not like him. Wright has a chance to sustain this position without incurring any parallel personal resentment, so what he needs from you is a careful statement of the policy of very good manners and very clear control over U.S. decisions which you personally have established in dealing with the GRC for over two years.[2]

McG.B.[3]

---

Source: Kennedy Library, National Security Files, Countries Series, China. The source text bears no classification marking and no indication of the drafter.

[1] Wright was appointed Ambassador to the Republic of China on May 3. According to Kennedy's Appointment Book, he met with Wright with Forrestal present from 10:20 to 10:42 a.m. on May 27. (Kennedy Library) No record of the meeting has been found.

[2] Airgram A–183 to Taipei, June 13, transmitted a message from Kennedy to Chiang, which Wright was to convey orally during his initial interview. It states that Kennedy "attaches the greatest importance" to maintaining the Republic of China's international position and its position in the United Nations, that "we shall continue to offer all appropriate support to this end," and that Kennedy "understands completely the great importance of the mutual defense agreements and understandings" between the two countries. (Department of State, Central Files, POL 15–1 CHINAT) See the Supplement. Wright presented his credentials to Chiang on June 29. The only record of their meeting that has been found is an unclassified account transmitted in airgram A–2 from Taipei, July 3. (Department of State, Central Files, POL 17–1 US–CHINAT)

[3] Printed from a copy that bears this typed signature.

## 180.  Editorial Note

Tripartite negotiations among the United States, United Kingdom, and the Soviet Union were held in Moscow, July 15–25, 1963, leading to the initialing on July 25 of a treaty banning nuclear weapons tests in the atmosphere, in outer space, and under water. Under Secretary of State for Political Affairs W. Averell Harriman represented the United States in the talks. The subject of Chinese nuclear weapons development arose on several occasions, especially in a July 15 conversation among Harriman, British representative Lord Hailsham, and Chairman of the Soviet Council of Ministers Nikita S. Khrushchev and a July 26 conversation between Harriman and Khrushchev.

A July 15 message from Kennedy to Harriman, sent in telegram 191 to Moscow of that date, reads in part as follows:

"I remain convinced that Chinese problem is more serious than Khrushchev comments in first meeting suggest, and believe you should press question in private meeting with him. I agree that large stockpiles are characteristic of US and USSR only, but consider that relatively small forces in hands of people like ChiComs could be very dangerous to us all. Further believe even limited test ban can and should be means to limit diffusion.

"You should try to elicit Khrushchev's view of means of limiting or preventing Chinese nuclear development and his willingness either to take Soviet action or to accept US action aimed in this direction." (Department of State, Central Files, DEF 18–4)

Telegram 191 is scheduled for publication in volume VII, along with further documentation on the background of the test ban treaty and records of Harriman's discussions in Moscow.

A memorandum from John J. de Martino of the Department of State Executive Secretariat to Executive Secretary Benjamin H. Read, dated October 2, 1964, reads as follows:

"A search of our records of the Test Ban Treaty negotiations in Moscow fails to reveal any Harriman proposal for a joint US-USSR effort to slow down Red China's nuclear weapons development. On the other hand the question of Chinese nuclear capacities came up in various Harriman/Khrushchev conversations. Harriman probed USSR knowledge of Chinese capacities and its attitude toward them. He expressed our concern regarding this matter and said he hoped that the problem would be solved by eventual Chinese adherence to the Treaty or by disarmament. Khrushchev was obviously unwilling to talk at much length on the question and he tried to give the impression of not being greatly concerned.

"One of the reasons that the Chinese issue was raised with Khrushchev was Harriman's theory that Khrushchev's interest in a test ban treaty flowed from his desire to isolate Red China in the international communist movement. Aside from this Harriman was also under instructions to express the President's great concern over Chinese development of nuclear weapons." (Library of Congress Manuscript Division, Harriman Papers, Kennedy–Johnson Administrations, Trips and Missions, Test Ban Treaty, Background)

## 181. Summary Record of the 516th Meeting of the National Security Council

Washington, July 31, 1963, 4:30–5:30 p.m.

*Chinese Communist Intentions*

Mr. Ray Cline of CIA summarized SNIE 13–4–63, "Possibility of Greater Militancy by the Chinese Communists."[1] The President asked about the Acting Director of Intelligence and Research of the Department of State who had noted his disagreement with parts of the Estimate.[2] Mr. McGeorge Bundy said Mr. Hilsman was prepared to speak to the minority views of the State Department Intelligence officers. Mr. Hilsman responded that he was prepared to speak to the policy implications of the SNIE.[3]

---

Source: Kennedy Library, National Security Files, Meetings and Memoranda Series, NSC Meetings, No. 516. Secret; Sensitive. The time of the meeting's conclusion was taken from Kennedy's Appointment Book. (Kennedy Library) A list of those in attendance is filed with the source text. McCone's record of the meeting is in Central Intelligence Agency, DCI (McCone) Files, Job 80–B01285A, Box 6, DCI Meetings With the President) The meeting was held at the President's direction; see Document 312.

[1] Dated July 31; it addressed the possibility of "more assertive Chinese Communist actions in the near future, arising from the coincidence of deepening Sino-Soviet dispute and recent Soviet negotiations with the West." It predicted that the Chinese would not "act recklessly or run very great risks" but might undertake "somewhat more assertive initiatives," the most likely of which would be "new pressures or incursions on the Indian border and in Laos." (Department of State, INR/EAP Files: Lot 90 D 110, SNIE 13–4–63) See the Supplement.

[2] Footnotes to the estimate noted that the INR Acting Director (Deputy Director George C. Denney, Jr.) was more skeptical of the likelihood of Chinese initiatives.

[3] McCone's record of the meeting, cited in the source note, states that Rusk and Harriman both endorsed the estimate without reservation and did not support the footnotes; Rusk stated that he not heard of the reservations before the meeting and did not support them. Rostow concurred and proposed to Rusk that the State Department consider the matter and withdraw the reservations if they were inconsistent with Rusk's thinking. They were not withdrawn; the final estimate cited in footnote 1 is unchanged from the advance copy filed with the source text. An INR memorandum of August 7 and a CIA memorandum of August 12 laid out the differing views on this subject in more detail. (Department of State, INR/EAP Files: Lot 90 D 110, SNIE 13–4–63)

*[5 paragraphs (27 lines of source text) not declassified]*

Secretary Rusk asked whether we have any hard evidence that there were significant movements of Chinese Communist troops anywhere along their borders. Mr. Cline responded that the answer depended on the definition of the word "significant." He then summarized the hard evidence on troop activity contained in the SNIE. He described the logistic improvements being made by the Chinese Communists along the Tibetan border consisting primarily of work on local roads.

Secretary Rusk asked whether it was agreed that we could only speculate as to what effect the Sino-Soviet split has had on military deployments on both sides. Mr. Cline agreed, adding that the SNIE stated that the Chinese probably anticipated less political support from the Russians than they had received in the past.

The President asked whether the recent military crisis in Korea should be viewed as an isolated incident or as part of a broader military pattern. Mr. Cline replied that no one could say with certainty. General Wheeler said that incidents similar to those which took place this week in Korea occur every summer. Citing officers with combat experience in Korea, he said at this time of year for several years past there have been instances of line-crossing activity. This year's incident is similar to last year's, although no one can say positively that the recent ambushes are not part of a larger pattern.

Secretary Rusk then asked Mr. Hilsman to discuss the actions which we were taking in anticipation of Chinese Communist initiatives. Mr. Hilsman had earlier circulated copies of a memorandum to Secretary Rusk (copy attached).[4] Secretary Rusk suggested that there was no need to review policy contingencies in Laos because the President had been thoroughly briefed on this subject earlier.

Mr. Hilsman said that Ambassador Cabot in Warsaw would be instructed to warn the Communist Chinese not to take actions which would prompt immediate U.S. response in the area. He mentioned the two recommendations in his paper; i.e. a request to the Department of Defense to comment on U.S. military responses to possible renewal of Chinese Communist militancy on the Indian front, and a request for a JCS military evaluation of the potential for increased infiltration into South Vietnam and of the means available to deal with it within the territory of South Vietnam.[5] An additional problem is how to reinforce against Communist subversion inside India.

---

[4] Hilsman's July 31 memorandum on the subject "Suggested United States Responses to Likely Chinese Communist Initiatives," was not attached to the source text. (Ibid., Central Files, POL 1 CHICOM).

[5] Rusk initialed Hilsman's July 31 memorandum on August 1, indicating his approval of these recommendations.

Mr. Hilsman also mentioned a draft statement for the President to use at his press conference in response to questions about Korea. Secretary Rusk noted that he wished to rework the statement before discussing it with the President.

The President called attention to a press story in the Philadelphia Inquirer which appeared to have been based on a statement made by a State Department spokesman to the effect that we were anticipating serious trouble with Communist China. Secretary Rusk responded by recalling the warning the U.S. had given Communist China two days before the outbreak of the Korean War. In his view, if our warning to the Chinese had been sent earlier, the Korean War might not have taken place. Because the warning reached Peiping only two days before the offensive began in Korea, the Chinese were so fully committed to the attack that it was too late for them to consider the warning.

Mr. Hilsman said the story the President referred to raised the problem of how to deal with press speculation. He said the State Department spokesman had not volunteered the statement but had merely said that the reports which the reporter had of Chinese Communist military activity were known to the Government and were being studied. The reporter had written the story as if the Department had confirmed the reports.

Mr. McCone referred to the Special Estimate and called attention to the majority USIB view; i.e. the possibility of Communist Chinese activity is greater than that expressed by the State Department.

The President asked whether the Indian army was any better off this year than it had been last year when the Communists attacked. General Wheeler responded that the Indians were better off because of our military assistance. He noted, however, that no Indian military force was in the NEFA, so that if the Chinese Communists chose to take this area, they could do so without military opposition.

Secretary Rusk concluded the discussion by expressing his belief that we should maintain a state of considerable alert during the next few weeks. He pointed out that the Chinese Communists could cause grave trouble from a standing start; i.e. without reinforcements, on several fronts at the same time. The military capability on their frontiers is great. The troops in front of them are very thin and totalitarian regimes can reverse their courses very quickly. Thus, some Chinese initiative might suddenly reveal that the Russians and the Chinese were back together again.

Mr. McCone added that although the differences between the Russians and the Chinese are very great, he did not think they were very deep or that a final break between the two powers would occur.

Mr. Harriman said he did not think the two powers would break, but he believed that Khrushchev would not back China in any wild adventure. Khrushchev would not react if the Chinese got into a small military fight, but if Chiang Kai-shek landed on the Mainland, the Russians would support the Chinese Communists fully.

Secretary Rusk said that during the period ahead of us, we should not contemplate reductions in the indigenous force levels of either Korea or Nationalist China. There was no comment on this suggestion.

In response to the President's question, Secretary Rusk said he was asking no action by the President on the matters discussed today.[6]

Mr. Murrow asked for Presidential approval of the way USIA is handling the Sino-Soviet split. He said existing guidance forbade polemics and attempts to exacerbate relations between Communist China and the Soviet Union. The Voice of America is playing straight the comments on the split coming out of both Peking and Moscow, but it does not attempt to exploit the difference. The President agreed that this was the proper way to handle the current situation.

[Here follows discussion concerning Vietnam, Ceylon, and Pakistan.]

**Bromley Smith**[7]

---

[6] NSC Action No. 2469, July 31, reads as follows:

"Chinese Communist Intentions.

"The Director of Central Intelligence presented SNIE 13–4–63, 'Possibilities of Greater Militancy by the Chinese Communists.' There followed a discussion of the Estimate and of responses to contingencies which might arise." (Kennedy Library, National Security Files, Meetings and Memoranda Series, NSC Meetings, No. 516)

[7] Printed from a copy that bears this typed signature.

## 182. Letter From Secretary of State Rusk to Secretary of Defense McNamara

Washington, August 1, 1963.

DEAR BOB: We have given careful consideration to the points you raise in your letter of June 20[1] concerning certain aspects of the employment of GRC forces. We believe that GRC forces available as a strategic reserve of conventional force in the Far East would contribute to the support of U.S. objectives of deterring Chinese Communist aggression and under certain circumstances of countering such aggression if it should occur. At the same time we do not agree with the JCS recommendation that U.S. policy favor the principle of employment of GRC units in conflicts in Southeast Asia, though as will be noted subsequently there is one set of circumstances where such employment might be feasible.

It seems to me that we must be quite realistic in understanding that the Nationalist Government of China would not commit its military forces except as a part of a major engagement whose objective is the return of that Government to full control on the mainland of China. Conversely, the use of Nationalist Chinese forces in Southeast Asia, in the absence of Chinese Communist forces in that area, would almost inevitably result in the commitment of Chinese Communist forces to meet them. The Nationalist Chinese forces are of great importance to the United States in the event of a major Chinese Communist aggression, and I would think that we would wish to be very cautious about reducing those forces during the present period of uncertainty about Peiping's intentions following their break with Moscow. In evaluating the role of Chinese Nationalist forces, particularly ground forces, I also feel that we must assess their capabilities in the most rigorous professional manner and not be unduly influenced in this regard by mere hope or traditional goodwill.

---

Source: Department of State, Central Files, DEF 6 CHINAT. Top Secret. Drafted by W.C. Magathan of the Office of Politico/Military Affairs and by Rusk, who, according to a note attached to the source text, added the second paragraph. A copy of the previous draft, attached to the source text, does not include the second paragraph but includes the following sentence at the end of the first paragraph: "Finally, our judgment as to the utility of GRC forces does not imply support for a specific force level."

[1] McNamara's letter of June 20 to Rusk enclosed a JCS memorandum of May 23 (JCSM–387–63) and a JCS study entitled "Effect on Force Requirements of US Use of Nuclear Weapons at Outset of ChiCom Aggression Against Taiwan or Southeast Asia." McNamara noted that the JCS conclusions included the argument that GRC forces should not be reduced because, among other considerations, they represented a strategic reserve "available for support of U.S. Objectives in the Far East" or "meeting contingency military requirements." He requested Rusk's views on this and on a JCS proposal of January 1963 supporting the possible use of GRC forces up to three divisions in Southeast Asia. (Ibid., DEF 12 US)

With respect to the strategic reserve concept, from the Chinese Communist viewpoint, the existence of these GRC forces must be regarded as providing the United States and its allies with a number of options, all of which the Chinese Communists would have to take into account in planning aggressive action anywhere in Asia. The Joint Chiefs' study points out that the GRC forces keep large Communist forces tied down on the mainland opposite Taiwan. The forces so tied down would presumably be unavailable to support a major Chinese Communist aggression in Korea or in Southeast Asia. Moreover, given the presence of the GRC strategic reserve force on Taiwan, one can imagine that in the event of Chinese Communist aggressive action in Korea or Southeast Asia, GRC feints against various points along the mainland China coast might serve to draw Chinese Communist forces off from their main point of attack or at least to restrain the Chinese Communists from developing their attack to major proportions which would require U.S. employment of nuclear weapons.

However, the only situation in which, from a political point of view, we can clearly visualize the actual introduction of GRC troops in Southeast Asian countries (or in the territory of any other free Asian nation) would be in the case of large-scale Chinese Communist aggression, as such aggression is defined in the Chiefs' study. There are two reasons why, except in the case of large-scale Chinese Communist attack, it would be infeasible to introduce GRC forces into Southeast Asia. The first is that the countries concerned would be strongly opposed to the introduction of GRC forces. Second, the introduction of GRC forces would almost certainly provoke the introduction of Chinese Communist forces. Consequently, while we support the concept of a GRC strategic reserve, we would not support the establishment of a general policy of favoring the use of GRC forces in Southeast Asia.

Conceivably, GRC troops might be used to help meet a limited Chinese Communist action against Southeast Asian countries, but this seems undesirable. If the limited Chinese Communist attack were of a probing nature designed to test our reactions, or if the attack could be adequately met by conventional U.S. and other allied forces (SEATO and indigenous), GRC troops should not be introduced. The use of GRC troops could have an important effect on the Chinese Communist estimate of our intentions. If no GRC troops were brought in, the Chinese Communists might consider that our intention was only to stop their probe and drive the Communist forces back behind existing borders. If GRC divisions were brought in, even if initially in only limited numbers, the Chinese Communists might consider that the ultimate intention was to reinforce and thence to try to drive into mainland China. Peiping could believe that American forces would be used only to achieve limited objectives whereas they would be more likely to judge that GRC troops would participate only as a means of facilitating their return to power on the mainland. The Chinese Communists would go all out to meet what they regarded as a serious threat to their security. Consequently, the introduction of GRC divisions might transform what was initially intended only as a limited Chinese Communist probing action into a large-scale Chinese Communist aggression.

In all the spectrum of conflict which ranges below these upper levels of intensity, it clearly would be infeasible to use GRC troops in Southeast Asia. And, it is in the lower part of the spectrum—subversion, guerrilla warfare, clandestine introduction of North Vietnamese cadres and troops—that the principal Communist threat to Southeast Asia is manifested.

One point which ought to be noted in this consideration of GRC strategic reserve divisions is the attitude of the GRC itself toward the actual employment of these divisions. Chinese Nationalist interest in such employment would probably vary directly with the opportunity afforded them to confront the Chinese Communists. In any event, before the GRC would make available divisions of their better trained troops for use on the Asian mainland, they would weigh very carefully the effect of such action on their own security and aspirations.

Aside from these questions of the use of GRC forces, I was much interested in the Study's presentation of the pros and cons on the use of nuclear weapons at the outset of large-scale Chinese Communist aggression. It seemed to us that CINCPAC's views, as set forth in the study on pages 8 and 9,[2] were particularly pertinent. Politically and psychologically it will become even more important after a Chinese Communist nuclear detonation, to have adequate U.S. conventional capability in the Pacific so that free Asian nations will believe that we can assist in defending them against at least limited Chinese Communist attack without necessarily involving them in nuclear war.

I should appreciate being kept abreast of your consideration of these matters in order that there may be ample opportunity for mutual con-

---

[2] The quotation of CINCPAC's views, which occurs in an annex to the study headed "Discussion," reads: "I will not comment on the political aspects that militate against making such a critical assumption. However, from purely a military point of view, the resulting inflexibility evolving from such a concept is one which causes me great concern. Should such a concept result in a force incapable of conducting successful operations against Chi-Com aggression without resort to the use of nuclear weapons, we would indeed have created conditions which would impose a degree of rigidity in our military forces which is undesirable and unwarranted."

sultation about the development of our nuclear weapons policy in the Pacific area.

With warm regards,

Sincerely,

Dean[3]

---

[3] Printed from a copy that indicates Rusk signed the original.

---

## 183.    Telegram From the Embassy in Poland to the Department of State

Warsaw, August 7, 1963, 8 p.m.

255. Cabot–Wang Talks. 116th Meeting. 3 hours, 35 minutes.[1] Deptels 138 and 184.[2]

(1) Wang opened referring to his Government statement July 31 advocating prohibition nuclear weapons and proposing conference Government Heads all countries[3] and to Chou En-lai message delivered me for transmission.[4] Expressed aspiration Chinese people prevent nuclear war. Said he must point out August 5 tripartite test ban treaty goes against aspirations people of world because it can be used by nuclear powers consolidate their nuclear monopoly. It legalizes continued manufacture, transportation, underground testing and use of weapons by US while binding hands of peace-loving countries, denying them adequate means protect selves against nuclear threat. Treaty thereby actually increases hazard of nuclear war and is fraud menacing world peace. Asked how a few nuclear powers could take into own hands seri-

---

Source: Department of State, Central Files, POL CHICOM–US. Confidential; Priority; Limit Distribution. Repeated to Taipei, Hong Kong, Stockholm, Moscow, and Geneva and passed to the White House on August 8.

[1] Cabot commented and sent recommendations for the next meeting in telegram 258, August 8. Noting that the meeting was the longest in over 4 years, he stated that Wang spoke "at times more emotionally than he has for some time." (Ibid.) He sent a detailed, apparently verbatim report of the meeting in airgram A–124, August 10. (Ibid.)

[2] Telegram 138 to Warsaw, July 26, provided guidance for the meeting on various subjects. Telegram 184, August 3, instructed Cabot to urge that Wang's side reconsider its public rejection of the test ban treaty. (Both ibid.)

[3] For text, see Documents on Disarmament, 1963, pp. 268–272.

[4] Reference is to an August 2 letter from Chou to Kennedy, identical to letters sent to other heads of government, which reiterated the proposal set forth in the Chinese statement of July 31. It was delivered to the Embassy in Warsaw with an August 2 covering letter from Wang to Cabot. The text was transmitted in telegram 221 from Warsaw, August 2. (Department of State, Central Files, DEF 18–3)

ous issues affecting human destiny. How can desire of people of whole world be ignored and a few nuclear powers be permitted monopolize everything. Without participation China no major questions in international affairs can be settled in our times. Said President Kennedy had gone out of his way to resume tone and airs of world overlord presuming describe non-nuclear powers as stable or unstable, responsible or irresponsible.[5] This was outright imperialistic attitude. Even Kennedy cannot deny that far from prejudicing nuclear strength of USG, treaty makes possible carrying on of nuclear race. If US sincere in wanting take first step, should first remove nuclear threat it now possesses by dismantling all overseas bases and reaching an accord establishing nuclear-free zones. Said Chinese Government hoped every government would give favorable response its proposal (Chou's letter) and that USG also will be favorable. Said if we desired consult with Chinese on this question, he was at my disposal any time to enter on this discussion.

(2) Wang said US should remove its nuclear threat to China and the Far East. This threat much felt in China and entire Far East. Spoke of Guam fortifications, units with nuclear weapons in Korea and Taiwan, important cities and hinterland of his country under direct threat of our nuclear forces, air force in Pacific deployed many nuclear-capable planes, attack aircraft carriers and subs with nuclears in Pacific. In short, eastern and southern flanks of China covered by our nuclear weapons and we held maneuvers in adjacent areas with nuclear weapons. Said Kennedy statement at press conference China determined on war as means bringing about ultimate success[6] was calumny and slander. Said it was only US which relied on nuclear blackmail as means bringing about its own ultimate success.

(3) Wang said he was instructed put forth draft agreed announcement at this meeting designed reduce nuclear threat. Hoped USG would give careful study and consideration. (Text pouched.)[7]

---

[5] Reference is to a statement by Kennedy in a July 26 radio and television address referring to the danger of nuclear weapons "in so many hands, in the hands of countries large and small, stable and unstable, responsible and irresponsible, scattered throughout the world." (*Public Papers of the President of the United States: John F. Kennedy, 1963*, p. 604)

[6] Reference is to a statement by Kennedy at an August 1 press conference that if in 10 years China still had 700 million people with a Stalinist regime, was still surrounded by weak countries, still had "a government determined on war as a means of bringing about its ultimate success," and was also a nuclear power, the situation would be potentially more dangerous than any since the end of World War II. (Ibid., p. 616)

[7] It would have declared that (1) the PRC and U.S. Governments would jointly propose the establishment of a nuclear-free zone in the Asia and Pacific region, including China, the United States, the Soviet Union, and Japan, and (2) the U.S. Government would "withdraw all its military bases, including nuclear bases, from the areas surrounding the People's Republic of China, and withdraw all its nuclear weapons and their means of delivery from these areas." The text was transmitted in telegram 259 from Warsaw, August 8. (Department of State, Central Files, POL CHICOM–US)

(4) I handed Wang information six deportee cases paragraph 6 first reference telegram. Wang said would study and respond later. Followed with substance paragraph 8 re President's speech, newsmen, imprisoned Americans, and helicopter personnel.[8] Also mentioned general incursions south of Korean truce line which scarcely could be assumed not deliberate.

(5) I spoke at some length on our policy to promote general disarmament, pointing out number of factors on which this complex question must depend.

(6) I continued quoting from ChiCom June 14 letter[9] at some length and saying nothing could be better designed renew vigilance of those wishing retain freedom. Said many people believe there are halting and tentative but nonetheless promising evidences of forces at work which could lead to peaceful and prosperous world as a whole. If great and talented Chinese people not permitted make their contribution in such cooperation, this would constitute one of saddest chapters in history of our times.

(7) I expressed regret at ChiCom rejection test ban treaty, pointing out its wide acceptance already indicated. Said we earnestly hoped nuclear power would never again be used and have striven since 1946 reach agreement this end.

(8) Wang said he had nothing new to say re newsmen or American prisoners in absence new developments. Said as for missing servicemen in Korea, all such matters whether previous or latest cases are matters between USG and Korean Peoples Republic, and not appropriate discussion here. Claimed Kennedy speech had been fully covered by Chinese press. Said they regarded it as important because revealed US strategy in staging fake peace. People of world coming to conclusion US actually has policy of war. Said my quotations June 14 letter represented scientific evaluation social development in world. However change within a given country is for the people to decide and also whether it is to be by peaceful or other means. Returning to test ban, said people of world do not want prevention proliferation nuclear power but prevention nuclear war and complete destruction nuclear weapons. July statement his government designed meet this question.

---

[8] Paragraph 8 of telegram 138 to Warsaw instructed Cabot to draw attention to "misquotes and misinterpretations" in the Chinese press of President Kennedy's June 10 speech calling for "a strategy of peace." It also instructed Cabot to propose new efforts to relax tensions: an agreement on exchange of newsmen, release of U.S. nationals in Chinese prisons, and release of two U.S. Army helicopter personnel whose aircraft strayed on May 17 into Korean territory under KPA/CPV control.

[9] Reference is to a June 14 letter from the Central Committee of the Chinese Communist Party to the Central Committee of the Soviet Communist Party; for text, see *Peking Review*, vol. VI, No. 25, pp. 6–22.

(9) I said our basic policy was seek general and complete disarmament but this was impossible without verification. We had been negotiating on this point at length. Our President's speech attempted to contribute toward this goal. Said could not reconcile Wang's statements today with clear purport June 14 letter, giving examples inconsistencies. Said I hoped Wang's statements re peaceful intent represented government policy and June 14 letter did not. Spoke further on "first step" aspects test ban treaty.

(10) Wang spoke at some length on alleged subversive activities against China on part US. Referred again to test ban treaty as "dirty fraud." Accused US of backing GRC acts on mainland, saying recently Chiang had tried so-called "climax" in activities but plot was thoroughly exposed. Said results had proven his oft-stated warnings in these meetings that our support of Chiang would do no good. In June alone, Chi-Com wiped out six commando groups and shot down P2V. Said we were held answerable for all Chiang's acts. Said precisely because we ourselves aware of this responsibility that I felt it necessary give him assurance we were not supporting Chiang but said our performance hardly supports the assurances given.

(11) Wang referred to two cases alleged ramming and sinking Chinese fishing vessels by American ships. First boat belonged to Ningpo Marine Fisheries Co. of Chekiang province. On 15 May 1961 rammed and sunk by SS *Letitia Lykes* of Lykes Bros. SS Co., at position 29 degrees 12 minutes north and 123 degrees 15 minutes east. Second boat on 19 September 1962, fishing vessel of Chia Tsu Commune, in Luk Fung county, Kwangtung province, fishing northeast of Chia Tsu port, sunk by SS *President Hoover* of American President Line. On 24 September 1962 Chinese gave us message on this matter.[10] Wang said these cases were result of faulty navigation and US companies therefore should compensate. Hoped we would intervene and hasten results.

(12) Refuted charges of intervention and occupation of Taiwan. Said re ship sinkings I was without instructions as far as compensation concerned but wondered whether his side would be interested in general discussion of material claims which each side has against the other. (Wang did not bite at this.)

(13) Had expected propose October 2 for next meeting but Wang said his side very anxious for earlier meeting in order receive response from USG on proposal joint statement handed me today. After some dis-

---

[10] Telegram 582 from Warsaw, September 24, 1962, reported that Cabot had received a letter from Wang concerning the latter incident. Telegram 451 to Warsaw, September 26, 1962, informed Cabot that the surviving crew members were being returned to mainland China via Hong Kong. (Both in Department of State, Central Files, 611.93/9–2462)

cussion settled on September 11 with my promise if I received word earlier I would get in touch with him.

(14) After meeting had adjourned, Wang stopped me to ask whether I had had vacation. I said understood he had also. He said he had just come from China where his people were working hard in constructing their country. They had much to do and would never attempt to break out of their own borders into other areas. Said I should not believe newspaper accounts in the US which claimed China was a peril in the Far East.

**Cabot**

---

### 184.  Telegram From the Embassy in the Republic of China to the Department of State

Taipei, September 6, 1963, noon.

177. Reference: Embassy's telegram 119.[1] As reported in Embassy's fortnightly "indications" telegrams and A–227 of September 3,[2] we see little indication that GRC is planning or preparing for any military or paramilitary action against China mainland in near future except small team probes similar to others attempted this summer. Atmosphere in this respect much more relaxed than spring of 1962 or early this year. Moreover, evidence is accumulating that GRC high command presently very much concerned with assessing implications for GRC policy of Sino-Soviet split and possible developments in US-USSR relations following test-ban treaty. Views on these matters have not crystallized and we believe situation therefore exceptionally favorable for influencing GRC thinking.

---

Source: Department of State, Central Files, DEF 1 CHINAT. Secret; Limit Distribution.

[1] In telegram 119, August 20, Wright sent recommendations for Chiang Ching-kuo's pending visit to the United States. Noting that Chiang would almost certainly play a crucial role after his father's death, he recommended explanation of U.S. global policies by top U.S. officials and firm assurances of continuing U.S. support. Concerning GRC mainland recovery aspirations, he commented that it would be important to "strike good balance between expressions U.S. confidence in ultimate casting off of Communist rule by Chinese people and view that time not ripe for any large-scale GRC action to this end." (Ibid., POL 15–1 CHINAT)

[2] Not printed. (Ibid.)

Recent conversations between [*less than 1 line of source text not declassified*] and Chiang Ching-kuo suggest that latter more inclined than previously to give serious attention to improving GRC political action and psychological warfare directed at mainland. Therefore recommend that in discussions with him opportunities be found to urge importance and timeliness of vigorous GRC political action program to take advantage of increasing Chinese Communist isolation in world community and probable internal stresses in Chinese Communist Party resulting from Sino-Soviet split. Believe careful steering of discussions away from military and toward political action would serve our long-term interests better than repeating blunt warnings against rash military action which do not seem called for by current situation, unless latter are needed to meet proposals Chiang Ching-kuo may make.

Clough

## 185.    Draft Minutes

Washington, September 10, 1963.

SUBJECT

Meeting Between Mr. McGeorge Bundy and General Chiang Ching-kuo, 10 September 1963[1]

*Summary*

On 10 September 1963, General Chiang Ching-kuo met with Mr. McGeorge Bundy. Also present at the meeting were Mr. Ray Cline, Mr.

---

Source: Kennedy Library, National Security Files, Countries Series, China. Secret. Filed with a September 19 covering memorandum from William E. Colby of the Central Intelligence Agency to Bundy, with the notation in Bundy's handwriting: "OK as amended. MB." See the Supplement.

[1] Chiang Ching-kuo visited Washington September 6–13. He met with Cline on September 8 and with Harriman, Hilsman, and Hughes the next day. According to Cline's September 9 memorandum for the record Chiang told him that President Chiang had authorized him to state that no military invasion would be made during the next 18 months unless there was a rebellion on the mainland; in return, he wanted U.S. cooperation and support for Nationalist clandestine operations and an effort to increase considerably the scale of paramilitary team infiltration. (Kennedy Library, President's Office Files, China Security, 1962–63, Memoranda for Meeting with Chiang Ching-kuo) Memoranda of Chiang's meetings with Harriman, Hilsman, and Hughes are in Department of State, Central Files, POL 2 CHINA, POL CHICOM–USSR, and POL 1 CHICOM, respectively.

384 Foreign Relations, 1961–1963, Volume XXII

William Nelson, Mr. James Shen, Mr. Cal Mehlert, and Mr. Donald Duffey.[2] After an exchange of amenities, General Chiang Ching-kuo said that, although the Government of the Republic of China (GRC) understood the reasons why the United States had signed the nuclear test ban treaty and the GRC shared the U.S. desire to ease world tensions and preserve world peace, the treaty alone would not solve all the problems. The GRC is encouraged by President Kennedy's public acknowledgement of the potential threat of continued Chinese Communist growth; but, Chiang emphasized, the Chinese Communist regime at the present time is weaker than it has ever been since its 1949 takeover of the China mainland. On the assumption that the U.S. and the U.S.S.R. will maintain the status quo in their mutual relations, the GRC feels that now is the time for the U.S. and the GRC to establish a formula aimed at solving the problem of the China mainland without triggering a major war. The GRC is prepared to assume full political responsibility for such action with U.S. support. President Chiang Kai-shek is positive that if the GRC acts now, the Soviet Union will not go to the aid of the Chinese Communists. Time is the key element, however, since new factors could change the situation in the future. According to Chiang Ching-kuo, it is important that the U.S. and the GRC take joint action immediately to enhance the difficulties now facing the Chinese Communists and make it impossible for them to consolidate their position. Chiang Ching-kuo re-emphasized that the GRC recognizes the leading role of the United States and accepts the assumption that no action will be taken which would risk war. The GRC is willing to discuss ways and means to weaken the Chinese Communist regime and eventually overthrow it and feels that the solution to the problem must be more political than military. Chiang's definition of political devices included political warfare, psychological warfare, diplomatic action and paramilitary operations such as maritime raids on the coast and airdrops of paramilitary teams. The GRC plans for the maritime raids and airdrops were to escalate from small and medium teams to large teams in three stages, six months apart. Chiang Ching-kuo claimed that the GRC has located missile sites and atomic installations on the China mainland and desires to work with the United States on ways and means to remove these and restrain their expansion. Chiang promised to discuss details of the ways and means to achieve this goal on other levels and reiterated that the GRC would assume full political responsibility for this action, expecting only transportation and technical assistance from the United States. In conclusion, Chiang repeated the contention that the GRC is not planning a large scale attack on the China

---

[2] Shen was Chiang's interpreter; Mehlert was Bundy's interpreter. A memorandum of Chiang's meeting with Harriman on September 9 identifies James D. Duffey as the Deputy Chief of the CIA Taiwan Desk. (Ibid., Central Files, POL 2 CHINA)

mainland and that the Chinese Communists must not be permitted to solve their present difficulties to become an even greater menace in the future.

In reply, Mr. Bundy told Chiang that the United States places a high priority on measures to weaken the Chinese Communist regime, particularly its nuclear growth, and assured him that the U.S. Government would examine most carefully any possibilities advanced. Mr. Bundy stressed the United States Government's aversion to triggering a major conflict and expressed the view that the split between the Soviet Union and Communist China would probably widen unless extreme forces of great magnitude drove them back together again. He said that one example of such a force would be any major attack against the China mainland in which the United States would be a dominant factor. Mr. Bundy emphasized that the moment when major action against the mainland can be taken without danger of Soviet intervention is not yet here and may never arrive.[3] In view of the lack of success of the small GRC operations of the past two and three years, Mr. Bundy felt there was a question of whether larger operations would be productive and said the U.S. and the GRC must work together on the problem. In Mr. Bundy's opinion, any action against the China mainland should depend on three factors: (1) a sound intelligence estimate of Chinese Communist strength and capabilities; (2) the degree of political usefulness of such operations; and (3) the hazards and repercussions of failure to the U.S. and GRC. In passing, Mr. Bundy mentioned the U.S. admiration of the GRC's accomplishments in its social and economic growth and assured Chiang that the success and effectiveness of such growth is of great interest to the United States Government. (End of summary)

[Here follows a more detailed record of the conversation; see the Supplement.]

---

[3] The words "when major" and "danger of" appear in Bundy's handwriting on the source text.

## 186.   Memorandum of Conversation

Washington, September 11, 1963, 10–10:25 a.m.

SUBJECT

United States Relations with the Republic of China

PARTICIPANTS

President Kennedy

General Chiang Ching-kuo, Minister without Portfolio, Executive Yuan, Republic of China

Mr. Michael Forrestal, Senior Staff Member of the National Security Council

Mr. James Shen, General Chiang's interpreter

Mr. Calvin Mehlert, Department of State interpreter

*Summary:*

General Chiang opened the interview by handing the President a letter from President Chiang Kai-shek.[1]

General Chiang then told the President:

—that the GRC wants additional aircraft (five C–130's) and landing craft to conduct commando raids, in units of up to 500 men, against the China mainland,

—that the 28 landings conducted since last October disrupted the Chinese Communists to some extent, and more and larger raids would cause commensurately greater disruption,

—that President Chiang's idea is to seize one or more of the provinces south of the Yangtze when the time is ripe,

—that President Chiang believes the Chinese Communists must be denied a respite to overcome their present serious difficulties.

The President responded:

—that we lack sufficient hard intelligence on conditions on the mainland,

---

Source: Kennedy Library, National Security Files, Countries Series, China. Top Secret. Drafted by Popple and approved in the White House September 20. The time of the meeting's conclusion was taken from Kennedy's Appointment Book. (Ibid.) Briefing memoranda for the meeting are ibid., National Security Files, Countries Series, China, and ibid., President's Office Files, China Security, 1962–1963, Memoranda for Meeting with Chiang Ching-kuo. Secretary of State Rusk met with Chiang on September 13; a memorandum of that conversation is in Department of State, Central Files, POL 2 CHINA. See the Supplement.

[1] Dated September 5; it enclosed a memorandum declaring that the time had come to take action by guerrilla airdrops and commando raids which would "ignite an explosion on the Chinese mainland" and stating that U.S. involvement would be unnecessary and that "there will be no question of our not abiding by the mutual defense pact." (Kennedy Library, President's Office Files, China General, 1963) See the Supplement. An additional aide-mémoire addressed to Kennedy elaborated on this and requested that the U.S. Government provide means of transport for maritime and airdrop operations and expedite delivery of weapons and equipment already allocated and approved but not yet delivered. (Kennedy Library, President's Office Files, China Security, 1962–1963, Memoranda for Meeting with Chiang Ching-kuo) See the Supplement.

—that we do not wish to become involved in military operations where our role would inevitably become known and which would end in failure,
—that we had one bad experience in Cuba where operations had been based more on hope than on a realistic appraisal of the situation,
—that we both agree that we wish to weaken and, if possible, to destroy Communist China, but undertaking actions which failed would result in a setback for the cause of freedom everywhere,
—that we would carefully study the GRC's proposals for use of additional ships and planes,
—that United States officials would work closely with GRC officials to develop detailed intelligence so that any action would fit the actual situation. End Summary.

1. General Chiang opened the substantive part of the conversation by presenting to the President a letter from President Chiang Kai-shek. After reading the letter, the President asked Chiang what he felt were the military prospects for intensified GRC raids on the Chinese mainland, such as the letter was suggesting, in view of the GRC experience with small scale raids in the recent past. The President asked what was the basis for the GRC belief that airdrop operations of 100 to 300 men and sea-borne landings of 300 to 500 men would be successful.

2. General Chiang replied that President Chiang had asked him to present the following views:

a. The signing of the Partial Nuclear Test Ban Treaty is a diplomatic victory for the United States which will help to preserve world peace. (President Kennedy then expressed appreciation for the signing by the Republic of China of the Treaty.)

b. The Sino-Soviet dispute is a favorable development because, within the premises of maintenance of the status quo and the preservation of peace, it gives us a chance to use the forces now available to us to weaken the Chinese Communists.

c. The Sino-Soviet dispute is primarily a personal one between Mao and Khrushchev. Thus, the dispute could continue to worsen or there could be a 180-degree change.

d. President Chiang greatly admires President Kennedy's foresight in predicting in a recent speech that by 1970 the Chinese Communists could become a much greater menace.[2] President Chiang believes that the Chinese Communists must not be allowed to recover from their present difficulties but that advantage should be taken of the present situation to harass and disrupt them, to weaken them so that it will be possible to launch a successful counterattack sometime in the future.

3. The President asked Chiang what weight he gave to historical and geographic factors in the Sino-Soviet dispute, noting his own feeling that the geographic factors had considerable importance. Chiang replied that while geography was important, in the Orient personality was a more

---

[2] Reference is to Kennedy's August 1 press conference; see footnote 6, Document 183.

important factor. This was especially true of the Communist party on the mainland.

4. Chiang said that President Chiang feels that the United States and the GRC should get together to take advantage of the present situation. Fully aware of the peace policy of the United States, President Chiang feels that this is not the time for large-scale military operations against the mainland. But if lesser attacks are not made against the mainland, if the Chinese Communists are left in peace to overcome their present serious difficulties, if means are not found to disrupt, disturb and disorganize them, the Chinese Communists will be able to develop into a far greater international menace than they have been in the past. Even though Soviet military aid has been discontinued, the Chinese Communists will be able to consolidate. While political and psychological warfare is important, it will not be effective unless military measures are carried on simultaneously. The GRC envisages an augmented program of attacks by airdrop operations and seaborne commando landings, but not a large-scale invasion.

5. President Kennedy inquired about the degree of success of the guerrilla raids carried out in the recent past, and asked for details concerning the number of raids and percentage of casualties involved.

Chiang replied that as military operations these raids had not seen much success, but from the point of view of their disruptive effect on the Chinese Communists, there had been much better results. Since last October, 28 raids had been carried out, involving teams ranging from six to 28 men. Most of the raiders were recent refugees from the areas attacked. Half of four teams were able to return to Taiwan. All other personnel became casualties. This meant a casualty rate of 85 percent. The significance of these raids lies not in the percentage of casualties but rather in the disruptive effect on the Chinese Communists, as demonstrated by Chinese Communist broadcasts themselves. For example, on July 28 of this year, a ten-man team was landed and suffered 100 percent casualties. But according to Chinese Communist radio broadcasts, 3,000 troops were mobilized to deal with the team and 205 officers and men were later rewarded for their part in the operations against the raiders. Similarly, according to the Chinese Communist radio, 1,500 CPR troops fought for three days to deal with a team which landed in Chekiang June 27.

These examples illustrate that, although most of the raiders may be casualties, the raids achieve their purposes: i.e., to cause trouble on the mainland, to raise the morale of the people, who hope for liberation, and to upset the organization of the army. The ability of the GRC to carry out these raids, however, is hindered by lack of transport and other factors.

6. The President asked what the GRC had in mind with regard to airdrops.

Chiang replied that the numbers involved would range from 20 to 100 or more depending upon the situation. Such operations would not lead to a world war, but would serve to keep the Chinese Communists on the defensive. Also, atomic research and development installations and missile emplacements might be likely targets for airborne raids. The purpose of these operations would be to weaken the strength of the Chinese Communists progressively over the next 12 to 18 months, to see what the result would be. President Chiang's idea is to proceed to establish a foothold on the continent, when the time is ripe, through the occupation of one or more provinces south of the Yangtze River.

The frequency and size of the airdrops would depend upon the situation, the target, and upon joint discussions with your officials. The size of the teams might range from 50 to 300 men. Both sides would have to study this.

7. The President asked what Chiang thought would be the result of such airdrops.

Chiang replied that likely targets would be in more inaccessible areas where communications were poor, where there were relatively few garrison troops, and where unrest was more pronounced. If 200 to 300 men were dropped, they might be able to seize a county, in which case the people would be likely to rally around them.

8. The President asked what information had been gathered from the recent landings or from intelligence sources which led the GRC to believe that the people would support such operations or that there would be defections in the Chinese Communist army.

Chiang replied that the overall picture on the mainland was one of growing unrest. Raiding operations would be carried out in areas where this unrest was marked; for example, slave labor camps would be ideal targets.

9. The President asked concerning the nature of GRC intelligence contacts on the mainland.

Chiang replied that the GRC had many intelligence sources. In July there had been a revolt of slave laborers in Chung-shan County, Kwangtung province. The GRC had dispatched a team of ten men to stimulate revolt there, but the timing had been poor and too few were involved.

10. The President asked how many intelligence agents the GRC had on the mainland.

[1-1/2 lines of source text not declassified] The GRC depends to a considerable extent on persons travelling to and from the mainland and on clandestine correspondence for intelligence.

11. The President emphasized that the United States felt there was a particular lack of hard intelligence from the China mainland. United States actions in Cuba, for example, had suffered for lack of hard intelli-

gence. We feel that there is insufficient detailed and reliable intelligence from the China mainland. If the GRC has such intelligence, the President hoped that it would be made available to us.

Chiang replied that, on this point, the President should understand a special characteristic of the Chinese people. The latter want to be rid of the Communists, but without anyone to lead and to organize them, they are reluctant to act. Throughout Chinese history, troops have hesitated to take action to revolt unless there were assurances of an external source of help. The same consideration applies to the Chinese people. The most important thing is not to allow the Chinese Communists to consolidate and to have peace and quiet over the next year. To let them alone for the coming year would be to permit them to survive this critical period and to advance to greater strength. What methods are to be used to prevent this consolidation is another matter, one which the United States and the GRC should discuss.

12. The President agreed that under the Communist control apparatus the people have no means to express their dissatisfaction. But it is an extremely serious matter for the United States to become involved in support of the operations suggested by General Chiang, particularly in view of the fact that the United States part would inevitably become public knowledge. There is no doubt that it is to our common advantage to weaken the Chinese Communists, but we do not want to become involved in operations which could be regarded as attacks on the mainland and which would fail. Thus, detailed and accurate intelligence is extremely important. Our intelligence people feel that there is a considerable lack of such intelligence. We need to know definitely the extent of unrest on the mainland and, for example, whether or not major officials are likely to defect. The United States is not sure that the operations can be successful until the whole mainland is ready for revolt.

13. Chiang stated that the question is one of how to deny the Chinese Communists a period of peace and quiet which would enable them to survive their present difficult situation. In this regard, aside from political and psychological warfare, it is important to step up raids by air and sea.

14. The President observed that 28 small-scale raids were not very significant. It did not appear that these raids had disrupted the mainland regime in any large degree.

Chiang replied that the need now was to increase the size of the raids, and that the GRC needed more transport and technical help to do this. The goal of these larger raids would be to multiply the disruption which had already been caused. Since the Chinese Communists had been obliged to use 3,000 men to deal with a small raid, more and larger raids would force them to use greater forces, and would cause commensurately greater disruption.

15. The President asked what the GRC wanted over the next 12 months in this regard.

Chiang replied that over the next 12 to 18 months the GRC would need to use the four C–123's which it now has, but is not using, and an additional five C–130's. It would also need additional landing craft. If agreement could be reached on principle, details can be determined at the working level.

16. The President noted that he felt the Chinese Communists pose a tremendous danger to world peace, and that the United States is willing to do any reasonable thing which would weaken their power. Our concern is that our policy should be determined by reality and not by our hopes or by our optimism. Thus, we feel that we should concentrate on improvement in the intelligence gathering field. With better intelligence and more facts, we can be more sure that our actions suit the situation. The small raids which have been carried out, for example, would appear to have been useful in teaching us a lesson concerning the feasibility of such operations. The sacrifice made by the many brave men who took part shows that the Chinese Communists still exercise effective control on the mainland.

For our part, we shall study carefully the GRC proposal for use of additional ships and planes. But such a study will depend upon more intelligence from the GRC. We would request that the GRC make sure that its plans are in fact realistic. The United States suffered a setback in the Cuban affair, because of insufficient intelligence, a setback we would not want to repeat.

Chiang replied that he hoped the President would authorize United States organizations to go into details on the requests made during this visit, and that planning could continue after Chiang's return to Taiwan. President Chiang feels that efforts must be coordinated. The Chinese Communists are like a starving tiger. The tiger should be killed now, when he is weak, and before he has a chance to regain his strength.

17. The President asked if Chiang thought it would be possible to send 300 to 500 men by air to such distant Chinese Communist atomic installations as that at Pao-t'ou, and whether it was not likely that the planes involved would be shot down.

Chiang replied that this had been discussed [*less than 1 line of source text not declassified*] yesterday and that [*less than 1 line of source text not declassified*] such an operation was feasible.

18. President Kennedy stated that the United States agreed that the Chinese Communist regime should be weakened, and even destroyed, if that were possible. The GRC wishes to return to its home, and we wish to ensure peace in the world. But we must be realistic. If operations which failed were to be undertaken, then we would be in a worse position than before. An example of this took place in 1961 in Cuba when the opera-

tions there were based more on hope than on realistic appraisals. We must be cold-blooded in our assessments. The United States cannot be involved in losing operations. If four to six divisions were put ashore on the China mainland and were defeated, this would be a setback for the cause of freedom everywhere.

The President then summarized the United States position: the need now was for better intelligence, more detailed information about conditions on the China mainland, so that we might be assured that whatever action is undertaken would fit the actual situation. He promised that the United States would work closely with Chinese officials for these ends.

19. The meeting concluded with the usual courtesies and an exchange of gifts. Chiang presented the President with a Chinese translation of his Inaugural Address and a copy of a Chinese translation of his book "Profiles in Courage." The President presented Chiang with an autographed photograph of himself.

---

**187.  Telegram From the Embassy in Poland to the Department of State**

Warsaw, September 11, 1963, 7 p.m.

513. Cabot–Wang Talks. 117th meeting.[1] Two hours 35 minutes. Deptel 390.[2]

(1) I opened with substance paragraphs 1, 2, and 3 reference telegram on deportees, claims against shipping companies, and Howden,[3]

---

Source: Department of State, Central Files, POL CHICOM–US. Confidential; Priority; Limit Distribution. Repeated to Taipei, Hong Kong, Stockholm, Moscow, and Geneva.

[1] Cabot commented and sent recommendations for the next meeting in telegram 516, September 12. He commented that in view of the Sino-Soviet rift, the Department was presumably considering whether a "more conciliatory tone on our part in talks might pay off." He stated that he saw "no signs whatever as yet it would", but he thought the Department "should study situation in light its overall knowledge to judge whether any change in atmospherics of the talks would be worthwhile experiment." (Ibid.) He sent a detailed, apparently verbatim report of the meeting in airgram A–235, September 14. (Ibid.)

[2] Telegram 390, September 4, provided guidance for the meeting. (Ibid.)

[3] Paragraph 1 concerned arrangements for the return of six deportees. Paragraph 2 stated that discussions were to take place in Hong Kong between the parties involved in one of the shipping incidents raised at the previous meeting. Paragraph 3 instructed Cabot to request information concerning Robert Howden, reported by a French journalist to be an American in prison in China.

adding to paragraph 3 that we still hoping for release other imprisoned Americans in accordance with agreed announcement. Said I mentioned this particularly in light newspaper reports Bishop Walsh ill. Said did not need tell Wang what painful impression would be caused in US if Bishop Walsh should die in Chinese jail. Continued with substance paragraphs 4 and 5 with some embellishment and handed Wang copy of *Documents on Disarmament 1961*.[4] Concluded opening statement with substance paragraph 7 on our defense commitments in area.

(2) Wang said he had listened with regret because he thought after more than month of consideration my government would have reacted favorably to Chou's August 2 letter and to draft agreed announcement. Said my statement showed once more we not sincerely interested preventing nuclear war. Wang said his government position clear and consistent, always standing for general disarmament and complete ban nuclear weapons. Gave lengthy review in most general terms of his government's "unremitting efforts for general disarmament and destruction nuclear weapons". Wang said his government convinced mankind will destroy nuclear weapons and nuclear weapons will not destroy mankind. Said his government had put forth both general objectives and concrete measures to reach general disarmament and destruction nuclear weapons. Said there was sharp contrast between his proposal and tripartite treaty which "divorced discontinuance of nuclear tests from total banning nuclear weapons". Alleged only by adopting Chinese proposal could real progress be made. Referred to ChiCom call for conference heads of all nations of world and said facts have shown that without participation China no major international question can be settled. Era when handful of big powers take all in their hands is passed. Said proposal for nuclear-free zone in accord with overwhelming desire people of Asia. Enumerated various provisions called for in Chou letter and draft announcement. Said it was high time we took action extricate ourselves from difficult situation posed by fact people of countries where we had military bases opposed our presence. Wang said believed agreement on draft presented last meeting would facilitate smooth settlement other disputes between China and US. Said draft was only statement of principle not containing any complicated technical questions and therefore agreement should be reached in a relatively short time. Said once agreement in principle reached, technical questions such as verification and

---

[4] Paragraph 4 instructed Cabot to call attention to discrepancies in Chinese statements on disarmament. Paragraph 5 instructed him to call attention to various U.S. statements and suggested that he give Wang a copy of *Documents on Disarmament, 1961;* it stated that the Department did not intend to answer Chou's letter or comment further on the agreed announcement Wang had proposed at the August 7 meeting (see Document 183), since it believed the Chinese might be hoping for an outright U.S. rejection of their proposals used to justify their own nuclear tests.

control could be settled through further negotiations between the two sides.

Said we had even got "Chiang clique" sign tripartite treaty.[5] This showed hostility to his country and was new plot to create two Chinas. Said nuclear fraud of USG could not succeed. Said he was calling on me to "reconsider" their proposal but immediately started his sentence over saying "give careful consideration" to proposal for it was major question which we called on to discuss seriously in this meeting. Invited constructive views on it.

(3) Wang said report by French correspondent of fifth American allegedly imprisoned was complete fabrication.

(4) I said disarmament was very complicated subject on which we have negotiated in Geneva for very long time. This suggests Wang incorrect in saying we not interested in elimination threat nuclear war. Fact we have been able sign treaty with USSR and UK is step forward and at least 88 nations have signed treaty. Said we had given detailed documents on our position re disarmament while Chinese proposal was vague and certainly not clear to us. Said his side had repeatedly talked of anxiety to reach general disarmament and prohibition nuclear weapons—why then did they not sign test ban treaty which is important step in that direction. Reminded him he had said number of nations had expressed sympathy for his side's proposals and inquired which these were. Said he had mentioned so-called Vietnam Democratic Republic support. Considering blatant intervention that regime in Laos and South Vietnam, I did not think this was good endorsement for proposals. Said while we shared to considerable extent basic objectives as he had described them in connection his side's proposals, we were far from convinced deeds matched words his side and certain care was essential in any scheme for disarmament to make sure there was no cheating.

(5) I continued with substance paragraph 9 reftel re firmness without hostility[6] and gave answer redraft agreed announcement as instructed paragraph 5 (C).[7]

(6) Wang continued with long dissertation peaceful intent his Government and USG obstruction to disarmament efforts. Listed testing and other activities by USG which he thought inconsistent with spirit recently signed treaty. Again asked for serious consideration draft

---

[5] The Republic of China signed the treaty on August 23.

[6] Paragraph 9 instructed Cabot that the United States intended to maintain an attitude of firmness without hostility and was prepared to "wait patiently until Wang's side is willing to cooperate in lessening tensions."

[7] Paragraph 5 (C) summarized U.S. criteria concerning nuclear-free zones. For a statement of U.S. views on this subject as set forth on October 29 in Committee I of the U.N. General Assembly by Charles C. Stelle, see Department of State *Bulletin*, November 18, 1963, pp. 797–798.

agreed announcement and returned to theme of convocation of Heads of Nations for conference on total disarmament. Said that proposal had been endorsed by many countries including North Korea, North Vietnam, Cambodia, Burma, Indonesia, Laos, Albania, Ethiopia and Sierra Leone. Read at length endorsements by Prince Sihanouk, Emperor Haile Selassie, and Bertrand Russell, and numerous editorials from newspapers (some of which I recognized as being pro-Commie). Said fact so many countries had signed tripartite treaty shows US authorities have abused innocent peaceful wishes of people of these countries in order serve selfish interest USG and was continuance policy of satellization. Quoted *Time* magazine saying, "effect of treaty negligible."

(7) I expressed regret Wang had not spelled out more fully what was meant by his side's proposals and recalled we had not received comments from their side on our explicit and detailed positions re disarmament which earlier passed him.

Reminded Wang actions we had taken since tripartite treaty had been in accord with that treaty and we had no intention accept moratoria as we did before and find ourselves surprised by nuclear testing. Asked Wang whether his side when able would test in air and under sea, and whether reports true his side working hard as it could to get nuclear power at same time talking nuclear diaramament.

(8) Wang simply replied by saying mankind confronted with serious nuclear threat and specifically his country now faced with nuclear threat coming from US. Therefore necessary put forward draft agreed announcement which is not vague but specific, practical and feasible and formed useful basis for negotiations.

Next meeting November 13.

Before talk I told correspondents at entrance that no significance should be read into presence of photographers who in view of precedents were briefly admitted by mutual consent. After talk I said to correspondents that no inference should be drawn from length of talk. This was because there seemed to be impression among correspondents that something important was impending. At end of talk one correspondent asked whether atmosphere was cordial and I, knowing correspondent was well aware that Wang and I are very blunt with each other, said ironically that atmosphere was always cordial.

**Cabot**

## 188. Memorandum for the Record

Washington, undated.

The following summarizes certain discussions with General Chiang Ching-kuo during the General's visit to Washington.

The present moment is an important one in world history particularly in relation to the future course of events in the Far East and in Communist China. In order to weaken the Chinese Communist regime, it is desirable for the Government of the Republic of China and the United States to consult closely and carry out such actions as we mutually agree will serve this end.

Both governments wish to avoid action which would run the risk of precipitating a world conflict or action which, by failure or otherwise, would be detrimental to their joint interests. [2 *lines of source text not declassified*]

[1 *paragraph (8 lines of source text) not declassified*]

There was discussion of a proposal [*less than 1 line of source text not declassified*] to study and develop more effective operations. This group would develop plans and programs for consideration by both sides to improve capabilities to hurt the Chinese Communist regime. It was agreed that this subject would be discussed further [*less than 1 line of source text not declassified*]. In general the plans and programs might cover:

1. *The Political Path to Mainland Resistance*—It is important to develop ways and means to win the political allegiance of individuals on the mainland and to properly indoctrinate agents who were sent there. President Chiang's "Ten Pledges to the Mainland People" might well form a basis for the political program.

2. *Penetration and Subversion*—Equally important is the weakening of the Chinese Communist control apparatus by the recruitment and subversion of individuals in the government, the Party, and the Communist Army.

3. *Strategic Targets*—Study would be given to paramilitary sabotage operations directed at key Chinese Communist military and industrial installations.

The United States will provide adequate support for use when necessary in mutually agreed operations.

---

Source: Kennedy Library, National Security Files, Countries Series, China. Secret. No drafting information appears on the source text. Filed with a covering memorandum of September 16 from Department of State Executive Secretary Benjamin H. Read to Bundy, which states that it reflected the substance of a September 14 discussion between McCone and Chiang Ching-kuo and that the CIA wanted to send it to Wright for transmittal to the GRC. Read's memorandum requested Bundy's clearance both on the substance of the attachment and the decision to give a copy to the GRC and bears Forrestal's handwritten "OK" and initials. A transcript of McCone's September 14 conversation with Chiang is in Central Intelligence Agency, DCI (McCone) Files, Job 80–B01285A, Box 7, DCI Meeting Transcripts)

China 397

The basic policy set forth in the Seven Points memorandum[1] will continue to guide the actions of both sides.

---

[1] Document 98.

---

**189. Editorial Note**

At a meeting of the Special Group on September 19, 1963, William Colby of the Central Intelligence Agency referred to a detailed review of Agency operations in several areas including China and Tibet. According to a memorandum of the meeting by Thomas A. Parrott, Colby stated that the review had shown those activities were "not especially productive." The memorandum continues: "Therefore, the responsible operators have come to the conclusion that probably a change of approach is indicated. This would restrict targets to those of real significance, and would provide sufficient agent forces to accomplish the objective. Sizeable losses would have to be anticipated." (Central Intelligence Agency, DCI (McCone) Files, Job 80–B01285A, Box 1, 303 Committee Meetings)

---

**190. Paper Prepared in the Bureau of Far Eastern Affairs**

Washington, undated.

FE—OFFICE OF ASIAN COMMUNIST AFFAIRS

Current trends underline the need for taking a new look at the problem of Communist China in a changing world: the deepening of the Sino-

---

Source: Department of State, FE Files: Lot 65 D 6, ORG—Organization and Administration. Limited Official Use. The source text is an attachment to a memorandum of October 8 from Hilsman to Deputy Under Secretary for Administration William O. Crockett proposing the establishment of an Office of Asian Communist Affairs in the Bureau of Far Eastern Affairs. Neither bears any drafting information.

Soviet rift, the growing triangulation of the Cold War, the new diffusion of power and authority in the Communist world, progress in arms control counter-balanced by evidence that a truculent China may soon enter the nuclear club, and signs that Peiping baffled by the great leap backward and the enormity of China's long-term economic problems is casting about for new solutions which could involve dangers and/or opportunities for us.

In this situation there is a need to lay the foundation for a longer-range China policy, for a better coverage of North Korea, North Vietnam and Outer Mongolia, for closer attention to the world-wide implications for US policy of the Sino-Soviet split and for new focus on Subcontinent affairs as they affect China. This Bureau must share responsibility for developing policy affecting Communist Asia and must assume the main responsibility for carrying out these policies.

Although Mainland China, North Vietnam, North Korea and Outer Mongolia comprise two-thirds of the land area of the Far East and have over two-thirds of the population of the Far East, it is a fact that at present there are only two officers in the Bureau of Far Eastern Affairs who spend full time on Mainland Chinese affairs, working under an officer in charge who devotes perhaps two-thirds of his time to Mainland China. These three officers comprise a sub-section of the Office of East Asian Affairs which is responsible for Japan, Korea, and Taiwan as well as Mainland China. Obviously, the Office's overwhelming concern is with operational problems affecting Korea, Taiwan and Japan, the first two of which are major recipients of our aid with the largest armed forces in free Asia while Japan is by far the most important nation of the free Far East. The Office has little capacity left for Mainland China. Besides this, there is no officer in the Bureau dealing full time with North Vietnamese or North Korean affairs while Mongolia is almost totally ignored.

We, therefore, believe it essential to make certain adjustments in the structure of the Bureau to permit more adequate coverage and handling of Asian Communist affairs. (We recognize that we should avoid creating any public impression of change in our China policy, but we feel there may be advantage in acknowledging efforts being made to follow more closely Asian Bloc developments and implications for the US.)

We propose to establish an Office of Asian Communist Affairs which will have the responsibility within the Bureau of reinvigorating our China policy and meeting all other requirements for increased attention to Asian Communist affairs. The new Office will be small, consisting of a Director and five or six officers with area and functional specialties. Three of these would be taken from the Mainland China desk of the Office of East Asian Affairs thus relieving that Office of responsibility for Mainland China affairs. Additional officers would include a Sino-Soviet specialist, a specialist in South and Southeast Asia, and people to work on North Korea and North Vietnam.[1]

---

[1] Establishment of the office was authorized in a November 14 memorandum from Assistant Secretary for Administration Dwight J. Porter to Hilsman. Telegram 470 to Taipei, December 4, informed the Embassy that the office had been established effective November 27. (Both ibid., Central Files, ORG 8 FE)

---

## 191.  Highlights From Secretary of State Rusk's Policy Planning Meeting

Washington, October 15, 1963.

SUBJECT

A Chinese Communist Nuclear Detonation and Nuclear Capability

[Here follows a distribution list, including the Secretary of State and 21 other high-level officials of the Department, the Agency for International Development, the Arms Control and Disarmament Agency, and the United States Information Agency.]

The paper under discussion[1] was favorably commented upon as a fine example of creative and imaginative thinking. There was consensus with the paper's thesis that the advent of a ChiCom nuclear capability would heighten already existing issues rather than pose wholly new problems.

Reference was made to the possibility that a ChiCom nuclear capability might create rather more difficulty with respect to the position of the Republic of China than the paper concluded. For example, it could

---

Source: Department of State, S/P Files: Lot 70 D 199, Secretary's Policy Planning Meetings. Secret. The source text does not indicate the drafter, although it was drafted on October 24. Nor does it list the participants at the meeting.

[1] Reference is to a draft policy statement entitled "A Chinese Communist Nuclear Detonation and Nuclear Capability," circulated with a summary, headed "A Chinese Communist Nuclear Detonation and Nuclear Capability: Major Conclusions and Key Issues." (Ibid., S/P Papers) A revised draft, also with a summary, is dated October 15. (Ibid.) For the October 15 summary, see the Supplement. An October 18 memorandum from Rostow to Planning Group members states that the paper was prepared in an interdepartmental group, including the Departments of State, Defense, CIA, and USIA. (Kennedy Library, National Security Files, Countries Series, China)

significantly affect morale on Taiwan, help undermine international support for the GRC (either as a result of international reaction to mainland raids or of pressures for expanded communication with Peiping) and create difficulties through Peiping's possible exploitation of the offshores situation.

The Soviet estimate puts a later date upon the development of Chi-Com advanced weapons capabilities than U.S. estimates; the possibility exists that we have overestimated the extent of Soviet technical aid to the ChiComs. U.S. intelligence may, however, now be better than that of the USSR on the ChiCom program. Prevention of a ChiCom nuclear capability is one important goal that we share in common with the Soviets. The USSR may mobilize all the means at its disposal to forestall the ChiComs from acquiring a nuclear capability. The test ban treaty may have been a step in this campaign.

There was discussion of how the Chinese Communist nuclear capability would affect the Moscow–Peiping alliance. In September the Soviets made it clear that there were at least two areas in which the USSR would not feel obliged to honor the treaty: in the event of ChiCom aggression against India, or in the Taiwan Straits. Thus, the Soviet nuclear umbrella over the "Socialist camp" does not mean unqualified support for ChiCom aggression.

There was discussion of whether a ChiCom nuclear capability would cause other Asian nations to move closer to either China or the U.S. (in the light of the estimate in the paper that Asian countries were likely, at least initially, to be confirmed in their present policies). It was pointed out that it did not require a large nuclear arsenal to terrorize Asian neighbors and coerce them into political compromises favorable to Peiping. The threat of one nuclear bomb on Calcutta could conceivably give Communist China considerable political leverage. The ChiComs might also hope to use their nuclear capability as a deterrent to response to major conventional aggression. On the other hand, the fear of a U.S. nuclear response to a nuclear attack would act as a major restraint on Communist China. U.S. countermoves and the U.S. military posture in the area will go far to determine the course which China's Asian neighbors will adopt once China has the bomb. For reasons developed in the paper, including effects on the willingness of Asian countries to seek U.S. aid, the emphasis should be on a strong U.S. conventional capability.

Question was raised as to whether we should reject outright as a future course of action the possibility of bringing Communist China into

the Eighteen Nation Disarmament Commission (ENDC) (Issue No. 3).[2]
In the second stage of the disarmament plans discussed at Geneva the
adherence of the ChiComs, France and others would be needed. It was
agreed that Issue 3 should be revised to make it clear that exclusion of
Communist China from the ENDC referred only to the immediate
future.

Regional disarmament arrangements were unrealistic because
there was little prospect that China's neighbors could reduce arms below
present levels without endangering internal security needs. It was suggested that we should attempt to divert Peiping from regional solutions,
nuclear free zones, etc. (It was noted that it was for this reason that the
paper proposed development of the Asian components of the Outline
Treaty rather than a separate Asian disarmament scheme.)

The difficulties of providing even "temporary limited" increases in
military assistance to Asian countries as a form of reassurance following
ChiCom detonation of a nuclear device were discussed. It was emphasized that the paper did not contemplate a massive increase in aid, but
only modest increases. Nonetheless even the provision of modest additional MAP could become very difficult or impossible in view of the rapidly decreasing availabilities of MAP funds. Such increase would
require, at a minimum, hard planning of MAP programs and hard selling
to Congress.

It was questioned whether military assistance for conventional military equipment would be a relevant form of response to a ChiCom
nuclear capability; it was pointed out that we did not want to burden
ourselves with needless additional assistance requirements. In answer it
was noted that assistance in air defense was likely to be considered relevant so long as the ChiComs depended upon aircraft for delivery. India
was cited as a case where assistance to air defense probably increased the
will to resist. Moreover, the real threat would continue to be conventional
rather than nuclear in character and Asian countries were likely to seek
additional U.S. aid as a form of general reassurance of the U.S. commitment to their defense.

It was suggested that the colored peoples of the world might rally to
a nuclear-armed China. However, the colored peoples would also tend
to fear China and to press a settlement on her rather than to rally to her
standard. It was partly for this reason that Communist China could be

---

[2] Reference is to Issue No. 3 in the summary, which asked how the United States could
meet probable Chinese Communist efforts to demonstrate peaceful intentions through
proposals for Asian nuclear-free zones and the like with positive initiatives, without taking
actions seriously unsettling to its Asian allies or inconsistent with other U.S. policies. Several actions were proposed, but bringing Communist China into the Eighteen-Nation Disarmament Commission was specifically rejected.

expected to emphasize its defensive and peaceful purposes in the post-detonation period.

ChiCom acquisition of the bomb will pose immediate problems that are diplomatic or political, rather than military, in nature. China is likely to strike a conciliatory stance from her new position of strength and wait for her neighbors to rush to the bargaining table. A good example of this tactic was China's sudden acceptance of a cease-fire and partial withdrawal after the invasion of India.

The question of the nuclear threshold was discussed and the similarity to the problem in Germany suggested. Just as the Germans demand an unambiguous commitment to nuclear defense, so the Asians might want to lower the nuclear threshold, rather than raise it as the paper advocates. We may well be put in the same position as in Europe–that of asking our allies to increase their conventional forces while they prefer to solve defense problems through greater nuclear protection. However, it was pointed out that the Germans, when it comes to cases rather than questions of general defense theory, admit the need of a conventional response as less likely to lead to obliteration of their country. Similar attitudes may be expected in Asia where, in any event, attitudes toward nuclear weapons are somewhat different.

There are few real targets for nuclear attack by Communist China in the area. In the Korean War we were ourselves faced with a similar situation: outside of the mass bombing of cities, there were no targets in China whose destruction would affect matters on the battlefield. Japan would present targets, but some of the most important targets in Asia would be U.S. military installations and the Chinese were most unlikely to attack these with nuclear weapons.

It was suggested that the statement of the second major conclusion in the summary paper[3] was somewhat misleading. As the basic paper itself made clear, a "pre-emptive" counter-force strike by the U.S. was ruled out. While the conclusion intended only to refer to the ChiCom perception of their situation and to the concern that perception could generate, it might be misinterpreted to imply the possibility of such a pre-emptive strike. It was agreed that the paper should be revised to avoid any such implication.[4]

---

[3] It reads:

"Whatever U.S. intentions, so long as the ChiComs have only soft, vulnerable delivery means, they will have to take account of the danger of pre-emptive U.S. counterforce action in military crisis situations. This could increase ChiCom caution."

[4] The second major conclusion in the revised paper of October 15 reads:

"Whatever actual U.S. intentions, so long as the ChiComs have only soft, vulnerable delivery means, they will have to take account of the danger of a U.S. nuclear or non-nuclear counterforce attack as a possible U.S. response to major ChiCom aggression. This could increase ChiCom caution."

## 192. Memorandum From the Assistant Secretary of State for Far Eastern Affairs (Hilsman) to Secretary of State Rusk

Washington, October 22, 1963.

SUBJECT

Consideration of (1) Restriction on Travel of American Citizens; and (2) Recognition of Mongolia

Two memoranda, both addressed to you through Governor Harriman, accompany this memorandum.[1] The first is entitled "Revision of Travel Regulations Governing American Citizens", with an annex providing talking points detailing our reasons for believing that a change in the travel rules is desirable. The second is entitled "Diplomatic Recognition of Mongolian People's Republic"; it also is annexed with talking points.

These two subjects seem unconnected. However, there are real advantages for taking action on both issues more or less simultaneously: the combined effect would be that we are trying to keep ourselves as well informed as possible on Communist Asia, siding neither with Moscow nor Peiping.

Recognition of Mongolia is a tactical decision, and we believe the national interest justifies it. A more basic issue is involved in the travel question: If we are interested in freedom, we have an interest in holding restriction on travel to a minimum. We believe that only in the case of Cuba are the foreign policy considerations so clear as to require that we continue to forbid travel by Americans. To other areas wherein we have no representation, we will discourage travel but not forbid it.

Our principal problem with recognition of Mongolia will be the GRC's reaction. The principal problem with the change of the travel rules will be domestic charges that "the Administration is going soft on Communism". Answers to these and other criticisms will be found in the annexed talking papers.

Both actions should be done before the 1964 election campaign reaches full crescendo. The proposal on travel is consistent with the policies which have been stated by this Administration, and the net effect on the electorate may well be favorable, but the announcement should be made in a relatively calm atmosphere, sufficiently well in advance of the

---

Source: Department of State, FE Files: Lot 65 D 6, POL 16, Independence, Recognition. Secret. Drafted by Grant. The memorandum was routed through Harriman, who did not initial it and it was thus apparently not sent to Rusk. Neither the memorandum nor its attachments bear any indication of the reason why they were not sent forward.

[1] Neither printed.

1964 elections to permit a sober consensus to have developed as to the advantages of the action.

If the recommendation to go ahead with the change in travel rules is accepted, there would appear to be no requirement for extra-Departmental clearances (since Justice has already cleared the original proposal), though we might check with Defense and CIA as a courtesy. CIA would probably be delighted over the change. Once it had been decided by the Administration to move on the travel question, there would be advance consultations with key Congressional leaders. Preparation should be made to notify interested governments shortly before the travel changes go into effect. The line for responding to press inquiries will need to be considered. A background briefing for selected members of the press might help to launch the new regulations properly.

### 193. Memorandum From Robert W. Komer of the National Security Council Staff to the President's Special Assistant for National Security Affairs (Bundy)

Washington, November 5, 1963.

Mac—

The PG lunch[1] on how to deal with a ChiCom nuclear capability was the usual disorderly affair.

The paper itself[2] is far more interesting. As I read it, the essential conclusion is that ChiCom acquisition of a semi-nuclear capability will not have much more than a marginally significant impact and can probably be coped with by some marginal stepping up of existing programs. Its major emphasis is on a variety of reassurances which we can give our Asian friends; in no case do these involve radical departures from existing policy.

Source: Kennedy Library, National Security Files, Countries Series, China. Secret.

[1] The Planning Group was an interdepartmental group of high-level officials who met regularly for informal discussions. Most of their discussions were apparently not recorded.

[2] Reference is to the October 15 draft paper cited in footnote 1, Document 191. The October 18 Rostow memorandum cited in that same footnote transmitted a copy of the paper, including the summary, for discussion at the Planning Group meeting. Both are filed with the source text.

The consensus was that the Chinese would remain basically cautious in the overt use of force even after they acquired a few nucs; first use by them would be highly unlikely—instead they would see their nucs as a deterrent to escalation by us.

There was much discussion on how to "strangle the baby in the cradle" before the Chinese developed a capability, but if my reading of the thrust of the paper (above) is correct, there would seem to be less incentive for us to do so.

Walt wants to move this paper forward for NSC review, once JCS comment on it.[3] I entered usual demur that paper still far from being in a form productive of useful discussion. But Walt asked me to raise with you, though conceding that paper was probably better suited in present form for weekend reading.[4]

RWK

[3] A copy of the October 15 paper was sent to the Joint Chiefs of Staff with a November 5 memorandum from William Bundy, requesting JCS comments. (Washington National Records Center, RG 330, Records of the Office of the Secretary of Defense, OASD/ISA Files: FRC 67 A 4564, 47/16 Communist China) A December 13 memorandum from Gilpatric to McCone enclosed a copy of a JCS paper, noting that it recommended establishing an interagency group "to consider ways and means for impeding the Chinese Communist nuclear development program." Gilpatric stated that he and William Bundy thought the 5412 Group would be an appropriate forum for considering the proposal. (Ibid., OSD/ISA Files: FRC 69 A 926, 092 Communist China) The JCS comments have not been found, but a related JCS paper of December 14 (JCSM–986–63) is ibid.

[4] The paper was apparently not sent to Kennedy. An attached handwritten note from Bromley Smith to Bundy states, "This event is so far down the road I doubt JFK should be given this this year."

## 194. Telegram From the Embassy in Poland to the Department of State

Warsaw, November 13, 1963, 7 p.m.

926. Cabot–Wang Talks. Deptel 799.[1] 118th meeting two hours 10 minutes.[2]

Source: Department of State, Central Files, POL CHICOM–US. Confidential; Priority; Limit Distribution. Repeated to Taipei, Hong Kong, Stockholm, Moscow, and Geneva.

[1] Telegram 799, November 6, provided guidance for the meeting. (Ibid.)

[2] Cabot commented on the meeting in telegram 928, November 14, and sent a detailed, apparently verbatim report of the meeting in airgram A–416, November 21. (Both ibid.)

1.   Wang opened with U–2 incident[3] asserting that second such incident was part and parcel plot harass mainland and constituted additional evidence US hostility and aggression. Stated he instructed lodge strong protest which he hoped I would transmit. Claimed facts proved President and State Department spokesman were wrong when they stated only 2 U–2s had been sold. He cited UPI story of crash on Taiwan and Reuter's December 19, 1962 story re replacements as proof there is agreement between intelligence agencies that there will always be U–2s on Taiwan. Also claimed these aircraft under US control and supply, maintenance, use, and authority solely in US hands.

2.   Wang then referred my statement last meeting[4] re our attitude of firmness without hostility and stated our recent behaviour had given lie this statement. Cited infringement China's territorial airspace and waters, guerrilla group parachuted onto Hainan Island, "summoning" of Chiang Ching-kuo to Washington, joint exercises involving Chiang clique with 173rd Airborne Brigade and 503rd Infantry Combat Group, and air support by 5th and 13th Air Forces as wanton military provocations. He instructed lodge serious protest these activities and demand that they cease immediately.

3.   Wang also alleged US had been using territories adjacent China for military activities. "Puppets" in South Vietnam and South Korea have launched agent operations. We have goaded India into provocations by equipping 6 divisions for Himalayan fighting, considering equipping two additional mountain divisions, and engaging in joint maneuvers.

4.   Wang referred to our obstructive tactics in UN and Ambassador Stevenson's statements there[5] noting his Foreign Ministry had issued statement of condemnation and protest.[6] He concluded with reference to Alsop tonsilectomy article as further evidence our aggressive conduct.

---

[3] A U.S.-made, Chinese Nationalist-piloted U–2 aircraft was shot down over the China mainland on November 1.

[4] See Document 187.

[5] On October 21, by a vote of 41 to 57 (U.S.), with 12 abstentions, the General Assembly rejected a draft resolution sponsored by Albania and Cambodia calling for the immediate removal of "the representatives of Chiang Kai-shek" and an invitation to the People's Republic of China to send representatives to occupy China's place in the United Nations and all its organs. (U.N. doc. A/L.427 and Add. 1) For text of Stevenson's statement before the General Assembly on October 16, see Department of State Bulletin, November 11, 1963, pp. 755–758.

[6] A statement issued by the PRC Foreign Ministry on October 24 is quoted in the Peking Review, vol. VI, No. 44 (November 1, 1963), pp. 3–4.

5. I expressed disappointment concerning his statements and reminded him we were allies of Republic of China. Replied U–2 accusations along lines paragraph 2 reference telegram.[7] Stated would refer protest to Washington but expressed belief it was uncalled for in circumstances. Added that in view consistently aggressive attitude his side it natural that nations on borders would take protective actions. Explained we did not "summon" officials of other sovereign governments. Re maneuvers pointed out these designed to protect against further aggression. Re territorial infringements and guerrilla activity I replied along lines paragraph 3 reference telegram. Denied knowledge Alsop story emphasizing he obviously private individual.

6. I then raised prisoner issue (paragraph 7) reference telegram, exchange of newsmen (paragraph 8), deportees (paragraph 9) and missing servicemen (paragraph 10).[8]

7. Wang rejoined by stating my justification for hostile acts would not hold hot water. My reference to Republic of China could not give legal basis our occupation of Taiwan. Defenses re U–2 described as futile. Claimed we use U–2s all over and such espionage flights now part of US national policy. Claimed we intentionally aggravating tension and conducting consistent smear campaign. Cited statements by Sihanouk, former Japanese Prime Minister Ishibashi, Chairman Nepalese National Assembly Bendudapa, a Kenyan Senator, a Deputy in Pakistan National Assembly and the Vice President of the Peoples Organization in Southwest Africa to prove false nature our alleged smear campaign.

8. Wang stated his side had first put forward exchange of personnel idea and had attempted promote this matter but US had placed obstacles in path by policy of hostility, relations could be normalized and obstacles in path exchange of persons could be eliminated.

9. Wang said he did not think it appropriate to discuss prisoners in North Korea and Laos at this meeting.

---

[7] Paragraph 2 of telegram 799 stated that if Wang reiterated New China News Agency charges that the U–2s were under U.S. control, Cabot should state that in view of Chinese Communist previous attacks and hostility toward the GRC, the United States had authorized the sale of U–2 planes to the GRC; if Wang referred to the statements cited in footnote 5 and asked if other U–2s had been or would be supplied, he should reply that he could not discuss U.S.-GRC mutual defense plans.

[8] Paragraph 7 stated that release of the U.S. prisoners would bring a strong response from the American public and expressed the hope that Wang's side would intercede with the Pathet Lao and North Korea for the release of Americans. Paragraph 8 reiterated that it would be in the interest of both sides to seek greater understanding through an exchange of newspapermen. Paragraph 9 instructed Cabot to ask Wang if his side would accept three additional deportees. Paragraph 10 stated that a recently returned Korean War nonrepatriate said he had seen American personnel identification tags from the Korean war on display at the Peking War Museum and requested that if this were true, the names and numbers from those tags should be provided.

10. Wang expressed hope that nothing will prevent return to China of 3 deportees already accepted.

11. Wang said he would look into cases of additional 3 deportees and hoped give a reply in a few days.

12. I expressed regret we seemed be far apart on most matters this meeting. Reiterated Republic of China operating U–2s and saw no reason for responsibility to be placed on US. With reference his quotation opinions prominent individuals I affirmed their right their own opinions. I then referred to recent Soviet-Chinese exchange of communications and said that Chinese statements themselves showed that his side was aggressive. Agreed we had worked against admission to UN in belief his side not peace-loving and majority of nations agreed with us. Regretted he no longer appeared willing exchange newsmen. Re deportees I stated we did not want them to remain but they themselves had raised obstacles to their immediate deportation.[9]

13. Wang misunderstood my comments about Sino-Soviet communications and thought I had referred to Soviet not Chinese statements. He stated it was inappropriate in these talks to refer to third countries and expressed view it was futile to cite Soviet statements as defense our own hostile policy. He described Soviet Union as great Socialist country whose people had glorious revolutionary tradition and said it would be premature for anyone to show delight or to attempt to profit from dispute.

14. Wang claimed our obstructive tactics UN becoming more unpopular each year and it was not up to US to determine unilaterally which countries are peace-loving. Said our obstructive tactics would go bankrupt.

15. I straightened out his confusion re my reference to Soviet and Chinese statements emphasizing the manner and reasonable man would interpret Chinese statements regarding their attitude towards matters which impinge on our interests.

16. I suggested next meeting be held January 8 but Wang requested it be January 29. I agreed.

**Cabot**

---

[9] Telegram 823 to Warsaw, November 12, reported that one deportee had failed to surrender himself and two had reopened their legal cases. (Department of State, Central Files, POL CHICOM–US)

## 195. Telegram From Secretary of State Rusk to the Department of State

Paris, December 16, 1963, 10 p.m.

Secto 25. Eyes only for the President.[1] Accompanied by Bohlen and Tyler I had about forty minutes with de Gaulle this morning. Also present were Couve de Murville, Alphand and de la Grandville who served as interpreter.

[Here follows discussion of other subjects, including Southeast Asia.]

I then reverted to the subject of the Communist world and relations between the Soviet Union and China. I said we were concerned at the evidence of Chinese militancy—one aspect of the dispute with the Soviet Union—and that in our talks at Warsaw they were insistent that we should give up Formosa. There had also been the Indian attack and we felt that Hanoi and Peking together had blocked the implementation of the Laotian accords. There was also some evidence that the Chinese were stimulating Sukarno in his present courses of action; they were active in Latin America, particularly with Castro; and finally Chou En-lai was at present in Africa. We felt it important that Peking not be given any impression that any such policy would pay dividends. I mentioned that we had been very glad to hear that France had no intention of recognizing China[2] but felt it was worthwhile keeping in contact on such developments. De Gaulle then made rather a long statement that with the Chinese-Soviet dispute the Soviets seemed to have calmed down while Peking was taking on "as a trial gallop" the task of promoting revolution, but he doubted if they would be any more successful than the Soviets had been except in Eastern Europe where the armies controlled. He said the question was how the West could turn this to its advantage, whether it was best to leave China alone completely or have certain contacts. He felt that such contacts had helped in the past with Soviet Russia. I replied I could not see much evidence of our influence in our contacts with the Soviets and I had felt that the change in Soviet attitude was due to the confrontation with military power in the West, possibly increased by the

---

Source: Department of State, Conference Files: Lot 66 D 110, CF 2345. Secret; Immediate. Rusk was in Paris to attend a NATO Ministerial meeting.

[1] President Lyndon B. Johnson; President Kennedy was assassinated in Dallas, Texas, on November 22.

[2] Reference is to a conversation on November 5 between de Gaulle and Ambassador Bohlen, reported in telegram 2222 from Paris, November 5. When Bohlen asked de Gaulle about his views on Communist China, he replied that he had no intention of proceeding with any such step as diplomatic relations "at this time" but that he thought "sooner or later" some relationships would have to be worked out. (Ibid., Central Files, POL 16 CHI-COM)

attitude of their own people and from the Eastern European countries. After all Moscow had been the most dangerous on Berlin and Cuba. Furthermore there had been no signs that the contacts with Peking such as the extremely friendly ones on the part of India and more informal ones on the part of Japan had had any effect on the Chinese. I told him I thought it would be a great mistake to let the Chinese or their Communist allies get any idea that such policies paid off.

De Gaulle agreed that the Soviets had been the more dangerous of the two but questioned whether they would not have been more so if we allowed them to "stew in their own juice", offering no alternative except war. He felt that the contacts had certainly not been unuseful. He agreed that India's and Japan's contacts had not changed the Chinese very much, but after all these were "poor" countries which had little to offer China whereas if at some time in the future the West might be in a position to establish relations with China this might be another story.

I pointed out that in Warsaw in nine years of contacts we had seen no interest insofar as Chinese trying to improve relations except at the cost of abandonment of Formosa. De Gaulle significantly said that Formosa would have to be sacrificed by the West (by implication in any agreement with the ChiComs).

In order to button down the French position further I inquired of de Gaulle whether he had any judgment as to the timing of any relationship with ChiComs and how far in the future this was to be since I understood that France was thinking of diplomatic relations for the future. De Gaulle said he could not answer this since it was a question for the future, and it depended on others and not France alone, but wished to assure me "as Secretary of State" that they would talk to the U.S. before any action was taken.

The conversation concluded with a mutual agreement to keep in touch on matters of the Soviet Union and particularly in regard to the Sino-Soviet dispute; and an exchange of amenities including a personal message of regards and good will to you.

**Rusk**

## 196. Letter From the Assistant Secretary of State for Far Eastern Affairs (Hilsman) to the Representative to the United Nations (Stevenson)

Washington, December 19, 1963.

DEAR ADLAI: Here is the brief rationale for my San Francisco speech[1] you requested in case you are questioned on its content and implications.

*1. The Policy*

a) Our policy towards Communist China is one of firmness, flexibility and dispassion. We are firm in our commitment to the government of the Republic of China and people of Taiwan and in our resistance to all forms of aggression by the Chinese Communists. We are flexible in our readiness to respond to a significant change in the behavior of the Peiping regime. We are dispassionate in our refusal to substitute cliches and polemical rhetoric for cool, objective analysis.

One parallel to this policy can be found in our recent relations with the USSR. When the Soviets placed missiles in Cuba, we responded with firmness; but six months later, when the Soviets sought a Test Ban agreement, we were willing to negotiate.

b) On the specific point of the Peiping regime's viability, we doubt the possibility of its overthrow for two reasons:

—Police states of such a far-reaching nature are notoriously invulnerable to uprisings by an inadequately armed populace;
—China's leaders, despite their intensive dogmatism, have shown a tendency to pull back and become pragmatic in the face of serious internal or external resistance.

Hence, as I concluded in my speech: "We hope that, confronted with firmness which will make foreign adventure unprofitable, and yet offered the prospect that the way back into the community of man is not closed to it, the Chinese Communist regime will eventually forsake its

---

Source: Princeton University, Seeley G. Mudd Manuscript Library, Stevenson Papers, Box 860, Chinese Representation. Limited Official Use; Official–Informal. Drafted by Thomson, according to Hilsman's copy. (Kennedy Library, Hilsman papers, Box 1, Communist China—Policy Speech, 12/13/63)

[1] For text of Hilsman's address to the Commonwealth Club of San Francisco on December 13, see Department of State *Bulletin*, January 6, 1964, pp. 11–17. According to James C. Thomson, Jr., Special Assistant in the Bureau of Far Eastern Affairs, it was drafted by Grant, with additions and revisions by Green, Deputy Assistant Secretary for Far Eastern Economic Affairs Robert W. Barnett, Director of the Office of Research and Analysis for the Far East in the Bureau of Intelligence and Research Allen Whiting, and himself. (Memorandum of May 6, 1964, by Thomson; Kennedy Library, Thomson Papers, Box 9, Hilsman Speech, Thomson Notes on Genesis and Reaction) See also Hilsman, *To Move a Nation*, pp. 350–357, and Thomson, "On the Making of U.S. China Policy, 1961–9: A Study in Bureaucratic Politics," *The China Quarterly*, No. 50, April/June 1972, pp. 230–231.

present venomous hatreds which spring from a rigid class view of society."

### 2.   The Implications

The speech signifies no change in U.S. policy, no new departure.[2]

It is significant primarily as the first attempt in some time to articulate the policies we have been pursuing toward Communist China for several years.

It should be added that we have similarly pursued a policy of firmness and flexibility toward the Soviet Union.

### 3.   The Timing

The speech was given at this time for the following reasons:

a)  The Commonwealth Club of San Francisco asked me to—early this autumn.

b)  No full-scale rational analysis of U.S. China policy has been available for public information since Mr. Dulles' speech in San Francisco of June 28, 1957.[3]

c)  There was a need to clarify the reasons for the apparent divergence between U.S. treatment of Moscow and U.S. treatment of Peiping. As the Soviets have begun to behave more responsibly, the U.S. has become more responsive to Soviet initiatives; but with Peiping continuing to hew to a bellicose Stalinist line, we have been unresponsive to the Chinese. This apparent divergence stems from a consistent policy of firmness and flexibility, as applied to two regimes whose behavior currently differs.

I hope that these points will be of use to you.

With my best wishes,

Sincerely,

**Roger**

---

[2] For text, see *Foreign Relations, 1955–1957*, vol. III, pp. 558–566.

[3] At President Kennedy's press conference on November 14 in response to a question under what conditions the United States might resume "some sort of trade with Red China," he replied in part as follows: "We are not planning to trade with Red China in view of the policy that Red China pursues. When the Red Chinese indicate a desire to live at peace with the United States, with other countries surrounding it, then quite obviously the United States would reappraise its policies. We are not wedded to a policy of hostility to Red China." (*Public Papers of the Presidents of the United States: John F. Kennedy, 1963*, pp. 845–846)

## 197. Letter From the Ambassador to the Republic of China (Wright) to the Assistant Secretary of State for Far Eastern Affairs (Hilsman)

Taipei, December 19, 1963.

DEAR ROGER: Having been on the job here for six months, I feel that I have my teeth reasonably dug into the situation. I am, therefore, compiling a brief summary of important aspects of recent developments which I think should be elaborated in a personal exchange with you.

*Mainland Recovery Activities*

With respect to the most delicate problem which has concerned us over the past two years—GRC preparations for military action against the mainland—we seem to be in a prolonged quiescent period. Statements to President Chiang, and to Chiang Ching-kuo during the latter's visit to the United States, reaffirming United States opposition to any overt military action by the GRC under present circumstances, combined with assurances of continued United States support for the GRC and acquiescence in small-scale clandestine operations plus study of other possibilities, appear to have served their purpose. Even though small-scale raids continued through October and November, accompanied by much high-flown publicity, there is little evidence that President Chiang contemplates cranking up the military machine for any early large-scale action.

The GRC sees little prospect of any significant economic recovery on the China mainland in the near future or any patching up of the Sino-Soviet dispute. These conclusions have tended to keep down the feeling of urgency here. However, there is a risk that this feeling may build up again over the next few months stimulated by the rush of European countries and Japan to do business with Communist China and by the downward trend of United States economic and military aid to the GRC. There is no sign yet that we are likely to run into a rising curve of secret military preparations here such as occurred in the spring of 1961 and to a lesser degree early in 1962, but we will keep our eyes open for indications.

*Japan-GRC Relations*

In the political field we have devoted considerable time in the past few weeks to the question of relations between the Republic of China and

Source: Department of State, FE/EA Files: Lot 66 D 224, R.C., ORG 1. Secret; Official–Informal. Wright sent a copy of the letter to Harriman. (Library of Congress Manuscript Division, Harriman Papers, Kennedy–Johnson Administrations, Subject Files, Box 524, Whf-Wz miscellaneous, 1961–1969)

Japan. The basic disquiet here arising from expanding Japanese trade with the Chinese mainland and the political implications of this expansion have been exacerbated by statements by Prime Minister Ikeda questioning the return-to-the-mainland policy and by the case of the ChiCom defector, Chou Hung-ching, still in Japan.

The GRC has been somewhat encouraged by the success of its protests in delaying Chou's repatriation, but continues to press for access to him. If the Japanese Government gives the GRC access to Chou, as it now seems inclined to do, and provides a further breathing spell before he is repatriated, reaction here may not be too serious. There is some evidence that the Chinese are endeavoring to prepare a situation in which the return of the defector to the mainland could be treated with measures short of either disruption of trade relations or impairment of diplomatic relations with Japan.

Recent press treatment of the subject has been moderate and it has been emphasized that Chou has been "brainwashed" by the ChiComs and is being forced to return to protect his family's safety. In these terms it could be demonstrated that he would not have made an unfettered decision not to come to Taiwan. The Japanese, of course, would continue to be castigated for permitting leftist influences access to him.

*Cabinet*

Recent government changes here in Taipei will not, we think, result in fundamental changes in the direction of GRC policies. C.K. Yen, the new Premier, can be expected to devote major energies to continuing economic development, financial stability and continuation of necessary United States aid arrangements, to the extent he is permitted to do so by the Gimo and the hard-line "return-to-mainland" supporters. There is general agreement he will not be a strong premier and his policies will be heavily dependent on presidential guidance and backing. The resignation of Chen Cheng as premier generally is interpreted as portending a long-term diminution of his influence in the GRC and this probably will, in fact, be the case. At the same time, the President's son, General Chiang Ching-kuo, is very likely to achieve greater influence. However, the full implications of the new government are not yet discernible.

*Representation at Funeral*

The GRC has been subject, as you know, to some criticism because of an allegedly inadequate response to President Kennedy's assassination. Our assessment is that the question was fumbled until the point had been reached where there was insufficient time to send someone, even after realization that a special delegation from the GRC would be conspicuous by its absence.

I see no important political significance in this matter and I think we should make every effort, as we have endeavored to do, to help mitigate

Chinese embarrassment on this score. The Japanese seem inclined to "make something" out of this blunder, but Reischauer is on top of the situation.

*Relations with President*

I have taken advantage of the visits of various prominent Americans recently and their calls on the President to take him aside briefly for discussions and presentations of interest to us. I believe that I am achieving a useful relationship with him and, for my part, I believe that these brief exchanges have served constructive purposes.

*Reduction in FY 64 Program and FY 65 Military Aid Plan*

The FY 64 Program as revised at CINCPAC in November and forwarded to the Department of Defense reduced the MAAG China ceiling from $133.8 million to $94.8 million. The FY 65 ceiling was reduced from $163.0 million to $108.4 million. The reduction in ceilings and in investment funds available for force modernization will increase the shortfall which must be funded in later years. Modernization of F–86F and C–46 squadrons and purchase of destroyers, tanks and armored personnel carriers, in addition to any minor but essential items, will not be possible under this reduced funding.

The second battalion of Nike-Hercules missiles is still funded in FY 64. However, the President has authorized deletion of this item under provisions which will be difficult to accept. CINCPAC's action has gone to Defense. If the deletion is approved, the FY 64 program will be reduced accordingly since it is very doubtful we will recoup any of these funds. The prospect is for a gradual decline in the overall capabilities of GRC forces, as equipment will not be modernized or replaced as rapidly as it wears out.

*F/RF–104G*

One squadron of eight RF–104G aircraft and seven F–104G aircraft have arrived in Taiwan. All F/RF–104G's will be initially based at Kung Kuan. Upon receipt of additional facilities and equipment, the reconnaissance models will move to Taoyuan.

*Economic Aid*

Progress is being made by the GRC in obtaining loans from international sources to replace the inflow of United States funds as the economic aid program is phased out. The World Bank made a loan to the GRC of almost $8 million repayable on commercial terms (5-1/2 percent interest, 15-year term). Burke Knapp, Vice President of the World Bank, told us and the Chinese on a visit here that the Bank was anxious to expand its lending program here.

Another favorable development has been the rapid increase in GRC exports to US$295 million in the first ten months of 1963 as compared with a preliminary Chinese estimate of US$270 million for the entire year. It appears that exports may well reach US$330–350 million for the year. This increase resulted largely from the fortuitous rise this year in the price of sugar, but other exports also increased by an impressive 22 percent. The government is concentrating increasing effort on the promotion of exports.

[Here follows brief discussion of copyright problems, the preparation of a national policy paper (not completed until 1964), Wright's interest in encouraging visits to Taiwan by high-level U.S. officials, pending military exercises, Hilsman's Commonwealth Club speech, and personnel matters.]

Sincerely yours,

**Jerauld Wright**[1]

---

[1] Printed from a copy that bears this typed signature.

# Mongolia

## 198. Memorandum From Secretary of State Rusk to President Kennedy

Washington, May 23, 1961.

SUBJECT

Diplomatic Recognition of Outer Mongolia (the Mongolian People's Republic)

In our staff memorandum of February 4 to General Goodpaster[1] I promised to review our policy toward Outer Mongolia and recommend a course of action.

The matter has now been thoroughly reviewed[2] and I believe that we should be prepared to extend diplomatic recognition to Outer Mongolia if we can reach agreement on an exchange of diplomatic missions and obtain specific assurance that our mission in Ulan Bator would be able to operate in a reasonably normal fashion. In arriving at this position I have given particular weight to the utility of that mission as a source of information. Ulan Bator would be a most useful place from which to observe and evaluate differences between the Soviet Union and Communist China, and these differences, of course, have significant and far-reaching implications for our foreign policy. Furthermore, the presence of a mission in Ulan Bator would provide improved access to some areas of the Soviet Union. We would plan to accredit our Ambassador in Moscow also to Ulan Bator and assign officers there for one year tours largely from Embassy Moscow. Travel of these officers and of couriers to and from Ulan Bator would traverse sectors of the Soviet Union now usually inaccessible.

---

Source: Kennedy Library, National Security Files, Countries Series, Outer Mongolia. Secret. The source text does not indicate the drafter; the Department of State file copy indicates that it was drafted by Officer in Charge of Multilateral Political Relations in the Office of Soviet Union Affairs John A. Armitage. (Department of State, Central Files, 793C.02/5–2361) A note on the source text in Bundy's handwriting indicates that the President approved it.

[1] Reference is to a February 4 memorandum from Department of State Executive Secretariat Director Walter J. Stoessel, Jr., to General Andrew J. Goodpaster, enclosing an undated paper prepared in the Department of State headed "United States Policy Toward Outer Mongolia." The paper discussed the possibility of U.S. recognition of Mongolia but recommended against it; Stoessel's memorandum states that Secretary Rusk was sending the paper to President Kennedy for his information but wished to review the matter before making a recommendation. (Kennedy Library, President's Office Files, Outer Mongolia)

[2] A May 4 memorandum from Assistant Secretary of State for European Affairs Foy D. Kohler to Rusk discussed the question and recommended recognition and establishment of diplomatic relations. (Department of State, Central Files, 611.93C/5–461)

417

I have taken into account the counterargument that recognition of Outer Mongolia would have adverse effects throughout the Far East and particularly on our relations with the Republic of China. We have already received indications of that government's displeasure over the possibility, and our Ambassador in Taipei has commented that the difficulties of reaching an accommodation with the Republic of China over the issue of Chinese representation in the United Nations will be greatly increased if we proceed with our recognition of the Outer Mongolian regime.

However, I believe the course of recent events in the United Nations has affected these objections. The Brazzaville group of African states and the French agreed to go along with the Soviet idea of a package deal involving admission of both Outer Mongolia and Mauritania. We concluded that if we followed this course we would find ourselves in the position of appearing to have been entrapped by a Soviet maneuver and would also have less likelihood of obtaining Outer Mongolian agreement to the establishment of a U.S. mission in Ulan Bator under satisfactory operating conditions. Moreover, we fear that a veto of Outer Mongolia by the Republic of China would have adverse effects on the Republic of China's position in the UN. Consequently, we are seeking to mobilize sufficient abstentions in the Security Council to block Outer Mongolian membership and will probably be successful in this effort.

We explained in the General Assembly that we are reexamining the question of Outer Mongolian sovereignty and if our examination discloses that that country has the attributes of sovereignty, including the ability and willingness to establish normal diplomatic and cultural relations with other countries, we will be prepared to support and even cosponsor Outer Mongolian application for UN membership.

I believe that our position at the UN affords us the most advantageous grounds on which to make an approach to the Outer Mongolians. However, I would recommend that we proceed no matter what the outcome of the anticipated proceedings in the Security Council.

We have discussed our proposed line of action with both the Senate Foreign Relations Committee and the House Foreign Affairs Committee in formal executive sessions,[3] as well as with Senators Mansfield and Fulbright and Congressman Morgan in private. These consultations went very well. Only Congressmen Judd and Zablocki[4] offered any criticism of the plan. I believe we can proceed without fear of significant Congressional difficulties.

---

[3] Under Secretary of State Chester Bowles raised the subject with the Senate Foreign Relations Committee in an executive session on May 17. See *Executive Sessions of the Senate Foreign Relations Committee (Historical Series)*, vol. XIII, Part 1, Eighty-seventh Congress, First Session, 1961, p. 563.

[4] Representatives Walter H. Judd of Minnesota and Clement J. Zablocki of Wisconsin.

We are now in the process of consulting with our allies to ascertain their views. If you approve the extension of diplomatic recognition to Outer Mongolia in the event we are able to reach agreement providing for normal operating conditions for our mission, I would recommend that we authorize Ambassador Thompson to inform the Soviets of our intentions and to make the approach to the Mongolian Ambassador in Moscow, as soon as the consultations with our allies are completed.

**Dean Rusk**

---

### 199.    Telegram From the Department of State to the Embassy in the Soviet Union

Washington, May 29, 1961, 8:05 p.m.

2088. Moscow for Ambassador. Ref Department's 1753 to Moscow, 521 Taipei, 2022 USUN.[1] President  has approved Department's staff study re US relations with Outer Mongolia,[2] together with my recommendation we now implement course of action outlined Department's 1753. Accordingly, after completion consultation with friendly governments, you will be requested take following action immediately in order avoid any suggestion that change of US policy vis-à-vis Outer Mongolia is related to agreement of President Kennedy and Premier Khrushchev to meet in Vienna.[3]

1.    Inform appropriate Soviet official that you are under instruction to initiate talks with Outer Mongolian Ambassador Moscow to ascertain whether conditions for establishing diplomatic relations now exist. You may state US envisages mutual establishment of Missions at Embassy level and that you would be accredited as Ambassador having concur-

---

Source: Department of State, Central Files, 611.93C/5–2961. Secret; Priority. Drafted by William O. Anderson of the Office of Soviet Union Affairs; cleared by Kohler, Assistant Secretary of State for Far Eastern Affairs Walter P. McConaughy, and Deputy Assistant Secretary of State for International Organization Affairs Woodruff Wallner; and approved for transmission by Rusk.

[1] Dated April 14. (Ibid., 793C.02/4–1461)

[2] The President approved Document 198. The reference to a staff study is unclear. The only staff study located in White House files was the paper cited in footnote 1, Document 198.

[3] Telegram 2090 to Moscow, May 30, instructed Ambassador Thompson to implement immediately the course of action outlined in telegram 2088. (Department of State, Central Files, 611.93C/5–3061)

rent assignment both Moscow and Ulan Bator. However, for foreseeable future US Mission Ulan Bator would be headed by Chargé with small staff. You should also state US consideration of this matter took note of Ambassador Menshikov's indication to Senator Mansfield Soviet Govt would welcome establishment diplomatic relations between US and OM.

2. After informing Sovs, initiate talks with OM Ambassador Moscow, making it clear that your approach is not for purpose of giving advance notice of US decision to extend recognition but is designed ascertain whether both governments mutually desire establish diplomatic relations and can reach agreement on conditions under which those relations (political, economic, cultural) will be maintained. Assuming OM Ambassador will wish to communicate urgently with his Govt before engaging in further talks re foregoing "conditions," I believe it highly desirable he clearly understand during this initial conversation that US not prepared proceed further if OM Govt unable agree to prompt establishment US diplomatic Mission in Ulan Bator. You are authorized to inform OM Ambassador US for its part is prepared agree to establishment OM Mission in Washington provided OM Govt grants reciprocal rights Ulan Bator and two Govts have clear-cut agreement on conditions (including normal diplomatic privileges) under which Missions will operate. You may note we would also be prepared to support OM membership application in UN provided these conditions are met. You may tell Ambassador US envisages giving our Ambassador Moscow additional accreditation to Ulan Bator and placing US Mission Ulan Bator under resident Chargé with small staff.[4]

FYI. Dept is taking immediate steps to inform NATO members through NAC of nature of these instructions. Similar action being taken through US reps in consulting with SEATO and OAS members. In each instance, will be made clear that US recognition not yet granted OM and that your talks this stage will be exploratory to ascertain whether satisfactory agreements can be reached on which establishment diplomatic relations can be based. End FYI.

*For Tokyo:* Embassy should inform Foreign Ministry of intended course of action, emphasizing conditional nature of approach to OM.

**Rusk**

---

[4] Telegram 2972 from Moscow, May 31, reported that Thompson had informed Deputy Prime Minister Vasily Vasilevich Kuznetsov of the proposed approach to the Mongolian Embassy. (Ibid., 611.93C/5–3161) Telegram 2997, June 2, reported that Edward L. Freers, who was acting as Chargé during Thompson's absence for the Kennedy–Khrushchev meeting in Vienna, had met with the Mongolian Ambassador that day. (Ibid., 611.93C/6–261) Telegram 3163 from Moscow, June 20, transmitted the text of an oral statement that the Mongolian Ambassador made to Freers in a meeting that day expressing readiness to establish diplomatic relations and to negotiate specific questions concerning this. (Ibid., 611.93C/6–2061)

## 200.    Editorial Note

A letter of July 20, 1961, from Deputy Assistant Secretary of State for European Affairs Richard H. Davis to Ambassador Thompson reads in part as follows:

"Since you are no doubt wondering what has happened to the detailed negotiating instructions for your dealings with the Outer Mongolian Ambassador, I thought I had better let you know where the matter stands. At present the package is in suspense, physically resting in Alex Johnson's In-box. I am sure you are aware of the fuss which Chiang Kai-shek has kicked up over the prospect of our recognizing the MPR. This has apparently had some effect in Congress and has spilled over to involve passage of foreign aid legislation and our public stance vis-à-vis the Berlin crisis. Thus, there appears to have been a decision to do nothing further with regard to Outer Mongolia for an indefinite period." (Department of State, Central Files, 793C.02/7–2061)

Correspondence with a number of members of Congress on this issue is ibid., 793C.02.

Further documentation concerning the possibility of U.S. recognition of Mongolia is in the China compilation; see especially Documents 32, 42, 44, and 46.

On August 11 Director of the Department of State's Office of News Lincoln White read a statement in response to a query by correspondents declaring that although the United States had for some time been exploring the question of the establishment of relations with Mongolia, "We believe that in view of the existing world situation, it is in the best interests of the United States to suspend further exploration of that matter at this time." (Department of State *Bulletin*, September 4, 1961, pages 408–409)

On October 25 the United Nations Security Council recommended the admission of the Mongolian People's Republic to the United Nations by a vote of 9–0; the United States abstained, and the Republic of China did not participate in the vote. Documentation concerning U.S. efforts to prevent the Republic of China's use of the veto on this question is in the China compilation.

Assistant Secretary of State for Far Eastern Affairs Roger Hilsman recommended the renewal of action leading toward recognition and establishment of diplomatic relations with Mongolia in a memorandum to Rusk of October 22, 1963, but no action was taken; see Document 192.

# Korea

## 201. Letter From Secretary of State Rusk to Secretary of Defense McNamara

Washington, March 2, 1961.

DEAR BOB: I am most anxious to draw your personal attention to a problem which all of us here regard as of great and urgent importance to our relations with Korea. The Korean Government has intermittently raised the subject of a status of forces agreement since 1955, and in recent times this has developed into a major popular issue with increasingly serious implications.[1] As things stand now, this issue essentially involves two basic questions: The Korean Government apparently wants us to pay some compensation to private Korean owners of facilities used by our forces in Korea; and it desired to have at least partial, and presumably nominal, criminal jurisdiction over our troops there. Korea is the only nation where we have exclusive jurisdiction over our forces, except for Taiwan, where this subject is under negotiation.

We have always held, and, I believe, should continue to insist that the Korean Government take full responsibility for any property claims involving our forces in Korea. I am convinced, however, that the time has come when we should proceed to negotiate promptly a full status of forces agreement with Korea, including some politically realistic formula on criminal jurisdiction which would in actual practice preserve for us a maximum degree of jurisdiction over our forces in Korea. In my view the foregoing conclusion remains valid despite the fact that a technical state of suspended hostilities still exists in Korea.

The Koreans are well aware that we have status of forces agreements with many other countries around the world, and believe that their sovereign status should be treated with equal consideration. They are especially sensitive over the fact that we have concluded a status of forces agreement with Japan including an agreement on criminal jurisdiction

---

Source: Washington National Records Center, RG 330, OSD Files: FRC 66 A 3542, Korea 013. Confidential.

[1] In telegrams 1063, 1087, and 1088 from Seoul, February 22, 28, and 28, the Embassy in Korea reported growing public pressure for a status of forces agreement and recommended high-level exploratory talks with the ROK as a prelude to opening negotiations on the issue. In telegram 1087 Ambassador McConaughy reported that CINCUNC General Magruder thought that the Embassy was exaggerating the force of the public pressure for a status of forces agreement, but agreed with the Embassy's recommendation about the need for preliminary discussion. (Department of State, Central Files, 611.95B7/2–2261 and 611.95B7/2–2861)

comparable with those signed with our European allies.[2] Inevitably, many Koreans regard our present position as one of discrimination against a country which has shed more blood than any other since World War II in the common cause of resisting Communist aggression.

In view of the fact that in Korean eyes the conclusion of a status of forces agreement has now come to be a real symbol of Korean sovereignty and legitimate nationalism, I am convinced that in the long run it will best serve our national interests to reach such an agreement with the present ROK Government. This Government is moderate, conservative, and striving to meet the natural and justifiable expectations of its people. It is currently under heavy pressure in connection with the series of vital but unpopular economic reforms which we have insisted are necessary for further progress. It would be a disservice to our interests to attempt to place such a Government in the impossible position of resisting strong popular opinion on the status of forces issue and at the same time to expose our own Government to increasing criticism by broad and important segments of the Korean public, as well as a large and vocal parliamentary opposition. I think there is good reason to hope that, if we move now in a resolute and constructive way, we will be able to arrive at an agreement more advantageous to us than any we could reach later with any succeeding Korean administration, when nationalist sentiments would surely have become stronger in Korea.

I hope that you will agree that we should commence negotiations with the Republic of Korea as soon as possible on a full status of forces agreement, and look forward to an occasion to talk with you further about this matter in the very near future.[3]

With warm personal regards,

Sincerely,

**Dean Rusk**

---

[2] At a State–JCS meeting on March 17, Chairman of the Joint Chiefs of Staff General Lemnitzer expressed strong opposition to a status of forces agreement that would include provisions on criminal jurisdiction. Lemnitzer stated that a "suspended state of war" existed in Korea and that the American people would rather see U.S. forces withdrawn from Korea than agree to turning U.S. servicemen over to Korean courts. (Ibid., State–JCS Meetings: Lot 70 D 328)

[3] Responding for the Department of Defense in a March 10 letter to Rusk, Deputy Secretary of Defense Roswell Gilpatric agreed that, "to the extent possible, Korea should be accorded the same treatment as our other allies." The problem the Department of Defense forsaw was the Korean desire for criminal jurisdiction over U.S. personnel in Korean courts. The Department of Defense was engaged in a study of whether it was possible to work out a satisfactory agreement on that issue with the ROK. Until that study was concluded, the Department of Defense could not agree to negotiations. (Washington National Records Center, RG 330, OSD Files: FRC 66 A 3542, Korea 013)

202.    **Report by Hugh D. Farley of the International Cooperation Administration to the President's Deputy Special Assistant for National Security Affairs (Rostow)**

Washington, March 6, 1961.

THE SITUATION IN KOREA, FEBRUARY 1961

Summary

There are three basic circumstances prevailing in Korea today, the conjunction of which makes it imperative that the U.S. Government recognize the gravity of the situation and act promptly to remedy it. The existence of any one or two of these elements without the third would be serious, to be sure, but not such as to warrant emergency consideration and immediate action. The three together, however, are compelling reasons for alarm, for they seriously endanger the whole U.S. position in Korea, and threaten to discredit, not only the aid program in Korea, but the Mutual Security program as a whole.

The three elements are these:

A.  The extent and depth of graft, corruption and fraud in the major institutions of Korean society today and the consequent lack of confidence on the part of Koreans, high and low, in these institutions, in themselves, in their own future, and—because of the absence of a U.S. posture on integrity—an increasing loss of confidence in the U.S. The receptivity of a people in such a frame of mind to Communist and other extremist influence, after 15 years of American presence, is natural.

B.  The dangerously deteriorating direction of the dynamics of the situation in South Korea, particularly over the next several months—with the economic and social phase of the April 1960 unfinished revolution still to be initiated, with the Government increasingly powerless to take the necessary actions because of its involvement in corruption, and with the probability, in the light of the current U.S. posture, that reaction

---

Source: Kennedy Library, President's Office Files, Countries Series, Korea, Security 1961–1963. No classification marking. In a covering letter to Rostow, Farley explained that he was submitting this report at the request of Arthur Schlesinger after a discussion with McGeorge Bundy. No other record of that discussion has been found. Farley told Rostow that the following read, contributed to, and supported his conclusions: Donald MacDonald, Department of State Officer in Charge of Korean Affairs; Major General Charles E. Bonesteel, Secretary of the General Staff; Robert Kinney, Korean Civilian Intelligence Officer, Department of Defense; Robert M. Macy, Chief of the International Division, Bureau of the Budget; William J. Sheppard, Regional Director for Far Eastern Operations, International Cooperation Administration; and James Cooley, Special Assistant to the Director of ICA. Farley stated that JCS Chairman General Lemnitzer would strongly support his conclusions, and that the CIA was concerned about Korea. According to Farley, the new ICA Director, Henry R. Labouisse, had heard an oral briefing, but was not prepared to support the report until further study.

against the Government, possibly even revolution, will be strongly anti-American.

C. The indecisive and inadequate leadership of the USOM in Korea, its critical role at this time, and the lack of a rapport between the USOM and the decision-makers in the ROK Government.

Following an exposition of these elements, a strategy is outlined for U.S. moves to change radically the present direction of events in Korea, and thus to serve basic Korean and U.S. security interests.[1]

[Here follows an 18-page report, which included four sections: "Integrity," in which Farley stated that the whole fabric of Korean life was "shot through with graft, corruption, and fraud"; "Dynamics," in which Farley predicted an explosion of popular discontent on April 19, the anniversary of the Rhee overthrow; "The U.S. Responsibility," in which Farley criticized USOM operations in Korea; and "Action," in which Farley recommended a "crash program" that would include a Presidential letter, a special envoy with a staff, authority over USOM and economic reporting, instructions to work with Prime Minister Chang and the rest of Korean society, and follow-up visits to the ROK by U.S. Cabinet heads and high officials. See the Supplement.]

---

[1] Hugh D. Farley was Assistant Director of USOM in Korea until February 24, when his stand on corruption in Korea and his criticism of USOM operations convinced him to submit his resignation. Farley returned to Washington where ICA did not immediately accept his resignation. Instead it asked him to put his criticisms on paper and discuss them with ICA and Department officials. (Memorandum from Parsons to Hare, February 28; Kennedy Library, President's Office Files, Countries Series, Korea, Security 1961–1963)

### 203. Memorandum From Robert W. Komer of the National Security Council Staff to the President's Deputy Special Assistant for National Security Affairs (Rostow)

Washington, March 15, 1961.

SUBJECT

Action in Korea

Agree completely that gut issue is not whether violence likely on 19 April[1] (Farley merely made himself vulnerable to State riposte by hinging too much on this).[2] The real issue is whether Korean picture, with which we have failed to come to grips for eight years, is really serious enough to warrant urgent action.[3]

Look at the basic problems of the ROK: (a) a poor country with few resources and skills; (b) saddled with staggering task of supporting a far larger military establishment than it really able to (or than is needed); (c) corruption feeding on inexperience in democratic government; and (d) a rising nationalism and expectancy frustrated by what the ROKs increasingly believe is US disinclination to accord them full equality, push for unification, or change overwhelming military emphasis in ROK.

Underlying ills and needs are *economic.* Major thrust of US effort over next decade must be:

a.  Substantial cutback in ROK military establishment, with diversion of US funds thus released to crash economic development. Defense of ROK could be met by ROK plus US forces in Korea and reminders to Bloc of US intent instantly to protect from outside Korea.

---

Source: Kennedy Library, National Security Files, Countries Series, Korea, General, 1/61–3/61. Secret. In a March 9 memorandum to Rostow, Komer suggested that the Kennedy administration not confine itself "to the political-economic aspects Hugh Farley dusts off so nicely, but hit the military angle too. For too many years a disportionate share of MAP dollars has been going to maintain huge ROK forces far beyond the likely need." (Ibid.)

[1] In telegram 1142 from Seoul, March 11, the Embassy presented a long analysis to support its conclusion that the "popular mood in Korea seems to be one of disenchantment rather than angry protest." The Embassy continued, "despite significant elements of instability in internal situation, they are not of a volume or character which would lead to general, spontaneous disturbances such as occurred in March–April 1960." (Department of State, Central Files, 795B.00/3–1161)

[2] William Sheppard of ICA agreed that Farley was too anxious over the April 19 date. He did not agree with Farley's proposed crash program or the reorganization of USOM. (Memorandum from Sheppard to Labouisse, March 10; ibid., 811.0095B/3–861)

[3] In a March 5 memorandum to Bacon, Deputy Assistant Secretary Avery Peterson, commenting on Farley's report, observed that "there are fundamental elements of truth in Mr. Farley's assessment but as a general statement [it is] too seriously overdrawn and emotional rather than rational." Bacon sent Steeves a memorandum on March 10 briefing him on Farley's report. (Ibid., 811.0085B/3–561 and 811.0095B/3–1061)

b. Buildup of ROK economy, stressing public sector, creation of light labor-intensive industry, and full utilization of main ROK resource—people.

c. Much more vigorous, imaginative US action in directing and supervising ROK economic development. In addition to basic long-term projects, the undertaking as well of a number of high-impact, short-term projects for political effect. Closer and more active instruction and supervision of ROK government, in such projects, but also more attribution to ROK government of their benefits.

d. Insistence on much more vigorous ROK crackdown on corruption, smuggling, illegal profiteering *wherever found;* similar US action against US nationals guilty of these; strong steps towards a more spartan US standard of life in ROK to avoid present embarrassing disparity.

Political actions also imperative:

a. Move forcefully to get a satisfactory *status of forces* agreement. By so doing we can buy public acceptance that our greater involvement in ROK economic direction will require.

b. Get ROK to take offensive on unification issue, with ROK public a major target. Unification is an abiding yearning of the Korean people, founded in both nationalistic and economic impulses. The US must present itself at the forefront of those favoring unification, making sure in the process that terms protect ROK and Free World interests.

c. Sharply reduce political role in ROK of US military and its spokesmen; make US Ambassador undisputed spokesman of US policy in Korea; greatly expand educational and labor contacts, leader grants, etc., between US and ROK.[4]

**Bob K.**

---

[4] Komer attached a CIA memorandum prepared for the DCI and asked Rostow to "use w. discretion." It was an advance copy of Document 206.

### 204.    Memorandum From the President's Deputy Special Assistant for National Security Affairs (Rostow) to President Kennedy

Washington, March 15, 1961.

SUBJECT

Korea

You may have read the paper written by Hugh Farley, the ICA officer until recently in charge of the Technical Assistance Program in Korea. He returned to try to communicate to the town a sense of the dangers and instability in the Korean situation and especially to urge the Government to act before the April 19 anniversary of the Seoul student demonstrations.

The Department of State has reviewed his paper and received an evaluation from the Ambassador in Seoul (1142, March 11, 1961).[1] Both the Department of State and the Ambassador, while recognizing the dangers in the present situation, believe it more likely than Farley does, that we can get through the Spring without a Korean explosion. The underlying fact is that all hands agree the situation in Korea is not good; and American policy in Korea requires a fresh look. Mac Bundy and I have indicated, through Mr. Battle, that the White House would like the State Department to come up with an indication of what it proposes to do in both the short run and the longer run in Korea.[2]

Fundamentally, the problem is to get our massive aid to Korea shifted around in a way which would not merely keep Korea from going down for the third time, but would begin to get Korea moving forward. There are in Korean politics, in the post-Rhee situation, elements who might join us in such a forward effort; but, equally, these elements could turn against us. We wish you to be informed of this situation. You may wish to discuss it directly with Mr. Rusk.

---

Source: Kennedy Library, National Security Affairs, Countries Series, Korea, General, 1/61–3/61. Confidential. Rostow had asked Robert Johnson of the NSC Staff for advice on Korea in light of Farley's report. Johnson responded in a March 15 memorandum to Rostow supporting Farley's proposals. Johnson wondered if Farley's "procedural device of sending a special emissary" was as important as it was for the United States to identify itself dramatically with reform and progress in Korea. If the President agreed, Johnson recommended that the Department of State be asked to make recommendations on how to approach the ROK on reform. (Ibid.)

[1] See footnote 1, Document 203.

[2] Rostow called Executive Secretary Lucius Battle on March 15 and told him that the President had seen Farley's report. Rostow asked that the Department prepare recommendations on Korea as soon as possible. (Note by Battle, March 15; Department of State, Central Files, 795B.00/3–1561)

## 205.  Memorandum From the Under Secretary of State for Economic Affairs (Ball) to the President's Deputy Special Assistant for National Security Affairs (Rostow)

Washington, March 20, 1961.

SUBJECT

Appraisal of Farley on Korea

Enclosed you will find memoranda relating to the analysis and rec-ommendations made by Mr. Hugh Farley about Korea.[1] The Department concurs in the general conclusion reached by the Special Committee that Mr. Labouisse established to inquire into Mr. Farley's proposal. You will note that the conclusion might be summarized as follows: we do not dis-agree with the broad outlines of the problem as set forth by Mr. Farley; we do not feel that the courses of action proposed are likely to achieve the results that he desires—and which the Department desires as well.

I am proposing that a further step be taken, however—one which was discussed with you the other night at dinner.

A special mission should be sent to Korea headed by Max Millikan, a mission patterned on the Presidential Special Mission that is now in Bolivia. The purposes of the special mission to Korea would be these:

(a) Drawing on the useful report of the Inspector General and Comptroller of January 1961 as a point of departure (the conclusions of this report preceded but coincide fairly closely with the analysis in Mr. Farley's memorandum), the mission should endeavor to translate the report's conclusions into action at the earliest possible date. It should also consider carefully the type of organization needed and the numbers and quality of personnel required to carry out an effective aid program.
(b) Using as a point of departure the new aid concepts now decided upon by the President, the special mission should attempt a revamping of the economic effort in Korea consistent with these proposals.
(c) The two elements of reform and new program that would be the principal purposes of the special mission would contribute to a third

---

Source: Department of State, Central Files, 795B.5–MSP/3–2061. No classification marking. Drafted by J. Robert Schaetzel of Ball's office.

[1] Enclosed was a March 16 memorandum from the Special Executive Committee (Sheppard of ICA, Steeves of the Department of State, and James Cooley of ICA) to Labouisse. This committee concluded that the problems described by Farley were "seri-ous," but were well-known in Seoul and Washington. The report continued that "Mr. Farley's diagnosis of Korea's ills is too largely centered on the issues of corruption and that the remedies he prescribes are in a major degree too sweeping and too likely to be counter-productive." It concluded: "In short, we cannot agree with the extent, the nature, and the timing of the measures proposed by Mr. Farley to cope with the problem." Also attached, but not printed, was a report on Korea by the Assistant Deputy Director and Controller for Mutual Security, Edward F. Tennant, who spent several weeks in Korea in January 1961.

highly desirable result, namely the building of a body of evidence which would be of great value in the course of presenting the new aid program to Congress. It would be a concrete case study in the application of new development principles.

Mr. Labouisse will take responsibility for moving this project along in my absence. I hope that it will be possible to call on the President to induce Dr. Millikan to accept this assignment.

**George W. Ball**[2]

---

[2] Printed from a copy that indicates Ball signed the original.

---

### 206.   Special National Intelligence Estimate

SNIE 42–61                                         Washington, March 21, 1961.

SHORT-RANGE OUTLOOK IN THE REPUBLIC OF KOREA

The Problem

To estimate the likelihood of a major political crisis in the Republic of Korea (ROK) over the next month or so.

Conclusion

1. The April anniversary of the fall of President Rhee will be marked by demonstrations and, probably, some acts of violence. In view of present grievances among opposition groups and the public at large,

---

Source: Kennedy Library, National Security Files, Countries Series, Korea, General, 1/61–3/61. Secret. According to a note on the cover sheet, the Central Intelligence Agency and intelligence organizations of the Departments of State, Defense, the Army, the Navy, the Air Force, and the Joint Staff participated in the preparation of this estimate. All members of the USIB concurred with this estimate on March 21 except the representatives of the AEC and the FBI, who abstained on the grounds that the subject was outside their jurisdiction.

A note on this special estimate indicates that it supplemented NIE 42.1–2–60, "Prospects for Korea," November 22, 1960. See Foreign Relations, 1958–1960, vol. XVIII, pp. 697–698.

these demonstrations could be converted—by design or accident—into a major political explosion of some kind in the next month or so. However, the odds appear to be against such an explosion, since present grievances are not as intense or focused as those which gave rise to the 1960 revolution. Nevertheless, the ROK will continue to be plagued by formidable economic and political problems, and the long-term outlook for the ROK is bleak.[1]

## Discussion

### I.  Introduction

2.  April 1961 will mark the first anniversary of the revolution that felled Syngman Rhee and swept his government and his followers from the political scene. Police terrorism and press censorship have been eliminated, but little real progress has been made in the past year on the basic social and economic problems which confront the ROK Government and people. Prime Minister Chang Myon has succeeded in consolidating a slim majority in Parliament and some reforms have been accomplished. However, as the anniversary approaches, there are mounting signs of frustration and resentment directed at the government and, increasingly, at the US, over the slow pace of reform and progress in South Korea. Public demonstrations, which succeeded so well a year ago, have continued to mark the ROK scene, especially in the nerve center of Seoul. Although the tempo of demonstration activity declined somewhat during the winter, there is a possibility that anniversary demonstrations will erupt—by design or accident—and confront the ROK Government and the US with a major crisis in the next month or so. This estimate seeks to assess the chances of such a crisis and the conditions which might spark it.

### II.  The Possible Sources of Crisis

#### A.  Political Weaknesses

3.  The new government has indicated an awareness of basic problems and has taken some steps to cope with them. Nevertheless, the seven months of Prime Minister Chang Myon's government, formed last autumn, have been expended largely in customary Korean politicking, and the government's position is none too strong. In the July 1960 elections, the ruling Democratic Party had won 174 of the 233 seats in the House of Representatives. However, the deep divisions within the party

---

[1] In a March 23 memorandum to Rostow, Robert Johnson comented on this SNIE and sent it to Rostow. Johnson noted that Rostow had seen it in what was "in effect, an initial draft form." Johnson stated that "if a further needle is needed for the skeptics who doubt the urgency of the situation, this is a good one. It does say that the 'odds appear to be against' an explosion on the anniversary of Rhee's overthrow, but the rest of the estimate is hardly reassuring." (Kennedy Library, National Security Files, Countries Series, Korea, General, 1/61–3/61)

showed up almost immediately and led to a prolonged struggle for party control. Chang was confirmed as Prime Minister by the House of Representatives only after Kim Toyon, a fellow Democrat, had been nominated but rejected by a very narrow margin. The faction led by Kim finally broke away completely, formed the New Democratic Party, and is now the major opposition, with about 61 adherents, in the House of Representatives. Chang's Democratic Party has about 128 seats (117 are needed for a majority) and he can increase the number slightly on certain issues by scattered support among the 37 independents in the House. However, potential schisms exist even within Chang's own Democratic Party, the most significant being a group of 25–30 younger men who believe Chang's leadership is not sufficiently imaginative or vigorous.

4.  The opposition in Parliament is made up of the conservative New Democratic Party, the independent group, and a few members of left-of-center parties. The opposition has enjoyed the full exercise of its constitutional rights of expression and parliamentary interpellation. Though fragmented and divided, it has been highly vocal and quick to take advantage of any opportunity to embarrass the government and demand the resignation of individual cabinet members. The opposition in Parliament is backed by a substantial segment of the press which has taken advantage of the new freedom from censorship to indulge in generally antigovernment, often irresponsible journalism. The government has come under increasing criticism from student, labor, veteran, and other groups as well, who feel that the reforms and improvements which should have followed upon Rhee's expulsion have been all too slow in coming about. Demonstrations and mass meetings have become a characteristic of Korean public life over the past year.

5.  In the past year the Communists have increased their efforts to subvert the ROK. North Korean broadcasts aimed at the South have increased in number and intensity, and there has been a greater North Korean effort of late to increase the influx of subversive literature and support into the ROK, largely by way of Japan. Some of the present political unrest in the ROK is almost certainly attributable to Communist efforts. However, we believe that this unrest for the most part would exist without Communist instigation.

6.  The National Police and security services were a primary target of the popular revulsion that led to last April's revolution. Since that time, purges and reorganizations have gone on repeatedly, causing a serious drop in the capabilities and morale of the police. Despite current antiriot training, there is little likelihood that they could function effectively against organized mass riots of the scale of 1960. In such circumstances, the army would become the most important element in the maintenance of order. We believe that the government would call on the

army in an extreme situation, and that the army would respond to the call but might be reluctant to fire on demonstrators.

7. Public resentment over corrupt practices played an important part in the making of the 1960 revolution. Corruption continues to be a major problem for the government, although by itself it is not likely to cause revolutionary action in present circumstances. Student groups in particular have continued to lead the outcry against corruption. Although Prime Minister Chang and the government generally have thus far escaped serious attack on this score, petty graft at lower government and military levels and among much of the public is as widespread as ever. The exposure of continuing corruption in the police has caused new public concern over the issue and forced the government to intensify its efforts to stamp it out. Solution of the problem will be difficult, especially as long as civil and military pay scales remain at their present low levels.

8. On balance, the Chang government has achieved certain limited goals but has not sparked any broad degree of public enthusiasm or support. As the government in power, it bears responsibility for the absence of significant political or economic advances. Well aware of increasing nationalist feeling, Chang has sought to avoid becoming too closely identified with the US. This has been difficult, however, as the government has recognized the necessity also of cooperating with the US on the solution of its economic problems. Although the Korean public probably does not regard Chang as a US puppet, it almost certainly believes that, under his government, the US has taken a more direct hand than previously in the conduct of the government's economic affairs and that the US therefore shares responsibility for existing economic conditions.

*Economic Grievances*

9. Underlying the political unrest in South Korea is the weak and uncertain state of an economy poor in natural resources and diverted from the major problems of reconstruction by the requirements of one of the largest military establishments in proportion to population in the entire world. Although the goverment's efforts at economic reform may yield some long-term benefits, there has in general been no significant improvement in the lot of the individual citizen since Chang's government took power last August. Indeed, some problems have become more serious.

10. The annual food shortage, which the rural areas normally experience in April and May before the early planting is harvested, has already hit many districts. There has been no starvation, but rations in many areas have been sharply reduced. The urban population has been subjected to a general rise in prices; in Seoul the wholesale price index rose by about 10 percent in January alone. This rise has slowed somewhat since, but the Korean public remains apprehensive over continuing

inflationary trends. The situation has already produced strikes, demonstrations, and petitions among the laboring groups. There has been no improvement in the employment situation, and unemployment and serious underemployment continue to affect about 20 percent of the labor force. This number will soon be swelled by most of this year's 45,000 college and vocational school graduates. In seeking to fix responsibility, the Korean public, through demonstrations and the press, blames not only the government but also, to an increasing extent, the US. In particular, the upward push of prices is ascribed to US-sponsored measures, namely the recent revision of exchange rates and a 50 percent increase in utility rates now awaiting enactment by the Parliament.

11. The Chang government is aware of the dissatisfaction caused by the state of the economy and is making efforts to remedy the situation. One important government measure is the National Construction Service program, a large-scale public works project being undertaken jointly with the US in an attempt to alleviate unemployment, particularly in the outlying provinces. The recent increase of US surplus food shipments has contributed to an easing of hunger in the drought-hit districts in the south. Chang is hopeful that such measures will at least tide the government over until longer term economic reforms begin to take hold. Although these short-term measures will probably have little practical effect on the economic situation within the period of this estimate, they may have some beneficial psychological result.

*C. Grievances Against the US*

12. The South Koreans have long resented the reluctance of the US to conclude an administrative agreement providing for the legal status of US armed forces in Korea. Under Rhee, public expression on this subject was channeled and controlled. Since his departure, public interest in such an agreement has mounted greatly, in keeping with the general rise of nationalist sentiment. The Koreans hold that whatever reason excused the absence of a status of forces agreement in the past, the end of Rhee and the virtual restoration of peacetime conditions—this latter recognized in the conclusion of a US-ROK bilateral economic aid agreement—no longer justify US reluctance to meet ROK desires on this issue. On 2 March 1961, the Assembly unanimously passed a resolution urging "the earliest conclusion" of such an agreement, and Chang has been urging on the US the immediate necessity of such a step.

13. Considerable controversy developed over the bilateral economic aid agreement. Opponents of the agreement alleged that, under it, the US was "interfering" in the operations of the government, infringing Korean sovereignty, and treating South Korea as a client state. In spite of this charge, the measure was supported by a substantial majority in the National Assembly. The US and the ROK Government also continue to be criticized, sporadically, for being "pro-Japanese."

## D. The Unification Issue

14. Although Korean unification has not become a burning issue, interest in it has increased considerably over the past year, at least in part as a consequence of dissatisfaction over conditions in the ROK. Student groups have been in the forefront of those calling for a re-examination of past stands and for new initiatives to end the division of the country. The government itself would like to take the propaganda initiative on unification from North Korea but has put off any new action until after the UN consideration of the Korean question this spring. The unification issue will almost certainly become an increasingly serious problem for the ROK and the US.

## III. The Prospects for a Major Crisis

15. Combustible materials are present. Design, incident, or a combination of accidents could ignite street demonstrations, converting them into destructive mob action and a major crisis. The Communists would, of course, exploit such an event. At a minimum, there will be considerable noise over the next month or so. Some acts of violence are probable and a major explosion of some kind is possible.

16. However, the odds appear to be against such an explosion this spring. Despite the factors present which could spark a new revolution, the situation in April 1961 is different in many respects from that of April 1960. Present frustrations are not as severe as those so long suppressed by Rhee. Moreover, although demonstrators may once again take to the streets, there is at present no single, emotion-packed focus for discontent comparable to last year's election frauds and police brutality. Finally, the government is alert to the danger and has publicized its preparations for coping with disturbances.

17. In any event, South Korea's fundamental problems will continue to plague any ROK leadership. Faced with an impoverished economy, drained by defense costs, and handicapped by inexperience in self-government, South Korea will remain heavily dependent on outside economic and military assistance for the foreseeable future. There will, moreover, be increasing political pressures arising out of growing nationalist spirit and incipient neutralist sentiment. In short, South Korea is basically so weak economically and unsteady politically that internal crisis or threat of crisis will be the norm, not the exception, over the years ahead.

## 207.   Telegram From the Department of State to the Embassy in Korea

Washington, April 1, 1961, 5:03 p.m.

1123. One of greatest concerns you will continue face when you assume your leadership of FE[1] is very dubious future free Korea so long as ROK lacks forceful leadership, exhibits serious weakness in moral fiber, and permits graft and corruption on scale equalling if not excelling that during moral nadir of Rhee regime. Evidence is clear that youth and intelligentsia most Asian countries are in no mood in latter 20th Century to continue stomaching "typically Asian" accommodation to graft, nepotism and apathy of past centuries; and history has shown that they are more ready to accept the high costs in human values exacted by communism (even when these are understood fully, and all the more when they are not) then we tend to find credible before the fact. When sufficiently revolted by apathetic drifting and by illegal gains for the elite, the totalitarian aspects of communism appear less fearsome and its austerity and determined purposes may become positively attractive, in the hunger for national material progress leading, they hope, to national dignity at last. You will be able to draw on your uncommonly thorough knowledge of the antecedents to the China mainland collapse in developing this troublingly recurrent theme in post-war Asian realities. Unfortunately we are having similar problems in Laos, Viet-Nam, and in varying degrees elsewhere. US wealth and military might will prove unavailing in situations where indigenous motivation is weak and governmental actions and self-discipline desultory. Repose of many KMT mainland leaders in childish confidence that "our friend, the great US cannot afford to let the communists take China" comes to mind.

Department hopes that in final talks with ROK leaders you will make occasion for earnest, unhurried exposition of above theme, adapted as you deem most effective and appropriate. We offer below additional points directed more specifically to Korean scene. It is recognized that you have made frequent representations along these lines, but it may be helpful to cite Washington view to lend additional emphasis to seriousness of need for far more resolute leadership in national development if disaster is to be averted in next few years or sooner. Your new position should add considerable weight to the seriousness of your presentations. While we deal below primarily with deficiencies, Depart-

---

Source: Department of State, Central Files, 795B.00/4–161. Confidential; Priority. Drafted by Peterson, Jenkins, and MacDonald; cleared in substance with Vettel and Bane of NA, and in draft by Bacon; cleared by Steeves; and approved by Peterson.

[1] On April 18 McConaughy became Assistant Secretary of State for Far Eastern Affairs.

ment does not overlook positive contributions which Chang government has made and are well known to you. You will wish to interlard these, but restrainedly.

1.  ROKG seems unduly concerned with press reactions and postures taken by elements in Korean political scene which deserve examination ascertain whether they are still of importance. Too often it seems here that Chang Govt has plotted its course from old landmarks which are no longer controlling and has failed to recognize the commanding importance of youthful element in the political spectrum which accomplished the April revolution and gave the new ROKG power to move in an area formerly completely stratified. Thus bemused ROKG may overlook salient fact that it must make some visible progress toward the improvement of life and prospects of the youthful element in Korea and their descendants if Administration is to remain in power. Otherwise it might be replaced by some political element equally myopic which if in turn thrown out could leave a highly volatile dangerous situation in which the appeal of unification of the country might be so great as to tempt the South Korean people to enter the Communist crab pot.

2.  It must be recognized that with principal exception of National Construction Service, actions so far have generally been removal of past abuses. But even the Construction Service is in urgent need, not only of funds (which may be voted this weekend), but of good planning and energetic follow-through. This imaginative and obviously useful program is of type to win popular support for ROKG and to meet in a tangible way demands of ROK unemployed and underemployed for some progress toward a better life and better use of human resources which comprise ROK greatest asset. Its resolute implementation will benefit all Koreans through irrigation, reclamation, reforestation, highway construction, etc. Its failure will only heighten public sense of frustration and weaken confidence in the effectiveness of the revolutionary government.

3.  Department notes mounting signs of frustration and resentment directed at government,and at US as well, over slow pace of reform and progress. Apparent acceptance by ROKG of legislative practice of politics-as-usual feeds fires of press and popular criticism and tends undermine faith in democratic mechanisms for national development. We do not believe that Chang goverment will fail survive critical month ahead, but we are convinced that its strength will be eroded unless it adopts programs and policies which can command general support of people and pursues them with energy, thereby turning the tables on the venal, malicious, or ambitious opposition it presently faces in the legislature and in its own party.

4.  In Washington view recent attempt to widen National Security Law is symptomatic of negative approach to present danger—an

approach which will create more problems that it solves. What Korea needs is informed, cohesive society moving in agreed directions toward defined goals. Social discipline and order comes from basic convictions and understanding of men; laws and regulations are of no value without broad popular support and effective social agencies to apply and enforce them.

5.   US believes that following points demand immediate attention and action by ROKG:

a.   National planning, both economic and social, on practical concepts, with effective participation by leading Korean personalities and promising younger people. Planning activities to be supported by public information program.

b.   Energetic, non-political promotion of National Construction Service as a matter of greatest national urgency, and which presents opportunity to train and use practical skills in highway engineering, building and mechanical trades, agriculture and forestry.

c.   Removal of police from politics and promotion of its morals and esprit de corps as dignified, self-contained public service agency.

d.   Civil Service reform.

e.   Continued emphasis on tax reform, including equitable and effective collection.

6.   USG prepared to assist to fullest possible extent in planning and implementation and also recognizes that as Korean War era recedes into history US programs must put far more emphasis on development. Nevertheless initiative in planning and implementation must come from Korean leadership if it is to be meaningful for Korean people. USG will continue support for Korean economic and political development and looks forward to continuation this cordial relationship in future and to steadily increasing effectiveness of ROKG in directing and promoting national development to meet popular aspirations for well-being, security and freedom. In last analysis the future of Korea as reunified and sovereign member of Free World community depends upon success of national leadership in bringing about this development. Assistance from other nations can supplement but never replace progress of Korean people themselves and can be effective only when such progress is being made.

**Rusk**

**208.    Memorandum From Robert H. Johnson of the National
Security Council Staff to the President's Deputy Special
Assistant for National Security Affairs (Rostow)**

Washington, April 3, 1961.

SUBJECT

Korea

I talked this morning with the Korean desk officer in State, Donald
Macdonald, in an informal effort to learn something of the status of work
on Korea. He has impressed me in the past as a very able officer. He indicated that he is presently working on a paper which is intended for you.
It will deal with the question of what should be done about Korea's economic situation and will contain an analysis of Mr. Farley's political conclusions.

He said that he did not know the exact status of the recommendation
for a special mission to Korea which was being handled elsewhere in the
Department. He was himself very much in favor of such a mission but
feared that the idea, after starting "in a burst of glory," was now being
downgraded. Everyone concerned with Korean problems agreed that
some such action was needed. The psychology that had guided U.S. aid
programs in Korea since 1945 had been one which emphasized stopgaps.
If there was famine you provided food, but you didn't look beyond that
to what you should do about the food problem. The Koreans themselves
now recognize that this is an inadequate approach and are receptive to
change. Through no fault of any particular individual, our aid mission in
Korea had been characterized by too many indians, too few chiefs. There
were too many people in Korea and they were of the wrong kind. The
mission was characterized by too much concern with bureaucracy and
petty detail, too little with the larger aspects of the program.

An adequate approach to the problem would have three characteristics:

a.    A special mission to Korea made up of really able people. The
people sent should have real ability and prestige. We should not send
retired businessmen, but people who are equipped by background for a
rapid insight into Korea's political and economic problems. I inferred
that he thought that present planning in State was inadequate in this
respect.

b.    Provision should be made for follow-through on the special mission's recommendations. This was a defect of the Farley proposals; that

---

Source: Kennedy Library, National Security Files, Countries Series, Korea, General,
4/1/61–5/25/61. Confidential.

he made no recommendations for bringing people in with the special mission who would stay on and see that recommendations are carried out.

    c.   A smaller group of higher-level people was needed to run the aid program in Korea.

He indicated that he thought that an inquiry by you as to the status of planning for a special mission would be highly desirable.

In view of the character of some of Mr. Macdonald's comments, they should obviously be treated confidentially.

Bob

---

### 209.   Telegram From the Department of State to the Embassy in Korea

Washington, April 5, 1961, 9:49 p.m.

1133. Joint State–Defense message. Embtel 1088.[1] In view political climate in Korea and strong desire of ROKG which we wish support to fullest extent consistent with US interests as well as rapidly increasing and potentially dangerous popular pressures encompassing practically all segments ROK governmental, political and public opinion, we have come to conclusion we should no longer refuse to negotiate full status of forces agreement with ROK. Accordingly, Ambassador authorized to inform PriMin that US now prepared open such negotiations. At same time Ambassador should warn PriMin again that we are not willing to pay compensation for any facilities used by US forces in Korea and shall continue to insist that ROKG be responsible for any and all such claims, public or private, although USG will cooperate to maximum extent in releasing such facilities as may be no longer needed and in accepting satisfactory alternative facilities offered by ROKG.

---

Source: Department of State, Central Files, 611.95B7/2–2861. Confidential. Repeated to CINCPAC for POLAD. Drafted by Manhard and William Lang of DOD/ISA; cleared by Bane, Steeves, Salans of L/FE, Huang of L/SFP, and Gilpatric of Defense; and approved by Ball.

[1] See footnote 1, Document 201.

Ambassador should also indicate to PriMin subject of criminal juris-diction is matter which must be handled most carefully.[2] US Government is under Congressional mandate to insure that US personnel subject to the jurisdiction of foreign courts will be assured fair trial guarantees comparable to those which would obtain in trials before US courts. Of necessity, this entails a study of the host state judicial system which the US has done in all countries where its personnel are subject to local juris-diction and which it has undertaken with respect to Korea. When results of Korean law study are known, we will then be able to determine on what basis a solution to the criminal jurisdiction problem might be pos-sible. Since all systems of criminal law are not identical, it may be neces-sary to take special steps to provide the assurances which we would require. FYI. As a result of the Chinese law study, we found it necessary to include fair trial guarantees additional to those found in the NATO SOF which the Chinese have informally implied might require certain revisions to their legal system. End FYI. Unless arrangements can be worked out which would ensure that US personnel would be assured of trials comparable to US standards, no agreement on criminal jurisdiction can be reached.

In addition, Ambassador should also indicate to PriMin that under any arrangements concerning criminal jurisdiction we consider it essen-tial that in actual practice the US exercise jurisdiction over our forces in the maximum number of cases, since we believe such course will best promote continued cordial ROK-US relations.

As to agenda and negotiating tactics, we have no objection to suggestion reftel that such aspects as entry and exit, customs, duties and taxation be negotiated first, although we see no reason why these sub-jects could not be handled simultaneously. While we recognize that ROKG desire for some compensation could make facilities and areas agreement difficult and controversial, we believe that question could logically be separated from other elements of such agreement, especially if ROKG aware we prepared to proceed in due course on criminal juris-diction. We expect to have draft of proposed facilities and areas agree-ment (excluding any provision for compensation of property claims) ready for transmittal soonest.

---

[2] In a March 30 memorandum to McNamara, JCSM–195–61, the JCS stated that it was their opinion that "negotiation of a criminal jurisdiction arrangement should not be com-menced until such time as the ROK has demonstrated a stable government, capable of judi-cious administration of a criminal jurisdictional arrangement." The JCS also stated that, if the Department of State insisted on initiating a full SOFA with the ROK, the Department of Defense should take the issue to the President. (Washington National Records Center, RG 330, OSD Files: FRC 66 A 3542, Korea 013) This message was revised by Department of State and Defense officials to take into consideration JCS objections, but the JCS refused to con-cur with the message as revised. (Memorandum from William Bundy to Gilpatric, March 27; ibid.)

Since rentals and criminal jurisdiction are clearly principal issues as far as ROK Government and public are concerned, we do not believe it in our best interest to postpone consideration these aspects too long and thereby raise risk of increased popular pressures on ROKG in meantime. Now that we have decided negotiate full SOFA we believe best course of action is to proceed with negotiations as quickly as normal and prudent procedures allow.

We believe Ambassador, accompanied by CINCUNC, should meet with PriMin as authorized first paragraph above and report ROKG reaction soonest.[3]

**Rusk**

---

[3] In telegram 1351 from Seoul, April 12, McConaughy reported that he and General Magruder had informed Prime Minister Chang Myon on April 10 that the United States was initiating negotiations for a full SOFA. Chang was very pleased, calling it the "best news ever." McConaughy also stressed to Chang the sensitive nature of criminal jurisdiction. (Department of State, Central Files, 611.95B7/4–1261)

---

## 210. Telegram From the Embassy in Korea to the Department of State

Seoul, April 11, 1961, 8 p.m.

1349. Embtel 742.[1] As termination of my mission here approaches, I would single out four paramount questions not susceptible to ready conclusive answers which point to actions and postures I believe we should take over extended period. At same time reftel continues to represent comprehensive and current summation Emb's views on Korean scene.

(1) *How best to bring our influence to bear on ROKG in order to have Koreans take measures we believe decidedly in their as well as in our interests?*

Press stories to the contrary notwithstanding, these past several months in Korea have seen considerable accomplishment, including

---

Source: Department of State, Central Files, 795B.00/4–1161. Confidential; Priority. Repeated to Tokyo and to CINCPAC for POLAD.

[1] Reference should be to telegram 942, January 31, which was the Embassy's "comprehensive and current summation" of the Korean scene. (Ibid., 795B.5–MSP/1–3161)

such basic reforms as institution of realistic unitary exchange rate, conclusion of new bilateral aid agreement,[2] measures to put "sick" industries on their feet, to raise transportation power rates, as well as rationalize the electric power industry. These important products of "Dillon Package"[3] required a lot more cooperative resolve and effective background political action than the Chang Myon govt has been given credit for. Moreover, these measures, taken as a whole and particularly in context Jan–Feb food shortages and resulting rising price trends, imposed short-term hardships and inevitable popular reactions which ROKG and ROK-US relations had to weather.

Rigors of these accomplishments put our relationships and ROK constitutional system to new trial and highlighted question of ROK sovereignty and question of US respect for ROK sovereignty. ROK sensitivities particularly stirred up as result of conclusion by end of February of new bilateral aid agreement which somewhat irrationally regarded by ROKs as derogatory of their sovereignty and language of which gave considerable offense. Incident brought out fact that nationalism in Korea, delayed by war and reconstruction, now becoming an important factor in Korean life. Moreover, pressures on ROKs to normalize aid procedures and economic relationships with US gave new prominence to status of force question on which no action was taken.

Yet our general approach of holding out additional assistance to ROKG only in return for ROK compliance with specific conditions seems to have been highly successful in achieving results we had sought unavailingly for years. Question arises therefore how in period of rising nationalism and of perhaps declining overall US assistance US can nevertheless pursue same general tactic as reflected in Dillon letter, exerting greater influence on ROKs to place their house in order. Tremendous tasks lie ahead, including spurring economic development, eliminating corruption, promoting the austerity movement, etc., without taking steps which involve "interference" from US, these things likely not to be done in time, yet if we overplay our hand and stir up serious ROK resentment, our efforts could be danerously counter-productive.

---

[2] Officially "Agreement providing for economic, technical and related assistance, with agreed minute and exchange of notes," which entered into force on February 28, 1961. (TIAS 4710)

[3] The "Dillon Package" was embodied in a letter with two annexes from the Under Secretary of State Dillon to Prime Minister Chang Myon, October 25, 1960. Dillon's letter offered the ROK $165 millon of Defense Support Assistance plus $7.3 million in Technical Cooperation Assistance, but required the ROK to make a series of reforms in its exchange rate, to normalize its aid procedures, to raise significantly public utility and transportation rates, and to resolve outstanding problems related to effective use of aid. Dillon's letter plus two annexes are in telegram 382 to Seoul, October 25, 1960. (Department of State, Central Files, 795B.5–MSP/10–2560)

Basic answer lies in being firm in our councils, yet never treating ROKs as less than equal, of consulting them properly on international issues, and of maintaining sympathetic understanding for a nation which has gone through great agony, remains divided, and has enormous economic and political problems. ROKs are tested friends looking to US leadership and guidance but not wishing to be reminded of dependency on US. In present nationalistic setting, bringing our influence to bear more effectively on ROKG will take some doing. Answer would seem to lie in exerting more influence by doing it less conspicuously. Aware of this problem for some time, Embassy has already devised many techniques for quietly influencing legislators and ROKG executive branch. More and more and more meetings with PriMin have been held without knowledge of press through rendezvous at my home or elsewhere. Visits to Korea of influential US officials would be helpful in this regard, assuming, of course, that our counsels would be discreetly conveyed; and visits to US of key ROK officials (like FinMin Kim last fall) should be utilized to maximum effect. Above all, it will require hard, sustained efforts applied widely but with the ultimate in diplomacy, tact and patience.

*(2) How to make the ROK democratic system more effective?*

Here I feel we must do more to influence PriMin Chang Myon to exercise leadership—an ingredient definitely lacking at present in Korean political scene. He is no dynamic leader by nature and it will be difficult to alter this style which reflects PriMin's own personality and character. However, we should continue to urge that PriMin act decisively to get through important bills or act on other needed measures, bearing in mind that when he has acted in a forthright, forceful way, results have been good for country and party. This is not to suggest that he should act autocratically or without proper consultation with opposition. Indeed one of his faults has been failure on occasion to prepare groundwork for more expeditious legislative action through adequate consultation with opposition leaders as well as elements his own party.

Particularly in these challenging times, PriMin and his cohorts cannot afford to act in politics-as-usual manner. They should recognize that semi-emergency times call for statesmanship, greater unity and concerted effort.

We have also counselled PriMin—although he seems to have been unresponding so far and therefore our counsels should perhaps be more strongly accentuated—to get out among his own people, to break free from the chrysalis of Seoul politics and identify himself as the kind of leader of the people who understands their problems and spearheads their interests. For example, PriMin and Cabinet members never visited areas reported to be suffering from famine during past several months.

We would also hope to induce PriMin to show better judgment in some of his appointments, notably in the diplomatic field, and to show greater disposition for drawing younger leaders into top positions— particularly younger leaders pledged to integrity and austerity in Korean life. In latter regard, pervading effects of oriental family system and traditional respect for elders is going to make it difficult to achieve quick progress in having wider, more influential participation of younger leaders in politics, business and society. Nevertheless, it is apparent that there is sharp divergency between the convictions, training and values of the Korean under thirty as compared with his elders. It is obviously to our advantage that these younger elements be able make their contributions through the established conservative political parties. We should not try to force them into a premature prominence but we should be alert for opportunities to assist them to gain experience and public recognition. The emergence of such younger elements might also provide a factor which at present time is sadly lacking in Korea, i.e. a group which knows that a modern state can limit graft and corruption in both govt and business and that South Korea can hardly hope survive unless it does take such measures.

Furthermore, we must discourage any ROKG tendency to rely on repression as means of retaining power. While there is need for tightening up security laws in Korea, communism and leftism will be far more effectively counteracted by positive measures to improve national well-being (such as National Construction Service) than by anti-Communist laws. Accent must be upon the positive, not upon the negative. Korea must be made to look forward rather than backward.

*(3) How to inculcate greater hope among ROK in their own future and greater mutual trust and confidence among themselves?*

I am increasingly persuaded that this is the basic psychological problem here. Stark, bleak facts of economic life and frustrations over continued divisions of Korea are prominent among factors explaining widespread feelings of hopelessness in future, continuing mutual recriminations among Koreans who as a people have been traditionally addicted to distrust of fellowman, and all this creates an atmosphere wide open to exploitation by enemies of a free Korea. To overcome this deeply disturbing state of national mind involves improvement of conditions of life and closing the widening gap between ROK expectations and the actual rate of progress toward those aspirations.

A carefully conceived and rigorously pursued long-range economic development plan is an absolute necessity, providing not only the blueprint for action but also the grounds for hope and a sense of achievement that would go with the formulation and execution of such a program. ROK increasingly aware of importance such planning and govt busy on developing plans in consultation with US advisers. ROKG has hailed new US administration's recent announcement of proposal to give US economic aid programs on long-term basis for economic development purposes and in harmony with recipient countries on long-range development programs. This announcement in itself injected a new ray of hope in ROK community.

If National Construction Service proves to be the important benefit to Korea which I believe it will be, its continuation should be encouraged and supported by US.

Japan, longtime and natural trading partner of ROK, offers great possibilities for developmental aid to Korea—at least in form of long-term investment loans—and for furnishing technological assistance which Korea eminently requires. Recent efforts of Italian and German private interests (backed by their respective govts) to enter Korean development with long-term credits for industrial projects have been welcomed by ROKG and should be encouraged by US. On other hand, although ROK foreign investment law has now been in effect for over 15 months, there has been no rush of foreign private investors to Korea and not one capital investment project has actually been initiated under this law. Since the law itself appears to provide adequate safeguards for investment, political and social instability seem to be main inhibiting factors.

Also needed to counteract lack of faith and hope among Koreans is more responsible press and a far better govt information service. We are working hard in encouraging progress in these fields. Press, of course, responds best to advice from newspaper contacts from abroad. A recent letter from IPI Director criticizing Korean press irresponsibility had deep impact. This kind of approach should be repeated.

(4) *How to bring about soonest normalization ROK-Japanese relations and establishment of mutually beneficial ties between ROK and Japan?*[4]

Past few months marked by discouragingly slow pace in this direction. ROKG at last realizes time is working against it and, within limitations set by Korean political scene, is working hard for early settlement. Unless improved progress in current ROK-GOJ talks is not soon forthcoming, I believe we should consider whether US taking more active role in trying to induce settlement might not be less risky than permitting situation continue to drift. There may be temptation to transfer this middle-man responsibility to another third party such as ICJ or neutral group but it is doubtful that any outside group could be as efficacious in bringing ROK and GOJ together as US.

---

[4] At the 476th meeting of the National Security Council on February 9, Secretary of State Rusk stated that he attached great importance to encouraging the ROK to reopen relations, particularly trading relations, with Japan. (NSC Action No. 2402–b, approved by the President on February 11; ibid., S/S–NSC (Miscellaneous) Files: Lot 66 D 95, NSC Record of Actions)

So much for the four main questions emerging from events of past few months. Additional to these and to recommendations contained in reftel, I feel that there are two basic problems which have received inadequate attention and need redressing. I refer to problem of excessive population growth and to problem of excessive numbers of unemployed college graduates. These phenomena, if unmitigated, are going to be dangerously compromising to the viability, stability and security of free Korea. Korea would do well to examine and emulate, as valid and desirable, family planning methods being pursued in India and elsewhere. High literacy and educational system in Korea furnish useful background in this regard. As to unemployed graduates of higher institutes, I believe we should exert influence to encourage more vocational technical and scientific training at expense of liberal arts and law, plus higher entrance and graduation requirements for college students.

In relinquishing my duties here, I wish to thank those many able colleagues of all US agencies represented in Seoul who, reinforced by excellent guidance and backstopping from Dept and other agencies in Washington, are so effectively promoting US interests in this strategic peninsula.

McConaughy

## 211.  Editorial Note

On April 24–25, 1961, Republic of Korea Foreign Minister Yil Hyung Chyung visited Washington for discussions with Department of State officials. On April 24 Yil Hyung Chyung met with Assistant Secretary McConaughy and other members of the Bureau of Far Eastern Affairs. Although there was one discussion, two memoranda of conversation were produced on separate topics: "Korean Item at the United Nations" and "ROK-Japan Relations." (Department of State, Central Files, 795B.00/4–2461 and 694.95B/4–2561, respectively)

The following day the Korean Foreign Minister met with Secretary Dean Rusk at 11:30 a.m. for approximately 1 hour. The record of the conversation was divided into five separate memoranda of conversation covering the following topics: "United States Approach to Countries Seeking Economic Development," "ROK–Japan Relations," "Status of Forces Agreement with Korea," "Anti-Americanism in the Republic of Korea," and "Communist Subversion in the Republic of Korea." The five memoranda are ibid., 795B.5–MSP/4–2561, 694.95B/4–2561, 795B.5/4–2561, 795B.00/4–2561, and 795B.00/4–2561, respectively. Foreign Minister Yil Hyung Chyung also met with under Secretary of State Chester Bowles on April 25 for a discussion on U.S. economic aid. (Memorandum of conversation, April 25; ibid., Secretary's Memoranda of Conversation: Lot 65 D 330)

## 212.  Editorial Note

At the 483d meeting of the National Security Council on May 5, 1961, with President Kennedy in attendence, the Council "agreed that a Task Force under the Assistant Secretary of State for Far Eastern Affairs should be established to prepare and circulate a report on the subject [U.S. policy toward Korea] by May 15 for discussion by the Council on May 19." The President approved this as National Security Action No. 2421 on May 16. (Kennedy Library, National Security Files, Meetings and Memoranda Series, NSC Meetings, No. 483) In his brief memorandum for the record of this meeting, Chief of Naval Operations Admiral Arleigh Burke noted that the task force would include representatives of the Departments of Defense (tentatively William P. Bundy), the Treasury, and State, and the Central Intelligence Agency. Burke also noted that Under Secretary Bowles had planned to go to Korea, but would be replaced by "a Senator." (Naval Historical Center, Burke Papers, Area Files, Bumpy Road)

Deputy Assistant Secretary Avery Peterson told Assistant Secretary of State Walter McConaughy that he had information from White House staffers that President Kennedy "was concerned with Korea in the sense that the situation might be one in which real trouble could arise and he wants to plan to head off that contingency." Another concern reportedly expressed by the President was that the Korea Task Force study should be "focused on important problems and should propose action within known limitations." (Memorandum from Peterson to McConaughy, May 9; Department of State, FE/EA Files: Lot 65 D 235, K6.8 Korea Task Force, Jan–June 1961)

No complete record of Task Force discussions has been found. The best source for documentation on the Task Force, including agenda, related papers, and draft minutes of some meetings, is ibid.

**213.    Telegram From the Commander in Chief, U.S. Forces Korea (Magruder) to the Joint Chiefs of Staff**

Seoul, May 16, 1961, 5:45 p.m.

EUSA JOC 70305. 1.(C) At approximately 3:00 am on the morning of 16 May 1961, General Magruder was called on the telephone by Lt General Chang Do Young, Chief of Staff, ROKA, who informed General Magruder that an attempted military coup of the ROK Government was in progress. At this time, he requested that US MPs be committed against ROK Marines. General Magruder refused.

2.(C) General Chang stated that the coup was led by Maj General Pak Jung Hui and that also involved were elements of the 1st Marine brigade from Kimpo Peninsula, the 30th, 31st, 33d reserve divisions, and the ROK Special Forces.

3.(C) Later information indicated that Maj General Pak Jung Hui, Deputy CG, SROKA, assumed command at 6th Military District Headquarters at approximately midnight. At approximately 0300 hours, the reserve battalion of the 1st Marine Brigade of Kimpo peninsula started north across the Soul Han River bridge where a fire fight developed with ROKA MPs. It later developed that the battalion was led by Brig Gen Kim Yun Geun, CG of the 1st Marine brigade.

4.(C) Maj Gen Pak Jung Hui then proceeded to treat with Lt Gen Chang Do Young, in an effort to get Lt Gen Chang to lead the military coup. The KBS radio facilities in the hands of Maj Gen Pak Jung Hui forces, starting at 0500 hours KST, began to make broadcasts in the name of the Revolutionary Committee. The broadcast was made in the name of Lt Gen Chang. It is not believed that Lt Gen Chang authorized the use of his name for this purpose.

5.(C) The Military Revolutionary Committee released a statement that the committee had assumed control of the legislative, executive, and judicial branches of the ROK Government. The action was taken to terminate corruption and overcome the difficult situation facing the nation. The committee promised that the new government will (1) be strictly anti-Communist, (2) root out corruption, (3) observe the UN Charter and all international agreements and cooperation with the US and all other free nations, (4) endeavor to stabilize the national economy, (5) unify Korea as an anti-Communist nation, and (6) turn over the reins of gov-

---

Source: Kennedy Library, National Security Files, Countries Series, Korea, Cables, 1/20/61–5/17/61. Confidential. Repeated to the White House, which is the source text, and passed to Ottawa, where President Kennedy was making a State visit to Canada May 16–18. Also repeated to CINCPAC, the Embassy, USIS, and USOM in Seoul, and 16 U.S. military commanders in East Asia.

ernment to "honest and competent political leaders." The statement concluded with an appeal to citizens to report for work as normal.

6.(C) At Gen Magruder's request, Gen Chang visited Gen Magruder in his office at approximately 0630 hours. At this time Chang gave Gen Magruder the impression that he was not a party to the revolution, but desired to negotiate with the revolutionaries to prevent bloodshed. Chang stated he wished to talk to military cmdrs to get assurance they would back him in opposing revolution. He was reluctant to call in ROKA troops.

7.(C) In later talk with Magruder, Chang indicated he was still negotiating with Pak in an endeavor to get Pak to operate through the ROK Government. Chang requested Pak to make his demands known to the government.

8.(C) Chang indicated to Gen Magruder he would request the President to declare martial law with Chang as martial law cmdr thus enhancing Chang's position vis-à-vis Pak.

9.(C) As of 160900 May 61, "the Military Revolution Committee" announced over the radio that the entire nation had been place under emergency martial law. Composition of the committee as announced over the Korean radio was: Lt Gen Chang Do Young, Chairman; Maj Gen Pak Jung Hui, Vice Chairman; Lt Gen Yi Han-im, CG, FROKA; Lt Gen Ch'oe Kyong-nok, CG SROKA; Maj Gen So Chong-ch'oi, CG IV MDC; Maj Gen Kim Kye-won, CG III MDC; Maj Gen Pak Ki-pyong, CG V MDC; and Maj Gen Pak Hyon-su, CG log comd. The announcement prohibited all public gatherings and travel to foreign countries; set curfew hours from 1900 to 0500 hours; froze all bank assets; closed all airports and harbors; and established censorship of all publications.

10.(C) by 1000 hours most of downtown Seoul was under control of the Military Revolutionary Committee employing elements of the ROK MC 1st Brigade. The 30th and 33d ROK Reserve Divs, VI Corps Arty Units, and of the 1st Combat Team (Airborne).

11.(C) At approx 1018 hours, the following statement was released by PIO EUSA: General Magruder, in his capacity as Commander in Chief of the UNC, calls upon all military personnel in his Command to support the duly recognized Government of the ROK headed by Prime Minister Chang Myon. General Magruder expects that the Chiefs of the Korean Armed Forces will use their authority and influence to see that control is immediately turned back to the government authorities and that order is restored in the armed forces.

12.(C) Almost concurrently the following statement of Minister Marshall Green, Chargé d'Affaires, American Embassy. The position taken by the Commander in Chief UNC in supporting the freely elected and constitutionally established Government of the ROK is [one with] which I fully concur. I wish to make it emphatically clear that the US supports the constitutional Government of the ROK as elected by the people of the Republic last July and as constituted by the election last August of a Prime Minister.

13.(C) After reading General Magruder's statement, Gen Lee Han Lim, CG FROKA, stated that he will obey the ROK Government. That if his troops were called upon to put down the insurrection, there might be a few who would not fight the insurrectionists, but most would. Gen Lee has alerted certain troops for possible movement. FROKA has not been alerted.

14.(C) At approx 1030 hours KST Lt General Chang, Chief of Staff, ROKA, went to visit the President of the Republic of Korea who is under no restriction and the Minister of National Defense, who is under house arrest. The President told General Chang that he does not desire martial law to be established in Korea and that he does not desire any firm action to eliminate the revolutionary movement. The Minister of National Defense stated that he does not desire that FROKA troops be used to put down the revolutionary movement.

15.(C) At about 1115 hours, Lt Gen Choi Kyung-muk, CG ROKA, was in communication with General Magruder. He advised that he remained loyal to and would support the government; further he had recalled to their barracks elements of 2 engineer bns which had taken control in Taegu and they had withdrawn.

---

214.  Telegram From the Chairman of the Joint Chiefs of Staff (Lemnitzer) to the Commander in Chief, U.S. Forces Korea (Magruder)

Washington, May 16, 1961, 11:20 a.m.

SSO JCS 686–61. Exclusive for Gen Magruder from Gen Lemnitzer, info Adm Felt.

1.  I have just returned from a White House meeting[1] the purpose of which was to assist in preparing suitable answers to questions on the situation in Korea which were likely to be directed at President's press sec-

---

Source: Kennedy Library, National Security Files, Countries Series, Korea, Cables, 1/20/61–5/17/61. Secret. Repeated to CINCPAC.

[1] No other record of this meeting has been found.

retary Salinger at his regular press briefing at 1130 hours today. McConaughy attended also.

2.   One of the questions that required most of our time was "Does the President fully indorse the statements released by General Magruder and DCM Green?"[2] As you know, CJCS Kim is reported to have stated that both statements went too far. Answer proposed by White House group was that you and Green had issued statements appropriate to your assigned responsibilities.

3.   The purpose of this message is to let you know that the consensus of opinion at the White House meeting was that your statement went just about as far as you can possibly go without becoming seriously involved in the internal affairs of the ROK. Therefore, I suggest that insofar as possible you avoid issuing any further statements and concentrate any comments you may have to make on importance of the mission assigned to CINCUNC, i.e., maintenance of the defense of the ROK against Communist attack.

---

[2] The statements by Magruder and Green are in Document 213. According to a telephone conversation between Acting Secretary Bowles and President Kennedy in Ottawa, May 16, 6:05 p.m.:

"The President asked if there was anything on the Korean business. CB said a cable came in a little while ago saying the coup was successful as far as they could see. He said they are aware that we are disturbed and they say full cable will follow tomorrow. The President said he would like to hear their explanation and said he wanted it when he got back. The President asked if there were two statements. CB said Magruder made a statement and the Embassy made one." (Department of State, S/S Files: Lot 66 D 147, Chester Bowles Telephone Conversations)

---

## 215.   Telegram From the Department of State to Secretary of State Rusk at Geneva

Washington, May 16, 1961, 7:52 p.m.

Tosec 137. Following is first sitrep on coup d'état in Republic of Korea subsequent to information contained Seoul's 1524 previously

---

Source: Department of State, Central Files, 795B.00/5–1661. Confidential; Niact. Drafted by Manhard; cleared by Bacon and William B. Coolidge, Chief of the East Asia Division of INR; and approved by McConaughy. Repeated to Ottawa, Bangkok for Vice President Johnson, Athens, Taipei, Tokyo, and Paris TOPOL. Rusk was in Geneva for the opening sessions of the Geneva Conference on Laos.

passed Secretary in Geneva.[1] Subsequent sitreps will be transmitted as need arises and also rptd info Ottawa for President during his visit there.

Military coup d'état began in Seoul pre-dawn May 16, carried out by few ROK Army airborne units and elements first ROK Marine Brigade under leadership Maj Gen Pak Chong-hui, Deputy CG Second ROK Army. These military units swiftly took over ROK military headquarters, principal communications and governmental centers. Indications also that coup has affected some other urban centers. Coup group made its first broadcast over Seoul radio 5 AM May 16 in name of Military Revolutionary Committee "which is revolutionary govt" stating Chairman is Lt Gen Chang To-yong, Chief of Staff ROK Army, and Deputy Chairman Maj Gen Pak. So far seven decrees known to have been issued ordering martial law throughout ROK, night curfew, full censorship, restricted use of airports and seaports, ban on travel out of Korea by Koreans, ban on public meetings, dissolution of National Assembly and local councils, arrest of all Cabinet Ministers and Vice Ministers, freezing of all banking activities, and protection of lives and property of foreign troops and diplomatic personnel. Coup group also broadcast six-point program calling for continuation anti-Communist policy, support for US and UN, "economic revolution," preparations for unification of country and turning over govt to "new and honest" politicians.

With less than 4000 ROK military personnel estimated to comprise coup units controlling Seoul, bulk of regular ROK armed forces have apparently made no attempt either assist or interfere with coup operations. First ROK Army CG, Lt Gen Yi Han-lim, and Second ROK army CG (formerly ROK Army Chief of Staff) Lt Gen Choe Kyong-nok reportedly not in sympathy with coup leaders. Position of present Chief of Staff Gen Chang To-yong seems equivocal. He has reportedly declined call on other ROK Army units to put down coup, presumably on ground this would cause considerable bloodshed. On other hand Gen Chang has apparently not cast his lot with coup group. Latter's use of Gen Chang's name as coup leader appears unauthorized and incorrect.

On morning May 16 Gen Magruder, as CINCUNC, issued statement calling on all military personnel his command to support ROK Govt headed by PriMin Chang Myon and expressing CINCUNC's expectation that chiefs ROK forces "will use their authority and influence to see that control is immediately turned back to lawful governmental authorities" and that order restored in armed forces. Chargé Green issued statement concurring in above position and saying US supports constitutional government of ROK. Texts of both statements carried over US

---

[1] Telegram 1524, May 16, received in the Department of State on May 15 at 5:21 a.m., was the first notice of the coup. Chargé Green stated that he approved Magruder's decision not to release U.S. forces to put down the coup. (Ibid.)

Armed Forces Korea radio network, but reportedly carried by only one domestic Korean newspaper as result censorship. Dept has issued brief official statement and has given press brief factual résumé of events and political backgrounders indicating, however, Dept not yet in position make any assessments of future prospects. Dept has also told press there are no indications that American lives or property are in imminent danger.

Chargé Green and Gen Magruder mid-day May 16 had three-hour meeting with ROK President Yun Po-sun.[2] Gen Magruder told President he believed Chief of Staff Chang loyal to ROKG and that Chang had urged insurgent leader Pak insure order, safeguard public officials and submit rebel group's complaints to duly constituted govt. Magruder also emphasized any usurpation of govt authority by insurgent group at gunpoint would be disastrous for future of Korea. Green stressed constructive achievements present govt and that any change in govt by force would jeopardize survival of hard-won ROK democratic institutions, takeover by military clique in defiance of law would harm ROK's international prestige. Green recognized that many officers involved in coup might be motivated by patriotism, however misdirected.

President Yun in taking partial issue with Magruder and Green said popular dissatisfaction and disillusionment with Chang administration widespread, corruption extensive and extended to high places in govt, ROK needed strong govt and Chang Myon had proven incapable of providing such leadership. Yun believed solution would have to come through establishment supra-partisan national cabinet including leaders from both within and without National Assembly. He did not specify whether he envisaged his solution as taking place inside or outside existing Constitutional framework.

PriMin Chang's whereabouts uncertain, but he believed to be in hiding since coup began.

**Bowles**

---

[2] As reported in telegram 1536 from Seoul, May 16, 9 p.m., received in the Department of State on May 15 at 11 a.m. (Ibid.)

## 216.  Telegram From the Department of State to the Embassy in Korea

Washington, May 16, 1961, 10:45 p.m.

1316. White House, Department, and other interested agencies closely following reports Embassy and CINCUNC on coup crisis. You are to be commended on alertness, initiative and timeliness characteristic of your reporting.

We recognize desirability of restoring authority of lawful government against reckless challenge of military clique invoking force to upset government freely chosen by Korean people under their own constitutional system. Even though no ideological issue apparently involved, our assessment is that coup attempt undermines stability and reputation of ROK and therefore is contrary to our joint interests.

However, the strange unwillingness of the President, armed forces leaders and other key officials to take any action to suppress coup or to take sides at all, with disappearance from public view of Prime Minister and other members of Cabinet, does not encourage view that Chang government can survive crisis unscathed. Irresolution of those officials who have it in their power to deal with uprising and apparent indifference general public to fate of Chang government provide poor foundation for exertion U.S. influence in behalf Chang Myon.

Therefore cautious attitude of wait-and-see has been adopted pending clarification of situation. We will continue to hope Government can reestablish itself and we will avoid any action which would adversely affect its prospects. On the other hand, in absence some indication government able and willing put forth some effective effort save itself, we will refrain from additional public identification of U.S. with fate of what may be a lost cabinet.[1]

---

Source: Department of State, Central Files, 795B.00/5–1661. Secret; Niact. Drafted by McConaughy, cleared with Bacon and Jenkins, and approved by McConaughy. Repeated to Tokyo, Geneva for Rusk, and Ottawa for the Presidential visit.

[1] The following morning at the Secretary's staff meeting, McConaughy explained that "the President was disturbed by the Green–Magruder statements of support for the Chang Government and said the President has given Green approval for his exercise of necessary discretion but cautioned against further comment." McConaughy said that the situation was difficult because the government was discredited by weak performance but the coup group did not offer promising leadership. Cleveland suggested the use of U.N. machinery, and Bowles asked Cleveland and McConaughy to confer with him that afternoon. (Department of State, S/S Files: Lot 66 D 147, Secretary's Staff Meetings)

It was this line of reasoning which prompted high-level decision to take position reflected in May 16 noon press briefing (Deptel 1311).[2] This is in no sense a repudiation of public statements made May 16 by you and General Magruder, which are approved.

While it is too early to spell out U.S. course to be followed event Chang Government not restored to power, thought is being given to this question. Recommendations from Embassy would be useful.

**Bowles**

---

[2] In telegram 1311, May 16, the Department sent the Embassy a statement made by the Director of News, Lincoln White, at the noon briefing that day. The statement reads: "We continue to receive reports which are under study. The situation, however, is so fluid and unclear that we are unable to make substantive comment. The statements by General Magruder and Chargé d'Affaires Marshall Green were made within the scope of their authority in their posts." (Ibid., Central Files, 795B.00/5–1661)

---

### 217.   Memorandum From Director of Central Intelligence Dulles to President Kennedy

Washington, May 16, 1961.

SUBJECT

   CIA Korea Coup Reports dated 21 through 26 April 1961

[less than 1 line of source text not declassified] CIA commencing 21 April reported on plans for a coup d'état in Korea by Major General Pak Chong-hui as follows:

> 21 April—[less than 1 line of source text not declassified] reports that one of two existing coups to overthrow ROK Government is led by Major General Pak Chong-hui, Deputy Commanding General, Second ROK Army. The other is led by Yi Pom-sok and members of the Racial Youth Corps. Plans discussed throughout ROK Army down to and including division commanders. Army leaders look upon the present politicians as corrupt and weak and believe they have either caused or permitted situations to exist whereby the military, collectively and individually, have been hurt.

---

Source: Central Intelligence Agency, DCI/ER Files, Job 80–B0176R, White House, Jan.–June 1961. Secret. Drafted by [text not declassified] Directorate of Plans, Far East Division, [text not declassified], on May 15. Sent to the White House under cover of a May 16 memorandum from J.S. Earman to Clifton.

21 April—[*less than 1 line of source text not declassified*] summary on possibility of a military coup. Definite threat exists; however, increased political stability, absence of violence and civil disorder and strengthening of the police would tend to thwart any coup attempt.

23 April—[*less than 1 line of source text not declassified*] believes there is sufficient evidence to gauge that a significant grouping exists which is actively and seriously talking and planning a coup and that the grouping is largely made up of elements which are bitter, rash, purposeful and quite capable of abrupt and violent action.

23 April—The plot is supported by ROK Army, student groups and reformists. Leader believed to be General Pak Chong-hui, and General So Chong-ch'ol, Commanding General of VI Military District Command is also a close supporter. Much detail contained on military supporters.

24 April—Views of ROK Army Chief of Staff, Chang To-yong on military plot. Chang desires arrest Pak Chong-hui but has lack of evidence. Believes arrest might trigger coup. Chang believes Racial Youth Corps and Yi Pom-sok may support coup.

25 April—ROK Army CIC is investigating the coup. If the coup is not attempted on 26 April, group will await a more opportune time. As of 24 April, according to Chang, Chang Myon was unaware of the coup; however, newspaper publisher planned to advise him on 25 April.

25 April—[*less than 1 line of source text not declassified*] had one-hour meeting with ROK Army Chief of Staff Chang To-yong on 24 April and told Chang that information on coup had been volunteered our office, that General Magruder would be advised at first opportunity and that thereafter General Magruder would probably discuss this matter with Chang. Chang mentioned that Pak had talked to him one week earlier. Chang states that he believes no action imminent.

26 April—Prime Minister Chang Myon is aware of rumors circulating to the effect that a group of malcontents within the Army may be plotting some kind of coup. He attaches little importance to these stories and believes that the situation is by no means dangerous. Chang Myon is satisfied with the performance of ROK Army Chief of Staff Chang To-yong. He believes that General Chang is forceful and able and enjoys the respect of his American counterparts. He plans to retain General Chang for a full two-year tour.

**Allen W. Dulles**[1]

---

[1] Printed from a copy that indicates Dulles signed the original.

## 218.   Telegram From the Commander in Chief, United Nations Command (Magruder) to the Chairman of the Joint Chiefs of Staff (Lemnitzer)

Seoul, May 17, 1961, 11:40 a.m.

From General Magruder. My personal summary of the situation after the first twenty four hours is set forth below.

The Prime Minister continues to remain in hiding and does not reveal himself to us. He does not have a reputation for personal courage.

The strength behind the military coup is still unclear but appears to be growing. Only a few troops have moved into Seoul, probably about 3600. They have been essentially unopposed. More have not been needed so we cannot be sure whether more are available. The troops actually available and those reported to be available come from Korean reserve and corps artillery units under the operational control of the US I Corps Group.

A US Army CIC poll of casual bystanders along the streets indicates an average for each ten questioned of four in favor of the uprising, two in favor but consider timing too early, and four opposed.

I am not fully confident in the loyalty of the Chang Myun government of any of the chiefs of staff. Chairman of JCS Kim Chong Oh appears to be neutral with some leaning toward loyalty but exercises little influence. Kim Shin, Lee Sung Ho and Kim Sung Eun appear to be neutral.

Chang Do Young has represented himself as loyal but claimed that he did not take decisive action because he wished to avoid bloodshed. There is much to indicate he is two faced. He is in a state of mental depression which makes it particularly hard to analyze his actions. He is unwilling to bring troops even to the outskirts of Seoul. He had at least some previous knowledge of the uprising. In the propaganda of the insurgents he was cited as the head of the Revolutionary Committee. He said he was not but he was unwilling to deny it publicly. He has now accepted this position for the purpose (so he states) of securing authority to move the insurgent troops out of Seoul.

President Yun Po Sun while giving lip service to the constitution initially, appeared to consider a coup as an acceptable method of getting rid of his political opponent Chang Myun and establishing a new kind of government. He still probably wants to replace Chang Myun and seems

Source: Kennedy Library, National Security Files, Countries Series, Korea, Cables, 1/20/61–5/17/61. Secret. Repeated to CINCPAC and to the Department of State as UK 70316CC. (Department of State, Central Files, 795B.00/5–1761)

to be seeking most legally correct way of achieving this. Both President Yun and Chairman of the House of Councillors George Paik oppose bringing in troops to suppress the uprising.

I have not seen the MND who is confined in the City Hall by the insurgents but Chang Do Young stated he urged no troops be brought in to quell the uprising lest there be bloodshed.

In summary all the powerful men in and around the Seoul government appear to have had knowledge of the plan for the coup and at least have not opposed it. The people appear to be divided for and against but they do not appear to be sufficiently concerned at this time to take any active part.

The basic purpose of the uprising appears to be the elimination of the Chang Myun government and probably the elimination of the cabinet responsive system. There has been no evidence of anti-American or pro-Communist feeling. The actual leader is Major General Pak Chong Hui, a forceful officer tainted in the past with Communism and who was convicted by the Rhee government as a Communist. Subsequently he collaborated with the ROK in eliminating some Communists. Since that time he has a reputation of being anti-Communist. There appear to be no known Communists among the other members of the coup group nor are there any who are known to be anti-American. It must be realized that if the coup is permitted to be successful, Pak, whose real loyalty remains to be determined, may emerge as the most powerful man in Korea.

The insurgents have possession of the radio stations and have a censorship on the press. They are broadcasting propaganda and suppressing everything unfavorable to their cause. Given time, this may convert many individuals who up to now have been neutral into supporters of the uprising.

On the advice of General Lee Han Lim in order to help hold the First ROK Army in line and in an effort to stop all the neutrals from going over to the insurgents I have broadcast my support of the constitutionally elected government as has Chargé d'Affaires Marshall Green. This appears to have had some effect but it can not be expected to endure indefinitely. However, at minimum, it will emphasize need to return to civilian, legally constituted government as soon as possible.

We are seeking to undermine the uprising by pressing the responsible commanders, from whose commands came the insurgent troops now in Seoul, to endeavor to get their troops to return to their duty. Success appears probable with the Marine Battalion. It appears improbable with the artillery battalion of the VI ROK Corps. Other troops are still in doubt.

General Chang, in his presumably new position as Martial Law Commander, states that he will order the insurgent troops out of Seoul. If they go under these circumstances it will presumably be with some assurance that the Chang Myun government will be replaced although the insurgents have not made known whatever demands they have. The replacement of the Chang Myun government is the publicly stated reason for the uprising.

Lee Han Lim and his First ROK Army are the force which can probably suppress the uprising by bringing to Seoul such an overwhelming force as to make it hopeless for the insurgents to fight. General Lee states that his troops, with few exceptions, will do as they are ordered. He has four Divisions now in reserve alerted. I believe he would accept and carry out instructions if they were given by Chang Myun to suppress the uprising. I believe he would accept and carry out such instructions if given by me. The longer the above action is delayed the less likely is the prospect of success.

I have hoped that Chang Myun would reveal his whereabouts last night but it is now 0900 KST and he has not yet done so. Some of his people have been contacted but none admit knowing where he is. We urged to have him get in touch with us but he has not responded.

If the Prime Minister will assert himself and direct the use of FROKA to suppress the uprising I propose to support him. Unless and until he does, I will seek to hold FROKA available for use. I do not know how long I can hold FROKA in this situation available to support Chang Myun by suppressing the uprising. The longer the Prime Minister remains in hiding the less are his chances of returning to power.

A possible course of action is for me to direct Lee Han Lim to suppress the uprising even though the President, the Chairman of the House of Councillors, the MND and the CS ROKA oppose use of the FROKA for this purpose. If I should do so and were successful we might restore a government with no one to run it and lacking popular support. Basically my mission is to protect Korea from external aggression. To this end the Korean Forces appear to be steadfast. I feel that it is also a part of my mission to protect Korea from internal subversion by the Communists. The uprising does not appear to be Communist inspired although the leader is a former Communist and any uprising against the duly elected government may react to the advantage of the Communists. Accordingly, I do not propose to direct FROKA to suppress the uprising on my own authority only.

*Addendum:*

Just as the above message was about to be dispatched, I received Lemnitzer's message of 16 May.[1] This message confirms my intention not to direct FROKA, on my own authority, to suppress the uprising. It

---

[1] Document 214.

puts me in some doubt as to the degree of support I should give the Prime Minister if he comes out of hiding. I visualize the support I would propose to give as my personally urging Lee Han Lim and all other officers of the ROK Military Forces to comply with the orders of the Prime Minister if the prospects of success are favorable.

If the above line of action is not acceptable request further guidance.

## 219. Telegram From the Department of State to the Embassy in Korea

Washington, May 17, 1961, 11:23 p.m.

1321. Handling of current situation by you and General Magruder has our full endorsement. We want to give you maximum latitude within following framework in meeting fast breaking developments which may call for immediate responses on your part. We recognize that tactical moves in this emergency can not be best directed from this distance. We have full confidence in sound judgment yourself and General Magruder.[1]

If it is your finding that Chang Myon government has disintegrated irretrievably you are authorized to work along lines which you consider best calculated to encourage early emergence of broadly based, responsible non-partisan government of national unity and of predominantly civilian composition with which we can work constructively and cooperatively in atmosphere of mutual trust. While Revolutionary Committee as presently constituted may appear to offer scant promise of developing in this direction, you are authorized in your discretion to work as you deem necessary with that Committee as starting point, seeking to bring to bear all available moderating, balancing and restraining influences. Possible utility of General Lee Han Lim, Commander First ROK Army, in this connection might be considered.

Source: Department of State, Central Files, 795B.00/5–1761. Secret; Niact. Repeated to Ottawa for the Presidential visit and Geneva for Rusk.

[1] In JCS 996156 to CINCUNC, May 18, the JCS informed Magruder that in light of telegram 1321 to Seoul and "the currently developing situation, agree you should contact General Chang Do Young and General Pak Chang Hui soonest and emphasize in strongest terms necessity of reestablishing command relationship as soon as possible and the vital importance of maintaining ROK Armed Forces at a high state of combat readiness responsive to the Commander-in-Chief, United Nations Command." (Ibid., 795B.00/5 1861)

It is highly important to confer on successor government to maximum attainable extent an aura of legality, continuity and legitimate constitutional succession. Presumably this can best be achieved by continuation in office of Yun Po Sun as President who would use his prestige and office to bring about selection of generally acceptable candidate for Prime Minister.

It our tentative impression here that coup group has no very clear idea exactly where it wants to go after having overthrown Chang government. If this impression correct and Yun Po Sun willing assert leadership inherent in his office at such period of crisis, suggest possibility of Yun calling in coup group leaders together with a few widely respected military and civilian figures of national stature and attempting obtain immediate agreement on selection Prime Minister and full cabinet slate who could reassert governmental authority. Even though such action may not be possible strictly within constitutional framework seems from here some such action within spirit orderly governmental processes might offer best hope of preventing degeneration into chaotic situation which communists might attempt to exploit or into out-and-out military dictatorship. This offered only as suggested line of approach within foregoing framework. There may well be other such lines not apparent to us here.

If in your judgment situation calls for radically different approach, you should outline it soonest for our urgent consideration.[2]

**Bowles**

---

[2] In telegram 1579 from Seoul, May 19, Green proposed to enter into discussions with ROK President Yun Po-sun supplemented by Magruder's discussions with the ROK Chief of Staff and "discreet discussions" with General Pak Chung-hui and the Revolutionary Committee. Green hoped to achieve "the emergence soonest of a ROK Government which is broadly based, responsible, non-partisan government of national unity and of predominantly civilian composition determined to defend Korea against communist aggression external or internal." Green went on to list six suggested expectations of the new ROK Government: "Cooperation with the United States; continued recognition of existing treaties and agreements; restoration of operational control of ROK armed forces to CINCUNC; return of ROK forces to pre-coup roles and positions; release of political prisoners without reprisals; anti-corruption and nepotism policies; and economic stablity, development, and efficient use of U.S. aid. (Ibid., 795B.00/5–1961)

## 220.    Memorandum From Acting Secretary of State Bowles to President Kennedy

Washington, May 18, 1961.

SUBJECT

Background of Statements by American Representatives in Korea

On the morning of May 15 during the early hours of the Korean coup, General Carter Magruder, Commander in Chief, UN Command, Republic of Korea, issued a statement calling on all military personnel under his command to support the Government of the Republic of Korea headed by Prime Minister Chang Myon and restore order in the Korean armed forces. This statement was made in collaboration with our Chargé d'Affaires, Marshall Green, whose parallel statement fully concurred in General Magruder's position and emphasized that the United States supports the constitutional government of the Republic of Korea as elected by the Korean people and duly constituted under legal procedures.[1]

These statements were not authorized in advance by the Department of State; but in the Korean context, they were justified as affirmations of established policy for the purpose of strengthening and maintaining democratic institutions. The United States enjoys an unusual role in Korea because of our long association with the country as liberator, defender, and source of economic and military support. The Korean people and government, since the founding of the Republic, have continued to look to the United States for guidance in hours of crisis. Public statements by our Embassy at Seoul during the April 1960 revolution were extremely important in preventing further bloodshed during the student demonstrations and preparing for an orderly transfer of power from the Rhee administration to that of the interim government under Korean constitutional procedures. The Department of State believes that it is especially important that the Republic of Korea maintain its adherence to democratic procedures and constitutional processes, which are among the Republic's chief assets in its struggle against Communism. In these circumstances, it was a proper decision to throw our influence on the side of the legitimate government, in the belief that the domestic forces supporting this government would be strengthened. Not to have done so would have strengthened the revolutionists' hand.

General Magruder has also informed us that his statement and that of the Chargé d'Affaires were made on the advice of General Lee Han

---

Source: Department of State, Central Files, 795B.00/5–1861. Secret. Drafted by James A. Klemstine of NA and cleared by Bacon, McConaughy, William Bundy, and Lemnitzer.

[1] See Document 213.

Lim in order to help hold the First ROK Army in its position on the demarcation line and in an effort to prevent those neutrally inclined from joining the insurgents' case. General Magruder has noted that these statements emphasized the need of the ROK to return to civilian constitutional government as soon as possible and remove the Army from any political power struggle. General Magruder has also commented that apparently these statements had some effect, which could not be expected, however, to endure indefinitely.

Our representatives in Korea also felt that it was necessary for the United States Government immediately to make clear that it was not involved in a revolutionary group, in order to forestall speculation such as the rumors prevalent in France following the abortive coup of rightist forces in Algeria.

**Chester Bowles**[2]

---

[2] Printed from a copy that indicates Bowles signed the original.

---

### 221. Memorandum From Robert H. Johnson of the National Security Council Staff to the President's Deputy Special Assistant for National Security Affairs (Rostow)

Washington, May 23, 1961.

SUBJECT

Immediate Actions in Korea

I believe that there are three kinds of actions that we should seek to obtain from the Koreans in the immediate future:

1. Maximum possible civilianization of the regime and a clear distinction between officers engaged in political and administrative responsibilities and those engaged in military responsibilities.

---

Source: Kennedy Library, National Security Files, Countries Series, Korea, General, 4/1/61–5/25/61. Secret. A note by Johnson on the source text indicates that he discussed the action described here with McConaughy in a telephone conversation on May 23.

2.  Make it absolutely clear that U.S. assistance in the future, above a minimum maintenance level, will be conditional upon Korean performance, in accordance with this Administration's new aid concepts.

3.  Actions to deal with corruption. This involves inter alia Civil Service and police reform, reform of the tax collection system, reform of government budgeting procedures, improving contracting procedures, and action to rationalize interest rates.

**Bob**

---

## 222.  Telegram From the Department of State to the Embassy in Korea

Washington, May 24, 1961, 9:13 p.m.

1377. For Green.

1.  We strongly concur with approach you have taken in your talks with General Chang Do Young and Foreign Minister Kim Hong-il. We are also in substantial accord with your analysis and policy suggestions contained your 1579[1] and 1640.[2] The sound judgment and sense of balance and proportion you have shown are heartily commended.

2.  Department not particularly inclined to issue further circumstantial policy and operating directives at this time unless you feel the need of such additional detailed guidance. Such guidance would almost inevitably have effect of cementing close relations with new regime and thereby increasing their confidence that they can count on full US support, at a time when various disturbing actions taken by them indicate that they should be kept under some indirect pressure from us and in

---

Source: Department of State, Central Files, 795B.00/5–2361. Secret; Niact. Drafted and approved by McConaughy.

[1] See footnote 2, Document 219.

[2] In telegram 1640 from Seoul, May 23, Green described the approaches that he, Magruder, and other members of the Country Team made in line with the guidelines he suggested in telegram 1579 from Seoul. Green stated that the Embassy was more convinced than ever that President Yun Po-sun was able "to exercise little influence and almost no authority." Green proposed to concentrate his efforts on the new Foreign Minister, Kim Hong-il, who not only was the correct channel, but "one of the principal holders of power in new regime." (Department of State, Central Files, 795B.00/5–2361)

some suspense as to our future course. Possibility that General Chang may pursue application to come to US for consultations is a further reason for refraining from more detailed negotiations at this moment. We are also influenced by adverse results General Magruder's May 23 meeting with General Pak Chung-hui, amounting to ROK refusal to return ROK armed forces to operational control of CINCUNC.

3. If you nonetheless feel that you need more comprehensive guidance at this stage, you should so indicate, setting forth any new operational areas in which you believe Departmental instructions would be useful. Bear in mind that we believe we can best test bona fides of regime by observing their actions in response to representations made by you and General Magruder and that we would not want to take any new initiatives at this stage which might embolden them to withhold actions responsive to our known wishes. We believe you have ample authority for maintaining all contacts which you consider desirable.

**Rusk**

---

### 223. Telegram From the Commander in Chief, United Nations Command (Magruder) to the Chairman of the Joint Chiefs of Staff (Lemnitzer), in Paris

Seoul, May 25, 1961.

[KRA] 306. Yesterday, through an indirect approach, I was informed that former Lieutenant Colonel Kim Chong Pil had stated that the entire joint statement as drafted by General Pak Chung Hi and me could be approved by the Supreme Council for National Reconstruction if they were really satisfied that I would not use my operational control in an attempt to break the revolution. I sent back word that I would be glad to talk to Kim.

Former Lieutenant Colonel Kim Chong Pil was perhaps the foremost of the young officers who agitated for the elimination of senior officers after the April revolution that overthrew President Rhee. He was one of the group that waited on Chief of Staff General Song Yo Chan to

---

Source: Kennedy Library, National Security Files, Countries Series, Korea, Cables, 5/25/61–5/31/61. Secret; Exclusive. Also sent to General Bonesteel in Washington. Lemnitzer was in Paris for discussions at SHAPE Headquarters May 22–26. (National Defense University, Lemnitzer Papers, Journal, L–419–71)

demand his resignation. He was the moving spirit that activated the group of sixteen officers who waited on Chief of Staff General Choi Young Hi to demand his resignation. Kim did not actually enter Choi Young Hi's office with the sixteen officers, he brought them to the office and remained outside himself. He was perhaps the foremost of the agitators whose elimination from the ROK Army I have sought over the past year. He was eliminated from the Army in February 1961. I am now informed that he is reinstated as a Lieutenant Colonel although he called on me today dressed in civilian clothes.

Col Kim called on General Meloy and me this morning. Colonel Kim reviewed the justification for the revolution, regretted that the only method of conducting the revolution required a violation of my operational control and assured me of the good intentions of the new government. He said nothing new but followed the same line that the group have pursued in all their propaganda.

I accented to Col Kim that my mission was to defend Korea, not to determine what kind of a government Korea had. I explained each of my important actions in the past based upon carrying out my mission of defending Korea. I sought by implication to make it crystal clear that as long as the revolutionary government took no action that would prejudice the defense of Korea they had nothing to fear from me.

I reviewed the specific actions that the coup group had taken that prejudiced my ability to accomplish my mission and that I therefore opposed, namely:

A. They have deprived me of some of the means for accomplishing my mission by withdrawing troops assigned in the forward areas.

B. They have weakened my ability to get my orders carried out by relieving and appointing senior commanders without my consent.

C. They have weakened the authority of their own commanders by the organization of officers who are loyal to the coup group instead of to their own commanders and who stay ready to act against their own commanders when they feel those commanders are taking actions that would not be approved by the coup group.

Our meeting concluded without any specific conclusions or agreements. I therefore have no idea as to whether Colonel Kim will use his influence to seek reconsideration of the disapproval by the Supreme Council for National Reconstruction of the draft proposed by Major General Pak Chung Hi and myself.[1]

---

[1] In telegram KRA 309 to Lemnitzer, May 26, Magruder stated that after protracted negotiations with Major General Pak Chung-hui and Lieutenant Colonel Kim Chin-pil, he had agreed to an exchange of letters returning operational control of all ROK forces to CINCUNC and restablishing consultation on high-ranking military personal assignments. The letters were contained in telegram KRA 309 and were subsequently released to the public in Seoul on May 26. (Kennedy Library, National Security Files, Countries Series, Korea, General, 5/26/61–5/31/61)

## 224.  Special National Intelligence Estimate

SNIE 42–2–61                                    Washington, May 31, 1961.

### SHORT-TERM PROSPECTS IN SOUTH KOREA

#### The Problem

To assess the significance of the military coup d'état in the Republic of Korea (ROK), and to estimate probable trends over the next few months.

#### Conclusions

1.  We believe that the present coup group dominated by Major General Pak Chong-hui will retain the principal elements of power in South Korea over the next few months at least, whether or not nominal civilian rule is re-established. (Paras. 9, 13)

2.  The coup group will probably inject a new sense of drive and discipline into the ROK Government's economic and administrative efforts, and may make some headway, especially in curbing corruption. However, in view of the magnitude of the problems the new leaders are inheriting and are themselves creating, we believe they will not make much progress, and because of their inexperience and a probable reluctance to accept outside advice, may make matters even worse. (Para. 16)

3.  The coup group is composed of divergent elements and interests. Unless Pak and his colleagues can generate and enforce a greater unity than appears likely, ROK politics will probably follow a pattern of constant factional maneuvering and periodic shifts in power within the ruling military group. (Paras. 9–10, 14)

4.  South Korea's coup leaders are a new and different breed from the civilian and the more senior military people with whom the US has had most contact. Their authoritarian and nationalistic stamp suggests that they will be less receptive to US guidance. Furthermore, they will be tough, determined, and difficult to deal with. They will probably continue South Korea's alignment with the US, recognizing their country's dependence on the US, but at the same time will seek to assert South Korea's independence in military, economic, and political affairs. ROK-

---

Source: Department of State, INR/EAP Files: Lot 90 D 110. Secret. According to a note on the cover sheet, the Central Intelligence Agency and intelligence organizations of the Departments of State, Defense, the Army, the Navy, the Air Force, and the Joint Staff participated in the preparation of this estimate. All members of the USIB concurred with this estimate except the representatives of the AEC and the FBI, who abstained on the grounds that the subject was outside their jurisdiction.

UN military command relationships will probably be a source of continuing difficulty. (Paras. 17–20)

5. The declared position of the regime is anti-Communist, and available evidence does not support allegations of Pak's continuing ties with the Communists. However, we cannot rule out the possibility that he is a long-term Communist agent, or that he might redefect. Also, Communist ends in South Korea could be advanced in the event of student and public uprisings against repressive government measures and probable deteriorating economic conditions. (Para. 21)

6. The coup leaders have been preoccupied with internal matters and have not yet given clear definition of their intended foreign policies. (Para. 22)

[Here follows the "Discussion" section of the estimate; see the Supplement.]

## 225.  Memorandum by Robert H. Johnson of the National Security Council Staff

Washington, June 6, 1961.

### THE TASK FORCE REPORT ON KOREA

*A Note on the Manner in Which the Report was Prepared*

Successive drafts of the report were prepared in a drafting group consisting of the Deputy Assistant Secretary of State for Far Eastern Economic Affairs (Peterson), the State and ICA desk officers and me. Discussion in the Task Force was confined to major issues and, except in one case, never got down to specifics of language. The final draft of the Introduction and Recommendations was prepared by the new ambassa-

---

Source: Kennedy Library, National Security Files, Countries Series, Korea, General, 6/61. Secret. The 85-page long Task Force Report is ibid., 6/5/61, Task Force Report. For a summary and revision of the recommendations of the report as approved by the President and the National Security Council, see Document 230.

At the Under Secretary of State's staff meeting on June 5, McConaughy told Bowles that the Task Force Report was complete and ready for the NSC. Bowles had read it and believed it was "an excellent report." McConaughy reported that General Pak Chung-hui would replace General Chang Do-yong as chairman of the Supreme Committee for National Rehabilitation. McConaughy noted that "the military junta appears to be adopting a more moderate approach and to be moving in a better direction from our viewpoint." (Department of State, Secretary's Staff Meetings: Lot 66 D 147)

dor (Berger) in the light of the last Task Force discussion and was reviewed by Mr. Peterson and me. The paper is, therefore, primarily a State Department product, though State did, after argument, accept language from DoD and ICA on key paragraphs dealing with ROK military forces and electric power. The acceptance of the ICA language on power occurred following the review of Ambassador Berger's draft.

*Rationale*

When the Task Force began its work prior to the coup the U.S. was endeavoring, in the words of the report, "to spur a liberal and well-intentioned, but weak, administration into more resolute action on basic economic and social problems". Now we are faced by a tough, authoritarian, nationalistic regime which may be capable of overriding the political obstacles to action on Korean problems, but which is inexperienced, likely to be plagued by continued factionalism, and clearly less amenable to U.S. influence.

Yet in its fundamentals the Korean situation has not changed as a result of the coup. Both the overthrow of the Rhee regime and the overthrow of the Chang Myon regime were, at root, expressions of the rising forces of nationalism in Korean society. Both reflected dissatisfaction on the part of a younger generation with the lack of direction and progress and with corruption in Korean society.

The basic economic problems remain: resources are limited, population growth rapid, and unemployment, a major problem; industry is hamstrung by power and water shortages and by inadequate management and financing: farmers are burdened with debt and high interest rates; corruption is endemic. Our own economic assistance programs have lacked a clear economic development purpose and had been inadequately administered.

Our general policy prescription both before and after the coup was to harness the forces of nationalism by giving Korean society a new sense of purpose. This requires a new thrust and developmental purpose in our own programs (adequately dramatized by new U.S. actions) and at the same time demands Korean action to begin serious economic planning and to undertake a whole series of reform measures.

In the case of the old Chang Myon regime we were more confident about its good intentions than about its political capabilities. In the case of the new military regime we are somewhat more confident about capabilities, at least to initiate reform measures, and less confident of intentions. Thus the strategy outlined in the report is one designed to elicit indications of the purposes of the new group and its willingness to act and to give the ambassador considerable discretion in determining when performance merits responsive action on our part. Three stages in the interchange of views are proposed: (a) the ambassador's initial talks with the ROK Government leadership; (b) a visit by the ROK Chief of State to Washington; and (c) the dispatch of a special envoy and mission to Korea. Initiation of each successive step is contingent upon satisfactory response under the one before.

*Major Suggestions with Respect to the Report*

1. *Power.* A U.S. commitment to meet Korean power needs is one of the most effective means we could use to demonstrate quickly the seriousness of our intent with respect to long range development and to get off to a new start in our relations on economic matters. That this is one of the most important bottlenecks is recognized by all; we do not need a five year plan before we move ahead on it. Responsibility for past inaction must be shared by the ROK and U.S. Governments. The ROK has failed to raise rates sufficiently to pay power costs; we have taken much more time than we should to decide whether we will support particular projects, notably the proposed hydro project at Chongju.

The language of present par. f–(3) (p. 6)[1] goes further in the direction of a long term commitment than we have been willing to go in the past according to ICA. It is not nearly as strong language as that contained in the penultimate draft of the report. ICA objected to the stronger language on the grounds that a firm and long range commitment of the kind proposed had to be made strictly conditional upon more specific Korean performance on reform measures. I recommend that present par. f–(3) be deleted and that the following paragraph, based upon the version in the last Task Force draft, be added to "Category 2", following present subpar. c (p. 7). The revisions I have made, plus the placement in category 2 would recognize the ICA concern (which is to some degree legitimate) without completely watering down the commitment we would make.

"d. Subject to action by the Korean Government to rationalize the corporate structure and rates in the power industry, and to other clear evidence of Korean action to undertake fundamental economic reform measures, announce U.S. willingness to provide, subject to Congressional appropriation, the external resources required to carry out an agreed five- or ten-year plan of power development, including prompt implementation of the Chungju hydro-electric project."

This is the most important change that needs to be made in the report; all other proposed changes below are of less importance.

2. *Use of Korean forces for economic development purposes.* Under the Defense draft of par. e on p. 8, now incorporated in the report, U.S. action to permit increased use of ROK armed forces for economic development purposes subpars. (3) and (4) must await the study of force goals.[2] The

---

[1] Summarized in paragraph a–7 of Document 230.

[2] Summarized in paragraph a–9 of Document 230.

argument for this approach is that we cannot commit ourselves on the increased use of ROK forces for civilian purposes (particularly for training) until we are clear as to whether we wish to maintain ROK forces at existing levels and with existing missions. We might desire, for example, to reduce ROK forces and to use the savings for economic development rather than to employ some of a larger ROK force in economic development activities.

Since I am not optimistic that our review of force goals is likely to produce a significant change (much as I would like to see one), I am rather reluctant to see any action to plan for increased use of ROK forces for economic development purposes delayed for the force goal review. The U.S. military commander in Korea has, I understand, been reluctant to permit use of ROK forces in the National Construction Service and on other works projects. A clear directive to the U.S. commander to "encourage and support greater participation, etc. (par. (3))" would be desirable even before the review of force goals is completed.

We should not only make an assessment of the implications of a program for using the armed forces for training in civilian skills, but should, if possible, *simultaneously* develop a *proposed program* for such use so that, if our assessment of the implications is favorable, we will be ready to move ahead.

3. *Category 3: Required Korean actions.* I would favor deletion in the final NSC action document of the introduction to "Category 3", (p. 10) because it weakens the whole section. It is much weaker than the characterization of this category contained in par. 7 of the Introduction.[3]

4. *USOM leadership and organization.* The terms of reference for the proposed high-level mission to Korea include (Appendix A, p. 2, par. 5–(e)) reference to review of the administrative structure of the USOM. This was the only reference I was able to obtain to what is a most important problem. There is a good deal of evidence that USOM leadership and organization leaves much to be desired. State has wished to avoid reference to it. It is most important, however, that Mr. Labouisse and Ambassador Berger be impressed with the necessity for early and major action to improve the USOM situation.

*Other Problems*

*Military involvement in civil affairs.* Up to the final draft, the report also contained the following language which I drafted:

"Maximum possible effort [should be made by the military regime][4] to insulate from direct involvement in military matters those military

---

[3] Johnson's suggestion was accepted.

[4] Brackets in the source text.

officers who are engaged in political and civilian administrative functions."

This was viewed by CIA as reflecting an unrealistic hope; and Ambassador Berger concurred. Admittedly you cannot hope to separate the top military people in the government from command responsibility, but it does seem to me that those engaged in work at lower levels could be so separated. If they are not, we are going to have some difficult problems in Korea because of the peculiar UN Command relationship.

*Korean action to improve ROK-Japanese relations.* Though par. f on p. 9 calls for U.S. encouragement to the Japanese to improve their relations with Korea, there is no comparable requirement that we put pressure on the Koreans. Such a requirement was included in an earlier draft but it is State's view that we need to know more about the attitude of the new regime toward Japan before we can decide how far and how fast we should go in applying pressure on the ROK's to act.[5]

*Objectives.* There was some complaint in the Task Force that we had failed to state clearly our objectives with respect to Korea. It is true that there is no specific objectives statement. The efforts to produce one seemed to me rather sterile. It seems to me that in par. 2 of the Introduction and elsewhere our general purposes come through clearly enough. And our basic approach is to get the Koreans to define their own objectives with some help and guidance from us.

*Relations between Americans and Koreans in Korea.* It is generally recognized that the high standard of living and the separateness of the Americans from the Korean population is an important problem. It is difficult to draft a meaningful recommendation on the subject. The Ambassador, I am informed, is very much aware of it and is working out his own plans to deal with it.

*Procedural Matters*

*The NSC action on the report.* As the need to include an increasing element of tactics that became evident, the recommendations grew in length so that they are probably no longer brief enough to be included in an NSC action. Though I would like to see the Council and President approve them all, I recognize that they will have to be briefed down for NSC action purposes and plan to begin work immediately on the draft for the Council action.

[2 *paragraphs (15 lines of source text) not declassified*]

---

[5] This paragraph was crossed out by Johnson.

### 226. Memorandum From Robert W. Komer of the National Security Council Staff to the President's Special Assistant for National Security Affairs (Bundy)

Washington, June 12, 1961.

*Relative Priority of Military vs. Reconstruction Focus in Korea*

Admittedly, the question of MAP aid for Korea needs further study, but it is discouraging that Korean TF report[1] goes no further in flagging this issue.

A real ROK development program will involve staggering costs over the next decade. The ROK has so many handicaps, it is so far from self-sustaining growth, its governmental structure is so feeble that we will be spending billions more there during the 60s. Because of this, I feel a hard new look should be taken at whether we want to spend even the $1.6 billion currently projected for maintaining ROK forces 1962–66.

In my opinion, one of the basic reasons why we have accomplished so little in Korea since 1953 has been our predominantly military focus. We have spent more money on MAP 1953–60 than on the domestic economy. This mal-focus arose largely from the fiction that there was only a truce on the "38th parallel" and that hostilities might reopen at any time. As a result, we did little more than keep the economy afloat, while focussing our main effort on maintaining very substantial ROK forces.

Obviously, there is a risk of renewed local aggression. But I would argue that it is less than almost any place else around the Bloc periphery. Given the consequences of its last miscalculation, would the Bloc leadership really regard it as sensible to reopen the Korean war? Look at the deterrents! There still exist a series of condemnatory resolutions and a UN Command (even though in attenuated form). On top of the direct UN role in Korea, we have far more than a plate glass window, in the form of two divisions of US troops with nuclear capabilities. Add to this ten regular and nine reserve ROK divisions and you have a greater deterrent capability than any place but perhaps the Taiwan Strait. Moreover, the Chinese forces have long since withdrawn from North Korea, although the CPR divisions in Manchuria are still close at hand.

Given all these deterrents, the risk of the ROK being attacked again is far less than that of its being subverted because of internal weakness. The North Koreans are already beginning to play the siren song of reunification, and it may have increasing appeal in a weak and disunited south. If South Korea goes, it will go this route and not that of local war.

---

Source: Kennedy Library, National Security Files, Meetings and Memoranda Series, Staff Memoranda, Komer. Secret. Also sent to Rostow.

[1] See the source note, Document 225.

Of course with a hard-nosed military regime now in the saddle, it may be difficult to talk about reducing MAP. I would argue, however, that this might be a good means of forcing the young colonels to face up to the hard realities of domestic reconstruction instead of letting them talk us into continuing to foot huge military as well as civilian bills.

Hence I urge flagging this issue for the President. Korea's domestic needs are so great that we may have to take risks in other categories to find the resources necessary to do the job. A gradual cut in ROK forces to around 14 and ultimately 12 divisions would still give us quite a deterrent, and free substantial resources to meet the real problems facing us in the ROK.

**Bob K.**

### 227. Memorandum by Robert H. Johnson of the National Security Council Staff

Washington, June 13, 1961.

THE TASK FORCE REPORT ON KOREA

*I.  Key Issues*

*To what extent should U.S. aid be contingent upon Korean performance?* To give the Korean people a sense of progress and a realization that the U.S. is shifting its emphasis to economic development and reform may require certain quite dramatic U.S. actions. But unhappy experience with past Korean inaction and the toughness of the new regime suggest the importance of making U.S. offers of assistance contingent upon specific Korean performance on needed reform measures. Under such circumstances, the dramatic impact of the U.S. action may be dissipated.

In general the revised recommendations call for a fairly tough U.S. policy of making our commitments to provide economic development assistance contingent upon Korean performance with considerable discretion left to the Ambassador to determine when performance is adequate (pars. 4, 6, 7, 12).[1] Once the Koreans have taken action on a

---

Source: Kennedy Library, National Security Files, Countries Series, Korea, General, 6/61. Secret.

[1] All references to paragraphs and subparagraphs of the revised recommendations are to those in Document 230.

series of reform measures we would be quite forthcoming in offering U.S. support for economic development, including specifically power development.

*How much of a commitment should the U.S. make toward meeting Korea's electric power needs?* This question is a particular variant of the question above. Power is a serious bottleneck in Korea preventing full utilization of existing industrial plant capacity. The U.S. estimates five year power needs at 480,000 kw of installed capacity. Action is underway to provide 80,000 kw of this amount, in part through emergency measures such as provision of power barges.

Debate in the Task Force centered upon the question of how far the U.S. should go in committing itself to meeting the remaining power requirement of 400,000 kw until there was concrete action by the Korean government to increase rates, to consolidate the power companies and to eliminate power losses. The revised recommendations propose (par. 4(b)) that we indicate a willingness to undertake *specific projects* provided action on reform measures is begun, and (par. 7) that we commit ourselves to an agreed *five year program* when concrete action has been completed.

*Should missions and force levels for ROK armed forces be revised?* The revised recommendations call for a review of missions and of alternative force and equipment structures (par. 8). The arguments of proponents and opponents of reduction are described in an attachment to this paper. ROK force levels seem better suited to meeting the Communist threat as we perceived it in the 1950's than to dealing with present dangers and politico-economic needs.

All JCS-proposed changes in the recommendations of the report have been accepted in the revised recommendations except for two proposed changes in par. 8. One of these (JCS memo, par. 2) would make it clear that the Secretary of Defense would make the assessment of Korean force and equipment levels and that the Secretary of State would be limited to coordinating political and economic factors with this assessment. The suggestion implies too clean a distinction between the two processes. The other change (Appendix to JCS memo, par. f) would delete the word "substantial" from par. 8 (b) of the revised recommendations on the grounds that it prejudges the outcome of the force level review.[2] But the wording of 8 (b) makes clear that a "substantial reduction in forces" is only one alternative that would be studied.

*To what extent should we encourage and support the use of ROK armed forces for economic development purposes?* The question has two aspects: (a)

---

[2] The views of the Joint Chiefs of Staff are in a June 12 memorandum from Lemnitzer to McNamara. (Kennedy Library, National Security Files, Countries Series, Korea, General, 6/61)

use of ROK forces to provide the leadership in the National Construction Service (a kind of CCC) and in similar public works activities; and (b) use of the ROK forces for expanded training in civilian skills. The armed forces now participate in the National Construction Service. However, it is alleged that the U.S. military in Korea has been less than completely enthusiastic about such use. The first sentence of par. 9 of the revised recommendations would direct the U.S. military to encourage greater participation. The U.S. military is very reluctant to give up time from military duties for training in civilian skills. The second sentence of par. 9 of the recommendations calls for preparation of a proposed program of increased training and the assessment of its economic and military implications.

## II.    Other Matters

1. Until the final draft, the revised recommendations made the invitation to the Korean Chief of Government to visit Washington contingent upon some Korean action on reform measures. At the request of Secretary Rusk the contingent feature of the invitation was eliminated (par. 3 of recommendations) on the grounds that we were committed to an invitation and that it should not be delayed unduly.

2. The new Korean regime seems, on present evidence, much more anti-Japanese than its immediate predecessor. Therefore, though we believe that ROK-Japanese rapprochement is of great economic importance to Korea, State is not optimistic that Japanese investment in, or economic aid to, Korea is an immediate prospect. When the Japanese seemed, just after the recent coup, to want to rush in with substantial economic aid, State suggested that they go slow fearing a Korean rebuff which would seriously set back relations.

3. Present at the NSC meeting today will be the new first team in Korea: Mr. Samuel Berger, the new U.S. Ambassador; General Guy Meloy, presently Deputy United Nations Commander who will take over as the UN Commander on July 1; and Mr. James Killen, presently USOM Director in Pakistan who is to be designated the new USOM Director in Korea. You may wish to have a brief talk with these three immediately following the Council meeting.

### Attachment

### THE PROS AND CONS OF A REDUCTION IN ROK FORCES

## I.    Existing Forces in Korea

The ROK army of 525,000 men consists of 18 divisions plus artillery, anti-aircraft, heavy mortar and tank battalions. In addition the ROKs have one marine division and ten reserve army divisions. Two U.S. Army divisions are in Korea. The North Koreans maintain a total of 355,000 men under arms (compares with 600,000 for ROK), including a 22 division army. The ChiComs have no forces in North Korea but could deploy 6–8 divisions to the Demilitarized Zone within 10 to 14 days. Neither North nor South Korea has much of a navy; the North Korean air force is somewhat superior to the ROK air force.

## II.   The Arguments For a Reduction in ROK Forces

The direct threat of military aggression across the 38th Parallel is slight. We have a political and military plate-glass window in place there. The border is clearly demarked; the U.S. divisions are in place; the UN Command provides the structure for an international response to aggression. The Communists have greater opportunities for gains with less risk in other areas of Asia.

U.S. aid to Korea, partly because of a mistaken focus on a military threat, has been concentrated upon the support of ROK military forces and upon repairing war damage, with very little left for economic development. Meanwhile, the new tide of Korean nationalism and the submerged, but clearly present, desire for unification pose, in the face of the economic stagnation and poverty of the ROK and North Korea's considerable economic progress, important long-run political dangers. To harness the forces of Korean nationalism to the constructive ends of economic development will require either still more massive U.S. aid (which the Korean economy would have difficulty absorbing) or a substantial shift of U.S. and Korean resources from military support to economic development.

The Chang Myon government exerted pressure on the United States to agree to Korean force reductions, but we made only minimal concessions. Though it may be difficult to force it to do so, the new military regime must be made to face Korea's real economic problems and to recognize that existing ROK force levels make poor military and economic sense.

## III.   The Arguments Against a Reduction in ROK Forces

The military situation is stable in Korea because the level of U.S. and ROK forces is adequate to deter attack. [6-1/2 lines of source text not declassified]

The ROK is an abundant source of low-cost military manpower which, if we continue to utilize it fully, will continue to give greater strategic flexibility to U.S. forces in coping with pressures elsewhere on the ChiCom periphery. Moreover, a considerable reduction in the level of ROK forces would be required to produce any real saving of resources. This is partly because, unless we permit ROK capabilities to decline, any substantial reduction in forces would have to be accompanied by increased modernization. The ROKs would probably also demand such modernization as a price for agreement to force reductions. In addition, because of the unemployment problem in South Korea, release of men from the armed forces would only transfer the burden of maintaining them to the civilian economy. Finally, it seems most unlikely that a force reduction would be politically acceptable to the new Korean military regime.

## 228.  Editorial Note

At 3 p.m. on June 13, 1961, the National Security Council met in the Cabinet Room of the White House for its 485th meeting. With the President presiding, 32 people attended the meeting including Secretary of State Dean Rusk, Secretary of the Treasury Douglas Dillon, Attorney General Robert Kennedy, Deputy Secretary of Defense Roswell Gilpatric, Chairman of the Joint Chiefs of Staff General Lyman Lemnitzer, Under Secretary of State Chester Bowles, Assistant Secretary of State for Far Eastern Affairs Walter McConaughy, Ambassador-designate to Korea Samuel Berger, the President's Special Assistant for National Security Affairs McGeorge Bundy, and his Deputy, Walt Rostow. The first part of the meeting was taken up with a report by the President on his European trip, including the summit meeting at Vienna with Soviet Chairman Nikita Khrushchev. The other topic of discussion was Korea.

According to cryptic notes by Lemnitzer, Rusk began by reviewing past events in South Korea. He stressed that the current government had "no experience" and "no honest administrators." The question of the invitation of the leader of the Supreme Council for National Reconstruction to visit the United States was discussed. Ambassador Berger would assess the prospects. Lemnitzer's notes outlined his presentation of the military problem: South Korea was in a suspended state of war; in light of U.S. lives and money expended during the Korean war, the United States had a great stake in Korea: and, there was "great pressure" for subversion and infiltration, "like Vietnam and Laos." Lemnitzer noted that South Korea had a 155-mile front line. He highlighted substantial problems with the flow of refugees from north to south (presumably during the Korean war) and the problem of unemployment. Dillon raised the issue of South Korean economic viability and Rostow stated that Korea was "not as hopeless" as it might seem. The revised recommendations of the Task Force were approved as amended and deemed "adequate." (Lemnitzer's handwritten notes of the June 13 NSC meeting; National Defense University, Lemnitzer Papers, L–215–71)

## 229.  Notes of the 485th Meeting of the National Security Council

Washington, June 13, 1961.

[Here follows discussion unrelated to Korea.]

In taking up the report of the Task Force on Korea,[1] Rusk summarized the history of political development of that country and outlined U.S. aims and intentions. He also cited certain economic figures. In response to a question by the President about the relative status of North and South Korea, Mr. McConaughy replied that approximately 35% of the working force is unemployed or only partially employed in South Korea, in contrast to no unemployment in North Korea. He added quickly that this figure for North Korea was deceiving because of the Communist methods of utilizing labor, frequently under slave conditions. Although agriculture is better in South Korea, manufacturing is more highly developed in the north where the gross national product is rising, but only to be plowed back into the industrial base and war potential. He went on to say that the greatest hindrance to Korean development was the continued animosity between Japan and South Korea and the failure to re-establish relations which would prove mutually beneficial. He said that one of the principal missions of Ambassadors Berger and Reischauer should be to attempt to establish a reconciliation between the two countries.

McNamara wanted to go on record as opposing any decrease in the level of the armed forces of Korea at this time. He felt that any proposed decrease would first of all alienate the new military leadership; secondly, it would contribute further to the serious unemployment problem; and thirdly, it was well worth keeping effective troops on the front line at a cost of only $5 per month, especially when a decrease of approximately 100,000 soldiers would save only $6 million per year.

The President asked if it would be possible to increase to any measurable extent the contribution of the armed forces to civilian work. The Deputy Commander-in-Chief, UNC, replied that road and mining projects are presently being performed by certain units of the armed forces, but expressed the opinion that little more could be done without an unacceptable decrease in military effectiveness. Lemnitzer interrupted with the observation that from a military standpoint force levels are presently below that which is necessary for an adequate defense of Korea. He said that he is simply repeating the views which he and Generals Taylor and

---

Source: Johnson Library, Vice Presidential Security File, National Security Council (III). Although no drafter is indicated on the source text, these notes were prepared by Howard L. Burris, Vice President Johnson's military aide.

[1] See the source note, Document 225.

Decker have expressed previously. He cited the 157-mile front which must still be defended against the same threat and even against a more highly efficient North Korean force than existed during wartime—all this even without regard to the fact that a state of war technically still exists.

The President expressed the view that the economic and political situation in and about Korea were such as to present a hopeless situation. McConaughy confirmed that it was bad and perhaps would not improve principally because of an unstable economy, limited resources and an explosive population. Rostow disagreed with the acceptance of a hopeless economic situation and cited the following three factors as the basis for a certain degree of optimism:

1. New effective economic and social planning.
2. Young, aggressive, capable people in government.
3. Better relations with Japan.

The President concluded that the best opportunity for improvement among those mentioned would appear to be the improvement of Korean-Japan relations and directed Ambassador Berger to concentrate on the issue. The President suggested that the U.S. should also have a look at its own program and position and asked what we should demand of the Koreans. McConaughy and Berger agreed that a start should be made by demanding a decrease in corruption. The President stated that he would take up the subject of improvement in relations with Korea with the Japanese Prime Minister next week.

General Decker stated that in his view the most ominous and difficult problem in Korea is the control of the country by a bunch of junior officers and suggested that the United States demand the return of control of the armed forces and the country immediately to senior officers "rather than to a bunch of lieutenant colonels." He went on to say that he had already conveyed this idea to the Korean officer who has just departed the U.S. to become the new Defense Minister. The President disagreed with General Decker and expressed the opinion that the United States had no alternative except to deal with the people in power.

## 230.   Record of National Security Council Action No. 2430

Washington, June 13, 1961.

*Korea (NSC Action No. 2421;[1] SNIE 42–2–61;[2] Report of the Task Force on Korea, dated June 5, 1961[3])*

a.   Discussed the Report of the Task Force on Korea and concurred in the following recommendations:

*U.S. Actions to be Undertaken Immediately*

1.   The new U.S. Ambassador to Korea should undertake early discussions with the appropriate leaders of the Supreme Council for National Reconstruction along the lines described in paragraphs a[4] and c through e[5] (pp. 5–6) of the report.

2.   With reference to paragraph b (p. 5),[6] in these early discussions and subsequently the Ambassador should seek to create a gradual recognition among the leaders of the Supreme Council that it is in their interest and in the interest of their country that they from time to time publicly reaffirm their intention eventually to restore representative government and constitutional liberties; and that failure over the long run to demonstrate their good faith in this matter will compromise them in the eyes of the people of the United States and other Free World countries and in the United Nations.

---

Source: Kennedy Library, National Security Files, Meetings and Memoranda Series, NSC Meeting No. 485. Secret. This NSC action was taken at the 485th meeting of the Council on June 13 and approved by the President that same day. NSC Action No. 2429 was taken at the same meeting.

[1] See Document 212.

[2] Document 224.

[3] See the source note, Document 225.

[4] Paragraph a on page 5 of the report reads: "To inform them that the U.S. is prepared to deal on a friendly and cooperative basis with the new regime;".

[5] Paragraphs c–e on pages 5–6 of the report read: "c. To affirm the intention of the U.S. to continue supporting assistance to the civilian economy and defense establishment; d. To make clear that the higher levels of assistance to support a National Development Plan will be provided only as the Korean Government enters into and carries out firm and specific commitments of reform, including certain reforms which have been under consideration for a long time. In this connection, the U.S. is prepared to offer technical and managerial experts to the Supreme Council; e. To obtain renewed assurance that the SCNR will recognize the authority of CINCUNC to exercise operational control over Korean Armed Forces, as a constituent element of the UN Command."

[6] Paragraph b on page 5 of the report reads: "To impress upon them that it is in their own national interest that the Supreme Council publicly and repeatedly affirm its adherence to the principle of representative government and constitutional liberties and its intention to restore these at the earliest possible time; and that the failure to demonstrate their good faith in this matter will ultimately compromise them in the eyes of the Untied States, and in the forum of the United Nations."

3. The Ambassador is authorized to invite the Chief of Government to Washington for an informal visit including conferences with the President and the Secretary of State.

4. Provided assurances are given in respect to the matters to be discussed under 1 and 2 above and that the Korean Government undertakes actions immediately with respect to certain essential reforms, including the completion of fiscal, foreign exchange and stabilization reforms, the rationalization of the corporate structure and rates in the power and transportation industries, and the bringing into production of certain factories already built; and provided the Ambassador is satisfied with evidences of Korean willingness and capacity to carry out mutually agreed plans and programs, then the Ambassador is authorized:

(a) to indicate U.S. willingness to release approximately $28 million in remaining defense support funds for FY 1961;
(b) to state that the United States is willing to enter into agreed commitments for specific projects for expansion of the power industry, immediately upon appropriation of funds;
(c) to indicate U.S. willingness to support through U.S. aid the expansion and intensification of the National Construction Service on a long-term basis;
(d) to offer technical experts to assist the Korean Government in preparation of its Five-Year Development Plan; and
(e) to state that, provided substantial progress is made in the next few months, the United States will be prepared to provide resources to the Korean Government to help carry out a Five-Year Development Plan. As a long-term policy, U.S. influence should be reinforced by making economic development assistance (as distinguished from supporting assistance) available in increments which can be withheld in the event of Korean failure to carry out agreed programs.

5. The Director of the International Cooperation Administration should take immediate measures to improve the administration of the United States Operations Mission in Korea, including action to concentrate the U.S. effort on the most essential projects and to reduce or eliminate others.

*Subsequent U.S. Actions*

6. Upon a determination of the Secretary of State that the Korean Government is sufficiently stable and cooperative to justify provision of long-range development assistance to it, the actions specified in para-

graphs a through d[7] (pp. 7–8) should be taken, including the appointment of a Special Envoy of the highest stature to visit Korea at a time recommended by the Ambassador. The Envoy will be accompanied by a group of economic advisers to perform functions along the lines of those described in Appendix A to the report, including assistance in the definition of Korean economic goals. While the Koreans must establish and take responsibility for their own goals, the United States can, having defined its goals, help advise the Koreans toward goals that are realistic and consistent with our own. The economic goals which the United States should seek to achieve in Korea include: (1) reversal of the present downward trend in the rate of economic growth and establishment of a specific target of an average annual growth rate for the first five-year plan (rate in 1960: 2.3 per cent); (2) reduction of the present unemployment and underemployment rate (estimated at 35 per cent); (3) increase in average real farm income; and (4) consistent with (1)–(3) above, reduction of the present wide gap between imports and exports ($30 million v. $345 million) in a staged progression toward an eventual balance in Korea's international accounts.

7.  Subject to concrete action by the Korean Government to increase electric power rates, consolidate the power companies and eliminate power losses, announce U.S. willingness to provide, subject to Congressional appropriation, the external resources required to carry out an agreed five-year plan of electric power development. In addition announce that Korean power requirements for the next ten years will be further reviewed and the level of U.S. support re-examined following development of an adequate Korean Five-Year Development Plan.

8.  The Secretaries of State and Defense should conduct an urgent review of the force and equipment levels of Korean Armed Forces, including in the first instance a military assessment of (a) the missions of these forces, in the context of overall U.S. Far East strategy and in the light of the Communist threat and of the anticipated deployment and use of U. S. forces; and (b) the strategic implications of alternative force and equipment structures, including the adequacy of the existing level of forces. Such a military assessment should then be keyed to political and

---

[7] Paragraphs a–d on pages 7–8 of the report read: "a. Authorize the Secretary of State to determine when the Korean Government is sufficiently stable and cooperative to justify long-range development assistance; b. Upon such finding, and at a time recommended by the Ambassador, appoint a Special Envoy of the highest stature to visit Korea. This envoy would be accompanied by a group of economic advisers and would carry out the terms of reference set forth in Appendix A. c. Announce, on the recommendation of the Special Envoy and the Ambassador, the readiness of the U.S. to make available, in concert with other nations of the Free World, external resources to support a Korean Five-Year National Development Plan; d. Authorize the Secretary of State to explore with nations most likely to make a contribution to Korean developments (e.g. Japan and Germany), their willingness to contribute to such a program."

economic factors, to produce a recommendation for long-term force goals and for immediate actions, as necessary and practical, to move toward these goals. This review should be completed in time for use as a basis for allocation of FY 1962 military assistance funds.

9. U.S. military personnel should be directed to encourage and support greater participation by Korean armed forces in the work of the National Construction Service and in other appropriate civil works projects. The review referred to in 8 above should also include the preparation, and the assessment of the economic and military implications, of a program to place far greater stress than heretofore on the training of Korean military personnel in skills and vocations which will permit them to make a greater contribution to the development of Korean infrastructure and the civilian economy.

10. The improvement of Japanese-ROK relations, along the lines called for in paragraph f (p. 9),[8] should be discussed with the Japanese Prime Minister during his visit to Washington and should be urged upon the new regime in Korea. (It is recognized that this is an extremely sensitive issue with the present ROK regime.)

11. The Director of the U.S. Information Agency should arrange for USIS to assist the Korean Government, as may be appropriate, in defining and propagating national ideals and goals and in improving the Korean image abroad.

*Required Korean Actions*

12. The following basic requirements must be pressed upon the Koreans from the outset if they are to achieve meaningful progress and to make profitable use of U.S. development assistance:

(a) Formulation and implementation of a National Development Plan, with short-range, measurable elements susceptible of prompt fulfillment; and in conjunction therewith, undertaking long-range social planning including definition and public promulgation by national leaders of national goals and ideals; reform of civil service and police (including salary increases); achievement of better relations with students, intellectuals, and the press; and enhancement of Korea's national image;

(b) Consideration of the preconditions for the eventual return to civilian rule;

---

[8] Paragraph f on page 9 of the report reads: "Discuss with the Japanese Minister during his forthcoming visit, the U.S. planning for Korea and the ways in which economic and political differences between Korea and Japan can be bridged, despite recent changes of government. It should be understood that while the U.S. will not participate actively in negotiations, it should be prepared to act as a catalyst in seeking a settlement. The Prime Minister should be encouraged to continue efforts recently begun to develop Japanese trade with Korea, and to provide economic assistance for Korean development coordinated with American programs. It should be made clear that Japanese settlement of GARIOA is not to be related to U.S. and Japanese aid to Korea. (The U.S. should also urge the SCNR to be responsive to Japanese overtures.)"

(c) Assurances that the new regime does not interfere with CINC-UNC in the discharge of its military responsibilities;

(d) Endorsement by deed and word of the constitutional freedoms of individuals to the maximum extent consistent with the emergency nature of the government, and avoidance of promiscuous abuse of power, ex post facto laws, blood-purges, or other excesses;

(e) Protection of the rural population against the exhorbitant interest rates of the money-lenders; and

(f) Formulating and implementing a thorough anticorruption program along the lines outlined in Appendix B to the report.

b. Agreed that NSC 6018/1, "U.S. Policy Toward Korea", is no longer applicable.[9]

c. Noted that the Task Force would remain in being for such follow-through action on the above directives as its Chairman deems appropriate.

---

[9] NSC 6018 is printed in *Foreign Relations*, 1958–1960, vol. XVIII, pp. 699–707.

---

## 231.  Telegram From the Embassy in Korea to the Department of State

Seoul, June 13, 1961, 8 p.m.

1798. Embtels 1771,[1] 1764.[2] My recent conversations with ROKG leaders and trend of events here lead me to certain tentative conclusions and policy implications which will have, of course, to be tested against future developments.

*A. Conclusions:*

(1) Junta has no intention of relinquishing power to civilian authority for long time—perhaps years. Moreover, deeply distrustful of civil-

---

Source: Department of State, Central Files, 795B.00/6–1361. Confidential. Repeated to Tokyo, CINCPAC for POLAD, Taipei, Manila, Canberra, and London.

[1] In telegram 1771 from Seoul, June 11, Green reported an hour-long conversation he had with the Chairman of the SCNR, General Chang To-yong (Chang Do Young), which covered the spectrum of U.S.-Korea issues, with the exception of a possible visit by Chang To-yong to the United States. (Ibid., 611.95B/6–1161)

[2] In telegram 1764 from Seoul, June 9, Green reported on his hour-long conversation with Major General Pak Chung-hui. During this meeting Green made five specific points to Pak Chung-hui as instructed in telegram 1465 to Seoul, June 8. They were that the United States considered the SCNR the established government; it welcomed the SCNR's stated objectives; it hoped for a "fruitful relationship," which would serve the Korean people and U.S. interests; it hoped the SCNR would move forward with economic reforms; and it welcomed the reaffirmation of CINCUNC operational control of ROK Armed Forces. (Ibid., 795B.00/6–961 and 611.95B/6–861, respectively)

ians and bent on achieving its aims by rigidly enforced national discipline, junta members are unwilling at present, despite yesterday's regimented "citizens rally" (Embtel 1786),[3] to undertake any real broadening of government's base by bringing civilian leaders into authoritative positions. In refusing make such concessions they not only disregard our urging but put themselves in position of opposition to main stream Korean public thought which, as near as we can judge, desires fairly early return civil authority or, at minimum, establishment of target date for such return.

(2) It is still unclear where new regime is moving. Junta indicates its intention eradicating communism, corruption and social evils, but it may well pursue these worthy objectives by self-defeating means. Excessively narrow, repressive, end-justifies-means tactics will weaken Korea's capability to cope with the fundamental problems of instability, mutual distrust, poverty, backwardness, surplus population and underemployment. Junta seems poorly organized at present in terms of structure as well as competency of military to deal with nation's staggering economic problems despite plain evidence that economic disorder is principal cause of political instability here.

(3) Divisions among junta members and within ROK military may become accentuated in months ahead. In absence single strong leader commanding national respect, factionalism and old loyalties, as well as basic differences in outlook between senior and junior officers, will be all the greater obstacles to cohesive operations by junta. Continuation of junta as now constituted is not assured and, particularly, General Chang Do-young's future is insecure. So far junta has been engaged in denouncing and tearing down the old order, but it now faces the far more difficult job of constructing a viable social-political order, advancing the national economy and ensuring stability. Difficulties of this task will impose new and greater strains on the group holding power.

(4) Junta outwardly appears confident that US gives and will give it full support, and indeed increased economic aid, as long as junta demonstrates it is clearly anti-Communist. Up to present, junta's principal argument for full or increased US support, usually made in private conversations, is that this will help put government in strong position from which it (especially younger military officers will feel they) can afford be less repressive and more attentive to broadening base of government. In absence full support and assistance in future, however, junta will seek to intimidate us into giving such support on grounds that only alternative to continuation of junta is a Communist takeover.

---

[3] Dated June 12. (Ibid., 795B.00/6–1261)

*B. Policy Implications:*

I believe that we should continue along general policy lines which we have pursued over past several weeks. Although many of our counsels seem to have been ignored, I nevertheless feel that our efforts have not been all in vain. We have undoubtedly averted perpetrations of greater excesses by regime. Moreover, US press and Congressional reactions have not gone unnoticed, and ROKG leaders are acutely aware of necessity for continued military and economic aid from us. Despite surface appearances, junta is probably far from feeling secure. In final analysis this uncertainty is probably our most useful short-range means of preventing regime from riding roughshod over Korean people and of moving it in direction of positive program for coping with national problems which could enlist true public support at home and abroad. Under these conditions, a position of friendly reserve is infinitely preferable to expressions of complete confidence and support which reduce our ability to influence situation and, in event regime becomes dangerously repressive and discredited with people, would resound only to advantage of the ever-ready Communists and to permanent detriment of US standing with the Korean people.

US friendship and prestige in Korea should not stand or fall with this present regime. Our time-tested friends in Korea are still the Korean people, not necessarily those few who arrogate power to speak for them, who may be corrupted by the power they too long wield, and who may fail to hold this nation's confidence and support.

**Green**

## 232.  Memorandum of Conversation

Washington, June 20, 1961, 10:30–11:55 a.m.

SUBJECT

Korea

PARTICIPANTS

*Japan*
Prime Minister Hayato Ikeda
Foreign Minister Zentaro Kosaka
Kiichi Miyazawa, Member of the Upper House of the Japanese Diet
Shigenobu Shima, Deputy Vice Minister for Foreign Affairs
Koichiro Asakai, Japanese Ambassador to the United States
Toshiro Shimanouchi, Counselor, Ministry of Foreign Affairs, Interpreter

*United States*
The President
The Secretary of State
George W. Ball, Under Secretary of State for Economic Affairs
Edwin O. Reischauer, United States Ambassador to Japan
FE—Walter P. McConaughy, Assistant Secretary
Walt W. Rostow, Deputy Assistant to the President for National Security Affairs
NA—Richard L. Sneider, Officer in Charge of Japanese Affairs
LS—James J. Wickel, Interpreter

Prime Minister Ikeda said that a question of utmost difficulty for Japan is the problem of Korea. From its own experience of governing Korea for 40 years, Japan recognizes that the Koreans are difficult to deal with, being exclusive and self-willed. The problem is what to do at the present time. The Prime Minister claimed that Japanese relations had not been formalized with the Republic of Korea and as a result of the recent coup there is very little that Japan can do. The Japanese people do not like the recent developments and would like to see an early restoration of civil government. However, since the coup is an accomplished fact, the situation must be dealt with as it now stands. The Prime Minister pointed out that the Japanese are powerless to influence Korean political developments and therefore hope that the U.S. will restore civil government. To do so, however, Japan feels that it is necessary first to restore economic stability and is prepared to cooperate with external assistance to Korea to accomplish this objective.

The President said that the United States had been hopeful regarding the ability of the former regime to gain increasing popular support.

Source: Kennedy Library, National Security Files, Countries Series, Japan, Ikeda Trip, Memcons and Follow Up. Confidential. Drafted by Richard L. Sneider. The time of the meeting is from the President's Appointment Book. (Ibid.) Korea was one of the topics discussed at the meeting. For additional information on Ikeda's visit, see Documents 330–339.

We now face a very difficult situation which concerns us greatly, particularly in the light of the large scale unemployment and discontent in Korea. He said that we intend to use our influence to move the new regime to a restoration of constitutional methods and civil rule, but this will be a slow process. The President pointed out that the United States has spent a considerable amount of money in Korea with little to show for it in view of the serious economic difficulties and discontent. However, we intend to continue aid to this country. He said it would be most helpful to bring about agreement between Japan and Korea, although we recognize this is difficult due to the nationalistic flavor of the coup group and the popular dislike in Japan for militaristic regimes. One aim of our policy in Korea is to attempt to establish close relations between Japan and Korea. We also consider that Japanese assistance, particularly for power development, would be very helpful.

The President asked whether, in the Prime Minister's judgment, a communist seizure of control of South Korea would have an extremely adverse effect on Japan. The Prime Minister replied that the record of Japan's long history testifies to the fact that the security of Korea is, in effect, a domestic problem for Japan. Japan has a very vital stake in Korea. Japan is willing to accept even the present regime since it is anticommunist. Although it is important to bring about an improvement in the present situation, it is even more essential to prevent a communist takeover of South Korea.

The President suggested that there be further talks with the Secretary on the Korean question, and the Prime Minister agreed.

---

### 233.  Memorandum From Robert H. Johnson of the National Security Council Staff to the President's Deputy Special Assistant for National Security Affairs (Rostow)

Washington, June 28, 1961.

SUBJECT

Korea Task Force Meeting on Thursday, June 22, 1961

Mr. McConaughy called a meeting of the Korea Task Force on June 22, 1961 to discuss a message from Seoul (No. 1840 of June 17)[1] and a

---

Source: Kennedy Library, National Security Files, Countries Series, Korea, General, 6/61. Secret.
[1] Not printed. (Department of State, Central Files, 795B.00/6–1761)

related army message[2] which raised the question of whether there was significant Communist influence in the new military regime in Korea. Mr. McConaughy indicated that the Secretary was very disturbed by the embassy message.

The message reported a conversation between Chargé Green and Lieutenant General Choi Kyong Nok in which the latter stated that Communists were behind the coup. General Choi based his belief on his personal knowledge of officers within the coup group, on information he had received from friends within the group, and on his examination of the past records of individuals within the coup group which indicated connections with the North Korean regime during the period 1945–49. He stated that he did not know whether General Pak was a Communist. He did identify four other generals by name as Communists and claimed that an additional three or four unnamed colonels were Communists.

Mr. McConaughy said that he had high regard for General Choi, but noted that General Choi had never got along well with General Pak who was at one time his deputy. Moreover, General Choi was related to the Foreign Minister of Chang Myon's government. It was, therefore, necessary to take his allegations with a grain of salt.

Mr. FitzGerald of CIA indicated that CIA had examined biographical information on the members of the group, [*less than 1 line of source text not declassified*] and had consulted with one of its best sources [*3 lines of source text not declassified*]. He said that all of CIA's evidence indicated that the officers in SCNR are highly motivated individuals who were disgusted with the Chang Myon government and who had engaged from time to time in plotting. CIA does not think that they are Communists although there may be some Communist agents in the substructure of the coup group. A greater danger, in CIA's opinion, is the possibility that the coup group may, through naiveté, be led to believe that unification with the North is both feasible and desirable. In conclusion, Mr. FitzGerald stated that the main stream of the coup group is not Communist.

Mr. Hilsman noted that these cables had been discussed at the USIB meeting the previous day and that USIB had also concluded that the coup group was not Communist.[3] It was possible that the idea of adopting a Nasser-type approach might cross the minds of members of the coup group though we consider it unlikely that the regime will move in that direction. There is also some danger of penetration of the coup group by the Communists for intelligence purposes.

Admiral Heinz, while not commenting on the allegations of Communism, expressed concern over the growing power of Lieutenant Colonel Kim Chong-pil (head of ROK intelligence and one of those accused

---

[2] Not further identified.

[3] No record of the USIB meeting has been found.

by Choi) who, he feared, might be setting the stage for ruthless one-man rule. If this kind of rule were established, it might make it easier for the Communists to take over in the future.

Mr. McConaughy agreed that the repressive acts of the new regime could produce a future explosion. He thought that General Choi may have been influenced in his view by the fact that the methods being used by the new regime were, in certain respects, similar to those used by the Communists. He mentioned specifically the parading of hoodlums through the streets. It was subsequently pointed out that this had been a common practice in China long before the Communists took over there.

Mr. Sheppard said that the only evidence that ICA had that was conceivably relevant was the fact that, in conferences with economic officials of the new regime, there was an increasing emphasis on the "socialist character" of the new regime. When pressed for details, these officials become quite vague. Mr. FitzGerald suggested that it was important for all agencies that had contacts with the military to look for evidences of attitudes that might have a bearing on the question of Communist influence.

Roger Hilsman pointed out that a number of those who were accused by General Choi had tangled with him at one time or another.

Mr. McConaughy asked what Mr. Sheppard made of the fact that we had had almost no contact with the people on the economic side of the new regime. Mr. Sheppard attributed this to three causes: (a) organizational confusion; (b) the fact that the ministries were headed by military officers and that officials below the top level had inhibitions about talking; and (c) of the fact that there were various apparently influential economic committees under the SCNR with which we had so far been unable to establish effective contact.

In conclusion it was agreed that the coup in Korea had not been the "cleverest Communist coup" ever pulled off. It was also agreed that there was some possible danger, as a result of a power struggle within the SCNR, that a group that was losing out might attempt a unification maneuver in cooperation with the North as a means of salvaging its position. Mr. FitzGerald suggested that the country team be asked to prepare a contingency plan against such possibility. I suggested that contingency planning be broadened to cover various other sorts of situations that might develop out of a power struggle within the SCNR. Mr. McConaughy agreed that, as a first step in developing such a contingency plan, it would be desirable to ask for the views of the country team.

At the end of the meeting Mr. McConaughy raised the question of progress reports to the NSC. As a result of the discussion that I had with the State people at the meeting and subsequently with Brom Smith, it was agreed that progress reports would be prepared, in accordance with existing State procedure, for the Operations Center and that a copy of these reports would be sent to Mr. Bundy.

**Bob**

---

## 234. Memorandum of Conversation

Washington, July 7, 1961, 2:30–3 p.m.

SUBJECT

New Korean Government and ROK-U.S. Relations

PARTICIPANTS

*Koreans*
Ambassador Yang Soo Yoo, Chief of Korean Good Will Mission[1]
Ambassador Il Kwon Chung, Korean Ambassador to the United States
Mr. Yun Yong Lim, Political Counselor, Korean Embassy

*Department of State*
The Secretary
Mr. Walter P. McConaughy, Assistant Secretary of State for Far Eastern Affairs
Mr. Leonard L. Bacon, Acting Director, Office of Northeast Asian Affairs
Mr. Philip W. Manhard, International Relations Officer, Office of Northeast Asian Affairs

In the course of an official ROK good will mission to Washington July 5–9, 1961, the chief of the mission, Special Ambassador Yang Soo Yoo, accompanied by the Korean Ambassador, Il Kwon Chung, and the Korean Embassy Political Counselor, Mr. Yun Yong Lim, called on the Secretary. Although Ambassador Yoo's English is fairly good and he

---

Source: Department of State, Central Files, 795B.00/7–761. Confidential. Drafted by Manhard and approved in S on July 31.

[1] Major General Yang Soo Yoo was the Chairman of the Foreign Affairs and Defense Committees of the SCNR. A briefing memorandum for the meeting was sent from McConaughy to Rusk on July 7. It noted that the Department just learned that Special Ambassador Soo would be returning to Seoul because "the situation required his presence," and Ambassador Il Kwon Chung would continue the mission to New York, Canada, and Central and South America. In Seoul SCNR Chairman General Chang To-yong had been ousted and replaced by General Pak Chung-hui. Chang To-yong was detained and charges of Communist collaboration were brought against the former Chang Myon government and its members. (Ibid., 033.95B11/7–761)

required no interpreting from English into Korean, Counselor Lim interpreted for him from Korean into English.

Ambassador Yoo said that his Government and people have been extremely gratified by the assurances given by Ambassador Berger that the United States Government would continue its keen interest in Korea and cooperate with the new ROK Government for the welfare of Korea. Ambassador Yoo trusted that the Secretary understood the extremely difficult situation the ROK faced from the political, economic, and national security points of view prior to the military takeover, which the junta considered essential as possibly the last opportunity for the salvation of the country. Expressing deep gratitude for the "'sympathetic understanding" shown by the U.S. Government, Ambassador Yoo affirmed that the new ROK regime intends to make every effort to sustain the "sympathy and expectations" of the U.S. Yoo stressed that among the announced objectives of the new Government the most important are (1) strengthening national security against subversion and aggression, (2) eradicating all forms of corruption and inefficiency, and (3) turning over the Government to civilian control as soon as the regime's pledges are achieved. Yoo emphasized that his Government has every intention to return to civilian control as soon as the "opportune time arrives when we can turn over the government to conscientious, clean civilians". The new ROK leaders realize the importance of continued close relations with the U.S. and the need to promote even closer ties.

Ambassador Yoo said he recognized that recent events in Seoul have placed the executive branch of the U.S. Government, particularly the State Department, in a difficult position, and remarked that Senator Morse had told him that the Secretary had been hard pressed by Congress on foreign aid including the Korean aid program. Yoo stated that in this initial stage the new government has many obstacles to overcome and some actions have not met with U.S. approval, but the Korean leaders are aware of "what is required of them" and realize that in trying to achieve their objectives it is of prime importance not to "place a curtain across Korean-American friendship".

The Secretary pointed out that since 1945 the U.S. and Korean peoples had shared a great deal, fighting a war and struggling to rebuild the ROK together. The American people have accepted large sacrifices in the interest of Korean independence. Although we understand some of the problems which led the ROK military leaders to consider a coup necessary, we are concerned about the future. The Secretary stated that the defense of the ROK depends on (1) its military strength and the determination of the Korean people to defend themselves, and (2) the attitude of the rest of the world toward Korea.

The Secretary said that we are frankly puzzled and uncertain about the future course of events in Korea.[2] We have not felt that our representatives in Korea or here were in intimate contact with those exercising real power and authority in Korea. The Secretary stressed the need to discuss many important problems with those in power and hoped that we could stimulate such contact in the near future. We desire to show a spirit of cooperation and partnership. There are points on which we would like to offer advice, areas in which we feel we can assist progress in the ROK. However we need to know that we are working with those in real authority, and it is difficult for us to know how best to proceed. Ambassador Berger has taken the initiative to consult with Korean leaders and we hope they will discuss with him their plans and intentions. The Secretary also emphasized that Ambassador Berger enjoys the full confidence of the President and himself and that the ROK leaders can rely on Ambassador Berger to work for the best relations between the ROK and the U.S.

The Secretary thought that it would be useful if in the next few weeks the Korean leaders could show that they are prepared to exercise authority through processes of law and through the application of procedures and standards general to constitutional governments elsewhere in the world. If the impression is given that the new ROK Government is acting arbitrarily or taking actions not based on generally recognized concepts of legality and justice, the result might well be to undermine confidence in the ROK and alienate the sympathy of many who wish Korea well. The ROK has enjoyed considerable international support over the years. This is a valuable resource which we hope will not be dissipated. Our own policy, interests, military forces and reputation are deeply involved in the success or failure of the ROK.

Ambassador Chung said that Ambassador Yoo during his visit here had been able to gain a clear understanding of the views of the U.S. Government, Congress and people and his imminent return to Seoul would ensure the prompt transmittal of our views to the Korean Government. Ambassador Chung said that he was very hopeful that a "good reaction" would ensue for both the U.S. and the ROK. Ambassador Yoo said that "weak as my position is" he would do whatever he could to impress on his colleagues what needs to be done in the future.

---

[2] At 4:05 p.m. Rusk met with British Ambassador Caccia and French Ambassador Alphand and confided to them that the United States was "very much disturbed by the present situation in Korea. We are puzzled by the present exercise of powers of state in that country." Rusk noted that the Department had always had doubts about the durability of General Chang To-yong and discounted rumors of Pak Chung-hui's contacts with North Korea. Rusk hoped that the British, French, and U.S. Ambassadors in Seoul could work closely together. Rusk stated that there might be some danger of the ROK military taking over the country without the knowledge of the U.N. Commander. (Memorandum of conversation; ibid., 795.00/7–761)

### 235.   Telegram From the Embassy in Korea to the Department of State

Seoul, July 9, 1961, 4 p.m.

45. Deptel 32.[1]

1. This is interim evaluation in response your telegram.

2. Revolution now in its second stage with General Pak Chung-hui increasing his authority and control within Supreme Council and engaged in eliminating elements which he thinks threatening him.

A. His aim clearly is to unify Supreme Council into homogeneous group loyal to him and what he hopes to achieve.

B. At same time he is taking steps to break up possible anti-Pak combinations in armed forces which he thinks could threaten him from outside.

C. He is also continuing to move against civilian leaders and organizations which he believes could become centers of organized opposition. (For example after announcing three days ago four relief pension and loan measures for veterans and their survivors, Supreme Council dissolved National Veterans' Organization.)

3. For better or for worse we must let this phase of revolution work itself out. Inexorable forces are at work and no useful purpose would be served at this juncture by our trying apply heavy pressure to alter play of these forces. First of all, Pak literally fighting for his life and we would almost certainly not be listened to. Secondly, assuming we successful in moderating or slowing down purges it would merely result in continuation of internal factionalism and postponement of eventual showdown inside Supreme Council, perpetuation and possibly accentuation of division in armed forces, and further delays in taking economic decisions, which now an immediate necessity if whole economy, already staggering under impact of revolution, is not to collapse. Thirdly, undue pressures on Pak at this critical juncture might lead him take more repressive measures that would separate this government further from its citizens and from U.S. and might invite countercoups and bloody civil strife with

---

Source: Department of State, Central Files, 795B.00/7–961. Confidential; Limited Distribution. Repeated to CINCPAC for POLAD and Tokyo.

[1] In telegram 32 to Seoul, July 6, the Department stated that recent events in Korea—the ouster and detention of General Chang To-yong, his replacement by Pak Chung-hui, and sweeping government accusations against the former Chang Myon government of Communist connections—were causing concern in Washington. The tentative Department assessment was that Chang's ouster was inevitable and the accusations against Chang Myon and associates were an attempt to weaken the opposition to the junta. The Department worried about the loss of Chang To-yong's moderating influence on the SCNR and asked for the Embassy's assessment. (Ibid., 795B.00/7–761)

no acceptable politicians and few institutions to salvage ruins. What Pak ultimately aims for or will be able to accomplish, I do not know, but he is strongest figure in situation, has a clear sense of nature and use of power, and seems genuinely motivated by patriotic ideals. He nevertheless will bear watching.

4. Meanwhile, Pak is fully aware of importance restoring CINC-UNC and ROK forces command authority, has taken some constructive steps in this direction (see Embtel 35, paras 3 and 4)[2] and has given General Meloy and me assurances this whole problem must be and will be resolved soon. But he cannot in my opinion resolve command authority problem without regard to his own problems described in para 2 above. Pak has also taken some constructive measures to cope with corruption and social evils.

5. Supreme Council charges of Communist associations levelled against Chang Myon and some of his ministers and senior officials is a serious tactical mistake both from domestic and international point of view and is of questionable utility in terms of consolidating revolution. (Quite apart from fact that published evidence is unconvincing, these charges merely deepen prevailing atmosphere of apprehension and add to public concern here and abroad over how far Pak is going in direction of retaliation and repression.)

6. It is clear Pak's purpose in bringing charges is to discredit Chang Myon government but why he chose this means when he could have charged them with corruption or tolerating corruption, ineffectiveness, incompetence, etc. is less clear. Probably he not only wants discredit them, but means to get them out of way. Additionally, I think Pak genuinely convinced that Communist propaganda and neutralism were making an impression in South Korea under Chang Myon govt. especially among students, labor unions and intellectuals, and he means use any evidence, however tenuous, to prove his case and to display his anti-communism.

7. Green and I feel that in formulating our public position and approach we must be ever mindful of our relations with Koreans as a whole and that Pak may be passing phenomenon. At same time we face fact there is no alternative at present to giving Pak our support and trying to encourage restraint and wisdom in his exercise of his growing power. In dealing with this dilemma our tactic at this end up to now has been to

---

[2] Paragraph 3 of telegram 35 from Seoul, July 7, reported that General Pak told Berger, General Meloy, and General McNamara that with the ouster of 30 General Army officers the purge of the ROK Armed Forces was over, that military officers assigned to civilian duties would be replaced by civilians, that the ROK military chain of command was in effect, and that soldiers charged with police functions had been ordered to stop browbeating the public. In paragraph 4 Meloy welcomed these assurances, which he believed would help reestablish command authority. (Ibid.)

avoid public statements, and to try to moderate Pak through my personal talks with him, Foreign Minister and economic ministers; through Green's contacts with one or two who are close to Pak; through [*less than 1 line of source text not declassified*] talks with Col. Kim, head of Intelligence, and apparently second strongest man in junta.

8.   We feel that we must now give some public indication of our concern. Accordingly suggest following procedure:[3]

A.   Secretary call in Korean Ambassador and state that we prepared and want to work with ROK Govt. on friendly and cooperative basis toward achievement of govt's worthy goals and we recognize govt. has made some constructive reforms. At same time certain actions such as continued detention of certain ROK Army officers (FYI, officers who were loyal to Gen. Magruder's orders on May 16. End FYI) and charges of Communist associations leveled against Chang Myon and some of his people well known to us are causing apprehension among U.S. public, Congress and in executive branch, including U.S. military. While we do not wish prejudge these matters, want to convey importance of speedy investigation and early public trials. Moreover, we would strongly urge ROK Govt. avoid retaliation, vindictiveness and repression which can only sow seeds of national bitterness and future disunity, and observe policy of clemency and magnanimity in order unite country and enlist popular support and confidence. We do not believe govt. can achieve its declared objectives and gain US understanding without this.

B.   Secty should also refer to our concern over gap which still remains in CINCUNC's Command authority.

C.   That I be authorized in name of Secretary to make simultaneous official representations here.

D.   That Dept. Spokesman make general public statement on Secty's meeting with Amb Chang along lines A above for replay here. Since Pak has given me his assurances there would be public trials, Spokesman can also refer to this assurance in his statement.

Berger

---

[3] In telegram 129 to Seoul, July 13, the Department stated that Rusk made such a statement to ROK good will Ambassador Yang Soo Yoo and Ambassador Il Kwon Chung. (Ibid., 795B.00/7–961) See Document 234.

## 236.  Special National Intelligence Estimate

SNIE 42–3–61                                  Washington, July 18, 1961.

THE CURRENT REGIME IN THE REPUBLIC OF KOREA

The Problem

To assess the character and intentions of the Korean military junta.[1]

The Estimate

*I.   Introduction*

1.  The members of the military junta now ruling the Republic of Korea (ROK) are tough, nationalistic, and ambitious. They have all spent their adult lives in military service and most of them have had extensive combat experience. Their approach is not that of the intellectual or the professional politician. They are activists who have demonstrated an understanding of the instruments and techniques for political control. They have long been disgusted with corruption and inefficiency in the government and the military establishment and disillusioned with the lack of progress under civilian rule. Their approach to government is authoritarian and they are convinced that the solution of the ROK's many economic, political, and social ills requires rigid public discipline and firm, centralized government control.

2.  The members of the military junta still feel that their position is insecure. Consequently, they are suspicious and quick to suppress any potential source of opposition. There are almost certainly elements of vindictiveness and bitterness in their attitude toward Korean politicians and military officers who have served as tools of the politicians.

3.  The ROK's new ruling group intends to bring a new order and discipline into Korean life and to initiate a major economic development effort. While the ruling group desires close relations with the US, it intends to run Korean affairs in its own way and to assert Korean inde-

---

Source: Department of State, INR/EAP Files: Lot 90 D 110, SNIE 42–3–61. Secret. According to a note on the cover sheet, the Central Intelligence Agency and intelligence organizations of the Departments of State, Defense, the Army, the Navy, the Air Force, and the Joint Staff participated in the preparation of this estimate. All members of the USIB concurred with this estimate on July 18 except the representatives of the AEC and the FBI, who abstained on the grounds that the subject was outside their jurisdiction.

[1] This estimate should be read in conjunction with SNIE 42–2–61, "Short-Term Prospects for South Korea," dated 31 May 1961. A more detailed estimate on both North and South Korea is scheduled to be completed in August 1961. [Footnote in the source text. For SNIE 42–2–61, see Document 224.]

pendence. At least for the near future, the group has no intention of turning the government back to civilian control or of reinstating institutions of representative government despite assurances to the contrary. They are only beginning to realize the complexities of the tasks which face them and the limitations of their own training and experience. Frustration of their efforts is likely to cause them to resort to ill-considered or repressive acts.

II.   *Locus of Power*

4.   Major General Pak Chong-hui is the dominant figure in the military junta, but his control of the group is neither absolute now nor certain to continue. The recent removal of Lt. Gen. Chang To-yong eliminated the most likely member of the coup group around whom antijunta military elements might have gathered. Chang's departure, however, did little to resolve the basic problem of control within the coup group. We believe that conflicts are continuing within the junta concerning policies and tactics, and perhaps, objectives.

5.   Although there are various possible factional alignments within the junta based on regional origin or service, the potential division which is most apparent at present lies in the difference between the general officers and the field grade officers. There is a group of some 10 or 12 members of the junta—most of them Colonels—who provided much of the coup's initial impetus and planning and who probably differ with Pak on junta policies. In general, these officers tend to favor drastic measures to achieve their objectives and to suppress opposition.

6.   [*8 lines of 2-column source text not declassified*] Pak has indicated that he intends to curb the influence of the Colonels, possibly by ousting them altogether or by assigning them to army commands with promotions. Pak may be sufficiently adroit to accomplish this without causing the Colonels to turn against him. There is, however, a possibility that there may be an open break between Pak and the Colonels group. If such a break occurred, the outcome would depend on whether [*less than 1 line of source text not declassified*] chose to support Pak or the field grade officers in the junta and in the army with whom he has close ties.

7.   There will probably be a continuing struggle for power within the junta as various factions vie for influence and as Pak strives to consolidate his position. Besides the Colonels faction, there is a Marine Corps group, headed by Major General Kim Tong-ha, and other opposition groups may emerge. There will probably be efforts to compromise and settle differences, but if open conflict breaks out, we cannot exclude the possibility that the various faction leaders would call upon their supporters in the armed forces. This in turn would be likely to create an opening for action by ROK military commanders who disapprove of the junta. This could result in armed clashes and even civil war.

## III. The Communism Issue

8. Despite the accusations that have been leveled against Pak and some of the other members of the junta, we still have no hard evidence from credible, disinterested sources that they are in fact Communists or are consciously acting as North Korean agents. In its statements and actions to date, the regime has taken a strong anti-Communist stand. Moreover, Bloc press reports and broadcasts have bitterly attacked the junta, its actions, and Pak personally. We recognize that the junta position and Bloc reaction could be an attempt to conceal the true character of the regime. We cannot rule out the possibility that the coup was Communist inspired and directed, but presently available evidence leads us to the view that the junta as a whole was, and continues to be, motivated primarily by personal ambition, intense nationalism, and a strong desire to impose discipline and force development on the ROK.

## IV. National Attitude Toward the Junta

9. The junta has passed a new basic law, virtually suspending the Constitution of the Second Republic and setting itself up as both the maker and executor of the nation's laws. Under this law, the junta's Supreme Council for National Reconstruction is to approve the appointment of all judicial officials and all formerly elected local governing officers, such as province governors and town mayors. The civil rights of the people are guaranteed only as long as they do not conflict with the accomplishment of the Supreme Council's program. At the same time, the Supreme Council has restored much of their previous authority and power to the National Police and other control organs.

10. When it first seized control, the coup group enjoyed some measure of acceptance from the Korean public which had grown weary of the Chang Myon government's inability to subordinate politicking to economic and political reform. Over the past two months, however, public disenchantment with the new regime has appeared in the cities. Some of the junta's early administrative acts favored the farmers and in the rural areas a favorable attitude toward the junta can still be found. The economic dislocation resulting from the coup has not yet had a measurable political effect on the public, but it will almost certainly add to other causes of public dissatisfaction with the junta if not soon rectified. The increasing authoritarianism and resort to police rule is adversely affecting the junta's standing among intellectuals and students. Many of the latter now regard the military junta as little or no better than the Rhee regime they overthrew.

11. The junta has made full use of its powers under martial law to close newspapers, jail politicians, educators, and businessmen, and impose curfews and censorship. The atmosphere of fear and intimidation thus created has so far prevented demonstrations of public opposi-

tion to the junta. The junta's campaign against potential opposition leaders has greatly reduced the chances for organized resistance. Another student-led uprising is possible. If it were to take place, the junta would probably attempt to put it down quickly and violently, and follow up with increased repressive measures.

### V.   Relations With the US

12. With the assumption of power by the military junta, US-ROK relations have entered a new phase. The cooperativeness of the Chang Myon government has been replaced by suspicion and distrust. Being personally convinced of the imperative need to rid the country of rule by ineffectual and corrupt politicians, the members of the junta probably were dismayed by and resentful of the initial US opposition to the take-over. Much of this sentiment still remains and the coup group probably feels that its cool, reserved, and suspicious attitude toward the US is but a reflection of the official US attitude toward them. [*5 lines of source text not declassified*]

13. The members of the military junta are fully aware of Korean dependence upon the US and will seek a relationship with the US which will not endanger the country's major source of economic, military, and diplomatic support. At the same time, the military junta probably intends to develop a new and different US-ROK relationship in which South Korea's leaders will feel that they are in full control of Korean affairs. The junta will be less responsive to US advice in political matters, and almost certainly intends to go about the tasks of reform and political control in its own way. US appeals for leniency for individuals or groups considered by the junta to be corrupt or to be opponents of its regime might be interpreted as interference in Korean affairs.

14. The junta has accepted the principle of the subordination of the ROK Army to the UN Command. However, their willingness to implement fully agreements on the command structure cannot be taken for granted. US forces in the ROK probably will be faced with increasing restrictions and problems of maintaining good relations with the Korean authorities. While recognizing the military necessities of the situation, the junta probably intends to maintain a large degree of independence in its command of the ROK Army, at least in peace time.

## 237. Telegram From the Department of State to the Embassy in Korea

Washington, July 20, 1961, 9:35 p.m.

125. Ref: (A) Seoul's 88,[1] (B) Seoul's 89,[2] (C) Seoul's 90,[3] (D) Seoul's 94.[4]

1. Appreciate incisive appraisal Korean situation ref A, in which Dept generally concurs. Necessary of course bear in mind that opportunism and thirst for power, believed originally large factor in coup along with patriotic motives, may grow stronger with passage of time, thus complicating US relationships with SCNR.

2. Dept however encouraged by indications para 10 ref A that problems facing ROK military government increasingly better understood by Pak Chong-hui and others. Also welcome indications para 7 ref A that relationships between Korean and US leaders and agencies improving. Believe Ambassador's skillful application Task Force Report guidelines, and his and Green's effective dealings with ROK leaders, largely responsible for improvement thus far.

3. Dept prepared accept as working hypothesis that new ROK leadership essentially anti-Communist. Embassy requested, however, continue giving priority attention to indications bearing on validity this hypothesis, whether tending to support or contradict.

Source: Department of State, Central Files, 795B.00/7–1861. Confidential. Drafted by Macdonald; cleared by Bacon, Abram E. Manell of FE/P, Jenkins, and Peterson; and approved by Steeves. Repeated to Tokyo and CINCPAC for POLAD.

[1] In telegram 88 from Seoul, July 15, the Embassy reported the results of an investigation of the May 1961 military coup. The investigation found that the "mainsprings" of the revolt were "patriotic, nationalistic, and anti-communist." Disgust with corruption, incompetence, and ineffectiveness of the civilian government and fear of possible Communist subversion caused the revolt. Although the Embassy did not discount the possibility of "communist sleepers" among the revolutionary leaders and their civilian advisers, it felt that General Pak Chun-hui's defection from communism was legitimate. (Ibid., 795B.00/7–1561)

[2] In telegram 89 from Seoul, July 17, the Embassy reported that the ROK had granted amnesty to 1,293 persons held in jail. This was precisely the kind of act of clemency that the Embassy had been encouraging the SCNR to make. Berger hoped the U.S. Government could make a statement welcoming this action. (Ibid., 795B.00/7–1761) Rusk's statement at a news conference on July 27 is printed in American Foreign Policy: Current Documents, 1961, p. 483.

[3] In telegram 90 from Seoul, July 17, Berger reported his efforts to encourage better press coverage of the Military Government by The New York Times journalist in Seoul. (Department of State, Central Files, 795B.00/7–1761)

[4] In telegram 94 from Seoul, July 18, Berger explained that he had made a statement welcoming the amnesty for political prisoners. (Ibid., 795B.00/7–1861)

4. In regard Embassy recommendations para 12 reftel A[5] Dept recognizes importance US role in critical Korean situation and need for constructive application of influence. (See para 7 below.) Ambassador's statement reported reftel D believed useful expression US interest, sympathy and support in response to specific constructive ROKG action.

5. Dept believes however it important to avoid impression of unconditional US support for present ROK regime, as pointed out in para 13 reftel A, and to key our statements to ROKG actions clearly in our mutual interests. Accordingly, in view of lack detailed information here on nature and affiliations of persons released, Dept did not issue statement concerning Constitution Day amnesty as suggested ref B.

6. Dept will however be prepared make appropriate statements related to specific and concrete events and actions ROKG which clearly evidence progress toward mutually desired goals, and invites further recommendations from Embassy this connection.

7. Ambassador requested obtain advance Dept concurrence where possible for statements indicating US approval ROKG or its actions. Importance time factor mentioned para 12 ref A nonetheless recognized and Ambassador authorized make appropriate statements such as reported ref D on own initiative if in his judgement such action necessary and time does not permit advance clearance.

8. In regard press reporting on ROK developments and US attitude toward ROKG, Dept believes your guidance to American reporters such as Rosenthal is very useful.

**Rusk**

---

[5] In paragraph 12 of telegram 88, Berger stated that the Embassy might have to come out publicly in favor of the ROK Government even in the absence of desired actions. Berger would keep the Department informed in advance of his intentions in this respect, but quick and timely action could be of the essence.

## 238. Letter From Secretary of State Rusk to the Ambassador to Korea (Berger)

Washington, August 1, 1961.

DEAR SAM: One of the continuing problems which has concerned the President, Secretary McNamara, and me for some time is how to assure that the effectiveness and cost of our military assistance programs are consistent with the role to be played by U.S. forces and our major new efforts in other foreign programs, including economic aid. Our recent experience in presenting the President's new aid legislation to the Congress[1] indicates that influential members of the legislative branch are similarly concerned.

We recognize the need to provide military assistance where necessary in our continuing security interests. In our view, however, many of our country programs reflect habits of thinking and methods of operation built up over the years which do not come fully to grips with the range of problems and opportunities which confront us. A realistic reassessment of these country programs in context of our political, economic, and military policies is imperative, bringing the whole spectrum of external and internal threats and capabilities into focus to determine the optimum thrust and balance of our overall effort.

The military review must be also related specifically to the current major reassessment of our economic aid activities requested in my Circular Airgram 1065 of June 23, 1961.[2] Our real military requirements must be evaluated before our economic judgments can become final, just as we must know probable economic resource capabilities and demands thereon before we decide on our military programs.

As a first major step in this process, Mr. McNamara and I have determined that a special priority should be given to a review of our programs in seven major aid-recipient countries—Korea, China, Vietnam, Pakistan, Iran, Turkey, and Greece. An interagency Steering Group, chaired by State, with representatives from Defense, AID, and the Joint Staff, has been established to supervise this review separate from the FY 1962–67 military assistance planning now in progress (CW–608 of July 21, 1961).[3]

---

Source: Department of State, Central Files, 795B.5–MSP/8–161. Secret. Drafted by Martin M. Tank of the Office of the Deputy Coordinator for Foreign Assistance on July 25. Cleared by Peterson, George A. Morgan of S/P, Deputy Coordinator for Foreign Assistance John O. Bell, William Bundy, William A. Ellis of ICA, Jeffrey C. Kitchens of the Office of the Deputy Under Secretary for Political Affairs, Assistant Director of Bureau of the Budget Kenneth R. Hansen, Komer, and General Counsel for the newly created AID, Seymour J. Rubin.

[1] Which became Public Law 87–195, the Foreign Assistance Act of 1961, approved September 4. (75 Stat 424)

[2] Not printed. (Department of State, Central Files, 700.5–MSP/6–2361)

[3] Not printed. (Ibid., 700.5–MSP/7–2161)

As you are aware from your participation in the Korean Task Force meetings our recently established policy assumes that, in both U.S. and Korean activities, priority should be given to the crucial internal problems and to the contributions which the Korean military establishment might make to economic development. Also as indicated in the Task Force Report,[4] the JCS is reviewing ROK force levels and assessing their missions and strategic implications of alternative force structures. It is our hope that you will be in a position to provide a background combining all factors relevant to U.S. interests and decisions on longer term goals. In addition, this re-evaluation of military assistance would extend the review period to FY 1967, stressing the need to examine the policy alternatives both for the U.S. and those which may be feasible for Korea, and would seek to evaluate the risks and consequences of those alternatives and the military and economic aid measures related thereto, and to point up the optimum distribution of total resources in the U.S. and Korean interest.

For this review to be effective, your personal appraisal beyond the contributions of your associates, will be required and should be directed primarily at long-term aspects of our military assistance policies. While short-run considerations must be included in our planning, we are chiefly interested in where you believe we should be by 1967.

To this end we are seeking the most informed answers to the types of questions, among others, presented for Korea in the first enclosure to this letter to assure ourselves that we are following the most promising course in relating military assistance to our overall objectives and other U.S. programs over the next few years. The answers may, of course, be provided separately or within the framework of a general response to the issues raised, whichever is considered to be most effective. I hope as well that the particular questions will not limit the scope of the response.

Perhaps the most important question is whether, despite the continuing risk of renewed local aggression, we should not somewhat reduce the size of the military aid insurance policy we are buying in South Korea in order to direct greater U.S. and indigenous resources to meet the crucial need for dynamic social and economic growth. Though to do so might involve taking greater calculated risks with respect to ROK military defenses, the continued presence of substantial U.S. forces plus the UN umbrella might suffice to reduce this risk to acceptable proportions. These are questions for your judgment.

Alternatives to the basic guidance used in preparation of the revised FY 62–67 plan, attached as enclosure 2 of this letter, have been formulated to provide a practical framework for judging the consequences of

---

[4] See the source note, Document 225.

military program adjustments on costs and other factors in the context of other programs. Your views on these alternatives will also be solicited directly by CINCPAC through regular military assistance channels. A copy of your reply should go to him for consideration of the military consequences. These are clearly not the only possible alternatives, and we would welcome your views on any other you think desirable. All of this, of course, must be treated as an internal U.S. exercise.

I realize that this intensive review, coming on top of other requests for economic analyses and regular military assistance program reviews, will put a heavy burden on you and your associates since I would appreciate having your response by September 1 if possible. I also realize, however, the particular difficulties you are now facing and can well understand that you may feel a look into the next five years would not appear either practicable or worthwhile at this moment. If such should be the case, I would appreciate your view of an appropriate time to accomplish this task. I would hope on the other hand that this would not be too long delayed for we are faced with the need very soon to take a number of basic decisions on the nature and volume of military and economic aid to be programmed in FY 62 and that to be requested of the Congress in FY 63.

With warmest personal regards,
Sincerely,

**Dean**[5]

Enclosure 1[6]

PROPOSED MAP QUESTIONNAIRE FOR KOREA

I.   What alternative political developments may occur in Korea in the planning period with respect to such issues as unification, alliances, form of government?

A.   How do these relate to U.S. national interest?

B.   How do they relate to policy goals of the communist bloc?

C.   What military and economic requirements are associated with such developments?

---

[5] Printed from a copy that indicates Secretary Rusk signed the original.
[6] Secret.

II.  How can military assistance policies and programs contribute to overall U.S. aims in Korea?

A.  What are the military, economic, political, and social threats to U.S. interests in Korea over the planning period; which of these are likely to be the most serious; against which should (a) U.S., and (b) Korean resources be focused?

B.  What positive contributions can ROK forces make to the healthy development of Korea in the next few years and how can MAP programs encourage such contributions?

C.  Can MAP policy have any influence with the SCNR on the issue of civilian participation in government?

D.  What are the probable future military command relationships (UN, US, ROK) and how will these relationships affect military requirements and MAP policy?

III.  What role for ROK forces will best serve U.S. interests?

A.  Should this role be limited to meeting the threat from North Korea and maintaining internal security?

B.  If larger forces are to be maintained what considerations should limit their size.

C.  Does the "UN umbrella"—UN command structure, demilitarized zone, and U.S. forces in Korea and nearby—contribute a sufficient deterrent to communist attack even if the ROK forces were to be considerably reduced.

D.  Should ROK forces be considered for deployment outside of the area?

IV.  In the context of fundamental internal problems, what should be our approach to the threat of communist aggression against Korea from North Korea and Communist China?

A.  How might the chances of successful aggression relate to the internal situation?

B.  To what extent is Korea capable of developing forces to defeat such aggression?

C.  What risks are involved in maintaining an imbalance in ROK forces (e.g., lack of air force strength) and do U.S. policy considerations justify a continuation of this imbalance. Will U.S. and UN forces continue to be required in support of the ROK to meet external aggression in any event?

D.  What limits should be placed on the provision of modern and dual-capable weapons to ROK armed forces? What are the costs and risks in such a military emphasis?

E.  What added local facilities and military capabilities would be required to permit the introduction of larger UN or U.S. forces in defense of Korea?

V. How should the U.S. approach areas of difference between the U.S. and ROK views on military requirements and priorities?

A. What are the prospects of current ROK thinking on defense policies changing over the next five years?

B. What are the consequences and risks involved if divergent US/ROK views on military policies developed, e.g., is the ROK likely to launch an attack against North Korea; rely on its own resources in the event of a withdrawal or reduction in military assistance at the expense of ROK economic and social development?

C. What risks are involved for the U.S. if we accept fully ROK views on military requirements and priorities?

D. What are the prospects for changing the primary emphasis of U.S. programs from military to economic and what U.S. measures would be required to do this.

VI. Faced with severe limitations of local human, material, financial and institutional resources, how should local and external resources be distributed across the spectrum of possible uses (military, economic, and social) to achieve the desired long-term results of national strength and independence?

**Enclosure 2[7]**

ALTERNATIVES TO MILITARY ASSISTANCE FOR KOREA

I.  *Alternatives:*

The following proposals are alternatives to guidance used in preparation of the FY 62–67 MAP as per CW 608 of July 21, 1961 which includes, inter alia, retaining ground forces at the current level and providing equipment comparable in effectiveness to that possessed by forces of neighboring communist states. Further it should be assumed that there will be progressive reductions in supporting assistance throughout this period.

A.  *Alternative #1:*

Provide only maintenance support for current ROK Armed Forces for period 62–67, thus deferring currently planned force improvements, including the provision of complex and sophisticated weapon systems; i.e., missile systems and F–104 aircraft.

---

[7] Confidential.

B.  *Alternative #2:*

Reduce the current 600,000 ROK Armed Force by 50,000 men annually during the planning period FY 62–67; thus limiting U.S. military assistance support of ROK armed forces to 350,000 men commencing FY 68. This reduction in force and loss in combat capability is to be effected without off-setting modernization.

II.    *Assessment of Alternatives:*

For each alternative under I above, a summary of Country Team assessments should be provided covering as a minimum the following:

A.  The estimated political, military, and economic consequences of each alternative.

B.  A determination of the U.S. and country political, military, and economic measures which would be necessary if the alternatives were to be implemented.

C.  A feasible time schedule for the implementation of the alternatives.

D.  The order of magnitude costs of each alternative on the country and on military assistance, and supporting and other economic assistance programs for the period FY 62–67.

E.  An estimate of the interrelationship of each alternative with currently proposed development assistance requirements (CG 1066 of 23 June 61 and replies thereto).

---

**239.    Telegram From the Department of State to the Embassy in Korea**

Washington, August 5, 1961, 5:53 p.m.

222. Seoul's 236 rptd info Tokyo 105.[1]

1.  Dept concurs your comments para 4 reftel and believes clarification by Ambassador Berger of our position on return to civilian govt in

---

Source: Department of State, Central Files, 795B.00/8–461. Confidential; Priority; Limited Distribution. Drafted by Manhard, cleared by Koren, and approved by McConaughy.

[1] In telegram 236 from Seoul, August 4, the Embassy reported that it had indications that the younger members of the SCNR, Prime Minister Song, and KCIA Director Kim Chong-pil were resisting the idea of relinquishing military rule during the next 2 years. The Embassy also received an indication that Pak Chung-hui would welcome a private statement that the United States hoped for a quick return to civilian goverment. (Ibid.)

reasonably near future without pressing for specific date would be useful.[2]

2. If Embassy thinks it would be helpful in order disabuse PriMin Song and SCNR Colonels of notion that US favors prolonged military rule, Dept prepared to consider, upon Secretary's return, a letter from him to Song along line of Ambassador's intended clarification,[3] perhaps in reply Song's letter thanking Secretary for his July 27 press statement.[4]

---

[2] On August 12 the SCNR announced a program for eventual return of the government to civilian control under revised constitutional provisions. The government would begin drafting a new constitution and electoral law in October 1962, hold a referendum on the constitution in March 1963, and hold general elections for a president and a unicameral legislature in May 1963. Included in the program was an "Qualifications Examination Board" to approve candidates for elections. Berger advised the SCNR that the board was a poor idea as it would be open to manipulation. (Telegram 269 from Seoul, August 9; ibid., 795B.00/8–961)

[3] Berger met separately with Pak Chong-hui and Prime Minister Song over the weekend and used the opportunity to talk about restoration of civilian rule. Pak claimed there was no difference of opinion in the SCNR about the principle of restoration, just about timing. He promised to send Berger a plan for restoration. Song thought the restoration's timing was a difficult matter. If it came too soon, it would only restore incompetent and corrupt politicans and encourage factionalism. In light of Pak's promise of a plan, Berger thought that the Department should hold the Secretary's letter in abeyance. (Telegram 250 from Seoul, August 7; ibid., 795B.00/8–761)

[4] See footnote 2, Document 237.

**Ball**

---

## 240. Memorandum From Robert H. Johnson of the National Security Council Staff to the President's Deputy Special Assistant for National Security Affairs (Rostow)

Washington, August 9, 1961.

SUBJECT

Korea

During the last two or three days I have been trying to catch up on the situation with respect to the implementation of the Task Force report on Korea. It is very difficult, on the basis of available telegrams, to get any clear picture of where we stand in the implementation of the Task Force recommendations. The best message on this subject is the attached For-

---

Source: Kennedy Library, National Security Files, Countries Series, Korea, General, 7/61–2/62. Secret.

eign Service Despatch summarizing a conference between the Ambassador and the Economic Ministers of the Korean Government on June 29.[1]

You will note from this message that we have released the $28 million in remaining defense support assistance funds for FY 1961. We are currently involved in consideration of who should provide an economic team to go to Korea. We have not, so far as I have been able to determine, indicated our general willingness to aid the power industry and to support the National Construction Service. I am sure that we have had some discussion of these subjects in ICA channels, but to my knowledge they have not been raised in the manner authorized by Task Force recommendations in conversations between the Ambassador and Korean officials.

On the matter of an economic team, as I indicated to you earlier, there has been a controversy between State and ICA as to whom should be chosen. ICA has preferred the Arthur B. Little Company (economists named Cleveland and Bryce have been mentioned); State has preferred RAND primarily because of the apparent Korean preference for RAND. However there has been a recent message[2] indicating that now the Koreans may prefer Arthur B. Little (perhaps as a result of ICA–USOM missionary work in Korea). State and ICA agreed yesterday that RAND should do the job, subject however, to verifying that RAND is preferred by the Koreans. Charles Wolfe is in Washington today and tomorrow, discussing possible RAND participation with State and ICA. The ICA case against retention of RAND is contained in the attached telegram.[3]

In view of the lack of clarity as to where we stand on some of the Task Force recommendations, I have been pressing State to prepare a status report on the recommendations which could be circulated to the Task Force and which could be the basis for a Task Force discussion.

It is anticipated that the Task Force will have a meeting some time next week to discuss a JCS paper on Korean military forces.[4] Although

---

[1] Despatch 10 from Seoul, July 11. (Department of State, Central Files, 895B.00/7–1161)

[2] Not attached and not further identified.

[3] Johnson added the following handwritten note at this point: "I believe Carl Kaysen will put in a plug with the State people in support of RAND." The attached telegram was not identified further.

[4] JCSM–512–61, August 2, to Secretary McNamara, in which the Joint Chiefs presented a military assessment of the Communist threat to South Korea and ROK ability to defend itself. The Joint Chiefs concluded that although the threat in Korea remained strong, there was no evidence that the Communists would attack. ROK forces were capable of maintaining internal security and defending against minor incursions without assistance, but a successful defense of South Korea would require the use of allied forces already deployed there, PACOM air, and other support. A successful counteroffensive could not be carried out with existing forces. Current ROK force levels of 600,000 were the "minimum acceptable" as was current military assistance support. The Joint Chiefs recommended no changes in ROK force missions, U.S. and ROK force structure, or military assistance. (Washington National Records Center, RG 330, OSD Files: FRC 65 A 3464, Korea 091)

the latter paper has not yet been circulated, my general feeling about it is that any action on ROK forces must await the outcome of the general MAP review now going on.

**Bob**

---

## 241.  Memorandum of Conversation

Washington, August 11, 1961.

SUBJECT

Program for Return to Civilian Control of the Government of the Republic of Korea[1]

PARTICIPANTS

The Secretary
Mr. Il Kwon Chung, Korean Ambassador to the United States
Mr. Walter P. McConaughy, Assistant Secretary for Far Eastern Affairs
Mr. H. L. T. Koren, Director, Office of Northeast Asian Affairs

The Secretary called in Ambassador Chung this afternoon and said he wished to make some comments as a friend on some matters the Korean Government was going to decide in the next few days, emphasizing he did not wish to presume in questions which were of course for decision by the ROKG.

The Secretary referred to the conversations President Kennedy had last June with Chairman Khrushchev.[2] Khrushchev made the point that the Soviet Government was going to back popular regimes all over the world and that it was historically inevitable that Communism would

---

Source: Department of State, Central Files, 795B.00/8–1161. Confidential. Drafted by Koren and approved in S on August 17.

[1] In an August 11 memorandum drafted by Manhard and sent by McConaughy to Rusk FE recommended that he make four main points to Ambassador Il Kwon Chung: elections should be held earlier, the United States appreciated Pak's confidence in Berger and his frankness, the United States welcomed the ROK desire to reopen negotiations with Japan for better relations, and the U.S. desire to assist Korean economic development was undiminished. (Ibid., 601.95B11/8–1161)

[2] For documentation on the Kennedy–Khrushchev discussions at Vienna in June 1961, see volume V.

triumph in these countries. Khrushchev said that the U.S. finds itself the "gendarme of the status quo" and the U.S. would inevitably lose if we took this role against the will of the peoples. The President, in turn, pointed out the hypocrisy of this statement in that there was no Communist government currently in power which had achieved its status through free elections. Khrushchev had pointed to Korea as being vulnerable to his kind of penetration and that the military orientation of the present government made it susceptible to pressures from underneath such as would be stimulated by Khrushchev himself.

The Secretary stated that the ROK has a stake in the opinions of other states forming the body of the UN. The importance of the UN to Korea has been demonstrated over a considerable period, particularly in 1950, when a number of members joined the U.S. in resisting invasion not just for policy reasons, but also reflecting the general sentiment and opinion of the peoples. ROK has needed UN support in the past and may need it in the future. It is, therefore, vital for the safety and security of the ROK that it engender respect among the UN peoples.

The foregoing two comments, the Secretary said, were connected with the moves presently contemplated by the ROK toward reestablishment of constitutional government, and have a bearing on what will be shortly announced regarding elections. The Secretary expressed concern should elections be announced for as far away as 1963. Such a date would raise doubts whether this was indeed a serious proposal and whether the step was actually contemplated by the government.

The Secretary suggested consideration by ROKG of scheduling elections before the 1962 General Assembly meeting. He said that how the Korean question came before this year's General Assembly was not particularly serious, it being understood that the new government must have time to formulate and begin implementation of its governmental planning. It was reasonable to expect other governments would adopt a wait-and-see policy; however, this attitude would undoubtedly run out by the end of one year.

Indicating he had not discussed this idea with his colleagues, the Secretary wondered whether, if the ROKG did not feel it could announce elections before 1963, it might consider not specifying a date. The date of May 1963 might give the impression that the ROK feared elections. Mr. McConaughy thought there was something to be said for deferring announcing a specific date, but that it was our understanding that the Korean public were eagerly anticipating a specific announcement on August 14, and omitting a timetable would be a great disappointment. Ambassador Chung seconded this and the idea was dropped. In this connection, the Secretary inquired of the Ambassador how he felt the Korean people would react to the 1963 date. Ambassador replied it was hard to answer this definitely. He had been away on a trip until a few days ago and he had left Korea over four years ago, so he did not feel in a position to make a judgment.

The Secretary emphasized the spirit in which he made his comments. It was not up to the U.S. to say "when" but he considered it a friendly act to point out to the Ambassador the effect of the proposed election date on other countries and on the ROKG's international relations. Such a long postponement would undoubtedly be picked up by the communists and used in their propaganda. We have been encouraged by the progress made so far by the present government but he felt he ought to express our feeling of concern over the matter of election date. The decision was, however, entirely an ROK matter. The Secretary realized the great concern the ROKG felt on this matter, and the fact that it must balance many things. He hoped that the ROKG would take into account the fact that the date for elections will have an influence on the international position of the ROK. Many governments to whom the ROK has and will turn to for friendship are concerned over this matter, have consulted with us, and are anxious to see a steady progression to constitutional status.

The Ambassador thanked the Secretary for his advice. He did not feel in a position to give a definite answer, but he would try his best to influence his government and advise it in accordance with the Secretary's wishes.[3]

---

[3] On August 21–22 Major General Kim Dong Ha, Chairman of the Steering Committee of the SCNR, met with McConaughy and Under Secretary for Economic Affairs Ball during a visit to Washington. Both McConaughy and Ball stressed in their talks with General Kim the need for unity in the junta, fair and free elections in 1963, and continued economic reform. (Memoranda from Koren to McConaughy and McConaughy to Ball, both August 21; memoranda of conversation, August 21 and 22; ibid., 795B.00/8–2161 and 611.95B/8–2261)

## 242.   Progress Report

Washington, August 24, 1961.[1]

REVISED PROGRESS REPORT ON FOLLOW UP ACTIONS
RESPONSIVE TO RECOMMENDATIONS OF KOREA TASK
FORCE REPORT

(Keyed to Summary and Revision of Recommendations, dated
June 13, 1961)[2]

*Category I: U.S. Actions to be Undertaken Immediately*

1 a. Ambassador Berger and DCM Green have so informed the new
Korean leaders at the highest levels and on a number of occasions. Secretary Rusk issued a full statement along these lines to the press on July 27.[3]

1 b. See paragraph 2 below.

1 c. Done by Ambassador Berger and by the Secretary in his July 27
press statement (see 1 a above).

1 d. Ambassador Berger has made this clear to Korean leaders and
has provided a senior U.S. economic adviser to General Pak Chong-hui,
i.e., in mid-July Mr. Albert Boucher of USOM was temporarily detailed
to this advisory position on a full-time basis. At Ambassador Berger's
request, the State Department is actively recruiting the services of a team
of top-flight economic advisers to assist the Supreme Council in the formulation of Korea's long-range development program (also see 4 d).

1 e. The new Korean Government on May 26 agreed to restore
CINCUNC's operational control over the ROK armed forces, and CINC-
UNC's operational control appears to be essentially restored in practice.
Moreover, Embassy Seoul has recently reported that General Meloy is
receiving "excellent cooperation" in this field.

2. On August 12, Chairman Pak announced that the Korean Government would be turned back to civilian control in 1963 under a presidential system with a smaller unicameral legislature in accordance with
a time schedule calling for a new constitution before March 1963 and

---

Source: Kennedy Library, National Security Files, Countries Series, Korea, General,
7/61–2/62. Secret. Drafted by Manhard and Elizabeth Gallagher of NA.

[1] Based upon a draft submitted to the Task Force Meeting of August 17, revised by
State:FE:NA in accordance with ICA comments. [Footnote in the source text. The revisions
were apparently incorporated into this report on August 25, but the date of the memorandum remained August 24. No record of the Task Force meeting has been found.]

[2] See Document 230.

[3] See footnote 2, Document 237.

general elections in May 1963. Although this timetable is somewhat slower than we would have preferred, General Pak's announcement does represent a step in the right direction in that it provides a public commitment to return to representative constitutional government by a specific time.

3. The authorization to invite the chief of Government to Washington was originally prepared in the context of the announced desire of the previous Prime Minister, General Chang Do-young, to do so and has since been held in abeyance until the attitude of his successor should become clear. The new Prime Minister, General Song Yo-chan, is at present only a front man and completely subordinate to Supreme Council Chairman Pak, who has now indicated that he would like to visit Washington, briefly and informally, perhaps in late October or early November. In the meantime the Department has informed Embassy Seoul that we would be prepared to consider such a request, but that the President's schedule would probably preclude a visit before November. We are now awaiting Ambassador Berger's further recommendations.

4. The Korean Government has publicly expressed its intention to carry out the economic reform program agreed to by the previous regime, including maintenance of a unified exchange rate at 1300 hwan per dollar. (The new exchange rate system has not yet been implemented to the Embassy's complete satisfaction—see Embtel 106, July 19).[4] The electric power industry has been reorganized into a single corporation for improved administration. New and improved credit facilities have been established, banking and price controls generally eliminated, leading businessmen released from detention, and other actions taken to engender business confidence and stimulate the economy. In a recent message (Deptel 165, August 1)[5] Ambassador Berger stated: "Recent actions of military government leave little doubt of its ability to develop and instate measures and establish machinery to deal with present economic problems." However, economic confusion and stagnation continue; the private business sector has still not regained confidence to move ahead; the ROKG has still not fully complied with the economic undertakings of October, 1960; tax collections are lagging; and increases in money supply may lead to inflation.

4 a. The residual FY 1961 aid funds were released ($28 million, of which $25 million was for fertilizer) in the closing days of the '61 fiscal

---

[4] Not printed. (Department of State, Central Files, 895.B00/7–1961)

[5] The quote is not from telegram 165 to Seoul, July 26, in which the Department asked the Embassy for its current evaluation of the SCNR's ability to develop and implement promptly effective measures to solve Korea's economic problems. (Ibid.) The quote is taken from the Embassy's response to telegram 165, telegram 206 from Seoul, August 1. (Ibid., 895B.00/8–161)

year. Ambassador Berger has requested waiver of the preferential U.S. procurement policy for fertilizer; this matter is under ICA consideration.

4 b. Expansion of electric power will receive high priority as soon as Ambassador Berger makes a determination as to the eligibility of Korea for continuing developmental assistance, based upon Korean willingness and ability to carry out a long-range development program. Meanwhile, DLF has undertaken preliminary work on several proposed power projects, in order to be in a position to take immediate action on all pending loan applications as soon as the "go-head" decision is taken. USOM is engaged in preparing a long-range power development plan in conjunction with the ROKG and Commonwealth Associates.

4 c. Although the new regime has indicated plans to expand the National Construction Service, the Embassy has reported that the program is not fully under way; local currency financing appears to be the bottleneck. Under present circumstances, it is doubtful that additional U.S. support of the program is necessary or practicable. If and when it appears that additional U.S. support can be advantageously utilized, it will be made available to the ROKG.

4 d. The ICA is urgently attempting to contract for a team of specialists to assist the ROKG in preparation of its Five-Year Development Plan (see 1d above). The choice appears to be between the RAND Corporation and the Arthur D. Little Company; a decision is expected to be made within the next few days and the team should be in Seoul within the next few weeks.

4 e. Ambassador Berger has on several occasions informed the Korean Government of the terms on which developmental funds will be available. Commitments to the support of specific undertakings necessarily await formulation of an agreed Five-Year Development Plan. The draft plan prepared by the ROKG, as it now stands, is hastily prepared, and contains unrealistic assumptions.

5.   Over the past year and one-half, USOM/Korea has made a considerable reduction in its staff, and it is considered desirable to await the new Director's arrival in Korea (in early September) before undertaking further actions to streamline USOM operations with a view to eliminating unessential projects.

*Category II: Subsequent U.S. Actions*

6.   The proposal to send a Special Envoy accompanied by a group of economic advisers was directed toward a contingency situation which has not yet arisen. In a recent cable (Embtel 146, July 24)[6] Ambassador Berger stated that he was not prepared to recommend at this time that the Department send a Special Envoy and team on long-range economic

---

[6] Not printed. (Ibid., 795B.00/7–2461)

program as visualized in the NSC Paper, adding that this is something we can do, if at all, later when we see how situation evolves and what effect emergency economic measures have on the economy.

In regard to the question of consulting other Free World nations about the possibility of contributing to a Korean Five-Year Development Plan, Embassy Bonn has been alerted to our interest, but we feel that it is premature to approach Japan on this subject, at least until ROK receptivity to such Japanese assistance can be ascertained. It is doubtful that the Korean Government will be willing to entertain Japanese offers of economic assistance until and unless at least most of the basic issues outstanding between the two countries have been resolved, particularly Korean claims against Japan. (Our Embassy has recently reported a serious resolve on the part of the ROKG to resume negotiations with Japan in the near future aimed at a settlement of basic issues.)

7.  These announcements have not yet been made, not only because Congressional appropriations have not yet been determined, but also because while the Korean Government has consolidated the power companies, administration of the power industry and its financial and rate structure is still under Embassy/USOM observation.

8.  The question of ROK force levels has been reviewed by Defense on the basis of a preliminary assessment from the field, and the Defense Department assessment thereof will be transmitted to the State Department in the very near future.

9.  This subject is included in the Defense assessment referred to in paragraph 8 above.

10. The improvement of ROK-Japan relations was discussed with the Japanese Prime Minister during his visit to Washington and has been discussed in a similar vein by Ambassador Berger in Seoul. It has been made clear to the Japanese and Korean Governments that the Japanese settlement of GARIOA is not to be related to U.S. and Japanese aid to Korea. We anticipate that ROK-Japanese relations will be resumed in September or October. There are indications that the Korean Government may have decided to seek solutions to outstanding issues, but it is not clear whether the ROK is prepared to make realistic compromises with the Japanese or whether the Japanese Government is yet prepared to reach settlements with the new Korean Military Government so soon after the military coup.

11. These activities are subject to further review by USIA in the light of our developing overall policy toward the new ROK Government.

*Category III: Required Korean Actions*

12 a. The Korean Government has issued a preliminary Five-Year Economic Plan which is to be reviewed by a team of experts who will advise the ROK Government in the plan's implementation.

12 b. The SCNR Chairman, General Pak, issued a statement on this subject on August 12, in which general elections were scheduled for May 1963.

12 c. The Korean Government has indicated its intention to cooperate fully with CINCUNC, who has stated that he is now receiving "excellent cooperation" from Korean military leaders.

12 d. General Pak has indicated that he intends to grant a large-scale amnesty to many of those imprisoned after the coup and to deal leniently with military leaders who did not cooperate with the coup. Moreover on August 12 he promised to return the Government to civilian control in 1963 (see paragraph 2 above). In this connection, over 5,000 prisoners were released on August 15, including former First Army Commander Lee Han-lim.

12 e. The Korean Government has taken a number of actions specifically designed to reduce usurious practices among the rural population.

12 f. The Korean Government has issued many decrees and taken many actions which appear sincerely designed to root out corruption throughout the Korean society.

---

### 243.  National Intelligence Estimate

NIE 14.2/42–61                      Washington, September 7, 1961.

#### THE OUTLOOK FOR KOREA

#### The Problem

To estimate the major trends and prospects in South Korea, with particular attention to the impact of North Korea on the south over the next two or three years.

#### Conclusions

1.  In its push to unify Korea under Communist control, the North Korean regime will continue to depend primarily on subversive tactics

---

Source: Department of State, INR/EAP Files: Lot 90 D 110. Secret. According to a note on the cover sheet, the Central Intelligence Agency and intelligence organizations of the Departments of State, Defense, the Army, the Navy, and the Air Force, and the Joint Staff participated in the preparation of this estimate. All members of the USIB concurred with this estimate on September 7 except the representatives of the AEC and the FBI, who abstained on the grounds that the subject was outside their jurisdiction.

and propaganda appealing to nationalistic sentiments and stressing the economic benefits of unification. Although these efforts have had little effect, the Communists probably believe their longer term prospects for a favorable response to its unification appeals are good and improving. In view of this and the automatic involvement of US forces in any resumption of hostilities in Korea, we believe the Communists are not likely to assume the grave risks of armed action against South Korea over the next several years. (Paras. 12–25, 50–53)

2.  The greatest threat to South Korea, at least in the near term, comes from within South Korea. The country lacks a sense of national purpose and faces both tremendous economic problems and a brittle political situation. The military junta seeks to provide the drive and stability which was lacking in the previous civilian government but is subject to internal factionalism and lacks general public support in confronting these enormous problems. (Paras. 28–38, 54)

3.  The prospect for South Korea over the next few years is therefore very cloudy and uncertain. US aid will probably succeed in preventing economic collapse. However, even under the most favorable circumstances, progress will be slow and South Korea will continue to require large-scale foreign aid for the indefinite future if it is to remain an independent nation allied with the West. (Paras. 39–42, 55)

4.  The political situation is subject to sudden and rapid change. Much depends on future actions of the junta, in particular, on its capacity to establish a sense of forward momentum among the Korean people. If the overall situation in South Korea fails to improve significantly and the people lose hope for national progress, the continued enticements offered by the North Korean regime could lead to some movement in the south toward an accommodation with the north. (Paras. 23–33, 56)

[Here follows the Discussion section of the estimate.]

## 244.  Telegram From the Embassy in Korea to the Department of State

Seoul, October 28, 1961, 6 p.m.

640. Department pass Defense, AID. This tel in two parts. This is part one.

1. This message is further response I promised in my reply of September 14[1] to Secretary's letter of August 1.[2] It identifies and defines the basic problems involving our economic and military aid programs for Korea. It represents distillation many hours of study and discussion by Country Team members and staff and is a joint and agreed message from General Meloy, Killen and me. This part of message gives immediate political background of problems. Second part deals with economic aspects.[3]

2. Military government has now been in power five months. It has taken hold with energy, earnestness, determination and imagination, albeit with certain authoritarian and military characteristics which have hampered its public image. Though it has no popular base and there is little evidence of positive popular enthusiasm, it is nonetheless a genuine revolution from the top trying to introduce sweeping reforms of a most fundamental kind. Projects of reform long talked about or under actual consideration by previous governments are becoming realities in banking and credit policy, foreign trade, increased public works for unemployed, tax evasion, agriculture, trade union organization, education, public administration, social welfare (prison reform, rehabilitation of prostitutes, birth control information, assistance to veterans and their survivors) and other fields. Many reforms are constructive and some long urged by American advisors. Others while well-intentioned have been too hastily developed or are poorly implemented. Some of these latter already undergone correction, for government, at least in some cases, prepared admit and correct mistakes.

3. Military government's efforts to deal with wholesale graft, bribery and corruption in government and business, smuggling, large-scale diversion of military supplies, hoodlum terror, and police and press

---

Source: Department of State, Central Files, 795B.5–MSP/10–2861. Secret. Also sent to Tokyo and CINCPAC for POLAD.

[1] Not found.

[2] Document 238.

[3] Telegram 642, October 28, in which the Embassy defined the basic unresolved problem of U.S. assistance to Korea. U.S. policy sought to replace supporting assistance and P.L. 480 aid with development loans to encourage economic independence. Because of the scale of U.S. assistance, however, the goal of economic independence would take much longer in Korea. (Department of State, Central Files, 795B.5–MSP/10–2861)

blackmail of individuals are genuine and are producing results. Vigilance against communist subversion and quality and volume anti-communist propaganda have greatly improved.

4.  Government administration, while improved in sense now possible get rapid top-side decisions, suffering from continuous changes in intermediate and senior personnel, but situation gradually stabilizing this regard. Majority of Cabinet ministers with military background have impressed us with their competence and effectiveness for administration. Others less so. Physical breakdowns from overwork becoming problem. PriMin has not been well for a month; Min of Comm and Ind Maj Gen Chonghmae-hyok, one of ablest, collapsed from exhaustion at Cabinet meeting but now back to work after two weeks rest. Chairman Economic Planning Board and Vice Premier, Kim Yu-taek, ordered take two months off. Chairman Pak himself showing some signs of strain from overwork.

5.  Increase in administrative efficiency arising from competence of able ministers is handicapped by absence of clear division of responsibility and functions between Supreme Council and Cabinet. Some Supreme Council members are interfering and overriding Cabinet decisions and some military ministers by-passing PriMin. This is producing frictions and in some cases erratic decisions involving increased government expenditures.

PriMin endeavoring establish that Supreme Council limit itself to legislative functions and leave executive functions to Cabinet. He is also endeavoring stop ministers from by-passing Cabinet. He is having difficulty establishing these principles. One reason for this is he not one of original coup group, is tainted by service during Rhee regime, and is suspected of harboring personal political ambitions.

6.  Military government has its enemies, but it is not without support. If it has little positive support, it can claim with justice that it does considerable mass good will on part of many who fear a return to instability and drifting and who hope it will succeed in laying foundation for regeneration of Korea before it returns government to civilian hands in spring-summer of 1963 in accordance August 12 promise Chairman Pak. Very large part of population, however, remain non-committal, and "wait and see" remains most characteristic attitude of majority of Koreans. This attitude, almost indistinguishable from skepticism, springs from traditional lack of confidence that Koreans and especially those who govern Korea can be effective for long, will not succumb to corruption and factionalism, or can contain their urge to dominate once they are in power.

7.  Too soon to say where this revolution will end. There is evidence traditional propensity for factionalism is asserting itself inside Supreme Council. Most serious case occurred during September and first week of

October when bitter internal power struggle was initiated by Kim Chong-p'il, Director ROK CIA, and some young Colonels aimed at purging Generals from Hamgyong Province. But there also evidence that Chairman Pak and others are determined to prevent this and internal power situation has become a little more stable in last couple weeks. However, long-term problem far from resolved. There are also a few signs of corruption and graft again appearing in high places. Here again Pak and others are determined to expose and deal with it ruthlessly. At this writing cannot be said with any certainty that military government will not succumb to endemic factionalism or financial scandals during two years it has set for its term of office. Much will depend on Chairman Pak, who is coolest head and most reliable and stable of leaders. We shall better be able assess these dangers in course of next three months or so.

8.   Second threat to stability of government stems from possibility of spiraling price inflation next year. In its determination to make fundamental reforms before it returns power civilian hands, government is trying to do too much too quickly. Public works to relieve unemployment, farm reforms (high and stable rice prices by means of rice supports, refinancing usurious loans, fertilizer subsidies), prospective increases next year in pay rates of government employees and military in order give these dignity and reduce temptation for graft, provision of loan capital at reasonable rates to small and medium industry, and step-up in capital investment in public sector are all worthy objectives. But they are all being pursued simultaneously and government borrowing and money in circulation have expanded rapidly with prospects of further increases next year. Manufacturing and trade only gradually reviving from summer low.

9.   Here too there are offsetting factors so that situation not entirely one-sided. Tax evasion has been curtailed, and if manufacturing and trade expand, collections should be much better in future. Higher interest rates on time deposits are encouraging savings. Economic cost of doing business should be reduced with reduction in heavy political contributions and bribes. All or nearly all government enterprises have in past run with heavy losses and subsidies. Most flagrant cases being reorganized and if efforts successful should cut losses substantially. Improved government systems of purchasing, audit, and inventory control in both civilian and military sectors promise considerable savings. High level of foreign exchange reserves will enable government to import if necessary to hold down price inflation. Forced saving measures under consideration. Prices have remained fairly stable since May 16. Finally there is growing awareness by top leaders of need for restraint in government expenditures and greater selectivity in their program priorities.

10. In final analysis ability control price inflation will depend on more rapid revival of manufacturing and trade to meet potential demand which has been created. This in turn requires government settlement with illicit profiteers and tax evaders who control Korean industry and who have been dragging their heels in effort obtain better terms on their assessments and fines. Pak decided settlement imperative, and supported proposal made by profiteers to PriMin Song to pay their assessments over period of years in form of capital investment in new industries, with government holding equity. This has now received SCNR approval. There is therefore chance price inflation may not get out of hand. We will be in better position to assess this danger in two or three months.

11. Further source of danger to stability of government is more intangible and more difficult to assess. It arises from activities of Kim Chong-p'il and ROK CIA. This organization is watchdog of government, has extensive organization, which also embraces military, holds great power. Use of wire-tapping, informers and mail censorship widespread. Practice of "taking people into custody for questioning"—local euphemism for arrest without warrant—(sometimes for weeks) and practice of midnight arrests and reports of strong-arm methods to extract confessions, still occur with sufficient frequency to maintain atmosphere of insecurity and fear. Many Koreans in public or business circles have blemished records in respect to graft or bribes, dealing in diverted military supplies, evading taxes, or smuggling, have associations with past governments or with men under arrest or suspicion which could be invoked against them. Many have reservations about this government or some facets of it and have been indiscreet in expressing them. All this combines to produce pervasive tension that cannot be ignored in our calculations. It clearly plain in government, in active military service, in and outside Embassies, and even the Supreme Council members and the Cabinet.

12. Pak and Supreme Council have taken some steps to deal with this fear. Announcements have been made that certain offenses committed prior to the coup and persons who have not been investigated for certain illegalities before certain dates will not be prosecuted. Certain arrests now require warrants and high level arrests need personal approval of Pak. "Habeas corpus" is still in the law and in use, although it is being suspended in particular cases.

13. Despite above limitations and considerable pressure both in and out of government to limit CIA's power, power of Kim Chong-p'il is still great enough to represent serious unsettling element in situation, and is a factor in factional fight in Supreme Council. There will be no relaxation in this country until CIA's power is contained or more judiciously exercised. Pak aware that Kim Chong-p'il is capable of excesses arising from

his exuberance for power and his inexperience, but Pak relies heavily on Kim Chong-p'il to detect subversion, disloyalty, dishonesty and conspiracy, and these are four factors in situation which cannot be brushed away. It is our hope that when present Revolutionary Court trials are finished, which is planned for end of this year, atmosphere will become much less tense.

15. From United States point of view, despite above dangers, this government still offers much hope. Gen Meloy, Killen and I are encouraged by fact we have access to top leaders and they are often responsive to our private counsel and advice and sensitive to United States and world opinion. They are determined to establish Korea on far sounder basis in all respects and if they can deal successfully with above dangers, there could be established a stable political and economic environment for progress over next few years. In this event, basic economic growth, which has top priority in their thinking, could be rapid. This however, will be strongly influenced by solutions to problems posed in part two this tel.

**Berger**

## 245.  Memorandum of Conversation

Seoul, November 5, 1961, 9:30 a.m.

SUBJECT

The Secretary's Call on Chairman Park Chung Hee[1]

PARTICIPANTS

Chairman Park Chung Hee[2]
The Secretary of State
Ambassador Samuel D. Berger

1.  The Chairman welcomed the Secretary to Seoul.

2.  The Secretary said President Kennedy was looking forward with pleasure to the Chairman's visit,[3] and the Chairman and his colleagues could be assured of a friendly welcome. The American Government was greatly impressed by the military government's efforts to deal with corruption, and with the energy with which it was tackling many Korean problems. He knew that the American Government had made many mistakes in Korea, at the same time it must be said that the performance of past Korean Governments has been disappointing and unsatisfactory. The military government was doing many things to establish economic, political and social life on a new basis, and the Secretary wished the Chairman to know that we supported these efforts.

3.  The Secretary asked if there was anything the Chairman wished him to convey to the President in advance of the visit. Chairman Pak said he was sure General Meloy, Mr. Killen and Ambassador Berger had made the necessary reports on the situation in Korea so that he knew the President would be fully informed in advance, and he had nothing to suggest.

4.  The Secretary said the President would want to talk with him about the dangerous world situation which exists over Berlin. Khru-

---

Source: Department of State, Central Files, 795B.00/11–561. Secret. Drafted by Berger and approved in S on November 11. The meeting was held at Park Chung Hee's residence.

[1] Rusk had just attended a meeting of the Joint U.S.-Japan Committee on Trade and Economic Affairs in Japan November 2–5. He was in Seoul November 5 and returned to Washington on November 6. Rusk also met with President Po Sun-yun at 9 a.m. A record of that meeting is in a November 5 memorandum of conversation. (Ibid., 795B.11/11–561) At 2:15 p.m. Rusk met with Prime Minister Song Yo-chan and members of the ROK Cabinet responsible for economic affairs to discuss U.S. aid to Korea. Rusk reiterated U.S. determination to aid Korea, but stressed that resources were limited. (Memorandum of conversation, November 5; ibid., 795B.00/11–561)

[2] In August 1961 Pak Chung-hui requested that his name be spelled in correspondence and publications as Park Chung Hee. The spelling used within Department of State internal and telegraphic correspondence remained the standard McCune–Reischauer transliteration of Korean characters: Park Chung-hui or Pak Chong-hui.

[3] See Document 247.

shchev was set on a course which unless he changed was headed for collision. The effects could be immediately felt everywhere including the Korean front. He was sure the Chairman, as a military man, realized that the Korean and U.S. forces must be on the alert. Moreover, it was important during this period of crisis to maintain Korean military forces at their present strength. The Chairman said the Korean Government had every intention of maintaining its military forces at full strength.

5.  The Secretary congratulated the Chairman on his promotion to full General.

6.  The Chairman said it was 10:00 a.m. and the Republic of Korea was observing a minute of silence in protest against Soviet nuclear tests.

7.  Resuming, the Secretary said he had talked with Prime Minister Ikeda on the need for a Korean-Japanese settlement.[4] Ikeda had a full appreciation both of the need for and the importance of a settlement. Ikeda, as the Chairman knew, had domestic opposition to a settlement from the Socialists. In his talks with Ikeda, it was evident that he realized that the Chairman also had his domestic problems. The Secretary said he was pleased that the Chairman was stopping in Tokyo en route to the U.S. for a long talk with Ikeda. Face-to-face talks and quiet diplomacy were the only way to deal with problems as emotionally loaded as this one was. The Secretary said he was confident that only good could come from these talks, and he hoped that a new chapter was about to be written in Korean-Japanese relations. The Secretary said the U.S. Government could not and should not involve itself directly as a mediator or intermediary in these negotiations, but he wished to say to the Chairman that if he thought we could be helpful we would be ready to do what we could.

8.  The Chairman nodded approvingly while these remarks were made. The Chairman said he thought the Japanese sincerely wished a settlement and he hoped in his direct talks with Ikeda to establish the basis for successful negotiations. He hoped that an understanding could be reached soon, and thanked the Secretary for his offer to be helpful.

*Note:* Chairman Park's Aide Col Cho interpreted. Mr. Campen of the Embassy stood by to check the interpretation.

---

[4] A memorandum of that discussion, November 2, is in Department of State, Central Files, 694.95B/11–261.

## 246.  Memorandum of Conversation

Washington, November 14, 1961, 10 a.m.

SUBJECT

Korean-United States Tour d' Horizon

PARTICIPANTS

| | |
|---|---|
| Gen. Chung Hee Park, Chairman | The Secretary of State |
| Maj. Gen. Yang Soo Yoo, Chairman, | Ambassador Samuel D. Berger |
| Foreign Affairs Natl. Defense | Mr. W.P. McConaughy, Assistant |
| Duk Shin Choi, Foreign Minister | Secretary for Far Eastern Affairs |
| Byung Kyu Chun, Finance Minister | Mr. J.S. Killen, Director, USOM/Korea |
| Byeng Kwon Bak, Minister of Defense | Mr. H.L.T. Koren, NA Director |
| Chung Pum Song, Deputy Chairman, | Mr. D.S. Macdonald, NA |
| Economic Planning Board | Dr. Paul S. Crane, Interpreter |
| Il Kwon Chung, Korean Ambassador | Mr. Avery F. Peterson, Deputy |
| Sang Ho Cho, Interpreter | Assistant Secretary for Far Eastern |
| | Affairs |

The meeting convened in the Secretary's Conference Room at ten o'clock Tuesday, November 14. The Secretary extended a warm welcome to Chairman Park and his party, and expressed his appreciation for his reception in Korea on the occasion of his recent visit there.[1] He said that the United States was impressed with the Chairman's accomplishments and those of his Government in Korea at present, and that he looked forward to an opportunity to make the current series of talks as profitable as possible for both sides.

Chairman Park said he appreciated the warm welcome he had received. Referring to the ceremony at the Tomb of the Unknown Soldier, from which he had just come, he said he had been deeply touched at this recollection of American sacrifice for Korea, and appeared at the conference table with deep feeling. The Secretary said he had been struck by a small but significant incident at the airport: Chairman Park's thoughtful greeting for the Korean community after the welcoming ceremony was a simple but expressive gesture and the first such action that he had observed.

---

Source: Department of State, Central Files, 895B.00–FIVE YEAR/11–1461. Confidential. Drafted by Macdonald and approved in S on November 28. McConaughy proposed to Rusk on August 31 that Pak undertake an informal working visit to Washington in November. McConaughy noted that the visit would be in keeping with the recommendations of the Korean Task Force Report and pointed out the advantages for Pak of meeting with senior U.S. officials. (Memorandum from McConaughy to Rusk, August 31; ibid., 933.95B11/8–3161) Pak was in Washington November 14–16.

[1] See Document 245.

Continuing, the Secretary said he attached the highest importance to the forthcoming talks with the Administrator of AID[2] and with the President.[3] The purpose of the present meeting would be to review matters in a preliminary way; he would like the Chairman to raise any points he might wish on his side, following which the Secretary might have a few to raise for his part.

Chairman Park said that the first purpose of his visit was to convey thanks for United States assistance. He wished also to take the opportunity to present his views on the problems of Korea and his recommendations. He believed the Secretary was already familiar with most of the major problems since he had visited Korea and had been briefed by the Government Ministers there; moreover, Ambassador Berger and Mr. Killen had reported to him in Washington. In a way it was odd to reiterate this material, but he would like to re-emphasize the points the Secretary already knew. The Secretary replied that he would be happy to hear the Chairman's views and recalled his long association with Korea.

The Chairman stated that in view of the Communist threat, Korea must maintain her armed forces strength of 600,000, but at the same time Korea must develop economically. These two major problems must go together. The United States was aware of the decrease in force maintenance assistance since 1960, with the consequent increase in the Korean proportion of force maintenance. Korea was making all possible efforts on its own to take over America's share of the burden, because the problem affected the over-all defense posture throughout the Free World. However, the Korean Government had prepared a five-year economic development program. The increase in the defense budget imposed a burden on economic development. Therefore, until the economy was stabilized to a certain extent, he hoped the level of United States military assistance would be maintained at the level of 1959 for force maintenance.

The Chairman pointed out that to remain as the staunchest anti-Communist country, for which an armed forces strength of 600,000 men was imperative, it was necessary to obtain as much economic aid as possible until the five-year program was completed. It had been reported, although not verified, that supporting assistance was to be decreased. If true, this fact would reflect a great deal on the economic program. Accordingly, the Chairman requested that this year's level be maintained.

---

[2] Pak met the Administrator of the Agency for International Development, Fowler Hamilton, at 11 a.m., and discussed assistance and development. Pak stressed the need for maintaining at the current level U.S. support for the ROK's 600,000-man armed forces and strong and positive support for its Five-Year Plan. (Memorandum of conversation, November 14; Department of State, Central Files, 811.0095B/11–1461)

[3] See Document 247.

The Chairman continued that, in order to carry out the five-year economic program for the next year, Korea had planned to invite large foreign investment loans. Korea was faced with a shortage of hwan to meet the local currency requirements associated with such loans. It was, therefore, necessary to ask for a loan of $100 million as a special, or stabilization fund plus $70 million from DLF, and technical assistance of $8 million. Of course, this might seem a large request, and the Chairman recognized that the United States had its own problems; but to maintain a strong anti-Communist nation and 600,000 troops, Korea needed this amount of United States assistance. The Chairman said he recognized that he had reiterated items the Secretary had already known about, but wished nonetheless to repeat them.

The Secretary replied that he was glad to discuss the policy aspects of Korea's requirements with the Chairman; there would be opportunity during the visit to discuss the subject in more detail.[4] He continued that, first, the American people and Government felt a strong commitment to uphold the safety and independence of the Republic of Korea. This feeling was not based solely upon the Mutual Defense Treaty. The United States had already made a very large investment in Korea's independence and security in terms of men and resources. Moreover, in the present world situation, the facts of international life gave the United States a powerful interest in the security of the Republic of Korea. In this connection, the Secretary said that the United States had had some extremely dangerous questions on its agenda this year which touched closely the Sino-Soviet bloc—Berlin, Southeast Asia, the Congo, and other points of immediate friction, of which the Chairman was aware. The United States had not thought it wise on its side to inflame other issues and points of friction, such as the Middle East, Iran, and Korea, by making speeches about them. The United States had a direct and fundamental commitment to Korea, but we did not think it wise to make speeches on Korea vis-à-vis the communists at this time.

The Free World will go through a period of great danger in the next few months. In the case of Berlin, although there had been some apparent reduction of tension in one or two procedural matters, there was still conflict between the powers concerned on the basic issues. Speaking to the

---

[4] Pak met with Walt Rostow, Hamilton, McConaughy, and others for an informal discussion of ROK economic planning on November 16. (Memorandum of conversation, November 16; Department of State, Central Files, 895B.00/11–1661) He also met with Secretary of Defense McNamara and Defense officials on November 15. (Memorandum of conversation, I–17979/61; Washington National Records Center, RG 330, OASD/ISA Files: FRC 64 A 2382, 333 Korea) William Bundy also sent a letter to Felt and Meloy, November 18, describing the contacts between Pak and the Koreans and the Department of Defense during the visit. (Ibid.) Pak also met Secretary of Commerce Luther H. Hodges on November 15 at 2:30 p.m. They discussed mutual trade and ROK development. (Memorandum of conversation, November 15; Department of State, Central Files, 795B.00/11–1561)

Chairman in the most private possible sense, the Secretary wished to say that Khrushchev was still on a collision course in respect to Berlin. Similarly, in Southeast Asia it was apparent that the Sino-Soviet bloc was engaged in a "sacred war of liberation," which the Free World would define as an illegal war of enslavement. In respect to Viet-Nam, the United States would be taking basic measures which would become apparent in the future. The Secretary explained that he was saying this to the Chairman because it was important to him even though these points were distant from Korea; it was unlikely there could be tension in troubled areas without having effects all around the Sino-Soviet bloc. Accordingly, the Secretary said, he agreed with the Chairman that Korean and United States forces in Korea should be in a good state of readiness and preparation in the months ahead. The Chairman could rely completely on the presence of American armed forces in Korea as tangible and, the Secretary thought, convincing evidence of the United States commitment in Korea.

In respect to assistance, both military and economic, the Secretary recalled that an Englishman once termed economics "the dismal science," because those on the policy side demanded more than those on the resource side could furnish. This was surely true in Korea as in the United States. He wished to give background on one special part of the problem: The Kennedy administration and Congress felt it necessary to review in broadest terms the experience of fifteen years with United States foreign aid, because it was felt that the American people had become weary of foreign aid and needed a new program they could support with good conscience and some degree of enthusiasm. Great emphasis had been put in the administration's foreign aid program on long-term economic development and support for such programs as Korea's five-year development plan. Unfortunately, the Congress had taken up the idea of long-range development, but at the same time had put pressure on reducing military assistance, supporting assistance, and short-term assistance generally. He wished to say with great sincerity and without giving offense that it seemed some aid given on a short-term basis had not been used to best advantage in some countries, including Korea. The same reasons which had led Chairman Park and his Government to take power led the United States to believe that aid had not been used to best advantage. The attitude of Congress was heavily influenced by the past, and it had not been able to take into account developments at the present time. Korea had problems but the United States had also, such as those just stated. The United States would endeavor to work out solutions realistically and speedily with Chairman Park and his Government, taking account of defense needs, not only in Korea but in the entire world, and of the need also for economic and social development.

The Secretary continued that there were one or two points he would like to make which had bearing on the question of need: first, whether there were aspects of economic development where added assistance might be provided by the armed forces as a part of their training operations without interfering with their combat readiness—in such fields as engineering, signal communications, and health. The Secretary said that the Prime Minister had pointed to the limitations on armed forces participation because of the unemployment problem, but he left it as something to consider, based on his own armed forces experience. He realized that soldiers in all countries felt it their duty to fight, not to work, but he still supported the possibility. A second possibility, the Secretary said, was the contribution which might result from relations with Japan. He would welcome the observations which the Chairman might wish to make. A third point was that, although there might be legal limits on various categories of United States assistance, there were "many ways to skin a cat," and the United States would work with Korea to find solutions to problems.

Chairman Park responded that, as a citizen of Korea, he wished to express his deep regret that United States assistance had not always been utilized to best effect. The Secretary interjected that it would be better to say that there had been mistakes on both sides. The Chairman continued that he also fully realized the United States, as leader of the Free World, must give consideration to many countries other than Korea. All came to the United States and looked to the United States for assistance and support; if it continued, the United States would exhaust its resources for aid. Unless they attained self-sufficiency one by one, eventually Free World strength would deteriorate. He noted the Secretary had pointed out that one of the reasons for the recent revolution was ineffective use of United States assistance. The present revolutionary government was fully aware it must strive for self-sufficiency so that gradually United States aid could be decreased. Also, the Secretary had pointed out the orientation of United States policy toward long-term loans rather than grant assistance; however, in Korea it was impossible to switch from one to the other at once. The Secretary responded that he recognized Korea's problem in this regard.

However, if present United States assistance was continued for the next few years, Korea would be able to lay the foundations for transition to long-term loans.

The Chairman referred to questions raised by the Secretary. Regarding the Secretary's suggestion on the utilization of the armed forces in economic development, the Government was planning to make maximum utilization of them and had already started in that direction. In his opinion, it was mandatory so to use the armed forces, so long as their primary duty was not imperiled.

In respect to his meeting with Prime Minister Ikeda en route to the United States, the Chairman keenly felt it was necessary to normalize relations between the two countries to assure peace and security for the Far East. This was the consensus of himself and other Government leaders, but he could not say Korean public opinion was the same as theirs. In order to satisfy public sentiment, it was necessary to solve a couple of pending issues before the relationship between the two countries was normalized. On this point, he had had an exchange of frank views with Prime Minister Ikeda at an exclusive private interview. Both men had agreed the two countries must normalize diplomatic relations at the earliest opportunity. To attain this, a couple of problems remained to be solved; administrative and technical details had to be ironed out at working levels. This done, economic relations between Korea and Japan could be taken into consideration. It was a fact that some knowledgeable people in Korea expressed concern at possible Japanese economic aggression if relations were normalized, especially in view of past history. The Government was using all prudence in normalizing relations with Japan.

The Secretary said he wanted to repeat what he had said to the Prime Minister—that he did not expect settlement with Japan to provide a substitute for United States aid, but rather a supplementary resource. Though it was a matter for the experts, the Secretary felt some aspect of a Korea–Japan settlement might provide a hwan contribution, perhaps through some interlocking arrangement with the United States.

Chairman Park said that this matter was too technical to answer, but asked the Secretary whether he could give the Korean side some hope in respect to the question that he had raised. The Secretary said he would rather let Mr. Hamilton discuss these questions, and perhaps he himself could talk to the Chairman before he left.[5] There would also be conversations with the President. He wished to make clear that this response should not be taken as a negative answer.

In concluding, the Secretary expressed his belief that the amnesty measures taken by the Korean Government would contribute to the international standing of Korea and stated his view that the Chairman was to be congratulated on this step.

---

[5] See Document 248.

## 247.  Memorandum of Conversation

Washington, November 14, 1961, 3:30–4:50 p.m.

SUBJECT

U.S.-Korean Relations

PARTICIPANTS

*Korea*
Gen. Chung Hee Park, Chairman, Supreme Council for National Reconstruction
Major Gen. Yang So Yoo, Foreign Affairs National Defense Committee, SCNR
Minister Duk Shin Choi, Foreign Minister
Minister Byung Kyu Chun, Finance Minister
Minister Byeng Kown Bak, Defense Minister
Minister Chung Pum Song, Deputy Chairman, Economic Planning Board
Ambassador Il Kwon Chung, Korean Ambassador to the United States
Lt. Col. Sang Kuh Han, Interpreter

*United States*
The President
Secretary Rusk
Secretary McNamara
Ambassador Samuel D. Berger, United States Ambassador to Korea
Dr. Walt Rostow
Mr. Fowler Hamilton, Administrator, Agency for International Development
Mr. Walter P. McConaughy, Assistant Secretary of State for Far Eastern Affairs
Mr. James S. Killen, Director, USOM Korea
Mr. H. L. T. Koren, Director, Northeast Asian Affairs
Dr. Paul S. Crane, Interpreter

The President read the joint communiqué and said it appeared satisfactory to him. If it were equally so to Chairman Park, he thought they could go ahead and issue it.[1] The Chairman indicated agreement, and the President directed that it be issued.

The President mentioned that he and the Chairman had discussed at lunch in considerable detail the matter of ROK-Japan relations. Also, with the Foreign Minister he had discussed the situation in Viet-Nam. The Foreign Minister had promised to give him a memorandum of what, in his judgment, might be useful to us to do in that difficult crisis. The President spoke of our great concern over how to prevent the collapse of

---

Source: Kennedy Library, National Security Files, Countries Series, Korea, Park Visit, 11/61–12/61. Secret. Drafted by Koren and approved in S on December 5 and in the Department of Defense on December 6. The closing time of the meeting, which was held in the White House, is from the President's Appointment Book. (Ibid.) Extensive briefing material for Pak's visit is ibid., National Security Files, Countries Series, Korea, Park Visit, 11/61–12/61, and ibid., Park Briefing Book, 11/14/61–11/15/61, Parts I–III.

[1] The communiqué, which was negotiated in advance of Pak's visit, is in *American Foreign Policy: Current Documents, 1961*, pp. 979–980.

Viet-Nam. The ultimate step was the use of U.S. troops. However, the real answer was for the Vietnamese to do for themselves and not rely heavily on help from abroad. The President said that Viet-Nam was a common problem, not just a U.S. one, and he wondered whether the Chairman might have some ideas on this score.

Chairman Park began by expressing his appreciation for the time the President was able to give him and also for U.S. support for Korea in these difficult days. As he had said to Secretary Rusk and Mr. Hamilton earlier, he realized the heavy burden the U.S. was bearing and he felt that each nation of the Free World must do its best to decrease this burden by its own efforts, thereby increasing the strength of the Free World. This was the reason why he laid such stress on the ROK-Japan settlement.

With regard to Southeast Asia, particularly Viet-Nam, the Chairman stated that, as a firm anti-Communist nation, Korea would do its best to contribute to the security of the Far East. North Viet-Nam had well-trained guerrilla forces. Korea had a million men well trained in this type of warfare. These men had been trained in the regular forces and were now separated. With U.S. approval and support, Korea could send to Viet-Nam its own troops or could recruit volunteers if regular troops were not desired. Such action would prove that there was unity of action among the nations of the Free World. Just before departure he had discussed this question with his senior ROK officers. All were enthusiastic. He suggested that the President ask his military advisers to study this offer and let him know the results.

The President expressed deep appreciation, noting that the U.S. was carrying the burden from Berlin all the way around the globe. He would talk with Secretary McNamara and the Chairman might have some more detailed discussions with him and General Lemnitzer tomorrow. The President speculated that it would probably be a good idea to talk also with the Filipinos. There was a limit, as the French found out, on what an occidental could do in a situation like this.

Turning to economic matters, the President spoke of his regret at having to institute the "Buy American" policy, which limited the effectiveness of our aid by closing cheaper supply sources to us. He then outlined in some detail for Chairman Park the Congressional alarm over the flight of gold and the alternative posed by the Congress, i.e., either it would drastically cut aid appropriations or the Administration must limit where the funds would be spent. The President had chosen the latter course, but he hoped in a couple of years the situation would be corrected, and, when this occurred, the first step would be a reversal of "Buy American." Chairman Park appreciated this explanation and said that he was not asking revocation of the whole policy, only certain specific exceptions important to Korea. The President went into some further details on the U.S. payments difficulties and Secretary Rusk suggested that the Korean waiver request might be pursued at dinner that night.

Chairman Park said that he had brought some documents with him concerning the events before and after the May revolution and what had been accomplished. He had discussed this matter with Secretary Rusk and Mr. Hamilton. The President said both Ambassadors had presented to him very convincing stories of the accomplishments of the revolutionary group. He had been impressed and assured the Chairman the U.S. would give him the maximum support possible. He drew attention to the fact that we had had to spend a great deal more money in Southeast Asia (Laos and Viet-Nam) than originally planned. However, we knew the importance of aid to Korea; if Korea were not free, Japan would not be free and that would mean the whole Pacific area would go too, so Korea had a vital interest for us. In this connection, the President thought it would interest Chairman Park if Secretary McNamara gave him an assessment of U.S. military strength in light of the recent Soviet atmospheric testing.

Secretary McNamara described how the U.S. military budget had been increased by $6 billion over the previous administration's planning figure primarily to increase nuclear military power, and non-nuclear strength such as ground and air support forces. Of our 1700 total nuclear-equipped bomber strength, 850 could be in the air in 15 minutes. The Polaris and Minuteman missile programs had been increased by 50 percent. 300,000 men had been added, mostly to the ground forces. A billion and a half dollars had gone into increased logistic capabilities. In sum, our over-all military strength was greater than that of the Communist Bloc and the President had instructed him to keep it that way. With regard to nuclear strength, the U.S. was substantially superior to the Soviets despite their recent test series. We were three to eight times better off quantitatively and far ahead quality-wise. The Soviets, for example, could only place 200 to 300 nuclear bombers over North America at present. As for ICBM, the Secretary noted that we now had 5 Polaris submarines carrying 80 nuclear missiles.

The President said we were faced with the challenge of maintaining our strategic position and being prepared to fight guerrilla wars—"wars of liberation," as Khrushchev called them in stating the Soviets would back these types of wars. However, the President said, he was confident we could deliver, even after an initial Soviet attack, a more crippling blow to the Soviets than they had originally launched against us. Secretary Rusk repeated this, because he said he wanted it absolutely certain that Chairman Park and his party understood what the President had just said.

The President said our most difficult task right now was the other kind of struggle, such as that going on in Iran, Viet-Nam and Cuba. Secretary Rusk asked Chairman Park if there were Communist infiltration across the 38th parallel. The Chairman replied that there was none now across the parallel. They had tried by every means to infiltrate but they had been rooted out. The President invited the Chairman to give his estimate of the state of morale and political orientation of the North Koreans. The Chairman replied that their daily food consumption was low and civilian living standards very poor. They were, of course, superior in basic industries and mineral resources to South Korea. Likewise, their electric power output was now 1,100,000 k.w. whereas the ROK goal in their 5-year plan was only 1,030,000. The President asked about the possibility of atomic generation of electric power in Korea. The Chairman replied that construction costs were so high they had given it no thought, but (smiling) if U.S. support were forthcoming, they would certainly consider it. North and South Korean ground forces and navy were about even in potential, according to Chairman Park, but in air power the Communists were 4 times as strong. Secretary Rusk asked whether this was strictly North Korean air power or ChiCom and Soviet air power. The Chairman said it was strictly North Korean; however, the U.S. air forces in Korea and Japan equalized the situation.

North Korea was putting great emphasis on industrialization and South Korea was in danger of falling far behind. His most urgent task was to maintain his armed strength and at the same time to build up the economy. He compared the situation in Korea today to Germany, saying that in a divided country, unless each side maintained economic strength equal to the other, one side would fall far behind in many respects. The Chairman did not want South Korea caught this way and his primary objective in coming here was to seek the President's positive support for the maintenance of the Korean armed forces at their present strength and also for the implementation of economic reforms and regeneration. The Chairman inquired whether the words of the communiqué meant that that support would be forthcoming. Secretary Rusk reassured the Chairman that we recognized the importance of maintaining armed strength throughout the Free World and at the same time generating economic, social progress. Our experts would work with his and the Secretary felt sure we could move forward with confidence together.

The President said he wanted no misunderstanding between himself and the Chairman. As he had already indicated, he considered the safety and security of Korea vital to the U.S. We would do the very best we could but the Chairman must realize that we had not been too successful in the aid appropriations this year and he wanted the Chairman to have a very clear idea of our problems and responsibilities and why we cannot do as much as we would like. The Chairman said that he wished to reiterate his conviction that it was most important that the developing nations of the Free World be able to stand on their own feet.

He felt the emphasis should be on those nations that could accomplish the most in the shortest time. The President said that we shared that thought. Our Congress and people felt most strongly that aid should go where it would do the most good. Laos had been most distressing because we had put a lot of aid in there that seemed to have gone down the drain. One of our disappointments had been that the economically sound European nations had not assumed more of the aid burden. They were ready to make loans, but at 6 percent or higher. The President added that, as far as Berlin was concerned, he could give no assurances of successful negotiations, so that we might be faced with a serious problem of access to the city after the peace treaty had been signed. In fact, we might be hard pressed in Berlin and Viet-Nam at the same time.

The Chairman said he thought he had taken enough of the President's time and wanted to say good-bye, but could he have before leaving a "refreshing answer" to his request for support? The President replied that we would far rather do what we said we would, rather than say something we could not fulfill. As a matter of fact, he had wished someone would give him something refreshing, and he had been refreshed by the Chairman's offer of help in Viet-Nam. The President said that perhaps he had given the Chairman some encouragement by telling him we had enough atom bombs to blow us all up. Seriously, he did not want the Chairman to leave with a feeling of not having achieved what he had come here for, but he was sure the Chairman realized now the grave problems facing us. The President hoped that Ambassador Chung would be able to elaborate on these for the Chairman.[2]

[2] President Kennedy met Pak Chung-hui for a farewell call at the White House on November 15 from 4 to 4:35 p.m. When Kennedy remarked that he hoped that his visit assured Pak of U.S. interest in Korea, Pak asked for special foreign aid assistance during the next year. Kennedy suggested that the situation should be reviewed in 6 months. Pak reiterated his offer of ROK troops for Vietnam or guerrilla wars elsewhere. Kennedy suggested that the time was not right for such a commitment, but he promised to keep in touch on the issue through Ambassador Berger. (Memorandum of conversation, November 15; Kennedy Library, National Security Files, Countries Series, Korea, Park Visit, 11/61–12/61)

## 248.   Memorandum of Conversation

Washington, November 16, 1961.

SUBJECT

U.S. Assistance to Korea (Secretary's Farewell Call on Chairman Park)

PARTICIPANTS

*Korea*
Gen. Chung Hee Park, Chairman, Supreme Council for National Reconstruction
Ambassador Il Kwon Chung, Korean Ambassador to the U.S.
Lt. Col. Sang Kuh Han, Interpreter

*United States*
The Secretary
Ambassador Samuel D. Berger, United States Ambassador to Korea
Mr. H. L. T. Koren, Director, Northeast Asian Affairs
Dr. Paul S. Crane, Interpreter

The Secretary began by saying that, while he would have the privilege of bidding the Chairman good-bye at the airport the next day, he wanted to have a few minutes conversation with him, as he had mentioned at their first meeting on November 14. The Secretary said he also wanted to take advantage of the opportunity to congratulate the Chairman on his appearance at the National Press Club, which he understood had gone off extremely well. The Chairman thanked the Secretary and said he thought the Press Club meeting had been all right.

The Secretary want on to say that he had reviewed the discussions the Chairman had had with the President, Secretary McNamara, himself, and others, and he hoped the Chairman understood that he could go back with full confidence of U.S. determination to do what the President said we would. There was one particular point he wished to mention and that was he had gained the impression that the figure of $90 million Supporting Assistance had perhaps assumed more importance during the visit than it deserved. He felt he had sensed some disappointment regarding this figure among the Chairman's colleagues. He himself had discussed with the Chairman the difficulties we encountered in dealing with so many different countries and endeavoring to meet their needs for varying types of aid such as supporting assistance, technical cooperation, development loans, etc.

The Secretary said that he was concerned that, if a member of the Chairman's party on his return should speak of the $90 million in terms of disappointment, it would be harmful to public understanding on both

---

Source: Department of State, Central Files, 033.95B11/11–1661. Confidential. Drafted by Koren and approved in S on December 1. The meeting was held at the Korean Embassy.

sides, since this figure might not be related to the total amount of aid received. For example, regular military assistance committed to Korea would be very substantial, even though, for policy reasons, there was never any public announcement of the total figure. Likewise, there were the development loans whose purpose was to initiate and sustain specifically the kind of economic development the Chairman had spoken of during his stay. The Secretary said that he had the impression that a given amount of assistance to Korea would now produce more results than the same amount given to previous governments. In other words, a dollar in the Chairman's hand was worth more than in the hands of previous governments, but the Chairman must have the profit and not the U.S. Specifically in regard to the questions of offshore procurement and "Buy American" policy, the Secretary reiterated our determination to do our best to make adjustments favorable to Korea.

The Secretary emphasized that Ambassador Berger had the full backing of the President and the other interested Department heads as well as a full understanding of the significance of the President's assurances to the Chairman of our determination to assist the Republic of Korea and his Government to progress in accordance with the Chairman's plans. The Chairman's visit and the opportunity it had afforded the top echelon of our Government of becoming personally acquainted with the Chairman and his colleagues had given us a deep sense of assurance. He hoped the Chairman would go back with a deeper assurance on his side of our interest and determination to assist him and his country. Finally, the Secretary remarked that he had been privileged to receive a number of foreign guests, but it was his opinion that no other visitor had more right to return to his country with confidence. The Secretary had lived through a good part of the recent history of Korea, and he wanted the opportunity to say this simply and directly to the Chairman.

Chairman Park said he fully appreciated and understood the Secretary's remarks and was grateful for the hospitality extended to him. He had been deeply impressed and encouraged by the assurances of friendship and help which had been conveyed to him. He took pride in sharing the responsibility of meeting the great tasks ahead. He also wished to thank the Secretary for coming to see him with the message that he had just given him. He agreed that if the $90 million figure was singled out it might become some sort of symbol, but it would not represent the truth of the deep relations between the two countries. It would, therefore, perhaps be better to forget the figure in terms of trying to measure U.S. interest in Korea.

In closing the meeting, the Secretary said the Chairman was very strongly represented in Washington, not only by Ambassador Chung but by Ambassador Berger as well.

### 249. Letter From the Ambassador to Korea (Berger) to Secretary of State Rusk

Seoul, December 15, 1961.

DEAR DEAN: I have now had time to reflect on the situation here in the light of Park Chung Hee's visit to the United States, and am able to send you the appraisal you requested.[1]

2. I believe the political situation is now fairly well stabilized, and we can count on this continuing for at least six months. I would not yet venture to say it will remain stable until the election promised for May 1963 because there are still some uncertainties, especially in the economic field, but I think it possible. (All this presupposes that Park will escape an assassin's bullet.)

3. I attribute this stabilization to five principal factors:

a. When the Junta took power in May almost no one knew who they were or what they were up to. They have now established themselves as a group of capable, energetic and dedicated men, determined to make genuine reforms, to lay foundations for honest and effective government, and devoted to the return of representative government. They have produced convincing evidence that they will not tolerate corruption, graft, bribes, smuggling, tax evasion, or political blackmail in government, military or civilian life. They are introducing long overdue reforms in agriculture, industry, banking, education, and social welfare. They are reorganizing public administration at all levels. While there is skepticism in some quarters that they will succeed, bitterness on the part of those who have been hurt, and criticism that in some respects they have moved too fast and often too arbitrarily, no honest person here now questions their motives, and most people are impressed with their dedication and an increasing number with the results already achieved.

b. The emergency stage of the revolution is now practically over, and the early atmosphere of tension and personal fear and insecurity has virtually disappeared. People are now beginning to relax and speak more freely, and the press, while still inhibited by self-censorship, puts out a surprising amount of critical comment. There are two main reasons for this improved atmosphere:

i. The government has announced there will be no further indictments after December 11 before the Special Revolutionary Courts, which hope to wind up their trials of those indicted prior to that date by Febru-

---

Source: Department of State, Central Files, 795B.00/12–1561. Confidential; Official–Informal.

[1] Rusk's request has not been found.

ary or earlier, and people who have not been charged for past offenses can now breathe easy.

ii. The government policy of amnesty or leniency toward all but principal offenders—in the interests of national unity—has been greeted with relief.

However, even though arrests from now on will normally require warrants, habeas corpus will be restored, and future trials will generally take place in the regular courts, the government is not yet ready to restore full "due process." The right of peaceful assembly is still restricted by martial law; the midnight to 4 a.m. curfew is still in effect; and under a special law which went into effect December 11 persons who obstruct revolutionary tasks, initiate disturbance or civil war, or join anti-state organizations will be subject to court-martial. These may be subject to arrest without warrant and may not be protected by habeas corpus. Sentences for such activities may be as severe as death.

c.  Chairman Park Chung Hee has established himself in Republic minds as a forceful, fair and intelligent leader who can be trusted with power, trusted to keep the revolution on the path of decency and moderation, and trusted to abide by the pledge he gave on August 12 to return to civilian government after the election in May 1963. Park, therefore, represents a most important link between the government and the people, and a most important stabilizing element in the situation. Moreover, the vigor with which Park has fought against factionalism in the Supreme Council has so far served to keep this endemic disease under control.

d.  The bumper 1961 crop, the gradually accelerating economic revival since July, public works to help relieve unemployment, and the government's farm reform measures are beginning to give new hope to the people. Earlier fears of inflation have somewhat subsided; civil servants, teachers and soldiers are looking forward to a promised pay increase in 1962; and the farmers, after an initial skepticism, are beginning to believe that perhaps this government is different from its predecessors and that there will be real reforms to the benefit of agriculture.

e.  The public support given the military government by the United States and the friendly reception of Park during his visit to the United States have, however, been perhaps the decisive factors in stabilizing the situation. One Korean put it to me in a sentence, "Since the United States is impressed with Park, we Koreans value him more."

4.  As a result of the above any immediate danger of an attempted counter coup has receded; the government is growing every day in self-confidence; false rumors about corruption and incompetence in government, directed partly at American ears, have almost ceased circulating; and the threat that the government would be torn to pieces by factionalism has subsided.

5.  Thus, as I see it, we shall enter 1962 with fairly promising prospects:

a.  Our economic aid and loan and military assistance programs for FY 1962 will be more effectively used than by any previous government and should provide enough to produce substantial economic progress next year. There is the prospect that the International Development Association may soon make its first loan to Korea—for railway rolling stock. The West German government has just announced that $37 million in government and private funds will be made available for capital investment. If there is a settlement with Japan in the current negotiations—and the military government is determined to achieve this and is prepared to make reasonable concessions—this will bring great benefits to the Korean community and give them even more hope for their future. Indeed without a normalization of Korean-Japanese relations, I can see little hope for the economic future of South Korea.

b.  The United States Operations Mission, under Mr. Killen's able direction, is being rapidly whipped into shape, both in terms of policies and staff, so as to concentrate our aid and our energies in the vital sectors. Mr. Killen will also reduce his staff by September 1, 1962, from about 475 direct hire and contract employees to about 225. If more US economic aid and loans can be effectively utilized, Mr. Killen and I will not hesitate to ask for them.

c.  Our United States military are encouraged by the vigor with which the government is eliminating corrupt practices in the military and reducing the volume of pilfering and diversion of military supplies. Improvements in auditing, inspection and inventory control in the ROK military establishment are also producing good results, and many of these practices are now being introduced in the civilian government sector.

6.  Against this rosy background there are, however, certain potential dangers in the situation:

a.  The government is trying to do too much too fast, as a result of which its calendar 1962 budget, now under consideration, is not only very much larger than last year but provides for an excessive amount of deficit financing. It is quite clear they are assuming the United States will make up most of this deficit. Mr. Killen and I are doing everything possible to persuade them to reduce their planned expenditures. We are making clear that we will take no responsibility for making up any such deficit as they have budgeted for nor bail them out if unwise policies set off a serious price inflation. We are asking them to come up with a more prudent and better balanced budget at this stage, and to resort to supplemental budgets if the situation develops more favorably than we now think. At this writing I cannot tell you what success we will have.

b.  Since the low point of economic activity in June when only $7.4 million of foreign exchange were sold, there has been an encouraging improvement:

| | |
|---|---|
| July | $10 million |
| August | $12.6 million |
| September | $21.3 million |
| October | $27.6 million |
| November | $32.9 million |

Part of this rise is healthy, but part can be attributed to forward speculative buying in anticipation of price inflation, for the revival of production and trade has lagged behind foreign exchange sales. This forward buying, of course, has the advantage of bringing goods into the pipeline—now somewhat depleted as a result of the summer slump in foreign exchange sales—and will serve to moderate the upward price movement that it anticipates. Happily, foreign exchange reserves have been climbing, and this provides a potential weapon against inflationary pressures. To keep prices from spiralling in 1963, however, there will need to be a much faster pickup in production. It is not yet possible to say whether this will take place.

c.  The Korean Business Community is still lukewarm, at best, in its support of the military government and its economic program. Among the pending problems assumed by the new government was a group of old cases of tax evasion, profiteering by illicit means and related offenses involving most of the country's leading industrialists. This posed a real dilemma, since the offenses were so flagrant and well-known that they could not be allowed to go unpunished, yet the people and corporations concerned represented a very substantial portion of the industrial plant and experience essential to economic recovery and expansion. The government moved rapidly and forcefully to dispose of the problem and acted with moderation and understanding of the economic as well as the political issues which it entailed. The businessmen, however, after their initial fright, have realized the strength of their own bargaining position and have been jockeying for advantage, protesting their support for the government's program but delaying the action and decisions that would start wheels turning. Success in dealing with this problem will require just the right combination of incentives and pressure and this combination has not yet been worked out.

d.  Unemployment, underemployment, and low wages are still pervasive, and we are beginning to get a few reports of restlessness among urban workers. So far this has been held in check by stable prices, but if price inflation should get its head, there could be public demonstrations and strikes next year.

e. Factionalism, which has plagued Korean governments for hundreds of years, remains a latent threat to the stability of the government. That factionalism has been kept under control up to now is due largely to Park's determination to fight those of his colleagues who are so motivated. He has been successful so far, and at the moment the situation is fairly quiet, but there may well be a renewal of factional fighting in the Supreme Council and it cannot yet be said with any certainty that Park will be able to contain it during the whole period of his government's tenure in power.

f. Corruption, the other endemic disease of Korean governments, has been sharply curtailed, but there have already been a few confirmed cases of corruption involving military officers in the government, including some very close to those at the top. These have been immediately and severely dealt with, and Park hopes this will be a warning to others. There is good evidence that the great majority of leaders on the Supreme Council will not hesitate to punish any offender no matter how high. While leaders at the top are likely to keep their hands clean, the danger is that corruption will gradually begin to creep back in the lower military ranks of the Junta and among civil servants. The extent is not likely to be anything like as great as in the past, because people are being very much more careful. The outlook, therefore, is for less corruption, but those who engage in it will play for bigger stakes. Fewer but bigger scandals are therefore a possibility and could do damage to the good reputation of the government.

g. The educational community is in turmoil because of a radical educational reform that provides for a reduction in university and college intake from about 40,000 to 11,000 a year so as to reduce the total enrollment over four years from about 156,000 to about 44,000. There are a number of other educational measures, including the compulsory retirement of teachers and professors at 60, the organization of teachers and students into associations under government auspices, reduction in liberal art and expansion of technical education, engineering and science enrollment, scholarships for poor students (this for the first time), et cetera. These measures, some still tentative, have been applauded in some circles, but they have also engendered bitterness, criticism, and some resistance among those who have been hurt. There is general agreement among most Koreans that reforms are needed to get at profit-making "diploma mills," bribery to get into and out of universities and inferior teaching, but in developing its programs the Ministry of Education has done too little spadework with those interested or affected, and in general has been pre-emptory in putting through its measures. There have already been two public protest meetings among university groups in violation of the government ban on meetings, and these have led to threats of prosecution, and there could be trouble from this quarter. The government is aware of this, is keeping the educational community under close surveillance, and is determined to act forcibly to break up any disturbance.

h.  The government requirement that all voluntary organizations be investigated and cleaned up before they will be re-registered and allowed to function normally is still in effect. Trade unions, business and professional associations, charity, welfare, sports, and numerous other organizations are all involved. Many have already been cleared and are functioning normally, although subject to irksome surveillance. However, a good many organizations, still awaiting clearance, are operating in low gear. Dissatisfaction hits many groups and individuals, and here too, unless the situation is rectified this could become a breeding ground for trouble.

I have discussed this situation with a number of leaders of these organizations. With few exceptions they applaud the government's efforts at reform and would support the government if given a chance. I have urged key government leaders to try to enlist their positive cooperation by consultation and by giving them more freedom of action, but while I have been thanked for this counsel and been assured it will be done, the government, and especially the ROK CIA, remains suspicious and fearful of organized groups, and improvement in the situation has been slow.

i.  Political parties are banned, and unless government policy is changed they will not be allowed to become active until January 1963. However, politicians are meeting more or less secretly to plan their tactics and strategy. Most of them are waiting to see how the situation develops over the next six months. If it develops unfavorably they will continue to sit in the wings. If it develops favorably, many of them plan to offer their support and services to the government, hoping in such an alliance to get into the public eye in advance of January 1963 so as to present themselves as the leaders best able to carry on with the revolutionary reforms when the military government retires. We may assume that there are a number of military leaders who are toying with the idea of taking off their uniforms and running for office, and that they will not be averse to alliances with selected politicians whose reputations are not too tarnished. Factionalism in the Supreme Council could be enhanced by this development, because military leaders with political ambitions will be jockeying for position and may differ on which politicians and political groupings to join up with.

7.  To summarize, I think there are good prospects for 1962, as well as dangers. We shall know a lot more in the course of the next three to six months. Meanwhile I think it safe to say that despite certain important shortcomings and certain dangers, the record of reform and improvement which has taken place is heartening and suggests we can go to Con-

gress this spring in good conscience that this has been a constructive year and that our continuing massive support is well justified.

8.    There are certain aspects of American aid policy based on world wide considerations and which do not take into account certain special problems in Korea, which are disturbing General Meloy, Mr. Killen and me, for they hamstring what we are trying to achieve here. I have already analyzed them in Embassy telegram No. 642 of October 28,[2] and there is no point in going over the ground again. I mean, however, to write you about these when we can see more clearly the shape of the Korean budget, now under consideration.

I hope you will find these observations helpful.[3]

Sincerely,

**Sam**

---

[2] See footnote 3, Document 244.

[3] On January 10, 1962, Assistant Secretary of State for Far Eastern Affairs Harriman sent a memorandum to Rusk summarizing Berger's letter and suggesting a reply in which Rusk stated that he shared Berger's "cautious optimism." The Rusk letter also suggested that the success that the military in Korea had enjoyed was due in good part to the encouragement and assistance of Berger and his team. The letter was sent to Berger on January 19, 1962. (Department of State, Central Files, 795B.00/1–1062 and 795B.00/1–1862)

---

## 250.    Memorandum From Robert W. Komer of the National Security Council Staff to the President's Special Assistant for National Security Affairs (Bundy)

Washington, December 20, 1961.

Berger's dispute with General Meloy over how to divide our budget support for ROK between economic and military sectors (Seoul's 817, Eyes Only)[1] bears directly on the MAP turn-around. Let's weigh in on this issue, if necessary.

In briefest compass, Berger wants to divide the 275 billion hwan in US controlled local currency with which we expect to support the ROK

---

Source: Kennedy Library, National Security Files, Countries Series, Korea, General, 7/61–2/62. Secret. Also sent to Kaysen.

[1] Komer wrote "815, 816" in the margin, a reference to telegrams 815 and 816 from Seoul, both December 19. Telegram 817 is dated December 20. (All in Department of State, Central Files, 895B.10/12–1961 and 895B.10/12–2061)

1962 budget, 150 military to 125 economic. This is a change from the country team view last spring that 173 should go to the defense budget and 102 to the rest. The ROK military is very unhappy with Berger's apportionment, and is being backed by Meloy. In fact, Meloy wants a 180/85 split, and has referred the dispute to Washington.

Berger feels that we must give greater emphasis to economic development. He thinks that the ROK has padded its defense budget and that in any case if we keep financing some 95 per cent of it through US generated local currency, we will never get the Koreans to put their own house in order. He says we're facing a ROK squeeze play and must be prepared for a ROK threat to cut its forces unless we give it relief.

Meloy argues that present 600,000-man ROK force level is sacred; it was "developed by the US Joint Chiefs of Staff and approved by the UN [US?] National Security Council." To him, 180 billion hwan in defense budget support is "vital" to Korea.

This issue is giving Berger a liberal education. He has discovered that the old five-year plan for MAP gives defense such a high priority that by 1965 almost all US-controlled hwan would be going into the military budget, leaving nothing for support of economic growth. The only trouble is that even Berger seems horrified by the thought that ROKs might cut their forces if they can't get what they and Meloy want. For my money, we should welcome such a ROK decision; it would begin the turn-around the Steering Group recommends,[2] and (better still) place responsibility for it on them rather than on us.

State, and I suspect even DOD, will back Berger.[3] If not, however, this is one of issues President might want discussed in connection with NSC review of SG Report. In meantime, why not indicate to McNamara that WH much interested in this test of whether we really want a MAP turn-around in the largest MAP client country?

**Bob K.**

---

[2] The Military Assistance Steering Group, established by agreement between Secretaries Rusk and McNamara on July 8, was an inter-agency group responsible for reshaping the military assistance program. The Steering Group focused on six nations—of which Korea was one—which absorbed 50 percent of the U.S. Military Assistance Program. The Steering Group recommended that the mix of aid in the ROK be re-examined, but Berger, McConaughy, and William Bundy agreed that the United States should not open up the question of ROK force levels (the basic factor on which the MAP was based) until June 1962 when there would be a better appreciation of the economic situation in South Korea. (Memorandum from William Bundy to Komer, December 12; Washington National Records Center, RG 330, OASD/ISA Files: FRC 64 A 3282) Regarding the Steering Group's report, see Document 251.

[3] The Departments of State and Defense agreed to apportion U.S. supporting assistance to Korea for fiscal year 1962 in the form of U.S. aid-generated currency on the basis of 150 million hwan for ROK Defense budget support and 125 million hwan for economic development. (Telegram 709 to Seoul and letter from Gilpatric to Rusk, both December 29; Department of State, Central Files, 895B.10/12–2061 and 895B.10/12–2961)

## 251.  Editorial Note

On January 18, 1962, the National Security Council, with President Kennedy presiding, discussed the report of the Military Assistance Steering Group. The Steering Group was established on July 8, 1961, by Secretary of State Rusk and Secretary of Defense McNamara to reshape the U.S. military aid program. It its report, the Steering Group focused on six key U.S. allies: Korea, the Republic of China, Pakistan, Iran, Greece, and Turkey, which absorbed about 50 percent of the U.S. Military Assistance Program. According to the report, the bulk of this aid went to equip and maintain large armed forces well beyond the abilities of these developing countries to maintain. At his 496th meeting the National Security Council noted the President's request for further prompt reviews of military and economic aspects of long-range U.S. military aid planning with the assumptions that resources would be limited and that military assistance programs and economic aid programs were competitive as well as complementary. The President specifically asked the Joint Chiefs of Staff to look again at the issue, bearing in mind that decreases in military aid would be compensated by increases in economic aid.

The National Security Council agreed that for Korea—as for Iran, Greece, and Turkey—proposed Military Assistance Plans for fiscal years 1964–1968, as well as a final proposed plan for fiscal year 1963, should be submitted by July 15. It required similar plans for the Agency for International Development's programs for the comparable periods. For Korea the Council required military and political studies in order to recommend a desirable Korean force level and structure, including a desirable level of U.S. forces in Korea, by June 15.

The Administrator of the Agency for International Development was responsible for these studies and for determining by May 15 how to improve planning and programming techniques so that military and economic aid could be effectively coordinated to ensure that the total aid given to a recipient country was used to best overall advantage. (NSC Action No. 2447, January 18; Department of State, S/S–NSC (Miscellaneous) Files: Lot 66 D 95, NSC Actions) Documentation on the work of the Steering Group and the Kennedy administration's reappraisal of military and economic aid is in volume IX, pages 648 ff.

252. Telegram From the Embassy in Japan to the Department of State

Tokyo, March 18, 1962, 10 p.m.

2586. From Harriman.[1] Have asked Ambassador Berger to report on my conversations ROK officials while in Seoul. Was impressed by determination and present sincerity of group to eliminate corruption and raise moral tone of government and country in all fields. There is determination of revolutionary atmosphere which is leading them to questionable methods as in case of new law on political activity.[2] Was assured that probably not more than 20 percent of four thousand affected individuals would be disqualified from political activity though not disqualified from government employment. This revolutionary group, including Chairman Pak, undoubtedly looking to United States for moral as well as material support. Therefore believe our Ambassador and other American representatives in Korea, can influence to some extent future actions. Will reserve further comment until I hear from Berger. In any event, I believe we are fortunate in having in this Asian country a group dedicated to personal integrity and opposed to corruption as well as strongly anti-Communist, though the road to satisfactory democracy may be a bit rough. Therefore, recommend we do not change for the present our aid policies on account of this latest political action. Ambassador Berger should, however, be fully supported in his protest against this type of action without prior consultation.

Reischauer

---

Source: Department of State, Central Files, 795B.00/3–1862. Secret. Repeated to Geneva for Rusk, Seoul, and CINCPAC.

[1] After the Far Eastern Chiefs of Mission conference in Baguio, the Philippines, Assistant Secretary Harriman visited Taipei March 15, Seoul March 16–17, and Tokyo March 17–19. Accounts of his discussions with Korean Government officials are in telegrams 1041 and 1047 from Seoul, March 17 and 18. (Ibid., 110.15–HA/3–1763 and 795B.00/3–1962) While in Tokyo, Harriman discussed Korean-Japanese relations with Japanese leaders. An account is in telegram 2618 from Tokyo, March 20. (Ibid., 110.15–HA/3–2062)

[2] The Political Purification Law, announced by the SCNR on March 16, applied to a diverse group of former government officials, politicians, party functionaries, illicit fortune makers, and staff members of certain social organizations as well as those "conspicuously responsible" for political corruption from February 4, 1960, to May 15, 1961. (Airgram A–308 from Seoul, March 20; ibid., 795B.00/3–2062)

## 253.  Special National Intelligence Estimate

SNIE 42–62                                          Washington, April 4, 1962.

### THE OUTLOOK FOR SOUTH KOREA

#### The Problem

To assess the prospects for political and economic stability in South Korea through 1970, with particular reference to the impact of major changes in the level and type of US support and assistance.

#### Note

The last estimate on Korea was NIE 14.2/42–61, "The Outlook for Korea," dated 7 September 1961.[1] It dealt with the major trends and prospects in South Korea, with particular attention to the impact of North Korea on the south over the next two or three years. That estimate remains substantially valid, in our opinion, and it should be consulted for the background of the present estimate.

The introduction to the present estimate is intended to bring NIE 14.2/42–61 up to date in the briefest possible manner. Parts II through V assess the prospects for South Korea through 1970. Part VI discusses the probable impact of a substantial reduction of South Korean armed force strengths and, concurrently, a substantial increase in the amount of US economic aid. For the purpose of this section it is assumed that US aid during the period FY 1964–1968 would be based upon a phased reduction of about one-third in present Republic of Korea (ROK) armed force strength and, concurrently, an increase in assistance for a comprehensive and balanced economic development program on the order of $50–$100 million per year.

#### Conclusions

1.  As far as we can see at present, the political situation in South Korea during the period of this estimate will probably be characterized by vigorous dissension and factionalism in both military and civilian circles. We believe that the military will continue to dominate the state,

---

Source: Department of State, INR/EAP Files: Lot 90 D 110, SNIE 42–62. Secret. According to a note on the cover sheet the Central Intelligence Agency and the intelligence organizations of the Departments of State, Defense, the Army, the Navy, and the Air Force, and the Joint Staff participated in the preparation of this estimate. All members of the USIB concurred with this estimate on April 4 except the representatives of the AEC and the FBI, who abstained on the grounds that the subject was outside their jurisdiction.
[1] Document 243.

even though the government may be ostensibly civilian. Occasional abrupt changes of leadership by coup d'état may be in prospect. (Paras. 9–13)

2.  The economic outlook is grim but not hopeless. Assuming a continuance of US aid at approximately present levels and a reasonable degree of political stability, there will probably be some improvement. An increase in the amount of US aid, if effectively used, could speed up the rate of economic growth and in the long run would probably contribute to political and social stability. At best, however, economic advance will be slow. (Paras. 14–17, 27–29)

3.  The Communist powers will continue their attempts to destroy the independence of South Korea by various forms of political warfare and subversion. The greatest threat to the country lies in the possibility that political dissension, economic stagnation, and social unrest will render it increasingly vulnerable to this Communist effort. (Paras. 21–23)

4.  As long as the Communist powers believe that the US will defend South Korea, they will almost certainly not launch an overt military invasion.[2] Accordingly, a reduction of strength of the South Korean armed forces, by anything up to about one-third of present numbers, would probably not in itself increase the likelihood of invasion from the north. It would, however, produce considerable political unrest within the country, which would possibly be great enough to endanger any government initiating the measure.[3] (Paras. 24–26, 30–33)

[Here follows the "Discussion" section of the estimate, comprising 7 pages.]

---

[2] The Assistant Chief of Staff, Intelligence, USAF, would state this sentence as follows: As long as the Communist powers believe that the US will defend South Korea with the kind and degree of force necessary quickly to defeat any invasion, they will almost certainly not launch an overt military invasion. [Footnote in the source text.]

[3] For the positions of the Director, Defense Intelligence Agency; the Assistant Chief of Staff for Intelligence, Department of the Army; and the Assistant Chief of Naval Operations (Intelligence), Department of the Navy; see the footnote to paragraph 25. [Footnote in the source text. The footnote to paragraph 25 stated that the above officials believed that the chief deterrent to military and paramilitary action against South Korea was a "combination of the Communist belief that the US will defend South Korea, present US-ROK military capability in South Korea and the additional military strength the US can immediately bring to bear in that area." These officials opposed any reduction in ROK forces on the grounds that it would have serious and unassessable consequences for the strategic balance in the Far East.]

### 254.    Memorandum From the Joint Chiefs of Staff to Secretary of Defense McNamara

JCSM–265–62                                    Washington, April 10, 1962.

SUBJECT

Strategic Appraisal of US Position in Korea 1962–1970

1.  Reference is made to your memoranda of 26 January 1962 and 30 January 1962 to the Chairman of the Joint Chiefs of Staff and the Assistant Secretary of Defense (ISA), respectively, concerning certain studies to be made on Korea.[1]

2.  In response to the above, the Joint Chiefs of Staff have conducted a study of Korea from a military standpoint. This study is appended hereto[2] and includes an assessment of the communist military threat to the Republic of Korea (ROK), roles and missions of both US and ROK forces together with the necessary ROK force levels and equipment over the period extending approximately to 1970.

3.  The Joint Chiefs of Staff have re-examined the present threat; have scrutinized the relationships between the military posture in Korea and the threat to Korea and Northeast Asia; have noted the relationship of actions in Northeast Asia to those in Southeast Asia; have challenged and redetermined the minimum acceptable US/ROK military strength and structure; have re-examined the precarious balance in which the new ROK military/politico/economic structure still finds itself in this first year in power and have projected all of these considerations through 1970.

4.  The Joint Chiefs of Staff consider that the ROK is an essential element of our forward defense strategy in Northeast Asia. A reduction in ROK forces could encourage the very aggression we seek to deter. The net result of any significant reduction of ROK forces below their present levels would be increased military risk in Northeast Asia; lowering of US influence in Asia; decreasing the capability of keeping a limited war at a nonnuclear level; increasing the requirement for the augmentation of US forces and shortening the time by which these forces must be available; and encouragement of the communists to undertake further aggression.

5.  In view of the above, the Joint Chiefs of Staff agree that a reduction in ROK military strength by lowering Military Assistance would be

---

Source: Washington National Records Center, RG 330, OSD Files: FRC 66 A 3542, Korea 320.2. Top Secret. A stamp on the source text reads: "Dep Sec has seen."

[1] The January 26 memorandum to the Chairman of the JCS has not been found; the January 30 memorandum to the Assistant Secretary of Defense (ISA) is ibid.

[2] The appended paper, not printed, is 53 pages long.

directly and fundamentally counter to the US interests in Korea and Northeast Asia. It cannot be emphasized too strongly that current US/ROK force levels in Korea are the minimum acceptable for assuring the long-term security of Northeast Asia.

For the Joint Chiefs of Staff:
**L.L. Lemnitzer**[3]
*Chairman*
*Joint Chiefs of Staff*

---

[3] Printed from a copy that indicates Lemnitzer signed the original.

---

**255. Memorandum From Robert W. Komer of the National Security Council Staff to President Kennedy**

Washington, April 23, 1962.

An expression of your concern over the apparent new impasse in the ROK/Japanese negotiations would be highly desirable at this point.

These talks have dragged on fitfully since 1951. ROK animosity stemming from thirty-five years of Japanese rule in Korea was long the chief obstacle; ROK claims were ridiculously high. The new ROK military regime, however, is interested in an early settlement because General Pak needs money for his ambitious development program. But his effort, sparked by his talks with Ikeda last November, has now run into Japanese stalling.

Ikeda has been fighting a balance of payments problem brought on partly by his own ten-year development plan. He foresees little relief before November and hesitates to arouse public criticism by new foreign obligations. He also faces upper house elections and wants reelection as Liberal Democratic Party chief this summer. Leftist opponents are looking for an issue with which to embarrass Ikeda. Moreover, Ikeda's recognition of the need to stabilize the ROK political and economic situation is still not strong enough to overcome his suspicion that the US may be

---

Source: Kennedy Library, National Security Files, Meetings and Memoranda Series, Staff Memoranda, Komer. Secret.

gradually withdrawing support for South Korea in the expectation that Japan will assume responsibility. Reischauer says it may be late autumn before Tokyo is willing to consider serious talks again. But the Koreans threaten "other action" if a settlement is not reached by the end of the year.

As the attached cables[1] indicate, the issues still dividing the two countries are exceedingly complex. State has been reluctant to see us get involved too directly, lest we incur the onus of an unpopular settlement or end up paying a large portion of the bill. Nonetheless, our interests dictate an early resolution of this issue in a manner which will bring Japan to assume a greater share of the burden of subsidizing South Korea—a matter at least as important to Japan's security as to ours.

State is working up an action program to get things moving again. However, I recommend the attached nudge from you[2] to put steam behind this exercise and to let the ambassadors know of White House interest. At least some quarters in State would not be at all averse to such a nudge.

**R.W. Komer**

---

[1] Telegrams 2617, 2901, and 2933 from Tokyo, March 20, April 18 and 21, telegram 966 to Seoul, April 12, and airgram A–321 from Seoul, March 29, were indicated as attachments, none found attached. (All in Department of State, Central Files, 294.9541/3–2062, 294.9541/4–1862, 294.9541/4–2162, 294.9541/4–562, and 794.56211/3–2962, respectively)

[2] Document 256.

---

## 256.   National Security Action Memorandum No. 151

Washington, April 24, 1962.

MEMORANDUM FOR

The Secretary of State

Having read the recent dispatches from Seoul and Tokyo,[1] I am concerned over the apparent impasse which has again developed between Japan and South Korea over the issues which they have been discussing for so long. Since these negotiations have been progressing fitfully for

---

Source: Department of State, FE Files: Lot 65 D 25, National Security Action Memorandum. Secret. A copy was sent to McNamara.

[1] See footnote 1, Document 255.

over a decade, I believe that we must make every effort to bring them to a prompt and successful conclusion.

One facet of the problem which particularly worries me is that time does not seem to be on the Korean side; as time passes, the Japanese will probably see less and less incentive to agree to a settlement which will provide as much help as we desire toward strengthening the South Korean economy.

I recognize the complexities involved in this painful negotiation, and the undesirability of the US being put in the middle. On the other hand, if certain pressures or inducements from the US turn out to be essential to bring the two parties together, we may want to run these risks. I also note that the Department of State may recommend messages from me to both parties at an appropriate time. I would be happy to weigh in if necessary.

While recognizing the need for tactical flexibility as to timing, particularly in view of Ikeda's reluctance to proceed much further until after the Diet session, his upper house elections, and his own re-election as party chief, I hope that we can try to keep up momentum toward a settlement, using US good officers to the extent required. Therefore, may I have a report by *15 May* on what plan of action you consider would most effectively bring the negotiations to a successful conclusion.

**John F. Kennedy**

---

### 257. Memorandum From Harold H. Saunders of the National Security Council Staff to President Kennedy

Washington, April 25, 1962.

SUBJECT

Japanese Assistance to South Korea[1]

The Japanese government has given *no assistance to South Korea* since the end of World War II. The governments still have not established nor-

---

Source: Kennedy Library, National Security Files, Countries Series, Japan. Secret. A note, on the source text indicates that the memorandum was pouched to Palm Beach, Florida, on April 26 for the President.

[1] According to an April 23 memorandum from the President's secretary, Evelyn Lincoln, to McGeorge Bundy, President Kennedy wanted "an up to date report on the assistance Japan is giving to South Korea." Bundy wrote the following note on the memorandum, "Mr. Komer, have we responded adequately? MB." (Ibid.)

mal diplomatic relations, although a Korean mission in Tokyo remains from US occupation days. A few private business deals may bring some Japanese investment to Korea soon, but amounts will be negligible until normal relations are established.

Trade has been small ($22.8 million to Japan, $123.8 million to Korea in 1961). Although the above amounts to over half of Korea's puny exports, the balance has heavily favored Japan. A desire for Japanese development assistance is the chief reason why General Pak wants a settlement with Japan.

It is also *why we feel the success of the present round of Jap-ROK negotiations is so important*, and have suggested to you an NSAM asking State to consider what we can do to bring the two together. It won't be easy to talk the Japanese into assuming their share of the burden in aiding the underdeveloped world—except where they see profit. But history and geography make Jap-ROK cooperation essential, if we can just break through the emotionalism and animosity dating from 35 years of Japanese rule in South Korea.

Harold H. Saunders[2]

---

[2] Printed from a copy that bears this typed signature.

---

### 258.   Letter From Secretary of Defense McNamara to the Administrator of the Agency for International Development (Hamilton)

Washington, April 27, 1962.

DEAR FOWLER: As you know, the Department of Defense has set up two major studies directed to the final decision on Korean force levels to be reached in accordance with NSC Action No. 2447.[1]

---

Source: Washington National Records Center, RG 330, OSD Files: FRC 66 A 3542, Korea 320.2. Top Secret. Drafted by William Bundy on April 19.

[1] See Document 251.

One of these studies is a JCS analysis from a purely military stand-point.[2] I expect to confer on this in the near future and will then forward it to you with my statement of the final Defense position. I am, however, attaching at this time the parallel study performed by a special group under Paul Nitze's office, headed by Major General John B. Cary, USAF (Ret.), who was borrowed from the Institute of Defense Analyses for the purposes of this study.[3] I am anxious that your staff review this study, on a limited circulation basis because of its sensitive nature, in order to be sure that we are not in any serious divergence concerning the economic analyses contained therein. It is also, of course, appropriate that you yourself should have this basic input to the total problem.

Paul Nitze's office would welcome informal staff contact and comment either through him or directly to the action officer, Mr. Stephen Loftus.

I propose to proceed at this point by conferring with the JCS and with the interested parties in my office to arrive at a firm Defense Department position on this matter. I hope to do so early in May, and will then be in touch with you about the next steps to be taken.

Sincerely,

**Bob**[4]

**Attachment**

Washington, April 1962.

KOREA: A POLITICAL-MILITARY STUDY OF SOUTH KOREAN
FORCES

[Here follow pages 1–35, which comprise sections I–VII: "Introduction," "Underlying Factors," "Political Environment," "Economic Environment," "Subversion and Insurgency," "Military Environment," and "Total Environment."]

---

[2] Document 254.

[3] As outlined in the introduction of the report the task of the study group under Cary was to determine the most desirable force posture for the ROK for 1962–1970. The group was specifically enjoined to consider possible alternative basic policies for the defense of Korea.

[4] Printed from a copy that indicates McNamara signed the original.

*VIII—Alternative Defense Policies*

1. Of the many possible variations, three alternative defense policies were adopted for investigation. These are described in some detail in Annex M. They are summarized in the following paragraphs.

*Option A*

2. This option involves the provision of in-place forces in South Korea, which, together with available U.S. and ROK reinforcements, can contain, on a non-nuclear basis, an attack by North Korea alone. Since any major North Korean military operation requires Chinese Communist support and agreement, and at least tacit assent by the USSR, and since the Chinese have previously demonstrated their willingness to intervene if necessary to preserve North Korea as a Communist state, the question immediately arises as to what is necessary to keep the Chinese out. Since, under this assumed defense policy, it is not in-place military forces in South Korea, it follows that there must be some other military sanction available of sufficient strength and credibility to cause the Chinese to refrain from open intervention. This military sanction now exists. It is visible to the Chinese in the form of U.S. [*less than 1 line of source text not declassified*] forces now in the area.

*Option C*

3. This option is essentially the present defense policy of the U.S. with regard to South Korea—that is, to be able to contain, on a non-nuclear basis, open aggression by combined ChiCom/KorCom forces. [*2 lines of source text not declassified*]

*Option B*

4. This assumed defense policy is identical with Option C, except that it envisages immediate use [*less than 1 line of source text not declassified*] by the defending forces. It was assumed that the Chinese would retaliate with whatever indigenous [*less than 1 line of source text not declassified*] they might have after the U.S. initiated [*less than 1 line of source text not declassified*] operations. In view of the very few weapons estimated to be available to the Chinese, this assumption would result in one-sided use of [*less than 1 line of source text not declassified*] except for a very few, area-type weapons deliverable by Red China. (Section VI above)[5]

5. Sub-studies made by or for the Study Group clearly indicate that there would be an appreciable reduction in force requirements under this Option as compared with Option C. The Study Group was unable, however, to assess with any precision the impact of [*3 lines of source text not declassified*]. No further attention, therefore, has been devoted to this Option.

---

[5] Section VI was "Military Environment."

*General*

6. In all three Options, it has been assumed that the mission of the defending forces is limited to containment of the initial Communist offensive. No geographic requirement is assumed except that there be retained sufficient depth to permit a further UN buildup if that should be necessary. It will be noted that this mission is somewhat at variance with the present mission of UN forces, which at least implies a requirement to retain Seoul, and which requires readiness to conduct a subsequent counter-offensive.

7. Two analytical sub-studies were made for the Study Group to serve as yardsticks for air and ground force requirements under Options A and C. Air considerations are covered in WSEG Staff Study No. 88 (available in draft form to the Study Group)[6] which has been taken into consideration. A study limited to ground combat operations in the Korean environment is attached at Annex O.

8. Analyses of the two alternative defense policies follow in Sections IX and X. Option C is considered first, so that a situation which represents essentially the present defense policy can serve as a basis for analysis of change.

9. The methods used for these analyses are the product of the Study Group and do not represent either the methods of analysis nor the judgments of the responsible Commanders. It is emphasized that these analyses are based upon the large number of assumptions and estimates, some of a highly tenuous nature, set forth elsewhere in this study and particularly in Annex L. Even though the results of the analyses are set forth in direct terms, they are not intended and should not be construed to be of an absolute or categorical nature, since they are highly sensitive to the validity of the assumptions and estimates used.

[Here follow pages 39–55, which comprise sections IX "Option C," X "Option A," and XI "Implications of Major Force Reductions in ROK Forces."]

*XII—Over-All Conclusion*

1. The Study Group, in comparing the two assumed defense policies (Options A and C) examined in this study, believes that Option A—if its adoption were linked to some highly significant and publicly evident change in the political or military situation, and if based on firm U.S. resolve to use its nuclear strength as necessary—would provide strong assurance that South Korea would not be attacked, and probably that it could not be successfully attacked. If it had been adopted earlier (in con-

---

[6] Apparent reference to "Some Aspects of Force Posture in Northeast Asia," prepared by the Weapons Systems Evaluation Group (WSEG), April 25, and sent to the Director of Defense Research and Engineering on April 27. (Washington National Records Center, RG 330, OASD/ISA Files: FRC 66 A 3501, Korea 1962 320.2 (Cary Study))

nection, say, with the withdrawal of Red Chinese forces from North Korea), political and economic advantage would probably have ensued.

2.  The Study Group considers that a reduction in ROK forces of the magnitude which would result from adoption of Option A, would, under present circumstances, entail risks and disadvantages which far outweigh any potential economic advantage which might ensue.

3.  Circumstances which would permit the early adoption of a defense policy entailing dramatic reductions in ROK military strength, without jeopardy to U.S. objectives and position, must include a prior, major improvement in the political and economic environments within South Korea, and additionally some visible political or military event at least approaching the significance of the ROK force reduction.

4.  The Study Group concludes, therefore, that the defense policy of the U.S. for the security of South Korea should not now undergo drastic revision and that the armed forces of the Republic of Korea should remain at approximately the level now programmed.

[Here follow 18 annexes.]

---

### 259.  Memorandum for the Record

Washington, May 4, 1962.

SUBJECT

Cary Report on ROK Force Levels[1]

This is a fascinating document. The Cary group agrees that "Option A" (a six division cut) is *militarily* reasonable if some sanction exists to keep Communist China from attacking the ROK and that this sanction does exist in the form of US [*less than 1 line of source text not declassified*] forces in the area (pp. 36 and 56).[2] Indeed, it says that if such a cut had been made at the time of withdrawal of ChiCom forces from Korea, it would have been advantageous, and might again be feasible in the future if events provide some similar justification.

---

Source: Kennedy Library, National Security Files, Countries Series, Korea, General, 3/62–7/62. Top Secret.

[1] For extracts, see the attachment to Document 258.

[2] The new SNIE 42–62 also concludes that a one-third reduction in ROK forces "would probably not in itself increase the likelihood of invasion from the north," although some military members of the USIB take a more alarmist view. [Footnote in the source text. SNIE 42–62 is printed in part as Document 253.]

However, the report opposes such a cut at present, primarily, because it would upset Pak's regime and secondarily because it would have adverse repercussions on US allies throughout East Asia, who would see in it a reduced US interest in their defense as well. The main argument seems to be that the Pak regime would naturally be quite upset by a major cut in its main base of support, the Army. Great political instability might ensue. Thus the Cary Report *seems to make its case against a force cut not on military grounds but on the grounds that it would have political repercussions* undermining ROK political (and by extension) economic stability.

This conclusion seems contestable on three grounds:

(1) It is supported primarily by some rather scary speculation. I am not persuaded that a 135,000 man cut over three years, leaving ROK forces at a still sizable 460,000, would create such dire risks. The new SNIE (42–62) seems to take a less gloomy view of these repercussions, although not minimizing them. But the SNIE concludes that the Pak regime would accept a force cut if pressed, and if adequate US reassurances were given. Indeed, no one has assessed whether Pak himself might not prefer a force cut *if the hwan released plus dollars saved could be used to support his new five year plan.* It might be interesting to put this proposition up to General Pak. Moreover, are we sure that a force cut would be so politically unpopular as to promote instability, rather than the reverse? Recall that Chang Myon campaigned in 1960 on a platform of reducing the ROK army by 200,000 men, and got elected. Then he attempted to press a 100,000 man force cut; the opposition was from the US, not the ROK. Finally in December 1960 the US agreed to a T/O cut from 630,000 to 600,000. I also recall seeing a paper written by General Chung Il-Kwon, three times ROK Chief of Staff, in which he too argued for a much smaller ROK army. The initiation of a major development program along the lines suggested by Pak might be the dramatic and significant event which the Cary group says would be necessary to justify a force cut.

(2) While the Cary Report devotes some attention to the subversive threat, it makes no analysis of the comparative seriousness of internal and external threats which is the guts of the problem. The Steering Group argued (based on NIE 14.2/42–61)[3] that the greatest threats to the security and stability of South Korea were not overt attack but domestic weaknesses which would be politically exploited by the NK Communists.[4] Therefore, while recognizing that an external threat still existed, it argued for reducing somewhat our insurance against this contingency in order to back adequately an intensified development effort. The new

---

[3] Printed in part as Document 243.
[4] In the report of the Military Assistance Steering Group; see Document 251.

SNIE (42–62) bears out this need. In effect, we face a necessity for choice in Korea between two legitimately competing views.

(3) My third reservation applies to the economic argument. The Report makes much of the limited capacity of the ROK economy to absorb new outside capital. Maybe so, but it also emphasizes the constant ROK problem of avoiding large government deficits which create inflation. It notes that to do so will require either substantial hwan diversions from the military budget or substantial reductions in government investment for economic development below the level projected in the five year plan (p. 18). Thus we do have a real competition for resources. Incidentally, the report dismisses the argument that force cuts would seriously complicate the unemployment problem by pointing out that to add 135,000 to 2.7 million already unemployed, would not be an economic catastrophe (p. 52).

It is also notable that the military analysis indicates that Communist air superiority would be of very short duration in any conflict (p. 42). Indeed, by employing US forces available in the theatre we could build up to an 800-plane offensive air strength by D plus 8. Of course, this is based on providing the ROK air defenses called for in current MAP planning.

The Report simply dismisses the likelihood of a successful NK attack against even a 12-division force (pp. 45–46). Thus the real military issue is whether we want to maintain the present much larger ROK force against the contingency of a combined ChiCom/NK attack. Is this remote contingency sufficient military rationale for the present ROK force structure? [5 *lines of source text not declassified*]

In sum, therefore, the Cary Report can be read as justification for a six division cut in ROK forces unless the *political* repercussions are too great. This is a question of judgment, on which the Cary group's pronouncements do not seem to me to be particularly compelling and on which other judgments exist (e.g. those in the NIEs and those of State in endorsing the Steering Group Report last year).

**R.W. Komer**[5]

---

[5] Printed from a copy that bears this typed signature.

## 260.  Memorandum From Secretary of State Rusk to President Kennedy

Washington, May 17, 1962.

SUBJECT

  Korean-Japanese Relations

Your memorandum to me of April 24, 1962 (National Security Action Memorandum No. 151),[1] asks for a report on appropriate action to bring the negotiations between Japan and the Republic of Korea to a successful conclusion.

Governor Harriman discussed this problem at length with our Ambassadors in Tokyo and Seoul, and with Japanese and Korean Government leaders, during his recent trip to the Far East. It was evident from these conversations, as well as from the subsequent reporting of both Embassies, that the principal obstacle to a settlement at present is the gap between unrealistically high Korean claims against Japan, arising out of the Japanese occupation, and unrealistically low Japanese counter-offers. The Koreans have indicated to us a willingness to settle for considerably less than they have previously asked, but the Japanese seem less willing to settle than they were at the end of last year.

United States influence toward a settlement should, therefore, be exerted at this stage more on the Japanese than on the Koreans. However, our ability to influence the Japanese on the question of their relations with Korea is limited. Prime Minister Ikeda is reluctant to take the political risks which he believes such a settlement would involve for him, especially before the House of Councillors and Liberal-Democratic Party elections in July of this year. The Japanese, however, may be willing to raise their offer and pursue a settlement more actively after their elections are out of the way.

Moreover, I understand that former Prime Minister Yoshida in a conversation with you on May 3 agreed as to the importance of a settlement with Korea, although he, too, felt it must wait until those elections have taken place.[2] Therefore, I would assume that Mr. Yoshida's consid-

---

Source: Kennedy Library, National Security Files, Meetings and Memoranda Series, NSAM 151. Confidential.

[1] Document 256.

[2] According to the memorandum of conversation of the Kennedy–Yoshida meeting on May 3: "The President underlined the importance he placed on the settlement of Japanese/Korean relations and urged that this be done. Mr. Yoshida said he fully agreed that the question ought to be settled and settled promptly, but that it should wait until after the senatorial elections in June. The President underlined that we had protected the security of Korea largely because of its importance to the security of Japan. Korea could not achieve healthy economic growth without close economic relations with Japan, and the President implied that now was the time for Japan to do her share." (Department of State, Central Files, 611.94/5–362)

erable prestige and influence may prove helpful in inducing Prime Minister Ikeda to move decisively toward a rapprochement with Korea, beginning sometime this summer.

In the interim we hope to utilize possibilities for Korean development now being explored by third countries to stimulate interest of the two sides, and particularly of the Japanese, in a settlement. We have in mind interest the Germans are showing in giving supplier credits for a steel mill, perhaps to be followed by credits for a fertilizer plant, shipyard, coal mines and coal cars. Moreover, at the present time a group led by General Van Fleet is in Korea investigating possibilities for investment by a number of important American firms. We hope that the Japanese will decide they do not want to be left behind. In any case, Mr. Janow, Assistant Administrator of AID, is shortly to visit Japan and Korea, perhaps accompanied by a political officer. There he is to assess developing attitudes, ask questions and stimulate interest. We hope that this also will help allay the restiveness of the Koreans by giving some sense of forward motion. AID is also studying incentives which we might offer the two Governments to encourage a settlement. Such a settlement, required by the self-interest of both parties, will of course require that each move toward the other's position on Korean claims and, we think, that Korea accept Japanese loans as part of the settlement "package". Messages from you to both parties might at some point help materially to precipitate a settlement. For the present, however, I believe we should keep such possible measures in reserve for a time when they may be expected to have the desired effect.[3]

Dean Rusk

---

[3] At the White House staff meeting of May 18, Komer stated that "the ROK/Japanese negotiation problem was still hung up." McGeorge Bundy told Komer to turn this problem over to Michael Forrestal as it was more properly in his area. Komer returned to the issue, remarking that "we need a policy on the negotiation problem after the Japanese elections on 1 July. The fear is that the Japanese will just walk off and drop any attempt to reach an agreement with the Koreans." Bundy remarked that he had spoken to Vice President Johnson about going to Japan and hoped he could do something. (Memorandum of White House Daily Staff Meeting, May 18; National Defense University, Taylor Papers, Daily Staff Meetings, May–September 1962)

## 261. Memorandum Prepared in the Department of State

Washington, May 17, 1962.

### KOREAN-JAPANESE RELATIONS

(Background paper for use in connection with the meeting of the
NSC Standing Group, May 18, 1962)

*I.    General Considerations*

1. Prospects for early normalization of relations between the Republic of Korea and Japan are not bright. From 1952 to 1960, normalization was impossible because of Korean ex-President Rhee's intransigent anti-Japanese position. A new Korean administration gave hope that a settlement could be achieved, although its expectations were unrealistically high. Japanese conservative leaders in 1961 apparently decided in favor of a settlement. Now, however, the Japanese wish to "go slow" because of domestic political pressures and current balance of payments difficulties. They also believe that time is on their side. Nevertheless, despite lack of progress, neither the Koreans nor the Japanese seem to contemplate a rupture in negotiations, which are continuing at working levels.

2. It continues to be in the United States interest to promote an early settlement of differences between the Republic of Korea and Japan, for the following reasons:

a. Rapid Korean economic development, crucially necessary for stability, would be materially accelerated by Japanese economic aid additive to continued U.S. aid.

b. Korea would gain greater access to Japanese markets for her exports, thus providing further major stimulus to Korean economic development.

c. A significant impediment to Free World unity and strength in Asia would be removed.

d. ROK prestige would be bolstered in the increasingly serious competition with the Communist North Korean regime.

3. United States leverage to induce a settlement is limited by the following factors:

---

Source: Kennedy Library, National Security Files, Meetings and Memoranda Series, Standing Group Meetings, 5/18/62–8/3/62. Confidential. Drafted by Macdonald for use at the NSC Standing Group meeting at 3 p.m. on May 18. The Standing Group, an interagency group, was the precursor of the more significant EXCOM (Executive Committee) of the National Security Council, which came into ad hoc existence during the Cuban missile crisis of October 1962 and was later formalized.

a.  The Japanese believe the U.S. must support Korea in any event, and see no reason for haste in assuming any portion of the economic burden themselves, especially since they suspect that we are trying to reduce our own burden thereby, and believe that passage of time will make a cheaper settlement possible.

b.  The Japanese Prime Minister is reluctant to proceed with a settlement because (1) he believes that any large contribution to Korea would be unpopular in Japan because of popular prejudice against the Koreans; (2) the Japanese Left is opposed to any settlement with the anti-Communist Republic, and would use the issue against the Government; (3) elements within the ruling conservative party in Japan seek to use the Korean problem as a device for weakening the Prime Minister's leadership position. These factors carry particular weight with Ikeda prior to the Upper House and Conservative Party elections scheduled for July.

c.  The Koreans also fear we will sell them out to Japan economically in order to lessen our foreign aid burden.

d.  Both sides resent any American role that could be interpreted as interference (almost any overt U.S. role would be so interpreted by Communist propaganda and by the Japanese Left). At the same time, each side is constantly seeking to invoke U.S. influence and money against the other in a complex tangle of issues where a misstep for the U.S. would be very easy and could be quite damaging.

e.  With Japan once again a world power, and in the present state of Japan-U.S. relations, we cannot force Japan to act except in accordance with her own conception of her national interest.

f.  Despite the enormous leverage our aid gives us in Korea, our influence there would be seriously weakened by forcing the Koreans to settle with Japan at levels materially lower than they believe reasonable.

g.  Under these circumstances, United States pressure, if injudiciously applied, might well retard a settlement rather than promote it.

II.   *Issues between Korea and Japan*

4.  The principal issues outstanding between Korea and Japan are: (a) Korean claims for compensation, based on Japanese occupation from 1910 to 1945, including North as well as South Korea, (b) Korean claims of exclusive fishing rights within an extensive and legally untenable "Peace Line," 50 to 200 miles at sea. Other minor issues are: (c) Korean art objects in Japan, (d) status of Korean residents in Japan, (e) repatriation of Koreans to North Korea, (f) sovereignty over Tokto or Takeshima (Liancourt Rocks), an inconsequential islet in the Japan Sea, (g) claims for vessels taken by Japan from Korea in 1945. The occupation claims issue is the principal bone of contention, and if it can be settled, the other issues can also be settled.

*III. U.S. Policy and Objectives*

5.  United States policy has been, and continues to be, to "influence the ROK and Japan to negotiate a settlement of their differences through a realistic and forthcoming attitude on both sides, and to normalize their relations without, however, placing the United States in the position of mediator." To this end, the United States has the following immediate objectives:

a.  To keep contact between the Koreans and the Japanese, at least at the technical level, and avoid any rupture of negotiations.

b.  To persuade both sides that it is in their interest to settle now, and that delay will be contrary to their own interests.

c.  To convince both sides that Japanese economic aid (under whatever name) will not supplant, but supplement, continuing high-level U.S. assistance.

d.  To bring about the resumption of negotiations at a high political level as soon as possible, and to induce a reasonable over-all settlement of outstanding issues without public evidence of United States coercion or interference.

*IV.  Recent U.S. Actions*

6.  Our Ambassadors in Tokyo and Seoul, in continuing informal contacts with the Japanese and Korean governments at various levels, are urging flexibility, restraint, and a forthcoming attitude on both sides, looking toward a resumption of negotiations at a higher level in July or August after the Japanese elections. The Koreans are being urged to lower their figure for claims against Japan from the $700 million currently asked, and probably will do so if talks are resumed. The Japanese are being urged to raise their offer for compensation and economic assistance grants above the unrealistically low level of $70 million (made to the Koreans in negotiations between the Foreign Ministers last March).

7.  Meetings among senior officers in the Department of State (including AID) on April 16 and May 15[1] have considered means for applying American influence to bring about a settlement between Korea and Japan. The conclusions were reported in the Secretary's memorandum to the President (attached), responding to National Security Action Memorandum 151 of April 24, 1962.[2]

8.  AID is now studying possible incentives to offer the Japanese and Koreans through the economic assistance program to promote a settlement.

---

[1] The record of the April 16 meeting is attached to a May 14 memorandum from Bacon to Rice, prepared in anticipation of the May 15 meeting. No other record of the May 15 meeting has been found. (Department of State, Central Files, 694.95B/5–1462)

[2] Document 260.

## V.    The Current Situation

9. In a conversation with Ambassador Reischauer on April 18, Japanese Foreign Minister Kosaka made clear [1 line of source text not declassified] the lack of progress in the March talks. He added that Korean persistence in unreasonable claims "might create anti-American feeling in Japan because of the U.S. role in confiscating private Japanese property in Korea in violation of international law."

10. The ROK Foreign Minister, in a talk with Ambassador Berger on April 24, indicated that the Koreans would refrain from public statements on Korea–Japan relations, and intended to keep the door open to visits by Japanese officials and newsmen.

11. A four-man Japanese economic fact-finding mission, headed by Yoshihiro Nakayama, Director of the Foreign Ministry's Economic Affairs Bureau, visited Korea in late April. Nakayama had a frank discussion with Ambassador Berger in Seoul, which should do much to promote Japanese understanding of the Korean situation and our position.

12. In an appraisal on April 29, working-level Japanese Foreign Office officials reflected less gloom about the danger of a hostile rupture in negotiations. They were seeking ways in which both governments could foster a constructive atmosphere, pending a new impetus toward rapprochement. They stated, however, that the Japanese Government was proceeding on the assumption that Ikeda would not authorize any major negotiating effort before the Japanese elections.

13. On May 16, Japanese Foreign Office officials confidentially informed our Embassy that the Koreans had approved a small rotating Japanese mission in Seoul, to be staffed by a series of "visitors," beginning with Toshio Urabe, Counselor of the Foreign Ministry's Asian Affairs Bureau. Urabe may have access to Korean SCNR Chairman Park, in which case the locus of informal discussions may shift to Seoul. Such talks would be the best way to maximize prospects for subsequent high-level negotiations.

14. The Japanese have signed an agreement to import 40 thousand tons of Korean rice this year, in return for which the Koreans will purchase fertilizer.

15. The Koreans have recently seized additional Japanese fishing boats allegedly within the "Rhee Line," but the seizures have apparently not attracted major attention.

16. On balance, it appears that there is a continuing willingness on both sides to keep communication channels open; that the Koreans are willing to make a claims settlement at somewhat less than their asking figure (Ambassador Berger estimated $350–450 million in compensation and grants (exclusive of credits and loans) in his conversation with Nakayama); and that a settlement is possible if the Japanese leadership

can be motivated to make a decision in favor of a settlement at a higher cost than they have so far been prepared to accept.

---

262.  **Memorandum From the Executive Secretary of the Department of State (Brubeck) to the President's Special Assistant for National Security Affairs (Bundy)**

Washington, June 11, 1962.

SUBJECT

Reopening of Status of Forces Negotiations with Korea

Ever since the United States Government promised to negotiate "promptly" a status of forces agreement with the Republic of Korea in the Dulles–Rhee joint statement of August 1953,[1] every Korean Government has pressed for such negotiations. Meanwhile, the Commander of the U.S. forces in Korea has continued to exercise exclusive jurisdiction over U.S. military personnel under the "Taejon Agreement" of 1950[2] and the Economic Coordination Agreement of 1952.[3]

The Defense Department long opposed a status of forces agreement because of the unique state of suspended hostilities in Korea and the presumably unsatisfactory Korean legal system. In April 1961, however, with Defense Department agreement, negotiations for a full status of forces agreement were begun.[4] When the civil government was overthrown one month later, the talks were suspended.

In June 1961, the new military government requested that the United States reopen negotiations, but in view of the unstable situation and uncertainty at that time as to the intentions of the regime, this request was refused.

In March of this year, the ROK Government again requested the resumption of negotiations. On May 14, the ROK Government was

---

Source: Kennedy Library, National Security Files, Countries Series, Korea, General, 6/62. Confidential. The Department of State copy of this memorandum indicates Elmer Hulen of FE/EA is the drafter; Yager, Rice, and Harriman cleared in draft; and Robert M. Winfree of G/PM cleared in final. (Department of State, Central Files, 795B.5/6–1162)

[1] For text, see *American Foreign Policy: Basic Documents, 1950–1955*, pp. 2674–2676.

[2] Entered into force on July 28, 1950. (1 UST 705)

[3] Entered into force on May 24, 1953. (3 UST 4430)

[4] See footnote 3, Document 209.

informed that the United States Government would be willing to reopen negotiations provided it could obtain a written commitment in advance that the question of criminal jurisdiction would not be raised for discussion until a new constitutional government had been formed (scheduled for next year) and normal legal processes had been fully restored.[5] About two weeks later, the ROK Government rejected this proposal, contrary to earlier private assurances by the Foreign Minister that it would be accepted, offering instead to postpone the signing and putting into effect of any agreement reached until the above conditions had been met.

On June 9 the United States reiterated this basic proposal, but dropped the request for an advance written commitment.[6] This, too, was rejected by Chairman Pak, who speculated that the problem might be handled by placing the subject of criminal jurisdiction on the status of forces agenda but postponing discussion from time to time. The Foreign Minister later said that the government was prepared to pass a "special law" regarding the U.S. and UN forces in Korea which would meet U.S. standards. He indicated that this could be done during the coming year, apparently concurrently with status of forces negotiations.

In the last week, a number of Korean student demonstrations have occurred in Seoul and elsewhere, protesting recent unfortunate incidents involving U.S. military personnel, and demanding a status of forces agreement. These demonstrations apparently were not inspired by the government, and they reflect a genuine nationalistic feeling which regards a status of forces agreement as an essential symbol of sovereignty. The Koreans are well aware of the fact that the United States has, or is negotiating, status of forces agreements with other countries in which large U.S. forces are maintained.

In this connection, Koreans can point out that the United States has an agreement covering all its NATO allies, an agreement with Japan, and a base agreement with the Philippines. They know that the United States is negotiating an agreement with the Republic of China. Not unnaturally, they feel that the United States discriminates against the ROK.

We have requested Ambassador Berger's views on the current impasse with the ROK Government over the reopening of SOFA negoti-

---

[5] The Embassy was instructed in telegram 1041 to Seoul, May 11, to so inform the ROK Government. (Department of State, Central Files, 611.95B7/4–2761)

[6] This information was transmitted in telegram 1104 to Seoul, June 8. (Ibid., 611.95B7/5–2962)

ations.[7] When we have received the Ambassador's views, we will consult with the Defense Department on further steps that may be required in the present situation.

E.S. Little[8]

---

[7] In telegram 1277 from Seoul, June 12, the Embassy reported that the ROK Government "appears to have taken steps to calm press and public on SOFA issue, recognizing inherent danger to government stability as emotionalism generated got out of hand." Berger stated that the Department could "rely on ROKG assurances postpone discussions jurisdiction for some time and then discuss at leisurely pace." He proposed that the negotiations be resumed in July on this basis and with the understanding that an agreement could not be signed until normal constitutional and legal procedures were restored in South Korea. (Ibid., 611.95B7/6–1262)

[8] Little signed for Brubeck above Brubeck's typed signature.

---

**263. Memorandum From Michael V. Forrestal of the National Security Council Staff to the President's Special Assistant for National Security Affairs (Bundy)**

Washington, June 11, 1962.

SUBJECT

Status of Forces Agreement in Korea

I have discussed the progress of our negotiations on the Korean Status of Forces Agreement ("SOFA") with Messrs Rice and Yager in State and Mr. Lang in Defense (ISA).

Talks on this subject have been going on intermittently since August 1953 when Secretary Dulles agreed to prompt SOFA negotiations after the ROK signed a Mutual Defense Treaty.

In 1958 the Defense Department made a study of the criminal law and legal procedures of Korea and concluded that several important changes would have to be made both in the penal code and in the administration of justice before the United States could submit its personnel to Korean criminal jurisdiction. The results of this study have never been given to the ROK.

---

Source: Kennedy Library, National Security Files, Countries Series, Korea, General, 3/62–7/62. No classification marking. Copies were sent to Taylor and Kaysen.

In April 1961 actual negotiations were finally begun but with the understanding that there would be no agreement on criminal jurisdiction unless arrangements could be made to assure fair trials by U.S. standards to U.S. personnel. The Korean Government fell shortly after the opening of negotiations and was replaced by a military junta. Negotiations were thereupon suspended, both State and Defense agreeing that they should not be renewed until civil government and civil administration of justice was restored.

In May of this year we again agreed to start negotiations on a SOFA but only on the understanding that there would be no discussion of criminal jurisdiction. After the recent unpleasant incidents, we reaffirmed essentially this position, but the ROK has refused to negotiate without discussing what they consider the most important attribute of a status of forces agreement, i.e. criminal jurisdiction.

*Comment:* I asked both State and Defense to explain why it is not possible to begin discussions immediately on an overall SOFA including a criminal jurisdiction. State's position is a little wobbly. They mainly want to use the issue of the SOFA as a means of compelling the restoration of a civilian government. Governor Harriman, however, is inclined to go ahead with negotiations if Sam Berger, our ambassador, concurs.

Defense's position is clearer and tougher. They are unwilling to make even a first step towards an agreement covering criminal jurisdiction under the present circumstances. To do so, they think, would only make incidents like the recent ones even more dangerous, since they would increase the pressure for signing an agreement on criminal jurisdiction.

In light of the obvious political beating we appear to be taking in Korea now, I would think that we could agree to begin negotiations on a SOFA in Korea. We obviously should not sign an agreement until the military lawyers are satisfied that appropriate safeguards have been obtained; but I don't see how we can refuse even to negotiate.[1]

In the last analysis, I should think that what we really care about is the physical safety of our people. I wonder why it isn't possible when we have doubts about the local courts to agree to the criminal jurisdiction of the host country and also agree as an executive matter that U.S. personnel convicted of crimes and sentenced would be, at our request, expelled from the country. This would tend to solve the political problem while at

---

[1] In a memorandum to McGeorge Bundy, June 14, Executive Secretary Brubeck stated that the Department had authorized Ambassador Berger to inform ROK authorities that the United States was prepared to resume status of forces negotiations in July, provided that it was clearly understood that no agreement on criminal jurisdiction could be reached until after the re-establishment in South Korea of normal constitutional and judicial procedures. (Department of State, Central Files, 611.95B7/6–1462) Berger received these instructions in telegram 1126 to Seoul, June 14. (Ibid., 611.95B7/6–1262)

the same time protecting our people from the consequences of primitive and un-American legal systems.

MF

---

## 264. Memorandum of Discussion at a Department of State–Joint Chiefs of Staff Meeting

Washington, June 15, 1962, 11:30 a.m.

[Here follow a list of participants—18 people attended for the Joint Chiefs of Staff and Department of Defense, 8 for the Department of State, and General Marshall Carter for the Central Intelligence Agency—a table of contents, and discussion of item I on Vietnam, which is printed in volume II, pages 459–460.]

*II.   Korea*

Admiral Anderson said that the JCS would like to have a run down on the latest developments in Korea. Mr. Johnson then asked Mr. Yager to speak to cover this item. Mr. Yager said that the situation in Korea is a disturbing one. The present military government has the attributes of efficiency and is attempting progressive modernization. However, there are signs that the leaders are losing self-confidence. They are worried about their lack of effective progress and cliques are beginning to develop among the ruling classes. The ROK CIA is not acting properly; it is becoming involved in the economic field, and there are persistent reports that it is engaged in massive financial corruption. We had hoped to receive an overall situation report from Ambassador Berger by today, but he has deferred submitting his report in view of the fast moving situation. We hope to have this report in the near future.[1]

---

Source: Department of State, S/P Files: Lot 69 D 121, State–JCS Minutes. Top Secret. A note on the cover sheet indicates the memorandum was a Department of State draft, not cleared with the Department of Defense.

[1] The assessment was received in telegram 1312 from Seoul, June 19. In it the Country Team stated that the present situation in Korea was best described as a "power and policy struggle which has created a condition of instability in top leadership and tension in the country." The resignation of President Song Yo-chan, infighting within the SCNR, coup plotting outside and possibly inside the government, massive student demonstrations, stock market scandals, and corruption all contributed to the situation, but the Country Team considered KCIA Director Kim Chong-pil and his organization most responsible for the instability. The Country Team still considered Pak the dominant figure and believed Kim Chong-pil's influence could be diluted with the proper U.S. encouragement. (Ibid., Central Files, 795B.00/6–1962)

Mr. Johnson emphasized that the recent currency conversion and reform was undertaken without our knowledge and that this is a bad development. The ROK leaders knew that we would disapprove the proposal if they had discussed it with us in advance. We are still not clear on many of the detailed aspects of the new program. Mr. Yager said that there probably will be a heavy levy against capitalists and wealthy persons with a resultant harm to business and a slow down of capital investment and expansion. Mr. Johnson said that if the present trend continues with respect to our relations with the Korean Government, we may have to take a hard look at our policy vis-à-vis the Park Government. In response to Admiral Anderson's question, Mr. Johnson indicated that he was not prepared to say just what such a policy review would entail. Mr. Johnson also informed Admiral Anderson that the message to Ambassador Berger concerning the Korean SOFA negotiations had been dispatched (with information copies to DoD and JCS).[2]

[Here follows discussion unrelated to Korea.]

---

[2] See footnote 1, Document 263.

---

### 265.   Memorandum From the President's Military Representative (Taylor) to the President's Special Assistant for National Security Affairs (Bundy)

Washington, June 18, 1962.

SUBJECT

The Korean Military Assistance Program

I was recently briefed on the Cary Report[1] on the possible reduction of MAP supported military forces in Korea. I understand it has pleased no one since it does not come up with an easy solution to the problem of reducing force levels. I am also aware that the JCS have reviewed the matter and come out strongly for the maintenance of the present levels.

---

Source: Kennedy Library, National Security Files, Countries Series, Korea, General, 3/62–7/62. Secret.

[1] Printed in part as an attachment to Document 258.

I have three observations to make on the matter. The first is that it is highly unlikely that responsible U.S. military authorities will ever recommend a reduction in Korean force levels unless assured of the availability of [*less than 1 line of source text not declassified*] in case of the intervention in Korea of ChiCom forces in significant strength. With such an assurance, they would be justified in limiting the mission of South Korean forces to off-setting the North Korean establishment. Without that assurance [*1-1/2 lines of source text not declassified*] there is no military ground to support a substantial cut in Korean conventional forces.

[*1 paragraph (3-1/2 lines of source text) not declassified*]

A final comment is to wonder why, with all the pressure on the Department of Defense to support a reduction in the level of Korean forces, has the State Department never been asked to find a political solution to the armistice impasse? The North Koreans and their supporters must be just as tired of the present situation as we are. A minimum political objective would be to secure agreement on both sides to dismantle the fortified front and to maintain a frontier no more heavily defended than the frontier separating, say, Czechoslovakia from West Germany. Why do we not ask our diplomats to ply at their trade of negotiations?

MDT

---

## 266.  Memorandum From the President's Special Assistant for National Security Affairs (Bundy) to President Kennedy

Washington, June 20, 1962.

*Your Meeting With General Van Fleet et al.*[1]

Who is coming:

General Van Fleet—Head of the mission of businessmen to Korea

---

Source: Kennedy Library, President's Office Files, Korean Security, 1961–1963. No classification marking.

[1] President Kennedy met with General Van Fleet and his three colleagues as well as Seymour Janow of AID from 12:34 to 12:55 p.m. (Ibid., President's Appointment Book) No other record of the meeting has been found.

         Ernest  Barth—Vice  President—International  Agricultural Corp.
         Corde Snyder—Not known to me
         David Ginsburg—A very intelligent DC lawyer, and a good Democrat—counsel to the group

1.  You saw General Van Fleet's group May 3rd.[2] They have now been to Korea and come back with a warm welcome and some concrete proposals.[3]

2.  AID thinks they have done a good job but warns against any express or implied commitment of AID help at this time for these projects (Tab A)[4]

3.  Given recent reports of disturbance in Korea, you may want to ask General Van Fleet what he thinks of General Park and the SCNR (Supreme Council for National Reconstruction). Berger and our military in Korea are both troubled by

    a.  Evidence of economic naivete and mismanagement;
    b.  Increasing reluctance to consult fully with the U.S.;
    c.  The growing influence of Kim Chong Pil, the head of the Korean CIA and a fairly fancy operator;
    d.  Signs of disturbance in the recent resignation of the figurehead Prime Minister Song—whose place General Park has now taken.

All concerned still think Park is our best bet, but Berger thinks we may have to put some heat on soon to prevent a Rhee-like mess. (Tab B)[5]

4.  Finally, Berger has just asked that Vance Brand (a member of Van Fleet's group) be urged to go through with a planned visit to Korea because Brand is "sophisticated and will be able to bring home to them the significance of their action." This is worth repeating to Van Fleet and Ginsburg.

                                         **McG. B.**

---

[2] From 6:16 to 6:25 p.m. (Ibid.) Van Fleet was accompanied by 16 businessmen, members of a U.S. industrial mission to Korea to investigate possibilities in new or expanded ventures.

[3] In a memorandum from Brubeck to McGeorge Bundy, June 19, the Department of State described the mission of this private group and the enthusiastic welcome it received from the ROK Government. The concrete proposals included feasibility studies for investment of U.S. capital in various plants. (Department of State, Central Files, 895B.05111/6–1962)

[4] Tab A was a copy of the memorandum described in footnote 3 above. At the end of this paragraph, McGeorge Bundy wrote the following note: "Van Fleet's is a *private* group, & we want to avoid misunderstanding here or in Korea on this point."

[5] Tab B was telegram 1312 from Seoul, June 19; see footnote 1, Document 264. Tab C, telegram KA 41202 from Meloy, June 11, described approaching instability in the ROK and predicted a possible "sudden turn toward increased deterioration." (Department of State, Central Files, 795B.00/6–962)

## 267. Telegram From the Department of State to the Embassy in Japan

Washington, July 13, 1962, 8:30 p.m.

90. 1. This message for your comment constitutes policy directive being considered to govern US actions for promoting normalization of relations between Republic of Korea and Japan.

2. US objective is to bring about a settlement of outstanding differences and establishment normal diplomatic and economic relations between ROK and Japan, in order reduce tensions and promote security in Western Pacific and increase rate of Korean economic development.

3. General US course of action should be: (a) to stress to both sides the advantages of a settlement in their own respective national interests; (b) to use US influence and good offices with both sides to bring about settlement through realistic, forthcoming, and reasonable negotiation; (c) to suggest to both sides the use of well established Japanese-Korean practice of go-between for prior confidential exchange of information concerning range of settlement figures that will be acceptable at formal negotiations, and to act as go-between if requested; (d) if necessary to encourage both sides to look to US for confidential transmission of messages; (e) to seek discreetly to serve during course of negotiations as confidential informants to Chairman Pak and (if necessary) to Japanese Prime Minister on course of negotiations and conduct of negotiators; (f) to avoid rupture of negotiations or talks; (g) to maintain disinterested posture toward special interests of parties, playing role of catalyst but not acting as a party to negotiations. Specific actions are set forth in following paragraphs.

4. As soon as practicable following Ikeda's reappointment as Prime Min and formation new Japanese Cabinet, and subject to conditions reasonable political stability Korea, US Ambassador Tokyo will approach Prime Min and prevail upon him to set early date for resuming negotiations with Korea at political level, preferably in Seoul.

5. Subject to consultation between US Ambassadors Seoul and Tokyo, Seoul will approach ROKG at highest level, prevailing upon Koreans (a) to think in terms of claims settlement package of reasonable proportions including claims payments, grants, and long-term soft loans which can be accepted as package without emphasis on claims; (b) to name as their chief negotiator an individual who will deal effectively, reasonably and authoritatively with the Japanese.

Source: Department of State, Central Files, 694.95B/7–1362. Secret. Drafted by Macdonald; cleared by Yager, Peterson, Rice, Deputy Assistant Secretary for Economic Affairs Philip H. Trezise, and in draft by Janow; and approved by McGhee. Also sent to Seoul as telegram 40 and repeated to CINCPAC for POLAD and Paris for USRO.

6. In this connection, Embassies Tokyo and Seoul will immediately undertake review all outstanding issues between ROK and Japan, ascertaining positions of two sides and differences between them, with view to determining whether differences on fisheries or other issues aside from claims will impede overall settlement if claims issue resolved. Embassies should recommend possible US contribution toward settlement these issues, such as provision technical consultants from US or other countries.

7. As basis for influencing Japanese, Embassy Tokyo will stress in representations to GOJ officials the European and US business interest in Korean development.

8. Japanese officials should also be discreetly reminded of recent US cooperation in encouraging Korean-Japanese trade despite our own balance-of-payments problems—e.g., our facilitation of Korean nitrogenous fertilizer purchases; our provision of barley to Korea under PL 480 so that Korea could barter rice for additional fertilizer.

9. As basis for influencing Koreans, Embassy Seoul will stress in representations to ROKG officials that in joint consultation re Five Year Economic Development Plan, ROK and US must consider all potential capital resources additional to those of US, including Europe and particularly Japan, as well as export market opportunities in Japan. If additional pressure on the ROK Government is required to produce a bargain in the face of reasonable Japanese offer, US Development Lending may be related to this settlement.

10. Embassy Seoul will also point out to Koreans the desirability of publicity on fisheries issue designed to show (a) importance this issue to both countries, (b) Korean willingness to negotiate reasonable settlement. Such approach would give GOJ useful domestic argument for settlement with ROK, and would remind Japanese of Korean bargaining lever.

11. US Embassies Bonn, Paris, London, Rome and USRO will discreetly promote European government and business interests in investment Korea and offer US assistance in selecting suitable projects and examining possibilities for US public or private participation.

12. Department will approach suitable individual to travel to Korea as special representative to attend August 15 ceremonies Seoul and talk with ROKG leaders about development problems (contingent upon favorable political situation Korea). Assuming favorable reception by Koreans, same individual would visit Japan for talks with GOJ leaders and would thereafter be available on standby basis to be called in as consultant to both sides as appropriate. Representative could fulfill much of purpose envisaged in Embassy Seoul's proposal for high-level envoy (Seoul's telegram 1126)[1] thus cloaking his connection with ROK-Japan

---

[1] Dated April 26. (Ibid., 694.95B/4–2662)

negotiations but providing preliminary contacts as a basis for future good offices. He might carry Presidential letters to Ikeda and Pak, encouraging free and frank discussion with him on current issues and referring in passing to question ROK-Japan relations.[2]

Rusk

---

[2] In telegram 224 from Tokyo, July 24, the Embassy stated that while it endorsed the objectives of this telegram, its reaction was that the proposed policy "oversteps influence which we can exert on Japan in bringing about ROK-Japan settlement, and underestimates dangers, at least in Japan, if we were to press forward with expanded U.S. role." The Embassy recommended against any dramatic U.S. steps. (Ibid., 694.95B/7–2462)

---

268. **Telegram From the Embassy in Korea to the Department of State**

Seoul, July 23, 1962, 5 p.m.

66. Country Team has reviewed current situation and provides following assessment:

1. For almost two months military government has been undergoing its greatest crisis since taking power. Leadership struggle at highest levels has been coupled with economic dislocation stemming largely from ill-advised monetary reform and stock market fiasco. Embassy and USOM have taken firm position on failure of government to consult on matters of fundamental importance to our relationship, and we also expressed clearly unfavorable consequences if iniquitous aspects of monetary changes not removed. This has introduced measure of strain in Embassy-ROKG relations and a feeling which may border on frustration and even anger on part of certain people in ROKG, although others have welcomed our initiative. Additionally, a mood of pessimism and uncertainty has arisen in the country as result government's economic faltering, evidences instability in leadership, activities of ROK CIA, and concern over problem of transition to representative government.

2. It appears that worst of current crisis has passed. Undesirable features of monetary reform have been rescinded. Some minor changes

---

Source: Department of State, Central Files, 795B.00/7–2062. Secret; Priority. Repeated to Tokyo and CINCPAC for POLAD.

in SCNR have been effected, a new team of economic administrators has taken cabinet office and we are hopeful that more fruitful relationship between Embassy, USOM and their ROKG counterparts can be instituted. At the leadership level an uneasy truce seems to have been achieved but factional clash which pitted Kim Chong-p'il and some of young colonels against combination of Hamgyong and other anti-Kim elements hovers over scene.

3.  After wavering and despite heavy pressure Pak appears have decided retain Kim in some position of significance, whether as ROK CIA [omission—head or?] figure elsewhere in military government. While Kim may have his freedom of maneuver and his exercise of power restricted to some extent by Pak and may even be shifted, he still is a major force in military government. Kim has not given up his efforts to gain complete upper hand over his opponents, and this promises have continuing unsettling effects.

4.  Test of power between Kim and his opponents has left each side wary of other. Pak carefully avoided taking sides since he derives support from all contending elements. Nevertheless, he finds himself faced with classic Korean factional struggle which has roots in personal antipathies and ambitions and involves rival groups bound together by common regional or education ties. Factionalism also plays its part in bureaucratic rivalries, and is intensified by the overlapping and often conflicting jurisdiction of SCNR, cabinet and CIA.

5.  Factional fighting is deeply rooted in Korean national character and has been a continuous problem for Pak and this government. It played a part in Chang To-young case and was feature of illicit fortune committee case last [garble] Kim Chong-p'il attacked Yi Chu-il. Similar attacks and counter-attacks re-appeared in fight between Song Yo-chan and Kim early this year and again in June. Latest outbreak occasioned by economic activities of CIA gave Kim's opponents their first big chance move against him.

6.  Retention and exercise of power by Pak has always required restraint of factional fighting, and maintenance of balance between contending forces. While it is significant that outcome of most recent fracas finds most of young colonels and their leader Kim in strong position, Hamgyong and other factions have also emerged intact. In our opinion, conflict is only suspended and stability not assured through next year's election. Meanwhile, worthwhile achievements of regime have been obscured and its public reputation has suffered as charges and counter-charges of corruption, bad advice, shady-dealings, bad planning, economic retrogression, CIA repression, and coup-plotting have become common knowledge.

7.  Unsettling actions and disturbing tensions of past two months have shaken our confidence in government's judgment. They have also

thrown doubt on ability and willingness of military government to bring about satisfactory (tolerable for the US) political evolution in Korea. Military government has been approaching task of governing with dogmatic faith in their own sometimes ill-formed ideas and belief that since their ends are lofty, their means and even their mistakes are justified. Military government's political image is tarnished by recent events; its leadership is at odds; its opponents may seek capitalize on instability to bring about drastic change; and government measures to control thought and deed in Korea remains pervasive and could worsen.

8.   Outlook for military government has become clouded and consequences could be serious. We believe, however, that we must continue support Pak and continue behave toward him and his government in manner showing understanding of his problems and reflecting confidence in his leadership. We should not, however, take open and unquestioning public stance which will associate US without reservation with all actions and policies of military government. Our eyes should be focused on promoting peaceful transition to representative government while promoting economic progress in Korea.

We should work on assumption that transition and election will be carried out on schedule and successor government will have some measure of constitutional legitimacy. We can also assume that revolutionary leadership will seek perpetuate its objectives and control in any new government. This is not necessarily an undesirable prospect. We should, therefore, continue to work with present government but look forward to its replacement by government more popularly based and resting on a publicly approved constitution containing some measure of checks and balances. We should maintain this strategy unless it becomes unrealistic.

9.   Pak remains our best hope in this situation. He is in position maintain structure of government in transition period and through his leadership we can hopefully expect a measure of stability.

10. Pak's problem centers on the difficult task of gaining widest possible support in country, asserting his leadership of government, and recapturing momentum of revolution which has faltered. In relations with United States, Pak should appreciate and accept necessity of close cooperation and consultation, and be prepared enlarge area and content of consultation in economic and political spheres.

11. One consoling and stabilizing factor in midst this economic uncertainty and high level power play has been loyalty of military forces to government and also to United Nations Command. Chain of command and command relationships have been firm and reliable. This stability is anchor and foundation of military government's existence and an area in which we have considerable influence. We should use this to our advantage and avoid taking measures which would interrupt this influence. Such actions as excessive force reductions or sharp reductions

in MAP funds could cause trouble. (Indeed USFK believes any force reduction would cause trouble.)

12. We have put great pressure on military government over past weeks, with particular emphasis on undoing of monetary regulations. We have also rightfully insisted on need for consultation. We have been careful reiterate our confidence in Pak and readiness support his government in reasonable courses of action. While insisting on fundamental cooperation, and continuing offer objection to unreasonable actions, we are seeking achieve greater rapport between military government and United States, while pursuing Korean political and economic progress which desirable in any event.

13. United States should not at this time involve itself directly in factional power struggle among leaders. Resolution this problem should be left to Pak and we should be prepared accept his solution if at all possible, i.e., if it does not involve means or ends incompatible with our objectives. In a deteriorating situation, however, we may have to involve ourselves. For example, if Kim Chong-p'il's power and actions become intolerable we may have to throw our weight against him.

14. Probably best area for cooperation and obtaining forward momentum in immediate future lies in economic field. In this area, where we retain effective leverage, we can more readily assert ourselves in pursuit our policy objectives.

15. USOM has proposed and ROKG has agreed to a joint review of government's financial and economic development position as of now. This will involve full consideration of government's plans for CY 1962 and CY 1963. In this exercise we will continue press for sound ROKG economic policies, concentrating our efforts on shorter term and priorities which can be established for next two-three years.

16. In addition to above stated actions we propose:

A. Keep under review possible despatch of special envoy. We do not believe this is opportune time for such visit and will elaborate on this subject in separate message.

B. Low key, but steady expression of interest in problems surrounding political evolution involved in transition to representative government. We should exercise such influence as we can to obtain a tolerable political solution.

C. As required use such other means as are available, [less than 1 line of source text not declassified] to influence character and actions of this government.

17. As a final comment, we should accept fact that there is no overnight solution to political and economic problems plaguing Korea. We should recognize that cyclical variations in relationship between United States and Korea are endemic. We must face fact that judicious intervention in Korean internal affairs will continue be necessary. We will have to guide and sometimes lecture them and sometimes we are going to anger

or frustrate them. In process we have to be careful not alienate them, but we cannot sacrifice our principles or our objectives for sake of momentary solutions or transitory agreement. There is continuing test of will involved in our relations with this government and we should preserve a firm but reasonable posture.

**Berger**

### 269.  Memorandum of Conversation

Washington, July 24, 1962.

SUBJECT

The Korean Military Government

PARTICIPANTS

General James A. Van Fleet
Edward E. Rice, Deputy Assistant Secretary for Far Eastern Affairs
Donald S. Macdonald, Officer in Charge, Korean Affairs, Office of East Asian
    Affairs

General Van Fleet called by appointment at 10:00 a.m. With very few preliminaries he turned immediately to the subject of the Korean military government, of whom he said that "these are good boys". He stated that "everything is going fine" in Korea; and that the United States should give these leaders our support. He referred to the new Korean Cabinet appointments approvingly as bringing civilian bankers into key posts. He urged that now was the time for the State Department to make a suitable statement of United States support, to give encouragement to the Korean Government. He complained of the effect of Washington statements indicating lack of confidence in the military government, and cited a statement attributed to Secretary Dillon that if Korea were to become a state-run economy, it should not receive another dollar of aid. Mr. Rice commented that he had never heard or read of such a statement, and inquired what its source was. General Van Fleet stated that it came from "American sources."

---

Source: Department of State, Central Files, 795B.00/7–2462. Confidential; Limit Distribution. Drafted by Macdonald.

Turning to the subject of Colonel Kim Chong-p'il, Director of the Korean CIA, General Van Fleet said that he was indispensable to the Korean Government at the present time. He and Chairman Pak continued to be very close, and were working together; there was no real trouble within the regime. General Van Fleet had talked to "Tiger" Song (General Song Yo-ch'an, ex-Prime Minister), to Kim Chong-p'il and to Chairman Pak, and had heard the views of each. Mr. Rice inquired whether the Chairman's and Kim's reports had agreed. The General said they had. He continued that he had told both the Chairman and Colonel Kim that Kim should stay within his field, and not get beyond it, as he had with the Walker Hill project (a foreign tourist center) and the taxi import and assembly project. In the Walker Hill case, however, Colonel Kim had been asked to undertake it because he was the only man who could accomplish the job.

Mr. Rice asked about Kim's involvement in the stock market deal. The General answered, first, that Colonel Kim's involvement in it had never been proved; then, that opposition forces had endeavored to use the stock market for political fund-raising, against which countermeasures were necessary; finally, that business optimism, coupled with the scarcity of opportunities for investment, had forced the market up. Mr. Macdonald commented that the power available to the Korean Government should have enabled it to control the market and avoid a speculative spiral, if it had wished.

General Van Fleet commented [2 *lines of source text not declassified*] that the U.S. military intelligence sources were the best, and that we should look to them for information. Mr. Macdonald stated that both the Department and the Embassy in Seoul were receiving intelligence reports from the Eighth Army; that these reports were very helpful; but that they did not conflict in their general import with information from other sources.

Mr. Rice asked whether General Van Fleet had given the Ambassador his views and observations on Korea, and the General affirmed that he had done so.

General Van Fleet recalled his wartime experiences in Korea, when the Korean military were very eager to have American guidance and American approval. They would respond even to his unspoken thoughts—he would think, for example, that a hill should be taken, and before he knew it, it would be in ROK hands. Since then the Koreans had matured; they wanted to do things for themselves, in their own way; but they still wanted and needed American approval and commendation when they did well. Of course, they sometimes acted rashly, and made mistakes. The currency reform had been such a mistake. Nevertheless, the Koreans had been quick to acknowledge their error, and to correct it. Having done so, they expected our approval. We must understand the

Koreans' nature in our dealings with them. In this connection, it would be very desirable for the United States to make an appropriate public statement of our support. The Secretary, for example, might make a prepared statement.

Mr. Rice said that the United States had already made clear its support. Mr. Macdonald cited Ambassador Berger's May 16 statement for the Educational Radio Network,[1] and promised, at General Van Fleet's request, to send him a copy. Mr. Rice continued that he welcomed the General's strong partisan support of the military government, commenting that it was a needed source of help for the Koreans.

Mr. Rice continued that he had known Ambassador Berger and his work for some years, and had every confidence in him. He hoped that General Van Fleet, also, would cooperate with the Ambassador, give him his confidence and keep him informed. General Van Fleet agreed, and continued that while in Korea he had done his best to avoid creating difficulties for the Ambassador. He himself, although by nature a modest person, was willynilly a hero in Korea, and always received and treated as one, though he never wanted it. He had sometimes felt that this must make it difficult for the Ambassador.

The General wondered why Korea should have such a generally bad press in the United States. He had commented on this point to some of his friends, who agreed. Mr. Macdonald stated that the many achievements of Korea were unfortunately overshadowed by Korean crises, which appeared to be more newsworthy. General Van Fleet mentioned that he had heard of an American newspaper story that the level of U.S. economic aid to Korea was to be reduced. Mr. Macdonald said there had been some speculative stories, but he had seen no such report.

Turning to the question of military procurement in Korea, General Van Fleet urged that U.S. purchases be increased, and that Secretary McNamara's recent order not be allowed to affect procurement in Korea. He suggested that some procurement now being made in Japan might be made in Korea, referring as example to a suggestion by a U.S. military officer that trucks now being bought in Japan ready to run could be purchased in stripped form and assembled in Korea with Korean tires and batteries, which now are just as good as American makes. The Japanese had already benefited enormously by U.S. purchases there—for example, he himself had spent over $100 million in Japan for rehabilitating the Korean transportation system (while he was in command in Korea). Korean suppliers to U.S. procurement agencies were private firms, and loss of this business would be a terrible blow to them.

---

[1] Not further identified.

Mr. Rice assured General Van Fleet that he sympathized with this position and understood the prospective adverse effects of the directive on Korea, but pointed out that the directive had been issued in response to the need to redress the U.S. balance of payments.

In concluding pleasantries, General Van Fleet said he would go to New York to attend two directors' meetings—Twentieth Century Fox, in connection with the possible ouster of Mr. Skouros, and Webb–Knapp, in connection with a similar situation involving Mr. Zeckendorf. He had come back from Korea for these meetings, and would return to Korea after they were over.

### 270.   Memorandum From the Deputy Under Secretary of State for Political Affairs (Johnson) to Secretary of State Rusk

Washington, July 26, 1962.

SUBJECT

Redeployment of US Forces from Korea

1.   Consistent with your request I have been looking into implications of a redeployment of one of the US divisions in Korea. I discussed the matter briefly with Admiral Felt during my trip last week with Secretary McNamara and I have informed Ambassador Berger, Eyes Only, of our pending review.[1]

2.   In pursuing this question I have found that the interagency committee developing the report in response to NSC Action 2447 (Review of the Military Aid Program)[2] has moved rather far along in evolving proposals which relate to levels of Korean forces and of US aid in relation thereto. Though NSC Action 2447 is primarily addressed to US Military Assistance and its problems, the Action does direct that the review of

---

Source: Department of State, Central Files, 795.00/7–2662. Top Secret. Drafted by Seymour Weiss of G/PM. A note on the source text indicates Rusk saw the memorandum.

[1] Reference is to telegram 80 to Seoul, July 27, in which Weiss and Johnson informed Berger that the principal presumed advantages to the United States would be "increased tactical flexibility" and "balance of payment savings" by stationing the troops in a dollar area such as Okinawa. They stressed that they appreciated the disadvantages of the proposal and reiterated that no decision had been yet made. (Ibid., 795.00/7–2762)

[2] See Document 251.

Korean Military Assistance plans and programs should take into account and make recommendations in connection with "the desirable level of US forces in Korea." This latter point has not been adequately addressed in the work of the interagency committee developing the report in response to 2447. The issue has largely been assumed away, i.e., that the importance of the present levels of US forces in Korea is assumed to be manifest. The study then focuses on levels of Korean forces and related aid problems. Since NSC Action 2447 is cast in terms of a review of US foreign aid activities it is understandable why the basic strategic policy implications surrounding the US force commitment have not emerged clearly. As I see it, however, the preliminary direction in which that Report is moving would severely prejudice any serious consideration of a US force withdrawal since a large reduction in Korean forces will probably be recommended.

3. As a result of the foregoing I propose to discuss this matter with Fowler Hamilton, Paul Nitze and Governor Harriman with a view to seeing how the fundamental question which you raised, and which is explicitly raised by the NSC Action 2447, can best be brought into focus. I am also going to let McGeorge Bundy know what we are doing so as to assure full coordination with the White House.

### 271. Telegram From the Embassy in Korea to the Department of State

Seoul, July 27, 1962, 6 p.m.

85. 1. We have been having rocky time here during past couple months, and while situation is better in sense that new PriMin and Economic Ministers are working with us in fairly cooperative fashion, I am still not happy about certain aspects of situation.

2. Basic problem is power of Kim Chong Pil and ROK CIA. Kim was given severe shaking and for few days in June and again in July it looked as if his organization was going to be cut back to its basic intelligence mission. Pak gave me assurances of this on two occasions, but there is no sign this has been done.

Source: Department of State, Central Files, 611.95B/7–2762. Secret; Limit Distribution.

3. ROK CIA has curious set-up. One part devoted to usual activities. Second part consists of political, economic, legislative and public information divisions: which occupy themselves with major policy matters. Numbers employed in latter are large; we have no access to them; and some of their key people have record of past Communist or leftist associations or hold extreme anti-American views. Moreover ROK CIA is in "everything"—appointments, lodging their people in newspapers and business, deriving income from variety of sources from stock market to business deals, etc.

4. If Pak carries out his assurance to return ROK CIA to its proper function, or if its extra-curricular activities are separated from ROK CIA, we can then deal with Kim Chong Pil on a tidy basis. But there is a real possibility that Kim Chong Pil may continue in the same capacity with the same all-embracing functions, in which case we will have serious problem of whether and how to deal with him.

5. In a recent conversation with [*less than 1 line of source text not declassified*] Political Counselor, Kim Chong Pil expressed his resentment, frustration, and some bitterness [*2-1/2 lines of source text not declassified*] at our refusal to accept him as a major direct channel for communication with ROKG on other matters. He said he wears two hats which are completely separate, and we were to recognize this and deal with him on all matters, for he is the real power and policy maker in the government, and he is going to continue in that capacity. He asked them to convey his desire for direct and regular contact with me. He made it clear that anyone in or out of the mil govt who tries to take his power away had better watch out, and that he is going to "get" those on the Supreme Council who are trying to reduce his power. At same time he went to some length to try to assure us that stability had been reestablished at top leadership and contending factors had agreed work together in furtherance revolutionary goals.

6. In two conversations with him, once with me in March and once with one of our [*less than 1 line of source text not declassified*] officers in July, he said that if it ever becomes necessary to preserve the "revolution," (i.e. preserve his power, which he identifies with the revolution), he will do whatever is necessary, including even "toppling" Pak Chong-hui.

7. We will be analyzing the implications of foregoing in separate message.[1]

8. Meantime we are picking up rumors that there is resentment in some ROK Govt circles over my actions during past couple months. One such rumor has it that Kim Chong Pil is out to get "certain Americans." Another, that some weeks ago Pak wrote Amb Chong Il-kwon to arrange

---

[1] Not further identified.

for my recall. According this rumor, Chong replied this was impossible and he would resign if ordered to do so, after which Pak wrote back "to forget it." I cannot vouch for reliability latter rumor, but I believe that idea of declaring me PNG has been considered. [*3 lines of source text not declassified*] However, a recent report has it that some around Pak are anxious that close contact and good relations be reestablished between him and me.

9.  I should add that according reliable Korean source, Van Fleet made deprecating remarks about me to Pak and Kim Chong Pil, which has not helped matters, and I am thinking of discussing this with him when he returns in a few days.

**Berger**

## 272. Telegram From the Department of State to the Embassy in Korea

Washington, August 5, 1962, 12:38 p.m.

109. Ref: Seoul's 85.[1]

1.  Our problem with Kim Chong-p'il and CIA appears to Dept as crystallization more general problem we have all foreseen: How effectively to counter trends toward totalitarian control and ambitions of young colonels for political and personal power, and how to keep Korea somewhere near road toward democratic development.

2.  As you have pointed out, it is not realistic for us to insist on full-blown democracy and complete disappearance of military leadership in 1963. On other hand, continuing usefulness of Korea to us in terms our long-range objectives depends upon maintenance of some forward momentum toward evolution of free society. We can tolerate ups and downs, but not major reversal.

3.  Seems inescapable that we must be prepared accept either Pak Chong-hui or man selected by him as Korea's leader for next few years, subject to proviso that this leadership must be legitimated by people through processes sufficiently free and fair to be acceptable in Korea and world. Pak is only figure now in sight who seems to possess sufficient intelligence, vision, breadth of contact, forcefulness, personal reputa-

---

Source: Department of State, Central Files, 611.95B/7–2762. Secret; Priority; Limit Distribution. Drafted by Macdonald; cleared by Yager, U. Alexis Johnson, and Rice; and approved by Harriman.
[1] Document 271.

tion, and access to power (especially over military) to fulfill present leadership requirements.

4.  As you have recommended, we therefore should work with Pak, manifesting our support for him implicitly rather than explicitly, continuing to make clear that our support flows from our general policy toward Korea and not from commitment to any individual or group, and using our support for him as basis to influence his courses of action along lines acceptable to us.

5.  First course of action concerns Kim Chong-p'il. Just as we should not support any individual qua individual, we should not overtly so oppose anyone. However we can make it clear, as you already have done, that a director of espionage and secret police should not at same time be principal policy maker and second-ranking leader of modern state, even in transition period; nor should same man whose function it is to serve as watchdog over government and society serve also as head of vast and uncontrolled executive apparatus which is set above established governmental apparatus and stifles it. Hence if Kim is to continue run CIA, he should head his intelligence apparatus, make his recommendations, and limit himself to those roles, leaving policy decision and execution to established executive arm even when he believes his men might do it faster or better. Alternatively, Kim might be removed from picture gracefully, say as Ambassador to Japan where he seems to have been so successful in negotiations. Pak might be reminded that principal distinction between top leader and his associates is that former alone exercises jurisdiction over all aspects of national affairs while subordinates handle assigned parts. If this distinction is blurred, status of leader is also blurred, and consequently his power. Hence imperative that Kim accept his specialized role.

6.  As corollary to above, and as basis for continuity of revolution, power and effectiveness of executive branch of government should be enhanced, including greater role for Cabinet. This branch, with its organization and personnel, has legitimacy of centuries of history, constitutional sanction, and largely civilian staffing. It needs more motivation, discipline, esprit de corps, and efficiency; but if it is harassed and pushed aside by CIA and military, it can never hope to improve; and if its work is to be taken over by uncontrolled ad hoc organizations, these sooner or later will fall prey to same weaknesses as present bureaucracy, as well as lacking legitimacy and hence public acceptance. On other hand, if bureaucracy can be strengthened, motivated, and brought to support revolutionary objectives, it can be most powerful means of assuring continuation of revolution under successor civilian government. Effective bureaucracy with sense of pride, ideals, and esprit de corps can be much more immune to undesirable political pressures than weak and underpaid organization of past, and hence can be expected to remain on rea-

sonable course toward national development. Extra-legal executive agencies, such as those under CIA, should be either abolished or merged into established government structure.

7.   Second course of action concerns transition to civilian government. Following propositions suggested for comment:

a.   Eventual success of revolution depends upon consensus of Korean people that its goals desirable and attainable; that revolutionary program conceived and pursued for people's benefit, not that of junta alone or its individual members; that government is led by men best equipped to carry out this program; and that channels exist through which people can express views, exert influence, and have sense participation.

b.   This consensus can best be promoted by (1) protecting prestige and reputation of military leaders as able, sincere men dedicated to national welfare above all else; (2) legitimating government through legitimate expression of popular will in referendum and elections; (3) primary reliance on persuasion and firm leadership rather than terror; (4) avoidance of unreasonable promises or unreasonable demands.

c.   If revolutionary leaders are convinced that their goals and programs are valid, and that Free World ideals they profess to support are valid, then they should be willing accept challenges and risks of unrigged elections.

d.   On other hand, fraudulent election victory would negate everything they stand for.

e.   Such fundamental and far-reaching reforms as revolutionary leaders envisage cannot be accomplished overnight, except in their most superficial and least meaningful aspects; too much haste and pressure will actually retard social and economic progress; hence long view is essential, and setbacks are inevitable.

f.   Korean people are basically sensible, pragmatic, independent-minded, but suspicious of government; therefore if they are approached sincerely, sensibly, and pragmatically, and if their suspicions thus in some measure alleviated, they are most likely to support revolution at polls, while trickery, bribery and pressure will do lasting damage whatever statistical election outcome might be.

g.   Best way of dealing with expectable opposition vote is to split it among contending candidates rather than suppressing it. (This procedure would also shed useful light on relative popularity of opposition leaders.)

h.   Progressive increase in freedom of action and expression as election time approaches would be valuable demonstration of military leaders' good faith. Removal additional individuals from political purification lists, and termination martial courts and other emergency control measures, would be useful this connection. Skillful public debate on opposition political claims and pronouncements, based on objectives, background, and experience of military leaders with good public-relations counsel, could turn increased freedom to leaders' advantage.

8.  Third course of action concerns civilian participation, necessity of which you have emphasized. Believe Pak should open channel of communication with senior political leaders, inviting their suggestions, and in course of dialogue on future of country, endeavor to gain support of some of them by accepting at least portions of proferred advice, and possibly by constituting an informal council of elder statesmen which would have certain emoluments and status attached to it but would also have degree of independence. Senior leaders' nominees might be given Cabinet and sub-Cabinet positions as initial step in gaining their confidence.

9.  Fourth course of action concerns post-election control. Continuation of CIA-like apparatus in some form probably inevitable, regardless of U.S. arguments pro or con, but exclusive reliance must not be placed on it. Continued ties between military and civilian bureaucracy, perhaps with latter protected through some sort of civil service commission, plus plurality military government members and supporters in national assembly and Pak or his nominee as chief executive, backed by continued implicit power of armed forces, should insure continuity of revolution. Another possibility might be small legislative Upper House, half of whose members appointed for first term of, say, six years, and other half subjected to re-election after three years. Frank expression of military leadership's influence through such means might be preferable to rigging of elections for single legislation house.

10. You authorized approach Pak at appropriate time and in appropriate circumstances and discuss situation along foregoing lines in context US desire to be helpful, making above points as your own or as US Government's as seems most expedient, and emphasizing that our concern with specific problems or individuals, such as Kim Chong-p'il, is solely in context our general concern with Korean security, progress, and prosperity, which is in US interests as well as Korea's.

11. In regard your relations with military government, Dept continues to have utmost confidence your ability to handle situation, and is prepared to back you up in future as in past. Dept agrees with your policy of refusing deal with Kim Chong-p'il except on CIA matters, and not surprised that this policy, as well as your firmness on other matters, has resulted in some back-pressure and bitterness. Dept believes we are on right track and proposes we stay on it, having in mind of course the need for the eager, sensitive, and by now somewhat confused revolutionary leaders to have the sweet judiciously mingled with the sour.

**Rusk**

273.  **Memorandum From Robert W. Komer of the National
Security Council Staff to the President's Special Assistant for
National Security Affairs (Bundy)**

Washington, August 17, 1962.

McGB—

Sam Berger's return[1] offers a chance not to be missed of giving him our current thinking about ROK force and MAP cut-backs. This account costs a cool half billion a year in all forms of aid; as such, it deserves a long hard look because many of us can think of better ways to spend the last hundred million of this dough.

My sense is that DOD, State, and AID are moving toward some form of force and MAP cut. But this is such a longstanding, contentious issue, and vested interests are so firmly entrenched, that few are willing to bite the bullet. Moreover, I'm sure Berger will argue that current political uncertainty in Korea militates against upsetting ROK Army. He'd like at least to get rid of Kim Chong-pil first. However, my sense is that if we can offset force and MAP cut with promises of increased support for Korean development, Pak regime might snap at this option, because its political future depends largely on domestic record it makes.

I'd urge that you personally, along with Dave Bell, Carl, Ken Hansen, and Mike have a private session with Berger in order to get across that there is real desire in WH to do something about ROK problem. This might also provide occasion to lay out to Berger importance JFK personally attaches to quick ROK/Jap settlement (NSAM 151).[2] Wish I were here for this one.[3]

**Bob K.**

---

Source: Kennedy Library, National Security Files, Countries Series, Korea, General, 8/62–3/63. Secret. Copies were sent to David Bell, Kaysen, Hansen, and Forrestal.

[1] Berger returned to Washington for consultations on August 19.

[2] Document 256.

[3] Komer handwrote the following note at the end of this memorandum: "I'd also think it well worthwhile for President to spend half hour with Berger, *after being filled in.*" Bundy wrote the following note on the top of the memorandum: "This is no fortnight for a climax on this one." President Kennedy's Appointment Book has no record of a meeting with Berger. (Kennedy Library)

### 274. Letter From the Deputy Secretary of Defense (Gilpatric) to Secretary of State Rusk

Washington, August 28, 1962.

DEAR DEAN: As a result of a recent meeting in Alexis Johnson's office[1] regarding the pros and cons of redeploying one U.S. division from Korea to Okinawa, the JCS were asked to give their recommendations on the military and financial implications of such a move.[2]

Based on the following conclusions, the Chiefs believe that the redeployment of one division would not be in consonance with U.S. interests:

a.   Removal of a division not only would dilute our present deterrent to Communist aggression in Korea to an unacceptable level but could lead to an undesirable change in U.S./ROK command relationship. It would also result in ROK reluctance to continue U.S. operational control of ROK forces.

b.   Combat capability in Korea would be reduced without proportional increase in the general Pacific area.

c.   In view of the limited airfield and port facilities in Okinawa, redeployment could result in a decrease in flexibility of forces.

d.   Redeployment would require an additional one-time expenditure ranging from an order of magnitude of $87 million without dependents in Okinawa, to $138 million with dependents.

e.   The acquisition of the additional land which would be required in Okinawa would be extremely difficult in view of the attendant political implications.

f.   Transportation resources presently available in the Pacific Command would not support an immediate redeployment of a division from Okinawa to Korea during the initial phases of hostilities.

g.   Redeployment of a division to Okinawa, vis-à-vis having it in Korea, would affect the international balance of payments adversely by

---

Source: Department of State, Central Files, 795B.65311/8–2862. Top Secret.

[1] The meeting took place on August 2. According to a memorandum from Nitze to McNamara, August 24, Department of Defense officials were asked at this meeting to examine the possibilities of redeploying a division from Korea to Okinawa. The idea had been raised twice by Rusk who anticipated it would result in greater military flexibility and balance-of-payments relief. According to the memorandum, "Mr. Johnson suggested that from the standpoint of Communist intentions, one division should be sufficient to serve as a 'plate glass' and thus deter another attack. He presumed that sizeable savings of foreign exchange could be realized by shifting a division to a 'dollar area'; and that these 'savings' would reduce the need for cutting ROK forces." (Washington National Records Center, RG 330, OASD/ISA Files: FRC 65 A 3501, 320.2 Korea)

[2] The Joint Chiefs made these recommendations to McNamara in JCSM–622–62, August 15. (Ibid., OSD Files: FRC 66 A 3542, Korea 320.2)

approximately $1.1 million annually. This results from the fact that only some $9.3 million of the costs, including pay and allowances, of maintaining a division in Korea enter the balance of payments account each year, whereas the loss of dollars involved in maintaining a division in Okinawa would amount to approximately $10.4 million, because of the close association between the Okinawan and Japanese economies.

In addition to these views, we have had the benefit of several other studies conducted recently in DoD by special study groups regarding the situation in this area and the forces required to cope successfully with the several major contingencies. These studies generally agree that, while present forces in Korea are fully capable of inflicting a decisive defeat against North Korean forces alone, a combined North Korean Chi-Com attack would present a quite serious challenge to the ability of these forces to defend South Korea. Obviously, the gravity of this threat and the managing of a successful defense depend upon such critical elements as length of warning time, availability of bases in Japan, and events in other areas of the world, as well as the size and readiness of the defending forces.

In view of these considerations and the fact that no decision has yet been taken on the optimum balance between our economic and military assistance programs in Korea, we are not prepared at this time to recommend the withdrawal of one U.S. division from Korea.[3] In the event of a severe reduction in the FY '63 appropriations for the Military Assistance Program, we will reconsider the matter.

Sincerely,

**Ros Gilpatric**

---

[3] At the White House staff meeting on September 13, this letter was discussed as follows: "The Secretary of Defense has sent a letter to the Secretary of State stating that this is not a good time to cut down US forces in Korea. We have to keep three divisions in the Far East, and shifting the one from Korea to Okinawa would cost more gold as well as being very difficult to do politically. As far as the White House is concerned, this point is settled. Now comes the question of settling on a Korean force reduction, which has been agreed to a certain extent, but Harriman reports that Defense is cutting up about this reduction." (National Defense University, Taylor Papers, Daily Staff Meetings, May–September 1962)

## 275.  Special National Intelligence Estimate

SNIE 42–2–62                                    Washington, September 7, 1962.

### SHORT-TERM OUTLOOK FOR SOUTH KOREA

#### The Problem

To assess the political situation in South Korea and to estimate probable developments over the next few months.

#### Conclusions

A.  The recent outbreak of factional strife within the military junta which rules South Korea has been caused largely by controversy [5 lines of source text not declassified]. We believe that the junta, with General Pak Chong-hui as the key figure, will remain in power until the elections scheduled for 1963, and will exercise a large degree of control over the new civilian government. (Paras. 1–5, 9–12)

B.  The junta currently has little popular support. Blatantly rigged elections or further economic deterioration could cause riots and demonstrations. While the regime can suppress local outbursts, massive public demonstrations could trigger coup attempts by disgruntled military leaders, perhaps acting in concert with presently disbarred political elements. The outcome of such attempts cannot be estimated, but the government which emerged from such a situation would almost certainly require a large degree of backing from the ROK military. (Paras. 6–8, 11)

C.  ROK-US relations will continue to be difficult over the next few months. There will probably be some attempts to improve liaison with US officials in economic matters, although the CIA will continue its largely uncontrolled economic activities. In political matters, it is doubtful that either Pak or Kim will accept US suggestions which might impose limitations on their actions. Despite strong US pressures, it is doubtful that the issue of ROK-Japanese relations will soon be resolved. Only on the military plane will ROK-US relations remain reasonably open and friendly. (Paras. 13–17)

D.  Factional strife within the junta, increased public apathy and even hostility toward the regime, and strained relations with the US have

---

Source: Department of State, INR/EAP Files: Lot 90 D 110, SNIE 42–2–62. Secret. According to a note on the cover sheet, the Central Intelligence Agency and the intelligence organizations of the Departments of State, Defense, the Army, the Navy, and the Air Force, and the Joint Staff participated in the preparation of this estimate. All members of the USIB concurred with this estimate on September 7 except the representatives of the AEC and the FBI, who abstained on the grounds that the subject was outside their jurisdiction.

increased the danger of Communist subversive activities. Appeals to Korean nationalism and for peaceful unification may prove more effective than in the past. During the next few months, a real Communist threat to the regime is unlikely to develop, but if the political erosion, which has already commenced, is not halted and if economic stagnation persists, the problem of countering Communist subversion will become far more serious. (Paras. 18–20)

[Here follows the "Discussion" section of the estimate.]

## 276.  Memorandum From the Deputy Under Secretary of State for Political Affairs (Johnson) to Secretary of State Rusk

Washington, September 15, 1962.

SUBJECT

U.S. Force Level, Korea

I have examined the question of withdrawing a U.S. division from Korea as a means of increasing the flexibility of our military posture in the Western Pacific. Although the withdrawal of one division would probably not materially dilute the deterrent effect of the presence of U.S. forces, there are a number of negative considerations.

It appears that proximity to Korea is important in light of a finding by the JCS that in the event of a combined North Korean-ChiCom attack, the presence of two U.S. divisions would be necessary at the outset. Thus, Okinawa would provide the best alternate location for the division. Hawaii and the Philippines are both comparatively distant. Difficulties with this alternative are a) the present lack of sufficient transportation in the opening days of a conflict, and b) the lack of sufficient airfield and port facilities in Okinawa rapidly to effect the movement of the necessary size.

In addition, there are also a number of disadvantages of a political and economic nature. Such a withdrawal would likely have an unsettling effect on the Korean Government in its present stage of develop-

---

Source: Department of State, Central Files, 795B.56311/8–2862. Top Secret. Drafted by Wallace C. Magathan of G/PM and cleared by Peterson, Allen S. Whiting of INR, Joseph J. Wolf of AID, and "informally" by William Bundy of DOD/ISA.

ment and might trigger a demand by the ROKs for a change in command relationships which we would find unacceptable. It would militate against carrying out the reduction in ROK Army force levels which we are presently contemplating as a means of increasing the availability of local resources for economic development purposes. The concomitant loss of the 9.3 million dollars which accrues to Korea by virtue of the presence of a division would be equivalent to reducing Korea's export level by about 22.7 per cent. Accordingly, an increase in supporting assistance would be required, a doubtful possibility at best.

Acquisition of the necessary additional land in Okinawa (with 1539 persons per square mile already one of the most densely populated areas in the world) would likely produce political repercussions which might militate against continued U.S. use of that vital base.

In light of these arguments it would appear inadvisable to withdraw a U.S. division from Korea at this time.

The DOD position is at Tab B.[1] Departmental inputs are at Tabs C and D.[2]

*Recommendations:*

1.  That you approve this conclusion as a basis for current drafting on NSAM 2447 (study of future economic and military aid levels and U.S. force level, Korea).[3]

2.  That you sign a letter to Ros Gilpatric (Tab A)[4] which conveys this conclusion but raises questions regarding future possibilities.

---

[1] Document 274.

[2] Tab C was a memorandum from Jeffrey C. Kitchen of G/PM to Johnson, recommending that Johnson send the package forward to Rusk. Tab D was a memorandum from Wolf to Magathan, September 1, which has not been found.

[3] Rusk initialed his approval on September 19. Reference should be to NSC Action No. 2447.

[4] Tab A was a September 19 letter from Rusk to Gilpatric, agreeing that it was "inadvisable to withdraw a U.S. Division at this time," but suggesting that the Department of Defense improve sea and airlift capabilities in the Far East and then "examine alternative possibilities such as the Philippines." (Department of State, Central Files, 795B.56311/8–2862)

**277. Paper Prepared by the President's Military Representative (Taylor)**

September 20, 1962.

IMPRESSIONS OF KOREA[1]

*1.  Contradictory Factors*

In studying the economic/political problems and programs for South Korea, one is impressed with the conflicting factors which enter into a consideration of these matters. The following is a list of some of the things we would like to accomplish, yet which obviously can not be done at the same time and without mutual conflict.

a.  Effect a significant reduction in military spending in order to improve the ROK economy and, in so doing, to stabilize the ROK military budget.

b.  Make the ROK Government pay its own way to a greater degree, particularly in meeting the military costs of soft goods (MAP transfer).

c.  Restrain the gold dollar outflow.

d.  Anticipate the effects of a large cut in foreign aid by Congress.

e.  Increase the size of CINCPAC's general reserve, possibly from forces in Korea.

f.  Retain the confidence and friendship of the ROKs—particularly of the ROK military.

g.  Retain operational control of ROK military forces under the UN banner.

h.  Do all of the foregoing without running undue military risks.

*2.  New Approach*

To bring some order into this chaos of conflicting desiderata, we need to review from the beginning the goals of U.S. policy in South Korea. As a point of departure, we should begin with the fact that we must first meet the hard requirements of adequate defense before concerning ourselves with other things no matter how attractive and desirable. It is essential to be able to defend the ROK economy before building

---

Source: National Defense University, Taylor Papers, FE Trip September 1962, T–022–69. Top Secret. After being confirmed as the Chairman of the Joint Chiefs of Staff on August 9, but before taking up his post on October 1, Taylor took a trip to the Far East from August 31 to September 21. He explains in his memoirs, *Sword and Plowshares*, pp. 256–259, that it was a "refresher visit" and an examination of U.S. political-military policy in a key area threatened by the growing power of the People's Republic of China. Taylor visited Japan, Korea, Taiwan, South Vietnam, Thailand, Cambodia, and Indonesia.

[1] These impressions formed the substance of the Korea portion of Taylor's summarizing telegram on his trip, September 20, to Rusk, McNamara, Lemnitzer, and McGeorge Bundy. (Telegram DTG 200410Z, September; Department of State, Central Files, 120.1590/9–2362)

it into a lucrative, vulnerable target for Communist military aggression. After meeting the indispensable requirements of security, we are then ready to take those actions which will be most helpful to the ROK economy at least cost to the U.S., particularly in gold.

3.    *The Hard Requirements of Adequate Defense*

[*1 paragraph (12 lines of source text) not declassified*]

At the present time, and for several years until the effect of considerable additional MAP expenditures can be felt, this war plan would be implemented in the face of a greatly superior enemy air force. It is not difficult to visualize a surprise 1,000 plane air attack by the North Korean-ChiCom air forces on South Korean targets at the outset of hostilities, resulting in great damage to the S. Korean air defense system, the concentrated logistic facilities, and the ports and airfields necessary to receive the planned augmentation from outside Korea. Until some solution to the air defense problem is found, the successful execution of the war plan is doubtful—without any of the cuts in money and manpower discussed in the following paragraph.

4.    *Supporting Military Assistance Program*

The 5-year MAP program recommended by General Meloy, Admiral Felt and JCS (600,000 strength—$250 million a year MAP and 21 billion won—defense budget)—is designed to support the foregoing war plan. Particularly important to the MAP program are those measures to overcome the weaknesses in air defense mentioned above. They include an improved AC&W capability, the introduction of the F104G AW interceptor to replace the F86D, more SAM missiles (but not launchers), more air fields capable of receiving augmentation aircraft and possibly the F5A tactical fighter to replace the F86F. Deferment is possible in the F5A program as the F86F can still play a useful role in ground support.

5.    *Reduced MAP Program*

The Ambassador's proposal to set a ceiling on the ROK won defense budget would predictably result in a reduction of the ROKAF by 70,000 in the next two years. However, he does not recommend any decrease in the MAP program, because of the agreed Country Team position that any personnel reduction should be in part compensated by improvement of the remaining forces. As a separate matter, there are independent Washington proposals for reduced MAP programs which, regardless of the outcome of the Ambassador's proposals with respect to the won budget, would similarly result in reduction of the ROKAF. Two such programs are now being considered. One sets an annual MAP ceiling at $225 million and the other at $180 million. In both cases, the manpower cut would accomplish very little savings—about $9 million a year in the won defense budget and $10 million a year in annual MAP maintenance. The military effect would be a reduction of 4–5 ROK division equivalents if applied over a 2-year period and the serious diminution of the initial ground strength and logistical back-up necessary to execute the war plan. Any chance for ultimate success in the situation contemplated, i.e., massive North Korean-ChiCom conventional attack, would require a compensating increase in augmentation forces brought into Korea under hostile air attack which would make such augmentation slow and costly.

A MAP cut to $225 million would retard modernization of ROK forces undesirably, particularly in the fighter-interceptor program and would weaken logistical capabilities. However, the dollar cut in itself would not seriously affect the ability to execute the war plan.

On the other hand, a cut to $180 million would fail to fund about 48% of the force improvements and make impossible the correction of the weakness in air defense. If such a reduction of MAP were decided, it would be necessary to overhaul completely the ROK force structure and to make a new war plan consistent with this reduced force.

6.  *Interim Conclusions*

a. One reaches the conclusion that any large personnel cut is unproductive of savings which would justify weakening the defense posture and incurring the political and psychological problems which such proposals would create with the ROKs. Further, we should recognize that if we cut ROK manpower, the US force strength in Korea is nailed down for the indefinite future. If, in spite of these considerations, a large force cut is imposed we must change the concept of the war plan and the objectives of the MAP program.

b. Some dollar reduction in MAP may be accepted by way of stretchout and deferrals. However, air defense modernization is so important that most of it—certainly the AC&W and F104G parts— should be fully funded. My feeling is that $225 million is about the minimum figure to consider for reducing MAP.

c. The stabilization of the won defense budget is a desirable objective but should be defined in terms of % of GNP rather than as a fixed ceiling. This is an inflationary economy and defense costs seem certain to rise.

d. While a withdrawal of US forces would offer the possibility of improving CINCPAC's strategic posture, it would be hard to find a location for their redeployment in the Pacific. Their withdrawal would offer some reduction of the gold outflow in Korea but this might be offset by the need of greater dollar aid on the economic side to compensate for the dollars lost by the reduction of U.S. forces.

e. No real savings in Korean manpower and/or MAP can be achieved without changing one or more of the following basic factors:

The mission of forces in Korea.
The assumption with regard to the use of nuclear weapons.
The availability of space in PACOM for the redeployment of US forces from Korea.
The assumption as to availability of new and advanced weapons for Korea.

7.    *Possible Effect of Changing Basic Factors*

Let us take the following assumptions and then consider the effect on military plans and programs:

*New Assumptions:*

a. The mission of UN/ROK forces in Korea is to defeat without the use of nuclear weapons any aggression by N. Korean forces.

b. [3 *lines of source text not declassified*]

c. Space can be found for a U.S. division force in the Philippines, Guam or Okinawa, singly or in combination.

The effect of these assumptions would permit the change of the Korean force requirements along the following lines:

a. The Korean active armed forces could be safely reduced to some figure safely above the N. Korean strength of about 350,000 of which a significant number of Army units are tied down to coast defense missions. Obsolescent equipment made excess by this reduction could be stored for use by ROK reserve divisions.

b. Other forms of force modernization would continue at presently planned levels. The Air Defense component about as presently planned in the $250 million MAP program would still be required.

c. The MAP program would be reduced to conform to the requirements of the new force structure.

d. US Army forces in Korea could be reduced to a Task Force of about one division [*less than 1 line of source text not declassified*] (eventually to include the Pershing missile). In the period prior to receiving Pershing, the surface-to-surface capability of Nike Hercules would be fully exploited. The U.S. troops withdrawn from Korea would be redeployed to CINCPAC reserve and stationed in the Western Pacific.

8.    *Alternatives*

In summary, we are presented with these alternatives:

a. Stay with present assumptions, plans and programs essentially as recommended (600,000—$250 million).

b. Revise assumptions and restate missions along lines suggested in paragraph 7. Then reevaluate requirements and reshape the MA and AID programs.

c. Put out diplomatic feelers to the USSR to see if there is a possibility of normalizing North-South relationships in Korea, at least to point of easing the present defense requirements which are an increasingly heavy burden to both sides. This last course can be undertaken concurrently with either of the other alternatives.

### 278.   Memorandum From Michael V. Forrestal of the National Security Council Staff to President Kennedy

Washington, September 24, 1962.

REPORT FROM GENERAL TAYLOR

You are meeting with General Taylor at 5:00 p.m. on Tuesday, September 25th in the Cabinet Room. Others who have been asked are: Secretary Rusk (or Ball), Secretary McNamara (or Gilpatric), Governor Harriman, Messrs. Nitze, Sullivan, Forrestal and Komer.[1]

General Taylor will report on his trip to the Far East and will amplify the points made in his recent cable (CINCPAC 200410Z to Department), a copy of which was sent to you.[2]

You may wish to take advantage of the opportunity raised by General Taylor's concise statement of the issue of ROK force cuts in paragraph B of his cable. The JCS has been, as you know, strongly opposed to any consideration of such cuts on the grounds that the joint U.S.-ROK mission in Korea is to defend against a combined North Korean-ChiCom assault against the ROK.

It seems to me that such a contingency, if it occurred would raise a question which would go far beyond what we faced in Korea in 1950. If this is true, should we not re-examine our very expensive commitments in Korea to see if they still are based on realistic contingencies.

You might wish, for example, to ask the Joint Chiefs to examine what size ROK force would be necessary to hold South Korea against a non-

Source: Kennedy Library, National Security Files, Countries Series, Korea, General, 8/62–3/63. Top Secret.

[1] Forrestal drafted a memorandum for the record, September, 26, outlining the action requested by the President in light of his meeting with Taylor and others at 5 p.m. on September 25. According to Forrestal's memorandum: "The President authorized a re-study of force requirements in South Korea in light of a concurrent study on the advisability of using [text not declassified] in the event of a massive assault against South Korea by combined ChiCom and North Korean Forces." (Ibid., Meetings and Memoranda Series, Staff Memos, Forrestal)

[2] See footnote 1, Document 277. Part B of the telegram is similar to Document 277, but does not provide as much supporting analysis and detail.

nuclear attack by North Korean forces alone. Then they might consider what other military dispositions we might make both in Korea and outside it to deter the ChiComs from assisting the Koreans in such an attack.

### 279. Memorandum From Robert W. Komer of the National Security Council Staff to the President's Deputy Special Assistant for National Security Affairs (Kaysen)

Washington, September 26, 1962.

Carl—

President's view that we could limit US/ROK force mission to meeting North Korean attack alone, [1 line of source text not declassified] provides an opening to get our ROK force cut [1-1/2 lines of source text not declassified].[1]

I confess to a twinge as I heard the discussion, but on reflection it comes out this way:

(1) I may have misunderstood General Taylor, but I see no real difference between our strategic posture in Europe and that in FE. In either case we resist conventionally unless and until confronted with an overwhelming attack. To me, all-out ChiCom attack at outset would be comparable to all-out Soviet attack in Europe. [1 line of source text not declassified]

[5-1/2 lines of source text not declassified] Remember it was threat of nuclear escalation which led to Korean armistice.

(3) [2-1/2 lines of source text not declassified] This, together with US "tripwire" also there, is real deterrent which makes attack on Korea seem so poor a bet to Peiping. Thus the only circumstances under which the ChiComs would think of attacking would be firm conviction that we wouldn't end up using [less than 1 line of source text not declassified]. Cutting 6–8 ROK divisions wouldn't basically change this equation; indeed, it would only underline it more.

(4) Indeed we have a greater combination of deterrents against local aggression in Korea than anywhere else around the Bloc perimeter—not just the above but two plus US divisions, 19 ROK divisions, UN command and umbrella of UN resolutions, 10 mile demilitarized zone.

---

Source: Kennedy Library, National Security Files, Countries Series, Korea, General, 8/62–3/63. Top Secret. A copy was sent to Forrestal.

[1] See footnote 1, Document 278.

(5) Ergo, direct ChiCom attack on the ROK *is the least likely of all cases.* There has *never* been a direct Soviet or ChiCom local aggression. Even the one overt Communist local attack in the whole postwar period was an attack by proxy (North Korean).

(6) For all these reasons, I've never understood why we've tied up so much of our MAP (and US) assets in Korea. *We are militarily over-insured in this area,* by comparison to SEA, Middle East, even Europe. Why did we ever spend so much on ROK forces in 1953–62 instead of shoring up SEA more?

(7) As McNamara so cogently says, we're betwixt and between in Korea. We have a lot more than is needed to stop NKs conventionally, but not enough to do more than delay a massive ChiCom attack without either (a) mounting an even bigger Korean War style effort; or (b) *[less than 1 line of source text not declassified]*. So who are we kidding?

(8) Finally, I can't envisage the truly massive ChiCom buildup needed for attack occurring without lots of warning. We knew when ChiComs left Korea in 1956–59. We should be able to find out easily if 600,000 came back.

Thus to change the mission of the US/ROK forces in Korea would be essentially a bookkeeping transaction. It would *not* significantly lower the existing *[less than 1 line of source text not declassified]* threshold. It would *not* significantly increase the *[less than 1 line of source text not declassified]* risks. It would only make somewhat more explicit what is implicit now, i.e. if the almost inconceivable happened and the ChiComs launched a direct attack, we would have to decide whether to use *[less than 1 line of source text not declassified]* at some point. Since we have that capability now (and presumably have contingency plans for its use), I see no new policy issue.[2]

Therefore, I see no need for President, in authorizing change in conventional mission, to give any more authority to count on use of *[less than 1 line of source text not declassified]* than before. We would continue, as in so many other areas of the world, to be prepared against this contingency, for ultimate decision at the time. Have we decided to use *[less than 1 line of source text not declassified]* in case Iran is overwhelmed, in case ChiComs invade SEA, etc.? How is Korea different, especially when likelihood is so low?

**Bob K.**

---

[2] In an October 4 memorandum to McGeorge Bundy, Forrestal informed Bundy of the President's decision at the September 25 meeting. Forrestal noted that Carl Kaysen was "somewhat concerned about this, because it appears to him to be a change in policy, reversing in effect what we have tried to accomplish in Europe." Forrestal's own judgment was that "unless the military have something quite different in mind, this assumption does not really change the present situation, *[2 lines of source text not declassified]*" (Kennedy Library, National Security Files, Meetings and Memoranda Series, Staff Memos, Forrestal)

### 280. Memorandum of Conversation Between the President's Deputy Special Assistant for National Security Affairs (Kaysen) and the Korean Ambassador (Il Kwon Chung)

Washington, October 9, 1962.

The Ambassador and I talked for fifteen or twenty minutes while he was waiting to see the President. Mr. Norred, the Korean desk officer, was with us.

I raised the question of the possibility of reducing the size of the Korean army and transferring more resources to economic development. He agreed it would be desirable, if there was some way of doing it without increasing unemployment and if we in fact did sustain the total level of aid and transferred more for economic purposes. This much of the conversation took place in my office.

When Mr. Norred had left us and we were waiting in the Fish Room, the Ambassador said to me that he wanted to raise a question with me, speaking personally. He then spoke of the forthcoming visit of Colonel Kim, the head of the Korean CIA.[1] He expressed great concern about whether Kim might interfere with the forthcoming elections. He thought it would be highly useful to have the Secretary of State or the Vice President talk briefly, informally, and directly with Kim to indicate the value we place on democratic processes and orderly government, and the dangers of covert interference with electoral processes.[2]

He repeated his fears of Kim, who he said was into many things that were none of his business. He also remarked on his earlier relations with Kim when the latter was a mere lieutenant, and stated that he himself would like to be a candidate for the Presidency of Korea.

CK

---

Source: Department of State, Central Files, 611.95B/10–962. Secret. Drafted and initialed by Kaysen.

[1] Kaysen sent this memorandum and Document 281 under a covering memorandum to Harriman, October 9, noting that his conversation with Chung raised a "rather ticklish issue on Colonel Kim, the head of the Korean CIA. My own thought would be that it might indeed be very useful to have the Vice President talk with Kim when he is here, and if you like we can see what can be done about it." A note on the bottom of the page signed H.S. [Harold Saunders of the NSC Staff?] reads as follows: "Mr. Rice, Mr. Yager: Harriman called Kaysen & told him Kim should not see the Vice President (but OK to see Atty Genl) that it was wrong to grade him up to the V.P. level, etc. Kaysen agreed." (Department of State, Central Files, 611.95B/10–962)

[2] Ambassador Chung made a similar suggestion "as a private citizen" to Rice on September 28. (Memorandum of conversation, September 28; ibid., 033.95B11/9–2862) On October 15, Chung met with William Bundy and made similar points. (Ibid., 033.95B11/10–1562) On October 20, Chung met with Maxwell Taylor and asked him to see Kim, suggesting that Taylor encourage him to be flexible in negotiations for settlement of differences with Japan and to reiterate the need to allow the 1963 elections to be conducted in a democratic manner. (Memorandum for the record, October 23; Washington National Records Center, RG 330, OASD/ISA Files: FRC 65 A 3501, 333 Korea)

**281.  Memorandum of Conversation Between President Kennedy and the Korean Ambassador (Il Kwon Chung)**

Washington, October 9, 1962, 10:30 a.m.

After an exchange of courtesies, Ambassador Chung raised the question of whether or not our interest in the ROK-Japanese settlement presaged a reduction of U.S. commitments and an attempt to shift the responsibility to Japan.

The President assured the Ambassador that this was not the case. He said that the Korean economic problems were so great that Korea needed all the assistance that the U.S. and Japan could provide. Our hope was that Japan could play her part in addition to what the U.S. was able to furnish. Further, the President noted that the Japanese were in no sense prepared to take over our military commitments, and we had every intention of maintaining them. He urged the Ambassador to repeat these reassurances to Chairman Park.

Ambassador Chung showed the President some figures concerning present North Korean production levels in steel, cement, electric power and fertilizer, with South Korea goals for 1966, and pointed out the population discrepancies between the two parts of the country as well.

The President then handed Ambassador Chung his response to General Park's letter[1] and repeated his request that the Ambassador transmit to his government our assurances in the matter of continued help for Korea.

The meeting lasted about 15 minutes.

CK

---

Source: Department of State, Central Files, 611.95B/10–962. Confidential. Drafted and initialed by Kaysen.

[1] Pak's September 12 letter outlined the Korean position on settlement of the outstanding issues between Korea and Japan. (Kennedy Library, National Security Files, Countries Series, Korea, Park Correspondence—B) Kennedy's response of October 9, which encouraged Pak to be flexible and forthcoming in the negotiations, is ibid. According to an October 4 memorandum from Forrestal to Komer, Chung was given this "off the record" and unusual meeting with the President because of information received that Pak was annoyed that his letter of September 12 was not delivered in person by Chung to the President. (Ibid., General, 8/62–3/63)

## 282.   Memorandum of Conversation

Washington, October 29, 1962, 4 p.m.

PARTICIPANTS

Mr. Kim, Director of the ROK CIA
Ambassador Chung, Korean Ambassador
Colonel Kim (interpreter)
The Secretary
Governor Harriman, Assistant Secretary, FE
Mr. Nicholas A. Natsios, Special Assistant to Ambassador Berger
Mr. Yager, Director, EA

The Secretary remarked that Director Kim found the Department preoccupied with a major crisis.[1] The Secretary asked whether Mr. Kim saw any signs of significant activity in North Korea. Mr. Kim replied that he did not. He expressed his appreciation for the Secretary's giving his time at a time when he is so busy.

The Secretary said he would like to speak first on the possibility of a Japanese-Korean settlement. He said that it would be helpful to both countries to resolve their problems and establish normal political, economic and military relations. The Secretary said he understood that Mr. Kim had stopped in Tokyo on his way to the U.S. and that as a result of his talks there, there is some gleam of hope that a settlement can be reached.

Mr. Kim said that he met with Foreign Minister Ohira for two hours and with Prime Minister Ikeda for 2-3/4 hours. His purpose in meeting the Japanese leaders was to create a better atmosphere for the negotiations which have been underway in Tokyo. His discussions with Ohira and Ikeda concentrated on claims, fisheries, the peace line, and Tokto Island. The status of Korean residents and art treasures was also mentioned, but, Director Kim said, these were "small matters."

Concerning claims, Mr. Kim said that Ohira mentioned payment of $300 million over 12 years in installments of $25 million per year. Kim told Ohira that $300 million is not sufficient and that 12 years is too long. He said that he hoped for something more than $300 million plus loans which would bring the total to $600 million. Kim said that Ohira explained that even $300 million was only his own opinion and had not been discussed with Ikeda. Ohira also told Kim that annual payments to

---

Source: Department of State, Central Files, 694.95B/10–2962. Secret. Drafted by Yager and approved in S on November 7. On October 27 Harriman sent Rusk a briefing memorandum for this meeting stressing that the Secretary should encourage ROK-Japanese negotiations on outstanding issues, better Korean use of U.S. assistance, and the return to civilian government and free elections. (Ibid., 694.95B/10–2762)

[1] The Cuban missile crisis.

Korea could not exceed the $25 million paid annually under the reparations agreement with the Philippines. Ohira noted that Japan pays a total of $80 million per year for reparations. Kim said that Ohira also remarked that it was unrealistic to discuss a $600 million ceiling. He asked Kim to be more flexible about loans. Kim said that he replied that, in view of the anti-Japanese feeling among the Korean people fostered by the Rhee regime, $600 million was the least that could be accepted.

According to Kim, in concluding the talks Ohira said that the amount could be $300 million but could not be called reparations. He suggested that the payment be described as "congratulatory in recognition of Korean independence." Kim said that he replied again that $300 million would not be sufficient. The total must be $600 million including more than $300 for reparations with the remainder being made up of loans. Concerning what the non-loan portion would be called, Kim said he told Ohira that he would not insist on the term "reparations" so long as it was clear to the Korean public that the total included reparations. Kim said that he would refer the question to his Government.

The Secretary said he hoped that both sides would carefully study the problem. We have strongly urged both Korea and Japan to make the strongest possible effort. We believe that a settlement is of the highest importance to both countries and, therefore, to the U.S. Mr. Kim indicated that he would meet again with Ohira on his way back to Korea.

The Secretary said that his experience of the past two weeks, during which he has dealt with a dangerous problem involving governments that are not friends, has made problems between friends appear simple. In his present state of mind, he would simply urge both sides: agree, agree, agree.

Mr. Kim said he would like next to report on the peace line and fisheries. In his recent Tokyo talks, he said, he asked the Japanese not to be so sensitive about the peace line and to deal with it separately from the fisheries question. He pointed out that the line is directed at the Communists, not the Japanese. He also pointed out that the ROK is in a state of war and that 200 attempted infiltrations occurred last year. On fisheries, he suggested to the Japanese that an agreement beneficial to both sides be negotiated. He intended to be flexible and asked the Japanese to be flexible also.

Concerning Tokto Island, Mr. Kim said that this question was only recently introduced into the negotiations by the Japanese. In his recent talks in Tokyo, he urged that this question be put off until after a general settlement is reached.

The Secretary asked what the island is used for. Mr. Kim replied that it is "a place for sea gull droppings." He suggested to the Japanese that it be blown up. The Secretary commented that this solution had also occurred to him. Mr. Kim indicated that Ohira had apparently not been amused by this suggestion but replied that the Socialists would attack him on the issue.

Mr. Kim said that his talk with Prime Minister Ikeda revealed a somewhat different Japanese position on claims. Ikeda offered $150 million for claims. Kim said that when he told Ikeda that the Foreign Minister had spoken of $300 million, Ikeda had replied that this was a matter he would settle, not the Foreign Minister. Kim said that in response to his questions, Ikeda told him that the $150 million figure is not rigid, that loans above the $150 million claims payment could bring the total to about $600 million, and that these loans could be from government to government at very low interest rates. Kim said that Ikeda agreed with his approach to the peace line and fisheries questions.

Kim said that Ikeda confirmed Ohira's statement that Japanese-Korean political talks could be held by the end of 1962 and that an agreement could be signed next spring and ratified by the Japanese Diet in June or July.

On Tokto Island, Kim asked Ikeda whether referral to the International Court of Justice was the only solution seen by the Japanese. Ikeda indicated that possibly the matter could be delayed until after public interest had died down.

The Secretary commented that he would gather from Kim's report that some possibility of agreement exists. Kim replied that he would do his best to promote an early settlement when he stops in Tokyo on his way home.

The Secretary referred to the coming elections in South Korea and expressed the hope that these elections would give the Korean people a sense of real partnership in their government. Kim assured the Secretary that the Korean Government will do its best to have fair and just elections and would open the way more and more to public participation in public affairs. He questioned, however, whether it will be possible to move to a completely democratic government by next year.

The Secretary said that we will be in touch further with the Korean authorities on these questions through Ambassador Berger. He asked Mr. Kim to convey his personal greetings to Chairman Pak.

## 283. Memorandum of Conversation

Washington, October 29, 1962.

PARTICIPANTS

Mr. Kim
Ambassador Chung, Korean Ambassador
Colonel Kim (interpreter)
Governor Harriman, Assistant Secretary, FE
Mr. Natsios, Special Assistant to Ambassador Berger
Mr. Rady, CIA
Mr. Yager, Director, EA

Governor Harriman took Director Kim to his office to continue discussions after conclusion of Kim's call on the Secretary.

Governor Harriman said that the Secretary had spoken of plans for the elections in South Korea. The Governor commented that these elections can make a great difference in the confidence of the Korean people.

Mr. Kim asked in what respect Governor Harriman is particularly concerned about the elections. The Governor replied that he is concerned over the restriction of candidates. Mr. Kim said that the Korean authorities are not going to apply restrictions beyond those in the political purifications law, but candidates will not be allowed to run as independents. They must run as members of a political party because in the past independents have been corrupt and easily bought. In response to Governor Harriman's question, Mr. Kim said that all parties except the Communists and "socialistic elements" will be allowed to put up candidates.

Governor Harriman said that we greatly respect the determination of the Korean leaders to eliminate corruption but that political freedom is quite another matter. Mr. Kim said that it is necessary to avoid recurrence of the old evils that would threaten stability of the ROK and might block further progress toward freedom. The Korean Government however intends to develop a sound party system. Government and opposition parties will be given an equal chance.

Governor Harriman asked how soon free political discussion is to be permitted. Mr. Kim answered this will be done at the beginning of 1963, thereby providing five to five and one half months of free discussion before the elections.

Governor Harriman asked how many politicians on the proscribed list have been taken off. Mr. Kim replied that over 4,000 persons were listed at first. Between 2600 or 2700 remain on the list. More are to be taken off.

Source: Department of State, Central Files, 795B.00/10–2962. Secret. Drafted by Yager.

Governor Harriman asked Mr. Kim about his talks at the Pentagon. Mr. Kim replied that he had seen a number of people, including Deputy Assistant Secretary Bundy and Generals Wheeler, Fitch, Breitweiser, Carroll and Taylor.[1] He said that some of the discussions had been heated. Governor Harriman asked whether Mr. Kim wanted to maintain armed forces at 600,000. Mr. Kim replied "at least that large." Governor Harriman asked how long this would be necessary. Mr Kim replied "until we have driven the Communists out." Mr. Kim noted that former Premier Chang Myon had reduced the forces by 30,000 men. He described this action as a complete failure. The economy had not been helped. Unemployment had been increased.

Governor Harriman asked about the civic action program. Mr. Kim said that this program is very active. In the past it suffered from diversion of military supplies but this has been stopped. He said that good results have been obtained in training soldiers before their discharge in skills that they can use when they return home.

Governor Harriman asked Mr. Kim what activity he saw in the North Korean military. Mr. Kim recalled that he had told the Secretary that he had seen no significant North Korean activity because he understood the Secretary's question to refer to activity in response to the Cuban crisis. Mr. Kim said that there has been a significant development, however. A combined North Korean-Chinese Communist headquarters has been established. Also, the number of Chinese advisers in all fields: military, political and industrial has increased. There are more Chinese advisers than Russian advisers. Russian influence is declining and Chinese influence is increasing.

In response to Governor Harriman's question concerning conditions in North Korea, Mr. Kim said that although people there get enough to eat, life is miserable beyond description because of the lack of freedom. North Korea, however, is superior to South Korea in many economic fields. Mr. Kim commented that this is why the ROK is trying to advance in all economic fields. Governor Harriman said that we are very anxious that the ROK industrial program succeed. Mr. Kim said that the Korean Government is determined to do all it can to develop basic industry quickly.

---

[1] No other record of these talks has been found. On October 26 and 28 Kim had two hour-long discussions with Walt Rostow, Counselor and Chairman of the Policy Planning Staff. The first discussion dealt with problems of generating economic development and the second with how a military dictatorship disengages and moves a nation into a democracy. (Memorandum of conversation, October 28; ibid., 033.95B11/10–2862)

## 284. Memorandum From Michael V. Forrestal of the National Security Council Staff to President Kennedy

Washington, October 17, 1962.

*Visit of Korean CIA Director Kim*

You have been asked by General Van Fleet to receive Kim Chong P'il.[1]

Kim is the Director of the Korean CIA, and both he and his organization have been involved in practices which State considers questionable, among which was the heavy speculation on the Korean stock exchange several months ago which resulted in a financial crisis. In addition, the Department feels that Kim, who is the second most powerful man in the government, uses the secret police as a political tool.

Both Governor Harriman and Ambassador Berger strongly recommend against Kim's being received by you or the Vice President. They do recommend that he be received by the Secretary of State, the Attorney General and, possibly, the Secretary of Defense. The Attorney General will be asked by the Department to comment rather severely to him upon the proper role of the police in a democracy.[2]

---

Source: Kennedy Library, National Security Files, Countries Series, Korea, General, 8/62–3/63. No classification marking. Apparently attached to this memorandum was a memorandum from Clifton to Smith, October 17, indicating that the President read the Forrestal memorandum, but that in light of a letter from Van Fleet (see footnote 1 below) he wanted to see Kim Chong-p'il, barring recommendations to the contrary. A note, apparently by Clifton, on this memorandum states that Forrestal "strongly opposes appointment. The A.G. [Attorney General] is seeing him. The Korean's reputation is not good." (Ibid.)

[1] Van Fleet wrote the President on October 16. No copy of his letter has been found. McGeorge Bundy sent Van Fleet a response, on October 22, in which he stated that the President agreed with Van Fleet's view that Kim "is far more than the head of his agency in Korea." Bundy explained that since the President was restricting his official meetings during the next few weeks because of the Cuban missile crisis, he could not make an exception for Kim. However, Bundy continued, Kim would see Rusk, McNamara, McCone, and Robert Kennedy. (Ibid.)

[2] In a memorandum to James Symington of Robert Kennedy's office, October 24, Executive Secretary Brubeck attached a talking paper for the Attorney General's meeting with Kim Chong-p'il on October 26, at 10 a.m. The paper suggested that the Attorney General state that the United States considered it important for the ROK Government to carry out its pledge to restore constitutional government through free elections before the summer of 1963. In preparation, the government should broaden its civilian base, not restrict candidates for office without good cause, not restrict the right to criticise the government before and during the campaign, and terminate martial law well before the campaign began. (Department of State, Central Files, 033.95B11/10–2462) No record of the Robert Kennedy–Kim conversation has been found.

## 285.    Airgram From the Embassy in Korea to the Department of State

A–399                                                    Seoul, December 7, 1962.

SUBJECT
     The Political Outlook in Korea

*Summary*

The political process precedent to the establishment of an elected government under a revised constitution is getting underway in Korea. From now until the seating of a successor government in mid-summer 1963, political activity and elections will dominate the local scene.

The military government has been planning the transition with great care and attention to detail, seeking to ensure the perpetuation of power in the hands of those who made the revolution of May 16, 1961. To succeed they intend to secure the election of Pak Chong-hui as President and majority control of the National Assembly. Government plans include banning political activity by major ex-political leaders, certain restrictions on political party organizations, and constitutional provisions favoring government objectives. The government political party to be formed will be aided also by the natural advantages of a government in power, plentiful financial resources, a head-start in organization, and the absence of a cohesive opposition. We can expect a cleverly managed election rather than a crudely rigged one. Strong leadership within the junta is being exercised by Kim Chong-p'il with the support of Pak Chong-hui. Kim's power continues in the ascendancy, resting on good organization, dedication, great ambition and an extensive police network.

Opposition to the government's political plans and ambitions resides in dissident civilian and ex-military elements who see in the "mainstream" of the revolution a long-term threat to their own political survival and ambitions. There is also opposition within the junta to the dominant role played by Kim Chong-p'il and the "young colonels" in the government's plans: deep factional differences exist and intense political maneuvering is taking place. The students remain a latent force capable of action or manipulation when sufficiently stimulated and an opportunity arises.

The outcome of the ferment and political processes which are now beginning is by no means certain. The government party will probably win a contrived election, but there are a number of possible variations in what might follow:

---

Source: Department of State, Central Files, 795B.00/12–762. Secret. Drafted by Berger and Habib. Repeated to CINCPAC for POLAD and sent with instructions to pass to the Department of Defense.

a. Pak–Kim and the "core group" of the revolution would then govern in authoritarian fashion, gradually eliminating opposition threats to power;

b. Differences within the junta may erupt sooner or later in an all-out fight. If Kim and his faction win, they could hold power by extreme methods. If they lose, new alliances, possibly on a broader basis, would form but be plagued by factional differences;

c. The junta would hold together, but in the aftermath, the actions taken to gain victory would create schisms between the government and the people who would not accept continued rule by a narrow elite of military men;

d. After election, Korea would move toward increasingly successful representative government on an increasingly democratic basis. Instead of military authoritarianism there would be a gradual broadening of power and moderation in government over several years.

Political tension exists in Korea. There is apprehension, dissatisfaction and fear among articulate groups in and out of government. Any complacency as to stability of leadership is unwarranted. The Embassy is concerned that the political trend may move contrary to our objective of a politically stable Korea with an increasing capacity to govern itself on a democratic basis.

In the current situation the US should try to minimize the danger of sharp changes which would only replace the present uneasy and tense stability with irrational instability. We should concentrate on moderating government actions, but prepare for the contingency that may require a change in our attitude and policy toward the military regime.

For the immediate future we should urge the government to accept the need for taking measures to promote national unity and advise the widest possible clearance of people banned from political activity under the Political Purification Law. We should urge the need for the widest possible freedom of debate, assembly and press consistent with normal security considerations. We should not threaten specific action if our advice is not taken but should leave no illusion that the US supports all the political plans of the government. We should be prepared, if necessary, to issue a prudent statement setting forth US policy with respect to the return to representative government.[1]

---

[1] In airgram 404 from Seoul, also December 7, Berger reported on a conversation with Pak about the upcoming elections and the return to constitutional government. Pak stated that an effort would be made to avoid encouragement of splinter parties and to discourage vote buying and corruption. When Berger mentioned the need to clear currently proscribed politicans, Pak raised his voice in objection, stressing that the United States did not understand how unrepentant these politicans were. Berger encouraged Pak to create the broadest-based government political party possible. Berger asked Pak to stop other SCNR members and government officials from claiming that the United States endorsed the government's election plan. Berger stated that the United States was neither endorsing or not endorsing the plan, and would be neutral in the elections. Pak promised free and fair elections. (Ibid.)

We should begin to think in terms of a possible need for alternatives for leadership in Korea. At the moment, we do not have a clear idea of what these alternatives may be. As a prerequisite the Koreans themselves must coalesce into coherent groups and show readiness to work for their own political evolution without excesses. We should be cautious and not try to be the decisive internal political force ourselves. Many thoughtful Koreans believe the military government is embarked on a disastrous course. On the other hand, some continue to reserve judgment until after political activity gets under way. Others intend to reserve judgment until after elections. We, too, should wait. When we see our problem more clearly, it may be desirable for the Ambassador to return to Washington for consultation to consider new policy lines.

[Here follows the main text of the airgram, comprising 17 pages.]

---

### 286.  Telegram From the Department of State to the Embassy in Korea

Washington, January 24, 1963, 6:10 p.m.

448. Your 521.[1]

1.  Congratulations on your success in moderating Pak's plan for settling current crisis within ruling group. We agree optimism must be restrained until we see how events unfold in next few days. On basis your excellent reporting, however, it appears we may now pass through crisis and gain better relationship with Pak than previously existed.

2.  At appropriate time assume you will wish to make use of improved rapport with Pak to advise him further on transition to civilian rule.

3.  Line which you took with Pak in your talk January 16 (Embassy's 503) is in general accord with our thinking.[2] We recognize that if Korean

---

Source: Department of State, Central Files, 795B.00/1–2463. Secret; Niact; Limit Distribution. Drafted by Yager, cleared in draft with Rice, and approved by Harriman.

[1] In telegram 521 from Seoul, January 24, Berger reported that Chairman Pak had informed him through an emissary that he had taken the following positions to resolve the crisis of factionalism in the SCNR: Kim Chong-p'il would resign from the government's political party and leave Korea for an extended trip; Pak had withdrawn his plan to relieve five anti-Kim officers from the SCNR; the SCNR and its political party would be separated; and Pak would run for President in the promised elections later in the year. (Ibid.)

[2] In telegram 503, January 17, Berger reported the results of a 2-hour conversation on January 16 with Pak on the political situation. In telegram 504 from Seoul, January 18, Berger commented on this discussion. Telegram 504 was designated as "part two of two," while telegram 503 was "part one of two." (Ibid., 795B.00/1–1763 and 795B.00/1–1963)

people believe transition to civilian rule has been rigged, chances of popularly supported and stable government may well be lost. Your advice to Pak on need for broader base for ruling group and for effective opposition therefore remains valid if it is not interpreted as effort to push Korea with unrealistic rapidity into American style representative government. In current Korean situation, political forms are probably less important than effective government with broad popular support. We therefore suggest that in future you place comments on need for broadening base of regime in context of overriding need to gain popular support. Regime must make more active effort to reach and influence important groups such as students, intellectuals, labor and farmers, and broaden popular support by promulgating and vigorously pursuing policies which accord with popular needs and aspirations.

**Rusk**

---

## 287. Telegram From the Department of State to the Embassy in Korea

Washington, January 26, 1963, 2:03 p.m.

451. Reference Seoul's 527, repeated Tokyo 130, CINCPAC 115.[1]

1. Department commends your excellent handling and reporting of fast-changing situation.

2. We agree with your assessment (telegram 520)[2] that compromise solution of factional struggle within junta would offer best hope of

---

Source: Department of State, Central Files, 795B.00/1–2662. Secret; Niact; Limit Distribution. Drafted by Norred and approved by Harriman. Repeated to Tokyo and CINCPAC for POLAD.

[1] In telegram 527, January 26, the Embassy reported that after Berger and Meloy met with Pak and Kim Chong-p'il on January 25, they realized that the plan Pak outlined to Berger (see footnote 1, Document 286) to resolve the crisis within the SCNR was not working. The two problems were Kim Chong-p'il's resignation as chairman of the government's political party (Democratic Republican Party) and the reorganization of the junta to remove Kim Chong-p'il's appointees. What was really at stake, the Embassy reported, was a power struggle between Kim Chong p'il and his supporters versus most of the military men who led the revolution and wanted to reduce Kim's power in favor of their own. Should both sides refuse to compromise, there could be a showdown with possible armed clashes, and the plans for smooth transition to civilian government would be in a shambles. (Department of State, Central Files, 795B.00.1–2662)

[2] Dated January 24. (Ibid., 795B.00/1–2463)

peaceful transition to civilian rule under conditions favoring longer term political stability.

A. We hope Chairman Pak's maneuvering will not lead to victory and unchallenged leadership of Kim Chong-p'il, particularly if his victory left him free to carry out his plans for authoritarian-type political party.

B. Military coup by forces opposing Kim Chong-p'il would also be most undesirable. Unfortunate precedent of military intervention in politics would be strengthened, and transition to civilian government might be frustrated. Also if leadership such a coup were restricted to Hamgyong faction we would question whether it could command significant popular support.

3.   Your efforts to promote compromise solution have our full support.

**Rusk**

---

### 288.   Memorandum From Michael V. Forrestal of the National Security Council Staff to the Assistant Secretary of State for Far Eastern Affairs (Harriman)

Washington, February 12, 1963.

SUBJECT

ROK/Japan Settlement

Seoul's 558[1] is about as depressing a cable as I have seen. Is it possible that Sam Berger is in a temporary fit of depression brought about by the very difficult political situation he is facing?

All my information is to the effect that if we don't get this settlement agreed to very shortly, the occasion may pass away for the foreseeable

---

Source: Kennedy Library, National Security Files, Countries Series, Japan, 2/63. Confidential.

[1] In telegram 558 from Seoul, February 12, the Embassy reported that as a result of increasing strains within the ROK Government and within Korea as a whole, which arose from renewed political activity in preparation for elections and transfer of government, the short-term prospects for normalization of ROK-Japan relations were becoming dimmer by the day. (Department of State, Central Files, POL 33–4 JAP–KOR)

future. I also gather that a great deal is at stake here: almost half a billion dollars of Japanese capital coming into Korea in a way which makes it likely that it would be more effectively used for development than the equivalent amount of Aid funds.

Do you think we should go back at Sam Berger with a cable drafted to convince him of the utmost importance of getting the Koreans to move on this settlement before the election campaign and pointing out, perhaps, that the economic future of Korea is very much at stake?[2] I don't see how we can justify a U.S. effort at stimulating economic development in Korea if we cannot get them to take advantage of this opportunity for substantial and useful outside help.

I cannot estimate whether the President's personal leverage will have much effect in this area; but I am sure he would want to do anything he could to help bring these negotiations to an early and successful conclusion. Although I have no specific idea of my own to offer, I do think we must rack our brains to find the best method of making another attack upon the problem.

**Michael V. Forrestal**[3]

---

[2] In telegram 479 to Seoul, February 12, the Department urged Berger and the Embassy "to press Koreans hard" on ROK-Japanese relations. In telegram 480 to Seoul, February 12, Harriman sent Berger a message to "underline to you personally importance which is placed here at the highest level on ROK-Japanese settlement being achieved this spring." (Both ibid.)

[3] Printed from a copy that bears this typed signature.

### 289.   Telegram From the Embassy in Korea to the Department of State

Seoul, February 13, 1963, 6 p.m.

561. Policy. Ref: Embtel 557 rptd Tokyo 145 CINCPAC 128.[1]

1. It has become increasingly apparent that USG must within next few days make fundamental decision on our attitude toward Chairman Pak, his government and their plans for election and transition to civilian govt.

2. Fear of Kim Chong-p'il's power, dissension among revolutionary leaders, growing public knowledge of Kim's stock market operations, dissatisfaction with ROK CIA general record of interference, and growing opposition criticism of govt's policies and actions, have been combining to weaken govt's unity and discredit it in eyes of people, even in countryside where govt previously enjoyed considerable support. Economic situation involving rising prices and inflationary pressures being exaggerated beyond its real significance. Economy not in as bad condition as attributed, however, there has been loss of confidence which has added to political difficulties. Public apprehension that military govt is losing US confidence is also contributing to gradually rising atmosphere of uneasiness. There is probability of trouble in which students and even other groups will participate, Universities reopen March 1 and both govt and opposition leaders have indicated to US student political activity expected thereafter. Now apparent govt party will find it difficult to win a fair election. Pak reportedly showing signs of concern over his ability to resolve political and economic instabilities.

3. Two weeks ago there was outside chance that if Kim Chong-p'il left govt party country situation might remain reasonably stable during transition. It now appears that Kim's retirement from scene would be helpful but would not in itself suffice to deal with whole complex of fac-

---

Source: Department of State, Central Files, POL 12 S KOR. Secret; Priority; Limit Distribution. Repeated to Tokyo and CINCPAC for POLAD. Michael Forrestal sent a copy of this telegram to the President noting: "The political situation in Korea is reaching disturbing proportions." Forrestal wrote that telegram 561 summarized the situation, and that Harriman was in the process of formulating recommendations. When this was done, Forrestal would arrange a meeting with the President to hear the recommendations and the advice of other interested Departments. (Memorandum from Forrestal to Kennedy, February 14; Kennedy Library, National Security Files, Countries Series, Korea, General, 8/62–3/63)

[1] In telegram 557, February 11, Berger reported on a conversation that he had with Kim Chong-p'il, lasting over 2 hours. According to Kim, Pak was deeply discouraged and would not run for President, but Kim was trying to convince him to change his mind. Kim also said that he would retire from politics himself. Berger observed that Kim's motivation for imparting this information was subject to multiple interpretations. (Department of State, Central Files, POL 12 S KOR)

tors which are evolving. Yun Po-sun and Ho Chong have made strong pleas to us that both Kim and Pak must withdraw with Pak continuing in caretaker role until after election, or there will be no hope for political stability. A very different view is being advocated by some revolutionary leaders, who fear calling off election, reimposing martial law, and holding power for another year or two. These are symptoms of crisis, and it can only be resolved if USG throws full force of our position into situation.

4. In our view establishment of political and economic stability and restoration of public confidence now require fundamental actions:

A. On economic side, there must be immediate checks on inflationary pressure and moves to stabilize the won. Killen is working with new Chairman EPB to develop policies to accomplish this. The measures required would mean sharp modification of current govt economic policies re budget management, credit, and money supply, and trimming 5-year economic plan projects. These would probably be politically unpalatable, especially to Kim Chong-p'il and his govt party. Pak might more easily carry out these measures if he removed himself from political campaign and assumed caretaker role with our support.

B. On political side, threat to stability might be reduced if Pak announced that he will keep revolutionary pledge to return power to civilian hands, will not run as candidate and will assume caretaker role until transfer accomplished. With US support Pak could hold military forces together on side of orderly transition, and deal with any counter move against his decision. Such a decision by Pak would necessitate negotiations with party leaders, changes in political party law and election law (it is too late to change constitution), probable delay in elections until June or July, and lifting all political purification bans. Kim Chong-p'il would need to leave Korea.

5. I cannot go much further here on my own initiative without clear Dept decision and support. If Pak sees me, as I requested and tells me he has decided to withdraw from presidential race and assume caretaker role, this may be genuine, but he will be under most terrific pressure to reverse himself and almost certainly government party conference February 25 will seek to draft him. Alternately, he may tell me he has weighed all factors and decided no course is desirable, but one which promises to minimize instability is for him to run. If Pak is drafted or runs voluntarily for president, Kim Chong-p'il will stay. In any of these cases, I will urge him to talk to opposition leaders, especially Ho Chong and Yun Po-sun before making his decision final. In absence of Dept's instruction I do not feel that I can say anything more to him except that I will report his views to Dept.

6. It is evident from foregoing and our recent telegrams that Koreans heading for crisis. Everyone now speaks of "big trouble" ahead

soon, and we are getting appeals from all sides to bring our influence to bear and stabilize situation. There are now no simple solutions. We can do several things:

A. Not intervene and let situation develop. This I think dangerous, and an abdication of our responsibilities.

B. Encourage Pak to run for president, which means Kim Chong-p'il will stay. This will align US with a govt increasingly unpopular, alienate US from the people, and may involve US in support of a govt that may have to resort to force to deal with discontent both within its ranks and outside. I cannot see us following this course because it will probably fyt [not?] produce stability. It will produce a govt which will be basically undemocratic, even more difficult to work with, and will vest unacceptable power in hands of Kim Chong-p'il.

C. Tell Pak that Kim Chong-p'il must leave country for a year, and that he must negotiate with opposition leaders for adjustments in elevation [election?] law. That it would be preferable for him to retire to caretaker role, but if he feels this would create too much instability we will abide by his decision, and our further attitude toward situation and this govt will depend on conduct of elections and course of development. This may or may not be acceptable to opposition and may or may not produce stability, but it deals with some of basic problems in picture. This may involve a further postponement of the elections.

D. Tell Pak and opposition leaders that only solution is to form govt of national unity, that will govern say for one year, while new election laws, political party laws, and constitution are drafted for eventual transition. This would involve us in formation of a new govt in which Pak possibly could serve as Acting President, Ho Chong possibly as PriMin, etc. Kim Chong-p'il would have to leave country. There is much to be said for this but it will be almost impossible to realize.

7. Next two weeks are critical and I would urge Asst Secy Harriman to plan to come here next week in order to:

A. Establish USG position;

B. Emphasize to all parties here seriousness of our concern with situation;

C. Assist us in working out acceptable understanding between Pak and opposition for transition to civilian rule; and possible understanding on ROK-Japan settlement;

D. Throw full weight of US behind solution we decide on.

**Berger**

## 290.   Telegram From the Department of State to the Embassy in Korea

Washington, February 14, 1963, 3:25 p.m.

485. Seoul's 561, rptd Tokyo 147, CINCPAC 130.[1] For Berger from Harriman.

1.   You should not encourage Pak to run for presidency, for reasons stated reftel para 6(B). Approaches to you by Kim Chong-p'il and Yi Tongwon (your tels 557 and 563)[2] obviously intended elicit U.S. support, which you should not offer. On other hand, you should not counsel Pak against running. He must make this decision himself. You should underline his obligation to see that an orderly transition takes place.[3]

2.   You should not explicitly advise Kim Chong-p'il's departure. If Pak's vacillation on his candidacy proves to be only an exercise, and we tried unsuccessfully to remove Kim, our relations with regime would be difficult. You may, however, wish to repeat in strong terms advice that Kim's use of CIA apparatus to control Democratic Republican Party is destroying chance of Party's gaining genuine popular acceptance.

3.   You should emphasize overriding importance of developing government with strong popular support. We are less concerned with processes by which this is achieved than with achievement that objective.[4]

4.   FYI. If Pak decides not to run, we may need to use our influence with various Korean leaders to create stable situation for interim government under Pak if he willing continue until elections. We are inclined to

---

Source: Department of State, Central Files, POL 14 S KOR. Secret: Niact; Limit Distribution. Drafted by Norred, cleared by Yager, and approved by Harriman. Repeated to Tokyo and CINCPAC for POLAD.

[1] Document 289.

[2] See footnote 1, Document 289. In telegram 563, February 14, Yi Tongwon made a similar approach on behalf of Pak. (Department of State, Central Files, POL 12 S KOR)

[3] Berger met with Pak for 1-1/2 hours on February 14, which because of the time difference between Seoul and Washington occurred well before he received telegram 485. Pak stated he was leaning toward retirement from politics, but agreed to make no public statement until Berger had a chance to explore the situation and talk with a few key people. In commenting to the Department, Berger questioned whether Pak really planned to withdraw, but he saw no solution to the political instability as long as Kim Chong p'il remained in South Korea. (Ibid.)

[4] In telegram 570 from Seoul, February 15, sent after receiving telegram 485 to Seoul, Berger proposed to tell Pak that while only he could decide whether or not to withdraw, the United States agreed with his reasoning and thought his retirement offered the best hope of stabilizing the economic and political situation. Berger would not mention Kim and the KCIA to Pak who already knew the U.S. views on Kim and that agency. (Ibid.) In telegram 486 to Seoul, February 15, the Department of State concurred with this approach. (Ibid.) Berger talked to Pak again on February 17 and made these points during that conversation. (Ibid.)

believe strong government could be developed after elections without Pak, under leadership Ho Chung for example, and that military factions would support such government. End FYI.

5. Foregoing views transmitted for your guidance, not as detailed instructions in view of fast moving situation in which you are involved.

6. A visit by me at this time would not be appropriate and is out of question. Norred can come to help you for a time if his knowledge of Washington views and of Korean politics would be of use. Please advise.

**Ball**

## 291. Memorandum From the Director of Intelligence and Research (Hilsman) to Secretary of State Rusk

Washington, February 18, 1963.

INTELLIGENCE NOTE

Pak Proposes Solution of the South Korean Political Crisis

*Pak's Offer to Withdraw.* Chairman Pak Chong-hui today publicly proposed a compromise settlement. His crucial points were: in return for assurances of no retaliation against members of the junta and revolutionary government officials he would abstain from political activity; politicians still restricted under the Political Purification Law would, with some exceptions, be cleared; and the election would be postponed until after May. He gave all party leaders until February 23 to accept or reject the plan.[1]

*Expected Party and Junta Reactions.* The political leaders will be inclined to accept Pak's terms. They realize that the government-sponsored party will have little appeal if Pak does not run as its presidential candidate. Furthermore, postponing the elections would give the opposition parties a real opportunity to organize. Most members of the

---

Source: Kennedy Library, National Security Files, Countries Series, Korea, Cables, 2/63. Confidential.

[1] As reported in telegram 577 from Seoul, February 18. (Department of State, Central Files, POL 12 S KOR) See Document 292.

junta can probably accept the settlement proposed by Pak, but Kim Chong-p'il and his group might be justifiably fearful of their fate despite the non-retaliation proviso. Their reaction remains an unknown but probably unsettling factor.

*Intensified Maneuverings.* Pak may be merely attempting to gain a temporary respite or to provoke a reaction which would rationalize a thinly disguised continuation of the present military role. More probably he is really seeking a solution. During the next few days feverish negotiations among Pak, the junta factions, and the political leaders can be expected. Discussions will center on the commitment against retaliation and on the extent of the political clearance offered by Pak.

---

## 292.  Editorial Note

On February 18, 1963, Chairman Pak Chung-hui told Ambassador Berger that he was considering withdrawing from the presidential race. Pak noted the strong opposition within the military government to the Director of the Korean Central Intelligence Agency, Kim Chong p'il. Pak also told Berger he was disillusioned with politics and government and had met with political leaders on February 14 to discuss his future. Berger informed the Department of State of these developments and received instructions to inform Pak that the United States considered his withdrawal the best hope for political and economic stability.

Pak announced on February 18 that he was willing to withdraw from the presidential election, provided opposition political leaders would agree on a nine-point program featuring political harmony, continuation of certain basic political objectives, including normalization of relations with Japan. The U.S. Embassy immediately gave public support to the proposal, saying that it believed the plan provided a basis for the smooth transition to civilian government through the democractic process in an atmosphere of national unity and stability. The principal South Korean political leaders accepted the scheme formally on February 27.

Kim Chong p'il left the country on February 25 to become a roving Ambassador, and a former rival took over control of the Korean Central Intelligence Agency. (Memorandum by Norred, March 27, sent by Forrestal to McGeorge Bundy on March 28; Kennedy Library, National Security Files, Countries Series, Korea, General, 8/62–3/63)

### 293. Telegram From the Embassy in Korea to the Department of State

Washington, March 14, 1963, 10 p.m.

640. Ref: Embtel 639 rptd Tokyo 192.[1]

1. After seeing PriMin I went directly to Gen Meloy to discuss Pri-Min's alarming observations about extent of armed forces involvement in new coup plots. Gen Kim Chong-oh, C/S ROK Army, was with Gen Meloy and I asked him to join us.

2. They both expressed astonishment and disbelief in PriMin's information (para 3 reftel) discounted most of it, and wondered where he got his info. Gen Kim said he knew nothing of possible frontline unit defections.

3. I said I had to report PriMin's remarks to Washington, and while I welcomed these assurances, fact remained that two coup plots had been uncovered, that previous evening PriMin informed me of coup plot by rightist "Chokchong" and of reports that members of political party were organizing terrorist group to assassinate Park. With four major groups involved or allegedly involved in coup plots, I thought it essential Gen Meloy and I meet with Park, all Chiefs of Staff, Minister of Defense, and PriMin to discuss situation. I asked Gen Kim what would be impact on armed forces if substantial numbers from four major Korean factional or political groups were arrested. Could forces be kept united under these circumstances? Gen Kim said effect would be very serious.

4. I said if any person is really involved in a coup plot the Korean Govt must, of course, act. But speaking frankly I thought some of these reports of plots or involvement were fabricated for the clear purpose of creating turmoil in order force Chairman Park to reverse his Feb 18 decision.

5. I asked Gen Kim who was stimulating student anti-American demonstrations? Who was spreading propaganda about American intervention? Who encouraged Chairman Park to propose to introduce

---

Source: Department of State, Central Files, POL 26 S KOR. Confidential; Limit Distribution. Repeated to Tokyo and CINCPAC.

[1] In telegram 639, March 14, Berger reported a conversation he had with Prime Minister Kim Hyon-chol who informed Berger that the situation was becoming increasingly chaotic as a result of various coup and assassination plots. The Prime Minister expected large-scale student demonstrations in favor of Pak reversing himself and agreeing to run for President. He also predicted anti-American student demonstrations. Kim stated that plotting was widespread and the threat to the Military Government was serious. According to Kim Hyon-chol, many ROK army units were involved and there could even be defection of frontline ROK troops to North Korea. (Ibid.)

martial law, suspend political activity, and delay elections? Who planted the phony story that chief of air force had resigned? Who besides Communists had an interest in turmoil.

6.  I pointed out that it was Chiefs of Staff and Minister of Defense who gave Chairman Park ultimatum that Kim Chong-p'il must leave country and there must be an investigation into ROK-CIA scandals. This would not be forgiven by Kim Chong-p'il and his supporters. Did this mean that he and other Chiefs of Staff and Minister of Defense would before long find themselves on list of people accused of something or other and purged? We had much evidence that Kim Chong-p'il's machine in and out of Democratic Republican Party was still intact, well financed, and active, and he knew as well as we that they are determined to create confusion in order to force Park to call off his Feb 18 announcement.

7.  Gen Kim did not dissent, I asked where Korea was going, saying we want to help Chairman Park during transition and will do what we can to keep situation stable. But it is now in Korean hands whether some semblance of reason and order will be introduced into situation. Korean armed forces were only stable and stabilizing institution in Korea. He and other Chiefs of Staff had moved into chaotic situation in early February and brought some sense and stability into situation. Park's Feb 18 announcement and Kim Chong-p'il's departure were the result. Gen Meloy and I said that that achievement was now threatened. The situation was again disintegrating and he and his colleagues had once again to move in to make their weight and wisdom felt.

**Berger**

## 294.    Telegram From the Department of State to the Embassy in Korea

Washington, March 16, 1963, 5:58 p.m.

547. Seoul's 645 rptd Tokyo 196, CINCPAC 172.[1]

1.  In absence knowledge as to attitudes chiefs ROK armed services and conclusions country team we do not wish express final judgment. In meantime our tentative view is that we have no proper alternative but to oppose course of action Chairman Pak has announced in view of prospects continued military dictatorship would have of increasing instability, factional conflict, and unpopularity. If you believe immediate action necessary, you are authorized to inform Chairman Pak that U.S. Government:

(a) Cannot possibly approve and might be compelled openly to oppose continuation of military government for four more years;

(b) Considers this a violation of repeated pledges made by Chairman Pak, including that to President Kennedy in their joint communiqué of November 14, 1961;[2]

(c) Expects that this course of action will be condemned by world opinion and, if they are permitted freely to do so, by Korean people themselves, to whom he so recently promised an early and smooth transition to civilian government. (We do not consider that proposed referendum would provide Korean people truly meaningful choice.)

(d) Would make it inevitable that USG would have to review in most fundamental way degree and character of its support of Chairman Pak's government;

(e) Plans to make no public comment for moment on decision in hope that Chairman Pak will alter his decision.

---

Source: Department of State, Central Files, POL 15 S KOR. Secret; Operational Immediate; Limit Distribution. Drafted by Norred, cleared by Yager and Rice and in draft with William Bundy, and approved by Harriman. Repeated to Tokyo and CINCPAC for POLAD.

[1] In telegram 645, March 15, Berger reported that Pak Chung-hui had informed him that within the next few days he would announce a national referendum on whether the military government should continue in power for 4 more years. If the electorate rejected the proposal to continue the military government, Pak would proceed to turn the government over to civilians in August. Pak justified his decision as necessary to maintain stability. Berger asked if there would be a "national debate" on the referendum and whether opposition elements could observe balloting and ballot counting. Pak assured him the referendum would be fair, although the opposition would be under some limits. In commenting to the Department, Berger stated that he did not see how the outcome of the referendum could be anything but a continuation of military rule. He asked for the Department's immediate views. (Ibid.)

[2] The communiqué reads: "The Chairman [Pak] reiterated the solemn pledge of the revolutionary government to return the government to civilian control in the summer of 1963, as he declared in the statement made on August 12, 1961. The President [Kennedy] particularly expressed his satisfaction with the Korean government's intention to restore civilian government at the earliest date." (American Foreign Policy: Current Documents, 1961, pp. 979–980)

2.  FYI. We have in mind considering any or all of following actions:

(a) Possibility of Presidential letter to Chairman Pak pegged on November 14, 1961 joint communiqué;

(b) Public condemnation of Chairman Pak's decision not to restore civilian government;

(c) Suspension of consideration of any new economic development assistance;

(d) Suspension of certain categories of military assistance not immediately required to maintain minimum level of preparedness against possible Communist military action, such as large hardware items;

(e) Consultations with other governments to secure supporting representations on their part to Chairman Pak. End FYI.

3.  Request your comment on above possible actions.[3]

4.  Request your comment also on (a) possible means of inducing Pak to retreat at once or in several stages, and (b) potentials for our influence over service chiefs and other commanders actually controlling military forces. Have service chiefs taken any firm position or are they waiting for U.S. reaction?

5.  Report on present reactions and temper Korean public and manner it might be mobilized against Pak plan.

6.  Defense concurs.

**Rusk**

---

[3] In telegram 548 to Seoul, March 18, Harriman asked Berger "whether this Government can be held together for a period of time until we are reasonably sure conditions are right for the election of a competent civilian government." (Department of State, Central Files, POL 15 S KOR) A draft of this telegram was included in the President's weekend reading of March 17. (Kennedy Library, National Security Files, Countries Series, Korea, Cables, 3/1/63–3/21/63)

### 295.   Memorandum From Michael V. Forrestal of the National Security Council Staff to President Kennedy

Washington, March 17, 1963.

SUBJECT

Korea

I attach several messages regarding the situation in Korea.[1] Seoul's 645 describes the problem raised by Pak's decision to have a rigged referendum on the question whether to return to civilian government. The Department replied authorizing Berger to tell Pak we did not approve of this scheme *if Berger thought it necessary*. After telling Averell of my talk with you yesterday afternoon,[2] State sent out an additional question to Berger asking if the military government might be extended for a short time.[3]

This morning we had word from Berger that he wanted to go slow.[4] Everyone agrees we must rely on his judgment.

I think you will want to catch up with this in a meeting soon after you get back.[5]

**Mike**

---

Source: Kennedy Library, National Security Files, Countries Series, Korea, General, 9/62–3/63. Secret.

[1] Regarding telegram 645 from Seoul, which was attached, see footnote 1, Document 294. Also attached was telegram 547 (Document 294) and telegram 653 from Seoul, March 17, in which Berger stated that Pak's public announcement of a referendum on March 17 "was timed to force the U.S. to deal with a fait accompli." (Kennedy Library, National Security Files, Countries Series, Korea, General, 9/62–3/63) Berger then asked the Department for time for the Country Team to come up with an assessment. McGeorge Bundy also enclosed a memorandum from Hilsman, printed as an enclosure. All three cables and Hilsman's memorandum were part of the President's weekend reading of March 17. (Ibid.)

[2] No other record of that discussion has been found. Since the President was then in Palm Beach, Florida, it apparently was a telephone conversation.

[3] See footnote 3, Document 294.

[4] See footnote 1 above.

[5] President Kennedy was in San José, Costa Rica, March 18–20. Kennedy met with Rusk, U. Alexis Johnson, Yager, McGeorge and William Bundy, and Luther Heinz at 6 p.m. on March 26. Presumably they discussed Korea at their "off the record" meeting. Kennedy then met Harriman, Heinz, Frank Sloan, and Forrestal on March 28, 12:07 to 12:35 p.m., for an "off the record" meeting at which Korea was the topic. (Kennedy Library, President's Appointment Book) For a briefing memorandum for the March 28 meeting, see Document 298.

Enclosure[6]

INTELLIGENCE NOTE

Latest Indications from the Republic of Korea

*Concerted Moves to Purge Opposition.* There is evidence that some force, probably the organization which Kim Chong-p'il built around the CIA and the government political party, is moving to break the power of several possible opposition groups and prolong the period of military government. Many of the leaders of the Hamkyong Faction of the junta have been jailed. The Cabinet has resigned and it appears that the Minister of Defense—who last month joined with the ROK Chiefs of Staff in forcing Kim out of the country—will not be reappointed. Small groups of military demonstrators have demanded the extension of military rule; the demonstrations were probably inspired and were certainly tolerated by the regime. There are reports that the government is prepared to place charges of coup plotting against two or three other major factional groups within the armed forces and a number of politicians, including the heads of state during the interim government of 1960 and republic of 1960–61. Chairman Pak Chong-hui may again impose martial law.

*Changes in the Power Spectrum.* The government's actions seem to have at least temporarily stunned potential opposition. The Hamkyong Faction has been rendered harmless by the arrest of its leaders. The military leaders are not exerting their strength and seem bewildered by the pace of recent developments. Civilian politicians appear to be even further removed from positions of influence. The status of the Kim Chong-p'il organization is unknown; investigations of the many scandals in which Kim was involved have led to some arrests but it is not clear whether this has yet affected the basis of his power.

*Pak's Intentions Estimated.* It is clear that the actions already taken could not have been without Pak's acquiescence or, perhaps, cooperation. It is also clear that these actions involve real danger of chaos both within the political world and the armed forces, and aim at postponing civilian government.

Two opposite views are conceivable: 1) that Pak never intended to bow out of politics and contrived the entire coup plot situation as a cover to renege on his previous promises or 2) that Pak would like to carry through on his pledge, but is being used by Kim Chong-p'il's followers to promote their own cause. Another possibility is that Pak had believed that he could move toward a civilian government without sacrificing Kim—whom he has consistently protected—or greatly reducing his own

---

[6] Secret; No Foreign Dissem.

power. Finding this impossible in the situation which followed Kim's departure he may now be driven toward a desperate effort to regain control.

*United States Interests.* To turn back the clock at this point may be possible, briefly, but can hardly bring stability for any prolonged period. The Pak–Kim axis is too thinly based, and the knowledge of the military government's failures is now too widely known. The group pushing for such a reversal will be aware that the United States will not view such changes with equanimity and they will try to prevent the exercise of American influence by inspiring criticism of alleged US influence in Korean affairs. There are reports that some student demonstrations along this line are being inspired. In addition, the regime may seize upon the internal crisis to seek additional US aid as necessary to stabilize the situation.

---

### 296. Memorandum for the Record

Washington, March 21, 1963.

SUBJECT

Daily White House Staff Meeting, 21 March 1963

1. Mr. Kaysen presided throughout a rather desultory meeting, a large part of which was given over to possible items for President's press conference at 1800 today.

2. Forrestal is now shooting for next Wednesday as a date for a Korea "background and review" for the President.[1] One of the reasons for the Wednesday date is that Governor Harriman will be out of town until early next week. Kaysen referred to some meeting recently held in

---

Source: National Defense University, Taylor Papers, Chairman's Staff Group, T–210–69. Secret; Eyes Only. Drafted by Colonel Legere.

[1] March 27. See footnote 5, Document 295.

[2] The meeting took place in Meloy's office in Seoul on March 20 and was reported over military channels in telegram KRA 269, March 20, from Berger to Rusk, Taylor, and Felt. Berger reported that he and Meloy met with the four ROK Service Chiefs who had asked that the Kennedy administration make no public statements on the Korean situation to give them time to explore what could be done. Meloy and Berger urged the Chiefs to meet with other ROK military and civilian leaders to resolve the crisis. Meloy and Berger supported the Chiefs' request that the Kennedy administration make no public statement. (Kennedy Library, National Security Files, Countries Series, Korea, Cables, 3/1/63–3/21/63)

General Meloy's office[2] and remarked that this meeting had served to stress once more who was the "real head of the country team out there." Forrestal defended the ability and role of Ambassador Berger, but Kaysen went on to note that the two most meaty and urgent messages to come out of Korea recently had come from Meloy.[3] For some reason or other, possibly simply because of the weight Forrestal swings around here, the President will make a brief statement on the Korea situation at his press conference this afternoon.[4] My impression had been that this 1800 television appearance was to be devoted entirely to a statement or speech on Latin America, but the story is that the prepared statements will only take up half the time, with the remainder devoted to questions as usual.

[Here follow paragraphs 3–7 on other subjects.]

LJL

---

[3] Apparent references to KRA 269 cited in footnote 2 above and to KRA 0255 to Taylor and Felt, March 17. In KRA 0255, Meloy reported that coup plotting by many of the military officers and individuals arrested could have been an attempt to overthrow Kim Chong-p'il, but that after he resigned from the KCIA in January and left the country on February 25, it had turned against Pak. Meloy believed that Pak's referendum was a scheme to retain power, but the ROK Service Chiefs told Meloy that in order to maintain stability they would support Pak's referendum. Meloy observed: "The armed forces are the strongest and most reliable stablizing influence in Korea. It is wrong to mess around with aid and force levels." (Ibid.)

[4] President Kennedy answered a question on Korea at his press conference on March 21. He noted that the situation was in flux, and his statement could not be final. "We are continuing to maintain very close contact with what's going on there. We are anxious for stability in the area. We regard South Korea, of course, as an important interest in the security of Asia and therefore we are continuing to follow very closely the present discussions about the return of democratic government in South Korea. But as the situation is still not hardened, I don't think that anything I say on it would be very helpful, at least this week." (Public Papers of the Presidents of the United States: John F. Kennedy, 1963, p. 275)

## 297.  Telegram From the Department of State to the Embassy in Korea

Washington, March 28, 1963, 7:33 p.m.

1825. (A) Seoul's 710 rptd Tokyo 245, CINCPAC 216;[1] (B) Seoul's 728 rptd Tokyo 257, CINCPAC 226;[2] (C) Seoul's 736 rptd Tokyo 262, CINCPAC 231.[3]

1.  We consider it unwise tie ourselves any particular solution, especially at this time, because:

a.  We and Korean opposition have good cause be suspicious of good faith Chairman Pak and his advisors;
b.  We do not yet have views of principal opposition leaders;
c.  We are not clear concerning real views of Kim Chong-o and other service chiefs, despite their public support of Pak's March 16 decision.

2.  Our objectives are:

a.  Creation of stable government with sufficient base of political and popular support;
b.  Removal of Korean military from political arena; and
c.  Maintenance of international support of ROK and UNC.

3.  To these ends, we believe transition to civilian government should be effected through elections at earliest practical date. Military

---

Source: Department of State, Central Files, POL 15 S KOR. Secret; Operational Immediate; Limit Distribution. Drafted by Norred; cleared by Yager and Rice and in draft with William Bundy and Richard N. Gardener, Deputy Assistant Secretary of State for International Organizations Affairs; and approved by Harriman. Repeated to Tokyo and CINPAC for POLAD.

[1] In telegram 710 from Seoul, March 25, Berger suggested that Pak was under "heaviest pressure" from his supporters not to reverse his decision for a referendum. Berger doubted he wanted to reverse, but was also sure Pak could not do it even if he wanted to. Berger stated in paragraph 6 of the telegram that he read his instructions to mean that the United States did not find acceptable Pak's March 16 proposal for a referendum, even if Pak and the junta allowed wider latitude for free debate and a reduction of military rule to less than 4 years. Berger considered as the only solution an interim military-civilian government that would act as a transition to full civilian rule. (Ibid.) A copy of telegram 710 was sent by Forrestal to the President. (Kennedy Library, President's Office Files, Countries Series, Korea Security, 1961–1963)

[2] In telegram 728 from Seoul, March 27, Berger reported on separate conversations with ROK Chief of Staff of the Army General Kim Chong-o and Prime Minister Kim Chong-so covering the political impasse between junta and civilian politicians. Berger stated that he saw no solution until there were meaningful discussions between the two sides. Berger believed it possible that the situation would "go along in this confused fashion for awhile" with an uncertain outcome. (Department of State, Central Files, POL 15 S KOR)

[3] In telegram 736 from Seoul, March 28, Berger reported on a 2-hour conversation he had with Pak Chong-hui that day. Pak told Berger he was trying to negotiate with the politicians and asked that the United States help him by issuing a public statement in favor of an interim coalition government. Berger believed that the SCNR was looking toward such a coalition as a temporary solution. (Ibid.)

junta is broken by military factional quarrels and probably faces declining stability and popularity. Also, if repeatedly promised elections are not held before 1963 UNGA we will have hard time explaining and will run risk of losing much of international support that is vital for ROK and UNC.

4.  We agree you should give no encouragement to compromise on basis of making proposed referendum freer or shortening extension of military rule (para 6 ref A). Under present circumstances, it almost inconceivable any assurances of free political discussion would be fulfilled. Recent suspension political activity and arrest party leaders has created impossible atmosphere for referendum. As for mere shortening period of extension, we consider one or two year extension to have no greater justification and to be basically open to similar objections as four year extension. We do not believe atmosphere for smooth transition to effective civilian government likely improve with only passage of time.

5.  Prime emphasis should continue to be placed on need for genuine consultation by junta with civilian leaders, including necessarily opposition leaders Ho Chong and Yun Po-sun, who are obviously of greater stature than others on scene. We thoroughly approve your stressing this point in discussing plan for reorganizing SCNR with General Kim Chong-o (para 5 ref B).

6.  In order to be in better position to bring about meaningful consultation between junta and civilian opposition leaders, you should at earliest opportunity secure directly or indirectly views of major opposition leaders and report them with your recommendations and comment. Although we certainly would not support their arbitrary veto of a reasonable solution, we should be careful not undercut them in dealing with government side, since future government will almost surely sooner or later come from their camp. You should urge them make constructive approach and give junta leaders an honorable way out and assurances as to future role and safety.

7.  We would find return to February 27 formula thoroughly acceptable and believe best arrangement might be along those lines, if junta and opposition can agree upon it. Idea of compromise by returning to February 27 agreement if "corrupt" politicians withdraw is hard to understand. Who is to decide who is corrupt? You might point out entire political purification concept has been strongly censured outside Korea as well as inside, and ask specifically whether such men as Ho Chong, Yun Po-sun and Kim Pyong-no are judged to be corrupt and if so why. FYI. Despite lack of clarity in this compromise proposal, it should not be rejected out of hand. It might in fact be acceptable if only few second-rank politicians are required to retire. End FYI.

8.  We believe it important for you to continue your talks with General Kim Chong-o, since he played part in developing February 27 for-

mula and later opposed martial law and was not consulted regarding extension military rule, and since he is chief figure in group you consider new main military force. As for his ostensible support of junta's March 16 decision, we do not see how he could realistically be expected to do otherwise. Despite show of military unity on March 22, we have impression factionalism exists in military forces as a whole, that many military strongly believe military should not be involved in politics, and many still hold to long Korean tradition that armed forces do not have internal security role, especially against popular movements.

9. Although we are skeptical about practicability and durability civil-military combination, we recognize it has some potential as short interim arrangement pending elections. Under such arrangement Chairman Pak should, however, be bound by collegiate action of enlarged SCNR, and cease his recent practice of one-man decisions based apparently on advice from outside SCNR.

10. At appropriate point, you should let Chairman Pak know that in our view return of Kim Chong-p'il to Korea would be most unfortunate, both in terms of prospects for Korean political stability and international support of ROKG.

11. Defense concurs.[4]

**Rusk**

---

[4] Although he agreed with Berger's recommendations and the solution proposed in paragraph 6 of telegram 710, Meloy stated that his mission charged him with the security of South Korea and that he was particularly sensitive to the ROK Service Chiefs, who were unequivocal supporters of Pak. Meloy stated that the United States could not afford disunity in the ROK armed forces. While he approved of the solution of a mixed civilian-military government—with Pak at its head—as a transition to full civilian rule, he did not believe political issues should govern U.S. policy if it resulted in a loss of faith in the United States by the ROK military. (Telegram UK 50188, to Taylor and Felt, March 25; ibid.)

**298.   Memorandum From Michael V. Forrestal of the National
Security Council Staff to President Kennedy**

Washington, March 28, 1963.

## KOREA

Governor Harriman and Mr. Yager (Director of East Asian Affairs in
State), Mr. Sloan (deputy to Paul Nitze in Defense) and Admiral Heinz
will report to you on the current situation in Korea.[1] The purpose of this
meeting is to bring you up-to-date on developments in Korea in the past
few weeks.

As you will recall, the military junta, headed by Chairman Park,
came into power in Korea in May 1961. At the outset our attitude toward
the Government was equivocal; but Ambassador Berger, after several
months at his post, came to the conclusion that the military junta might
provide Korea with a stable, reasonably clean government and one that
we could work with.

The junta functioned well for the first year; but beginning in early
1962 a series of difficulties began to arise. In April of that year the junta
adopted a political Purification Law, which in effect banned political
activity by the opposition for a period of 6 years. In June of 1962 the junta
adopted a currency conversion program and froze private bank
accounts. The effect on the economy was depressing and confidence was
badly shaken. Shortly after this action, it became known that Kim
Chong-pil, head of the Korean CIA and Chairman Park's son-in-law, had
made the greatest financial coup in Korean history by manipulating the
stock market for a profit of approximately $20 to $30 million. There are
suspicions of other financial manipulations by the CIA.

The junta had announced at the beginning of its regime that it would
transfer power to a popularly elected civilian government in the summer
of 1963. It repeated this promise from time to time and secured the adoption of a new constitution by referendum. Last January a pro-junta political party was formed, headed by Kim Chong-pil with the purpose of
securing the election of Chairman Park as President and, it later turned
out, the maintenance of Kim Chong-pil in power. At this point the junta
began coming to pieces because of the conflict between Kim and other
factions of the military junta. On February 18th Chairman Park, having
become disillusioned with the military administration, announced that
he would withdraw from the presidential race provided the civilian

---

Source: Kennedy Library, National Security Files, Countries Series, Korea, General,
8/62–3/63. Secret.

[1] See footnote 5, Document 295.

political leaders would agree upon a 9-point program featuring political harmony and the continuation of certain basic political objectives, including the normalization of relations with Japan. The political leaders accepted and Kim Chong-pil left the country as a roving ambassador.

At the beginning of this month a series of coup plots and counter plots preceded an announcement by Chairman Park on March 16th that he considered it necessary for the military rule to be extended for four more years, and that a national referendum would be held on this subject in April. There is some evidence that some, if not all, of the coup plots were engineered to support Park's announcement.

At the moment the situation is still unclear. The Korean military leaders have apparently sided with Chairman Park, and the civilian politicians remain adamant in their refusal to accept what appears to them to be an indefinite extension of the military government. We have been pressing for a "pan-national" solution in which the civilians and the military would get together to agree on a compromise government which would represent a broader range of Korean political life. There has been some evidence that Chairman Park may be reconsidering his insistence on prolongation of military rule. In the meantime he has sent you a personal letter, which is reported in the attached cable.[2]

---

[2] In a March 19 letter to President Kennedy, Pak detailed his reasons for not transferring the government to "ever corrupt politicians." Pak cited the recent political situation, "the dishonorable feud among politicians," and "anti-state plots masterminded by certain radical elements as justifications for his decision. (Telegram 713 from Seoul, March 25; Department of State, Central Files, POL 15 S KOR) In telegram 712 from Seoul, March 25, Berger reported that the Acting Foreign Minister had informed the Embassy that a new transitional military government under Pak would consist of 50 persons, two-thirds of them civilians. Pak would also have an advisory board of 30 elder statesmen. (Ibid.)

---

## 299.    Memorandum for the Record

Washington, March 29, 1963.

SUBJECT

Call of the Korean Ambassador upon the President

The President received Ambassador Il Kwon Chung of Korea at 6 p.m. today. Ambassador Chung delivered to the President a letter from

---

Source: Kennedy Library, National Security Files, Countries Series, Korea, General, 8/62–3/63. Secret. Yager also attended this meeting between Kennedy and Ambassador Chung. According to a March 29 memorandum of conversation by Yager, the meeting took place in the President's office. (Ibid.)

Chairman Park explaining his reasons for deciding that it was necessary to extend military rule in Korea four more years.

The President remarked that he and the American people were concerned for the future of South Korea and were anxious to see the country successful. The President stressed the importance of avoiding political instability which would prevent an evolution into democratic procedures. The President said that Ambassador Berger spoke for the United States, and that the President shared the Ambassador's hope that the military and civilian leaders in Korea could reach an accord establishing a timetable for the smooth transition to civilian government.

Ambassador Chung responded that Chairman Park was doing his best, and said that the military leaders have stepped into the situation with a constructive program. The Ambassador said that he would convey the President's remarks to Chairman Park.

The President re-emphasized the importance of finding a Korean solution to the problem of transition to civilian government.[1]

**MVF**

---

[1] After consultation with the Embassy (telegrams 594 and 597 to Seoul, March 29 and 31; Department of State, Central Files, POL 15 S KOR), the Department of State and the White House sent a letter from Kennedy to Pak, March 31, which reads in part: "We believe that a solution to the current political problem in Korea is to be found through consultations between your government and political leaders with a view to reaching an accord on a procedure for transition that will be acceptable to the Korean nation as a whole." (Ibid.)

### 300. Telegram From the Department of State to the Embassy in Korea

Washington, April 8, 1963, 6:57 p.m.

624. Seoul's 789, rptd Tokyo 304, CINCPAC 264.[1]

1. For time being at least, we believe U.S. should minimize its involvement in junta's April 8 solution to political controversy for following reasons:

A. Solution must be a Korean solution.

B. As it now stands, suspension formula is not clear cut resolution of controversy, particularly since commitment to hold elections has not been voiced publicly or apparently even privately to opposition leaders.

C. Formula thus far represents unilateral action by junta rather than agreement with opposition.

2. Approve your discouragement of intransigent opposition by civilian leaders para 5 reftel,[2] but suggest you avoid endorsing April 8 formula or strongly encouraging them to accept it unqualifiedly. We agree it desirable that civilian leaders use April 8 statement constructively. It would now appear to be sound tactic for them to press for elections and for verification of govt's real intention regarding elections.

3. Dept plans make no early comment on April 8 formula and may hold to that position even after reaction of civilian political leaders has been clarified.

**Ball**

---

Source: Department of State, Central Files, POL 15 S KOR. Secret; Operational Immediate; Limit Distribution. Drafted by Norred, cleared in draft with Yager and with Gregory of FE/P, and approved by Rice. Repeated to Tokyo and CINCPAC for POLAD.

[1] In telegram 789, April 8, the Embassy commented on a plan, announced by the SCNR on April 8, to hold "in abeyance" until September the national referendum scheduled for April. During September the government would examine the political situation with representatives of political parties and decide whether to hold the referendum or go ahead with the presidential and National Assembly elections. In the meantime, the announcement continued, the government would concentrate on improving its administrative functions and deal with food shortages. Political activities by political parties would be allowed, but the government expected the parties to reform themselves. (Telegram 787 from Seoul, April 8; ibid.) The Embassy noted that there were three positive aspects of this announcement: postponement of the April referendum on continuation of military rule, the commitment to discuss the future with the opposition, and lifting the ban on political activity. (Ibid.)

[2] In paragraph 5 of telegram 789, Berger stated that although he felt unable to tell the opposition that the ROK Government had given him any assurances, he did not want to encourage the political opposition's intransigence. In his discussion with opposition leaders he would emphasize the positive. (Ibid.)

## 301. Memorandum From the Joint Chiefs of Staff to Secretary of Defense McNamara

JCSM–312–63                                      Washington, April 20, 1963.

[Source: Washington National Records Center, RG 330, OSD Files: FRC 71 A 3479, Korea. Top Secret. 5 pages of source text not declassified.]

---

## 302. Telegram From the Embassy in Korea to the Department of State

Seoul, April 29, 1963, 6 p.m.

838. For Hilsman and Bell from Berger. Reference: Aidto 1219.[1]

1. Since January we have been preoccupied with day-to-day aspects of political crises and negotiations on economic stabilization measures, punctuated by rapid changes in junta and cabinet membership. Sudden and dramatic changes in situation have made it all but impossible to put together political, economic and psychological assessments in kind of perspective necessary for Washington's understanding of situation here. With Pak's announcement on April 8 delaying until Sept decision on elections, and with Korean Govt's commitment to USOM last week to adopt certain anti-inflationary measures, it is now possible to provide an interim assessment which has immediate relevance to certain policy decisions Washington must make.

2. On political side I shall be sending this week Embassy's analysis of various elements now in motion and play of forces, issues and personalities. It is our present view that moderate elements in junta are making genuine and serious effort to find basis for holding elections this year, because they think referendum proposal to prolong military rule does not hold out prospect for stability in Korea. Our strong stand was an

---

Source: Department of State, Central Files, E 1–1 S KOR. Confidential; Limit Distribution. Repeated to Tokyo and CINCPAC for POLAD.

[1] Aidto 1219 to Seoul, April 16, stressed the need for completion and implementation of economic stabilization immediately or as soon after resolution of ROK political problems as possible. Otherwise the program would become lost in the face of demands for politically urgent aid commitments. (Ibid., E 2–2 S KOR)

important factor in this conclusion, but it was also determined by adverse action within Korea itself. Indeed I think latter was decisive reason for decision to abandon April referendum.

3. What is now going on is an examination and behind-the-scenes talks by moderate military and civilian leaders of the problems of providing Korea with a political solution that hopefully, through elections this year, will provide a stable and effective govt. It will be some weeks or months before results are discernible. Meanwhile tension has subsided and immediate danger of domestic collision has been averted.

4. With this easing of political situation country's attention now being concentrated more and more on economic instability, attributable in part to political uncertainties, but in the main to inflationary pressures generated during 1962 and continued in 1963. Industrial production, tax collections and exports have held well during first quarter, but the rise in domestic prices, fall in foreign exchange reserves, and growing propensity to hoard in anticipation of accentuated price inflation are now producing great nervousness in country. Govt took some steps in March to curb inflation by means of credit restrictions and last week agreed with USOM to cut budget and reduce deficit. They represent substantial measures in right directions. Whether Korea Govt can during balance of 1963 resist pressures to modify them, can be argued. Our immediate problem during next four critical months, while political solutions are being sought, is to encourage govt to hold to its stabilization plans and to take US actions that will help keep economic situation as stable as possible.

5. Current pressing problem is upward trend of rice prices. This arises in part from smaller crop in 1962 in part from natural inclination of farmers and merchants to hoard in anticipation of higher price rises this year, and in part from inflated incomes of largest segment of population during last eighteen months which they are using to buy more food. Only 400,000 tons of wheat provided under Nov 1962 PL 480 agreement, along with carryover of wheat and barley from June 1962 agreement, added to Korea's own grain supplies, would give Korean people during this year about same food intake as in 1961, but it does not reckon with psychological, inflationary and higher consumption patterns that are disturbing whole situation. From now until new rice crop harvested in November I anticipate serious pressure on rice prices as supplies thin out. I interpret govt's intention to import 50,000 tons of rice from Japan on deferred credit terms, as psychological moves to discourage hoarding and relieve pressure upon prices. It should have some effect but fear of inflation and worry over declining foreign exchange reserves are now so psychologically deep-seated in Korean community and these two measures may not be adequate to arrest further rises in price of rice.

6. Timing of our announcement of additional PL 480 wheat and cotton and additional SA as requested in reftel will have major psycho-

logical impact. I feel strongly that an immediate Washington decision supporting our request at least for PL 480 would contribute to political and economic stability during next four critical months.

7. To summarize I think Korea is now in period of restless insecurity and nervous instability. If we withhold PL 480 announcements until we have iron-clad guarantees as to elections or performance indications in respect to stabilization measures, it will only add to country's frustrations and worsen matters. If we announce aid now we have a better chance of influencing local personalities and local situation in political and economic directions we would like to see them proceed. Moreover Korean Govt is intent on settling with Japanese during these months and will go to some length to make concessions on fisheries. Evidences of our support of Korea during this period might be helpful in persuading Japanese to conclude with this govt.

**Berger**

---

### 303.  Memorandum From the Assistant Secretary of Defense for International Security Affairs (Nitze) to Secretary of Defense McNamara

I–35, 531/63                                    Washington, May 11, 1963.

[Source: Washington National Records Center, RG 330, OSD Files: FRC 71 A 3470, Korea. Top Secret. 4 pages of source text not declassified.]

---

### 304.  Letter From the Deputy Under Secretary of State for Political Affairs (Johnson) to the Chairman of the Joint Chiefs of Staff (Taylor)

Washington, May 28, 1963.

[Source: Department of State, Central Files, DEF 15 S KOR–US. Top Secret. 5 pages of source text not declassified.]

### 305.  Memorandum From the President's Special Assistant for National Security Affairs (Bundy) to President Kennedy

Washington, May 31, 1963.

SUBJECT

, Ambassador Berger's call at 12:00 noon today[1]

This is an informal call, with no immediate business. Berger has settled with Dave Bell's people the particular question of economic assistance funds for the current fiscal year which brought him to Washington. (He wished to keep a contingency bargain which he had made with the Koreans using funds already committed to him by Washington, while AID was trying to recapture the money as a windfall; Berger has won.)

You will probably want to hear from Berger about the current political situation in Korea which Roger Hilsman reports as "balanced on a knife edge." Roger and I agreed that Berger can tell you much more about it than we can.

For the long pull, you may want to raise with Berger the possible prospect of an urgent further need for further reductions in both military and economic assistance to Korea. He has been cooperative in responding to these pressures so far, and will no doubt point out that he is the most virtuous of ambassadors on this score. Nevertheless, programmed assistance for next year runs at $205 million for MAP and $125-to-$145 million on the economic side (of which 80 million is PL 480). You may want to point out to Berger that with the growing claims of India, and the possibility of major reductions in the overall appropriation, something may have to give, and Korea is necessarily a likely target. Berger understands economics better than most ambassadors, and anything you can do to get him thinking as a member of your own team on this problem will help.

McG. B.[2]

---

Source: Kennedy Library, National Security Files, Countries Series, Korea, General, 4/63–11/63. Confidential.

[1] Berger met the President from 12:06 to 12:20 p.m. (Ibid., President's Appointment Book) No record of their meeting has been found.

[2] Printed from a copy that bears these typed initials.

## 306. Memorandum From Robert W. Komer of the National Security Council Staff to President Kennedy

Washington, May 31, 1963.

When you see Sam Berger you might condition him to the prospect that we may need some deep cuts in Korean MAP.[1]

If Congress slashes the aid bill this year (or even if not) we'll have to do some extensive reprogramming to find enough MAP for India and other possible new accounts. Korea, with some $200 million MAP planned for FY 1964, is the logical source and that from which DOD has generally drawn in the past.

In fact, I'd argue that our investment in Korea far exceeds our strategic interest. On top of over $5 billion already invested *since* the end of the Korean War, we plan another billion in MAP alone over the next five years. Moreover, the ROK falls so far short of being able to fund even the local currency costs of its over-sized army that it's our biggest remaining SA account ($90 million in FY '63 and perhaps $400 million planned for FY 64–68).

Berger, State and DOD reportedly agree on a modest force cut over the next two years. But this will provide only marginal savings. If we gradually cut ROK forces back from 19 to 12 divisions, we might free as much as $50 million a year for use elsewhere (depending on the rate of modernization of remaining forces).

Obvious political factors make a force cut now a delicate operation, but a case can be made for squeezing the ROK military on political grounds. Aside from this, we have failed in the decade since 1963 to get the ROK economy moving at a pace which would offer reasonable prospect of eventually getting it off our backs. Maybe we should spend more on development, and less on the military.

---

Source: Kennedy Library, National Security Files, Countries Series, Korea, General, 4/63–11/63. Secret.

[1] At the White House staff meeting on May 31, the following related exchange took place:

"In connection with Ambassador Berger's call on the President this morning, Bundy asked if there were any ideas on how the President should handle him. For the most part, the President intends to tell him that he has been doing a good job out in Korea, but Komer and Kaysen, eventually supported by Bundy, felt that the President should at least indicate generally to the Ambassador a "clear line" to the effect that if, as is very likely, Congress gets tough on foreign economic and military assistance, the chances are high that a substantial portion of their economizing will have to come out of those areas where the programs continue relatively 'fat,' and over $200 million of military assistance to Korean forces is fat indeed." (Memorandum for the record; National Defense University, Taylor Papers, Chairman's Staff Group, May 1963, T–211–69)

In short, Korea continues to be our most expensive military satellite. Is it worth as much as it costs?

**R. W. Komer**[2]

---

[2] Printed from a copy that bears this typed signature.

---

### 307.  Memorandum From Secretary of Defense McNamara to President Kennedy

Washington, June 4, 1963.

[Source: Washington National Records Center, RG 330, OSD Files: FRC 71 A 3470, Korea. Top Secret. 3 pages of source text not declassified.]

---

### 308.  Memorandum From Colonel Lawrence J. Legere of the White House Staff to the Chairman of the Joint Chiefs of Staff (Taylor)

Washington, June 11, 1963.

SUBJECT

    Force Level in Korea

This subject arose at the staff meeting this morning, but is so sensitive that I have decided to treat it separately in this original-only memorandum.

---

Source: National Defense University, Taylor Papers, Chairman's Staff Group, March to June 1963, T–208–69. Top Secret. Taylor's intials apear on the source text.

Bundy announced that he had in his hand a "piece of paper from Bob McNamara which has not and never will be officially written."[1] This hot potato apparently indicates Secretary McNamara's intention to let force levels in Korea (surely Korean and maybe US also, I would say) reach lower levels through the operation of immutable forces over time, without, as Bundy put it, any formally "theological" structure of justification. Bundy stressed strongly (a) the sensitivity of this information and (b) the fact that no one anywhere should try to flush this issue onto the table for decision or even for serious discussion.

Bundy knew that Komer and Hansen would try to say something, and, sure enough, Komer did start to talk about MAP funds and the need for a rationale for lowering them in specific areas, but Bundy shut him off with an abruptness that I have seldom if ever seen Bundy indulge.

*Sic transit ratio* of the JCS. I would say that this "decision" reflects credit on the JCS because it indicates that no one wants to join logical battle with them.

LJL

---

[1] Apparently a companion document, which has not been found, to Document 307.

---

### 309.  Memorandum of Conversation

Washington, June 17, 1963.

SUBJECT

Presentation of Credentials by Korean Ambassador

PARTICIPANTS

The President
Ambassador Duke—U/PR[1]
Mr. Tonesk—U/PR
Ambassador Kim[2]
Joseph A. Yager, Director, EA

---

Source: Kennedy Library, National Security Files, Countries Series, Korea, General, 4/63–11/63. Confidential. Drafted by Yager and approved in the White House on June 20 according to the copy in Department of State, Central Files, POL 17–1 KOR-US. There is no record of this meeting in the President's Appointment Book. (Kennedy Library)

[1] Angier Biddle Duke was Chief of Protocol, Department of State, and William J. Tonesk was Deputy Chief of Protocol.

[2] Kim Chong-yul, Korean Ambassador to the United States since June 4.

After welcoming Ambassador Kim, the President remarked that he had been reading about the Ambassador's military career. The President said that he had noted also that the Ambassador had been born in an excellent year. The Ambassador agreed and added that not only were both he and the President born in 1917, but they were born on the same day of the month although four months apart.

After photographers were admitted to the President's office, the Ambassador handed the President his credentials, the letter recalling his predecessor and his prepared statement. After reading the Ambassador's statement, the President remarked that he had been pleased over recent reports of progress in solving the ROK's political problems. The President said that he is aware that Korea has serious economic problems. He said that the US will continue to help to the limit of its ability, but our resources must be spread over many countries. The Administration recently sent an aid program to Congress but does not yet know what action Congress will take.

Ambassador Kim said that the ROK's heavy military burden adds to its economic problems. The President asked whether it might be possible to reduce the ROK military forces. Ambassador Kim responded that this would be most difficult since the ROK forces are thinly spread over a long line facing the Communists.

The President inquired into the status of the two American Army helicopter pilots who were captured by the North Koreans last month.[3] Mr. Yager reviewed the efforts that are being made to obtain the release of these pilots and concluded with the judgment that we face a very difficult problem. Ambassador Kim agreed and said that we may expect the Communists to make the maximum propaganda exploitation of their seizure of the pilots.

The President said that we continue to be interested in the negotiations between Japan and the ROK. We believe that a settlement between Japan and Korea is most important. The extra resources which Korea will obtain by means of the settlement will be very useful in Korean economic development.

The President asked whether the fisheries question is the most important issue still being negotiated between Japan and the ROK.

---

[3] On May 17 Captain Ben W. Stutts of Florence, Alabama, and Captain Carleton W. Voltz of Frankfort, Michigan, were detained by North Korean authorities after their helicopter strayed into North Korea and made a forced landing. On May 28 Assistant Secretary of State Hilsman briefed Rusk on actions taken and plans to secure their release. (Memorandum from Hilsman to Rusk, May 28; Department of State, Central Files, POL 27–7 KOR N–US) On July 26 the Department of State suggested in a public statement that July 27, the tenth anniversary of the Korean armistice, would be an appropriate time to release the two Army captains. (American Foreign Policy: Current Documents, 1963, p. 788) They were not released by North Korea on that date.

Ambassador Kim and Mr. Yager confirmed that this is the case. Ambassador Kim remarked that both the Japanese and Korean fishermen are complaining about the negotiations. The President said that in his opinion this is a sign of progress. It would be much worse if only one group of fishermen was complaining.

Ambassador Kim said he has been instructed to do what he can to facilitate a settlement with the Japanese, working here in Washington with the USG and the Japanese Embassy. The President said that he is sure that the State Department is actively pursuing this problem.

### 310. Memorandum From Michael V. Forrestal of the National Security Council Staff to President Kennedy

Washington, July 3, 1963.

FAR EAST ROUNDUP

[Here follow sections on South Vietnam (for text, see volume III, pages 447–449) and Laos.]

*Korea*

The immediate problem in Korea is the shortfall in the current harvest, which amounts to approximately half a million tons of grain.[1] After some bureaucratic delay we have succeeded in making approximately $8,500,000 worth (about 160,000 tons) of grain available to the Koreans. It will be nip and tuck whether the food arrives in Korea in time to avert real shortages, and we have suggested strongly to the Japanese that they make an interim contribution of rice. The Japanese have agreed to contribute 40,000 tons.

Over Agriculture's objections, we allowed this emergency shipment to go forward under the current PL 480 agreement which provides

---

Source: Kennedy Library, National Security Files, Meetings and Memoranda Series, Staff Memoranda, M.V. Forrestal, 11/62–11/63. Secret.

[1] The Department of State sent McGeorge Bundy a memorandum explaining the grain crisis and the measures to cope with it. (Memorandum from Brubeck to Bundy, June 19; Department of State, Central Files, AID (US) 15–9 S KOR) Ball and Hilsman and later Ball and McNamara discussed the grain shortage problem on June 28, agreeing that the situation was worthy of U.S. action to allieviate it. (Memoranda of telephone conversations, June 28; Kennedy Library, Ball Papers, Telephone Conversations, Korea)

that only 10 percent of the local currency proceeds be devoted to U.S. uses. I have told Agriculture and Treasury that we would support them in an overall review of South Korean's dollar position when a new PL 480 agreement is negotiated this fall with a view to seeing whether we can increase the U.S.-use percentage.

The two American captains whose helicopter landed in North Korea near the Demarcation Line are alive but have not been released. Having exhausted diplomatic channels, we are beginning to take retaliatory action. We have asked Japan to deny North Korea any transit rights. Similar and increasingly severe measures are planned.

[Here follow sections on Indonesia, the Philippines, and Thailand.]

### 311.    Telegram From the Embassy in Korea to the Department of State

Seoul, July 15, 1963, 9 p.m.

64. Ref: Embtel 56 info Tokyo 8 CINCPAC 12.[1]

1. With Pak's latest moves (see reftel) hand of Pak–Kim Chong-p'il group has been strengthened, and Korea has moved into another period accentuated instability. We believe these moves were undertaken for following reasons:

A. Outright clash between junta moderates led by Kim Chae-ch'un and pro-Kim Chong-p'il group had reached acute stage which could not be resolved by compromise. In making decision Pak chose go along with pro-Kim hard core with which he is most closely linked.

B. Pak's growing concern he cannot win a free election owing to Korea's food difficulties, accelerating price inflation, and declining popular confidence in ability of military junta to govern effectively and honestly.

---

Source: Department of State, Central Files, POL 15 S KOR. Secret; Limit Distribution. Repeated to Tokyo and CINCPAC for POLAD.

[1] In telegram 56 from Seoul, July 12, the Embassy reported a series of ROK governmental changes announced by the SCNR, the most prominent of which was the replacement of Kim Chae-chun as KCIA Director by Kim Hyong-uk. The Embassy commented that these moves represented a strengthening of Kim Chong-p'il's forces and an "ominous indication" that Pak Chung-hui was preparing the ground for the return of Kim Chong-p'il. (Ibid.)

C. With this group in control it would be easier either to rig elections, if held this year, or to deal with reaction if Pak decides to postpone them again and prolong military rule. In latter event he will use excuse that "food crisis, irresponsible political criticism, and economic and political confusion and instability" do not permit elections to take place.

D. Probability of junta's need to toughen repressive policy to curb press and opposition criticism as well as criticism from within certain military elements in effort maintain Pak–Kim group in power.

E. Need to tighten control in order to cover up Pak and Kim Chong-p'il's responsibility for stock market scandal and other misdeeds.

F. Desire to set stage for Kim Chong-p'il's return when Pak decides the time is right or if he feels that he cannot manage the situation without Kim's presence.

2. Timing of latest developments worth mentioning. That they came after additional US food commitment and additional $15 million support assistance announced, and universities recessed for summer is probably not just coincidence. Pak knows US reaction to these moves will be adverse but, encouraged by Kim Chong-p'il, he believes that US is so committed in Korea that we will have to accept his actions. With enhanced control of the reins of power, we expect that Pak will now press ahead rapidly to try settle with the Japanese in order open up that line of aid and credit. He knows US must under any circumstances provide substantial SA, PL 480 and military assistance, and with this and Japanese contribution he believes he can manage to deal with rising economic difficulties, particularly if US begins go slow on support. However, he probably counts on US desire for ROK–Japan normalization to inhibit our opposition to junta actions.

3. Once again the small group that constitutes core of the original revolution have shown their determination to maintain power. Characteristics of this group have in course of last year become more and more apparent. These are:

A. A "will to power" and a willingness to be ruthless.

B. Frequent rejection of US advice on political matters and tendency to originate and support unsound economic policies.

C. Touchy ultra-nationalism and barely concealed anti-Americanism, which manifest themselves openly whenever we oppose a course of action taken by govt or fail to respond as they may wish.

D. Continued prominence within the group of political advisors with pro-Communist backgrounds who have extraordinary influence. Despite frequent US objection to these individuals and widespread criticism in Korean Govt and political circles, their influence has not diminished and they play an important role in Democratic-Republican Party.

E. Distrust and disregard of independent civilian political forces and of normal democratic processes.

F. Desire to concentrate greater power in hands of narrower leadership group with deliberate elimination of opposing elements within the junta, until in latest move power concentrated almost exclusively in Pak and Kim group.

4. We believe that military junta under this leadership will continue and intensify the attitudes and actions spelled out above. This likely lead to increasing repression of opposition, proposal of irresponsible economic policies, ever-widening gap between govt and people, accentuation of corrupt practices, and little chance of an election along acceptable lines if an election is held at all.

5. Now more clear than ever that junta will do anything necessary to hold power. With this latest drive for maintenance of power, the junta may have added to its problems and may have over-reached itself. The political and economic situation may worsen along following lines:

A. In face of prospect of repression and govt's failure to modify rigorous conditions preventing free elections, opposition is seriously considering active boycott elections and will increase anti-govt agitation. Up till now opposition has been weak and divided. More serious efforts to unify will be made.

B. Further purges may occur within govt and military to remove or neutralize anti Kim Chong-p'il elements and those moderates unwilling to go along with hard line. (We have already received reports of possibility further cabinet changes including key figures such as Prime Minister, Chairman Economic Planning Board, and Home Minister.)

C. Economic situation will remain difficult. Continued inflationary pressure with danger of further run-down foreign exchange reserves and resultant loss of business confidence may be anticipated.

D. Public attitude toward junta will become increasingly hostile in face of mounting political and economic problems.

6. If events unfold as now appears likely, we anticipate that we will soon find ourselves unable to support the junta not only because nature these actions is offensive to us, will generate increasing opposition from articulate elements and widen gap between govt and people, but also because their methods of governing do not give promise of avoiding confusion and greater economic and political difficulty.

7. We are moving into a period where we must consider what steps we take as this process unfolds. We must also consider the prospects of and the moves toward acceptable alternatives. We propose:

A. To guard against a close political identification with junta.

B. To constantly emphasize our position on the necessity of free public discussion and fair elections this year.

C. To increasingly associate our economic assistance with our requirements for improved ROKG performance on the economic front and be prepared to withstand the anticipated ROKG charges of interference for political reasons and indifference to their economic problems. In the process we should continue to supply essential food requirements and support of military forces.

D. To work more closely with opposition elements, especially those which we believe are best suited to our purpose and most responsive to our guidance. Our objective is not to stimulate opposition to overthrow govt by sudden action, but to try to help create opposition to which we can turn as an alternative to junta in any situation that may develop. An opposition is needed in Korea and our influence should be brought to bear as appropriate in order to help in its formation and survival.[2]

8. Specific actions should now be taken to make our position clear. As a beginning we should:

A. Adhere to decision (of which Killen has already informed ROKG) to withhold $15 million SA on grounds inadequate implementation stabilization measures until and unless adequate corrective action is taken. On same basis withhold DL approvals.[3]

B. Stimulate US press interest in junta's misdeeds, e.g. stock market scandal, use of torture to extract confessions from defendants in current coup plot trials, and expected repression of press and opposition.

C. Use occasion of Foreign Minister's visit to Washington to question him and ROK Ambassador Kim Chong-yol closely about govt's political intentions and when govt intends to announce date of elections. They should be asked whether govt intends allow opposition membership in election committees to count ballots and should be told that US considers this essential for fair election. Dept should make clear US opposition to return Kim Chong-p'il and our attitude toward elections and suppression of opposition or press in light take-over dominant role by Kim machine. Subject should also be discussed with Kim Chong-o before he returns to Korea.

9. We should work along these lines, recognizing that we will probably elicit a sharp reaction as junta seeks hold power, and that we may reach a point where we can no longer support Pak. There is always possibility of some sudden sharp actions by Korean elements which will bring

---

[2] In telegram 78 to Seoul, the Department of State stated that it concurred in the courses of action recommended in paragraphs A–D. The Department noted that in working closely with the opposition, the Embassy should avoid "identifying ourselves with opposition or giving the appearance of seeking overthrow of government." (Ibid.)

[3] In telegram 78 to Seoul, the Department indicated that these recommendations in paragraph A had already been approved. The Department noted that it was attempting to interest the press in Korean developments and that it was replying candidly to press questions without attempting to apologize for or to conceal the junta's deficiencies.

about immediate end of junta rule, but resort to intensified police state methods would make this more difficult.

10. We offer the above for Dept's consideration and comment. Recommend Tokyo not discuss foregoing analysis of situation with Japanese at this time.

**Berger**

---

312.   **Editorial Note**

On July 29, 1963, between 5:50 and 6 p.m. local time, an undetermined number of North Koreans ambushed three U.S. soldiers of the 1st Cavalry Division, killing two and wounding one. At 9:09 a.m. local time, July 30, 50 ROK National Police and a detail of U.S. troops skirmished with an estimated 5 North Korean soldiers, 7 miles south of where the July 29 incident took place. One U.S. soldier, one ROK policeman, and two North Korean soldiers were killed. (Telegrams KA 31348 GI–I and KA 920170 GI, July 29 and 30; Kennedy Library, National Security Files, Countries Series, Korea, Cables, 6/63–7/63) Public statements on the incidents read by the Director of the Office of News, Department of State, are in *American Foreign Policy: Current Documents, 1963*, pages 788–789.

President Kennedy called a meeting with the Joint Chiefs of Staff on July 30 at 11:30 a.m. Washington time to discuss the skirmishes between the North Koreans and U.S.-ROK forces in the Demilitarized Zone. The President decided at this meeting to hold a National Security Council meeting the following day to assess the meaning of the incidents in the Demilitarized Zone and apparently related movements by the People's Republic of China on its borders with India and Laos and in Manchuria. (Memorandum of conference with the President, July 31; Kennedy Library, National Security Files, Chester V. Clifton Series, JCS Conferences with the President, 2/28/63–9/9/63)

The 516th National Security Council meeting was held at 4:30 p.m. on July 31 to discuss Chinese Communist intentions. A summary record of that meeting is printed as Document 181. According to that record, the President asked "whether the recent military crisis in Korea should be viewed as a isolated incident or as part of a broader military pattern." Ray Cline of the Central Intelligence Agency stated that "no one could say with certainty," but General Earle G. Wheeler, Chief of Staff of the

Army, noted that similar incidents usually took place during summer. There had been evidence of North Korean violations of the Demilitarized Zone at this time of the year for the past several years. Still, Wheeler could not state that the recent attacks were not part of a larger pattern. (Memorandum of discussion by Bromley Smith, July 31; ibid., Meetings and Memoranda Series, NSC Meetings, No. 516)

At his press conference on August 1 President Kennedy answered a question about the seriousness of China's apparent hard line, the violence along the Demilitarized Zone in Korea, and reported troop movements on the Indian-Tibetan border. The President stated that there was always potential for trouble, but there had been danger for years. The United States would carry out its commitments if need be, but the President hoped and believed there would be no need. (*Public Papers of the Presidents of the United States: John F. Kennedy, 1963*, page 614)

---

### 313.   Telegram From the Embassy in Korea to the Department of State

Seoul, September 2, 1963, 2 p.m.

277. Re Embtel 64 rptd Tokyo 12. CINCPAC 4.[1]

1. Course of events in Korea since mid-July bears out assessment of situation contained reftel. This current review should be read against background analysis reported reftel which remains largely valid. Evidence continues to mount that junta is dominated by hard core elements in SCNR and Democratic-Republican Party and that they have extended and deepened their control while moderate elements are being neutralized or eliminated. Pak remains key figure and his association with hard core more confirmed than ever.

2. Certain actions planned by hard core have been forestalled, principally by reason of US position. Kim Chong-p'il's return appears once again to have been postponed, sweeping cabinet changes temporarily averted, and danger of repression of opposition criticism may have been lessened in short term by US stand taken in Song Yo-chan case. Neverthe-

---

Source: Department of State, Central Files, POL 15 S KOR. Secret; Priority. Repeated to Tokyo and CINCPAC for POLAD.

[1] Document 311.

less we remain convinced that hard core is determined perpetuate its power by any means.

3. This objective has become more difficult in face increased public criticism of regime, especially in urban areas. Earlier govt hopes for smoothly run elections, with victory for Pak and DRP through reasonably fair election process, are giving way to apprehension that victory will not be easy. As result junta is now reacting more sharply to criticism, harassing press and other critics and have plans to take even more repressive action to dampen criticism when necessary.

4. The dominant group in the junta, operating from a narrower power base, is increasingly preoccupied with internal factional maneuverings and the problem of maintaining power. ROK CIA has been reorganized by hard core elements, re-staffed with Kim Chong-p'il supporters in key positions, and is now working to reestablish its power over govt and political policy-making. Opposition to the hard core from members of the anti-Kim Chong-p'il group who have been ousted from positions of influence, continues to be manifested, but has not been effective nor cohesive.

5. Key to Pak remaining in power continues to rest in support of ROK military forces. Junta's prestige has doubtless suffered in armed forces over past months. A factor in this has been effect of rising prices on low paid officer and enlisted personnel. However, in absence some explosive situation which would galvanize public opposition (e.g., wholesale election rigging), the ROK Armed Forces appear likely remain responsive to junta leadership and senior commanders appear willing to go along with junta plans. Those commanders who show any sign of faltering or opposition will continue to be removed or shifted from key positions.

6. Civilian political opposition forces have been making strenuous efforts to unite against regime but continue to suffer badly from old ills of factionalism, personal ambition and short-sightedness. Ability of civilian politicans to organize against junta will be given decisive test during next two weeks. Prospects for effective unity have deteriorated with recent inter-party squabbling and public image of opposition leadership has suffered. With presidential election only about seven weeks away, opposition still has not settled on single candidate and party merger initiatives have been unsuccessful. Funds are short and competition among aspirants for presidency and Assembly strong and possibly even bitter. Moreover, realizing danger presented by opposition united behind single presidential candidate, govt is doing all it can to weaken, divide and harass opposition. Although opposition leaders express confidence that tide is running in their favor, there is no evidence at this time that popular discontent with military govt has been converted into positive

support for opposition. If opposition closes ranks behind single candidate this could change.

7. Election campaign will be in full swing in few days. As things heat up regime will intensify efforts to promote Pak's candidacy, and denigrate opposition leaders and their capacity to govern. Govt is counting heavily on bumper rice crop which appears in making to reverse decline in govt's popularity and to create favorable public attitude at election time. A promising crop already doing much to remove the pressure on food prices and the food shortage psychology which have continuously plagued govt since February. Junta will seek to capitalize on Pak's prestige and constructive achievements of past two years while playing down failures. Success in elections will be sought through good party organization, use of govt administrative organs, plentiful funds and use of ordinary powers of govt. If this is not enough, hard core determined to take whatever other measures needed. However, the job today is too divided politically and the opposition too active to predict that resort to repressive measures will not back-fire. Extreme repression on the part of the regime could set off chain reaction of opposition-public defiance, especially in cities.

8. Political differences built up over past year have an air of permanence about them which presents us with outlook for protracted period of political struggle. Opposition now has only one purpose in mind, downfall of military govt and junta leadership as soon as possible. If that not possible by means of elections, and many opposition leaders believe junta's policies preclude such possibility, then opposition will lie in wait for whatever occasion or events can speed up the process of change.

9. In present circumstances, outlook is for Pak victory but DRP chances of winning majority in Assembly are poor. With tougher prospects in Assembly elections, junta will be inclined to tougher measures in effort secure majority. A substantial Pak victory could have significant effect on Assembly elections and the interval between presidential and Assembly elections would be used by DRP to develop more enthusiasm for its candidates.

10. Whichever way one looks at the situation, the prospect for emergence stable and effective govt is not apparent:

A. A Pak victory with no majority in the Assembly would create a troublesome problem of governing. Normally in such a situation the solution would lie in a coalition, but the hostility and lack of trust on both sides is such that this will not be easy and may not be possible.

B. Pak and Govt Party may win majority in Assembly and if the elections were not flagrantly rigged there may be no serious public protest.

C. In either above cases, return of Kim Chong-p'il at some stage is inevitable, and he together with hard core, would dominate govt. This could produce renewal of fighting within regime between pro and anti-Kim Chong-p'il elements.

D. If by any outside chance opposition succeeded in presidential and Assembly elections, they would be plagued by internal divisions, and there would be a struggle between civilians and the defeated junta with danger of another coup.

11. At this stage of Korea's political development it is too much to expect that any govt could be stable or effective in a Western sense or that economic and political actions would not be sometimes erratic. It remains our judgment that the resolution of Korean political problems should continue to be left primarily to the interplay of domestic political forces. There is not much we can do at the moment to change things without precipitating a sharp upheaval which would not resolve conflict at this stage and might set off chain reaction of disorders. We must be guided by patience and principles; patience to allow Korean dynamics to work out their own solutions; and principles to set limits of behavior as well as targets for achievement. We should avoid interjecting ourselves prematurely into internal political affairs or become too committed to a given solution. We should remain wedded to the principle of fair elections, and assume a critical stance when that principle is threatened.

12. There are those in junta who believe US will have to go along with anything which they may do. We have taken pains to prove them wrong on a number of occasions (e.g., currency reform, extension military rule, Kim Chong-p'il, Song Yo-chan). In future we must be sure to exert immediate pressure when junta moves off course which we consider acceptable. Repressive political actions need to be exposed and criticized, and irresponsible economic policies penalized. We should do this not only because of our natural distaste for repressive or irresponsible actions, but also because our long term interests are not served by US acquiescence in unpopular, unjustified acts. This may increase the risk of open confrontation with junta, which has shown its dissatisfaction when crossed, but we should be prepared ride out any repercussions however sharp.

13. In these circumstances we continue believe US policy should be geared to preparing for various possible alternatives in fluid situation. We are still of the opinion expressed in para 7 reftel that US for time being should continue to:

A. Guard against a close political identification with junta, while at the same time seeking to influence their actions when these are unacceptable;

B. Constantly emphasize our position on necessity free public discussion and fair elections;

C. Increasingly associate our economic assistance with our requirements for improved ROKG performance on the economic front;

D. Maintain a close association with responsible opposition elements and as appropriate use our influence to support development of a viable opposition.

E. Maintain a close association and influence with armed forces leaders who in the end may prove to be the arbiters should there be internal upheaval.[2]

14. General Howze and Killen have seen this message.

**Berger**

---

[2] In telegram 206 to Seoul, September 11, the Embassy concurred in recommendations A–E. The Department suggested that it would "not be overly troubled" by the election of Pak as President if the opposition controlled the National Assembly. Unlike the Embassy's assessment the Department did not believe that Pak Chung-hui was supported by the ROK military, but rather that he was not opposed by it. (Department of State, Central Files, POL 15 S KOR)

---

### 314. Telegram From the Embassy in Korea to the Department of State

Seoul, October 9, 1963, noon.

450. Reference Department telegram 288 repeated Tokyo 873 CINCPAC unnumbered.[1]

1. With presidential election campaign entering final week, two of three main opposition candidates have dropped out and Yun Po-son has emerged as only serious challenge to Pak. Opponents of regime are falling in behind him adding to his vote-getting power. This, plus forcefulness of Yun's campaign and large turnouts at his meetings are beginning to worry junta. Opposition efforts so far confined mainly to urban cen-

---

Source: Department of State, Central Files, POL 14 S KOR. Secret; Priority; Limit Distribution. Repeated to Tokyo and CINCPAC for POLAD.

[1] In telegram 288 to Seoul, October 4, the Department of State suggested that the "hard slugging campaign of the opposition" and the withdrawal of presidential candidate Ho Chang in favor of Yun Po-sun appeared to be bordering on an "opposition boom." While not predicting victory for the opposition in the October 15 presidential elections, the Department could not rule it out provided balloting and counting were relatively honest. Still, the hard-core elements in the military government were capable of harsh and antidemocratic countermeasures. The Department suggested contingency countermeasures for possible actions by the hardliners. (Ibid.)

ters, campaign in rural areas getting underway as speakers fan out in crucial final week.

2. Despite substantial hostility to junta, especially in urban areas, and rising interest created by opposition oratory, we still do not characterize situation as "opposition boom." Facing single major opposition candidate, Pak now running harder than before and still enjoys advantages of money, organization, use of govt administrative apparatus, an assured bumper crop and a solid core of popular support.

3. So far govt side has responded with restraint to hard-hitting opposition campaign. Amidst back-room threats of widescale arrests, martial law and election postponement, plus murmurings of assassination possibilities, junta keeping to original election strategy which aims to assure Pak victory in a quiet campaign with minimum of public disturbance. However, signs of growing opposition strength during remaining week could lead junta to change strategy. Concern about outcome of election or civil disturbance could provoke junta to take various actions which would arouse adverse opinion domestically and internationally. Junta's actions so far to harass and hamstring opposition and its abundant funds, far in excess of legal limits, have stretched credibility in fairness of elections. However, despite its handicaps opposition has managed recently to mount a vigorous campaign with Yun Po-son hitting on two main themes that aim to discredit Pak: his Communist past and the allegation that he is unable to command the support and confidence of the US.

4. We agree with Dept's view expressed para 3 reftel and to need formulate contingencies and possible lines of action open to US. We tend, however, to formulate such contingencies differently than set forth para 4 reftel.

A. On basis present indications we do not believe junta will postpone or cancel presidential election. In discussions with key leaders we have made clear adverse Korean and foreign reaction that would occur and have found no readiness to take such drastic step.

B. We do not believe junta will arrest Yun Po-son before presidential election. Consequences such action have also been discussed with govt leaders and to date such hard line has been rejected.

5. In our view should contingencies arise in connection with elections they more likely take following form:

A. Opposition boom develops and threatens Pak victory. Junta will react by severe repression opposition campaigning and then stuff ballot boxes or falsify count.

B. If by some freak junta's plans go awry and opposition wins presidential election, govt would charge election irregularities and seek invalidate result in courts.

C. In addition to, or in place of, legal maneuvering in (B) above, junta would simply declare unwillingness accept unfavorable result and try to continue military govt by decree backed by force of arms.

6. We do not believe junta prepared accept defeat even though mindful of consequences of resort to extreme measures (paras 2 and 6 A reftel). They know blatantly rigged election or use of force to maintain power as military govt could set off public reaction but this would not deter them. We have repeatedly made clear to leaders importance we attach to proper conduct of elections and acceptance of election results, but there are those in ROKG who believe we have to support Korea whatever they may do.

7. Re para 6 reftel, Pak, Kim Chong-p'il and hard core of junta are not interested in compromise with opposition. The opposition on other hand is completely at odds with junta. While publicly promising abstain from political retaliation, if opposition comes to power, we can expect they will not hesitate to purge revolutionaries.

8. If presidential election takes place and Pak can make his victory stick without upheaval, there will still remain the uncertainties in connection with Assembly elections and establishment of govt power within a constitutional frame-work. Opposition will attack Pak victory as rigged and seek arouse public feeling. If serious disturbances occur, junta may be tempted hold off Assembly elections and continue authoritarian rule by an "elected" president. If Assembly elections are held country will go through another bitter campaign, in which govt's chances are not so good and tendency to resort to unfair practices will be even greater. For example junta has threatened arrest and try (after October 15 elections) opposition politicians for "illegal" actions in presidential campaign. This maneuver, if carried out, would inhibit electioneering in Assembly campaign while also removing from field prominent opposition activists.

9. Our problem is constantly to weigh acceptability and consequences govt's actions. We may at some time be faced with a clearcut issue, e.g., postponement of elections, martial law, or widescale arrests, and our actions in such cases can be more easily planned. In these circumstances the reactions of Korean people would be discernible and could be taken into account in deciding what actions we should take. We might however be faced with a series of less dramatic actions, no one of which is sharp or drastic enough to create a crisis within Korea or a collision with US, but which cumulatively would produce restiveness in important segments of the population and a generally unhealthy political environment. In such a situation the nature and timing of any decision the US might take would be more difficult to arrive at because it would have no clearcut focal point.

10. We have tended to rely greatly on private advice and carefully weighed public statements to encourage responsible political behavior in hope of building a more or less stable government structure in the wake of revolution. We have also counted on the rise of political forces within the Korean context which could take care of problems without overly active US intervention. While we must continue to rely on advice and official comments in dealing with or seeking to prevent contingencies of the sort laid out in the preceding discussion, such expressions may not be sufficient. We accept the lines of action proposed by Dept in paras 4, 5, and 6 of reftel and in fact have been following those courses as appropriate. However, in certain contingencies, we believe that more fundamental decisions may need to be taken.

11. The lines of action proposed by Dept in reftel are in nature of US reactions to a set of possible extreme measures by junta which we would find undesirable, which would confirm that US unable to deal with junta except on latter's own terms, and which probably would be unacceptable to a substantial proportion if not a majority of the Korean public. We would therefore be setting the US in opposition to the junta, and in effect instituting a course of action which could have either of two basic objectives:

A. To force a change in junta policy to one which would be acceptable to us and suitable to local situation;

B. To begin process of withdrawing support from junta with purpose of replacing it with an acceptable govt.

Either of these objectives would call forth actions and counteractions involving the full range of complex relations and strategic interests which face US in Korea.

12. Alternative A above is not as harsh or difficult as alternative B, but if faced with intransigence on the part of the junta and a rising tide of public hostility to junta inside Korea it might inevitably lead to alternative B. We would need, therefore, to consider carefully the ultimate objectives we would have in mind and weigh the consequences, risks and alternatives. In dealing with various contingencies it is difficult to decide at what stage it is prudent as well as possible to move from the mild to the more drastic courses. No complete answer can be given in advance of events and the way in which situation develops.

13. We would welcome Dept's comments on foregoing soonest. We also urge that in event contingencies of sort feared arise, there be close consultation and coordination prior to development our position or any public statement. While fully aware of possible need for quick US reaction, we believe such reaction should not be automatic but should develop in light of actual events and be based upon deliberate and recognized objectives.

**Berger**

315. **Telegram From the Embassy in Korea to the Department of State**

Seoul, October 16, 1963, 1 a.m.

515. 1. Election returns have astonished all observers.[1] While it is true opposition gained on Pak in last week, extent of vote for Yun, especially in armed forces, generally remarkable. Equally remarkable, and to surprise everyone (including Embassy), was junta's apparent willingness to take chance of free balloting. That it may have been overconfident is true, but nevertheless by conscious decision govt did its best insure an orderly election day and efficient conduct of balloting.

2. We do not intend in this message to analyze complete campaign and probable future consequences. It is a little too soon for that, and we want to watch a few days to see popular and organized political reaction.[2] At this point, however, it is clear that Pak did not achieve decisive victory which he expected. Yun's hard-hitting personal campaign attacks took their toll, but dissatisfaction with military govt on economic and political grounds and with its style of governing, and was more fundamental. Much of Yun's vote was not so much pro-Yun as anti-military govt. The opposition vote was registered in face of a govt machine which had money and organization. Pak won a personal victory but his opponents have a moral victory and with it perhaps a new sense of confidence which they may use to their advantage in the future.

3. Our preliminary evaluation of the vote count runs like this. Pak's ability to hold Yun to a surprise draw in Pusan, rack up a big majority in his home Kyongsany provinces and overturn Yun's hopes in normally opposition Cholla provinces carried the day. A decisive factor in holding down Yun's vote was the 800,000 odd votes picked up by the three minor candidates. Undoubtedly a majority of these would otherwise have gone to Yun and would have made the difference between defeat and victory.

4. Another factor significance of which we not able yet judge is the large number of invalid votes and their locale. Vote tallies as announced so far do not provide the necessary statistics evaulate this element. What data we have show large numbers of invalid votes (perhaps as many as one million) particularly in areas where Yun ran strong. These may be votes cast for Song Yo-chan in addition to ballot otherwise spoiled but

---

Source: Department of State, Central Files, POL 14 S KOR. Confidential; Immediate. Repeated to CINCPAC for POLAD and Tokyo.

[1] The final total vote count was: Pak Chung-hui, 4,702,640; Yun Po-sun, 4,546,614; three other minor candidates, a total of 1,031,944. There were 954,977 invalid ballots and 1,948,840 abstentions. (Telegram 525 from Seoul, October 18; ibid.)

[2] The Embassy sent a long appraisal of the elections in airgram 346 from Seoul, October 29. (Ibid.)

that is only speculation. We will have to await opposition and press initiatives to probe this. If spoilage is overwhelmingly and disproportionately large in Yun strongholds, the opposition will have something critical to say.

5.  So far opposition comment on Pak's vote in Pusan is surprise [garble] with snide reference to power failure when vote counting [garble]. Pak's vote in the Chollas is being attributed to strong campaigning by the DRP with plenty of money and liberal use of govt favors in an area where the govt knew Pak might have trouble.

6.  More than anything the military vote will be debated back and forth. It was not rigged, that is sure. That it favored Yun is also sure. Inflationary pressure and consequent discontent help to explain it.

7.  We do not know how either junta or the opposition will react in the immediate future. Pak's first reaction has been statesmanlike and moderate. Some of his associates have not been as forthright. That Pak did not win either outright majority or sizeable margin over his nearest opponent may have restraining effect on junta's actions. An important test in next few days will be how govt behaves toward election and "violators."

Pak reaffirmed in post-election statement he intends no retaliation.

8.  Opposition has said very little so far about election, preliminary statements moderate. Too early to say if this will last.

9.  Both we and ROK face difficult few days followed by period uncertainty until Assembly elections over. However, country appears have taken a major step, in which it might easily have stumbled, towards transfer to civil govt. We will do an assessment of the outlook as soon as we can draw a fine bead.

**Berger**

316.    Telegram From the Department of State to the Embassy in
         Korea

Washington, October 22, 1963, 2:17 p.m.

335. Reference A) Seoul's 361 rptd Tokyo 136, CINCPAC 140;[1] B)
Seoul's 64 rptd Tokyo 12, CINCPAC 14.[2]

1. Following are some preliminary views on post-election scene
and implications for our policies. Your comments invited.

2. Democratic election was held in orderly manner. Flagrant
repression and wholesale rigging which we feared did not occur. U.S.
posture of neutrality regarding presidential candidates appears to be
well established publicly. For these and other beneficial developments
referred to below credit is due in large part to effective efforts of Embassy.
You and your staff are warmly commended.

3. Although narrow Pak victory with less than majority of valid
votes was unexpected and creates complex political situation, situation
has certain compensations from our viewpoint. Had Pak secured strong
popular mandate, he could more easily justify repressive trends set forth
para 3 reftel B than he can as plurality victor. Had opposition won, particularly by narrow margin, there would have been period of widespread
uncertainty, instability, and possibly violence as it sought to establish its
authority.

4. Our preliminary and tentative interpretation of election is that
opposition won moral victory. Even without evaluating high number
invalid votes, it seems clear that genuine support for Chairman Pak was
relatively narrow. Vote for opposition in certain military areas makes
apparent that support for junta within military cannot now be taken for
granted.

5. We are encouraged by talk of moderation on both sides, but especially with Kim Chong-p'il returning there is danger of his baleful
repressive influence being reflected in government actions. Beginning of
Assembly elections probably will regenerate political controversy, with
at least temporary impairment of atmosphere of moderation and cooperation. Our preliminary guess is that Democratic-Republican Party is
unlikely win majority of constituencies in Assembly although it could

---

Source: Department of State, Central Files, POL 14 S KOR. Secret; Immediate; Limit
Distribution. Drafted by Norred; cleared by Fearey, Green, and Harriman, in draft by Ives
of AID and Colonel Moorman of OSD/ISA, and in substance by Hulen of INR/RFE; and
approved by Hilsman.

[1] In telegram 361, September 18, the Embassy predicted Pak's election as a "virtual
certainty" in light of the failure of the opposition to unite and the junta's determination to
win the election. (Ibid., POL S KOR)

[2] Document 311.

gain majority of seats as consequence of new proportional representation system. Assembly election seems unlikely to have any marked effect on present political balance of power.

6.  We believe paras 7 A, B, C, and D reftel B still afford sound guidance for U.S. policy, despite some changes in situation. Strength of opposition vote underlines importance of 7 A and 7 D. Need for pressing for freedom of elections (para 7 B) still pertinent with respect to Assembly elections, especially in view return of Kim Chong-p'il to scene. Linkage of assistance with Korean performance (para 7 C) remains essential. We believe these policies are becoming well understood at present in Korea, largely as result of Embassy–USOM steadfast adherence to them.

7.  We suggest three special points of emphases at this juncture:

A.  Encouragement of moderation, tolerance, and cooperation on part of both government and opposition. Although we must recognize need for continued political conflict and should not help ROKG subvert opposition in guise of developing cooperation, we should endeavor to move their political dialogue into constructive channels. To this end, we should consult with opposition as well as government on such problems as Korean-Japanese normalization of relations, and economic stabilization.

B.  Encouragement of Pak to make best selections possible for cabinet and other key positions on basis of competence and of promoting national interests. We should work to establish authority and responsibility in cabinet and ministries rather than continued behind-scenes activities. Canadian grain purchase could be made case in point. We should also refuse help Korean activities in which Korean CIA improperly involved.

C.  Renewed focus on threat of Kim Chong-p'il and his supporters in government. We hope that his prolonged absence from Korea, opposition's show of strong popular support, and our cold-shoulder treatment may have impaired his political strength in Korea. We strongly question, however, whether he has changed, and regard him as still a dangerous unstabilizing force. In working to counter him, Embassy could truthfully say that Dept has received many inquiries about scandal cases, including quite a few from Congress.

8.  At appropriate occasion in course of coming week Hilsman proposes publicly to refer to orderly conduct of election and encouraging post-election developments.

**Rusk**

## 317.  Editorial Note

On November 18, 1963, Korean Foreign Minister Kim Yong-sik, who was attending the U.N. General Assembly session in New York, arrived in Washington for talks with Department of State officials. At 11 a.m. on November 19 Kim met with Secretary of State Rusk and then had lunch at the Department of State. A memorandum of conversation of the Rusk–Kim conversation, November 19, covered the following topics: the incidents of violence in the demilitarized zone, the Korean question in the United Nations, transition to civilian government, economic assistance for Korea, Korean-Japanese talks, U.S. representation at Korean presidential inauguration ceremonies, reports of withdrawals of U.S. forces, the Communist threat, and the Military Assistance Program. (Department of State, Central Files, POL KOR–US)

After lunch Assistant Secretary of State for Far Eastern Affairs Roger Hilsman met with Kim. The two men discussed many of the same topics that Rusk and Kim had raised that morning. In addition, Kim expressed hope that if President Kennedy visited the Far East, he would come to Korea. Christopher Norred, Jr., Officer in Charge of Korean Affairs, raised the question of status of forces negotiations. Kim responded that they were going well, but slowly, given their technical nature. Kim hoped that criminal jurisdiction could be discussed soon and assured Hilsman that there was no anti-Americanism among the Korean people. (Memorandum of conversation, November 19; ibid.) Foreign Minister Kim was scheduled to meet with Harlan Cleveland, Assistant Secretary of State for International Organization Affairs, on November 20, but no record of their discussion has been found.

## 318.   Memorandum of Conversation

Washington, November 25, 1963.

SUBJECT

United States-Korean Relations

PARTICIPANTS

| United States | Korea |
|---|---|
| The President[1] | Acting President Chung Hee Park[2] |
| Mr. Roger Hilsman, Assistant Secretary | Foreign Minister Young Shik Kim |
| of State for Far Eastern Affairs | Ambassador Yong Chul Kim |

President Park expressed the condolences of the Korean people on the death of President Kennedy, but their satisfaction that a man of President Johnson's stature had succeeded him.

President Johnson thanked the Korean President and stressed the regard of the American people for Korea and the continuity of United States foreign policy.

President Johnson noted United States pleasure at the fulfillment of the military junta's pledge to return to civilian rule and the moderation marking the recent elections in Korea.[3]

President Johnson mentioned our pleasure at indications that the negotiations for normalization of relations between Korea and Japan had been progressing and expressed the hope that the completion of elec-

---

Source: Department of State, Central Files, POL KOR–US. Confidential. Drafted by Hilsman and approved by the White House on December 2. The meeting was held at the President's reception at the State Department.

[1] Lyndon B. Johnson. President Kennedy was assassinated in Dallas, Texas, on November 22.

[2] Pak Chung-hui was Acting President until his inauguration on December 17.

[3] In telegram 470 to Seoul, the Department of State cabled an account of the Johnson–Pak conversation based on this memorandum. The Department thought that Korean journalists might have been given a "somewhat distorted account" by the Supreme Council Spokesman Yi Hu-rak. The Department asked for a summary of ROK press coverage. (Department of State, Central Files, POL 1 S KOR–US) According to telegram 742 from Seoul, November 27, the Johnson–Pak talk was reported prominently by all Seoul newspapers. The *Korea Times* and *Hankik Ilbo* carried accounts based on a Korean Embassy source, which stated that President Johnson had pledged renewed and strengthened cooperation between the ROK and the United States and had praised the October 15 presidential election as being democratic. Johnson also assured Pak of U.S. cooperation in matters of mutual interest. The *Korean Republic*, the government newspaper, claimed that Pak had received assurances from President Johnson that the United States would continue its policies of military and economic support. (Ibid.)

tions in both Japan and Korea would set the stage for a rapid and successful completion of the negotiations.[4]

---

[4] On November 26 Rusk discussed normalization of Japanese-Korean relations with
Japanese Prime Minister Ikeda and Foreign Minister Ohira, both in Washington for President Kennedy's funeral. Rusk suggested joint utilization of fisheries resources; Ohira
thought the fisheries issue capable of solution if the Koreans were willing. (Memorandum
of conversation, November 26; ibid., POL JAP–US)

---

### 319. Memorandum From the Deputy Under Secretary of State for Political Affairs (Johnson) to the President's Special Assistant for National Security Affairs (Bundy)

Washington, December 18, 1963.

SUBJECT

Force Reduction in Korea

I refer to our conversation on force reduction in Korea and the task
Ros Gilpatric and I were given in this regard.[1] For your background
information, the Howze recommendations,[2] on which Ambassador
Berger based the view in his 784 that the time was ripe to come to grips
with planning for an ROK and U.S. force reduction in Korea, did not
envisage any American unit withdrawal until at least the end of 1965.
However, the Howze recommendations have not been accepted even by
the Army, much less the JCS.[3] Thus, we are faced, not with reacting to the

---

Source: Department of State, Central Files, DEF 6 S KOR. Secret. Drafted by U. Alexis
Johnson.

[1] Johnson wrote the following marginal note at this point: "Assigned by President to
Secretaries Rusk & McNamara. No details known as of now. 12/18. UAJ."

[2] According to telegram 784 from Seoul, December 6, General Hamilton H. Howze,
CINCUNC, had submitted proposals that would permit a modest reduction in both
Korean and U.S. forces in Korea based on a restructuring of U.S. forces in Korea. U.S. forces
would also be unlocked from their forward positions on the DMZ. The reductions would
be small and would probably be acceptable to the ROK. (Department of State, Central Files,
DEF 6 S KOR)

[3] During a White House staff meeting on October 21 Kenneth Hansen of the Bureau of
the Budget reported on a recent trip he made to the Far East, including Korea. Hansen
expressed disappointment that Howze did not produce an "independent appraisal" as
promised. McGeorge Bundy stated that one could not expect a commander in the field to
come up with a fresh look at a problem that had existed for 10 years. Bundy suggested that
reductions would be handled by the appropriation process anyway. (Memorandum for the
record by Smith, October 21; National Defense University, Taylor Papers, Chairman's Staff
Group, October 63, T–205–69)

plan that Ambassador Berger had in mind, but rather constructing a political-military plan to give effect to the purposes of the President.

I believe that we can do this in a matter of weeks based upon the previous work that was accomplished last summer. In order to do the thorough job required for a decision by the President on this important subject, including the economic factors and the ramifications throughout the Far Eastern area, I would hope that we could have until the middle of January. In any event, we are proceeding as urgently as possible, with the full cooperation of DOD, and I will keep you informed of our progress.

U. Alexis Johnson[4]

---

[4] Printed from a copy that indicates Johnson signed the original.

---

### 320.   Memorandum From the President's Special Assistant for National Security Affairs (Bundy) to the Deputy Under Secretary of State for Political Affairs (Johnson)

Washington, December 20, 1963.

SUBJECT

Korea

I have your memorandum of December 18 on force reduction in Korea.[1] I agree that we need to develop a political-military plan of U.S. action which will deal with all of the implications of U.S. and ROK force reduction.

The President is most anxious that we get some action on this matter which has been hanging fire for so long; and in this connection I assume that State will want to consider not only how to convey to the Koreans the rationale for the suggested force reductions, but would also want to formulate a diplomatic plan for achieving an ROK-Japanese peace treaty in the very near future. This is especially important in light of the economic impact of a U.S. force reduction and the diminished funds we will have available for economic assistance to Korea in the coming year.

McGeorge Bundy[2]

---

Source: Johnson Library, National Security File, Aides Files, McGeorge Bundy, Chron Dec. '63. Secret.

[1] Document 319.

[2] Printed from a copy that bears this typed signature.

# Japan

[The Office of the Historian prepared a compilation for Japan of 65 documents, 3 for the 1958–1960 period and 62 for 1961–1963. Nine documents were denied declassification, despite full use of the appeal process for 3 of the documents (see the Preface, page III). The Advisory Committee on Historical Diplomatic Documentation has examined the denied documents and concluded that this published compilation does not constitute a "thorough, accurate, and reliable documentary record of major United States foreign policy decisions," the standard set by Public Law 102–138 of October 28, 1991 (22 USC 4351, *et seq.*). The Advisory Committee will continue to seek declassification of the documents withheld.]

---

### 321. Memorandum From the Chief, Far East Division (Ulmer) to Director of Central Intelligence Dulles

Washington, June 24, 1958.

[Source: Central Intelligence Agency, History Staff Historical Files, Job 83–0036R. Secret. 3 pages (including 2-page attachment) of source text not declassified.]

---

### 322. Memorandum From the Chief, Far East Division (Ulmer) to the Chief, Psychological and Paramilitary Staff, Central Intelligence Agency

Washington, June 25, 1958.

[Source: Central Intelligence Agency, History Staff Historical Files, Job 83–0036R. Secret. 2 pages of source text not declassified.]

### 323.  Memorandum From the Chief, Far East Division (FitzGerald) to Acting Director of Central Intelligence

Washington, June 20, 1960.

[Source: Central Intelligence Agency, History Staff Historical Files, Job 83–0036R. Secret. 7 pages of source text not declassified.]

---

### 324.  National Intelligence Estimate

NIE 41–61                                         Washington, February 7, 1961.

PROSPECTS FOR JAPAN

The Problem

To analyze the political situation in Japan in the light of developments during 1960 and to estimate the general outlines of probable developments over the next year or so.

Conclusions[1]

1.  Although Japan will almost certainly remain aligned with the US over the next year or so, it will continue slowly to grow more assertive of

---

Source: Central Intelligence Agency Files, Job 79–R01012A, ODDI Registry. Secret. According to a note on the cover sheet, the Central Intelligence Agency and the intelligence organizations of the Departments of State, Defense, the Army, the Navy, the Air Force, and the Joint Staff participated in the preparation of this estimate. All members of the USIB concurred with this estimate on February 7 except the representatives of the AEC and the FBI, who abstained on the grounds that the subject was outside their jurisdiction.

[1] NIE 41–63, October 9, 1963, reached largely similar conclusions regarding Japan: The outlook for continued political stability appeared favorable. The economy, while growing rapidly, was "exceptionally vulnerable to threats to its export markets." Although the economy would continue to expand, it would probably not be "at the remarkable rate of recent years." The Security Treaty would remain the "keystone" of Japan's defense and military planning, but the Japanese would be "particularly edgy about their use in connection with hostilities which Japan did not see as an immediate threat to itself." NIE 41–63 placed greater emphasis than its predecessor on an expected increase in Japanese international assertiveness. (Central Intelligence Agency Files, Job 79–R01012A, ODDI Registry) See the Supplement.

its own independent interests and more active in world affairs. The conservative elements will almost certainly continue to control Japanese governments for the foreseeable future and Ikeda will probably retain the Premiership for the next year, at least. Japan's economy will probably continue to expand at a rapid rate although it will remain sensitive to adverse actions abroad beyond the control of the Japanese. (Paras. 15–22)

2.   Ikeda will almost certainly have his hands full coping with dissension within his party and with an irresponsible and increasingly aggressive opposition in the Diet. Consequently, he will probably exercise extreme caution in dealing with sensitive domestic or foreign policy issues and will emphasize domestic economic measures of popular appeal to the Japanese. He will seek to avoid accusations of highhandedness or subservience to foreign pressures. (Para. 16)

3.   Pacifist and neutralist sentiment, born of Japan's [less than 1 line of source text not declassified] fear of involvement in another war, will almost certainly continue to influence the government's execution of its pro-Western policies. In addition, there will probably be strong domestic pressures for the regularization of Japanese relations with Communist China. However, if the US maintains its opposition to recognition of Communist China, the Ikeda government probably will not take any serious steps in this direction. (Paras. 23–27)

4.   The Left will seize any opportunity to agitate the public and to maintain pressure upon the Japanese Government to obstruct effective implementation of the US-Japan security arrangements. In most circumstances, the Ikeda government will probably take fairly vigorous steps to oppose leftist efforts to obstruct operation of the US bases. [12 lines of source text not declassified] In addition, the utility of the bases would almost certainly be impaired by leftist mass demonstrations and labor boycotts, and possibly by sabotage.[2] (Para. 28)

[Here follow the Discussion section of the estimate, a political annex, and an economic annex.]

---

[2] The Director of Intelligence and Research, Department of State, the Assistant Chief of Staff, Intelligence, USAF, the Director for Intelligence, Joint Staff, and the Assistant to the Secretary of Defense, Special Operations, would substitute the following text for the last four sentences of this paragraph:

[19-1/2 lines of 2-column source text not declassified] barring an unexpected change in Japan's leadership, we believe that the Japanese Government would not stand in the way of US use of Japanese bases for logistical purposes in support of security operations elsewhere in the Far East during the next year or so, although it would expect to be informed in advance of our intentions. [Footnote in the source text.]

### 325.    Memorandum From the Acting Director of the Office of Foreign Military Rights Affairs (Bronez) to the Deputy Assistant Secretary of Defense for International Security Affairs (Williams)

I–18423/61                                    Washington, April 27, 1961.

[Source: Washington National Records Center, RG 330, OSD Files: FRC 64 A 2382, 471.6–Japan. Top Secret. 2 pages of source text not declassified.]

### 326.    Memorandum From the Deputy Secretary of Defense (Gilpatric) to the Secretary of the Navy (Connally)

Washington, May 19, 1961.

[Source: Washington National Records Center, RG 330, OSD Files: FRC 64 A 2382, 471.6–Japan. Top Secret. 1 page of source text not declassified.]

### 327.    Memorandum for the Record

Washington, May 29, 1961.

[Source: Washington National Records Center, RG 330, OSD Files: FRC 71 A 6489, 471.61(SENS). Top Secret. 1 page of source text not declassified.]

## 328.   Editorial Note

From May 29 through June 30, 1961, Japanese and U.S. delegations met in Washington to negotiate a Japanese request that Japan Air Lines be allowed a route Japan/Honolulu/San Francisco/New York "and beyond." After the United States refused to grant this request, Japan asked for a similar route via Seattle instead of San Francisco. The United States countered with the offer of a polar route from Japan to New York provided certain existing routes were modified. Japan was willing to negotiate on this basis provided the United States granted the polar route to New York "and beyond." Upon U.S. refusal to concur with the request for the right to fly "beyond" New York, the delegations agreed to recess the talks "until an appropriate date in the near future." (Summary of the Civil Aviation Consultations between Japan and the United States, June 30, 1961; Department of State, Central Files, 611.9494/6–3061)

When Secretary Rusk and Foreign Minister Kosaka discussed the matter in Washington on June 22, Rusk stated that no U.S. airline had "rights such as we are now discussing," pointed out the President "had only recently refused trans-Pacific route applications from certain United States air lines because it would be disadvantageous to Japan," and declined to be drawn into detailed discussion on the subject on the ground the formal negotiations were the proper channel. (Memorandum of conversation by Richard L. Sneider; ibid., Secretary's Memoranda of Conversation: Lot 65 D 330)

On January 25, 1962, Edward A. Bolster, Director of the Office of Transport and Communications, told Hisaharu Kajita, First Secretary of the Japanese Embassy, that the United States did not wish to resume air route negotiations "next summer" because successful discussions were "highly improbable." (Memorandum of conversation by Bolster; ibid., Central Files, 611.9494/1–2562) Additional documentation on the negotiations and the general question of expanded Japanese air routes is ibid., Central File 611.9494 for March through December 1961.

## 329.    Memorandum From Secretary of State Rusk to President Kennedy

Washington, June 9, 1961.

SUBJECT

U.S.-Japan Committee on Trade and Economic Affairs

We have had under consideration, in connection with the forthcoming visit of Prime Minister Ikeda, the advisability of establishing a Joint United States-Japan Committee on Trade and Economic Affairs. This would follow the pattern of the Joint United States-Canadian Committee established in 1953.

Prime Minister Ikeda's visit provides an opportunity to set the pattern for our relations with Japan during your Administration. It will permit us to dispel lingering Japanese doubts about the importance we attach to Japan as compared with our major allies in Europe, as well as Japanese doubts about the relative weight we give to our economic relationship as opposed to our military security relationship. I believe the establishment of a joint committee on the United States-Canadian pattern will do a great deal to accomplish these objectives by giving public recognition to the importance we attach to close and mutually beneficial trade and economic relations. It would also be a logical development in view of Article II of the Treaty of Mutual Cooperation and Security between the United States and Japan in which the two Governments agree that "They will seek to eliminate conflict in their international economic policies and will encourage economic collaboration between them." We believe the Committee would also serve the following specific purposes:

1.  It would provide a medium, now lacking, for periodic high level economic discussions with our second largest trading partner.

2.  It would counteract the Japanese impression that their economic interests are overshadowed in U.S. policy determination as a result of our close ties with our Western European allies and the forums provided by these close ties in NATO and OECD for regular high level discussions within the Atlantic Community.

3.  It would provide an interim organ for the discussion of economic and trade problems of mutual interest as long as Japan is not a full member of OECD.

---

Source: Kennedy Library, National Security Files, Countries Series, Japan, 6/61. No classification marking.

4.   It would permit an annual high level review of economic development questions, particularly such joint programs as may be developed for Korea and other areas.

The proposal has been discussed with Ambassador Reischauer, who considers it a most constructive step. It has also been discussed with other interested Departments (Treasury, Interior, Agriculture, Commerce, and Labor). They have approved the establishment of the Committee, subject to your approval. The Secretaries of the Interior and Labor[1] are not regular members of the United States-Canadian Committee, but have expressed a strong desire to participate in the United States-Japan Committee. I accordingly recommend that you authorize me to conclude an agreement with the Government of Japan along the lines of the enclosed draft notes.

We would hope to conclude an agreement establishing this Committee on the occasion of Prime Minister Ikeda's visit, June 20–23, 1961. I would propose to exchange notes without public ceremony along the lines of the enclosed drafts with the Japanese Foreign Minister during the visit. The establishment of the Committee would be announced in your joint communiqué with Prime Minister Ikeda and the notes published with the communiqué.[2]

**Dean Rusk**

---

[1] Stewart Udall and Arthur Goldberg.

[2] A marginal note reads: "OK by JFK 12 June 1961 McG B."

## 330.  Memorandum of Conversation

Washington, June 20, 1961, 10:30–11:55 a.m.

SUBJECT

Communist China

PARTICIPANTS

*Japan*
Prime Minister Hayato Ikeda
Foreign Minister Zentaro Kosaka
Kiichi Miyazawa, Member of the Upper House of the Japanese Diet
Shigenobu Shima, Deputy Vice Minister for Foreign Affairs
Koichiro Asakai, Japanese Ambassador to the United States
Toshiro Shimanouchi, Counselor, Ministry of Foreign Affairs, Interpreter

*United States*
The President
The Secretary of State
George W. Ball, Under Secretary of State for Economic Affairs
Edwin O. Reischauer, United States Ambassador to Japan
FE—Walter P. McConaughy, Assistant Secretary
Walter W. Rostow, Deputy Special Assistant to the President for National Security
   Affairs
NA—Richard L. Sneider, Officer-in-Charge of Japanese Affairs
LS—James J. Wickel, Interpreter

The President, in opening the discussion of Communist China, said that the problem of Communist China, and particularly the United Nations aspects of this issue, is a matter of concern on which we wish the Prime Minister's opinion. He added that he understands the Japanese do not believe the moratorium procedure would be successful at the next United Nations General Assembly. He said that the handling of the Chinese representation to the United Nations seriously concerns the United States since we wish to assure that the Chinese Communists do not gain U.N. membership while the Republic of China does not lose its member-

Source: Department of State, Central Files, 611.94/7–1861. Confidential. Drafted by Sneider and approved in S on July 14 and in the White House on July 20. The time of the meeting, which was held at the White House, is taken from the President's Appointment Book. (Kennedy Library) This is one of six memoranda of this conversation: one summarized the opening remarks; the other four concerned Japanese-Korean relations (Document 232), Berlin, Laos, and nuclear testing. (All in Department of State, Central Files, 611.94/7–1861)

In his openings remarks, the Prime Minister stated his appreciation for the reception accorded him in Washington. Kennedy welcomed Ikeda to the United States, stated his extreme interest in relations with Japan, and "pointed out that the security interests of the United States extend to the south to Latin America, to the east to Europe and to the west to Japan. Happy relations with Japan are a fundament on which United States security rests. The President expressed the hope that the Japanese people, likewise, would consider that their security depends on good relations with the United States." (Ibid.)

ship. We are particularly anxious, he said, for the Japanese views on this problem.

The Prime Minister said that China posed a difficult problem for Japan since there are strong feelings in Japan on this issue. Unlike the United States, the Japanese people feel a sense of kinship to Mainland China due to geographic propinquity, long historical ties, and a sense of guilt regarding the last war. Furthermore, many Japanese consider it unrealistic to keep a country with 600 million people out of the U.N. The Prime Minister pointed out, however, that this viewpoint does not mean that public opinion favors recognition of Communist China. Public opinion is not, in fact, unified on the recognition question. First, Japan has a peace treaty with the GRC. Secondly, there is a strong feeling in Japan that Taiwan must be held by the Free World and under no circumstances returned to Communist China. The Japanese, the Prime Minister explained, feel assured regarding the stability and safety of Taiwan so long as Chiang Kai-shek is in control. They are most anxious, however, about what will happen after Chiang dies since they do not trust his son, Chiang Ching-kuo, due to the nature of his background and character. Further, out of the 9 million people on Taiwan, 7 million are native Formosans who cherish freedom and independence and whose desires should not be ignored. The Prime Minister concluded that it may not be proper to seek a solution to the problem of Chinese Communist admission to the U.N. before taking action on the broader Taiwan question and securing this area for the Free World. He thought most Free World countries would agree on this approach. Further, since both Chinas insist on a "One China" policy, the Chinese Communists would not come into the U.N. if we secure Taiwan now.

The President told the Prime Minister that Khrushchev in Vienna had informed him of Chinese Communist unwillingness to enter the United Nations if the GRC remains a member. This has continually been the Chinese Communist line. He felt, however, that it is difficult to agree on a formula which appears to indicate a willingness to take Communist China into the U.N. and to embrace in effect a "Two-China" policy. This will require a great deal of work in order to reach the right conclusion.

The President emphasized that the Chinese representation question posed a particularly difficult problem for the United States since there is a great deal of emotional interest in this problem among the American people and there are also very strong feelings in Congress on this issue. He said that it was difficult for us to enter into a maneuver in which the U.S. appears to be willing to accept Chinese Communist entry into the United Nations since this is perhaps the most sensitive foreign policy issue in the United States. He suggested that the Secretary discuss the details of the China representation question with the Foreign Minister and attempt to reach a more precise understanding with the Japanese

Government before the Prime Minister's departure. Prime Minister Ikeda agreed and said that he understood the feeling of the United States on this issue quite well.[1]

---

[1] In a discussion of Chinese issues that afternoon, Rusk and Foreign Minister Kosaka agreed that recognition of the PRC was not contemplated by either country, but that the U.N. representation issue was crucial. Rusk stated that the GRC needed to acquire more tactical flexibility to retain its seat. Kosaka advised that the question of Chinese Security Council membership should be divorced from General Assembly discussion of Chinese representation and that "the status of the Taiwan Government should be limited to only the areas under its control. For Japan, the crux of the problem is keeping Taiwan free from Chinese Communist control." Rusk stressed that he hoped a new formula on U.N. representation could develop through multilateral discussion. (Department of State, Secretary's Memoranda of Conversation: Lot 65 D 330)

---

## 331.  Memorandum of Conversation

Washington, June 20, 1961, 4 p.m.

SUBJECT

United States and Japanese Balance of Payments Problems

PARTICIPANTS

*Japan*
Prime Minister Hayato Ikeda
Foreign Minister Zentaro Kosaka
Kiichi Miyazawa, Member of the Upper House of the Japanese Diet
Shigenobu Shima, Deputy Vice Minister for Foreign Affairs
Koichiro Asakai, Japanese Ambassador to the United States
Teshiro Shimanouchi, Counselor, Ministry of Foreign Affairs, Interpreter
Nobuhiko Ushiba, Director, Economic Affairs Bureau, Ministry of Foreign Affairs
Akira Nishiyama, Minister, Embassy of Japan
Tadao Kato, Counselor, Embassy of Japan

*United States*
The Secretary of State
Douglas Dillon, Secretary of the Treasury
Chester Bowles, Under Secretary of State

---

Source: Department of State, Secretary's Memoranda of Conversation: Lot 65 D 330. Confidential. Drafted by Swayne and approved in S and B. The time of the meeting, which was held at the Department of State, is taken from Rusk's Appointment Book. (Johnson Library) This is one of six memoranda of this conversation: the memorandum on GARIOA is cited in footnote 1 below; the memoranda on trade liberalization and textiles are Documents 332 and 333; the memoranda on the Administrative Agreement and the Peace Corps are not printed. (All in Department of State, Secretary's Memoranda of Conversation: Lot 65 D 330)

Edward Gudeman, Under Secretary of Commerce
Rowland Burnstan, Assistant Secretary for International Affairs, Department of
    Commerce
George W. Ball, Under Secretary of State for Economic Affairs—B
R. Sargent Shriver, Director of the Peace Corps
Edwin O. Reischauer, United States Ambassador to Japan
FE—Walter P. McConaughy, Assistant Secretary
NA—Leonard L. Bacon, Acting Director
NA—Richard L. Sneider, Officer-in-Charge of Japanese Affairs
Edgar J. Gordon, Acting Chief, FE Division, Office of International Finance,
    Treasury Department
NA—Kingdon W. Swayne, International Relations Officer
James J. Wickel, Interpreter, Department of State

The Secretary called on Secretary Dillon to speak on the subject of the United States balance of payments. Secretary Dillon opened his remarks by stating that he would like to associate himself with the statement made earlier by Secretary Rusk about the GARIOA settlement.[1] He expressed great pleasure that a mutually satisfactory settlement of this difficult and vexing problem had been reached.

Turning to the United States balance of payments situation, Secretary Dillon noted that there has been a considerable improvement in the first few months of this year, the upturn having begun late last year. For the past three years there have been very substantial deficits; for 1960 the figure was $3.8 billion. However, an analysis of this figure discloses that there was a great improvement in the basic trade deficit, from $4 billion in 1959 to $1.9 billion in 1960; the remaining $1.9 billion in 1960 was the result of short term capital movements.

In the first quarter of 1961 the overall deficit was at the annual rate of $1.2 billion, made up of a deficit from short term capital movements at an annual rate of $1.9 billion (identical to 1960) and a *surplus* in the basic trade account at an annual rate of $700 million (compared with the 1960 figure of $1.9 billion).

Several points should be made about these figures. The surplus in the basic account is not as favorable as it appears. It is largely the result of a decline in imports due to our business recession which reached the low point of the cycle during the first quarter. Imports (annual rate) were $1.3 billion less than last year. Thus, if imports had equalled those of last year, the basic trade account would show a deficit of $600 million (annual rate) instead of a surplus of $700 million. The business upswing has now begun and we should begin to see higher import levels in the fall. We expect that they will return to the December 1959 level which was $2 bil-

---

[1] After the Prime Minister expressed appreciation for the GARIOA settlement, which had been initialed in Tokyo on June 9, Rusk stated that the United States had been very satisfied with the settlement and planned to use some of the proceeds for financing aid to less developed counties. See Document 353.

lion over the level of the first quarter of 1961. This level of imports would create a deficit in the basic trading account of about $1.25 billion.

While our imports have been temporarily low because of the business recession in the United States, the economies of Europe and Japan have been booming and our exports have been good. We hope this will continue. On the other hand, the temporary drop in our import level should soon be corrected and this will produce a continued imbalance in our international payments. We therefore believe we must continue with the President's program to preserve a reasonable balance in our international payments, for such a balance is essential to the maintenance of the value of the dollar.

Looking to the future, we hope, by carrying out the President's program, to reduce our out-payments by $1 billion to $1.5 billion. At the same time we expect our commercial imports will increase by about $2 billion so that the other trading nations of the world will not be hurt by our reduced out-payments under the President's program.

With respect to the short term capital flow, the rate of the outflow for the first quarter of 1961 was the same as for the whole of 1960, but was much less than the very high rate reached last fall. This year the components of the short term capital outflow are also different. Last year there was a combination of substantial capital outflows for business reasons, such as the search for higher interest rates, plus large speculative outflows. The latter have all but disappeared, but the outflow for business reasons continued during the first quarter of 1961 at approximately the same level as 1960.

The short term capital outflow in the first quarter of 1961 had some interesting aspects. The largest amount went to Japan as financing for Japanese imports from the United States. The next largest amount went to Germany, where German businessmen were borrowing dollars in New York as a hedge against a possible further revaluation of the German mark. (We do not think the Germans will revaluate the mark again.) Because of these special factors, we think the short term capital outflow situation during the first quarter of 1961 is better than it appears on the surface. Greater confidence is also being shown in the value of the dollar. There has been a net gold inflow of more than $100 million since February.

Prime Minister Ikeda expressed his appreciation for Secretary Dillon's analysis of the balance of payments situation. He had watched the situation very closely and considered that it was no longer a cause for great concern. On the Japanese side, gold and dollar reserves have been built up to about $2 billion but there have been deficits on merchandise account of about $600 million so far this year. This is a matter of considerable concern and is a question which the Japanese view as a real test for the Ikeda Cabinet. The Prime Minister said he anticipated that business conditions would improve in the United States in the second half of 1961 and expected that Japan's situation would be helped by substantially greater United States imports from Japan later this year. He expressed the hope that the United States could assist Japan in balancing its payments by continuing to make purchases in Japan from ICA and DLF funds.

Prime Minister Ikeda noted that there are two primary reasons for the imbalance in the Japanese payments situation. First, Japan has liberalized the importation of cotton and wool, and purchases of these commodities have increased considerably. Second, as a result of Japan's trade liberalization program, Japanese manufacturers feel they must improve the productivity of their plants by importing large quantities of expensive industrial equipment. Japan is devoting 20 percent of its GNP to capital investment. It needs this high rate of investment because it is the least developed of the well-developed countries. The rising imports are not for luxury goods but for raw materials and a greatly increased quantity of industrial machinery. Most of this machinery is being bought in the United States.

## 332.  Memorandum of Conversation

Washington, June 20, 1961.

SUBJECT

Liberalization of Trade and Payments

PARTICIPANTS

[Here follows the same list of persons as Document 331.]

The Secretary said that we would appreciate the observations of the Prime Minister regarding Japan's plans to liberalize its trade and payments restrictions. The United States has a very lively interest in this problem as do other countries. We recognize that trade liberalization becomes involved in domestic political problems in the United States and perhaps likewise in Japan. In the United States, exporters tend to take for granted their export markets and are not politically vocal. On the

Source: Department of State, Secretary's Memoranda of Conversation: Lot 65 D 330. Confidential. Drafted by Swayne and approved in S and B. See the source note, Document 331.

other hand, those manufacturers affected by imports become politically vocal, creating difficult domestic problems for trading countries such as the United States. The Secretary said that we feel Japan's trade policies are somewhat restrictive and hope that the Prime Minister might comment on the possibility of greater liberalization.

Prime Minister Ikeda said that there is considerable opposition to liberalization from certain segments of Japan industry. Nevertheless, two years ago, when he was Minister of International Trade and Industry, he insisted upon undertaking liberalization of trade and payments so that the Japanese economy could stand on its own feet. Japan now plans virtually full liberalization by 1963. This target takes into account that some industries are well developed, while others, such as the automobile industry, are lagging behind. The Prime Minister thought that by 1963 Japanese industry as a whole would be prepared for liberalization.

The Secretary commented that the trade liberalization question is very timely for the U.S. Next year, Congress will consider the renewal of U.S. trade legislation. There has been a steady increase in protectionist pressures in the U.S., the Secretary explained, due to several internal economic factors: (1) the movement of industry into traditional free trade areas of the United States; and (2) the growing pressure for protection on the part of the trade union movement due to fears of unemployment resulting from imports. Opponents of liberal trade legislation are seeking every possible rationalization for defeating renewal of our current trade agreements legislation. In particular, they are canvassing the positions of other governments with a view to using foreign efforts to restrict imports from the U.S. to support opposition to liberal U.S. trade legislation. The Secretary concluded that this is a matter of real concern to us and that we would appreciate anything the Prime Minister can do to accelerate Japanese trade liberalization.

Mr. Ball commented that, as the Prime Minister recognized, Japan had a greater number of quantitative restrictions on imports than any major trading country. The U.S., he said, is doing its best to persuade other nations not to invoke GATT Article 35[1] against Japan. We are basically seeking to create an international trading system in which most favored nation treatment is accorded all countries and there are no quantitative restrictions against imports. Mr. Ball pointed out that the items liberalized by Japan are mostly agricultural products and U.S. manufacturing interests have complained about restrictions against their products. We hope, therefore, with the general upswing in the Japanese balance of payments and the increase in their reserves, Japan will see its

---

[1] For text of the Protocol of Provisional Application of the General Agreement on Tariffs and Trade, signed at Geneva October 30, 1947, see TIAS 1700 (two volumes), or 61 Stat. (pts. 5 and 6). Aricle XXXV provides for non-application of the Agreement between particular contracting parties.

way clear to accelerate the pace of its liberalization program and go fairly far to full liberalization by the end of 1961.

Prime Minister Ikeda replied that invocation of GATT Article 35 creates problems for Japan in trade liberalization. In addition, there are domestic problems since 40 per cent of population is employed in the agricultural sector where productivity is low. There are also many small and medium-sized industries with low productivity. Nevertheless, Japan intends to accelerate its liberalization program to achieve 90 per cent liberalization by 1963.[2]

---

[2] In a further discussion of this subject the morning of June 21, Foreign Minister Kosaka stated that U.S. protectionist measures such as those then contemplated on tile and glass made trade liberalization more difficult for Japan, and he pointed out that the United States had a favorable merchandise trade balance of some $5 billion yearly. Rusk responded that although protectionist pressures had risen in the United States since the immediate postwar period, there was no question as to the policy the United States wished to pursue. (Department of State, Secretary's Memoranda of Conversation: Lot 65 D 330)

---

### 333.    Memorandum of Conversation

Washington, June 20, 1961.

SUBJECT

Textiles

PARTICIPANTS

[Here follows the same list of persons as Document 331.]

Prime Minister Ikeda pointed out that Japan has a system of voluntary controls over exports to the U.S., including textiles. Forty per cent of the goods exported to the United States are now under the voluntary control system. In 1957, the Japanese undertook the textile control program in good faith. However, the Japanese share of textiles imported into the United States declined from 75 per cent in 1957 to 18 per cent at the present time. Meanwhile, as a result of the self-control exercised by

---

Source: Department of State, Secretary's Memoranda of Conversation: Lot 65 D 330. Confidential. Drafted by Swayne and approved in S and B. See the source note, Document 331.

Japan, other countries expanded their textile exports to the United States. The Prime Minister stressed that Japan was concerned not only by the textile problem per se, but by the fear that the same process could occur with respect to other items presently under voluntary control by Japan. Japan does not wish to create a situation whereby the application of self-control in good faith results in a loss of United States markets to other countries. It hopes this situation can be borne in mind during the multilateral textile discussions.

Mr. Ball replied that the United States fully appreciates the unfairness of the situation created by Japanese self restraint in the textile field which has permitted other producing areas, particularly Hong Kong, to increase their imports into the United States to the point where Hong Kong's imports are now greater than Japan's. This situation is the major factor underlying our recent proposal for a multilateral agreement.

Mr. Ball said that there were a number of elements and considerations involved in the United States initiative for a multilateral textile arrangement. First, we wish to use as much pressure as possible against the nations invoking GATT Article 35 against Japan's textiles or placing severe quantitative restrictions against Japanese textiles. We desire to persuade these countries to accept Japanese textiles without restriction. Mr. Ball mentioned that the United States is meeting tomorrow for two or three days with representatives of the seven principal importing countries: the United Kingdom, Canada, France, Italy, West Germany, Belgium, and the Netherlands. In this meeting we will seek an agreement that all nations should accept textiles at an increasing rate on the basis of a certain, still not decided, percentage of domestic consumption.

Mr. Ball said that the second step in our multilateral approach is to bring together the major producing and consuming nations. The GATT Council has accepted in principle a meeting of these nations to be called by the Secretary General of GATT. At this meeting, we hope to reach an understanding calling for acceptance of textiles by the consuming nations under agreed limits.[1] We hope the producing nations will agree on these limits as well. In fixing the limits for the United States, we intend to take into account the helpful self-restraints imposed by Japan during the last few years. The third element in the multilateral arrangement is a formula for annual increases of imports into consuming nations. The fourth element would be steps to prevent circumventing the agreement by the substitution of other fibers. The fifth element would be measures to limit imports from producing nations not parties to the agreement.

Mr. Ball concluded that we are seeking in the multilateral arrangement full protection for Japan against the situation created by the unilat-

---

[1] See footnote 2, Document 371.

eral Japanese voluntary control system. We are seeking increased imports of textiles but in a manner designed to avoid market disruption. Basically, the United States wishes to bring rationality and order into the international cotton and textile market. The Secretary concluded that we believe the record demonstrates that Japan has earned real consideration. He recalled that President Kennedy had made this point to the Japanese Economic Mission and that Ambassador Asakai had made a very effective case in his conversations with the Department. Nevertheless, there are limits due to political factors as to what the United States can do. The Secretary said that we will do what we can and suggested that Mr. Ball and the Japanese discuss how best we can proceed. Mr. Ball expressed the hope that the Japanese Government could give us full support in the multilateral textile discussions.

The Prime Minister expressed his appreciation for our frank discussion of the textile problem. He said the textile industry is a central industry in Japan and also the industry most friendly to the United States. He felt that he had not, until the discussions with the Secretary, understood the deep consideration given to the Japanese problem by the United States in the formulation of its plans for a multilateral arrangement. He assured the Secretary that Japan, in the interest of free trade, would cooperate fully with the United States.

## 334. Memorandum of Conversation

Washington, June 21, 1961, 10 a.m.

SUBJECT

Visit of Nuclear Powered Submarines to Japan

PARTICIPANTS

*Japan*
Foreign Minister Zentaro Kosaka
Shigenobu Shima, Deputy Vice Minister for Foreign Affairs
Toshiro Shimanouchi, Counselor, Ministry of Foreign Affairs
Koichiro Asakai, Japanese Ambassador to the United States
Nobuhiko Ushiba, Director, Economic Affairs Bureau, Ministry of Foreign Affairs
Akira Nishiyama, Minister, Embassy of Japan
Tadao Kato, Counselor, Embassy of Japan

*United States*
Dean Rusk, Secretary of State
Chester Bowles, Under Secretary of State
Edwin O. Reischauer, U.S. Ambassador to Japan
Paul Nitze, Assistant Secretary of Defense for International Affairs
FE—Walter P. McConaughy, Assistant Secretary
NA—Leonard L. Bacon, Acting Director, Office of Northeast Asian Affairs
Captain John J. Reidy, USN, Assistant to Director, FE Region, International Security Agency, Department of Defense
NA—Richard L. Sneider, Officer in Charge, Japanese Affairs
James J. Wickel, Interpreter

The Secretary said that he wished to raise the possibility of visits to Japan by Nautilus-type nuclear-powered submarines. The submarines are engaged in long cruises and it would be helpful if they could visit Japan occasionally for crew rest and provisioning. The United States recognizes the sensitivity of this issue to Japan but these vessels have nuclear power plants as differentiated from the Polaris-type submarines. He asked whether the visit of nuclear-powered submarines would create much of a problem for Japan.

The Foreign Minister said that while the Japanese people support peaceful uses of atomic energy, they are behind the times both technically

---

Source: Department of State, Secretary's Memoranda of Conversation: Lot 65 D 330. Secret. Drafted by Sneider and approved in S and U on July 17. The time of the meeting, which was held at the Department of State, is from Rusk's Appointment Book. (Johnson Library) This is one of nine memoranda of this conversation: regarding the discussion of Chinese representation at the United Nations, see footnote 1, Document 330; the discussion of trade liberalization is cited in footnote 2, Document 332; regarding the discussion of Japan Air Lines routes, see Document 328; the discussion of cultural relations is summarized in footnote 1 below; and memoranda of the discussion of Korea, shipping, offshore procurement, and pending claims under the Administrative Agreement are not printed. (All in Department of State, Secretary's Memoranda of Conversation: Lot 65 D 330)

and in understanding of the problem. The public still tends to relate anything atomic to nuclear weapons and thereby to the possibility of involvement in a nuclear war. The Japanese Government would therefore like to give further study to this problem before agreeing to the visits of nuclear-powered submarines.

The Secretary said that we would return to this question at some future time. He felt that the key to the problem is gaining greater public familiarity with the normal uses of nuclear energy, as distinct from nuclear weapons, by demonstrating the potential of nuclear power plants in ships. We hope eventually nuclear-powered vessels, including submarines, would be accepted in Japan.

The Foreign Minister said that the Japanese Government could well understand the desirability of inviting nuclear-powered submarines to Japan. However, in all frankness, he felt that considerable groundwork must be laid first among the public. At present, public opinion is not sufficiently aware of the potential uses of atomic energy; and there is also a lack of understanding in the Japan Science Council which has close ties to the left. At present, there is certain to be a great deal of opposition to almost any step relating to atomic energy, including a visit by nuclear-powered submarines. He said that it was a matter of timing and method in Japan so that a situation could be created publicly whereby United States proposals on such subjects would be acceptable. The Secretary said that we would be in touch with the Japanese Government again on the problem.[1]

---

[1] At the close of their morning meeting, Rusk and Kosaka agreed to set up three binational committees, each with both private and official members, to consider means of expanding cultural, educational, and scientific exchanges between the two countries. (Memorandum of conversation by Sneider; Department of State, Secretary's Memoranda of Conversation: Lot 65 D 330)

## 335. Memorandum of Conversation

Washington, June 21, 1961, 3:15 p.m.

SUBJECT

    Political Consultation

PARTICIPANTS

| U.S. | Japan |
|------|-------|
| The President | Prime Minister Ikeda |
| James J. Wickel—LS/I | Mr. Miyazawa, Member, House of |
| |     Councillors, Japan |

The Prime Minister advanced the request that the United States undertake to establish with the Japanese in Asia a relationship similar to that enjoyed by Britain, under which the two Governments consult continuously on foreign policy problems of common concern.

The President noted that the United States does indeed prize her good relations with Japan, especially since she and India play such influential roles in Asia. The United States does appreciate the advantages of consulting on foreign policy matters with the British. Therefore, the President agreed that the establishment of some form of consultative machinery between Japan and the United States would be mutually beneficial, particularly on such problem areas as China, Southeast Asia, Laos, Viet-Nam and any others which affect our mutual security in Asia and the Pacific.

The Prime Minister expressed his appreciation for past American aid to Japan as well as his hopes for cooperation in jointly devising a policy for Asia which would be responsive to the need for maintaining peace.

The President noted that our two governments had already agreed to establish a Joint Cabinet-level Economic Committee[1] and a Committee

---

Source: Department of State, Central Files, 611.94/6–2161. Secret. Drafted by Wickel and approved in S on August 8 and by the White House on August 11. The time of the meeting, which was held aboard the *Honey Fitz* during a cruise on the Potomac River, is taken from Kennedy's Appointment Book. (Kennedy Library) This is one of four memoranda of the private talk between Kennedy and Ikeda: the memoranda of discussion on economics and Sino-Japanese relations are Documents 336 and 337; the memorandum of the discussion on Berlin is not printed. (Department of State, Presidential Memoranda of Conversation: Lot 66 D 149)

[1] At a meeting between Rusk and Foreign Minister Kosaka also held aboard the *Honey Fitz*, at 3 p.m., Kosaka expressed appreciation for the U.S. proposal to set up this Committee and stated that the Japanese Government proposed to have six Cabinet members represent it on the Committee. He extended an invitation to have it meet in Tokyo some time during 1961. (Memorandum of conversation by Sneider; ibid., Secretary's Memoranda of Conversation: Lot 65 D 330)

for Scientific, Cultural and Educational Exchanges. Therefore, the President felt that it would be possible to establish consultative machinery, perhaps at the level of our Ambassadors, in the absence of other suggestions. Further, this consultative organization need not limit itself to Asian and Pacific problems, but could also consider global matters, such as Berlin.

Following discussions of other matters, the President said he had the impression that our two countries did agree to the desirability of developing consultative machinery to consider global matters of common interest, not merely those of the Asian-Pacific area.

To this the Prime Minister expressed great satisfaction, since, he indicated, he himself had been ready to request this type of bilateral consultation.[2]

---

[2] At a meeting with Ikeda and a larger group of officials held that afternoon after the private talk, Kennedy reported on this discussion and expressed the intention of the United States "to consult whenever possible in advance with Japan, particularly in instances where there are serious threats to the international peace and where the interests of both countries are involved, in the same manner as we now consult with the British and the French." (Memorandum of conversation by Sneider; ibid., Central Files, 611.94/7–1861)

---

### 336.  Memorandum of Conversation

Washington, June 21, 1961.

SUBJECT

International Economic Groupings and US-Japan Economic Relationships

PARTICIPANTS

[Here follows the same list of persons as Document 335.]

The President introduced the subject of the OECD, pointing out that the United States consulted fully with Japan before becoming a member. In spite of Japan's great desire to enter the OECD the President did not

---

Source: Department of State, Central Files, 611.94/6–2161. Secret. Drafted by Wickel and approved in S on August 8 and in the White House on August 11. See the source note, Document 335.

think this to be the best time to press for admission.[1] The President described the European nature of the institution and its attempt to involve the United States and Canada in its affairs, but pointed out that Japanese membership in the OECD would naturally lead to a demand by the British for admission of Commonwealth nations such as India, Pakistan and Australia, thus destroying its basic character. The President expressed a preference for leaving the matter in abeyance for awhile.

The President commented on the role of the OECD in promoting the flow of capital among its members and wondered if it might not be desirable to establish a similar organization to do the same in non-European areas. The President indicated that the United States would consider such a proposal carefully.

The President noted that an inquiry by Japan on the question of Japanese admission to the OECD had been received prior to the Prime Minister's visit but pointed out again that the Atlantic nature of the organization would be basically altered by the admission of Japan, which would open the door for applications by other Commonwealth nations.

He explained that most European peoples view the OECD as a means to promote greater unity in the Atlantic Community. Therefore, he concluded that it might be better to leave the matter in abeyance and instead, during the summer and fall, consider the establishment of a similar organization for the other Free World nations.

The Prime Minister noted that Japan is asked to join organizations which finance projects in underdeveloped nations, for example the DAG, but is excluded from trading blocs. He considers this to be most unfair. Should Britain enter the Common Market he feels that Japan's trade position will deteriorate since such membership will no doubt lead to greater restrictions against her.

The President noted that British membership would pose a problem for the United States as well as Japan, as would the development of a Latin American trading bloc, both of which would decrease America's export market. Perhaps trade could be increased with the former French colonies of Africa in place of the Latin American market.

---

[1] According to a memorandum of a telephone conversation between Heller and Ball on June 14, Dillon had assured the British that the United States would not regard admission of Japan into the Development Assistance Group as a first step toward getting Japan into the OECD. Ball commented: "We are in a bad situation. The President is strong to get the Japanese in." Heller stated that the OECD was based "on an assumption that we recognize" a "community of dedicated people in this business" who "in an organization like the OECD" find "themselves plotting against their own government to force a change. Whether you could get Japan in that frame of mind he does not know—the Oriental mind." (Memorandum of telephone conversation by VH; Kennedy Library, Ball Papers, Japan)

However, the President felt that the integration of West Germany into the economic life of Europe is sufficient reason to support the development of the Common Market, because the orientation of post-Adenauer Germany is as yet unknown. He admitted that the United States would have to make a sacrifice to achieve this purpose and recognized that Japan's sacrifice might be greater. In any event, these matters could be discussed with Mr. Ball.

The Prime Minister expressed particular pleasure with the establishment of the Joint Economic Committee. He also expressed his own and his nation's appreciation for the generous manner in which the United States had negotiated a settlement of the troublesome GARIOA problem. Referring to the importance of Japanese-American trade the Prime Minister emphasized his view that the United States offers the greatest possibility for expansion of Japan's export market.

The President assured the Prime Minister that the United States values all trade, including that with Japan. He reaffirmed the free-trade position of his administration and his intention to encourage trade liberalization. The President noted that American reciprocal trade legislation will be up for renewal by Congress next year, and observed that American cotton exporters do not articulately support such legislation despite the fact that they export more cotton to Japan than this country's total cotton textile imports. Since those American manufacturers who are affected by imports are most articulate and energetic in their public opposition to it, the President forecast difficulty in securing renewal of the legislation next year. He emphatically stated his endorsement of liberal trade and promised to do his utmost to secure passage of the extension.

(At this point the President himself drew a graph, charting the constant level of Japanese imports from 1957 to 1961 under voluntary export controls in contrast to the sharply ascending line of imports from Hong Kong, which have this year surpassed those from Japan.)

The President considered this to be a most serious situation because of its inherent inequity. He indicated that demands for relief by the depressed American textile industry are a source of concern to him, for these articulate demands are focused on Congress. He promised to do his best to maintain a liberal trade policy in both the national and the world interest.[2]

---

[2] At a meeting held with the President and a larger group of officials later that afternoon, the Prime Minister "expressed fears that the importing countries would gang up on the exporting countries in the multilateral [textile] talks. The President commented that the best protection for the exporting countries would be an effort to provide a mechanism for the orderly expansion of their markets. Under these circumstances, individual countries would not be hurt such as Japan had been by its multilateral restrictions." Ball then described U.S. efforts to bring this about. Ikeda stated that Japan considered these efforts favorably. (Memorandum of conversation by Sneider; Department of State, Central Files, 611.94/7–1861)

The Prime Minister explained that Japan has embarked on a ten year program to double the national income. As advances are made Japan will increase her imports from the United States from the present $1.5 billion level annually to $3 billion annually at the completion of the program. The Prime Minister doubted that Japan could increase her purchases in the United States without reciprocal sales.

The President promised that Under Secretary Ball would maintain a continuing interest in this matter. He regretted again that those who benefit from liberal trade policies remain silent in politics while only those who are adversely affected are articulate. He hoped to find a way to stimulate and articulate reaction by those who benefit from their exports to Japan.

---

### 337.  Memorandum of Conversation

Washington, June 21, 1961.

SUBJECT

Sino-Japanese Relations

PARTICIPANTS

[Here follows the same list of persons as Document 335.]

The President acknowledged the importance of Japan's relationship with the United States, for which reason we watch closely internal developments there. At present the pull toward neutralism, the attraction of Communist China, the desire for non-involvement in the East-West struggle, and the influence of communism and socialism pose a challenge to the Government of Japan. The President assured the Prime Minister that the United States intended to adopt policies which would not embarrass his regime or expose it to political danger. He is aware that American policy decisions do affect free world governments, for example, a decision to resume nuclear tests would have a most serious effect not only in Japan but also in Britain. Therefore, the effect of every American act on the nations of the Free World must be considered most closely.

---

Source: Department of State, Central Files, 693.94/6–2161. Secret. Drafted by Wickel and approved in S and by the White House on August 11. See the source note, Document 335.

The President pointed out that Communist China poses the most difficult problem faced by his Administration in terms of its internal consequences.

The President recalled that Peiping had attempted to license certain "friendly" companies in Japan for trade and asked the Prime Minister for his assessment of the attraction exerted toward Japan by Communist China. The Prime Minister, in reply, denied that this attraction is as great as the Japanese press indicates. He reassured the President that the great majority of Japanese people are most friendly toward the United States. Even the press favors strong ties between Japan and the United States. In fact at a recent round-table discussion of foreign policy problems by journalists Japanese recognition of Peiping under present conditions was rejected.

None of Japan's big companies has been licensed by Peiping to trade with her; only small and medium size firms with leftist tendencies have been so licensed. The Japanese Government hopes to establish an export-import organization to trade with Communist China under government subsidy in an attempt to prevent that regime from channeling Sino-Japanese trade through selected friendly companies.

The Prime Minister characterized the attraction of Communist China as one of "mood". He asserted that Japan does not wish to disturb her economic relations with the United States merely for trade with Peiping, for such a move would lead to a Japanese economic collapse. He reviewed the Chinese Communist attempt to license "friendly" firms for trade in the same way some British firms are so licensed. He felt that this type of classification of trading firms as "friendly" and by implication "unfriendly" would divide the business community of Japan much as Korea is divided by the 38th parallel.

He explained that Japanese trade with the Peiping regime through private companies is of slight scale and value. Since the big companies, such as those in the steel industry, experienced an arbitrary cancellation of contract by China in 1958 there need be no concern about their position on the resumption of trade.

The Prime Minister reaffirmed the Japanese Government's position on the China problem, which he had explained on June 20.[1] He expected that concrete discussions would take place between Foreign Minister Kosaka and Secretary Rusk.[2] He also pointed out that the Foreign Minister would shortly visit London to exchange views with Prime Minister Macmillan, who is scheduled to visit Japan in September of this year. He hoped that a mutually agreeable policy could be achieved by that time. In any event, he promised to continue to consult fully on this matter.

---

[1] See Document 330.
[2] See footnote 1, Document 330.

The President explained that the United States views the problem of recognition of Outer Mongolia with gravity. Since the USSR insists on Outer Mongolian admission to the United Nations as a quid pro quo for Mauritania's admission, the Republic of China stands to lose at least 6 or 7 African votes in the General Assembly should she veto the admission of that regime. Unfortunately, the GRC has already announced her intention to veto Outer Mongolia's application for admission.

The Prime Minister suggested that the Republic of China must somehow be brought to view this matter in proper perspective. He recalled that the legal status of the island of Formosa was not determined at the San Francisco Peace Conference, at which Japan merely renounced her sovereignty. He repeated a suggestion he had made to Ambassador Stevenson, that a conference of those nations which attended the San Francisco Conference be called to determine the legal status of Formosa.

The President commented that both Mao and Chiang are bitterly opposed to any "two-Chinas" solution and expressed doubts that both parties could be brought to agree to a solution.

---

### 338.  Memorandum of Conversation

Washington, June 21, 1961.

SUBJECT

The Ryukyu Islands

PARTICIPANTS

*Japan*
Mr. Hayato Ikeda—Prime Minister
Mr. Zentaro Kosaka—Foreign Minister
Mr. Koichiro Asakai—Japanese Ambassador to the United States
Mr. Kiichi Miyazawa—Member of the Upper House of the Japanese Diet
Mr. Shigenobu Shima—Deputy Vice Minister for Foreign Affairs
Mr. Toshiro Shimanouchi—Counselor, Ministry of Foreign Affairs

---

Source: Department of State, Central Files, 611.94/6–2161. Confidential. Drafted by Sneider. Approved in S and B on July 14 and by the White House on July 20. This is one of five memoranda of the discussion between Ikeda and Kennedy aboard the *Honey Fitz* with a larger group of officials after their private meeting at 3:15 p.m. The discussion of U.S.-Japanese consultation is cited in footnote 2, Document 335; the talk on trade and textiles is summarized in footnote 2, Document 336; the memorandum on the Japanese relationship to the OECD is a report of the discussion of that subject at the private meeting, see Document 336. The fifth topic was an inconclusive discussion of the timing of the projected first meeting of the Joint U.S.-Japan Committee on Trade and Economic Affairs.

United States
The President
Mr. Dean Rusk—Secretary of State
Mr. George W. Ball—Under Secretary for Economic Affairs
Mr. Walter W. Rostow—Deputy Assistant to the President for National Security
Affairs
Mr. Walter P. McConaughy—Assistant Secretary for Far Eastern Affairs
Mr. Edwin O. Reischauer—U.S. Ambassador to Japan
Mr. Paul Nitze—Assistant Secretary of Defense for International Affairs
Mr. Richard L. Sneider—Officer in Charge, Japanese Affairs

The Secretary reviewed for the President and the Prime Minister his discussions with the Foreign Minister on the flying of the Japanese flag over public buildings in the Ryukyus on the New Year's holiday.[1] He said it was agreed that the High Commissioner would announce this action since this would support the High Commissioner's position in the area. The Foreign Minister asked whether permission could be granted to fly the Japanese flag on other national holidays as well as the New Year's holiday. He thought this would not be contrary to U.S. administration over the area and would have a good psychological effect on the Ryukyuans, demonstrating that their interests were considered in the meetings with the President. The President said that he would speak to the Secretary of Defense on this matter and reply on the following day to the Prime Minister's suggestion.[2]

The Prime Minister explained the Japanese Government's position on the Ryukyus. He said that he had no intention of seeking restoration to Japan of civil administration over the Islands or interfering in any way with U.S. administration. He felt, however, that within the framework of continued U.S. administration it was important to minister to the economic needs of the people and give them treatment at least equivalent to that accorded Japanese nationals in the poorer prefectures of Japan. He pointed out that the tax burden of the Okinawa citizens was far higher than that borne by the people of the poorer Japanese prefectures. He mentioned that in Tottori prefecture grants by the central government

---

[1] Rusk and Kosaka met earlier aboard the *Honey Fitz* during the President's private meeting with the Prime Minister. Rusk stated that although the United States wanted "to leave no doubt as to the clarity" of its "administrative control" over the Ryukyus, it was prepared to do everthing possible to improve its administration of them and economic and educational standards in them. (Memorandum of conversation by Sneider; ibid., Secretary's Memoranda of Conversation: Lot 65 D 330)

[2] On the morning of June 22 Rusk informed Kosaka that the United States was agreeable to his suggestion that the Japanese flag fly over public buildings on all Ryukyuan holidays. Rusk cautioned that this action would solely serve to confirm Japan's residual sovereignty over the Ryukyus and meant no change in U.S. responsibilities in them. Kosaka "expressed complete agreement." Rusk then stated that Kennedy had agreed to flying the Japanese flag on the Prime Minister's assurance at their final meeting on June 21 that it would help stabilize the situation in the Ryukyus. (Memorandum of conversation by Sneider; ibid.)

provide 90 per cent of the prefectural revenues, with only ten per cent derived from local taxes. In contrast, 80 to 90 per cent of the Ryukyuan expenditures are paid for by local taxes, with the remainder coming from U.S. assistance. This situation creates pressures in the Ryukyus for return of Japanese administration. The Prime Minister concluded that the best way to diminish reversionist desires is to provide the Ryukyuans with treatment comparable to that which they would receive if residing in a Japanese prefecture.

The President said that the only interest of the U.S. in the Ryukyus is to support our security position in Southeast Asia and Korea. Okinawa, for example, was the main staging base for possible operations in Laos. It is a key military base in the Far East and the U.S. and Japan have a common interest in maintaining this base as a powerful center for possible military operations, both in Southeast Asia and Korea. If the U.S. were forced to give up Okinawa as a military base, quite possibly we might have to deploy all the way back to Hawaii. The President said that we agree fully with the need to better living conditions in the area and recognize the sensitivity of this issue for Japan. The Japanese suggestions for improving conditions there and Japanese assistance in the area were much appreciated. The President said we ought to make the maximum effort to raise the standards in the Ryukyus. He reiterated that our interest in the area is not colonial, but flows purely from security considerations. He suggested that Ambassador Reischauer discuss further with the Japanese Government steps to improve the livelihood of the Ryukyuans and report these views back.

Prime Minister Ikeda raised the possibility of setting up a round table group consisting of the U.S., Japan, and the GRI to provide the Ryukyuans with an avenue of expression. The President said he would review this with the Department of Defense and the High Commissioner, and following this review have Ambassador Reischauer discuss the problem further with the Japanese Government. The President concluded that he felt the U.S. and Japan shared a common interest in the Ryukyus, both in improving the livelihood of the Ryukyuan people and in avoiding pressures for reversion. He was certain the Communist powers wished to push the U.S. out of Okinawa, and if this occurred it would be very difficult to maintain the Free World position in Asia.

The Prime Minister said he fully appreciated and understood the very important security requirements of the U.S. in Okinawa. He recognized that [there] was considerable opposition in Japan to bringing nuclear weapons into his country, so that he fully understood the need to maintain the U.S. position on Okinawa as a base for such weapons.

## 339.   Memorandum of Conversation

Washington, June 22, 1961, 10 a.m.

SUBJECT

Communiqué and Concluding Remarks

PARTICIPANTS

*Japan*
Foreign Minister Zentaro Kosaka
Koichiro Asakai, Japanese Ambassador to the United States
Shigenobu Shima, Deputy Vice Minister for Foreign Affairs
Nobuhiko Ushiba, Director, Econ Affairs Bureau, Min of Foreign Affairs
Akira Nishiyama, Minister, Embassy of Japan
Toshiro Shimanouchi, Counselor, Ministry of Foreign Affairs, Interpreter
Tadao Kato, Counselor, Embassy of Japan

*United States*
The Secretary of State
Edwin O. Reischauer, United States Ambassador to Japan
FE—Walter P. McConaughy, Assistant Secretary
NA—Richard L. Sneider, Officer-in-Charge of Japanese Affairs
P—Robert J. McCloskey, Press Officer
James J. Wickel, Interpreter, Department of State

The Secretary and the Foreign Minister agreed on the draft communiqué prepared for their consideration. They also agreed to issue the communiqué at 1:45 PM.[1]

The Foreign Minister expressed his gratification for the constructive, frank, and productive exchanges of views with the Secretary. He said the talks in Washington had been very favorably received in Tokyo and that they further consolidated the understanding and friendship between Japan and the United States. He pointed out that both he and the Prime Minister had sought to reflect in their conversations the views of various segments of opinion in Japan. He hoped the Secretary would understand that Japanese public opinion was not united and there were some elements in Japan who sought to distort the truth. However, the Government was making every effort to enlighten the public and unify Japanese opinion.

The Secretary responded that he considered the discussions with the Prime Minister and the Foreign Minister extraordinarily important

---

Source: Department of State, Secretary's Memoranda of Conversation: Lot 65 D 330. Confidential. Drafted by Sneider and approved in S on July 17. The time of the meeting, which was held at the Department of State, is taken from Rusk's Appointment Book. (Johnson Library)

[1] For text, see Department of State *Bulletin*, July 10, 1961, pp. 57–58. Text of the exchange of notes establishing the Joint United States–Japan Committee on Trade and Economic Affairs, signed that day by Rusk and Kosaka, is ibid., p. 58.

and helpful and that a fresh, new step forward has been made in United States-Japanese relations. He expressed great personal satisfaction with the talks in view of his personal involvement with Japanese matters since 1941 and the great change in relations between the countries over the last 20 years. He remarked that while on occasion we may be disturbed by the attitudes of some segments of Japanese opinion, we recognize that United States people also do not speak as a single voice. He concluded that the visit had served to consolidate relations between the two countries at the official level and to encourage better relations between private citizens in both countries. He hoped that from the visit would flow increased consultation between the two governments and he urged the Japanese Government to take the initiative in expressing its views on important international matters even if the United States Government is not in a position to express its position definitively.[2]

---

[2] At 11 a.m. Rusk held a final brief conversation with Prime Minister Ikeda, also at the Department of State. (Memorandum by Sneider; Department of State, Secretary's Memoranda of Conversation: Lot 65 D 330) The Prime Minister left Washington on June 23 after a farewell morning visit to President Kennedy at the White House.

---

### 340.    National Security Action Memorandum No. 68

Washington, August 11, 1961.

TO

The Secretary of State
The Secretary of Defense
The Director, International Cooperation Administration

SUBJECT

Task Force on the Ryukyus

1.  In his recent talks with Prime Minister Ikeda, the President indicated that the United States was determined to examine and recommend action on the sources of dissatisfaction which exist among the Ryuky-

---

Source: Department of State, NSAM Files: Lot 72 D 316, NSAM 68. Secret. Copies were sent to Dillon, David E. Bell (Bureau of the Budget), Allen Dulles, Elvis J. Stahr (Secretary of the Army), Ball, Nitze, and Kaysen.

uans. The United States Ambassador to Japan and the High Commissioner of the Ryukyus Islands welcome this initiative.

2.   A Task Force will be established to examine the present situation and U.S. programs in the Ryukyus Islands. The Task Force will investigate the extent to which economic and social conditions contribute to the dissatisfaction of the Ryukyuans, what measures can we undertake to improve economic and social conditions, and what specific steps are needed to make such a program effective. In carrying out its task the group will bear in mind the importance to us of (a) Okinawa as a military base, (b) continued friendly relations with Japan, and (c) our responsibility to the people of the Ryukyus under the peace treaty with Japan.

3.   The Task Force on the Ryukyus will be chaired by a representative of the White House[1] and will be composed of representatives of the Department of State, the Department of Defense and the International Cooperation Administration.

**McGeorge Bundy**

---

[1] Carl Kaysen. The Task Force held its organizational meeting on August 25. (Memorandum from W.O. Baxter of G/PM to Jeffrey Kitchen of G/PM, August 25; ibid., Central Files, 794C.0221/8–2561)

---

## 341.   Memorandum From the Deputy Assistant Secretary of State for Far Eastern Economic Affairs (Peterson) to the Under Secretary of State for Economic Affairs' Special Consultant (Christopher)

Washington, August 18, 1961.

SUBJECT

Possible Basic Line to be Taken in Japanese Cotton Textile Negotiations[1]

1.   While the United States is in no way ashamed of its offer on cotton textiles which represents an 8–10% increase in Japan's export oppor-

---

Source: Department of State, Central Files, 611.9441/8–1861. A marginal note reads: "OK'd by Mr. Ball 19 Aug."
[1] See Document 342.

tunities at a time when other import suppliers are to be cut back (e.g. a 30% rollback for Hong Kong)—the increase being accepted at a time when the domestic industry is encountering unemployment—the agreement is proposed without a contention that in itself it is attractive or perhaps wholly palatable to the Japanese Government and the Japanese industry.

2.   Rather, it is proposed for acceptance by Japan as one of the essential preconditions to the maintenance of an economic policy in the United States which is a prerequisite of well-founded relationships between the two countries. In the absence of a bilateral agreement with Japan, the possibilities of achieving some sort of rollback with Hong Kong, thus to restore some equity in the positions, becomes remote. Without U.S. bilateral understandings with these two important suppliers, the prospects of the Geneva multilateral agreement fade.[2] If the Geneva agreement fails to come to fruition, domestic pressures are certain to seek in the United States unilaterally imposed specific quantitative restrictions, commodity by commodity, country by country.

3.   Such a result would mean the torpedoing of a commercial policy which has been pursued since the time of Cordell Hull and which was reaffirmed in our wartime agreements with the United Kingdom, which in turn started the undertaking to create an international trade organization which in its final form is the GATT. The institution of quantitative restrictions on cotton textiles would generate insuperable pressures from a wide range of other domestic interests which find imports from Japan disturbing or disruptive. The range of Japanese exports now subject to voluntary controls needs only to be recalled. The pressures will range from wire nails, pipe fittings, plywood, chinaware, woolen suits, steel flatware, optical goods, electronic items, basic and finished steel, ad infinitum. The whole spectrum of Japanese exports of manufactured goods which provide employment for such an important sector of the Japanese people and provide its treasury with foreign exchange for essential needs from abroad will be threatened. This in turn cannot fail to undermine the degree of political and military understanding between the two countries which happily now prevails.

4.   In the light of these predictable consequences, it therefore behooves Japan and the United States to work in partnership to protect the institutions and policies which permit a logical mutually advantageous exchange of goods and in turn a political rapport which provides a basis for free institutions and avoids the coercive. Japan is urged therefore to accept what can be offered now which must be admitted as a step in the right direction, albeit not wholly palatable—this in the much larger interests of the two countries which clearly are endangered.

---

[2] For text of the Geneva Cotton Textile Agreement dated July 21, 1961, see Department of State *Bulletin*, August 21, 1961, p. 336.

## 342.    Editorial Note

On August 22, 1961, a Japanese Delegation led by Minoru Seki, Director of the Economic Affairs Bureau in the Ministry of Foreign Affairs, and a U.S. Delegation led by Warren Christopher met in Tokyo to negotiate a bilateral cotton textile agreement as permitted by the Geneva Cotton Textile Agreement of July 21, 1961.

Documentation in Department of State, Central Files 611.9441 and 411.946 for June through September 1961 indicates that Japan wanted an increase in its cotton textile quota for 1962 of approximately 30 percent and that the Bureau of Far Eastern Affairs believed this to be a reasonable figure in view of the facts that Japan had received an increase of only 5 percent since the quota program was initiated in 1957 and that its share of cotton fabric imports had fallen from 70 percent to 18 percent of all U.S. imports of these items during the same period. FE nonetheless believed that U.S. domestic political considerations made it unfeasible for the United States to meet Japanese wishes and on June 7 Under Secretary Ball offered Japan 5 percent plus some flexibility among various categories of items. By the time the two delegations met in Tokyo, the United States had increased its offer. Regarding conclusion of the negotiations in Tokyo on September 8 with agreement at a figure of 7.8 percent, see Document 343.

## 343.    Telegram From the Embassy in Japan to the Department of State

Tokyo, September 9, 1961, 3 p.m.

823. Reference: Embtel 820.[1] After day of stormy negotiations, marked by frequent outbursts by Seki and sharp attacks US position by other members Japanese delegation, basic understanding on textile bilateral reached in late afternoon session, with Ushiba supplanting Seki as chief Japanese negotiator. While USDel caucaused, Ushiba obtained authority from Kosaka, Sato concurring, to proceed along lines of understanding. Detailed discussions which followed were completed at 3:45

---

Source: Department of State, Central Files, 611.9441/9–961. Official Use Only. Repeated to Hong Kong.

[1] Not printed. (Ibid.)

a.m. September 9. Agreement, full text of which given in reference telegram, to be initialed by Foreign Office and Embassy September 11, in order permit Foreign Office and MITI Ministers read and approve.

Although over-all ceiling raised by 7.8 per cent and concessions made to Japan on total number categories, GOJ committed adhere Geneva multilateral, categories were added for sensitive items not previously specified, "item veto" provision included which not only permits US call for consultation whenever export concentration occurs (including case if woven trousers quota becomes concentrated in either men's or women's categories but also obliges GOJ undertake holding action at 110 percent level preceding 12 months, and GOJ agreed act to prevent circumvention of arrangement by substitution of directly competitive textiles. Flexibility provision wound up with proviso for 5 percent across the board but applicable only to basket categories, this after hardest kind of bargaining.

Discussions were intensive and often on Japanese side, bitter, with MITI official Matsumura[2] complaining US argued at some points about volume of imports, at others on "political realities", giving GOJ no consistent reasons for requests made on it. Seki accused USG of "hypocrisy" in claims to adherence liberal trade policy and at one point said emotionally he would resign from diplomatic service if overruled on his recommendation against agreement. Ambassador saw Foreign Minister, MITI Minister,[3] and Prime Minister to urge agreement on them and Embassy obtained intervention powerful Japanese business figures in favor understanding USG position. USDel consulted industry and labor advisers daily and in depth on all developments and in final stages negotiations advisers were fully briefed on all concessions USDel proposed make.

Separate codicils to basic agreement[4] cover: (1) provision for consultation on concentration in either mens or womens trousers; (2) clauses making GOJ adherence contingent on restraints on Hong Kong and absence further US restraints (except equalization fee), which specified "will not make agreement inoperative" (3) Geneva adherence; (4) typewriter ribbon cloth (terms not yet settled)

**Reischauer**

---

[2] Keichi Matsumura, Director of the Textile Bureau of the Japanese Ministry of International Trade and Industry.

[3] Eisaku Sato.

[4] For text of the Arrangement Concerning the Export of Cotton Textiles from Japan to the United States, effected by an exchange of notes dated October 16, 1961, entered into force on January 1, 1962, see TIAS 4908. Texts of the ancillary codicils, which were embodied in two side agreements, are enclosures to despatch 338 from Tokyo, October 17. (Department of State, Central Files, 611.9441/10–1761) The agreement regarding item 2 was originally classified.

344. **Telegram From the Embassy in Japan to the Department of State**

Tokyo, September 12, 1961, 6 p.m.

842. Reference: Embtel 823 repeated 58 Hong Kong.[1] With achievement cotton textile agreement I wish express appreciation for work USDel, members of which conducted difficult negotiation with extraordinary skill and patience, particularly deserving commendation is USDel Head Warren Christopher who devoted himself unsparingly to obtaining agreement acceptable US. In my view public service indeed fortunate at being able recruit for cotton textile assignment man of such outstanding intelligence and ability. Embassy of course gave all possible support to obtaining agreement meeting US needs on requirements and I believe our efforts, particular those treaties, usefully supplemented USDel.

Now that negotiations sucessfully concluded, however I would be remiss if I did not call attention costs we incurred in getting this agreement. I do not refer to strains placed on our relationships with senior Japanese civil servants or to heavy expenditure our Embassy influence, including my representations to Prime Minister. These are more or less normal aspects difficult negotiation. I am ready also discount decline in our moral position in respect trade liberalization (although I am compelled say we can expect future representations this subject be received with little grace by GOJ) since Japan obviously intends proceed according its own liberalization schedule anyway.

What is of concern is extent to which agreement was at expense Ikeda's political position and general cordial atmosphere US Japanese relations. For Ikeda, whose prestige enormously enhanced by reception given him in Washington, new agreement was obviously unpalatable and unhelpful. It was taken by many Japanese as a slap in face after warm handshake. Moreover his government has grave balance payments problem on its hands which makes anything bearing on exports especially sensitive subject. Although Sato his chief political rival, eventually went along with Ikeda's decision that an agreement necessary in Japan's own interests, it would be beyond ordinary self restraint if he did not seize on this "unfavorable" and "imposed" accord to present himself to textile interests and business community generally as leader more capable than Ikeda standing up to "unreasonable" US demands. This is first opportunity since Washington visit make factional gains against Ikeda and Sato, as well as other ambitious politicians, is not likely overlook it.

Source: Department of State, Central Files, 611.9441/9–1261. Confidential.
[1] Document 343.

Of considerably more importance for long run is fact US has been portrayed ever since Geneva as single mindedly committed impose on GOJ and Japanese industry unfair terms. Emotion generated around this issue by no means confined Osaka textile merchants. There is widespread belief in Japan that US, through superior economic power, forced Japan "surrender" on matter basic importance to Japanese economy. Strong feelings on this broke out in negotiations themselves, with so senior official as Foreign Office Economic Affairs Chief Seki evidently convinced Japan should on principle refuse sign "another unfavorable" textile quota agreement no matter what reprisals might follow.

It is true that background textile problem was unusually conducive to emotional Japanese response. For example on numerous occasions GOJ delegate harked back to 1956 discussions[2] when at last moment by White House fiat, already agreed velveteen quota was slashed by one million units. Moreover Japanese apparently believe US intended provide much more generous recompense for period vol[untary] restraint. There was and is real and deep rooted unhappiness among textile people at what is considered failure do so.

Moreover we should not consider textiles isolated and unique problem. Over recent years we have badgered GOJ and Japanese industries to impose quotas and set minimum export prices on numerous commodities as condition continued access our market. In most cases we (or our industries) asked Japanese establish export restraints on items which presumably could not be shown as causing our producers damage under procedures Trade Agreements Act. Implicit and sometimes explicit in this has been assumption Japan must be treated as special and somewhat disreputable kind of trading partner, to be trusted in US market only under differential arrangement. This is all the more galling since US usually has favorable balance trade with Japan which this year will reach massive proportions. There little doubt that these small and large humiliations have now accumulated to point where many Japanese, in out of government, have come hold real bitterness toward US.

I do not wish exaggerate matters (our position here is not so fragile that it will be shaken seriously by aftermath textile agreement). At same time I fear that if we continue along path charted over past few years, our relationship may eventually be damaged irreparably. Trade is so close to problem Japanese survival that we cannot hope enjoy full Japanese friendship and partnership if we continue treat Japan as not fully suitable for polite trading society. In my opinion we urgently need trade policy that will give USG sufficient authority and flexibility in domestic

---

[2] For information on these discussions, see *Foreign Relations, 1955–1957,* vol. XXIII, Part 1, pp. 247–249.

handling difficult import problems to enable us deal with country like Japan on some more acceptable and thereby more durable basis.

**Reischauer**

## 345.  Editorial Note

The First Meeting of the Joint U.S.-Japan Committee on Trade and Economic Affairs was held at Hakone, Japan, November 2–4, 1961.

Prime Minister Ikeda opened the meeting. Cabinet ministers attending for Japan were Zentaro Kosako, Foreign Affairs; Eisaku Sato, International Trade and Industry; Ichiro Kono, Agriculture and Forestry; Mikio Mizuta, Finance; Aiichiro Fujiyama, Economic Planning; Kenji Fukunaga, Labor; and Masayoshi Ohira, Chief Cabinet Secretary. Ambassador Asakai also attended. Representing the United States were Secretary Rusk; Stewart Udall, Interior; Orville Freeman, Agriculture; Luther Hodges, Commerce; Arthur Goldberg, Labor; Henry Fowler, Treasury Under Secretary; Myer Feldman, Deputy Special Counsel to the President; and Ambassador Reischauer.

Agenda topics included: general survey and outlook for the Japanese and U.S. economies, balance of payments, wage systems and productivity in Japan and the United States, expansion of trade and promotion of economic relations between Japan and the United States, promotion of Japanese and U.S. economic and commercial relations with other parts of the world, economic assistance to less developed countries, proposals for stabilizing primary commodity prices and their relationship to terms of trade, the Sino-Soviet economic offensive, U.S. economic polices towards the Sino-Soviet bloc, and Japanese trade relations with the Sino-Soviet bloc.

Scheduling information, briefing papers, talking papers, and memoranda of conversation are in Department of State, Conference Files: Lot 65 D 366, CF 1981–1988. Despatch 416 from Tokyo, November 13, contains a comprehensive summary of all the sessions of the meeting. (Ibid., Central Files, 411.9441 / 11–1361) For text of the communiqué of the meeting, issued November 4, see Department of State *Bulletin*, November 27, 1961, page 891. Additional information on the meeting is in Documents 346 and 347.

## 346.  Memorandum of Conversation

Hakone, Japan, November 3, 1961, 1 p.m.

SUBJECT

1) Domestic Political Context and Impact of Hakone Meeting;
2) Nuclear Weapons; and
3) Japan's Role in Foreign Affairs

PARTICIPANTS

| United States | Japan |
|---|---|
| The Secretary | Prime Minister Hayato Ikeda |
| David L. Osborn, First Secretary, | |
| Embassy Tokyo | |

1. *Domestic Political Context and Impact of Hakone Meeting:* The Secretary described in general terms his meeting with former Prime Minister Yoshida on November 1,[1] and said he had felt some puzzlement at Yoshida's offer to convey his views to Prime Minister Ikeda, in view of the close personal relationship and the direct contact existing between the Secretary and the Prime Minister. The Prime Minister explained that Yoshida's remark had been in the nature of a formal courtesy. He said he enjoyed Yoshida's full confidence and support; after the Secretary's meeting with Yoshida, Ikeda had had a three-hour tete-à-tete with him on the subject of the Hakone Conference and his talk with the Secretary.

The Prime Minister emphasized the unity and stability of his "strong-man cabinet." He attributed his success in organizing this cabinet in good part to his trip to Washington. Following this trip he had had no trouble in getting the factional leaders to join the cabinet. This contrasted with the difficulties experienced by previous Prime Ministers in lining up the more powerful political figures for their cabinets. It had taken former Prime Minister Kishi two hours to persuade Ikeda to join the Kishi cabinet, for example.

When Ikeda formed his cabinet last July, the factional leaders had practically fallen over themselves in their eagerness to join.

One incident related by the Prime Minister (in response to the Secretary's request for comment on Finance Minister Mizuta's background) illustrated both the eagerness of the present cabinet ministers to join the cabinet and the personal relationship between Ikeda and Mizuta.

Source: Department of State, Secretary's Memoranda of Conversation: Lot 65 D 330. Confidential. Drafted by David L. Osborn, Political Officer and First Secretary of Embassy and approved by S on November 27. The meeting was held at the Kansui Inn.

[1] No memorandum of this conversation has been found.

Mizuta, although technically a member of the Ohno faction, had been willing to defy the dictates of his faction (which had been holding out for more representation in the cabinet) or even to leave it if necessary to join the cabinet.

The Prime Minister noted that in the greetings which he had exchanged with the Secretary at the beginning of the lunch, he had expressed the intention of sending the present cabinet members to the United States for the next meeting of the Joint Committee. This Joint Committee meeting would occur after the party elections of next July, so that the Prime Minister's remarks were in effect serving notice on the strongmen present at the lunch that Ikeda intended to stay in power with his strongman Cabinet following the party elections. The Prime Minister said that if he did stay in after next July, then his cabinet would run for three years. He hoped within those three years to be able to reform the political character of the Japanese population, reducing the ratio of "un-Japanese" from the present roughly one-third to one-fourth or one-fifth. Ikeda said that the Hakone meeting might have advanced the target date for the completion of this transformation by a year or so.

2. *Nuclear Weapons:* The Prime Minister said the very fact that there is a debate in Japan on the problem of nuclear weapons for Japan reflected the fact that at least a minority considered it necessary for Japan also to have nuclear weapons. This minority, he indicated, included people in his own cabinet and party. The Secretary made it clear that the United States was opposed to the proliferation of nuclear powers, with the tremendous waste of resources and the other difficulties and dangers this would entail. He said that the United States remained as firmly committed as it had been in 1946 to the principle of effective international control over nuclear armaments. He mentioned the almost inconceivable destruction that would be caused by a nuclear war, not only on the belligerents but on all other countries of the world. It was enough to make one consider seriously the possibility of emigration to the moon, he remarked. He did not think that any rational world leader could take the responsibility of initiating a nuclear war. The Prime Minister replied that he had not been thinking so much of Japan's going into the production of nuclear weapons, but of the argument that the presence of nuclear weapons in Japan might be necessary for its defense. He indicated that he would be interested in learning more about the broader aspects of the nuclear armaments question.

3. *Japan's Role in Foreign Affairs:* The Secretary complimented the Prime Minister on Japan's increasing willingness to take the initiative in foreign affairs, both in the United Nations and in other fields. The Prime Minister said this was perhaps attributable in part to the growth of Japan's real power. He also said that Japan's representative in the United Nations, Mr. Okazaki, was extremely well qualified and that Ambassa-

dor Asakai in Washington was one of Japan's best Ambassadors. The Secretary commented that Mr. Okazaki had given a good demonstration of his qualifications as a negotiator during the negotiations for the Administrative Agreement in 1951.[2]

The Prime Minister remarked ruefully that he seemed to be achieving considerable success in the foreign policy field, where he was a rank amateur, but encountering difficulties in the economic field, where he considered himself an expert.

---

[2] Rusk and Kazuo Okazaki negotiated the original Administrative Agreement (operative until 1960) in January and February 1952. It was signed at Tokyo on February 28, 1952, and entered into force that same day; for text, see 3 UST (pt.3) 3341.

---

### 347.  Telegram From Secretary of State Rusk to the Department of State

Hakone, Japan, November 4, 1961, 11 a.m.

Secto 17. Eyes only for President from Secretary. Cabinet conference adjourns today, having accomplished its broader purpose of improving background of understanding among cabinet officers two sides involved in US-Japanese trade relations.[1] Suggest briefing meeting US cabinet officers with you to report impressions. No negotiations or particular points taken up at conference, although cabinet officers did discuss particular transactions with opposite numbers privately.

In a long private talk with Ikeda[2] I mentioned the possibility your visit. He was deeply gratified your interest but wished to think it over and be in touch with you again. It is obvious that he wants to be certain that there would be no possibility of revival anti-Eisenhower demonstra-

---

Source: Department of State, Central Files, 411.9441/11–461. Secret. No Other Distribution.

[1] In an October 12 memorandum to Frederick Dutton of the White House Staff, Ball wrote that he was "persuaded that the agenda and the specific papers to be discussed are far less important than the fact that the discussions take place" and that they were to be considered talks among "political people having political responsibilities for economic questions." (Kennedy Library, National Security Files, Countries Series, Japan, 10/61)

[2] The memorandum of the Secretary's conversation with Ikeda held November 2 is not printed. (Memorandum by Osborn; Department of State, Secretary's Memoranda of Conversation: Lot 65 D 330) During their conversation on the morning of November 4, Rusk discussed with Kosaka Korea, the work of the Ryukyu Task Force, the introduction of Mace missiles into Okinawa, and nuclear testing. (Memorandum by Osborn; ibid.)

tions. One troubling aspect is that he anticipates serious domestic difficulties, including violent reactions 200,000 Koreans in Japan in
connection his determination establish good relations ROK.

I gave Ikeda[3] full briefing on nuclear test situation happily prior to
arrival your statement. Ikeda said that as Prime Minister Japan he could
not officially approve US nuclear testing but that "in my heart I believe
that the President must do what has to be done." Your excellent statement was received here about as well as could be expected in Japan. Official government statement was masterpiece of combining Japanese
viewpoint in low key with tactful indication Japanese understanding
our problem. Ikeda told me privately that he expects to remain in office
for another three years. This of some significance since at least two members his present cabinet are standing in the wings ready to succeed. Incidentally, Yoshida told me that Ikeda had been a new man since his visit to
Washington and was moving in foreign affairs with a confidence and
ability which had greatly enhanced his strength and position in Japan.

Ikeda is taking the Korean matter with great seriousness and will do
everything possible to put relations on normal basis and find means of
substantial assistance to Korea. Pak will visit Ikeda on way to Washington.

Ikeda was optimistic about prospects of bringing Burma further
into free world and away from Communist China. Through close personal friends in Burmese Government, Ikeda is trying to work out Japanese aid to Burma which would divert latter from large ChiCom
assistance.

In keeping his general interest in fresh Japanese initiatives throughout Asian free countries, Ikeda will try to smooth over Cambodian-Thai
problem prior to and during his forthcoming visit India and Southeast
Asia.

Although he may not know critical nature present situation in Vietnam, Ikeda showed great misgivings about introducing US combat
forces in that country. He seems to think that economic assistance was
what was required. My guess is that he needs more factual information
about Vietnam and will arrange to provide this through Embassy.

I was impressed with general atmosphere here of need and opportunity for Japan to play a much more active role in Asia, a mood prompted
both by political and economic considerations. It is obvious that Reischauer has gotten off to an excellent start and that he and his wife are
highly regarded both in official circles and publicly.

**Rusk**

---

[3] Reference is to the President's November 2 statement on possible resumption of
nuclear testing; see Department of State *Bulletin*, November 20, 1961, p. 844.

## 348.   Telegram From the Department of State to the Embassy in Japan

Washington, December 7, 1961, 8:50 p.m.

1465. Embtel 1625.[1] Department concerned at adverse Japanese Government and public reaction to request for Tariff Commission investigation regarding equalization fee on cotton textiles.[2]

Suggest following points be used in response protest by Takeuchi:

(1) This Government considers Japanese participation in international textile discussions most useful and looks forward to its continued cooperation in attempts work out solution to problems international trade in cotton textiles which will accord with basic interests both countries.

(2) President's November 21 request for Tariff Commission investigation was in accordance Section 22 Agricultural Adjustment Act which provides for full investigation and opportunity all interested parties present their views. We note from Takeuchi statements that Japanese business interests will actively oppose fee at hearings and we would anticipate such opposition. Assume arguments regarding Japanese purchases raw cotton and others outlined reftel would be used as appropriate by Japanese interests in their appearance before Tariff Commission. Tariff Commission recommendation, after full study all facts, will be based on its conclusion as to whether case has in fact been made under provision Section 22.

(3) President's May 2 program of assistance to US textile industry directed Department of Agriculture to explore and make recommendations to eliminate or offset cost to US mills of adverse differential in raw cotton costs between domestic and foreign textile producers. Since that date, Department of Agriculture has been working in consultation with interested groups in effort develop recommendations for changes in cotton production adjustment and price support system that would better

---

Source: Department of State, Central Files, 411.006/12–561. Confidential. Drafted by Edelen M. Fogarty of E/OR, cleared by E/OT and Avery Peterson, and approved by Philip H. Trezise, Deputy Assistant Secretary of State for Economic Affairs.

[1] Telegram 1625, December 5, reported a protest by Ryuji Takeuchi, Japanese Vice Minister of Foreign Affairs, against the U.S. action described in footnote 2 below. (Ibid.)

[2] Reference is to President Kennedy's letter to Ben B. Dorfman, chairman of the U.S. Tariff Commission, requesting the Commission to make an immediate investigation under Section 22 of the Agricultural Adjustment Act to determine whether a fee equivalent to the per pound U.S. cotton export subsidy (the difference between the U.S. and world price) on the cotton content of imported fabric should be levied to prevent such imports from interfering with the cotton support program or from reducing substantially the processing of U.S. cotton products. Text is in *Public Papers of the Presidents of the United States: John F. Kennedy, 1961*, p. 736.

meet various objectives deemed desirable. These consultations are continuing. If program developed to eliminate present two price system for cotton, need for equalization fee would of course also be eliminated.

(4) Regarding confidential letter exchanged connection 1962 US-Japan bilateral,[3] we agree that this letter does not mean GOJ has abandoned right to object to imposition equalization fee. However, we are concerned at statement[4] that if fee imposed, bilateral textile agreement would be dead. Letter provides that application of non-discriminatory fee to compensate for US two price cotton system should not cause arrangement to become inoperative. We believe Takeuchi statement inconsistent this provision.

(5) Re query concerning US plans for consultation with GOJ in case imposition equalization fee approved, suggest Takeuchi be informed that USG would be prepared consult with GOJ and give prompt and sympathetic consideration to appropriate remedies any adverse effect resulting from equalization fee, if such fee were to be imposed. However, Tariff Commission recommendation impossible forecast, and we believe it premature to enter into consultation at this time.

Department has not received formal protest from Japanese Embassy in Washington this regard although Asakai made representations shortly after November 21 announcement. If such protest received we plan reply above lines.[5]

**Rusk**

---

[3] See footnote 4, Document 343.

[4] By Takeuchi, as reported in telegram 1625.

[5] Reischauer reported carrying out this instruction in telegram 1681 from Tokyo, December 12. Takeuchi responded by asking for U.S.-Japan consultations on the matter even though the Tariff Commission's recommendation would not be known for several months. (Department of State, Central Files, 411.006/12–1261)

## 349.    Memorandum of Conversation

Tokyo, February 5, 1962.

PARTICIPANTS

The Attorney General[1]                 Prime Minister Hayato Ikeda
Ambassador Reischauer              Chief Cabinet Secretary Masayoshi Ohira
David L. Osborn                            Member, House of Councillors, Kiichi
                                                        Miyazawa

PLACE

Prime Minister's Residence, Shinanomachi

After an exchange of greetings, the Attorney General said that President Kennedy had asked him to tell the Prime Minister that he feels their meetings in Washington last year were most beneficial; that a great deal has been accomplished by the economic, scientific, and cultural conferences, and that a great deal more can be accomplished in the future. The President had also asked the Attorney General to reassure the Prime Minister that the arrangements and agreements which the United States is attempting to make with the members of the EEC will benefit not only the United States and the Western European countries, but also Japan. The President has emphasized again and again to the representatives of the countries concerned that it is not enough, for the sake of the strength of the EEC and the United States, and they become fortresses in isolation; they must share with others the benefits that they produce for themselves.

The Attorney General said he had also discussed with the President the cotton equalization fee. The Administration is in the midst of a major domestic struggle with some very important economic groups over its efforts to lower trade barriers. However, the President wanted to assure the Prime Minister that the trend in the United States is toward lower tariffs, and that as far as the equalization fee is concerned, all that has been done so far is to request the Tariff Commission to make a study of the program. The Attorney General explained that this problem presented some internal difficulty for the United States. There is unemployment in the textile industry, and a number of companies have gone out of business,

---

Source: Department of State, Central Files, 033.1100–KE/2–2862 Confidential. Drafted by Osborn. This memorandum is enclosure 11 to despatch 731 from Tokyo, February 28.

[1] Attorney General Robert F. Kennedy visited Japan February 4–10 for a good will visit in the course of a world tour. Extensive documentation on his trip is ibid., 033.1100–KE. An evaluation and summary of the trip, along with memoranda of Kennedy's principal conversations while in Japan, are in despatch 731.

with some economic upheaval and attendant problems for ordinary citizens. The President and the Attorney General, being natives of Massachusetts, which lost its textile mills to the South, are particularly aware of these problems. However, the President feels that the way to progress lies not in raising tariffs, but in lowering them. The Attorney General said the President was of course free to accept or reject the recommendation of the Tariff Commission after it had made its study.[2]

The Prime Minister expressed his appreciation for the President's message. He went on to explain the sensitivity of current problems in United States-Japanese economic relations and the adverse reaction of Japanese businessmen to any signs of protectionism on the part of the United States, such as the "Buy American" policy and the AID purchases of fertilizer, which were undermining the natural development of Japanese markets in Southeast Asia. He criticized the "stereotyped" character of United States aid.

The Attorney General said that in view also of the problems on the American side, including the loss of gold, there are bound to be disagreements between Japan and the United States; but he said it was the judgment of the United States Government that there is so much good will between the two Governments and peoples that as a general matter difficulties can be resolved. Perhaps the particular difficulty mentioned by the Prime Minister was not going to be resolved, but in general the President was trying to move in the direction of closer relations with Japan.

The Prime Minister recalled that when he was in the United States in 1960 he had told Mr. Rockefeller that he thought it was premature to start working on a broader economic framework for Asia. Conditions have changed in the past year, however, and he thought the idea of an Asian Economic Community deserved more careful attention. He asked what the United States felt about the possibility of closer United States-Japanese cooperation in the development of Southeast Asia.

The Attorney General said the President is very much interested in this area; he thought that if Japan and the United States as partners can work jointly to develop this kind of cooperation, it would be very helpful in years to come.

The Prime Minister suggested that the United States ought to put more emphasis on Burma in its aid program (and perhaps less on India) and said that this was an area in which Japanese cooperation in economic assistance could be most helpful. He knew from close personal acquaint-

---

[2] On September 6 President Kennedy announced that the Tariff Commission had rejected the Agriculture Department's recommendation for an import fee of 8.5 cents a pound on the cotton content of textile imports. He stated also his intention to recommend to the next Congress "legislation designed to remove the inequity created by the present two-price cotton system." For text of this statement, see *Public Papers of the Presidents of the United States: John F. Kennedy, 1962*, pp. 664–665.

718 Foreign Relations, 1961–1963, Volume XXII

ance with Burmese Chief of Staff Aung Gyin and other Burmese that the military there are anti-Communist. However, loans from Communist China totaling £160 million exert a powerful attraction. The Prime Minister mentioned the Burmese four-year economic development plan, and referred to the mission which Japan was about to send to Burma to assist in the development of this plan.

The Attorney General said he would mention the Prime Minister's point to the President and to Mr. Hamilton of the AID program. He commented on the similarity of the developmental problems of Southeast Asia to those of South America, and hoped that Japan could take a more active part in sending expertise and technological assistance to these areas. He felt that the United States-Japanese partnership could play a most important part in planning and assisting the development of the less-developed countries. The Prime Minister agreed, but thought a concentrated effort should be made along these cooperative lines in Southeast Asia.

[Here follows discussion of Berlin, Laos, Vietnam, and Korea.]

### 350. Telegram From the Department of State to the Embassy in Japan

Washington, February 8, 1962, 9:17 p.m.

1999. Attorney General visit. Embtel 2212.[1] For Attorney General from Kaysen. I appreciate your interest in work of Task Force Ryukyus[2] and will be glad to see that final action by President on Task Force report[3] is held up until your return. While consideration of Okinawa by UN Committee of Seventeen is definite possibility for which we must be prepared, and specific provisions for greater Japanese interest in Okinawa

---

Source: Department of State, Central Files, 033.1100–KE/2–862. Confidential; Niact; Limit Distribution. Drafted by Swayne, cleared with McGeorge Bundy and the Department of the Army, and approved by Rice.

[1] In telegram 2212, February 8, the Embassy reported that the Attorney General had many questions on Okinawa during his visit and wished to have the Task Force's key recommendations telegraphed to him in Tokyo. (Ibid.)

[2] Documentation on the work of the Ryukyu Task Force, September 1961–March 1962, is ibid., 794C.0221, and in the Kennedy Library, National Security Files, Countries Series, Ryukyu Islands.

[3] Text of a draft report at this stage not found. The final text, dated March 1962, is ibid.

and greater local autonomy appear best way of meeting anticipated "anti-colonialist" criticism in this forum, do not anticipate need for action in next few weeks.

Expect report will remain internal US Govt document, with substance made public by various means, including possible Presidential announcement of acceptance recommendations, legislative proposals to Congress, and in connection negotiations with Japan.

Report has been submitted by Task Force to State and Defense for comment.[4] Believe State will recommend its approval by President without change, but formal approval by SecState has not been sought pending conclusion current review in Defense, where concern has been expressed particularly with recommendations for increased autonomy for GRI, organizational changes in US administration and civil rights (see High Commissioner's HCRI 1–125, repeated Tokyo).[5]

Text of report pouched Embassy early December[6] is unchanged except for minor amendments and addition of "summary and recommendations" section at beginning of paper. Following is summary of recommendations:

A. Future US-Japan relationship would be based on economic cooperation agreement by which Japan would contribute perhaps one third of cost of US-approved economic and social development aid programs in Ryukyus. If necessary agreement could specifically mention eventual reversion of Ryukyus to Japan. (See text of illustrative agreement among Task Force working papers pouched Embassy.)[7] Cooperation with Japan would be developed to maximum degree consistent with retaining control of base, recognizing that this will mean greater Japanese influence but need not impair US control.[8]

B. GRI should be given as much autonomy as possible consistent with security of base in order develop its responsibility and establish more viable relation between it and US. Report suggests as examples but not as specific recommendations: (1) nomination of Chief Executive by

---

[4] Dated November 30, 1961. (Department of State, Central Files, 794C.0221/11–3061)

[5] Not found.

[6] Apparently the same as that cited in footnote 4 above.

[7] Not found attached. A copy of the draft, December 15, is attached to a memorandum from Harriman to U. Alexis Johnson, April 16. (Department of State, Central Files, 794C.0221/4–662)

[8] An undated copy of these recommendations points out that the Japanese Government had "no desire to push us out of Okinawa," but instead welcomed the U.S. base there, which contributed to Japanese security "without creating the political problems which would follow if the base were situated in Japan." Nevertheless, the Japanese Government would "continue to speak publicly in favor of returning administration of the Ryukyus to Japan" while recognizing that the United States would not do so in the "foreseeable future." (Kennedy Library, President's Office Files, Countries Series, Ryukyu, Task Force Report, 11/61–12/61)

legislature, subject to HICOM approval; (2) severely limiting prior coordination of legislation with USCAR and placing coordination at initiative of majority party in legislature, and a few others.

C. US-Japan and US-Japan-GRI consultative arrangements would be for purpose of implementing economic cooperation agreement, with policy matters considered in Tokyo between Ambassador and FonMin and technical questions in Naha by US-Japan-GRI Committee. (See illustrative agreement.)

D. Aid programs would concentrate on providing short range benefits in areas where Ryukyuans are clearly worse off now than they would be under Japan and on long range economic development. Cost of recommended programs would rise from $17 million to $27 million over five years, with US share dependent on outcome negotiations with Japan.

E. Reorganization of administration to vest in a civilian Civil Administrator, appointed by SecDef in consultation with SecState and with approval of President, all administrative functions retained by US except ultimate authority of veto over acts of GRI, promulgation of basic ordinances and liaison with State and Embassy Tokyo in conduct foreign relations. Latter functions would remain with High Commissioner, who would continue to be military officer. Under Civil Administrator there would be clear division between supervision and control function on one hand and technical assistance function on other. Report emphasizes importance of attracting competent civilian personnel for USCAR.

F. Civil rights questions were also found by Task Force to be significant source of irritation and report recommends less restrictive policy in control of publications, travel and labor unions.

**Rusk**

351.   Letter From the Ambassador to Japan (Reischauer) to the
       Under Secretary of State (Ball)

Tokyo, February 12, 1962.

DEAR GEORGE: I trust that the furor over the *Wall Street Journal* rewrite
of the Beecher article on the Attorney General's so-called "hint" about
the equalization fee[1] has quieted down long before this letter arrives. But,
in case it has not, I feel that you should know one matter that was not
brought out in the telegraphic exchanges for fear that it might leak.

The Attorney General was supposed to have a personal message
from the President for Ikeda (in fact, he had none), and we were informed
(I cannot remember who in his party transmitted the information) that,
before the Attorney General left Washington, Ambassador Asakai had
been given a broad hint or even more that the President as of now did not
intend to apply the equalization fee, whatever the Commission's recommendation might be. Since there was every reason to believe Asakai had
sent this information to Ikeda, the Attorney General and I decided that it
would look most curious to Ikeda if the Attorney General did not mention this point as part of the President's personal message. Under the circumstances, in fact, silence on this point might have seemed like a
rupture of the close relationship Ikeda feels he established with the President in June. Consequently, the Attorney General, after giving Ikeda the
President's assurances of his determination to move toward more liberal
international trade and to exert his energies to see that Japan was not economically isolated, told the Prime Minister that the President as of now
did not expect to apply the equalization fee, but hoped to rectify the
inequalities of the two-price system in some other way.

Ikeda's reaction showed that it would indeed have been most unfortunate if the Attorney General had not made this statement. Ikeda said
that he himself already knew of this from Asakai, that he had felt all
along the President would not apply the equalization fee, but that he felt
it would be most undesirable if this information leaked out at this time
and that he, therefore, hoped the Attorney General would not tell anyone, including the Foreign Minister, of the President's thinking on this
matter. Only six persons were in the room at the time—Ohira, the Cabi-

---

Source: Department of State, Central Files, 033.1100–KE/2–1262. Secret; Eyes Only.
[1] Reference is to an article by Henry Beecher which appeared in *The Wall Street Journal*
on February 10. The article stated that Attorney General Kennedy had hinted while in
Japan that the United States would not impose the cotton equalization fee with regard to
Japan. After receiving representations from Ball, *The Wall Street Journal* printed a partial
retraction on February 13. Further documentation on this incident is ibid.,
033.1100–KE/2–1062, and in the Kennedy Library, Ball Papers, Telephone Calls, Japan,
February 10–12, 1962.

net Secretary, Miyazawa of the Upper House (both close aides of the Prime Minister), Osborn of the Embassy and myself. My wording in Embassy telegram #2234[2] ("At no time did he make any statement or observation that could reasonably have provided basis even for Beecher's original implications, much less *Journal*'s further distortions.") was meant to exclude this conversation with the Prime Minister, since it obviously could not "have provided basis" for story. The statements in this telegram, therefore, are absolutely correct in my judgment.

There is one other point about the equalization fee problem I might as well bring up now. When a final decision is made by the President, whatever it may be, it would be highly desirable to have it passed to Ikeda before it is made public in Washington. This would strengthen his feeling of closeness to the President and would give him a chance to assume a suitable posture for the moment when the news breaks. A day or two in advance would probably be adequate, and the most intimate and therefore desirable way of passing the news to him would, I feel, be through me.

I sometimes despair of our American newsmen over here. They know so little of Japan that they get things wrong constantly. In the light of what has already been said between us and the Japanese and what is in their minds, the Attorney General (except for his Ikeda talk) was constantly throwing water on their hopes that the equalization fee would not be imposed. Despite this fact, I cannot overemphasize what a tremendous success the Attorney General's visit was, especially the incident at Waseda University.[3] While the latter skirted the thin edge of disaster, it turned out to be a resounding triumph that may well have a lasting effect on the student movement in Japan.[4]

Sincerely,

Ed

---

[2] Dated February 10. (Department of State, Central Files, 033.1100–KE/2–1062) It was sent for the Department's use in denying the statement in the original *Wall Street Journal* article concerning the interest equalization tax.

[3] According to telegram 2183 from Tokyo, February 6, the Attorney General dealt effectively with "Communist-sponsored" hecklers during a visit to Waseda University that day, and his handling of the incident favorably impressed the Japanese public. (Ibid., 033.1100–KE/2–662)

[4] The Embassy's lengthy telegraphic summary of the Attorney General's visit concluded that the "outpouring of good will during this visit was on a scale unique in history of US-Japan relations." (Telegram 2261 from Tokyo, February 15; ibid., 033.1100–KE/2–1562)

## 352.    National Security Action Memorandum No. 133

Washington, March 5, 1962.

TO

The Secretary of State
The Secretary of Defense
The Director, Bureau of the Budget

SUBJECT

Ryukyus Action Program

The Secretaries of State and Defense have concurred in the recommendations of the Ryukyu Task Force[1] on the steps it is now desirable to take to improve the security of our tenure in the Ryukyus and our relations with Japan as they are affected by that tenure.

*Section I*[2]

Accordingly, I am requesting the Secretary of State to take responsibility for the following measures:

1.    Initiation of negotiations with the Government of Japan to provide a framework for a continuing Japanese contribution to economic assistance to the Ryukyus that minimizes interferences with our administrative control and that recognizes, at least tacitly, our intention to continue to administer the Ryukyus for the foreseeable future.[3] In the conduct of these negotiations, Ambassador Reischauer should maintain close contact with General Caraway, the High Commissioner of the Ryukyus so that he can play his appropriate part.

2.    Presentation to the appropriate members of the Congress of the need for these negotiations and the goals we are seeking to achieve. Also, provision of such assistance to the Secretary of Defense as he may request in supporting his requests to the Congress for legislative changes and increased appropriations in accordance with the recommendations of the Report.

---

Source: Department of State, NSAM Files: Lot 72 D 316, NSAM 133. Confidential. Copies were sent to Robert Kennedy, the Director of USIA, and General Taylor. The President discussed some of the subject matter of this memorandum with McNamara and the JCS on March 1. (Memorandum of conference with the President by Clifton; Kennedy Library, National Security Files, Clifton Series, Conferences with the President, 10/61–11/62)

[1] See footnote 2, Document 350.

[2] The numbered sections are handwritten on the source text.

[3] Instructions for these negotiations are in telegrams 2684 to Tokyo, April 28; 2697 to Tokyo, April 30; and in airgram CW–9871 to Tokyo, June 11. (Department of State, Central Files, 794C.0221/4–2862, 794C.0221/4–2692, and 611.944/6–1162, respectively)

3.  A report to me of the earliest possible time at which you think it is suitable to make a public announcement, which would include the recommended changes in the Executive Order, as well as a general statement of our intentions of future action.[4]

If at all possible, I think it desirable to notify the Government of Japan of our desire to initiate this negotiation by the time Assistant Secretary Harriman reaches Tokyo on his present trip.[5]

*Section II*

In addition, I am requesting the Secretary of Defense to take responsibility for the following measures:

1.  Presentation to the Congress of an amendment to the Price Bill,[6] raising the ceiling on aid to the Ryukyus to a level consistent with the purposes of our proposed program.

2.  Adjustment by the Services of their wage policies in accordance with the recommendations of the Report.[7]

3.  Selection, in consultation with my office and the Department of State, of a suitable civilian to fill the post of Civil Administrator as soon as practicable, preferably at the retirement of the present Administrator.

4.  Instruction to the High Commissioner of the Ryukyus to:

a.  speed up the process of giving responsibility and autonomy to the Government of the Ryukyu Islands and extending the liberties of the Ryukyuans to the greatest extent consistent with his fundamental responsibilities, and

b.  examine the organization of his own staff with respect to both the problem of encouraging the growth of responsibility in the GRI and assisting in the economic development program recommended in the Report.

In both these actions, the High Commissioner should take the Task Force Report as a policy guide.

---

[4] In a statement issued on March 19, the President recognized the Ryukyus "to be a part of the Japanese homeland" and looked "forward to the day when the security interests of the Free World will permit their restoration to full Japanese sovereignty." He stated that he was asking the Congress to raise the $6 million ceiling on U.S. assistance to the Ryukyus and to "provide over future years a steady increase in loan funds" for Ryukyuan development. The United States would discuss with Japan means for the two countries to cooperate in promoting Ryukyuan economic development. For text, see *Public Papers of the Presidents of the United States: John F. Kennedy, 1962,* pp. 247–248.

[5] Harriman was in Japan March 15–16 and 17–20.

[6] Apparent reference is to P.L. 86–629, approved July 12, 1960 (74 Stat. 462), and known as the Price Act after Representative Melvin Price of Illinois. It set a ceiling of $6 million per annum on U.S. economic assistance to the Ryukyus.

[7] The Task Force Report recommended an increase in wages of Ryukyuan employees of the United States.

c.   report to you[8] in six months and each year thereafter his progress in carrying out the policies of the Report.

5.   Initiation of the detailed studies required to carry out the recommendations of the Task Force in respect to social welfare and economic assistance.

6.   Preparation of a supplemental budget request for the Ryukyu Islands for FY 1963 covering those items in the recommended program which can most suitably be dealt with now.

*Section III*

Also, I am requesting the Director of the Bureau of the Budget to prepare an amendment to Executive Order 10713[9] which gives effect to the following recommendations of the Report: (a) that the Civil Administrator be a civilian appointed by the Secretary of Defense with the approval of the President, after consultation with the Secretary of State; (b) that the chief executive of the Government of the Ryukyu Islands be nominated by the legislature to the High Commissioner; (c) that the term of office of the legislature be three years; (d) that the number of members of the legislature and the boundaries of election districts be made a matter for determination by the legislature, with the approval of the High Commissioner; and (e) that the purposes of the High Commissioner's use of the veto power be empahsized, and he be required to report his reasons for each veto to the Secretary of Defense.[10]

**John F. Kennedy**[11]

---

[8] "SecDef" is handwritten at this point on the source text.

[9] Dated June 5, 1957. (22 Fed. Reg. 4007)

[10] On March 19 the President signed E.O. 11010 (27 Fed. Reg. 2621) amending E.O. 10713 along the lines set forth above.

[11] Printed from a copy that indicates the President signed the original.

## 353.  Paper Prepared in the Department of State

Washington, March 22, 1962.

### SETTLEMENT OF THE UNITED STATES CLAIM FOR POSTWAR ECONOMIC ASSISTANCE TO JAPAN (GARIOA)

On January 9, 1962, the Agreement between the United States and Japan for the Settlement of Postwar Economic Assistance to Japan (GARIOA) was signed in Tokyo.[1] It formalizes the Memorandum of Understanding initialed in Tokyo on June 10, 1961,[2] prior to Prime Minister Ikeda's visit to Washington. The Agreement is now pending before the Japanese Diet for ratification.

The Agreement provides for payment to the United States by Japan of the principal sum of $490 million over a period of 15 years in semi-annual installments, with interest at 2-1/2 percent per annum on the unpaid balance. Accompanying exchanges of notes provide that 1) the United States intends, subject to appropriate legislation, to use the major portion of the payments to further its economic assistance programs and 2) the United States will accept $25 million of the total repayment in yen to be used for educational and cultural exchange between the two countries. A letter handed to the Japanese Foreign Minister on January 9 states the U.S. intention to accept this $25 million in yen from the first two installments.

The bulk of the assistance to Japan covered by this Agreement was provided under U.S. Appropriations Acts for Government and Relief in Occupied Areas (GARIOA) for fiscal years 1947 through 1952, plus assistance provided on an emergency basis by the Army prior to the GARIOA appropriations. Total disbursements for Japan under these

---

Source: Kennedy Library, National Security Files, Countries Series, Japan, 3/62. Confidential. Attached to a covering note from Battle to McGeorge Bundy. A handwritten note, signature illegible, indicates that this paper was prepared pursuant to the President's request for information on the subject.

[1] For text of the Agreement regarding the settlement of postwar assistance to Japan with exchanges of notes, signed at Tokyo on January 9, 1962, and entered into force on September 11, 1962, see 13 UST 1957.

[2] A text of the Memorandum of Understanding is attached to despatch 1391 from Tokyo, June 12, 1961. (Department of State, Central Files, 294.1141/6–1261) A memorandum from McConaughy to Rusk, June 6, 1961, contains a summary of the negotiations leading up to the memorandum. (Ibid., 294.1141/6–661) Additional documentation is ibid., 294.1141 for 1961, 1962, and January 1963; documentation for the remainder of 1963 is ibid., FN 14 JAPAN.

appropriations were about $1.99 billion. After deductions for U.S. administrative expenses, counterpart funds not of direct benefit to the Japanese economy, etc. the U.S. claim for GARIOA assistance to Japan was about $1.8 billion.

Formal negotiations with Japan on this claim began in May 1954. Settlement has been delayed to await the settlement of Japan's reparations obligations and because of a series of difficult political and economic problems in Japan. Since the opening of the negotiations this claim settlement has been a major political issue in Japan, where many people have considered this assistance to be a gift. Although each succeeding Japanese Prime Minister since 1952 has publicly and privately recognized GARIOA as a "debt of honor," Prime Minister Ikeda is the first to take steps to make a settlement.

The Socialist Party, the Democratic Party and certain elements of the Liberal Democratic Party have opposed settlement of GARIOA from the beginning. The government in power has been subjected to questioning on this matter at each succeeding session of the Diet since 1954. With the Agreement now pending before the Diet for ratification, the Socialist Party is organizing its opposition to it. All opposing factions are expected to seek to use the coincidence of the settlement with Japan's present deteriorating foreign exchange position to embarrass Ikeda. The Ikeda government appears to have prepared well for debate on this issue and to date appears to be handling it with considerable skill. Although particularly acrimonious debate centering on U.S.-Japanese relations is expected, present estimates are that the Agreement will be ratified in May.[3]

In accordance with U.S. intention expressed in one of the exchanges of notes, the proposed Foreign Assistance Act of 1962 contains a provision making available for appropriation the dollar repayments of Japanese GARIOA for the purposes of the Act.[4]

---

[3] By May 1962 the GARIOA Agreement had been approved by Parliament, but domestic enabling legislation (for which the Japanese Government preferred to wait until exchanging notes putting the Agreement into effect) would not be passed until September. Documentation is ibid., 294.1141.

[4] Once the GARIOA Agreement had gone into effect on September 11 the United States and Japan negotiated further regarding the method of repayment under it. Documentation on these negotiations is ibid. For text of the Agreement relating to the payment by Japan of the first and second installments under the agreement of January 9, regarding the settlement of postwar assistance, see 14 UST 202.

## 354. Department of State Guidelines Paper

Washington, undated.

### GUIDELINES OF U.S. POLICY AND OPERATIONS TOWARD JAPAN

#### I. Basic Approach

1. We see Japan as our principal ally in East Asia, our second largest world trading partner, the host for important forward U.S. military facilities, and a source of technical skill and capital contributing to the economic development of South and Southeast Asia. Japan offers the prospect of development as an increasingly important political, economic and, possibly, military counterweight to the rising power of Communist China.

2. Japan's continued control by moderate elements, its readiness to cooperate with the United States in foreign policy, and its ability in the future to play a more constructive role in Asian and world affairs depend on many factors but primarily on the maintenance of a high level of economic activity, which, in turn depends to an unusual extent upon access to world markets. As a reaction to defeat and occupation, there is a profound wish to avoid military involvement and great sensitivity to the risks of nuclear warfare. Recently there has been a growing nationalist sentiment and an increasing desire for independent self-assertion and leadership.

3. Accordingly, as Japan attempts with our help to play a more positive role in Asian affairs, U.S. and European economic and trade policies

---

Source: Department of State, S/S Country Files: Lot 70 D 209, Japan. Secret. Fearey was the principal drafter. In connection with preparation of this paper, the NSC rescinded NSC 6008/1, "U.S. Policy Toward Japan," June 11. (Memorandum from Bromley Smith to holders of NSC 6008/1, January 2, 1962; ibid.) By approving on April 18 a memorandum dated April 12 from Harriman to Rusk, McGhee authorized the publication and distribution of this paper. (Ibid.) CA–6760 to Tokyo, December 21, 1962, enclosed the paper and termed it "the primary formulation of U.S. policy toward Japan." (Ibid., Central Files, 611.94/12–2162) For text of NSC 6008/1, see Foreign Relations, 1958–1960, vol. XVIII, pp. 335–349.

A draft of this paper, dated October 1961, was circulated to 10 Departments and agencies and to the Embassy in Tokyo for comment. The draft and several replies are in Department of State, S/S Country Files: Lot 70 D 209, Japan. In a March 16 memorandum to Rice, Leonard Bacon of EA/RA wrote that although the "question of concurrence did not arise" in interagency discussions subsequent to the replies, CIA and DOD representatives "could formally state that they did not find the revised paper objectionable in any important respect." (Ibid.) See the Supplement. Of the replies from other agencies, the memorandum dated December 12, 1961, from Robert Amory, Deputy Director (Intelligence) of the CIA, to Battle, and the memorandum dated December 13, 1961, from William Bundy to McGhee, are also in the Supplement.

must be responsive to Japanese marketing needs, and defense links must infringe as little as possible on Japanese prerogatives and sensibilities.

## II. Background

1.  Japan stands today as a fully independent and influential member of international society. Its recovery since 1945 has been most impressive in the economic sphere and least impressive in the military field. Japan has enjoyed one of the fastest rates of economic growth in the world, averaging nine percent annually during the past ten years; trade has increased to record levels; foreign exchange reserves reached a post-war peak of $2 billion in April, 1961, since reduced to $1.5 billion, and per capita income (about $350) is now the highest in Asia, though still low by the standards of Western industrialized nations.

2.  The continued rapid rate of economic growth has reinforced the firm grasp over political power in Japan held during the post-war period by the moderate conservative forces (Liberal-Democratic Party), which are supported by over 60 percent of the electorate and have large majorities in both houses of the Diet. The 1960 elections, however, showed a rise of 3.7% since 1958 in the opposition vote. Population shifts partially accounting for this rise seem likely to continue. Major scandals, significant foreign policy failures, or a radical curtailment of the rate of economic growth would accelerate the apparent gradual shift of political power to the left. If as a result of the current economic boom Japan's balance of payments situation should further deteriorate, the Ikeda Government might be faced with the necessity of taking counter-measures of such severe character that economic growth would be seriously retarded. In such case the position of his Government and the Liberal-Democratic Party would be seriously weakened, particularly in view of promises to double the income of Japanese wage earners within ten years. The conservatives, moreover, have been unable to give Japan the kind of stable, firmly Western-oriented government warranted by their large parliamentary majority, due to certain weaknesses in Japan's post-war structure, principally:

a.  Factionalism is endemic to the Japanese conservative movement and breeds ineffectual governments if not curbed. Although the leaders of all factions of the Liberal-Democratic Party in varying degrees recognize the necessity of close ties with Western countries, some have shown serious political irresponsibility in their intra-party struggles for power. As a consequence, conservative governments in Japan have been tempted occasionally to sponsor opportunistic policies, to be less cooperative with the United States, and to be susceptible to appeals based on emotionally-tinged nationalism.

b.  Conservative parties have failed to develop genuine grassroots support for their policies, relying instead on traditional patron-voter relationships, particularly in rural areas where their main source of strength lies. This failure could become increasingly serious for them with the steady shift of population to the cities and the gradual erosion of traditional political patterns throughout Japan.

c. Japan is extremely vulnerable to external economic influences, because the health of its economy is heavily dependent upon a high level of international trade. Conservative public appeal, however, rests increasingly on the "bread and butter" issues and its demonstrated ability to guide an economic growth which has brought steady improvement in living standards. If their economic policies falter, the conservatives could be in very serious difficulties. Therefore, the maintenance of a high level of trade with the West, particularly the United States, is virtually a life or death issue for the conservatives.

d. Japan has failed to digest fully the major political and social reforms of the occupation or to develop a solid sense of national purpose. Pre-war totalitarian institutions and national goals are largely discredited. However, the new postwar democratic institutions have shallow roots and are not fully understood by any segment of Japanese society on the right or the left. Furthermore, the Japanese people have not recovered fully from the tremendous social upheaval of the last twenty years or developed a new social equilibrium.

e. The urge for neutralism and for disengagement from alignment with the U.S. has a major impact on Japanese policy. Japan is under constant pressure to assume a neutral stance both from Sino-Soviet sources and from left-wing elements in Japan. These appeals often strike a responsive chord: Japan's long isolation from the West ended only a little over 100 years ago; Japanese nationalism is introverted and places great value on "national independence"; and the memories of defeat in World War II and particularly of the atom bombings of Hiroshima and Nagasaki are still intense. While successive conservative governments have rejected a policy of disengagement without election defeat, in deference to these public sentiments they must trim their sails by demonstrations of Japanese independence particularly on such sensitive issues as the Ryukyus and China policy, and by limiting Japanese security ties particularly through the refusal to enter into regional security commitments. Although aware of the United Nations' present limitations, Japan places great store by that body and participates actively in efforts to make it a more effective instrument of peace and progress. The Japanese remain unwilling, however, because of Constitutional considerations, to contribute troops or logistic support to UN emergency operations.

f. The Japanese people are haunted by the fear of involvement in another nuclear war, to the point where all manifestations of military activity, whether U.S. or Japanese, are at most acquiesced in by substantial segments of the nation. The conservatives cannot afford to flout these fears and must tailor their security policies so as to avoid, when possible, heated public debate on military-security issues and particularly must oppose storage of nuclear weapons in Japan. Such storage, however, remains an important U.S. military objective to be pursued when politically feasible.

g. The left has demonstrated its capabilities for effective exploitation of Japan's political weaknesses and fears of involvement in a nuclear war, and is often able to handcuff completely government initiatives having large parliamentary support. The left has developed extra-parliamentary means of frustrating the conservative majority through the use of violence to impede or interrupt the normal legislative processes. The Government is deterred from the use of its full powers to override these tactics by the fear of adverse public reaction weakening its mandate, or of the creation of a situation of disorder bordering on the revolutionary. The left, for its part, is restrained by the fear of jeopardizing public support, or at least tolerance, of its activities. Since the left is particularly well entrenched in the communications media and labor circles, it has been able to secure very broad tolerance for its actions, and to impede the efforts of the Government to gain support for its own policies. This situation is particularly dangerous because the Communists have shown themselves capable of effectively influencing left-wing actions to the benefit of the Sino-Soviet bloc.

3. Continued conservative rule can, therefore, not be taken for granted. Its vulnerabilities are most evident on issues involving Japan's security ties with the U.S., the status of the Ryukyus, policy toward the Communist bloc, particularly Communist China, and, most importantly, the expansion of Japan's trade and economy. However, the only current alternative is rule by the Japan Socialist Party (JSP), which seeks not only drastic social revolution in Japan, but a neutralist policy leaning very much in the direction of the Sino-Soviet bloc. There are forces at work within Japanese society which may in time effect a change in the orientation of the JSP, and a closer approach to the responsibilities of a ruling party might of itself have a sobering effect; however, rule by the Socialists as now oriented would not only completely reverse the present trend of U.S.-Japan relations but could also precipitate a major and decisive power shift in Asia toward the Communist bloc with other Asian nations also swinging to a Communist-oriented neutralism.

4. Given this situation, U.S. policy toward Japan must necessarily depend upon maintenance of a moderate, conservative government for the time being. The day may come when this is no longer feasible. Looking toward this day, it is vitally important to seek a gradual moderation of left-wing views, but not at the expense of accelerating or condoning an early accession to power of the left. At the same time, U.S. policy toward Japan must recognize the limitations on the conservatives for actions in

the security field and their most vital dependence on trade as a means of promoting Japan's continued economic growth. This dependence on trade, however, provides the United States with very considerable leverage in Japan. If trade with Japan can be maintained at a growing level over the next decade, Japan's alliance with the U.S. and its inter-dependence with the West can become so intimate and responsive to Japanese interests as to discourage thoroughly any Japanese government, whether left or right, from reversing this course.

### III. Objectives

*A.  Long-Term Goal*

The long-term goal of U.S. policy toward Japan is the development of Japan as a major power center in Asia acting in concert with U.S. and Free World interests.

*B.  Short-Term Objectives—(Objectives realistically attainable during the period 1962–64)*

1.  Continuation in power of a moderate, Western-oriented government.

2.  Maintenance of a U.S.-Japanese alliance based on the political, economic and security provisions of the Treaty of Mutual Cooperation and Security.

3.  Maintenance of our base structure in Japan, primarily to assist in the defense of Japan and to provide logistic support for the U.S. military forces in the Far East.

4.  A Japanese defense effort capable of maintaining internal security against Communist-inspired subversion and insurgency and capable of assuming increasing responsibility for the defense of the Japan area and thereby, together with U.S. forces, of coping with and deterring Communist aggression in the Pacific.

5.  Continuation of Japanese acquiescence in the U.S. administration of the Ryukyu and Bonin Islands.

6.  Growth of a more healthy and moderate outlook on the part of the Japanese intellectual community.

7.  Development of closer links with the U.S. and other non-Communist nations, particularly developed countries, based on increased trade and greater coordination of economic policies.

8.  An increasing Japanese contribution to economic growth in non-Communist Asia.

9.  An expanding international role for Japan, particularly among the Asian and African nations.

## IV. Lines of Action

In the short-term, U.S. policy toward Japan will be dominated by achievement of two objectives: continuation in power of a moderate government and the development of an expanding level of trade between Japan and other non-Communist countries. A fundamental reorientation of Japan's position in the world and its relationship to the U.S. will result from failure to achieve either objective.

### A.   U.S.-Japanese Alliance

1.  Move quickly to resolve differences between Japan and the U.S.

2.  Maintain a pattern of consultation with Japan consonant with its status as the major partner of the U.S. in Asia, paralleling such consultations with top Western European leaders.

3.  Seek broader public support in Japan for the U.S.-Japan alliance:

a) By expeditious settlement of security and base problems.

b) By minimizing overt U.S. pressures on the Japanese Government in security matters.

c) By implementing and emphasizing the non-security provisions of Article II of the Treaty of Mutual Cooperation and Security, particularly in the field of trade and economic cooperation.

d) By fostering both the concept and reality of equal partnership and interdependence with the U.S. and Free World.

e) By promoting ideological identification with the Western democracies and encouraging closer ties with the NATO countries.

### B.   Moderate Government

4.  Support the continuation in power of a moderate, Western-oriented conservative government in Japan.

5.  Encourage—without alienating conservative support—the development of moderating trends among the opposition Socialists and their trade union supporters, by such steps as:

a) Showing sympathetic interest in Zenro and the Democratic Socialist Party;

b) Stimulating broader contacts between non-Communist Sohyo, Zenro and other labor leaders and the U.S. and other Western union leadership, by inter alia continuing a sizeable labor exchange program, while encouraging privately financed programs; and

c) Encouraging West European Socialist interest in and contact with the Democratic Socialist Party and the Japan Socialist Party.

6.  Encourage discreetly Japanese initiatives to strengthen their democratic institutions, and in particular to reduce the government's vulnerability to extra-parliamentary pressures and violence.

7.  Strengthen systematically cultural and intellectual relations with Japan on a long-term and largely non-governmental basis by:

a) Stimulating and supporting private American and other Western efforts to increase greatly Japanese intellectual, cultural, and youth contacts with democratic societies on the lines recommended at the first meeting of the U.S.-Japan Committee on Cultural and Educational Cooperation.[1]

b) Maintaining an expanded U.S. Government educational and cultural exchange program, with emphasis on the areas of political theory, law, social sciences and welfare, communications media, education and labor.

c) Stepping up U.S. cultural presentations in Japan, and Japanese cultural presentations in the U.S., by actively encouraging private sponsorship and by providing increased U.S. financial assistance.

d) Promoting scientific exchanges, both government and non-government, in non-defense areas, on the lines initiated at the first meeting of the U.S.-Japan Committee on Scientific Cooperation.

C.   *Economic Relations*

8. Promote closer economic relations and expanded trade between the U.S. and Japan through such actions as:

a) Generally maintaining a liberal trade policy and urging Japan and other trading nations to maintain in practice such a policy.

b) Consulting through normal diplomatic channels and through the joint U.S.-Japan Committee on Trade and Economic Affairs on problems of trade, aid, investment, regional groupings, technical assistance, economic relations with the Communist bloc, and other economic matters.

c) Resisting pressures to establish U.S. import restrictions, or to "negotiate" Japanese "voluntary" export quotas, except where absolutely essential; when Japanese export quotas to the U.S. are unavoidable they should be negotiated on a multilateral basis.

d) Handling all specific import commodity problems through the "Escape Clause" or other available legal mechanisms.

e) Urging Japan not to raise tariffs solely for protection purposes, or as a means of avoiding the consequences of trade liberalization.

f) Urging Japan to take steps toward more meaningful liberalization of items of interest to the United States under its trade and exchange control system with the objective of eliminating all but a "hard core" of non-discriminatory import restrictions.

9. Seek Japan's cooperation in the alleviation of the United States balance of payments problem, while avoiding actions in this connection which would have a serious or abrupt adverse effect on Japan's own balance of payments position, trading position, or economic strength generally, through such actions as:

a) Pressing vigorously for Japan's trade liberalization (see 8.f above).

---

[1] Held in Tokyo January 25–31. See Department of State *Bulletin*, January 22, 1962, p. 142.

b) Promoting increased Japanese assistance to less-developed countries.

c) Seeking Japanese understanding of the changed U.S. balance of payments position and of its necessary effect on U.S. economic policy.

10. Promote a broadening economic relationship between Japan and Western Europe through such actions as:

a) Continuing strongly to urge a liberalization of Western Europe trade policy toward Japan, including the disinvocation of Article XXXV of the GATT.

b) Promoting at the highest levels of government in Japan and Western Europe understanding of the need for closer economic ties between the two areas.

c) Studying the possibility of organizational ties between Japan, Western Europe, Canada, the U.S. and other developed nations.

d) Continuing to support as appropriate Japan's efforts to secure full membership in OECD.

D.    *Japan's International Role*

11. Encourage and assist Japan to exercise a moderating and constructive influence in the UN, particularly with the Afro-Asian nations, but avoid efforts to overidentify Japan with Western positions to the extent that its usefulness and influence among Afro-Asians is undermined and to this end accept occasional divergencies of viewpoint.

12. Seek to increase Japan's contribution to and assumption of responsibility for the economic development of the less-developed countries through such actions as:

a) Encouraging a large-scale economic assistance program to ROK;

b) Coordinating, through such mechanisms as DAC and multilateral consortia, U.S. and Japanese economic assistance programs;

c) Seeking with Japanese agreement a selective acceleration of utilization by recipient countries of Japan's reparations payments, including urging recipients to make increased use of the loan portions of such payments.

d) Encouraging and facilitating, at every opportunity, increased Japanese technical assistance to less-developed countries generally and, in particular, seeking to increase the scope of and Japan's contribution to the Asian Productivity Organization.

13. Seek an early settlement of ROK-Japanese differences with such steps as:

a) Establishment of reciprocal official relations.

b) Japanese economic assistance for the ROK.

c) A fisheries conservation agreement in the Korean straits.

14. Coordinate closely with Japan on policy toward the Sino-Soviet bloc and particularly Communist China, but recognize that Japanese policy toward Communist China may diverge from U.S. policy in certain

respects. In this connection, encourage Japan to hamper and weaken ties between the Japan Communist Party and the Soviet Union and Communist China.

### E.  Security-Military Relations

15. In public statements generally avoid reference to the military-security aspects of U.S.-Japanese relations. In such public references to this subject as are appropriate, accentuate the mutually supporting aspects of U.S.-Japanese security relations and seek to reduce fears that U.S. military bases in Japan will increase the risk of Japanese involvement in a nuclear conflict.

16. Maintain with Japanese agreement a level of U.S. military facilities and forces in Japan as required to provide primarily logistic support for U.S. forces in the Far East, and to demonstrate our determination to fulfill U.S. treaty commitments to Japan.

17. In U.S.-Japanese security relations:

a)  Assist in the defense of Japan in the event of an armed attack against the territories of Japan.

b)  Adhere rigidly to the provisions of the consultation arrangements, avoiding actions contrary to the wishes of the Japanese Government as expressed in such consultations.

c)  Implement the [less than 1 line of source text not declassified] response to an attack against the United Nations Forces in Korea only with the authorization of the President.

d)  Inform the Japanese Government confidentially in advance regarding major United States logistic operations from bases in Japan to areas outside of Japan and regarding any major withdrawal of United States forces from Japan.

e)  Implement U.S.-Japan administrative arrangements in a manner best calculated to obtain maximum cooperation and support from the Japanese Government and public and to avoid publicly-inflamed base rights issues, being prepared to adjust existing military bases when overall political considerations are believed to outweigh purely military considerations.

18. Encourage Japan to increase its defense effort and to modernize its military forces, while avoiding pressures and other actions prejudicial to Japanese political and economic stability. Continue U.S. military assistance for specific projects designed primarily to stimulate the expansion and modernization of Japanese forces. U.S. assistance should be predominantly in the form of U.S. contributions to cost-shared projects, with the Japanese providing approximately 75% of the total cost, and should normally not include items which the Japanese are capable of producing for themselves. Assistance should be gradually phased down with the objective of ultimate termination.

*F.   Ryukyus, Bonins and other U.S.-Administered Pacific Islands*

19. Attempt to keep pressures in Japan and in the Ryukyus for reversion within manageable proportions by developing a cooperative relationship with Japan with respect to the Ryukyus to the degree consistent with the indefinite continuation of exclusive U.S. jurisdiction over the islands. Acknowledge the inevitability of substantial Japanese influence in the Ryukyus, and seek to use it constructively to enhance the security of the U.S. bases. Be prepared to accept a substantial Japanese contribution to the economic and social development of the Ryukyus, preferably through the medium of an economic cooperation agreement. The agreement would define, channel and limit the levels and types of Japanese aid activities, while creating the political basis in Japan for Japanese Government acquiescence in continued U.S. administration.

20. Conduct our administration of the Ryukyus so as to promote political stability, economic advancement and reasonable satisfaction with continued United States rule. To this end,

a)  Speed up the process of giving responsibility and autonomy to the Government of the Ryukyu Islands and extending the liberties of the Ryukyans to the greatest extent consistent with the High Commissioner's fundamental responsibilities, using the report of Task Force Ryukyus as a policy guide.

b)  Seek amendment of the Price Act[2] to remove the $6 million ceiling on assistance to the Ryukyus.

c)  Provide assistance, in conjunction with Japanese contributions which are agreed upon, at a level substantially higher than in past years as a supplement to local resources in order to support effective administration and long-term economic development of the islands.

21. Permit the selective entry of Japanese nationals into U.S. administered territories in the Pacific.

## V. Contingencies

Achievement of U.S. policy objectives in Japan, particularly the maintenance of a close alliance, could be seriously frustrated in the event of the following contingencies:

A.  A split in the conservative Liberal-Democratic Party or a sustained period of intense factional conflict within the Party, leading to prolonged ineffective conservative rule and greatly intensified vulnerability to leftist extra-parliamentary pressures.

B.  Socialist assumption of power, followed by neutralization of Japan in accord with current Socialist policies.

---

[2] See footnote 6, Document 352.

C. An open and violent conflict for power between the left and the right, precipitated by continued leftist resort to extra-parliamentary pressures and violence.

D. A failure to achieve adequate trade levels with the U.S., Western Europe and other non-Communist countries, particularly as a result either of restrictions against Japanese imports by these countries or of a major world-wide economic recession.

E. Major pressures in Japan and the Ryukyus for reversion of the Ryukyus to Japanese administration.

## 355.    Memorandum From the Assistant Secretary of State for Far Eastern Affairs (Harriman) to the Deputy Under Secretary of State for Political Affairs (Johnson)

Washington, April 6, 1962.

SUBJECT

Negotiations with Japan Regarding the Ryukyus

Mr. Gilpatric's letter of March 22 to you (Tab A)[1] presents a basic issue which will have to be resolved before we can proceed further with a negotiation with Japan over the Ryukyus.

Underlying the Defense position is a fear that Congress will not provide the funds necessary to carry out the programs recommended by the Task Force. There appears to be some basis for this fear, since we understand that Representative Passman[2] has taken a very negative view of the Army's request for even $6 million for FY 1963. This request was sub-

---

Source: Department of State, Central Files, 794C.0221/4–662. Confidential. Drafted by King Swayne.

[1] This letter, not attached, reports that the primary objective in the negotiations, "from the Defense viewpoint, is to maintain the unhampered use of our forces and facilities on Okinawa" and that the proposed agreement should "provide an arrangement for defining, controlling, limiting and channeling Japanese aid activities, in return for U.S. agreement to permit increased Japanese aid." The letter concludes that a Japanese commitment subject to annual review by the High Commissioner would be desirable. (Ibid., 794C.0221/3–2262)

[2] Otto Passman of Louisiana, member of the House Appropriations Committee and Chairman of its Foreign Aid Subcommittee.

mitted before the Task Force recommendations for annual programs in the $20 million range were accepted in the Executive Branch.

If congressional resistance to increased US assistance to the Ryukyu Islands becomes a serious obstacle, it will be necessary for us to re-think the entire approach to Ryukyuan problems taken by the Task Force. Our failure in the past to provide adequate assistance to the Ryukyus has resulted in Japanese offers of assistance to make up the deficit. This in turn has produced what is in effect a US-Japanese competition for the favor of the Ryukyuan people, with the size of prospective aid programs taken as the measure of concern for Ryukyuan welfare and well-being. If the Executive Branch is unable to obtain the funds from Congress that will permit us to demonstrate that our interest in Ryukyuan welfare more than matches that of Japan, our position in the islands may well become untenable. I consider it essential that we assure ourselves of the congressional support necessary to carry out the Task Force recommendations before entering into negotiations with Japan.

The fear of failure with Congress that underlies the Defense position has also produced an unrealistic request to the Department that we try to eliminate competitive undercutting of the US position in the Ryukyus by Japan, while suggesting arrangements for Japanese assistance programs which would have precisely the undesired effect. We agree with Defense that Japanese efforts to outbid us annually for Ryukyuan favor are undesirable and should be eliminated. However, the internal pressures on any Japanese Government are such that it seems highly unlikely that we can eliminate this kind of competitive bidding (1) if Japanese aid programs are determined on an annual basis and (2) if, in Mr. Gilpatric's words, "Japanese aid must be kept in a sound relationship to annual US aid programs." The Defense suggestion (see paragraph 6 of the attachment to Mr. Gilpatric's letter)[3] that we obtain an over-all five-year commitment from the Japanese as to their aid program, with this commitment subject to annual renegotiation (probably downward to keep it well below the US aid figure), seems guaranteed to increase Ryukyuan dissatisfaction with our administration as well as expose as a sham our profession of a desire to cooperate with Japan.

The concept of working by five-year periods, incorporated in the draft agreement used by the Task Force in its deliberations, would largely eliminate this concern with competitive bidding, but it would require an advance five-year commitment by the US on aid programs to the Ryukyus, a commitment Defense seems reluctant to undertake. If we feel we cannot generate the necessary support in Congress and must

---

[3] This attachment sets forth specific comments on the draft U.S.-Japan agreement on Ryukyus assistance. The draft is dated December 15 and is attached to Harriman's memorandum as Tab C.

therefore tailor Japanese aid levels to our own on an annual basis, I see no prospect of avoiding annual Japanese efforts to outbid us as benefactors of the Ryukyus.

There are two other aspects of Mr. Gilpatric's letter that deserve mention. First, the philosophy underlying the letter is clearly out of phase with the spirit of the President's statement of March 19 (Tab B).[4] Language identical to that in the President's statement acknowledging our responsibility to "minimize the stresses that will accompany the anticipated eventual restoration of the Ryukyu Islands to Japanese administration" has been deleted by Defense from the proposed draft agreement (Tab C) "to avoid creating any new basis for increased reversionism." (See paragraph 1 of the attachment to Mr. Gilpatric's letter.) The President's statement reflects the belief that reversionsim can best be contained by recognizing the inevitability of close ties between the Ryukyus and Japan and tailoring our policies accordingly. It appears that the Department of Defense has not yet accepted this change in US policy. Secondly, the Department of Defense suggests that specific arrangements on the agreement with Japan be worked out by Ambassador Reischauer and General Caraway on the basis of criteria agreed between the Departments of State and Defense. This position is not inconsistent with our own thinking, but overlooks the fact that the Department of State cannot delegate to an ambassador abroad responsibility for all aspects of an international agreement. The Defense position does, however, lay the basis for the type of State–Defense coordination recommended to you in our memorandum of March 9 (Tab D).[5] This would involve close contacts between Ambassador Reischauer and General Caraway in the field, with disagreements between them resolved by the Department of State, after receiving Defense's views as appropriate, in accordance with the intent of the President's directive to the Secretary of State on the conduct of the negotiation (Tab E).[6]

I recommend that the following steps now be taken:[7]

1.  A discussion with Defense and the White House of the prospects for congressional support, of possible means for insuring greater congressional support if this appears necessary, and of the implications for our position in the Ryukyus if such support is not forthcoming.

---

[4] See footnote 4, Document 352.

[5] Memorandum to Johnson from Rice, not printed. (Department of State, Central Files, 794C.0221/3–962)

[6] Dated March 5; this directive incorporates the the first section of NSAM No. 133, Document 352.

[7] Johnson approved only the first of these options. An April 19 memorandum from Joseph A. Yager of EA to Rice states that Johnson deferred approval of the second two "pending the outcome of consideration of the question of gaining congressional support." (Department of State, Central Files, 811.0094C/4–1962)

2. If the necessary assurances of congressional support are received, we should proceed with plans for a negotiation with Japan on the basis of five-year aid commitments by both parties. If not, our whole Ryukyuan policy will have to be reviewed.

3. Assuming a positive outcome, we should seek Defense concurrence to an initial negotiating instruction which would incorporate as far as possible the concerns expressed in Mr. Gilpatric's letter but would thereafter leave the conduct of the negotiations firmly in the hands of the Department of State, with General Caraway playing his appropriate role in the field. A proposed instruction to Embassy Tokyo to this effect is attached at Tab F.[8]

---

[8] Not printed. Kaysen eventually worked out with the Department of Defense, and Harriman accepted, the following sentence regarding potential State–Defense disagreements during the course of the negotiations with Japan: "In resolving such differences, the two Departments will be guided by the directives of the President as embodied in NSAM 133." (Memorandum from Harriman to U. Alexis Johnson, May 29: ibid., 794C.0221/5–2962) As a preliminary to U.S.-Japan negotiations, Japanese Government "survey teams" visited Okinawa June 15–August 8.

---

## 356.  Editorial Note

In CINCPAC message 200410Z September 20, 1962, JCS Chairman-designate Maxwell Taylor, during an inspection tour of East Asia, commented on U.S. military policy in a number of Asian countries. The section on Japan reads:

"I looked at Japan primarily from the point of view of the military asset which it represents for the U.S. Its principal value lies in the military facilities which are made available to the U.S. forces, rather than in the possible participation of its forces in combined operations. In peace, these bases make in important contribution to the efficiency and economy of operation of all U.S. Services. In war, the continuing value of these bases is uncertain. In limited war, it is likely that the Japanese would permit the U.S. to continue to use these facilities provided the U.S. moves no nuclear weapons into or out of Japan. Since our primary enemy in the Far East is Red China and it would probably be necessary to use atomic weapons in an all-out war with that enemy, the foregoing is a serious limitation on the usefulness of Japanese bases. In case of general nuclear war of the kind envisaged in the SIOP, the contribution of the Japanese bases would have little significance on the world-wide situation.

"If the foregoing evaluation is correct, there is no justification for the U.S. to pay any great price for U.S. bases in Japan. This fact, plus the continued apathy of the Japanese toward the requirements of their own self defense makes Japan a poor bet as a military ally, and causes one to conclude that military considerations need not shape U.S. relations with Japan."

After reading this cable, President Kennedy sent NSAM No. 188 to Secretary McNamara: "General Taylor's summary about the limited benefit of bases in Japan reinforces, I believe, the necessity for tightening dollar expenditures there where, I understand, we spend $350 million per year. I know this is a matter the Department of Defense is looking into. Does it appear that a saving can be made?"

On October 1 McNamara replied that he was convinced savings could be made, although while studies were underway, it was too early to be precise about the amounts. Regarding "the basic issue" raised by Taylor, McNamara was asking the Joint Chiefs of Staff for their views. (All in Kennedy Library, National Security Files, Meetings and Memoranda Series, NSAM No. 188)

## 357.  Editorial Note

On October 4, 1962, the President signed Public Law 87–746, which raised the annual authorization ceiling on U.S. economic aid to the Ryukyus from $6 to $12 million. The lower ceiling, far short of the $25 million authorization ceiling that the administration had requested, came at the initiative of the Senate Armed Services Committee, which was "inclined to believe that the level of assistance [was] being accelerated too rapidly" and hoped that there would be "no [administration] proposal to increase the authorization ceiling next year." (Quotations from the Committee's report to the full Senate as reported in telegram 663 to Tokyo, September 21; Department of State, Central Files, 811.0094C/9–2162)

Although the administration had requested $12 million in FY 1963 appropriations for Ryukyuan aid, the House Appropriations Committee recommended only $6 million and the Senate Appropriations Committee recommended $9 million. After the respective Houses had approved these figures, a conference committee set a final total, excluding administrative expenses, of $6,95 million, only $950,000 over the previous ceiling.

In an October 6 letter to U. Alexis Johnson, Gerald Warner, Political Adviser to the High Commissioner in the Ryukyus, stated that the congessionally approved amounts, although lower than the administration's requests, did not necessarily mean that the President's policy for the Ryukyus had been undercut: "For one thing the GOJ is not too anxious to have the Ryukyus revert too quickly. They know a good thing defense wise and economy wise when they see it. They don't want to have the Okinawans living too high off the hog while we are here, and thus have the Okinawans squealing even louder after reversion than they do now. So all in all the situation does not look too bad. I think we can and should put a favorable face on it." (Ibid., 811.0094C/10–662)

In an October 30 memorandum to the Secretary Harriman recommended that "in view of the disappointingly small aid appropriation for the Ryukyus" Rusk issue a statement stressing that there had been no change in the President's policy as announced March 19 (see Document 352) and that U.S.-Japanese discussions on the subject would continue. (Ibid., 794C.0221/10-3062) After White House approval, such a statement was issued November 1. For text, see Department of State *Bulletin*, November 19, 1962, page 770.

---

### 358. Memorandum From the Chairman of the Working Group of the United States–Japan Joint Committee on Trade and Economic Affairs (Yager) to the Working Group

Washington, October 15, 1962.

SUBJECT

Under Secretary Ball's Comments on Japanese Trade Restrictions

Under Secretary Ball believes that, during the coming Cabinet Committee[1] discussions, we should be much more on the offensive vis-à-vis Japan and its trade restrictions than we have in the past. We should make it clear that if Japan is to be a leading and active participant among the developed nations of the world, it must pursue liberal trade policies. The Under Secretary has noted that the Japanese record of restrictions is in many ways worse than the situation prevailing in the European countries. He hopes that the briefing papers now in preparation will reflect this point of view.

---

Source: Department of State, Conference Files: Lot 65 D 533, CF 2189. Confidential.
[1] See Document 361.

### 359. Letter From the Ambassador to Japan (Reischauer) to the Assistant Secretary of State for Far Eastern Affairs (Harriman)

Tokyo, October 22, 1962.

DEAR GOVERNOR HARRIMAN: During his recent brief visit to Tokyo, General Maxwell Taylor startled us by his suggestion in a briefing session with Embassy officers that the value of our bases in Japan might be open to question. General Smart,[1] who has mentioned to me his conversation with you in Washington, has now provided me with a brief summary of General Taylor's report to the President.[2] He has also shown me a telegram from Admiral Felt to the Joint Chiefs of Staff[3] which makes a forceful and convincing military case for the retention of bases in Japan. I have no doubt that you share Admiral Felt's misgivings over General Taylor's thesis, but I thought that it might be of some use to you if your man on the spot provided you with his view of the question.

It seems to me that General Taylor has asked himself the wrong question and has therefore come up with the wrong answer. The question he seems to be asking is. *"Disregarding Japan itself,* of what value to the United States defense position *are* our bases in Japan?"* Even accepting his question in this form, I would not myself be in agreement with his answer. I have been given to understand by many military authorities, including General Taylor's immediate predecessor as Chairman of the Joint Chiefs of Staff,[4] that without the Japanese bases our military position in Korea would be quite impossible to maintain and our positions further to the south would be seriously weakened.

The real problem, however, is the nature of the question to which General Taylor has addressed himself. For one thing, are we concerned only with the immediate value of our bases and not with their potential value in the foreseeable future? Even accepting General Taylor's low estimate of the current value of the bases—and I for one would rate their deterrent value much more highly than he does—should this estimate automatically apply to their value five years or even two years hence? I think not. The outbreak of warfare, whether non-nuclear, limited, or universal, would have its special background, and depending on what that background is and what the public and official reaction to this is in Japan, our bases here may prove to have much greater utility than General Taylor estimates. Moreover, there is good reason to believe that the general drift of Japanese attitudes is in the right direction and that, as a result,

---

Source: Department of State, Central Files, 102.201/8–2261. Top Secret.

[1] General Jacob Smart, USAF, COMUSJAPAN.

[2] See Document 356.

[3] Not found.

[4] General Lyman L. Lemnitzer, USA.

two years from now our bases will be of greater value in a war situation than they are today and that five years from now they will be of even greater value.

What basically bothers me, though, is General Taylor's apparent omission in his calculations of the importance of these bases in the defense of Japan itself and in the developing political situation here. Friendly Japanese cooperation with the United States seems to me central to our whole position—military, political and economic—in the Far East, or, to put it negatively, Japan's adherence to the Communist bloc or even strict neutralism on its part would play havoc with our whole position in this part of the world. The primary role of our bases in Japan, I feel, is to help insure that this country does not fall or gravitate into Communist hands or into a neutralist position, but General Taylor seems to be judging them solely on their secondary value as bases for the defense of other areas in the Far East.

Even if it were established that our bases are not needed for the defense of Japan—and General Taylor apparently is not even raising this question—there would still be strong political reasons for moving with great caution in reducing their size and number, because any action of this sort would be likely to make the Japanese feel that we were abandoning them and would thus encourage a movement toward neutralism or alignment with the Communist camp. Without doubt such action would seriously damage the position of the present pro-American conservative leadership in Japan, and it probably would set in motion a train of adverse reactions here that could not be easily stopped. Parenthetically, I might add that any drift of the Japanese away from us would have serious repercussions in Okinawa which would, in my opinion, seriously impair the value of our bases there.

I could say a great deal more about the grave political as well as military consequences to Japan and to our whole position in the Far East if any decision were taken to cut down significantly on our bases here. The main point I wish to make, however, is that, if such a decision were taken without due consideration of the military and political bearing of these bases on Japan's future, it would indeed be a case of throwing out the baby with the bath water.

In view of the sensitivity of the subject, I have discussed this letter only with John Emmerson,[5] who concurs fully in it, but I am sure that there would be no essential disagreement anywhere in the Embassy on the points I have made.

Sincerely,

**Ed**

---

[5] John K. Emmerson succeeded William Leonhart as Counselor of Embassy with the personal rank of Minister in July 1962.

**360.   Position Paper**

JAE/D–21                                    Washington, November 26, 1962.

UNITED STATES–JAPAN COMMITTEE ON
TRADE AND ECONOMIC AFFAIRS
Washington, December 3–5, 1962

Position Paper
(To be raised at U.S. or Japanese Initiative)[1]

*United States Investment in Japan*

Although U.S. investment interest in Japan has been and continues
to be active, the Japanese Government has been successful in restricting
and channeling such investments to fields and levels considered by the
Government to be consistent with its economic and commercial objectives. The Government has thus tended to encourage technological
assistance contracts at the same time that only a minimum amount of
equity investment has been approved.

*United States Position*

1.   The United States believes that the growth in the Japanese economy and in Japanese exports over the past decade has been due in great
measure to the large number of technological assistance contracts concluded with American companies. Benefits have also been derived from
American equity investment, which unfortunately has not been of the
magnitude which would have been possible had Japanese regulations
been administered in a less restrictive manner.

2.   Now that Japan has a strong economy and has succeeded in
vastly improving its balance-of-payments position, such limitations on
foreign equity investment can no longer be considered justified. Nor, in
view of the worldwide movement on the part of developed countries
toward a freer flow of trade and capital, can Japan afford to continue to
isolate its business from the benefits which such investment can provide.
Japan is a capital-short country and many mutually profitable enterprises have been under consideration. American investors cannot be

---

Source: Department of State, Conference Files: Lot 65 D 533, CF 2187. Limited Official
Use. Drafted by R.M. Klein of the Department of Commerce and cleared at the Depart-
ments of Agriculture, Labor, and the Treasury, and with the Council of Economic Advisers.
Cleared by Tresize in the Department of State. This paper was prepared for the Second
Meeting of the U.S.-Japan Committee on Trade and Economic Affairs; see Document 361.
   [1] It was not raised during the Second Meeting of the Committee.

expected to provide capital to Japan unless they are assured of the right to convert income into dollars and ultimately to repatriate capital.

3. In this connection, the United States would consider modification of Article XII of the Treaty of Friendship, Commerce and Navigation,[2] or the equivalent through less formal means, to be a regressive step. Publicity accompanying such a restrictive effort on Japan's part would undoubtedly have an adverse effect on Japan's economic relations with both the United States and other free world countries.

*Japanese Position*

1. The question of relaxing controls on the entry of private foreign equity investment is a difficult one for the Japanese Government. If, as a result of an IMF decision, Japan is classified as an "Article VIII country,"[3] it may be anticipated that the inflow of foreign investments will rise substantially because Japan will no longer be able to restrict the outflow of current earnings from such investments. Some transitional arrangements would be necessary to assist Japanese industries in adjusting to the new situation.

2. Contrary to some opinions, there are many weak points in the Japanese economy, and the Japanese Government considers it essential to the future economic growth of the country that foreign capital not be permitted entry on an indiscriminate basis. For this reason, the Government hopes that Japan will be enabled to continue reasonable restrictions on foreign equity investment, particularly since soundness of the Japanese economy is a matter of much concern not only to the Japanese Government but to the United States Government as well.

---

[2] For text of this treaty, signed at Tokyo on April 2, 1953, and entered into force on October 30, 1963, see 4 UST (pt. 2) 2063. Article XII requires the parties not to impose restrictions on transfers of foreign exchange except when necessary to prevent monetary reserves from "falling to a very low level" or to effect "a moderate increase in very low reserves." It sets guidelines for foreign exchange restrictions when imposed. Documents in Department of State, Central Files 611.9442 and 394.41 for the fall of 1962 indicate the interest of some Japanese officials in a revision of the FCN Treaty that would allow the parties greater power to regulate direct investment and other capital transfers.

[3] Reference is to Article VIII of the Articles of Agreement of the International Monetary Fund, signed at Washington on December 27, 1945, and effective for the United States that day. For text, see 60 Stat. (pt. 3) p. 1411. Article VIII pledges members to avoid multiple exchange rates and other restrictions on foreign exchange and to make their currencies freely convertible. Many members of the fund, including Japan, were able to join it in advance of full adherence to Article VIII.

**361.    Editorial Note**

The Second Meeting of the Joint U.S.-Japan Committee on Trade and Economic Affairs was held at Washington December 3–5, 1962.

Cabinet Ministers attending for Japan were Masayoshi Ohira, Foreign Affairs; Hajime Fukuda, International Trade and Industry; Seishi Shigemasa, Agriculture and Forestry; Kakuei Tanaka, Finance; Kiichi Miyazawa, Economic Planning; and Takeo Ohashi, Labor. Ryuji Takeuchi, Vice Minister of Foreign Affairs, and Ambassador Asakai also attended. Representing the United States were Secretary Rusk; Stewart Udall, Interior; Orville Freeman, Agriculture; Edward Gudeman, Acting Secretary of Commerce; Willard Wirtz, Labor; C. Douglas Dillon, Treasury; Walter Heller, Chairman of the Council of Economic Advisers; and Ambassador Reischauer.

Agenda topics included: review of the current economic situation in Japan and the United States; review of current financial, monetary, and balance of payments situation in Japan and the United States; economic growth in Japan and the United States; expansion of trade and promotion of economic relations between Japan and the United States; trends in international trade and economic relations; and problems of economic development in less-developed countries.

A "Scope Paper," dated November 26, states that the three main U.S. objectives at the meeting were to obtain full Japanese participation on a broad basis in the proposed GATT negotiations for tariff reductions under the new U.S. Trade Expansion Act; more substantial and meaningful progress toward full Japanese liberalization of its restrictive trade and exchange controls, with emphasis on early liberalization of commodities of importance to U.S. exporters; and increased Japanese assistance to the less-developed countries and continued improvement in the terms of such assistance. (JAE/D–22, drafted by Thelma Vettel of FE/EA; Department of State, Conference Files: Lot 65 D 533, CF 2187) For the Trade Expansion Act, approved October 11, 1962, as P.L. 87–794, see 76 Stat. 872.

Scheduling information, briefing papers, talking papers, extensive summaries of the sessions, and memoranda of conversation are in Department of State, Conference Files: Lot 65 D 533, CF 2187–2192. Additional documentation is ibid., Central File 411.9441 for November and December 1962.

In a memorandum for the file prepared on January 8, 1963, P.W. Kriebel of the Executive Secretariat wrote that "according to FE/EA the main accomplishment of the recent meetings with the Japanese was a commitment by the Japanese Cabinet to take full part in the proposed negotiations under the U.S. Trade Expansion Act." (Ibid., Conference Files: Lot 65 D 533, CF 2187)

Additional information on the meeting is in Documents 358 and 362–364. For text of the communiqué of the meeting, issued November 4, see Department of State *Bulletin*, December 24, 1962, page 959. The documents printed here should be read in conjunction with the text of the communiqué.

## 362.  Memorandum of Conversation

Washington December 3, 1962, 5:30 p.m.

SUBJECT

The Japanese Defense Effort and Military Offsets

PARTICIPANTS

The Secretary
Masayoshi Ohira, Minister of Foreign Affairs, Japan
Kakuei Tanaka, Minister of Finance, Japan
Ryuji Takeuchi, Vice Minister for Foreign Affairs, Japan
Koichiro Asakai, Ambassador, Embassy of Japan
Douglas Dillon, Secretary of the Treasury
Roswell L. Gilpatric, Deputy Secretary of Defense
Edwin O. Reischauer, American Ambassador to Japan
Leonard Lee Bacon, Deputy Director, Officer of East Asian Affairs
Michio Mizoguchi, Third Secretary, Embassy of Japan
James J. Wickel, Language Services

The Secretary remarked that there was one matter he would like to discuss in a very discreet way and not as part of the Joint Committee conference or to be mentioned in the Communiqué. It was a matter to which the President had referred at lunch today.[1] We are very much concerned about the over-all defense effort of the free world especially as it relates to Asia. While we are endeavoring to press our NATO friends to increase

---

Source: Department of State, Central Files, 794.5/12–362. Confidential. Drafted by Leonard Bacon of FE/EA; and approved in S on December 9. The conversation was held in the Secretary's Office at the Department of State.

[1] In his public remarks at the luncheon Kennedy referred to the problem of containing "the expansion of Communism in Asia, so that we do not find the Chinese moving out into a dominant position in all of Asia, with its hundreds and hundreds of millions of people in Asia, while Western Europe is building a more prosperous life for themselves." China was in a "belligerent phase" of "national development," and Kennedy expressed hope that thought could be given to what role the United States and Japan could play as "partners" to "attempt to prevent the domination of Asia by Communist movement." For text, See *Public Papers of the Presidents of the United States: John F. Kennedy, 1962*, pp. 850–851.

their efforts in Europe the threat is now growing in Asia and the resources to meet that threat are not nearly as strong as they ought to be.[2]

As we look ahead into the immediate future it appears that it is now Peiping which will pose a grave problem with respect to security in the far Pacific area. As the influence of Communist China increases it can exert more pressure through North Korea and North Viet Nam and its increasingly aggressive attitude toward India as well as the nature of its differences with the USSR all indicate a growing threat to security. If, in addition, Peiping acquires a nuclear weapons capacity—and we are fully confident they are trying to do so—the danger which now exists in the Pacific area will be immeasurably increased. We fear we must all take this threat seriously. President Kennedy, after taking office, has increased the Eisenhower defense budget almost 25 percent or $10 billion. We have 16,000 men in Southeast Asia and are taking casualties almost every week in the struggle to protect the security of that area. We might hope to obtain a test-ban treaty which could forestall Chinese development of nuclear weapons or an agreement under which other nations would not supply nuclear weapons to China. But even if we would get an international agreement calculated to forestall the Communist Chinese, there is every indication that China would under no circumstances subscribe to any such agreement. I realize these are matters on which you would want to confer with Prime Minister Ikeda because of their extreme gravity. We do wish, however, to raise the possibility of Japan increasing her defense contribution faster than is planned at present; not just because we all need all the strength we can muster, but also because such an increase would serve as a signal to Moscow and Peiping that Japan, the United States, and the free world would resist any attempt by them to embark on aggression. It would help contribute to maintaining peace while Peiping and Moscow are determining what to do.

We shall be called upon to increase our own effort overseas during this period. Governor Harriman's report of his trip to India makes it quite clear that India will require large scale assistance.

We would like to see Japan minimize the cost to the United States of the increased Japanese defense program because of the increasing major burdens the United States is now called upon to carry both internally and externally. To me personally, it is a tragedy for the United States and Japan to be obliged to discuss this problem with each other—we have

---

[2] During a luncheon discussion with Rusk on December 4 Ohira stated "that it was his personal opinion that the United States should leave Communist China alone. Making too much fuss about it only served to raise its prestige." Rusk "responded that the United States will leave the Chinese Communists alone when the Chinese Communists leave others alone. When they put pressures on India or Southeast Asia, the United States must be concerned." (Memorandum of conversation by Swayne; Department of State, Secretary's Memoranda of Conversation: Lot 65 D 330)

both been working for a world in which this problem ought not to arise. But because Moscow and Peiping present an increasingly serious danger, if we are to prevent a catastrophe we must let the other side know that their aggression cannot succeed.

I fully understand the long and special history of this subject in Japan. As a matter of fact I negotiated in 1952 the first administrative agreement relating to our defense forces in Japan. Since then I have followed this subject closely. Could you indicate what significance is accorded in Japan to these security developments in the Pacific area?

The Foreign Minister said that President Kennedy had asked him a similar question at luncheon. The Japanese know that the time has come to consider this problem separately, because apart from receiving aid from the United States Japan herself must consider her own defense. Both the Finance Minister and I replied in that sense to the President's question. In summary, up until now, it has been the Japanese view that if Japan maintains internal peace and economic stability that this self-sufficiency would in itself serve the purposes of the free world and would contribute to stabilization of countries in the Far East. But as I just said we realize the time has come for Japan to reconsider this problem. As you know, we developed our second defense plan last year under which there would be an annual increase of more than $50 million in our defense expenditures. This was done with the approval of the Finance Minister but there will be some difficulties with this plan because our original plan has not been "digested" that is, completed, as yet; consequently, there is some discrepancy between the two plans. As you know, there has been a wage increase for the self-defense forces and perhaps half of our military budget increase will be absorbed by it. Through the MAAG, the Pentagon has been gradually cutting down on its assistance to us. Therefore we must reconsider our second defense plan. At this time we must regard the problem, as the Secretary has indicated, as a most serious one. I would like to discuss it with the Finance Minister and we must ask the Prime Minister to consider it.

Minister Tanaka said he was in agreement with Minister Ohira's expression of the need to strengthen Japan's defenses. He, Tanaka, understood the problem quite well and wondered whether the United States had a proposal to make on what Japan might do. In making up the Japanese budget they would give such a proposal emphatic consideration.

The Secretary said that the United States had in mind, first, whether Japan could increase its total defense effort at a rate faster than presently planned so as to contribute to the general strength of the free nations; second, whether Japan could find a way to relieve the United States of the military assistance increments—this would be helpful at a time when we must try to increase our aid efforts in India and South Viet Nam; and third, whether Japan could find a way to take into account the local costs borne by the United States in maintaining its forces in Japan.

Since there were important matters requiring close study by both our governments, he had no wish to formulate proposals at this time, considering the great delicacy which the subject has in Japanese political life. Ambassador Reischauer could discuss later in Tokyo the details of what we have in mind. If further meetings are needed, we can hold them but we want to do this in a manner most convenient to you because of the internal political situation which we understand quite well.

The Secretary added with a smile that the President and he had not concerted to take up this matter both at lunch and here. The fact that both did so was only an indication of how much the matter was on their minds.

Secretary Dillon observed that if Japan should reach a decision to increase its defense effort we would think it possible to find various items which could be purchased in the United States more cheaply than they could be manufactured in Japan, particularly in fields such as aircraft, electronics and anti-aircraft missiles.[3] Corresponding arrangements have been made by the United States with Germany and Italy. In their negotiation the Treasury took no part, considering the Pentagon was in a better position to determine what was the best course.

Our Mutual Defense program has developed this way in Europe and one incidental effect has been to relieve our balance of payments problem. That, however, is not the approach we used in making the arrangements, which were undertaken with the intention of helping Germany and Italy. It might work the same way in Japan if we should decide to move ahead. Our Pentagon and your defense officials might well make the same type of arrangements.

Secretary Rusk commented that Prime Minister Ikeda should be briefed on the growing sophistication of weapons in Mainland China and that it would be desirable to arrange such a briefing for him.

Deputy Secretary Gilpatric wished to make two points: first, in this era of nuclear weapons there is an even greater need for conventional weapons. In increasing our own defense budget there has been a 10 percent increase for conventional arms. The Pentagon views the future threat not so much as nuclear as one involving conventional weapons—witness the recent events on the Sino-Indian frontier and in the Caribbean area. What Japan faces is not primarily a nuclear threat. There does

---

[3] According to telegram 895 to Tokyo, October 19, marked "Joint State–Defense–Treasury message," the U.S. Government tentatively hoped by a combination of reduced defense expenditures in Japan and an increase in Japanese purchases of U.S. military equipment to improve the balance of payments by $100 million in FY 1963, $200 million in FY 1964, and $300 million in FY 1965. (Ibid., Central Files, 794.5/10–1962)

exist in the free world a United States nuclear deterrent which serves all of the free nations, but in the conventional weapons field each nation should provide for some of its own defense, as Japan has done, for example, with Hawk missiles and other advanced non-nuclear weapons systems. (The Secretary here mentioned in addition anti-submarine equipment.) The Soviet Union is putting 20 percent of its military budget into conventional weapons systems and our NATO allies are pursuing a similar course. Therefore we think you need to spend more on conventional weapons.

As a second consideration, Secretary Gilpatric said, he wished to emphasize the real benefit of cooperative logistic arrangements such as had been set up with Germany and Italy—joint planning, training, and development of weapons systems. Then if we had to use the weapons for defense your weapons and ours could be used interchangeably. In the case of Germany and especially Italy we have gained over the past two years major results at a lower cost than either could have achieved alone. In the same sense your military colleagues will find that these cooperative logistic arrangements will permit our two nations to work closely toward the common purpose of national defense.

The Secretary said that the United States was not raising the possibility of Japan preparing an expeditionary force to serve outside of Japan but had in mind only the question of the defense of Japan, Even that, however, is a problem. In 1954 the United States had a practical monopoly of nuclear weapons, under which we could always say that if Japan is the victim of aggression the United States will retaliate. Now the other side also has the means of delivery, in Asia as well as in Europe. A nuclear exchange is not a defense operation we would want to undertake. Consequently the separate threat of superiority in conventional weapons means that Japan is in effect held a hostage while China moves in Southeast Asia and elsewhere. Therefore he wanted a review for the Prime Minister of the changes in the past 4 or 5 years. The Secretary regretted that he had no words of comfort to give the Finance Minister, Mr. Tanaka, except to point out that Secretary Dillon himself is facing a $7 billion deficit while Secretary Gilpatric is taking $10 billion more for the defense budget.

Vice Minister Takeuchi asked whether the Japanese military had been briefed on the new development of sophisticated weapons on the mainland. The Secretary said that the subject had not been previously raised with the Japanese Government. Minister Takeuchi pointed out that if Prime Minister were briefed on such a technical subject he would have to seek advice of his military advisors. Secretary Rusk agreed that the Prime Minister would certainly wish to consult Director-General Shiga of the Defense Agency.

It was agreed that the conversation would not be considered a part of the Joint Committee conference and would not figure in the record of the conference; and that there should be no disclosure that any substantive conversations at all had been held.

## 363.  Memorandum of Conversation

Washington, December 4, 1962, 1 p.m.

SUBJECT

Japanese Copper Ore Purchases; Trade Liberalization by Japan; Trade Expansion Act

PARTICIPANTS

Mr. Hajime Fukuda, Minister of International Trade and Industry
Mr. Akira Nishiyama, Minister, Embassy of Japan
Mr. Keiichi Matsumura, Director, Bureau of International Trade, Ministry of International Trade and Industry
Mr. Tetsuro Ohata, Commercial Counselor, Embassy of Japan
Mr. Akira Harada, Bureau of International Trade, Minister of International Trade and Industry
Mr. Michiyoshi Kawada, Commercial Secretary, Embassy of Japan
Mr. Makoto Watanabe, Attaché, Embassy of Japan

Mr. Edward Gudeman, Acting Secretary of Commerce
Mr. Clarence D. Martin, Under Secretary of Commerce
Mr. Jack N. Behrman, Assistant Secretary of Commerce for Domestic and International Business
Mr. Eugene M. Braderman, Director, Bureau of International Commercial Affairs
Mr. Richard Holton, Economic Advisor to the Secretary of Commerce
Mr. Saul Baran, Director, Far Eastern Division, Bureau of International Commerce
Mr. John S. Stillman, Deputy to the Under Secretary
Mr. Robert M. Klein, Chief, Japan-Korea Section, Far Eastern Division
Mr. John F. Knowles, Department of State

A friendly and relaxed atmosphere prevailed throughout the luncheon. The only specific problem discussed at significant length concerned the American side's request that Japan take action to relieve the distress of American copper smelting companies.[1] Minister Fukuda said he had not been aware of this problem, promising to look into it and try

---

Source: Department of State, Central Files, 411.9441/12–462. Confidential. Drafted by John F. Knowles of EA/J.

[1] Documentation on this problem is ibid., 494.004, 494.006, 494.42, and 894.2542 for 1961 and 1962.

and do something upon his return to Tokyo. Otherwise, discussion of a substantive nature focussed upon the American desire that Japan take further action to liberalize trade and the Japanese desire for information on American trade policy and how it would be implemented in the future.

[Here follows discussion of Japanese purchase of copper ores and concentrates.]

*United States Foreign Trade Policy and Trade Liberalization by Japan*

As the luncheon began, Secretary Gudeman alluded briefly to the investment made by Bell and Howell in a Japanese firm as an example of mutually beneficial American investment in Japan.

A question from Fukuda about pictures on the wall of vintage American automobiles led to some discussion of automobile prices in Japan and Japanese duties on imports of American cars, particularly on compacts as compared with the German Volkswagen. Secretary Gudeman took the opportunity of casually pointing out that American car imports are one item which the United States would like Japan to liberalize. Fukuda responded by citing the narrow and congested condition of Japanese roads as one reason why Japan is restricting American car imports. In response to a question from Fukuda, Matsumura said that American compacts are being imported by Japan and commented that the base price of American compacts is higher than that of the Volkswagen. Assistant Secretary Behrman observed that the American compact is placed in a higher domestic Japanese tax category than the Volkswagen. Fukuda then expressed, in Japanese, some doubt to Matsumura as to the reasonableness of the Japanese policy of determining the automobile tax on the basis of horsepower.

In offering a toast at the end of the luncheon, Secretary Gudeman emphasized the American belief that trade and economic relations should be viewed as having two aspects: short-range and long-range. There is often a conflict between the two, exemplified at present by the measures which the United States feels obliged to take in view of its balance of payments problem. The Trade Expansion Act, on the other hand, is an example of long-range United States policy. The United States is aware of Japan's disagreement with short-range United States policies in such areas as the Buy American policy, shipping, and textiles but hopes Japan will understand why these policies have had to be adopted. The United States and Japan each wish the other to be its leading customer. Both countries have a common interest in freer trade as the means of achieving higher standards of living and have a common interest in partnership vis-à-vis the totalitarian world.

Fukuda, in his toast, said the relationship between Japan and the United States is such that the two countries cannot be separated, whatever happens. Japanese deeply regret Pearl Harbor and are very grateful for the generosity which the United States showed, in spite of Pearl Harbor, during the Occupation of Japan. Japan, he said, well knows how much the Japanese economy depends upon the United States. He shares Secretary Gudeman's view of the importance for the future of cooperation between the two countries in order to raise standards of living. Regardless of problems existing between Japan and the United States at present, they do not and ought not interfere with United States-Japan friendship and with their long-term relations.

In the discussion which followed the luncheon, Secretary Gudeman offered to answer any questions the Japanese might have regarding the Trade Expansion Act. Fukuda then asked to what extent adjustment assistance would be provided to American companies. Secretary Gudeman pointed out that this is a new law and that negotiations under the Act with foreign countries have not as yet begun. It is our hope, he said, that any adjustments in the United States will be made under the trade adjustment part of the Act rather than through increases in tariffs. We recognize that higher tariffs protect the least efficient manufacturers and for this reason the new law contains no peril point provision, unlike previous legislation. We also recognize that, to a degree as yet unknown, certain American companies will be hurt by the negotiation of lower tariffs. Companies which are injured through the action of the United States Government and not through any action of their own must be given assistance. Assistance to labor, such as labor retraining programs, is the responsibility of the Department of Labor. The Department of Commerce is responsible for assistance to business and is all ready for the problem when it arises, having put a man on the staff 6–7 months ago to study methods of assistance.

Assistant Secretary Behrman pointed out that there are many in the American business community who do not like the system of adjustment assistance provided for by the Act. They can be expected to press for higher tariffs. In this connection, the Japanese should be aware that the new Act provides for an industry-wide investigation whenever one company appeals for a rise in tariff. Japanese should not be concerned when they hear of such investigations because it is the final decision, and not the investigation, which truly reflects current United States trade policy.

Secretary Gudeman then described the steps whereby the Tariff Commission investigates an appeal for a higher tariff and submits a recommendation to the President who makes the final decision whether or not to change a tariff or, alternatively, to provide adjustment assistance under the Act. Mr. Braderman then emphasized to the Japanese guests his observation over twelve years that Japanese concern over protectionism in the United States has been sparked by sensational and inaccurate

Japanese press reports of Tariff Commission recommendations and not by the final decisions that were taken.

Minister Fukuda replied by saying that Japan is prepared to cooperate in the implementation of the Trade Expansion Act. He wished, however, to reiterate one point; namely, the cooperation of the maximum number of countries would be needed in order to realize the purpose of the Act to the fullest extent. He understood the principle of expanding trade on the basis of lower tariffs and higher consumption. The United States should recognize, however, that the various countries have different problems according to their stage of economic development. In this connection, he referred to Japan as being in the category of middle development. In illustration, he suggested the possible analogy of the movement of a fleet wherein the pace must be set by the slowest ship and not by the fastest in order that the fleet move together. He hoped the United States would give further study to this point in its implementation of the Act.

Secretary Gudeman responded with the hope that Japan would liberalize its view of worldwide trade and jokingly accused Minister Fukuda of not giving due credit to Japan in placing Japan in the category of middle development.

Assistant Secretary Behrman observed that there are times when a country can benefit from unilateral tariff concessions; namely, under conditions of full employment and a worldwide growth in trade. The United States intends to lead the world toward a worldwide reduction in tariffs but, since it has problems of its own, it is not in a position to lead without assistance from other countries.

---

### 364.   Telegram From the Department of State to the Embassy in Japan

Washington, December 5, 1962, 9:09 a.m.

1062. Joint ECONCOM. Based on uncleared memo of conversation.[1] Discussions second day of conference continued in atmosphere of candor and friendliness.

---

Source: Department of State, Central Files, 411.9441/12–562. Confidential; Limit Distribution. Drafted by Vettel and approved by Yager.

[1] Two papers drafted by Fearey record the material summarized in this telegram. JAE/R–10 covers Agenda Item IV, "Expansion of Trade and Promotion of Economic Relations between Japan and the U.S," discussed the morning of December 4. JAE/R–15 records the afternoon discussion of Item V, "Trends in International Trade and Economic Relations." (Both ibid., Conference Files: Lot 65 D 533, CF 2191)

1. *Agenda Item IV.* In prepared statement MITI Minister Fukuda emphasized various restraints on Japanese trade. Cited voluntary controls and variety of means by which US can "restrict" imports. Observed real question is what attitude of USG will be, characterizing example of blouses and trousers as indication of USG reaction to industry pressures which distressing to Japanese. Welcomed Trade Expansion Act. Noting apparent US dissatisfaction with Japanese liberalization, pointing to rapid pace of liberalization and to difficulties faced by Japan because of small scale and dual nature of economy, underemployment, relatively low level of technology, etc. Said Japan endeavoring to diversify markets to avoid undue concentration on single market but cited European QR's and limitations of LDC markets as difficulties. Referring to recent European countries agreement disinvoke Article XXXV[2] pointed to "safeguards" requested in return. Requested US support for Japanese efforts.

MAF Minister Shigemasa reviewed nature Japanese agriculture and fishery industries citing difficulties in expanding and diversifying agricultural production. Stated agricultural and fishery commodities 74 percent liberalized. Emphasized importance of Japan as the leading market for US agriculture (paying cash) and expectation of its further growth. Expressed Japanese intention to cooperate in conservation and development of marine resources but stressed Japanese concern over Bartlett Amendment.

Commerce Acting Secretary Gudeman discussed scope and extent of US market, Japanese complaints of "protectionism" in US, Tariff Reclassification Act,[3] US dedication to freer trade.[4]

Interior Secretary Udall made statement on trade and investment in natural resources. Cited recent Reclamation Bureau purchases from Mitsubishi and Hitachi. Pointed out opportunities for Japanese investment in resources of US giving examples. Expressed hope both countries can continue cooperation in conservation of marine resources. Cited large Japanese fish product exports to US.

In prepared statement Agriculture Secretary Freeman emphasized need for reduction of trade barriers. Stated US has fewer protections of farmer than most countries. Emphasized US efforts make effective use of abundance of food (e.g. Food for Peace) but pointed out limitations on use of food in economic development. Observed that in passing TEA Congress stressed its use to gain improved access to foreign markets for

---

[2] For text of this Article of the GATT, see 62 Stat. (pt. 2) 1994.

[3] For the Tariff Classification Act of 1962, P.L. 87–456, approved on May 24, 1962, see 76 Stat. 72.

[4] In Gudeman's prepared statement the perceived inadequacies of the Japanese import liberalization program received an analysis similar to that in Document 366. The statement is in Department of State, Conference Files: Lot 65 D 533, CF 2187.

US farm products. Pointed out that US is world's second largest agricultural importer and one-half of $4 billion US agricultural imports compete directly with US products. Expressed hope that problem of import of Kobe beef could be solved by early 1963. While mandarin orange problem more difficult US working on it. Said US supported GATT sponsored conference in early 1963 to develop international grain agreement and sought Japan's support. Pointed out, however, such agreements did not constitute panacea.

*Discussion.* In response to Gudeman statement Fukuda said Japan would like to act on liberalization in accordance US views. Agreed with Gudeman that voluntary controls had benefited Japan by avoiding clash of interest with US. But would hope voluntary controls could be gradually relaxed. Re TEA said if only tariffs reduced while other restrictions (QR's and voluntary controls) remain Japan could see little hope of expanded trade.

Ohira requested on behalf of absent Minister of Transportation that US give careful consideration to Japanese statements re shipping and aviation problems.

In response to Fukuda's request Udall said present outlook for tobacco-ferroalloy barter not good in view present status US stockpile.

In response to Fukuda's question re possibility US would propose long-term woolen fabric arrangement, Secretary said we had reached no decision to request such an agreement. Gudeman added that we are pressed, however, for some relief for short term.

2. *Agenda Item V.* (afternoon December 4)

Under Secretary Ball made initial statement this item. Characterizing present free world situation as process of redrawing trade patterns and habits involving development of EEC itself, inclusion of UK (followed by 2 to 4 Scandinavian countries) and resultant realignment of trade of Commonwealth countries, stressed need for initiative by other trading nations, particularly US, Canada and Japan to bring about redrawing of trade lines before restrictive patterns become solidified. US initiative through enactment TEA can be effective only if all work together to reduce trade barriers. US hopes begin consultations early 1963 with Japan and other trading countries in preparation for formal negotiations. Stressed US intention to negotiate across the board on broad categories and urged Japanese participation on that basis. Stressed importance rapid removal of QR's during preparatory year (1963), including disinvocation Article XXXV by European countries and Japan's movement toward greater liberalization in manufactured as well as raw materials. Congratulated Japan on Ikeda's success in Europe. Discussed development of OECD and Japan's relationship thereto. Said US has told European members we look forward to Japan's full OECD membership. Said we look forward to expanding role and full membership for Japan soon as possible (in his view should be realized before too long) and assured Japanese US feels strongly this matter and will do all we can to bring it about.

Ohira reviewed Japan's general trade problems emphasizing LDC's foreign exchange shortage and consequent need expand Japan's trade with US and Europe. Characterized results of Ikeda visit as encouraging re expansion of trade with Europe but not optimistic re removal discrimination against Japan. Said to extent possible Japan would participate in across the board negotiations and consider liberalization of remaining items. Said on many items of interest to Japan would prefer removal other restrictions rather than tariff reductions.

In response to Ohira's questions Ball said US equally concerned that EEC be outward looking and we would exert every effort to see that its policies nondiscriminatory. Responded re difference between OECD and GATT. Re questions on "restrictive" provisions TEA Ball said this Act most liberal ever enacted in US stressing choice given President as to remedies which may be applied. Said he could not envisage situation where US would accord anything but MFN treatment to Japan.

In response to Secretary's question regarding Japan's willingness participate in across the board negotiations Fukuda said unable to answer without further study. At Miyazawa's urging Fukuda explained nature and place in Japanese economy of small and medium sized industry and difficulty presented by US objective of 50 percent tariff reduction over 5 years with only 10 percent reservation. Also said Japanese industry does not have access to assistance such as trade adjustment provision of TEA. Therefore matter required further study.

Ohira interposed to say there no doubt Japan willing to participate.[5]

Further discussion Items IV and V deferred to December 5.[6]

**Rusk**

---

[5] JAE/R–15 reports Fukuda as saying "at this meeting I can say that we will cooperate with you, but I cannot positively say under what terms and conditions and by what methodology, pending a little more study and investigation." JAE/R–15 also indicates Tanaka added his assurances of Japanese participation in an across-the-board tariff reduction to Ohira's.

[6] According to telegram 1072 to Tokyo, December 6, there was no further discussion of Items IV and V in the concluding day of the meeting; instead the Committee considered Agenda Item VI on foreign aid. (Department of State, Central Files, 411.9441/ 12–662)

### 365.   Memorandum From the Joint Chiefs of Staff to Secretary of Defense McNamara

JCSM–967–62                                              Washington, December 7, 1962.

SUBJECT

US Bases in Japan (U)

1.   Reference is made to your memorandum, dated 1 October 1962,[1] subject as above, in which you requested the views of the Joint Chiefs of Staff on the role of US bases in Japan in peacetime, and in sub-limited, limited, and general war.

2.   The Joint Chiefs of Staff have examined the role of these bases in peacetime and in the various conditions of war. The results of this examination are detailed in the Appendix hereto.[2] It is concluded that the principal roles of US bases in Japan are as follows:

a.   Essential to the maintenance of the US deterrent posture in the Far East; required for the support of the US position in Korea; permit rapid tactical deployment of forces in the Western Pacific.

b.   Provide primary logistic support to the entire Far East area and key repair facilities not available elsewhere in the area.

c.   Provide essential intelligence gathering and reporting facilities and opportunities, as well as communications for command and control.

d.   Provide facilities in northeast Asia necessary to maintain and support the SIOP posture.

e.   Provide dispersion of stocks and bases for projection of residual power after an initial nuclear exchange.

f.   Complicate the Soviet nuclear targeting problem.

g.   Provide an important link in the maintenance and improvement of US-Japanese political, economic, and military relations.

3.   In examining the desirability of retaining the Japanese bases, the unfavorable aspects of their continued use, as set forth hereinafter, must be weighed against the disadvantages associated with a withdrawal therefrom. The most important of these are:

a.   It would reduce the forward strategy deterrent posture in the Far East with possible attendant loss of confidence by US Allies and non-aligned neutrals.

---

Source: Washington National Records Center, RG 330, OSD/ISA Files: FRC 65 A 3501, 680.1 Japan 7 December 62. Top Secret. Attached to a December 17 memorandum to the President in which Gilpatric noted his concurrence "in the judgment of the Joint Chiefs of Staff that U.S. strategic interests require the retention of our bases in Japan in essentially their present status," described the U.S. proposal to Japan set forth in Document 362, and stated that the next steps would be taken by himself or McNamara during a trip to Japan in January or February. See Document 368.

[1] See Document 356.

[2] See the Supplement.

b. A victory would result for neutralist forces in Japan and for the Communist world-wide drive against US overseas bases with concomitant unfavorable effect on our Allies.

c. Dispersal of forces which Japan now affords would be lost.

d. The Japanese commitment on military force levels would be jeopardized and a neutral Japan could result.

e. The ability of military forces to operate in northeast Asia and contiguous waters would be significantly reduced, particularly their capability to react quickly to contingency situations.

f. The logistic and combat support of Korea would be extremely difficult.

g. Japanese repair facilities and skilled Japanese labor now available would be lost.

h. The cost of replacing the present extensive facilities in Japan in other areas would be very great.

i. The only large-capacity industrial base in the Far East would not be available for the support of US forces.

j. Long lines of communication and difficulties in obtaining real estate and base rights complicate the relocation of these bases to other areas.

4. Although, as indicated above, there are a number of important reasons for the maintenance of US bases in Japan, there are also factors which affect the continued maintenance of these bases. The most important of these are:

a. US bases in Japan are vulnerable to strikes by those Japanese laborers who are Communist-controlled and the capabilities of the bases might thus be impaired when they are most needed.

b. The introduction of nuclear weapons into Japan has not been politically feasible and the prospects of their introduction in peacetime are not promising.

c. The cost of maintaining US bases in Japan results in a continuing unfavorable balance of military payments.

d. The Japanese have demonstrated apathy toward shouldering the obligations for their own defense.

e. The Japanese Security Treaty restricts the deployment of US forces to combat areas without "prior consultation." This could be a serious limitation on the usefulness of the bases, particularly in limited war where the vital interests of the Japanese were not involved.

5. The Joint Chiefs of Staff believe the US bases in Japan contribute significantly to the over-all strategic US posture in the Pacific. On balance, they conclude that the reasons for maintaining these bases outweigh the factors militating against their retention. If a major change were made in US strategy for the Far East, then it might be possible to reduce bases in Japan.

6. It is the judgment of the Joint Chiefs of Staff that US strategic interest requires the retention of the US bases in Japan in essentially their present status.

For the Joint Chiefs of Staff:
**Maxwell D. Taylor**[3]
*Chairman*
*Joint Chiefs of Staff*

---

[3] Printed from a copy that indicates Taylor signed the original.

---

### 366. Airgram From the Embassy in Japan to the Department of State

A-827                                                    Tokyo, December 28, 1962.

SUBJECT

Japan's Import Liberalization: Further Steps

With the removal of import quota restrictions on 230 items on October 1, 1962, the Government of Japan came within two percentage points of the 90% liberalization target which it had committed itself to attain by that date. A further slight gain was registered on November 21, with the liberalization of an additional eight items. Since the 68% liberalization level at the time of the first meeting of the US-Japan Committee on Economics and Trade in November 1961, successive transfers from the restrictive Fund Allocation System have shifted some 728 items to the Automatic Fund Allocation System or to the Automatic Approval list. Two hundred and fifty-four (254) items remain unliberalized.

Despite the substantial progress indicated above, Japan still maintains a greater degree of import restrictions than any other major trading nation in the Free World. The measure of liberalization employed by the Government of Japan, through the bias of a weighting system based on

---

Source: Department of State, Central Files, 494.0012/12–2862. Official Use Only. Drafted by Andrew B. Wardlaw, Commercial Attaché; Millard L. Gallop, Commercial Officer; and Clyde R. Keaton, an attaché in the Agricultural Section.

1959 imports, seriously understates the proportion of import trade still subject to quota restrictions. A somewhat more realistic measure of the relative importance of the restricted sector of imports is given by the proportion of the most recent commodity import budget under the Fund Allocation System. For the period October 1, 1962—March 31, 1963, 26% of the commodity import budget falls under FA control.

Although Japan has made some progress in the liberalization of manufactured goods, many of the manufactured items which offer the greatest possibilities to American exporters remain on the Negative List. In some of these cases, import license can often be obtained fairly readily, but in others licenses are not obtainable at all or only with much difficulty. It is obvious that in general the remaining controls offer a substantial impediment to American exports.[1]

[Here follows a detailed description of the degree of import restriction on items on which the Embassy had previously made representations, together with suggestions for future representations.]

For the Ambassador:
**A.Z. Gardiner**
*Minister for Economic Affairs*

---

[1] Among the items listed in the portion of the airgram not printed as being still subject to heavy quotas and other import restrictions were bulldozers; turbines, compressors and some other heavy machinery items; digital computers, typewriters and electric cash registers; color film; antibiotics and most insulins; automobiles; industrial and chemical testing equipment; private aircraft; and a wide variety of agricultural products such as fresh lemons, hog and cattle breeding stock, nonfat dry milk, and fruit juices.

### 367. Memorandum From the Assistant Secretary of State for Far Eastern Affairs (Harriman) to Secretary of State Rusk

Washington, December 28, 1962.

SUBJECT

Japanese Budget Provision for Assistance to Ryukyus[1]

The following information is for use in your discussions at 11:00 today with Secretary McNamara.[2]

The GOJ on December 6 proposed a list of projects totalling $5.1 million to be included in the budget (for the fiscal year to begin April 1), for presentation to the Diet, in assistance to the Ryukyus. (This was a reduction from $7.7 million contemplated earlier, which Ambassador Reischauer believed to be too much above the figure the High Commissioner would regard as acceptable.)

On December 27 the High Commissioner made counter-proposals which would have had the effect of reducing the total to about $4.7 million.[3] This was to be achieved by eliminating a proposed mental hospital; reducing a public housing program; and cutting down projects for training and technical assistance. A Japanese offer of alternative projects was made and rejected, as HICOM was not prepared to accept the overall figure of $5.1 million. Since the Japanese budget must be ready for presentation December 29, the Embassy asked for instructions to be sent niact (Tab A—Tokyo's 1529).[4]

We felt that the US Government should not get into disagreement with the GOJ by obstructing Japanese generosity to Okinawans, thereby

---

Source: Department of State, Central Files, 794C.0221/12–2862. Confidential. Drafted by Rice.

[1] Before U.S.-Japanese discussions on aid to the Ryukyus resumed on November 2, the Embassy recommended in telegram 1000, October 5, that the proposal for a 5-year aid plan be dropped and that the discussions resume on the basis of annual consultations. An October 15 memorandum from Yager to U. Alexis Johnson indicates that this suggestion was accepted. (Telegram 1000 is attached to the October 15 memorandum; ibid., 794C.0221/10–1562)

[2] No memorandum of this discussion has been found, but see footnote 7 below.

[3] According to a December 31 letter from First Secretary of Embassy, James S. Sutterlin to Fearey, General Caraway's basic reason for wanting to limit the Japanese contribution "was his continuing fear that a Japanese program which was above the 2 to 1 ratio foreseen for US and Japanese aid would seriously jeopardize U.S. administrative authority in the Ryukyus." (Department of State, Central Files, 794C.0221/12–362)

[4] Dated December 28; in it Reischauer strongly recommended the $5.1 million figure because to lower it would render the "U.S. again vulnerable to charges both in Okinawa and Japan of seeking restrict Japanese 'generosity.'" $5.1 million was less than half of what the United States would request for FY 1964, and "we have had remarkable success in conveying impression in Japan that U.S. wishes cooperate with GOJ on Okinawa and welcomes GOJ aid." This positive factor would be jeopardized if the United States insisted on a further reduction. (Ibid., 894.0094C/12–2862)

negating a cooperative relationship envisaged in the President's program for the Ryukyus established last March. At about 8 P.M. last night we consulted Mr. Kaysen, who promised White House support for this position. We accordingly instructed Ambassador Reischauer to inform the GOJ we accept the $5.1 million budget figure, adding that some modification might be necessary in respect of individual proposed projects within that total (Tab B—Deptel 1184).[5]

The Congress approved $6.9 million for US aid to Okinawa in FY 1963 and we are asking for $12 million in FY 1964 which overlaps nine months of the Japanese fiscal year in question.[6] In addition we are in the final stages of negotiating a three year $18 million PL 480 Title IV (loan capital) agreement with the Government of the Ryukyus.

*Recommendation:*

We recommend you support the thesis that a Japanese contribution of $5.1 million is in the US interest, and that the High Commissioner should be instructed to accept projects totalling that amount from among those already agreed to plus others to be negotiated.[7]

---

[5] Not printed. (Ibid.)

[6] At this time the U.S. Government's fiscal year began on July 1, while Japan's began on April 1.

[7] Telegram 1188 to Tokyo, December 28, reported that Rusk had raised the matter with McNamara that morning and that the latter had "agreed that we should not get into argument with GOJ over $400,000 but should accept $5.1 million aid offer." (Ibid.)

---

### 368.    Memorandum From the Deputy Secretary of Defense (Gilpatric) to President Kennedy

Washington, February 8, 1963.

SUBJECT

U.S./Japanese Defense Relationships

In my memorandum to you to December 17, 1962,[1] I referred to the proposal, which Secretaries Rusk and Dillon broached to Foreign Minis-

---

Source: Department of State, Central Files, ORG 7 OSD. Secret. Attached to a copy of Document 369.

[1] See the source note, Document 365.

ter Ohira last December, that either Mr. McNamara or I visit Tokyo early this year for the purpose of briefing high Japanese officials on the military threat to the Japan area and of raising the question of how to solve the U.S. balance of payments problem arising out of its military expenditures in Japan. In accordance with arrangements worked out by Ambassador Reischauer, I met with Prime Minister Ikeda and Foreign Minister Ohira in Japan on February 6–7.[2] The attached memorandum, which was reviewed and approved by the Japanese Foreign Office, summarizes the discussions which took place at those meetings.

You will note from the memorandum that Prime Minister Ikeda and Foreign Minister Ohira specifically agreed to the following two positions:

1. The importance of increasing the Japanese defense budget; and

2. The desirability of establishing a defense study group, within the framework of the Security Consultative Committee, to pursue our further defense cooperation, including the study of balance of payments effects on our respective foreign exchange expenditures.

Based on these discussions and my own assessment of the Japanese/U.S. defense relationships, it is my conclusion that the objective of entirely offsetting the present U.S. adverse balance of military expenditures in Japan, now running at well over $300 million a year, through the purchase by the Japanese of U.S. military equipment is unlikely of achievement in the near future, primarily for two reasons:

1. The increase in the Japanese defense budget to a level which would permit any large-scale purchasing of U.S. equipment will take a period of years because of the necessity for creating political support by the Japanese people for a sharp acceleration of its defense buildup.

2. Even were the necessary funds available to the Japanese defense authorities, there may not be a sufficient amount of U.S. military hardware that the Japanese are likely to purchase to offset our total expenditures. Much of the materiel they need can be supplied out of indigenous production. For example, since the Japanese do not require sophisticated or high performance aircraft they can produce their own fighter and transport planes with the technology they presently possess. Similarly their shipyards are capable of designing and constructing patrol craft, minesweepers and small submarines, the only naval vessels which are planned for the Japanese maritime defense forces. Only for such advanced antiaircraft missile systems as Nike–Ajax, Nike–Hercules and Hawk and electronic gear for ground environment ACW Systems have the Japanese turned to U.S. sources. Consideration of price has not been a

---

[2] A lengthy review of Gilpatric's visit is contained in airgram A–1195 from Tokyo, February 20; a set of memoranda of his conversations during the trip is in airgram A–1215, February 25. (Both Department of State, Central Files, ORG 7 OSD)

major factor in Japanese procurement planning in the past. Thus, much of their local production is at prices far in excess of U.S. production costs. If it does become a factor in the future as a result of greater demands on their budget, there may be a larger potentiality for Japanese procurement in the U.S. This possibility, however, cannot be expected to have an effect on the procurement level in the immediate future.

Accordingly, under existing circumstances the fastest way that I see for the U.S. to reduce or eliminate its current adverse balance of military expenditures in Japan would be through a series of additional measures, of which the following are examples, aimed at cutting down U.S. dollar outlays in Japan:

1.  Decreasing the numbers of Air Force personnel and dependents in Japan by rotating, instead of permanently stationing, the U.S. tactical units now in Japan or by repositioning those units in a dollar area such as Okinawa;

2.  Transferring to the U.S. the home-porting in Japan of naval vessels whose crews with their families now are on permanent station in Japan;

3.  Thinning out the present Army logistics base in Japan by returning to the continental U.S. support units that would not be needed there prior to D-day; and,

4.  Removing, transferring to the Japanese, the depot operation now used for MAP support in Japan.

Such measures, while reducing the U.S. gold flow to Japan, would undoubtedly increase the U.S. military budget and might impair the capabilities and readiness of U.S. forces in the Far East.

A possible alternative course of action for reducing U.S. defense expenditures in Japan would be through a major redeployment of U.S. forces there. This step, however, could lead to the loss of our U.S. bases in Japan which, in the judgment of the Joint Chiefs of Staff, should be retained in their present status barring a major change in U.S. strategy for the Far East.

In the light of the foregoing analysis of the Japanese situation, it appears that we should revise our goals there as follows:

1. We should continue our efforts to persuade the Japanese Government, as rapidly as possible within the political realities that it faces, to increase its defense budget and at the same time to develop those elements of a cooperative logistics plan which would serve to maximize the offsetting of our defense expenditures through Japanese military procurement in the U.S. and sharing of U.S. facilities in Japan. Realistic military sales/cooperative logistics goals for offset would be $50 million for FY 64, $100 million for FY 65, and $150 million for FY 66.

2. We should redouble our efforts to find ways and means of reducing the balance of payments costs of U.S. military forces in Japan short of a major redeployment of forces. Such efforts would be aimed at achieving a $50 million reduction in FY 64, $100 million in FY 65, and $150 million in FY 66. These actions will undoubtedly affect military readiness and therefore the options available to us to accomplish this end should be carefully considered, along with the recommendations of the Joint Chiefs of Staff, before selecting the particular actions to achieve these goals.

With your approval, we will press forward on the following line of action to meet the above objectives:

1. The State Department will be requested to follow up on my discussions immediately for the establishment of a bilateral defense study group which will consider all aspects of our cooperative defense program including those related to balance of payments. This group would include representatives from Defense, State and Treasury and appropriate Japanese

2. The Defense Department will undertake an analysis of options available to us, by priority, to achieve the U.S. support reductions required to meet the above stated goals.

3. The Defense Department will develop an analysis of Japan's defense force missions throughout the period 1964–70 and related modernization requirements as a basis for future bilateral discussions. This analysis will include suggested goals for an accelerated Japanese buildup program and a plan of cooperative logistics including sales designed to achieve the FY 64–66 desired offset goals.

4. The Defense Department, in conjunction with State and Treasury, will aim at another series of meetings with the Japanese Government by April, hoping to achieve more specific commitments from the Japanese prior to their '64 budget cycle which starts in the fall of '63.

**Roswell Gilpatric**

Attachment[3]

Tokyo, February 7, 1963.

MEMORANDUM

I.

In my meetings with the Prime Minister and the Foreign Minister of Japan to review with them in behalf of the President of the United States the general status of international security affairs and the defense of the United States and Japan, I made the following points as reflecting the thinking of the United States Government:

—The security of the United States and Japan is a matter of mutual concern to both nations. Unity in developing and maintaining such security over the long run requires a coordinated effort by each nation in a manner commensurate with its political and economic posture in the world.

—Japan is one of the most vital strategic centers of the world and as such is a target for Communist attack of both a direct and an indirect nature. A Japan inadequately defended against Communist air or naval blockade might lose much of its independence and could be utilized to project Communist power decisively into the Pacific.

—The nuclear power of the U.S. should serve to deter any Communist atomic attack on Japan. However, Soviet and Chinese Communist conventional military forces, including submarines and aircraft, are deployed around waters and land immediately contiguous to Japan. Such forces represent Communist ability to test the strength and resolution of Japan and the U.S. to resist Communist attempts to dominate Japan through limited and conventional means of warfare.

—Japan's own self defense, as well as its need to back up its political and economic posture in the world with greater defensive power, make it increasingly necessary that Japan develop as a stronger member of the U.S./Japan partnership.

—An expanded Japan/U.S. defense system of cooperation in all matters related to defense and logistic support activities in Japan should be developed. This system of cooperation can be built on the foundations of the existing mutual security agreements and on the close associations previously developed with Japanese authorities.

—It is hoped that a defense study group composed of representatives of both governments will be set up to advise their political execu-

---

[3] Confidential.

tives of both immediate and long term actions which can be taken to develop this system of defense cooperation. Such advice would cover force missions, force requirements, equipment, supporting facilities, supply sources, cost and timing.

—It is recognized that defense strength rests on the economic health of both nations. In addition to the other very great costs of maintaining the United States defense posture in and around Japan, over the past ten years we have spent more than $7 billion in procurement by U.S. forces of Japanese equipment, material and services. At the present time, balance of payments has become an economic problem of great significance to both nations. It is therefore hoped that Japan and the U.S. will strive to equalize each other's defense foreign exchange expenditures through reciprocal procurement or barter programs or take other actions designed to minimize the balance of payments effects of the U.S./Japan defense partnership.

—The United States Government recognizes that defense expenditures are a problem of particular political sensitivity in Japan and that it would be politically infeasible for Japan to attempt to equal the 9-1/2 percent of the gross national product that the United States devotes to defense expenditures or even the somewhat smaller percentages attained by our major European allies. We do, however, believe that it would not be unrealistic for the Government of Japan to aim at an appreciable acceleration of its defense buildup.

## II.

In my conversations with the Prime Minister and Foreign Minister they assured me that they were in agreement with the points I had made and were themselves determined to build up Japanese defense capabilities to the maximum that political and economic conditions in Japan would permit. Specifically we agreed on the following two positions:

1. The importance of increasing the Japanese defense budget;

2. The desirability of establishing a defense study group within the framework of the Security Consultative Committee to pursue our further defense cooperation, including the study of balance of payments effects on our respective foreign exchange expenditures.

**Roswell Gilpatric**

### 369. Letter From Secretary of State Rusk to the Deputy Secretary of Defense (Gilpatric)

Washington, February 25, 1963.

DEAR ROS: Thank you for your letter of February 8, 1963,[1] enclosing a copy of a memorandum to the President setting forth the conclusions reached during your recent meetings in Tokyo.

I am pleased to learn that your visit to Tokyo went so well. Ambassador Reischauer shares your belief that substantial progress has been made in our efforts to stimulate a greater Japanese defense effort.[2] I believe the decision to form a defense study group holds particular promise, and we are already working to establish it. I understand it is your intention that the additional series of meetings mentioned in the final paragraph of your memorandum to the President would be held in this forum.

I believe our efforts so far have demonstrated that we must approach the objective of greater military offsets in Japan by going back to fundamentals—agreeing on the threat and developing therefrom missions, then requirements, then equipment lists, from which will finally emerge opportunities for sales of U.S. military materiel easing our balance of payments situation. The defense study group should be an ideal forum for this approach.

The Department of State would of course wish to be consulted about any significant alteration in the U.S. military posture in Japan. As Ambassador Reischauer has pointed out,[3] reductions producing even relatively small balance of payments savings might severely undermine the confidence of Japan in our determination to maintain strong defenses in the Far East, and thus weaken its desire to maintain its Free World alignment.

Finally, I think it should be borne in mind that Japan represents a highly favorable market for United States civilian exports. The principal limiting factor to steadily expanding United States civilian exports to Japan will continue to be Japan's ability to earn the foreign exchange nec-

---

Source: Kennedy Library, National Security Files, Countries Series, Japan, 2/63. Drafted by Kingdon W. Swayne of EA/J and cleared in FE/EA, U, and G/PM. Attached to a covering note from Brubeck to McGeorge Bundy, February 25.

[1] Document 368.

[2] Telegram 1848 from Tokyo, February 8. (Department of State, Central Files, DEF 1 JAPAN)

[3] In telegram 1904 from Tokyo, February 14. (Ibid.)

essary to pay for them.[4] This element in our economic relations with Japan should be kept in mind as we deal with the balance of payments drain associated with our forces there.[5]

With warm regards,
Sincerely,

**Dean**[6]

---

[4] Dillon, who had received a copy of this letter, stated in a March 8 letter to Rusk that this paragraph implied a direct link between the level of U.S. military expenditures in Japan and Japan remaining a favorable market for U.S. exports, but that such a direct link was "contrary to the principle of multilateral trade and payments" that was "the foundation of our entire international trade and financial policy." He believed there was no question of the overall adequacy of Japan's foreign currency earnings and its foreign exchange reserves were increasing, and he suggested a State–Defense–Treasury meeting once the JCS had completed its analyses of possible reductions in Japan. (Kennedy Library, National Security Files, Countries Series, Japan, 3/63)

[5] A note from Michael Forrestal of the NSC Staff to Bundy dated February 26 noted: "It is pretty obvious that State is the Department which wants to go easy on reduction of military expenditures in Japan. I have commented to Gilpatric that we thought Defense might move more briskly. Unless you think this is enough, I will take the matter up with Averell [Harriman] who may not be sympathetic." (Ibid.)

[6] A handwritten postscript reads: "This supplements my earlier note! DR" The earlier handwritten note, February 9, reads: "Dear Ros—many thanks for your trip to Japan—it was a great help to us and you handled it magnificently. Dean" (Ibid.)

---

## 370.  Editorial Note

In a memorandum for the record of the meeting of the Joint Chiefs of Staff with the President on February 28, 1963, the section relating to discussion of Okinawa reads as follows: "General Wheeler led a discussion of the Chiefs' views on the continued strategic essentiality of Okinawa to the U.S. military posture in the Pacific. The President expressed no disagreement, indicating that he had no intention of giving up the island." (Memorandum by Taylor, March 1; Kennedy Library, National Security Files, Clifton Series, JCS Meetings with the President, 2/63–11/63)

### 371.   Memorandum From the Director of the Office of East Asian Affairs (Yager) to the Assistant Secretary of State for Far Eastern Affairs (Harriman)

Washington, March 15, 1963.

SUBJECT

Japanese Cotton Textile Exports

*Problem:*

On December 28 we levied on Japan a request[1] for export restraints in 36 categories (in addition to 3 categories agreed last fall) of cotton textiles for 1963 on the basis of market disruption as provided in Article 3 of the Long-Term Cotton Textile Arrangement (LTA).[2] The Japanese have rejected the allegation of market disruption except in 4 categories. There has been a series of exchanges in Washington and Tokyo, the net result of which has left us far from agreement. Our allegation of market disruption on a broad scale has touched off a storm of protest in Japan which has acquired wide political proportions actually threatening damage to our relations with Japan. Moreover, failure to reach early agreement would undoubtedly lead to a confrontation in the GATT which probably would destroy the LTA itself, cause an unpleasant and destructive exchange regarding U.S. trade policy, and seriously affect the prospects for a successful Kennedy Round of Tariff negotiations under the TEA. We must quickly find a solution which will avoid a confrontation with Japan on issues of principle and permit us to negotiate on the actual level of exports for 1963, such a solution must, of course, provide adequate safeguards and assurance to the U.S. industry.

*The Issues*

The basis for Japanese indignation is the fact that the U.S. has "accused" Japan of market disruption on a broad scale (about 90 percent of its exports to the U.S.) in the face of its long record as the only country to exert rigorous restraints on textile exports to the U.S., all of which were worked out in close consultation with the U.S. They are also conscious of the key role they played in support of the U.S. in bringing about the LTA. Except for 4 categories they do not agree that the LTA definition of mar-

---

Source: Department of State, EA/J Files: Lot 68 D 373, Cotton Textiles January–June 1963. Confidential. Drafted by Vettel.

[1] The previous agreement expired on December 31, 1962; see footnote 4, Document 343.

[2] Dated February 9, 1962; for text of this multilateral arrangement, see 13 UST (pt. 3) 2672. The arrangement entered into force for the United States on October 1, 1962.

ket disruption has been met. It is now apparent that continued efforts to negotiate restraints with the Japanese on the basis of the market disruption principle (Article 3) will not be successful. In the end we would probably be required to take unilateral action to impose import restrictions, which would undoubtedly lead to a confrontation with Japan in the GATT.

After extensive exchanges in Washington and Tokyo regarding interpretation of the LTA, no agreement in principle has been reached and the Japanese have refused to discuss restraint levels under Article 3. On the basis of a Cabinet decision, which over-rode a Foreign Office recommendation to move directly to negotiation of restraint levels, the Japanese requested U.S. agreement to six points of principle regarding the LTA, after which they would be willing to negotiate restraint levels under Article 4 of the LTA (which provides for bilateral agreements) (attached).[3] It is the consensus in this office and in E that efforts to come to agreement on the six points would be interminable.

The Commerce Department prefers the use of Article 3 because of its provision for the imposition of unilateral controls in the event of lack of agreement or breach of agreed ceilings. This they consider to be a valuable "lever" which they do not believe a bilateral agreement under Article 4 would provide. Naturally the Commerce Department feels its responsibility to provide adequate safeguards for the U.S. industry.

*Proposed Solution*

We believe that the best solution lies in our moving away from the market disruption principle and presenting a proposal for agreed restraints under a bilateral agreement. Recent private discussions with the Japanese both here and in Tokyo lead us to the conclusion that a U.S. proposal for negotiation that meets the Japanese objection to the market disruption "accusation" may result in avoidance of a clash on the issues of principle. It is obvious that the Japanese Government's interests lie in avoiding further prolongation of this issue in the public domain, but that it must find a solution which "saves face" on the market disruption issue.

A bilateral agreement which provides agreed specific ceilings on all sensitive categories together with an over-all ceiling on all Japanese exports to the U.S. (which is not provided under the market disruption method), would safeguard the U.S. industry against unforeseen disruptive imports from Japan. Although we deal with almost all other countries under Article 3, the unique record of bilateral textile arrangement with Japan since 1957 should adequately explain this departure.

We have suggested that a proposal be made to the Japanese for a bilateral agreement with 1) an over-all restraint level of about 290 million

---

[3] Not found attached.

square yards (Commerce's estimate of total Japanese exports under our original proposal),[4] 2) specific ceilings on the 39 categories, and 3) a residual basket ceiling for the remaining 25 LTA categories. Both parties would reserve their rights under the LTA and the GATT.

We have discussed this proposal with Mr. Philip Trezise, who has taken over Mr. Blumenthal's duties regarding textiles, and are in basic agreement with him. He is now preparing to take up the proposal with Commerce and other interested agencies as soon as possible. His problem will be to convince the other Departments that such a proposal will break the impasse and, at the same time, provide adequate safeguards for U.S. industry.

Mr. Trezise wishes to discuss this matter with you and Mr. Ball before taking it up with the other agencies.[5]

---

[4] At a background press briefing held February 26 W. Michael Blumenthal, Deputy Assistant Secretary of State for Economic Affairs, stated that 1962 shipments in the affected categories, according to figures submitted by the Japanese Government, were 262.5 million yards. (Department of State, EA/J Files: Lot 68 D 373, Cotton Textile Consultation 1963)

[5] Negotiations were successfully concluded under Article 4 of the LTA. (Ibid.) Other documentation on this topic prior to January 31, 1963, is ibid., Central File 611.9441; for the remainder of 1963 it is ibid., Central File FT 11–5 JAPAN. For text of the notes effecting the arrangement between Japan and the United States concerning trade in cotton textiles, exchanged at Washington on August 27, 1963, and entered into force that day (operative from January 1, 1963), see 14 UST 1078. Text of the August 27 joint announcement on the arrangement is in Department of State *Bulletin*, September 16, 1963, p. 440. A review of the bilateral cotton textile trade is in Contingency Paper KEA/C–3, November 15; Department of State, Conference Files: Lot 66 D 110, CF 2361. See the Supplement.

---

### 372.    Memorandum for the Record

Washington, March 26, 1963.

[Source: Kennedy Library, National Security Files, Meetings and Memoranda Series, Meetings with the President, 3/63. Top Secret. 2 pages of source text not declassified.]

### 373. Telegram 1810 From the Department of State to the Embassy in Japan

Washington, March 27, 1963, 9:38 p.m.

[Source: Kennedy Library, National Security Files, Countries Series, Japan, 3/63. Secret; Operational Immediate. 4 pages of source text not declassified.]

---

### 374. Telegram 2335 From the Embassy in Japan to the Department of State

Tokyo, April 4, 1963, 7 p.m.

[Source: Kennedy Library, National Security Files, Countries Series, Japan, 4/63. Secret; Operational Immediate; Limit Distribution. 5 pages of source text not declassified.]

---

### 375. Memorandum of Conversation

Washington, April 25, 1963, noon.

SUBJECT

Japan's Role on the World Scene and US-Japan Relations

PARTICIPANTS

The President
Ambassador Ryuji Takeuchi of the Embassy of Japan
Mr. Duke, Chief of Protocol
Mr. Rice, Deputy Assistant Secretary, FE

After an exchange of amenities, the President commented that a remark he had made to Japanese cabinet ministers during a luncheon last

---

Source: Department of State, Central Files, POL JAPAN-US. Confidential. Drafted by Rice and approved by the White House on April 30. The meeting was held at the White House. Ryuji Takeuchi succeeded Koichiro Asakai as Japanese Ambassador to the United States.

December[1] about China, had evidently created quite a stir in Japan. He added that he had merely expressed how he felt, and that he still felt the same way. The Ambassador said he recalled the occasion (which was on December 3 in connection with the second meeting of the Joint US-Japan Committee on Trade and Economic Affairs), as he was among those present. The Japanese press, he commented, had examined every word to see what it could read into the statement. (Later on he commented that few Americans realize how free the Japanese press is, and that it is uniformly anti-government—though people have learned to read between the lines.) The President said that some had thought his remarks were intended to be taken in the context of trade, but that this was not what he had in mind.

The President adverted to Japan's remarkable economic resurgence and asked the Ambassador what he envisages the role of Japan to be on the world scene, in the years ahead. Ambassador Takeuchi replied that Japan should serve as an example of economic stability and of successful democratic government. Without social, economic and political progress and stability in Japan, the countries of the area would look elsewhere (by implication, to Communist countries) for their model.

There were but passing references to the question of outstanding problems in US-Japan relations: The Ambassador characterized our relations as good, at the same time suggesting by waggles of head and hand that they are not entirely problem-free. At this point the President rose to close the interview and, as if reading the Ambassador's mind, he laughingly commented that there is the matter of textiles which, it seems, will always be with us.

---

[1] See footnote 1, Document 362.

## 376.  Memorandum of Conversation

Washington, August 1, 1963.

SUBJECT

The Under Secretary's Meeting with the Japanese Foreign Minister[1]

PARTICIPANTS

Under Secretary Ball
Foreign Minister Ohira
Ambassador Takeuchi
Mr. Taketoshi Yamashita, Financial Minister, Embassy of Japan
Mr. Yoshihiro Nakayama, Director of Economic Affairs Bureau, Japanese Ministry
   of Foreign Affairs
Mr. Michio Mizoguchi, Interpreter (Second Secretary, Embassy of Japan)
Mr. Roger Hilsman, Assistant Secretary for Far Eastern Affairs
Ambassador Reischauer
Mr. Benjamin Caplan, Director, Office of International Finance and Analysis
Mr. Leonard L. Bacon, Acting Director for East Asian Affairs
Mr. M. D. Goldstein, Deputy Director, Office of International Finance and
   Analysis
Mr. James Wickel, Department of State Interpreter

The Under Secretary explained to the Foreign Minister the American thinking underlying the proposal of an interest equalization tax.[2] He referred to the increase in the outflow of long-term capital at a time when foreign short-term claims against the dollar were also increasing. To meet this situation Secretary Dillon had pursued the least restrictionist policy, preferring the mechanical method of an interest equalization tax to any form of direct controls. The proposed tax afforded the best method, short of direct controls, of equating U.S. interest rates with the world level while permitting our friends to have continued access to the U.S. capital market with the least harmful effect on their economies. We believed that the tax, the equivalent of a 1 percent increase in U.S. long-term interest rates, would eliminate marginal borrowing, particularly in areas like Europe where interest rates were close to those of the United

---

Source: Department of State, Central Files, POL JAPAN–US. Confidential. Drafted by Wickel and John F. Knowles of EA/J and approved in U on September 18.

[1] Ohira had arrived in Washington August 1 to make representations regarding the proposed interest equalization tax.

[2] President Kennedy had presented this proposal to the Congress on July 18 in a special message to the Congress on the balance of payments. For text, *see Public Papers of the Presidents of the United States: John F. Kennedy, 1963*, p. 580. Purpose of the proposed tax was to effect an increase of about 1 percent in the cost to foreigners of capital raised in the United States, and thereby to help bring the U.S. balance of payments into equilibrium without raising domestic interest rates. It was approved on September 2, 1964, as P.L. 88–563; see 78 Stat. 809.

States and where capital would be available were the capital markets better organized. The tax would, in effect, spread the burden of providing capital for world-wide economic expansion. The best advice of the New York financial community was that while the tax might reduce access to the U.S. capital market, it would not seriously interfere, for example, with Japan's ability to finance her programs. No long-term restrictive effect was anticipated in view of the difference in Japan's equity and interest rate structure even though the immediate effect would be an increase in interest and equity costs for Japan. The Under Secretary recognized that Japanese financial experts disagreed with these views and suggested that the experts explore the question.

The Foreign Minister replied that Japanese financial experts were aware of the American belief that the tax would not interfere with normal Japanese access to the American capital market. He pointed out that investment in Japanese stocks came to an almost complete standstill when the new tax was announced.[3] Should the tax be imposed, little return could be expected from Japanese bonds; the return was so slight already that hardly any difference existed between American and Japanese bonds.

The Foreign Minister stated that Japan had based her economic policies on the premise that the United States was firmly committed to the maintenance of a free dollar and would take no steps to control access to the American capital market. In his view, the new policy would have serious effects in Japan and, unless changed, could have serious political consequences. Japan understood that the new policy had been formulated because of the need to protect the dollar. He hoped that the talks between the experts could be expedited with a view toward reaching, as rapidly as possible, a resolution of differences which would spare Japan from unfavorable consequences of the proposed tax.

The Under Secretary assured the Foreign Minister that all concerned desired a solution which met Japan's financial and political problems as well as our own balance of payments problem. We were, however, restricted in our search for an easy solution by the tensions existing in world capital markets; he noted the growing movement against the dollar in the previous week, particularly in Switzerland. This results from the belief in financial circles that the United States must consider political affairs in the world as carefully as the strength of the dollar. Scepticism about American efforts to stem the outflow of capital was a factor which

---

[3] In a telephone conversation between Dillon and Ball at 10:15 a.m. on July 27, Ball agreed with Dillon's statement that "it is very clear that their [Japan's] problem [with the interest equalization proposal] is more face and that sort of stuff than it is economic." Dillon also asserted that "we" had received a telegram stating that the Bank of Japan did not believe the proposal would really hurt Japan but that it didn't want this statement attributed to it. (Notes of telephone conversation; Kennedy Library, Ball Papers, Japan)

could not be ignored in seeking a solution which would demonstrate our sympathetic understanding of Japan's situation.

The Foreign Minister said there had been no change in the Japanese Government's position of cooperating in the defense of the dollar. He understood that the United States Government must be firm in this purpose. He did not intend to advocate a change in this basic policy. However, within the framework of this policy and U.S.-Japan cooperation, he felt that the two countries can, and indeed must, achieve an adjustment of their differences.

Ambassador Takeuchi inquired whether any estimate of Japanese needs to borrow in the American market had been made in the course of the U.S. Government's study of the effect of the tax on Japanese borrowing. The Under Secretary replied that he did not know, adding that Secretary Dillon would discuss this question. The Treasury conducted these studies in which, because of the sensitivity of the matter, the Department of State did not participate until just before the proposal was advanced.

Ambassador Takeuchi asked whether the United States Government had any intention of reducing the amount of money which Japan can borrow in the United States. He said that the dollar had not been endangered by Japanese borrowing in spite of an increase of $100 to $150 million over 1962.

The Under Secretary replied that market forces would determine the flow of capital which would continue to go to those countries having the greatest differential in interest rate. If the differential was less than 1 percent, then capital flow would be reduced. The out-flow of long-term capital, he believed, would ultimately be reduced to $400 to $600 million a year, the same result as would be obtained from a 1 percent increase in interest rates.

Ambassador Takeuchi said that many Japanese feel that the impact of the proposed tax on Japanese borrowing needs had not been studied carefully. This feeling had been strengthened by the action taken with regard to Canada,[4] a country about which the United States should have known more. Apparently something happened to occasion an exemption for Canada. Many Japanese feel that the same situation applies to Japan.

The Under Secretary commented that this question should be raised with the Treasury which undertook the studies. The studies themselves were global and not national in nature. European interest rates had been studied and it was felt that the tax would divert borrowing from the American to the European market, provided the 1 percent tax equalized the interest rate differential.

---

[4] Concerning the nature of the "exemption" granted Canada, see the joint U.S-Canadian communiqué, dated July 21, in Department of State *Bulletin*, August 12, 1963, p. 256.

The Foreign Minister observed that his Prime Minister and Government believed that Japan, by leaving her earnings and borrowings in the United States to finance imports from the United States, had not aggravated the outflow of capital. Japan has cooperated with the United States in this matter and was dismayed at this step taken by the United States.

The Under Secretary said it was his impression that part of Japan's dollar holdings had gone to finance Japan's adverse trade balance with Europe. He felt that the U.S.-Japan trade balance might have reached a state of equilibrium. However, the tax was directed at Europe rather than elsewhere. While there might be some reduction in the flow of American capital to Japan, he felt there would still be a substantial flow, particularly in the form of portfolio investment. There is no desire to impair the development of the Japanese economy. The American interest is in the solution of the political and economic problem, which is difficult to achieve in view of the sensitivity of the world financial markets.

Ambassador Takeuchi asked whether the United States would consider measures which would permit Japanese borrowing if it can be proved in the near future that the tax would prevent Japan from financing her programs, thereby endangering both the programs and the government itself. He said he was not seeking a guarantee but he wondered whether the logic of Japan's position was not evident.

Ambassador Reischauer commented that this was precisely the question under discussion.

Ambassador Takeuchi asked whether the same result might not be achieved by voluntary controls rather than by a tax. In reply, the Under Secretary said that was a matter to be explored with the Treasury. The problem was extremely sensitive and must be handled without leading to further erosion in the position of the dollar.

Ambassador Reischauer asked what Japan's capital needs were expected to be. The Foreign Minister replied that the need was great from the standpoint of Japan's balance of payments and economic growth. Japan's current transactions were generally in balance but there was a deficit of about $400 million in invisibles which was covered by capital borrowing. $300 million would be the minimum required for investments which would permit a continuation of Japan's growth rate. When Mr. Kaplan pointed out that the tax would apply to portfolio but not direct investments, the Foreign Minister said that $600 million was the figure for all capital borrowing, including direct investment.

Ambassador Takeuchi wondered whether the new policy was not successful in Europe in view of the absence of any protests against it. The Under Secretary agreed that there did not seem to be so much concern in European nations which could find capital at home and have turned to the United States only out of convenience. Japan and Canada had been the countries of greatest concern to the United States in this matter.

The Under Secretary assured the Foreign Minister of our desire to be helpful, adding that the Treasury should take the lead since it is responsible for the United States balance of payments. Policy would be guided, he cautioned, by the impact of any decision on the financial community.

Ambassador Takeuchi noted that the draft legislation was general in terminology and did not exclude the possibility of an exemption for Japan. Should Administration officials make any statement in their testimony before Congress advocating excluding Japan from exemption, this would have a very adverse effect in Japan leaving no room for improvement of the situation. The Ambassador pointed out that the Japanese stock market had taken a downturn immediately following a press article attributing to a high United States official the view that Japan was not to be exempted from the tax.

The Under Secretary concluded the meeting by noting that some possibilities might come to light during subsequent discussions by the experts. These could be reviewed before the Foreign Minister's meeting with the President.[5]

---

[5] See Document 377. Ohira also met with Rusk on August 1. (Memorandum by Wickel and Knowles; Department of State, Central Files, POL JAPAN–US) See the Supplement.

---

## 377.  Memorandum of Conversation

Washington, August 2, 1963, 11:30 a.m.

SUBJECT

The President's Meeting with the Japanese Foreign Minister

PARTICIPANTS

The President
Foreign Minister Ohira
Ambassador Takeuchi
Mr. Michio Mizoguchi, Interpreter (Second Secretary, Embassy of Japan)
The Secretary of the Treasury
Under Secretary of State Ball
Mr. Roger Hilsman, Assistant Secretary for Far Eastern Affairs

---

Source: Department of State, Presidential Memoranda of Conversation: Lot 66 D 149. Confidential. Drafted by Wickel and Knowles. Approved in S and the White House on August 28.

Ambassador Reischauer
Mr. Robert Barnett, Deputy Assistant Secretary for Far Eastern Economic Affairs
Mr. William J. Tonesk, Deputy Chief of Protocol
Mr. James Wickel, Department of State Interpreter

The President said he was pleased to have an opportunity to meet the Foreign Minister again, and expressed regret if any actions taken by the United States caused the Foreign Minister to come to Washington at this time.

The Foreign Minister thanked the President for receiving him on such short notice and expressed appreciation for the President's leadership of the Free World.

The discussion then turned to the subject of U.S. balance of payments measures. The President began by expressing regret that U.S. actions had created difficulties for Japan and by assuring the Foreign Minister that the United States wishes to lessen the impact of these measures on Japan to the extent possible. We recognize that Japan has not actually contributed to our difficulties and has refrained from taking gold from the United States. If the problem concerned only Japan, Canada and the United States, a solution could easily be reached since the American dollar is almost the common currency of these three countries. However, the problem is common to all of us in the Free World. In taking these measures to defend the integrity of the dollar, the United States feels it is acting in the interests of the entire Free World. The great number of dollars outstanding which can be converted into gold is alarming. This outflow of dollars and consequent claims against the U.S. gold reserve cannot be allowed to continue, the United States having already suffered a gold outflow of $15 billion in the last ten years. The American dollar is the very basis for the entire financial system of the West and the cooperation of all parties is required if the dollar is to continue to serve that function. If the value of the dollar were not maintained, then a new monetary system would have to be invented since there is obviously not enough gold to maintain world trade at its present level. This is an area, however, where nations guard their sovereignty most jealously.

The Foreign Minister assured the President that Japan understands the necessity of safeguarding the value of the dollar to maintain the prosperity of the Free World. Japan has cooperated to this end in the past and desires to work even more closely with the United States to help overcome the present difficulties. There will be no change in this basic policy of the Japanese Government. The Foreign Minister expressed confidence that the U.S. balance of payments would be successfully resolved under the fine leadership of the President.

The President expressed appreciation for Japan's cooperation in a number of problem areas, such as textiles, which has helped to maintain an even flow of trade.

The President repeated assurances that the United States is anxious to explore means of minimizing the unfavorable impact on Japan of the U.S. balance of payments measures. He noted that the joint communiqué[1] was being drafted with a view to inspiring confidence in Japan, halting the decline of the Japanese stock market.

The Foreign Minister handed to the President a letter from Prime Minister Ikeda,[2] a copy of which the President had already read. The President remarked that he appreciated the Prime Minister's concern over the impact on Japan of U.S. balance of payments measures. We recognize that Japan requires a regular inflow of capital.

The Foreign Minister expressed appreciation for U.S. efforts in GATT and for the assistance rendered Japan by the United States with respect to Japan's entry into the OECD and IMF.

The President inquired whether reference might be made in the joint communiqué to matters other than the balance of payments. Under Secretary Ball said it might be useful to mention the importance of the partial test ban treaty and Japan's announced intention to adhere. The Foreign Minister replied that Japan had not considered going so far in the communiqué. Ambassador Takeuchi added that inserting an additional paragraph on the treaty in the already long communiqué would make it unmanageable in length and suggested that consideration be given to a separate communiqué covering other matters. The President said he would leave it up to the others present to decide.

In response to a question by the President, Ambassador Takeuchi said there had been an overall drop of 10 percent in the Tokyo stock market since the President's speech of July 18. Secretary Dillon compared this to the decline from 734 to 640 in the index of U.S. stock prices in the past year.

As the Foreign Minister rose to leave, the President inquired about the reaction of the Japanese Communist Party (JCP) to the Sino-Soviet split. The Foreign Minister explained that the JCP is basically sympathetic to Communist China but that there is severe internal strife between pro-Peiping and pro-Moscow factions. The JCP has about 100,000 mem-

---

[1] The joint communiqué has not been found, but a joint communiqué issued at the conclusion of a meeting of the U.S.-Japan Committee on Trade and Economic Affairs on January 28, 1964, quoted a portion of it as follows: "if contrary to U.S. expectations, serious economic difficulties were to arise in Japan, the United States would consider appropriate measures that might then be taken to meet the problem, including some form of exemption from the proposed interest equalization tax for new issues of securities." (*American Foreign Policy: Current Documents, 1964*, p. 911)

[2] Dated July 31, it deals with the interest equalization proposal. (Attached to an August 21 memorandum from Benjamin Read, Executive Secretary of the Department, to McGeorge Bundy; Department of State, Central Files, E 1 JAPAN–US; also enclosed is Kennedy's formal note of reply to Ikeda, dated August 26.) See the Supplement for all.

bers and polls about 2 percent of the popular vote in Japanese elections. Its real strength, however, is greater than these statistics suggest.

The President asked for the Foreign Minister's views on the possible course of Communist China in the near future. The Foreign Minister said he believes Communist China will become more active in promoting its ideological position, particularly in Southeast Asia, but will probably remain cautious about undertaking any actions in Southeast Asia.

### 378.  Memorandum of Conversation

Washington, August 5, 1963.

SUBJECT

    US-Japan Defense Problems

PARTICIPANTS

    *US*
    Deputy Secretary of Defense Gilpatric
    Ambassador Reischauer
    Deputy Assistant Secretary of Defense Frank K. Sloan
    R/Adm. L. C. Heinz, DoD
    Mr. Robert A. Fearey, State Department
    Capt. W. M. Carpenter, USN, DoD

    *Japan*
    Foreign Minister Ohira
    Ambassador Takeuchi
    Mr. Mizoguchi (Interpreter)
    Mr. Kikuchi, Secretary to Mr. Ohira
    Col. Mai, Military Attaché

Mr. Gilpatric opened the conversation by saying that he was glad to have the opportunity to talk with the Foreign Minister, since some of the aspects of the U.S. balance of payments problem have defense implications.

Mr. Ohira responded that he had come to Washington primarily to discuss the balance of payments question and the equalization tax, but

---

Source: Kennedy Library, National Security Files, Countries Series, Japan, 8/63. Secret. No drafter is indicated on the source text but it was approved by Gilpatric on August 6.

was grateful for the opportunity to continue discussions begun in meetings in Tokyo last February with Mr. Gilpatric. He inquired if the President's message had caused any change in U.S. Department of Defense expenditure policies.

Mr. Gilpatric replied that when he had talked with Mr. Ohira in Tokyo he had said that the U.S. would not reduce its power base in the Far East and that this intent was as valid now as then. In February the threat of the Chinese Communists was considered a real and present danger and is so regarded now, as President Kennedy had mentioned in his press conference last week.[1] Although there seems to be a possibility for some kind of détente with the Soviets, our assessment of the risk of Chinese militancy is not lessened over the long run.

Adverting again to his February statements about the U.S. power base in the Far East, Mr. Gilpatric said that his remarks at the time were not meant to rule out some future readjustment of our force dispositions, so long as our over-all capability was not impaired. He said that several developments have occurred over the past year. For one thing, the U.S. has greatly improved its airlift capability and by 1966 will have a 300% increase over its 1961 airlift strength. Further, the range of our tactical fighters has been increased to the point where rapid deployment over the Atlantic and Pacific is possible. The U.S. now has the capability to deploy a division to Europe or the Far East in days rather than weeks and, by prepositioning the heavy equipment, can have a division combat ready at a distant location much more rapidly than in the past. As a consequence of these developments, and as the President said in his July 18th message, the U.S. expects by adjusting force levels in the Far East and elsewhere to save about $300 million a year in defense expenditures overseas.

With respect to the proposed adjustments in Japan, the U.S. will, through Ambassador Reischauer and U.S. military personnel, discuss with their Japanese counterparts the specifics involved. Mr. Gilpatric said that, although we were not yet ready to discuss details,[2] we have in mind such actions as returning some of our transport aircraft, and some of the tactical aircraft, since replacements for these types are capable of long-range deployment. The U.S. also has in mind that some of our squadrons in Japan will be deployed without dependents and that some of our bases there may be put on a "joint-use" status, manned by U.S. and Japanese personnel, rather than in a full operating status. To demon-

---

[1] For the President's remarks on China made at his press conference on August 1, see *Public Papers of the Presidents of the United States: John F. Kennedy, 1963*, p. 614.

[2] Documentation on U.S. efforts to reach an agreed U.S. Government position on the nature of its force reductions is in Department of State, Central Files DEF 1 JAPAN, DEF 19–3 JAPAN, and FN 12 JAPAN for 1963.

strate our capability for rapid deployment of aircraft earmarked for bases in Japan we plan to hold large-scale military exercises, and have in mind one such exercise in the Far East next spring if we can work out the necessary arrangements. For logistic support of Far East forces we would continue to use ships as floating depots, to back up rapid force deployments. Mr. Gilpatric emphasized that all these projected actions are part of a world-wide effort to reduce overseas expenditures without affecting combat effectiveness, and that the effort relates particularly to the logistics and support areas. Our Ambassador and military personnel will be working out these moves with Japanese representatives. As the President has said, we do not want to weaken, or to give the appearance of weakening, U.S. strength and resolution to meet the threat in any area.

Mr. Gilpatric pointed out that the U.S. is aware that the moves he had described are recognized as politically sensitive matters to both countries and that he felt neither the U.S. nor the Japanese side would want to discuss them publicly at this time. Mr. Gilpatric added that these moves are but a natural evolution of the U.S. total defense posture, planned when President Kennedy took office and now coming into being.

Mr. Ohira replied that he appreciated Mr. Gilpatric's frank remarks and that he would see that no leaks were made to the press.

Mr. Ohira went on to a related question. He said that press reports have said the U.S. is withdrawing a division from Korea, and he wondered if this were part of the U.S. balance of payments actions, or perhaps an erroneous report.

Mr. Gilpatric replied that the press statements were at least premature. He explained that the U.S. is in a paradoxical situation in Korea. The US/ROK forces there are more than sufficient for dealing with a North Korean attack but inadequate without reinforcement for containing a North Korean/ChiCom attack. He said that ever since he was Under Secretary of the Air Force ten years ago, the U.S. has had the same force deployed to Korea. Speaking personally, since no decision has yet been made, Mr. Gilpatric said he predicted that we would not make any immediate change in Korean forces—the situation is too uncertain—but that in the long run we will be thinking of some readjustment of forces in Korea as our capability to redeploy will permit.

Mr. Ohira had a second question. He asked when the US-Japan talks could take place, inasmuch as he could foresee a curtailment on Japanese income from U.S. forces and some effect on Japanese defense budget planning. He said it was necessary to put next year's Japanese defense budget together about November of this year.

Mr. Gilpatric replied that he could foresee some such effects from the moves of U.S. dependents, but he hoped these would be temporary. He said that after the Ambassador returns at the end of August and sometime within the next two months or so we should be ready for discussions. On the U.S. military side General Smart, although he has just moved to Hawaii, would take an active interest in talks, as would Admiral Felt. The full implications of the U.S. moves (FY 64 and later) should be discussed with Japan before the latter had to make budget decisions. Mr. Gilpatric went on to say that the U.S. has its budget problems too. Indeed, some of the projected actions will cost the U.S. more in budget dollars, e.g., to fly out aircraft to the Far East, but that this is a way to save gold.

Mr. Ohira went to a third point, concerning the Japan Second Defense Five-Year Build-up Plan (1962–1966). This plan, which called for Japanese expenditures of about $3-1/3 billion, was drafted with the expectation of receiving about $50 million per year in U.S. grant aid. Of the $250 million anticipated, Japan had received about one fourth. Japan wants to cooperate in the U.S. program to save dollars but is concerned that in the portion of grant aid not yet received is the U.S. portion for BADGE (air defense system),[3] and for naval ships and helicopters (ASW). Mr. Ohira said he realized what U.S. thinking was from the President's message and from Senator Church's amendment, but he wondered just what to expect from U.S. military assistance.

Mr. Gilpatric said that our position on military assistance to Japan has not changed from that discussed with Mr. Shiga in Tokyo and that the U.S. still intends to share in the cost of BADGE. He said that we have studied the Japanese choice of Hughes as contractor for BADGE, and noted that these projects always cost more than anticipated. As to support for ASW, we can make no commitment in the FY 64 MAP until Congress acts on the appropriation (about two months from now). As to the Church amendment, we hope for a Foreign Relations Committee interpretation that will be helpful.

Mr. Ohira said he wished to conclude with a reference to the proposed entry into Japanese ports of U.S. nuclear-powered submarines.[4] He said he understood that the U.S. Navy might be impatient, but that it was his idea that it was politically wise to have the Japan AEC make a favorable recommendation to the Japanese Government. For this reason Dr. Kaneshige, JAEC Commissioner, was in Washington to discuss technical matters and that he hoped this would be helpful. Ambassador Rei-

---

[3] U.S.-Japanese agreement relating to a joint cost-sharing program for the production of equipment and the provision of technical assistance for the base air defense ground environment (BADGE) system was effected by an exchange of notes at Tokyo on December 4, 1946. It entered into force that same day. For text, see 15 UST 2339.

[4] The United States and Japan did not reach agreement on entry of nuclear-powered submarines into Japanese ports until 1964. Documentation in Department of State, Central Files DEF 7 JAPAN–US and AE 10–2 JAPAN indicates that a stumbling block throughout 1963 was the inability of the United States under existing security regulations to furnish Japan with information that would answer Japan's concerns over safety of the vessels.

schauer said that he and Dr. Kaneshige had met with V/Adm. Rickover earlier that morning for a useful discussion.

Mr. Ohira's final question was to ask if there are any new developments in the Far East.

Mr. Gilpatric said that President Kennedy had held a meeting last week to consider the implications of recent international incidents, such as the shootings in Korea, a possible Chinese Communist build-up on the border of India, and the uncertain truce in Laos, and that at the moment the consensus was that, although the situation was threatening, no major moves are foreseen. Mr. Gilpatric assured Mr. Ohira that if any such moves are anticipated, the U.S. will consult with Japan.

Mr. Gilpatric closed by saying that he believes these talks are quite useful and that there should be regular exchanges of views between Defense officials of the two countries.

It was agreed that statements to the press regarding Mr. Ohira's call would be limited to saying that the latter was a follow-up of Mr. Gilpatric's visit to Tokyo in February, 1963.

---

## 379.  Briefing Paper Prepared in the Embassy in Japan

BB–21                                          Tokyo, November 1, 1963.

### US–JAPAN COMMITTEE ON TRADE AND ECONOMIC AFFAIRS
Tokyo, November 25–27, 1963[1]

*US–Japan–Okinawa*

The United States administration of Okinawa and other islands in the Ryukyus is provided for by Article 3 of the Treaty of Peace with Japan, entered into in 1952, which states that Japan will concur in any proposal of the United States to place the Ryukyu Islands under UN trusteeship with the US as the sole administering authority. The Article also gives the

---

Source: Department of State, Central Files, E 1 JAPAN–US. Limited Official Use. The paper was transmitted as enclosure 1 to airgram A–549 from Tokyo, November 15. Drafted by William H. Bruns, First Secretary and Political Officer, and Chadwick Johnson, Second Secretary and Industrial Officer.

[1] Concerning postponement of this meeting, see Document 385.

United States the right to exercise all governmental powers pending such a proposal. The US has not made any proposal for trusteeship but has retained its control over the Ryukyus, and has developed, principally on Okinawa, extensive military bases of major importance.

During the Occupation and the period immediately following the Peace Treaty, Japan's interest in the US administration was minimal and Ryukyuan issues had little or no bearing on political developments in Japan. This interest increased markedly, however, in 1955 when Ryukyuan dissatisfaction with US land rental policies assumed serious proportions. Although this dissatisfaction was alleviated by changes in US policies, Japanese interest in the welfare of the Ryukyuans has continued and problems in US administration are frequently used by Japanese leftist elements for their own political ends and for the purpose of arousing sentiment against the continued use of the Islands for US military bases.

Responsible LDP leaders recognize that US bases in Okinawa are vital to defense of Japan and free Asia but at same time they must take into consideration wide feeling among Japanese that the Ryukyus should be returned to Japan in the not too distant future. As result GOJ "in principle" desires return of the Ryukyus. Since the US, for security reasons, cannot comply, it inevitably is placed in a position of public "disagreement" with its Japanese partner even though the present Japanese Government understands and tacitly accepts need for retention of Okinawan bases by US.

As nationalism revives in Japan Okinawa can, unless wisely handled, become cause of serious trouble between US and Japan even if Japan continues to have a conservative government.

The problem we face is to prevent a situation from arising in which GOJ will be under such domestic pressure on the Okinawan issue that in the interest of self-preservation it will feel required to place serious pressure on its US partner to return the Ryukyus. It already faces constant agitation on the issue from the Left. If this should combine with pressure on right from renascent nationalism, the results could be extremely serious.

The new policy announced by President Kennedy on March 19, 1962[2] constitutes an effort to meet this challenge. Under it we hope (a) to work out a cooperative relationship which will permit Japan to provide more aid for the Ryukyus and generally work *with* us in the best interests of the Ryukyuans; and (b) to reduce dissatisfaction in the Ryukyus by providing more economic assistance, by permitting gradually increased autonomy for the GRI and by eliminating grievances to the extent possible in the field of civil rights. The GOJ can thus evidence its concern for

---

[2] See footnote 4, Document 352.

the Ryukyus and increase its role there, and thereby meet the requirements of nationalism and reduce its vulnerability to Leftist pressures without compromising our administrative authority. Moreover, the Ryukyuans can be kept relatively content.

For the past year the US and Japanese Governments have been engaged in negotiations, in accordance with the Presidential statement of March 19, 1962, to implement a cooperative relationship in providing assistance to promote the welfare of the inhabitants of the Ryukyu Islands and their economic development. The negotiations are directed toward the establishment of a Consultative Committee in Tokyo which will plan and coordinate aid policies and a Technical Committee in Okinawa to implement programs. The Embassy in July, 1963 submitted to the Foreign Office the USG draft of an agreement for the establishment of the two committees. In late September it received the GOJ counterdraft which it forwarded to Washington for review. The Embassy is now awaiting Washington advice prior to resuming negotiations with the Foreign Office, and anticipates that a considerable amount of negotiation will be required to arrive at mutual agreement.[3]

[Here follows an analysis of economic problems in the Ryukyus.]

------

[3] A detailed Embassy analysis of U.S. and Japanese objectives in the Ryukyus and the Bonins is in airgram A–1677 from Tokyo, May 24. (Department of State, Central Files, POL JAPAN–US) See the Supplement. Other documentation on this topic during 1963 is in Department of State, Central Files POL 19 RYU IS, POL RYU IS–US, and DEF 15 RYU IS–US. An agreement providing economic and technical assistance to promote the economic development of the Ryukyu Islands was concluded by an exchange of notes at Tokyo April 25, 1964, and entered into force that day. For text, see 15 UST 1371.

------

**380.    Telegram From the Embassy in Japan to the Department of State**

Tokyo, November 1, 1963, 9 p.m.

1356. Joint ECONCOM. Deptel 1004[1] and Emb's A–1734, June 17, 1963.[2] Following is summary politico-economic assessment as of Nov. 1,

------

Source: Department of State, Central Files, E 1 JAPAN–US. Confidential; Priority.
[1] Dated October 30. (Ibid.)
[2] Not printed. (Ibid.)

1963 (more comprehensive political comment prepared for use ECON-COM,[3] and complete politico-economic assessment, being submitted separately):

[Here follow sections on the current Japanese economic situation and on prospects for the Japanese economy.]

C. Current situation of economy as affecting U.S.-Japanese relationship.

Despite general health of economy, with expanding production and exports, climate of Japanese/American economic relations has worsened since last assessment for period ending May 1963. Prevailing tone in press more often bitter than mellow; govt officials more skeptical than receptive to U.S. démarches on economic subjects.

Following developments are favorable, however, both to Japan-U.S. relationships and to fortunes of Liberal Democratic Party: (1) Japan's invitation from OECD to full membership;[4] (2) some reduction of discrimination against Japanese trade by European countries and Australia, as credit for acceptance of Japan given U.S. to considerable extent; (3) Japan's increasing confidence in her role in Asia, again because encouragement by America has contributed to Japan's confidence to take more initiative; (4) close consultation between two countries on matters affecting restoration of relations with Korea, enabling hopefully Japan to play major role in developing Korea's economy, also drew Japan and America closer together; (5) visits of Ministers Ohira and Tanaka to U.S.

Unfavorable developments in our economic relationships however appear to outweigh favorable factors, insofar as Japanese public is concerned, and change in mood for worse is pronounced also in business, finance and government. Unfavorable factors include: (1) proposed interest equalization tax, which came as surprise and shock to Japan, especially when Canada was granted exception. It led to fears that denial of U.S. funds would seriously impede growth of Japan's economy and that tax itself was prelude to still more drastic U.S. action; (2) continued reduction offshore and MAP procurement, and "Buy American" and "Ship American" policies: (3) fears that America embarking on protectionist course despite Kennedy Round stimulated by (A) protracted negotiations on cotton textiles; (B) unsatisfied Japanese aspirations on

---

[3] Regarding postponement of the Third Meeting of the Joint U.S.-Japan Committee on Trade and Economic Affairs, see Document 385. The "comprehensive political comment" is Document 381.

[4] The OECD issued this invitation on July 26. Regarding U.S. support for Japanese admission, see Rusk's March 28 statement in Department of State *Bulletin,* April 15, 1963, p. 572. Japan's admission to the OECD was completed April 28, 1964.

revision North Pacific Fisheries Treaty;[5] (C) rumblings of possible restraints on woolen textiles; (D) anti-trust investigation of steel operations; (E) charges that steel products are still being dumped and demands for "audit" of steel companies books to verify information voluntarily provided by steel companies; (F) use of licensing powers of Dept Commerce in attempt enforce east-west trade restrictions in manner which Japanese considered unreasonable; and (4) apprehension over U.S. attitudes toward Japanese trade with Sino-Soviet Bloc countries, particularly ChiComs.

Joint ECONCOM scheduled for late November can materially improve climate of opinion in Japan if U.S. delegation can look forward with Japanese colleagues to remove misapprehensions and reassure Japanese of momentum of U.S. liberal trade policies. Despite problems, trade of Japan is flourishing with U.S., and Japanese economy is moving toward new highs. Furthermore, U.S. remains far and away most liked foreign country among Japanese, according to public opinion polls. Long list of contentious points should not obscure reality of fundamentally friendly attitude despite increasing number minor divergencies.

[Here follows a section on the current situation of the Japanese economy as it affected the domestic political scene.]

E.  Problems for Japan's future.

Japan's leadership must plan for future that will be heavily dependent on overseas sources for raw materials, markets for exports, and capital funds which are essential if Japan is to continue to develop her social and economic structure. Circumstances dictate that Japan's headlong growth rate is bound in long run to slow down, and that more attention must be given to improvements in Japan's infrastructure, roads, schools, water and sewage systems. Diversion of labor, capital and management from expansive industry to these areas will have a dampening effect on economic growth that has made such startling advance in last decade. Japan's need for raw materials appears today to present no special problems, except perhaps in case of sugar; shortage of world supplies and sharp price increases have increased substantially Japan's bill for sugar and future supplies available to Japan cause her great concern. Japan's problems, however, center on need for expanding export markets rather than on intensive search for imports and on her recent dependence on

---

[5] For the joint press release issued at the close of the tripartite (United States, Japan, Canada) fisheries negotiations, which took place at Tokyo September 16–October 7, see ibid., November 4, 1963, p. 709. Documentation on the talks is in Department of State, Central File INCO 4 FISH for 1963. A review of the problems involved in revision is in Embassy Brief BB–2, November 2. (Ibid., FE/EA Files: Lot 66 D 225, Embassy Briefings) See the Supplement. For text of the international convention for the high seas fisheries of the North Pacific Ocean, with annex and protocol, signed at Tokyo on May 9, 1952, and entered into force for the United States on June 12, 1953, see 4 UST 380.

capital from overseas to finance continued growth which her people have come to demand and to expect. At Joint ECONCOM Embassy would expect Japanese side to stress this dependence and to seek U.S. guidance and advice on trends in U.S. and elsewhere which would affect Japanese prospects for expanding her exports of merchandise and her imports of capital.

**Reischauer**

## 381. Telegram From the Embassy in Japan to the Department of State

Tokyo, November 1, 1963, 10 p.m.

1357. Ref: Deptel 1004 and Embtel 1356.[1] Joint Econ Com. Following is Japan political assessment as of November 1, 1963:

*I.    Summary*

Japan continues on course as political, economic and defense partner of U.S., as increasingly important member free world, as contributor to UN objectives, and as active member Asian-African bloc where it plays ever more prominent role. Partly because of lingering, pacifistic yearning for neutralism growing out of Japan's experience World War II, recent Limited Nuclear Test Ban Agreement and impression resulting improved east-west atmosphere have paved way for mood of détente in Japan. At same time USSR and CPR have in variety of ways redoubled blandishments to GOJ. Govt meeting situation with eyes open, well aware that eternal vigilance continues be price safety in Communist-threatened world. Fact is, however, détente mood militates against too abrupt assumption higher "posture" by Ikeda and GOJ and precludes, for example, any dramatic defense build-up early assumption full defense burden.

Source: Department of State, Central Files, E 1 JAPAN–US. Secret. Repeated to Seoul, Taipei, Hong Kong, Manila, Saigon, Vientiane, Bangkok, Phnom Penh, Kuala Lumpur, Djakarta, Canberra, Wellington, Rangoon, New Delhi, Karachi, Colombo, London, Paris, Moscow, Bonn, and Rome.
[1] Document 380 and footnote 1 thereto.

LDP will almost certainly be returned to power in general elections scheduled Nov 21 though probably with slightly diminished support as result of continuation of slow, long-term political trend. Moderately successful LDP record in election could consolidate Ikeda's position in both Diet and own party and permit if not abandonment of "low posture" approach at least a degree of added initiative in moving Japan toward more responsible role on world scene.

Japan's foreign policy reflects definite intention play greater role in field foreign economic assistance particularly Asian LDC's. US-Japan security arrangements well established. Prevailing harmony affected to some extent dissonance over force readjustment and other relatively minor problems.

[Here follow sections on Japan's domestic affairs and external relations.]

*IV. Security Affairs*

*A. General*

US-Japan relations under 1960 Security Treaty have steadily improved over past two years, characterized by increasingly closer coordination and consultation on security problems between Embassy and FonOff on other. [*sic*] On Japanese side strong pacifistic, anti-militarist feelings, which have been characteristic of the Japanese people since World War II and are somewhat less intense and over past year there has been distinct trend toward greater Japanese acceptance of realities of world strategic situation. PriMin and FonMin, both in public and private statements, have affirmed principle that Japan must greatly increase its own defense efforts if it is to assume its rightful role as a world power. While defense trend therefore favorable, should be borne in mind that neither Japanese Govt nor public is yet ready to undertake defense program of magnitude which US considers desirable. Present favorable trend in defense field has been accomplished with minimal pressures from US and adherence to our low pressure approach to Japanese continues offer by far safer and better course of action. Japanese will be more inclined accept unpalatable actions in defense area if GOJ takes these actions on own steam while we for our part keep them fully informed on our own defense thinking and planning and otherwise treat them as true and equal partners in defense problems of this area.

At present time there are four outstanding problems under active discussion and consideration by US and GOJ in defense field. These are: (1) US force readjustments; (2) military offset agreements; (3) cut-back and eventual elimination of US military assistance and (4) calls at Japanese ports by US atomic-powered submarines. These four questions are discussed in order below:

(1) Main thrust US force readjustment proposals currently being discussed with Japanese Govt is reduction in US Air Force presence in Japan, both aircraft and civilian personnel. Of paramount concern to Emb is proposal for complete withdrawal by July 1, 1965 of all US fighter interceptor aircraft presently stationed Japan (GOJ not informed this aspect readjustment). Withdrawal these aircraft (3 squadrons F–102s) will leave void in air defense of Japan which Japanese cannot fill from own defense resources by July 1, 1965. Of even greater concern to Emb is fear that withdrawal of all US defensive aircraft will leave US open to charge by opposition elements that US not fulfilling its commitments re defense of Japan under Security Treaty; and instead utilizing Japan only as base for US forward strategic air strike forces. This aspect of problem still under consideration in Washington.

(2) As result Deputy Secretary Defense Gilpatric's February discussions defense problems with PriMin, in Tokyo, special US-Japan study group has discussed military offset purchase arrangements. Extensive lists of available US military equipment were submitted to GOJ for consideration in connection preparation JFY 64 defense budget. However, while GOJ increasing budget by estimated 40 billion yen ($112 million), no additional US equipment (beyond some items deleted from MAP) is to be included in JFY 64 program. Budget increase rather is being [utilized?] by GOJ to refurnish and improve existing badly dilapidated GOJ defense facilities, to accommodate rising defense costs, including pay increase for self defense forces, and cover cost certain US items originally scheduled be furnished by US under MAP. Hopefully, following elections, JFY 64 defense budget may be stretched to include purchase small amount additional US equipment. However, Japanese obviously not keen about entering into any large-scale military offset agreement with US. Primary GOJ interest lies in building up its own defense production base by producing its own military equipment in Japan. In this context, our best chance for achieving offset arrangement benefiting [garble] appears to lie in negotiating agreements permitting Japanese produce US equipment under licensing arrangements.

(3) Military assistance to Japan will apparently be drastically curtailed in US FY 64 and will be terminated in 1965 except for continuation certain small training programs. Since second Japanese defense buildup plan (now in its second year) was formulated by GOJ on basis approximate $50 million annual MAP contribution from US, curtailment of MAP poses serious problems for Japanese in carrying out second defense plan. This, in combination with proposed US force adjustments, will compel Japanese face up to realities own defense needs much sooner than they originally planned.

(4) Question port calls by US atomic-powered submarines has been under discussion with GOJ during most of year and has become class

one political problem. While Ikeda govt accepts US might bring such submarines into Japan under security treaty and both Ideda and FonMin have publicly affirmed intention allow entry these vessels at conclusion discussions with US regarding safety these ships and agreement on compensation arrangements in case of accident, opposition elements are continuing campaign arouse Japanese public to oppose entry SSNs on grounds ships constitute nuclear hazard to public and would involve Japan in US nuclear strategy. We expect soon finalize exchange official documents with GOJ and following GOJ approval eventual entry of first SSN.[2]

**Reischauer**

---

[2] See footnote 4, Document 378.

---

### 382.    Briefing Paper Prepared in the Embassy in Japan

BB–18                                                    Tokyo, November 14, 1963.

US-JAPAN COMMITTEE ON TRADE AND ECONOMIC AFFAIRS
Tokyo, November 25–27, 1963[1]

*Treatment of U.S. Investment in Japan: Recent Developments*

*Embassy Recommendations:*

It is recommended that the Government of Japan be urged to modify its screening procedures and criteria for approving foreign investment so as to enable American investors to obtain the national treatment to which they are entitled under Article VII of the FCN Treaty. Specifically, we should request: (a) that American firms making application for investment in an industry in which all investment is restricted by the Japanese Government be treated on the same basis in all respects as a Japa-

---

Source: Department of State, Central Files, E 1 JAPAN–US. Limited Official Use. Transmitted as enclosure 1 to airgram A–549 from Tokyo, November 15. Drafted by Millard L. Gallop, Second Secretary and Commercial Officer, and Keld Christensen, Counselor for Economic Affairs.

[1] Concerning postponement of this meeting, see Document 385.

nese firm; and (b) that restrictions placed on American firms to which Japanese firms are not subjected (e.g., limited equity participation and limitations on the number of Americans on the board of directors) be removed.

*Background:*

On July 1, 1963, the Government of Japan amended its foreign investment and foreign exchange laws[2] so as to eliminate the right of foreigners to invest in Japan on a non-validated basis, thereby eliminating the possibility for foreigners to invest in Japan on the same basis as Japanese nationals. This change was accompanied by the announcement of new, more liberal criteria for the validation of foreign investments: the amendments to the Japanese law were referred to by the Government of Japan as a liberalization. The Government declared that in the future, direct foreign investment such as joint ventures would be presumed approved in principle and disallowed only in exceptional cases deemed to have "conspicuously adverse effects on the national economy." Criteria for such a determination were declared to be: extreme disruption of the industrial order; extremely adverse effects on the domestic financial and economic conditions as well as on the balance of payments; and unfair pressure on small or medium enterprises.

Despite the emphasis given in the announcement to relaxing the criteria for approval, there has been no indication in the several months since July 1 that the treatment of new foreign investment has been liberalized. Changes in screening procedures have been apparent only for approval of new funds for investments which previous to July 1 did not need validation. As long as American firms could make such "yen-basis" investments, no discrimination in treatment between American and Japanese firms was involved in the Government of Japan's failure to approve a joint venture or to approve the percentage of participation desired by a United States firm. However, since the foreclosing of the option of "yen-basis" investment, the Japanese Government's current investment screening practices appear to constitute discrimination against American firms.

Although ostensibly designed to limit calls on foreign exchange reserves, the screening of foreign investment has been administered particularly to limit the extent of foreign control in Japanese enterprises and to prevent upsetting the establishment pattern of competition in an industry.

Foreign Office officials, in discussions with the Embassy, have suggested that if American firms bring complaints of discriminatory treat-

---

[2] A detailed description of these changes is in airgram A–10 from Tokyo, July 17. (Department of State, Central Files, FN 5 JAPAN)

ment of investment applications, such cases should be called to the attention of the Foreign Office. The Embassy has sought to obtain from American business evidence of discrimination on which a protest could be based. However, since American firms operating in Japan are dependent in manifold ways on the good will of the bureaucracy, such firms are understandably reluctant to allow their names to be used in a specific protest to the Japanese Government. In the one instance in which an American firm (the American Cyanamid Company) authorized the Embassy to use its name in representations to the Government of Japan, the Foreign Office indicated that the failure to approve the application was not discriminatory since the Japanese Government is restricting all investment whether domestic or foreign, in the particular industry (see Embassy's A–499 of November 6, 1963, attached).[3]

A talking paper delivered to the Foreign Office on August 14[4] noted that the abolition of "yen-basis" investment introduced a distinction between the treatment afforded Japanese and American investors and that this difference in treatment appeared to constitute a possible denial to American investors of "national treatment." It was pointed out to the Foreign Office that whether the loss by American investors of the option to invest on a "yen-basis" resulted in practice in a denial of national treatment would depend on how the new criteria for the approval of foreign investment were applied.

*Anticipated Japanese Position:*

It must be recognized that the Japanese economy has many weak points, and that the Japanese officials believe it is essential for economic growth that foreign capital not be permitted entry on an entirely indiscriminate basis. In spite of this, the Japanese Government has obligated itself to approve foreign investment in all but exceptional cases. Exceptions would involve cases which would have a serious effect on small and medium size industry and where an adverse effect on the existing "industrial order" might be anticipated. Since approval of investments under the new regulations, dated July 1, will be given in all but exceptional cases, Japan will not consider the "yen-basis" option to be necessary.

---

[3] Not printed.
[4] Not found.

### 383. Letter From Secretary of Defense McNamara to Secretary of State Rusk

Washington, November 16, 1963.

DEAR DEAN: Ambassador Reischauer has reminded us that the subject of defense will inevitably arise while you, Doug Dillon and other Cabinet Members are in Tokyo.[1] Perhaps it would be useful if I gave you my views as to what we might achieve in moving the U.S./Japan defense relationship forward during your trip.

In his report to the President after his trip to Tokyo last February,[2] Ros Gilpatric reported that Prime Minister Ikeda and Foreign Minister Ohira agreed to a Memorandum prepared by the U.S. side which expressed among other things the hope "that Japan and the U.S. will strive to equalize each other's defense foreign exchange expenditures through reciprocal procurement. . . or take other actions designed to minimize the balance of payments effects of the U.S./Japan defense partnership" and the following two specific positions:

(1) The importance of increasing the Japanese Defense budget; and
(2) The desirability of establishing a Defense Study Group, within the framework of the Security Consultative Committee, to pursue our further defense cooperation, including the study of balance of payments effects on our respective foreign exchange expenditures.

Mr. Gilpatric's report, which was approved by the President, indicated further that, based on his assessment of Japanese/U.S. relationships, it was his conclusion that the objective of entirely offsetting the present U.S. adverse balance of military expenditures in Japan, running at well over $300 million a year, through the purchase by the Japanese of U.S. military equipment was unlikely of achievement in the near future. In addition to proposed methods of reducing our costs in Japan, the Memorandum concluded that we should revise our military sales goals for offset to $50 million for FY 64, $100 million for FY 65 and $150 million for FY 66. To date the Defense Study Group meetings have been largely unproductive in achieving any long range agreement on offset in Japan or any basis on which detailed procurement planning could proceed with the Japanese Ministry of Defense. Meetings have been so highly secretive and in such small groups that it has really been impossible to utilize Government channels as a principal means of relating Japanese

---

Source: Department of State, Central Files, E 1 JAPAN–US. Secret. A copy was sent to Dillon. Attached to a December 6 letter from Rusk to McNamara; see footnote 3 below.

[1] For the projected Third Meeting of the U.S.-Japan Committee on Trade and Economic Affairs, scheduled for November 25–27, see Document 385.

[2] Document 368.

military requirement to U.S. export potential. However, there have been sufficient contacts between U.S. and Japanese industry as well as between U.S. and Japanese Armed Forces representatives, with the coordination of the MAAG, that the offset procurement picture which presents itself to us prior to your meetings in Japan appears as follows:

(1) In comparison with the $50 million objective for FY 64, the Japanese Government currently estimates that purchases of military equipment from the U.S. will total $64.7 million during FY 64, most of which will be through direct transactions with U.S. defense industry.
(2) In comparison with $100 million for FY 65, current Japanese Government estimates and purchases suggest a total of $100 million of which $36 million will be government-to-government transactions and $64 million directly with U.S. defense industry.

It would thus appear from an analysis of Japanese sales forecasts that the very modest steps envisaged for FY 64 and FY 65 towards offsetting procurement have been accomplished and that the principal remaining questions concern:

(1) Completion of the third step of FY 66 planning for $150 million; and
(2) Extension of the scope of the discussions undertaken through the Defense Study Group in such a way as to provide better possibilities for increasing the offset procurement program in the future.

We believe that your meetings in Tokyo offer an opportunity to make some progress on these two points. We recommend that you try to reach a bilateral agreement along the lines of the attached draft Memorandum of Understanding[3] during your visit which would serve to formalize Japanese agreement to the Memorandum prepared by Mr. Gilpatric during his visit to a greater extent than was possible at that time. Such agreement, taking advantage of the fact that good progress is being made and offering U.S. credit assistance as a means of achieving the $150 million goal for FY 66, might now establish a more workable basis for future offset procurement planning.

If you agree, I propose that Mr. Leonard A. Alne of my negotiating staff be in Tokyo during your visit for the purposes of consulting with MAAG Japan and establishing a follow-up plan of action to carry out the

---

[3] This draft included reaffirmation of the agreement in principle on offsets reached by Ikeda and Gilpatric in February 1963; a summary of anticipated Japanese equipment purchases in the United States, and of anticipated reductions in U.S. military expenditures in Japan, in FYs 1964 and 1965; and a list of more vigorous efforts to be taken to increase offsets.

arrangements of Part III of the proposed Memorandum of Understanding.[4]

Sincerely,

Bob

---

[4] In his reply Rusk agreed to discuss offsets and more vigorous action to achieve them during his January trip to Japan, but left open the question of whether a formal Memorandum of Understanding would be necessary. He cautioned that U.S. plans to remove USAF F–102s from Japan as part of the U.S. effort to reduce expenditures might affect the negotiating atmosphere because F–102s were the backbone of the Japanese all-weather interception system. Documentation on U.S.-Japanese discussion of U.S. plans for removal of all F–102s from Japan by July 1, 1965, and of proposals for alternative air defense for Japan is in Department of State, Central Files DEF 6 US and DEF 15 JAPAN–US, and in Washington National Records Center, RG 330, OASD/ISA Files: FRC 67 A 4564, 333 Far East 12/9/63.

---

### 384. Telegram From the Embassy in Japan to the Department of State

Tokyo, November 20, 1963, 6 p.m.

1567. Joint ECONCOM. On Nov 19 senior MITI officials took initiative with EmbOffs to request that questions relating to liberalization of US investment in Japan not be raised by Cabinet members in joint ECONCOM to the extent of involving the FCN Treaty. MITI officials said that approach to Emb being made quite independently of FonOff and Ministry of Finance. Confidential and sensitive nature of subject was emphasized. MITI officials stated that basic policy of GOJ with respect to foreign investment is to offer treatment as liberal as possible. To raise the question of the treaty in the Joint Committee could very well, it was asserted, lead to political consequences domestically and to complications in US-Japanese relations. Reference was also made to new legislation governing Japan's trade, invisible, and capital transactions now being drafted by MITI. This legislation accepts, according to MITI officials, the principle that all external economic transactions are to be "free." The proposed law would introduce the so-called "automatic

---

Source: Department of State, Central Files, E 1 JAPAN–US. Confidential. Repeated to CINCPAC for POLAD.

authorization system" in which an application for investment will be considered approved if a certain period has passed without any decision having been taken. Restrictions would be limited to exceptional cases specified by law.

EmbOffs responded that MITI's request would be discussed within the Embassy and with Dept, but no hope was held out that MITI's suggestion would be accepted.

Emb feels that MITI's approach, far from suggesting that we should refrain from any initiative, underscores the importance of having the subject (i.e., the problems facing American investors in Japan and their difficulties in obtaining national treatment under the FCN Treaty) raised by U.S. Cabinet officers in the Joint Committee. The Emb has reliable information to the effect that the FonOff and the Ministry of Finance are opposed to the draft legislation proposed by MITI and instead wish to see a regime which would be more beneficial and attractive to foreign investors (the proposed legislation will not, insofar as the Emb has been able to ascertain, be a liberalization helpful to U.S. business). Moreover the fact that MITI officials raised this subject with the Emb without the knowledge of other govt ministries (MITI officials insisted on a discreet meeting with EmbOffs in a private club) indicates that MITI is in a very weak position on this subject within the GOJ. The difficulties which American business has encountered with respect to investment in Japan may to a great extent be laid at the door of the bureaucrats in MITI. If we wish to achieve any progress in this field, either on behalf of American business or in the interests of a further opening up and a liberalizing of Japanese economy, action on our part at the highest levels is required. In economic terms further liberalization of foreign investment in Japan would benefit the Japanese economy by serving to break down emerging old and traditional oligopolistic forms and draw the Japanese business community closer to its Western counterparts. Emb believes that suggestions by the Japanese (essentially MITI officials on this and previous occasions) that pressure on this subject from the U.S. side would force Japan into the position of being obliged to request a revision of the FCN Treaty should be taken with a grain of salt. Such action on the part of Japan would have such far-reaching consequences for the U.S.-Japanese partnership that it is doubtful the step would be taken only on the issue of the terms of U.S. investment.

Emb accordingly urges that the entire subject in terms of the FCN Treaty be raised by the U.S. side (in line with existing briefing papers) in Joint ECONCOM.[1] Significantly, senior FonOff official without prompting took same line with Emb officer very recently.

**Reischauer**

---

[1] See Document 385.

## 385.  Memorandum of Conversation

Washington, November 25, 1963.

SUBJECT

United States-Japan Relations

PARTICIPANTS

*Japanese side*
Prime Minister Hayato Ikeda
Foreign Minister Masayoshi Ohira
Ambassador Ryuji Takeuchi
Genichi Akatani, Ministry of Foreign Affairs (Interpreter)

*United States side*
President Johnson
Secretary Rusk
Richard W. Petree, International Relations Officer (EA/J)
James Wickel, LS, (Interpreter)

President Johnson extended warm congratulations to Prime Minister Ikeda for the recent election victory of his party in Japan and went on to ask if the Prime Minister could give him a secret formula for electoral success. The President said he would be able to use such a formula in next year's elections. The Prime Minister responded that he believes his party's success owes to a tip he received from President Johnson during the Prime Minister's visit to the United States two and a half years ago. President Johnson at that time had emphasized the great assistance he received from Mrs. Johnson in political campaigns, that in fact most American politicians received invaluable help from their wives. Prime Minister Ikeda said he went home and immediately put his own wife to work and instructed his cabinet officers to do the same. The recent election victory reflected the valuable help of these wives.

President Johnson expressed deep regret that the tragedy[1] had at the last moment forced postponement of the Third Meeting of the United

---

Source: Department of State, Central Files, POL JAPAN–US. Confidential. Drafted by Petree on November 26 and approved in S on November 26 and by the White House on December 2.

[1] Reference is to President Kennedy's assassination in Dallas, Texas, on November 22. Documentation in Kennedy Library, National Security Files, Countries Series, Japan, for 1963 indicates that the White House considered several proposals for a Presidential visit to Japan in the months prior to the President's death. On November 19 Kennedy discussed with Hilsman and Howard Jones, Ambassador to Indonesia, a possible visit in April or May 1964 to several Asian countries including Japan, of which the centerpiece was to be a trip to Indonesia, should the United States succeed in efforts to improve Indonesian-Malaysian relations. (Memorandum of conversation by Jones; Department of State, FE Files: Lot 65 D 6, POL 7, Visits and Meetings, Oct–Dec 1963)

States-Japan Joint Economic Committee.[2] The meeting has economic significance for us, but it also has great political significance, with the presidential election to be held in November 1964. He said we need the meeting now more than ever. He assured Prime Minister Ikeda that it is the intent of the United States to arrange for the mission to return to Japan, possibly early next year, and when the mission does go we hope Japan will remember our problem.

Prime Minister Ikeda expressed sympathy for and understanding of the reasons for the postponement. He said Japan wishes to continue in its relationship with the United States as before, emphasized complete cooperation in United States-Japan relations, in both economics and diplomacy.

President Johnson expressed thanks and said that despite this tragedy the bonds of friendship between Japan and the United States will not be weakened, but rather will be strengthened. He then spoke of the United States hope that relations between Japan and the Republic of Korea can be normalized as soon as possible[3] after elections in both Japan and Korea are finished. Prime Minister Ikeda said he feels that it is doubtful that under the present circumstances the party of Acting President Park of the Republic of Korea can win a majority of the seats of the National Assembly in this week's general election in Korea. He points out, however, that if Park worked out a coalition of conservative and moderate elements more or less aligned with his objectives he would have a workable majority in the National Assembly and have a good chance to stabilize the situation in the Republic of Korea. Japan would hope that Park will seek this course of action following the elections. The Prime Minister said that if Park is able to stabilize the political situation along these lines, Japan would hope to move toward complete normalization of relations as quickly as possible.

Prime Minister Ikeda went on to remark that the Republic of Korea is a nation of 25 million well-educated and hardworking people. A healthy development of the Republic of Korea is, in the Prime Minister's opinion, essential for the security of Japan. Japan and the Free World cannot afford to sit back and allow the Republic of Korea to degenerate into Communism. Therefore, Japan believes it must do everything possible to achieve normalization of relations with the Republic of Korea.

President Johnson said that since World War II the United States has spent over $100 billion dollars to help other nations to stand on their own

---

[2] This meeting, originally scheduled to take place in Tokyo November 25–27, was postponed to January 27–28.

[3] Documentation on U.S. interest in improved relations between Japan and the Republic of Korea is in the Korea compilation. Rusk and Ikeda discussed this topic on November 26; see footnote 4, Document 318.

feet and regain their productivity. Now, however, the Administration is facing increasing problems in Congress, not because of any lack of prosperity in the United States, but because Congressmen feel strongly that others must now assume a larger share of the burden than they have. Congress has made severe and radical reductions in the appropriations for overseas aid programs. We therefore look forward especially to a fruitful exchange between our Cabinet officers and the Ministers of Japan, for Japan is one of the major industrial nations of the world. We hope that we can work together to influence and to assist the less fortunate nations in the world.

The President said the fate of the aid bill in Congress represents a very serious problem. He said the Administration wants to tell Congress that the United States will have the help of other nations in carrying the load of overseas assistance programs, in the hope that Congress will provide a stronger aid bill than it so far has appeared willing. The President told Prime Minister Ikeda that we hope we can receive help from Japan in this problem.

Prime Minister Ikeda responded that the general direction of United States policy in this field (i.e. reducing its share of the worldwide burden) appears to him unavoidable. For this reason Japan both understood and acceded readily in the severe reduction in Military Assistance Program expenditures in Japan. The Prime Minister expressed the belief that rather than largescale dollar aid, we should concentrate together on broader economic assistance to underdeveloped areas such as Southeast Asia. He said he agrees with present United States policy trends.

Secretary Rusk noted to the President that Japan under Prime Minister Ikeda has made remarkable progress in claiming its rightful place among nations, particularly in such areas as the United Nations, the OECD community, and Southeast Asia. He said the United States values its close partnership with Japan because Japan has great power and can make a great contribution in these areas.

Prime Minister Ikeda said he personally believed much of this success owes to the help of the United States. He said the direction of emphasis of Japanese policy originated in the urging of former President Kennedy on the occasion of the Prime Minister's visit to Washington two and a half years ago. When Japan first surveyed its chances of admission into the OECD it looked like an impossible challenge. Great Britain in particular appeared to Japan to pose considerable resistance to the entry of Japan into the community. Prime Minister Ikeda visited England, France, Germany and Benelux last year, however, and as he held talks in the various capitals he sensed an improved climate, which he credited to the help of the United States, which obviously paved the way for achievement of greater success than Japan had hoped for. He again termed Japan's progress in Europe a result of work of the United States.

The Prime Minister went on to state he firmly believes that the frankest United States–Japan consultation is essential, particularly concerning Southeast Asia,[4] where there are problems in Burma and Malaysia and elsewhere requiring such close collaboration. He felt such close consultation is the best form of diplomacy in United States–Japan relations.

The President said it was impossible to hold detailed talks at this time, but the United States intends to follow just that kind of policy in the future. He said we hope for close consultations, frank and above-board, recognizing our great mutuality of interests.

In closing the meeting, Prime Minister Ikeda expressed the sincere honor he felt at being received by the President when President Johnson is so tired and pressed for time. The Prime Minister said that as a politician and statesman he had learned a great deal through his participation in the ceremonies surrounding President Kennedy's funeral. He said he had learned more of the political attitude of President Kennedy. He said he intended to take these thoughts home with him, to review his own outlook and performance, and to try to apply the Kennedy spirit in a renewal of relations between Japan and the United States.

President Johnson thanked the Prime Minister for meeting with him and assured him of the continued friendship and cooperation of the United States.

---

[4] On November 26 Rusk discussed with Ikeda a possible Japanese role in easing the confrontation between Indonesia and Malaysia. (Memorandum by Ainsworth; ibid., Secretary's Memoranda of Conversation: Lot 65 D 330)

# Index

*U.S. G.P.O.:1996-301-429:00006

ISBN 0-16-045206-6

9 780160 452062

90000